9e

Cost Accounting Principles

Cecily A. Raiborn, Texas State University—San Marcos

Michael R. Kinney, Texas A&M University

SOUTH-WESTERN
CENGAGE Learning

Australia • Brazil • Japan • Korea • Mexico • Singapore • Spain • United Kingdom • United States

SOUTH-WESTERN
CENGAGE Learning

Cost Accounting Principles, Ninth International Edition
Cecily A. Raiborn, Michael R. Kinney

Vice President of Editorial, Business: Erin Joyner
Editor-in-Chief: Rob Dewey
Executive Editor: Sharon Oblinger
Developmental Editor: Jeffrey L. Hahn
Editorial Assistant: Courtney Doyle Chambers
Associate Marketing Manager: Heather Mooney
Content Project Manager: Darrell E. Frye
Media Editor: Anita Verma
Manufacturing Planner: Doug Wilke
Marketing Communications Manager: Libby Shipp
Production Service: LEAP Publishing Services, Inc.
Compositor: Cenveo Publisher Services
Sr. Art Director: Stacy Jenkins Shirley
Cover Designer: Patti Hudepohl
Internal Designer: Mike Stratton
Cover Photo Credits:
B/W Image: Getty Images/Rubberball
Color Image: Shutterstock Images/Menna
Rights Acquisitions Director: Audrey Pettengill

Library of Congress Control Number: 2012934883

International Edition:
ISBN-13: 978-1-111-97210-3
ISBN-10: 1-111-97210-9

Cengage Learning International Offices

Asia
www.cengageasia.com
tel: (65) 6410 1200

Australia/New Zealand
www.cengage.com.au
tel: (61) 3 9685 4111

Brazil
www.cengage.com.br
tel: (55) 11 3665 9900

India
www.cengage.co.in
tel: (91) 11 4364 1111

Latin America
www.cengage.com.mx
tel: (52) 55 1500 6000

UK/Europe/Middle East/Africa
www.cengage.co.uk
tel: (44) 0 1264 332 424

Represented in Canada by
Nelson Education, Ltd.
tel: (416) 752 9100/(800) 668 0671
www.nelson.com

Cengage Learning is a leading provider of customized learning solutions with office locations around the globe, including Singapore, the United Kingdom, Australia, Mexico, Brazil, and Japan. Locate your local office at:
www.cengage.com/global

For product information: **www.cengage.com/international**
Visit your local office: **www.cengage.com/global**
Visit our corporate website: **www.cengage.com**

Printed in Canada
1 2 3 4 5 6 7 16 15 14 13 12

BRIEF CONTENTS

CONTENTS

PREFACE

Cost accounting is a dynamic discipline that is constantly responding to the needs of managers in a highly competitive and global business world. While the primary use of cost accounting is to determine product costs for internal management and external financial reporting, managers also need cost accounting information to develop, implement, and evaluate strategy. The ninth edition of *Cost Accounting Principles* covers the fundamental cost accounting procedures and calculations as well as the more strategic cost management concepts needed for planning and decision making.

A text is valuable only when students find the subject matter applicable to their business or personal lives. Through the use of a straightforward, readable approach, *Cost Accounting Principles* engages students by highlighting the real-world relevance of each topic. The text encourages students to expand their capabilities beyond merely computing answers to critically thinking about a variety of business issues.

HALLMARK FEATURES

This edition provides in-depth, current coverage of cost management concepts and procedures, while integrating relevant, real-world business examples and ethical considerations, in a straightforward, logical, and student-friendly framework. The unique hallmark features of this text that have been retained include the following.

Streamlined, Student-Friendly Approach

The book's thought-provoking writing keeps concepts intriguing and easy to comprehend. This edition's solid blend of concepts and practices will help students clearly understand how to solve actual business problems. Always praised for its engaging, student-friendly writing style, the authors have further enhanced the text's unmatched readability by breaking lists and equations out of text narrative for a clean presentation that's easy to read.

The text is well written, and students like it.

Gary L. Bridges, University of Texas at San Antonio

Clarity for Complex Topics

Building on the text's proven strength of helping faculty effortlessly teach fundamental cost accounting concepts with precision, we have taken extra care to clarify the topics—such as equivalent units for process costing, cost allocation under ABC, and overhead variances—with which your students are most likely to struggle. Many of these topics have been rewritten to make the issues more easily comprehended by students with limited familiarity with manufacturing environments. Wherever possible, additional service and not-for-profit examples have been provided. New exhibits have been added throughout to help students make visual connections with the concepts.

Relevance in Today's Business World

Real-world examples that appeal to today's students and clearly exemplify the chapter's concepts are integrated throughout the main body of the text to immediately connect today's business world with the classroom experience. Care has been taken to include relevant sustainability and environmental issues to cost/management accounting topics.

> *The Raiborn/Kinney book does a great job on more modern topics such as ABC, TQM, and JIT.*
>
> *Alan D. Campbell, Troy University*

Comprehensive Review Modules

A Comprehensive Review Module for each chapter ensures your students' mastery of concepts. The module provides an overview of key terms, succinct chapter summaries, solution strategies that highlight key equations and concepts, and a demonstration problem that students can use as a framework for solving similar examples in homework assignments or exams. These modules reinforce the critical concepts from the chapters and show how to apply those concepts to particular situations.

In addition to the chapter opening learning objectives (which are linked within the chapter to guide students through the material), learning objective links are included in the chapter summary to help students close the loop and easily identify areas that require additional attention or practice. Page references have also been added to the Solution Strategies at the end of the chapter, so students can quickly reference the text for additional explanations when necessary.

Developing Ethical Business Leaders

ETHICS

The need for students to analyze business situations and make informed, ethical decisions is essential in today's world. *Cost Accounting Principles* weaves ethical considerations throughout each chapter so that students learn to continually incorporate ethical reasoning into their cognitive processes. At the end of each chapter, a section entitled Potential Ethical Issues emphasizes cost and management situations that students may encounter in their future business endeavors. These scenarios illustrate the potential for information manipulation that could be a precursor to unethical behavior. Exercises and problems involving ethical considerations are marked with an ethics icon.

High-Quality End-of-Chapter Assignments

The end-of-chapter (EOC) materials provide a wide array of assignment types that allow students to practice their cost/management accounting skills. New problems have been added and nearly 50 percent of this edition's end-of-chapter assignments have been updated or modified. Clarification on rounding has been included in the EOC materials to reduce the potential for answer differences due solely to rounding.

The EOC items include not only procedural computations but also Excel templates, writing, Internet research, and group activities. Questions test basic chapter comprehension; Exercises offer short procedural and conceptual checkpoints; and Problems delve deeper into the issues to challenge students' comprehension of critical topics and procedures. Writing labels have been added to better identify which assignments build written communication and research skills.

> *A strength of the textbook is the quality of the exercises and problems at the end of each chapter. These items . . . do a good job of reinforcing important concepts in the chapter. Furthermore, most chapters have one or two broad-scope problems that integrate many of the concepts presented in that chapter and, in some cases, also integrate concepts from preceding chapters.*
>
> *Nace R. Magner, Western Kentucky University*

Advanced Technology Solutions

This edition includes an updated CengageNOW package that provides ultimate control and customization to ensure that your students are mastering the procedural and decision-making skills needed for future success. This integrated, online course management system saves you time by making your course planning more efficient, and by taking the work of grading out of your hands. It also encourages students to work smarter, by reinforcing course content through an integrated eBook, interactive learning tools, and Personalized Study Plans that are automatically developed for each student based on results of the included pre- and post-tests. CengageNOW allows you to assign tests, homework, quizzing, and more, then automatically grades those assessments, and posts grades to an internal gradebook. The gradebook in CengageNOW gives you the capability to run multiple reports so you can better evaluate student progress and track and report on outcomes.

SIGNIFICANT REVISIONS IN THE NINTH EDITION

In addition to updating and changing examples, references, and end-of-chapter items, some significant changes to the ninth edition include the following:

Chapter 1

- Included the concept of sustainability as part of environmental constraints and the value chain
- Consolidated all ethics information at the end of the chapter

Chapter 3

- Moved regression analysis to an appendix
- Streamlined discussion of over- and underapplied overhead

Chapter 5

- Moved the discussion about the use of standard costs in job order costing to an appendix

Chapter 6

- Included journal entries with the discussion of weighted-average process costing
- Added an exhibit to illustrate multidepartment process costing
- Moved the discussion about the use of standard costs in process costing to an appendix
- Reordered the chapter discussion to place why standards are used and considerations in establishing standards at the beginning of the chapter

Chapter 8

- Included chart on sources of information for sales forecasting
- Expanded the retail company demonstration problem

Chapter 10

- Added a section on the necessity of relevant costing in decision making
- Eliminated the appendix on linear programming

Chapter 11

- Provided additional clarification distinguishing net realizable and realized value approaches
- Included new exhibits for the net realizable value and realized value approaches

Chapter 12

- Added discussion of the role of social media in gathering external information

Chapter 13

- Added a new exhibit about decentralization/centralization of environmental decisions
- Updated the transfer pricing section

Chapter 14

- Adapted Exhibits 14.1 and 14.3 and the related discussion to include sustainability issues
- Clarified the topic of throughput
- Included a new exhibit incorporating green information technology initiatives into the balanced scorecard

Chapter 15

- Increased the discussion of post-investments audits and added two exhibits on the topic
- Revised the demonstration problem to include profitability index and accounting rate of return

Chapter 17

- Modified Exhibit 17.2 to include a discussion on where quality costs might be "buried"

End of Text

- Included a acronym list for reference

INSTRUCTOR SUPPORT MATERIALS

A comprehensive instructor support package is provided for this text, including the following.

Text Companion Web Site

http://login.cengage.com

This Web site provides immediate access to an extensive array of teaching and interactive learning resources—including chapter-by-chapter online tutorial quizzes, a final exam, online learning games, flashcards, and more! Easily download the instructor resources such as the Solutions Manual, Instructor's Manual, PowerPoint® Presentation slides, and Excel® Spreadsheet Templates with Solutions from the password-protected, instructor-only section of the site.

Solutions Manual

Find full solutions for all end-of-chapter assignment items, including questions, exercises, and problems. Complete computations allow you to demonstrate clearly how to reach the correct answers. All solutions were developed by the authors of the textbook.

Instructor's Manual

Access the tools you need in the Instructor's Manual, which provides the resources to streamline and maximize the effectiveness of your course preparation. The Instructor's Manual presents an overview of the learning objectives, a chapter-by-chapter glossary of terminology, and a detailed lecture outline.

Test Bank

Efficiently assess your students' understanding as this edition's Test Bank offers an extensive selection of questions for quizzes, tests, and exams. AICPA and IMA tags help you quickly identify problems that have been used on professional accounting exams. Also, all test items have now been tied directly to Bloom's Taxonomy of Learning. The Test Bank is also available in ExamView® for customized electronic testing.

ExamView Pro® Testing Software

This edition's electronic Test Bank offers a variety of class-tested multiple-choice problems, short problems, and essay problems. Designed to make exam preparation as convenient as possible, each Test Bank chapter contains enough questions and problems to prepare several exams without repeating material. Tests can be instantly customized with this easy-to-use software. AICPA and IMA tags help you quickly identify problems that have been used on professional accounting exams. Also, all test items have now been tied directly to Bloom's Taxonomy of Learning.

PowerPoint® Slides

Make your lectures come to life and clarify difficult concepts with slides designed to complement your lecture and focus student attention. A free student version of the slides is also available online.

Excel® Spreadsheet Solutions

These templates provide the solutions for the problems and exercises that have Excel Spreadsheet Templates. Through these files, instructors can see the solutions in the same format as the students. All problems with accompanying templates are marked in the book with an icon.

CengageNOW

Ensure that your students have the understanding of accounting procedures and concepts they need to know with CengageNOW. This integrated, online course management and learning system combines the best of current technology to save time in planning and managing your course and assignments. You can reinforce comprehension by creating customized student learning paths, and efficiently test and automatically grade assignments. Access is available through a printed access card or electronic access code that can be bundled with this edition or purchased separately. See your sales representative for details.

Experience Accounting Video Series

Included within the Study Tools available in CengageNOW for Cost Accounting Principles, 9e, these videos provide students with an inside look into the unique decision making of top companies—including BP, Hard Rock Café, Coldstone Creamery, Boyne Resorts, and more—to better illustrate how accounting information is used.

STUDENT SUPPORT MATERIALS

Text Companion Web Site

Master the procedures and concepts of accounting and earn the grade you want in your accounting course with the learning resources at the *Cost Accounting Principles, 9e* interactive companion Web site. Designed specifically for your success, this Web site features chapter-by-chapter online tutorials, quizzes and solutions, learning games, flash cards, and more. To access these materials, visit www.cengagebrain.com and search by ISBN number.

PowerPoint® Slides

Take notes easily and study or review difficult concepts with the student version of this edition's PowerPoint® slides, available online at www.cengagebrain.com.

Excel® Spreadsheet Templates

Save time and ensure accuracy with online Excel® templates on the text's companion Web site that help you solve selected end-of-chapter exercises and problems, while gaining valuable experience with Excel® software. Download these templates through the Free Study Tools link at www.cengagebrain.com.

CengageNOW

CengageNOW is an easy-to-use online resource that helps you study more effectively in less time so that you can get the grade you want. This integrated system helps you efficiently manage and complete your homework assignments from the text. Take pre-tests to determine the areas in which you require more practice, receive direction about what you still need to review and focus on, and take a post-test to continuously revise your Personalized Study Plan. CengageNOW includes additional assets, like games and videos, to help you review key content in multiple ways. Ask your instructor about using CengageNOW in your course!

ACKNOWLEDGMENTS

We would like to thank all the people who have helped us during the revision of this text. The constructive comments and suggestions made by the following reviewers were instrumental in developing, rewriting, reorganizing, and improving the quality, readability, accuracy, and student orientation of *Cost Accounting Principles.* The reviewers of the ninth edition are:

Gregory Haselde,
Furman University

David Laurel,
South Texas College

Nace R. Magner,
Western Kentucky University

Herbert L. Martin,
Hope College

Dennis P. Moore,
Worcester State University

David Ozag,
Kaplan University

Grace Peng,
Zane State College

Donald Pomeroy,
Trine University

Robert Rambo,
Roger Williams University

George Starbuck,
McMurry University

Kanaiya Sugandh,
La Sierra University

Wallace Wood,
University of Cincinnati

Reviewers of the previous editions were:

Gary L. Bridges
University of Texas at San Antonio

Alan D. Campbell
Troy University

Charles R. Chambers
University of Toledo

Beatrix DeMott
Park University

Rita L. Dufour
Northeast Wisconsin Technical College

Richard D. English
Augustana College

Dennis J. George
University of Dubuque

Elsayed Kandiel
State University of New York, Plattsburgh

Howard Lawrence
University of Mississippi

David J. Medved
Thomas Edison State College

Philip W. Morris
Sam Houston State University

Letitia Meier Pleis
Metropolitan State College of Denver

William R. Rhodes
University of Mississippi

Larry L. Simpson
Davenport University

Jan Smolarski
University of Texas–Pan American

Ron Stunda
Birmingham-Southern College

Timothy J. Swenson
Sullivan University

Ara G. Volkan
Florida Gulf Coast University

Theodore N. Wood
Gordon College

Wallace R. Wood
University of Cincinnati

We thank the Institute of Management Accountants, American Institute of CPAs, and various periodical publishers for use of materials that have contributed significantly to making this text a truly useful learning tool for the students. The authors also thank all the people (especially Jeffrey Hahn, Developmental Editor; Darrell Frye, Content Project Manager; and Sharon Oblinger, Executive Editor) at South-Western, a part of Cengage Learning, who have helped us on this project. Special thanks go to Erin Tilley, at LEAP Publishing Services, for her time and effort on this edition.

Additionally, thanks are extended to the following supplement preparers who have provided high-quality content and to the verifiers for ensuring the accuracy of this text and its supplements:

Supplement Preparers:

Test Bank:
Edward R. Walker
University of Central Oklahoma

Instructor's Manual:
Dennis J. George
The University of Dubuque

PowerPoint Slides:
Herb Martin
Hope College

CengageNOW Content & Excel Templates
Barbara J. Muller
Arizona State University

Verifiers:

James M. Emig
Villanova University

Dennis J. George
The University of Dubuque

Cecily Raiborn & Mike Kinney

Wavebreakmedia ltd/Shutterstock.com

1

Introduction to Cost Accounting

LEARNING OBJECTIVES

After completing this chapter, you should be able to answer the following questions:

1. What are the relationships among financial, management, and cost accounting?
2. What are the sources of authoritative pronouncements for the practice of cost accounting?
3. What is a mission statement, and why is it important to organizational strategy?
4. What must accountants understand about an organization's structure and business environment to perform effectively in that organization?
5. What is a value chain, and what are the major value chain functions?
6. How is a balanced scorecard used to implement an organization's strategy?
7. What are the sources of ethical standards for cost accountants?
8. Why is ethical behavior so important in organizations?

INTRODUCTION

Starting a career as a staff accountant with the goal of becoming a partner in a public accounting firm is the dream of many accounting majors. However, a career goal of becoming a chief financial officer or controller in the private sector is just as viable, and the end result can be equally rewarding. This text presents techniques that will help cost and management accountants solve problems and make decisions necessary to achieve corporate goals. Such knowledge is important to anyone who wants to become a Certified Public Accountant (CPA) and/or a Certified Management Accountant (CMA). The first part of this text presents the traditional tools of cost and management accounting, which are the building blocks for generating information used to satisfy internal and external user needs. The second part of the text presents innovative cost and management accounting topics and methods used in many organizations.

1 What are the relationships among financial, management, and cost accounting?

COMPARISON OF FINANCIAL, MANAGEMENT, AND COST ACCOUNTING

Accounting is called the language of business. As such, accounting can be viewed as having different "dialects." The financial accounting "dialect" is often characterized as the primary focus of accounting. Financial accounting is concentrated on the preparation and provision of financial statements: the balance sheet, income statement, cash flow statement, and statement of changes in stockholders' equity. Financial accounting information is typically historical, quantitative, monetary, and verifiable. Such information usually reflects activities of the whole organization.

The second "dialect" of accounting is that of management and cost accounting. **Management accounting** is concerned with providing information to parties inside an organization so that they can plan, control operations, make decisions, and evaluate performance, while **cost accounting** is directly concerned with the determination and use of product or service costs.[1]

Financial Accounting

The objective of financial accounting is to provide useful information to external parties, including investors and creditors. Financial accounting requires compliance with generally accepted accounting principles (GAAP), which are primarily issued by the Financial Accounting Standards Board (FASB), the International Accounting Standards Board (IASB), and the Securities and Exchange Commission (SEC). Most large, and many small, businesses are required to use GAAP to prepare their financial statements, which may be audited by an independent public accounting firm. Oversight of auditing standards for public companies is the responsibility of the Public Company Accounting Oversight Board (PCAOB).[2]

In the early 1900s, financial accounting was the primary source of information for evaluating business operations. Companies often used **return on investment (ROI)** to allocate resources and evaluate divisional performance. ROI is calculated as income divided by total assets. Using a single measure such as ROI for decision making was considered reasonable when companies engaged in one type of activity, operated only domestically, were primarily labor intensive, and were managed and owned by a small number of people who were very familiar with the operating processes.

As the securities market grew, so did the demand by stockholders for audited financial statements. Preparing financial reports was costly, and information technology was limited. Developing a management accounting system separate from the financial accounting system would have been cost prohibitive at that time, particularly given the limited benefits that would have accrued to managers and owners who were intimately familiar with their organization's narrowly focused operating activities. Collecting information and providing reports to management on a real-time basis would have been impossible in that era.

[1] Other accounting "dialects," such as tax and auditing, are beyond the scope of this text.

[2] The PCAOB was created by the Sarbanes-Oxley Act of 2002.

Management Accounting

By the mid-1900s, managers were often no longer owners but, instead, were individuals who had been selected for their positions because of their skills in accounting, sales, finance, or law. These managers frequently lacked in-depth knowledge of an organization's underlying operations and processes. Additionally, businesses began operating in multiple states and countries and began manufacturing many products in a non-labor-intensive environment. Further, service entities became more prevalent and not-for-profit organizations (NFPs) were developing and donors trying to evaluate where to engage in philanthropic efforts wanted better information from these NFPs.

Business managers needed an accounting system that could help implement and monitor organizational goals in a globally competitive, multiple-product or multi-service environment. NFP managers needed an accounting system that focused on the manner in which resources were used and measured the benefits provided by such use. Introduction of affordable information technology allowed management accounting to develop into a discipline independent from financial accounting.

Management accounting is used to gather the financial and nonfinancial information needed by internal users. In a production environment, managers are concerned with fulfilling organizational goals, communicating and implementing strategy, and coordinating product design, manufacturing, and marketing while simultaneously operating distinct business segments. Except for manufacturing issues, similar concerns exist in a business service environment. In a not-for-profit organization, the focus is still on strategy and goal fulfillment, but managers are also extremely concerned with budgeting, controlling costs, and determining the cost of providing distinct organizational services. Management accounting information commonly addresses individual or divisional concerns rather than those of the organization as a whole. Management accounting is not required to adhere to GAAP but provides both historical and forward-looking information for managers.

The primary differences between financial and management accounting are shown in Exhibit 1.1.

Exhibit 1.1 Financial and Management Accounting Differences

	Financial Accounting	Management Accounting
Primary users	External	Internal
Primary organizational focus	Whole (aggregated)	Parts (segmented)
Information characteristics	Must be • Historical • Quantitative • Monetary • Verifiable	May be • Current or forecasted • Quantitative or qualitative • Monetary or nonmonetary • Timely and, at a minimum, reasonably estimated
Overriding criteria	Generally accepted accounting principles	Situational relevance (usefulness)
	Consistency Verifiability	Benefits in excess of costs Flexibility
Recordkeeping	Formal	Combination of formal and informal

As organizations grew and were organized across multiple locations, financial accounting became less appropriate for satisfying management's internal information needs. To prepare plans, evaluate performance, and make more complex decisions, management needed forward-looking information rather than only the historical data provided by financial accounting. The **upstream costs** (research, development, product design, and supply chain) and **downstream costs** (marketing, distribution, and customer service) incurred were becoming a larger percentage of total enterprise costs. When making pricing decisions, managers needed to add these upstream and downstream internal costs to the GAAP-determined product cost. The various types of costs associated with products are shown in Exhibit 1.2.

Exhibit 1.2 Organizational Costs

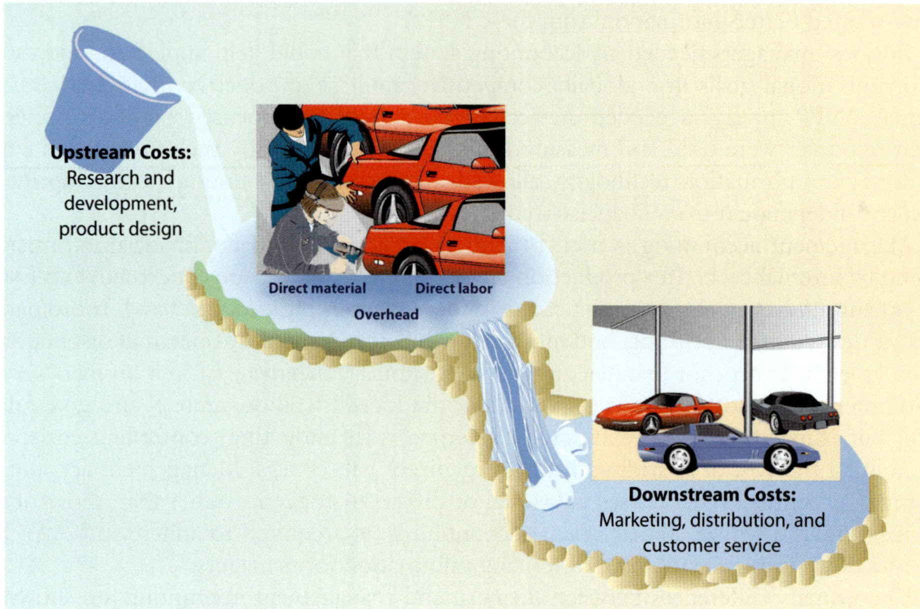

Cost Accounting

Cost accounting can be viewed as the intersection between financial and management accounting (see Exhibit 1.3). Cost accounting addresses the informational demands of both financial and management accounting by providing product or service cost information to

- external parties (stockholders, creditors, regulatory bodies, and donors) for investment and credit decisions and for reporting purposes, and
- internal managers for planning, controlling, decision making, and evaluating organizational performance.

Exhibit 1.3 Relationship of Financial, Management, and Cost Accounting

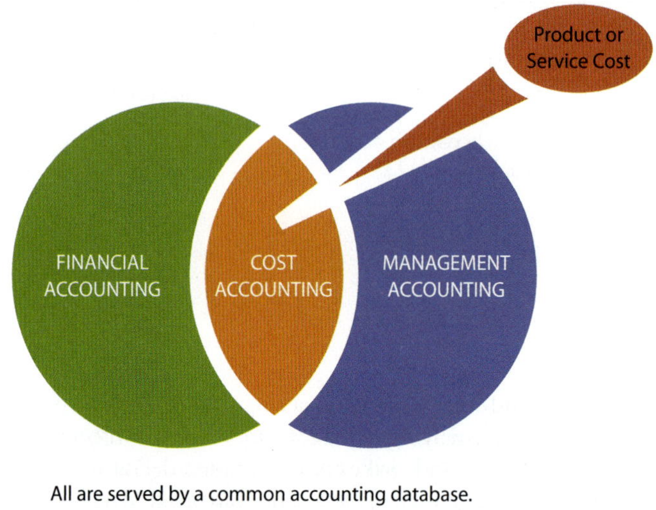

For a manufacturing company, **product cost** consists of the sum of all factory costs incurred to make one unit of product and is developed in compliance with GAAP for financial reporting purposes. In nonmanufacturing companies or NFPs, a **service cost** is more likely to be computed. But product/service cost information can also be developed outside of the constraints of GAAP to assist management in its needs for planning and controlling operations.

As companies expand operations, managers recognize that a single cost can no longer be computed for a specific product or service. For example, a company's Asian operations could be highly labor intensive, whereas its North American operations could be highly capital intensive. Product costs cannot be easily compared between the two locations because their production processes are not similar. Such complications have resulted in the evolution of expanded accounting databases, which include not only financial accounting information but also cost and managerial accounting information.

COST ACCOUNTING STANDARDS

2 What are the sources of authoritative pronouncements for the practice of cost accounting?

Although internal accounting reports need not comply with GAAP, three bodies (Institute of Management Accountants, Society of Management Accountants of Canada, and Cost Accounting Standards Board) issue cost accounting guidelines or standards.

The Institute of Management Accountants (IMA) is a voluntary membership organization of accountants, finance specialists, academics, and others. The IMA issues directives on the practice of management and cost accounting called Statements on Management Accounting (SMAs). SMAs are not legally binding, but their rigorous developmental and exposure process helps ensure their wide support. The Society of Management Accountants of Canada (CMA-Canada), which is similar to the IMA, issues Management Accounting Guidelines (MAGs). Like SMAs, MAGs are not mandatory for organizational accounting but suggest high-quality accounting practices. The Cost Accounting Standards Board (CASB) is part of the U.S. Office of Federal Procurement Policy. The CASB's purpose is to issue cost accounting standards for defense contractors and federal agencies to help ensure uniformity and consistency in government contracting. Compliance with CASB standards is required for companies bidding on or pricing cost-related contracts of the federal government.

Although the IMA, CMA-Canada, and CASB have been influential in standards development, most management accounting procedures have been developed within industry and influenced by economic and finance theory. Thus, no "official" agency publishes generic management accounting standards for all companies, but there is wide acceptance of (and, therefore, authority for) the methods presented in this text.

Because accounting and other types of information are used to measure an organization's performance, managers may be tempted to manipulate the information to alter others' perceptions about an organization's performance. A strong organizational commitment to ethical behavior can curb deceptive uses of information.

Cost accounting information is needed by both financial and management accountants. Although financial accounting must be prepared in compliance with GAAP, management accounting must be prepared in accordance with management needs. Managers need information to develop mission statements, implement strategy, control the value chain, measure and assess personnel performance, and set balanced scorecard goals, objectives, and targets.

ORGANIZATIONAL STRATEGY

3 What is a mission statement, and why is it important to organizational strategy?

Each organization (whether for-profit or not-for-profit) should have a **mission statement** that expresses the purposes for which the organization exists, what the organization wants to accomplish, and how its products and services can uniquely meet its targeted customers' needs. These statements are used to develop the organization's **strategy** or plan for how the firm will fulfill its goals and objectives by deploying its resources to create value for customers and shareholders. Mission statements are modified over time to adapt to the ever-changing organizational environment.

Each organization is unique; therefore, even organizations engaged in selling similar products or providing similar services have unique strategies that are feasible and likely to be successful. In Exhibit 1.4 is a model of the major factors that influence an organization's strategy. These factors include organizational structure, core competencies, organizational constraints, management style and organizational culture, and environmental constraints.

Exhibit 1.4 Factors Influencing Organizational Strategy

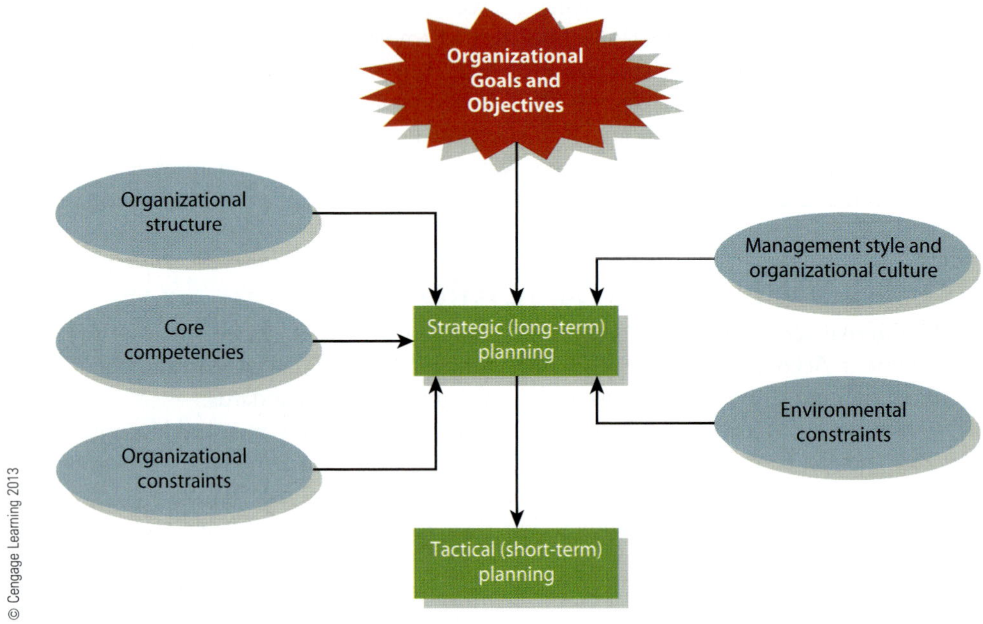

Organizational strategy should be designed to help the firm achieve an advantage over its competitors. For instance, the trend towards producing books on digital platforms has seen phenomenal growth: according to the February 2011 sales report of the **Association of American Publishers**, e-books grew over 200 percent since the 2010 report and downloadable books increased almost 37 percent during the same period.[3] **Amazon**'s strategic choice of producing Kindle e-book readers was well in advance of the marketplace. That company's customer-based mission statement is: "to be earth's most customer-centric company; to build a place where people can come to find and discover anything they might want to buy online."[4] When opportunities to serve new customers in new ways (be that through e-books or video streaming) are presented, Amazon conceives and builds new business models to exploit those opportunities.[5]

Small organizations frequently develop only a single strategy, whereas large organizations often design an overall entity strategy as well as individual strategies for each organizational unit (such as a division or a location). Unit strategies flow from the organization's overall strategy to ensure effective and efficient resource allocations that are compatible with corporate goals.

Strategy decisions should reflect the organization's core competencies. A **core competency** is any critical function or activity in which an organization seeks a higher proficiency than its competitors, making that function or activity the root of competitiveness and competitive advantage. Technological innovation, engineering, product development, and after-sales service are examples of core competencies. **Apple** believes it has two distinctive core competencies: innovative design and technology. In contrast, **Disney** asserts its six core competencies are leadership excellence, people management, quality service, loyalty, organizational creativity, and value chain management. The **M.D. Anderson Cancer Center** in Houston, Texas, believes its

[3] Andi Sporkin, "Popularity of Books in Digital Platforms Continues to Grow, According to AAP Publishers February 2011 Sales Report," *Association of American Publishers* (April 14, 2011); http://publishers.org/press/30/.

[4] Amazon.com FAQs; http://phx.corporate-ir.net/phoenix.zhtml?c=97664&p=irol-faq (accessed 1/13/12).

[5] Mark W. Johnson, "Amazon's Smart Innovation Strategy," *Bloomberg Businessweek* (April 12, 2010); http://www.businessweek.com/innovate/content/apr2010/id20100412_520351.htm.

core competency is patient care in the form of cancer surgery, therapy, research, education, and prevention.

Regardless of the type of organization, managers are concerned with formulating strategy, and cost accountants are charged with providing management with the information necessary for making choices about, and assessing progress toward, strategic achievement. Most companies employ either a cost leadership or a product (or service) differentiation strategy. **Cost leadership** refers to a company's ability to maintain its competitive edge by undercutting competitor prices. Successful cost leaders sustain a large market share by focusing almost exclusively on manufacturing products or providing services at a low cost. For example, **Walmart**, **Volkswagen**, and **Rent-a-Wreck** primarily compete in their markets based on price. **Product** or **service differentiation** refers to a company's ability to offer superior quality products or more unique services than competitors. Such products and services are generally sold at premium prices. **Nordstrom**, **BMW**, and **Beverly Hills Rent-a-Car** compete on quality and features. Successful companies usually focus on one strategy. However, some firms focus on more than one strategy (possibly for different product lines) simultaneously, but one strategy is often more dominant. Exhibit 1.5 provides a checklist of questions that help indicate whether an organization has a comprehensive strategy in place.

Exhibit 1.5 Strategy Checklist

1. What are the most important factors in your organization's operating environment? These factors could include the economy, population demographics, competitors, suppliers, resource availability, innovation, and the environment.
2. What are your organization's core competencies? These items could include human resources, product/service quality, innovation, speed to market, cost control, pricing, environmental policies, marketing skills, customer service, and organizational culture and ethics.
3. Have your organization's core competencies become competitive advantages? If yes, can these competitive advantages be maintained and how? If not, why has the organization failed to capitalize on those core competencies?
4. What is your organization's current position relative to your competitors? Factors to consider include cost structure, product/service lines, ability to innovate and adapt to change, market share, market "reach," customer perceptions of quality and service, and profitability. Analyze similarities and weaknesses.
5. What are your customers' purchase or selection criteria? Are your products or services designed to fit these criteria as well as or better than your competitors' products or services?
6. What is the organizational vision identified by your management, shareholders, and other internal and external stakeholders? Is the vision supported by identifiable goals and objectives? Is the vision amenable to change with a changing environment?
7. Does your organization have the appropriate resources (financial, personnel, and technological) to fulfill its vision? If not, what else is needed, and how can it be obtained?
8. Have appropriate performance measurements been established to determine if progress is being made toward your organization's mission and vision?
9. Are operating conditions continuously monitored to detect changes so that your organization can adapt with flexibility and sensitivity, especially to new trends in technology?

ORGANIZATIONAL STRUCTURE

4 What must accountants understand about an organization's structure and business environment to perform effectively in that organization?

An organization is composed of people, resources other than people, and commitments that are acquired and arranged to achieve organizational strategies and goals. The organization evolves from its mission, strategies, goals, and managerial personalities. **Organizational structure** reflects the way in which authority and responsibility for making decisions are distributed among personnel. **Authority** refers to the right of an individual or team (usually by virtue of position or rank) to use resources to accomplish a task or achieve an objective.

Responsibility is the obligation of an individual (or team) to accomplish a task or achieve an objective.

Every organization contains management and nonmanagement line and staff personnel. **Line personnel** work directly toward attaining organizational goals. Persons in these positions are held responsible for achieving performance targets or budgeted income for their departments, divisions, or geographic regions. **Staff personnel** give assistance and advice to line personnel. Relative to top accounting jobs, the treasurer and controller are staff positions. Treasurers are generally responsible for achieving short- and long-term financing, investing, and cash management goals, while controllers are responsible for delivering financial reports in conformity with GAAP to management. The CFO, who oversees all financial activities of an organization, is considered a member of line personnel.

Given the need for global personnel access, the distinction between line and staff positions sometimes becomes blurred. For example, in 2006, **IBM** launched a worldwide "innovation portal" in which any employee having a product idea can use online chat rooms to organize a team, obtain resources, gain access to market research, and collaborate on prototypes and testing. One concept developed from this portal project was "Blue Cloud" which is "a series of cloud computing offerings that will allow corporate data centers to operate more like the Internet by enabling computing across a distributed, globally accessible fabric of resources, rather than on local machines or remote server farms."[6]

Organizational Constraints

A variety of organizational constraints may affect a firm's strategy options. Most constraints exist only in the short term because they can be overcome by existing business opportunities. Four common organizational constraints are monetary capital, intellectual capital, technology, and the environment. Although additional monetary capital can almost always be acquired through debt (short- or long-term borrowings) or equity (common or preferred stock) sales, management should decide

- whether the capital can be obtained at a reasonable cost and/or
- a reallocation of current capital would be more effective and efficient.

Intellectual capital encompasses all of an organization's intangible assets: knowledge, skills, and information. Companies rely on their intellectual capital to create ideas for products or services, to train and develop employees, and to attract and retain customers. As for technology, companies must adopt emerging technologies to stay at the top of their industry and achieve an advantage over competitors.

Environmental constraints also impact organizational strategy. An **environmental constraint** is any limitation caused by external cultural, fiscal (such as taxation structures), legal/regulatory, or political situations and by competitive market structures. One cultural constraint that is becoming more prevalent in its effects on organizational strategy is sustainability. More organizations are becoming aware of the need to integrate economic longevity with ecological longevity, often referred to as the triple bottom line of people, profits, and planet. Some of the pressure for sustainability considerations comes from legal requirements, while other pressure has been exerted by internal and external organizational stakeholders. Because environmental constraints cannot be directly controlled by an organization's management, they tend to be long- rather than short-run influences.

Going global, expanding core competencies, and investing in new technology require organizational change, and an organization's ability to change depends heavily on its management style and organizational culture. Different managers exhibit different preferences for interacting with the entity's stakeholders, especially employees. Management style is exhibited in decision-making processes, risk taking, willingness to encourage change, and employee development, among other issues. Typically, management style is also reflected in

[6] IBM Media Relations, "IBM Introduces Ready-to-Use Cloud Computing," *IBM Press Release* (November 15, 2007); http://www-03.ibm.com/press/us/en/pressrelease/22613.wss.

an organization's culture: the basic manner in which the organization interacts with its business environment, the manner in which employees interact with each other and with management, and the underlying beliefs and attitudes held by employees about the organization. Culture plays a significant role in determining whether the communication system tends to be formal or informal, whether authority is likely to be concentrated in management or distributed throughout the organization, and whether organizational members are experiencing feelings of well-being or stress.

VALUE CHAIN

5 What is a value chain, and what are the major value chain functions?

Strategic management's foundation is the value chain, which is used to identify the upstream and downstream organizational processes that lead to cost leadership or product differentiation. The **value chain** is a set of value-adding functions or processes that convert inputs into products and services for company customers. The following definitions are contained in the generic value chain shown in Exhibit 1.6. Examples from **General Motors** (GM) are used to illustrate the functions within the value chain.

Exhibit 1.6 Components of a Value Chain

- Research and Development—experimenting to reduce costs or improve quality. GM can experiment with various paint formulas to produce the most lasting exterior paint finish.
- Design—developing alternative product, service, or process designs. In 2012, GM made design changes to the seats and increased the number of **Bose** speakers to nine from seven in the Corvette; new options for the car included choices of traction systems, tires, and trim packages. In 2006, GM also changed, in part, its manufacturing process by building one of the world's most environmentally advanced manufacturing plants in Lansing, Michigan; energy savings at the plant have been estimated at 45 percent above the industry average or about $1 million annually.[7]

[7] General Motors, "GM Opens First-Ever LEED-Gold Certified Automobile Manufacturing Facility," *Press Release* (August 3, 2006); http://archives.media.gm.com/archive/documents/domain_2/docId_27772_pr.html.

- Supply—managing raw materials received from vendors. Companies often develop long-term alliances with suppliers to reduce costs and improve quality. Bose, a long-time GM partner, produced a sound system specifically for the electric Volt that is 30 percent smaller, weighs 40 percent less, and uses 50 percent less energy than conventional Bose systems.[8]
- Production—acquiring and assembling resources to manufacture a product or render a service. For GM, production reflects the acquisition of tires, metal, paint, fabric, glass, electronics, brakes, and other inputs and the assembly of those items into an automobile.
- Marketing—promoting a product or service to current and prospective customers. Promotion at GM could involve developing a Super Bowl half-time commercial, placing automobiles on a showroom floor, designing a billboard advertisement, or recording a radio announcement to inform customers about the company's products or services.
- Distribution—delivering a product or service to a customer. GM uses trains and trucks to deliver automobiles to dealerships. Other companies could use airlines or couriers to distribute their products.
- Customer Service—supporting customers after the sale of a product or service. GM provides an 800 number for its customers to call if they have questions or need roadside service. Other companies may require customers to return a product if it needs repair.

Company managers communicate organizational strategy to all members in the value chain so that the strategy can be effectively implemented. The communication network needed for coordination among internal functions is designed in part with input from cost accountants who integrate information needs of managers of each value chain function.

BALANCED SCORECARD

6 How is a balanced scorecard used to implement an organization's strategy?

Accounting information helps managers to measure dimensions of performance that are important in accomplishing strategic goals. In the past, management spent significant time analyzing historical financial data to assess whether organizational strategy was effective. Today, firms use a variety of information to determine not only how the organization has performed but also how it is likely to perform in the future. Historical financial data reflect **lag indicators** or outcomes that resulted from past actions, such as installing a new production process or implementing a new software system. For example, an increase in operating profits (lag indicator) could occur after a new production process is installed. Unfortunately, lag indicators are often recognized and assessed too late to significantly improve current or near-future actions.

In contrast, **lead indicators** project future outcomes and thereby help assess strategic progress and guide decision making before lag indicators are known. For example, a lead indicator is the number of employees trained on a new accounting information system. The expectation is that the more employees who are trained to use the new system, the more rapidly orders will be processed, the more satisfied customers will be with turnaround time after placing an order, and the more quickly profits will be realized. If training (lead indicator) was provided to fewer employees than planned, future profits (lag indicator) will decrease (or not increase as expected) because some customers will be unhappy with sales order turnaround time.

Lead and lag performance indicators can be developed for many performance aspects and to assess strategy congruence. The **balanced scorecard (BSC)** is a framework that translates an organization's strategy into clear and objective performance measures (both leading and lagging) that focus on customers, internal business processes, employees, and

[8] General Motors, "General Motors, Goodyear, and Bose Collaborate to Boost Chevrolet Volt's Efficiency," *Press Release* (February 10, 2009); http://www.qualitychevy.com/carresearch/Press-Release/make_Chevrolet/id_1514/confid_qualitychevrolet/.

shareholders. Thus, the BSC provides a means by which actual business outcomes can be evaluated against performance targets.

The BSC includes short- and long-term, internal and external, and financial and nonfinancial measures to balance management's view and execution of strategy. As illustrated in Exhibit 1.7, this simplified BSC has four perspectives:

- learning and growth,
- internal business,
- customer value, and
- financial performance.

Each of these perspectives has a unique set of goals and measures.

Exhibit 1.7 Simplistic Balanced Scorecard

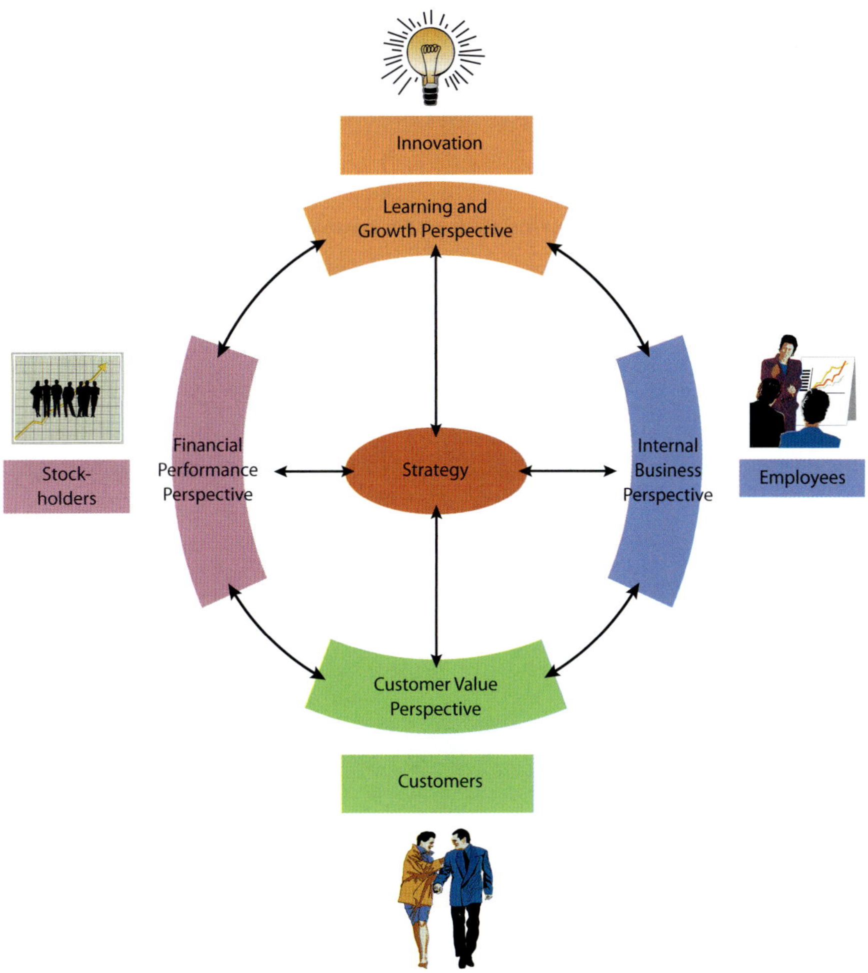

The **learning and growth perspective** focuses on using the organization's intellectual capital to adapt to changing customer needs or to influence new customers' needs and expectations through product or service innovations. This perspective addresses whether a company can continue to progress and be seen by customers as adding value. The **internal business perspective** focuses on those things that the organization must do well to meet customer needs and expectations. This perspective concentrates on issues such as employee satisfaction, product quality control, and cost management. The **customer value perspective** addresses how well the organization is doing relative to important customer criteria such as speed (lead time), quality, service, and price (both purchase and after purchase). Customers must believe that, when a product or service is purchased, the value received was worth the price paid. Finally, the **financial performance perspective** addresses the concerns of stockholders and other stakeholders about profitability and organizational growth. A performance measurement in this perspective might address the savings provided from outsourcing decisions—an amount that has declined since 2006 because of increases in ocean freight costs, the global commodity price index, the value of the Chinese yuan relative to the U.S. dollar, and Chinese labor costs.[9]

Exhibit 1.8 illustrates a more realistic balanced scorecard than the one shown in Exhibit 1.7 and provides some performance measures for the various goals.

Exhibit 1.8 Balanced Scorecard and Perspectives

Learning and Growth Perspective

Goals	Measures	TARGET
Technology leadership	Time to develop next generation	
Manufacturing learning	Process time to maturity	
Product focus	Percent of products that equals 80% of sales	
Time to market	New product introduction versus competition	

↑ ↓

Internal Business Perspective

Goals	Measures	TARGET
Technology capability	Manufacturing ability versus competition's	
Manufacturing excellence	Cycle time	
	Unit cost	
	Yield	
Design productivity	Engineering efficiency	
New product introduction	Actual production schedule versus plan	

↑ ↓

Customer Value Perspective

Goals	Measures	TARGET
New products	Percent of sales from new products	
	Percent of sales from proprietary products	
Responsive supply	On-time delivery (defined by customer)	
Preferred supplier	Share of key accounts' purchases	
Customer partnership	Number of cooperative engineering efforts	

↑ ↓

Financial Performance Perspective

Goals	Measures	TARGET
Survive	Cash flow	
Succeed	Quarterly sales growth and operating income by division	
Prosper	Increased market share and return on equity (or investment)	

Source: Robert S. Kaplan and David P. Norton, "The Balanced Scorecard—Measures That Drive Performance," *Harvard Business Review* (January–February 1992), pp. 72–76.

[9] Archstone Consulting, "Does Offshoring Still Make Sense?" *Area Development Online* (February 17, 2009); http://www.areadevelopment.com/StudiesResearchPapers/2-17-2009/manufacturing-supply-strategy-offshoring.shtml.

PROFESSIONAL ETHICS

7 What are the sources of ethical standards for cost accountants?

ETHICS

Most businesses participate in the global economy, which encompasses the international trade of goods and services, movement of labor, and flows of capital and information. The world has essentially become smaller through technology advances, improved communication capabilities, and trade agreements that promote international movement of goods and services among countries. Multinational corporation managers must achieve their organization's strategy within a global structure and under international regulations while exercising ethical behavior.

In business, managers need to attain their financial targets by concentrating on acquiring a targeted market share and achieving desired levels of customer satisfaction. However, executives at many companies have exhibited unethical behavior in trying to "make their numbers." **Earnings management** is any accounting method or practice used by managers or accountants to deliberately "adjust" a company's profit to meet a predetermined internal or external target. Earnings management allows a company to meet earnings estimates, preserve a specific earnings trend, convert a loss to a profit, increase management compensation (tied to stock performance), or hide illegal transactions. When the boundaries of reason are exceeded in applying accounting principles, companies are said to be engaging in "aggressive" accounting. Such aggression may range from simply stretching the limits of legitimacy all the way to outright fraud. **WorldCom**, **Enron**, **Tyco**, and **HealthSouth** are but a few of the many companies whose managers faced criminal penalties from acting unethically within the parameters of their jobs. Some of the aggressive accounting practices that have been exposed involved the manipulation of cost accounting information.

In 2002, as a result of many large financial frauds, the U.S. Congress passed the Sarbanes-Oxley Act of 2002 (SOX). This act holds chief executive officers (CEOs) and chief financial officers (CFOs) personally accountable for their organizations' financial reporting. In addition, the accounting profession promotes high ethical standards for accountants through several of its professional organizations. The IMA administers the CMA exam, which is focused on the professional expertise required by accounting and financial management professionals. The CMA credential demonstrates expertise in financial planning, analysis, control, decision support, and professional ethics.[10] CMAs are required to adhere to the IMA's *Statement of Ethical Professional Practice*. This set of standards (shown in Exhibit 1.9) focuses on competence, confidentiality, integrity, and credibility. Adherence to these standards helps

Exhibit 1.9 Statement of Ethical Professional Practice

COMPETENCE

Each member has a responsibility to:

- Maintain an appropriate level of professional expertise by continually developing knowledge and skills.
- Perform professional duties in accordance with relevant laws, regulations, and technical standards.
- Provide decision support information and recommendations that are accurate, clear, concise, and timely.
- Recognize and communicate professional limitations or other constraints that would preclude responsible judgment or successful performance of an activity.

CONFIDENTIALITY

Each member has a responsibility to:

- Keep information confidential except when disclosure is authorized or legally required.
- Inform all relevant parties regarding appropriate use of confidential information. Monitor subordinates' activities to ensure compliance.
- Refrain from using confidential information for unethical or illegal advantage.

(*Continued*)

[10] The CMA Exam is comprised of two parts: Part 1 covers financial planning, performance, and control; Part 2 covers financial decision making. Additional information about the CMA can be found at http://www.imanet.org/cma_certification/become_a_cma.aspx.

Exhibit 1.9 Statement of Ethical Professional Practice (*Continued*)

INTEGRITY

Each member has a responsibility to:

- Mitigate actual conflicts of interest. Regularly communicate with business associates to avoid apparent conflicts of interest. Advise all parties of potential conflicts.
- Refrain from engaging in any conduct that would prejudice carrying out duties ethically.
- Abstain from engaging in or supporting any activity that might discredit the profession.

CREDIBILITY

Each member has a responsibility to:

- Communicate information fairly and objectively.
- Disclose all relevant information that could reasonably be expected to influence an intended user's understanding of the reports, analyses, or recommendations.
- Disclose delays or deficiencies in information, timeliness, processing, or internal controls in conformance with organization policy and/or applicable law.

RESOLUTION OF ETHICAL CONFLICT

In applying the Standards of Ethical Professional Practice, you may encounter problems identifying unethical behavior or resolving an ethical conflict. When faced with ethical issues, you should follow your organization's established policies on the resolution of such conflict. If these policies do not resolve the ethical conflict, you should consider the following courses of action:

- Discuss the issue with your immediate supervisor except when it appears that the supervisor is involved. In that case, present the issue to the next level. If you cannot achieve a satisfactory resolution, submit the issue to the next management level. If your immediate superior is the chief executive officer or equivalent, the acceptable reviewing authority may be a group such as the audit committee, executive committee, board of directors, board of trustees, or owners. Contact with levels above the immediate superior should be initiated only with your superior's knowledge, assuming he or she is not involved. Communication of such problems to authorities or individuals not employed or engaged by the organization is not considered appropriate, unless you believe there is a clear violation of the law.
- Clarify relevant ethical issues by initiating a confidential discussion with an IMA Ethics Counselor or other impartial advisor to obtain a better understanding of possible courses of action.
- Consult your own attorney as to legal obligations and rights concerning the ethical conflict.

Source: Institute of Management Accountants, IMA Statement of Ethical Professional Practice (2000). Copyright by Institute of Management Accountants, Montvale, NJ; http://www.imanet.org/PDFs/Statement%20of%20Ethics_web.pdf.

management accountants attain a high level of professionalism, thereby facilitating the development of trust from people inside and outside the organization.

Competence means that individuals will develop and maintain the skills needed to practice their profession. For instance, cost accountants working in companies involved in government contracts must be familiar with both GAAP and CASB standards. **Confidentiality** means that individuals will refrain from disclosing company information to inappropriate parties (such as competitors). Acting with **integrity** means that individuals will not participate in organizationally or professionally discreditable actions. Integrity, for example, would preclude cost accountants from accepting gifts from suppliers because such gifts could bias (or be perceived to bias) the accountants' ability to fairly evaluate the suppliers and their products. **Credibility** means that individuals will provide full, fair, and timely disclosure of all relevant information. For example, a cost accountant should not intentionally miscalculate product cost data to materially misstate a company's financial position or results of operations.

Cost and management accountants may find that others within the organization have acted illegally or immorally; such actions could include financial fraud, theft, environmental violations, or employee discrimination. As indicated in Exhibit 1.9, the IMA's code of ethical conduct provides guidance on what to do when confronted with ethical issues. Accountants should document what (if any) regulations have been violated, obtain evidence of violation of such actions, and research and record the appropriate actions that should have been taken. This information should be kept confidential but be reported and discussed with a superior who is not involved in the situation—meaning that it could be necessary to communicate up the corporate ladder, even as far as the audit committee. If accountants cannot resolve the matter, their only recourse could be to resign and consult a legal advisor before reporting the matter to regulatory authorities.

Jacob Wackerhausen/iStockphoto.com

Management accountants must focus on competence, confidentiality, integrity, and credibility in order to attain a high level of professionalism and trust.

Managers and accountants who knowingly provide false information in public financial reports can be severely punished. For example, a CEO or CFO who knowingly certifies false financial reports may be punished with a maximum penalty of a $5 million fine, 20 years in prison, or both under SOX. Accountants who believe that a fraudulent situation exists should evaluate that situation and, if appropriate, "blow the whistle" on the activities by disclosing them to appropriate persons or agencies. Federal laws, including SOX, provide for some legal protection of whistle-blowers. The False Claims Act (FCA) allows whistle-blowers to receive 15 to 30 percent of any settlement proceeds resulting from the identification of such activities related to fraud against the U.S. government. In 2010, the Dodd-Frank Wall Street Reform and Consumer Protection Act (Dodd-Frank) was passed with several provisions to encourage whistle-blowing by persons who provide original information to the SEC. Awards can range from 10 to 30 percent of the amount recouped.

All accountants, regardless of organizational or geographical placement, should recognize their obligations to their profession and to professional ethics. Ethics is one aspect of business that should be practiced consistently worldwide.

ETHICS IN MULTINATIONAL CORPORATIONS

8 Why is ethical behavior so important in organizations?

Accountants and other individuals should be aware of not only their company's and profession's codes of ethical conduct but also the laws and ethical parameters within any countries in which their company operates. After some American companies were found to have given substantial bribes in connection with business activities, the United States passed the Foreign Corrupt Practices Act (FCPA), which prohibits U.S. corporations (and certain other foreign issuers of securities that are sold in the United States) from offering or giving bribes (directly or indirectly) to foreign officials to influence those individuals (or cause them to use their influence) to help companies obtain or retain business. In 1998, the FCPA was amended to apply to foreign entities that make bribes or corrupt payments within the United States. The FCPA is directed at payments that cause officials to perform in a way specified by the firm rather than in a way prescribed by their official duties. Both the frequency and severity of FCPA enforcement activity directed at companies and individuals has been increasing in recent years.[11]

In a recent FCPA case, the SEC filed suit against **Siemens AG** (a German manufacturer of industrial and consumer products) for paying approximately $1.4 billion in bribes to government officials around the world. Admitting guilt, Siemens agreed to pay $1.6 billion in fines, penalties, and disgorgement of profits; $800 million of that amount is to be

ETHICS

[11] Shearman & Sterling LLP, *Recent Trends and Patterns in the Enforcement of the Foreign Corrupt Practices Act* (July 2011); http://shearman.symplicity.com/files/ef6/ef696d76ef6a9b953f4cf5c1aeb3910a.pdf.

paid to U.S. authorities. This is the largest monetary sanction ever imposed in an FCPA case.[12] The largest FCPA settlement received from a U.S. company was $579 million from KBR/Halliburton.[13]

Globally, the Organisation of Economic Co-operation and Development (OECD) issued an Anti-Bribery Convention in February 1999 to combat bribery. This document criminalizes any offer, promise, or giving of a bribe to a foreign public official so as to obtain or retain international business deals. As of mid-2011, 39 countries (shown in Exhibit 1.10) had signed this document, and the United States had modified the FCPA to conform to several of the document's provisions. By signing the OECD convention, a country acknowledges that bribery should not be considered an appropriate means of doing business.

Exhibit 1.10 Countries Signing the OECD Anti-Bribery Convention (as of July 2011)

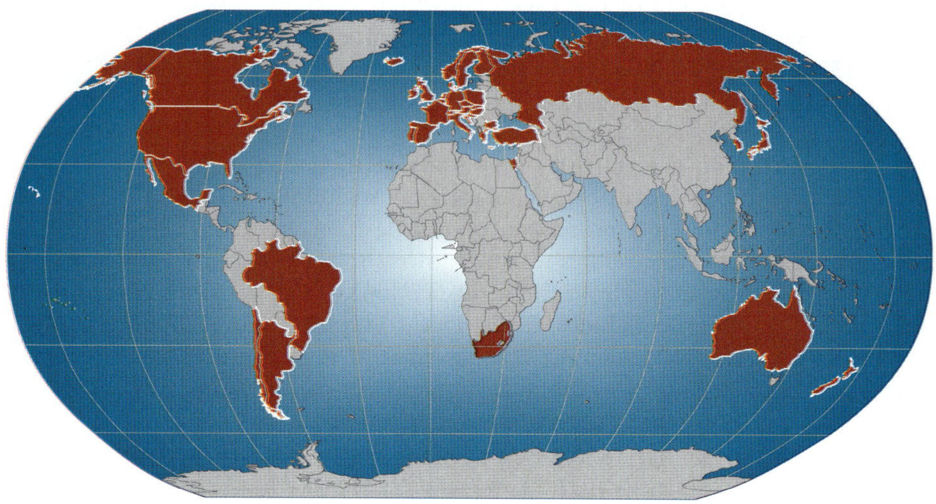

Argentina (2/01)
Australia (10/99)
Austria (5/99)
Belgium (7/99)
Brazil (8/00)
Bulgaria (12/98)
Canada (12/98)
Chile (4/01)
Czech Republic (1/00)
Denmark (9/00)
Estonia (11/04)
Finland (12/98)
France (7/00)
Germany (11/98)
Greece (2/99)
Hungary (12/98)
Iceland (8/98)
Ireland (9/03)
Israel (3/09)
Italy (12/00)
Japan (10/98)
Korea (1/99)
Luxembourg (3/01)
Mexico (5/99)
Netherlands (1/01)
New Zealand (6/01)
Norway (12/98)
Poland (9/00)
Portugal (11/00)
Russia (5/11)
Slovak Republic (9/99)
Slovenia (9/01)
South Africa (6/07)
Spain (1/00)
Sweden (6/99)
Switzerland (5/00)
Turkey (7/00)
United Kingdom (12/98)
United States (12/98)

Slovenia has not yet enacted full implementing legislation.

Source: OECD (Organisation for Economic Co-operation and Development) Convention on Combating Bribery of Foreign Public Officials in International Business Transactions: Ratification Status as of March 2009; http://www.oecd.org/dataoecd/59/13/40272933.pdf (copyright © 2009 OECD) and Khristina Narizhnaya, "Russia Signs OECD Anti-Bribery Convention," *The Moscow Times* (May 26, 2011); http://www.themoscowtimes.com/business/article/russia-signs-oecd-anti-bribery-convention/437585.html.

[12] U.S. Securities and Exchange Commission, Litigation Release No. 20829 (December 15, 2008) and Accounting and Auditing Enforcement Release No. 2911 (December 15, 2008); http://www.sec.gov/litigation/litreleases/2008/lr20829.htm.

[13] M. Goozner, "The 10 Largest Global Business Corruption Cases," *The Fiscal Times* (December 13, 2011); http://www.thefiscaltimes.com/Articles/2011/12/13/The-Ten-Largest-Global-Business-Corruption-Cases.aspx#page1.

Comprehensive Review Module

KEY TERMS

authority, p. 7
balanced scorecard (BSC), p. 10
competence, p. 14
confidentiality, p. 14
core competency, p. 6
cost accounting, p. 2
cost leadership, p. 7
credibility, p. 14
customer value perspective, p. 11
downstream costs, p. 4
earnings management, p. 13
environmental constraint, p. 8
financial performance perspective, p. 12
integrity, p. 14
intellectual capital, p. 8
internal business perspective, p. 11
lag indicators, p. 10
lead indicators, p. 10
learning and growth perspective, p. 11
line personnel, p. 8
management accounting, p. 2
mission statement, p. 5
organizational structure, p. 7
product cost, p. 5
product differentiation, p. 7
responsibility, p. 8
return on investment (ROI), p. 2
service cost, p. 5
service differentiation, p. 7
staff personnel, p. 8
strategy, p. 5
upstream costs, p. 4
value chain, p. 9

CHAPTER SUMMARY

1 Accounting Information, Types

- Accounting
  - provides information to external parties (stockholders, creditors, and various regulatory bodies) for investment and credit decisions.
  - helps an organization estimate the cost of its products and services.
  - provides information useful to internal managers who are responsible for planning, controlling, decision making, and evaluating performance.
- The purposes of financial, management, and cost accounting are as follows:
  - financial accounting is designed to meet external information needs and to comply with generally accepted accounting principles;
  - management accounting is designed to satisfy internal users' information needs; and
  - cost accounting overlaps financial accounting and management accounting by providing product costing information for financial statements and quantitative, disaggregated, cost-based information that managers need to perform their responsibilities.

2 Cost Accounting Standards

- Generally accepted cost accounting standards
  - do not exist for companies that are not engaged in contracts with the federal government; however, the Statements on Management Accounting and Management Accounting Guidelines are well-researched suggestions related to high-quality management accounting practices.
  - are prepared by the Cost Accounting Standards Board for companies engaged in federal government cost/bidding contracts.

3 Mission Statements, Organizational Strategy

- The organizational mission and strategy are important to cost accountants because such statements help to
  - indicate appropriate measures of accomplishment.
  - define the development, implementation, and monitoring processes for the organizational information systems.

- Two common corporate strategies are
  - cost leadership, which refers to maintaining a competitive edge by undercutting competitor prices, and
  - product/service differentiation, which refers to offering (generally at a premium price) superior quality products, more unique services, or a greater number of features than competitors.
- Organizational strategy may be constrained by
  - monetary capital, intellectual capital, and/or technology.
  - environmental factors, such as external cultural, fiscal, legal/regulatory, or political situations (including sustainability concepts).
  - competitive market structures.

4 Organizational Structure

- The organizational structure
  - is composed of people, resources other than people, and commitments that are acquired and arranged relative to authority and responsibility to achieve the organizational mission, strategy, and goals.
  - is used by cost accountants to understand how information is communicated between managers and departments as well as the level of each manager's authority and responsibility.
  - has line personnel who seek to achieve the organizational mission and strategy through balanced scorecard targets.
  - has staff personnel, such as cost accountants, who advise and assist line personnel.
  - is influenced by management style and organizational culture.

5 Value Chain

- The value chain is a set of value-adding functions or processes that convert inputs into products and services for company customers.
- Value chain functions include
  - research and development,
  - product design,
  - supply,
  - production,
  - marketing,
  - distribution, and
  - customer service.

6 Balanced Scorecard

- A balanced scorecard
  - indicates critical goals and targets needed to operationalize strategy.
  - measures success factors for learning and growth, internal business, customer satisfaction, and financial value.
  - includes financial and nonfinancial, internal and external, long- and short-term, and lead and lag indicators.

7 Ethical Standards

- Ethical behavior in organizations is addressed in part in the following items:
  - IMA's *Statement of Ethical Professional Practice*, which refers to issues of competence, confidentiality, integrity, and credibility.
  - Sarbanes-Oxley Act, which requires corporate CEOs and CFOs to sign off on the accuracy of financial reports.
  - False Claims Act, which provides for whistle-blowing protection related to frauds against the U.S. government.

8 Ethical Behavior

- Accountants need to be aware of ethical conduct and laws globally, not just in the United States.
- Ethical behavior has been addressed internationally:
  - The Foreign Corrupt Practices Act and the OECD's Anti-Bribery Convention prohibit companies from offering or giving bribes to foreign officials to influence those individuals to help obtain or retain business.
  - The OECD's Anti-Bribery Convention has been adopted by almost 40 countries worldwide.

POTENTIAL ETHICAL ISSUES

ETHICS

1. Using earnings management techniques to generate materially misleading financial statements
2. Achieving the "low-cost producer" strategy at any sacrifice
3. Retaliating against whistle-blowers within an organization
4. Developing a strategic alliance with another organization that would restrict fair trade (such as by fixing prices)
5. Engaging in bribery or other forms of corruption to obtain or retain business
6. Using accounting practices that hide illegal or improper managerial acts

QUESTIONS

1. Flexibility is said to be the hallmark of modern management accounting, whereas standardization and consistency describe financial accounting. Explain why the focus of these two accounting systems differs.
2. Why are legally binding cost accounting standards more critical for defense contractors than for other entities?
3. Why is a mission statement important to an organization?
4. What is organizational strategy? Why would each organization have a unique strategy or set of strategies?
5. What is a core competency, and how do core competencies impact the feasible set of alternative organizational strategies?
6. Why should a business be concerned with "being green" when polluting might be substantially less expensive—thereby helping in the pursuit of a "low-cost producer" strategy and making that organization's products less expensive for consumers? ETHICS
7. Differentiate between *authority* and *responsibility*. Can a manager have one without the other? Explain.
8. "If an organization can borrow money or sell stock, it does not have a capital constraint." Is this statement true or false? Discuss the rationale for your answer.
9. How does workplace diversity affect organizational culture? Include in your answer a discussion of both the potential benefits and the potential difficulties of hiring workers with diverse backgrounds.
10. How can a change in governmental laws or regulations create a strategic opportunity for an organization? Give an example.
11. What is an organization's value chain, and how does it interface with strategy?
12. What is a balanced scorecard? How is a balanced scorecard more useful than return on investment in implementing and monitoring strategy in a global economy?
13. Why would operating in a global (rather than a strictly domestic) marketplace create a need for additional information for managers? Discuss some of the additional information managers would need and why such information would be valuable.
14. What ethical issues might affect a U.S. company considering opening a business in Venezuela? ETHICS

EXERCISES

15. **LO.1 (Interview; research)** Call a local company and set up an interview with the firm's cost or management accountant. The following questions can be used as starting points for the interview:
    - What is your educational background?
    - What was your career path to attain this position?
    - What are your most frequently recurring tasks?
    - What aspects of your job do you find to be the most fun? The most challenging?
    - What college courses would be the most helpful in preparing a person for your job? Why did you select these courses?

    a. Compare and contrast your interview answers with those of other students in the class.
    b. Which one or two items from the interview were of the most benefit to you? Why?

16. **LO.1 (Organizational accountants; research; writing)** Use library or Internet resources to find how the jobs of management accountants have changed in the past 10 years. INTERNET

    a. Prepare a "then-versus-now" comparison.
    b. What five skills do you believe are the most important for management accountants to possess? Discuss the rationale for your choices. Do you think these skills have changed over the past 10 years? Why or why not?

17. **LO.1 (Accounting information; writing)** You are a partner in a local accounting firm that does financial planning and prepares tax returns, payroll, and financial reports for

medium-size companies. Your monthly financial statements show that your organization is consistently profitable. Cash flow is becoming a small problem, however, and you need to borrow from your bank. You have also been receiving some customer complaints about time delays and price increases.

a. What accounting information do you think is most important to take with you to discuss a possible loan with your banker?
b. What accounting information do you think is most important to address the issues of time delays and price increases in your business? What nonaccounting information is important?
c. Can the information in parts (a) and (b) be gathered from the organization's books and records directly? Indirectly? If the information cannot be obtained from internal records, where would you obtain such information?

INTERNET

18. **LO.3 (Strategic information; research; writing)** Select a multinational manufacturing company and access its three most recent annual financial reports. Assume that you have just been offered a position as this company's CFO. Use the information in the annual report (or 10-K) to develop answers to each of the following questions.
    a. What is the company's mission?
    b. What is the company's strategy? Does it differ from the strategy of two years ago?
    c. What are the company's core competencies?
    d. What are the value chain processes for this company?
    e. What products (services) does the company manufacture (offer)?
    f. What is the company's organizational structure? Prepare an organizational chart.
    g. What would be your top priorities for this company in the coming year?
    h. Based on your findings, would you accept employment? Why or why not?

19. **LO.3 (Mission statement; writing)** You have managed Indiana's Best Appliances franchises for 15 years and have 100 employees. Business has been profitable, but you are concerned that the Indianapolis locations could soon experience a downturn in growth. You have decided to prepare for such an event by engaging in a higher level of strategic planning, beginning with a company mission statement.
    a. How does a mission statement add strength to the strategic planning process?
    b. Who should be involved in developing a mission statement and why?
    c. What factors should be considered in the development of a mission statement? Why are these factors important?
    d. Prepare a mission statement for Best Appliances and discuss how your mission statement will provide benefits to strategic planning.

20. **LO.3 (Mission statement; research; writing)** Obtain a copy of the mission statement of your college or university. Draft a mission statement for this cost accounting class that supports the school's mission statement.
    a. How does your mission statement reflect the goals and objectives of the college mission statement?
    b. How can the successful accomplishment of your college's objectives be measured?

21. **LO.3 (Strategy; writing)** You are the manager of a small restaurant in your hometown.
    a. What information would you obtain for making the decision of whether to add quiche and rack of lamb to your menu?
    b. Why would each of the information items in (a) be significant?

22. **LO.3 (Core competencies; group activity; research)** In a team of three or four people, list the core competencies of your local public school district and explain why these items are core competencies. Make an appointment with the principal of one of the high schools or the superintendent of the public school system and, without sharing your team's list, ask this individual what he or she believes the core competencies to be and why. Prepare a written or video presentation that summarizes, compares, and contrasts all of the competencies on your lists. Share copies of your presentation with the individuals whom you contacted.

23. **LO.3 (Organizational constraints; writing)** Three common organizational constraints are monetary capital, intellectual capital, and technology. Additionally, the environment in which the organization operates may present one or more types of constraints: cultural, fiscal, legal/regulatory, or political.

    a. Discuss whether each of these constraints would be influential in the following types of organizations:

        (1) city hall of a major metropolitan city
        (2) a franchised quick-copy business
        (3) a new firm of attorneys, all of whom recently graduated from law school
        (4) an international oil exploration and production company

    b. For each of the previously listed organizations, discuss your perceptions about which of the constraints would be most critical and why.

INTERNET

24. **LO.3 (Strategy; research; writing)** Choose a company that might use each of the following strategies relative to its competitors and discuss the benefits that might be realized from that strategy. Indicate the industry in which the company does business, the company's primary competitors, and whether a code of conduct or corporate governance appears on its Web site.

    a. Differentiation
    b. Cost leadership

ETHICS

25. **LO.3 (Mission statement; writing)** Mission statements are intended to indicate what an organization does and why it exists. Some of them, however, are simply empty words with little or no substance used by few people to guide their activities.

    a. Does an organization really need a mission statement? Explain the rationale for your answer.
    b. How could a mission statement help an organization in its pursuit of evoking ethical behavior from employees?
    c. How could a mission statement help an organization in its pursuit of making high-quality products and providing high levels of customer service?

INTERNET

26. **LO.3 (Strategy; research; writing)** Select a major manufacturing company. Use library, Internet, or other resources to answer as completely as possible the questions in Exhibit 1.5 about the manufacturer you have chosen.

27. **LO.3 (Strategy; writing)** You are the manager of a large home improvement store. What are the five factors that you believe are most critical to your store's success? How would these factors influence your store's strategy?

28. **LO.4 (Organizational structure; writing)** Early this year, you started a financial planning services firm and now have 20 clients. Because of other obligations (including attending classes in pursuit of an advanced degree), you have hired three employees to help service the clients.

    a. What types of business activities would you empower these employees to handle and why?
    b. What types of business activities would you keep for yourself and why?

29. **LO.5 (Value chain; writing)** Strategic alliances represent an important value chain arrangement. In many organizations, suppliers are beginning to provide more and more input into customer activities.

    a. In the United States, would a strategic alliance ever be considered illegal? Explain.
    b. What do you perceive are the primary reasons for pursuing a strategic alliance?
    c. With whom might the manager of a catalog company selling flowers and plants want to establish strategic alliances? What issues might the manager want to consider prior to engaging in the alliance?

30. **LO.5 (Value chain; writing)** You are the management accountant for a small company that makes and distributes hot sauce. You have been asked to prepare a presentation that will illustrate the company's value chain.
    a. What activities or types of companies would you include in the upstream (supplier) part of the value chain?
    b. What activities would you include in the internal value chain?
    c. What activities or types of companies would you include in the downstream (distribution and retailing) part of the value chain?

31. **LO.6 (Balanced scorecard; writing)** You attended a conference on the balanced scorecard last week and your manager has asked you to prepare a short report to answer the following questions.
    a. Why is a balanced scorecard used in a business?
    b. What are some benefits of a balanced scorecard approach to measuring organizational performance?
    c. What are some disadvantages of using a balanced scorecard approach?

ETHICS

32. **LO.7 (Ethics; writing)** In pursuing organizational strategy, cost and management accountants want to instill trust between and among themselves and their constituents, including other organizational members and the independent auditing firm. The IMA has a code of conduct for management accountants.
    a. List and explain each of the major guidelines of the IMA's code.
    b. What steps should a cost or management accountant who detects unethical behavior by his or her supervisor take before deciding to resign?

ETHICS

33. **LO.8 (Ethics; writing)** Accounting has a long history of being an ethical profession. In recent years, however, some companies have asked their accountants to help "manage earnings."
    a. Who is more likely to be involved in managing earnings: the financial or management accountant? Why?
    b. Do you believe that "managing earnings" is ethical? Discuss the rationale for your answer.

ETHICS

34. **LO.8 (Ethics; writing)** You are a senior manager at Giganto Inc. All senior managers and the board of directors are scheduled to meet next week to discuss some questionable manipulations of earnings that were found by the outside independent auditors. The CEO has asked you to be prepared to start the discussion by developing questions that should be addressed before responding to the auditors.
    a. Why would the CEO be concerned about earnings management? After all, it is the auditor who attests to the fair presentation of financial reporting.
    b. If the earnings management were deemed to be "abusive" and you decided to resign and blow the whistle, would you have any protection? Explain.

ETHICS

35. **LO.8 (Ethics; writing)** "Few trends could so thoroughly undermine the very foundation of our free society," wrote Milton Friedman in *Capitalism and Freedom* (Chicago: University of Chicago Press, 1962), "as the acceptance by corporate officials of a social responsibility other than to make as much money for their shareholders as possible."
    a. Discuss your reactions to this quote from a legal standpoint.
    b. Discuss your reactions to this quote from an ethical standpoint.
    c. How would you resolve any conflicts that exist between your two answers?

ETHICS

36. **LO.8 (Ethics; writing)** Intellectual capital is extremely important to an organization's longevity. There are, however, "intellectual capital pirates" who make their living from stealing.
    a. Assume you have made several popular music recordings that are being pirated overseas. Discuss your feelings about these intellectual capital pirates and what (if anything) should be done to them.

b. Copying a copyrighted computer software program is also intellectual capital piracy. Do you perceive any difference between this type of copying and the copying of music recordings? Discuss the rationale for your answer.

37. **LO.8 (Ethics)** The Foreign Corrupt Practices Act prohibits U.S. firms from giving bribes to officials in foreign countries, although bribery is customary in some countries. Non-U.S. companies operating in foreign countries are not necessarily similarly restricted; thus, adherence to the FCPA could make competing with non-U.S. firms more difficult in foreign countries. Do you think bribery should be considered so repugnant that American companies should be asked to forgo a foreign custom and, hence, the profits that could be obtained through observance of the custom? Prepare both a pro and a con position for your answer, assuming you will be asked to defend one position or the other.

ETHICS

38. **LO.8 (Ethics; writing)** You have recently been elected president of the United States. One of your most popular positions is that you want to reduce the costs of doing business in the United States. When asked how you intend to accomplish this, you reply, "By seeking to repeal all laws that create unnecessary costs. Repealing such laws will be good not only for business but also for the consumer since product costs, and therefore selling prices, will be reduced." Congress heard the message loud and clear and has decided to repeal all environmental protection laws.

ETHICS

   a. Discuss the short- and long-term implications of such a policy.
   b. How would such a policy affect the global competitiveness of U.S. companies?
   c. What reactions would you expect to such a policy from (1) other industrialized nations and (2) developing countries?

39. **LO.8 (Ethics; research; writing)** Use library or Internet resources to find the major international stock exchanges on which **Volkswagen AG** is listed. Write a short paper on the complexities relative to ethics of listing on stock exchanges across multiple countries.

ETHICS

INTERNET

2

Cost Terminology and Cost Behaviors

LEARNING OBJECTIVES

After completing this chapter, you should be able to answer the following questions:

1. Why are costs associated with a cost object?
2. What assumptions do accountants make about cost behavior, and why are these assumptions necessary?
3. How are costs classified on the financial statements, and why are such classifications useful?
4. How does the conversion process occur in manufacturing and service companies?
5. What are the product cost categories, and what items comprise those categories?
6. How and why does overhead need to be allocated to products?
7. How is cost of goods manufactured calculated and used in preparing an income statement?

INTRODUCTION

No product can be produced without the incurrence of costs for material, labor, and overhead. At a minimum, no service can be produced without the incurrence of costs for labor and overhead; a cost for material may or may not be involved. **Cost** reflects the monetary measure of resources consumed to attain an objective such as making a good or performing a service. However, the term *cost* must be defined more specifically before "the cost" of a product or service can be determined and communicated to others. Thus, a clarifying adjective is generally used to specify the type of cost being considered. For example, the balance sheet value of an asset is an **unexpired cost**, but the portion of an asset's value consumed or sacrificed during a period is an expense or **expired cost**, which is shown on the income statement. Thus, when supplies are purchased, they represent an asset and an unexpired cost. As the supplies are consumed, the fact is recorded in supplies expense, an expired cost.

To effectively communicate information, accountants must clearly understand the differences among various types of costs, how those costs are computed, and how those costs are used. This chapter provides the necessary terminology for understanding and communicating cost and management accounting information. Additionally, cost flows and the process of cost accumulation in a production environment are presented.

COST TERMINOLOGY

A **cost management system** is a set of formal methods developed for planning and controlling an organization's cost-generating activities relative to its strategy, goals, and objectives. This system is designed to communicate all value chain functions about product costs, product profitability, cost management, strategy implementation, and management performance. Cost concepts and terms have been developed to facilitate this communication process. Some important types of costs are summarized in Exhibit 2.1.

Exhibit 2.1 Cost Classification Categories

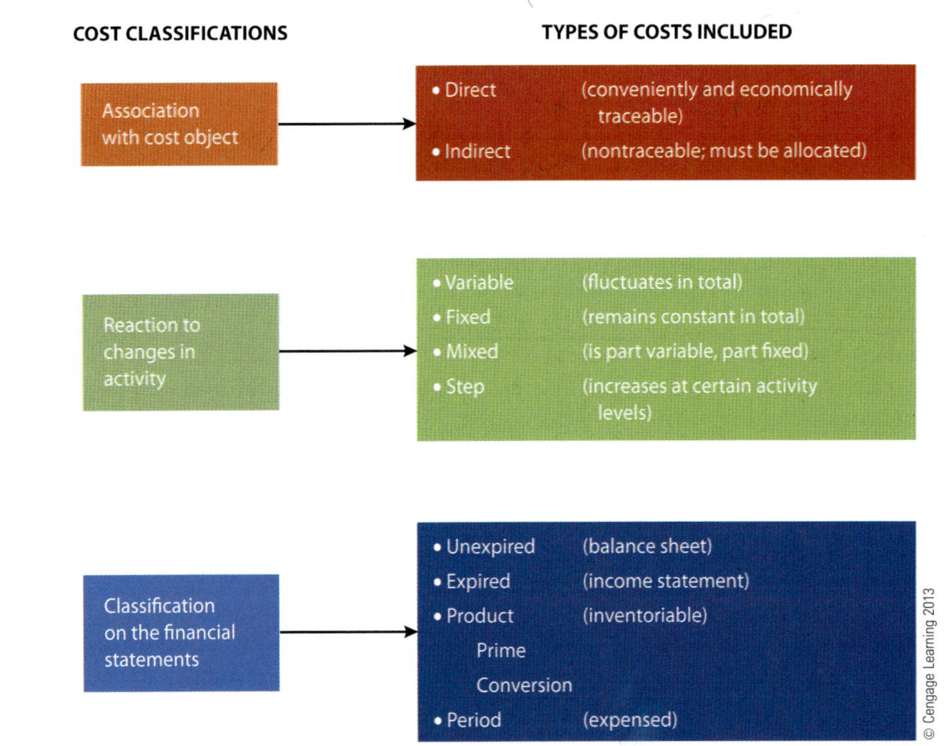

Association with Cost Object

1 Why are costs associated with a cost object?

A **cost object** is anything for which management wants to collect or accumulate costs. Production operations and service lines are common cost objects. For example, **Toyota**'s Princeton, Indiana, plant makes Highlander and Sequoia SUVs and Sienna minivans.

Company managers could define the plant as the cost object and request information about production costs for a specific period; alternatively, managers could define the Highlander SUV as the cost object and request information about production costs during the same period. In the first situation, production costs of all types of vehicles would be included in the information report, whereas in the second situation, production costs for Sequoia SUVs and Sienna minivans would be excluded from the report. Collecting costs in different ways can help management make decisions regarding the efficiency of operations at the Princeton plant or the cost management effectiveness in producing the Highlander or other types of vehicles.

Costs of making a product or performing a service are appropriately labeled product or service costs. The costs associated with any cost object can be classified according to their relationship to the cost object. **Direct costs** are conveniently and economically traceable to the cost object. If management requested cost data about the Highlander, direct costs would include tires, sheet metal, CD player, leather, paint, and production line labor.

Indirect costs cannot be economically traced to the cost object but instead are allocated to the cost object. For example, Toyota uses glue in manufacturing Highlanders, but tracing that material would not be cost effective because the cost amount is insignificant. The clerical and information-processing costs of tracing the glue cost to products would exceed any informational benefits that management might obtain from the information. Thus, glue cost for each SUV would be classified as an indirect cost.

Classification of a cost as direct or indirect depends on the cost object specification. For example, if the Princeton plant is specified as the cost object, then the plant's depreciation is directly traceable. However, if the cost object is specified as the Highlander, then the plant's depreciation cost is not directly traceable, in which case the depreciation is classified as indirect and must be allocated to the cost object.

Reaction to Changes in Activity

2 What assumptions do accountants make about cost behavior, and why are these assumptions necessary?

To manage costs, accountants must understand how total (rather than unit) cost behaves relative to a change in a related activity measure. Common activity measures include production volume, service and sales volumes, hours of machine or service time consumed, pounds of material moved, and number of purchase orders processed.

Every organizational cost will change if sufficient time passes or if an extreme shift in activity level occurs. Thus, to properly identify, analyze, and use cost behavior information, a time frame is specified to indicate how far into the future a cost should be examined and a particular range of activity is assumed. For example, the cost of a set of Highlander tires might be expected to increase by $25 next year but by $80 in the year 2016. When Toyota estimates production costs for next year, the $25 increase would be relevant, but the $80 increase would be irrelevant. The assumed range of activity that reflects the company's normal operating range is referred to as the **relevant range**. Within the relevant range, the two primary cost behaviors are variable and fixed.

A cost that varies in total proportionately with activity is a **variable cost**. Accordingly, a variable cost is a constant amount per unit. Relative to volume of product or number of customers serviced, examples of variable costs include the costs of material, hourly wages, and sales commissions. Variable costs are extremely important to a company's total profitability because each time a product is produced or sold, or a service is rendered, a specific amount of variable cost is incurred.

Although accountants view variable costs as linear relative to activity volume, economists view these costs as curvilinear as shown in Exhibit 2.2. The cost line slopes upward at a given rate until a volume is reached at which the unit cost becomes fairly constant. Within this relevant range, the firm experiences stable effects on costs such as material price discounts and worker skill and productivity. Beyond the relevant range, the slope becomes quite steep as the firm enters a range of activity in which operations become inefficient and production capacity is overutilized. In this range, the firm finds that costs rise rapidly because of worker crowding, equipment shortages, and other operating inefficiencies. Although the curvilinear graph is more correct, it is awkward to use in planning or controlling costs. Accordingly, accountants choose the range in which these variable costs are assumed to behave as they are defined, and as such, the assumed cost behavior is an approximation of reality.

Exhibit 2.2 Economic Representation of a Variable Cost

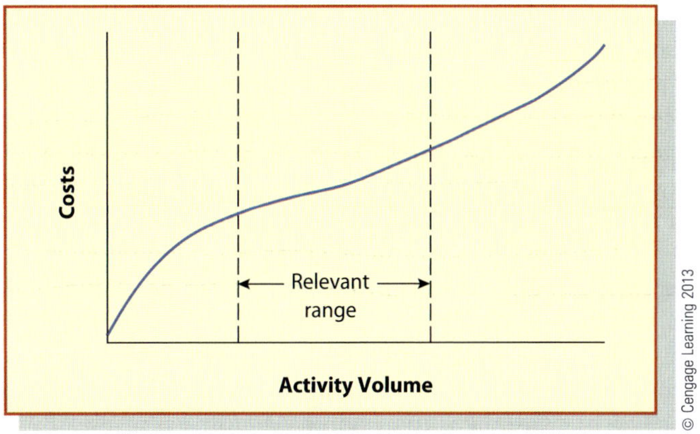

To illustrate a variable cost, assume that the battery used in Highlanders costs $50 within the relevant production range of 0–120,000 SUVs annually. (At higher levels of activity, the price could decrease because of a volume discount from the supplier or increase because the supplier's capacity would be exhausted.) Within this relevant range, total battery cost can be calculated as $50 times the number of Highlanders produced. For instance, if 15,000 Highlanders were produced in October, total variable cost of batteries would be $750,000 ($50 × 15,000).

In contrast, a cost that remains constant in total within the relevant range of activity is considered a **fixed cost**. Many fixed costs are incurred to provide a firm's production capacity. Fixed costs include salaries (as opposed to hourly wages), depreciation (computed using the straight-line method), and insurance. On a per-unit basis, a fixed cost varies inversely with changes in the level of activity: the per-unit fixed cost decreases with increases in the activity level and increases with decreases in the activity level.

To illustrate how to determine the total and unit amounts of a fixed cost, suppose that Toyota rents some Highlander manufacturing equipment for $12,000,000 per year. The equipment has a maximum annual output capacity of 150,000 Highlanders. If Toyota expects to produce 120,000 Highlanders per year, its annual equipment rental is a fixed cost of $12,000,000 and its equipment rental expense per Highlander is $100 ($12,000,000 ÷ 120,000). However, if Toyota produces 125,000 Highlanders in a year, total equipment rental expense remains at $12,000,000, but rental expense per SUV decreases to $96 ($12,000,000 ÷ 125,000). The total equipment rental cost remains constant as the level of activity changes within the relevant range of production, but equipment rental cost per unit declines from $100 to $96 as the level of Highlanders produced increases from 120,000 to 125,000. The respective total cost and unit cost definitions for variable and fixed cost behaviors are presented in Exhibit 2.3.

Exhibit 2.3 Comparative Total and Unit Cost Behavior Definitions

	Total Cost	Unit Cost
Variable Cost	Varies in direct proportion to changes in activity	Is constant throughout the relevant range
Fixed Cost	Remains constant throughout the relevant range	Varies inversely with changes in activity throughout the relevant range

From period to period, fixed costs may change. Business volume will increase or decrease sufficiently that production capacity will be added or sold. Alternatively, management could decide to "trade" fixed and variable costs for one another. For example, a company installing new automated production equipment would incur a substantial additional fixed cost for depreciation but would eliminate (or reduce) the variable cost for hourly production workers' wages. In contrast, a company outsourcing its data processing function would eliminate the fixed costs of data processing equipment depreciation and personnel salaries but incur a variable cost based on transaction volume. Whether variable costs are traded for fixed costs or vice versa, a shift from one type of cost behavior to another type changes a company's basic cost structure and can have a significant impact on profits.

Other costs exist that are not strictly variable or fixed. A **mixed cost** has both a variable and a fixed component. On a per-unit basis, a mixed cost does not fluctuate proportionately with changes in activity nor does it remain constant with changes in activity. An electric bill that is computed as a flat charge for basic service (the fixed component) plus a stated rate for each kilowatt hour of usage (the variable component) is an example of a mixed cost. Exhibit 2.4 graphs a firm's electric bill, assuming a cost of $5,000 per month plus $0.018 per kilowatt hour (kWh) consumed. In a month when the firm uses 80,000 kWh of electricity, the total electricity bill is $6,440 [$5,000 + ($0.018 × 80,000)]. If the firm uses 90,000 kWh, the total electricity bill is $6,620 [$5,000 + ($0.018 × 90,000)].

Exhibit 2.4 Graph of a Mixed Cost

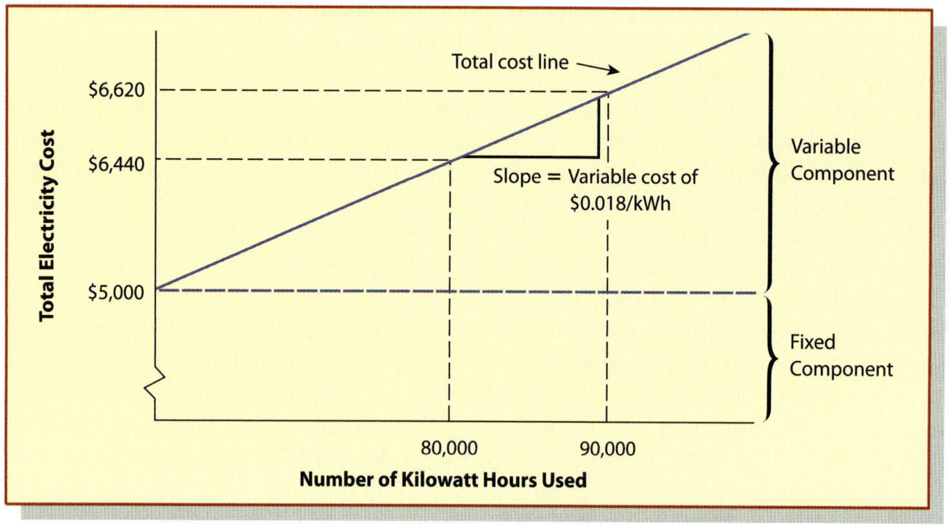

A **step cost** shifts upward or downward when activity changes by a certain interval or "step." A step cost can be variable or fixed. Step variable costs have small steps; step fixed costs have large steps. For instance, a water bill computed as $0.002 per gallon for up to 1,000 gallons, $0.003 per gallon for 1,001–2,000 gallons, and $0.005 per gallon for 2,001–3,000 gallons is a step variable cost. In contrast, the salary cost for airline reservations agents is a step fixed cost. Assume that each agent is paid $3,200 per month and can serve a maximum of 1,000 customers per month. If airline monthly volume increases from 3,500 customers to 6,000 customers, the airline will need six reservations agents rather than four. Each additional 1,000 customers will result in an additional step fixed cost of $3,200.

Understanding the types of behavior exhibited by costs is necessary to make valid estimates of total costs at various activity levels. Variable, fixed, and mixed costs are the typical types of cost behavior encountered in business. Cost accountants generally separate mixed costs into their variable and fixed components so that the behavior of these costs is more readily apparent.[1] For step variable or step fixed costs, accountants must choose a specific relevant range of activity to use for analysis so that the step variable costs can be treated as variable and step fixed costs can be treated as fixed.

By separating mixed costs into their variable and fixed components and by specifying a time period and relevant range, cost accountants force all costs into either variable or fixed categories. Assuming a variable cost is constant per unit and a fixed cost is constant in total

[1] Separation of mixed costs is discussed in Chapter 3.

within the relevant range can be justified for two reasons. First, if a company operates only in the relevant range of activity, the assumed conditions approximate reality. Second, selection of a constant per-unit variable cost and a constant total fixed cost provides a convenient, stable function for use in planning, controlling, and decision-making activities.

Accountants use activities as predictors of cost changes. A **predictor** is an activity that, when changed, is accompanied by a consistent, observable change in a cost item. However, simply because two items change together does not prove that the predictor causes the change in cost. For instance, assume that every time you see a Highlander commercial during a sports event, the home team wins the game. If this is consistent, observable behavior, you can use a Highlander commercial to predict the winning team—but viewing the commercial does not cause the team to win!

In contrast, a predictor that has an absolute cause-and-effect relationship to a cost is called a **cost driver**. For example, production volume has a direct effect on the total cost of raw material used and can be said to "drive" that cost. Exhibit 2.5 plots production volume on the *x*-axis and raw material cost on the *y*-axis to show the linear cause-and-effect relationship between production volume and total raw material cost. This exhibit also illustrates the variable cost characteristic of raw material cost: the same amount of raw material cost is incurred for each unit produced. If the raw material is assumed to be engines and the units produced are assumed to be Highlanders, this illustration shows that as total Highlander production rises, total engine cost also rises proportionally. Thus, planned Highlander production volume could be used to predict total engine cost.

Exhibit 2.5 Total Raw Material Cost Relative to Production Volume

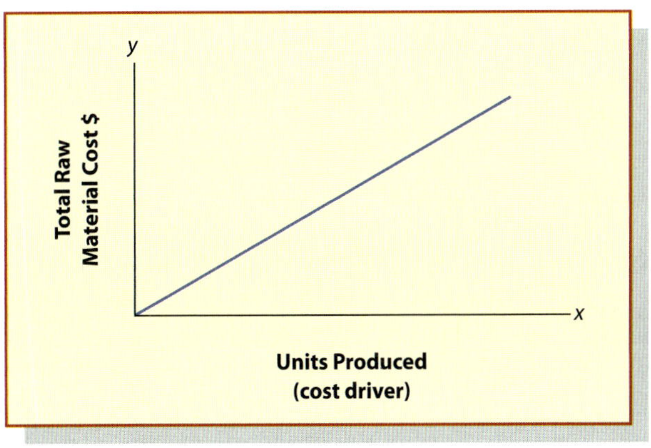

In most situations, the cause-and-effect relationship between a cost and a driver is less clear than as illustrated by engine cost and Highlander production because multiple factors commonly cause cost incurrence. For example, in addition to production volume, factors such as material quality, worker skill levels, and level of automation affect product spoilage cost. Although determining which factor actually caused a specific change in spoilage cost can be difficult, any of these factors could be chosen to predict that cost if confidence exists about the factor's relationship with cost changes. To be used as a predictor, the factor and the cost need only change together in a reliable manner.

Traditionally, a single predictor was often used to predict costs, but accountants and managers have realized that single predictors do not necessarily provide the most reliable forecasts. This realization has caused a movement toward activity-based costing (covered in Chapter 4), which uses multiple cost drivers to predict different costs. Production volume, for instance, would be a valid cost driver for Highlander rearview mirrors, but sales volume would be a more realistic driver for Toyota's sales commissions cost.

Classification on the Financial Statements

3 How are costs classified on the financial statements, and why are such classifications useful?

The balance sheet and income statement are two basic financial statements. The balance sheet is a statement of unexpired costs (assets), liabilities, and owners' equity; the income statement is a statement of revenues and expired costs (expenses and losses). The concept of matching revenues and expenses on the income statement is central to financial accounting.

The matching concept provides a basis for deciding when an unexpired cost becomes an expired cost and is moved from an asset category to an expense or loss category.

Expenses and losses differ because expenses are intentionally incurred in the process of generating revenues, but losses are unintentionally incurred in the context of business operations. Cost of goods sold, advertising, and estimated product warranty costs are examples of expenses. Costs incurred for fire damage or abnormal production waste are examples of losses, as is selling a machine for less than book value.

When a product is the cost object, all costs can be classified as either product or period. **Product costs** are related to making or acquiring the products or providing the services that directly generate the revenues of an entity; **period costs** are related to business functions other than production, such as selling and administration.

Product costs are also called **inventoriable costs** and include direct costs (direct material and direct labor) and indirect costs (**overhead**). Precise classification of some costs into one of these categories can be difficult and requires judgment; however, the following definitions (with Highlander examples) are useful. Any material that can be easily and economically traced to a product is a **direct material**. Direct material includes raw material (sheet metal), purchased components from contract manufacturers (batteries), and manufactured subassemblies (engines and transmissions). **Direct labor** refers to the time spent by individuals who work specifically on manufacturing a product or performing a service. The people bolting the chassis to the frame are considered direct labor, and their associated wages are direct labor costs. Any production cost that is indirect to the product or service is considered overhead. This cost element includes Toyota factory supervisors' salaries as well as depreciation, insurance, and utility costs on production machinery, equipment, and facilities. The sum of direct labor and overhead costs is referred to as **conversion cost**—those costs that are incurred to convert materials into products. The sum of direct material and direct labor cost is referred to as **prime cost**.[2]

Period costs are associated with a particular time period rather than with making or acquiring a product or performing a service. Period costs that have future benefit are classified as assets, whereas those having no future benefit are expenses (or losses). Prepaid insurance for an administration building represents an unexpired cost; when the insured period ends, the insurance becomes an expired or period cost (insurance expense). Salaries paid to the salesforce and depreciation on computers in company headquarters are also expired period costs.

One important type of period cost is that of distribution. A **distribution cost** is any cost incurred to warehouse, transport, or deliver a product or service. Financial accounting rules require that distribution costs be expensed as incurred. However, managers should remember that these costs relate directly to products and services and should not adopt an "out-of-sight, out-of-mind" attitude about these costs simply because of the way they are handled under generally accepted accounting principles (GAAP). Distribution costs must be considered in relationship to product/service volume, and these costs must be managed well for profitability to result from sales. Thus, even though distribution costs are not technically product costs, they can have a major impact on management decision making. For example, **Teevin Bros. Land and Timber Company** views its rail, water, and interstate access as providing a cost advantage for its timber and rock products over its competitors.

THE CONVERSION PROCESS

4 How does the conversion process occur in manufacturing and service companies?

To some extent, all organizations convert or change inputs into outputs. Inputs typically consist of material, labor, and overhead. In general, product costs are incurred in the production (or conversion) area and period costs are incurred in all nonproduction (or nonconversion) areas.[3] Conversion process outputs are usually either products or services.

[2] In the past, direct material and direct labor cost represented the largest percentage of production cost. In the current automated production environment, direct labor cost has become a very low percentage of product cost, and thus, "prime cost" has lost much of its significance.

[3] It is less common but possible for a cost incurred outside the production area to be in direct support of production and therefore considered a product cost. An example of this situation is the salary of a product cost analyst who is based at corporate headquarters; this salary would be considered part of overhead.

See Exhibit 2.6 for a comparison of the conversion activities of different types of organizations. Note that many service companies engage in a high degree of conversion. Firms of professionals (such as accountants, architects, or attorneys) convert labor and other resource inputs (material and overhead) into completed services (audit reports, building plans, or contracts).

Exhibit 2.6 Degrees of Conversion in Firms

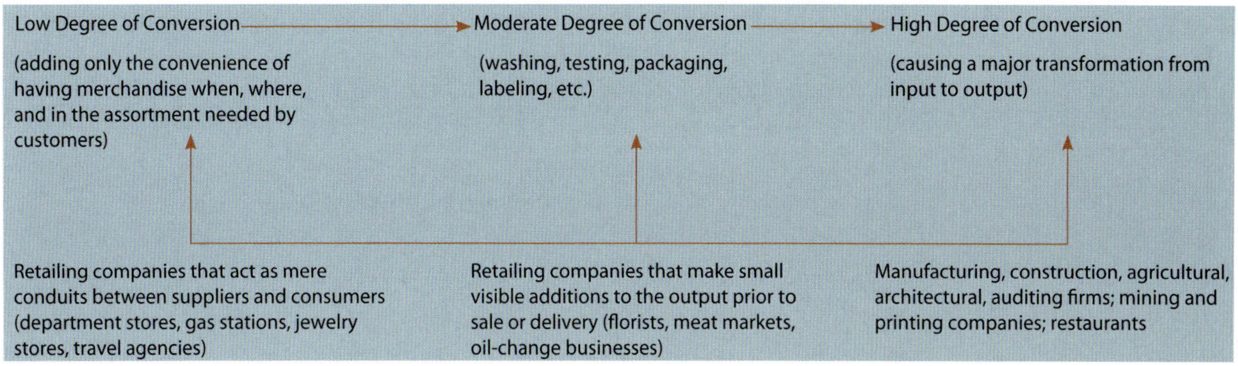

Firms that engage in only low or moderate degrees of conversion can conveniently expense insignificant conversion costs of labor and overhead as period costs. The clerical cost savings from expensing outweigh the value of any slightly improved information that might result from assigning such costs to products or services. For example, when retail employees open shipping containers, hang clothing on racks, and tag merchandise with sales tickets, a labor cost for conversion is incurred. However, clothing stores do not attach the stock workers' wages to inventory; such labor costs are treated as period costs and expensed when incurred. The major distinction of retail firms relative to service and manufacturing firms is that retailers have much lower degrees of conversion than the other two types of firms.

In contrast, in high-conversion firms, the informational benefits gained from accumulating the material, labor, and overhead costs incurred to produce output significantly exceed clerical accumulation costs. For instance, when constructing a house, certain types of costs are quite significant (see Exhibit 2.7). The exhibit indicates that the clerical cost of accumulating direct labor costs is only \$165 (0.22 × \$750). Direct labor cost of \$50,000 (0.25 × \$200,000) is accumulated as a separate component of product cost because the amount is material and requires management's cost-control attention. Furthermore, direct labor cost is inventoried as part of the cost of the construction job until the house is complete.

Exhibit 2.7 Building Construction Costs

	Manufacturing Cost	Clerical Cost
Direct material	40%	34%
Direct labor	25%	22%
Manufacturing overhead	35%	44%
Total cost	$200,000	$750

A **manufacturer** can be defined as any company engaged in a high degree of conversion of raw material input into a tangible output. Manufacturers typically use people and machines to convert raw material to output that has substance and can, if desired, be physically inspected. A **service company** is a firm that uses a significant amount of labor to engage in a high or moderate degree of conversion. A service company's output can be tangible (an architectural drawing) or intangible (insurance protection). Service firms can be either for-profit businesses or not-for-profit organizations.

Retailers versus Manufacturers/Service Companies

Retail companies purchase goods in finished or almost finished condition, so that little, if any, conversion is needed before the goods are sold to customers. Costs associated with such inventory are usually easy to determine, as are the valuations for financial statement presentation. Retail stores that engage in only low or moderate degrees of conversion ordinarily have only one inventory account (Merchandise Inventory).

In comparison, manufacturers or service companies engage in activities that involve the physical transformation of inputs into finished products or services. The materials or supplies and conversion costs of manufacturers and service companies must be assigned to output to determine the cost of both inventory produced and goods sold or services rendered. Cost accounting provides the structure and process for assigning material and conversion costs to products and services. The production or conversion process occurs in three stages:

1. work not started (**raw material**),
2. work started but not completed (**work in process**), and
3. work completed (**finished goods**).

Thus, manufacturers normally use three types of inventory accounts to accumulate costs as goods flow through the manufacturing process:

1. Raw Material Inventory (may include direct and indirect materials, e.g., supplies),
2. Work in Process Inventory (for partially converted goods), and
3. Finished Goods Inventory.

Exhibit 2.8 compares the input–output relationships of a retail company with those of a manufacturing/service company. This exhibit illustrates that the primary difference between retail companies and manufacturing/service companies is the absence or presence of the area labeled "The Production Center." In a production center, input factors (raw material, supplies, and parts) enter, are transformed, and are stored until the goods or services are completed. If the output is a product, it can be warehoused or displayed until sold. Service outputs are directly provided to the client commissioning the work. Retail companies normally incur very limited conversion time, effort, and cost compared to manufacturing or service companies. Thus, although a retailer could have a department (such as one that adds store name labels to goods) that might be viewed as a "mini" production center, most often retailers have no designated "production center."

Costs are associated with each processing stage. The stages of production in a manufacturing firm and some of the costs associated with each stage are illustrated in Exhibit 2.9 (on page 34). In the first stage of processing, the costs incurred reflect the prices paid for raw materials and/or supplies and quantities purchased. As work progresses through the second stage, accrual-based accounting requires that labor and overhead costs related to the conversion of raw materials or supplies be accumulated and attached to the goods. Accumulating costs in appropriate inventory accounts allows businesses to match the costs of buying or manufacturing a product or providing a service with the revenues generated when the goods or services are sold. The total costs incurred in stages 1 and 2 equal the total production cost of finished goods in stage 3. At the point of sale, these product or service costs will flow from an inventory account to Cost of Goods Sold or Cost of Services Rendered on the income statement.

Manufacturers versus Service Companies

Several differences in accounting for conversion activities exist between a manufacturer and a service company. Whereas manufacturers normally use three inventory accounts, service firms may have either one or two inventory accounts. The "work not started" stage of processing normally consists of the cost of supplies needed to perform the services; these costs are accounted for in a Supplies Inventory account. When supplies are placed into work in process, labor and overhead are added to complete the conversion process; all of these costs may be accumulated in a Work in Process Inventory account. However, service firms do not normally have a Finished Goods Inventory account because most services cannot be warehoused. If collection is yet to be made for a completed and delivered service

Exhibit 2.8 Business Input–Output Relationships

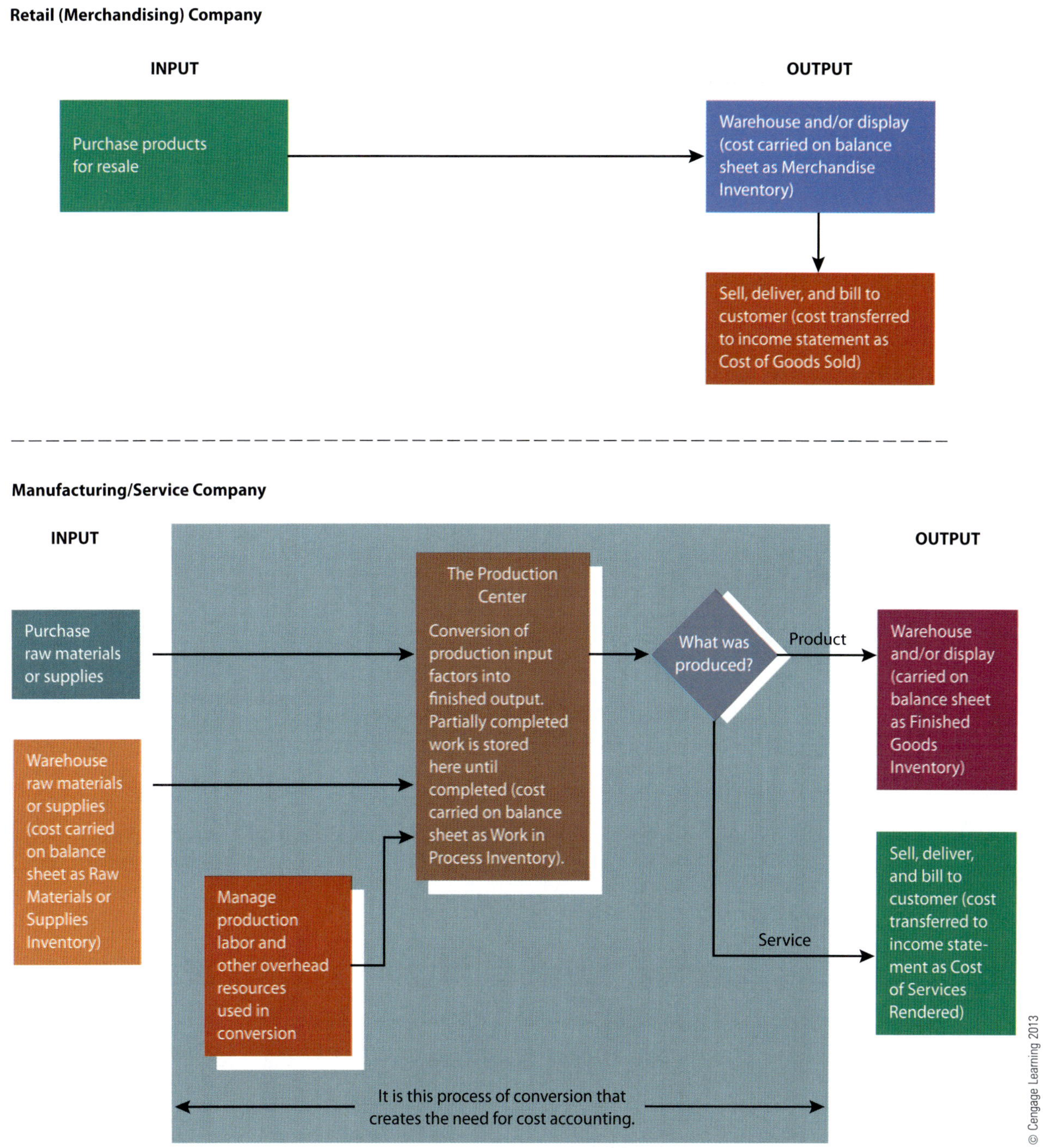

engagement, the service firm has a receivable from its client but no Finished Goods Inventory. The costs of finished jobs are usually transferred immediately to the income statement to be matched against service revenue. Determining the cost of services provided is extremely important in both profit-oriented service businesses and not-for-profit entities. For instance, architectural firms need to accumulate the costs incurred for designs and models of each project, and hospitals need to accumulate the costs of x-rays, MRIs, or other medical treatments for each patient.

Despite the accounting differences among retailers, manufacturers, and service firms, each type of organization can use management and cost accounting concepts and techniques, although to a different degree. Managers in all firms engage in planning, controlling, performance evaluation, and decision making. Thus, management accounting is

Exhibit 2.9 Stages and Costs of Production

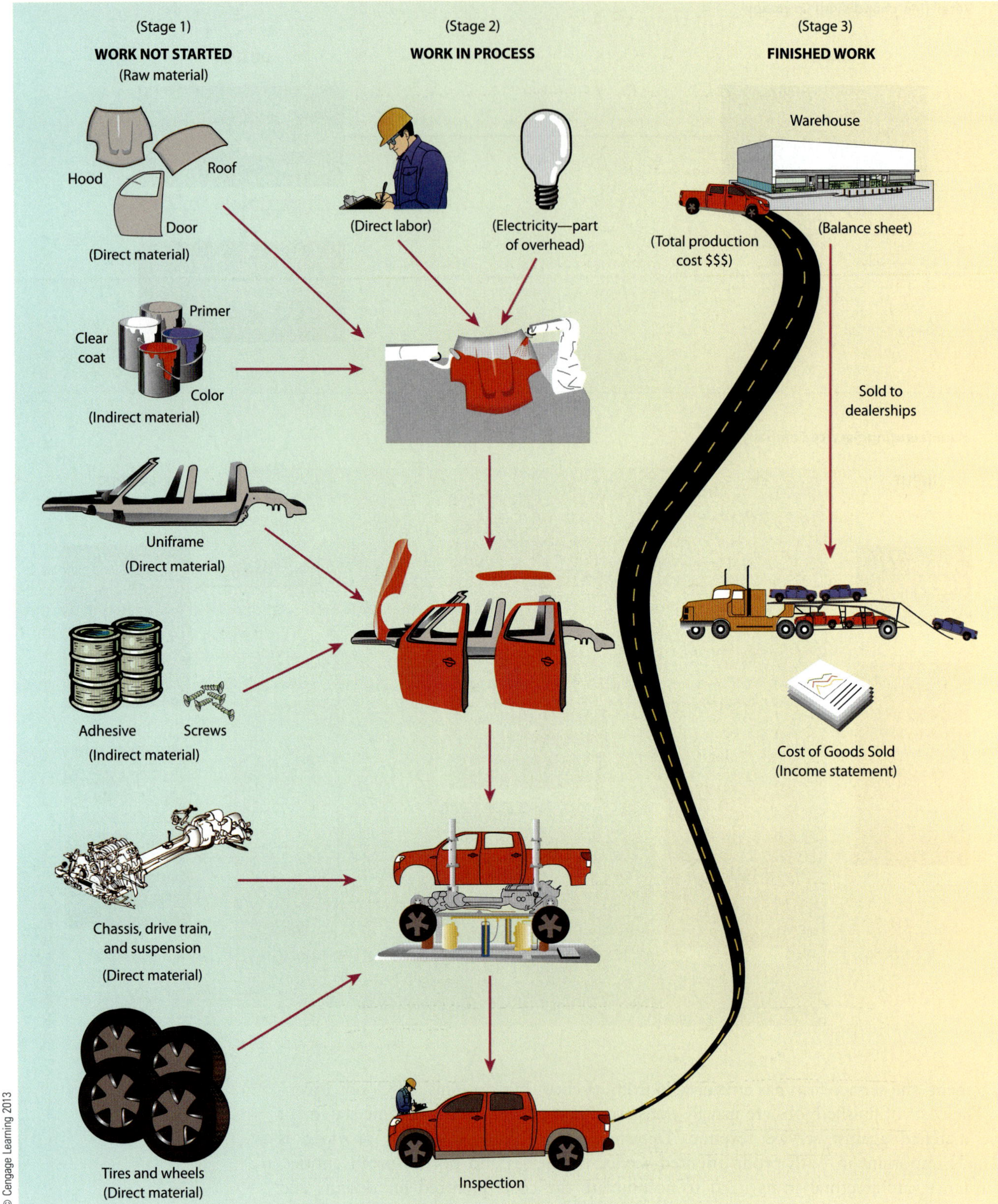

appropriate for all firms. Cost accounting techniques are essential to all firms engaged in significant conversion activities. In most companies, a main focus of managers is finding ways to reduce costs without sacrificing quality or productivity; both management and cost accounting techniques are used extensively in this pursuit.

COMPONENTS OF PRODUCT COST

5 What are the product cost categories, and what items comprise those categories?

Product costs are related to items that generate an entity's revenues. These costs can be separated into three components: direct material, direct labor, and production overhead.[4]

Direct Material

Any readily identifiable part of a product is a direct material. Theoretically, direct material cost should include the cost of all materials used to manufacture a product or perform a service. However, some material costs are not conveniently or economically traceable to the final product. Such costs are treated and classified as indirect costs. For instance, the cost of the paper on which an architect prepares building plans is very small relative to the plans' overall value. Accordingly, even though the paper can easily be traced to the final product (the actual blueprints), paper cost is so insignificant that tracking it as a direct material is not justified.

Zsolt Nyulaszi/iStockphoto.com

Service firms, such as hospitals, account for conversion activities differently because most of their services cannot be warehoused.

Direct Labor

Direct labor refers to the effort of individuals who manufacture a product or perform a service. Direct labor could also be considered effort that directly adds value to the final product or service. Direct labor cost is the total wages or salaries paid to direct labor personnel. Direct labor cost should include basic compensation, production efficiency bonuses, and the employer's share of Social Security and Medicare taxes. In addition, if a company's operations are relatively stable, direct labor cost should include all employer-paid insurance costs, holiday and vacation pay, and pension and other retirement benefits.[5]

As with materials, some labor costs that theoretically are direct costs are treated as indirect. One reason for this treatment is that specifically tracing certain labor costs to production is inefficient. For instance, fringe benefit costs should be treated as direct labor cost, but the time, effort, and clerical expense of tracing this cost might not justify the additional accuracy such tracing would provide. Thus, the treatment of employee fringe benefits as indirect costs is often based on clerical cost efficiencies.

A second reason for not treating certain labor costs as direct is that doing so could result in erroneous information about product or service costs. Assume that Langley Corporation employs 20 assembly department workers who are paid \$12 per hour; overtime wages are \$18 (or time and a half) per hour. One week, the employees worked a total of 1,000 hours (including 200 hours of overtime) to complete all production orders. Of the total employee labor payroll of \$13,200, only \$12,000 (1,000 hours × \$12 per hour) is classified as direct labor cost. The remaining \$1,200 (200 hours × \$6 per hour) is considered overhead. If the overtime cost were assigned to products made during the overtime hours, those products would have a labor cost 50 percent higher than items made during regular working hours. Because products are assigned to regular or overtime shifts randomly, items completed during overtime hours should not be forced to bear overtime charges. Thus, overtime or shift premiums are usually considered overhead rather than direct labor cost and are allocated among all units.

On some occasions, however, overtime or shift premiums should be considered direct labor cost. For example, if a customer is in a rush and requests a job to be scheduled during overtime or a night shift, overtime or shift premiums should be considered direct labor cost and attached to the customer's job that created the costs. Assume that on a Friday in July, Rosa Company asked Langley Corporation to deliver 100 units of product the following Monday. Because the order's completion requires employees to work overtime, Langley

[4] This traditional definition of product cost is referred to as absorption cost. Another product costing method, called *variable costing*, excludes the fixed overhead component. Absorption and variable costing are compared in Chapter 3.

[5] Institute of Management Accountants (formerly National Association of Accountants), *Statements on Management Accounting Number 4C: Definition and Measurement of Direct Labor Cost* (Montvale, N.J.: NAA, June 13, 1985), p. 4.

Corporation should charge Rosa Company a higher selling price for each unit and, additionally, the overtime costs should be included as part of the direct labor cost of the Rosa Company order.

There are occasions when labor costs are being incurred but no work is being performed. For example, workers may be idle while they are waiting for machines to be maintained or for materials to arrive on the production floor. This cost of idle time should be assigned to overhead.

Because people historically performed the majority of conversion activity, direct labor once represented a large portion of total manufacturing cost. In highly automated work environments, direct labor often represents only 10–15 percent of total manufacturing cost.

Overhead

Overhead is any factory or production cost that is indirect to manufacturing a product or providing a service. Accordingly, overhead excludes direct material and direct labor costs, but includes indirect material and indirect labor costs as well as all other production costs.[6] Automated technology has made manufacturing significantly more capital intensive than in the past, and overhead has become a progressively larger proportion of total cost. As such, overhead costs merit much more attention today than in the past.

Overhead costs can be variable or fixed based on how they behave in response to changes in production volume or other activity measure. Variable overhead includes the costs of indirect material, indirect labor paid on an hourly basis (such as wages for forklift operators, material handlers, and other workers who support the production, assembly, and/or service process), lubricants used for machine maintenance, and the variable portion of factory utility charges. Depreciation calculated using either the units-of-production or service-life method is also a variable overhead cost; these depreciation methods reflect a decline in machine utility based on usage rather than time passage and are appropriate in an automated plant.

Fixed overhead includes costs such as straight-line depreciation on factory assets, factory license fees, and factory insurance and property taxes. Fixed indirect labor costs include salaries for production supervisors, shift superintendents, and plant managers. The fixed portion of factory mixed costs (such as maintenance and utilities) is also part of fixed overhead.

Investments in new equipment can create significantly higher fixed overhead costs but can also improve product or service quality—and thus reduce another overhead cost, that of poor quality. Quality costs are an important component of overhead cost. Quality is a managerial concern for two reasons. First, high-quality products and services enhance a company's ability to generate revenues and produce profits. Consumers want the best quality product for the money they spend. Second, managers are concerned about production process quality because higher process quality leads to shorter production time and reduced costs for spoilage and rework. The level of customer satisfaction with a company's products and services is usually part of the customer perspective in the balanced scorecard.

Quality costs usually refer to either costs of controlling quality or costs of failing to control quality. Costs of controlling quality include prevention and appraisal costs. **Prevention costs** are incurred to improve quality by precluding product defects and improper processing from occurring. Amounts spent to implement training programs, research customer needs, and acquire improved production equipment are prevention costs. Amounts incurred for monitoring or inspecting are called **appraisal costs**; these costs are incurred to find mistakes not eliminated through prevention efforts.

The inability to control quality results in **failure costs**, which may be internal (such as scrap and rework) or external (such as product return costs caused by quality problems, warranty costs, and complaint department costs). Amounts spent for prevention costs minimize the costs incurred for appraisal and failure. Management techniques to improve quality are discussed in greater depth in Chapter 17.

[6] Another term used for overhead is *burden*. Although this is the term under which the definition appeared in *Statements on Management Accounting Number 2, Management Accounting Terminology*, the authors believe that this term is unacceptable because it connotes costs that are extra, unnecessary, or oppressive. Overhead costs are essential to the conversion process but simply cannot be traced directly to output.

Quality costs, like other costs, may have variable, fixed, mixed, or step behaviors. Some quality costs are variable in relation to the quantity of defective output, some are step fixed with increases at specific levels of defective output, and some are fixed for a specific time. For example, rework cost could vary directly with the total quantity of production and, therefore, be a variable cost. In contrast, training expenditures are fixed costs if set by management because they will not vary regardless of the quantity of output produced in a given period.

ACCUMULATION AND ALLOCATION OF OVERHEAD

6 How and why does overhead need to be allocated to products?

Direct material and direct labor are easily traced to a product or service. Overhead, on the other hand, must be accumulated throughout a period and allocated to the products manufactured or services rendered during that period. **Cost allocation** refers to the assignment of an indirect cost to one or more cost objects using some reasonable allocation base or driver. Cost allocations can be made across time periods or within a single time period. For example, in financial accounting, a building's cost is allocated through depreciation charges over its useful or service life. This process is necessary to satisfy the matching principle. In cost accounting, production overhead costs are allocated within a period through the use of allocation bases or cost drivers to products or services. This process reflects application of the cost principle, which requires that all production or acquisition costs attach to the units produced, services rendered, or units purchased.

Overhead costs are allocated to cost objects for three reasons:

1. to determine the full cost of the cost object;
2. to motivate the manager in charge of the cost object to manage it efficiently; and
3. to compare alternative courses of action for management planning, controlling, and decision making.[7]

The first reason relates to financial statement valuations. Under GAAP, the "full cost" of a cost object must include allocated production overhead. In contrast, the assignment of nonmanufacturing overhead costs to products is not normally allowed under GAAP.[8] The other two reasons for overhead allocations are related to internal purposes, and thus no specific rules apply to the allocation process.

Regardless of the reason overhead is allocated, the method and basis of allocation should be rational and systematic so that the resulting information is useful for product costing and managerial purposes. Traditionally, the information generated for satisfying the "full cost" objective was also used for the second and third objectives. However, because the first purpose is externally focused and the others are internally focused, different methods can be used to provide different costs for different purposes.

Overhead can be allocated to products or services in one of two ways. In an **actual cost system**, actual direct material and direct labor costs are accumulated in Work in Process Inventory as the costs are incurred. Actual production overhead costs are accumulated separately in an Overhead Control account and are assigned to WIP Inventory either at the end of a period or at completion of production. Use of an actual cost system is impractical because all production overhead information must be available before any cost allocation can be made to products or services. For example, the cost of products manufactured or services rendered in May could not be calculated until the May electricity bill is received in June.

An alternative to an actual cost system is a **normal cost system**, which combines actual direct material and direct labor costs with overhead that is assigned using a predetermined rate or rates. A **predetermined overhead rate** (or overhead application rate) is a charge per unit of activity that is used to allocate (or apply) overhead cost from the Overhead Control account to Work in Process Inventory for the period's production or services. Predetermined overhead rates are discussed in detail in Chapter 3.

[7] Institute of Management Accountants, *Statements on Management Accounting Number 4B: Allocation of Service and Administrative Costs* (Montvale, N.J.: NAA, June 13, 1985), pp. 9–10.

[8] Although potentially unacceptable for GAAP, certain nonmanufacturing overhead costs must be assigned to products for tax purposes.

Product costs can be accumulated using either a perpetual or a periodic inventory system. In a perpetual inventory system, all product costs flow through Work in Process (WIP) Inventory to Finished Goods (FG) Inventory and, ultimately, to Cost of Goods Sold (CGS); this cost flow is diagrammed in Exhibit 2.10. The perpetual inventory system continuously provides current information for financial statement preparation and for inventory and cost control. Because the cost of maintaining a perpetual system has diminished significantly as computerized production, bar coding, radio-frequency identification, and information processing have become more pervasive, this text assumes that all companies discussed use a perpetual system.

Exhibit 2.10 Illustration of a Perpetual Inventory Accounting System

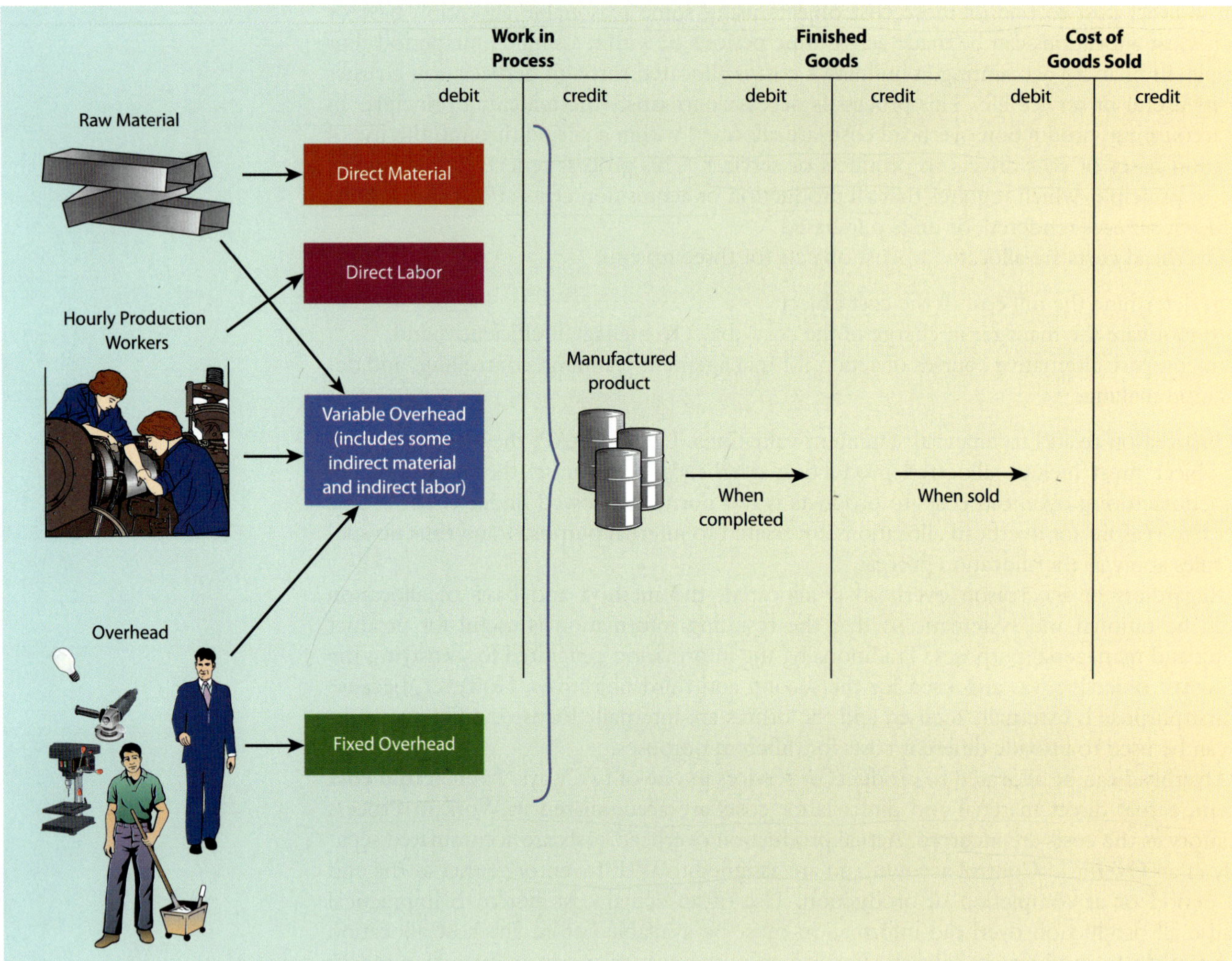

Langley Corporation is used to illustrate the flow of product costs in a manufacturing company's actual cost system. The April 1, 2013, inventory account balances for the company were as follows:

Raw Material (RM) Inventory (all direct)	$ 73,000
WIP Inventory	145,000
FG Inventory	87,400

Langley Corporation uses separate variable and fixed accounts to record overhead costs. In this illustration, actual overhead costs are used to allocate overhead to WIP Inventory. The journal entries in Exhibit 2.11 are keyed to the following transactions representing Langley Corporation's activity for April.

Exhibit 2.11 Langley Corporation—April 2013 Journal Entries

	Account	Debit	Credit
(1)	Raw Material Inventory	280,000	
	Accounts Payable		280,000
	To record cost of raw material purchased on account		
(2)	Work in Process Inventory	284,000	
	Raw Material Inventory		284,000
	To record cost of raw material transferred to production		
(3)	Work in Process Inventory	436,000	
	Variable Overhead Control	94,000	
	Salaries & Wages Payable		530,000
	To accrue factory wages for direct and indirect labor		
(4)	Fixed Overhead Control	20,000	
	Salaries & Wages Payable		20,000
	To accrue production supervisors' salaries		
(5)	Variable Overhead Control	16,000	
	Fixed Overhead Control	12,000	
	Utilities Payable		28,000
	To record mixed utility cost in its variable and fixed amounts		
(6)	Variable Overhead Control	5,200	
	Supplies Inventory		5,200
	To record supplies used		
(7)	Fixed Overhead Control	7,000	
	Cash		7,000
	To record payment for factory property taxes for the period		
(8)	Fixed Overhead Control	56,880	
	Accumulated Depreciation—Equipment		56,880
	To record depreciation on factory assets for the period		
(9)	Fixed Overhead Control	3,000	
	Prepaid Insurance		3,000
	To record expiration of prepaid insurance on factory assets		
(10)	Work in Process Inventory	214,080	
	Variable Overhead Control		115,200
	Fixed Overhead Control		98,880
	To record the assignment of actual overhead costs to WIP Inventory		
(11)	Finished Goods Inventory	1,058,200	
	Work in Process Inventory		1,058,200
	To record the transfer of work completed during the period		
(12)	Accounts Receivable	1,460,000	
	Sales		1,460,000
	To record total sales of goods on account during the period		
(13)	Cost of Goods Sold	1,054,000	
	Finished Goods Inventory		1,054,000
	To record cost of goods sold for the period		

During the month, Langley's purchasing agent bought $280,000 of raw material on account (entry 1), and the warehouse manager transferred $284,000 of direct material to the production area (entry 2). April's wages for hourly employees in the factory totaled $530,000, of which $436,000 was for direct labor (entry 3). April salaries for the production supervisors were $20,000 (entry 4). April utility cost of $28,000 was accrued; cost analysis indicated that $16,000 was variable and $12,000 was fixed (entry 5). Langley maintains a separate inventory account for supplies. Supplies costing \$5,200 were transferred from supplies inventory to production (entry 6). Supplies are a type of indirect material. Langley paid \$7,000 for April's property taxes on the factory (entry 7), depreciated the factory assets \$56,880 (entry 8), and recorded the expiration of \$3,000 of prepaid insurance on the factory assets (entry 9). Entry 10 shows the assignment of actual overhead cost to WIP Inventory for April. During the month, \$1,058,200 of goods were completed and transferred to FG Inventory (entry 11). Total April sales were \$1,460,000 and these were all on account (entry 12); goods that were sold had a total cost of \$1,054,000 (entry 13). An abbreviated presentation of the cost flows is shown in selected T-accounts in Exhibit 2.12.

Exhibit 2.12 Selected T-Accounts for Langley Corporation's April 2013 Production and Sales

Raw Material Inventory

Beg. bal.	73,000	(2)	284,000
(1)	280,000		
End. bal.	69,000		

Variable Overhead Control

(3)	94,000	(10)	115,200
(5)	16,000		
(6)	5,200		

Work in Process Inventory

Beg. bal.	145,000	(11)	1,058,200
(2) DM	284,000		
(3) DL	436,000		
(10) OH	214,080		
End. bal.	20,880		

Fixed Overhead Control

(4)	20,000	(10)	98,880
(5)	12,000		
(7)	7,000		
(8)	56,880		
(9)	3,000		

Finished Goods Inventory

Beg. bal.	87,400	(13) CGS	1,054,000
(11) CGM	1,058,200		
End. bal.	91,600		

Cost of Goods Sold

(13) CGS	1,054,000		

7 How is cost of goods manufactured calculated and used in preparing an income statement?

COST OF GOODS MANUFACTURED AND SOLD

The T-accounts in Exhibit 2.12 provide detailed information about the cost of material used, goods transferred from work in process, and goods sold. This information is needed to prepare financial statements. A schedule of cost of goods manufactured is prepared as a preliminary step to the determination of cost of goods sold. **Cost of goods manufactured (CGM)** is the total production cost of the goods that were completed and transferred to FG Inventory during the period. This amount is similar to the cost of net purchases in the cost of goods sold schedule for a retailer. A service business prepares a schedule of cost of services rendered.

Formal schedules of cost of goods manufactured and cost of goods sold are presented in Exhibit 2.13 using the amounts from Exhibits 2.11 and 2.12. The schedule of cost of goods manufactured starts with the beginning balance of WIP Inventory and details all product cost components. The cost of material used in production during the period is equal to the beginning balance of RM Inventory plus raw material purchased minus the ending balance of RM Inventory. If RM Inventory includes both direct and indirect materials, the cost of direct material used is assigned to WIP Inventory and the cost of indirect material used is included in variable overhead. Because direct labor cannot be warehoused, all charges for direct labor during the period are part of WIP Inventory. Variable and fixed

Exhibit 2.13 Cost of Goods Manufactured and Cost of Goods Sold Schedules

LANGLEY CORPORATION
Schedule of Cost of Goods Manufactured
For the Month Ended April 30, 2013

Beginning balance of work in process inventory, 4/1/13			$ 145,000
Manufacturing costs for the period			
Raw material inventory (all direct)			
Beginning balance	$ 73,000		
Purchases of material	280,000		
Raw material available	$353,000		
Ending balance	(69,000)		
Total raw material used		$284,000	
Direct labor		436,000	
Variable overhead			
Indirect labor	$ 94,000		
Utilities	16,000		
Supplies	5,200	115,200	
Fixed overhead			
Supervisors' salaries	$ 20,000		
Utilities	12,000		
Factory property taxes	7,000		
Factory asset depreciation	56,880		
Factory insurance	3,000	98,880	
Total current period manufacturing costs			934,080
Total costs to account for			$1,079,080
Ending balance of work in process inventory, 4/30/13			(20,880)
Cost of goods manufactured			$1,058,200

LANGLEY CORPORATION
Schedule of Cost of Goods Sold
For the Month Ended April 30, 2013

Beginning balance of finished goods inventory, 4/1/13	$ 87,400
Cost of goods manufactured	1,058,200
Cost of goods available for sale	$1,145,600
Ending balance of finished goods inventory, 4/30/13	(91,600)
Cost of goods sold	$1,054,000

overhead costs are added to direct material and direct labor costs to determine total manufacturing costs.

Beginning WIP Inventory cost is added to total current manufacturing costs to obtain a subtotal amount referred to as **total cost to account for**. After the value of ending WIP Inventory is calculated (through techniques discussed in Chapters 5–7), it is subtracted from the subtotal to provide the CGM for the period. The schedule of cost of goods manufactured is an internal schedule and is not provided to external parties.

In the schedule of cost of goods sold, the CGM is added to the beginning balance of FG Inventory to find the cost of goods available for sale during the period. Ending FG Inventory is calculated by multiplying a physical unit count by a unit cost. If a perpetual inventory system is used, the actual amount of ending FG Inventory can be compared to the amount shown in the accounting records; any differences can be attributed to losses that could have arisen from theft, breakage, evaporation, or accounting errors. Ending FG Inventory is subtracted from the cost of goods available for sale to determine the CGS.

Comprehensive Review Module

KEY TERMS

actual cost system, p. 37
appraisal cost, p. 36
conversion cost, p. 30
cost, p. 25
cost allocation, p. 37
cost driver, p. 29
cost management system, p. 25
cost object, p. 25
cost of goods manufactured (CGM), p. 40
direct cost, p. 26
direct labor, p. 30
direct material, p. 30
distribution cost, p. 30
expired cost, p. 25
failure cost, p. 36
finished goods, p. 32
fixed cost, p. 27
indirect cost, p. 26
inventoriable cost, p. 30
manufacturer, p. 31
mixed cost, p. 28
normal cost system, p. 37
overhead, p. 30
period cost, p. 30
predetermined overhead rate, p. 37
predictor, p. 29
prevention cost, p. 36
prime cost, p. 30
product cost, p. 30
raw material, p. 32
relevant range, p. 26
service company, p. 31
step cost, p. 28
total cost to account for, p. 41
unexpired cost, p. 25
variable cost, p. 26
work in process, p. 32

CHAPTER SUMMARY

1 Cost Classification

- Direct or indirect, depending on the cost's relationship to a cost object.
- Variable, fixed, or mixed depending on the cost's reaction to a change in a related activity level.
- Unexpired (assets) or expired (expenses or losses) depending on whether the cost has a future value to the company.
- Product (inventoriable) or period (selling, administrative, and financing) depending on the cost's association with the revenue-generating items sold by the company.

2 Assumptions Used to Estimate Product Cost within Relevant Range of Activity

- Variable costs are constant per unit and will change in total in direct proportion to changes in activity.
- Fixed costs are constant in total and will vary inversely on a per-unit basis with changes in activity.
- Mixed costs fluctuate in total with changes in activity and can be separated into their variable and fixed components.
- Step costs are either variable or fixed, depending on the size of the changes (width of the steps) in cost that occur with changes in activity.

3 Conversion Process Differences

- Manufacturers require extensive activity to convert raw material into finished goods; the primary costs in these companies are direct material, direct labor, and overhead; manufacturers use three inventory accounts (Raw Material, Work in Process, and Finished Goods).
- Service companies often require extensive activity to perform a service; the primary costs in these companies are direct labor and overhead; service companies may use Supplies Inventory and Work in Process Inventory accounts but typically have no Finished Goods Inventory.
- Retailers require little, if any, activity to make purchased goods ready for sale; the primary costs in these companies are prices paid for goods and labor wages; retailers use a Merchandise Inventory account.

4 Product Cost Categories

- Direct material, which is the cost of any item that is physically and conveniently traceable to the product or service.
- Direct labor, which is the wages or salaries of the people whose work is physically and conveniently traceable to the product or service.
- Overhead, which is any cost incurred in the conversion (or production) area that is not direct material or direct labor; overhead includes indirect material and indirect labor costs.

5 Cost of Goods Manufactured

- CGM equals the costs that were in the conversion area at the beginning of the period plus production costs (direct material, direct labor, and overhead) incurred during the period minus the cost of incomplete goods that remain in the conversion area at the end of the period.
- CGM is shown on an internal management report called the schedule of cost of goods manufactured; it is equivalent to the cost of goods purchased in a retail company.
- CGM is added to beginning Finished Goods Inventory to determine the cost of goods available (CGA) for sale for the period; CGA is reduced by ending Finished Goods Inventory to determine cost of goods sold on the income statement.

SOLUTION STRATEGIES

Product Cost, p. 30

	Direct Material
+	Direct Labor
+	Overhead
=	Total Product Cost

Schedule of Cost of Goods Manufactured, p. 40

Beginning balance of work in process inventory			$ XXX
Manufacturing costs for the period:			
Raw material (all direct):			
Beginning balance	$ XXX		
Purchases of material	XXX		
Raw material available for use	$ XXX		
Ending balance	(XXX)		
Direct material used		$XXX	
Direct labor		XXX	
Variable overhead		XXX	
Fixed overhead		XXX	
Total current period manufacturing costs			XXX
Total cost to account for			$ XXX
Ending balance of work in process inventory			(XXX)
Cost of goods manufactured			$ XXX

Cost of Goods Sold, p. 41

Beginning balance of finished goods inventory	$ XXX
Cost of goods manufactured	XXX
Cost of goods available for sale	$ XXX
Ending balance of finished goods inventory	(XXX)
Cost of goods sold	$ XXX

DEMONSTRATION PROBLEM

Latourneau Company had the following account balances as of August 1, 2013:

Raw Material (direct and indirect) Inventory	$20,300
Work in Process Inventory	7,000
Finished Goods Inventory	18,000

During August, the company incurred the following factory costs:

1. Purchased $164,000 of raw material on account.
2. Issued $180,000 of raw material to production. Of this amount, $134,000 was for direct material and the remainder was for production supplies.
3. Accrued $88,000 in factory payroll costs; $62,000 was for direct labor and the rest was for supervisors' salaries.
4. Accrued $7,000 of utility costs; of this amount, $1,600 was a fixed cost and the remainder was variable.
5. Accrued $2,000 of property taxes on the factory.
6. Recorded the expiration of $1,600 of prepaid insurance on factory equipment.
7. Recorded $40,000 of straight-line depreciation on factory equipment.
8. Applied actual overhead to Work in Process Inventory.
9. Transferred goods costing $320,000 to Finished Goods Inventory.
10. Recorded total sales of $700,000; of these, $550,000 were on account.
11. Recorded cost of goods sold of $330,000.
12. Recorded selling and administrative costs of $280,000 (credit "Various accounts").

Required:

a. Journalize the transactions for August.
b. Post transactions to T-accounts for Raw Material Inventory, Work in Process Inventory, Finished Goods Inventory, and Cost of Goods Sold.
c. Prepare a schedule of cost of goods manufactured for August using actual costing.
d. Prepare an income statement, including a detailed schedule of cost of goods sold.

Solution to Demonstration Problem

a.

		Debit	Credit
(1)	Raw Material Inventory	164,000	
	Accounts Payable		164,000
	To record raw material purchased on account		
(2)	Work in Process Inventory	134,000	
	Variable Overhead Control	46,000	
	Raw Material Inventory		180,000
	To transfer direct and indirect materials to production		
(3)	Work in Process Inventory	62,000	
	Fixed Overhead Control	26,000	
	Salaries and Wages Payable		88,000
	To accrue factory wages and salaries		
(4)	Variable Overhead Control	5,400	
	Fixed Overhead Control	1,600	
	Utilities Payable		7,000
	To accrue factory utility expenses		
(5)	Fixed Overhead Control	2,000	
	Property Taxes Payable		2,000
	To accrue property tax		
(6)	Fixed Overhead Control	1,600	
	Prepaid Insurance		1,600
	To record expired insurance on factory equipment		

		Debit	Credit
(7)	Fixed Overhead Control	40,000	
	Accumulated Depreciation—Factory Equipment		40,000
	To record depreciation on factory equipment		
(8)	Work in Process Inventory	122,600	
	Variable Overhead Control		51,400
	Fixed Overhead Control		71,200
	To assign actual overhead to WIP Inventory		
(9)	Finished Goods Inventory	320,000	
	Work in Process Inventory		320,000
	To record cost of goods manufactured		
(10)	Accounts Receivable	550,000	
	Cash	150,000	
	Sales		700,000
	To record sales on account and for cash		
(11)	Cost of Goods Sold	330,000	
	Finished Goods Inventory		330,000
	To record cost of goods sold for the period		
(12)	Selling & Administrative Expenses	280,000	
	Various accounts		280,000
	To record selling and administrative expenses		

b.

Raw Material Inventory

BB	20,300	(2)	180,000
(1)	164,000		
EB	4,300		

Work in Process Inventory

BB	7,000	(9)	320,000
(2)	134,000		
(3)	62,000		
(8)	122,600		
EB	5,600		

Finished Goods Inventory

BB	18,000	(11)	330,000
(9)	320,000		
EB	8,000		

Cost of Goods Sold

(11)	330,000		

where BB = beginning balance

EB = ending balance

c.

LATOURNEAU COMPANY
Schedule of Cost of Goods Manufactured
For the Month Ended August 31, 2013

Balance of work in process inventory, 8/1/13			$ 7,000
Manufacturing costs for the period			
Raw material			
Beginning balance		$ 20,300	
Purchases of material		164,000	
Raw material available		$184,300	
Indirect material used	$46,000		
Ending balance	4,300	(50,300)	
Total direct material used		$134,000	
Direct labor		62,000	
Variable overhead		51,400	
Fixed overhead		71,200	
Total current period manufacturing costs			318,600
Total cost to account for			$325,600
Balance of work in process inventory, 8/31/13			(5,600)
Cost of goods manufactured*			$320,000

*Note the similarity between the schedule of CGM and the WIP Inventory T-account.

d.

LATOURNEAU COMPANY
Income Statement
For the Month Ended August 31, 2013

Sales		$ 700,000
Cost of goods sold		
Finished goods, 8/1/13	$ 18,000	
Cost of goods manufactured	320,000	
Cost of goods available	$338,000	
Finished goods, 8/31/13	(8,000)	
Cost of goods sold		(330,000)
Gross margin		$ 370,000
Selling and administrative expenses		(280,000)
Income from operations		$ 90,000

POTENTIAL ETHICAL ISSUES

ETHICS

1. Leaving expired costs on the balance sheet as assets, thereby not recognizing expenses or losses that would reduce net income
2. Treating period costs as product costs to inflate inventory assets and increase net income
3. Treating product costs as period costs to reduce the cost of goods manufactured and increase gross profit on the income statement, thereby making the conversion area appear more profitable than it actually was
4. Attaching the "random" costs of direct labor (such as overtime) to specific production units to inflate the cost of those units—especially if the buyer is required to pay for production cost plus a specified profit percentage
5. Overstating the cost of ending inventory accounts to reduce the cost of goods manufactured, reduce the cost of goods sold, and increase net income
6. Moving manufacturing operations to countries with weak environmental protection to reduce operating costs

QUESTIONS

1. Why must the word *cost* be accompanied by an adjective to be meaningful?
2. Why is it necessary to specify a cost object before being able to distinguish between a direct cost and an indirect cost?
3. Why is it necessary for a company to specify a relevant range of activity when making assumptions about cost behavior?
4. How do cost drivers and cost predictors differ, and why is the distinction important?
5. How do a product cost and a period cost differ?
6. What are conversion costs? Why are they called this?
7. In recent years, which product cost category has been growing most rapidly? Why?
8. How does an actual costing system differ from a normal costing system? What advantages does a normal costing system offer?
9. What is meant by the term *cost of goods manufactured*? Why does this item appear on an income statement?

EXERCISES

10. **LO.1 (Association with cost object)** Morris & Assoc., owned by Cindy Morris, provides accounting services to clients. The firm has two accountants (Jo Perkins, who performs basic accounting services, and Steve Tompkin, who performs tax services) and

one office assistant. The assistant is paid on an hourly basis for the actual hours worked. One client the firm served during April was Vic Kennedy. During April 2013, the following labor time was incurred. Classify the labor time as direct, indirect, or unrelated based on whether the cost object is (1) Kennedy's services, (2) tax services provided, or (3) the accounting firm.

a. Four hours of Perkins's time in preparing Kennedy's financial statements
b. Six hours of the assistant's time in copying Kennedy's tax materials
c. Three hours of Morris's time playing golf with Kennedy
d. Eight hours of continuing education paid for by the firm for Tompkin to attend a tax update seminar
e. One hour of the assistant's time spent at lunch on the day that Kennedy's tax return was prepared
f. Two hours of Perkins's time spent with Kennedy and his banker discussing Kennedy's financial statements
g. One-half hour of Tompkin's time spent talking to an IRS agent about a deduction taken on Kennedy's tax return
h. Forty hours of janitorial wages
i. Seven hours of Tompkin's time preparing Kennedy's tax return

11. **LO.1 (Association with cost object)** Chase University's College of Business has five departments: Accounting, Economics, Finance, Management, and Marketing. Each department chairperson is responsible for the department's budget preparation. Indicate whether each of the following costs incurred in the Accounting Department is direct or indirect to the department:

a. Accounting faculty salaries
b. Accounting chairperson's salary
c. Cost of computer time of university server used by members of the department
d. Cost of office assistant salaries (office assistants are shared by the entire college)
e. Cost of travel by department faculty paid from externally generated funds contributed directly to the department
f. Cost of equipment purchased by the department from allocated state funds
g. Depreciation allocation of the college building cost for the number of offices used by department faculty
h. Cost of periodicals/books purchased by the department
i. Cost of software on faculty computers

12. **LO.1 (Association with cost object)** Following is a list of raw materials that might be used in the production of a notebook computer: touch pad and buttons, glue, network connector, battery, paper towels used by line employees, AC adapter, CD drive, motherboard, screws, and oil for production machinery. The notebooks are produced in the same building using the same equipment that produces desktop computers and servers. Classify each raw material as direct or indirect when the cost object is the

a. notebook.
b. computer production plant.

13. **LO.2 (Cost drivers)** Assume that Dover Hospital performs the following activities in providing outpatient service:

a. Verifying patient's insurance coverage
b. Scheduling patient's arrival date and time
c. Scheduling staff to prepare patient's surgery room
d. Scheduling doctors and nurses to perform surgery
e. Ordering patient's tests
f. Moving patient to laboratory to administer lab tests
g. Administering laboratory tests
h. Moving patient to the operating room
i. Administering anesthetic
j. Performing surgery

k. Administering postsurgical medications
l. Moving patient to recovery room
m. Discharging patient
n. Billing patient's insurance company

Assume that the patient is the cost object and determine the appropriate cost driver or drivers for each activity.

14. **LO.2 (Predictors and cost drivers; team activity)** Lawrence & Sluyter CPAs often use factors that change in a consistent pattern with costs to explain or predict cost behavior.

    a. As a team of three or four, select factors to predict or explain the behavior of the following costs:

        (1) Staff accountant's travel expenses
        (2) Office supplies inventory
        (3) Notebook computers used in audit engagements
        (4) Maintenance costs for the firm's lawn & grounds service

    b. Prepare a presentation of your chosen factors that also addresses whether the factors could be used as cost drivers in addition to cost predictors.

15. **LO.2 (Cost behavior)** Flaherty Accounting Services pays $2,000 per month for a tax preparation software license. In addition, variable charges incurred average $9 for every tax return the firm prepares.

    a. Determine the total cost and the cost per unit if the firm expects to prepare the following number of tax returns in March 2013:

        (1) 200
        (2) 500
        (3) 800

    b. Why does the cost per unit change in (1), (2), and (3) of (a)?
    c. The owner of Flaherty Accounting Services wants to earn a margin (excluding any other direct costs) on tax returns of $15,000 during March. If 200 returns are prepared, what tax return preparation fee should be charged? If that fee is charged and 800 returns are prepared, what is the margin in March?

16. **LO.2 (Cost behavior)** The next winner of *America's Idol* will perform at your fraternity's charity event for free at your school's basketball arena (25,000-person capacity) on January 28, 2014. The school is charging your fraternity $37,500 for the facilities and $10 for each ticket sold. The fraternity asks you, their only numbers-astute member, to determine how much to charge for each ticket. The group wants to make a profit of $8 per ticket sold. You assume that 15,000 tickets will be sold.

    a. What is the total cost incurred by the fraternity if 15,000 tickets are sold?
    b. What price per ticket must be charged for the fraternity to earn its desired profit margin?
    c. Suppose that on the morning of January 28, 2014, a major snowstorm hits your area, bringing in 36 inches of snow and ice. Only 5,000 tickets are sold because most students were going to buy their tickets at the door. What is the total profit or loss to the fraternity?
    d. What assumptions did you make about your calculations that should have been conveyed to the fraternity?
    e. Suppose instead that fair weather prevails and, by show time, 20,000 concert tickets are sold. What is the total profit or loss to the fraternity?

17. **LO.2 (Cost behavior)** Merry Olde Games produces croquet sets. The company makes fixed monthly payments to the local utility based on the previous year's electrical usage. Any difference between actual and expected usage is paid in January of the year following usage. In February 2013, Merry Olde Games made 2,000 croquet sets and incurred the following costs:

Cardboard boxes (1 per set)	$ 1,000
Mallets (2 per set)	12,000
Croquet balls (6 per set)	9,000
Wire hoops (12 per set, including extras)	3,600
Total hourly wages for production workers	8,400
Supervisor's salary	2,600
Building and equipment rental	2,800
Utilities	1,300
Total	$40,700

a. What was the per-unit cost of each component of a croquet set?
b. What was the total cost of each croquet set?
c. Production for March 2013 is expected to be 2,500 croquet sets. Last November, when 2,500 sets were made, utility cost was $1,400. There have been no rate changes at the local utility companies since that time. What is the estimated cost per set for March?

18. **LO.2 (Cost behavior)** Spirit Company produces baseball caps. The company incurred the following costs to produce 12,000 caps last month:

Cardboard for the brims	$ 4,800
Cloth	12,000
Plastic for headbands	6,000
Straight-line depreciation	7,200
Supervisors' salaries	19,200
Utilities	3,600
Total	$52,800

a. What did each cap component cost on a per-unit basis?
b. What is the probable type of behavior that each of the costs exhibits?
c. The company expects to produce 10,000 caps this month. Would you expect each type of cost to increase or decrease? Why? Can the total cost of 10,000 caps be determined? Explain.

19. **LO.2-LO.3 (Cost behavior and classification)** Classify each of the following costs incurred in manufacturing bicycles as variable (V), fixed (F), or mixed (M) cost (using number of units produced as the activity measure). Also indicate whether the cost is direct material (DM), direct labor (DL), or overhead (OH).

a. Factory supervision
b. Aluminum tubing
c. Rims
d. Emblem
e. Gearbox
f. Straight-line depreciation on painting machine
g. Fenders
h. Raw material inventory clerk's wages
i. Quality control inspector's salary
j. Handlebars
k. Metal worker's wages
l. Roller chain
m. Spokes (assuming cost is considered significant)
n. Paint (assuming cost is considered significant)

20. **LO.2-LO.3 (Cost behavior and classification)** Indicate whether each of the following items is a variable (V), fixed (F), or mixed (M) cost and whether it is a product/service (PT) or period (PD) cost. If some items have alternative answers, indicate the alternatives and the reasons for them.

a. Wages of factory maintenance workers
b. Wages of forklift operators who move finished goods from a central warehouse to the outbound loading dock

c. Insurance premiums paid to insure the headquarters of a manufacturing company
d. Cost of labels attached to shirts made by a company
e. Property taxes on a manufacturing plant
f. Paper towels used in factory restrooms
g. Salaries of office assistants in a law firm
h. Freight costs of acquiring raw material from suppliers
i. Computer paper used in an accounting firm
j. Cost of wax to make candles
k. Freight-in on a truckload of furniture purchased for resale

21. **LO.3 (Financial statement classification)** Babineaux Company incurred the following costs in May 2013:

- Paid a six-month (May through October) premium for insurance of company headquarters, $18,600.
- Paid $1,000 fee for a salesperson to attend a seminar in July.
- Paid three months (May through July) of property taxes on its factory building, $15,000.
- Paid a $10,000 bonus to the company president for his performance during May 2013.
- Accrued $20,000 of utility costs, of which 40 percent was for the headquarters and the remainder was for the factory.

a. What expired period costs are associated with the May information?
b. What unexpired period costs are associated with the May information?
c. What product costs are associated with the May information?
d. Discuss why the product cost cannot be described specifically as expired or unexpired in this situation.

22. **LO.3 (Financial statement classification)** Wayside Machine Tool Company purchased a $600,000 welding machine to use in production of large machine tools and robots. The welding machine was expected to have a life of 10 years and a salvage value at time of disposition of $60,000. The company uses straight-line depreciation. During its first operating year, the machine produced 600 product units, of which 480 were sold.

a. What part of the $600,000 machine cost expired?
b. Where would each of the amounts related to this machine appear on the financial statements at the end of the first year of operations?

23. **LO.4 (Degrees of conversion)** Indicate whether each of the following types of organizations is characterized by a high, low, or moderate degree of conversion.

a. Textbook publisher
b. Convenience store
c. Sporting goods retailer
d. Christmas tree farm
e. Custom print shop
f. Bakery in a grocery store
g. Greek restaurant
h. Jelly manufacturer
i. Auto manufacturer
j. Concert ticket seller

24. **LO.4 (Company type)** Indicate whether each of the following terms is associated with a manufacturing (Mfg.), a retailing or merchandising (Mer.), or a service (Ser.) company. There can be more than one correct answer for each term.

a. Depreciation—factory equipment
b. Prepaid rent
c. Auditing fees expense
d. Merchandise inventory
e. Sales salaries expense
f. Finished goods inventory

g. Cost of services rendered
h. Cost of goods sold
i. Direct labor wages

25. **LO.5 (Labor cost classification)** Tidy House produces a variety of household products. The firm operates 24 hours per day with three daily work shifts. The first-shift workers receive "regular pay." The second shift receives an 8 percent pay premium, and the third shift receives a 12 percent pay premium. In addition, when production is scheduled on weekends, the firm pays an overtime premium of 50 percent (based on the pay rate for first-shift employees). Labor premiums are included in overhead. The October 2013 factory payroll is as follows:

Total wages for October for 32,000 hours	$435,600
Normal hourly wage for first-shift employees	$12
Total regular hours worked, split evenly among the three shifts	27,000

a. How many overtime hours were worked in October?
b. How much of the total labor cost should be charged to direct labor? To overhead?
c. What amount of overhead was for second- and third-shift premiums? For overtime premiums?

26. **LO.5 (Product cost classifications)** In June 2013, Carolyn Gardens incurred the following costs. One of several projects in process during the month was a landscaped terrace for Pam Beattie. Relative to the Beattie landscaping job, classify each of the costs as direct material, direct labor, or overhead. The terrace required two days to design and one five-day work week to complete. Some costs may not fit entirely into a single classification; in such cases, and if possible, provide a systematic and rational method to allocate such costs.

Mulch purchased for Beattie's landscaping	$ 320
June salary of Z. Trumble, the landscape designer, who worked 20 days in June	3,000
Construction permit for Beattie's landscaping	95
Gardeners' wages; all worked on Beattie's landscaping; gardeners work eight hours per day, five days per week; there were 20 working days in June	3,840
June depreciation on the company loader, driven by a gardener and used on Beattie's landscaping one day	200
Landscaping rock purchased for Beattie's landscaping	1,580
June rent on Carolyn Gardens offices, where Z. Trumble has an office that occupies 150 square feet of 3,000 total square feet	2,400
June utility bills for Carolyn Gardens	1,800
Plants and pots purchased for Beattie's landscaping	1,950

27. **LO.5 (Labor cost classification)** Woodlands Restaurant Supply operates in two shifts, paying a late-shift premium of 10 percent and an overtime premium of 75 percent. The May 2013 payroll follows:

Total wages for 6,000 hours	$54,000
Normal hourly employee wage	$9
Total regular hours worked, split evenly between the shifts	5,000

All overtime was worked by the early shift during May. Shift and overtime premiums are considered part of overhead rather than direct labor.

a. How many overtime hours were worked in May?
b. How much of the total labor cost should be charged to direct labor? To overhead?
c. What amount of overhead was for second-shift premiums? For overtime premiums?

28. **LO.5 (Product cost classifications)** Forham Inc. manufactures stainless steel knives. Following are factory costs incurred during 2013:

Material costs	
Stainless steel	$800,000
Equipment oil and grease	6,000
Plastic for handles	5,600
Wood blocks for knife storage	24,800

Labor costs	
Equipment operators	$500,000
Equipment mechanics	82,000
Factory supervisors	272,000

a. What is the direct material cost for 2013?
b. What is the direct labor cost for 2013?
c. What is the total indirect material cost and the indirect labor cost for 2013?

29. **LO.5 (Product cost classifications)** Barbieri Co. makes aluminum canoes. The company's June 2013 costs for material and labor were as follows:

Material costs	
Janitorial supplies	$ 1,800
Chrome rivets to assemble canoes	12,510
Sealant	1,230
Aluminum	1,683,000
Labor costs	
Janitorial wages	$ 9,300
Aluminum cutters	56,160
Salespeople's salaries	43,050
Welders	156,000
Factory supervisors' salaries	101,250

a. What is the direct material cost for June?
b. What is the direct labor cost for June?

30. **LO.6 (OH allocation)** Tamra Corp. makes one product line. In February 2013, Tamra paid $530,000 in factory overhead costs. Of that amount, $124,000 was for January's factory utilities and $48,000 was for property taxes on the factory for the year 2013. February's factory utility bill arrived on March 12, 2013, and was only $81,000 because the weather was significantly milder than in January. Tamra Corp. produced 50,000 units of product in both January and February 2013.

a. What were Tamra's actual factory overhead costs for February 2013?
b. Actual per-unit direct material and direct labor costs for February 2013 were $24.30 and $10.95. What was actual total product cost for February?
c. Assume that, other than factory utilities, all direct material, direct labor, and overhead costs for Tamra Corp. were the same for January and February 2013. Will product cost for the two months differ? How can such differences be avoided?

31. **LO.7 (Cost of services rendered)** The following information is related to North Zulch Veterinary Clinic for April 2013, the firm's first month of operation:

Veterinarian salaries for April	$8,100
Assistants' salaries for April	3,140
Medical supplies purchased in April	2,400
Utilities for month (90% related to animal treatment)	2,000
Office salaries for April (20% related to animal treatment)	1,900
Medical supplies on hand at April 30	1,200
Depreciation on medical equipment for April	3,700
Building rental (80% related to animal treatment)	3,100

Compute the cost of services rendered.

32. **LO.7 (Cost of goods manufactured)** The Work in Process Inventory account of Phelan Corporation increased $23,000 during November 2013. Costs incurred during November included $24,000 for direct material, $126,000 for direct labor, and $42,000 for overhead. What was the cost of goods manufactured during November?

EXCEL

33. **LO.7 (CGM; CGS)** Irresistible Art produces collectible pieces of art. The company's Raw Material Inventory account includes the costs of both direct and indirect materials. Account balances for the company at the beginning and end of July 2013 follow:

	July 1	July 31
Raw Material Inventory	$ 93,200	$ 69,600
Work in Process Inventory	146,400	120,000
Finished Goods Inventory	72,000	104,800

During the month, the company purchased $656,000 of raw material; direct material used during the period amounted to $504,000. Factory payroll costs for July were $788,000, of which 75 percent was related to direct labor. Overhead charges for depreciation, insurance, utilities, and maintenance totaled $600,000 for July.

a. Prepare a schedule of cost of goods manufactured.
b. Prepare a schedule of cost of goods sold.

34. **LO.7 (CGM; CGS)** The cost of goods sold in March 2013 for Targé Co. was $2,644,100. The March 31 Work in Process Inventory was 25 percent of the March 1 Work in Process Inventory. Overhead was 225 percent of direct labor cost. During March, $1,182,000 of direct material was purchased. Other March information follows: EXCEL

Inventories	March 1	March 31
Direct Material	$ 30,000	$42,000
Work in Process	90,000	?
Finished Goods	125,000	18,400

a. Prepare a cost of goods sold schedule for March.
b. Prepare the March cost of goods manufactured schedule.
c. What was the amount of prime cost incurred in March?
d. What was the amount of conversion cost incurred in March?

35. **LO.7 (Service industry; journal entries and CSR)** Kalogrides & McMillan CPAs incurred the following costs in performing audits during September 2013. The firm uses a Work in Process Inventory account for audit engagement costs and records overhead in fixed and variable overhead accounts. EXCEL

a. Prepare journal entries for each of the following transactions:
   - Used $5,000 of previously purchased supplies on audit engagements.
   - Paid $8,000 of partner travel expenses to an accounting conference.
   - Recorded $6,500 of depreciation on laptops used in audits.
   - Recorded $1,800,000 of annual depreciation on the Kalogrides & McMillan Building, located in downtown New York; 65 percent of the space is used to house audit personnel.
   - Accrued audit partner salaries, $200,000.
   - Accrued remaining audit staff salaries, $257,900.
   - Paid credit card charges for travel costs for client engagements, $19,400.
   - One month's prepaid insurance and property taxes expired on the downtown building, $17,300.
   - Accrued $3,400 of office assistant wages; the office assistant works only for the audit partners and staff.
   - Paid all accrued salaries and wages for the month.

b. Determine the cost of audit services rendered for September 2013.

36. **LO.7 (CGM; CGS)** Wasik Company had the following inventory balances at the beginning and end of August 2013:

	August 1	August 31
Raw Material Inventory	$ 58,000	$ 84,000
Work in Process Inventory	372,000	436,000
Finished Goods Inventory	224,000	196,000

All raw material is direct to the production process. The following information is also available about August manufacturing costs:

Cost of raw material used	$612,000
Direct labor cost	748,000
Manufacturing overhead	564,000

a. Calculate the cost of goods manufactured for August.
b. Determine the cost of goods sold for August.

PROBLEMS

37. **LO.1-LO.3 (Cost classifications)** Joe Reynolds painted four houses during April 2013. For these jobs, he spent $2,400 on paint, $160 on mineral spirits, and $300 on brushes. He also bought two pairs of coveralls for $100 each; he wears coveralls only while he works. During the first week of April, Reynolds placed a $200 ad for his business in the classifieds. He hired an assistant for one of the painting jobs; the assistant was paid $25 per hour and worked 50 hours.

    Being a very methodical person, Reynolds kept detailed records of his mileage to and from each painting job. The average operating cost per mile for his van is $0.70. He found a $30 receipt in his van for a metropolitan map that he purchased in April. He uses the map as part of a contact file for referral work and for bids that he has made on potential jobs. He also had $30 in receipts for bridge tolls ($2 per trip) for a painting job he completed across the river.

    Near the end of April, Reynolds decided to go camping, and he turned down a job on which he had bid $6,000. He called the homeowner long distance (at a cost of $2.20) to explain his reasons for declining the job.

    Using the following headings, indicate how to classify each of the April costs incurred by Reynolds. Assume that the cost object is a house-painting job.

Type of Cost	Variable	Fixed	Direct	Indirect	Period	Product

ETHICS

38. **LO.2 (Cost behavior; cost management; ethics)** An extremely important and expensive variable cost per employee is employer-provided health care. This cost is expected to rise each year as more and more expensive technology is used on patients and as the costs of that technology are passed along through the insurance company to the employer. One simple way to reduce these variable costs is to reduce employee insurance coverage.

    a. Discuss the ethical implications of reducing employee health-care coverage to reduce the variable costs incurred by the employer.
    b. Assume that you are an employer with 600 employees. You are forced to reduce some insurance benefits. Your coverage currently includes the following items: mental health coverage, long-term disability, convalescent facility care, nonemergency but medically necessary procedures, dependent coverage, and life insurance. Select the two you would eliminate or dramatically reduce and provide reasons for your selections.
    c. Prepare a plan that might allow you to "trade" some variable employee health-care costs for a fixed or mixed cost.

39. **LO.2 (Cost behavior)** Mason Company's cost structure contains a number of different cost behavior patterns. Following are descriptions of several different costs; match these to the appropriate graphs. On each graph, the vertical axis represents cost, and the horizontal axis represents level of activity or volume.

    Identify, by letter, the graph that illustrates each of the following cost behavior patterns. Each graph can be used more than once.

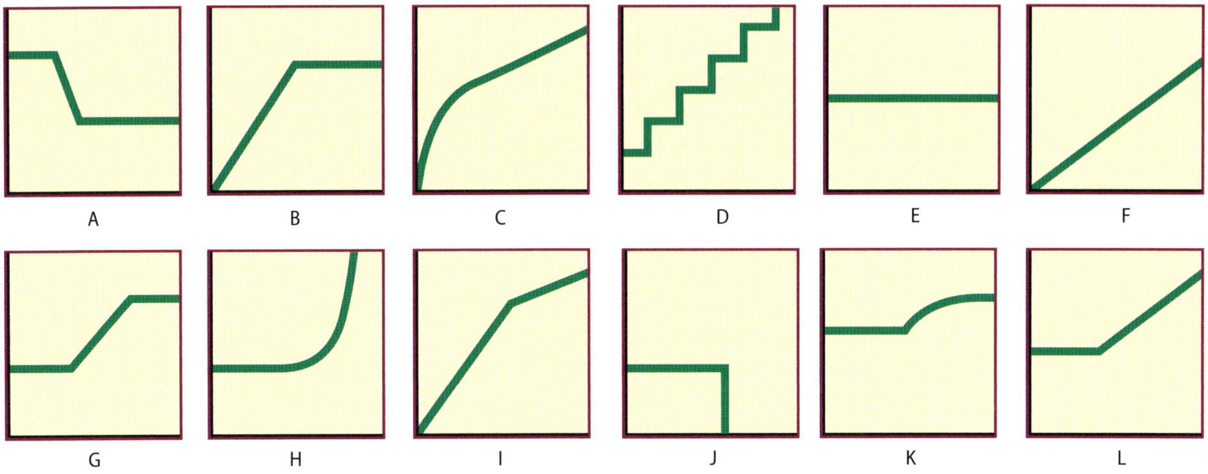

1. Cost of raw material, where the cost decreases by $0.06 per unit for each of the first 150 units purchased, after which it remains constant at $2.75 per unit.
2. City water bill, which is computed as follows: first 750,000 gallons or less, $1,000 flat fee; next 15,000 gallons, $0.002 per gallon used; next 15,000 gallons, $0.005 per gallon used; next 15,000 gallons, $0.008 per gallon used; and so on.
3. Salaries of maintenance workers, assuming one maintenance worker is needed for every 1,000 hours or less of machine time.
4. Electricity rate structure—a flat fixed charge of $250 plus a variable cost after 150,000 kilowatt hours are used.
5. Depreciation of equipment using the straight-line method.
6. Rent on a machine that is billed at $1,000 for up to 500 hours of machine time. After 500 hours of machine time, an additional charge of $1 per hour is paid up to a maximum charge of $2,500 per period.
7. Rent on a factory building donated by the county; the agreement provides for a monthly rental of $100,000 less $1 for each labor hour worked in excess of 200,000 hours. However, a minimum rental payment of $20,000 must be made each month.
8. Cost of raw material used.
9. Rent on a factory building donated by the city with an agreement providing for a fixed-fee payment unless 250,000 labor hours are worked, in which case no rent needs to be paid.

AICPA ADAPTED

40. **LO.2 (Cost behavior)** Creative Catering prepares meals for several airlines, and sales average 150,000 meals per month at a selling price of $25.32 per meal. The significant costs of each meal prepared are for the meat, vegetables, and plastic trays and utensils; no desserts are provided because the airlines are concerned about cost control. The company prepares meals in batches of 2,000. The following data are shown in the company's accounting records for June 2013:

Cost of meat for 2,000 meals	$3,600
Cost of vegetables for 2,000 meals	1,440
Cost of plastic trays and utensils for 2,000 meals	480
Direct labor cost for 2,000 meals	3,800

Monthly overhead charges amount to $1,200,000 and are fully fixed. Company management has asked you to answer the following items.

a. What is the cost per meal based on average sales and June costs?
b. If sales increase to 300,000 meals per month, what will be the cost per meal (assuming that the cost behavior patterns remain the same as in June)?

c. Assume that sales increase to 300,000 meals per month. Creative Catering wants to provide a larger meat portion per meal and has decided that, since the airlines are willing to incur the cost determined in (a), the company will simply increase its per-unit spending for meat. If all costs other than meat remain constant, how much can Creative Catering increase its cost per meal for meat?

d. The company's major competitor has bid a price of $21.92 per meal to the airlines. The profit margin in the industry is 100 percent of total cost. If Creative Catering is to retain the airlines' business, how many meals must the company produce and sell each month to reach the bid price of the competitor and maintain the 100 percent profit margin? Assume that June cost patterns will not change and meals must be produced in batches of 2,000.

e. Consider your answer to (d). Under what circumstances might the manager for Creative Catering retain the airlines' business but cause the company to be less profitable than it currently is? Show calculations.

41. **LO.2 (Cost drivers and predictors)** Customers now demand a wide variety of "personalized" products and want those products delivered quickly. Factory automation is replacing the traditional labor-intensive production lines. Thus, product costs are determined when they are "on the drawing board" because, once they are designed, it is difficult to change the method of production or product components.

a. Why is determining the cost to manufacture a product quite a different activity from determining how to control such costs?

b. Why has the advancement of technology made costs more difficult to control?

c. For many production costs, why should "number of units produced" not be considered a cost driver even though it is certainly a valid cost predictor?

42. **LO.2 (Cost behavior)** Toni Rankin has been elected to handle the local Little Theater summer play. The theater has a maximum capacity of 1,000 patrons. Rankin is trying to determine the price to charge Little Theater members for attendance at this year's performance of *The Producers*. She has developed the following cost estimates associated with the play:

- Cost of printing invitations will be $360 for 100–500; cost to print between 501 and 1,000 will be $450.
- Cost of readying and operating the theater for three evenings will be $900 if attendance is 500 or less; this cost rises to $1,200 if attendance is above 500.
- Postage to mail the invitations will be $0.60 each.
- Cost of building stage sets will be $1,800.
- Cost of printing up to 1,000 programs will be $350.
- Cost of security will be $110 per night plus $30 per hour; five hours will be needed each night.
- Cost to obtain script usage, $2,000.
- Costumes will be donated by several local businesses.

The Little Theater has 300 members, and each member is allowed two guests. Ordinarily only 60 percent of the members attend the summer offering. Of those attending, half bring one guest and the other half bring two guests. The play will be presented from 8 to 11 P.M. each evening. Invitations are mailed to those members calling to say they plan to attend and also to each of the guests they specify. Rankin has asked you to help her by answering the following items.

a. Indicate the type of cost behavior exhibited by each of the items Rankin needs to consider.

b. If the ordinary attendance occurs, what will be the total cost of the summer production?

c. If the ordinary attendance occurs, what will be the cost per person attending?

d. If 90 percent of the members attend and each invites two guests, what will be the total cost of the play? The cost per person? What primarily causes the difference in the cost per person?

43. **LO.2 (Cost behavior)** PlumView Printers makes stationery sets of 100 percent rag content edged in 24 karat gold. In an average month, the firm produces 80,000 boxes of stationery; each box contains 100 pages of stationery and 80 envelopes. Production costs are incurred for paper, ink, glue, and boxes. The company manufactures this product in batches of 500 boxes of a specific stationery design. The following data have been extracted from the company's accounting records for June 2013:

Cost of paper for each batch	$10,000
Cost of ink and glue for each batch	1,000
Cost of 1,000 gold boxes for each batch	32,000
Direct labor for producing each batch	16,000
Cost of designing each batch	20,000

Overhead charges total $408,000 per month and are considered fully fixed for purposes of cost estimation.

a. What is the cost per box of stationery based on average production volume?
b. If sales volume increases to 120,000 boxes per month, what will be the cost per box (assuming that cost behavior patterns remain the same as in June)?
c. If sales volume increases to 120,000 boxes per month but the firm does not want the cost per box to exceed its current level [based on (a)], what amount can the company pay for design costs, assuming all other costs are the same as June levels?
d. Assume that PlumView Printers is now able to sell, on average, each box of stationery at a price of $195. If the company is able to increase its volume to 120,000 boxes per month, what sales price per box will generate the same per-unit gross margin that the firm is now achieving on 80,000 boxes per month?
e. Would it be possible to lower total costs by producing more boxes per batch, even if the total volume of 80,000 is maintained? Explain.

44. **LO.5 (Journal entries)** The following transactions were incurred by Dimasi Industries during January 2013:

EXCEL

(1) Issued $800,000 of direct material to production.
(2) Paid 40,000 hours of direct labor at $18 per hour.
(3) Accrued 15,500 hours of indirect labor cost at $15 per hour.
(4) Recorded $102,100 of depreciation on factory assets.
(5) Accrued $32,800 of supervisors' salaries.
(6) Issued $25,400 of indirect material to production.
(7) Completed goods costing $1,749,300 and transferred them to finished goods.

a. Prepare journal entries for these transactions using a single overhead account for variable and fixed overhead. The Raw Material Inventory account contains only direct material; indirect material costs are recorded in Supplies Inventory.
b. If Work in Process Inventory had a beginning balance of $18,900 and an ending balance of $59,600, what amount of manufacturing overhead was included in Work in Process Inventory during January 2013?

45. **LO.5 (Ethics)** You are the chief financial officer for a small manufacturing company that has applied for a bank loan. In speaking with the bank loan officer, you are told that two minimum criteria for granting loans are (1) a 40 percent gross margin and (2) operating income of at least 15 percent of sales. Looking at the last four months' income statements, you find that gross margin has been between 30 and 33 percent, and operating income ranged from 18 to 24 percent of sales. You discuss these relationships with the company president, who suggests that some of the product costs included in Cost of Goods Sold should be moved to the selling and administrative categories so that the income statement will conform to the bank's criteria.

ETHICS

a. Which types of product costs might be most easily reassigned to period cost classifications?
b. Because the president is not suggesting that any expenses be excluded from the income statement, do you see any ethical problems with the request? Discuss the rationale for your answer.

c. Write a short memo to convince the banker to loan funds to the company in spite of its noncompliance with the specified loan criteria.

46. **LO.5 (Direct labor; writing)** A portion of the costs incurred by business organizations is designated as direct labor cost. As used in practice, the term *direct labor cost* has a wide variety of meanings. Unless the meaning intended in a given context is clear, misunderstanding and confusion are likely to ensue. If a user does not understand the elements included in direct labor cost, erroneous interpretations of the numbers may occur and can result in poor management decisions. In addition to understanding the conceptual definition of direct labor cost, management accountants must understand how direct labor cost should be measured. Discuss the following issues:

a. Distinguish between direct labor and indirect labor.

b. Discuss why some nonproductive labor time (such as coffee breaks and personal time) can be and often is treated as direct labor whereas other nonproductive time (such as downtime and training) is treated as indirect labor.

c. Following are labor cost elements that a company has classified as direct labor, manufacturing overhead, or either category depending on the situation.

- *Direct labor:* Included in the company's direct labor are production efficiency bonuses and certain benefits for direct labor workers such as FICA (employer's portion), group life insurance, vacation pay, and workers' compensation insurance.
- *Manufacturing overhead:* Included in the company's overhead are costs for wage continuation plans in the event of illness, the company-sponsored cafeteria, the personnel department, and recreational facilities.
- *Direct labor or manufacturing overhead:* Included in this category are maintenance expenses, overtime premiums, and shift premiums.

Explain the rationale used by the company in classifying the cost elements in each of the three categories.

d. The two aspects of measuring direct labor costs are (1) the quantity of labor effort that is to be included, and (2) the unit price by which the labor quantity is multiplied to arrive at labor cost. Why are these considered separate and distinct aspects of measuring labor cost?

CMA ADAPTED

47. **LO.4-LO.7 (Cost flows; CGM; CGS)** For each of the following cases, compute the missing amounts.

	Case 1	Case 2	Case 3
Sales	$9,300	$ (g)	$112,000
Direct material used	1,200	(h)	18,200
Direct labor	(a)	4,900	(m)
Prime cost	3,700	(i)	(n)
Conversion cost	4,800	8,200	49,300
Manufacturing overhead	(b)	(j)	17,200
Cost of goods manufactured	6,200	14,000	(o)
Beginning work in process inventory	500	900	5,600
Ending work in process inventory	(c)	1,200	4,200
Beginning finished goods inventory	(d)	1,900	7,600
Ending finished goods inventory	1,200	(k)	(p)
Cost of goods sold	(e)	12,200	72,200
Gross profit	3,500	(l)	(q)
Operating expenses	(f)	3,500	18,000
Net income	2,200	4,000	(r)

48. **LO.5 & LO.7 (CGM; journal entries)** DeeZees makes evening dresses. The following information was gathered from the company records for 2013, the first year of company operations. Work in Process Inventory at the end of 2013 was $15,750.

Direct material purchased on account	$ 555,000
Direct material issued to production	447,000
Direct labor payroll accrued	322,500
Indirect labor payroll accrued	93,000
Prepaid factory insurance expired	3,000
Factory utilities paid	21,450
Depreciation on factory equipment recorded	32,550
Factory rent paid	126,000
Sales (all on account)	1,431,000

The company's gross profit rate for the year was 35 percent.

a. Compute the cost of goods sold for 2013.
b. What was the total cost of goods manufactured for 2013?
c. What is Finished Goods Inventory at December 31, 2013?
d. If net income was $125,000, what were total selling and administrative expenses for the year?
e. Prepare journal entries to record the flow of costs for the year, assuming the company uses a perpetual inventory system and a single Manufacturing Overhead Control account and that actual overhead is included in WIP Inventory.

49. **LO.5-LO.7 (CGM; journal entries)** Weatherguard manufactures mailboxes. The following data represent transactions and balances for December 2013, the company's first month of operations.

Purchased direct material on account	$248,000
Issued direct material to production	186,000
Accrued direct labor payroll	134,000
Paid factory rent	3,600
Accrued factory utilities	16,200
Recorded factory equipment depreciation	15,800
Paid supervisor salary	6,400
Ending work in process inventory (6,000 units)	35,000
Ending finished goods inventory (3,000 units)	?
Sales on account ($24 per unit)	648,000

a. How many units were sold in December? How many units were completed in December?
b. What was the total cost of goods manufactured in December?
c. What was the per-unit cost of goods manufactured in December?
d. Prepare the journal entries to record the flow of costs for December. Weatherguard uses a perpetual inventory system and a single Manufacturing Overhead Control account. Assume that actual overhead is included in WIP inventory.

50. **LO.6 (OH allocation; writing)** In a manufacturing company, overhead allocations are made for three reasons: (1) to determine the full cost of a product, (2) to encourage efficient resource usage, and (3) to compare alternative courses of action for management purposes.

a. Why must overhead be considered a product cost under generally accepted accounting principles?
b. Ryan Company makes plastic dog carriers. The manufacturing process is highly automated and the machine time needed to make any size carrier is approximately the same. Ryan's management decides to begin producing plastic lawn furniture, and to do so, two additional pieces of automated equipment are acquired. Annual depreciation on the new pieces of equipment is $38,000. Should the new overhead cost be allocated over all products manufactured by Ryan? Explain.
c. What one specific reason would make the use of a normal cost system more logical for a business located in Michigan than for one located in Hawaii?

51. **LO.7 (CGM; CGS)** Flex-Em began business in July 2013. The firm makes an exercise machine for home and gym use. Following are data taken from the firm's accounting records that pertain to its first month of operations.

Direct material purchased on account	$ 900,000
Direct material issued to production	377,000
Direct labor payroll accrued	126,800
Indirect labor payroll paid	40,600
Factory insurance expired	6,000
Factory utilities paid	17,800
Factory depreciation recorded	230,300
Ending work in process inventory	51,000
Ending finished goods inventory (30 units)	97,500
Sales on account ($5,200 per unit)	1,040,000

a. How many units did the company sell in July 2013?
b. Prepare a schedule of cost of goods manufactured for July 2013.
c. How many units were completed in July?
d. What was the per-unit cost of goods manufactured for the month?
e. What was the cost of goods sold in the first month of operations?
f. What was the gross margin for July 2013?

52. **LO7. (CGM; CGS)** August 2013 inventory and cost data for Petersham Company are as follows:

Direct labor	$182,400
Direct material purchased	196,300
Direct material used	195,800
Selling and administrative expenses	171,200
Factory overhead	205,700

	8/1/13	8/31/13
Direct material	$12,300	$?
Work in process	25,900	33,300
Finished goods	62,700	55,500

a. Compute the inventory value for direct materials at August 31, 2013.
b. Compute total product costs for August 2013.
c. Prepare a schedule of cost of goods manufactured for August 2013.
d. Compute cost of goods sold for August 2013.
e. Prepare an income statement for August 2013. Assume that Petersham's income tax rate is 40 percent. Sales for August 2013 were $985,000.

EXCEL

53. **LO.3-LO.7 (Product and period costs; CGM; CGS)** On August 1, 2013, Sietens Corporation had the following account balances:

Raw Material Inventory (both direct and indirect)	$ 72,000
Work in Process Inventory	108,000
Finished Goods Inventory	24,000

During August, the following transactions took place:

(1) Raw material was purchased on account, $570,000.
(2) Direct material ($121,200) and indirect material ($15,000) were issued to production.
(3) Factory payroll consisted of $180,000 for direct labor employees and $42,000 for indirect labor employees.
(4) Office salaries totaled $144,600 for the month.
(5) Utilities of $40,200 were accrued; 70 percent of the utilities cost is for the factory.
(6) Depreciation of $60,000 was recorded on plant assets; 80 percent of the depreciation is related to factory machinery and equipment.
(7) Rent of $66,000 was paid on the building. The factory occupies 60 percent of the building.
(8) At the end of August, the Work in Process Inventory balance was $49,800.
(9) At the end of August, the balance in Finished Goods Inventory was $53,400.

Sietens Corporation uses an actual cost system and debits actual overhead costs incurred to Work in Process Inventory.

a. Determine the total amount of product cost (cost of goods manufactured) and period cost incurred during August 2013.
b. Compute the cost of goods sold for August 2013.

54. **LO.5-LO.7 (Missing data)** Grand Rapids Industrial suffered major losses in a fire on June 18, 2013. In addition to destroying several buildings, the blaze destroyed the company's Work in Process Inventory for an entire product line. Fortunately, the company was insured; however, it needs to substantiate the amount of the claim. To this end, the company has gathered the following information that pertains to production and sales of the affected product line:

(1) The company's sales for the first 18 days of June amounted to $230,000. Normally, this product line generates a gross profit equal to 40 percent of sales.
(2) Finished Goods Inventory was $29,000 on June 1 and $42,500 on June 18.
(3) On June 1, Work in Process Inventory was $48,000.
(4) During the first 18 days of June, the company incurred the following costs:

Direct material used	$76,000
Direct labor	44,000
Manufacturing overhead	42,000

a. Determine the value of Work in Process Inventory that was destroyed by the fire, assuming Grand Rapids Industrial uses an actual cost system.
b. What other information might the insurance company require? How would management determine or estimate this information?

Pi-Lens/Shutterstock.com

3

Predetermined Overhead Rates, Flexible Budgets, and Absorption/Variable Costing

LEARNING OBJECTIVES

After completing this chapter, you should be able to answer the following questions:

1. Why and how are overhead costs allocated to products and services?
2. What causes underapplied or overapplied overhead, and how is it treated at the end of a period?
3. What impact do different capacity measures have on setting predetermined overhead rates?
4. How is the high–low method used in analyzing mixed costs?
5. How do managers use flexible budgets to set predetermined overhead rates?
6. How do absorption and variable costing differ?
7. How do changes in sales or production levels affect net income computed under absorption and variable costing?
8. (*Appendix*) How is least squares regression used in analyzing mixed costs?

INTRODUCTION

Any cost incurred to make products or perform services that is not direct material or direct labor is overhead. Overhead costs are incurred both in the production area and in selling and administrative departments. Manufacturers traditionally considered direct material and direct labor as the primary production costs, and overhead was often an "additional" cost that was necessary but not of an exceptionally significant amount. However, many manufacturing firms have begun to heavily invest in automation, which has increased the costs of manufacturing overhead.

Regardless of where costs are incurred, a simple fact exists: for a company to be profitable, product or service selling prices must cover all costs. Direct material and direct labor costs can be easily traced to output and, as such, create few accounting challenges. In contrast, indirect costs (overhead) cannot be traced directly to separately distinguishable outputs.

Whereas Chapter 2 discusses and illustrates actual cost systems in which actual direct material, direct labor, and manufacturing overhead are assigned to products, this chapter discusses normal costing and its use of predetermined overhead rates to determine product cost. Separation of mixed costs into variable and fixed elements, flexible budgets, and various production capacity measures are also discussed.

In addition, this chapter discusses two methods of presenting information on financial reports: absorption and variable costing. Absorption costing is commonly used for external reporting; variable costing is commonly used for internal reporting. Each method uses the same input data but accumulates and presents those data differently. Either method can be used in job order or process costing (discussed in Chapters 5 and 6) and with actual, normal, or standard costs.

NORMAL COSTING AND PREDETERMINED OVERHEAD

1 Why and how are overhead costs allocated to products and services?

An alternative to actual costing is normal costing, which assigns actual direct material and direct labor to products but allocates manufacturing overhead (OH) to products using a predetermined rate (see Exhibit 3.1). The overhead allocation can occur in real time as products are manufactured or as services are delivered. Many accounting procedures are based on allocations. Cost allocations can be made across time periods or within a single time period. For example, in financial accounting, a building's cost is allocated through depreciation charges over its useful life. This process is necessary for fulfilling the matching principle. In cost accounting, manufacturing OH costs are allocated to products or services within a period using cost predictors or cost drivers. Such allocations reflect the cost principle requiring all production or acquisition costs to be attached to the units produced, services rendered, or units purchased.

Exhibit 3.1 Actual versus Normal Costing Systems

	Actual Cost System	Normal Cost System
Direct material	Assigned to product/service	Assigned to product/service
Direct labor	Assigned to product/service	Assigned to product/service
Overhead	Assigned to product/service	Assigned to overhead (OH) control account; predetermined OH rate is used to allocate overhead to product/ service

There are four primary reasons for using predetermined OH rates in product costing.

- First, predetermined OH rates facilitate overhead assignment during a period as goods are produced or sold and services are rendered. Thus, predetermined OH rates improve the timeliness of information.

- Second, predetermined OH rates adjust for variations in actual overhead costs that are unrelated to fluctuations in activity. Overhead can vary monthly because of seasonal or calendar (days in a month) factors. For example, factory utility costs could be highest in summer because of the necessity to run air conditioning. If monthly production were constant and actual overhead were assigned to production, the increase in utilities would cause product cost per unit to be higher in summer than during the rest of the year as illustrated in the following example.

  Monthly production = 3,000 units

	March	July
Utility costs	$1,200	$1,800
Divide by units	3,000	3,000
Utility cost per unit	$0.40	$0.60

- Third, predetermined OH rates overcome the problem of fluctuations in activity levels that do not impact fixed overhead costs. Even if total manufacturing overhead were the same for each period, changes in activity levels between periods would cause a per-unit change in fixed overhead cost as illustrated in the example that follows.

  Monthly production = 3,000 units; 3,750 units

	October	November
Utility costs	$600	$600
Divide by units	3,000	3,750
Utility cost per unit	$0.20	$0.16

  As mentioned earlier, many such overhead cost differences could create major variations in unit cost. Establishing a uniform annual predetermined OH rate for all units produced during the year overcomes the problems illustrated in these examples.
- Finally, using predetermined OH rates—especially when the bases for those rates truly reflect overhead cost drivers—often allows managers to be more aware of individual product or product line profitability as well as the profitability of business with a particular customer or vendor. For instance, assume that a gift shop purchases a product from Vendor X for $20; the gift shop will sell that product to customers for $40. If the gift shop manager has determined that a reasonable OH rate per hour for vendor telephone conferences is $5 and that she often spends three hours on the phone with Vendor X because of customer complaints or shipping problems, the gift shop manager could decide that the $5 profit on the product [$40 selling price − ($20 product cost + $15 in overhead)] does not make it cost beneficial to continue working with Vendor X.

Formula for Predetermined Overhead Rate

With one exception, normal cost system journal entries are identical to those made in an actual cost system. In both systems, overhead is debited during the period to a manufacturing overhead account and credited to the various accounts that "created" the overhead costs. In an actual cost system, the total amount of actual overhead cost is then transferred from the overhead account to Work in Process (WIP) Inventory. In contrast, a normal cost system assigns overhead cost to WIP Inventory using a predetermined OH rate.

To calculate a predetermined OH rate, total budgeted overhead cost at a specific activity level is divided by the related activity level:

$$\text{Predetermined OH Rate} = \frac{\text{Total Budgeted OH Cost at a Specified Activity Level}}{\text{Volume of Specified Activity Level}}$$

Overhead cost and its related activity measure are typically budgeted for one year, although a longer or shorter period could be more appropriate in some organizations' production cycles. For example, a longer period is more appropriate in a company that constructs ships, bridges, or high-rise office buildings.

Companies should use an activity base that is logically related to actual overhead cost incurrence. Although production volume might be the first activity base considered, this base is reasonable only if the company manufactures one type of product or renders just one type of service. If a company makes multiple products or performs multiple services, production or service volumes cannot be summed to determine "activity volume" because the products and services are dissimilar.

To effectively allocate overhead to heterogeneous products or services, a measure of activity that is common to all output must be selected. The activity should be a cost driver that directly causes the incurrence of overhead costs. Direct labor hours and direct labor dollars are common activity measures; however, these bases could be inappropriate if a company is highly automated. Using any direct labor measure to allocate overhead costs in automated plants results in extremely high overhead rates because the costs are applied over a relatively small activity volume. In automated plants, machine hours could be a more appropriate base for allocating overhead. Other possible measures include the

Photolink/Photodisc/Getty Images

A company that builds high-rise office buildings will likely budget overhead cost for a period longer than one year.

- number of purchase orders,
- product-related physical characteristics such as tons or gallons,
- number of, or amount of time used performing, machine setups,
- number of parts,
- material handling time,
- product complexity, and
- number of product defects.

Applying Overhead to Production

2 What causes underapplied or overapplied overhead, and how is it treated at the end of a period?

Once calculated, the predetermined OH rate is used throughout the period to apply overhead to WIP Inventory. Applied overhead is calculated as the predetermined OH rate multiplied by the actual activity volume. Thus, **applied overhead** is the dollar amount of overhead assigned to WIP Inventory using the activity measure that was selected to develop the OH rate. Overhead can be applied when goods or services are transferred out of WIP Inventory or at the end of each month if financial statements are to be prepared. Or, under the real-time systems currently in use, overhead can be applied continuously as production occurs.

For convenience, both actual and applied overhead are recorded in a single general ledger account.[1] Debits to the account represent actual overhead costs, and credits represent applied overhead. Variable and fixed overhead may be recorded either in a single account or in separate accounts, although separate accounts provide better information to managers. Exhibit 3.2 presents the alternative overhead recording possibilities.

Exhibit 3.2 Cost Accounting System Possibilities for Manufacturing Overhead

Single overhead account for variable and fixed overhead:

Manufacturing Overhead Control	
Total actual OH incurred	Total OH applied

Separate overhead accounts for variable and fixed overhead:

Manufacturing Variable Overhead (VOH) Control	
Total actual VOH incurred	Total VOH applied

Manufacturing Fixed Overhead (FOH) Control	
Total actual FOH incurred	Total FOH applied

[1] Some companies may use separate overhead accounts for actual and applied overhead. In such cases, the actual overhead account has a debit balance and the applied overhead account has a credit balance. The applied overhead account is closed at the end of the year against the actual overhead account to determine the amount of underapplied or overapplied overhead.

If variable and fixed overhead are applied using separate rates, the general ledger will have separate variable and fixed OH accounts. Because overhead represents an ever-larger part of product cost in automated factories, the benefits of separating OH according to its variable or fixed behavior are thought to be greater than the time and effort needed to make that separation. Separation of mixed costs is discussed later in this chapter.

Regardless of the number of predetermined OH rates used, actual overhead is debited to the general ledger overhead account and credited to the source of the overhead cost. Overhead is applied to WIP Inventory as production occurs, and as measured by the activity identified in the denominator in the predetermined OH rate formula. Applied overhead is debited to WIP Inventory and credited to the overhead general ledger account.

Assume that Tri-State Industrial, a manufacturer of children's car seats, budgeted and then experienced the following amounts for the current year:

	Variable Overhead	Fixed Overhead
Budgeted amount	$375,000	$630,000
Budgeted machine hours	÷ 50,000	÷ 50,000
Predetermined overhead rate	$7.50	$12.60
Actual January machine hours	× 4,300	× 4,300
Applied January overhead	$32,250	$54,180
Actual January overhead	$31,385	$55,970

Journal entries to record the actual and applied overhead for this example follow.

Variable Manufacturing Overhead	31,385	
Fixed Manufacturing Overhead	55,970	
Various accounts		87,355
To record actual manufacturing overhead		
Work in Process Inventory	86,430	
Variable Manufacturing Overhead		32,250
Fixed Manufacturing Overhead		54,180
To apply variable and fixed manufacturing overhead to WIP		

At year-end, total actual overhead will differ from total applied overhead. The difference is called underapplied or overapplied overhead. **Underapplied overhead** occurs when the OH applied to WIP Inventory is less than the actual OH cost. **Overapplied overhead** occurs when the OH applied to WIP Inventory is more than actual OH cost. Underapplied or overapplied overhead must be closed at year-end because the overhead account is temporary.

Under- or overapplication is caused by two factors that can work independently or jointly. These two factors are cost differences and capacity utilization differences. For example, if actual fixed overhead (FOH) cost differs from expected FOH cost, a fixed manufacturing overhead spending variance is created. If actual capacity utilization differs from expected utilization, a volume variance arises.[2] The independent effects of these differences (or for similar differences related to variable OH) are as follows:

Actual FOH Cost > Expected FOH Cost = Underapplied FOH
Actual FOH Cost < Expected FOH Cost = Overapplied FOH
Actual Utilization > Expected Utilization = Overapplied FOH
Actual Utilization < Expected Utilization = Underapplied FOH

In most cases, however, both cost and capacity utilization differ from estimates. When this occurs, no generalizations can be made as to whether overhead will be underapplied or overapplied.

Disposition of Underapplied and Overapplied Overhead

Overhead accounts are temporary accounts and are closed at period-end. Closing the accounts requires disposition of the underapplied or overapplied OH. Disposition depends on the materiality of the amount involved. If the amount is immaterial, it is closed to Cost of Goods Sold. As shown in Exhibit 3.3, when overhead is underapplied (debit balance), an

[2]These variances are covered in depth in Chapter 7.

insufficient amount of OH was applied to production and the closing process causes Cost of Goods Sold to increase. Alternatively, overapplied overhead (credit balance) reflects the fact that too much OH was applied to production, so closing overapplied OH causes Cost of Goods Sold to decrease.

Exhibit 3.3 Effects of Underapplied and Overapplied Overhead

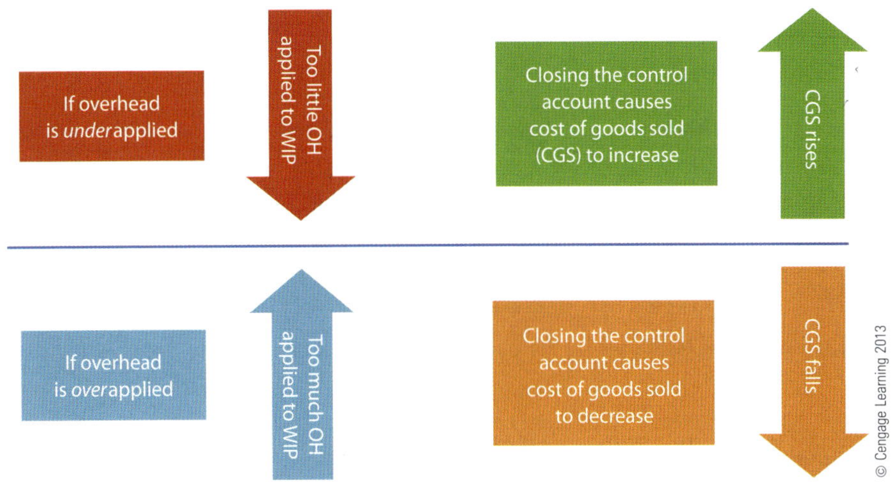

To illustrate the closing process in the case that the underapplied or overapplied overhead is immaterial, assume that Tri-State Industrial incurred and applied overhead as follows.

ACTUAL AND APPLIED OVERHEAD BASED ON 51,500 HOURS FOR THE YEAR

	Variable Overhead	Fixed Overhead
Actual (assumed)	$383,000	$657,000
Applied		
Variable ($7.50 × 51,500)	386,250	
Fixed ($12.60 × 51,500)		648,900
Over- (under-) applied amount	$ 3,250	$ (8,100)

Each amount is immaterial, so the journal entries to close these amounts are:

Variable Manufacturing Overhead	3,250	
Cost of Goods Sold		3,250
To close overapplied VOH		
Cost of Goods Sold	8,100	
Fixed Manufacturing Overhead		8,100
To close underapplied FOH		

If the amount of applied OH differs materially (significantly) from actual overhead costs, it should be prorated among the accounts in which applied OH resides: Work in Process Inventory, Finished Goods Inventory, and Cost of Goods Sold. Proration of the underapplied or overapplied overhead makes the account balances conform more closely to actual historical cost as required by generally accepted accounting principles (GAAP) for external reporting. Exhibit 3.4 (p. 68) uses assumed data for Tri-State Industrial to illustrate proration of a material amount of overapplied fixed overhead to the accounts based on their year-end account balances.[3] If the OH had been underapplied, the accounts debited and credited in the journal entry would be reversed.

[3]Theoretically, underapplied or overapplied OH should be allocated based on the amounts of applied OH contained in each account rather than on total account balances. Use of total account balances could cause distortion because they contain direct material and direct labor costs that are not related to actual or applied OH. In spite of this potential distortion, use of total balances is more common in practice for two reasons. First, the theoretical method is complex and requires detailed account analysis. Second, overhead tends to lose its identity after leaving Work in Process Inventory, thus making the determination of the amount of overhead in Finished Goods Inventory and Cost of Goods Sold account balances more difficult.

Exhibit 3.4 Proration of Overapplied Fixed Overhead

Fixed Manufacturing Overhead		Account Balances	
Actual FOH	$220,000	Work in Process Inventory	$ 45,640
Applied FOH	260,000	Finished Goods Inventory	78,240
Overapplied FOH	$ 40,000	Cost of Goods Sold	528,120

STEP 1: Add balances of accounts and determine proportional relationships:

Balance		Proportion	Percentage
Work in Process	$ 45,640	$45,640 ÷ $652,000	7
Finished Goods	78,240	$78,240 ÷ $652,000	12
Cost of Goods Sold	528,120	$528,120 ÷ $652,000	81
Total	$652,000		100

STEP 2: Multiply percentages by the overapplied overhead amount to determine the adjustment amount:

Account	%	×	Overapplied FOH	=	Adjustment Amount
Work in Process	7	×	$40,000	=	$2,800
Finished Goods	12	×	$40,000	=	$4,800
Cost of Goods Sold	81	×	$40,000	=	$32,400

STEP 3: Prepare the journal entry to close manufacturing overhead account and assign adjustment amount to appropriate accounts:

	Debit	Credit
Fixed Manufacturing Overhead	40,000	
Work in Process Inventory		2,800
Finished Goods Inventory		4,800
Cost of Goods Sold		32,400
To close overapplied fixed overhead		

3 What impact do different capacity measures have on setting predetermined overhead rates?

Alternative Capacity Measures

The activity level used in setting the predetermined OH rate generally reflects a consideration of organizational capacity. The estimated maximum potential activity for a specified time is the **theoretical capacity**. This measure assumes that all production factors are operating perfectly. Theoretical capacity disregards realities such as machinery breakdowns and reduced or stopped plant operations on holidays. Choosing this activity level for setting a predetermined OH rate nearly guarantees a significant amount of underapplied overhead cost. The amount by which overhead is underapplied reflects the difference between actual capacity and theoretical capacity.

Reducing theoretical capacity by ongoing, regular operating interruptions (such as holidays, downtime, and start-up time) provides the **practical capacity** that could be achieved during regular working hours. Consideration of historical and estimated future production levels and the cyclical fluctuations provides a **normal capacity** measure that encompasses the firm's long-run (5–10 years) average activity and represents an attainable level of activity. Although it may generate substantial differences between actual and applied overhead in the short run, use of normal capacity has been required under GAAP.[4]

[4] FASB Statement No. 151, titled *Inventory Costs*, was issued in November 2004 (Codification 330-10-30). The statement indicates that variations in production levels from period to period are expected and establish the normal capacity range. This capacity range will vary based on business- and industry-specific factors. The actual production level may be used if it approximates normal capacity. In periods of abnormally high production, the amount of fixed overhead allocated to each unit of production is decreased so that inventories are not measured above cost. The amount of fixed overhead allocated to each unit of production is not increased as a consequence of abnormally low production or an idle plant.

Expected capacity is a short-run concept that represents the firm's anticipated activity level for the coming period based on projected product demand. Expected capacity level is determined during the budgeting process, which is discussed in Chapter 8. If actual results are close to budgeted results (in both dollars and volume), this measure should result in product costs that most closely reflect actual costs and, thus, generate an immaterial amount of underapplied or overapplied overhead.[5]

See Exhibit 3.5 for a visual representation of capacity measures. Although expected capacity is shown in this diagram as much smaller than practical capacity, it is possible for expected and practical capacity to be more equal—especially in a highly automated plant.

Regardless of the capacity level chosen for the denominator in calculating a predetermined OH rate, any mixed overhead costs must be separated into their variable and fixed components.

SEPARATING MIXED COSTS

As discussed in Chapter 2, a mixed cost contains both a variable and a fixed component. For example, a cell phone plan that has a flat charge for basic service (the fixed component) plus a stated rate for each minute of use (the variable component) creates a mixed cost. A mixed cost does not remain constant with changes in activity, nor does it fluctuate on a per-unit basis in direct proportion to changes in activity.

Exhibit 3.5 Measures of Capacity

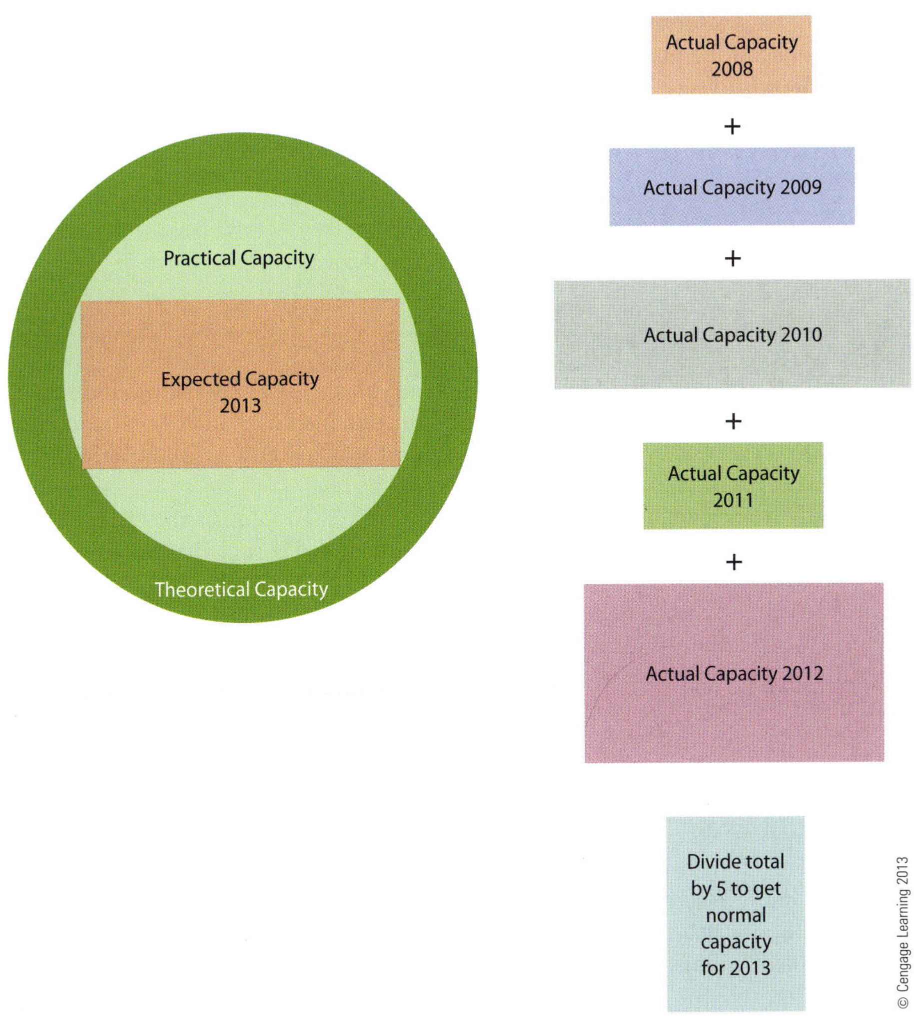

[5]Except where otherwise noted in the text, expected capacity has been chosen as the basis for calculating the predetermined fixed manufacturing overhead rate because it is believed to be the most prevalent practice. This choice, however, may not be the most effective for planning and control purposes as is discussed further in Chapter 7 with regard to standard cost variances.

To simplify estimation of costs, accountants typically assume that costs are linear rather than curvilinear. Because of this assumption, the general formula for a straight line can be used to describe any type of cost within a relevant range of activity. The straight-line formula is

$$y = a + bX$$

where y = total cost (dependent variable),
a = fixed portion of total cost,
b = unit change of variable cost relative to unit changes in activity, and
X = activity base to which y is being related (the predictor, cost driver, or independent variable).

If a cost is entirely variable, the a value in the formula is zero. If the cost is entirely fixed, the b value in the formula is zero. If a cost is mixed, it is necessary to determine formula values for both a and b. Two methods of determining these values—and thereby separating a mixed cost into its variable and fixed components—are the high–low method and least squares regression analysis.

High–Low Method

4 How is the high–low method used in analyzing mixed costs?

The **high–low method** analyzes a mixed cost by first selecting the highest and lowest levels of activity in a data set if these two points are within the relevant range. Activity levels are used because activities cause costs to change, not vice versa. Occasionally, operations occur at a level outside the relevant range (a special rush order could require excess labor or machine time), or cost distortions occur within the relevant range (a leak in a water pipe could go unnoticed for a period of time). Such nonrepresentative or abnormal observations are called **outliers** and should be disregarded when analyzing a mixed cost.

Next, changes in activity and cost are determined by subtracting low values from high values. These changes are used to calculate the b (variable unit cost) value in the $y = a + bX$ formula as follows:

$$b = \frac{\text{Cost at High Activity Level} - \text{Cost at Low Activity Level}}{\text{High Activity Level} - \text{Low Activity Level}}$$

$$b = \frac{\text{Change in Total Cost}}{\text{Change in Activity Level}}$$

The b value is the unit variable cost per measure of activity. This value is multiplied by the activity level to determine the total variable cost contained in the total cost at either the high or the low level of activity. The fixed portion of a mixed cost is found by subtracting total variable cost from total cost.

As the activity level changes, the change in total mixed cost equals the change in activity multiplied by the unit variable cost. By definition, the fixed cost element does not fluctuate with changes in activity.

Exhibit 3.6 illustrates the high–low method using machine hours and utility cost information for Tri-State Industrial. In November 2013, the company wanted to calculate its predetermined OH utility rate to use in calendar year 2014. Tri-State Industrial gathered information for the prior ten months' machine hours and utility costs. During 2013, the company's normal operating range of activity was between 3,500 and 9,000 machine hours per month. Because May activity is substantially in excess of normal activity levels, that observation is viewed as an outlier and should not be used in the analysis of utility cost.

One potential weakness of the high–low method is that outliers can inadvertently be used in the calculation. Estimates of future costs calculated from a line drawn using such points will not indicate actual costs and probably are not good predictions. A second weakness of this method is that it considers only two data points. A more precise method of analyzing mixed costs is least squares regression analysis. This method is discussed in the chapter appendix.

Once a method has been selected and mixed overhead costs have been separated into fixed and variable components, a flexible budget can be developed to estimate overhead at various levels of the denominator activity.

Exhibit 3.6 Analysis of Mixed Utility Cost for Tri-State Industrial

The following machine hours and utility cost information is available:

Month	Machine Hours	Utility Cost
January	7,260	$2,960
February	8,850	3,410
March	4,800	1,920
April	9,000	3,500
May	11,000	3,900 *Outlier*
June	4,900	1,860
July	4,600	2,180
August	8,900	3,470
September	5,900	2,480
October	5,500	2,310

STEP 1: Select the highest and lowest levels of activity within the relevant range and obtain the costs associated with those levels. These levels and costs are 9,000 and 4,600 hours, and $3,500 and $2,180, respectively.

STEP 2: Calculate the change in cost compared to the change in activity.

	Machine Hours	Associated Total Cost
High activity	9,000	$3,500
Low activity	4,600	2,180
Changes	4,400	$1,320

STEP 3: Determine the relationship of cost change to activity change to find the variable cost element.

$$b = \$1{,}320 \div 4{,}400 \text{ MH} = \$0.30 \text{ per machine hour}$$

STEP 4: Compute total variable cost (TVC) at either level of activity.

$$\text{High level of activity: TVC} = \$0.30(9{,}000) = \$2{,}700$$
$$\text{Low level of activity: TVC} = \$0.30(4{,}600) = \$1{,}380$$

STEP 5: Subtract total variable cost from total cost at the associated level of activity to determine fixed cost.

$$\text{High level of activity: } a = \$3{,}500 - \$2{,}700 = \$800$$
$$\text{Low level of activity: } a = \$2{,}180 - \$1{,}380 = \$800$$

STEP 6: Substitute the fixed and variable cost values in the straight-line formula to get an equation that can be used to estimate total cost at any level of activity within the relevant range.

$$y = \$800 + \$0.30X$$

where X = machine hours

FLEXIBLE BUDGETS

5 How do managers use flexible budgets to set predetermined overhead rates?

A **flexible budget** is a planning document that presents expected variable and fixed costs at different activity levels. Activity levels shown on a flexible budget usually cover the contemplated range of activity for the current or future period. If all activity levels are within the relevant range, costs at each successive level should equal the previous level plus an increment for each variable cost. The increment is equal to variable cost per unit of activity times the quantity of additional activity.

Expected cost information from the flexible budget is used for the numerator in computing the predetermined OH rate. Exhibit 3.7 illustrates a flexible overhead budget for Tri-State Industrial at selected levels of activity. All amounts have been assumed. Note that the variable overhead cost per machine hour (MH) does not change within the relevant range, but the fixed overhead cost per machine hour varies inversely with the level of activity. Given that the company selected 50,000 machine hours as the denominator level of annual activity, the variable and fixed predetermined OH rates were $7.50 and $12.60, respectively.

Exhibit 3.7 Flexible Overhead Budget for Tri-State Industrial

	NUMBER OF MACHINE HOURS (MHs)				
	40,000	**45,000**	**50,000**	**55,000**	**75,000**
Variable OH (VOH)					
Indirect material	$ 60,000	$ 67,500	$ 75,000	$ 82,500	$112,500
Indirect labor	120,000	135,000	150,000	165,000	225,000
Utilities	14,000	15,750	17,500	19,250	26,250
Other	106,000	119,250	132,500	145,750	198,750
Total	$300,000	$337,500	$375,000	$412,500	$562,500
VOH rate per MH	$ 7.50	$ 7.50	$ 7.50	$ 7.50	$ 7.50
FOH					
Factory salaries	$215,000	$215,000	$215,000	$215,000	$215,000
Depreciation	300,000	300,000	300,000	300,000	300,000
Utilities	9,600	9,600	9,600	9,600	9,600
Other	105,400	105,400	105,400	105,400	105,400
Total	$630,000	$630,000	$630,000	$630,000	$630,000
FOH rate per MH	$ 15.75	$ 14.00	$ 12.60	$ 11.45	$ 8.40

Plantwide versus Departmental Overhead Rates

Because most manufacturing companies make many different kinds of products, calculation of a plantwide predetermined OH rate generally does not provide the most useful information. Assume that Tri-State Industrial has two departments: Assembly and Finishing. Assembly is highly automated, but Finishing requires significant direct labor. As such, it is highly probable that machine hours would be the more viable overhead allocation base for Assembly, and direct labor hours would be the better allocation base for Finishing.

Exhibit 3.8 uses a single product (Part #AB79Z) to show the cost differences that can be created by using a plantwide predetermined OH rate. Production of this part requires one hour of machine time in Assembly and five hours of direct labor time in Finishing. The departmental cost amounts shown in Exhibit 3.8 have been assumed so that they will balance with information provided in Exhibit 3.7. Notice that the $20.10 plantwide OH rate using machine hours in Exhibit 3.8 is the same total rate implied in Exhibit 3.7: a variable rate of $7.50 per MH plus a fixed rate of $12.60 per MH. For purposes of this illustration, the use of separate variable and fixed OH rates is ignored.

Exhibit 3.8 shows how product cost can change dramatically depending on the predetermined OH rate. A company with multiple departments that use significantly different types of work effort (such as automated versus manual or diverse materials that require considerably different processing times in those departments should use separate departmental predetermined OH rates to attach overhead to products to derive the most rational product cost. Homogeneity more likely exists within a department than across departments. Thus, separate departmental OH rates generally provide better information for management

Exhibit 3.8 Plantwide versus Departmental Predetermined OH Rate for Tri-State Industrial

	Plantwide	Assembly	Finishing
Budgeted annual overhead	$1,005,000	$724,500	$280,500
Budgeted annual direct labor hours (DLHs)	13,000	3,000	10,000
Budgeted annual machine hours (MHs)	50,000	45,000	5,000

Departmental overhead rates

Assembly (automated): $724,500 ÷ 45,000 = $16.10 per MH
Finishing (manual): $280,500 ÷ 10,000 = $28.05 per DLH

Plantwide overhead rates

Using DLHs: $1,005,000 ÷ 13,000 = $77.31 per DLH (rounded)
Using MHs: $1,005,000 ÷ 50,000 = $20.10 per MH

Part #AB79Z

Overhead assigned using departmental rates

Assembly	1 MH × $16.10	$ 16.10
Finishing	5 DLHs × $28.05	140.25
Total		$156.35

Total overhead assigned using plantwide rates

Based on DLHs	5 DLHs × $77.31	$386.55
Based on MHs	1 MH × $20.10	$ 20.10

Using assumed direct material and direct labor costs, the total cost of Part #AB79Z is

	Using Departmental OH Rates	Using a Plantwide Rate Based on DLHs	Using a Plantwide Rate Based on MHs
Direct material	$110.00	$110.00	$110.00
Direct labor	36.00	36.00	36.00
Overhead	156.35	386.55	20.10
Total cost	$302.35	$532.55	$166.10

planning, control, and decision making than do plantwide OH rates. Computing departmental OH rates allows each department to select the most appropriate measure of activity (or cost driver) relative to its operations.

Additionally, the use of variable and fixed categories within each department lets management understand how costs react to changes in activity. The use of variable and fixed categories also makes it easier to generate different reports for external and internal reporting purposes.

OVERVIEW OF ABSORPTION AND VARIABLE COSTING

6 How do absorption and variable costing differ?

In preparing financial reports, costs can be accumulated and presented in different ways. The choice of cost accumulation method determines which costs are recorded as part of product cost and which are considered period costs. In contrast, the choice of cost presentation method determines how costs are shown on external financial statements or internal management reports. Accumulation and presentation procedures are accomplished using one of two methods: absorption costing or variable costing. Each method accumulates and presents the same basic data differently, and either method can be used in job order or process costing and with actual, normal, or standard costs.

Absorption costing treats the costs of all manufacturing components (direct material, direct labor, variable overhead, and fixed overhead) as inventoriable, or product, costs in accordance with GAAP. Absorption costing is also known as **full costing**, and this method fits the product cost definition given in Chapter 2. Under absorption costing, costs incurred in the nonmanufacturing areas of the organization are considered period costs and are expensed in a manner that properly matches them with revenues. Exhibit 3.9 depicts the absorption costing model. In addition, absorption costing presents expenses on an income statement according to their functional classifications. A **functional classification** is a group of costs that were incurred for the same principal purpose. Functional classifications generally include cost of goods sold, selling expense, and administrative expense.

Exhibit 3.9 Absorption Costing Model

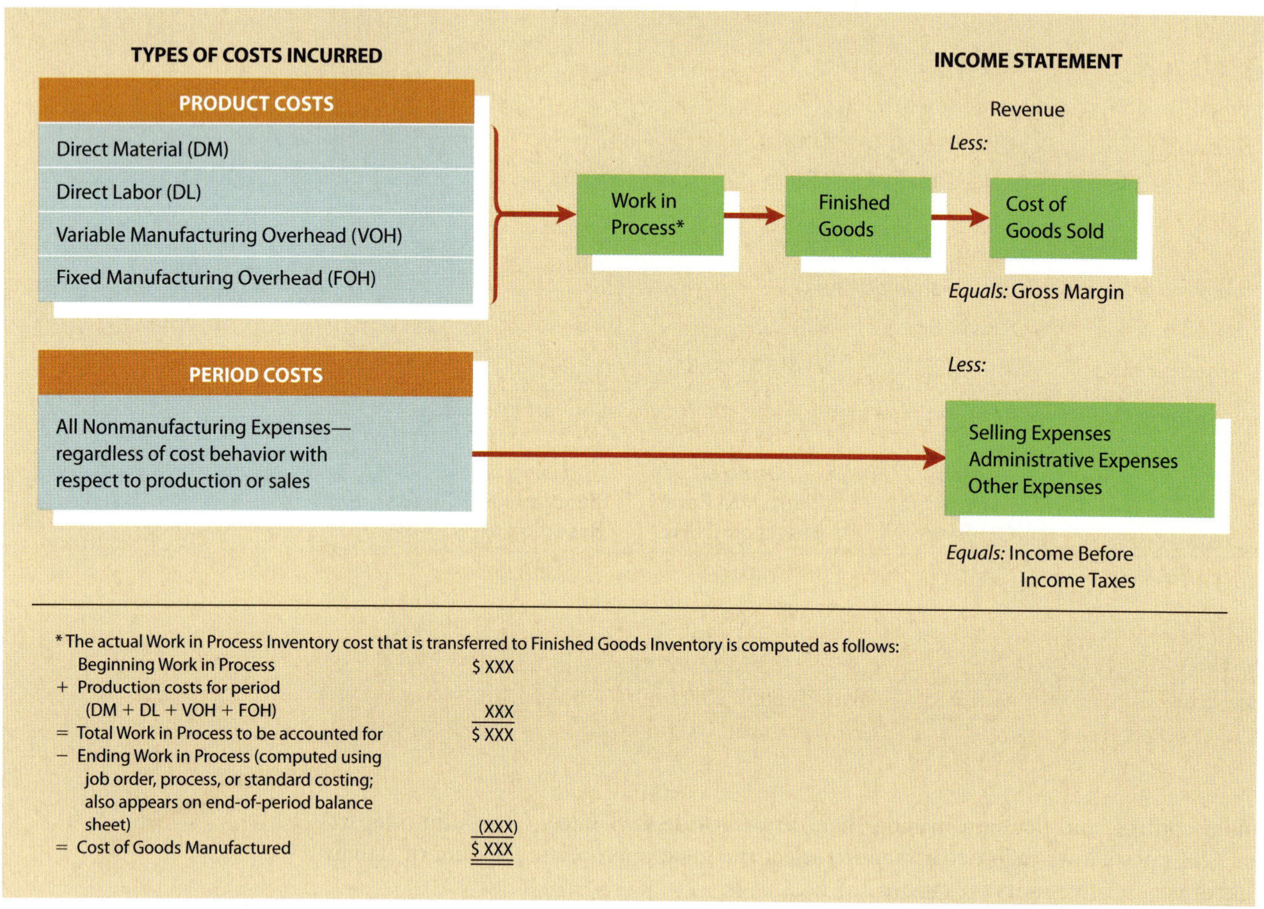

In contrast, **variable costing** (also known as **direct costing**) is a cost accumulation method that includes only direct material, direct labor, and variable overhead as product costs. This method treats fixed manufacturing overhead (FOH) as a period cost. Like absorption costing, variable costing treats costs incurred in the organization's selling and administrative areas as period costs. Variable costing income statements typically present expenses according to cost behavior (variable and fixed), although expenses can also be presented by functional classifications within the behavioral categories. See Exhibit 3.10 for the variable costing model.

Two differences exist between absorption and variable costing: one relates to cost accumulation and the other relates to cost presentation. The cost accumulation difference is that absorption costing treats FOH as a product cost; variable costing treats it as a period cost.

Exhibit 3.10 Variable Costing Model

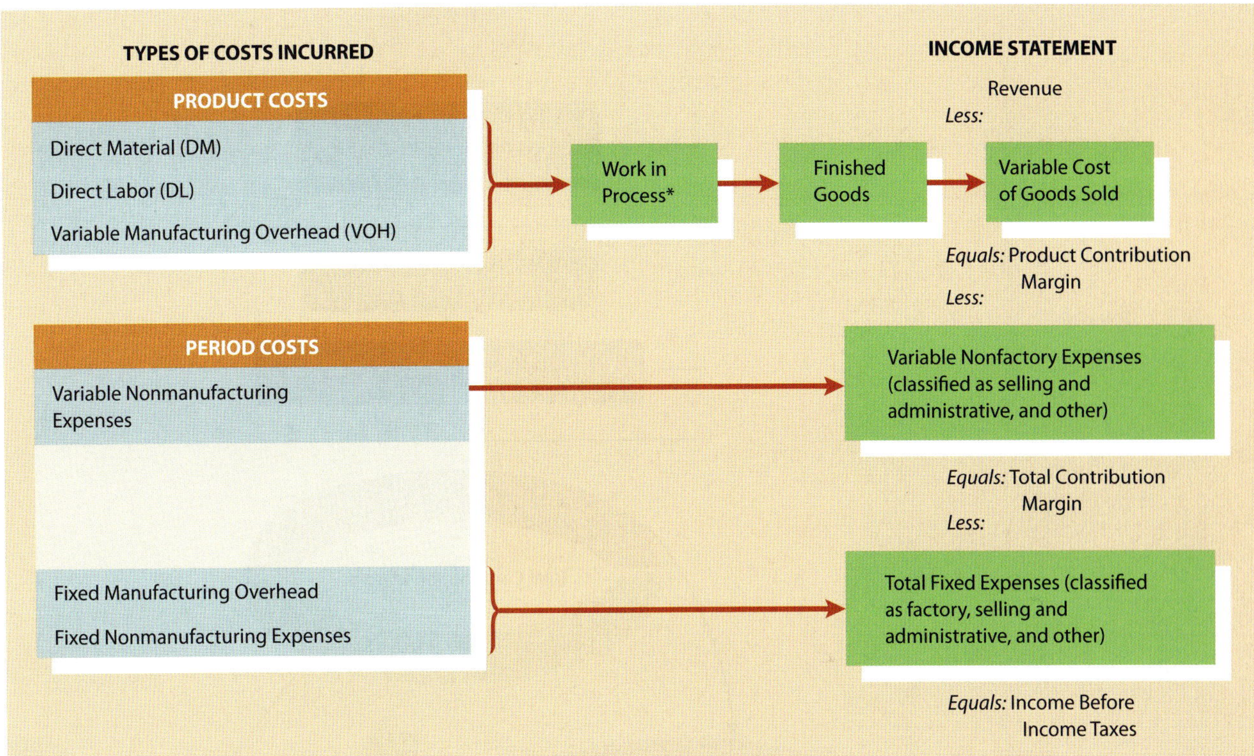

* The actual Work in Process Inventory cost that is transferred to Finished Goods Inventory is computed as follows:

Beginning Work in Process	$ XXX
+ Production costs for period (DM + DL + VOH)	XXX
= Total Work in Process to be accounted for	$ XXX
− Ending Work in Process (computed using job order, process, or standard costing; also appears on end-of-period balance sheet)	(XXX)
= Cost of Goods Manufactured	$ XXX

Absorption costing advocates contend that products cannot be made without the production capacity provided by fixed manufacturing overhead costs, and, therefore, these costs "belong" to the product. Variable costing advocates contend that FOH costs would be incurred whether any products are manufactured; thus, such costs are not caused by production and cannot be product costs.

The cost presentation difference is that absorption costing classifies expenses by function on both the income statement and management reports, whereas variable costing categorizes expenses first by behavior and then, possibly, by function. Under variable costing, cost of goods sold is more appropriately called variable cost of goods sold because it is composed only of variable production costs. Sales minus variable cost of goods sold is called **product contribution margin** and indicates how much revenue is available to cover all period expenses and to provide net income.

Variable nonmanufacturing period expenses, such as sales commissions set at 10 percent of product selling price, are deducted from product contribution margin to determine the amount of total contribution margin. Total **contribution margin** is the difference between total revenues and total variable expenses. This amount measures the dollars available to "contribute" to cover all fixed expenses, both manufacturing and nonmanufacturing, and to provide net income A variable costing income statement is also referred to as a contribution income statement. See Exhibit 3.11 (p. 76) for a diagram of these variable costing relationships.

Major authoritative bodies of the accounting profession, such as the Financial Accounting Standards Board and the Securities and Exchange Commission, require the use of

Exhibit 3.11 Variable Costing Relationships

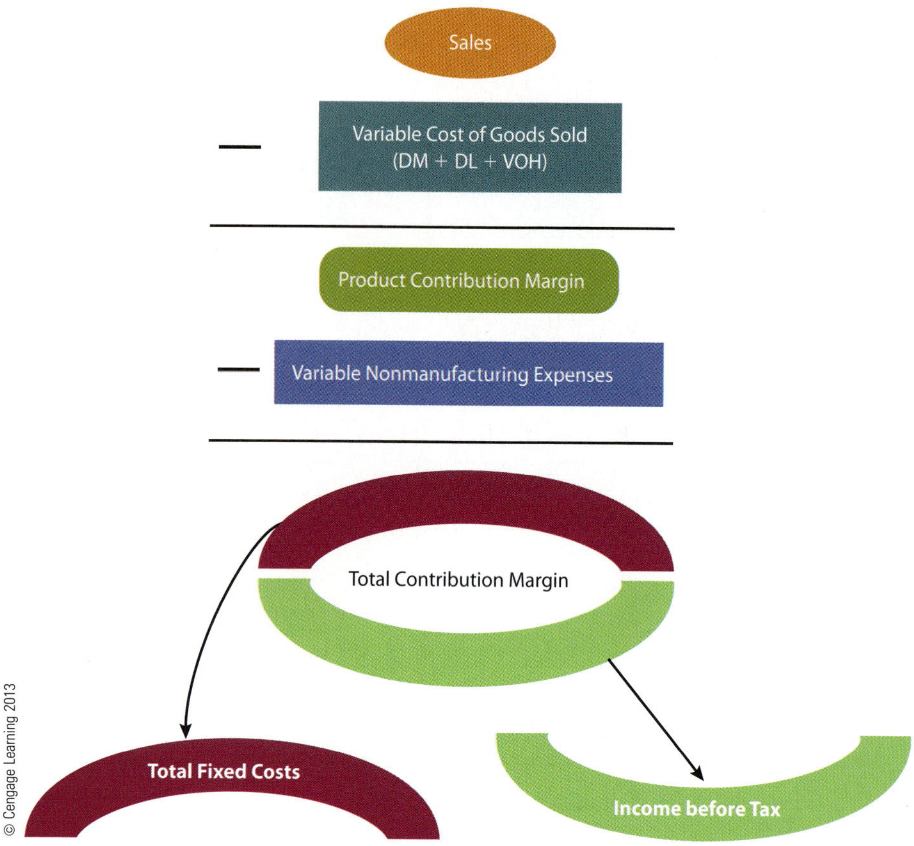

absorption costing to prepare external financial statements. Absorption costing is also required for filing tax returns with the Internal Revenue Service. The accounting profession has, in effect, disallowed the use of variable costing for external reporting purposes.

Because absorption costing classifies expenses by functional category, cost behavior (relative to changes in activity) cannot be observed from an absorption costing income statement or management report. Understanding cost behavior is extremely important for many managerial activities including budgeting, cost-volume-profit analysis, and relevant costing.[6] Thus, internal financial reports distinguishing costs by behavior are often prepared for use in management decision making and analysis. The next section illustrates both absorption and variable costing.

Absorption and Variable Costing Illustrations

Custom Covers began operations in 2012 and has been hired by Tri-State Industrial to make car seat cushions. Product specifications are likely to be constant at least until model year 2015. Data for this product are used to compare absorption and variable costing procedures and presentations.

The company uses standard costs for material and labor and predetermined rates for variable and fixed overhead.[7] Exhibit 3.12 presents unit production costs, annual budgeted nonmanufacturing costs, and other basic operating data for Custom Covers. The predetermined fixed OH rate of $0.54 per unit is computed by dividing budgeted annual FOH ($162,000) by expected capacity (300,000 units). All costs are assumed to remain constant over the three years 2012 through 2014, and, for simplicity, Custom Covers is assumed to

[6] These topics are covered in Chapters 8 (budgeting), 9 (cost-volume-profit analysis), and 10 (relevant costing).

[7] Actual costs can also be used under either absorption or variable costing. Standard costing was chosen for these illustrations because it makes the differences between the two methods more obvious. If actual costs had been used, production costs would vary each year, and such variations would obscure the distinct differences caused by the use of one method, rather than the other, over a period of time. Standard costs are also treated as constant over time to more clearly demonstrate the differences between absorption and variable costing and to reduce the complexity of the chapter explanations.

complete all units started and, therefore, will have no WIP Inventory at the end of a period. Also, all actual costs are assumed to equal the standard and budgeted costs for the years presented. The bottom section of Exhibit 3.12 is a comparison of actual unit production with actual unit sales to determine the change in inventory for each of the three years.

Exhibit 3.12 Custom Covers Basic Data for 2012, 2013, and 2014

Sales price per unit	$6.00	
Variable manufacturing cost per unit		
Direct material	$2.04	
Direct labor	1.50	
Variable manufacturing overhead	0.18	
Total variable manufacturing cost per unit	$3.72	

$$\text{Predetermined Fixed Manufacturing Overhead Rate} = \frac{\text{Budgeted Annual Fixed Manufacturing Overhead}}{\text{Budgeted Annual Capacity in Units}}$$

FOH rate = $162,000 ÷ 300,000 = $0.54

Total absorption cost per unit	
Variable manufacturing cost per unit	$ 3.72
Fixed manufacturing overhead per unit	0.54
Total absorption cost per unit	$ 4.26
Budgeted nonproduction expenses	
Variable selling expense per unit	$ 0.24
Fixed selling and administrative expense	$23,400

Total budgeted selling & administrative expenses = ($0.24 per unit sold + $23,400)

	2012	2013	2014	Total
Actual units made	300,000	290,000	310,000	900,000
Actual unit sales	(300,000)	(270,000)	(330,000)	(900,000)
Change in finished goods inventory	0	+20,000	(20,000)	0

Because Custom Covers began operations in 2012, there is no beginning finished goods inventory for that year. The next year, 2013, also has no beginning inventory because all units produced in 2012 were also sold in 2012. In 2013 and 2014, production and sales quantities differ, which is a common situation because production frequently "leads" sales so that inventory can be stockpiled to satisfy future sales demand. Refer to Exhibit 3.13 (p. 78) for Custom Covers' operating results for the years 2012 through 2014 using both absorption and variable costing. This example assumes that Custom Covers had no beginning inventory and that cumulative units of production and sales for the three years are identical for both methods. Under these conditions, the data in Exhibit 3.13 demonstrate that, regardless of whether absorption or variable costing is used, the cumulative income before tax will be the same ($1,279,800). Also, as in 2012, for any year in which there is no change in inventory from the beginning to the end of the year, both absorption and variable costing methods will result in the same net income.

Actual production and operating costs have been assumed to equal the budgeted costs for years 2012 through 2014. However, differences in actual and budgeted capacity utilization occurred for 2013 and 2014, which created a volume variance for each of those years under absorption costing. A **volume variance** reflects the monetary impact of a difference

Exhibit 3.13 Custom Covers' Absorption and Variable Costing Income Statements for 2012, 2013, and 2014

ABSORPTION COSTING PRESENTATION

	2012	2013	2014	Total
Sales ($6 per unit)	$ 1,800,000	$ 1,620,000	$ 1,980,000	$ 5,400,000
Cost of goods sold (CGS) ($4.26 per unit)	(1,278,000)	(1,150,200)	(1,405,800)	(3,834,000)
Gross margin	$ 522,000	$ 469,800	$ 574,200	$ 1,566,000
Volume variance (U)	0	(5,400)	5,400	0
Adjusted gross margin	$ 522,000	$ 464,400	$ 579,600	$ 1,566,000
Selling and administrative expenses	(95,400)	(88,200)	(102,600)	(286,200)
Income before tax	$ 426,600	$ 376,200	$ 477,000	$ 1,279,800

VARIABLE COSTING PRESENTATION

	2012	2013	2014	Total
Sales ($6 per unit)	$ 1,800,000	$ 1,620,000	$ 1,980,000	$ 5,400,000
Variable CGS ($3.72 per unit)	(1,116,000)	(1,004,400)	(1,227,600)	(3,348,000)
Product contribution margin	$ 684,000	$ 615,600	$ 752,400	$ 2,052,000
Variable selling expenses ($0.24 × units sold)	(72,000)	(64,800)	(79,200)	(216,000)
Total contribution margin	$ 612,000	$ 550,800	$ 673,200	$ 1,836,000
Fixed expenses				
Manufacturing	$ 162,000	$ 162,000	$ 162,000	$ 486,000
Selling and administrative	23,400	23,400	23,400	70,200
Total fixed expenses	$ (185,400)	$ (185,400)	$ (185,400)	$ (556,200)
Income before tax	$ 426,600	$ 365,400	$ 487,800	$ 1,279,800
Differences in income before tax	$ 0	$ 10,800	$ (10,800)	$ 0

between the budgeted capacity used to determine the predetermined FOH rate and the actual capacity at which the company operated. Thus, for Custom Covers, there is no volume variance for 2012 because 300,000 units were both budgeted and produced. For 2013, the volume variance is calculated as [$0.54 × (290,000 − 300,000)] or $5,400 unfavorable. For 2014, it is calculated as [$0.54 × (310,000 − 300,000)] or $5,400 favorable. Each of these variance amounts is considered immaterial and is shown as an adjustment to the year's gross margin. No volume variances are shown under variable costing because fixed manufacturing overhead is not applied to products; the FOH is deducted in its entirety as a period expense.

The income statements in Exhibit 3.13 show that absorption and variable costing provide different income figures in some years. Comparing the two sets of statements indicates that the difference in income arises solely from the different treatment of fixed overhead. If no beginning or ending inventories exist, cumulative total income under both methods will be identical. Over the three-year period, Custom Covers produced and sold 900,000 units. Thus, all the costs incurred (whether variable or fixed) are expensed in one year or another under either method. The income difference in each year is caused solely by the timing of the expensing of fixed manufacturing overhead.

In Exhibit 3.13, absorption costing income before tax for 2013 exceeds that of variable costing by $10,800. This difference is caused by the FOH assigned to the 20,000 units made but not sold (\$0.54 × 20,000) and, thus, placed in inventory in 2013. Critics of absorption costing refer to this phenomenon as creating illusionary or phantom profits. **Phantom profits** are temporary absorption costing profits caused by producing more inventory than is sold. When previously produced inventory is sold, the phantom profits disappear. In contrast, variable costing expenses all FOH in the year it is incurred.

In 2014, inventory decreased by 20,000 units. This decrease, multiplied by the FOH rate of \$0.54, explains the \$10,800 by which 2014 absorption costing income falls short of variable costing income in Exhibit 3.13. For 2014, not only is all current year fixed manufacturing overhead expensed through Cost of Goods Sold, but also the \$10,800 of FOH that was retained in 2013's ending inventory is shown in 2014's Cost of Goods Sold. Only 2014 fixed manufacturing overhead is shown on the 2014 variable costing income statement.

Comparison of the Two Approaches

7 How do changes in sales or production levels affect net income computed under absorption and variable costing?

Whether absorption costing income is more or less than variable costing income depends on the relationship of production to sales. In all cases, to determine the effect on income, it must be assumed that unit product costs are constant over time. See Exhibit 3.14 for the possible relationships between production and sales levels and the effects of these relationships on income. These relationships are as follows:

- If production equals sales, absorption costing income will equal variable costing income.
- If production is more than sales, absorption costing income is greater than variable costing income. This result occurs because some fixed manufacturing overhead cost is included in inventory cost on the balance sheet under absorption costing, whereas the total amount of fixed manufacturing overhead cost is expensed as a period cost under variable costing.
- If production is less than sales, income under absorption costing is less than income under variable costing. In this case, absorption costing expenses all of the current period fixed manufacturing overhead costs and releases some fixed manufacturing overhead cost from the beginning inventory where it had been deferred from a prior period.

Exhibit 3.14 Production/Sales Relationships and Effects on Income and Inventory

where P = Production and S = Sales
AC = Absorption Costing and VC = Variable Costing

	Absorption vs. Variable Income Statement Income before Taxes	**Absorption vs. Variable Balance Sheet Ending Inventory**
P = S	AC = VC No difference from beginning inventory $FOH_{EI} - FOH_{BI} = 0$	No additional difference $FOH_{EI} = FOH_{BI}$
P > S (Stockpiling inventory)	AC > VC By amount of fixed OH in ending inventory minus fixed OH in beginning inventory $FOH_{EI} - FOH_{BI} = +$ amount	Ending inventory increased (by fixed OH in additional units because P > S) $FOH_{EI} > FOH_{BI}$
P < S (Reducing inventory)	AC < VC By amount of fixed OH released from balance sheet beginning inventory $FOH_{EI} - FOH_{BI} = -$ amount	Ending inventory difference reduced (by fixed OH from BI charged to cost of goods sold) $FOH_{EI} < FOH_{BI}$

The effects of the relationships presented here are based on two qualifying assumptions:
(1) that unit costs are constant over time and
(2) that any under- or overapplied fixed overhead is written off when incurred rather than being prorated to inventory balances.

This process of deferring FOH costs into, and releasing FOH costs from, inventory makes it possible to manipulate income under absorption costing by adjusting levels of production relative to sales. For this reason, some people believe that variable costing is more useful for external reporting purposes than absorption costing. For internal reporting, variable costing information provides managers information about the behavior of the various product and period costs. To plan, control, and make decisions, managers must understand and be able to project how costs will change in reaction to changes in activity levels. Variable costing, through its emphasis on cost behavior, provides that necessary information.

APPENDIX

LEAST SQUARES REGRESSION ANALYSIS

8 How is least squares regression used in analyzing mixed costs?

Least squares regression analysis is a statistical technique that analyzes the relationship between independent (causal) and dependent (effect) variables. The least squares method is used to develop an equation that predicts an unknown value of a **dependent variable** (cost) from the known values of one or more **independent variables** (activities that create costs). When multiple independent variables exist, least squares regression also helps to select the independent variable that is the best predictor of the dependent variable. For example, managers can use least squares to decide whether machine hours, direct labor hours, or pounds of material moved best explain and predict changes in a specific overhead cost.[8]

Simple regression analysis uses one independent variable to predict the dependent variable based on the $y = a + bX$ formula for a straight line. In **multiple regression**, two or more independent variables are used to predict the dependent variable. All text examples use simple regression and assume that a linear relationship exists between variables so that each one-unit change in the independent variable produces a constant unit change in the dependent variable.[9]

A **regression line** is any line that goes through the means (or averages) of the independent and dependent variables in a set of observations. As shown in Exhibit 3.15, numerous straight lines can be drawn through any set of data observations, but most of these lines would provide a poor fit to the data. Actual observation values are designated as y values; these points do not generally fall directly on a regression line. The least squares method mathematically fits the best possible regression line to observed data points. The method fits this line by minimizing the sum of the squares of the vertical deviations between the actual observation points and the regression line. The regression line represents computed values for all activity levels, and the points on the regression line are designated as y_c values.

The regression line of best fit is found by predicting the a and b values in a straight-line formula using the actual activity and cost values (y values) from the observations. The equations necessary to compute b and a values using the method of least squares are as follows:[10]

$$b = \frac{\sum xy - n(\bar{x})(\bar{y})}{\sum x^2 - n(\bar{x})^2}$$

$$a = \bar{y} - b\bar{x}$$

where $\bar{x}$ = mean of the independent variable
$\bar{y}$ = mean of the dependent variable
n = number of observations

[8] Further discussion of finding independent variable(s) that best predict the value of the dependent variable can be found in most textbooks on statistical methods treating regression analysis under the headings of dispersion, coefficient of correlation, coefficient of determination, or standard error of the estimate.

[9] Curvilinear relationships between variables also exist. For example, quality defects (dependent variable) tend to increase at an increasing rate in relationship to machinery age (independent variable).

[10] These equations are derived from mathematical computations beyond the scope of this text but can be found in many statistics books. The symbol Σ means "the summation of."

Exhibit 3.15 Illustration of Least Squares Regression Line

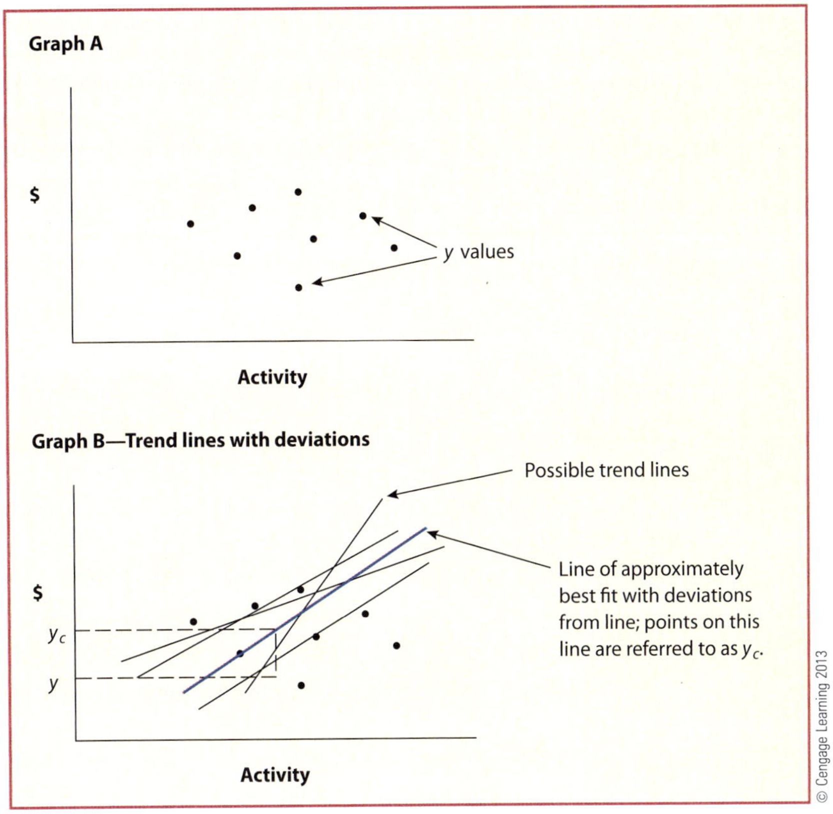

Using the machine hour and utility cost data for Tri-State Industrial (presented in Exhibit 3.6 and excluding the May outlier), the following calculations can be made:

x	y	xy	x^2
7,260	$ 2,960	$ 21,489,600	52,707,600
8,850	3,410	30,178,500	78,322,500
4,800	1,920	9,216,000	23,040,000
9,000	3,500	31,500,000	81,000,000
4,900	1,860	9,114,000	24,010,000
4,600	2,180	10,028,000	21,160,000
8,900	3,470	30,883,000	79,210,000
5,900	2,480	14,632,000	34,810,000
5,500	2,310	12,705,00	30,250,000
59,710	$24,090	$169,746,100	424,510,100

The mean of x (or $\bar{x}$) is 6,634.44 (59,710 ÷ 9), and the mean of y (or $\bar{y}$) is $2,676.67 ($24,090 ÷ 9). Thus,

$$b = \frac{\$169{,}746{,}100 \times 9(6{,}634.44)(\$2{,}676.67)}{424{,}510{,}100 - 9(6{,}634.44)(6{,}634.44)} = \frac{\$9{,}922{,}241}{\$28{,}367{,}953} = \underline{\underline{\$0.35}}$$

$$a = \$2{,}676.67 - \$0.35(6{,}634.44) = \$2{,}676.67 - \$2{,}322.05 = \underline{\underline{\$354.62}}$$

The b (variable cost) and a (fixed cost) values for the company's utility costs are $0.35 and $354.62, respectively. These values are close to, but not exactly the same as, the values computed using the high–low method.

By using these values, predicted costs (y_c values) can be computed for each actual activity level. The line drawn through all of the y_c values will be the line of best fit for the data. Because actual costs do not generally fall directly on the regression line and predicted costs naturally do, these two costs differ at their related activity levels. It is acceptable for the regression line not to pass through any of the actual observation points because the line has been determined to mathematically "fit" the data.

Like all mathematical models, regression analysis is based on certain assumptions that produce limitations on the model's use. Three of these assumptions follow; others are beyond the scope of the text. First, for regression analysis to be useful, the independent variable must be a valid predictor of the dependent variable; the relationship can be tested by determining the coefficient of correlation. Second, like the high–low method, regression analysis should be used only within a relevant range of activity. Third, the regression model is useful only as long as the circumstances existing at the time of its development remain constant; consequently, if significant additions are made to capacity or if there is a major change in technology usage, the regression line will no longer be valid.

Comprehensive Review Module

KEY TERMS

absorption costing, p. 74
applied overhead, p. 65
contribution margin, p. 75
dependent variable, p. 80
direct costing, p. 74
expected capacity, p. 69
flexible budget, p. 71
full costing, p. 74
functional classification, p. 74
high–low method, p. 70
independent variable, p. 80
least squares regression analysis, p. 80
multiple regression, p. 80
normal capacity, p. 68
outliers, p. 70
overapplied overhead, p. 66
phantom profit, p. 79
practical capacity, p. 68
product contribution margin, p. 75
regression line, p. 80
simple regression, p. 80
theoretical capacity, p. 68
underapplied overhead, p. 66
variable costing, p. 74
volume variance, p. 77

CHAPTER SUMMARY

1 Overhead Cost Allocation

- Manufacturing overhead costs are allocated to products to
  - eliminate the problems caused by delays in obtaining actual cost data.
  - make the overhead allocation process more effective.
  - allocate a uniform amount of overhead to goods or services based on related production efforts.
  - allow managers to be more aware of individual product or product line profitability as well as the profitability of doing business with a particular customer or vendor.
- Cost allocations can be made using actual or normal costing; normal costing necessitates the computation of one or more predetermined overhead rates.
- A predetermined OH rate is calculated as total budgeted OH cost at a specified activity level divided by the volume at that specified activity level.
- Applied OH is the amount of overhead debited to Work in Process Inventory using the actual volume of the specified activity measure multiplied by the predetermined OH rate.

2 Underapplied and Overapplied Overhead

- Underapplied (actual is more than applied) or overapplied (actual is less than applied) overhead is

- caused by a difference between actual and budgeted OH costs and/or a difference between the actual and budgeted level of activity chosen to compute the predetermined OH rate.
- closed at the end of each period (unless normal capacity is used for the denominator level of activity) to
  - ➢ Cost of Goods Sold (CGS) if the amount of underapplied or overapplied overhead is immaterial (underapplied will cause CGS to increase, and overapplied will cause CGS to decrease)

    or
  - ➢ Work in Process Inventory, Finished Goods Inventory, and Cost of Goods Sold (based on their proportional balances), if the amount of underapplied or overapplied overhead is material.

3 Predetermined Overhead Rates and Capacity

- Capacity measures affect the setting of predetermined OH rates because the use of
  - expected capacity (the budgeted capacity for the upcoming year) will result in a predetermined OH rate that would likely be most closely related to an actual OH rate.
  - practical capacity (the capacity that allows for normal operating interruptions) will generally result in a predetermined OH rate that is substantially lower than an actual OH rate would be.
  - normal capacity (the capacity that reflects a long-run average) can result in an OH rate that is higher or lower than an actual OH rate, depending on whether capacity has been over- or underutilized during the years under consideration.
  - theoretical capacity (the estimated maximum potential capacity) will result in a predetermined OH rate that is substantially lower than an actual OH rate; however, this rate reflects a company's utopian use of its capacity.

4 High–Low Method

- Mixed costs may be separated into their variable and fixed components using the high–low method.
  - The change in cost between the highest and lowest activity levels in the data set (excluding outliers) is used to compute a variable cost per unit.
  - Fixed cost is determined by subtracting total variable cost at either the highest or the lowest activity level from total cost at that level.

5 Predetermined Overhead Rates and Flexible Budgets

- Flexible budgets are used by managers to help set predetermined OH rates by
  - allowing managers to identify the manufacturing OH costs to be incurred and what the behaviors (variable, fixed, or mixed) of those costs are.
  - allowing managers to separate mixed costs into their variable and fixed elements.
  - providing information on the budgeted costs to be incurred at various levels of activity.
  - providing the impacts on the predetermined fixed OH rate (or on a plantwide rate) from changing the denominator level of activity.
- If an organization's departments use significantly different types of work effort or material processing, flexible budgets and predetermined OH rates generally should be computed using departmental rather than plantwide information.

6 Absorption and Variable Costing

- Absorption and variable costing differ in that
  - absorption costing
    - ➢ includes all manufacturing costs, both variable and fixed, as product costs.
    - ➢ presents nonmanufacturing costs on the income statement according to functional areas.
  - variable costing
    - ➢ includes only the variable costs of production (direct material, direct labor, and variable manufacturing overhead) as product costs.
    - ➢ presents both nonmanufacturing and manufacturing costs on the income statement according to cost behavior.

7 Changing Sales or Production Levels in Absorption and Variable Costing

- Differences between sales and production volume result in differences in income between absorption and variable costing because
  - absorption costing requires fixed costs to be expensed as a function of the number of units sold;
    - ➢ if production volume is higher than sales volume, some fixed costs will be deferred in inventory at year-end, making net income higher than under variable costing.
    - ➢ if sales volume is higher than production volume, the deferred fixed costs from previous periods will be expensed as part of Cost of Goods Sold, making net income lower than under variable costing.
  - variable costing requires all fixed costs to be expensed in the period incurred, regardless of when the related inventory is sold;
    - ➢ if production volume is higher than sales volume, all fixed manufacturing costs are expensed in the current period and are not deferred until the inventory is sold, making net income lower than under absorption costing.
    - ➢ if sales volume is higher than production volume, only current period fixed manufacturing costs are expensed in the current period, making net income higher than under absorption costing.

SOLUTION STRATEGIES

Predetermined Overhead Rate, p. 64

$$\text{Predetermined OH Rate} = \frac{\text{Total Budgeted OH Cost at a Specified Activity Level}}{\text{Specified Activity Level}}$$

(Can use separate variable and fixed rates or a combined rate)

High–Low Method, p. 70

(Using assumed amounts)

	(Independent Variable) Activity	(Dependent Variable) Total Cost	–	Total Variable Cost (Rate × Activity)	=	Total Fixed Cost
"High" level	14,000	$18,000	–	$11,200	=	$6,800
"Low" level	9,000	14,000	–	7,200	=	6,800
Differences	5,000	$ 4,000				

$0.80
variable cost per unit of activity

Underapplied and Overapplied Overhead, p. 66

Manufacturing Overhead Control	XXX	
Various accounts		XXX
To record actual overhead costs		
Work in Process Inventory	YYY	
Manufacturing Overhead Control		YYY
To apply overhead to WIP		

A debit balance in Manufacturing Overhead at the end of the period is underapplied overhead; a credit balance is overapplied overhead. The debit or credit balance in the overhead account is closed at the end of the period to Cost of Goods Sold or is prorated to Work in Process Inventory, Finished Goods Inventory, and Cost of Goods Sold.

Flexible Budget, p. 71

To prepare a flexible budget,

1. separate mixed costs into variable and fixed elements;
2. determine the $a + bX$ cost formula for each budgetary item (for example, all items creating manufacturing overhead);
3. select several potential levels of activity within the relevant range; and
4. use the cost formulas to determine the total cost expected at each of the selected levels of activity.

Absorption and Variable Costing, p. 74

1. Determine which method is being used (absorption or variable). The following abbreviations are used: VOH, variable manufacturing overhead; FOH, fixed manufacturing overhead; DM, direct material; DL, direct labor.
   a. If absorption:
      - Determine the FOH application rate.
      - Determine the denominator capacity used in determining FOH.
      - Determine whether production was equal to the denominator capacity. If not, a FOH volume variance must be properly assigned to CGS and, possibly, inventories.
      - Determine the cost per unit of product, which consists of (DM + DL + VOH + FOH).

b. If variable:
   - Determine the cost per unit of product, which consists of (DM + DL + VOH).
   - Determine the total FOH and assign that amount to the income statement as a period expense.

2. Determine the relationship of production to sales.
   a. If production = sales, then absorption costing income = variable costing income.
   b. If production > sales, then absorption costing income > variable costing income.
   c. If production < sales, then absorption costing income < variable costing income.
3. The dollar difference between absorption costing income and variable costing income equals FOH rate × change in inventory units.

DEMONSTRATION PROBLEM

White Plasto Company management uses predetermined VOH and FOH rates to apply overhead to its products. For 2012, the company budgeted production at 27,000 units, which would require 54,000 direct labor hours (DLHs) and 27,000 machine hours (MHs). At that level of production, total variable and fixed manufacturing overhead costs were expected to be $13,500 and $105,300, respectively. Variable overhead is applied to production using direct labor hours, and fixed overhead is applied using machine hours. During 2012, White Plasto Company produced 23,000 units and experienced the following operating volumes and costs: 46,000 direct labor hours; 23,000 machine hours; $11,980 actual variable manufacturing overhead; and $103,540 actual fixed manufacturing overhead. By the end of 2012, all 23,000 units that were produced were sold; thus, the company began 2013 with no beginning finished goods inventory.

In 2013 and 2014, White Plasto Company management decided to apply manufacturing overhead to products using units of production (rather than direct labor hours and machine hours). The company produced 25,000 and 20,000 units, respectively, in 2013 and 2014. White Plasto's budgeted and actual fixed manufacturing overhead for both years was $100,000. Production in each year was projected at 25,000 units. Variable production cost (including variable manufacturing overhead) is $3 per unit. The following absorption costing income statements and supporting information are available:

	2013	2014
Net sales (20,000 units and 22,000 units)	$ 300,000	$ 330,000
Cost of goods sold (a)	(140,000)	(154,000)
Volume variance (0 and 5,000 units × $4)	0	(20,000)
Gross margin	$ 160,000	$ 156,000
Operating expenses (b)	(82,500)	(88,500)
Income before tax	$ 77,500	$ 67,500
(a) Cost of goods sold		
Beginning inventory	$ 0	$ 35,000
Cost of goods manufactured[a]	175,000	140,000
Goods available for sale	$ 175,000	$ 175,000
Ending inventory[b]	(35,000)	(21,000)
Cost of goods sold	$ 140,000	$ 154,000

[a]CGM
25,000 units × $7 (of which $3 are variable) = $175,000
20,000 units × $7 (of which $3 are variable) = $140,000

[b]EI
25,000 − 20,000 = 5,000 units; 5,000 × $7 = $35,000
5,000 + 20,000 − 22,000 = 3,000 units; 3,000 × $7 = $21,000

	2013	2014
(b) Analysis of operating expenses		
Variable	$ 50,000	$ 55,000
Fixed	32,500	33,500
Total	$ 82,500	$ 88,500

Required:

a. Determine the predetermined variable and fixed overhead rates for 2012, and calculate how much underapplied or overapplied overhead existed at the end of that year.
b. Recast the 2013 and 2014 income statements on a variable costing basis.
c. Reconcile income for 2013 and 2014 between absorption and variable costing.

Solution to Demonstration Problem

a. VOH rate = $13,500 ÷ 54,000 DLHs = $0.25 per DLH
FOH rate = $105,300 ÷ 27,000 MHs = $3.90 per MH

Actual VOH	$ 11,980	Actual FOH	$103,540
Applied VOH (46,000 × $0.25)	(11,500)	Applied FOH (23,000 × $3.90)	(89,700)
Underapplied VOH	$ 480	Underapplied FOH	$ 13,840

Note that the large underapplication of FOH was caused mainly by a difference between the number of machine hours used to set the rate (27,000) and the number of machine hours that were actually worked (23,000): 4,000 × $3.90 = $15,600. The underapplication of FOH was constrained by the fact that the company incurred only $103,540 of FOH rather than the $105,300 the company expected to incur. The total underapplication is the combination of the negative machine hour effect and the positive total expenditure effect: $15,600 – ($105,300 – $103,540) = $13,840.

b.

	2013	2014
Net sales	$ 300,000	$ 330,000
Variable cost of goods sold	(60,000)	(66,000)
Product contribution margin	$ 240,000	$ 264,000
Variable operating expenses	(50,000)	(55,000)
Total contribution margin	$ 190,000	$ 209,000
Fixed costs		
Manufacturing	$ 100,000	$ 100,000
Operating	32,500	33,500
Total fixed costs	$(132,500)	$(133,500)
Income before tax	$ 57,500	$ 75,500

c. Reconciliation 2013

Absorption costing income before tax	$ 77,500
– Fixed manufacturing overhead in ending inventory ($4.00 × 5,000)	(20,000)
Variable costing income before tax	$ 57,500

Reconciliation 2014

Absorption costing income before tax	$ 67,500
+ Fixed manufacturing overhead released from beginning inventory ($4.00 × 2,000)	8,000
Variable costing income before tax	$ 75,500

POTENTIAL ETHICAL ISSUES

ETHICS

1. Using an inappropriately high normal capacity activity level to compute the predetermined OH rate, thereby reducing product cost and increasing operating income upon the sale of inventory—given that the closing of the underapplied manufacturing OH account would be deferred for multiple periods
2. Producing significantly more inventory than is necessary to meet current and anticipated sales, thereby lowering the predetermined FOH rate per unit, while increasing reported operating income
3. Treating period costs as product costs rather than expenses to inflate inventory (assets) and increase reported net income
4. Manipulating sales around the end of an accounting period to shift revenues and expired product costs into the current period or into the following period
5. Choosing a method of OH allocation that distorts the "true" profitability of specific products or specific subunits

QUESTIONS

1. What is the difference between variable and mixed costs, considering that both change in total with changes in activity levels?
2. The high–low method of analyzing mixed costs uses only two observation points: the high and the low points of activity. Are these always the best points for prediction purposes? Why or why not?
3. Discuss the reasons a company would use a predetermined overhead rate rather than actual overhead to determine cost of products or services.
4. Why are departmental predetermined OH rates more useful for managerial decision making than plantwide OH rates? Why do firms use separate variable and fixed rates rather than a total overhead rate?
5. How does absorption costing differ from variable costing in cost accumulation and income statement presentation? Why is FOH treated differently in the methods?
6. What is meant by classifying costs (a) functionally and (b) behaviorally? Why would a company be concerned about functional and behavioral classifications?
7. Is variable or absorption costing generally required for external reporting? Why is this method preferred to the alternative?
8. Why does variable costing provide more useful information than absorption costing for making internal decisions?
9. What are the income relationships between absorption and variable costing when production volume differs from sales volume? What causes these relationships to occur?
10. (*Appendix*) Why would regression analysis provide a more accurate cost formula than the high–low method for a mixed cost?

EXERCISES

11. **LO.1 (Plantwide vs. departmental OH rates)** Roddickton Manufacturing Co. has gathered the following information to develop predetermined OH rates for 2013. The company produces a wide variety of energy-saving products that are processed through two departments, Assembly (automated) and Finishing (labor intensive).

    Budgeted total overhead: $600,400 in Assembly and $199,600 in Finishing
    Budgeted total direct labor hours: 10,000 in Assembly and 40,000 in Finishing
    Budgeted total machine hours: 76,000 in Assembly and 4,000 in Finishing

    a. Compute a plantwide predetermined OH rate using direct labor hours.
    b. Compute a plantwide predetermined OH rate using machine hours.
    c. Compute departmental predetermined OH rates using machine hours for Assembly and direct labor hours for Finishing.
    d. Determine the amount of overhead that would be assigned to a product that required five machine hours in Assembly and one direct labor hour in Finishing using the answers developed in (a), (b), and (c).

12. **LO.1 (Predetermined OH rate)** For 2013, Omaha Mechanical has a monthly overhead cost formula of $42,900 + $6 per direct labor hour. The firm's 2013 expected annual capacity is 78,000 direct labor hours, to be incurred evenly each month. Making one unit of the company's product requires 1.5 direct labor hours.

    a. Determine the total overhead to be applied per unit of product in 2013.
    b. Prepare journal entries to record the application of overhead to Work in Process Inventory and the incurrence of $128,550 of actual overhead in January 2013, when 6,390 direct labor hours were worked.
    c. Given the actual direct labor hours in (b), how many units would you have expected to be produced in January?

13. **LO.1 (Predetermined OH rate)** Langston Automotive Accessories applies overhead using a combined rate for fixed and variable overhead. The rate is 250 percent of direct

labor cost. During the first three months of the current year, actual costs incurred were as follows:

	Direct Labor Cost	Actual Overhead
January	$180,000	$440,000
February	165,000	420,400
March	170,000	421,000

a. What amount of overhead was applied to production in each of the three months?
b. What was the underapplied or overapplied overhead for each of the three months and for the first quarter?

14. **LO.1 (OH application)** Use the information in Exercise 15 and assume that Lansing Mfg. has decided to use units of production to apply overhead to production. In April 2013, the company produced 900 units and incurred $7,500 and $26,500 of variable and fixed overhead, respectively.

    a. What amount of variable manufacturing overhead should be applied to production in April 2013?
    b. What amount of fixed manufacturing overhead should be applied to production in April 2013?
    c. Calculate the under- or overapplied variable and fixed overhead for April 2013.

15. **LO.1 (Predetermined OH rates)** Lansing Mfg. prepared the following 2013 abbreviated flexible budget for different levels of machine hours:

	40,000	44,000	48,000	52,000
Variable manufacturing overhead	$ 80,000	$ 88,000	$ 96,000	$104,000
Fixed manufacturing overhead	325,000	325,000	325,000	325,000

Each product requires four hours of machine time, and the company expects to produce 10,000 units in 2013. Production is expected to be evenly distributed throughout the year.

    a. Calculate separate predetermined variable and fixed OH rates using as the basis of application (1) units of production and (2) machine hours.
    b. Calculate the combined predetermined OH rate using (1) units of product and (2) machine hours.
    c. Assume that all actual overhead costs are equal to expected overhead costs in 2013, but that Lansing Mfg. produced 11,000 units of product. If the separate rates based on units of product calculated in (a) were used to apply overhead, what amounts of underapplied or overapplied variable and fixed overhead exist at year-end 2013?

16. **LO.2 (Predetermined OH rates and underapplied/overapplied OH)** Davidson's Dolls had the following information in its Work in Process Inventory account for June 2013:

Work in Process Inventory

Beginning balance	10,000	Transferred out	335,000
Materials added	150,000		
Labor (5,000 DLHs)	90,000		
Applied overhead	120,000		
Ending balance	35,000		

All workers are paid the same rate per hour. Factory overhead is applied to Work in Process Inventory on the basis of direct labor hours. The only work left in process at the end of the month had a total of 2,860 direct labor hours accumulated to date.

    a. What is the total predetermined OH rate per direct labor hour?
    b. If actual total overhead for June is $121,500, what is the amount of underapplied or overapplied overhead?
    c. Given your answer to (b), how would you recommend the over- or underapplied overhead be closed?

17. **LO.2 (Underapplied or overapplied overhead)** At year-end 2013, Dub's Wind Generator Co. had a $40,000 debit balance in its Manufacturing Overhead Control account. Overhead is applied to products based on direct labor cost. Relevant account balance information at year-end follows:

	Work in Process Inventory	Finished Inventory	Cost of Goods Sold
Direct material	$20,000	$ 80,000	$120,000
Direct labor	10,000	40,000	50,000
Factory overhead	20,000	80,000	100,000
	$50,000	$200,000	$270,000

a. What predetermined OH rate was used during the year?
b. Provide arguments to be used for deciding whether to prorate the balance in the overhead account at year-end.
c. Prorate the overhead account balance based on the relative balances of the appropriate accounts.
d. Identify some possible reasons that the company had a debit balance in the overhead account at year-end.

18. **LO.2 (Underapplied or overapplied overhead)** At the end of 2013, Jackson Tank Company's accounts showed a $66,000 credit balance in Manufacturing Overhead Control. In addition, the company had the following account balances:

Work in Process Inventory	$384,000
Finished Goods Inventory	96,000
Cost of Goods Sold	720,000

a. Prepare the necessary journal entry to close the overhead account if the balance is considered immaterial.
b. Prepare the necessary journal entry to close the overhead account if the balance is considered material.
c. Which method do you believe is more appropriate for the company, and why?

19. **LO.3 (Predetermined OH rates; capacity measures)** Alberton Electronics makes inexpensive GPS navigation devices and uses a normal cost system that applies overhead based on machine hours. The following 2013 budgeted data are available:

Variable factory overhead at 100,000 machine hours	$1,250,000
Variable factory overhead at 150,000 machine hours	1,875,000
Fixed factory overhead at all levels between 10,000 and 180,000 machine hours	1,440,000

Practical capacity is 180,000 machine hours; expected capacity is two-thirds of practical.

a. What is Alberton Electronics' predetermined VOH rate?
b. What is the predetermined FOH rate using practical capacity?
c. What is the predetermined FOH rate using expected capacity?
d. During 2013, the firm records 110,000 machine hours and $2,710,000 of overhead costs. How much variable overhead is applied? How much fixed overhead is applied using the rate found in (b)? How much fixed overhead is applied using the rate found in (c)? Calculate the total under- or overapplied overhead for 2013 using both fixed OH rates.

20. **LO.3 (Capacity measures)** For 2013, Milltown Iron Manufacturing has estimated its production capacities as follows:

Theoretical capacity	400,000 units
Practical capacity	300,000 units
Normal capacity	260,000 units
Expected capacity	200,000 units

Milltown is trying to choose which capacity measure it should use to develop its predetermined OH rates for 2013.

a. Why does the choice of capacity measure affect the amount of under- or overapplied overhead the firm will have at the end of 2013?
b. Which capacity measure choice would likely result in the least amount of under- or overapplied overhead?
c. Which of the alternative capacity measures makes allowances for possible cycles in the industry?

21. **LO.4 (High–low method)** Wyoming Wholesale has gathered the following data on the number of shipments received and the cost of receiving reports for the first seven weeks of 2013.

Number of Shipments Received	Weekly Cost of Receiving Reports
50	$175
44	162
40	154
35	142
53	185
58	200
60	202

a. Using the high–low method, develop the equation for predicting weekly receiving report costs based on the number of shipments received.
b. What is the predicted amount of receiving report costs for a week in which 72 shipments are received?
c. What are the concerns you have regarding your prediction from (b)?

22. **LO.4 (High–low method)** La Mia's Casas builds replicas of residences of famous and infamous people. The company is highly automated, and the new accountant-owner has decided to use machine hours as the basis for predicting maintenance costs. The following data are available from the company's most recent eight months of operations:

Machine Hours	Maintenance Costs
4,000	$1,470
7,000	1,200
3,500	1,680
6,000	1,100
3,000	1,960
9,000	880
8,000	1,020
5,500	1,200

a. Using the high–low method, determine the cost formula for maintenance costs with machine hours as the basis for estimation.
b. What aspect of the estimated equation is bothersome? Provide an explanation for this situation.
c. Within the relevant range, can the formula be reliably used to predict maintenance costs? Can the a and b values in the cost formula be interpreted as fixed and variable costs? Why or why not?

23. **LO.4 (High–low method)** Information about Indiana Industrial's utility cost for the last six months of 2013 follows. The high–low method will be used to develop a cost formula to predict 2014 utility charges, and the number of machine hours has been found to be an appropriate cost driver. Data for the first half of 2013 are not being considered because the utility company imposed a significant rate change as of July 1, 2013.

Month	Machine Hours	Utility Cost
July	33,750	$13,000
August	34,000	12,200
September	33,150	11,040
October	32,000	11,960
November	31,250	11,500
December	31,000	11,720

a. What is the cost formula for utility expense?
b. What is the budgeted utility cost for September 2014 if 31,250 machine hours are projected?

24. **LO.4 & LO.5 (High–low method; flexible budget)** Tijuana Tile has gathered the following information on its utility cost for the past six months.

Machine Hours	Utility Cost
1,300	$ 940
1,700	1,075
1,250	900
1,800	1,132
1,900	1,160
1,500	990

a. Using the high–low method, determine the cost formula for utility cost.
b. Prepare a flexible budget with separate variable and fixed categories for utility cost at 1,325, 1,500, and 1,675 machine hours.

25. **LO.5 (Flexible budget; variances; cost control)** The Sioux City Storage System's plant prepared the following flexible overhead budget for three levels of activity within the plant's relevant range.

	12,000 units	16,000 units	20,000 units
Variable overhead	$48,000	$64,000	$ 80,000
Fixed overhead	32,000	32,000	32,000
Total overhead	$80,000	$96,000	$112,000

After discussion with the home office, the plant managers planned to produce 16,000 units of its single product during 2013. However, demand for the product was exceptionally strong, and actual production for 2013 was 17,600 units. Actual variable and fixed overhead costs incurred in producing the 17,600 units were $69,000 and $32,800, respectively.

The production manager was upset because the company planned to incur $96,000 of costs and actual costs were $101,800. Prepare a memo to the production manager regarding the following questions.

a. Should the $101,800 actual total cost be compared to the $96,000 expected total cost for control purposes? Explain the rationale for your answer.
b. Analyze the costs and explain where the company did well or poorly in controlling its costs.

26. **LO.5 (Flexible budget)** Tom's Shoe Repair provides a variety of shoe repair services. Analysis of monthly costs revealed the following cost formulas when direct labor hours are used as the basis of cost determination:

EXCEL

Supplies: $y = \$0 + \$4.00X$
Production supervision and direct labor: $y = \$500 + \$7.00X$
Utilities: $y = \$350 + \$5.40X$
Rent: $y = \$450 + \$0.00X$
Advertising: $y = \$75 + \$0.00X$

a. Prepare a flexible budget at 250, 300, 350, and 400 direct labor hours.
b. Calculate a total cost per direct labor hour at each level of activity.
c. Tom's employees usually work 350 direct labor hours per month. The average shoe repair requires 1.25 labor hours to complete. Tom wants to earn a 40 percent margin on his cost. What should be the average charge per customer, rounded to the nearest dollar to achieve Tom's profit objective?

27. **LO.6 & LO.7 (Variable and absorption costing; writing)** Because your professor is scheduled to address a national professional meeting at the time your class ordinarily meets, the class has been divided into teams to discuss selected issues. Your team's assignment is to prepare a report arguing whether fixed manufacturing overhead should be included as a component of product cost. You are also expected to draw your own conclusion about this issue and provide the rationale for your conclusion in your report.

28. **LO.6 & LO.7 (Variable and absorption costing)** Porta Light manufactures a high-quality LED flashlight for home/office use. Data pertaining to the company's 2013 operations are as follows:

Production for the year	45,000 units
Sales for the year (sales price per unit, $8)	48,750 units
Beginning 2013 inventory	8,750 units
Costs to produce one unit (2012 & 2013):	
Direct material	$3.60
Direct labor	1.00
Variable overhead	0.60
Fixed overhead	0.40
Selling and administrative costs:	
Variable (per unit sold)	$0.40
Fixed (per year)	$150,000

The FOH rate is based on units of production based on an expected production capacity of 100,000 units per year.

a. What is budgeted annual fixed manufacturing overhead?
b. If budgeted fixed overhead equals actual fixed overhead, what is underapplied or overapplied fixed overhead in 2013 under absorption costing? Under variable costing?
c. What is the product cost per unit under absorption costing? Under variable costing?
d. How much total expense is charged against revenues in 2013 under absorption costing? Under variable costing?
e. Is income higher under absorption or variable costing? By what amount?

29. **LO.6 & LO.7 (Net income; absorption vs. variable costing)** Tennessee Tack manufactures horse blankets. In 2013, fixed overhead was applied to products at the rate of $8 per unit. Variable cost per unit remained constant throughout the year. In July 2013, income under variable costing was $188,000. July's beginning and ending inventories were 20,000 and 10,400 units, respectively.

a. Calculate income under absorption costing assuming no variances.
b. Assume instead that the company's July beginning and ending inventories were 9,000 and 12,000 units, respectively. Calculate income under absorption costing.

30. **LO.6 & LO.7 (Convert variable to absorption)** The April 2013 income statement for Fabio's Fashions has just been received by Diana Caffrey, Vice President of Marketing. The firm uses a variable costing system for internal reporting purposes.

Fabio's Fashions
Income Statement
For the Month Ended April 30, 2013

Sales		$14,400,000
Variable cost of goods sold		(7,200,000)
Product contribution margin		$ 7,200,000
Fixed expenses		
Manufacturing (budget and actual)	$4,500,000	
Selling and administrative	2,400,000	(6,900,000)
Income before tax		$ 300,000

The following notes were attached to the statements:

- Unit sales price for April averaged $144.
- Unit manufacturing costs for the month were:

Variable cost	$ 72
Fixed cost	30
Total cost	$102

- The predetermined FOH rate was based on normal monthly production of 150,000 units.

- April production was 7,500 units in excess of sales.
- April ending inventory consisted of 12,000 units.

a. Caffrey is not familiar with variable costing.
   1. Recast the April income statement on an absorption costing basis.
   2. Reconcile and explain the difference between the variable costing and the absorption costing income figures.

b. Explain the features of variable costing that should appeal to Caffrey. **CMA ADAPTED**

31. **LO.6 & LO.7 (Production cost; absorption vs. variable costing)** Ollie's Olive Oil began business in 2013, during which 104,000 quarts of olive oil were produced. In 2013, the company sold 100,000 quarts of olive oil. Costs incurred during the year were as follows:

Ingredients used	$228,800
Direct labor	104,000
Variable overhead	197,600
Fixed overhead	98,800
Variable selling expenses	50,000
Fixed selling and administrative expenses	20,000
Total actual costs	$799,200

a. What was the actual production cost per quart under variable costing? Under absorption costing?
b. What was variable cost of goods sold for 2013 under variable costing?
c. What was cost of goods sold for 2013 under absorption costing?
d. What was the value of ending inventory under variable costing? Under absorption costing?
e. How much fixed overhead was charged to expense in 2013 under variable costing? Under absorption costing?

32. **LO.6 & LO.7 (Absorption vs. variable costing)** Reese's Tot Toy Boxes uses variable costing to manage its internal operations. The following data relate to the company's first year of operation, when 25,000 units were produced and 21,000 units were sold.

Variable costs per unit	
Direct material	$50
Direct labor	30
Variable overhead	14
Variable selling costs	12
Fixed costs	
Selling and administrative	$750,000
Manufacturing	500,000

How much higher (or lower) would the company's first-year net income have been if absorption costing had been used rather than variable costing? Show computations.

33. **LO.6 & LO.7 (Absorption vs. variable costing)** Pete's Plant Stands manufactures wooden stands used by plant nurseries. In May 2013, the company manufactured 18,000 and sold 16,560 stands. The cost per unit for the 18,000 stands produced was as follows:

Direct material	$ 9.00
Direct labor	6.00
Variable overhead	3.00
Fixed overhead	4.00
Total	$22.00

There were no beginning inventories for May and no work in process at the end of May.

a. What is the value of ending finished goods inventory using absorption costing?
b. What is the value of ending finished goods inventory using variable costing?
c. Which accounting method, variable or absorption, would have produced the higher net income for May?

EXCEL

34. **LO.8 (Appendix; Least squares regression)** Refer to the information in Exercise 21 for Wyoming Wholesale.
   a. Using the least squares method, develop the equation for predicting weekly receiving report costs based on the number of shipments received.
   b. What is the predicted amount of receiving report costs for a month (assume a month is exactly four weeks) in which 165 shipments are received?

EXCEL

35. **LO.8 (Appendix; Least squares regression)** UpTop Mining has compiled the following data to analyze utility costs:

Month	Machine Hours	Utility Cost
January	200	$300
February	325	440
March	400	480
April	410	490
May	525	620
June	680	790
July	820	840
August	900	900

Use the least squares method to develop a formula for budgeting utility cost.

PROBLEMS

36. **LO.1 (Overhead application)** Last June, Lacy Dalton had just been appointed CFO of Garland & Wreath when she received some interesting reports about the profitability of the company's three most important product lines. One of the products, GW1, was produced in a very labor-intensive production process; another product, GW7, was produced in a very machine-intensive production process; and the third product, GW4, was produced in a manner that was equally labor and machine intensive. Dalton observed that all three products were produced in high volume and were priced to compete with similar products of other manufacturers. Prior to receiving the profit report, Dalton had expected the three products to be roughly equally profitable. However, according to the profit report, GW1 was actually losing a significant amount of money and GW7 was generating an impressively high profit. In the middle, GW4 was producing an average profit. After viewing the profit data, Dalton developed a theory that the "real" profitability of each product was substantially different from the reported profits. To test her theory, Dalton gathered cost data from the firm's accounting records. Dalton was quickly satisfied that the direct material and direct labor costs were charged to products properly; however, she surmised that the manufacturing overhead allocation was distorting product costs. To further investigate, she gathered the following information:

	GW1	GW4	GW7
Monthly direct labor hours	8,000	1,600	400
Monthly machine hours	800	2,400	12,800
Monthly allocated overhead cost	$80,000	$16,000	$4,000

Dalton noted that the current cost accounting system assigned all overhead to products based on direct labor hours using a predetermined overhead rate.

   a. Using the data gathered by Dalton, calculate the predetermined OH rate based on direct labor hours.
   b. Find the predetermined OH rate per machine hour that would allocate the current total overhead ($100,000) to the three product lines.
   c. Dalton believes the current overhead allocation is distorting the profitability of the product lines. Determine the amount of overhead that would be allocated to each product line if machine hours were the basis of overhead allocation.
   d. Why are the overhead allocations using direct labor hours and machine hours so different? Which is the better allocation?

37. **LO.1 & LO.3 (Plant vs. departmental OH rates)** Red River Farm Machine makes a wide variety of products, all of which must be processed in the Cutting and Assembly departments. For the year 2013, Red River budgeted total overhead of $993,000, of which $385,500 will be incurred in Cutting and the remainder will be incurred in Assembly. Budgeted direct labor and machine hours are as follows:

	Cutting	Assembly
Budgeted direct labor hours	27,000	3,000
Budgeted machine hours	2,100	65,800

Two products made by Red River are the RW22SKI and the SD45ROW. The following cost and production time information on these items has been gathered:

	RW22SKI	SD45ROW
Direct material	$34.85	$19.57
Direct labor rate in Cutting	$20.00	$20.00
Direct labor rate in Assembly	$ 8.00	$ 8.00
Direct labor hours in Cutting	6.00	4.80
Direct labor hours in Assembly	0.03	0.05
Machine hours in Cutting	0.06	0.15
Machine hours in Assembly	5.90	9.30

a. What is the plantwide predetermined OH rate based on (1) direct labor hours and (2) machine hours for the upcoming year? Round all computations to the nearest cent.
b. What are the departmental predetermined OH rates in Cutting and Assembly using the most appropriate base in each department? Round all computations to the nearest cent.
c. What are the costs of products RW22SKI and SD45ROW using (1) a plantwide rate based on direct labor hours, (2) a plantwide rate based on machine hours, and (3) departmental rates calculated in (b)?
d. A competitor manufactures a product that is extremely similar to RW22SKI and sells each unit for $310. Discuss how Red River's management might be influenced by the impact of the different product costs calculated in (c).

38. **LO.1 & LO.3 (Plant vs. departmental OH rates)** Montana Metal Works has two departments: Fabrication and Finishing. Three workers oversee the 25 machines in Fabrication. Finishing uses 35 crafters to hand-polish output, which is then run through buffing machines. Product CG9832-09 uses the following amounts of direct labor and machine time in each department:

	Fabrication	Finishing
Machine hours	10.00	0.30
Direct labor hours	0.02	2.00

Following are the budgeted overhead costs and volumes for each department for the upcoming year:

	Fabrication	Finishing
Budgeted overhead	$635,340	$324,000
Budgeted machine hours	72,000	9,300
Budgeted direct labor hours	4,800	48,000

a. What is the plantwide OH rate based on machine hours for the upcoming year? How much overhead will be assigned to each unit of Product CG9832-09 using this rate?
b. The company's auditors inform management that departmental predetermined OH rates using machine hours in Fabrication and direct labor hours in Finishing would be more appropriate than a plantwide rate. Calculate departmental overhead rates for each department. How much overhead would have been assigned to each unit of Product CG9832-09 using departmental rates?
c. Discuss why departmental rates are more appropriate than plantwide rates for Montana Metal Works.

39. **LO.1-LO.3 (Predetermined OH rates; flexible budget; capacity)** Battle Creek Storage Systems budgeted the following factory overhead costs for the upcoming year to help calculate variable and fixed predetermined overhead rates.

Indirect material	\$2.50 per unit produced
Indirect labor	\$3.00 per unit produced
Factory utilities	\$3,000 per year plus \$0.02 per unit produced
Factory machine maintenance	\$10,000 per year plus \$0.50 per unit produced
Material handling	\$8,000 per year plus \$0.12 per unit produced
Machine depreciation	\$0.03 per unit produced
Building rent	\$12,000 per year
Supervisors' salaries	\$72,000 per year
Factory insurance	\$6,000 per year

The company produces only one type of product that has a theoretical capacity of 100,000 units of production during the year. Practical capacity is 80 percent of theoretical, and normal capacity is 90 percent of practical. The company's expected production for the upcoming year is 70,000 units.

a. Prepare a flexible budget for the company using each level of capacity.
b. Calculate the predetermined variable and fixed overhead rates for each capacity measure (round to the nearest cent when necessary).
c. The company decides to apply overhead to products using expected capacity as the budgeted level of activity. The firm actually produces 70,000 units during the year. All actual costs are as budgeted.
   1. Prepare journal entries to record the incurrence of actual overhead costs and to apply overhead to production. Assume cash is paid for costs when appropriate.
   2. What is the amount of underapplied or overapplied fixed overhead at year-end?
d. Which measure of capacity would be of most benefit to management, and why?

40. **LO.1-LO.3 (Overhead application)** Sunny Systems manufactures solar panels. The company has a theoretical capacity of 50,000 units annually. Practical capacity is 80 percent of theoretical capacity, and normal capacity is 80 percent of practical capacity. The firm is expecting to produce 30,000 units next year. The company president, Deacon Daniels, has budgeted the following factory overhead costs:

Indirect material	\$2.00 per unit
Indirect labor	\$144,000 per year plus \$2.50 per unit
Utilities for the plant	\$6,000 per year plus \$0.04 per unit
Repairs and maintenance for the plant	\$20,000 per year plus \$0.34 per unit
Material handling costs	\$16,000 per year plus \$0.12 per unit
Depreciation on plant assets	\$210,000 per year
Rent on plant building	\$50,000 per year
Insurance on plant building	\$12,000 per year

a. Determine the cost formula for total factory overhead in the format of $y = a + bX$.
b. Determine the total predetermined OH rate for each possible overhead application base.
c. Assume that Sunny Systems produces 35,000 units during the year and that actual costs are exactly as budgeted. Calculate the overapplied or underapplied overhead for each possible overhead allocation base.

41. **LO.2 (Under/overapplied OH; OH disposition)** Grand Island Brake Co. budgeted the following variable and fixed overhead costs for 2013:

Variable indirect labor	\$100,000
Variable indirect material	20,000
Variable utilities	80,000
Variable portion of other mixed costs	120,000
Fixed machinery depreciation	62,000
Fixed machinery lease payments	13,000
Fixed machinery insurance	16,000
Fixed salaries	75,000
Fixed utilities	12,000

The company allocates overhead to production using machine hours. For 2013, machine hours have been budgeted at 50,000.

a. Determine the predetermined variable and fixed OH rates for Grand Island Brake Co. The company uses separate variable and fixed manufacturing overhead control accounts.
b. During 2013, the company used 53,000 machine hours during production and incurred a total of $273,600 of variable overhead costs and $185,680 of fixed overhead costs. Prepare journal entries to record the incurrence of the actual overhead costs and the application of overhead to production.
c. What amounts of underapplied or overapplied overhead exist at year-end 2013?
d. The company's management believes that the fixed overhead amount calculated in (a) should be considered immaterial. Prepare the entry to close the Fixed Overhead Control account at the end of the year.
e. Management believes that the variable overhead amount calculated in (c) should be considered material and should be prorated to the appropriate accounts. At year-end, balances were as follows for inventory and Cost of Goods Sold accounts:

Raw Material Inventory	$ 25,000
Work in Process Inventory	234,000
Finished Goods Inventory	390,000
Cost of Goods Sold	936,000

Prepare the entry to close the Variable Overhead Control account at the end of the year.

42. **LO.4 (Analyzing mixed costs)** Wisconsin Dairy determined that the total predetermined OH rate for costing purposes is $26.80 per cow per day (referred to as an animal day). Of this, $25.20 is the variable portion. Overhead cost information for two levels of activity within the relevant range are as follows:

	4,000 Animal Days	6,000 Animal Days
Indirect material	$25,600	$38,400
Indirect labor	56,000	80,000
Maintenance	10,400	13,600
Utilities	8,000	12,000
All other	15,200	21,600

a. Determine the fixed and variable values for each of the preceding overhead items, and determine the total overhead cost formula.
b. Assume that the total predetermined OH rate is based on expected annual capacity. What is this level of activity for the company?
c. Determine expected overhead costs at the expected annual capacity.
d. If the company raises its expected capacity by 3,000 animal days above the present level, calculate a new total overhead rate for product costing.

43. **LO.4 & LO.8 (High–low; appendix)** Sympco Glass manufactures insulated windows. The firm's repair and maintenance (R&M) cost is mixed and varies most directly with machine hours worked. The following data have been gathered from recent operations: EXCEL

Month	MHs	R&M Cost
May	1,400	$ 9,000
June	1,900	10,719
July	2,000	10,900
August	2,500	13,000
September	2,200	11,578
October	2,700	13,160
November	1,700	9,525
December	2,300	11,670

a. Use the high–low method to estimate a cost formula for repairs and maintenance.
b. Use least squares regression to estimate a cost formula for repairs and maintenance.
c. Does the answer to (a) or to (b) provide the better estimate of the relationship between repairs and maintenance costs and machine hours? Why?

EXCEL

44. **LO.5 (Flexible budgets)** Joe's Lawn Care Service primarily mows lawns for residential customers. Management has determined direct labor hours is the primary cost driver and has developed the following cost equations based on direct labor hours:

Lawn supplies (variable)	$y = \$0 + \$4.00X$
Direct labor (variable)	$y = \$0 + \$12.00X$
Overhead (mixed)	$y = \$8{,}000 + \$1.00X$

a. Prepare a flexible budget for each of the following activity levels: 550, 600, 650, and 700 direct labor hours.
b. Determine the total cost per direct labor hour at each of the levels of activity.
c. The company normally records 650 direct labor hours during June. Each job typically requires 1.45 hours of labor time. If management wants to earn a profit equal to 40 percent of the costs incurred, what should the charge be to an average lawn-care customer?

45. **LO.1 & LO.5 (Flexible budgets; predetermined OH rates)** The Splash makes large fiberglass swimming pools and uses machine hours and direct labor hours to apply overhead in the Production and Installation departments, respectively. The monthly cost formula for overhead in Production is $y = \$7{,}950 + \$4.05$ MH; the overhead cost formula in Installation is $y = \$6{,}150 + \$14.25$ DLH. These formulas are valid for a relevant range of activity up to 6,000 machine hours in Production and 9,000 direct labor hours in Installation.

Each pool is estimated to require 25 machine hours in Production and 60 hours of direct labor in Installation. Expected capacity for the year is 120 pools.

a. Prepare a flexible budget for Production at possible annual capacities of 2,500, 3,000, and 3,500 machine hours. Prepare a flexible budget for Installation at possible annual capacities of 6,000, 7,000, and 8,000 machine hours.
b. Prepare a budget for next month's variable, fixed, and total overhead costs for each department assuming that expected production is eight pools.
c. Calculate the total overhead cost to be applied to each pool scheduled for production in the coming month if expected capacity is used to calculate the predetermined OH rates.

46. **LO.5 (Flexible budgets)** Tom Snider is a staff accountant for BigBiz. Snider was recently given the task of developing a monthly flexible budget formula for several manufacturing costs. He was told that his equations would be used as an aid in developing future budgets for these manufacturing costs and he was told to put his results into an equation in the form $y = a + bX$ for each cost. Snider gathered data and used high–low analysis to obtain the flexible budget formulas. Rather than using a single activity measure, he decided to use two. Thus, for each manufacturing cost analyzed, he developed two equations. However, after analyzing several equations, Snider became perplexed over his results because the results from the two equations were very different in some cases. Snider has asked you, his colleague, how he should decide which of the two estimated equations for each manufacturing cost he should submit to his boss. To illustrate his dilemma, Snider provided you with his two equations for repairs and maintenance expense, which follow.

Using machine hours:	$y = \$15{,}000 + \$20X$
Using direct labor hours:	$y = \$450{,}000 + \$4X$

What advice will you give Snider?

47. **LO.6 & LO.7 (Absorption costing vs. variable costing)** Since opening in 2012, Akron Aviation has built light aircraft engines and has gained a reputation for reliable and quality products. Factory overhead is applied to production using direct labor hours and any underapplied or overapplied overhead is closed at year-end to Cost of Goods Sold. The company's inventory balances for the past three years and income statements for the past two years follow.

Inventory Balances	12/31/12	12/31/13	12/31/14
Direct Material	$22,000	$30,000	$10,000
Work in Process			
Costs	$40,000	$48,000	$64,000
Direct labor hours	1,335	1,600	2,100
Finished Goods			
Costs	$25,000	$18,000	$14,000
Direct labor hours	1,450	1,050	820

COMPARATIVE INCOME STATEMENTS

	2013		2014	
Sales		$ 840,000		$1,015,000
Cost of goods sold				
Finished goods, 1/1	$ 25,000		$ 18,000	
Cost of goods manufactured	556,000		673,600	
Total available	$581,000		$691,600	
Finished goods, 12/31	(18,000)		(14,000)	
CGS before overhead adjustment	$563,000		$677,600	
Underapplied factory overhead	17,400		19,300	
Cost of goods sold		(580,400)		(696,900)
Gross margin		$ 259,600		$ 318,100
Selling expenses	$ 82,000		$ 95,000	
Administrative expenses	70,000		75,000	
Total operating expenses		(152,000)		(170,000)
Operating income		$ 107,600		$ 148,100

The same predetermined OH rate was used to apply overhead to production orders in 2013 and 2014. The rate was based on the following estimates:

Fixed factory overhead	$ 25,000
Variable factory overhead	$155,000
Direct labor cost	$150,000
Direct labor hours	25,000

In 2013 and 2014, actual direct labor hours expended were 20,000 and 23,000, respectively. Raw material costing $292,000 was issued to production in 2013 and $370,000 in 2014. Actual fixed overhead was $37,400 for 2013 and $42,300 for 2014, and the planned direct labor rate per hour was equal to the actual direct labor rate. Actual variable overhead was equal to applied variable overhead.

For both years, all of the reported administrative costs were fixed. The variable portion of the reported selling expenses results from a commission of 5 percent of sales revenue.

a. For the year ending December 31, 2014, prepare a revised income statement using the variable costing method.
b. Describe both the advantages and disadvantages of using variable costing.

48. **LO.6 & LO.7 (Convert variable to absorption; ethics)** Georgia Shacks produces small outdoor buildings. The company began operations in 2013, producing 2,000 buildings and selling 1,500. A variable costing income statement for 2013 follows. During the year, variable production costs per unit were $800 for direct material, $300 for direct labor, and $200 for overhead.

ETHICS

Georgia Shacks
Income Statement (Variable Costing)
For the Year Ended December 31, 2013

Sales		$ 3,750,000
Variable cost of goods sold		
Beginning inventory	$ 0	
Cost of goods manufactured	2,600,000	
Cost of goods available for sale	$2,600,000	
Less ending inventory	(650,000)	(1,950,000)
Product contribution margin		$ 1,800,000
Less variable selling and administrative expenses		(270,000)
Total contribution margin		$ 1,530,000
Less fixed expenses		
Fixed factory overhead	$1,500,000	
Fixed selling and administrative expenses	190,000	(1,690,000)
Income before taxes		$ (160,000)

The company president is upset about the net loss because he wanted to borrow funds to expand capacity.

a. Prepare a pre-tax absorption costing income statement.
b. Explain the source of the difference between the pre-tax income and loss figures under the two costing systems.
c. Would it be appropriate to present an absorption costing income statement to the local banker, considering the company president's knowledge of the net loss determined under variable costing? Explain.
d. Assume that during the second year of operations, Georgia Shacks produced 2,000 buildings, sold 2,200, and experienced the same total fixed costs as in 2013. For the second year:
    1. Prepare a variable costing pre-tax income statement.
    2. Prepare an absorption costing pre-tax income statement.
    3. Explain the difference between the incomes for the second year under the two systems.

49. **LO.6 & LO.7 (Absorption and variable costing)** Bird's Eye View manufactures satellite dishes used in residential and commercial installations for satellite-broadcasted television. For each unit, the following costs apply: $50 for direct material, $100 for direct labor, and $60 for variable overhead. The company's annual fixed overhead cost is $750,000; it uses expected capacity of 12,500 units produced as the basis for applying fixed overhead to products. A commission of 10 percent of the selling price is paid on each unit sold. Annual fixed selling and administrative expenses are $180,000. The following additional information is available:

	2013	2014
Selling price per unit	$ 500	$ 500
Number of units sold	10,000	12,000
Number of units produced	12,500	11,000
Beginning inventory (units)	7,500	10,000
Ending inventory (units)	10,000	?

Prepare pre-tax income statements under absorption and variable costing for the years ended 2013 and 2014, with any volume variance being charged to Cost of Goods Sold. Reconcile the differences in income for the two methods.

ETHICS

50. **LO.1, LO.6, & LO.7 (Overhead application; absorption costing; ethics; writing)** Prior to the start of fiscal 2013, managers of MultiTech hosted a web conference for its shareholders, financial analysts, and members of the financial press. During the conference, the CEO and CFO released the following financial projections for 2013 to the attendees (amounts in millions):

Sales	$ 40,000
Cost of goods sold	(32,000)
Gross margin	$ 8,000
Operating expenses	(4,000)
Operating income	$ 4,000

As had been their custom, the CEO and CFO projected confidence that the firm would achieve these goals, even though projections had been significantly more positive than the actual results for 2012. Not surprisingly, the day following the web conference, MultiTech's stock rose 15 percent.

In early October 2013, the CEO and CFO of MultiTech met and developed revised projections for fiscal 2013, based on actual results for the first three quarters of the year and projections for the final quarter. Their revised projections for 2013 follow:

Sales	$ 38,000
Cost of goods sold	(30,500)
Gross margin	$ 7,500
Operating expenses	(4,000)
Operating income	$ 3,500

Upon reviewing these numbers, the CEO turned to the CFO and stated, "I think the market will be forgiving if we come in 5 percent light on the top line (sales), but if we miss operating income by 12.5 percent ($500 ÷ $4,000) our stock is going to get hammered when we announce fourth quarter and annual results."

The CFO mulled the situation over for a couple of days and started to develop a strategy to increase reported income by increasing production above planned levels. She believed this strategy could successfully move $500 million from Cost of Goods Sold to Finished Goods Inventory. If so, the firm could meet its early profit projections.

a. How does increasing production, relative to the planned level of production, decrease Cost of Goods Sold?
b. What other accounts are likely to be affected by a strategy of increasing production to increase income?
c. Is the CFO's plan ethical? Explain.
d. If you were a stockholder of MultiTech and carefully examined the 2013 financial statements, how might you detect the results of the CFO's strategy?

51. **LO.6 & LO.7 (Absorption vs. variable costing)** Tomm's T's is a New York–based company that produces and sells t-shirts. The firm uses variable costing for internal purposes and absorption costing for external purposes. At year-end, financial information must be converted from variable costing to absorption costing to satisfy external requirements.

At the end of 2012, management anticipated that 2013 sales would be 20 percent above 2012 levels. Thus, production for 2013 was increased by 20 percent to meet the expected demand. However, economic conditions in 2013 kept sales at the 2012 unit level of 40,000. The following data pertain to 2012 and 2013:

	2012	2013
Selling price per unit	$ 22	$ 22
Sales (units)	40,000	40,000
Beginning inventory (units)	4,000	4,000
Production (units)	40,000	48,000
Ending inventory (units)	4,000	?

Per-unit production costs (budgeted and actual) for 2012 and 2013 were:

Material	$2.50
Labor	4.00
Overhead	1.75
Total	$8.25

Annual fixed costs for 2012 and 2013 (budgeted and actual) were:

Production	$120,000
Selling and administrative	130,000
Total	$250,000

The predetermined OH rate under absorption costing is based on an annual capacity of 60,000 units. Any volume variance is assigned to Cost of Goods Sold. Taxes are to be ignored.

a. Present the 2013 income statement based on variable costing.
b. Present the 2013 income statement based on absorption costing.
c. Explain the difference, if any, in the income figures. Assuming that there is no Work in Process Inventory, provide the entry necessary to adjust the book income amount to the financial statement income amount if an adjustment is necessary.
d. The company finds it worthwhile to develop its internal financial data on a variable costing basis. What advantages and disadvantages are attributed to variable costing for internal purposes?
e. Many accountants believe that variable costing is appropriate for external reporting; many others oppose its use for external reporting. List the arguments for and against the use of variable costing in external reporting.

CMA ADAPTED

52. **LO.4 & LO.8 (Appendix; least squares regression)** Bon Voyage provides charter cruises in the eastern Caribbean. Tina Louise, the owner, wants to understand how her labor costs change per month. She recognizes that the cost is neither strictly fixed nor strictly variable. She has gathered the following information and has identified two potential predictive bases, number of charters and gross receipts:

Month	Labor Costs	Number of Charters	Gross Receipts ($000)
January	$ 8,000	10	$ 12
February	9,200	14	18
March	12,000	22	26
April	14,200	28	36
May	18,500	40	60
June	28,000	62	82
July	34,000	100	120
August	30,000	90	100
September	24,000	80	96

Using the least squares method, develop a labor cost formula using

a. number of charters
b. gross receipts

Jenn Huls/Shutterstock.com

4

Activity-Based Management and Activity-Based Costing

LEARNING OBJECTIVES

After completing this chapter, you should be able to answer the following questions:

1. In an activity-based management system, what are value-added and non-value-added activities?
2. How do value-added and non-value-added activities affect manufacturing cycle efficiency?
3. Why must cost drivers be designated in an activity-based costing system?
4. How are product and service costs computed using an activity-based costing system?
5. Under what conditions is activity-based costing useful in an organization, and what information do activity-based costing systems provide to management?
6. What criticisms have been directed at activity-based costing?

INTRODUCTION

To succeed in today's global marketplace, companies must generate high-quality products or services and have competitive cost structures. Actions taken to create cost efficiencies require an understanding of the drivers, or underlying causes, of costs and not merely recognition of cost predictors. Chapter 3 discusses computation of predetermined overhead (OH) rates using traditional activity bases: direct labor costs, direct labor hours, and machine hours. However, many alternative activity bases are available to assign overhead to products and services. Using such "nontraditional" bases can improve management information about the cost of production or provision and enhance an organization's competitive advantage.

This chapter discusses activity-based management (ABM) and activity-based costing (ABC). These two concepts allow a more direct focus on organizational actions and the overhead costs created by those actions. Used together, ABM and ABC can help managers make better decisions about the design, production or performance, profitability, and pricing of products and services.

ACTIVITY-BASED MANAGEMENT

1 In an activity-based management system, what are value-added and non-value-added activities?

Although specifically designated as an accounting function, determination of product or service cost is a major concern for all managers. Pricing, profitability, and organizational investments to support production or service provision are issues that extend beyond accounting into the areas of corporate strategy, marketing, and finance. In theory, production or performance cost would not matter if a sufficient number of customers were willing to buy a product or service at a price that was high enough to cover that cost and provide a reasonable profit margin. However, in reality, customers purchase a product or service only if they perceive that it provides an acceptable value for the price. Given that reality, management must be concerned about an equitable relationship between selling price and value.

Activity-based management (ABM) is a business process model focusing on the control of production or performance activities so that they improve customer value and enhance profitability. In a business context, an **activity** is any repetitive action that is performed in fulfillment of a business function. As shown in Exhibit 4.1, ABM includes a variety of concepts that help companies to

- produce more efficiently,
- determine product or service costs more accurately, and
- control and evaluate performance more effectively.

A primary component of activity-based management is **activity analysis**, which is the process of studying activities to (1) classify them into one of the two following categories and (2) devise ways of minimizing or eliminating activities that increase costs but provide little or no customer value.

Value-Added versus Non-Value-Added Activities

If a black-or-white perspective is taken, activities are either value-added or non-value-added. A **value-added (VA) activity** increases the worth of a product or service to a customer and is one for which the customer is willing to pay. Alternatively, a **non-value-added (NVA) activity** increases the time spent on a product or service but does not increase its worth and, thus, is viewed as unnecessary from the customer's perspective. NVA activities can be reduced, redesigned, or eliminated without affecting the product's or service's market value or quality. Often an easy way to determine the value provided by an activity is to ask "why" five times: if the answers represent valid business reasons, the activity generally adds value; otherwise, the activity adds no value. Consider the following "conversation" about storing a large quantity of flour at a pizza restaurant.

- Why are we storing flour? Because it was acquired before it was actually needed.
- Why was the flour acquired prior to its need? Because it was acquired in a bulk purchase.
- Why was the flour bought in bulk? Because it is less expensive that way.
- Why is buying in bulk less expensive if doing so creates costs for storing and moving the flour as well as possible costs of spillage or spoilage? Because those costs never occurred to me ... maybe there's a better way. (In this case, only four "why" questions were needed!)

Exhibit 4.1 Components of Activity-Based Management

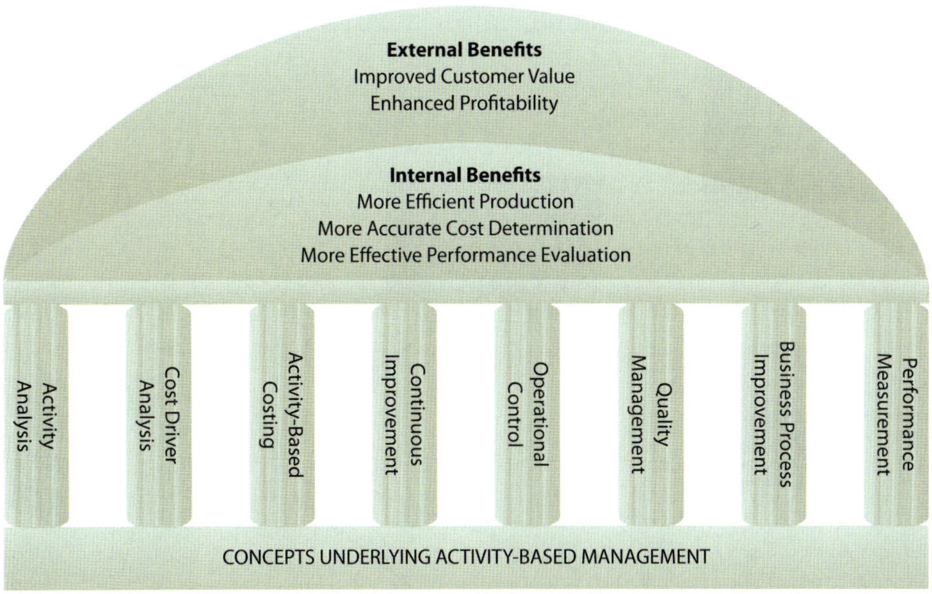

Businesses can also engage in some activities that are essential (or appear to be essential) to business operations but for which customers would not *willingly* choose to pay. These activities are known as **business-value-added (BVA) activities**. For example, companies must prepare invoices for documenting sales and collections. Customers realize invoice preparation creates costs, and that such costs must be covered by product selling prices. However, because invoice preparation adds no direct value to products or services, customers would prefer not to pay for this activity through a higher selling price.

Many product and service prices are set by the marketplace rather than by an individual organization attempting to cover its incurred costs. However, if the selling price of a product or service is insufficient to cover the cost of production or performance and produce a reasonable profit margin, management generally needs to find a way to reduce cost or, failing that, may need to exit the market for that product or service.[1] The easiest way to reduce cost is to minimize or eliminate the NVA activities that are incurred during the production or performance process. Such reductions will allow the company to obtain a larger profit margin when selling at market price than those companies with higher costs. Or cost reductions may allow the company to sell below the market price and thereby increase market share. Consider that the communications industry is heavily affected by customer turnover, so companies try to contain costs without negatively affecting customer sales and service—a difficult task when trying to "improve efficiency and reduce contact center costs, such as reducing call volume, handling time and overhead costs."[2] If companies can reduce operational support costs, profit margins can be increased even if prices are not raised.

To begin activity analysis, managers should first identify the organization's production or performance processes. A **process** is a series of activities that, when performed together, satisfy a specific objective. Companies engage in processes for production, distribution, selling, administration, and other company functions. Processes should be defined before a company tries to determine relationships among activities. Most processes occur horizontally across organizational functions and, thus, overlap multiple functional areas. For example, Exhibit 4.2 shows how a production process also affects engineering, purchasing,

[1] Occasionally, product or service prices may be set at a level that is insufficient to cover costs. Such a pricing structure usually is imposed to meet market competition, to establish a "presence" in a particular market segment, or to encourage the purchase of related products or services.

[2] Genesys, Customer Service Strategies for the Communications Industry (CA: Daly City, 2008), p. 5; www.genesyslab.com/system/files/2388_SG_US_Communica_screen.pdf.

Exhibit 4.2 Process Flow in an Organization

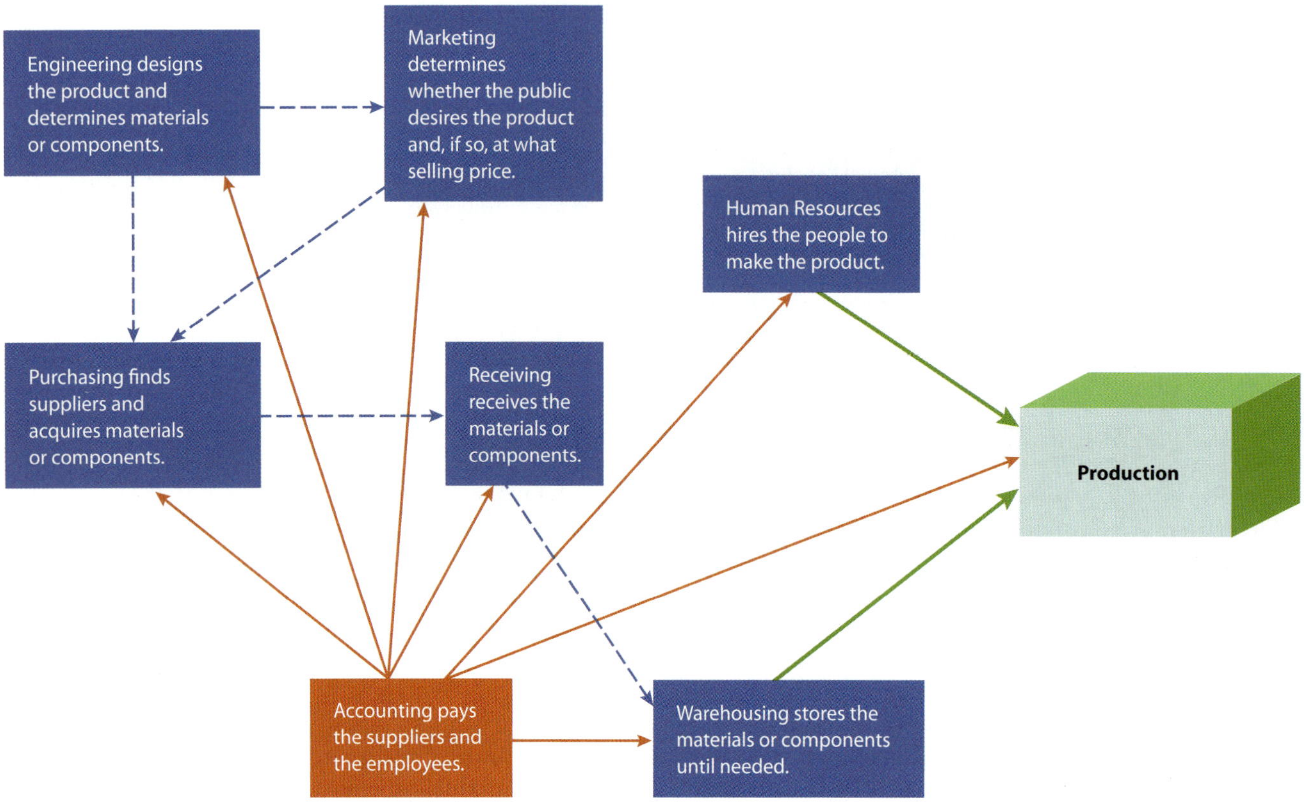

receiving, warehousing, accounting, human resources, and marketing. The exhibit's complexity indicates why a process should be defined relative to specific functions.

For each distinct process, a **process map** (or detailed flowchart) should be prepared to indicate *every* step in *every* area that goes into making or doing something. Some steps on the process map are necessary and, therefore, must be performed for the process to be completed. Other steps reflect those activities for which a valid business answer to the "why" question cannot be found and, as such, are unnecessary.

After a process map has been developed, the time needed to perform the activities should be noted and classified in one of four ways.

- **Processing (service) time**: the actual time spent performing all *necessary* functions to manufacture the product or to perform the service; this time is VA.
- **Inspection time**: the time required to perform quality control other than what is internal to the process; this time is usually considered NVA unless the consumer would actually be willing to pay for it (such as in the pharmaceutical or food industries).
- **Transfer time**: the time consumed moving products or components from one place to another; this time is NVA.
- **Idle time**: the time goods spend in storage or waiting at a production operation for processing; this time is NVA.

The time from the receipt to the completion of a product or service order is equal to value-added time plus non-value-added time or **cycle (lead) time**.

$$\text{Total Cycle (or Lead) Time} = \text{Value-Added Time} + \text{Non-Value-Added Time}$$

Packaging may be a VA activity for some companies and a NVA activity for others. Some products, such as liquids, require packaging; other products need little or no packaging. Because packaging takes up about a third of the U.S. landfills and creates a substantial amount of disposal cost, companies and consumers are beginning to focus their attention on reducing or eliminating packaging.[3]

Although viewing inspection time and transfer time as non-value-added activities is theoretically correct, few companies can completely eliminate all quality control functions and all transfer time. Understanding the NVA nature of these functions, however, should help managers strive to minimize such activities to the extent possible. Thus, companies should view VA and NVA activities as occurring on a continuum and strive to eliminate or minimize those activities that add the most time *and* cost and provide the least value.

Combining the process map and the time assessments produces a **value chart** that traces a process from beginning to end. Exhibit 4.3 provides a value chart for a liquid chemical produced by Prough Corporation. Value is added to a product only when processing actually occurs. Note the excessive time consumed by storing and moving materials. Out of a total maximum 64 days of cycle time, the VA time for the production of this chemical is four days.

Constructing a value chart for every product or service would be extremely time-consuming, but a few such charts can quickly indicate where a company is losing time and money through NVA activities. The cost of such activities can be approximated by using estimates for storage facility depreciation, property taxes and insurance charges, wages for employees who handle warehousing, and the capital cost of funds tied up in stored inventory. Multiplying these cost estimates by times shown in the value chart will indicate the amount by which costs could be reduced by eliminating NVA activities.

Exhibit 4.3 Value Chart for Prough Corporation

Assembling

Operations	Receiving	Quality control	Storage	Move to production	Waiting for use	Setup of machinery	Assembly	Move to inspection	Move to finishing
Average time (days)	1	.5	5–30	.25	.5	.25	2	.25	.25

Finishing

Operations	Receiving	Move to production	Waiting for use	Setup	Finishing	Inspection	Packaging	Move to loading dock	Storage	Ship
Average time (days)	.25	.25	5–10	.25	1	1	1	.25	3–7	2–8

Total time in Assembling:	10–35 days
Total time in Finishing:	14–29 days
Total processing time:	24–64 days
Total value-added time:	4–4 days
Total non-value-added time:	**20–60 days**

Assembling value-added time:	2 days
Finishing value-added time:	2 days
Total value-added time:	**4 days**

Non-value-added activities (green)

Value-added activities (gray)

[3]For instance, in 2006, Walmart began using a "packaging scorecard" to help meet its environmental sustainability goals. The scorecard measures multiple items including greenhouse gas emissions related to packaging production and transportation, product-to-packaging ratio, recycled content usage, quantity of renewable energy used in packaging production, raw materials recovery value, and distance required to transport the packaging materials. By 2010, Walmart indicated that reducing the packaging size of its Kid Connection line of toys had saved over $2.4 million in freight costs. Most of the company's cut fruit and vegetable trays are now packaged in a biodegradable polymer. That change alone saved about 800,000 gallons of gasoline and avoided more than 11 million pounds of greenhouse gas emissions. Source: http://www.associatedcontent.com/article/2614159/the_effects_of_walmarts_packaging_scorecard.html?cat=3.

Manufacturing Cycle Efficiency

2 How do value-added and non-value-added activities affect manufacturing cycle efficiency?

Dividing total value-added processing time by total cycle time results in a measurement referred to as **manufacturing cycle efficiency (MCE)**.

Manufacturing Cycle Efficiency = Total Value-Added Time ÷ Total Cycle Time

Using the information from Exhibit 4.3, Prough Corporation's MCE is 17 percent (4 ÷ 24) if the company operates with the least amount of NVA time or 6 percent (4 ÷ 64) at the highest level of NVA time.

Although 100 percent efficiency can never be achieved, most production processes add value to products only approximately 10 percent of the time from raw material receipt until shipment to customers. In other words, about 90 percent of manufacturing cycle time is wasted or NVA time. But products act like magnets in regard to costs: the longer the cycle time, the more opportunity the product has to "pull" costs to it.

A just-in-time (JIT) manufacturing process (discussed in detail in Chapter 18) seeks to achieve substantially higher efficiency by producing components and goods at the precise time they are needed by either the next production station or the consumer. JIT also often relies on the use of automated, robotic technologies that minimize downtime and maximize quality. Thus, JIT eliminates a significant amount of idle time (especially in storage) and reduces processing time; both of these types of NVA activities substantially decrease MCE.

In a retail environment, cycle time relates to time between ordering and selling an item. NVA activities in retail include shipping time from the supplier, delays spent counting merchandise in the Receiving Department, and any storage time between receipt and sale. In a service company, cycle time refers to the time between service order and service completion. All time spent on activities that are not actual service performance or are "non-activities" (such as delays in beginning a job) are considered NVA activities for that job. A service company computes **service cycle efficiency (SCE)** by dividing total actual service time by total cycle time.

Service Cycle Efficiency = Total Actual Service Time ÷ Total Cycle Time

Non-value-added activities are attributable to three types of factors:

Factor	Example	Change
Systemic	The need to manufacture products in large batches to minimize setup cost; the need to respond to service jobs in order of urgency	Invest in new equipment that has shorter setup times or can be adapted to the production of multiple products; redesign products to reduce or eliminate the need for new setups; reduce situations that create urgency
Physical	The need to move goods because of inefficient plant or machine layout, especially in multistory buildings in which receiving and shipping are on the ground floor but storage and production are on upper floors	Redesign plant and/or reconfigure machinery to improve product flow and alleviate machine bottlenecks
Human	The need to rework products because of errors made by employees who have improper skills or received inadequate training; delays caused by people who waste time by socializing at work	Hire employees with the right skill set or train them in the right skills; have employees accept responsibility for their work and strive for total quality control; emphasize the proper performance measures related to production times

Attempts to reduce NVA activities should be directed at all of these factors, but management must concentrate on reducing or eliminating the NVA activities that create the highest costs. Doing so should cause product/service quality to increase with a simultaneous decrease in cycle time and cost.

COST DRIVER ANALYSIS

3 Why must cost drivers be designated in an activity-based costing system?

Companies engage in many activities that consume resources and cause costs to be incurred. All activities have cost drivers, which are the factors that have direct cause-and-effect relationships to a cost. Cost drivers are classified as either volume-related (such as labor or machine hours) or non-volume-related (such as setups, work orders, or distance traveled), which generally reflect the incurrence of specific transactions. Many cost drivers can be identified for an individual business unit. For example, primary cost drivers for factory insurance are total value of plant assets, number of accidents or claims occurring in a period, quantity of workers, and inventory size.

Generally, more cost drivers can be identified for a given activity than should be used in activity-based costing. **Activity-based costing (ABC)** is a cost accounting system that focuses on an organization's activities, collects costs on the basis of the underlying nature and extent of those activities, and uses the gathered information to determine product/service cost accumulation and assess the appropriateness of activity elimination. For these purposes, a cost driver should be easy to understand, directly related to the activity being performed, and appropriate for performance measurement. Only a limited number of cost drivers should be selected and the cost of measuring a driver should not exceed the benefit of using it. For example, Exhibit 4.4 shows six possible cost drivers for shipping cost, but the one that is the easiest to track and measure is trip distance.

Exhibit 4.4 Potential Cost Drivers for Shipping Cost

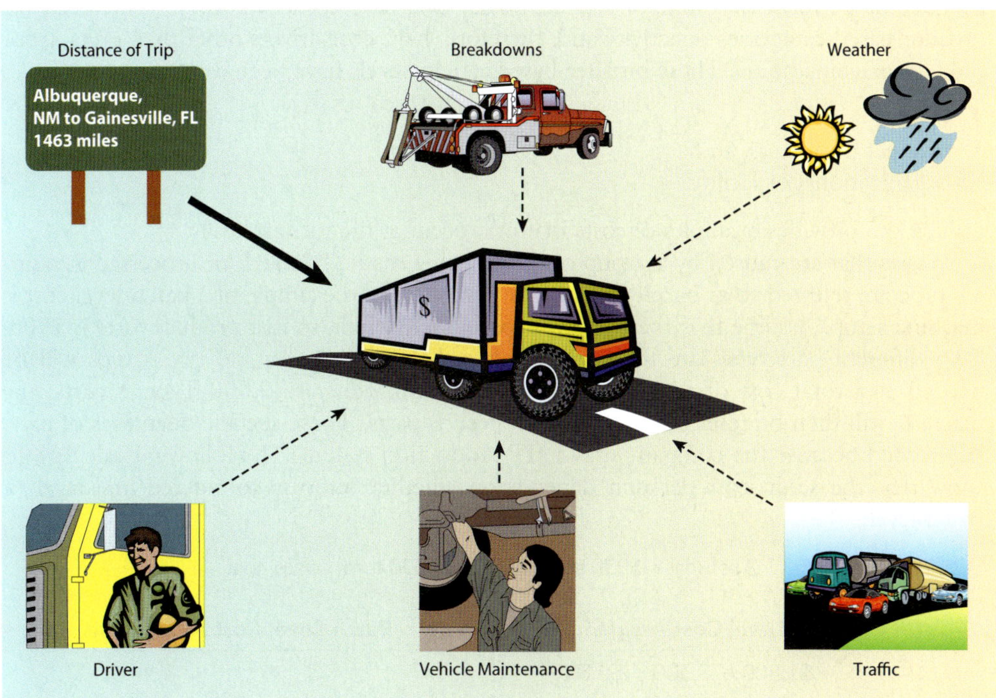

Product and service costs are commonly identified as direct material, direct labor, and overhead. Accountants have had little difficulty in tracing direct material or direct labor to products and services; the primary impediment to a fair determination of product or service cost has always been the assignment of overhead. As discussed in Chapters 2 and 3, OH has traditionally been accumulated as a single total overhead amount or as two (variable and fixed) overhead amounts. Such accumulations can be referred to as overhead "pools." The pooled costs are then assigned to products or services—often using only one driver, such as direct labor hours or machine hours or, possibly, a different driver for each of the variable and fixed overhead pools.

Such an allocation procedure causes few, if any, problems for financial statement preparation. However, the use of a minimal number of cost pools or cost drivers can produce illogical product or service costs for internal managerial use in complex production or service environments. However, organizations must limit the number of cost pools and cost drivers used so that the system will not become overly complicated and expensive. Thus, overhead should be divided into subgroups of costs that can be viewed as being primarily caused by one common or highly correlated cause.

Analyzing cost drivers in conjunction with activity analysis can highlight activities that do not add value and, as such, can be targeted for elimination to reduce costs and increase profitability. This information provides the basis for management's decisions for improving the process, benchmarking against competitors, and increasing profitability.

Levels at Which Costs Are Incurred

To reflect more complex environments, the accounting system must first recognize that costs are created and incurred because their drivers occur at different levels.[4] This realization necessitates using **cost driver analysis**, which investigates, quantifies, and explains the relationship of drivers to their related costs. Traditionally, cost drivers were viewed as existing only at the unit level: for example, the quantity of labor or machine time expended to make a product or render a service. Such **unit-level costs** are caused by the production or acquisition of a single unit of product or the delivery of a single unit of service. Direct material and direct labor are good examples of unit-level costs: each product uses a specific amount of raw material and requires a specific quantity of labor time to manufacture.

However, most overhead is not incurred on a per unit basis. There is no way to determine the exact amount of electricity or machine depreciation used to make one unit of product or perform one unit of service. Thus, overhead costs typically are incurred for broader-based categories of activity and, therefore, have cost drivers other than units, labor time, or machine hours. These broader-based activity levels have been categorized as

- batch,
- product or process, and
- organizational or facility.

Exhibit 4.5 provides examples of costs that may occur at the various levels.

Costs that are caused by a group of things being made, handled, or processed at a single time are referred to as **batch-level costs**. One overhead example of a batch-level cost is machine setup. Assume that the cost of preparing a machine to cast product parts is $900. Two different part types are to be manufactured during the day, so two setups will be needed at a total cost of $1,800. The first setup will generate 3,000 Type A parts; the machine will then be reset to generate 600 Type B parts. These specific quantities of parts are needed because the company uses a JIT production system. The following calculations show that the setup cost per unit depends on whether setup is considered unit-level or batch-level.

$$2 \text{ setups} \times \$900 \text{ per setup} = \$1{,}800 \text{ total setup cost}$$

	Unit-Level Cost Assignment			Batch-Level Cost Assignment			
	$1,800 ÷ 3,600 = $0.50						
	# of Parts	Cost per Part	Cost Assignment	Cost per Batch	# of Parts in Batch	Cost per Part	Cost Assignment
Type A	3,000	$0.50	$1,500	$ 900	3,000	$0.30	$ 900
Type B	600	$0.50	300	900	600	1.50	900
	3,600		$1,800	$1,800			$1,800

The unit-level method assigns the majority of setup cost to Type A parts. However, because setup cost is created by the incurrence of a batch being processed, the batch-level cost assignments are more appropriate. The batch-level perspective shows the commonality of

[4]This hierarchy of costs was introduced by Robin Cooper in "Cost Classification in Unit-Based and Activity-Based Manufacturing Cost Systems," *Journal of Cost Management* (Fall 1990), p. 6.

Exhibit 4.5 Levels of Costs

Classification Levels	Types of Costs	Necessity of Cost
Unit-Level Costs	• Direct material • Direct labor • Some machine costs, if traceable	Incur once for each unit produced
Batch-Level Costs	• Purchase orders • Setup • Inspection • Movement • Scrap, if related to the batch	Incur once for each batch produced
Product/Process-Level Costs	• Engineering change orders • Equipment maintenance • Product development • Scrap, if related to product design	Support a product type or a process
Organizational/Facility-Level Costs	• Building depreciation • Plant or division manager's salary • Organizational advertising	Support the overall production or service process

the cost to the parts within the batch and is more indicative of the relationship between the activity (setup) and the cost driver (different parts production runs).

A cost caused by the development, production, or acquisition of different items is called a **product-level (process-level) cost**. To illustrate this cost, assume that the engineering department issued five engineering change orders (ECOs) during May. Of these ECOs, four relate to Product R, one relates to Product S, and none relate to Product T. Each ECO costs $6,000 to issue, including charges for items such as labor review and redesign time, approval time, determination of new specifications, notification, and implementation. During May, the company made 7,500 products: 1,000 units of Product R, 1,500 units of Product S, and 5,000 units of Product T. If ECO costs are treated as unit-level costs, the following allocations would occur:

5 ECOs × $6,000 per ECO = $30,000 total ECO cost

	Unit-Level Cost Assignment			Product-Level Cost Assignment		
	$30,000 ÷ 7,500 = $4.00					
	# of Units	Cost per Unit	Cost Assignment	# of ECOs	Cost per ECO	Cost Assignment
Product R	1,000	$4.00	$ 4,000	4	$6,000	$24,000
Product S	1,500	$4.00	6,000	1	$6,000	6,000
Product T	5,000	$4.00	20,000	0		0
Total	7,500		$30,000	5		$30,000

Note that the unit-level method inappropriately assigns $20,000 of ECO cost to Product T, which had no ECOs!

This example indicates that using a product- or process-level driver (number of ECOs) for ECO costs would assign $24,000 of costs to Product R and $6,000 to Product S. However, the ECO costs should not attach solely to the current month's production. The ECO

William R. Minten/iStockphoto.com

General administration, rent, and building security costs are examples of organizational-level costs, which are incurred to support the facility operations in general.

cost should be allocated to all units of Products R and S that have been and will be manufactured while these ECOs are in effect because the changed design will benefit all that production. Since future production of Products R and S is unknown at the end of May, no per-unit cost is shown in the product-level cost assignment table. If product-level cost assignments are required, reasonable estimates can be made about future production levels so that no significant product cost distortions should arise for either internal or external reporting.

Organizational-level costs are incurred for the sole purpose of supporting facility operations. Such costs are common to many different products and services and should theoretically not be assigned to products and services at all because any such assignment would only be arbitrary. Many organizations, though, attach organizational-level costs to goods produced or services rendered because the amounts are insignificant relative to all other costs.

Accountants have traditionally (and incorrectly) assumed that when costs did not vary with changes in production at the unit level, those costs were fixed rather than variable. In reality, batch-, product/process-, and organizational-level costs are all variable, but they vary for reasons other than changes in production volume. Therefore, to determine a valid estimate of product or service cost, costs should be accumulated by cost level. Because unit-, batch-, and product/process-level costs are all associated with units of products or services (merely at different levels), these costs can be summed at the product/service level to match with the revenues generated by product sales. Organizational-level costs are not product or service related, so they should (again, in theory) be subtracted only in total from net product revenues.

Exhibit 4.6 shows how costs collected at the unit, batch, and product/process levels can be aggregated to estimate a total product cost. Each product or service cost is multiplied by the number of units sold, and that amount (cost of goods sold or cost of services rendered) is subtracted from total sales revenues to obtain a product or service line profit or loss amount. These computations would be performed for each product or service line and summed to determine net product or service income (or loss) from which the unassigned organizational-level costs would be subtracted to find company profit or loss for internal management use. In this model, the traditional distinction between product and period costs (discussed in Chapter 2) can be and is ignored. The emphasis is on modifying product or service profitability analysis to focus on internal management purposes rather than on external reporting. The approach in Exhibit 4.6 ignores the product/period cost distinction required by generally accepted accounting principles (GAAP) and, therefore, is not currently acceptable for external reporting.

Cost-Level Allocations Illustrated

Data for Bexar Manufacturing are presented in Exhibit 4.7 (p. 114) to illustrate the difference in information that would result from recognizing multiple cost levels. Prior to recognizing different levels of costs, Bexar accumulated and allocated its factory overhead costs among its three products (C, D, and E) on a machine-hour basis. Each product requires one machine hour, but Product D is a low-volume, special-order line.

The cost information in the first section of Exhibit 4.7 indicates that all three products are profitable for Bexar to produce and sell. After analyzing company activities, Bexar's cost accountant began capturing costs at the different levels and assigning those costs to products based on appropriate cost drivers. Individual details for this overhead assignment are not shown, but the final assignments and resulting product profitability figures are presented in the second section of Exhibit 4.7. This more refined approach to assigning costs shows that Product D is actually unprofitable for the company to produce.

Accountants have traditionally accumulated costs as transactions occurred and thus focused on the cost's amount rather than its source. However, this lack of consideration for

Exhibit 4.6 Determining Product Profitability and Company Profit

Product Unit Selling Price × Product Unit Volume = Total Product Revenue (1)

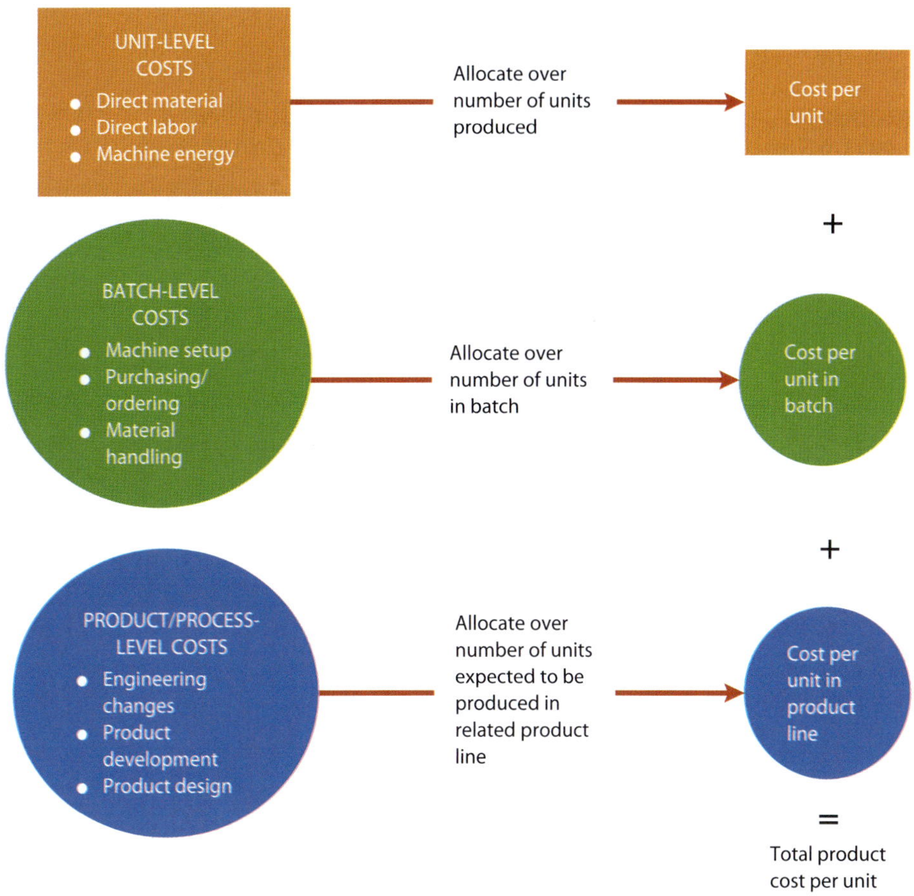

Total Product Cost per Unit × Product Unit Volume = Total Product Cost (2)

INTERNAL FINANCIAL STATEMENT PRESENTATION

	Total product revenue (1 above)
−	Total product cost (2 above)
=	Net product margin
±	All other net product margins[a]
=	Total margin provided by products
−	ORGANIZATIONAL- or FACILITY-LEVEL COSTS[b] • Corporate/divisional administration • Facility depreciation
=	Company profit or loss

[a]Calculations are made for each product line using the same method as above.
[b]Some of these costs could be assignable to specific products or services and would be included in determining product cost per unit.

underlying causes of costs has often resulted in a lack of ability to control costs as well as flawed cost data. Traditional cost allocations tend to subsidize low-volume specialty products by misallocating overhead to high-volume, standard products. This problem occurs because costs of the extra activities needed to make specialty products are assigned using the one or very few drivers of traditional costing—and usually these drivers are volume based.

Exhibit 4.7 Bexar Manufacturing Product Profitability Analysis

Total overhead cost $1,505,250
Total machine hours 111,500
Overhead rate per machine hour = $1,505,250 ÷ 111,500 = $13.50

Traditional Costing	PRODUCT C (5,000 UNITS)		PRODUCT D (1,500 UNITS)		PRODUCT E (105,000 UNITS)		
	Unit	Total	Unit	Total	Unit	Total	Total
Product revenue	$50.00	$250,000	$45.00	$67,500	$40.00	$4,200,000	$ 4,517,500
Product costs							
Direct	$20.00	$100,000	$20.00	$30,000	$ 9.00	$ 945,000	
Overhead (1 MH)	13.50	67,500	13.50	20,250	13.50	1,417,500	
Total	$33.50	$167,500	$33.50	$50,250	$22.50	$2,362,500	(2,580,250)
Net income		$ 82,500		$17,250		$1,837,500	$ 1,937,250

Activity-Based Costing	PRODUCT C (5,000 UNITS)		PRODUCT D (1,500 UNITS)		PRODUCT E (105,000 UNITS)		
	Unit	Total	Unit	Total	Unit	Total	Total
Product revenue	$50.00	$250,000	$45.00	$ 67,500	$40.00	$4,200,000	$ 4,517,500
Product costs							
Direct	$20.00	$100,000	$20.00	$ 30,000	$ 9.00	$ 945,000	
Overhead							
Unit level	8.00	40,000	12.00	18,000	6.00	630,000	
Batch level	9.00	45,000	19.00	28,500	3.00	315,000	
Product level	3.00	15,000	15.00	22,500	2.00	210,000	
Total	$40.00	$200,000	$66.00	$ 99,000	$20.00	$2,100,000	(2,399,000)
Product line income or (loss)		$ 50,000		$(31,500)		$2,100,000	$ 2,118,500
Organizational-level costs							(181,250)
Net income							$ 1,937,250

4 How are product and service costs computed using an activity-based costing system?

ACTIVITY-BASED COSTING

ABC focuses on attaching costs to products and services based on the activities conducted to produce, perform, distribute, and support those products and services. The three fundamental components of activity-based costing are

- recognizing that costs are incurred at different organizational levels,
- accumulating related costs into individual cost pools, and
- using multiple cost drivers to assign costs to products and services.

Two-Step Allocation

After being recorded in the general ledger and sub-ledger accounts, costs in an ABC system are accumulated in activity center cost pools. An **activity center** is any part of the production or service process for which management wants a separate reporting of costs. In defining these centers, management should consider the following issues:

- geographical proximity of equipment,
- defined centers of managerial responsibility,

- magnitude of product costs, and
- the need to keep the number of activity centers manageable.

Costs having the same driver are accumulated in pools reflecting the appropriate level of cost incurrence (unit, batch, or product/process). The fact that a relationship exists between a cost pool and a cost driver indicates that if the cost driver can be reduced or eliminated, the related cost should also be reduced or eliminated.

Gathering costs in pools having the same cost drivers allows managers to view an organization's activities cross-functionally. Companies not using ABC often accumulate overhead in departmental, rather than plantwide, cost pools. This type of accumulation reflects a vertical-function approach to cost accumulation; however, production and service activities are horizontal by nature. A product or service flows through an organization, affecting numerous departments as it goes. Using a cost driver approach to develop cost pools allows managers to more clearly focus on the cost effects created in making a product or performing a service than was traditionally possible.

After accumulation, costs are allocated out of the activity center cost pools and assigned to products and services by use of a second type of driver. An **activity driver** measures the demands placed on activities and, thus, the resources consumed by products and services. An activity driver often indicates an activity's output. The process of cost assignment is the same as the overhead application process illustrated in Chapter 3. Exhibit 4.8 illustrates this two-step allocation process of tracing costs to products and services in an ABC system.

Exhibit 4.8 Tracing Costs in an Activity-Based Costing System

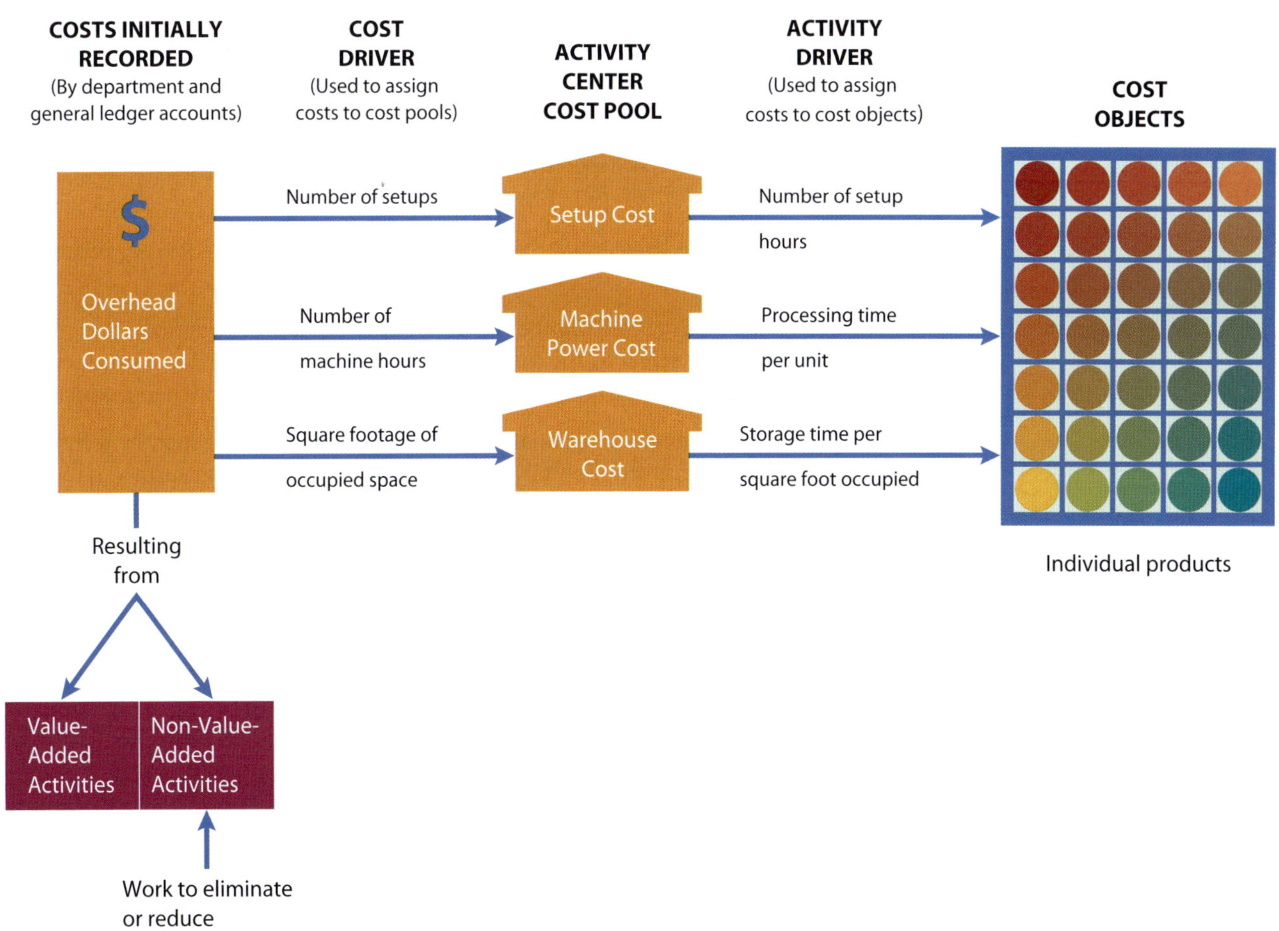

As illustrated in Exhibit 4.8, the cost drivers for the collection stage can differ from the activity drivers used for the allocation stage because some activity center costs are not traceable to lower levels of activity. Costs at the lowest (unit) level of activity should be allocated

to products by use of volume- or unit-based drivers. Costs incurred at higher (batch and product/process) levels can also be allocated to products by use of volume-related drivers, but the volume measure should include only those units associated with the batch or the product/process. Exhibit 4.9 provides some common drivers for various activity centers.

Exhibit 4.9 Activity Drivers

Activity Center	Activity Drivers
Accounting	Reports requested; dollars expended
Human resources	Job change actions; hiring actions; training hours; counseling hours
Data processing	Reports requested; transactions processed; programming hours; program change requests
Production engineering	Hours spent in each shop; job specification changes requested; product change notices processed
Quality control	Hours spent in each shop; defects discovered; samples analyzed
Plant services	Preventive maintenance cycles; hours spent in each shop; repair and maintenance actions
Material services	Dollar value of requisitions; number of transactions processed; number of personnel in direct support
Utilities	Direct usage (metered to shop); space occupied
Production shops	Fixed per-job charge; setups made; direct labor; machine hours; number of moves; material applied

Source: Michael D. Woods, "Completing the Picture: Economic Choices with ABC," *Management Accounting* (December 1992), p. 54. Reprinted from *Management Accounting*. Copyright by Institute of Management Accountants, Montvale, NJ.

Three significant cost drivers that have traditionally been disregarded are related to variety and complexity.

- **Product variety** refers to the number of different types of products made.
- **Product complexity** refers to the number of components included in a product.
- **Process complexity** refers to the number of processes through which a product flows.

Variety and complexity create additional overhead costs for activities such as warehousing, purchasing, setups, and inspections—all of which can be seen as "long-term variable costs" because they will increase as the number and types of products increase. Therefore, accountants should consider using items such as number of product types, number of components, and number of necessary processes as the cost drivers for applying ABC.

Activity-Based Costing Illustrated

A detailed ABC example is shown in Exhibit 4.10. The process begins by gathering information about the activities and costs for a factory maintenance department. Costs are then assigned to specific products based on activities. This department allocates its total human resources cost among the three activities performed in that department based on the number of employees in each area. This allocation reflects the fact that occurrences of a specific activity, rather than volume of production or service, drive work performed in the department. One of the company's products is Z4395, a rather complex unit with relatively low demand. Note that the cost allocated to it with the ABC system is 132 percent higher than the cost allocated with the traditional allocation system ($1.564 versus $0.675)!

Discrepancies in cost assignments between traditional and activity-based costing methods are not uncommon. Activity-based costing systems indicate that significant resources are consumed by low-volume products or services and complex production operations; some reasons for this conclusion are shown in Exhibit 4.11 (p. 118). Studies have shown

Exhibit 4.10 Illustration of Activity-Based Costing Allocation

Factory Maintenance Department: The conventional system assigns this department's human resources costs to products using direct labor hours (DLHs).

# of employees	9
Cost per employee	$50,000
Total departmental cost for 2013	$450,000
Expected DLHs in 2013	200,000
# of units of Z4395 produced in 2013	10,000
# of DLHs used to produce Z4395 in 2013	3,000

TRADITIONAL ALLOCATION

Traditional cost per DLH = $450,000 ÷ 200,000 = $2.25

Departmental cost allocation to Z4395 = (3,000 × $2.25) = $6,750; $6,750 ÷ 10,000 = $0.675 per unit

ABC ALLOCATION

Stage 1

Trace costs from general ledger and subsidiary ledger accounts to activity center pools according to number of employees:

- Regular maintenance—uses five employees; total cost pool for this activity = $250,000; second-stage allocation to be based on machine hours (MHs)
- Preventive maintenance—uses two employees; total cost pool for this activity = $100,000; second-stage allocation to be based on number of setups
- Repairs—uses two employees; total cost pool for this activity = $100,000; second-stage allocation is based on number of machine starts

Stage 2

Allocate activity center cost pools to products using cost drivers chosen for each cost pool. 2013 activity of second-stage drivers: 500,000 MHs; 5,000 setups; 100,000 machine starts

Step 1: Allocate costs per unit of activity of second-stage cost drivers.

- Regular maintenance: $250,000 ÷ 500,000 MHs = $0.50 per MH
- Preventive maintenance: $100,000 ÷ 5,000 setups = $20 per setup
- Repairs: $100,000 ÷ 100,000 machine starts = $1 per machine start

Step 2: Allocate departmental costs to products using quantity of second-stage cost drivers consumed in making these products. The following assumed quantities of activity are relevant to the 10,000 units of Z4395: 30,000 MHs; 30 setups; and 40 machine starts.

Departmental cost allocation to Z4395 = (30,000 × $0.50) + (30 × $20) + (40 × $1) = $15,640 for 10,000 units or $1.564 per unit

that, after an ABC implementation, the costs of high-volume standard products are often from 10 to 30 percent lower than the costs determined by traditional cost systems for the same products. Costs assigned to low-volume, complex specialty products tend to increase from 100 to 500 percent after implementing ABC. Thus, ABC typically shifts a substantial amount of overhead cost from standard high-volume products to premium special-order, low-volume products. The ABC costs of moderately complex products and services (those that are neither extremely simple nor complex nor produced in extremely low or high volumes) tend to remain approximately the same as costs calculated using traditional costing methods.

Managers in many companies are concerned about the product and service cost information provided by traditional cost accounting systems. Although reasonable for use in preparing financial statements, such costs often have limited value for managerial decision making and cost control—the latter being a high priority concern, especially in difficult economic times, for managers in all types of organizations.

Exhibit 4.11 Why Low Volume, Specialty Products/Services Cost More

Organizational Area	High Volume Items	Low Volume Items
Sales	Customers order from stock products.	Salespeople take extra time to help customers "create" specialty products that generate additional work for other areas.
Engineering	Design is known and kept current. Process has been kept current and adapted for new technology.	Design must be developed or reviewed for necessary changes. Process must be developed or reviewed to conform to new technology.
Purchasing	Suppliers are known. Raw material prices are standardized. Components are in stock.	New suppliers may have to be obtained. Price quotes may need to be evaluated or negotiated. Nonstandard raw materials may need to be found, ordered, and placed in stock.
Production or Performance	Setups are familiar and easily handled. Labor is familiar with the process, thereby reducing labor time. Changeovers from one process to another are scheduled in advance.	Setups are unfamiliar and take more time. Labor is unfamiliar with the process and must learn or relearn. Process changeovers may need to be expedited or randomly scheduled, creating delays, additional work orders, and confusion.
Quality Control	Potential problems are known and easily checked.	Problems are unknown and more inspection must be performed.

Activity-based costing is applicable to all organizational areas, including the selling and administrative departments. Many companies use an ABC system to allocate corporate overhead costs to their revenue-producing units based on the number of reports, documents, customers, or other reasonable activity measures.

DETERMINING WHETHER ABC IS USEFUL

5 Under what conditions is activity-based costing useful in an organization, and what information do activity-based costing systems provide to management?

Although not every accounting system using direct labor or machine hours to assign overhead costs produces inaccurate cost information, a great deal of information can be lost in the accounting systems of companies that ignore activity and cost relationships. Some general indicators can alert managers to the need to review the relevance of the cost information their system is providing. Several of these indicators are more relevant to manufacturing entities, whereas others are equally applicable to both manufacturing and service businesses. Factors to consider include the

- number and diversity of products or services produced,
- diversity and differential degree of support services used for different products,
- extent to which common processes are used,
- effectiveness of current cost allocation methods, and
- rate of growth of period costs.[5]

Additionally, if ABC is implemented, the new information will change management decisions *only* if management is able to set product/service prices, there are no strategic

[5]T. L. Estrin, Jeffrey Kantor, and David Albers, "Is ABC Suitable for Your Company?" *Management Accounting* (April 1994), p. 40. Copyright Institute of Management Accountants, Montvale, NJ.

constraints in the company, and the company has developed a culture of cost reduction. The following circumstances could indicate the need to consider using ABC.

Large Product or Service Variety

Product and service variety are commonly associated with the need to consider ABC. Whether items are variations of the same product line (such as **Hallmark**'s different types of greeting cards) or products are in numerous product families (such as **Procter & Gamble**'s detergents, diapers, fabric softeners, and shampoos), adding products causes numerous overhead costs to increase. Consider, for example, that **Walmart** has about 40 flat-panel television sets (out of its 142,000 SKUs per store), while a **Sally Beauty Salon** store carries between 5,000–10,000 SKUs of products.[6]

In the quest for product variety, many companies are striving for **mass customization** of products. Such personalized production can often be conducted at a relatively low cost. For example, **Mymüesli** lets customers create their own muesli from various ingredients and "566 quadrillon" possible combinations of base (starting at $6.44 for about 20 ounces), grains, fruits, nuts, seeds, and extras. **My Twinn** creates dolls to resemble photographs in about four weeks for about $150. Although such customization can please some customers, it has some drawbacks.

- There can be too many choices, creating confusion for customers.
- Mass customization creates a tremendous opportunity for errors.
- Most companies have found that customers, given a wide variety of choices, typically make selections based on the 20:80 **Pareto principle**. This principle suggests that, in many situations, it is common to observe that approximately 20 percent of "inputs" (choices) are responsible for 80 percent of "outputs" (selections).[7]

Most traditional cost systems do not provide information such as the number of different parts that are used in a product, so management cannot identify products made with low-volume or unique components. ABC systems are flexible and can gather such details so that persons involved in reengineering efforts have information about relationships among activities and cost drivers. With these data, reengineering efforts can be focused both on the primary causes of process complexity and on the causes that create the highest levels of waste.

High Product/Process Complexity

Companies with complex products, services, or processes should investigate ways to reduce that complexity. Management could review the design of the company's products and processes to standardize them and reduce the number of different components, tools, and activities. Products should be designed to consider the Pareto principle and take advantage of commonality of parts. For instance, if a company finds that 20 percent of its parts are used in 80 percent of its products, the company should ask where the remaining parts are being used.

- If the remaining parts are being used in key products, could equal quality be achieved by using the more common parts? If so, customers would likely be satisfied if more common parts were used and product prices were reduced.
- If the remaining parts are not being used in key products, will the customers purchasing the low-volume products be willing to pay a premium price to cover the additional costs of using low-volume parts? If so, the benefits from the complexity would be worth the cost. Complexity is acceptable *only* if it adds value from the customer's point of view.

[6] Greg Tarr, "Walmart TVs Up Close But Not So Personal," *Twice* (June 7, 2010), http://www.twice.com/article/453378-Walmart_TVs_Up_Close_But_Not_So_Personal.php; Tim Manners, "The Walmart Crapshoot," *The Hub Magazine* (June 2010), http://www.hubmagazine.com/2010/06/the-walmart-crapshoot-2/; Reuters, "Sally Beauty Holdings Inc.," *Profile* (August 19, 2011), http://www.reuters.com/finance/stocks/companyProfile?symbol=SBH.

[7] The Italian economist Vilfredo Pareto found that about 85 percent of Milan's wealth was held by about 15 percent of the people. The term *Pareto principle* was coined by Joseph Juran in relationship to quality problems. Juran found that a high proportion of such problems were caused by a small number of process characteristics (the vital few) whereas the majority of process characteristics (the trivial many) accounted for only a small proportion of quality problems.

Process complexity can develop over time, or it can exist because of a lack of sufficient planning in product development. Processes are complex when they create difficulties for the people performing the operations (such as physical straining, awkwardness of motions, and wasted motions) or using the machinery (such as multiple and/or detailed setups, lengthy transfer time between machine processes, and numerous instrument recalibrations). Process complexity is indicative of abundant non-value-added activities that cause time delays and cost increases.

Lack of Commonality in Overhead Costs

Certain products and services create substantially more overhead costs than others do. Although some of these additional overhead costs are caused by product variety or product/process complexity, others are related to support services. For instance, some products require high levels of advertising; some use expensive distribution channels; and some require the use of high-technology machinery. If only one or two overhead pools are used, overhead costs related to specific products will be spread over all products. The result will be higher costs for products that are not responsible for the increased overhead.

Similarly, some customers cost more to serve than others. Customers who buy in small quantities create additional processing and shipping costs. Customers who do not pay bills on time create additional accounts receivable costs. Customers who need too much personalized attention create additional sales or travel and entertainment costs. Determination of a "cost to serve" using ABC will help organizations identity the customers who are the most profitable and will also allow consideration of ways to generate additional revenue from the higher cost-to-serve customers. In general, cost to serve would include investigation of order size and frequency, sensitivity to price, level of repeat business, service requirements (especially in terms of time), return rates, and payment patterns; referral business from a customer should be considered a "negative cost" or an additional revenue from that client.

Irrationality of Current Cost Allocations

Companies that have undergone a significant change in their products or processes (such as increasing product variety or reengineering business processes) often recognize that existing cost systems no longer provide a reasonable estimate of product or service cost. For example, after automating production processes, many companies have experienced large reductions in labor cost with equal or greater increases in overhead. Continuing to use direct labor as an OH allocation base produces extraordinarily high application rates: some highly automated companies have predetermined OH rates ranging from 500 to 2,000 percent of direct labor cost. In such instances, products made using automated equipment tend to be charged an insufficient amount of overhead, whereas products made using high proportions of direct labor tend to be overcharged.

Traditional overhead cost allocations also reflect the financial accounting perspective of expensing period costs as they are incurred. ABC recognizes that some period costs (such as R&D and logistics) are distinctly and reasonably associated with specific products; ABC traces and allocates such costs to the appropriate products or services. Such a perspective modifies the traditional delineation between period and product cost.

Changes in Business Environment

A change in a company's competitive environment could also indicate a need for better cost information. Increased competition can occur because

- other companies have recognized the profit potential of a particular product or service,
- other companies now find the product or service has become cost feasible to make or perform, or
- an industry or market has been deregulated.

If additional companies are competing for the same "old" quantity of business, the best estimate of product or service cost must be available to management so that reasonable profit margins can be maintained or obtained. For instance, the U.S. jewelry and watch market's compound annual growth rate is expected to be a mere 1.6 percent through 2014, with buyers being extremely price sensitive.[8] Such companies must strictly control costs to achieve a profit margin level that allows them to remain in business.

Changes in management strategy can also signal the need for a new cost system. For example, if management wants to start a new production operation, the cost system must be capable of providing information on how costs will change. Showing costs as conforming only to the traditional unit-level variable and fixed classifications might not allow usable information to be developed. Viewing costs as batch level, product/process level, or organizational level focuses on cost drivers and on the changes the planned operations will have on activities and costs.

Eliminating NVA activities to reduce cycle time, making products (or performing services) with zero defects, reducing product costs on an ongoing basis, and simplifying products and processes reflect the concepts of continuous improvement. ABC, by promoting an understanding of cost drivers, allows the NVA activities to be identified and their causes eliminated or reduced.

CRITICISMS OF ACTIVITY-BASED COSTING

6 What criticisms have been directed at activity-based costing?

Realistically assessing new models and accounting approaches to determine what they can help managers accomplish is always important. However, no accounting technique or system provides management exact cost information for every product or the information needed to make consistently perfect decisions. For certain types of companies, ABC typically provides better information than that generated from a traditional overhead allocation process, but ABC is not a cure-all for all managerial concerns. Following are some shortcomings of ABC.

First, ABC requires a significant amount of time and cost to implement. If implementation is to be successful, substantial support is needed throughout the firm. Management must create an environment for change that overcomes a variety of individual, organizational, and environmental barriers, such as the following:

Individual Barriers	Organizational Barriers	Environmental Barriers
Fear of change	Territorial issues	Employee (often union) groups
Shift in status	Hierarchical issues	Regulatory agencies
Necessity to learn new skills	Corporate culture issues	Financial accounting mandates

To overcome these barriers, a firm must first recognize that these barriers exist, investigate their causes, and communicate information about the "what," "why," and "how" of ABC to all concerned parties. Top management must be involved with, and support, the implementation process; a shortfall in this area will make any progress toward the new system slow and difficult. Additionally, everyone in the company must be educated in new terminology, concepts, and performance measurements. Even if both of these conditions (support and education) are met, substantial time is needed to properly analyze the activities occurring in the activity centers, trace costs to those activities, and determine the cost drivers. One alternative to traditional ABC is time-driven ABC, which focuses only on the cost of supplying resources to activities and the time it takes to perform activities using the concept of available capacity.[9]

Another problem with ABC is that it does not conform specifically to GAAP. ABC suggests that some nonproduct costs (such as those for R&D) *should* be allocated to products, whereas certain other traditionally designated product costs (such as factory building depreciation) *should not* be allocated to products. Therefore, most companies have used ABC for internal reporting but continue to prepare their external financial statements with a more

[8] Datamonitor, *Industry Profile: Jewelry & Watches in the United States* (New York: Datamonitor, June 2010), pp. 8, 14.

[9] Robert S. Kaplan and Steven R. Anderson, "Time-Driven Activity-Based Costing," *Harvard Business Review* (November 2004).

traditional system—requiring even more costs to be incurred. As ABC systems become more accepted, more companies could choose to refine how ABC and GAAP determine product cost to make those definitions more compatible and, thereby, eliminate the need for two costing systems.

Companies attempting to implement ABC as a cure-all for product failures, sales volume declines, or financial losses will quickly find that the system is ineffective for these purposes. However, companies can implement ABC and its related management techniques in support of and in conjunction with total quality management, just-in-time production, or any of the other world-class methodologies. Companies doing so will provide the customer with the best variety, price, quality, service, and lead time of which they are capable—and, possibly, enjoy large increases in market share.

ABC and ABM are effective in supporting continuous improvement, short lead times, and flexible manufacturing by helping managers to

- identify and monitor significant technology costs;
- trace many technology costs directly to products;
- increase market share;
- identify the cost drivers that create or influence cost;
- identify activities that do not contribute to perceived customer value (i.e., non-value-added activities or waste);
- understand the impact of new technologies on all elements of performance;
- translate company goals into activity goals;
- analyze the performance of activities across business functions;
- analyze performance problems; and
- promote standards of excellence.

In summary, ABC assigns overhead costs to products and services differently from a traditional overhead allocation system. Implementation of ABC does not cause a company's overhead cost to be reduced; that outcome results from the implementation of ABM through its focus on identifying and reducing or eliminating non-value-added activities. Together, ABM and ABC help managers operate in the top right quadrant of the graph in Exhibit 4.12, so that they can produce products and perform services most efficiently and effectively and, thus, be highly competitive in the global business environment.

Exhibit 4.12 Efficiency and Effectiveness of Operations

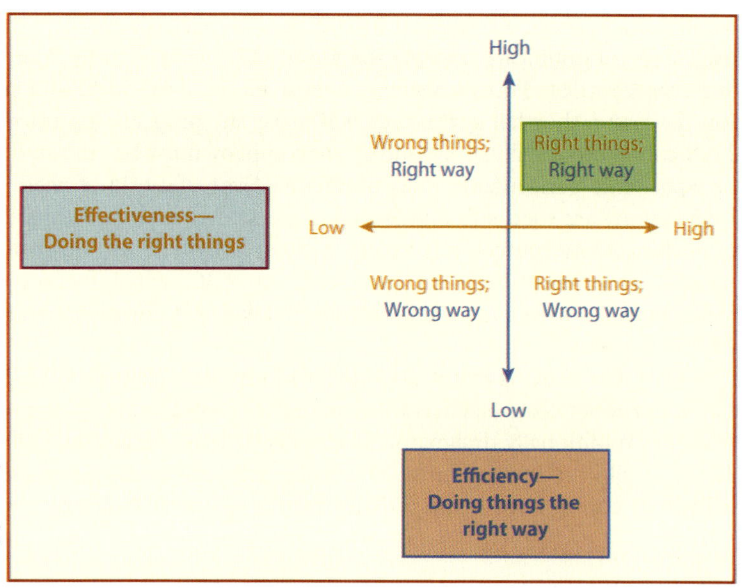

Comprehensive Review Module

KEY TERMS

activity, p. 104
activity analysis, p. 104
activity-based costing (ABC), p. 109
activity-based management (ABM), p. 104
activity center, p. 114
activity driver, p. 115
batch-level cost, p. 110
business-value-added (BVA) activity, p. 105
cost driver analysis, p. 110
cycle (lead) time, p. 106
idle time, p. 106
inspection time, p. 106
manufacturing cycle efficiency (MCE), p. 108
mass customization, p. 119
non-value-added (NVA) activity, p. 104
organizational-level cost, p. 112
Pareto principle, p. 119
process, p. 105
process complexity, p. 116
process map, p. 106
processing (service) time, p. 106
product complexity, p. 116
product-level (process-level) cost, p. 111
product variety, p. 116
service cycle efficiency (SCE), p. 108
transfer time, p. 106
unit-level cost, p. 110
value-added (VA) activity, p. 104
value chart, p. 107

CHAPTER SUMMARY

1 Activity-Based Management; Value-Added and Non-Value-Added Activities

- Activity-based management (ABM)
  - analyzes activities and identifies their cost drivers.
  - classifies activities relative to customer value and strives to eliminate or minimize those activities for which customers would choose not to pay.
  - helps assure that customers perceive an equitable relationship between product selling price and value.
  - improves processes and operational controls.
  - analyzes performance problems.
  - translates company goals into organizational activities.
- A value-added (VA) activity
  - increases the worth of a product or service.
  - is one for which the customer is willing to pay.
  - is an actual production or service task.
- A non-value-added (NVA) activity
  - lengthens the production or performance time.
  - increases the cost of product or services without adding product or service value.
  - is one for which the customer would not be willing to pay.
  - is created by
    - inspecting (except in certain industries such as food and pharmaceutical),
    - moving,
    - waiting,
    - packaging (unless essential to the convenient or proper delivery of a product), or
    - engaging in a task that is (or appears to be) essential to business operations but for which customers would not willingly choose to pay.

2 Manufacturing Cycle Efficiency

- Manufacturing cycle efficiency (MCE) is computed as total value-added time divided by total cycle time.
- MCE measures how well a company uses its time resources.
- VA activities increase MCE, while NVA activities decrease MCE.
- In a service company, cycle efficiency is computed as total actual service time divided by total cycle time (from original service order to service completion).

3 Importance of Cost Drivers

- Cost drivers identify what causes a cost to be incurred so that it can be controlled.
- Cost drivers should indicate at what level a cost occurs.
  - Unit costs are caused by the production or acquisition of a single unit of product or the delivery of a single unit of service.
  - Batch costs are caused by a group of things being made, handled, or processed at a single time.
  - Product/process costs are caused by the development, production, or acquisition of different items.
  - Organizational costs are caused by facility operations and the management of the organizational infrastructure.
- Cost drivers allow costs to be pooled together such that they have a common activity base that can be used to allocate those costs to products or services.
- Cost drivers promote the effective and efficient management of costs.
- Cost drivers help identify costs related to product variety and product/process complexity.

4 Computation of Costs in Activity-Based Costing

- Activity-based costing (ABC) is a cost accounting system that focuses on an organization's activities and collects costs on the basis of the underlying nature and extent of those activities.
- ABC is a process of overhead allocation.
- ABC differs from a traditional cost accounting system in that ABC
  - identifies several levels of costs rather than the traditional concepts of variable (at the unit level) or fixed.
  - collects costs in cost pools based on the underlying nature and extent of activities.
  - assigns costs within the multiple cost pools to products or services using multiple drivers (both volume- and non-volume-related) that best reflect the factor causing the costs to be incurred.
  - considers some costs that are considered product costs for external reporting as period costs.
  - considers some costs that are considered period costs for external reporting as product costs.
  - may, under certain conditions, provide a more realistic picture of actual production cost than has traditionally been available.

5 Conditions for Effective Use of ABC

- ABC is appropriate in an organization that
  - produces and sells a wide variety of products or services.
  - customizes products to customer specifications.
  - uses a wide range of techniques to manufacture products or to provide services.
  - has a lack of commonality in overhead costs of products or services.
  - has experienced problems with its current overhead allocation system.
  - has experienced significant changes in its business environment, including widespread adoption of new technologies.
- Installation of an ABM or ABC system allows management to
  - see the cost impact of an organization's cross-functional activities.
  - understand that fixed costs are, in fact, long-run variable costs that change based on an identifiable driver.
  - realize the value of preparing process maps and value charts.
  - determine that the traditional bases (direct labor and machine hours) might not produce the most logical costs for products or services.
  - recognize that standard products/services often financially support premium products/services.
  - set prices that reflect the activities needed to produce special or premium products.
  - decide whether premium or low-volume products are actually profitable for the company.
  - calculate MCE and measure organizational performance.
  - be aware that the most effective way to control costs is to minimize or eliminate NVA activities.
  - accept that customers who are not profitable should not necessarily be retained.

6 Criticisms of ABC

- ABC requires substantial time and cost to implement.
- ABC does not specifically conform to generally accepted accounting principles.
- ABC cannot "cure" product failures, sales volume declines, or financial losses.
- ABC does not reduce overhead costs.

SOLUTION STRATEGIES

Manufacturing Cycle Efficiency, p. 108

Total Cycle Time = Value-Added Processing Time + Inspection Time + Transfer Time + Idle Time

MCE = Value-Added Processing Time ÷ Total Cycle Time

Note: Depending on the organization, packaging time may be part of value-added processing time or a type of non-value-added time. In either case, packaging time will add to total cycle time. Business-value-added time may need to be included as NVA time for certain types of functions.

Activity-Based Costing, p. 109

1. Determine the organization's costs.
2. Determine the drivers creating the costs and aggregate the costs into "pools" based on levels of costs.
3. Determine the organization's activity centers and allocate costs to those centers using cost drivers.
4. Determine the activity drivers needed to assign costs to products and services.
5. Do not allocate organizational level costs to products and services unless those costs are immaterial in amount.

DEMONSTRATION PROBLEM

Potter Inc. manufactures wizard figurines. All figurines are approximately the same size, but some are plain ceramic whereas others are "fancy," with purple leather capes and a prism-headed wand. Management is considering producing only the fancy figurines because they appear to be substantially more profitable than the plain figurines. The company's total production overhead is $5,017,500. Some additional data follow.

	Plain	Fancy
Revenues	$15,000,000	$16,800,000
Direct costs	$ 8,050,000	$ 8,950,000
Production (units)	1,500,000	350,000
Machine hours	200,000	50,000
Direct labor hours	30,500	157,625
Number of inspections	600	6,900

Required:

a. Potter Inc. has consistently used machine hours to allocate overhead. Determine the profitability of each line of figurines, and decide whether the company should stop producing the plain figurines.

b. The cost accountant has determined that production overhead costs can be assigned to separate cost pools. Pool #1 contains $1,260,000 of overhead costs for which the most appropriate cost driver is machine hours; Pool #2 contains $2,257,500 of overhead costs for which the most appropriate cost driver is direct labor hours; and Pool #3 contains $1,500,000 of overhead costs for which the most appropriate cost driver is number of inspections. Compute the overhead cost that should be allocated to each type of figurine using this methodology.

c. Discuss whether the company should continue to manufacture both types of figurines.

Solution to Demonstration Problem

a. Overhead rate per MH = $5,017,500 ÷ 250,000 = $20.07 per MH
Overhead for plain figurines: 200,000 × $20.07 = $4,014,000
Overhead for fancy figurines: 50,000 × $20.07 = $1,003,500

	Plain		Fancy	
Revenue		$ 15,000,000		$16,800,000
Direct costs	$8,050,000		$8,950,000	
Overhead	4,014,000		1,003,500	
Total costs		(12,064,000)		(9,953,500)
Gross profit		$ 2,936,000		$ 6,846,500
Profit margin (rounded)		19.7%		40.8%

b.

	Plain	Fancy	Total
Machine hours	200,000	50,000	250,000
Rate per MH ($1,260,000 ÷ 250,000)	× $5.04	× $5.04	× $5.04
Pool #1 OH cost allocations	$1,008,000	$ 252,000	$1,260,000
Direct labor hours	30,500	157,625	188,125
Rate per DLH ($2,257,500 ÷ 188,125)	× $12	× $12	× $12
Pool #2 OH cost allocations	$ 366,000	$1,891,500	$2,257,500
Number of inspections	600	6,900	7,500
Rate per inspection ($1,500,000 ÷ 7,500)	× $200	× $200	× $200
Pool #3 OH cost allocations	$ 120,000	$1,380,000	$1,500,000
Total allocated overhead costs	$1,494,000	$3,523,500	$5,017,500

	Plain		Fancy	
Revenue		$15,000,000		$ 16,800,000
Direct costs	$8,050,000		$8,950,000	
Overhead	1,494,000		3,523,500	
Total costs		(9,544,000)		(12,473,500)
Gross profit		$ 5,456,000		$ 4,326,500
Gross profit margin		36.4%		25.8%

c. Given the new allocations, management should continue to produce both types of figurines because both appear to be profitable. However, the cost accountant could consider developing additional overhead pools because of the large number of costs charged to Pool #2.

POTENTIAL ETHICAL ISSUES

ETHICS

1. Ignoring non-value-added activities and times in the development of a value chart to improve cycle efficiency as a performance metric
2. Using an unsubstantiated designation of "non-value-added" for specific activities merely to justify the elimination of the jobs of the individuals performing those activities
3. Misclassifying batch- or product/process-level activities as unit-level to spread the costs of those activities to higher-volume products/services and, thereby, reduce the cost of lower-volume products so as to justify a reduced selling price on the lower-volume products/services
4. Selecting an inappropriate cost driver to allocate costs to products or services in a way that intentionally distorts realistic cost calculations
5. Using activity-based costing to unethically justify no longer purchasing from a particular vendor or selling to a particular customer
6. Using activity-based costing to justify not allocating corporate funds to social or environmental causes
7. Using distorted activity-based costing allocations to transfer costs from fixed-price contracts to cost-plus contracts

QUESTIONS

1. What is activity-based management (ABM), and what specific management tools are used in ABM?
2. What is activity analysis, and how is it used with cost driver analysis to manage costs and increase profits?
3. Why are value-added activities defined from a customer viewpoint?
4. According to a *Wall Street Journal* article, a three-hour televised football game boils down to 10 minutes and 43 seconds of actual playing time. [D. Biderman, "11 Minutes of Action," *WSJ* (January 15, 2010), W1] What other activities take place

during a televised football game? Of all the activities, which are value-added and which are non-value-added? Discuss whether everyone would agree with your choices. What is the cycle efficiency of the football game?

5. If five people from the same organization calculated manufacturing cycle efficiency for a specific process, would each compute the same MCE? Why or why not?
6. Why is service cycle efficiency generally a higher percentage than manufacturing cycle efficiency?
7. Do cost drivers exist in a traditional accounting system? Are they designated as such? How, if at all, does the use of cost drivers in a traditional accounting system differ from those in an activity-based costing system?
8. Why do more traditional methods of overhead assignment "overload" standard high-volume products or services with overhead costs? How does ABC improve overhead assignments?
9. Once an activity-based costing system has been developed and implemented in a company, will that system be appropriate for the long term? Why or why not?
10. Are all companies likely to benefit to an equal extent from adopting ABC? Discuss.
11. When Chrysler launched its Fiat 500 subcompact in 2011, the company offered three versions (Lounge, Sport, and Pop), having 14 exterior colors, 14 seat colors, six wheel styles, two transmission types, and a range of graphical designs that can be applied to the car's body panels—providing a total of about 500,000 combinations. [J. Bennett, "Options Overload for Fiat's 500," *WSJ* (November 10, 2010), B1] Discuss the additional costs that Chrysler might incur from having so many options for the Fiat 500. Do you think that customers will be willing to pay significantly different prices for option variations? Why or why not?
12. Significant hurdles, including a large time commitment, are often encountered in adopting ABC. What specific activities associated with ABC adoption require large investments of time?

EXERCISES

13. **LO.1 (Activity analysis)** The Raleigh plant manager of Allentown Corp. has noticed the plant frequently changes the schedule on its production line. He has gathered the following information on the activities, estimated times, and average costs required for a single schedule change.

Activity	Est. Time	Average Cost
Review impact of change on orders	30 min.–2 hrs.	$ 300
Reschedule production orders	15 min.–24 hrs.	875
Stop production and change over to new process	10 min.–3 hrs.	150
Locate inventory produced under old process	20 min.–6 hrs.	1,500
Remanufacture old inventory to conform to new process	3 hrs.–20 hrs.	6,000
Generate new production paperwork	15 min.–4 hrs.	500
Change purchasing schedule	10 min.–8 hrs.	2,100
Collect paperwork from the floor	5 min.–15 min.	75
Review new line schedule	15 min.–30 min.	100
Pay overtime premiums	3 hrs.–5 hrs.	1,000
Total costs required for a single schedule change.		$6,600

a. Which, if any, of these activities are value-added?
b. What is the cost driver in this situation?
c. How can the cost driver be controlled and the NVA activities eliminated?

14. **LO.1 (Activity analysis; research)** Go to a local department or grocery store.

a. List five packaged items for which it is readily apparent that packaging is essential and, therefore, would be considered value-added.
b. List five packaged items for which it is readily apparent that packaging is nonessential and therefore adds no value.
c. For each item listed in (b), indicate why you think the item was packaged rather than left unpackaged.

15. **LO.1 (Activity analysis)** The following activities are common at Pisana's Department Store. Goods are received with barcodes attached that can be read by scanners but not by customers.
    1. Attending trade shows to view new products
    2. Reviewing supplier catalogs
    3. Ordering merchandise
    4. Waiting for shipments to be received
    5. Inspecting goods for damage
    6. Matching receiving reports and purchase orders
    7. Placing customer-readable price tags on merchandise
    8. Moving goods to retail area
    9. Stocking shelves
    10. Training salespersons in store merchandise
    11. Checking out customer purchases
    12. Handing customer receipts
    13. Wrapping gift items when requested
    14. Helping customers with returns or exchanges

    a. Indicate which activities are value-added (VA), business-value-added (BVA), and non-value-added (NVA).
    b. How might some of the business-value-added activities be reduced or eliminated?

16. **LO.1 (Activity analysis)** Your boss wants to know whether quality inspections at your company add value. Use the "why" methodology to help your boss make this determination if you work at (a) a clothing manufacturer that sells to a discount chain and (b) a pharmaceutical manufacturer.

17. **LO.1 (Activity analysis; writing)** Choose an activity related to this class, such as attending lectures or doing homework. Write down the answers to the question "why" five times to determine whether your activity is value-added or non-value-added.

18. **LO.1 & LO.2 (Activity analysis; SCE)** Following are the activities that occur during a patient visit to a physician's office.

Step	Time Spent
Patient arrives at doctor's office and checks in with receptionist.	2 min.
Patient is asked to review previously provided information for changes; there are none.	3 min.
Patient returns forms to receptionist.	1 min.
Receptionist verifies patient insurance and collects co-pay.	5 min.
Patient waits in waiting room.	15 min.
Nurse escorts patient to exam room and takes vital signs.	3 min.
Patient waits in exam room.	7 min.
Physician examines and treats patient.	8 min.
Patient checks out with receptionist, if needed.	3 min.

    a. Classify each of the above activities as value-added or non-value-added.
    b. Determine the service cycle efficiency.

19. **LO.1 & LO.2 (Activity analysis; SCE)** The following activities take place at Lohman CPAs during a recurring external audit of Reliance Corp. Classify the activities as value-added or non-value-added from the perspective of Reliance Corp. and compute the service cycle efficiency.

Activity	Time (Hours)
Drafting engagement letter	4
Audit planning and discussion of audit risk	20
Internal control review	32
Preparing audit program	24
Fieldwork, transaction testing, completing work papers	125
Client discussions and rework	16
Drafting and issuing audit report; discussion with board of directors	23
Audit follow-up discussions	20

20. **LO.1 & LO.2 (Activity analysis; MCE)** Spice-a-licious produces creole seasoning using the following process for each batch:

Function	Time (Minutes)
Receiving ingredients	60
Moving ingredients to stockroom	80
Storing ingredients in stockroom	8,200
Moving ingredients from stockroom	8
Measuring ingredients	30
Mixing ingredients	60
Packaging ingredients	50
Moving packaged seasoning to warehouse	100
Storing packaged seasoning in warehouse	20,000
Moving packaged seasoning from warehouse to trucks	120

a. Calculate the total cycle time of this manufacturing process.
b. Which of the functions add value?
c. Calculate the manufacturing cycle efficiency of this process.
d. What could Spice-a-licious do to improve its MCE?

21. **LO.1 & LO.2 (Activity analysis; MCE)** Log Cabins Unlimited constructs vacation houses in the North Carolina mountains. The company has developed the following value chart:

Operations	Average Number of Days
Receiving materials	2
Storing materials	10
Measuring and cutting materials	9
Handling materials	7
Setting up and moving scaffolding	6
Assembling materials	3
Building fireplace	12
Pegging logs	8
Cutting and framing doors and windows	5
Sealing joints	4
Waiting for county inspectors	6
Inspecting property (county inspectors)	1

a. What are the value-added activities and their total time?
b. What are the non-value-added activities and their total time?
c. Calculate the manufacturing cycle efficiency of the process.
d. Explain the difference between value-added and non-value-added activities.

22. **LO.1 & LO.2 (Activity analysis)** Farrah Westin plans to build a concrete walkway for her home during her vacation. The following schedule shows how project time will be allocated:

Activity	Hours
Purchase materials	5
Obtain rental equipment	2
Remove sod and level site	20
Build forms for concrete	10
Mix and pour concrete into forms	5
Level concrete and smooth	6
Let dry	24
Remove forms from concrete	2
Return rental tools	1
Clean up	4

a. Identify the value-added activities. How much of the total time is value-added time?
b. Identify the non-value-added activities. How much total time is spent performing non-value-added activities?
c. Calculate the manufacturing cycle efficiency.

23. **LO.1 & LO.2 (Activity analysis; MCE)** Elaydo Inc. makes flavored water and performs the following tasks in the beverage manufacturing process:

	Hours
Receive and transfer ingredients to storage	9.0
Store ingredients	264.0
Transfer ingredients from storage to production area	3.5
Mix and cook ingredients	6.5
Bottle water	3.0
Transfer bottles to finished goods warehouse	5.0

a. Calculate the total cycle time of this manufacturing process.
b. Calculate the manufacturing cycle efficiency of this process.

24. **LO.2 (Value chart)** McAllen Co. manufactures special-order office cubicle systems. Production time is two days, but the average cycle time for any order is three weeks. The company president has asked you, as the new controller, to discuss missed delivery dates. Prepare an oral presentation for the executive officers in which you address the following:

a. Possible causes of the problem.
b. How a value chart could be used to address the problem.

25. **LO.2 (SCE)** When problems occur with products that are purchased, buyers contact the manufacturer's call center. After being notified of a problem and requesting assistance from the appropriate parties, a call center agent can create a solution document for the problem in 30 minutes. A supervisor then takes 15 minutes to review the document and verify the solution. The document is then routed to Marketing for review (30 minutes) and on to Legal (two hours) to make certain that the document is ready for publication. However, because of time lags between each step, the total cycle time takes 15 days from creation to publication. (Based on information at http://www.streetdirectory.com/travel_guide/16701/corporate_matters/increase_call_center_efficiency_with_knowledge_centered_support.html.)

a. Which of the activities in the correction process are value-added?
b. If the problem could not have been foreseen, how would you calculate the cycle efficiency for the correction process?
c. Assume again that the problem could not have been foreseen. After being notified of a problem and requesting assistance from the appropriate parties, a call center agent can create a solution document for the problem in 30 minutes. Call center agents are "licensed" to publish a solution document after placing it in a queue for four hours after development to allow Marketing and Legal the option of review. After four hours, the solution document is automatically posted on the company's Web site to assist customers. What is the new cycle efficiency?
d. Assume that the manufacturer sold 30,000 of the problem products just before Christmas. The first customer complaint call was received at 10 A.M. on December 25. The call center agent devised the solution document by 10:30 A.M.. If a call will be received every ten minutes until the support document is posted and each call costs the company $15, what is the call center cost related to this problem if the process is handled as originally discussed? As discussed in (c)?

26. **LO.3 (Levels of costs)** Three clients (A, B, and C) use Babineaux Call Service's call center. During October, Babineaux initiated four new equipment advancements. The following information indicates the cost and benefits of each service:

Service Type	Cost	Benefits Client	Estimated Calls Benefited
Service #359	$ 5,810	A	7,000
Service #360	7,085	A and	2,200
		B	4,300
Service #361	3,198	C	1,300
Service #362	4,887	C	2,700
	$20,980		17,500

a. If the total cost of new equipment is allocated to all units benefited, what is the cost per unit and total cost allocated to each client? (Round to the nearest cent.)
b. If the cost of new equipment is allocated to clients benefited, what is the cost per client and the cost per call benefited?
c. Assume that Babineaux Call Service charges the costs to the clients as indicated in (b). Client A estimates that a total of 30,000 calls will be processed by Babineaux over the life of the equipment advances. How should Client A allocate the new costs to its callers?

27. **LO.3 (Levels of costs)** Baldacci Inc. has a casting machine that is used for three of the company's products. Each machine setup costs $20,445, and the machine was set up in June for six different production runs. The following information shows the units of output from each of the setups.

Setup #	Product #453	Product #529	Product #663
1	22,800		
2			840
3		15,200	
4	27,900		
5			60
6	17,800		

a. If total machine setup cost is allocated to all units of product, what is the setup cost per unit and total setup cost for Products #453, 529, and 663 during June?
b. If machine setup cost is allocated to each type of product made, what is the setup cost per unit of Products #453, 529, and 663 and the total cost of those products during June? (Round to the nearest cent.)
c. If Baldacci Inc. had manufactured all similar products in a single production run, how would unit and total costs have changed during June? (Round to the nearest cent.)

28. **LO.3 (Levels of costs)** Carpenter Inc. designs industrial tooling parts and makes the molds for those parts. The following activities take place when the company creates a new mold. Classify each cost as unit level (U), batch level (B), product/process level (P), or organizational level (O).

a. Consulting with equipment manufacturer on design specifications
b. Engineering design of mold
c. Creating mold
d. Moving materials from warehouse for test quantity
e. Using direct materials for test quantity to judge conformity to design specifications
f. Inspecting test quantity
g. Preparing design specification changes based on test molds
h. Depreciating small kiln used solely for test quantities
i. Depreciating manufacturing building

29. **LO.3 (Levels of costs)** Leopold & Olney LLP has five partners and 12 staff accountants. The partners each work 2,100 hours per year and earn $350,000 annually. The staff accountants each work 2,600 hours per year and earn $80,000 annually. The firm's total annual budget for professional support available to partners and staff accountants is $312,750. The firm also spends $125,100 for administrative support that is used only by the partners.

a. Assume that total support cost is considered a unit-level cost based on number of work hours. What is the support rate per labor hour?
b. If one audit engagement requires 60 partner hours and 220 staff accountant hours, how much professional support cost would be charged to the engagement using the rate determined in (a)?
c. Assume that support costs are considered batch-level costs based on number of work hours. What are the professional and administrative support rates per labor hour? (Round to the nearest cent.)

d. If an audit engagement requires 60 partner hours and 220 staff accountant hours, how much support cost would be charged to the engagement using the rates determined in (c)?

30. **LO.3 (Levels of costs)** The following costs are incurred in a fast-food restaurant that relies on computer-controlled equipment to prepare customers' food. The majority of food is purchased daily for freshness. Classify each cost as unit level (U), batch level (B), product/process level (P), or organizational level (O):
    a. Maintenance of the restaurant building
    b. Store manager's salary
    c. Refrigeration of raw materials
    d. Oil for the deep-fat fryer (changed every four hours)
    e. Electricity expense for the pizza oven
    f. Ingredients for food orders
    g. Depreciation on equipment
    h. Cardboard boxes for food order
    i. Property taxes
    j. Frozen potatoes for french fries

31. **LO.3 (Cost drivers)** For each of the following costs commonly incurred in a manufacturing company, identify a cost driver and explain why it is an appropriate choice.
    a. Factory depreciation
    b. Freight costs for materials
    c. Machine setup cost
    d. Computer operations
    e. Material storage
    f. Material handling
    g. Engineering changes
    h. Advertising expense
    i. Building utilities
    j. Quality control
    k. Equipment maintenance

32. **LO.3 (Cost drivers)** For each of the following cost pools in a temporary employment agency, identify a cost driver and explain why it is appropriate.
    a. Advertising cost
    b. Accounts receivable department
    c. Property taxes and insurance on office building
    d. Information technology
    e. Payroll department
    f. Utilities

33. **LO.4 (ABC)** Briones Books is concerned about the profitability of its regular dictionaries. Company managers are considering producing only the top-quality, hand-sewn dictionaries with gold-edged pages. Briones is currently assigning the $2,000,000 of overhead costs to both types of dictionaries based on machine hours. Of the overhead, $800,000 is utilities related and the remainder is primarily related to quality control inspectors' salaries. The following information about the products is also available:

	Regular	Hand Sewn
Number produced	2,000,000	1,400,000
Machine hours	170,000	30,000
Inspection hours	10,000	50,000
Revenues	$6,400,000	$5,600,000
Direct costs	$5,000,000	$4,400,000

    a. Determine the total overhead cost assigned to each type of dictionary using the current allocation system.
    b. Determine the total overhead cost assigned to each type of dictionary if more appropriate cost drivers were used.
    c. Should the company stop producing the regular dictionaries? Explain.

34. **LO.4 (OH allocation using cost drivers)** Wambaugh Corp. has decided to implement an activity-based costing system for its in-house legal department. The legal department's primary expense is professional salaries, which are estimated for associated activities as follows:

Reviewing supplier or customer contracts (Contracts)	$270,000
Reviewing regulatory compliance issues (Regulation)	379,500
Court actions (Court)	862,500

Management has determined that the appropriate cost allocation base for Contracts is the number of pages in the contract reviewed, for Regulation is the number of reviews, and for Court is number of hours of court time. For 2013, the legal department reviewed 500,000 pages of contracts, responded to 750 regulatory review requests, and logged 3,750 hours in court.

a. Determine the allocation rate for each activity in the legal department.
b. What amount would be charged to a department that had 21,000 pages of contracts reviewed, made 27 regulatory review requests, and consumed 315 professional hours in court services during the year?
c. How can the developed rates be used for evaluating output relative to cost incurred in the legal department? What alternative does the firm have to maintaining an internal legal department and how might this choice affect costs?

35. **LO.4 (ABC)** Bernacke Corp. is instituting an activity-based costing project in its ten-person purchasing department. Annual departmental overhead costs are $731,250. Because finding the best supplier takes the majority of effort in the department, most of the costs are allocated to this activity area. Many purchase orders are received in a single shipment. EXCEL

Activity	Allocation Measure	Quantity	Total Cost
Find best suppliers	Number of telephone calls	75,000	$375,000
Issue purchase orders	Number of purchase orders	46,875	187,500
Review receiving reports	Number of receiving reports	28,125	168,750

One special-order product manufactured by the company required the following purchasing department activities: 25 telephone calls, 50 purchase orders, and 35 receipts.

a. What amount of purchasing department cost should be assigned to this product?
b. If 100 units of the product are manufactured during the year, what is the purchasing department cost per unit?
c. If purchasing department costs had been allocated using telephone calls as the allocation base, how much cost would have been assigned to this product?

36. **LO.4 (OH allocation using cost drivers)** Regis Place is a health-care facility that has been allocating its overhead costs to patients based on number of patient days. The facility's overhead costs total $3,620,400 per year and the facility (which operates monthly at capacity) has a total of 60 beds available. (Assume a 360-day year.) The facility's accountant is considering a new overhead allocation method using the following information:

	Cost	Cost Driver	Quantity
Rooms (depreciation, cleaning, etc.)	$ 504,000	# of rooms (25 double)	35
Laundry	151,200	# of beds	60
Nursing care	1,314,000	# of nurse-hours annually	43,800
Physical therapy	960,000	# of hours of rehab	8,000
General services	691,200	# of patient days	

Rooms are cleaned daily; laundry for rooms is done, on average, every other day.

a. How many patient days are available at Regis Place?
b. What is the current overhead rate per patient day? (Round to the nearest dollar.)
c. Using the individual cost drivers, what is the overhead rate for each type of cost? (Round to the nearest dollar.)
d. Assume a patient stayed at Regis Place for six days. The patient was in a single room and required six hours of nursing care and 30 hours of physical therapy. What

overhead cost would be assigned to this patient under the current method of overhead allocation? What overhead cost would be assigned to this patient under the ABC method of overhead allocation?

e. Assume a patient stayed at Regis Place for six days. The patient was in a double room and required six hours of nursing care but did not require any physical therapy. What overhead cost would be assigned to this patient under the current method of overhead allocation? What overhead cost would be assigned to this patient under the ABC method of overhead allocation?

ETHICS

37. **LO.5 (Decision making; ethics; writing)** Many manufacturers are deciding to service only customers that buy $10,000 or more of products from the manufacturers annually. Manufacturers defend such policies by stating that they can provide better service to customers that handle more volume and more diverse product lines.

a. Relate the concepts in the chapter to the decision of manufacturers to drop small customers.

b. Are there any ethical implications of eliminating groups of customers that could be less profitable than others?

c. Does activity-based costing adequately account for all costs that are related to a decision to eliminate a particular customer base? (*Hint:* Consider opportunity costs such as those related to reputation.)

38. **LO.5 (Benefits of ABC; writing)** The cost systems at many companies selling multiple products have become less than adequate in today's global competition. Managers often make important product decisions based on distorted cost information because the cost systems have been primarily designed to focus on inventory measurement. Current literature suggests that many manufacturing companies should have at least three cost systems, one each for inventory measurement, operational control, and activity-based costing.

a. Identify the purpose and characteristics of each of the following cost systems:

1. Inventory measurement
2. Activity-based costing

b. Discuss why a cost system developed for inventory valuation could distort product cost information.

c. Describe the benefits that management can obtain from using activity-based costing.

d. List the steps that a company using a traditional cost system would take to implement activity-based costing.

CMA ADAPTED

39. **LO.5 (Controlling OH; writing)** SailAway has changed its product line from general paints to specialized marine coatings, which has caused overhead costs to double. Costs affected include customer service, production scheduling, inventory control, and laboratory work. The company has decided to analyze and update its cost information and pricing practices. Although some large orders are still received, most current business is generated from products designed and produced in small lot sizes to meet specifically detailed environmental and technical requirements. Management believes that large orders are being penalized and small orders are receiving favorable cost (and, thus, selling price) treatment.

a. Indicate why the shift in product lines would have caused such major increases in overhead.

b. Is it possible that management is correct in its belief about the costs of large and small orders? If so, why?

c. Write a memo to management suggesting how it might change the cost accounting system to reflect the changes in the business.

40. **LO.5 (Product profitability)** Sandford Inc. manufactures lawn mowers and garden tractors. Lawn mowers are relatively simple to produce and are made in large quantities. Garden tractors are customized to individual wholesale customer specifications. The company produces and sells 300,000 lawn mowers and 30,000 garden tractors annually. Revenues and costs incurred for each product are as follows:

	Lawn Mowers	Garden Tractors
Revenue	$19,500,000	$17,850,000
Direct material	4,000,000	2,700,000
Direct labor ($20 per hour)	2,800,000	6,000,000
Overhead	?	?

Manufacturing overhead totals $3,960,000, and administrative expenses equal $7,400,000.

a. Calculate the profit (loss) in total and per unit for each product if overhead is assigned to product using a per-unit basis.
b. Calculate the profit (loss) in total and per unit for each product if overhead is assigned to products using a direct labor hour basis.
c. Assume that manufacturing overhead can be divided into two cost pools as follows: $1,320,000, which has a cost driver of direct labor hours, and $2,640,000, which has a cost driver of machine hours (totaling 150,000). Lawn mower production uses 25,000 machine hours; garden tractor production uses 125,000 machine hours. Calculate the profit (loss) in total and per unit for each product if overhead is assigned to products using these two overhead bases.
d. Does your answer in (a), (b), or (c) provide the best representation of the profit contributed by each product? Explain.

PROBLEMS

41. **LO.3 (Activity analysis)** Management at Glover & Lamb Inc. is concerned about controlling factory labor-related costs. The following summary is the result of an analysis of the major categories of labor costs for 2013:

EXCEL

Category	Amount
Base wages	$63,000,000
Health-care benefits	10,500,000
Payroll taxes	5,018,832
Overtime	8,697,600
Training	1,875,000
Retirement benefits	6,898,500
Workers' compensation	1,199,940

Following are some of the potential cost drivers identified by the company for labor-related costs, along with their 2013 volume levels:

Potential Activity Driver	2013 Volume Level
Average number of factory employees	2,100
Number of new hires	300
Number of regular labor hours worked	3,150,000
Number of overtime hours worked	288,000
Total factory wages paid	$71,697,600
Volume of production in units	12,000,000
Number of production process changes	600
Number of production schedule changes	375

a. For each cost pool, determine the cost per unit of the activity driver using the activity driver that you believe has the closest relationship to the cost pool.
b. Based on your judgments and calculations in (a), which activity driver should receive the most attention from company managers in their efforts to control labor-related costs? How much of the total labor-related cost is attributable to this activity driver?
c. In the contemporary environment, many firms ask their employees to work record levels of overtime. What activity driver does this practice suggest is a major contributor to labor-related costs? Explain.

42. **LO.3-LO.5 (Cost drivers; ABC; analysis)** Boerne Community Hospital has been under increasing pressure to be accountable for its patient charges. The hospital's current pricing system is ad hoc, based on pricing norms for the geographical area; only direct costs for surgery, medication, and other treatments are explicitly considered. The hospital's controller has suggested that the hospital improve pricing policies by seeking a tighter relationship between costs and pricing. This approach would make prices for services less arbitrary. As a first step, the controller has determined that most costs can be assigned to one of three cost pools. The three cost pools follow along with the estimated amounts and activity drivers.

Activity Center	Amount	Activity Driver	Quantity
Professional salaries	$13,125,000	Professional hours	75,000 hours
Building costs	6,187,500	Square feet used	56,250 sq. ft.
Risk management	850,000	Patients served	2,500 patients

The hospital provides service in three broad categories. The services follow with their volume measures for the activity centers.

Service	Professional Hours	Square Feet	Number of Patients
Surgery	3,750	12,500	500
Housing patients	70,000	27,500	1,250
Outpatient care	1,250	16,250	750

a. What bases might be used as cost drivers to allocate the service center costs among the patients served by the hospital? Defend your selections.

b. The hospital currently charges an "add-on" rate calculated using professional hours to patients' direct charges. What rate is Boerne Community Hospital charging per hour? (Round to the nearest dollar.)

c. Determine the allocation rates for each activity center cost pool.

d. Allocate the activity center costs to the three services provided by the hospital.

e. Boerne Community Hospital has decided to estimate costs by activity center using professional hours. What is the cost per professional hour of each service? What would cause the cost per hour difference for the three services? (Round to the nearest dollar.)

43. **LO.4 & LO.5 (ABC; decision making)** Casito Corp. manufactures multiple types of products; however, most of the company's sales are from Product #347 and Product #658. Product #347 has been a standard in the industry for several years; the market for this product is competitive and price sensitive. Casito plans to sell 65,000 units of Product #347 in 2014 at a price of $150 per unit. Product #658 is a recent addition to Casito's product line. This product incorporates the latest technology and can be sold at a premium price; the company expects to sell 40,000 units of this product in 2014 for $300 per unit.

Casito's management group is meeting to discuss 2014 strategies, and the current topic of conversation is how to spend the sales and promotion budget. The sales manager believes that the market share for Product #347 could be expanded by concentrating Casito's promotional efforts in this area. However, the production manager wants to target a larger market share for Product #658. He says, "The cost sheets I get show that the contribution from Product #658 is more than twice that from Product #347. I know we get a premium price for this product; selling it should help overall profitability." Casito has the following costs for the two products:

	Product #347	Product #658
Direct material	$80	$140
Direct labor	1.5 hours	4.0 hours
Machine time	0.5 hours	1.5 hours

Variable manufacturing overhead is currently applied on the basis of direct labor hours. For 2014, variable manufacturing overhead is budgeted at $1,120,000 for a total of 280,000 direct labor hours. The hourly rates for machine time and direct labor are $10 and $14, respectively. Casito applies a material handling charge at 10 percent of material cost; this material handling charge is not included in variable manufacturing overhead. Total 2014 expenditures for materials are budgeted at $10,800,000.

Marc Alexander, Casito's controller, believes that before management decides to allocate marketing funds to individual products, it might be worthwhile to look at these products on the basis of the activities involved in their production. Alexander has prepared the following schedule to help the management group understand this concept:

	Budgeted Cost	Cost Driver	Annual Activity for Cost Driver
Material overhead			
Procurement	$ 400,000	Number of parts	4,000,000 parts
Production scheduling	220,000	Number of units	110,000 units
Packaging and shipping	440,000	Number of units	110,000 units
	$1,060,000		
Variable overhead			
Machine setup	$ 446,000	Number of setups	278,750 setups
Hazardous waste disposal	48,000	Pounds of waste	16,000 pounds
Quality control	560,000	Number of inspections	160,000 inspections
General supplies	66,000	Number of units	110,000 units
	$1,120,000		
Manufacturing			
Machine insertion	$1,200,000	Number of parts	3,000,000 parts
Manual insertion	4,000,000	Number of parts	1,000,000 parts
Wave soldering	132,000	Number of units	110,000 units
	$5,332,000		

REQUIRED PER UNIT

	Product #347	Product #658
Parts	25	55
Machine insertions of parts	24	35
Manual insertions of parts	1	20
Machine setups	2	3
Hazardous waste	0.02 lb.	0.35 lb.
Inspections	1	2

Alexander wants to calculate a new cost, using appropriate cost drivers, for each product. The new cost drivers would replace the direct labor, machine time, and overhead costs in the current costing system.

a. Identify at least four general advantages associated with activity-based costing.

b. On the basis of current costs, calculate the total contribution expected in 2014 for

1. Product #347.
2. Product #658.

c. On the basis of activity-based costs, calculate the total contribution expected in 2014 for

1. Product #347.
2. Product #658.

d. Explain how the comparison of the results of the two costing methods could impact the decisions made by Casito's management group. **CMA ADAPTED**

44. **LO.4 (ABC)** Odyssey Inc. has a total of $2,362,500 in production overhead costs. The company's products and related statistics follow.

	Product A	Product B
Direct material in pounds	139,500	190,500
Direct labor hours	30,000	37,500
Machine hours	52,500	22,500
Number of setups	430	860
Number of units produced	15,000	7,500

Additional data: The 330,000 pounds of material were purchased for $544,500. One direct labor hour costs $12.

a. Assume that Odyssey Inc. uses direct labor hours to apply overhead to products. Determine the total cost for each product and the cost per unit.
b. Assume that Odyssey Inc. uses machine hours to apply overhead to products. Determine the total cost for each product and the cost per unit.
c. Assume that Odyssey Inc. uses the following activity centers, cost drivers, and costs to apply overhead to products:

Cost Pool	Cost Driver	Cost
Utilities	# of machine hours	$ 750,000
Setup	# of setups	193,500
Material handling	# of pounds of material	1,419,000

Determine the total cost for each product and the cost per unit.

EXCEL

45. **LO.4 (ABC)** Outdoor Texas makes umbrellas, gazebos, and chaise lounges. The company uses a traditional overhead allocation scheme and assigns overhead to products at the rate of $30 per direct labor hour. The costs per unit for each product group in 2013 were as follows:

	Umbrellas	Gazebo	Chaise Lounges
Direct material	$12	$120	$ 12
Direct labor	18	135	45
Overhead	24	180	60
Total	$54	$435	$117

Because profitability has been lagging and competition has been getting more intense, Outdoor Texas is considering implementing an activity-based costing system for 2014. In analyzing the 2013 data, management determined that its $12,030,000 of factory overhead could be assigned to four basic activities: quality control, setups, material handling, and equipment operation. Data for the 2013 costs associated with each of the four activities follow.

Quality Control	Setups	Material Handling	Equipment Operation	Total Costs
$630,000	$600,000	$1,800,000	$14,970,000	$18,000,000

Management determined that the following allocation bases and total 2013 volumes for each allocation base could have been used for ABC:

Activity	Base
Quality control	Number of units produced
Setups	Number of setups
Material handling	Pounds of material used
Equipment operation	Number of machine hours

Volume measures for 2013 for each product and each allocation base were as follows:

	Umbrellas	Gazebos	Chaise Lounges
Number of units	300,000	30,000	90,000
Number of setups	600	1,300	1,100
Pounds of material	1,200,000	3,000,000	1,800,000
Number of machine hours	600,000	1,100,000	1,300,000

a. How much direct labor time is needed to produce an umbrella, a gazebo, and a chaise lounge?
b. For 2013, determine the total overhead allocated to each product group using the traditional allocation based on direct labor hours.
c. For 2013, determine the total overhead that would have been allocated to each product group if activity-based costing were used. Compute the cost per unit for each product group.
d. Outdoor Texas has a policy of setting sales prices based on product costs. How would the sales prices using activity-based costing differ from those obtained using the traditional overhead allocation?

EXCEL

46. **LO.4 (ABC)** Reschman Co. manufactures two products. Following is a production and cost analysis for each product for 2013:

Cost Component	Product A	Product B	Both Products	Cost
Units produced	10,000	10,000	20,000	
Raw material used (units)				
X	50,000	50,000	100,000	$ 800,000
Y		100,000	100,000	$ 200,000
Labor hours used				
Department 1				$ 682,000
Direct labor	20,000	5,000	25,000	$ 375,000
Indirect labor				
Inspections	2,500	2,400	4,900	
Machine operations	5,000	10,000	15,000	
Setups	252	248	500	
Department 2				$ 462,000
Direct labor	5,000	5,000	10,000	$ 200,000
Indirect labor				
Inspection	2,680	5,000	7,680	
Machine operations	1,000	3,860	4,860	
Setups	250	310	560	
Machine hours used				
Department 1	5,000	10,000	15,000	$ 400,000
Department 2	5,000	20,000	25,000	$ 800,000
Power used (kW hours)				$ 400,000
Department 1			1,500,000	
Department 2			8,500,000	
Other activity data				
Building occupancy				$1,000,000
Purchasing				100,000
Number of purchase orders				
Material X			200	
Material			300	
Square feet occupied				
Purchasing			10,000	
Power			40,000	
Department 1			200,000	
Department 2			250,000	

Elysia Sanderson, the firm's cost accountant, has just returned from a seminar on activity-based costing. To apply the concepts she learned, she decides to analyze the costs incurred for Products A and B on an activity basis. In doing so, she specifies the following first and second allocation processes:

FIRST STAGE: ALLOCATIONS TO DEPARTMENTS

Cost Pool	Cost Object	Activity Allocation Base
Power	Departments	Kilowatt hours
Purchasing	Material	Number of purchase orders
Building occupancy	Departments	Square feet occupied

SECOND STAGE: ALLOCATIONS TO PRODUCTS

Cost Pool	Cost Object	Activity Allocation Base
Departments		
Indirect labor	Product	Hours worked
Power	Products	Machine hours
Machinery related	Products	Machine hours
Building occupancy	Products	Machine hours
Material purchasing	Products	Materials used

Source: Adapted from Harold P. Roth and A. Faye Borthick, "Getting Closer to Real Product Costs," *Management Accounting* (May 1989), pp. 28–33. Reprinted from *Management Accounting*. Copyright by Institute of Management Accountants, Montvale, NJ.

a. Determine the total overhead for Reschman Co.
b. Determine the plantwide overhead rate for the company, assuming the use of direct labor hours.
c. Determine the cost per unit of Product A and Product B, using the overhead rate found in (b).
d. Determine the cost allocations to departments (first-stage allocations). Allocate costs from the departments in the following order: building occupancy, purchasing, and power. Finish the cost allocations for one department to get an "adjusted" cost to allocate to the next department.
e. Using the allocations found in (d), determine the cost allocations to products (second-stage allocations).
f. Determine the cost per unit of Product A and Product B using the overhead allocations found in (e).

EXCEL

47. **LO.4 & LO.5 (ABC; pricing)** Chester Inc. has identified activity centers to which overhead costs are assigned. The cost pool amounts for these centers and their selected activity drivers for 2013 follow.

Activity Centers	Costs	Activity Drivers
Utilities	$1,800,000	90,000 machine hours
Scheduling and setup	1,638,000	1,170 setups
Material handling	3,840,000	2,400,000 pounds of material

The company's products and other operating statistics follow.

	PRODUCTS		
	A	B	C
Direct costs	$120,000	$120,000	$ 135,000
Machine hours	45,000	15,000	30,000
Number of setups	195	570	405
Pounds of material	750,000	450,000	1,200,000
Number of units produced	60,000	30,000	90,000
Direct labor hours	48,000	27,000	75,000

a. Determine unit product cost using the appropriate cost drivers for each product.
b. Before it installed an ABC system, Chester used a traditional costing system that allocated factory overhead to products using direct labor hours. The firm operates in a competitive market and sets product prices at cost plus a 25 percent markup.
   1. Calculate unit costs based on traditional costing. (Round to the nearest cent.)
   2. Determine selling prices based on unit costs for traditional costing and for ABC. (Round to the nearest cent.)
c. Discuss the problems related to setting prices based on traditional costing and explain how ABC improves the information.

EXCEL

48. **LO.4 & LO.5 (ABC; pricing)** Strickland Co. currently charges manufacturing overhead costs to products using machine hours. However, company management believes that the use of ABC would provide more realistic cost estimates and, in turn, give the company an edge in pricing over its competitors. Strickland's accountant and production manager have provided the following budgeted information for 2014, given a budgeted capacity of 1,000,000 machine hours:

Type of Manufacturing Cost	Cost Amount
Electric power	$ 500,000
Work cells	3,000,000
Material handling	1,000,000
Quality control inspections	1,000,000
Machine setups	350,000
Total budgeted overhead costs	$5,850,000

Type of Manufacturing Cost	Activity Driver
Electric power	200,000 kilowatt hours
Work cells	300,000 square feet
Material handling	200,000 material moves
Quality control inspections	50,000 inspections
Machine setups	25,000 setups

A national construction company approached Pete Lang, the VP of marketing, about a bid for 2,500 doors. Lang asked the cost accountant to prepare a cost estimate for producing the 2,500 doors; he received the following data:

Direct material cost	$ 50,000
Direct labor cost	$150,000
Machine hours	5,000
Direct labor hours	2,500
Electric power—kilowatt hours	500
Work cells—square feet	1,000
Number of material handling moves	20
Number of quality control inspections	15
Number of setups	6

Source: Adapted from Nabil Hassa, Herbert E. Brown, and Paul M. Saunders, "Management Accounting Case Study: Beaver Window Inc.," *Management Accounting Campus Report* (Fall 1990). Copyright Institute of Management Accountants, Montvale, NJ.

a. What is the predetermined overhead rate if the traditional measure of machine hours is used?
b. What is the manufacturing cost per door as presently accounted for?
c. What is the manufacturing cost per door under the proposed ABC method?
d. If the two cost systems will result in different cost estimates, which cost accounting system is preferable as a pricing base, and why?
e. If activity-based management were implemented prior to an ABC system, which of the manufacturing overhead costs might be reduced or eliminated? Why?

49. **LO.4 & LO.5 (ABC; pricing; writing)** McNeil Office makes standard metal five-drawer desks. Occasionally, the company takes custom orders. McNeil's overhead costs for a month in which no custom desks are produced are as follows:

Purchasing Department for raw material and supplies (20 purchase orders)	$10,000
Setting up machines for production runs (4 times per month after maintenance checks)	2,480
Utilities (based on 6,400 machine hours)	320
Supervisor salaries	16,000
Machine and building depreciation (fixed)	11,000
Quality control and inspections performed on random selection of desks each day; one quality control worker	5,000
Total overhead costs	$44,800

Factory operations are highly automated, and overhead is allocated to products based on machine hours.

In July 2013, six orders were filled for custom desks. Selling prices were based on charges for actual direct material, actual direct labor, and the overhead rate per machine hour. During July, the following costs were incurred for 6,400 hours of machine time:

Purchasing Department for raw material and supplies (44 purchase orders)	$12,400
Setting up machines for production runs (18 times)	3,280
Utilities (based on 6,400 machine hours)	320
Supervisor salaries	16,000
Machine and building depreciation (fixed)	11,000
Quality control and inspections performed on random selection of desks each day; one quality control worker	5,960
Engineering design and specification costs	6,000
Total overhead costs	$54,960

a. How much of the purchasing department cost is variable and how much is fixed? What types of purchasing costs would fit into each of these categories?
b. Why might the number of machine setups have increased from four to 18 when only six custom orders were received?
c. Why might the cost of quality control and inspections have increased?
d. Why were engineering design and specification costs included during July?
e. If McNeil Office were to adopt activity-based costing, what would you suggest as the cost drivers for each of the overhead cost items?
f. What is the current predetermined overhead rate based on machine hours? Do you think the custom orders should have been priced using this rate per machine hour? Explain the reasoning for your answer.

50. **LO.4 & LO.5 (ABC; pricing)** Craig Oldenettel owns and manages a commercial cold-storage warehouse that has 100,000 cubic feet of storage capacity. Historically, he has charged customers a flat rate of $0.16 per pound per month for goods stored.

In the past two years, Oldenettel has become dissatisfied with the profitability of the warehouse operation. Despite the fact that the warehouse remains relatively full, revenues have not kept pace with operating costs. Recently, Oldenettel asked his accountant, Pamela Beattie, to improve his understanding of how activity-based costing could help him revise the pricing formula. Beattie has determined that most costs can be associated with one of four activities. Those activities and their related costs, volume measures, and volume levels for 2013 follow:

Activity	Cost	Monthly Volume Measure	
Send/receive goods	$50,000	Weight in pounds	500,000
Store goods	16,000	Volume in cubic feet	80,000
Move goods	20,000	Volume in square feet	5,000
Identify goods	8,000	Number of packages	500

Source: Adapted from Harold P. Roth and Linda T. Sims, "Costing for Warehousing and Distribution," *Management Accounting* (August 1991), pp. 42–45. Reprinted from *Management Accounting*. Copyright by Institute of Management Accountants, Montvale, NJ.

a. Based on the activity cost and volume data, determine the amount of cost assigned to the following customers, whose goods were all received on the first day of last month:

Customer	Weight of Order in Pounds	Cubic Feet	Square Feet	Number of Packages
Barfield	40,000	3,200	1,100	15
Glover	40,000	800	600	10
Dozier	40,000	1,400	1,900	50

b. Determine the price to be charged to each customer under the existing pricing plan.
c. Determine the price to be charged using ABC, assuming Oldenettel would base the price on the cost determined in (a) plus a markup of 40 percent.
d. How well does Oldenettel's existing pricing plan capture the costs for providing the warehouse services? Explain.

51. **LO.4 & LO.5 (ABC; product profitability)** Delgado Design provides a wide range of engineering and architectural consulting services through its three offices in Altamont, Ballard, and Circleville. The company allocates resources and bonuses to the three offices based on the net income reported for the period. Following are the performance results for 2013:

	Altamont	Ballard	Circleville	Total
Sales	$1,500,000	$1,419,000	$1,067,000	$ 3,986,000
Less: Direct material	(281,000)	(421,000)	(185,000)	(887,000)
Direct labor	(382,000)	(317,000)	(325,000)	(1,024,000)
Overhead	(725,800)	(602,300)	(617,500)	(1,945,600
Net income	$ 111,200	$ 78,700	$ (60,500)	$ 129,400

Overhead items are accumulated in one overhead pool and allocated to the offices based on direct labor dollars. For 2013, this predetermined overhead rate was $1.90 for every direct labor dollar incurred. The overhead pool includes rent, depreciation, taxes, etc., regardless of which office incurred the expense. This method of accumulating costs forces the offices to absorb a portion of the overhead incurred by other offices.

Management is concerned with the results of the 2013 performance reports. During a review of overhead costs, it became apparent that many items of overhead are not correlated with direct labor dollars as previously assumed. Management decided that applying overhead based on activity-based costing and direct tracing, when possible, should provide a more accurate picture of the profitability of each office. An analysis of the overhead revealed that the following dollars for rent, utilities, depreciation, and taxes could be traced directly to the office that incurred the overhead:

	Altamont	Ballard	Circleville	Total
Office overhead	$195,000	$286,100	$203,500	$684,600

Activity pools and activity drivers were determined from the accounting records and staff surveys as follows:

			NUMBER OF ACTIVITIES BY LOCATION		
Activity Pools		**Activity Driver**	**Altamont**	**Ballard**	**Circleville**
General administration	$ 409,000	Direct labor	$ 386,346	$ 305,010	$325,344
Project costing	48,000	# of timesheet entries	6,300	4,060	3,640
Accounts payable/receiving	139,000	# of vendor invoices	1,035	874	391
Accounts receivable	47,000	# of client invoices	572	429	99
Payroll/mail sort & delivery	30,000	# of employees	34	39	27
Personnel recruiting	38,000	# of new hires	8	4	8
Employee insur. processing	14,000	# of insur. claims filed	238	273	189
Proposals	139,000	# of proposals	195	245	60
Sales meetings, sales aids	202,000	Contracted sales	$1,821,600	$1,404,150	$569,250
Shipping	24,000	# of projects	100	125	25
Ordering	48,000	# of purchase orders	126	102	72
Duplicating costs	46,000	# of copies duplicated	160,734	145,782	67,284
Blueprinting	77,000	# of blueprints	38,790	31,032	16,378
	$1,261,000				

a. How much overhead cost should be assigned to each office based on activity-based costing concepts?
b. What is the contribution of each office before subtracting the results obtained in (a)?
c. What is the profitability of each office using activity-based costing?
d. Evaluate the concerns of management regarding the traditional costing technique currently used.

IMA ADAPTED

52. **LO.1 & LO. 3-LO.5 (Activity analysis, ABC; pricing; cost drivers; decision making)** Jessica Corporation has identified the following overhead costs and cost drivers for the coming year:

Overhead Item	Cost Driver	Budgeted Cost	Budgeted Activity Level
Machine setup	Number of setups	$ 20,000	200
Inspection	Number of inspections	130,000	6,500
Material handling	Number of material moves	80,000	8,000
Engineering	Engineering hours	50,000	1,000
		$280,000	

The following information was collected on three jobs that were completed during the year:

	Job 101	Job 102	Job 103
Direct material	$5,000	$12,000	$8,000
Direct labor	$2,000	$ 2,000	$4,000
Units completed	100	50	200

(Continued)

	Job 101	Job 102	Job 103
Number of setups	1	2	4
Number of inspections	20	10	30
Number of material moves	30	10	50
Engineering hours	10	50	10

Budgeted direct labor cost was $100,000, and budgeted direct material cost was $280,000.

a. If Jessica Corp. uses activity-based costing, how much overhead cost should be assigned to Job 101?
b. If Jessica Corp. uses activity-based costing, compute the cost of each unit of Job 102.
c. Jessica Corp. prices its products at 140 percent of cost. If activity-based costing is used, what price should it set for each unit of Job 103?
d. If Jessica Corp. used a traditional accounting system and allocated overhead based on direct labor cost, by how much would each unit of Job 103 be over- or undercosted compared to activity-based costing? What would be the management implications of this difference?
e. Identify any non-value-added activities or activities that may be currently necessary but appear to be inefficient in Jessica Corp.'s production process. Explain what steps the company management could take to improve the production process and potentially lower manufacturing costs.
f. Jessica Corp. is considering outsourcing inspections to an outside company that would perform the inspections for $10 apiece. What are the potential total savings if Jessica outsources the inspections? What other factors should company management consider before making this decision?

CIA ADAPTED

53. **LO.1 & LO.3-LO.5 (Activity analysis, ABC; pricing; cost drivers)** Power Production manufactures two product models: Regular and Special. The following information was taken from the accounting records for the first quarter of 2013:

	Regular	Special	Total
Units produced	80,000	20,000	100,000
Material cost	$320,000	$180,000	$500,000
Labor cost	$480,000	$140,000	$620,000

Power currently uses a traditional cost accounting system where total overhead cost is assigned to products based on the total number of units produced. Company president Sue Power has approached the controller, Keisha Connaery, with concerns about sagging profit margins and his inability to explain competitors' pricing of similar products. Connaery suggests that the company explore the possibility of a costing system that is based less on volume and more on identifying the consumption of resources by products (given manufacturing process activities). Connaery identifies the following overhead costs related to the production process:

Wages and costs related to machine setups	$ 360,000
Material handling costs	480,000
Quality control costs	120,000
Other overhead costs related to units produced	240,000
Total	$1,200,000

During the quarter, there were 40 machine setups for production: 20 from Special to Regular and 20 from Regular to Special. Connaery believes that the number of setups is the most appropriate cost driver of machine setup costs and material cost is the primary indicator of material handling costs. The Special model uses more expensive and difficult-to-handle materials. Additionally, each Special unit is hand-inspected by quality control personnel because it is more complex and has more parts than a Regular unit. Quality control inspectors are paid $40 per hour; examination of payroll time sheets indicates that the inspectors spent 50 percent more hours inspecting Special units than Regular units. Finally, Connaery thinks the remaining 30 percent of overhead costs are related to the number of units produced.

a. Using a traditional, volume-based overhead rate, determine the overhead cost per unit of the Regular and Special units.
b. Using the information provided by Connaery, determine the overhead cost per unit of the Regular and Special Units using an activity-based costing system.
c. What is the total per-unit cost of the Regular and Special Units under each overhead costing system?
d. Compute the amount of product cross-subsidization per unit that was taking place under the traditional costing system.
e. Identify potential non-value-added activities in Power's current manufacturing system.
f. What suggestions would you have for Sue Power to improve the competitiveness of the company's products in the marketplace?

54. **LO.3 & LO.5 (ABC; pricing; cost drivers)** Believing that its traditional cost system may be providing misleading information, Missoula Corporation is considering an activity-based costing (ABC) approach. Missoula Corporation employs a full-cost system and has been applying its manufacturing overhead on the basis of machine hours. The organization plans on using 50,000 direct labor hours and 30,000 machine hours in 2014. The following data show the manufacturing overhead that is budgeted:

	Activity	Budgeted Cost Driver	Budgeted Activity Cost
Material handling	Number of parts handled	6,000,000	$ 720,000
Setup costs	Number of setups	750	315,000
Machining costs	Machine hours	30,000	540,000
Quality control	Number of batches	500	225,000
	Total manufacturing overhead cost		$1,800,000

Cost, sales, and production data for one of the company's products for the coming year are as follows:

Direct material cost per unit	$4.40
Direct labor cost per unit (0.05 DLH @ $15 per DLH)	0.75
	$5.15
Sales and production data:	
Expected sales	20,000 units
Batch size	5,000 units
Setups	2 per batch
Total parts per finished unit	5 parts
Machine hours required	80 MHs per batch

a. Compute the per-unit cost for this product for 2014 if Missoula uses the traditional full-cost system.
b. Compute the per-unit cost for this product for 2014 if the Missoula employs an activity-based costing system.
c. Assume the company wishes to achieve a gross profit rate of 40 percent. Determine the selling price that would be required based on your answers to (a) and (b). CIA ADAPTED

55. **LO.4 & LO.5 (ABC; pricing)** Treffle Molding Company manufactures two products: large jar covers and small bottle caps. Large jar covers require special handling. Each cover must be individually sanded on a special machine to remove excess material (referred to as "flash") from the units. Covers are sanded at the rate of 200 jar covers per hour. Jar covers also require special handling during the packaging process as they are hand-packed in special cartons with foam protection to avoid breakage during shipment. Special packaging materials are $5 per carton; each carton holds 250 jar covers.

Small bottle caps are processed in batches of 5,000 units and do not require use of the machine sander. One employee can process a load of small bottle caps in two hours.

The accounting department has established the following information related to overhead cost pools and cost drivers:

Overhead Cost Pool	Budgeted Annual Overhead Cost	Cost Driver	Budgeted Activity of Cost Driver
Engineering	$300,000	Engineering hours	3,000 hours
Machine setups	$ 50,000	Number of setups	100 setups
Material purchase and support	$200,000	Number of pounds of material	2,000,000 pounds
Machine sanding	$100,000	Machine hours	10,000 hours
Product certification	$270,000	Number of orders	6,000 orders

Treffle employs ten direct labor employees. Each employee averages 2,000 hours per year and is paid $25 per hour.

During August, Treffle received an order for 1,000 jar covers from Ravel Cosmetics and an order for 10,000 bottle caps from Nortell Skin Products. Additional information related to each order appears as follows:

	Ravel	Nortell
Machine setups	4	1
Raw material ($0.20 per pound)	$200	$500
Engineering hours	10	2
Direct labor hours	4	2

a. Compute the total overhead that should be charged to each order using activity-based costing.
b. Compute the total overhead that would be assigned to each order if Treffle uses a single, predetermined overhead rate based on direct labor hours.
c. Compute the full cost per unit under traditional costing and under activity-based costing. The company quotes all orders on a cost-per-1,000-units basis.
d. Analyze the difference in the cost per order between traditional and ABC. To what factors can the difference be attributed?
e. Based on the costs computed in (c), what selling price per unit would Treffle have to charge for each order to earn a gross profit of 40 percent on the order?
f. The president of Treffle Molding Company, James Mahoney, is upset that the buyer for Ravel Cosmetics insists on small deliveries of each order, resulting in frequent setups to complete each order. How can Mahoney improve this situation?

56. **LO.4 & LO.5 (ABC; pricing)** Classic Confections makes very elaborate wedding cakes to order. The company's owner, Sandra Tillson, has provided the following data concerning the activity rates in its activity-based costing system:

Activity Cost Pools	Activity Rate
Guest related	$0.90 per guest
Tier related	$34.41 per tier
Order related	$150.00 per order

The measure of activity for the size-related activity cost pool is the number of planned guests at the wedding reception. The greater the number of guests, the larger the cake. The measure of complexity is the number of cake tiers. The activity measure for the order-related cost pool is the number of orders. (Each wedding involves one order.) The activity rates include the costs of raw ingredients such as flour, sugar, eggs, and shortening. The activity rates do not include the costs of purchased decorations such as miniature statues and wedding bells, which are accounted for separately. The average wedding has 125 guests and generally requires a three-tiered cake.

Data concerning two recent orders appear below:

	Sacks Wedding	Nussbaum Wedding
Number of reception guests	50	164
Number of tiers on the cake	1	5
Cost of purchased decorations for cake	$22.50	$ 58.86

a. What amount would the company have to charge for the Sacks wedding cake to break even on that cake?
b. Assuming that the company charges $650 for the Nussbaum wedding cake, what would be the overall gross margin on the order?
c. Karen O'Brien wants to order a special cake for her 25th wedding anniversary celebration. She wants the cake to be four tiers but, in addition, would like 20 special flowers added to the top of the cake, which requires very intricate detailing instead of purchased decorations. O'Brien expects that attendance at the anniversary party will be 200 people. If Tillson decides to charge $5 for each special flower, which price should she quote? What price should be charged if the company wants to make an overall gross margin of 35 percent on the O'Brien order?
d. Suppose that the company decides that the present activity-based costing system is too complex and that all costs (except for the costs of purchased decorations) should be allocated on the basis of the number of guests. In that event, what would you expect to happen to the costs of cakes for receptions with more than the average number of guests and for receptions with fewer than the average number of guests? Explain your answer.

CIA ADAPTED

57. **LO.5 & LO.6 (Decision making; writing)** Companies that want to be more globally competitive can consider the implementation of activity-based management (ABM). Such companies often have used other initiatives that involve higher efficiency, effectiveness, or output quality. These same initiatives are typically consistent with and supportive of ABM.

a. In what other types of "initiatives" might such global companies engage?
b. How might ABM and activity-based costing (ABC) help a company in its quest to achieve world-class status?
c. For any significant initiative, senior management commitment is generally required. Would it be equally important to have top management support if a company were instituting ABC rather than ABM? Justify your answer.
d. Assume that you are a member of top management in a large organization. Do you think implementation of ABM or ABC would be more valuable? Explain the rationale for your answer.

58. **LO.5 & LO.6 (Decision making; ethics; writing)** As the chief executive officer of a large corporation, you have decided, after discussion with production and accounting personnel, to implement activity-based management concepts. Your goal is to reduce cycle time and, in turn, costs. A primary way to accomplish this goal is to install highly automated equipment in your plant, which would then displace approximately 60 percent of your workforce. Your company is the major employer in the area of the country where it is located.

ETHICS

a. Discuss the pros and cons of installing the equipment from the perspective of your (1) stockholders, (2) employees, and (3) customers.
b. How would you explain to a worker that his or her job is a non-value-added activity?
c. What alternatives might you have that could accomplish the goal of reducing cycle time but not create economic havoc for the local area?

59. **LO.5 & LO.6 (Product complexity; writing)** Strategic Supply is a world leader in the production of electronic test and measurement instruments. The company experienced almost uninterrupted growth through the 1990s, but in the 2000s, the low-priced end of its Portables Division's product line was challenged by the aggressive low-price strategy of several Japanese competitors. These Japanese companies set prices 25 percent below Strategic's prevailing prices. To compete, the division needed to reduce costs and increase customer value by increasing operational efficiency.

The division took steps to implement just-in-time delivery and scheduling techniques as well as a total quality control program and to involve people techniques that moved responsibility for problem solving down to the operating level of the division. The results of these changes were impressive: substantial reductions in cycle time, direct labor hours per unit, and inventory levels as well as increases in output dollars per person per day and in operating income. The cost accounting system was providing information, however, that did not seem to support the changes.

Total overhead cost for the division was $10,000,000; of this, 55 percent seemed to be related to materials and 45 percent to conversion. Material-related costs pertain to procurement, receiving, inspection, stockroom personnel, and so on. Conversion-related costs pertain to direct labor, supervision, and process-related engineering. All overhead was applied on the basis of direct labor.

The division decided to concentrate efforts on revamping the application system for material-related overhead. Managers believed the majority of material overhead (MOH) costs were related to the maintenance and handling of each different part number. Other types of MOH costs were driven by the value of parts, absolute number of parts, and each use of a different part number.

At this time, the division used 8,000 different parts, each in extremely different quantities. For example, annual usage of one part was 35,000 units; usage of another part was only 200 units. The division decided that MOH costs would decrease if a smaller number of different parts were used in the products.

Source: Adapted from Michael A. Robinson, ed., *Cases from Management Accounting Practice*, No. 5 (Montvale, NJ: National Association of Accountants, 1989), pp. 13–17. Copyright by Institute of Management Accountants (formerly National Association of Accountants), Montvale, NJ.

a. Why would MOH have decreased if parts were standardized?
b. Using the numbers given, develop a cost allocation method for MOH to quantify and communicate the strategy of parts standardization.
c. Explain how the use of the method developed in (b) would support the strategy of parts standardization.
d. Is any method that applies the entire MOH cost pool on the basis of one cost driver sufficiently accurate for complex products? Explain.
e. Are MOH product costing rates developed for management reporting appropriate for inventory valuation for external reporting? Why or why not?

5

Job Order Costing

LEARNING OBJECTIVES

After completing this chapter, you should be able to answer the following questions:

1. How do job order and process costing systems, as well as their related valuation methods, differ?
2. What are the distinguishing characteristics of a job order costing system?
3. What are the primary documents supporting a job order costing system, and what purposes are served by each of them?
4. How are costs accumulated in a job order costing system?
5. How does information from a job order costing system support management decision making?
6. How are losses treated in a job order costing system?
7. (*Appendix*) How are standard costs used in a job order costing system?

uniqueness of the jobs, costs of different jobs are maintained in separate subsidiary ledger accounts and are not added together in the ledger.

The logic of separating costs for individual jobs is illustrated by an example for Crown Fence Company, a firm that specializes in custom ornamental metal products. During February, the company completed three small contracts; each job required a different quantity and type of material, labor input, and conversion operations. Exhibit 5.2 provides Crown Fence Company's WIP Inventory control and subsidiary ledger accounts at the end of February. Crown uses normal costing valuation. Actual direct material and direct labor costs are fairly easy to identify and associate with particular jobs. However, overhead costs are usually not traceable to specific jobs and must be applied to production using a

Exhibit 5.2 Separate Subsidiary Ledger Accounts for Jobs

Job #412
Ornamental Fence

Job #414
Interior Railing

Job #417
Window Guards

GENERAL LEDGER

Work in Process Inventory Control

Direct material (actual)	XXX	Transferred to finished goods or next department	XXX
Direct labor (actual)	XXX		
Overhead (predetermined rate × actual activity)	XX		
Ending balance	25,400		

SUBSIDIARY LEDGER

Job #412, Ornamental Fence

Direct material (actual)	XXX	
Direct labor (actual)	XXX	
Overhead (predetermined rate × actual activity)	XX	
Ending balance	10,250	

Job #414, Interior Railing

Direct material (actual)	XXX	
Direct labor (actual)	XXX	
Overhead (predetermined rate × actual activity)	XX	
Ending balance	9,170	

Job #417, Window Guards

Direct material (actual)	XX	
Direct labor (actual)	XX	
Overhead (predetermined rate × actual activity)	X	
Ending balance	5,980	

predetermined OH rate multiplied by some actual cost driver (such as cost or quantity of materials used or number of direct labor hours required). For example, utility costs are related to all jobs worked on during that month. Accurately determining which jobs created the need for a given amount of water, heat, or electricity would be impossible. Because each job is distinctive, costs of the jobs cannot logically be averaged—a unique cost must be determined for each job.

Job order costing systems provide information important to managing profitability and setting prices for output. Custom manufacturers typically price their goods using two methods. A **cost-plus contract** allows producers to cover all direct costs and some indirect costs and to generate an acceptable profit margin. In other cases, producers may use a competitive bidding technique. In such instances, the company must accurately estimate the costs of making the unique products associated with each contract; otherwise, the company can incur significant losses when actual costs exceed costs estimated during the bidding process.

The trend in job order costing is to automate data collection and data entry functions supporting the accounting system. Automating recordkeeping functions relieves production employees of that task, and electronically stored data can be accessed to serve many purposes. For example, data from a completed job can be used as input to project the costs of a future job on which a bid is to be made, to understand a client's purchasing habits, or to estimate profit for next year. However, regardless of whether the data entry process is automated, virtually all product costing software, even very inexpensive off-the-shelf programs, contains a job costing module.

Many companies have created intranets to manage information, especially information pertaining to jobs produced. An **intranet** is a restricted network for sharing information and delivering data from corporate databases to local area network (LAN) desktops. Exhibit 5.3 illustrates types of information that can be accessed on an intranet. As shown

Exhibit 5.3 Project Management Site Content

Project Management Library
- Instructions on how to use the project intranet site
- Project manager manuals
- Policy and procedure manuals
- Templates and forms
- Project management training exercises

General Project Information
- Project descriptions
- Photos of project progress
- Contract information
- Phone and e-mail directories
- Project team rosters
- Document control logs
- Scope documents
- Closure documents
- Links to project control tools
- Links to electronic document retrieval systems

Technical Information
- Drawing logs
- Detailed budgets and physical estimates
- Specifications
- Bill of materials by department
- Punch lists
- Links to drawing databases

Management Information
- Meeting minutes
- Daily logs
- Project schedules
- Task and resource checklists
- Shutdown and look-ahead reports
- Work-hour estimates
- Change notices
- Labor hours worked
- Earned value

Financial Information
- Project cost sheet
- Funding requests for each cost account
- Cash flow projections and budgets
- Original cost budgets and adjustments
- Contract status reports
- Departmental budget reports
- Links to mainframe sessions for requisitions and purchase order tracking
- Companywide financial statements

Source: Lawrence Barkowski, "Intranets for Project and Cost Management in Manufacturing," *Cost Engineering* (June 1999), p. 36. Reprinted with permission of AACE International, 209 Prairie Ave., Suite 100, Morgantown, WV 25601 USA. Internet: http://www.aacei.org. E-mail: info@aacei.org.

in the exhibit, much information relevant to managing a particular job's production is available online to managers. Data related to contract information and technical specifications, budgeted costs, actual costs, and stage of production measurements are instantly available to managers. Because input functions are automated, the intranet data become more closely correlated with real time.

3 What are the primary documents supporting a job order costing system, and what purposes are served by each of them?

JOB ORDER COSTING: DETAILS AND DOCUMENTS

A job can be categorized by the stage of its production cycle. There are three stages of production:

- contracted for but not yet started,
- in process, and
- completed.[4]

The production stages are supported by various documents providing information about the job and supporting the journal entries related to the job.

Job Order Cost Sheet

The source document that provides virtually all financial information about a particular job is the **job order cost sheet**. The set of job order cost sheets for all incomplete jobs composes the WIP Inventory subsidiary ledger. Total costs contained on the job order cost sheets for all incomplete jobs should reconcile to the WIP Inventory control account balance in the general ledger (as shown in Exhibit 5.2).

A job order cost sheet includes a job number, job description, customer identification, scheduling information, delivery instructions, and contract price as well as details regarding actual costs for direct material, direct labor, and applied overhead. The form also might include budgeted cost information, especially if such information is used to estimate the job's selling price or to support a bid price. In bid pricing, budgeted and actual costs should be compared at the end of a job to determine any deviations from estimates. In many companies, job cost sheets exist only in electronic form.

Exhibit 5.4 illustrates a job order cost sheet for Crown Fence Company. The job is for the construction and installation of a decorative fence; the customer is the Willowdale Homeowners' Association. All of Crown Fence Company's job order cost sheets include a section for budgeted data so that budget-to-actual comparisons can be made for planning and control purposes. Direct material and direct labor costs are assigned and posted to jobs as work on the job is performed. Information to include on the job cost sheet is gathered from material requisition forms and from employee time sheets or labor tickets.

Material Requisitions

To begin a job, a **material requisition form** (shown in Exhibit 5.5 on page 156) is prepared so material can be released from inventory, or purchased, and sent to the production area. This source document indicates the types and quantities of material to be issued to production or used to perform a service job. Such documents are usually prenumbered and come in multiple-copy sets so that completed copies can be maintained in the warehouse, in the production department, and with each job. Completed material requisition forms verify material flow from the warehouse to the requisitioning department and allow responsibility for material cost to be traced to users. Although hard-copy material requisition forms may still be used, it is increasingly common for these documents to exist only electronically.

Because a company using job order costing makes products to user specifications, jobs occasionally require unique raw material. Thus, some raw material may not be acquired until a job is under contract and added to the production schedule. The raw material acquired, although often separately distinguishable and related to specific jobs, is accounted for in a single general ledger control account (Raw Material Inventory) with subsidiary

[4] In concept, there could be four categories. The third and fourth categories would distinguish between products completed but not sold and products completed and sold. However, firms using a job order costing system normally produce only products for which there is current demand. Consequently, there may be no need for an inventory of finished products awaiting sale.

Exhibit 5.4 Crown Fence Company Custom Fabricating Job Order Cost Sheet

Job #PF108

Customer Name and Address:
Willowdale Homeowners' Assoc.
200 Willow Avenue
Willow, Texas

Description of Job:
2,000 feet of 6′ steel fence per contract dated 8/13/2013

Contract Agreement Date: 8/13/13
Scheduled Starting Date: 9/01/13
Agreed Completion Date: 11/15/13
Actual Completion Date:
Delivery Instructions: Full installation per contract

Contract Price $35,250

FABRICATION

DIRECT MATERIAL			DIRECT LABOR			OVERHEAD BASED ON # OF LABOR HOURS			OVERHEAD BASED ON # OF MACHINE HOURS		
(EST. $5,000)			(EST. $7,200)			(EST. $3,000; $12 per DLH)			(EST. $2,000; $30 per MH)		
Date	Source	Amount	Date	Source	Amount	Date	Source	Amount	Date	Source	Amount

INSTALLATION
(SAME FORMAT AS ABOVE BUT WITH DIFFERENT OH RATES)

FINISHING
(SAME FORMAT AS ABOVE BUT WITH DIFFERENT OH RATES)

SUMMARY

	FABRICATION		INSTALLATION		FINISHING	
	Actual	**Budget**	**Actual**	**Budget**	**Actual**	**Budget**
Direct material		$ 5,000		$ 0		$1,500
Direct labor		7,200		1,800		3,000
Overhead (labor)		3,000		1,500		1,200
Overhead (machine)		2,000		2,000		
Totals		$17,200		$5,300		$5,700

		Actual	**Budget**
Final Costs:	Fabrication		$17,200
	Installation		5,300
	Finishing		5,700
	Totals		$28,200

ledger backup. The material may, however, be designated in the storeroom and possibly in the subsidiary records as being "held for use in Job #407." Such designations should keep the material from being used on a job other than the one for which it was acquired.

When the first direct material associated with a job is issued to production, that job enters the second stage of its production cycle: work in process. At this point, cost information begins to be accumulated on the job order cost sheet. Direct labor is the second element of the production process.

Exhibit 5.5 Material Requisition Form

Date ____________ No. 341

Job Number ____________ Department ____________

Authorized by ____________ Issued by ____________

Received by ____________ Inspected by ____________

Item No.	Part No.	Description	Unit of Measure	Quantity Required	Quantity Issued	Unit Cost	Total Cost

Employee Time Sheets

An **employee time sheet** indicates the jobs on which each employee worked and the direct labor time consumed. Exhibit 5.6 provides an illustration of a time sheet that would be completed manually by employees. Such time sheets are most reliable if the employees update the sheets as the day progresses. Work arriving at an employee station is accompanied by a tag or bar code specifying its job order number; the bar codes can be scanned as products pass through individual workstations. The times that work is started and stopped are noted on the time sheet.[5] These time sheets should be collected and reviewed by supervisors to ensure that the information is accurate.

Exhibit 5.6 Employee Time Sheet

For Week Ending ____________

Department ____________

Employee Name ____________

Employee ID No. ____________

TYPE OF WORK		Job Number	Start Time	Stop Time	Day (circle)	Total Hours
Code	Description					
					M T W Th F S	
					M T W Th F S	
					M T W Th F S	
					M T W Th F S	
					M T W Th F S	
					M T W Th F S	

____________ Employee Signature ____________ Supervisor's Signature (for overtime)

[5] Alternatives to daily time sheets are job time tickets that supervisors give to employees as they are assigned new jobs and supervisors record which employees worked on which jobs for what period of time. The latter alternative is extremely difficult if a supervisor is overseeing a large number of employees or if employees are dispersed through a large plant.

Large businesses often use electronic time-keeping software rather than manual time sheets. Employees simply swipe their employee ID cards and job cards through an electronic scanner when switching from one job to another. This software allows labor costs to be accumulated by both job and department. In highly automated factories, employee time sheets may not be used because of the low proportion of DL cost to total cost. However, machine time can be tracked through the use of machine clocks or counters in the same way as human labor is tracked. As jobs are transferred from one machine to another, the clock or counter can be reset to mark the start and stop times. Machine times can then be equated to employee-operator time.

Transferring employee time sheet (or alternative source document) information to the job order cost sheet requires knowledge of employee labor rates, which are found in employee personnel files. Time spent on the job is multiplied by the employee's wage rate, and the amounts are summed to find the job's total direct labor cost for the period.

Time sheets are filed and retained so they can be referenced for any future information needs. Following are three possible information uses of time sheets.

- If total actual labor costs for the job differ significantly from the original estimate, the manager responsible for labor cost control may be asked to explain the discrepancy.
- If a job is billed on a cost-plus basis, the number of hours worked may be audited by the buyer. This situation is quite common and especially important when dealing with government contracts. Hours not worked directly on the contracted job cannot be arbitrarily or incorrectly charged to the cost-plus job without the potential for detection.
- If there is a question about total time worked by an employee in a week, time sheets can provide information on overtime. Under the Fair Labor Standards Act, overtime must generally be paid at a time-and-a-half rate to all nonmanagement employees when they work more than 40 hours in a week.

Overhead

Overhead costs can be substantial in manufacturing and service organizations. Actual overhead incurred during production is debited to the Manufacturing Overhead control account. If actual overhead is applied to jobs, the cost accountant waits until the end of the period and divides the actual overhead incurred in each designated cost pool by a related measure of activity or cost driver to obtain an application rate. Actual overhead is applied to jobs by multiplying the actual OH application rate by the actual measure of activity associated with each job.

More commonly, normal costing is used, and overhead is applied to jobs with one or more annualized predetermined OH rates. Overhead is assigned to jobs by multiplying the predetermined OH rate by the actual measure of the activity that was recorded for each job during the period. If a job is completed within a period, OH is applied at completion of production so that a full product cost can be transferred to Finished Goods Inventory. If, however, a job is not complete at the end of a period, overhead must be applied at that time so that WIP Inventory on the period-end balance sheet contains costs for all three product elements (DM, DL, and OH).

Completion of Production

When a job is completed, its total cost is removed from Work in Process Inventory and transferred to Finished Goods Inventory. Job order cost sheets for completed jobs are removed from the WIP Inventory subsidiary ledger and become the subsidiary ledger for the Finished Goods Inventory control account. When a job is sold, its cost is transferred from Finished Goods Inventory to Cost of Goods Sold. The job cost sheet then becomes a subsidiary record for Cost of Goods Sold. This cost transfer presumes the use of a perpetual inventory system, which is common in a job order costing environment because goods are generally easily identified and tracked. Job order costing documents and cost flows are depicted in Exhibit 5.7 (p. 158).

Job order cost sheets for completed jobs are kept in a company's permanent files. A completed job order cost sheet provides management with a historical summary about total costs and, if appropriate, the cost per finished unit for a given job. The per-unit cost may be

Exhibit 5.7 Job Order Costing Documents and Cost Flows

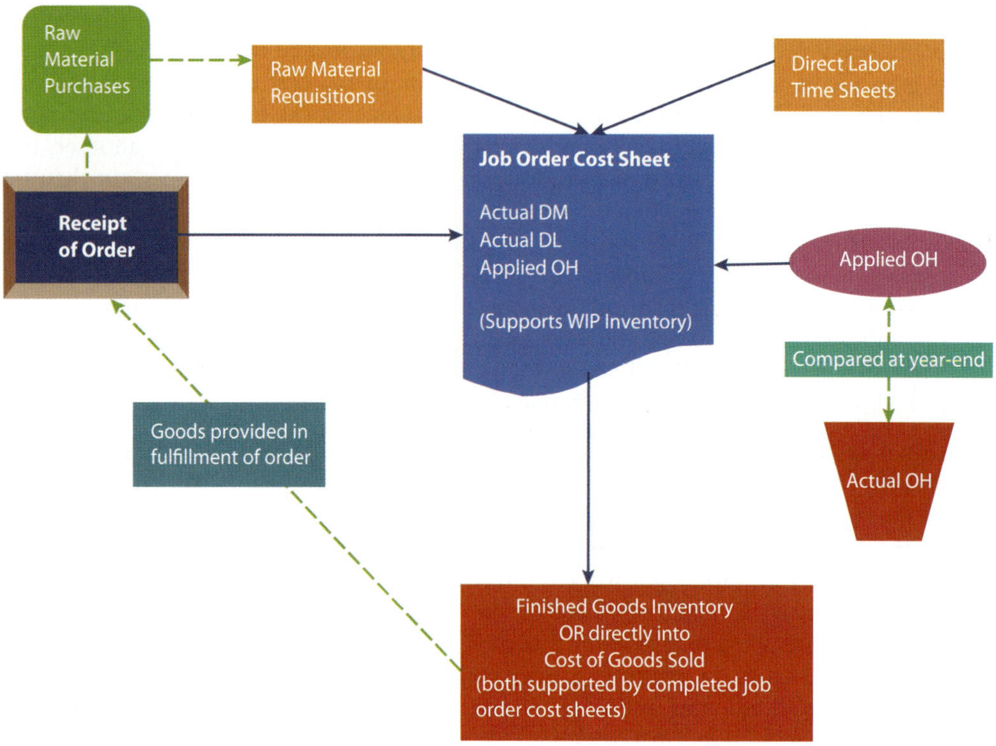

helpful for planning and control purposes as well as for bidding on future contracts. If a job was exceptionally profitable, management might decide to pursue additional similar jobs. If a job was unprofitable, the job order cost sheet may indicate areas in which cost control was lax. Such areas are more readily identifiable if the job order cost sheet presents the original, budgeted cost information.

Most businesses that use job order costing carry little or no Finished Goods Inventory because production occurs only when a specific customer contracts for a particular good or service. Upon completion, product or service cost may flow immediately to Cost of Goods Sold.

The next section presents a comprehensive job order costing situation using information from Crown Fence Company, the company introduced earlier.

JOB ORDER COSTING ILLUSTRATION

4 How are costs accumulated in a job order costing system?

Crown Fence Company establishes prices based on costs incurred. Over the long term, the company's goal is to realize a gross profit equal to 20 percent of sales revenue. This level of gross profit is sufficient to generate a reasonable profit after covering selling and administrative costs. In more competitive circumstances, such as when a company has too much unused capacity, prices and gross margin may be reduced to increase the likelihood of gaining job contracts. Crown Fence Company has little unused capacity, so the company sets prices somewhat high to reduce the possibility of successfully obtaining too many contracts.

To help in establishing the price for the Willowdale Homeowners' Association, Crown's cost accountant provided the sales manager with the budgeted cost information shown earlier in Exhibit 5.4. The sales manager believed that a normal selling price was appropriate and, thus, set the sales price to yield a gross margin of roughly 20 percent [($35,250 − $28,200) ÷ $35,250]. The customer agreed to this sales price in a contract dated August 13, 2013. Dean's production manager scheduled the job to begin on September 1, 2013, and to be completed by November 15, 2013. The job is assigned the number PF108 for identification purposes.

The following journal entries illustrate the flow of costs for the Fabrication Department during September 2013. Work on several jobs, including Job #PF108, was performed in Fabrication during that month. In entries 1, 2, and 4 in the list that follows, separate WIP Inventory accounts are shown for costs related either to Job #PF108 or to other jobs. In practice, the WIP Inventory account for a given department would be debited only once for all costs assigned to it. The details for posting to the individual job cost records would be presented in the journal entry explanations.

1. During September 2013, material requisition forms L40–L55 indicated that raw materials costing $5,420 were issued from the warehouse to the Fabrication Department. The Raw Material Inventory account may include the costs of both direct and indirect materials. When material is issued, its cost is released from Raw Material Inventory. If the material is considered direct to a job, the cost is assigned to WIP Inventory; if the material is indirect, the cost is assigned to Manufacturing Overhead Control. The raw material requisitioned in September included $4,875 of DM used on Job #PF108 and $520 of DM used on other jobs. The remaining $25 of raw materials issued during September were indirect.

Work in Process Inventory—Fabrication (Job #PF108)	4,875	
Work in Process Inventory—Fabrication (other jobs)	520	
Manufacturing Overhead Control—Fabrication (indirect material)	25	
Raw Material Inventory		5,420
To record direct and indirect materials issued per September requisitions		

2. The September time sheets and payroll summaries for the Fabrication Department workers were used to trace direct and indirect labor to that department. Total labor cost for the Fabrication Department for September was $9,599. Job #PF108 required $6,902 of DL cost combining the two biweekly pay periods in September. The remaining jobs in process required $1,447 of DL cost, and indirect labor cost for the month totaled $1,250.

Work in Process Inventory—Fabrication (Job #PF108)	6,902	
Work in Process Inventory—Fabrication (other jobs)	1,447	
Manufacturing Overhead Control—Fabrication (indirect labor)	1,250	
Wages Payable		9,599
To record direct and indirect labor wages for September		

3. The Fabrication Department incurred overhead costs in addition to indirect material and indirect labor during September. Factory building and equipment depreciation of $2,500 was recorded. Insurance on the factory building was prepaid and one month ($200) of that insurance had expired. A $1,900 bill for factory utility costs was received and would be paid in October. Repair and maintenance costs of $500 were paid in cash. Additional miscellaneous OH costs of $800 were incurred; these costs are credited to "Various accounts" for illustrative purposes. The following entry summarizes the accumulation of these other actual OH costs for September.

Manufacturing Overhead Control—Fabrication	5,900	
Accumulated Depreciation		2,500
Prepaid Insurance		200
Utilities Payable		1,900
Cash		500
Various accounts		800
To record actual September OH costs exclusive of indirect material and indirect labor wages		

4. Crown prepares financial statements monthly. To do so, WIP Inventory must include all production costs: DM, DL, and OH. Overhead is applied to production at Crown Fence Company based on departmental predetermined OH rates. The company is

organized into three departments: Fabrication, Installation, and Finishing. Each department may have more than one rate. In Fabrication, overhead is applied using two predetermined OH rates: $12 per direct labor hour and $30 per machine hour. In September, Fabrication employees committed 260 hours of direct labor time to Job #PF108, and 65 machine hours were consumed on that job. The other jobs worked on during September received total applied OH of $900 [25 direct labor hours (assumed) × $12] + [20 machine hours (assumed) × $30].

Work in Process Inventory—Fabrication (Job #PF108)	5,070	
Work in Process Inventory—Fabrication (other jobs)	900	
Manufacturing Overhead Control—Fabrication		5,970
To apply overhead for September using predetermined rates		

Notice that the $5,900 actual amount of September overhead in the Fabrication Department is not equal to the $5,970 of OH applied to that department's Work in Process Inventory. This $70 difference is the overapplied OH for the month. Because the predetermined OH rates were based on annual estimates, differences in actual and applied overhead accumulate during the year. Underapplied or overapplied overhead will be closed (as shown in Chapter 3) at year-end to Cost of Goods Sold (if the amount is immaterial) or allocated among Work in Process Inventory, Finished Goods Inventory, and Cost of Goods Sold accounts (if the amount is material).

The preceding entries for the Fabrication Department are similar to the entries made in each of the other departments of Crown Fence Company. Direct material and direct labor data are posted to each job order cost sheet frequently (usually daily or weekly); entries are posted to the general ledger control accounts for longer intervals (usually upon completion of a job or monthly, whichever occurs first).

Job #PF108 will pass consecutively through the three departments of Crown Fence Company. In other types of job shops, different departments may work on the same job concurrently. Similar entries for Job #PF108 are made throughout the production process, and Exhibit 5.8 shows the cost sheet at the job's completion. Note that DM requisitions, DL cost, and OH application shown previously in Entries 1, 2, and 4 are posted on the job cost sheet. The actual costs of Installation and Finishing are given in the job order cost sheet in Exhibit 5.8, but the details are omitted in this discussion.

When the job is completed, its costs are transferred to Finished Goods Inventory and, upon acceptance by the customer, to Cost of Goods Sold. The journal entries related to transfers among departments as well as the completion and sale of the goods follow.

Work in Process Inventory—Installation	16,847	
Work in Process Inventory—Fabrication		16,847
To transfer Job #PF108 from Fabrication to Installation		
Work in Process Inventory—Finishing	22,376	
Work in Process Inventory—Installation		22,376
To transfer Job #PF108 from Installation to Finishing		
Finished Goods Inventory—Job #PF108	28,091	
Work in Process Inventory—Finishing		28,091
To transfer completed Job #PF108 to FG Inventory		
Accounts Receivable—Willowdale Homeowners' Association	35,250	
Sales		35,250
To record the sale of goods on account		
Cost of Goods Sold—Job #PF108	28,091	
Finished Goods Inventory—Job #PF108		28,091
To record the CGS for the Willowdale sale		

Managers in all departments can use the completed job order cost sheet to determine how well costs were controlled. Overall, costs were slightly below the budgeted level, which is indicative of effective cost control, particularly in the Fabrication Department.

Job cost information is used by managers to make decisions and plan and control operations.

Exhibit 5.8 Crown Fence Company Completed Job Order Cost Sheet

Job #PF108

Customer Name and Address:		Description of Job:
Willowdale Homeowners' Assoc. 200 Willow Avenue Willow, Texas		2,000 feet of 6' steel fence per contract dated 8/13/2013
Contract Agreement Date:	8/13/13	
Scheduled Starting Date:	9/01/13	
Agreed Completion Date:	11/15/13	Contract Price $35,250
Actual Completion Date:		
Delivery Instructions:	Full installation per contract	

FABRICATION

DIRECT MATERIAL (EST. $5,000)			DIRECT LABOR (EST. $7,200)			OVERHEAD BASED ON # OF LABOR HOURS (EST. $3,000; $12 per DLH)			OVERHEAD BASED ON # OF MACHINE HOURS (EST. $2,000; $30 per MH)		
Date	Source	Amount	Date	Source	Amount	Date	Source	Amount	Date	Source	Amount
9/30	MR L40-L55	$4,875	9/30	payroll	$6,902	7/31	payroll	$3,120	9/30	Machine hour meters	$1,950
...	...	...	...	...	...	...	...	...	...	...	...

INSTALLATION
(SAME FORMAT AS ABOVE BUT WITH DIFFERENT OH RATES)

FINISHING
(SAME FORMAT AS ABOVE BUT WITH DIFFERENT OH RATES)

SUMMARY

	FABRICATION Actual	FABRICATION Budget	INSTALLATION Actual	INSTALLATION Budget	FINISHING Actual	FINISHING Budget
Direct material	$ 4,875	$ 5,000	$ 0	$ 0	$1,605	$1,500
Direct labor	6,902	7,200	1,805	1,800	2,970	3,000
Overhead (labor)	3,120	3,000	1,610	1,500	1,140	1,200
Overhead (machine)	1,950	2,000	2,114	2,000	0	0
Totals	$16,847	$17,200	$5,529	$5,300	$5,715	$5,700

Final Costs:		Actual	Budget
	Fabrication	$16,847	$17,200
	Installation	5,529	5,300
	Finishing	5,715	5,700
	Totals	$28,091	$28,200

JOB ORDER COSTING TO ASSIST MANAGERS

5 How does information from a job order costing system support management decision making?

Managers are interested in controlling costs in each department as well as for each job. Actual direct material, direct labor, and factory overhead costs are accumulated in departmental accounts and are periodically compared to budgets so that managers can respond to significant deviations. Transactions must be recorded in a consistent, complete, and accurate manner to have information on actual costs available for periodic comparisons.

Managers in different types of job order organizations may stress different types of cost control. Companies such as **Shaw Harley-Davidson** are extremely concerned about labor hours and their related costs required to build custom motorcycles: unlike most motorcycles that are built on a moving assembly line, each Shaw Harley-Davidson custom cycle takes up to 100 labor-hours to hand-make.[6] Other companies implement significant cost and physical controls for direct materials; for example, jewelers are concerned about the costs of platinum, gold, diamonds, and Australian black opals. Hospitals must be careful to control OH costs related to expensive but seldom-used equipment or to the processing of patient information.

One primary difference between job order costing for manufacturing and service organizations is that most service organizations use a fairly insignificant amount of material relative to the value of labor for each job. In such cases, only direct labor may be traced to each job and all material may be treated (for the sake of convenience) as part of OH. Overhead is then allocated to the various jobs, most commonly using a predetermined rate per direct labor hour or direct labor dollar. Other cost drivers that can effectively assign OH to jobs may also be identified.

Knowing the costs of individual jobs allows managers to better estimate future job costs and to establish realistic bids and selling prices. Using budgets in a job order costing system also provides information against which actual costs can be compared at regular time intervals for control purposes. These comparisons can also furnish some performance evaluation information. The following two examples demonstrate the usefulness of job order costing to managers.

Concrete Café

Concrete Café specializes in concrete structures. The firm has a diverse set of clients and job types. Its president, Joann Bradley, wants to know which of the firm's clients are the most profitable and which are the least profitable. To determine this information, she requested a breakdown of profit per job measured on both a percentage and an absolute dollar basis.

Bradley found that no client job cost records were kept. Costs had been accumulated only by type—travel, entertainment, and so forth. Stan Tobias, the sales manager, was certain that the largest profits came from Concrete Café's largest accounts. Careful job cost analysis found that the largest accounts contributed most of the firm's revenue but the smallest percentage and absolute dollars of incremental profit. Until Bradley requested this information, no one had totaled the costs of recruiting each client or the travel, entertainment, and other costs associated with maintaining each client.

A company that has a large number of jobs that vary in size, time, or effort may not know which jobs are responsible for disproportionately large costs. Job order costing can assist in both determining which jobs are truly profitable and helping managers to better monitor costs. As a result of the cost analysis, Bradley changed the company's marketing strategy. The firm began concentrating its efforts on smaller clients that were located closer to the primary office, causing a substantial increase in profit because significantly fewer costs were incurred for travel and entertainment. A job order costing system was implemented to track each client's costs. Unprofitable accounts were dropped, and account managers felt more responsibility to monitor and control costs related to their particular accounts.

Paul's Pirogues

Paul Boudreaux and his employees custom manufacture small wooden boats to customer specifications. Before completing his MBA and learning about job order costing, Boudreaux had merely "guess-timated" the costs associated with each boat's production. He would estimate selling prices by using vague information from past jobs and specifications for the new design and adding what he considered a reasonable profit margin. Often

[6] http://www.motorcyclenews.com/MCN/News/newsresults/Customs-modified-bikes/2011/April/apr2111-shaw-harley-davidson-custom-built-in-7-minutes/ (last accessed 9/28/11).

customers who indicated they thought the selling price was too high could convince Boudreaux to make price reductions.

Implementing the job order costing system provided Boudreaux with the following benefits:

- better cost control over the jobs that were in process;
- better inventory valuations for financial statements;
- better information with which to prevent part stockouts (not having parts in inventory) and production stoppages;
- a better ability to make certain that materials acquired for a particular custom boat were actually used for that job;
- more up-to-date information to judge whether to accept additional work and to determine when current work would be completed; and
- an informed means by which to understand how costs were incurred on jobs, to estimate costs that would be incurred on future jobs, and to justify price quotes on future jobs.

Job order costing information can help managers trace costs associated with specific jobs, like custom boats, to estimate costs for future jobs.

Whether an entity is a manufacturer or a service organization that tailors its output to customer specifications, company management will find that job order costing techniques help in performing managerial functions. This type of cost system is useful for determining the cost of goods produced or services rendered in companies that are able to attach costs to specific jobs. As product variety increases, the size of production lots for many items shrinks, and job order costing becomes more applicable. Custom-made goods may become the norm rather than the exception in an environment that relies on flexible manufacturing systems and computer-integrated manufacturing.

PRODUCT AND MATERIAL LOSSES IN JOB ORDER COSTING

6 How are losses treated in a job order costing system?

Production processes may result in losses of direct material or partially completed products. Some losses, such as evaporation, leakage, or oxidation, are inherent in the manufacturing process; such reductions are called **shrinkage**. Modifying the production process to reduce or eliminate shrinkage may be difficult, impossible, or simply not cost beneficial. At other times, production process errors (either by humans or machines) cause a loss of units through rejection at inspection for failure to meet appropriate quality standards or designated product specifications. Such units are considered either **defects**, if they can be economically reworked and sold, or **spoilage**, if such rework cannot be performed.

Units not meeting quality specifications may be reworked to meet specifications or may be sold as irregulars. Rework cost is a product or period cost depending on whether the rework relates to defective production that is considered to be normal or abnormal. A **normal loss** of units falls within a tolerance level that is expected during production. For example, if a company sets its quality goal as 99 percent of goods produced, the company expects a normal loss of 1 percent. Any loss in excess of the set expectation level is considered an **abnormal loss**. Thus, the difference between normal and abnormal loss is merely one of degree and is determined by management.

In a job order situation, the accounting treatment for lost units depends on two issues:

- Is a loss generally incurred for most jobs or is it specifically identified with a particular job?
- Is the loss considered normal or abnormal?

Generally Anticipated on All Jobs

If a normal loss is anticipated on all jobs, the predetermined OH rate should include an amount for the net loss, which equals the cost of defective or spoiled work minus any estimated disposal value of that work. This approach assumes that losses are naturally inherent and unavoidable in the production of good units, and the estimated loss should be allocated to the good units produced.

Assume that Kyndo Corp. produces special order cleaning compounds for use by manufacturers. Regardless of the job, some spoilage always occurs in the mixing process. In computing the predetermined OH rate related to the custom compounds, the following estimates are made:

Overhead costs other than spoilage		$ 121,500
Estimated spoilage cost	$10,300	
Sales of improperly mixed compounds to foreign distributors	(4,300)	6,000
Total estimated overhead		$ 127,500
Estimated gallons of production during the year		÷150,000
Predetermined OH rate per gallon		$ 0.85

During the year, Kyndo Corp. accepted a job (#38) from Husserl Co. to manufacture 100 gallons of cleaning compound. The compound is mixed in 20-gallon vats. In mixing the compound, one vat of ingredients was spoiled when a worker accidentally added a thickening agent meant for another job into a container of Job #38's cleaning compound. Actual cost of the defective mixture was $57, but it can be sold at an outlet market for $22. The following entry is made to account for the actual defect cost:

Disposal Value of Defective Work	22	
Manufacturing Overhead Control	35	
Work in Process Inventory—Job #38		57
To record disposal value of defective work incurred on Job #38 for Husserl Co.		

The estimated cost of spoilage was originally included when calculating the predetermined OH rate. Therefore, as defects or spoilage occur, the disposal value of nonstandard work is (if salable) included in Inventory, and the net cost of the normal, nonstandard work is charged to the Manufacturing Overhead Control account, as is any other actual OH cost.

Specifically Identified with a Particular Job

If losses are not generally anticipated but are occasionally experienced on specific jobs because of job-related characteristics, the estimated cost should *not* be included in setting the predetermined OH rate. Because the defect/spoilage cost attaches to the job, disposal value of such goods reduces the cost of the job that created those goods. If no disposal value exists for the defective/spoiled goods, the cost of those lost units is assigned to the job that caused the defect or spoilage.

Assume that Kyndo Corp. did not typically experience spoilage in its production process. The company's predetermined OH rate would have been calculated as $0.81 per gallon ($121,500 ÷ 150,000). Assume that more ammonia than normal was added to one vat of the batch at Husserl Co.'s request. After inspecting those 20 gallons, Husserl Co. was unsatisfied and asked Kyndo Corp. to keep the original formula for the remaining gallons. The 20 gallons could be sold to another company for $22; this amount would reduce the cost of the Husserl Co. job as shown in the following entry:

Disposal Value of Defective Work	22	
Work in Process Inventory—Job #38		22
To record disposal value of defective work incurred on Job #38 for Husserl Co.		

Abnormal Spoilage

The cost of all abnormal losses (net of any disposal value) should be written off as a period cost. This treatment is justified because asset cost should include only those costs that are necessary to acquire or produce inventory; unnecessary costs should be written off in the period in which they are incurred. Abnormal losses are not necessary to produce good units, and the cost is avoidable in the future. This cost should be separately identified and the cause investigated to determine how to prevent future similar occurrences.

The following entry assumes that Kyndo Corp. normally anticipates some losses on its custom orders and included the estimated cost of those losses in developing the predetermined OH rate. Job #135 produced defective units costing $198; however, a disposal value of $45 was associated with those units. Of the remaining $153 of cost, $120 was related to normal defects, and $33 was related to abnormal defects. The following journal entry records these facts.

Defective Work Inventory	45	
Manufacturing Overhead Control	120	
Loss from Abnormal Spoilage	33	
Work in Process Inventory—Job #135		198
To record reassignment of cost of defective and spoiled work on Job #135		

The first debit represents the defective inventory's disposal value; the debit to Manufacturing Overhead Control is for the net cost of normal spoilage. The debit to Loss from Abnormal Spoilage is for the portion of the net cost of spoilage that was unnecessary and unanticipated in setting the predetermined application rate. When the defective product is sold, Cash (or Accounts Receivable) is debited and Defective Work Inventory is credited.

APPENDIX

JOB ORDER COSTING USING STANDARD COSTS

7 How are standard costs used in a job order costing system?

The Crown Fence Company example illustrates the use of actual historical cost data for direct material and direct labor in a job order costing system. However, using actual DM and DL costs may cause the costs of similar units to fluctuate from period to period or from job to job because of changes in component costs. Use of standard costs for DM and DL can minimize the effects of such cost fluctuations in the same way that predetermined rates do for overhead costs.

A standard cost system uses predetermined norms in the inventory accounts for prices and/or quantities of cost components. After production is complete, standard production cost is compared to actual production cost to assess production efficiency. A difference between the actual quantity, price, or rate and its related standard is called a **variance**.[7]

Standards can be used in a job order system only if a company typically works jobs that produce fairly similar products. One type of standard job order costing system uses standards only for input prices of material or only for labor rates. Such an approach is reasonable if all output relies on similar kinds of material or labor. If standards are used for price or rate amounts only, the debits to WIP Inventory become a hybrid of actual and standard information: actual quantities at standard prices or rates.

A Coat of Many Colors, a house-painting company located in Denver, is used to illustrate the use of price and rate standards. Management has decided that, because of the climate, one specific brand of paint (costing $30 per gallon) is the best to use. Painters employed by the company are paid $18 per hour. These two amounts can be used as price and rate standards for A Coat of Many Colors. No standards can be set for the quantity of paint that will be used on a job or the amount of time that will be spent on the job. These items will vary based on the condition and texture of a structure's exterior as well as on the size of the structure being painted.

Assume that A Coat of Many Colors paints a house requiring 50 gallons of paint and 80 hours of labor time. The standard paint and labor costs, respectively, are $1,500 (50 × $30) and $1,440 (80 × $18). The paint was purchased at a sale price of $27 per gallon (a total of $1,350). The actual labor rate paid to painters was $19 per hour. Price and rate variances are calculated as follows:

Material: 50 × ($27 actual − $30 standard) = 50 × −$3 = −$150 price variance (favorable)

Labor: 80 hours × ($19 actual − $18 standard) = 80 × $1 = $80 rate variance (unfavorable)

The price variance is favorable because less was expended than what was expected. The rate variance is unfavorable because the amount spent is greater than what was expected.

[7] Standard costing is covered in detail in Chapter 7.

Other job order companies produce output that is homogeneous enough to allow standards to be developed for both quantities and prices of material and labor. Such companies usually use distinct production runs for numerous similar products. In such circumstances, the output is homogeneous for each run, unlike the heterogeneous output of A Coat of Many Colors.

Green Manufacturing Inc. is a job order manufacturer that uses both price and quantity material and labor standards. Green uses recycled wood to produce flower boxes that are retailed through several chains of garden supply stores. Retailers contract for the boxes on a job order basis because of the changes in style, color, and size with each spring gardening season. Green produces the boxes in distinct production runs each month for each retail chain. Price and quantity standards for direct material and direct labor have been established and are used to compare the estimated and actual costs of monthly production runs for each type of box produced.

Material and labor standards set for the boxes sold to Mountain Gardens were:

Material: 8 linear feet of 1″ × 10″ redwood plank at $0.60 per linear foot

Labor: 1.4 direct labor hours at $9.00 per direct labor hour (DLH)

In June, 2,000 boxes were produced for Mountain Gardens. The actual quantities and costs for wood and labor related to this job were:

Material: 16,300 linear feet used; purchased at $0.58 per linear foot

Labor: 2,700 actual hours worked at $9.10 per DLH

Given this information, the following variances can be calculated:

Material:

$16{,}300 \times (\$0.58 - \$0.60) = 16{,}300 \times -\$0.02 = \underline{\underline{-\$325}}$ price variance (favorable)

$16{,}300 - (8 \times 2{,}000) = 16{,}300 - 16{,}000 = 300$ linear feet above standard

300 ft. excess $\times$ \$0.60 standard cost $= \underline{\underline{\$180}}$ quantity variance (unfavorable)

Labor:

$2{,}700 \times (\$9.10 - \$9.00) = 2{,}700 \times \$0.10 = \underline{\underline{\$270}}$ rate variance (unfavorable)

$2{,}700 - (1.4 \times 2{,}000) = 2{,}700 - 2{,}800 = 100$ hours below standard

100 hours fewer $\times$ \$9.00 standard cost $= \underline{\underline{-\$900}}$ quantity variance (favorable)

A summary of variances follows:

Direct material price variance	$(326) favorable
Direct material quantity variance	180 unfavorable
Direct labor rate variance	270 unfavorable
Direct labor quantity variance	(900) favorable
Net variance (cost less than expected)	$(776) favorable

From a financial perspective, Green controlled its total material and labor costs well on the Mountain Gardens job.

Variances can be computed for actual-to-standard differences regardless of whether standards have been established for both quantities and prices or for prices or rates only. Standard costs for material and labor provide the same types of benefits as predetermined OH rates: more timely information and comparison benchmarks for actual amounts. In fact, a predetermined OH rate is simply a type of standard. It establishes a constant amount of overhead assignable as a component of product cost and eliminates any immediate need for actual overhead information in the calculation of product cost.

Standard cost job order systems are reasonable substitutes for actual or normal cost systems as long as the standards provide managers with useful information. Any cost accumulation system is acceptable in practice if it is effective and efficient in serving the company's unique production or performance needs, provides information desired by management, meets external reporting demands, and can be maintained at a cost that is reasonable when compared to the benefits received. These criteria apply equally well to both manufacturers and service companies.

Comprehensive Review Module

KEY TERMS

abnormal loss, p. 163
cost-plus contract, p. 153
defect, p. 163
employee time sheet, p. 156
intranet, p. 153
job, p. 150
job order cost sheet, p. 154
job order costing system, p. 150
material requisition form, p. 154
normal loss, p. 163
process costing system, p. 150
shrinkage, p. 163
spoilage, p. 163
standard cost system, p. 151
variance, p. 165

CHAPTER SUMMARY

1 Job Order vs. Process Costing; Valuation Systems

- Job order costing is used in companies that make limited quantities of customer-specified products or perform customer-specific services; process costing is used in companies that make mass quantities of homogeneous output on a continuous flow or batch basis.
- Job order costing requires the use of a job order cost sheet to track the direct material, direct labor, and actual or applied overhead to each customer-specific job; process costing accounts for direct material, direct labor, and actual or applied overhead by batch of goods per department.
- Job order costing does not allow for the computation of a cost per unit unless all units within the job are similar; process costing can and does create a cost per unit for each cost element.
- Job order costing may use an actual cost system, a normal cost system, or a standard cost system; process costing may use the same type of cost valuation systems but standard cost systems are significantly more prevalent in process costing than job order costing.
- There are three primary valuation systems.
    - An actual cost system combines actual direct material, direct labor, and overhead.
    - A normal cost system combines actual direct material and direct labor with applied overhead (which uses a predetermined OH rate).
    - A standard cost system combines budgeted norms (standards) for direct material, direct labor, and overhead.

2 Job Order Costing System Characteristics

- Costs are accumulated by job, which is a single unit or multiple similar or dissimilar units that has or have been produced to distinct customer specifications.
- Costs of different jobs cannot logically be averaged; a unique cost must be determined for each job.
- Custom manufacturers typically price their goods using either a cost-plus contract or competitive bidding.
- Job order costing modules are included in most basic accounting software packages.
- Operational and financial data about jobs are often disseminated throughout a firm over company intranets.

3 Job Order Costing Documents

- The job order cost sheet contains all financial information about a particular job.
    - Cost sheets for incomplete jobs serve as the Work in Process Inventory subsidiary ledger.
    - Cost sheets for completed jobs not yet delivered to customers constitute the Finished Goods Inventory subsidiary ledger.
    - Cost sheets for completed and sold jobs comprise the Cost of Goods Sold subsidiary ledger.
- Material requisition forms trace the issuance of raw material to the specific jobs in WIP Inventory so that direct material can be included on the job order cost sheets.
- Employee time sheets record the hours worked and jobs associated with work by employees so that direct labor cost can be included on the job order cost sheets.

4 Accumulating Costs in Job Order Costing

- Direct material and direct labor costs are included on the job order cost sheet.
- Indirect materials and indirect labor are included with other actual overhead costs in one or more Overhead Control accounts.
- Overhead is applied using predetermined overhead rates to jobs at completion or the end of the period, whichever is earlier.
- Jobs and their related costs are transferred between departments or, if completed, to Finished Goods Inventory.
- Goods are delivered to the requesting customers for cash or credit; the cost of those goods is removed from Finished Goods Inventory and expensed to Cost of Goods Sold.

5 Job Order Costing and Management Decision Making

- Job order costing assists managers in planning, controlling, decision making, and evaluating performance.
- Job order costing allows managers to trace costs associated with specific current jobs to better estimate costs for future jobs.
- Job order costing provides a means by which managers can better control the costs associated with current production, especially if comparisons with budgets or standards are used.
- Job order costing allows costs to be gathered correctly for jobs that are contracted on a cost-plus basis.
- Job order costing highlights those jobs or types of jobs that are most profitable to the organization.

6 Losses in a Job Order Costing System

- Defective production can be economically reworked; spoilage cannot be economically reworked.
- Both normal and abnormal losses may occur in a job order system.
  - Normal losses that are generally anticipated on all jobs are estimated and included in the development of the predetermined OH rate.
  - Normal losses that are associated with a particular job are charged (net of any disposal value) to that job.
  - Abnormal losses are charged to a loss account in the period in which they are incurred.

SOLUTION STRATEGIES

BASIC JOURNAL ENTRIES IN A JOB ORDER COSTING SYSTEM

	Debit	Credit
Raw Material Inventory	XXX	
Accounts Payable		XXX
To record the purchase of raw material		
Work in Process Inventory—Dept. (Job #)	XXX	
Manufacturing Overhead Control	XXX	
Raw Material Inventory		XXX
To record the issuance of direct and indirect material requisitioned for a specific job		
Work in Process Inventory—Dept. (Job #)	XXX	
Manufacturing Overhead Control	XXX	
Wages Payable		XXX
To record direct and indirect labor payroll for production employees		
Manufacturing Overhead Control	XXX	
Various accounts		XXX
To record the incurrence of actual overhead costs (Account titles to be credited must be specified in an actual journal entry.)		
Work in Process Inventory—Dept. (Job #)	XXX	
Manufacturing Overhead Control		XXX
To apply overhead to a specific job (This may be actual OH or OH applied using a predetermined rate. Predetermined OH is applied at job completion or end of period, whichever is earlier.)		
Finished Goods Inventory (Job #)	XXX	
Work in Process Inventory		XXX
To transfer completed goods to FG Inventory		

Accounts Receivable	XXX	
Sales		XXX
To record the sale of goods on account		
Cost of Goods Sold	XXX	
Finished Goods Inventory		XXX
To record CGS		

DEMONSTRATION PROBLEM

Modern Building Solutions (MBS) builds portable buildings to clients' specifications. The firm has two departments: Parts Fabrication and Assembly. The Parts Fabrication Department designs and cuts the major components of the building and is highly automated. The Assembly Department assembles and installs the components and this department is highly labor intensive. The Assembly Department begins work on the buildings as soon as the floor components are available from the Parts Fabrication Department.

In its first month of operations (March 2013), MBS obtained contracts for three buildings:

Job 1: a 20- by 40-foot storage building
Job 2: a 35- by 35-foot commercial utility building
Job 3: a 30- by 40-foot portable classroom

MBS bills its customers on a cost-plus basis, with profit set equal to 25 percent of costs. The firm uses a job order costing system based on normal costs. Overhead is applied in Parts Fabrication at a predetermined rate of $100 per machine hour (MH). In the Assembly Department, overhead is applied at a predetermined rate of $10 per direct labor hour (DLH). The following significant transactions occurred in March 2013:

1. Direct material was purchased on account: $80,000.
2. Direct material was issued to the Parts Fabrication Department for use in the three jobs: Job #1, $8,000; Job #2, $14,000; and Job #3, $45,000. Direct material was issued to the Assembly Department: Job #1, $500; Job #2, $1,200; and Job #3, $6,600.
3. Time sheets and payroll summaries indicated that the following direct labor costs were incurred:

	Parts Fabrication Department	Assembly Department
Job #1	$1,000	$2,400
Job #2	3,000	3,500
Job #3	5,000	9,500

4. The following indirect costs were incurred in each department:

	Parts Fabrication Department	Assembly Department
Labor	$ 4,200	$4,500
Utilities/Fuel	5,900	2,300
Depreciation	10,300	3,600

The labor and utilities/fuel costs were accrued at the time of the journal entry.

5. Overhead was applied based on the predetermined rates in effect in each department. The Parts Fabrication Department had 200 MHs (20 MHs on Job #1, 35 MHs on Job #2, and 145 MHs on Job #3), and the Assembly Department worked 950 DLHs (40 DLHs on Job #1, 110 DLHs on Job #2, and 800 DLHs on Job #3) for the month.
6. Job #1 was completed and sold for cash in the amount of the cost-plus contract. At month-end, Jobs #2 and #3 were only partially complete.
7. Any underapplied or overapplied overhead at month-end is considered immaterial and is assigned to Cost of Goods Sold.

Required:

a. Record the journal entries for transactions 1–7.
b. As of the end of March 2013, determine the total cost assigned to Jobs #2 and #3.

Solution to Demonstration Problem

	Debit	Credit
a. 1. Raw Material Inventory	80,000	
Accounts Payable		80,000
To record purchase of direct material		
2. WIP Inventory—Parts Fabrication (Job #1)	8,000	
WIP Inventory—Parts Fabrication (Job #2)	14,000	
WIP Inventory—Parts Fabrication (Job #3)	45,000	
Raw Material Inventory		67,000
To record requisition and issuance of direct material to Parts Fabrication Department		
WIP Inventory—Assembly (Job #1)	500	
WIP Inventory—Assembly (Job #2)	1,200	
WIP Inventory—Assembly (Job #3)	6,600	
Raw Material Inventory		8,300
To record requisition and issuance of direct material to Assembly Department		
3. WIP Inventory—Parts Fabrication (Job #1)	1,000	
WIP Inventory—Parts Fabrication (Job #2)	3,000	
WIP Inventory—Parts Fabrication (Job #3)	5,000	
Wages Payable		9,000
To record direct labor cost for Parts Fabrication Department		
WIP Inventory—Assembly (Job #1)	2,400	
WIP Inventory—Assembly (Job #2)	3,500	
WIP Inventory—Assembly (Job #3)	9,500	
Wages Payable		15,400
To record direct labor cost for Assembly Department		
4. Manufacturing Overhead Control—Parts Fabrication	20,400	
Manufacturing Overhead Control—Assembly	10,400	
Wages Payable		8,700
Utilities/Fuel Payable		8,200
Accumulated Depreciation		13,900
To record various overhead costs		
5. WIP Inventory—Parts Fabrication (Job #1)	2,000	
WIP Inventory—Parts Fabrication (Job #2)	3,500	
WIP Inventory—Parts Fabrication (Job #3)	14,500	
Manufacturing Overhead Control—Parts Fabrication		20,000
To apply overhead in Parts Fabrication Department		
WIP Inventory—Assembly (Job #1)	400	
WIP Inventory—Assembly (Job #2)	1,100	
WIP Inventory—Assembly (Job #3)	8,000	
Manufacturing Overhead Control—Assembly		9,500
To apply overhead in Assembly Department		
6. Finished Goods Inventory[a]	14,300	
WIP Inventory—Parts Fabrication		11,000
WIP Inventory—Assembly		3,300
To record completion of Job #1		
Cash	17,875	
Sales Revenue[b]		17,875
To record sale of Job #1		
Cost of Goods Sold	14,300	
Finished Goods Inventory		14,300
To record CGS for Job #1		
7. Cost of Goods Sold	1,300	
Manufacturing Overhead Control—Parts Fabrication		400
Manufacturing Overhead Control—Assembly		900
To assign underapplied overhead to CGS		

[a]Job #1 costs = $8,000 + $500 + $1,000 + $2,400 + $2,000 + $400 = $14,300
[b]Revenue, Job #1 = $14,300 × 1.25 = $17,875

b.

	Job #2	**Job #3**
Direct material—Parts Fabrication	$14,000	$45,000
Direct labor—Parts Fabrication	3,000	5,000
Overhead—Parts Fabrication	3,500	14,500
Direct material—Assembly	1,200	6,600
Direct labor—Assembly	3,500	9,500
Overhead—Assembly	1,100	8,000
Totals	$26,300	$88,600

POTENTIAL ETHICAL ISSUES

ETHICS

1. Inflating costs of cost-plus contracts so that the price of the contract increases as does the profit for the contract
2. Assigning costs from a fixed-fee contract to a cost-plus contract so that both contracts become more profitable
3. Substituting materials of a lower quality than specified in the contract to reduce costs and increase profits
4. Shifting costs from completed jobs (in Cost of Goods Sold) to incomplete jobs (in Work in Process Inventory) to both increase profits reported for financial accounting purposes and inflate assets on the balance sheet
5. Using manufacturing methods or materials that violate the intellectual property rights of other firms (e.g., patent rights of competitors)
6. Recording the disposal value from the sale of defective work in a cost-plus contract job as "Other Revenue" rather than reducing the inventory cost of the related job

QUESTIONS

1. In choosing a product costing system, what are the two choices available for a cost accumulation system? How do these systems differ?
2. In choosing a product costing system, what are the three valuation method alternatives? Explain how these methods differ.
3. In a job order costing system, what key documents support the cost accumulation process, and what is the purpose of each?
4. How can information produced by a job order costing system assist managers in operating their firms more efficiently?
5. If normal spoilage is generally anticipated to occur on all jobs, how should the cost of that spoilage be treated?
6. Why are normal and abnormal spoilage accounted for differently? Typically, how does one determine which spoilage is normal and which is abnormal?
7. (*Appendix*) In using standard costing in a job order costing system, are standards established for material and labor costs and quantities?
8. (*Appendix*) How can the variance information provided by standard costing be used to improve cost control?

EXERCISES

9. **LO.1 (Costing system/valuation method; writing)** Calista London, after spending 20 years working for a large engineering firm, has decided to start her own business. She has designed a product to remove jar lids with minimal physical effort. London believes this product will sell one million units per year. London has protected her design with appropriate patents, has acquired production space and required machinery, and is now training her newly hired employees to manufacture the product.

   London has been your friend for many years and has asked your advice about what type of product cost and valuation system she should use. Based on the limited information given here, what recommendation would you make to London? Why?

10. **LO.1 (Costing system choice)** For each of the following firms, determine whether it is more likely to use job order or process costing. This firm

a. provides legal services.
b. is a health-care clinic.
c. manufactures shampoo.
d. makes custom jewelry.
e. is an automobile repair shop.
f. provides landscaping services for corporations.
g. designs luxury yachts.
h. manufactures paint.
i. produces college textbooks.
j. produces candles.
k. provides property management services for real estate developers.
l. manufactures baby food.
m. manufactures canned vegetables.
n. makes wedding cakes.
o. designs custom software.
p. is a film production company.
q. manufactures air mattresses for swimming pool use.

INTERNET

11. **LO.1 (Costing system/valuation method; research; writing)** The six-acre facility of **Richmond Yachts** has the capacity to simultaneously build four composite yachts from 120 feet to 155 feet in length. Access the company's Web site (http://www.richmondyachts.com) and locate one of the yachts that is currently available for sale ("Our Yachts"). What features of this yacht indicate a critical need for the company to use job order costing?

ETHICS

12. **LO.3 (Job costing documents; ethics; writing)** Salem Corp. contracted for a specialized production machine from Quindo Industries, a tool company. The contract specified a price equal to "115 percent of production cost." A sales executive at Quindo told Salem's management that the machine's approximate price would be $1,725,000 based on the following estimates:

Direct material cost	$ 500,000
Direct labor cost	400,000
Manufacturing overhead (applied based on machine time)	600,000
Markup	225,000
Estimated price to Salem	$1,725,000

Two months later, Quindo Industries delivered the completed machinery, configured and manufactured as per the contract. However, the accompanying invoice caught Salem's executives by surprise. The invoice provided the following:

Direct material cost	$ 658,000
Direct labor cost	625,000
Manufacturing overhead (applied based on machine time)	640,000
Markup	288,450
Estimated price to Salem	$2,211,450

Upon receiving the invoice, Salem executives requested an audit of the direct material charges because they were more than 30 percent higher than the original estimate. Quindo Industries granted the request and Salem hired your firm to conduct the audit.

a. Describe your strategy for validating the $658,000 charge for direct material and discuss specific documents you will request from Quindo Industries as part of the audit.
b. Describe your strategy for validating the $625,000 charge for direct labor and discuss specific documents you will request from Quindo Industries as part of the audit.
c. How might Quindo Industries have manipulated the predetermined overhead rate?
d. Even if all of the charges are validated, do you perceive the tool company's behavior in this case as ethical? Explain.

13. **LO.3 (Job order costing documents; accounts)** Following are specific types of information that can be located in a particular account (such as WIP Inventory) or on a particular document (such as an employee time card). For each item listed, identify the account or document that would provide the relevant information.

a. Total hours worked on a job by a specific employee
b. Total cost of goods manufactured during a period
c. Total cost of material issued to production for a period
d. Total product cost assigned to a particular job
e. Total manufacturing overhead cost incurred for a period
f. Total overhead cost assigned to a particular job
g. Total cost of material purchased during a period
h. Total cost of goods sold during a period
i. Total indirect labor cost incurred during a period
j. Total direct labor cost incurred during a period

14. **LO.4 (Cost accumulation)** On September 25, 2013, a hurricane destroyed the work in process inventory of Biloxi Corporation. At that time, the company was in the process of manufacturing two custom jobs (B325 and Q428). Although all of Biloxi's on-site accounting records were destroyed, the following information is available from some backup off-site records:

- Biloxi Corp. applies overhead at the rate of 85 percent of direct labor cost.
- The cost of goods sold for the company averages 75 percent of selling price. Sales from January 1 to the date of the hurricane totaled $1,598,000.
- The company's wage rate for production employees is $12.90 per hour. A total of 25,760 direct labor hours were recorded from January 1 through September 25.
- As of September 25, $21,980 of direct material and 128 hours of direct labor had been recorded for Job B325. Also at that time, $14,700 of direct material and 240 hours of direct labor had been recorded for Job Q428.
- January 1, 2013, inventories were as follows: $19,500 of Raw Material and $68,900 of Finished Goods. Raw materials purchased during 2013 totaled $843,276.
- The amount of Work in Process Inventory at January 1, 2013, was $14,600. Jobs B325 and Q428 were not in process on January 1.
- One job, R91, was completed and in the warehouse awaiting shipment on September 25. The total cost of this job was $165,600.

Determine the following amounts.

a. Cost of goods sold for the year
b. Cost of goods manufactured during the year
c. Amount of applied overhead for each job in WIP Inventory
d. Cost of WIP Inventory destroyed by the hurricane
e. Cost of RM Inventory destroyed by the hurricane

15. **LO.4 (Cost accumulation; assigning costs to jobs)** The law firm of Taub & Lawson, LLP, currently has four cases in process. Following is information related to those cases as of the end of March 2013:

	Case #1	Case #2	Case #3	Case #4
Direct material	$480	$8,800	$3,700	$850
Direct labor hours ($190 per hour)	40	90	70	15
Estimated court hours	12	65	120	40

Taub & Lawson allocates overhead to cases based on a predetermined rate of $150 per estimated court hour.

a. Determine the total cost assigned to each case as of March 31, 2013.
b. Case #3 was completed at the end of April 2013. At that time, $10,100 of direct materials had been used and 174 direct labor hours had been incurred. Of the DLHs, 72 had been spent in court. Taub & Lawson's policy is to charge clients actual costs plus 45 percent. What amount will be billed to the client involved in Case #3?

16. **LO.4 (Cost accumulation; assigning costs to jobs)** Mystic Inc. uses a job order costing system and applies overhead to jobs at a predetermined rate of $4.25 per direct labor dollar. During April 2013, the company spent $29,600 on direct material and $3,900 on direct labor for Job #344. Budgeted factory overhead for the company for the year was $1,275,000.

    a. How did Mystic Inc. compute the predetermined overhead rate for 2013?
    b. Journalize the application of overhead to all jobs, assuming that April's total direct labor cost was $22,700.
    c. How much overhead was assigned to Job #344 during April?
    d. Job #344 had a balance of $18,350 on April 1. What was the April 30 balance?

17. **LO.4 (Cost accumulation in two departments)** Rio Valde Co. uses a normal cost, job order costing system. In the Mixing Department, overhead is applied using machine hours; in Paving, overhead is applied using direct labor hours. In December 2012, the company estimated the following data for its two departments for 2013:

	Mixing Department	Paving Department
Direct labor hours	12,000	28,000
Machine hours	60,000	12,000
Budgeted overhead cost	$480,000	$700,000

    a. Compute the predetermined OH rate for each department of Rio Valde.
    b. Job #220 was started and completed during March 2013. The job cost sheet shows the following information:

	Mixing Department	Paving Department
Direct material	$22,600	$3,400
Direct labor cost	$1,250	$4,050
Direct labor hours	24	340
Machine hours	290	44

    Compute the overhead applied to Job #220 for each department and in total.
    c. The president of Rio Valde suggested that, for simplicity, a single predetermined overhead rate be computed using machine hours. How much overhead would have been applied to Job #220 if that single rate had been used? Would such a rate have indicated the actual overhead cost of each job? Explain.

EXCEL

18. **LO.4 (Cost accumulation)** Barfield Mfg. Co. applies overhead to jobs at a rate of 140 percent of direct labor cost. The following account information is available.

Direct Material Inventory

Debit		Credit
Beg. balance	24,600	?
Purchases	?	
	4,100	

Work in Process Inventory

Debit		Credit
Beg. balance	56,000	?
Direct material	?	
Direct labor	395,000	
Overhead	?	
	27,640	

Finished Goods Inventory

Debit		Credit
Beg. balance	90,000	1,890,000
Goods completed	?	
	57,000	

Cost of Goods Sold

Debit	Credit
?	

Calculate the following items that are missing from Barfield's account information:

a. Cost of goods sold
b. Cost of goods manufactured
c. Amount of overhead applied to production

d. Cost of direct material used
e. Cost of direct material purchased

19. **LO.4 (Cost accumulation in two departments)** Country Products manufactures quilt racks. Pine stock is introduced in Department 1, where the raw material is cut and assembled. In Department 2, completed racks are stained and packaged for shipment. Department 1 applies overhead on the basis of machine hours; Department 2 applies overhead on the basis of direct labor hours. The company's predetermined overhead rates were computed using the following information:

	Department 1	Department 2
Expected overhead	$465,000	$380,600
Expected DLHs	4,000	22,000
Expected MHs	30,000	2,500

Sue Power contacted Country Products to produce 500 quilt racks as a special order. Power wanted the racks made from teak and to be made larger than the company's normal racks. Country Products designated Power's order as Job #462.

During July, Country Products purchased $346,000 of raw material on account, of which $19,000 was teak. Requisitions were issued for $340,000 of raw material, including all the teak. There were 285 direct labor hours worked (at a rate of $11 per DLH) and 2,400 machine hours recorded in Department 1; of these hours, 25 DLHs and 320 MHs were on Job #462. Department 2 had 1,430 DLHs (at a rate of $18 per DLH) and 180 MHs; of these, 158 DLHs and 20 MHs were worked on Job #462. Assume that all wages are paid in cash.

Job #462 was completed on July 28 and shipped to Power. She was billed cost plus 20 percent.

a. What are the predetermined overhead rates for Departments 1 and 2?
b. Prepare journal entries for the July transactions.
c. What were the cost and selling price per unit of Job #462? What was the cost per unit of the raw material?
d. Assume that enough pine had been issued in July for 20,000 quilt racks. The raw material inventory manager is Power's friend, who conveniently "forgot" to trace the teak's cost specifically to Job #462. What would the effect of this "error" be on the raw material cost, total cost, and selling price for each unit in Job #462? (Round to the nearest cent.)

20. **LO.4 (Cost accumulation)** Croftmark Co. began operations on May 1, 2013. Its Work in Process Inventory account on May 31 appeared as follows:

Work in Process Inventory

Direct material	138,600	Cost of completed jobs	??
Direct labor	96,000		
Applied overhead	134,400		

The company applies overhead on the basis of direct labor cost. Only one job was still in process on May 31. That job had $37,725 in direct material and $18,100 in direct labor cost assigned to it.

a. What was the predetermined overhead application rate?
b. What was the balance in WIP Inventory at the end of May?
c. What was the total cost of jobs completed in May?

21. **LO.4 (Cost accumulation)** Blaine Corp. makes floats for Mardi Gras in New Orleans. The company's fiscal year ends on March 31. On January 1, 2013, the company's WIP Inventory account appeared as follows:

Work in Process Inventory

Beginning balance	916,650	Cost of completed jobs	??
Direct material	589,670		
Direct labor	159,600		
Applied overhead	127,680		

The direct labor cost contained in the beginning balance of WIP Inventory was for a total of 15,200 direct labor hours (DLHs). During January, 7,600 DLHs were recorded. Only one job was still in process on January 31. That job had $73,250 in direct material and 2,850 DLHs assigned to it.

a. If overhead is applied on the basis of DLHs, what predetermined OH rate was in effect during the company's 2012–2013 fiscal year?
b. What was the average direct labor rate per hour?
c. What amount of direct material cost was in the beginning balance of WIP Inventory?
d. What was the balance in WIP Inventory at the end of January?
e. What was the total cost of jobs manufactured in January?

EXCEL

22. **LO.4 (Cost accumulation; assigning costs to jobs)** Entrada, an interior decorating firm, uses a job order costing system and applies overhead to jobs using a predetermined rate of $17 per direct labor hour. On June 1, 2013, Job #918 was the only job in process. Its costs included direct material of $8,250 and direct labor of $500 (25 hours at $20 per hour). During June, the company began work on Jobs #919, #920, and #921. Direct material used for June totaled $21,650. June's direct labor cost totaled $6,300. Job #920 had not been completed at the end of June, and its direct material and direct labor charges were $2,850 and $800, respectively. All other jobs were completed in June.

a. What was the total cost of Job #920 as of the end of June 2013?
b. What was the cost of goods manufactured for June 2013?
c. If actual overhead for June was $5,054, was the overhead underapplied or overapplied for the month? By how much?

23. **LO.4 (Journal entries; cost accumulation)** The following costs were incurred in February 2013 by Container Corp., which produces customized steel storage bins:

Direct material purchased on account		$ 76,000
Direct material used for jobs:		
Job #217	$44,800	
Job #218	7,200	
Other jobs	53,600	105,600
Direct labor costs for month:		
Job #217	$10,400	
Job #218	14,000	
Other jobs	19,600	44,000
Actual overhead costs for February		220,000

The balance in Work in Process Inventory on February 1 was $16,800, which consisted of $11,200 for Job #217 and $5,600 for Job #218. The February beginning balance in Direct Material Inventory was $44,600. Actual overhead is applied to jobs at a rate of $4.95 per dollar of direct labor cost. Job #217 was completed and transferred to Finished Goods Inventory during February. Job #217 was delivered to the customer at the agreed-upon price of cost plus 35 percent.

a. Prepare journal entries to record the preceding information.
b. Determine the February ending balance in WIP Inventory. How much of this balance relates to Job #218?

24. **LO.4 (Journal entries)** Nottaway Flooring produces custom-made floor tiles. The company's Raw Material Inventory account contains both direct and indirect materials. Until the end of April 2013, the company worked solely on a large job (#4263) for a major client. Near the end of the month, Nottaway began Job #4264. The following information was obtained relating to April production operations.

1. Raw material purchased on account, $204,000.
2. Direct material issued to Job #4263 cost $163,800; indirect material issued for that job cost $12,460. Direct material costing $1,870 was issued to start production of Job #4264.
3. Direct labor hours worked on Job #4263 were 3,600. Direct labor hours for Job #4264 were 120. All direct labor employees were paid $15 per hour.

4. Actual factory overhead costs incurred for the month totaled $68,700. This overhead consisted of $18,000 of supervisory salaries, $21,500 of depreciation charges, $7,200 of insurance, $12,500 of indirect labor, and $9,500 of utilities. Salaries, insurance, and utilities were paid in cash, and indirect labor charges were accrued.
5. Overhead is applied to production at the rate of $18 per direct labor hour.

Beginning balances of Raw Material Inventory and Work in Process Inventory were, respectively, $4,300 and $11,400. Of the beginning WIP balance, $800 was related to Job #4263. Job #4263 was completed during April.

a. Prepare journal entries for Transactions 1–5.
b. Determine the balance in Raw Material Inventory at the end of the month.
c. Determine the balance in Work in Process Inventory at the end of the month.
d. Determine the cost of the goods manufactured during April. If completed goods consist of 10,000 similar units, what was the cost per unit?
e. What is the amount of underapplied or overapplied overhead at the end of April?

25. **LO.5 (Job costing and pricing)** Attorney Maria Conroe uses a job order costing system to collect costs of client engagements. Conroe is currently working on a case for Stacie Olivgra. During the first three months of 2013, Conroe logged 95 hours on the Olivgra case.

In addition to direct hours spent by Conroe, her office assistant has worked 35 hours typing and copying 1,450 pages of documents related to the Olivgra case. Conroe's assistant works 160 hours per month and is paid a salary of $4,800 per month. The average cost per copy is $0.06 for paper, toner, and machine rental. Telephone and fax charges for long-distance calls on the case totaled $145. Last, Conroe has estimated that total office overhead for rent, utilities, parking, and so on amount to $9,600 per month and that, during a normal month, the office is open every hour that the assistant is at work. Overhead charges are allocated to clients based on the number of hours of assistant's time.

a. Conroe desires to set the billing rate so that she earns, at a minimum, $190 per hour, and covers all direct and allocated indirect costs related to a case. What minimum charge per hour (rounded to the nearest $10) should Conroe charge Olivgra? (Hint: Be sure to include office overhead.) What would be the total billing to Olivgra?
b. All the hours that Conroe spends at the office are not necessarily billable hours. In addition, Conroe did not consider certain other expenses such as license fees, country club dues, automobile costs, and other miscellaneous expenses when she determined the amount of overhead per month. Therefore, Conroe is considering billing clients for direct costs plus allocated indirect costs plus a 40 percent margin to cover nonbillable time as well as other costs. What will Conroe charge Olivgra in total for the time spent on her case?
c. Which billing method is more likely to be accepted by clients, and why?

26. **LO.5 (Cost control; writing)** Juneau Container makes steel storage canisters for various chemical products. The company uses a job order costing system and obtains jobs based on competitive bidding. For each project, a budget is developed.

One of the firm's products is a 55-gallon drum. In the past year, the company made this drum on four separate occasions for four different customers. Financial details for the four orders follow:

Date	Job No.	Quantity	Bid Price	Budgeted Cost	Actual Cost
Jan. 17	2118	60,000	$190,000	$120,000	$145,000
Mar. 13	2789	29,000	155,000	110,000	121,000
Oct. 20	4300	61,000	180,000	125,000	143,000
Dec. 3	4990	35,000	175,000	150,000	168,000

Assume that you are the company's controller. Write a memo to management describing any problems that you perceive in the data presented and the steps that should be taken to eliminate recurrence of these problems.

ETHICS

27. **LO.5 (Cost control; ethics; writing)** Companies use time sheets for two primary reasons: to know how many hours an employee works and, in a job order production situation, to trace work hours to products. An article (S. Greenhouse, "Altering of Worker Time Cards Spurs Growing Number of Suits," *New York Times*, 4/4/04) described a corporate practice of deleting worker hours to increase organizational profitability. Use your library database to obtain this article and discuss the following:
    a. What companies were mentioned as having been found to engage in this practice?
    b. Why is it easier now than in the past to engage in this practice?
    c. As a member of upper management, how would you respond to finding out that this practice was being used in some of your stores? Provide an answer that addresses both the short run and the long run.

28. **LO.5 (Job costing and decision making; writing)** Bonivo Inc. manufactures computers from commodity components to client specifications. The company has historically tracked only the cost of components to computers, and computer selling prices, or bids, have been based solely on the cost of components plus a markup sufficient to cover the other operating costs. In recent years, the company has encountered increasing price pressure from customers, and as a result, computers have often been sold at less than the full markup price—causing continually decreasing profits for the firm.

    As you have provided other financial services to Bonivo Inc. in the past, company management has asked you for guidance regarding approaches that could be taken to better manage the firm's profits and prices. You decide that a job order costing system could be helpful to Bonivo.
    a. Explain how a job order costing system could help Bonivo better control costs and profits.
    b. Explain why Bonivo should not base computer prices only on component costs plus a markup.

29. **LO.6 (Job order costing; rework)** Canyon City Co. uses a job order costing system that combines actual direct material and actual direct labor costs with a predetermined overhead charge based on machine hours. Expected overhead and machine hours of $1,421,000 and 145,000, respectively, were used in developing the predetermined rate for 2013.

    During 2013, the company worked on Job #876 and incurred the following costs and machine hours:

Direct material	$47,500
Direct labor	21,800
Machine hours	325

    a. What is the total cost of Job #876? What is the cost per unit if 1,500 units were made? (Round to the nearest cent.)
    b. In completing Job #876, 30 units were defective and had to be reworked at a cost of $25 each. Assume that spoilage and rework costs were included in the original estimated overhead costs. Where does the $750 rework cost appear in the accounts of Canyon City Co.?
    c. Disregard the facts in (b). Upon completing Job #876, the quality control inspector determined that 30 units were spoiled and would be unacceptable to the customer. Thirty additional good units were made at a total cost of $1,390. The spoiled units were sold for $240 as "seconds" to an outlet store. What is the total cost of Job #876?

30. **LO.6 (Accounting for losses; writing)** Describe how the following occurrences should be accounted for based on the fact pattern presented:
    a. Certain amounts of spoilage and waste are normal in the production system and affect all jobs.
    b. A certain amount of spoilage occurs that is unique to a particular job. There is no disposal value for the spoiled units.
    c. Because of a nonroutine malfunction in a production machine, a number of products in Work in Process Inventory were ruined. The quantity of work lost is assumed to be abnormal. There is some salvage value for the spoiled units.

31. **LO.6 (Job order costing; rework)** San Angelo Corp. uses a job order costing system for client contracts related to custom-manufactured pulley systems. Elmore Mechanical recently ordered 20,000 pulleys, and the job was assigned #BA468. Information for Job #BA468 revealed the following:

Direct material	$40,800
Direct labor	49,200
Overhead	36,800

Final inspection of the pulleys revealed that 230 were defective. In correcting the defects, an additional $1,150 of cost was incurred ($250 for direct material and $900 for direct labor). After the defects were corrected, the pulleys were included with the other good units and shipped to the customer.

a. Journalize the entry to record incurrence of the rework costs if San Angelo Corp.'s predetermined overhead rate includes normal rework costs.
b. Journalize the entry to record incurrence of the rework costs if rework is normal but specific to this job. If San Angelo Corp. prices jobs on a cost-plus basis, should the rework costs be considered in determining the markup?
c. Journalize the entry to record incurrence of the rework costs, assuming that all rework is abnormal.

32. **LO.7 (Appendix; standard costing)** Harvey Inc. uses a standard cost system for labor. Standard costs for material cannot be used because customers require unique materials and all jobs are different sizes. One of the company's jobs experienced the following results related to DL in December 2013:

Actual hours worked	9,000
Standard hours for production	8,600
Actual direct labor rate	$9.65
Standard direct labor rate	$9.85

a. Calculate the total actual payroll.
b. Determine the labor rate variance.
c. Determine the labor quantity variance.
d. What concerns do you have about the variances in (b) and (c)?

33. **LO.7 (Appendix; standard costing; writing)** Routine maintenance services are provided by Latamore Industries to oil and gas firms in their production facilities. Although many of the client services are relatively unique, some services are repetitive. The firm individually negotiates prices with each client. The CFO of Latamore Industries recently examined the profitability of a sample of the firm's service contracts and was surprised that contract profit amounts varied significantly. Additionally, production inputs (such as material and labor) often varied substantially from those budgeted at the time the service contracts were negotiated. The CFO has asked you, as a company intern, to write a memo describing how the adoption of standard costing could improve cost control and profit management for the firm's service contracts.

34. **LO.7 (Appendix; standard costing)** Weingold Inc. engages in routine and customer print jobs for customers. In November 2013, a client specified the use of one of the company's standard papers for a large job, but asked for a high level of customization relative to the print design. Thus, standard costs could be used for direct material but not for labor. The following DM costs were incurred for the client's job:

Actual unit purchase price	$0.032 per sheet
Standard unit price	$0.036 per sheet
Quantity purchased and used in November	980,000 sheets
Standard quantity allowed for good production	984,000 sheets

Calculate the material price variance and the material quantity variance for the client's job.

PROBLEMS

35. **LO.4 (Job cost sheet analysis)** You have applied for a cost accounting position with Chelsea Containers. The company controller has asked all candidates to take a quiz to demonstrate their knowledge of job order costing. Chelsea's job order costing system is based on normal costs, and overhead is applied based on direct labor cost. The following information pertaining to May has been provided to you:

Job No.	DM	DL	Applied OH	Total Cost
67	$ 35,406	$13,840	$15,916	$ 65,162
69	109,872	14,480	16,652	141,004
70	2,436	4,000	4,600	11,036
71	308,430	57,000	?	?
72	57,690	4,400	5,060	67,150

You are informed that Job #68 had been completed in April. You are also told that Job #67 was the only job in process at the beginning of May. At that time, the job had been assigned $25,800 for DM and $7,200 for DL. At the end of May, Job #71 had not been completed; all others were complete. Answers to the following questions are required.

a. What is Chelsea Containers' predetermined OH rate?
b. What was the total cost of beginning Work in Process Inventory?
c. What were total direct manufacturing costs incurred for May?
d. What was cost of goods manufactured for May?

36. **LO.4 (Departmental rates)** All jobs at Frankfurt Inc., which uses a job order costing system, go through two departments (Fabrication and Assembly). Overhead is applied to jobs based on machine hours in Fabrication and on direct labor hours in Assembly. In December 2012, corporate management estimated the following production data for 2013 in setting its predetermined OH rates:

	Fabrication	Assembly
Machine hours	104,000	44,000
Direct labor hours	50,400	320,000
Departmental overhead	$1,560,000	$1,760,000

Two jobs completed during 2013 were #2296 and #2297. The job order cost sheets showed the following information about these jobs:

	Job #2296	Job #2297
Direct material cost	$118,500	$147,200
Direct labor hours—Fabrication	900	460
Machine hours—Fabrication	1,800	900
Direct labor hours—Assembly	850	400
Machine hours—Assembly	108	46

Direct labor workers are paid $12 per hour in the Fabrication Department and $10 per hour in the Assembly Department.

a. Compute the predetermined OH rates used in Fabrication and Assembly for 2013.
b. Compute the direct labor cost associated with each job for both departments.
c. Compute the amount of overhead assigned to each job in each department.
d. Determine the total cost of Jobs #2296 and #2297.
e. Actual data for 2013 for each department are as follows:

	Fabricating	Assembly
Machine hours	103,200	43,200
Direct labor hours	47,800	324,000
Departmental overhead	$1,528,000	$1,790,000

What is the amount of underapplied or overapplied OH for each department for the year ended December 31, 2013?

37. **LO.4 (Simple inventory calculation)** Production data for the first week in November 2013 for Florida Fabricators were as follows:

WORK IN PROCESS INVENTORY

Date	Job No.	DM	DL	Machine Time (Overhead)
Nov. 1	411	$1,900	36 hours	50 hours
1	412	1,240	10 hours	30 hours
5	417	620	8 hours	16 hours

Finished Goods Inventory, Nov. 1: $23,800
Finished Goods Inventory, Nov. 5: $0

MATERIAL RECORDS

Type	Inv. 11/1	Purchases	Issuances	Inv. 11/5
Aluminum	$ 8,300	$98,300	$58,700	$?
Steel	12,800	26,500	34,200	?
Other	5,800	23,550	25,900	?

Direct labor hours worked in the first week of November were 680 at a cost of $15 per DL hour. Machine hours worked that week were 1,200. Overhead for the first week in November was as follows:

Depreciation	$ 9,000
Supervisor salaries	14,400
Indirect labor	8,350
Insurance	2,800
Utilities	2,250
Total	$36,800

Overhead is applied to production at a rate of $30 per machine hour. Underapplied or overapplied OH is treated as an adjustment to Cost of Goods Sold at year-end.

All company jobs are consecutively numbered, and all work not in ending Finished Goods Inventory has been completed and sold. The only job in progress on November 5 was #417.

Determine the following balances on November 5:

a. the three raw material inventory accounts
b. Work in Process Inventory
c. Cost of Goods Sold

38. **LO.4 (Comprehensive)** Edward Nabors owns Enclose, which designs and manufactures perimeter fencing for large retail and commercial buildings. Each job goes through three stages: design, production, and installation. Three jobs were started and completed during the first week of May 2013. No jobs were in process at the end of April 2013. Information for the three departments for the first week in May follows.

	DEPARTMENT		
Job #2019	**Design**	**Production**	**Installation**
Direct labor hours	800	NA	760
Machine hours	NA	720	NA
Direct labor cost	$81,600	$34,000	$10,080
Direct material	$9,600	$116,400	$10,400
Job #2020	**Design**	**Production**	**Installation**
Direct labor hours	680	NA	640
Machine hours	NA	2,400	NA
Direct labor cost	$69,360	$59,600	$11,520
Direct material	$8,200	$268,800	$36,800
Job #2021	**Design**	**Production**	**Installation**
Direct labor hours	720	NA	3,280
Machine hours	NA	960	NA
Direct labor cost	$73,440	$21,600	$15,200
Direct material	$17,600	$232,000	$10,400

Overhead is applied using departmental rates. Design and Installation use direct labor cost as the base, with rates of 30 and 90 percent, respectively. Production uses machine hours as the base, with a rate of $15 per hour. Actual OH for the month was $105,600 in Design, $60,000 in Production, and $31,200 in Installation.

a. Determine the overhead to be applied to each job. By how much is the overhead underapplied or overapplied in each department? For the company?
b. Assume that no journal entries have been made to Work in Process Inventory. Journalize all necessary entries to both the subsidiary ledger and general ledger accounts. Accrue direct labor costs.
c. Calculate the total cost for each job.

39. **LO.4 (Journal entries; cost accumulation)** Stockman Co. began 2013 with three jobs in process.

	TYPE OF COST			
Job No.	**Direct Material**	**Direct Labor**	**Overhead**	**Total**
247	$ 77,200	$ 91,400	$ 36,560	$ 205,160
251	176,600	209,800	83,920	470,320
253	145,400	169,600	67,840	382,840
Totals	$399,200	$470,800	$188,320	$1,058,320

During 2013, the following transactions occurred:

1. The firm purchased and paid for $542,000 of raw material.
2. Factory payroll records revealed the following:
   - Indirect labor incurred was $54,000.
   - Direct labor incurred was $602,800 and was associated with the jobs as follows:

Job No.	Direct Labor Cost
247	$ 17,400
251	8,800
253	21,000
254	136,600
255	145,000
256	94,600
257	179,400

3. Material requisition forms issued during the year revealed the following:
   - Indirect material issued totaled $76,000.
   - Direct material issued totaled $466,400 and was associated with jobs as follows:

Job No.	Direct Material Cost
247	$ 12,400
251	6,200
253	16,800
254	105,200
255	119,800
256	72,800
257	133,200

4. Overhead is applied to jobs on the basis of direct labor cost. Management budgeted OH of $240,000 and total DL cost of $600,000 for 2013. Actual total factory OH costs (including indirect labor and indirect material) for the year totaled $244,400.
5. Jobs #247 through #255 were completed and delivered to customers, who paid for the goods in cash. The revenue on these jobs was $2,264,774.
   a. Journalize all preceding events.
   b. Determine the ending balances for the jobs still in process.
   c. Determine the cost of jobs sold, adjusted for underapplied or overapplied overhead.

40. **LO.4 (Cost accumulation; assigning costs to jobs)** Gigi LeBlanc is an advertising consultant who tracks costs for her jobs using a job order costing system. During September, LeBlanc and her staff worked on and completed jobs for the following companies:

	Reliant Company	Dumas Manufacturing	Omaha Inc.
Direct material cost	$7,800	$14,200	$19,800
Direct labor cost	$5,580	$18,000	$28,350
Number of promotions designed	3	10	8

Direct material can be traced to each job because these costs are typically associated with specific advertising campaigns. Based on historical data, LeBlanc has calculated an overhead charge of $58 per direct labor hour. The normal labor cost per hour is $45.

a. Determine the total cost for each of the advertising accounts for the month.
b. Determine the cost per promotion developed for each client. (Round to the nearest dollar.)
c. LeBlanc charges $8,600 per promotion. What was her net income for the month, assuming actual overhead for the month was $50,000? Adjust for under- or overapplied OH.
d. You suggest to LeBlanc that she bill ads on a cost-plus basis and suggest a markup of 30 percent on cost. How would her income have compared to her income computed in (c) if she had used this method? How would her clients feel about such a method?

41. **LO.4 (Journal entries; assigning costs to jobs; cost accumulation)** Ialani Corp. uses a job order costing system for the yachts it constructs. On September 1, 2013, the company had the following account balances:

Raw Material Inventory	$ 332,400
Work in Process Inventory	1,512,600
Cost of Goods Sold	4,864,000

On September 1, the three jobs in Work in Process Inventory had the following balances:

Job #75	$586,400
Job #78	266,600
Job #82	659,600

The following transactions occurred during September:

Sept. 1 Purchased $1,940,000 of raw material on account.

4 Issued $1,900,000 of raw material as follows: Job #75, $289,600; Job #78, $252,600; Job #82, $992,200; Job #86, $312,400; and indirect material, $53,200.

15 Prepared and paid the $757,000 factory payroll for September 1–15. Analysis of this payroll showed the following information:

Job #75	9,660 hours	$ 84,600
Job #78	26,320 hours	267,200
Job #82	20,300 hours	203,000
Job #86	10,280 hours	110,800
Indirect labor wages		91,400

15 On each payroll date, Ialani Corp. applies manufacturing overhead to jobs at a rate of $12.50 per direct labor hour.

15 Job #75 was completed, accepted by the customer, and billed at a selling price of cost plus 30 percent. Selling prices are rounded to the nearest whole dollar.

20 Paid the following monthly factory bills: utilities, $39,600; rent, $70,600; and accounts payable (accrued in August), $196,800.

24 Purchased raw material on account, $624,000.

25 Issued $716,400 of direct material as follows: Job #78, $154,800; Job #82, $212,600; Job #86, $349,000; indirect material issued was $55,800.

30 Recorded additional factory overhead costs as follows: depreciation, $809,000; expired prepaid insurance, $165,400; and accrued taxes and licenses, $232,400.

(Continued)

Sept. 30	Recorded and paid the factory payroll for September 16–30 of $714,400. Analysis of the payroll follows:		
	Job #78	8,940 hours	$177,400
	Job #82	13,650 hours	228,400
	Job #86	9,980 hours	243,600
	Indirect labor wages		65,000
30	Applied overhead for the second half of the month to jobs.		

a. Journalize the September transactions.
b. Use T-accounts to post the information from the journal entries in (a) to the job cost subsidiary accounts and to general ledger accounts.
c. Reconcile the September 30 balances in the subsidiary ledger with the Work in Process Inventory account in the general ledger.
d. Determine the amount of underapplied or overapplied overhead for September.

EXCEL

42. **LO.4 (Comprehensive)** Birmingham Contractors uses a job order costing system. In May 2013, the company made a $3,300,000 bid to build a pedestrian overpass over the beach highway at Gulf Shores, Alabama. Birmingham Contractors won the bid and assigned #515 to the project. Its completion date was set at December 15, 2013. The following costs were estimated for completion of the overpass: $1,240,000 for direct material, $670,000 for direct labor, and $402,000 for overhead.

During July, work began on job #515; DM cost assigned to Job #515 was $121,800, and DL cost associated with it was $175,040. The firm uses a predetermined OH rate of 60 percent of DL cost. Birmingham Contractors also worked on several other jobs during July and incurred the following costs:

Direct material (including Job #515) issued	$579,300
Direct labor (including Job #515) accrued	584,000
Indirect labor accrued	55,800
Administrative salaries and wages accrued	39,600
Depreciation on construction equipment	26,400
Depreciation on office equipment	7,800
Client entertainment (on accounts payable)	11,100
Advertising for firm (paid in cash)	6,600
Indirect material (from supplies inventory)	18,600
Miscellaneous expenses (design-related; to be paid in the following month)	10,200
Accrued utilities (for office, $1,800; for construction, $5,400)	7,200

During July, Birmingham Contractors completed several jobs that had been in process before the beginning of the month. These completed jobs sold for $1,224,000, and payment will be made to the company in August. The related job cost sheets showed costs associated with those jobs of $829,000. At the beginning of July, Birmingham Contractors had Work in Process Inventory of $871,800.

a. Prepare a job order cost sheet for Job #515, including all job details, and post the appropriate cost information for July.
b. Prepare journal entries for the preceding information.
c. Prepare a Cost of Goods Manufactured Schedule for July for Birmingham Contractors.
d. Assuming that the company pays income tax at a 40 percent rate, prepare an income statement for Birmingham Contractors.

43. **LO.4 (Journal entries)** Polaski Inc. uses an actual cost, job order system. The following transactions are for August 2013. At the beginning of the month, Direct Material Inventory was $2,000, Work in Process Inventory was $10,500, and Finished Goods Inventory was $6,500.

- Direct material purchases on account totaled $90,000.
- Direct labor cost for the period totaled $75,600 for 8,000 DL hours; these costs were paid in cash.
- Actual overhead costs were $82,000 and are applied to production.
- The ending inventory of Direct Material Inventory was $3,500.
- The ending inventory of Work in Process Inventory was $7,750.
- Goods costing $243,700 were sold for $350,400 cash.

a. What was the actual OH rate per direct labor hour?
b. Journalize the preceding transactions.
c. Determine the ending balance in Finished Goods Inventory.

44. **LO.4 (Comprehensive; job cost sheet)** Lincoln Construction Company builds bridges. In October and November 2013, the firm worked exclusively on a bridge spanning the Calamus River in northern Nebraska. Lincoln Construction's Precast Department builds structural elements of the bridges in temporary plants located near the construction sites. The Construction Department operates at the bridge site and assembles the precast structural elements. Estimated costs for the Calamus River bridge for the Precast Department were \$1,550,000 for direct material, \$220,000 for direct labor, and \$275,000 for overhead. For the Construction Department, estimated costs for the Calamus River bridge were \$350,000 for DM, \$130,000 for DL, and \$214,500 for OH. Overhead is applied on the last day of each month. Overhead application rates for the Precast and Construction departments are \$25 per machine hour and 165 percent of direct labor cost, respectively.

Transactions for October

1	Purchased \$1,150,000 of material (on account) for the Precast Department to begin building structural elements. All of the material was issued to production; of the issuances, \$650,000 was considered direct.
5	Installed utilities at the bridge site at a total cost of \$25,000. This amount will be paid at a later date.
8	Paid rent for the temporary construction site housing the Precast Department, \$5,000.
15	Completed bridge support pillars by the Precast Department and transferred to the construction site.
20	Paid machine rental expense of \$60,000 incurred by the Construction Department for clearing the bridge site and digging foundations for bridge supports.
24	Purchased additional material costing \$1,485,000 on account.
31	Paid the following bills for the Precast Department: utilities, \$7,000; direct labor, \$45,000; insurance, \$6,220; and supervision and other indirect labor costs, \$7,900. Departmental depreciation was recorded, \$15,200. The company also paid bills for the Construction Department: utilities, \$2,300; direct labor, \$16,300; indirect labor, \$5,700; and insurance, \$1,900. Departmental depreciation was recorded on equipment, \$8,750.
31	Issued a check to pay for the material purchased on October 1 and October 24.
31	Applied overhead to production in each department; 6,000 machine hours were worked in the Precast Department in October.

Transactions for November

1	Transferred additional structural elements from the Precast Department to the construction site. The Construction Department incurred a cash cost of \$5,000 to rent a crane.
4	Issued \$1,000,000 of material to the Precast Department. Of this amount, \$825,000 was considered direct.
8	Paid rent of \$5,000 in cash for the temporary site occupied by the Precast Department.
15	Issued \$425,000 of material to the Construction Department. Of this amount, \$200,000 was considered direct.
18	Transferred additional structural elements from the Precast Department to the construction site.
24	Transferred the final batch of structural elements from the Precast Department to the construction site.
29	Completed the bridge.
30	Paid final bills for the month in the Precast Department: utilities, \$15,000; direct labor, \$115,000; insurance, \$9,350; and supervision and other indirect labor costs, \$14,500. Depreciation was recorded, \$15,200. The company also paid bills for the Construction Department: utilities, \$4,900; direct labor, \$134,300; indirect labor, \$15,200; and insurance, \$5,400. Depreciation was recorded on equipment, \$18,350.

Transactions for November

30 Applied overhead in each department. The Precast Department recorded 3,950 machine hours in November.

30 Billed the state of Nebraska for the completed bridge at the contract price of $3,450,000.

a. Journalize the entries for the preceding transactions. For purposes of this problem, it is not necessary to transfer direct material and direct labor from one department to the other.
b. Post all entries to T-accounts.
c. Prepare a job order cost sheet, which includes estimated costs, for the construction of the bridge.
d. Discuss Lincoln Construction Company's estimates relative to its actual costs.

45. **LO.4 (Journal entries)** Summer Shade installs awnings on residential and commercial structures. The company had the following transactions for February 2013:

- Purchased $790,000 of building (raw) material on account.
- Issued $570,000 of building (direct) material to jobs.
- Issued $120,000 of building (indirect) material for use on jobs.
- Accrued wages payable of $874,000, of which $794,000 could be traced directly to particular jobs.
- Applied overhead to jobs on the basis of 55 percent of direct labor cost.
- Completed jobs costing $1,046,000. For these jobs, revenues of $1,342,000 were collected.

Journalize the above transactions.

46. **LO.1 & LO.4 (Comprehensive)** Pip Squeaks Inc. is a manufacturer of furnishings for infants and children. The company uses a job order costing system. Pip Squeaks' Work in Process Inventory on April 30, 2013, consisted of the following jobs:

Job No.	Items	Units	Accumulated Cost
CBS102	Cribs	20,000	$ 900,000
PLP086	Playpens	15,000	420,000
DRS114	Dressers	25,000	1,570,000

The company's Finished Goods Inventory, carried on a FIFO (first-in, first-out) basis, consists of five items:

Item	Quantity and Unit Cost	Total Cost
Cribs	7,500 units × $64	$ 480,000
Strollers	13,000 units × $23	299,000
Carriages	11,200 units × $102	1,142,400
Dressers	21,000 units × $55	1,155,000
Playpens	19,400 units × $35	679,000
Total		$3,755,400

Pip Squeaks applies factory overhead on the basis of direct labor hours. The company's factory OH budget for the fiscal year ending May 31, 2013, totaled $4,500,000, and the company planned to work 600,000 DL hours during this year. Through the first 11 months of the year, a total of 555,000 DL hours were worked, and total factory OH amounted to $4,273,500.

At the end of April, the balance in Pip Squeaks' Raw Material Inventory account, which includes both raw material and purchased parts, was $668,000. Additions to and requisitions from the material inventory during May included the following:

	Raw Material	Parts Purchased
Additions	$242,000	$396,000
Requisitions:		
Job #CBS102	51,000	104,000
Job #PLP086	3,000	10,800

	Raw Material	Parts Purchased
Job #DRS114	124,000	87,000
Job #STR077 (10,000 strollers)	62,000	81,000
Job #CRG098 (5,000 carriages)	65,000	187,000

During May, Pip Squeaks' factory payroll consisted of the following:

Job No.	Hours	Cost
CBS102	12,000	$122,400
PLP086	4,400	43,200
DRS114	19,500	200,500
STR077	3,500	30,000
CRG098	14,000	138,000
Indirect	3,000	29,400
Supervision		57,600
Total		$621,100

The jobs that were completed in May and the unit sales for May are as follows:

Job No.	Items	Quantity Completed
CBS102	Cribs	20,000
PLP086	Playpens	15,000
STR077	Strollers	10,000
CRG098	Carriages	5,000

Items	Quantity Shipped
Cribs	17,500
Playpens	21,000
Strollers	14,000
Dressers	18,000
Carriages	6,000

a. Describe when it is appropriate for a company to use a job order costing system.
b. Calculate the dollar balance in Pip Squeaks' Work in Process Inventory account as of May 31, 2013.
c. Calculate the dollar amount related to the playpens in Pip Squeaks' Finished Goods Inventory as of May 31, 2013.
d. Explain the treatment of underapplied or overapplied overhead when using a job order costing system.

CMA ADAPTED

47. **LO.4 (Missing amounts)** Riveredge Manufacturing Company realized too late that it had made a mistake locating its controller's office and its electronic data processing system in the basement. Because of the spring thaw, the Mississippi River overflowed its banks on May 2 and flooded the company's basement. Electronic data storage was destroyed, and the company had not provided off-site storage of data. Some of the paper printouts were located but were badly faded and only partially legible. On May 3, when the flooding subsided, company accountants were able to assemble the following factory-related data from the debris and from discussions with various knowledgeable personnel. Data about the following accounts were found:

EXCEL

- Raw Material (includes indirect material) Inventory: Balance April 1 was $9,600.
- Work in Process Inventory: Balance April 1 was $15,400.
- Finished Goods Inventory: Balance April 30 was $13,200.
- Total company payroll cost for April was $58,400.
- Accounts payable balance April 30 was $36,000.
- Indirect material used in April cost $11,600.
- Other nonmaterial and nonlabor overhead items for April totaled $5,000.

Payroll records, kept at an across-town service center that processes the company's payroll, showed that April's direct labor amounted to $36,400 and represented 8,800 labor hours. Indirect factory labor amounted to $10,800 in April.

The president's office had a file copy of the production budget for the current year. It revealed that the predetermined OH rate is based on planned annual DL hours of 100,800 and expected factory OH of $302,400.

Discussion with the factory superintendent indicated that only two jobs remained unfinished on April 30. Fortunately, the superintendent also had copies of the job cost sheets that showed a combined total of $4,800 of DM and $9,000 of DL. The DL hours on these jobs totaled 2,144. Both of these jobs had been started during April.

A badly faded copy of April's Cost of Goods Manufactured and Sold Schedule showed cost of goods manufactured was $96,000, and the April 1 Finished Goods Inventory was $16,800.

The treasurer's office files copies of paid invoices chronologically. All invoices are for raw material purchased on account. Examination of these files revealed that unpaid invoices on April 1 amounted to $12,200; $56,000 of purchases had been made during April; and $36,000 of unpaid invoices existed on April 30.

a. Calculate the cost of direct material used in April.
b. Calculate the cost of raw material issued in April.
c. Calculate the April 30 balance of Raw Material Inventory.
d. Determine the amount of underapplied or overapplied overhead for April.
e. What is the Cost of Goods Sold for April?

ETHICS

48. **LO.5 (Ethics; writing)** One of the main reasons for using a job order costing system is to achieve profitability by charging a price for each job that is proportionate to the related costs. The fundamental underlying concept is that the buyer of the product should be charged a price that exceeds all costs related to the job contract; thus, the price reflects the cost.

However, there are settings in which the price charged to the consumer does not reflect the costs incurred by the vendor to serve that customer. A case heard by the U.S. Supreme Court involved the University of Wisconsin, which charged all students a user fee and then redistributed the fees to student organizations.

The purpose of collecting the fee is to ensure that money is available to support diversity of thought and speech in student organizations. The user fee supports even unpopular causes so that the students hear a variety of voices. In total, the fee subsidized about 125 student groups. However, a group of students filed suit, claiming that students should not be required to fund causes that are inconsistent with their personal beliefs.

a. In your opinion, how would diversity of thought be affected if a student were allowed to select the organizations that would receive the student's user fee (e.g., as with dues)?
b. Is the University of Wisconsin treating its students ethically by charging them to support student organizations for causes that conflict with their personal beliefs?

INTERNET

49. **LO.5 (Research; quality; writing)** Timbuk2 is a San Francisco company that makes a variety of messenger, cyclist, and laptop bags. The company's Web site (Timbuk2.com) allows customers to design their own size, color, and fabric bags with specific features and accessories; then the company sews the bags to the customers' specifications.

a. Visit the company's Web site and custom-design a bag. Compare the quoted price with a bag of similar quality and features at a local store. Explain whether you think the Timbuk2 bag is a good value.
b. Why would Timbuk2 be able to produce custom-made messenger bags for almost the same cost as mass-produced ones?
c. Would you expect the quality of the custom-produced messenger bags to be higher or lower than the mass-produced ones? Discuss the rationale for your answer.
d. Why would the custom-made messenger bags show a high profit margin?

ETHICS

50. **LO.5 (Ethics; writing)** Two types of contracts are commonly used when private firms contract to provide services to governmental agencies: cost-plus and fixed-price contracts. The cost-plus contract allows the contracting firm to recover the costs associated

with providing the product or service plus a reasonable profit. The fixed-price contract provides for a fixed payment to the contractor. When a fixed-price contract is used, the contractor's profits are based on its ability to control costs relative to the price received.

In recent years, a number of contractors have either been accused, or found guilty, of improper accounting or fraud in accounting for contracts with the government. One deceptive accounting technique that is sometimes the subject of audit investigations involves cases in which a contractor is suspected of shifting costs from fixed-priced contracts to cost-plus contracts. In shifting costs from the fixed-priced contract, the contractor not only influences costs assigned to that contract but also receives a reimbursement plus an additional amount on the costs shifted to the cost-plus contract.

a. Why would a company that conducts work under both cost-plus and fixed-price contracts have an incentive to shift costs from the fixed-price to the cost-plus contracts?
b. From an ethical perspective, do you believe such cost shifting is ever justified? Explain.

51. **LO.6 (Defective units and rework)** PlastiCo produces plastic pipe to customer specifications. Losses of less than 5 percent are considered normal because they are inherent in the production process. The company applies overhead to products using machine hours. PlastiCo used the following information in setting its predetermined OH rate for 2013:

Expected overhead other than rework	$850,000
Expected rework costs	75,000
Total expected overhead	$925,000
Expected machine hours for 2013	100,000

During 2013, the following production and cost data were accumulated:

Total good production completed	2,000,000 feet of pipe
Total defects	40,000 feet of pipe
Ending inventory	75,000 feet of pipe
Total cost of direct material for Job #B316	$687,100
Total cost of direct labor for Job #B316	$157,750
Total machine hours for Job #B316	3,080
Cost of reworking defects during 2013	$75,500
Total actual overhead cost for 2013	$862,000

a. Determine the overhead application rate for 2013.
b. Determine the cost for Job #B316 in 2013.
c. Assume that the rework is normal and those units can be sold for the regular selling price. How will PlastiCo account for the $75,500 of rework cost?
d. Assume that PlastiCo does not include rework costs in developing the overhead application rate because rework is related to specific jobs. Determine the cost of Job #B316.
e. Using the information from (d), assume that 20 percent of the rework cost was specifically related to 200 feet of pipe produced for Job #B316. The reworked pipe can be sold for $3.50 per foot. What is the total cost of Job #B316?

52. **LO.6 (Defective units and rework)** Prudoe Compounds produces a variety of chemicals used by auto manufacturers in their painting processes. With each batch of chemicals produced, some spoilage naturally occurs. Prudoe Compounds includes normal spoilage cost in its predetermined OH rate. For 2013, Prudoe Compounds estimated the following:

Overhead costs, other than spoilage	$600,000
Estimated spoilage cost	50,000
Estimated sales value of spoiled materials	20,000
Estimated direct labor hours	40,000

a. Prudoe Compounds applies overhead based on direct labor hours. Calculate the predetermined OH rate for 2013.

b. For a batch of chemicals mixed in May 2013, the firm experienced normal spoilage on Job #788. The cost of the spoiled material amounted to $1,730 and the company estimated the salvage value of those materials to be $496. Journalize the entry for the spoilage.

53. **LO.7 (Appendix; standard costing)** During July 2013, Pull-Along worked on two production runs (Jobs #918 and #2002) of the same product, a trailer hitch component. Job #918 consisted of 1,200 units of the product, and Job #2002 contained 2,000 units. The hitch components are made from sheet metal. Because this component is routinely produced for one of Pull-Along's long-term customers, standard costs have been developed for its production. The standard cost of material for each unit is $18; each unit contains six pounds of material at standard. The standard direct labor time per unit is 12 minutes for workers earning a standard rate of $20 per hour. The actual costs recorded for each job were as follows:

	Direct Material	Direct Labor
Job #918	(7,300 pounds) $23,525	(230 hours) $4,840
Job #2002	(11,900 pounds) 37,440	(405 hours) 7,850

a. What is the standard direct cost of each trailer hitch component?
b. What was the total standard direct cost assigned to each of the jobs?
c. Compute the variances for direct material and for direct labor for each job.
d. Why should variances be computed separately for each job rather than for the aggregate annual trailer hitch component production?

54. **LO.7 (Appendix; standard costing)** Modern Convenience specializes in making robotic conveyor systems to move materials within a factory. Model #89 accounts for approximately 60 percent of the company's annual sales. Because the company has produced and expects to continue to produce a significant quantity of this model, Modern Convenience uses the following standard costs to account for Model #89 production costs:

Direct material (28,000 pounds)	$ 56,000
Direct labor (1,720 hours at $20 per hour)	34,400
Overhead	76,000
Total standard cost	$166,400

For the 200 units of Model #89 produced in 2013, the actual costs were

Direct material (6,000,000 pounds)	$11,600,000
Direct labor (178,400 hours)	6,957,600
Overhead	14,800,000
Total actual cost	$33,357,600

a. Compute a separate variance between actual and standard cost for direct material, direct labor, and manufacturing overhead for the Model #89 units produced in 2013.
b. Is the direct material variance found in (a) driven primarily by the price per pound difference between standard and actual or the quantity difference between standard and actual? Explain.

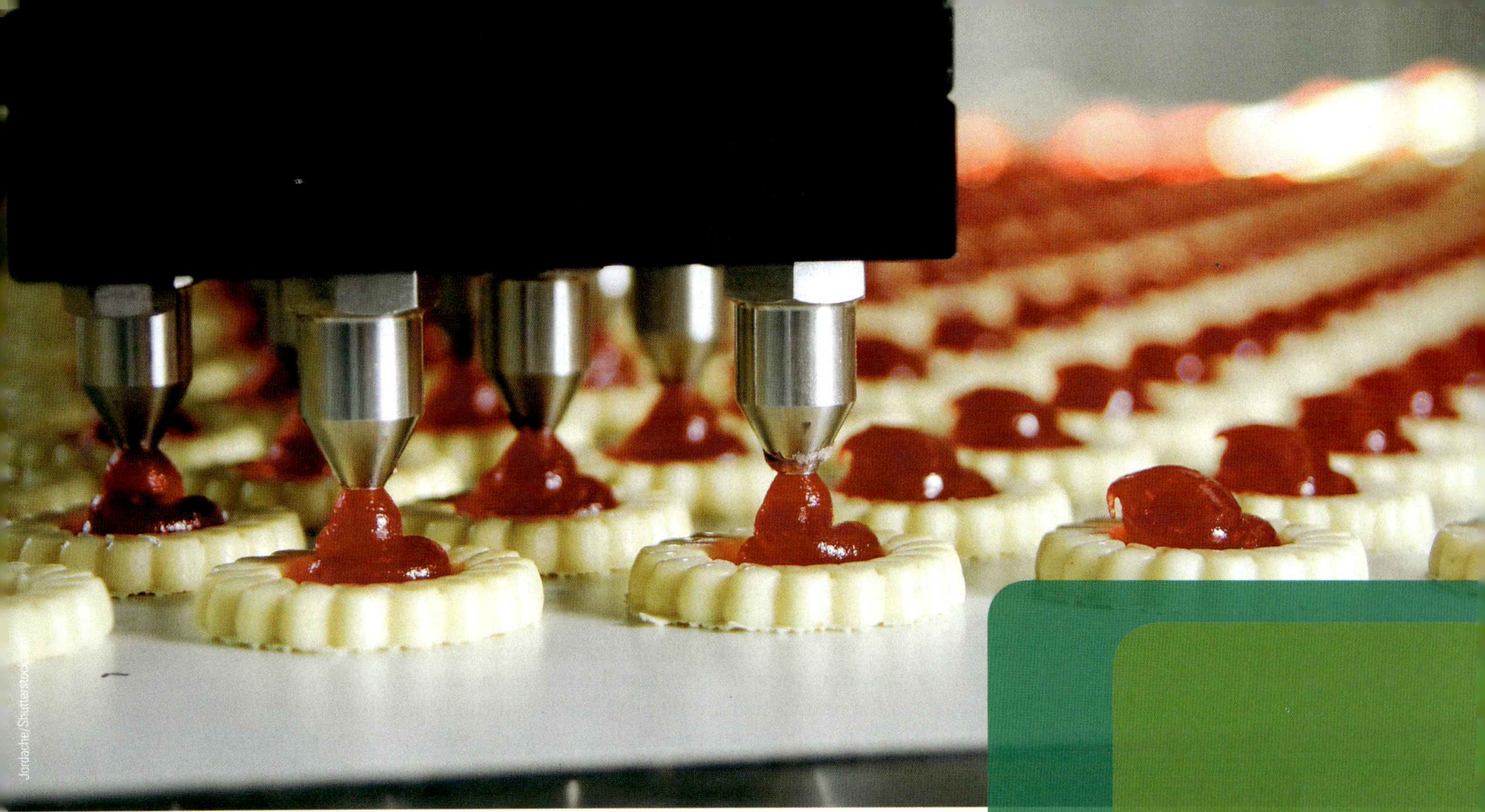

6

Process Costing

LEARNING OBJECTIVES

After completing this chapter, you should be able to answer the following questions:

1 Why are equivalent units of production used in process costing?

2 How are equivalent units of production, unit costs, and inventory values determined using the weighted average (WA) method of process costing?

3 How are equivalent units of production, unit costs, and inventory values determined using the first-in, first-out (FIFO) method of process costing?

4 How are transferred-in costs and units accounted for in a multidepartment production setting?

5 Why would a company use a hybrid costing system?

6 (*Appendix 1*) What alternative methods can be used to calculate equivalent units of production?

7 (*Appendix 2*) How are equivalent units of production, unit costs, and inventory values determined using the standard costing method of process costing?

8 (*Appendix 3*) How are normal and abnormal spoilage losses treated in an equivalent units of production schedule?

INTRODUCTION

Companies choose product costing systems based, in part, on the types of products manufactured and services offered. As discussed in Chapter 5, companies that manufacture products or perform services conforming to distinct customer specifications and made in limited quantities use job order costing. However, some companies manufacture products in a continuous flow process or in batches of output containing units that are identical. Manufacturers of food products, bricks, gasoline, candles, and paper, among many other types of firms, commonly use the process costing method. For example, **Kellogg's** produces Rice Krispies in batches, and all "rice puffs" in each batch are the same. For Kellogg's Pop-Tarts, the external pastry is the same for all batches, but the flavoring inside may differ or some external pastries may be frosted while others are not. Kellogg's uses a process costing rather than a job order costing system to accumulate and assign costs to units of production.

Both job order and process costing systems accumulate costs by cost component (direct material, direct labor, and overhead) in each production department. However, the two systems assign costs to departmental output differently. In a job order system, costs are assigned to specific jobs and, if possible, to the units contained within each job. Process costing uses an averaging technique to assign costs to all units produced during the period. In both systems, unit costs are transferred between departments as goods flow from one department to the next so that a total production cost can be accumulated.

This chapter first illustrates the weighted average (WA) and first-in, first-out (FIFO) methods of calculating unit cost in a process costing system. These two methods differ only in the treatment of beginning Work in Process (WIP) Inventory units and costs. After unit cost has been determined, a total cost is assigned to (1) units transferred out of a department and (2) that department's ending WIP Inventory.

The chapter also describes the use of process costing in multidepartment organizations and hybrid systems. Hybrid systems are used in some companies that customize products that would commonly be accounted for using a process costing system. Appendix 1 provides alternative computations for equivalent unit of product calculations. Appendix 2 describes how standard costing systems are used as a simplification of the FIFO process costing system. Appendix 3 briefly introduces the issue of accounting for spoilage in a process costing system.

INTRODUCTION TO PROCESS COSTING

Assigning costs to product units requires the use of an averaging process. In the easiest situation, a product's actual unit cost is found by dividing a period's departmental production costs by that period's departmental production quantity as expressed by the following formula:

$$\text{Unit cost} = \frac{\text{Production costs}}{\text{Production quantity}}$$

Production Costs: The Numerator

The formula numerator is obtained by accumulating departmental costs incurred in a single period. Because most companies make more than one type of product, costs must be accumulated by product within each department. The accumulation can occur by using either separate WIP Inventory accounts for each product or a single WIP Inventory control account that is supported by detailed subsidiary ledgers containing specific product information.

Cost accumulation in a process costing system differs from that in a job order costing system in two ways:

- the quantity of products for which costs are accumulated and
- the cost object to which the costs are assigned.

Production System	Quantity	Cost Object
Job Order	Small	Specific customer's job
Process	Large	Production run by department

The Candle Shop, which manufactures scented candles for two different customer groups, is used to illustrate the differences. In addition to its daily operations of making votive, 7-inch, and 12-inch taper candles, the company periodically contracts to make custom candles for client promotional activities. For its basic product lines, The Candle Shop uses a process costing system to accumulate periodic costs for each department and each product type. Because the company manufactures several types of candles each period, the costs assignable to each product type must be individually designated and attached to the specific production runs. Production run costs are then assigned to the units processed during the period. In contrast, for specialty candle production, The Candle Shop uses job order costing to accumulate direct material and direct labor costs associated with each distinctive order and assigns those costs directly to the individual customer's job; overhead is allocated using a predetermined overhead rate. After each job is completed, the total material, labor, and allocated overhead costs are known and job cost can be determined.

Exhibit 6.1 presents the source documents used to make initial cost assignments to production departments during a period. Costs are reassigned at the end of the period (usually each month) from the departments to the units produced. As goods are transferred from one department to the next, related departmental production costs are also transferred. When products are complete, their costs are transferred from WIP Inventory to Finished Goods (FG) Inventory.

Exhibit 6.1 Cost Flows and Cost Assignment

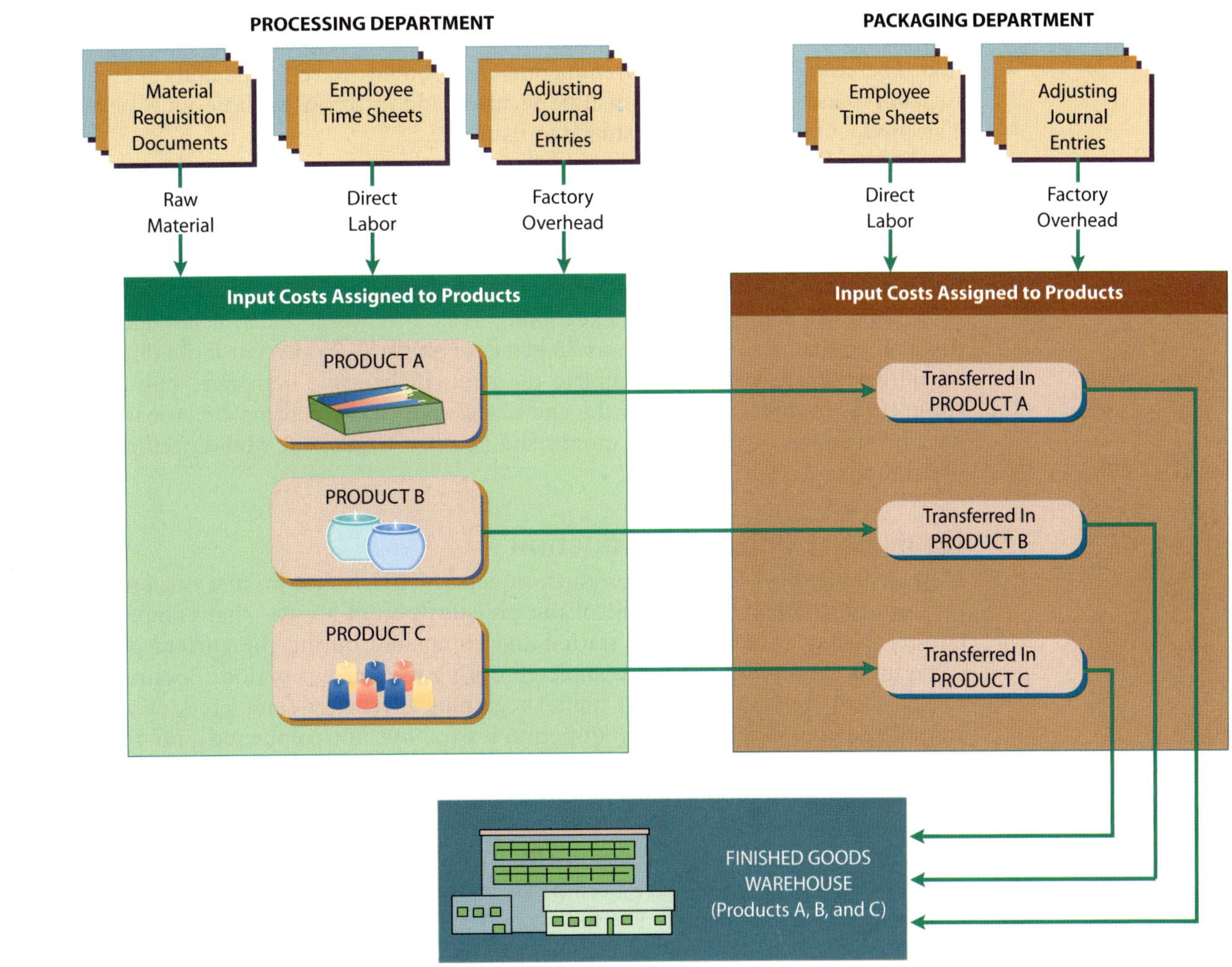

As in job order costing, direct material and direct labor costs present relatively few problems for cost accumulation and assignment in a process costing system. Direct material cost can be measured from material requisition slips; direct labor cost can be determined from employee time sheets (or time clock systems) and wage rates for the period. Overhead, however, must be allocated to output. If total overhead costs are relatively constant and production volume is relatively steady between periods, actual overhead costs may be used for product costing. Otherwise, as discussed in Chapter 3, using actual overhead for product costing would result in fluctuating unit costs, and therefore, usage of predetermined application rates is more appropriate. As costs and production activities change, the base on which overhead is assigned to production may shift. For example, as a production plant becomes less labor intensive and more automated, management should change from a labor-based to a machine-based overhead allocation.

Production Quantity: The Denominator

1 Why are equivalent units of production used in process costing?

The denominator in the unit cost formula represents total departmental production of a given product for the period. If all units started during a period were 100 percent complete at the end of the period, units could simply be counted to obtain the denominator. In most production processes, however, partially completed units comprise WIP Inventory at the end of one period and the beginning WIP Inventory of the next period. Process costing assigns costs to both fully and partially completed units by mathematically converting partially completed units to equivalent whole units.

Units in beginning WIP Inventory were started last period but will be completed during the current period. This two-period production sequence means that some costs for the units in beginning inventory were incurred last period and additional costs for those units will be incurred in the current period. Additionally, the partially completed units in ending WIP Inventory were started in the current period but will not be completed until next period. Therefore, some of the current period costs should attach to the units in ending WIP Inventory, and additional costs will be incurred and attached to those units next period. This production sequence is illustrated in Exhibit 6.2.

Ending WIP Inventory units must be physically inspected to determine the percentage of completion of each cost component (direct material, direct labor, and overhead) for the current period. One hundred percent minus each of these percentages represents the proportion of work to be completed on the different costs components in a future period. Inspection at the end of last period provided information on the proportion of work to be completed this period on beginning WIP Inventory. Thus, if last month it was determined that direct material was 75 percent complete, 25 percent more direct material would have been needed to complete the item. If the same item were only 90 percent complete as to direct material at the end of this month, 15 percent direct material would have been added in the current month and another 10 percent would need to be added next month.

Equivalent Units of Production

Units typically flow through a production department in first-in, first-out order. Goods that were incomplete at the end of the previous period are the first completed in the current period; other units are started and completed during the current period; and, some units are started but not completed during the current period. Because manufacturing efforts relate to different units (beginning inventory completed, current period started and completed, and current period started but not completed), production cannot be measured by counting only whole units. Accountants use a concept known as equivalent units of production to measure the quantity of production achieved during a period.

Equivalent units of production (EUP) are approximations of the number of whole units of output that could have been produced during a period from the actual resources expended during that period. The following simple example indicates how EUP are calculated. Assume The Candle Shop had no WIP Inventory on November 1. During November, the company worked on 220,000 units: 200,000 units were fully completed and

Exhibit 6.2 Two-Period Production Sequence

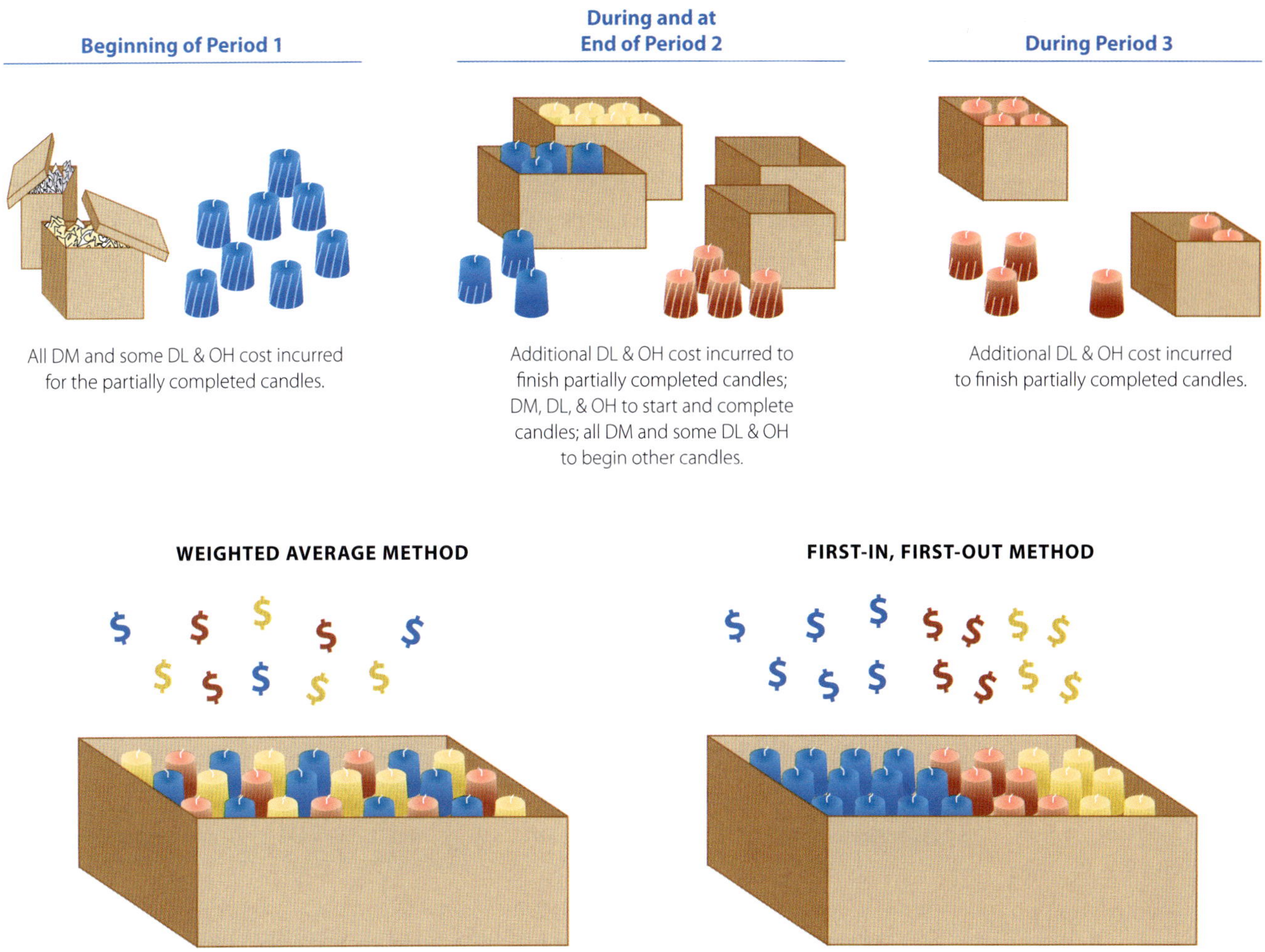

DM = Direct Material
DL = Direct Labor
OH = Overhead

20,000 units were 40 percent complete at the end of the period. The EUP for the period are as follows:

EUP = BI units completed + Units started and completed + EI units partially complete
EUP = 0 + [(200,000 × 100%)] + [(20,000 × 40%)]
EUP = 208,000

Some quantity of direct material must be introduced at the start of production to begin the conversion process. For example, to make its various products, The Candle Shop's production process begins with candle wax. Any material added at the start of production is 100 percent complete at the outset of the process, regardless of the percentage of completion of labor and overhead.

Most production processes require multiple direct materials. Additional materials may be added at any point or even continuously during processing. A direct material, such as a box, may even be added at the end of processing. Until the end of the production process, the product would be zero percent complete as to the box but may be totally complete with regard to other materials. The Candle Shop's production process occurs as follows:

- Wicks and wax are added at the beginning of the process. Thus, these materials are 100 percent complete at any point in the process after the start of production; no additional quantities of these materials are added later in production.

- When enough labor and overhead have been added to reach the 20 percent completion point, additional materials (color and scent) are added. Prior to 20 percent completion, these materials were 0 percent complete; after the 20 percent point, these materials are 100 percent complete.
- Almost at the end of the process, the candles are boxed and, after this step, the product is 100 percent complete. Thus, boxes are 0 percent complete until the candles are packaged; after packaging, the product is complete and transferred to the finished goods warehouse or directly to customers.

The production flow for candles is shown in Exhibit 6.3 and visually illustrates the need for separate EUP computations for each cost component.

Exhibit 6.3 Candle Manufacturing Process—Production Department

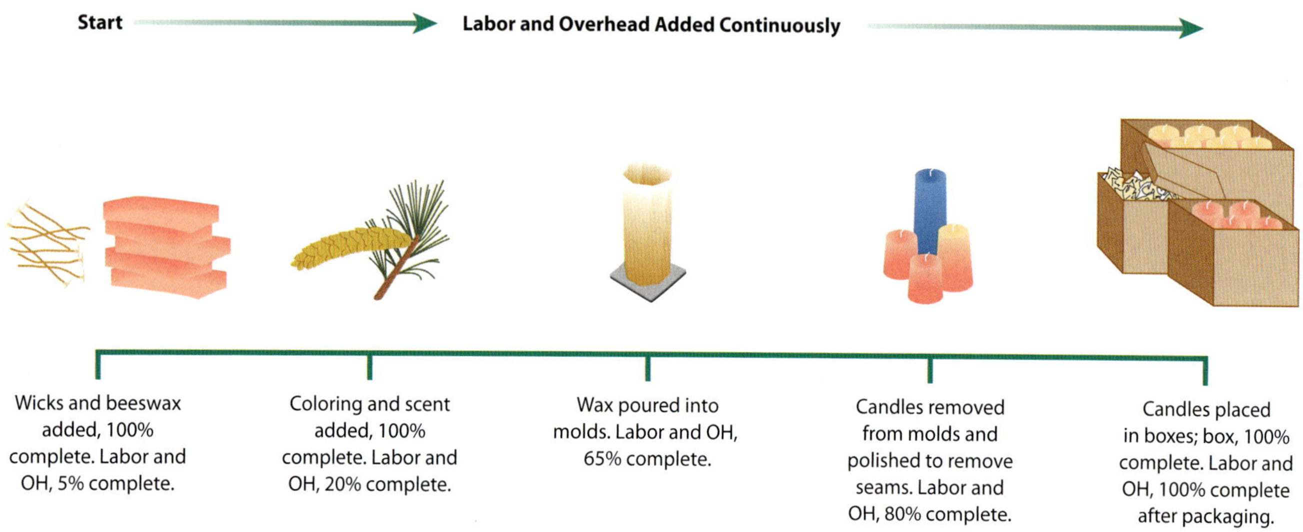

Assume that enough wicks and wax are started to make 8,000 candles. At the end of the period, the process is 75 percent complete as to labor and overhead. The candles are 100 percent complete as to wicks, wax, color, and scent, but 0 percent complete as to boxes. The materials EUP calculations indicate that there are 8,000 EUP for wicks, wax, color, and scent and 0 EUP for boxes. The labor and overhead (conversion) cost components have an equivalency of 6,000 candles because the candles are 75 percent complete and labor and overhead are added continuously during the process.[1]

When overhead is applied on a direct labor basis, or when direct labor and overhead are added to the product at the same rate, a single percentage of completion can be used for both conversion cost components. However, because cost drivers other than direct labor are increasingly being used to apply overhead costs, single computations for "conversion EUP" are being made less often. For example, the cost driver for the utilities portion of overhead cost may be machine hours and the cost driver for materials handling may be pounds of material. Accumulating costs using the activity-based costing concepts discussed in Chapter 4 makes it less likely that the degrees of completion for direct labor and overhead will be equal.

[1] Although the same number of equivalent units results for wicks, wax, color, and scent and for labor and overhead, separate calculations of unit cost may be desirable for each cost component. These separate calculations would give managers more information for planning and control purposes. Managers must weigh the costs of making separate calculations against the benefits of having the additional information. For illustrative purposes, however, single computations will be made when cost components are at equal percentages of completion.

WEIGHTED AVERAGE AND FIRST-IN, FIRST-OUT PROCESS COSTING METHODS

The two methods of accounting for cost flows in process costing are

- weighted average (WA) and
- first-in, first-out (FIFO).

These methods reflect the way in which cost flows are assumed to occur in the production process. In a very general way, these process costing approaches can be related to the cost flow methods used in financial accounting.

Some retail businesses use the WA method to determine an average cost per unit of inventory. This cost is computed by dividing the total cost of goods available for sale by the total units available for sale. Total cost and total units are found by adding the total purchase price and units purchased to those of beginning inventory. Costs and units of the current period are not distinguished in any way from those on hand at the end of the prior period. In contrast, other retail businesses use the FIFO method of accounting for merchandise inventory, which separates goods according to when they were purchased and at what cost.[2] Using the FIFO method, beginning inventory costs are the first sent to Cost of Goods Sold, with other costs following in the order in which they were incurred; units remaining in the ending inventory are assigned costs based on the most recent purchases.

Use of these methods for costing a manufacturing firm's production is similar to their use by a retailer. The **weighted average method** computes a single average cost per unit of the combined beginning WIP Inventory and current period production. The **first-in, first-out method** separates beginning WIP Inventory and current period production as well as their costs so that a *current period* cost per unit can be calculated. The denominator in the EUP cost formula differs, depending on which of the two methods is used.[3]

Costing Method	Units and Costs	Cost per Unit
Weighted average	BI + Current period production and costs	Average cost for all EUP worked on during the period
First-in, first-out	BI separated from current period production and costs	Separate costs for BI units and units started during the period

Calculation of a unit product cost is essential for determining the journal entry amount to be transferred as goods move between departments as well as for preparing the financial statements (containing WIP Inventory, FG Inventory, and Cost of Goods Sold). To make such a calculation requires the specification of either the WA or FIFO process cost flow method.

As with cost flow assumptions used in retail inventory, the choice to use the weighted average or first-in, first-out method depends on the type of information needed by management. The WA method provides a reasonable approximation of unit costs if inventory quantities are fairly constant and costs remain fairly steady over time. In such circumstances, the difference between the WA and FIFO inventory costs will be immaterial and management may choose the WA method because of its ease of calculation. If, however, inventory quantities and costs have a high level of variability, the FIFO method will provide better information about periodic changes on unit costs.

Exhibit 6.4 (p. 198) outlines the steps necessary in a process costing system for determining the costs assignable to the units completed and to those still in WIP inventory at the end of a period. Each of these steps is discussed, and then a complete example is provided for both WA and FIFO costing.

[2]Retail businesses also may use the last-in, first-out method. However, LIFO is not appropriate for process costing production environments.

[3]Note that the term *denominator* is used here rather than equivalent units of production. Based on its definition, EUP are related to current period production activity. Thus, for any given set of production facts, there is only one true measure of equivalent units produced—regardless of the cost flow assumption used—and that measure is FIFO EUP. However, this fact has been obscured over time due to the continued references to the "EUP" computation for weighted average. Thus, the term *EUP* has taken on a generic use to mean "the denominator used to compute the unit cost of production for a period in a process costing system." EUP is used in this generic manner throughout the process costing discussion.

Exhibit 6.4 Steps in Process Costing

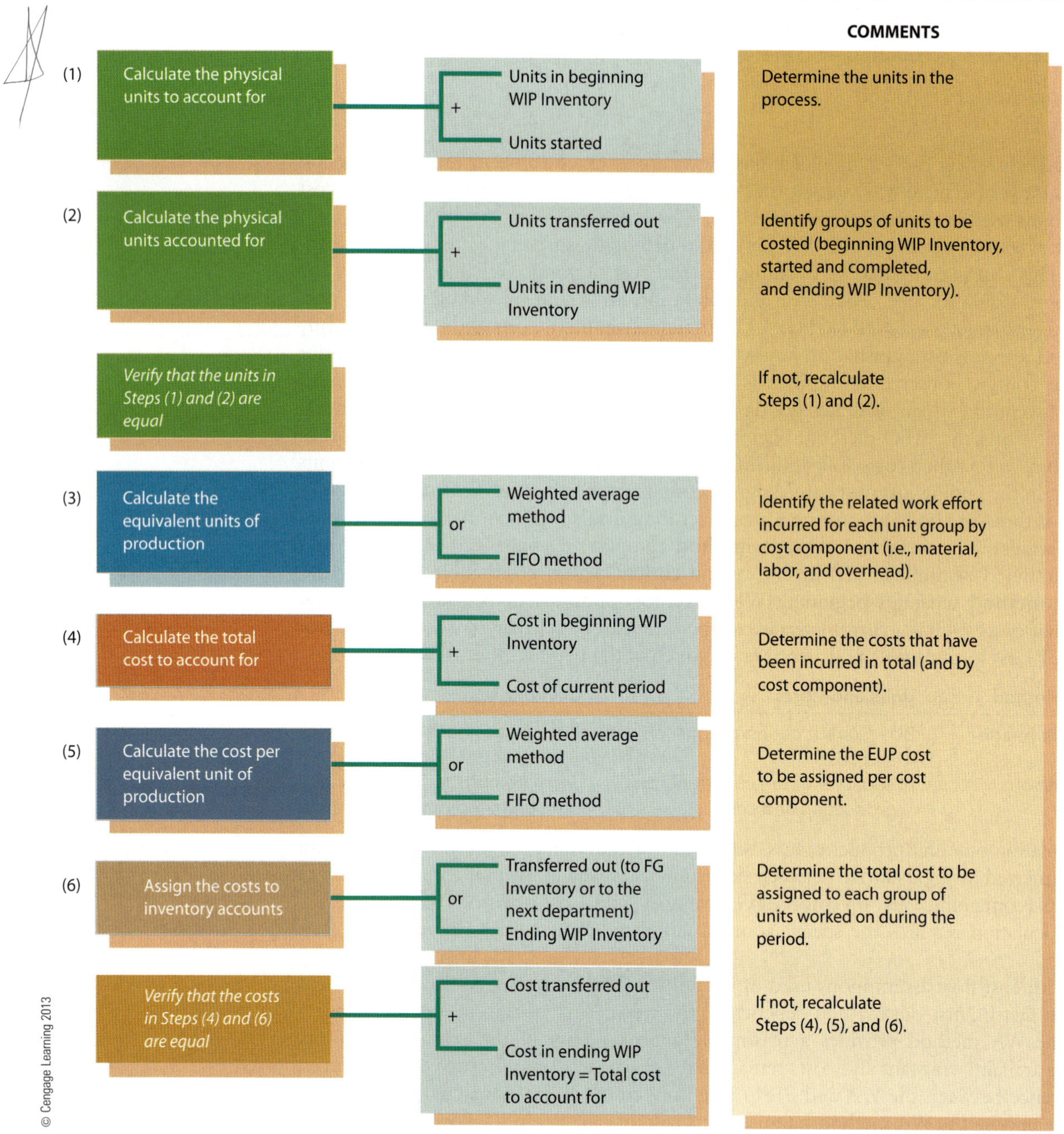

1. Determine the total actual physical (whole) units for which the department is responsible. This amount is the sum of fully and partially completed units processed in the department during the current period:

$$\text{Total units} = \text{Beginning WIP Inventory units} + \text{Units started this period}$$

2. Calculate the total physical units accounted for, which requires determining what happened to the units during the period. At period-end, the total physical units will be either (1) completed and transferred out or (2) partially completed and remaining in ending WIP Inventory.[4]

$$\text{Total units} = \text{Completed units} + \text{Partially completed units in ending WIP Inventory}$$

[4] A third category (spoilage/breakage) does exist. It is assumed at this point that no production losses occur. Appendix 3 to this chapter provides a discussion of spoilage in process costing situations.

Verify that the total physical units for which the department is responsible is equal to the total physical units accounted for. If these amounts are not equal, any additional computations will be incorrect.

3. At this point, because of the lack of similarity in the work performed on completed and partially completed units, physical units are converted (using either the WA or FIFO method) to equivalent units of production using the percentage of completion for each cost component. If all direct material is added at the same stage of completion, a single computation for direct material can be made. If multiple materials are used but placed into production at different points in the production process, multiple direct material EUP calculations are necessary. If overhead is based on direct labor or if these two factors are always at the same degree of completion, a single EUP can be computed for conversion. If neither condition exists, separate EUP schedules must be prepared for labor and overhead.[5]
4. Find the **total cost to account for**, which is the beginning balance in WIP Inventory plus all current costs for direct material, direct labor, and overhead.

   Total cost to account for = Beginning WIP \$ + Current \$ for DM, DL, and OH

5. Using either the WA or the FIFO equivalent units of production calculated in step 3, calculate the cost per equivalent unit for each cost component.
6. Use the unit costs computed in step 5 to assign production costs to units completed and transferred out of WIP Inventory and to units remaining in WIP Inventory.

   Total cost to account for = Total \$ transferred out of WIP + Ending WIP \$

   Verify that the total of the cost assigned to the units transferred out of WIP Inventory plus the cost of the units remaining in WIP Inventory is equal to the total cost to account for in step 4. If these amounts are not equal (with the exception of small rounding differences), an error has been made in the computations.

Production information for The Candle Shop is used to demonstrate the steps involved in EUP computation and cost assignment for both methods of process costing. The Candle Shop makes a 7-inch unscented pillar candle that is popular with restaurants and hotels because it minimizes customer allergy concerns. The company manufactures this product in one department with a single direct material: wax. Costs of wicks and coloring are insignificant and are considered indirect materials and part of overhead. Candles are shipped in reusable containers to a central warehouse. From there, candles are distributed to wholesalers and retailers who supply their own containers. Wax is added at the start of processing, so all units in process are 100 percent complete as to this material. Labor and overhead are assumed to be at the same degree of completion throughout the production process. Overhead costs for The Candle Shop are exceptionally stable, so actual overhead is assigned to production at the end of each period. Exhibit 6.5 (p. 200) presents April 2013 information regarding The Candle Shop's inventories and costs.

Although the exhibit provides information on both the quantity of candles transferred out and the quantity in the ending WIP Inventory, both quantities do not have to be explicitly stated. The number of candles remaining in the ending WIP Inventory can be calculated as total candles to account for minus the candles that were completed and transferred to FG Inventory during the period. Alternatively, the number of candles transferred to FG Inventory can be calculated as the total candles to account for minus the candles in ending WIP Inventory.

Next, The Candle Shop information is used to illustrate each step listed in Exhibit 6.4.

[5] As discussed in Chapters 3 and 4, overhead can be applied to products using a variety of traditional (e.g., direct labor hours or machine hours) or nontraditional (e.g., number of machine setups, pounds of material moved, or number of material requisitions) bases. The number of equivalent unit computations required depends on the number of different cost pools and overhead allocation bases established in the organization. In some highly automated manufacturers, a direct labor cost component may not be used because the cost is so nominal that it is included in a conversion category rather than being accounted for separately.

Exhibit 6.5 Production and Cost Information for The Candle Shop for April 2013

Candles in beginning WIP Inventory (40% complete as to labor and overhead or conversion)			10,000
Candles started during current period			401,400
Candles completed and transferred to FG Inventory			406,000
Candles in ending WIP Inventory (80% complete as to labor and overhead or conversion)			5,400
Costs of beginning WIP Inventory			
Direct material	$ 11,886		
Direct labor	5,658		
Overhead	19,858	$ 37,402	
Current period costs			
Direct material	$642,240		
Direct labor	122,638		
Overhead	385,262	1,150,140	
Total cost to account for		$1,187,542	

2 How are equivalent units of production, unit costs, and inventory values determined using the weighted average (WA) method of process costing?

Weighted Average Method

Step 1: Calculate the Total Physical Units to Account For The **total units to account for** is the sum of the physical units in the beginning inventory plus the physical units started during the current period.

Candles in beginning WIP Inventory	10,000
Candles started during current period	401,400
Candles to account for	411,400

Step 2: Calculate the Physical Units Accounted For The items detailed in this step indicate the categories, but not the quantities, to which costs will be assigned in the final step. Cost assignment will be based on equivalent units whereas this step is based on actual physical units. The number of candles accounted for in step 2 equals the number of candles to account for in step 1.

Candles completed and transferred to FG Inventory	406,000
Candles in ending WIP Inventory	5,400
Candles accounted for	411,400

Step 3: Calculate the Equivalent Units of Production The WA EUP computation focuses on two items: (1) the number of candles in the beginning WIP inventory and (2) the number of candles started and completed during the period. Of the total units transferred out of WIP Inventory, some units had been part of beginning inventory while others were started and completed within the current period. Thus, the **units started and completed** during a period equal the units completed during the period minus units in the beginning inventory. Units started and completed can also be computed as units started during the period minus the units in the ending inventory. Exhibit 6.6 illustrates the concepts of total units to account for, total units accounted for, and units started and completed.

For The Candle Shop, 396,000 candles were started and completed in April. This figure was calculated as either (406,000 units completed – 10,000 units in BI) or (401,400 units started during the period – 5,400 units in EI).

The ending WIP Inventory is 100 percent complete as to material because wax is added at the start of production. The ending WIP Inventory is 80 percent complete as to

Exhibit 6.6 Unit Concepts

Total units to account for =	Total units accounted for	Units started and completed
Beginning WIP Inventory units + Units started	Units completed + Ending WIP Inventory units	Units completed − Beginning WIP Inventory units OR Units started − Ending WIP Inventory units

labor and overhead (together referred to as conversion). One EUP computation can be made because these cost elements are assumed to be added at the same rate throughout the production process. The WA computation for equivalent units of production is as follows:[6]

	DM	Conversion
Candles in beginning WIP Inventory (physical units)	10,000	10,000
Candles started and completed (physical units)	396,000	396,000
Ending WIP Inventory (candles × % complete)	5,400	4,320
Equivalent units of production	411,400	410,320

Step 4: Calculate the Total Cost to Account For The total cost to account for equals beginning WIP Inventory cost plus current period costs. Exhibit 6.5 provides the cost for each component of production: direct material, direct labor, and overhead. Production costs can be determined from transfers of direct material from the warehouse, incurrence of direct labor, and either actual or applied overhead amounts. The sum of direct labor and overhead costs is the total conversion cost. For The Candle Shop, the total cost to account for is ($37,402 + $1,150,140) or $1,187,542.

	Total	DM	DL	OH
Beginning WIP Inventory costs	$ 37,402	$ 11,886	$ 5,658	$ 19,858
Current period costs	1,150,140	642,240	122,638	385,262
Total cost to account for	$1,187,542	$654,126	$128,296	$405,120

The total cost to account for must be assigned to two categories of goods: those transferred to FG Inventory (or, if appropriate, to the next department) and those in ending WIP Inventory. Assignments are made based on the whole or equivalent whole units contained in each inventory category.

Step 5: Calculate the Cost per Equivalent Unit of Production A cost per EUP must be computed for each component for which a separate calculation of EUP is made. Under the WA method, the costs of beginning WIP Inventory and of the current period are summed *for each cost component* and divided by that component's weighted average EUP to obtain the per-unit cost as follows:

$$\text{WA unit cost} = \frac{(\text{Beginning WIP Inventory cost} + \text{Current period cost})}{\text{Total WA equivalent units of production}}$$

$$= \frac{\text{Total cost incurred}}{\text{Total WA equivalent units of production}}$$

[6]Different approaches exist to compute equivalent units of production and unit costs under weighted average and FIFO. In addition to the computations shown within this chapter, two other valid and commonly used approaches for computing and reconciling WA and FIFO EUP are shown in Appendix 1 to this chapter.

This computation divides total cost by total units to produce an average component cost per unit. Because labor and overhead are at the same degree of completion, their costs can be combined and shown as a single conversion cost (CC) per equivalent unit. The Candle Shop's WA cost per EUP calculations for material and conversion follow.

	Total	DM	CC
Beginning WIP Inventory costs (Exhibit 6.5)	$ 37,402	$ 11,886	$ 25,516
Current period costs (Exhibit 6.5)	1,150,140	642,240	507,900
Total cost to account for	$1,187,542	$ 654,126	$ 533,416
Divided by EUP (step 3)		÷ 411,400	÷ 410,320
Cost per EUP	$2.89	$1.59	$1.30

The material and conversion cost amounts are summed to find the total production cost of $2.89 for equivalent whole candles completed during April by The Candle Shop. Note that the total cost of $1,187,542 cannot be divided by a quantity because each of the two cost components has a different number of equivalent units of production.

Step 6: Assign Costs to Inventories This step assigns total production costs to units of product by determining the cost of (1) goods completed and transferred out during the period and (2) units in the ending WIP Inventory.

Using the WA method, the cost of goods completed and transferred out is found by multiplying the total number of units transferred by the total cost per EUP:

$$\text{Total cost transferred} = 406{,}000 \text{ units} \times \$2.89 = \$1{,}173{,}340$$

Because the WA method is based on an averaging technique that combines both prior and current period work, the period in which the transferred units were started does not matter. All units and all costs, respectively, are commingled.

Ending WIP Inventory cost is calculated by multiplying the EUP for each cost component by the component cost per EUP computed in step 5. Cost of the ending WIP Inventory using the WA method is as follows:

Ending WIP Inventory	
Direct material (5,400 × $1.59)	$ 8,586
Conversion (4,320 × $1.30)	5,616
Total cost of ending WIP Inventory	$14,202

The total cost assigned to units transferred out and to units in the ending WIP Inventory must equal the total cost to account for. For The Candle Shop, total cost to account for (step 4) was determined as $1,187,542, which equals transferred-out cost ($1,173,340) plus the cost of the ending WIP Inventory ($14,202).

The steps just discussed can be combined into a **cost of production report**, which details all manufacturing quantities and costs, shows the computation of cost per EUP, and indicates the cost assigned to goods produced during the period. Exhibit 6.7 shows The Candle Shop's cost of production report using the WA method.

Information contained on the cost of production report indicates the actual flow of goods and dollar amounts through the general ledger accounting system. Exhibit 6.8 (p. 204) provides summary journal entries and related T-accounts that show how the information in Exhibit 6.7 is recorded in the WIP and FG Inventory accounts. Note that the total cost to account for must either be transferred out of WIP Inventory or remain as the ending balance of that account.

FIFO Method

3 How are equivalent units of production, unit costs, and inventory values determined using the first-in, first-out (FIFO) method of process costing?

Steps 1 and 2 are not repeated here because they use physical units and, as such, are the same in both the FIFO and WA methods.

Step 3: Calculate the Equivalent Units of Production Using the FIFO method, the work performed last period is not commingled with work performed in the current period. Only work completed on the beginning WIP Inventory during the current period is shown

Exhibit 6.7 The Candle Shop's Cost of Production Report for the Month Ended April 30, 2013 (Weighted Average Method)

		EQUIVALENT UNITS OF PRODUCTION	
Production Data	**Physical Units**	**Direct Material**	**Conversion**
Beginning WIP Inventory*	10,000		
Candles started	401,400		
Candles to account for	411,400		
Beginning WIP Inventory (completed)	10,000	10,000	10,000
Started and completed	396,000	396,000	396,000
Candles completed	406,000		
Ending WIP Inventory†	5,400	5,400	4,320
Candles accounted for	411,400	411,400	410,320

Cost Data	**Total Costs**	**Direct Material**	**Conversion**
Costs in beginning WIP Inventory	$ 37,402	$ 11,886	$ 25,516
Current period costs	1,150,140	642,240	507,900
Total cost to account for	$1,187,542	$ 654,126	$ 533,416
Divided by EUP		÷ 411,400	÷ 410,320
Cost per EUP	$2.89	$1.59	$1.30

Cost Assignment		
Transferred out (406,000 × $2.89)		$1,173,340
Ending WIP Inventory		
Direct material (5,400 × 100% × $1.59)	$8,586	
Conversion (5,400 × 80% × $1.30)	5,616	14,202
Total cost accounted for		$1,187,542

*Fully complete as to material; 40 percent complete as to conversion.
†Fully complete as to material; 80 percent complete as to conversion.

in the EUP schedule; this work equals the physical units in the beginning WIP Inventory times (1 – percentage of work done in the prior period). No additional material is needed in April to complete the 10,000 candles in the beginning WIP Inventory. Because the beginning WIP Inventory was 40 percent complete as to labor and overhead, the company will do 60 percent of the conversion work on those goods in the current period or the equivalent of 6,000 candles (10,000 × 60%). The computation for units started and completed is the same for both the FIFO and WA methods.

The EUP schedule for the FIFO method is:

	DM	**Conversion**
Candles in beginning WIP Inventory completed in the current period	0	6,000
Candles started and completed	396,000	396,000
Ending WIP Inventory (candles × % complete)	5,400	4,320
Equivalent units of production	401,400	406,320

Exhibit 6.8

Work in Process Inventory	642,240	
Raw Material Inventory		642,240
To record issuance of material to production (Exhibit 6.5)		
Work in Process Inventory	122,638	
Wages Payable		122,638
To accrue wages for direct labor (Exhibit 6.5)		
Manufacturing Overhead	385,262	
Various accounts		385,262
To record actual overhead costs (Exhibit 6.5)		
Work in Process Inventory	385,262	
Manufacturing Overhead		385,262
To apply actual overhead to production		
Finished Goods Inventory	1,173,340	
Work in Process Inventory		1,173,340
To transfer cost of completed candles to finished goods (Exhibit 6.7)		

Work in Process Inventory

Beginning balance	37,402	Cost of goods manufactured (transferred out)	1,173,340
Direct material	642,240		
Direct labor	122,638		
Overhead	385,262		
Total cost to account for	1,187,542		
Ending balance	14,202		

Finished Goods Inventory

Beginning balance	XXX	Cost of goods sold	$$$
Cost of goods manufactured	1,173,340		
Ending balance	YYY		

Except for the different treatment of units in the beginning WIP Inventory, the remaining amounts in the FIFO EUP schedule are the same as those for the WA method. Thus, the only difference between the EUPs of the two methods is that the FIFO method *does not* include the equivalent units of work performed on the beginning inventory in the EUP schedule while the WA method *does* include those equivalent units in the EUP schedule:

		DM	Conversion
	FIFO EUP	401,400	406,320
+	BI WIP (10,000 units × % work performed in prior period 100% DM; 40% conversion)	10,000	4,000
=	WA EUP	411,400	410,320

Step 4: Calculate the Total Cost to Account For This step is the same as it was for the WA method. The total cost to account for is $1,187,542.

Step 5: Calculate the Cost per Equivalent Unit of Production Because the FIFO EUP calculation ignores the work performed in the prior period on beginning WIP Inventory, the FIFO cost per EUP computation also ignores prior period costs in the current period computation. The calculation for each cost component at the end of the period is:

$$\text{FIFO unit cost} = \frac{\text{Current period cost}}{\text{Total FIFO equivalent units of production}}$$

Given that the EUP computations and the costs used to compute cost per EUP both differ between the FIFO and weighted average methods, different cost per EUP results will be obtained for the WA and FIFO methods. The FIFO cost per EUP calculations are as follows:

	Total	DM	CC
Current period costs	$1,150,140	$ 642,240	$ 507,900
Divided by EUP (Step 3)		÷ 401,400	÷ 406,320
Cost per EUP	$2.85	$1.60	$1.25

It is useful to understand the underlying difference between the WA and FIFO total cost computations. The WA total cost of $2.89 is the average cost of each candle *completed* during April, regardless of when production began. The FIFO total cost of $2.85 is the average cost of each candle *started and completed* during April. The $0.04 difference is caused solely by the difference in treatment of beginning WIP Inventory costs.

Step 6: Assign Costs to Inventories The FIFO method assumes that the units in beginning WIP Inventory are the first units completed during the current period and, therefore, are the first units transferred out. The remaining units transferred out during the period were both started and completed in the current period. As shown in the cost of production report in Exhibit 6.9 (p. 206), the two-step computation needed to determine the cost of goods transferred out distinctly presents this FIFO logic.

The first part of the cost assignment for units transferred out relates to beginning WIP Inventory units. Before April 1, these units had absorbed all material cost and some conversion (labor and overhead) cost in WIP Inventory. None of these prior period costs were included in the EUP cost calculations in step 5. These beginning inventory units were finished during the current period, so the cost of completion reflects only current period costs. Again, the BI units were complete as to material but needed an additional 60 percent of labor and overhead to be complete. Total cost of producing the units contained in the beginning WIP Inventory is equal to the beginning WIP Inventory costs plus the current period completion costs or $44,902. Next, the cost of units started and completed in the current period is computed using only current period costs. The total cost for all units completed and transferred to FG Inventory for April is $1,173,502.[7] This cost assignment process for The Candle Shop is as follows:

Transferred out	
(1) Beginning inventory (prior period costs)	$ 37,402
Completion of beginning inventory	
Direct material (10,000 × 0% × $1.60)	0
Conversion (10,000 × 60% × $1.25)	7,500
Total cost of beginning inventory transferred	$ 44,902
(2) Candles started and completed (396,000 × $2.85)	1,128,600
Total cost transferred	$1,173,502

[7] Because of FIFO's two-step process to determine cost of units transferred, a question exists as to how to calculate a per-unit cost for the units that were in beginning inventory and those that were started and completed in the current period. The resolution of this question is found in the use of either the strict or the modified FIFO method.

If strict FIFO is used, beginning inventory units are transferred out at their total completed cost; the units started and completed during the current period are transferred at a separate and distinct current period cost. For The Candle Shop, use of strict FIFO means that the 10,000 candles in beginning inventory are transferred at an approximate cost per unit of $4.49 ($44,902 ÷ 10,000). The candles started and completed in April are transferred at the current period cost of $2.85 (computed in step 5). If strict FIFO is used, the costs of these two groups should be reported separately, not added together to get a total transferred cost. Given the significance of the cost difference between March and April, strict FIFO would be most appropriate.

If the difference between the unit costs of beginning inventory and of units started and completed is not significant, there is no need to maintain the distinction. The costs of the two groups can be combined and averaged over all of the units transferred in a process known as the modified FIFO method. For The Candle Shop, modified FIFO assigns an approximate average cost of $2.89 per candle ($1,173,502 ÷ 406,000) to all candles transferred from the department. Modified FIFO allows the next department or Finished Goods Inventory to account for all units received during the period at the same cost per unit. This method is useful when products are processed through several departments so that the number of separate unit costs to be accounted for does not become excessive.

Exhibit 6.9 The Candle Shop's Cost of Production Report for the Month Ended April 30, 2013 (FIFO Method)

		EQUIVALENT UNITS OF PRODUCTION	
Production Data	**Physical Units**	**Direct Material**	**Conversion**
Beginning WIP Inventory*	10,000		
Candles started	401,400		
Candles to account for	411,400		
Beginning WIP Inventory (completed)	10,000	0	6,000
Started and completed	396,000	396,000	396,000
Candles completed	406,000		
Ending WIP Inventory†	5,400	5,400	4,320
Candles accounted for	411,400	401,400	406,320

Cost Data	**Total Costs**	**Direct Material**	**Conversion**
Costs in beginning WIP Inventory	$ 37,402		
Current period costs	1,150,140	$642,240	$507,900
Total cost to account for	$1,187,542		
Divided by EUP		÷ 401,400	÷ 406,320
Cost per EUP	$2.85	$1.60	$1.25

Cost Assignment		
Transferred out		
Beginning WIP Inventory costs	$37,402	
Cost to complete		
Conversion (10,000 × 60% × $1.25)	7,500	$ 44,902
Started & completed (396,000 × $2.85)		1,128,600
Total cost transferred		$1,173,502
Ending WIP Inventory		
Direct material (5,400 × $1.60)	$ 8,640	
Conversion (5,400 × 80% × $1.25)	5,400	14,040
Total cost accounted for		$1,187,542

*Fully complete as to material; 40 percent complete as to conversion.
†Fully complete as to material; 80 percent complete as to conversion.

The process of calculating the FIFO cost of the ending WIP Inventory is the same as under the WA method. Ending WIP cost using FIFO is as follows:

Ending WIP Inventory	
Direct material (5,400 × $1.60)	$ 8,640
Conversion (4,320 × $1.25)	5,400
Total cost of ending WIP Inventory	$14,040

The total cost of the candles transferred out ($1,173,502) plus the cost of the candles in the ending WIP Inventory ($14,040) equals the total cost to be accounted for ($1,187,542).

The journal entries provided for the issuance of direct material, accrual of direct labor wages, and recognition and application of actual overhead are the same as those shown in Exhibit 6.8 for the WA method. If FIFO were used, when completed goods are transferred from WIP Inventory to FG Inventory for April, the amount transferred would be \$1,173,502 rather than the \$1,173,340 shown in Exhibit 6.8. It is assumed that the company began April with no FG Inventory, 400,000 candles were sold on account for \$9 each, and a perpetual FIFO inventory system is used. Exhibit 6.10 provides the sale and cost of goods sold journal entries; inventory T-accounts are given for the FIFO information.

Exhibit 6.10 The Candle Shop's Sale Journal Entries (FIFO Method)

Accounts Receivable	3,600,000	
Sales		3,600,000
To record sales on account (400,000 candles \$9.00)		
Cost of Goods Sold	1,156,402	
Finished Goods Inventory		1,156,402
To transfer cost of goods sold, using strict FIFO:		

First 10,000 units	*\$ 44,902*
Remaining 390,000 units at \$2.85	*1,111,500*
	\$1,156,402

(Note: Using the information from Exhibit 6.7, this entry would be for \$1,156,000 if weighted average were used: 400,000 × \$2.89.)

Work in Process Inventory

Beginning balance	37,402	Cost of goods manufactured (transferred out)	1,173,502
Direct material	642,240		
Direct labor	122,638		
Overhead	385,262		
Total cost to account for	1,187,542		
Ending balance	14,040		

Finished Goods Inventory

Beginning balance	0	Cost of goods sold	1,156,402
Cost of goods manufactured	1,173,502		
Ending balance (6,000 × \$2.85)	17,100		

PROCESS COSTING IN A MULTIDEPARTMENT SETTING

4 How are transferred-in costs and units accounted for in a multidepartment production setting?

Most companies have multiple, rather than single, department processing facilities. In a multidepartment production environment, goods are transferred from a predecessor (upstream) department to a successor (downstream) department. Manufacturing costs always follow the physical flow of goods; thus, when goods are transferred from one department to another, costs are also transferred. Thus, if The Candle Shop decided to place candles (rather than send them to a central warehouse in reusable containers) in eight-unit boxes, production activities could be divided into two departments: Processing and Packaging. A new material (a box) would be added at the end of the Packaging Department.

Costs of the completed units of predecessor departments are treated as input costs in successor departments. Such a sequential treatment requires the use of an additional cost

Fertnig/iStockphoto.com

In multidepartment production, goods are transferred from one department to another before they are complete.

component called **transferred-in cost** or prior department cost. This cost component is always 100 percent complete because the goods would not have been transferred out of the predecessor department if processing there were not complete. The transferred-in cost component is treated the same as any other cost component in the calculations of EUP and cost per EUP.

A successor department might add additional raw material to the units transferred in or might simply provide additional labor with a corresponding incurrence of overhead. In some situations, addition or expansion of materials may cause the number of units accounted for to be higher than those to be accounted for originally or in a previous department. Anything added in the successor department requires its own cost component column for calculating EUP and cost per EUP (unless the additional components have the same degree of completion, in which case they can be combined).

Occasionally, successor departments change the unit of measure used in predecessor departments. For example, at The Candle Shop, production in the Processing Department might be measured as the number of candles but the production measure in the Packaging Department might be number of eight-unit boxes.

Exhibit 6.11 continues The Candle Shop example using the weighted average information from Exhibit 6.7. In Packaging, employees wrap each candle in transparent wrap and then place eight candles in a box. The wrap is considered an indirect material; the box is a direct material that is added at the end of the process. The following information is available:

Candles in beginning WIP inventory—Packaging Department (100% complete as to transferred in; 0% complete as to box; 45% complete as to conversion)	1,000
Candles transferred in from Processing	406,000
Candles in ending WIP Inventory—Packaging Department (100% complete as to transferred in; 0% complete as to box; 80% complete as to conversion)	2,800
Eight-pack boxes of candles sent to Finished Goods Inventory	50,525

	Transferred-In	DM	Conversion
Beginning WIP	$ 855	$ 0	$ 95
Current period	1,173,340*	20,210	10,066

*From Exhibit 6.7

HYBRID COSTING SYSTEMS

5 Why would a company use a hybrid costing system?

Many companies now customize what were previously mass-produced items. In such circumstances, neither a job order nor process costing technique is perfectly suited to attach costs to output. Thus, companies may design a hybrid costing system that is appropriate for their particular processing situation. A **hybrid costing system** combines characteristics of both job order and process costing systems. Such a system would be used, for example, in a manufacturing environment in which various product lines have different direct materials but similar processing techniques.

To illustrate the need for hybrid systems, assume that you order an automobile with the following options: heated leather seats, a Bose stereo system, an mp3 player plug, and pearlized paint. Costs of these options must be traced specifically to your car, but the assembly processes for all cars produced by the plant are similar. A hybrid system allows the job order costing feature of tracing direct material to specific jobs to be combined with the process costing feature of averaging labor and overhead costs over all homogeneous production to derive the total cost of your automobile. It would not be feasible to use a job order costing system to trace labor or overhead cost to your car individually, and it would be improper to average the costs of your options over all the cars produced during the period.

Exhibit 6.11 The Candle Shop Cost of Production Report for Packaging Department (Packaging) (WA Method)

		EQUIVALENT UNITS OF PRODUCTION		
Packaging Data	**Physical Units**	**Trans. In**	**DM**	**Conversion**
Beginning WIP Inventory*	1,000			
Candles started	406,000			
Candles to account for	407,000			
Beginning WIP Inventory (completed)	1,000	1,000	1,000	1,000
Started and completed	403,200	403,200	403,200	403,200
Candles completed (50,525 × 8)	404,200			
Ending WIP Inventory†	2,800	2,800	0	2,240
Candles accounted for	407,000	407,000	404,200	406,440
Candles per box		÷ 8	÷ 8	÷ 8
EUP in boxes		50,875	50,525	50,805

*100 percent complete as to transferred-in; 0 percent complete as to box; 45 percent complete as to conversion

†100 percent complete as to transferred-in; 0 percent complete as to box; 80 percent complete as to conversion

Cost Data	**Total Costs**	**Trans. In**	**DM**	**Conversion**
Costs in beginning WIP Inventory	$ 950	$ 855	$ 0	$ 95
Current period costs	1,203,616	1,173,340	20,210	10,066
Total costs to account for	$1,204,566	$1,174,195	$20,210	$10,161
Divided by EUP		÷ 50,875	50,525	50,805
Cost per box EUP	$23.68	$23.08	$0.40	$0.20

Cost Assignment		
Transferred out (50,525 × $23.68)		$1,196,432
Ending WIP Inventory (2,800 candles = 350 boxes)		
Transferred in (350 × 100% × $23.08)	$8,078	
Direct material (350 × 0% × $0.40)	0	
Conversion (350 × 80% × $0.20)	56	8,134
Total cost accounted for		$1,204,566

A hybrid costing system may be appropriate for companies producing items such as furniture, clothing, and special-order computers. In each instance, numerous kinds of raw materials could be used to create similar output. A table may be made from oak, teak, or mahogany; a blouse may be made from silk, cotton, or polyester; and computers may have different hard drives and other internal components. The material cost for a batch run would be traced separately, but the production process of the batch is repetitive.

Hybrid costing systems provide a more accurate accounting picture of the actual manufacturing activities in certain companies. Job order costing and process costing are two ends of a continuum and, as is typically the case for any continuum, neither end is necessarily the norm. As the use of flexible manufacturing processes increases, so will the use of hybrid costing systems.

APPENDIX 1

6 What alternative methods can be used to calculate equivalent units of production?

ALTERNATIVE CALCULATIONS OF WEIGHTED AVERAGE AND FIFO METHODS

Various methods can be used to compute equivalent units of production under the WA and FIFO methods. One common variation of the weighted average EUP calculation presented in the chapter is the following:

	Units transferred out (whole units)
+	Ending WIP Inventory (equivalent units)
=	WA EUP

The FIFO EUP can be quickly derived by subtracting the equivalent units in the beginning WIP Inventory that had been produced in the previous period from the WA EUP:

	WA EUP
−	Beginning WIP Inventory in equivalent units
=	FIFO EUP

This computation is appropriate because the WA method differentiates only between units completed and units not completed during the period. Since the WA method does not exclude the equivalent units in the beginning WIP Inventory, converting from WA to FIFO requires removal of the equivalent units produced in the previous period from beginning WIP Inventory.

The April production data for The Candle Shop are repeated here to illustrate these alternative calculations for the weighted average and FIFO methods.

Candles in beginning WIP Inventory (100% complete as to material; 40% complete as to conversion costs)	10,000
Candles started during the month	401,400
Candles completed during the month	406,000
Candles in ending WIP Inventory (100% complete as to material; 80% complete as to conversion costs)	5,400

Using these data, the EUP are computed as follows:

		DM	Conversion
	Candles transferred out	406,000	406,000
+	EI WIP (5,400 units × % work performed) (100% DM; 80% conversion)	5,400	4,320
=	**WA EUP**	411,400	410,320
−	BI WIP (10,000 units × % work in prior period) (100% DM; 40% conversion)	(10,000)	(4,000)
=	**FIFO EUP**	401,400	406,320

The distinct relationship between the WA and FIFO methods can also be used in another manner to generate EUP. This method begins with the total number of units to account for in the period. From this amount, the EUP to be completed next period are subtracted to give the WA EUP. As in the method just shown, the equivalent units completed in the prior period (the beginning WIP Inventory) are then deducted to give the FIFO EUP. Using The Candle Shop's data, these computations are as follows:

		DM	Conversion
	Total units to account for	411,400	411,400
−	EUP to be completed next period (5,400 EI units × % work not performed: 0% DM; 20% conversion)	0	(1,080)
=	**WA EUP**	411,400	410,320
	BI EUP (10,000 units × % work completed in prior period) (100% DM; 40% conversion)	(10,000)	(4,000)
=	**FIFO EUP**	401,400	406,320

These alternative calculations can be used either as a confirmation of answers found by using beginning WIP Inventory units, units started and completed, and ending WIP Inventory units or as a shortcut to initially compute EUP.

APPENDIX 2

PROCESS COSTING WITH STANDARD COSTS

7 How are equivalent units of production, unit costs, and inventory values determined using the standard costing method of process costing?

Companies may prefer to use standard rather than actual costs for inventory valuation purposes. Actual costing requires that a new production cost be computed each period. However, once a production process is established, the "new" costs are often not materially different from the "old" costs, so standards for each cost component can be developed and used as benchmarks to simplify the costing process and eliminate periodic cost recomputations. Standards should be reviewed, and possibly revised, at least once per year to keep quantities and costs current.

EUP calculations for standard process costing are identical to those of FIFO process costing. Unlike the WA method, the emphasis of both standard costing and FIFO are on the measurement and control of current production activities and current period costs. The WA method commingles prior and current period units and costs, which reduces the emphasis on current effort that standard costing is intended to represent and measure.

Use of standard quantities and costs allows material, labor, and overhead variances to be computed during the period. To illustrate the differences between using actual and standard process costing, The Candle Shop example is continued. When a standard cost system is used, inventories are stated at standard rather than actual costs. Therefore, although the EUP and current period costs remain the same as shown in Exhibit 6.8, the beginning inventory cost data must be restated to reflect standard costs and to demonstrate the effect of consistent use of standard costs over successive periods. Thus, the adjusted beginning WIP Inventory is a follows:

	Standard Cost per Unit	# of Units	% Completion	Cost
Direct material	$1.58	10,000	100%	$15,800
Direct labor	0.24	10,000	40%	960
Overhead	1.00	10,000	40%	4,000
Total standard cost	$2.82			$20,760

Although direct labor and overhead are at the same degree of completion, these amounts are not combined into a conversion cost category under standard costing. To do so would eliminate the benefit of observing cost variances by category.

Exhibit 6.12 (p. 212) presents the cost of production report using The Candle Shop's standard cost information.[8]

Summary journal entries for The Candle Shop's April production, assuming a standard cost FIFO process costing system and amounts from Exhibit 6.12, are as follows:

1. WIP Inventory is debited for $634,212: the standard cost ($625,680) of material used to complete 396,000 units started in April plus the standard cost ($8,532) for the material used to produce the units in ending WIP Inventory. Raw Material Inventory is credited for the actual cost of the material withdrawn during April ($642,240).

Work in Process Inventory	634,212	
Direct Material Variance	8,028	
Raw Material Inventory		642,240

To record issuance of material at standard and unfavorable direct material variance

[8] Total material, labor, and overhead variances are shown for The Candle Shop. Variances from actual costs must be closed at the end of a period. If the variances are immaterial, they can be closed to Cost of Goods Sold; otherwise, they should be allocated among the appropriate inventory accounts and Cost of Goods Sold.

Exhibit 6.12 The Candle Shop's Cost of Production Report for the Month Ended April 30, 2013 (Standard Costing)

		EQUIVALENT UNITS OF PRODUCTION		
Production Data	**Physical Units**	**DM**	**DL**	**OH**
Beginning WIP Inventory	10,000			
Candles started	401,400			
Candles to account for	411,400			
Beginning WIP Inventory (completed)	10,000	0	6,000	6,000
Started and completed	396,000	396,000	396,000	396,000
Candles completed	406,000			
Ending WIP Inventory†	5,400	5,400	4,320	4,320
Candles accounted for	411,400	401,400	406,320	406,320
Cost Data				
Total costs:				
Beginning inventory (at standard)	$ 20,760	$ 15,800	$ 960	$ 4,000
Current costs (actual)	1,150,140	642,240	122,638	385,262
(1) Total costs	$1,170,900	$658,040	$123,598	$389,262

Total Cost Assignment	**Costs**	**DM**	**DL**	**OH**
Costs in beginning WIP Inventory	$ 20,760	$ 15,800	$ 960	$ 4,000
Cost to complete BI:				
DL (6,000 × $0.24)			1,440	
OH (6,000 × $1.00)				6,000
Total cost to complete	7,440			
Started and completed:				
DM (396,000 × $1.58)		625,680		
DL (396,000 × $0.24)			95,040	
OH (396,000 × $1.00)				396,000
Total (396,000 × $2.83)	1,116,720			
Ending inventory:				
DM (5,400 × $1.58)		8,532		
DL (4,320 × $0.24)			1,037*	
OH (4,320 × $1.00)				4,320
Total EI costs	13,889			
(2) Total	$1,158,809	$650,012	$ 98,477	$410,320
Variances from actual (1 – 2)	12,091	8,028	25,121	(21,058)
Total costs accounted for	$1,170,900	$658,040	$123,598	$389,262

*Rounded to the nearest dollar.

NOTE: Favorable variances are shown in parentheses because they represent a cost reduction.

2. WIP Inventory is debited for the standard cost of labor allowed based on the equivalent units produced in April. The EUP for the month reflect the production necessary to complete the beginning WIP Inventory candles (6,000), the candles started and completed (396,000), and the work performed on the ending inventory candles (4,320), or a total of 406,320 EUP. Multiplying this equivalent production by the standard labor cost per candle of $0.24 gives a total of $97,517 (rounded).

Work in Process Inventory	97,517	
Direct Labor Variance	25,121	
Wages Payable		122,638
To accrue direct labor cost; assign labor cost to WIP Inventory at standard; record unfavorable direct labor variance		

3. Actual factory overhead incurred in April is $385,262.

Manufacturing Overhead	385,262	
Various accounts		385,262
To record actual overhead cost for April		

4. WIP Inventory is debited for the standard cost of overhead based on the EUP produced in April. Multiplying the 406,320 EUP by the standard overhead rate of $1.00 per candle gives $406,320.

Work in Process Inventory	406,320	
Manufacturing Overhead		385,262
Overhead Variance		21,058
To apply overhead to WIP Inventory and record the favorable overhead variance		

5. Finished Goods Inventory is debited for the total standard cost ($1,144,920) of the 406,000 candles completed during the month (406,000 × $2.82).

Finished Goods Inventory	1,144,920	
Work in Process Inventory		1,144,920
To transfer standard cost of completed candles to FG Inventory		

A standard costing system eliminates the need to differentiate between the per-unit cost of the beginning WIP Inventory units that were completed and the per-unit cost of the units started and completed in the current period. All units transferred out of a department are at the standard production cost for each cost component. Thus, recordkeeping is simplified, and variations from the norm are highlighted in the period of incurrence. Standard cost systems are discussed in depth in Chapter 7.

Standard costing not only simplifies the cost flows in a process costing system but also provides a useful tool to control costs. By developing standards, managers have a benchmark against which actual costs can be compared. Managers may also use these standards as targets for balanced scorecard performance measurements. For example, meeting standard costs 98 percent of the time may be set as a goal for the internal business process perspective. Variances serve to identify differences between the benchmark (standard) cost and the actual cost. By striving to control variances, managers control costs. Managers should also benchmark, to the extent possible, their firm's costs against costs incurred by other firms. Such information may help indicate the organization's cost strengths and weaknesses.

APPENDIX 3

SPOILAGE

8 How are normal and abnormal spoilage losses treated in an equivalent units of production schedule?

The chapter examples assumed that all units to be accounted for have been transferred out or are in the ending WIP Inventory. However, almost every process produces some units that do not meet production specifications. This appendix addresses two simple examples of spoilage in a process costing system.

Losses in a production process may occur continuously or at a specific point. For example, the weight loss in roasting coffee beans would be considered a **continuous loss** because it occurs fairly uniformly through the process. In contrast, a **discrete loss** is assumed to occur at a specific point and is detectable only when a quality check is performed. Control points can be either mechanically included in the production process or performed by inspectors.

Several methods can be used to account for units lost during production. Selection of the most appropriate method depends on whether the loss is considered normal or abnormal and whether the loss occurred continuously in the process or at a discrete point.[9] Exhibit 6.13 summarizes the accounting for the cost of lost units.

Exhibit 6.13 Continuous versus Discrete Losses

Type	Assumed to Occur	May Be	Cost Handled How?	Cost Assigned To?
Continuous	Uniformly throughout process	Normal or	Absorbed by all units in ending inventory and transferred out on an EUP basis	Product
		Abnormal	Written off as a loss on an EUP basis	Period
Discrete	At inspection point or at end of process	Normal or	Absorbed by all units past inspection point in ending inventory and transferred out on an EUP basis	Product
		Abnormal	Written off as a loss on an EUP basis	Period

The costs of normal shrinkage and normal continuous losses in a process costing environment are accounted for using the **method of neglect**, which excludes the spoiled units in the equivalent units of production schedule. Ignoring the spoilage results in a smaller number of EUP and dividing production costs by a smaller EUP raises the cost per equivalent unit. Thus, the cost of lost units is spread proportionately over the good units transferred out and those remaining in WIP Inventory.

Alternatively, the cost of normal discrete losses should be assigned only to units that have passed the inspection point. Such units should be good units (relative to the inspected characteristic), whereas the units prior to this point may be good or they may be defective or spoiled. Assigning loss costs to units that may be found to be defective or spoiled in the next period would not be reasonable.

The cost of all abnormal losses should be accumulated and treated as a loss in the period in which those losses occurred. Abnormal loss cost is always accounted for on an equivalent unit basis. Abnormal losses are extended in the EUP schedule at the percentage of completion at the end of production for continuous losses (100 percent complete for all cost elements) or at the point of inspection for discrete losses. For example, assume that a process added all direct material at the beginning of production and the inspection point for determining spoilage was at the 75 percent completion stage as to labor and overhead. If 100 units were found to be spoiled at the inspection point, the extension to the EUP schedule would be 100 EUP for DM and 75 EUP for conversion. The spoiled units would be removed at that point and no additional labor and overhead would be added to them.

Hanks Inc. will be used to illustrate the method of neglect for a normal loss and an abnormal loss. Hanks produces glass jars in a single department; the jars are then sold to

[9] Normal and abnormal losses are defined in Chapter 5.

candle manufacturers. All materials are added at the start of the process, and conversion costs are applied uniformly throughout the production process. Breakage commonly occurs at the end of the production process when a machine pushes air into the jars to form their openings. Hanks expects a maximum of 5 percent of the units started into production to be "lost" during processing. For convenience, quantities will be discussed in terms of jars rather than raw material inputs. Recyclable shipping containers are provided by buyers and, therefore, are not a cost to Hanks Inc. The company uses the WA method of calculating equivalent units. Exhibit 6.14 provides the basic information for June 2013.

Exhibit 6.14 Production and Cost Data for Hanks Inc. for June 2013

Jars			
Beginning WIP Inventory (60% complete)			12,000
Started during month			90,000
Jars completed and transferred			79,200
Ending WIP Inventory (75% complete)			15,000
Spoiled jars			7,800
Costs			
Beginning WIP Inventory			
Material	$ 16,230		
Conversion	3,459	$ 19,689	
Current period			
Material	$101,745		
Conversion	19,041	120,786	
Total cost to be accounted for		$140,475	

In June, Hanks had 12,000 jars in the beginning WIP Inventory and started 90,000 jars into production. At the end of June, the company accounted for 94,200 jars (79,200 completed and 15,000 in ending WIP Inventory).

Total jars to be accounted for (12,000 + 90,000)	102,000
Total jars accounted for (79,200 + 15,000)	(94,200)
Jars spoiled during processing	7,800
Normal spoilage (0.05 × 90,000)	(4,500)
Abnormal spoilage	3,300

Under the method of neglect, the normal spoilage is not included in the computation of EUP and, thus, simply "disappears" from the EUP schedule. Therefore, the cost per equivalent "good" jar made during the period is higher for each cost component.[10]

Exhibit 6.15 (p. 216) presents the cost of production report for Hanks Inc. for June 2013. Use of the FIFO process costing method by Hanks Inc. would have created differences in the number of equivalent units of production, cost per equivalent unit, and cost assignment schedule.[11]

[10]There is a theoretical problem with the use of the method of neglect when a company uses weighted average process costing. Units in the ending WIP inventory have spoiled unit cost assigned to them in the current period and will have lost unit cost assigned to them again in the next period. But even with this flaw, this method provides a reasonable measure of unit cost if the rate of spoilage is consistent from period to period.

[11]For FIFO costing, the EUP would be 85,500 and 86,550, respectively, for DM and Conversion. Cost per EUP would be $1.19 and $0.22, respectively, for DM and Conversion. Total cost transferred out would be $115,497; total cost of ending WIP Inventory would be $20,325; and cost of abnormal loss would be $4,653.

Exhibit 6.15 Hanks Inc.'s Cost of Production Report for the Month Ended June 30, 2013 (Normal and Abnormal Loss)

		EQUIVALENT UNITS OF PRODUCTION	
Production Data	**Physical Units**	**Direct Material**	**Conversion**
Beginning WIP Inventory (100%; 60%)	12,000		
Jars started	90,000		
Jars to account for	102,000		
Beginning WIP Inventory (completed)	12,000	12,000	12,000
Jars started and completed	67,200	67,200	67,200
Total jars completed	79,200		
Ending Inventory (100%; 75%)	15,000	15,000	11,250
Normal spoilage (not extended)	4,500		
Abnormal spoilage (100%; 100%)	3,300	3,300	3,300
Jars accounted for	102,000	97,500	93,750

Cost Data	**Total**	**Direct Material**	**Conversion**
Beginning WIP Inventory cost	$ 19,689	$ 16,230	$ 3,459
Current costs	120,786	101,745	19,041
Total cost to account for	$140,475	$117,745	$ 22,500
Divided by EUP		÷ 97,500	÷ 93,750
Cost per WA EUP	$1.45	$1.21	$0.24

Cost Assignment		
Transferred out (79,200 × $1.45)		$114,840
Ending WIP inventory:		
Direct material (15,000 × $1.21)	$18,150	
Conversion (11,250 × $0.24)	2,700	20,850
Abnormal loss (3,300 × $1.45)		4,785
Total costs accounted for		$140,475

Comprehensive Review Module

KEY TERMS

continuous loss, p. 213
cost of production report, p. 202
discrete loss, p. 214
equivalent units of production (EUP), p. 194
first-in, first-out (FIFO) method (of process costing), p. 197
hybrid costing system, p. 208
method of neglect, p. 214
total cost to account for, p. 199
total units to account for, p. 200
transferred-in cost, p. 208
units started and completed, p. 200
weighted average (WA) method (of process costing), p. 197

CHAPTER SUMMARY

1 Equivalent Units of Production (EUP)

- EUP approximate the number of whole units of output that could have been produced during a period from the actual effort expended during that period.
- EUP assign production costs for direct material, direct labor, and overhead to complete and incomplete output of the period; a separate EUP calculation is required for each cost component that is at a different percentage of completion in the production process.

2 Weighted Average (WA) Method

- WA combines the beginning WIP Inventory and current period production activity and costs.
- WA determines
  - EUP (by cost component) by adding the physical units in beginning WIP Inventory, physical units started and completed during the period, and equivalent units in the ending WIP Inventory.
  - average unit cost (per cost component) by dividing total cost (equal to beginning-of-the-period costs plus current period costs) by EUP.
  - transferred-out value by multiplying total units transferred out by total average cost per EUP.
  - ending WIP Inventory value by multiplying the EUP for each cost component by the related cost per EUP.

3 First-In, First-Out (FIFO) Method

- FIFO does not commingle beginning WIP Inventory and current period production activity or costs.
- FIFO determines
  - EUP (by cost component) by the equivalent units in beginning WIP Inventory that were completed during the current period, physical units started and completed during the period, and equivalent units in ending WIP Inventory.
  - average unit cost (per cost component) by dividing current period cost by EUP.
  - transferred-out value by adding the cost of beginning WIP Inventory, current period cost needed to complete beginning WIP Inventory, and cost of units started and completed in the current period.
  - ending WIP Inventory value by multiplying the EUP for each cost component by the related cost per EUP.

4 Multidepartment Production Setting

- Costs transferred from a predecessor department to a successor department are called Transferred In or Prior Department costs and these are always 100 percent complete.
- Successor departments may change the unit of measurement from the predecessor department; such changes will need to be reflected in the EUP schedule.

5 Hybrid Costing

- Hybrid costing combines the characteristics of both job order and process costing systems.
- Hybrid costing traces direct material and/or direct labor that is related to a particular batch of goods to those specific goods using job order costing.
- Hybrid costing uses process costing techniques to account for cost components that are common to numerous batches of output.

SOLUTION STRATEGIES

Steps in Process Costing Computations, p. 198

1. Calculate the physical units to account for:

   Beginning WIP Inventory in physical units
   + Units started (or transferred in) during the period

2. Calculate the physical units accounted for. This step involves identifying the groups to which costs are to be assigned (transferred out or remaining in ending WIP Inventory).

   Units completed and transferred
   + Units in ending WIP Inventory

3. Calculate the EUP per cost component. Cost components include transferred-in (if multidepartment), direct material, direct labor, and overhead. If multiple materials are used and have different degrees of completion, each material is considered a separate cost component. If overhead is applied on a direct labor basis or is incurred at the same rate as direct labor, the two cost elements can be combined as one cost component and referred to as conversion.

   a. WA

   Beginning WIP Inventory in physical units
   + Units started and completed*
   + (Ending WIP Inventory × % complete)

   b. FIFO

   (Beginning WIP Inventory × % not complete at start of period)
   + Units started and completed*
   + (Ending WIP Inventory × % complete)

   *Units started and completed × (Units transferred out × Units in beginning WIP Inventory)

4. Calculate total cost to account for:

   Cost in beginning WIP Inventory
   + Costs of the current period

5. Calculate cost per equivalent unit for each cost component:

   a. WA

   Cost of component in beginning WIP Inventory
   + Cost of component for current period
   = Total cost of component
   ÷ EUP for component
   = Cost per equivalent unit

   b. FIFO

   Cost of component for current period
   ÷ EUP for component
   = Cost per equivalent unit

6. Assign the costs to inventory accounts using the WA or FIFO method. The total cost assigned to units transferred out plus the units in the ending WIP Inventory must equal the total cost to account for.

   a. WA

      1. Transferred out:

      Units transferred out × Total cost per EUP for all components

2. Ending WIP Inventory:

   The sum of EUP for each component × Cost per EUP for each component

b. FIFO

1. Transferred out:

   Beginning WIP Inventory cost
   + (Beginning WIP Inventory × % not complete at beginning of period for each component × Cost per EUP for each component)

2. Ending WIP Inventory:

   The sum of EUP for each component × Cost per EUP for each component

DEMONSTRATION PROBLEM

Plaid-Clad manufactures golf bags in a two-department process: Assembly and Finishing. The Assembly Department uses weighted average costing; the percentage of completion of overhead in this department is unrelated to direct labor. The Finishing Department adds hardware to the assembled bags and uses FIFO costing; overhead is applied in this department on a direct labor basis. For June, the following production data and costs were gathered:

Assembly Department: Units	
Beginning WIP Inventory (100% complete for DM; 40% complete for DL; 30% complete for OH)	250
Units started	8,800
Ending WIP Inventory (100% complete for DM; 70% complete for DL; 90% complete for OH)	400

Assembly Department: Costs	**DM**	**DL**	**OH**	**Total**
Beginning WIP Inventory	$ 3,755	$ 690	$ 250	$ 4,695
Current period	100,320	63,606	27,681	191,607
Total costs	$104,075	$64,296	$27,931	$196,302

Finishing Department: Units	
Beginning WIP Inventory (100% complete for transferred in; 15% complete for DM; 40% complete for conversion)	100
Units transferred in	8,650
Ending WIP Inventory (100% complete for transferred in; 30% complete for DM; 65% complete for conversion)	200

Finishing Department: Costs	**Transferred In**	**DM**	**Conversion**	**Total**
Beginning inventory	$ 2,176	$ 30	$ 95	$ 2,301
Current period	188,570	15,471	21,600	225,641
Total costs	$190,746	$15,501	$21,695	$227,942

Required:

a. Prepare a cost of production report for the Assembly Department.
b. Prepare a cost of production report for the Finishing Department.
c. Prepare T-accounts to show the flow of costs through the Assembly and Finishing Departments.
d. Prepare the journal entries for the Finishing Department for June.

Solution to Demonstration Problem

a.

	Physical Units	EQUIVALENT UNITS OF PRODUCTION		
		DM	DL	OH
Beginning WIP Inventory	250			
Units started	8,800			
Units to account for	9,050			
Beginning WIP Inventory (completed)	250	250	250	250
Started and completed	8,400	8,400	8,400	8,400
Units completed	8,650			
Ending WIP Inventory	400	400	280	360
Units accounted for	9,050	9,050	8,930	9,010

Cost Data	Total	DM	DL	OH
Beginning WIP Inventory	$ 4,695	$ 3,755	$ 690	$ 250
Current period	191,607	100,320	63,606	27,681
Total cost to account for	$196,302	$104,075	$64,296	$27,931
Divided by EUP		÷ 9,050	÷ 8,930	÷ 9,010
Cost per EUP	$21.80	$11.50	$7.20	$3.10

Cost Assignment

Transferred out (8,650 × $21.80)		$188,570
Ending WIP Inventory		
DM (400 × $11.50)	$4,600	
DL (280 × $7.20)	2,016	
OH (360 × $3.10)	1,116	7,732
Total cost accounted for		$196,302

b.

	Physical Units	EQUIVALENT UNITS OF PRODUCTION		
		Transferred In	DM	Conversion
Beginning WIP Inventory	100			
Units started	8,650			
Units to account for	8,750			
Beginning WIP Inventory (completed)	100	0	85	60
Started and completed	8,450	8,450	8,450	8,450
Units completed	8,550			
Ending WIP Inventory	200	200	60	130
Units accounted for	8,750	8,650	8,595	8,640

Cost Data	Total	Transferred In	DM	Conversion
Beginning WIP Inventory	$ 2,301			
Current period	225,641	$188,570	$15,471	$21,600
Total cost to account for	$227,942			
Divided by EUP		÷ 8,650	÷ 8,595	÷ 8,640
Cost per EUP	$26.10	$21.80	$1.80	$2.50

Cost Assignment

Transferred out		
Beginning inventory cost	$2,301	
Cost to complete		
TI (0 × $21.80)	0	
DM (85 × $1.80)	153	
Conversion (60 × $2.50)	150	$ 2,604
Started and completed (8,450 × $26.10)		220,545
Ending inventory		
TI (200 × $21.80)	$4,360	
DM (60 × $1.80)	108	
Conversion (130 × $2.50)	325	4,793
Total cost accounted for		$227,942

c.

Work in Process Inventory—Assembly Dept.

Beginning balance:			Cost of Goods Transferred Out to Finishing Department	188,570
Direct material	3,755			
Direct labor	690			
Overhead	250	4,695		
Current costs:				
Direct material	100,320			
Direct labor	63,606			
Overhead	27,681	191,607		
Total cost to account for		196,302		
Ending balance				
Direct material	4,600			
Direct labor	2,016			
Overhead	1,116	7,732		

Work in Process Inventory—Finishing Dept.

Beginning balance:			Cost of Goods Manufactured (Transferred out to Finished Goods):		
Transferred in	2,176				
Direct material	30		Goods in BI completed	2,604	
Conversion	95	2,301	Goods Started & Completed	220,545	223,149
Current costs:					
Transferred in	188,570				
Direct material	15,471				
Conversion	21,600	225,641			
Total cost to account for		227,942			
Ending balance					
Transferred in	4,360				
Direct material	108				
Conversion	325	4,793			

Finished Goods Inventory

Beginning balance	XXX	Cost of Goods Sold	$$$
Cost of goods manufactured	223,149		
Ending balance	YYY		

d. **Assembly Dept.**

Account	Debit	Credit
Work in Process Inventory—Assembly	100,320	
Raw Material Inventory		100,320
To transfer in direct material		
Work in Process Inventory—Assembly	63,606	
Wages Payable		63,606
To record direct labor costs		
Work in Process Inventory—Assembly	27,681	
Factory Overhead Control—Assembly		27,681
To apply overhead costs to WIP		
Work in Process Inventory—Finishing	188,570	
Work in Process Inventory—Assembly		188,570
To transfer completed goods to next department		
Finishing Dept.		
Work in Process Inventory—Finishing	15,471	
Raw Material Inventory		15,471
To transfer in direct material		
Work in Process Inventory—Finishing	21,600	
Conversion Cost Control—Finishing		21,600
To apply direct labor and overhead costs to WIP		
Finished Goods Inventory	223,149	
Work in Process Inventory—Finishing		223,149
To transfer completed goods to FG		

POTENTIAL ETHICAL ISSUES

ETHICS

1. Estimating too high (or too low) a completion percentage for ending WIP Inventory to decrease (or increase) the cost per EUP and thereby distorting ending WIP and ending FG inventories on the balance sheet and Cost of Goods Sold on the income statement
2. Not updating standard costs to reflect new quantities or costs and thereby distorting ending WIP and ending FG inventories on the balance sheet and Cost of Goods Sold on the income statement and creating potentially significant variances that could be written off without management review
3. Ignoring the necessity to trace significant, direct costs to specific jobs in hybrid manufacturing situations and thereby understating the cost of products containing high-cost components or materials and overstating the cost of products containing low-cost components or materials
4. Treating abnormal spoilage as normal spoilage and thereby inflating the cost of "good" units and not reporting the abnormal spoilage as a current period loss on the income statement

QUESTIONS

1. What are the characteristics of a company that would be more likely to use process costing than job order costing?
2. How do the weighted average and first-in, first-out methods of process costing differ in their treatment of beginning Work in Process Inventory units?
3. What is an "equivalent unit of production," and why is it a necessary concept to employ in a process costing system?
4. Is one equivalent unit computation sufficient for all cost components? Explain your answer.
5. What is meant by the phrase *units started and completed*? Why is this phrase more closely associated with the first-in, first-out method of process costing than with the weighted average method?

6. What is meant by the phrase *transferred out cost*? Why does the transferred out cost under the WA method include only one computation, but the FIFO method includes multiple computations?
7. How is the cost of ending inventory calculated in a process costing system?
8. Which cost component can be found in a downstream department of a multidepartment production process that will not be present in the first upstream department? Discuss.
9. A company has two sequential processing departments. On the cost of production reports for the departments, will the cost per unit transferred out of the first department always be equal to the cost per unit transferred in to the second department? Explain.
10. What is a hybrid costing system? In what circumstances are hybrid costing systems typically employed?
11. (Appendix 2) Why does standard costing make process costing more clerically and computationally efficient?
12. (Appendix 3) In accounting for spoilage, what is meant by the "method of neglect"? How does the use of this method affect cost of good production?
13. (Appendix 3) In a process costing system, how are normal and abnormal spoilage typically treated? Why are normal and abnormal spoilage treated differently?

EXERCISES

14. **LO.1 (Research)** In a team of three or four people, choose a company whose mass production process you would like to study. Use the library, the Internet, and (if possible) personal resources to gather information. Prepare a visual representation (similar to Exhibit 6.3) of that production process. In this illustration, indicate the approximate percentage of completion points at which various materials are added and where/how labor and overhead flow into and through the process.

INTERNET

Assume that 1,000 units of product are flowing through your production process and are now at the 60 percent completion point as to labor. Prepare a written explanation about the quantity of direct material equivalent units that are included in the 1,000 units. Also explain how much overhead activity and cost have occurred and why the overhead percentage is the same as or different from the percentage of completion for labor.

15. **LO.2 (WA EUP)** In manufacturing its products, Trevano Corp. adds all direct material at the beginning of the production process. The company's direct labor and overhead are considered to be continuously at the same degree of completion. September production information is as follows:

INTERNET

Beginning WIP Inventory	24,000 pounds
Started during September	600,000 pounds
Completed during September	608,000 pounds

As of September 1, the beginning WIP Inventory was 45 percent complete as to labor and overhead. On September 30, the ending WIP Inventory was 65 percent complete as to conversion.

a. Determine the total number of pounds to account for if Trevano uses the weighted average process costing method.
b. Determine the equivalent units of production for direct material.
c. Determine the equivalent units of production for direct labor and overhead.

16. **LO.2 (WA EUP)** For each of the following situations, use the weighted average method to determine the equivalent units of production for labor and overhead, assuming that they are continuously at the same percentage of completion:

a. Beginning WIP Inventory (40% complete)	10,000
Units started in production	350,000

Units transferred out	344,000
Ending WIP Inventory (70% complete)	16,000
b. Beginning WIP Inventory (30% complete)	40,000
Units started in production	480,000
Units transferred out	?
Ending WIP Inventory (80% complete)	26,000
c. Beginning WIP Inventory (55% complete)	15,000
Units started in production	405,000
Units transferred out	415,800
Ending WIP Inventory (90% complete)	?
d. Beginning WIP Inventory (35% complete)	10,800
Units started in production	?
Units transferred out	351,600
Ending WIP Inventory (45% complete)	18,300

17. **LO.2 (WA EUP)** O'Malley Corp. uses a weighted average process costing system. Material is added at the beginning of the production process and overhead is applied on the basis of direct labor. O'Malley's records indicate that 70,000 units were in process at the beginning of May 2013; these units were 30 percent complete as to conversion. In May, the company started 445,300 and completed 427,500 units. May's ending inventory was 35 percent complete as to conversion.
    a. What are the equivalent units of production for direct material?
    b. What are the equivalent units of production for conversion?

18. **LO.3 (FIFO EUP)** Assume that O'Malley Corp. in Exercise 17 uses the FIFO method of process costing.
    a. What are the equivalent units of production for direct material?
    b. What are the equivalent units of production for conversion?

19. **LO.3 (FIFO EUP)** Using the information in Exercise 16 and assuming a FIFO method of process costing, determine the equivalent units of production for labor and overhead.

20. **LO.3 (FIFO EUP)** Assume that Trevano Corp. in Exercise 15 uses the FIFO method of process costing.
    a. What proportion of work needs to be performed on the beginning inventory units to complete them?
    b. What are the equivalent units of production for direct material?
    c. What are the equivalent units of production for conversion?

21. **LO.2, LO.3, & LO.6 (WA & FIFO EUP)** On April 30, 2013, Leander Co. had 21,600 units in process that were 85 percent complete as to material, 60 percent complete as to direct labor, and 45 percent complete as to overhead. During May, 561,000 units were started. The 13,700 units in ending inventory were 75 percent complete as to material, 25 percent complete as to direct labor, and 10 percent complete as to overhead.
    a. Calculate the physical units to account for in May.
    b. How many units were started and completed during May?
    c. Determine May's EUP for each category using the weighted average method.
    d. Determine May's EUP for each category using the FIFO method.
    e. Reconcile your answers to parts (c) and (d).

22. **LO.2 & LO.3 (WA & FIFO EUP)** Ramos Corp. uses a process costing system to assign costs to its steel production. During March 2013, Ramos had beginning Work in Process Inventory of 180,000 tons of steel (100 percent complete as to material and 65 percent complete as to conversion). During the month, the raw material needed to produce 3,400,000 tons of steel was started in process. At month-end, 165,000 tons remained in WIP Inventory (100 percent complete as to material and 40 percent complete as to conversion).
    a. Compute the total units to account for.
    b. Determine how many units were started and completed.

c. Determine the equivalent units of production using the weighted average method.
d. Determine the equivalent units of production using the FIFO method.
e. Reconcile your answers to parts (c) and (d).

23. **LO.2, LO.3, & LO.6 (WA & FIFO EUP)** Funtime Inc. makes small toys in a one-department production process. Plastic is added at the beginning of the process; all other materials are considered indirect. The following information is available relative to September 2013 production activities:

Beginning WIP Inventory: 15,000 toys (60 percent complete as to labor; 75 percent complete as to overhead)
Started into production: plastic for 620,000 toys
Ending WIP Inventory: 25,400 toys (35 percent complete as to labor; 60 percent complete as to overhead)

a. Compute the EUP for direct material, direct labor, and overhead using weighted average process costing.
b. Compute the EUP for direct material, direct labor, and overhead using FIFO process costing.
c. Reconcile the calculations in parts (a) and (b).

24. **LO.2 (Cost per WA EUP)** In October 2013, Pedraza Corp.'s production was 53,600 equivalent units for direct material, 48,800 equivalent units for direct labor, and 42,000 equivalent units for overhead. During October, direct material, conversion, and overhead costs incurred were as follows:

Direct material	$158,688
Conversion	189,648
Overhead	85,200

Beginning WIP Inventory costs for October were $26,232 for direct material, $19,504 for direct labor, and $20,640 for overhead.

a. How much did Pedraza Corp. spend on direct labor in October?
b. What was the October weighted average cost per equivalent unit for direct material, direct labor, and overhead?

25. **LO.3 (Cost per FIFO EUP)** Assume that Pedraza Corp. in Exercise 24 had 7,200 EUP for direct material in October's beginning WIP Inventory, 8,000 EUP for direct labor, and 7,920 EUP for overhead. What was the October FIFO cost per EUP for direct material, direct labor, and overhead?

26. **LO.2 & LO.3 (Cost per WA & FIFO EUP)** Pylonic Mfg. produces concrete garden border sections. All material is added at the beginning of processing. Production and cost information for May 2013 are as follows:

WA EUP	
Direct material	160,000 sections
Direct labor	152,000 sections
Overhead	150,000 sections
FIFO EUP	
Direct material	120,000 sections
Direct labor	124,000 sections
Overhead	132,000 sections
Beginning WIP Inventory costs	
Direct material	$19,600
Direct labor	6,320
Overhead	10,020
Current period costs	
Direct material	$54,000
Direct labor	34,720
Overhead	84,480

a. What is the total cost to account for?
b. Using weighted average process costing, what is the cost per equivalent unit for each cost component?
c. Using FIFO process costing, what is the cost per equivalent unit for each cost component?
d. How many units were in beginning inventory and at what percentage of completion was each cost component?

27. **LO.2 (WA EUP; cost per WA EUP)** Kahil Mfg. makes skateboards and uses a weighted average process costing system. On May 1, 2013, the company had 400 boards in process that were 70 percent complete as to material and 85 percent complete as to conversion. During the month, 3,800 additional boards were started, and 300 boards were still in process (40 percent complete as to material and 60 percent complete as to conversion) at the end of May. Cost information for May 2013 is as follows:

Beginning WIP Inventory costs	
Direct material	$ 4,349
Conversion	4,658
Current period costs	
Direct material	60,775
Conversion	46,750

a. Calculate EUP for each cost component using the weighted average method.
b. Calculate cost per EUP for each cost component.

28. **LO.2 (WA EUP; cost per WA EUP)** BeGone manufactures spray cans of insect repellent. On August 1, 2013, the company had 9,800 units in the beginning WIP Inventory that were 100 percent complete as to canisters, 60 percent complete as to other materials, 40 percent complete as to direct labor, and 20 percent complete as to overhead. During August, BeGone started 81,500 units in the manufacturing process. Ending WIP Inventory included 4,600 units that were 100 percent complete as to canisters, 40 percent complete as to other materials, 20 percent complete as to direct labor, and 10 percent complete as to overhead.

Cost information for the month is as follows:

Beginning WIP Inventory	
Canisters	$ 6,535
Other direct materials	6,174
Direct labor	5,594
Overhead	1,070
August costs	
Canisters	61,940
Other direct materials	86,793
Direct labor	82,026
Overhead	160,176

Prepare a schedule showing the BeGone August 2013 computation of weighted average equivalent units of production and cost per equivalent unit.

29. **LO.3 (FIFO EUP; cost per FIFO EUP)** Use the information in Exercise 27 except assume that Kahil Mfg. uses FIFO costing. Prepare a schedule showing the August 2013 computation of FIFO equivalent units of production and cost per equivalent unit.

30. **LO.3 (FIFO cost assignment)** In October 2013, Manchaca Company had the following production and cost data:

Beginning inventory units (80% complete as to DM; 45% complete as to DL; 30% complete as to OH)	42,600
October completed production	1,570,000

Units in ending inventory (35% complete as to DM; 15% complete as to DL; 25% complete as to OH)	28,400
Beginning inventory cost	$458,482
October direct material cost per EUP	$10.74
October direct labor cost per EUP	$13.88
October overhead cost per EUP	$24.80

a. What is the cost of the beginning inventory transferred out in October?
b. What is the total cost transferred out in October?
c. What is the cost of ending inventory at the end of October?
d. What is the total cost to account for during October?

31. **LO.2 (WA cost assignment)** The following production and cost per EUP data are available for Louvre Corp. for February 2013:

Units completed during February	390,000
Units in ending inventory (100% complete as to direct material; 30% complete as to direct labor; 25% complete as to overhead)	55,500
Direct material cost per EUP	$7.50
Direct labor cost per EUP	$9.00
Overhead cost per EUP	$10.20

a. What is the cost of the goods completed during February?
b. What is the cost of ending inventory at February 28, 2013?
c. What is the total cost to account for during February?

32. **LO.3 (FIFO cost assignment)** In November 2013, Lamb Co. computed its equivalent unit costs under FIFO process costing as follows:

Direct material	$29.50
Packaging	3.00
Direct labor	10.84
Overhead	7.68

Direct material and packaging are added at the start and end of processing, respectively. Beginning inventory cost was $1,026,810 and consisted of

- $789,040 direct material cost for 54,000 EUP.
- $91,862 direct labor cost for 16,200 EUP.
- $145,908 overhead cost for 18,900 EUP.

Lamb Co. transferred a total of 370,000 units to finished goods during November and had 12,000 units in ending WIP Inventory. The ending inventory units were 30 percent complete as to direct labor and 55 percent complete as to overhead.

a. What percentage complete were the beginning inventory units as to direct material? Packaging? Direct labor? Overhead?
b. What was the total cost of the completed beginning inventory units?
c. What was the cost of the units started and completed in November?
d. What was the cost of November's ending inventory?

33. **LO.3 (FIFO EUP; cost per FIFO EUP)** Use the information in Exercise 28 except assume that BeGone uses FIFO process costing. Prepare a schedule showing the BeGone August 2013 computation of FIFO equivalent units of production and cost per equivalent unit.

34. **LO.2 & LO.3 (EUP; cost per EUP; cost assignment; WA & FIFO)** Found Sound mass-produces miniature speakers for personal sound systems. The following cost information is available for June 2013:

Beginning inventory direct material cost	$ 4,133.20
Beginning inventory conversion cost	873.10
Direct material issued during June	62,928.00
Direct labor incurred during June	13,070.00
Overhead applied during June	10,356.00

On June 1, the company had 1,000 units in process, which were 60 percent complete as to material and 30 percent complete as to conversion. Found Sound started 8,400 units into process during June and had 300 units still in process on June 30. The ending WIP units were 80 percent complete as to material and 70 percent complete as to conversion.

a. Compute the unit costs for June under the weighted average method for direct material and for conversion.
b. Determine the cost transferred out for June using the weighted average method.
c. Determine the cost of June 30 ending inventory using the weighted average method.
d. Compute the unit costs for June under the FIFO method for direct material and for conversion.
e. Determine the total costs transferred to Finished Goods Inventory during June using the FIFO method.
f. Determine the cost of June 30 ending inventory using the FIFO method.
g. Prepare the entries for the direct material, direct labor, and overhead cost assigned to production during June as well as the transfer of the completed goods during June using the weighted average method.

35. **LO.2 & LO.4 (WA EUP; second department)** Angerstein Inc. produces calendars in a two-process, two-department operation. In the Printing Department, calendars are printed and cut. In the Assembly Department, the material received from Printing is assembled into individual calendars and bound. Each department maintains its own Work in Process Inventory, and costs are assigned using weighted average process costing. In Assembly, conversion costs are incurred evenly throughout the process; direct material is added at the end of the process. For September 2013, the following production and cost information is available for the Assembly Department:

Beginning WIP Inventory: 5,000 calendars (30 percent complete as to conversion); transferred in cost, $7,550; conversion cost, $1,093
Transferred in during September: 80,000 calendars
Current period costs: transferred in, $80,000; direct material, $10,270; conversion, $13,991
Ending WIP Inventory: 6,000 calendars (80 percent complete as to conversion)

For the Assembly Department, compute the following:

a. equivalent units of production for each cost component
b. cost per EUP for each cost component
c. cost transferred to Finished Goods Inventory
d. cost of ending WIP Inventory

36. **LO.2 & LO.4 (Second department)** During August 2013, Tibbetts's Casing Department equivalent unit product costs, computed under the weighted average method, were as follows:

Transferred in	$10
Material	2
Conversion	6

All material is introduced at the end of the process in the Casing Department. August's ending Work in Process Inventory contained 4,000 units that were 80 percent complete as to conversion. Twenty-five thousand units were transferred out during August to Finished Goods Inventory.

a. Compute the total costs that should be assigned to the August 31, 2013, Work in Process.
b. Compute the total cost of units transferred to finished goods.
c. Prepare the journal entry that Tibbetts's accountant should make at the end of August related to the units transferred out.

37. **LO.3 & LO.4 (FIFO EUP; second department)** Use the information in Exercise 35 and assume that Angerstein Inc. uses the FIFO method of process costing. For the Assembly Department, compute the following:

a. equivalent units of production for each cost component
b. cost per EUP for each cost component
c. cost transferred to Finished Goods Inventory
d. cost of ending WIP Inventory

38. **LO.2, LO.3, & LO.4 (WA & FIFO EUP; two departments)** Baum Co. has two processing departments: Fabrication and Assembly. In the Fabrication Department, metal is cut and formed into various components, which are then transferred to Assembly. The components are welded, polished, and coated with sealant in the Assembly Department. April 2013 production data for these two departments follow.

EXCEL

Fabrication

Beginning WIP Inventory (100% complete as to material; 25% complete as to conversion)	5,000
Units started during month	40,000
Ending WIP Inventory (100% complete as to material; 60% complete as to conversion)	6,800

Assembly

Beginning WIP Inventory (0% complete as to sealant; 35% complete as to conversion)	2,000
Units started during month	?
Ending WIP Inventory (0% complete as to sealant; 15% complete as to conversion)	6,100

a. Determine the equivalent units of production for each cost component for each department under the WA method.
b. Determine the equivalent units of production for each cost component for each department under the FIFO method.

39. **LO.5 (Hybrid costing)** Pat Koontz makes necklaces from glass beads, metal beads, and natural beads. After reading about hybrid costing, she realized that the different types of necklaces did not cost the same amount of money to make, even though they took the same amount of time and effort to assemble. Koontz developed the following standard costs for each type of necklace:

	Glass	Metal	Natural
Beads	$24	$15	$ 7
Direct labor (1.5 hours)	15	15	15
Overhead (based on 1.5 hours)	8	8	8
Total	$47	$38	$30

Koontz began 2013 with no beginning WIP Inventory after she experienced an extreme holiday rush. During January, 130 necklaces were started: 70 were glass, 25 were metal, and 35 were natural. At the end of January, 25 necklaces were not yet complete: 5 glass, 13 metal, and 7 natural. The stage of completion for each cost component for the 25 unfinished necklaces was as follows:

Material	100% complete
Conversion	60% complete

a. Calculate the cost of necklaces completed during January.
b. Calculate the cost of necklaces in ending WIP Inventory.

40. **LO.5 (Hybrid costing)** WrapAround makes one-size-fits-most capes. Each cape goes through the same conversion process, but three types of fabric (Dacron, denim, and cotton) are available. The company uses a standard costing system, and standard costs for each type of cape follow.

	Dacron	Denim	Cotton
Material (2 yards)	$10	$ 8	$12
Direct labor (1 hour)	9	9	9
Overhead (based on 1.5 machine hours)	6	6	6
Total	$25	$23	$27

Material is added at the start of production. In March 2013, there was no beginning WIP Inventory and 2,500 capes were started into production. Of these, 300 were Dacron, 500 were denim, and 1,700 were cotton. At the end of March, 100 capes (50 Dacron, 20 denim, and 30 cotton) were not yet complete. The stage of completion for each cost component for the 100 unfinished capes is as follows:

Material	100% complete
Direct labor	25% complete
Overhead	35% complete

a. Determine the total cost of the capes completed and transferred to Finished Goods Inventory.
b. Determine the total cost of the capes in the ending WIP Inventory.

41. **LO.7 (Appendix 2; standard process costing)** Cherbock Company uses a standard costing system to account for its pita bread manufacturing process. The bread is sold in packages of one dozen pieces. The company has set the following cost standards for each package:

Direct material—ingredients	$0.25
Direct material—packaging	0.05
Direct labor	0.07
Overhead	0.30
Total cost	$0.67

On June 1, the company had 12,000 pitas in process; these were 100 percent complete as to ingredients, 0 percent complete as to packaging, and 70 percent complete as to labor and overhead. During June, 310,000 pitas were started, and 314,000 were finished. Ending inventory was 100 percent complete as to ingredients, 0 percent complete as to the packaging, and 60 percent complete as to labor and overhead.

a. What were the equivalent units of production for June for each cost component?
b. What was the cost of the packages transferred to Finished Goods Inventory during June?
c. What was the cost of the ending WIP Inventory for June?

42. **LO.5 (Standard process costing; variances)** Reischman Co. uses a standard costing system to account for its production of toys. Plastic is added at the start of production; labor and overhead are incurred at equal rates throughout the process. The standard cost of one toy is as follows:

Direct material	$0.10
Direct labor	0.02
Overhead	0.09
Total cost	$0.21

The following production and cost data are applicable to April 2013:

Beginning WIP Inventory (45% complete)	180,000 units
Units started in April	1,300,000 units
Ending WIP Inventory (65% complete)	144,000 units
Current cost of direct material	$184,000
Current cost of direct labor	27,126
Current cost of overhead	118,500

a. What amount is carried as the April beginning balance of WIP Inventory?
b. What amount is carried as the April ending balance of WIP Inventory?

c. What amount is transferred to Finished Goods Inventory for April?
d. What are the total direct material, direct labor, and overhead variances for April?
e. Record the journal entries to recognize the direct material, direct labor, and overhead variances.

43. **LO.2 & LO.8 (Appendix 3; WA; normal vs. abnormal spoilage)** Hebert Industries uses a weighted average process costing system. Management has specified that the normal loss from shrinkage cannot exceed 3 percent of the units started in a period. All raw material is added at the start of the production process. Spoilage is determined upon inspection at the end of the production process. March processing information follows.

Beginning WIP Inventory (30% complete as to conversion)	20,000 units
Started during March	120,000 units
Completed during March	116,400 units
Ending WIP Inventory (20% complete as to conversion)	16,000 units

a. How many total units are there to account for?
b. How many units were spoiled during processing? Of the spoiled units, how many should be treated as a normal loss? As an abnormal loss?
c. What are the equivalent units of production for direct material? For conversion?
d. How are costs associated with the company's normal spoilage handled?
e. How are costs associated with the company's abnormal spoilage handled?

44. **LO.3 & LO.8 (Appendix 3; FIFO; normal loss)** Lilliputian Inc. produces dog food. All direct material is entered at the beginning of the process. Some shrinkage occurs during the production process, but management considers any shrinkage of less than 8 percent to be normal. October 2013 data are as follows:

EXCEL

Beginning WIP Inventory (45% complete as to conversion)	36,000 pounds
Started during the month	120,000 pounds
Transferred to FG Inventory	126,000 pounds
Ending WIP Inventory (15% complete as to conversion)	21,600 pounds
Loss	? pounds

The following costs are associated with October production:

Beginning WIP Inventory:		
Material	$14,000	
Conversion	10,800	$24,800
Current period:		
Material	$39,060	
Conversion	33,912	72,972
Total cost to account for		$97,772

Prepare an October 2013 cost of production report for Lilliputian Inc. using FIFO process costing.

45. **LO.3 & LO.8 (Appendix 3; FIFO EUP computations; normal loss)** Oehkle Inc. produces paint in a process in which spoilage occurs continually. Spoilage of 2 percent or fewer of the gallons of raw material placed into production is considered normal. The following operating statistics are available for June 2013:

Beginning WIP Inventory (60% complete as to material; 70% complete as to conversion)	16,000 gallons
Started during June	360,000 gallons
Ending WIP Inventory (40% complete as to material; 20% complete as to conversion)	8,000 gallons
Spoiled	2,800 gallons

a. How many gallons were transferred out?
b. What are the FIFO equivalent units of production for material? For conversion?

EXCEL

46. **LO.3 & LO.8 (Appendix 3; FIFO; normal and abnormal loss)** Omaha Foods manufactures corn meal in a continuous, mass production process. Corn is added at the beginning of the process. Normal losses are minimal and abnormal losses infrequently occur when foreign materials are found in the corn meal. Routine inspection occurs at the 95 percent completion point as to conversion.

During May, a machine malfunctioned and dumped salt into 8,000 pounds of corn meal. This abnormal loss occurred when conversion was 70 percent complete on those pounds of product. The error was immediately noticed, and those pounds of corn meal were pulled from the production process. Two thousand additional pounds of meal were detected as unsuitable at the routine inspection point; this amount was considered within normal limits. Production data for the month follow.

Beginning WIP Inventory (85% complete)	40,000 pounds
Started during the month	425,000 pounds
Ending WIP Inventory (25% complete)	10,000 pounds

a. Determine the number of EUP for direct material and for conversion, assuming a FIFO cost flow.

b. If the costs per EUP are \$0.08 and \$0.15 for direct material and conversion, respectively, what is the cost of the ending WIP Inventory?

c. What is the cost of abnormal loss? How is this cost treated in May?

PROBLEMS

47. **LO.2 (WA cost of production report; journal entries)** Delacroix Co. had 800 units of inventory at the beginning of March 2013. Other information about that beginning Work in Process Inventory is as follows:

Quantity: 800 units	Percent Complete	Costs Incurred
Direct material	45	\$ 6,748
Direct labor	65	8,680
Overhead	40	5,710
Total beginning inventory		\$21,138

Direct labor costs were extremely high during February, because the company had a labor strike and paid a high premium to get production workers that month.

During March, Delacroix Co. started production of 11,400 units of product and incurred \$259,012 for material, \$58,200 for direct labor, and \$188,210 for overhead. At the end of March, the company had 400 units in process (70 percent complete as to material, 90 percent complete as to direct labor, and 80 percent complete as to overhead).

a. Prepare a cost of production report for March using the weighted average method.

b. Journalize the March transactions.

c. Prepare T-accounts to represent the flow of costs for Delacroix Co. for March. Use XXX where amounts are unknown and identify what each unknown amount represents.

48. **LO.2 (WA cost assignment)** Fresh Seasons is a contract manufacturer for Delectable Dressing Company. Fresh Seasons uses a weighted average process costing system to account for its salad dressing production. All ingredients are added at the start of the process. Delectable provides reusable vats to Fresh Seasons for the completed product to be shipped to Delectable for bottling, so Fresh Seasons incurs no packaging costs. Production and cost information for Fresh Seasons during April 2013 follow.

Gallons of dressing in beginning WIP Inventory	36,000
Gallons completed during April	242,000
Gallons of dressing in ending WIP Inventory	23,500
Costs of beginning WIP Inventory	
Direct material	\$183,510
Direct labor	98,526
Overhead	78,273

Costs incurred in April	
Direct material	$1,136,025
Direct labor	451,450
Overhead	723,195

April beginning and ending WIP inventories had the following percentages of completion for labor and overhead:

	April 1	April 30
Direct labor	55%	15%
Overhead	70%	10%

a. How many gallons of dressing ingredients were started in April?
b. What is the total cost of the goods transferred out during April?
c. What is the cost of April's ending WIP Inventory?

49. **LO.2 (WA EUP; cost assignment)** Spangenberg Products manufactures computer cases. All material is added at the start of production and overhead is assumed to be incurred at the same rate as labor. Overhead is applied to each product at the rate of 70 percent of direct labor cost. At the beginning of July, there were no units in the Finished Goods Inventory. The firm's inventory cost records provide the following information:

	Units	DM Cost	DL Cost
Work in Process Inventory, 7/1 (70% complete as to labor)	100,000	$ 750,000	$ 215,000
Units started in production	1,500,000		
Costs for July		5,650,000	4,105,000
Work in Process Inventory, 7/31 (60% complete as to labor)	400,000		

At the end of July, the cost of the Finished Goods Inventory was determined to be $124,000.

a. Compute the following:
   1. Equivalent units of production using the weighted average method.
   2. Unit production costs for material, labor, and overhead.
   3. Cost of goods sold.

b. Prepare the journal entries to record the July transfer of completed goods and the July cost of goods sold.

50. **LO.2 (WA EUP & cost assignment)** GitAlong Inc. manufactures belt buckles in a single-step production process. The following information is available for June 2013:

	Physical Units	Cost of Material	Cost of Labor
Beginning work in process	200,000	$1,200,000	$ 671,875
Units started during period	1,000,000	7,800,000	3,976,250
Units in ending inventory	300,000		

All material is added at the start of the production process. Beginning and ending inventory units were, respectively 80 percent and 70 percent complete as to conversion. Overhead cost is applied to production at the rate of 60 percent of direct labor cost.

a. Prepare a schedule to compute equivalent units of production by cost component assuming the weighted average method.
b. Determine the unit production costs for material and conversion.
c. Calculate the costs assigned to completed units and ending inventory for August 2013.

51. **LO.3 (FIFO cost assignment)** Use the Fresh Seasons information from Problem 48, except assume that the company uses a FIFO process costing system.

a. How many gallons of dressing ingredients were started in April?
b. What is the total cost of the completed beginning inventory?
c. What is the total cost of goods completed during April?
d. What is the average cost per gallon of all goods completed during April? (Round to the nearest cent.)
e. What is the cost of April's ending WIP Inventory?

52. **LO.3 (FIFO cost of production report)** Use the information from Problem 47 for Delacroix Co.

a. Prepare a cost of production report for March using the FIFO method.
b. In general, what differences exist between the WA and FIFO methods of process costing and why do these differences exist?

53. **LO.3 (FIFO cost per EUP)** Itzgood makes a variety of healthy snack foods. The following information for January 2013 relates to a trail mix. Materials are added at the beginning of processing; overhead is applied based on direct labor. The mix is transferred to a second department for packaging. Itzgood's uses a FIFO process costing system.

Beginning WIP Inventory (40% complete as to conversion)	20,000 pounds
Mix started in January	321,600 pounds
Ending WIP Inventory (80% complete as to conversion)	16,000 pounds
Material cost incurred in January	$778,272
Conversion cost incurred in January	$277,536

Beginning inventory cost totaled $53,580. For January 2013, compute the following:

a. Equivalent units of production for material and conversion.
b. Cost per equivalent unit by cost component.
c. Cost of mix transferred to the packaging department in January.
d. Cost of January's ending inventory.

EXCEL

54. **LO.2 & LO.3 (WA & FIFO; cost of production report)** In a single-process production system, Phunky Phingers produces wool gloves. For November 2013, the company's accounting records reflected the following:

Beginning WIP Inventory (100% complete as to material; 30% complete as to direct labor; 60% complete as to overhead)	12,000 units
Units started during the month	90,000 units
Ending WIP Inventory (100% complete as to material; 40% complete as to direct labor; 80% complete as to overhead)	20,000 units

Cost Component	November 1	During November
Direct material	$13,020	$90,000
Direct labor	1,908	45,792
Overhead	4,636	70,824

a. For November, prepare a cost of production report, assuming that the company uses the weighted average method.
b. For November, prepare a cost of production report, assuming that the company uses the FIFO method.

EXCEL

55. **LO.2 & LO.3 (WA and FIFO; cost of production report)** Springtime Paints makes quality paint in one production department. Production begins with the blending of various chemicals, which are added at the beginning of the process, and ends with the canning of the paint. Canning occurs when the mixture reaches the 90 percent stage of completion. The gallon cans are then transferred to the Shipping Department for crating and shipment. Labor and overhead are added continuously throughout the process. Factory overhead is applied at the rate of $3 per direct labor hour.

Prior to May, when a change in the process was implemented, work in process inventories were insignificant. The change in process enables more production but results in large amounts of work in process. The company has always used the weighted average method to determine equivalent production and unit costs. Now production management is considering changing from the weighted average method to the first-in, first-out method.

The following data relate to actual production during May:

Work in process inventory, May 1	
Direct material—chemicals	$ 45,100
Direct labor ($10 per hour)	5,250
Factory overhead	1,550
Costs for May	
Direct material—chemicals	$228,900
Direct material—cans	7,000
Direct labor ($10 per hour)	35,000
Factory overhead	11,000
Units for May (Gallons)	
Work in process inventory, May 1 (25% complete)	4,000
Sent to Shipping Department	20,000
Started in May	21,000
Work in process inventory, May 31 (80% complete)	5,000

a. Prepare a cost of production report for May using the WA method.
b. Prepare a cost of production report for May using the FIFO method.
c. Discuss the advantages and disadvantages of using the WA method versus the FIFO method, and explain under what circumstances each method should be used. **CMA ADAPTED**

56. **LO.2 & LO.4 (Cost flows; multiple departments)** Elijah Inc. produces accent stripes for automobiles in 50-inch rolls. Each roll passes through three departments (Striping, Adhesion, and Packaging) before it is ready for shipment to customers. Product costs are tracked by department and assigned using a process costing system. Overhead is applied to production in each department at a rate of 80 percent of the department's direct labor cost.

The following T-account information pertains to departmental operations for June 2013:

Work in Process—Striping

	Debit		Credit
Beginning	20,000		
DM	90,000		?
DL	80,000		
Overhead	?		
Ending	17,000		

Work in Process—Adhesion

	Debit		Credit
Beginning	70,000		
Transferred in	?		
DM	22,600		480,000
DL	?		
Overhead	?		
Ending	20,600		

Work in Process—Packaging

	Debit		Credit
Beginning	150,000		
Transferred in	?		
DM	?	CGM	?
DL	?		
Overhead	90,000		
Ending	40,000		

Finished Goods

	Debit		Credit
Beginning	185,000		
TI	880,000		720,000
Ending	?		

a. What was the cost of goods transferred from the Striping Department to the Adhesion Department for the month?
b. How much direct labor cost was incurred in the Adhesion Department? How much overhead was assigned to production in the Adhesion Department for the month?

c. How much direct material cost was charged to products in the Packaging Department?

d. Prepare the journal entries for all interdepartmental transfers of products and the cost of the units sold during June 2013.

57. **LO.2 & LO.4 (WA; second department)** Octavia Corp.'s products are manufactured in three separate departments: Molding, Curing, and Finishing. Materials are introduced in Molding; additional material is added in Curing. The following information is available for the Curing Department for May 2013:

Beginning WIP Inventory (degree of completion: transferred in, 100%; direct material, 80%; direct labor, 40%; overhead, 30%)	8,000 units
Transferred in from Molding	40,000 units
Ending WIP Inventory (degree of completion: transferred in, 100%; direct material, 70%; direct labor, 50%; overhead, 40%)	4,000 units
Transferred to Finishing	? units

Cost Component	BI Cost	Current Period Cost
Transferred in	$200,160	$1,620,000
Direct material	42,504	333,300
Direct labor	31,360	517,880
Overhead	4,848	267,840

Prepare, in good form, a weighted average cost of production report for the Curing Department for May 2013.

CPA ADAPTED

EXCEL

58. **LO.2 & LO.4 (Two departments; WA)** Always Christmas makes artificial Christmas trees in two departments: Cutting and Boxing. In the Cutting Department, wire wrapped with green "needles" is placed into production at the beginning of the process and is cut to various lengths. The "branches" are then transferred to the Boxing Department, where the lengths are separated into the necessary groups to make a tree. The "limbs" are then placed in boxes and immediately sent to Finished Goods.

The following data are available related to the October 2013 production in each of the two departments:

		PERCENT OF COMPLETION		
	Units	Transferred In	Material	Conversion
Cutting Department				
Beginning WIP Inventory	8,000	N/A	100	40
Started in process	36,000			
Ending inventory	3,600	N/A	100	70
Boxing Department				
Beginning WIP Inventory	2,500	100	0	65
Transferred in	?			
Ending inventory	1,200	100	0	70

	COSTS		
	Transferred In	Material	Conversion
Cutting Department			
Beginning WIP Inventory	N/A	$ 293,000	$ 80,000
Current period	N/A	1,379,000	1,293,440
Boxing Department			
Beginning WIP Inventory	$166,420	$ 0	$ 6,993
Current period	?	383,640	246,120

a. Prepare a cost of production report for the Cutting Department assuming a weighted average method.

b. Using the data developed from (a), prepare a cost of production report for the Boxing Department assuming a weighted average method.

59. **LO.3 & LO.4 (FIFO; second department)** Use the information for Octavia Corp. in Problem 57, except assume that the company uses FIFO costing. Prepare, in good form, a FIFO cost of production report for the Curing Department for May 2013.

CPA ADAPTED

60. **LO.3 & LO.4 (Comprehensive; FIFO; two departments)** KeepIn makes fencing in a two-stage production system. In the Cutting Department, wood is cut and assembled into 6-foot fence sections. In the Coating Department, the sections are pressure-treated to resist the effects of weather and then coated with a preservative. The following production and cost data are available for March 2013 (units are 6-foot fence sections):

Units	Cutting Dept.	Coating Dept.
Beginning WIP Inventory (March 1)	1,300	900
Complete as to material	80%	0%
Complete as to conversion	75%	60%
Units started in March	4,800	?
Units completed in March	?	4,500
Ending WIP Inventory (March 31)	1,100	?
Complete as to material	40%	0%
Complete as to conversion	20%	40%
Costs		
Beginning WIP Inventory		
Transferred in	N/A	$11,840
Material	$ 8,345	0
Conversion	7,720	1,674
Current		
Transferred in	N/A	?
Material	35,200	4,950
Conversion	21,225	11,300

a. Prepare EUP schedules for both the Cutting and Coating Departments.
b. Determine the cost per EUP for the Cutting Department.
c. Assign costs to goods transferred out of and in ending WIP Inventory in the Cutting Department.
d. Determine the cost per EUP in the Coating Department. Use the modified FIFO basis and round to the nearest cent. (See footnote 7, page 205.)
e. Assign costs to goods transferred out of and in ending WIP Inventory in the Coating Department.

61. **LO.5 (Multiproduct; hybrid costing)** Be-at-Ease Industries manufactures a series of three models of molded plastic chairs: standard (without arms), deluxe (with arms), and executive (with arms and padding). All are variations of the same design. The company uses batch manufacturing and has a hybrid costing system.

Be-at-Ease has an extrusion operation and subsequent operations to form, trim, and finish the chairs. Plastic sheets are produced by the extrusion operation, some of which are sold directly to other manufacturers. During the forming operation, the remaining plastic sheets are molded into chair seats, and the legs are added; the standard model is sold after this operation. During the trim operation, the arms are added to the deluxe and executive models, and the chair edges are smoothed. Only the executive model enters the finish operation where the padding is added. All units produced complete the same steps within each operation.

The July production run had a total manufacturing cost of $898,000. The units of production and direct material costs incurred were as follows:

	Units Produced	Extrusion Materials	Form Materials	Trim Materials	Finish Materials
Plastic sheets	5,000	$ 60,000			
Standard model	6,000	72,000	$24,000		
Deluxe model	3,000	36,000	12,000	$ 9,000	
Executive model	2,000	24,000	8,000	6,000	$12,000
Totals	16,000	$192,000	$44,000	$15,000	$12,000

Manufacturing costs applied during July were as follows:

	Extrusion Operation	Form Operation	Trim Operation	Finish Operation
Direct labor	$152,000	$60,000	$30,000	$18,000
Factory overhead	240,000	72,000	39,000	24,000

a. For each product produced by Be-at-Ease during July, determine the
   1. Unit cost.
   2. Total cost.

   Account for all costs incurred during the month, and support your answer with appropriate calculations.

b. Without prejudice to your answer in (a), assume that only 1,000 units of the deluxe model remained in the Work in Process Inventory at the end of the month. These units were 100 percent complete as to material and 60 percent complete as to conversion in the trim operation. Determine the value of the 1,000 units of the deluxe model in Be-at-Ease's Work in Process Inventory at the end of July.

CMA ADAPTED

62. **LO.6 (Multiproduct; hybrid costing)** Randazzo Ltd. produces sports fan towels and uses the weighted average process costing method. All towels are cut to be the same size and from the same fabric but can be customized by adding one or more options: (1) embossed team logo, (2) streamers, and (3) a wooden handle. The following information is available for September 2013:

Towels	
BI (70% complete as to conversion)	15,000
Started	520,000
EI (95% complete as to conversion)	9,000
Cost data	
Beginning inventory DM	$ 13,250
Beginning inventory logos	4,035
Beginning inventory conversion	5,703
Current period DM	468,250
Current period embossed logos	298,735
Current period streamers	119,977
Current period wooden handles	1,312
Current period conversion	282,954

At the beginning of September, 40 percent of the towels had been embossed. At the end of September, 70 percent of the towels in work in process were plain, 25 percent had been embossed, and 5 percent had streamers. Conversion is applied to all items equally.

Randazzo's production and sales for the month were as follows:

	Production	Sales
Plain towels	60,000	58,000
Towels with logos and streamers	418,000	417,500
Towels with logos, streamers, and handles	25,000	24,800
Towels with streamers	15,200	15,175
Towels with streamers and handles	2,800	2,730
Towels with handles	5,000	4,350
Total production for September	526,000	522,555

a. Determine the cost of Randazzo's ending WIP Inventory of towels.
b. Determine the cost of Randazzo's ending FG Inventory of towels.
c. Determine the cost of goods sold for September.
d. Should the conversion cost for all towels be the same amount?

63. **LO.7 (Appendix 2; standard process costing)** MHR Inc. uses a standard process costing system. All material is added at the beginning of the production process. Per unit standard costs for one of the company's products are as follows:

Direct material	$ 8.25
Direct labor	1.60
Overhead	4.90
Total standard cost	$14.75

October 2013 production and cost information for MHR follow:

Units in beginning inventory (40% complete as to DL, 70% complete as to OH)	14,800
Units started	385,000
Units in ending inventory (60% complete as to DL, 85% complete as to OH)	4,300
Current period costs:	
Direct material	$3,201,032
Direct labor	625,510
Overhead	1,904,390

a. Prepare an equivalent units of production schedule.
b. Determine the cost of the beginning inventory (in total and by cost component).
c. Assign costs to goods transferred and to ending WIP inventory.
d. Calculate and label (F or U) the variances.

64. **LO.2, LO.4, & LO.8 (Appendix 3; WA; normal and abnormal loss)** Turkburg produces frozen turkey patties. In the Forming Department, ground turkey is formed into patties and cooked; an acceptable shrinkage loss for this department is 1 percent of the pounds started. The patties are then transferred to the Finishing Department where they are placed on buns, boxed, and frozen.

Turkburg uses a weighted average process costing system and has the following production and cost data for the Forming Department for May 2013:

Beginning WIP Inventory (80% complete as to conversion)	2,000 pounds
Started	250,000 pounds
Transferred to Finishing (357,300 patties)	238,200 pounds
Ending inventory (30% complete as to conversion)	6,000 pounds
Beginning inventory cost of turkey	$ 1,807
May cost of turkey	$240,208
Beginning inventory conversion cost	$ 150
May conversion cost	$ 24,380

a. What is the total shrinkage (in pounds)?
b. How much of the shrinkage is classified as normal? How is it treated for accounting purposes?
c. How much of the shrinkage is classified as abnormal? How is it treated for accounting purposes?
d. What are the May 2013 equivalent units of production in the Forming Department for direct materials and conversion?
e. What is the total cost of the patties transferred to the Finishing Department? Cost of ending inventory? Cost of abnormal spoilage?
f. How might Turkburg reduce its shrinkage loss? How, if at all, would your solution(s) affect costs and selling prices?
g. What might have been the cause of the abnormally high spoilage in May? Use calculations to support your answer.

65. **LO.7 (Appendix 2; standard process costing)** Donbrowski Co. manufactures reflective lenses and uses a standard process costing system. For May 2013, the following data are available:

Standard Cost of One Unit	
Direct material	$ 5.50
Conversion	12.50
Total manufacturing cost	$18.00

Beginning WIP Inventory	10,000	units (100% DM; 70% conversion)
Started in May	180,000	units
Completed in May	150,000	units
Ending WIP Inventory	?	units (100% DM; 60% conversion)
Actual costs for May:		
Direct material	$1,001,000	
Conversion	2,136,000	
Total actual cost	$3,137,000	

a. Prepare an equivalent units of production schedule.
b. Prepare a cost of production report and assign costs to goods transferred and to ending work in process inventory.
c. Calculate and label the variances and close them to Cost of Goods Sold.

66. **LO.2, LO.4, & LO.8 (Appendix 3; WA; normal and abnormal discrete spoilage)** Strongarm manufactures various lines of bicycles. Because of the high volume of each type of product, the company employs a process cost system using the weighted average method to determine unit costs. Bicycle parts are manufactured in the Molding Department and transferred to the Assembly Department where they are partially assembled. After assembly, the bicycle is sent to the Packing Department.

Annual cost and production figures for the Assembly Department follow:

Production Data	
Beginning WIP Inventory (100% complete as to transferred in; 100% complete as to material; 80% complete as to conversion)	3,000 units
Transferred in during the year (100% complete as to transferred in)	45,000 units
Transferred to Packing	40,000 units
Ending WIP Inventory (100% complete as to transferred in; 50% complete as to material; 20% complete as to conversion)	4,000 units

	COST DATA		
	Transferred In	Direct Material	Conversion
Beginning WIP Inventory	$ 82,200	$ 6,660	$ 13,930
Current period	1,237,800	96,840	241,430
Totals	$1,320,000	$103,500	$255,360

Damaged bicycles are identified on inspection when the assembly process is complete. The normal rejection rate for damaged bicycles is 5 percent of those reaching the inspection point. Any damaged bicycles above the 5 percent quota are considered to be abnormal. Damaged bikes are removed from the production process, and when possible, parts are reused on other bikes. However, such salvage is ignored for the purposes of this problem.

Strongarm does not want to assign normal spoilage cost either to the units in ending inventory (because they have not yet been inspected) or to the bikes that are considered "abnormal spoilage." Thus, the company includes both normal and abnormal spoilage in the equivalent units schedule (at the appropriate percentage of completion). The cost of the normal spoilage is then added to the bikes transferred to the Packing Department. Abnormal spoilage is treated as a period loss.

a. Compute the number of damaged bikes that are considered to be
   1. Normal spoilage.
   2. Abnormal spoilage.
b. Compute the weighted average equivalent units of production for the year for
   1. Bicycles transferred in from the Molding Department.
   2. Bicycles produced with regard to Assembly material.
   3. Bicycles produced with regard to Assembly conversion.
c. Compute the cost per equivalent unit for the fully assembled bicycle.
d. Compute the amount of total production cost that will be associated with the following items:
   1. Normal damaged units.
   2. Abnormal damaged units.
   3. Good units completed in the Assembly Department.
   4. Ending Work in Process Inventory in the Assembly Department.
e. What amount will be transferred to the Packing Department?
f. Discuss some potential reasons for spoilage to occur in this company. Which of these reasons would you consider important enough to correct and why? How might you attempt to correct these problems?

CMA ADAPTED

67. **LO.2 & LO.8 (Appendix 3; WA; normal and abnormal discrete spoilage)** LaToya Company produces door pulls, which are inspected at the end of production. Spoilage may occur because the door pull is improperly stamped or molded. Any spoilage in excess of 3 percent of the completed good units is considered abnormal. Direct material is added at the start of production. Labor and overhead are incurred evenly throughout production.

The company's May 2013 production and cost data follow:

Beginning WIP Inventory (50% complete)	5,600
Units started	74,400
Good units completed	70,000
Ending WIP Inventory (1/3 complete)	7,500

	DM	Conversion	Total
Beginning inventory	$ 6,400	$ 1,232	$ 7,632
Current period	74,400	31,768	106,168
Total	$80,800	$33,000	$113,800

Calculate the equivalent units schedule, prepare a weighted average cost of production report, and assign all costs. LaToya extends both the normal and abnormal spoilage units in the EUP schedule to all cost components that have been incurred to the point of detection (100 percent completion). The cost of normal spoilage is attached to the units transferred to Finished Goods Inventory; the cost of abnormal spoilage is considered a period loss.

68. **LO.3 & LO.8 (Appendix 3; FIFO; normal and abnormal discrete spoilage)** Use the LaToya Company data given in Problem 67. However, assume that the spoiled goods were detected when conversion was 30 percent complete. Prepare a May 2013 cost of production report using the FIFO method. The cost of normal spoilage is attached to the units transferred to Finished Goods Inventory; the cost of abnormal spoilage is considered a period loss. Round all cost calculations to the nearest penny.

69. **LO.2, LO.4, & LO.8 (Appendix 3; WA; normal and abnormal discrete spoilage)** Gary's Tools manufactures one of its products in a two-department process. A separate Work in Process Inventory account is maintained for each department, and the company uses a weighted average process costing system. The first department is Molding; the second is Grinding. At the end of production in Grinding, a quality inspection is made and then packaging is added. Overhead is applied in the Grinding Department

on a machine-hour basis. Production and cost data for the Grinding Department for August 2013 follow:

Production Data

Beginning WIP Inventory (percent complete: material, 0; labor, 30; overhead, 40)	1,000 units
Transferred in from Molding	50,800 units
Normal spoilage (found at the end of processing during quality control)	650 units
Abnormal spoilage (found at end of processing during quality control)	350 units
Ending WIP Inventory (percent complete: material, 0; labor, 40; overhead, 65)	1,800 units
Transferred to finished goods	? units

Cost Data

Beginning WIP Inventory		
Transferred in	$ 6,050	
Material (label and package)	0	
Direct labor	325	
Overhead	980	$ 7,355
Current period		
Transferred in	$149,350	
Material (label and package)	12,250	
Direct labor	23,767	
Overhead	50,190	235,557
Total cost to account for		$242,912

a. Prepare the August cost of production report for the Grinding Department. Gary's Tools assigns the cost of normal spoilage only to the products that are transferred out. As such, the company extends both the normal and abnormal spoilage units in the EUP schedule to all cost components except packaging (as packaging is not added to spoiled units). The cost of normal spoilage is attached to the units transferred to Finished Goods Inventory; the cost of abnormal spoilage is considered a period loss.

b. Prepare the journal entry to dispose of the cost of abnormal spoilage.

7

Standard Costing and Variance Analysis

LEARNING OBJECTIVES

After completing this chapter, you should be able to answer the following questions:

1. Why are standard cost systems used?
2. How are material, labor, and overhead standards set?
3. How are material, labor, and overhead variances calculated and recorded?
4. How have the setting and use of standards changed over time?
5. How does the use of a single conversion element (rather than the traditional labor and overhead elements) affect standard costing?
6. *(Appendix)* How are variances affected by multiple material and labor categories?

INTRODUCTION

As discussed in Chapter 5, a standard is a performance benchmark. Organizations, even those not involved in production activities, develop and use standards for almost all tasks. For example, businesses set standards for employee sales expenses; pizza restaurants set standards to prepare and bake a pizza; and casinos set standards for revenue to be generated per square foot of playing space. The MGM Grand in Las Vegas has standards for housekeeping (30 minutes), room service (maximum of 30 minutes to deliver), maintenance calls (15 minutes to be handled), and car valet delivery (8 minutes).[1] A Big Mac at McDonald's should be assembled in 15 seconds; Taco Bell requires that Crunchwrap Supremes get grilled for 27 seconds; and Wendy's has an average of 134 seconds per vehicle in the drive-through lanes.[2]

Because of the variety of organizational activities and information objectives, no single standard costing system is appropriate for all situations. Some systems use standards for costs but not for quantities; other systems (especially those in service businesses) use standards for labor but not material. Standards act as target measures of performance and therefore may be met, exceeded, or failed to be met. Accountants help explain the financial consequences of exceeding or failing to achieve standards. Without a predetermined measure, managers have no way of knowing what performance level is expected or gauging actual performance. And without comparing the actual result to the predetermined measure, managers have no way of knowing whether the company met expectations or exercised reasonable operational control.

This chapter discusses a traditional standard cost system that provides price and quantity standards for each cost component: direct material, direct labor, and manufacturing overhead. The chapter discusses why standard cost systems are used, how standards are developed, how variances from standards are calculated, and what information can be gained from variance analysis. Journal entries used in a standard cost system are shown. The chapter appendix covers mix and yield variances that can arise from using multiple types of materials or groups of labor.

USE OF STANDARD COST SYSTEMS

1 Why are standard cost systems used?

Although manufacturing companies originally initiated the use of standard cost systems, service and not-for-profit organizations also use standards. A standard cost system tracks both standard and actual costs in the accounting records. This dual recording provides an essential element of cost control: having norms against which actual operations can be compared. Actual costs may differ each time materials are acquired. Labor rates may be adjusted during a period. Overhead costs fluctuate for a wide variety of reasons, some of which are not controllable within the organization. Additionally, material quantities, labor times, and machine hours may vary with production or service activities. In an actual cost system, each difference will have an impact on product cost. With an actual cost system, product or service unit costs would change continuously with changes in prices and usage of inputs.

In contrast to an actual cost system, a standard cost system uses **standards** that specify the expected costs and quantities needed to manufacture a single unit of product or perform a single service. By holding unit costs constant for some period of time, the use of standard costs provides the same benefits as the use of predetermined overhead rates: a standard cost system allows (1) the allocation of costs in real time to products and services and (2) the ability to adjust for cost or quantity fluctuations unrelated to activity differences.

Although a substantial commitment of time and effort is required to implement and use a standard cost system, companies are willing to make such a commitment for a variety of reasons. Once in place, standard cost systems require less clerical time and effort than are necessary in an actual cost system because costs are assigned to the inventory and Cost of Goods Sold accounts at predetermined amounts per unit regardless of actual conditions. However, more importantly than the clerical efficiency provided, standard cost systems are designed to provide an assessment measure of performance to managers for use in performing their various functions.

[1] Andrea Petersen, "When 12,000 Guests Spend the Night," *Wall Street Journal* (September 22, 2011), p. D1.

[2] Karl Greenfeld, "Fast and Furious," *Bloomberg Businessweek* (May 9–May 15, 2011), pp. 64–69.

Motivating

Standards help communicate management's expectations to workers. When standards are achievable and rewards for attaining them are available, workers are likely to be motivated to strive to meet the targets that have been set. However, from a standpoint of organizational profitability and competitiveness, the standards must require a reasonable amount of effort on the worker's part.

Planning

Financial and operational planning requires estimates about future price and usage of inputs. Managers can use current standards to estimate future quantity needs and costs. These estimates help determine purchasing needs for material, staffing needs for labor, and capacity needs related to overhead and planning for company cash flows. Standards are also used to provide the cost basis needed to analyze relationships among the organization's costs, sales volume, and profits. But standards should not be considered long-term amounts and should be reviewed, and likely updated, at least annually, especially if an organization implements changes in production technology.

Controlling

The control process begins with the establishment of standards as a basis against which actual costs and quantities can be measured and variances calculated. **Variance analysis** is the process of categorizing the nature (favorable or unfavorable) of the differences between actual and standard costs/quantities and seeking explanations for those differences. A favorable variance indicates that actual costs or quantities were less than the standard, whereas an unfavorable variance indicates that actual costs or quantities were above the standard. A well-designed variance analysis system computes variances as early as possible, subject to cost–benefit assessments. The system should help managers determine who or what was responsible for each variance and who is best able to explain it. An early measurement and reporting system allows managers to quickly monitor operations and take corrective action if necessary.

In analyzing variances, managers must recognize that they have a specific scarce resource: their time. They must distinguish between situations that can be ignored and those that need attention. To do this, managers establish upper and lower tolerance limits of acceptable deviations from the standard. If variances are small and within an acceptable range, no managerial action is required. If a variance differs significantly from standard, the manager responsible for the cost is expected to identify the variance cause(s) and then take actions to eliminate future unfavorable variances or, perhaps, to perpetuate favorable variances.

Setting upper and lower tolerance limits for deviations (as illustrated in Exhibit 7.1) allows managers to implement the **management-by-exception** concept. In the exhibit, the

Exhibit 7.1 Illustration of Management-by-Exception Concept

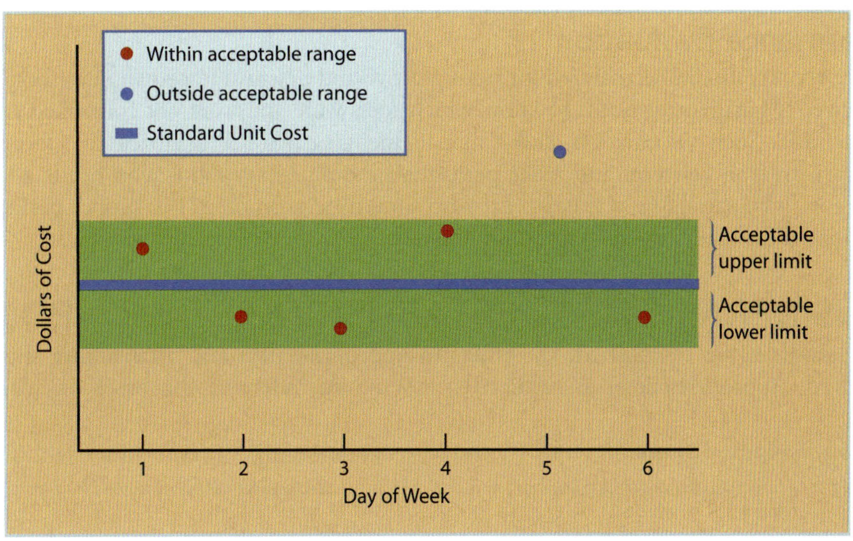

only significant deviation from standard occurred on Day 5, when the actual cost exceeded the upper limit of acceptable performance. An exception report describing the situation should be generated on this date so that the manager can investigate the underlying variance causes.

Variances large enough to fall outside the acceptability ranges often indicate problems. However, a mere computation of a variance does not reveal the variance's cause nor the person or group responsible for it. To determine variance causality, managers must investigate significant variances through observation, inspection, and inquiry. The investigation involves people at the operating level as well as accounting personnel. Operations personnel should spot variances as they occur and record the reasons for the variances to the extent that those reasons are discernible. For example, operating personnel could readily detect and report causes such as machine downtime or material spoilage.

One important point about variances must be made: a favorable variance is not necessarily a good variance. Although people often equate "favorable" with "good," an extremely favorable variance could mean that an error was made when the standard was set or that a related, offsetting unfavorable variance exists. For example, if low-grade material is purchased, a favorable price variance may result when the cost of the material is less than anticipated. However, use of the lower grade material may mean that more material than standard might have to be used to overcome defective production or that more labor time was required to complete a job as a result of using the inferior material—both results would create unfavorable variances. Another common situation begins with labor rather than material. Using workers who are lower paid but less skilled than others will result in a favorable wage variance but can cause an excessive, unfavorable use of raw material and of labor time. Managers must be aware that such relationships exist and that variances cannot be analyzed in isolation.

Variance computations are being made more often than in the past. Monthly variance reporting is still common, but there is movement toward shorter reporting periods. As more companies integrate total quality management (TQM) and just-in-time (JIT) production into their operations, variance reporting and analysis will become more frequent.[3]

Decision Making

Standard cost information facilitates decision making. For example, managers can compare a standard cost with a quoted price to determine whether an item should be manufactured in-house or purchased. Using actual cost information in such a decision could be inappropriate because the actual cost could fluctuate each period. Also, in deciding whether to offer a special price to customers, managers can use standard product cost to determine the lowest price limit. Similarly, a company bidding on contracts must have some idea of estimated product costs. Bidding too low and winning the contract could cause substantial operating income (and, possibly, cash flow) reduction; a bid that is too high could be noncompetitive and cause the contract to be awarded to another company.

Performance Evaluation

Variance reports should be analyzed for both positive and negative information as soon as they are received. Management needs to know which costs were and were not controlled and who is responsible. Such information allows management to provide feedback to subordinates, investigate areas of concern, and make performance evaluations about who needs additional supervision, who should be replaced, and who should be promoted. For proper performance evaluations to be made, variance responsibility must be traced to specific managers.[4]

CONSIDERATIONS IN ESTABLISHING STANDARDS

When standards are established, the issues of appropriateness and attainability should be considered. Appropriateness, in relation to a standard, refers to the bases on which the

[3]Total quality management is discussed in Chapter 17, and just-in-time production is discussed in Chapter 18.

[4]Responsibility accounting, performance evaluation, and cost control relative to variances are discussed in greater depth in, respectively, Chapters 13, 14, and 16.

standards are developed and how long they will be viable. Attainability refers to management's belief about the degree of difficulty or rigor that should be exerted in achieving the standard.

Appropriateness

Although developed from past and current information, standards must evolve to reflect relevant future technical and environmental factors. Consideration should be given to factors such as material quality, normal ordering quantities for material, expected employee wage rates, mix of employee skills, facility layout, and expected degree of plant automation. As mentioned earlier, standards will not remain useful forever. Current operating performance should not be compared to out-of-date standards because such comparisons will generate variances that are not logical bases for planning, controlling, decision making, or evaluating performance.

Attainability

Standards provide a target measure of performance and can be set at various levels of rigor that can affect employee motivation. Similar to the capacity levels discussed in Chapter 3, standards can be classified as expected, practical, and ideal. Depending on the rigor of standard in effect, the acceptable ranges used to apply the management-by-exception principle will differ—especially on the unfavorable side.

Type of Standard	Ability to Achieve	Types of Variances
Expected	Almost always	Almost always favorable
Practical	60–70% of the time	Favorable and unfavorable
Ideal	Rarely, if ever	Almost always unfavorable

Expected standards reflect what is actually expected to occur. Such standards anticipate future waste and inefficiencies and allow for them. As such, expected standards are not of significant value for motivating, controlling, decision making, or evaluating performance. A company using expected standards should set a very small range of acceptable variation because actual costs should conform closely to standards. Expected standards tend to generate favorable variances.

Standards that can be reached or slightly exceeded approximately 60–70 percent of the time with reasonable effort are called **practical standards**. These standards allow for normal, unavoidable delays such as those caused by machine downtime and worker breaks. Practical standards represent an attainable challenge and traditionally have been thought to be the most effective in motivating workers and determining their performance levels. Both favorable and unfavorable variances result from the use of such moderately rigorous standards.

Standards that provide for no inefficiency of any type are called **ideal** (or theoretical) **standards**. These standards are the most rigorous and do not allow for normal operating delays or human limitations such as fatigue, boredom, or misunderstanding. Unless a plant is entirely automated (and then the possibility of human error or power failure still exists), ideal standards are impossible to attain. Applying such standards has traditionally resulted in discouraged and resentful workers who ultimately ignored the standards. Variances from ideal standards were almost always unfavorable and were commonly not considered useful for constructive cost control or performance evaluation. However, as discussed in more depth later in the chapter, this perspective has begun to change.

DEVELOPMENT OF A STANDARD COST SYSTEM

2 How are material, labor, and overhead standards set?

A primary objective in manufacturing a product is to minimize unit cost while achieving certain quality and functionality specifications. Almost all products can be manufactured from a variety of alternative inputs that would generate similar output and output quality. The input choices that are made affect the standards that are set. Some possible input resource combinations are not necessarily practical or efficient. For instance, a labor team might consist only of craftspeople or skilled workers, but such a team might not be cost beneficial if the wage rates of skilled and unskilled workers differ significantly. Also, providing high-technology equipment to unskilled labor is possible, but doing so would not be an efficient use of resources. Developing a standard cost involves judgment and practicality in identifying the material and labor types, quantities, and prices as well as understanding the types of organizational overhead and how they behave.

After the desired output quality and the input resources needed to achieve that quality at a reasonable cost have been determined, price and quantity standards can be developed. Experts from cost accounting, industrial engineering, human resources, data processing, purchasing, and management contribute information and expertise toward developing standards. Inclusion of the various groups helps to ensure credibility of the standards and to motivate people to achieve the standards. The discussion of the standard-setting process begins with material.

Material Standards

The first step in developing material standards is to identify and list the specific direct material(s) needed to manufacture the product or provide the service.[5] This list is generally available on product specification documents prior to initial production. Without such documentation, material specifications can be determined by observing the production area, questioning production personnel, inspecting material requisitions, and reviewing the product-related cost accounts. Four things must be known about material inputs:

- type of material needed,
- quality (grade) of material needed,
- quantity of material needed, and
- price per unit of material (must be based on level of quality specified).

For example, the direct material used in producing a baseball glove is cured and tanned leather; indirect materials include nylon thread and small plastic reinforcements at the base of the thumb and small finger. Because only about 30 percent of a cowhide can actually be used to make baseball gloves, each cowhide provides enough leather for only three or four gloves—but actual output depends on the glove size being produced (from gloves worn to play T-ball to those worn in the major leagues). Buffalo hide, kangaroo hide, pigskin, and man-made materials may be substituted for cowhide, but choice of material will affect production cost.

In making quality decisions, managers should remember that as the material grade rises, so generally does price; decisions about material inputs usually seek to balance the relationships of price, quality, and projected selling prices with company objectives. The resulting trade-offs affect material mix, material yield, finished product quality and quantity, overall product cost, and product salability. Thus, quantity and cost estimates become direct functions of quality decisions. Only after the quality level is selected for each component can estimates be made for the physical quantity of weight, size, volume, or other input measure(s). These estimates are based on the results of engineering tests, opinions of managers and workers using the material, past material requisitions, and review of the cost accounts.

Most products require multiple direct material inputs. The specifications for materials, including quality and quantity, are compiled on a product's **bill of materials**. Exhibit 7.2 shows the bill of materials for one type of mountain bike manufactured by Salinas Corporation. Even companies without formal standard cost systems develop bills of materials for products as guides for production activity.

When converting quantities from the bill of materials into costs, companies often make allowances for normal waste of components.[6] After standard quantities have been developed, component prices must be determined. Purchasing agents may be able to exercise substantial influence on input prices in the following ways:

- understanding the quantity and timing of company purchasing;
- knowing what alternative suppliers are available;

[5] For the remainder of the chapter, the text discussion will assume that a product is being manufactured. The discussion, however, is equally appropriate for service provision.

[6] Although such allowances are often made, providing for them does not result in the most effective use of a standard cost system. Problems arising from including such allowances are discussed later in this chapter.

Exhibit 7.2 Salinas Corporation's Bill of Materials

Product Name: Mountain Bike (unassembled)

Product # 15

Date Established: January 10, 2013

Component ID#	Quantity Required	Description	Comments
WF-05	1	Front wheel, tire & tube	Stumpjumper
WR-05	1	Rear wheel, tire & tube	Stumpjumper
B-05	2	Front & rear brakes	Includes derailleur, levers, and calipers
HB-05	1	Handlebar and stem	Stainless steel
B-21	16	2.5″ × 5/16″ bolts	Includes nuts and flat washers
S-18	12	3″ clamps	Stainless steel
SPS-05	1	Seat post and seat	Nylon and black
P-05	2	Pedals	Black rubber
F-05	1	Frame	Fiberglass

- recognizing the economic climate under which purchases are being made;
- performing "due diligence" as to the input costs incurred and profit margins desired by suppliers; and
- seeking single source suppliers or partnership alliances with suppliers, when appropriate.

Rather than considering only the direct purchase price of an input, purchasing agents now try to estimate and minimize the **total cost of ownership (TCO)**, which includes price, freight, duty, tax charges, payment and discount terms, inventory storage costs, scrap rates, rebates or special incentives, warranties, and disposal costs. Incorporating such information into price standards should make it easier for the purchasing agent to later determine the causes of any significant differences between actual and standard prices.

When all quantity and price information is available, component quantities are multiplied by unit prices to obtain each component's total cost. These totals are summed to determine the total standard material cost of one unit of product.

Labor Standards

Developing labor standards requires the same basic procedures as those used for material. Each production operation performed by workers (such as bending, reaching, lifting, moving material, and packing) or by machinery (such as drilling, cooking, and assembling) should be identified. In specifying operations and movements, all necessary activities should be included when time standards are set, but all unnecessary movements of workers and material should be disregarded.[7]

To develop effective standards, a company obtains quantitative information for each production operation. Such information can be gathered from industrial engineering methods, in-house time-and-motion studies, or historical data. **Methods-time measurement (MTM)** is an industrial engineering process that analyzes work tasks to determine the time a trained worker needs to perform a given operation at a rate that can be sustained for an eight-hour workday. In-house studies may result in employees engaging in "slowdown" tactics when they are being monitored. Such tactics result in a longer time being established as the standard, which makes employees appear more efficient when actual results are

[7] Similar to making "normal" allowances for wasted material in setting material standards, companies also include certain often unnecessary activities such as rework in determining labor standards. Problems related to assessing production efficiency also arise with such inclusions.

measured. Slowdowns may also occur because employees, knowing they are being observed, want to make certain that they are performing the task correctly. Rather than monitoring task performance, the average time needed to manufacture a product during the prior year can be calculated from employee time sheets and used to set a current time standard. A problem with this method is that historical data can include inefficiencies. To compensate for biases in internal estimates, management and supervisory personnel normally adjust standards for slowdowns or past inefficiencies by making subjective adjustments to the internal information that has been gathered.

After all labor tasks have been analyzed, a company prepares an **operations flow document** that lists all tasks necessary to make one unit of product or perform a specific service. When products are manufactured individually, the operations flow document shows the time necessary to produce one unit. In a process that produces goods in batches, individual times cannot be specified accurately, and time is specified for the batch. Exhibit 7.3 presents the operations flow document for a mountain bike produced by Salinas Corporation.

Exhibit 7.3 Salinas Corporation's Operations Flow Document

Product: Mountain Bike

Product # 15

Date Established: January 10, 2013

Operation ID#	Department	Standard Time	Description of Task
009	Painting	3.00 hours	Spray primer, clear coat, and paint on frame
012	Assembly	5.00 hours	Assemble bike
015	Oiling	1.00 hour	Oil all gear parts
018	Testing	0.50 hour	Inspect and test bike
210	Packaging	0.25 hour	Place bike in corrugated packaging

Labor rate standards should reflect employee wages and related employer costs for fringe benefits, FICA (Social Security), and unemployment taxes. In the simplest situation, all departmental personnel are paid the same wage rate as, for example, when wages are task specific or tied to a labor contract. If employees performing the same or similar tasks are paid different wage rates, a weighted average rate (total wage cost per hour divided by the number of workers) must be computed and used as the standard. Differences in rates could be caused by length of employment or skill level.

Once time and rate information are available, job task times are multiplied by wage rates to generate each operation's total cost. These totals are summed to provide the total standard labor cost of one unit (or batch) of product.

Overhead Standards

Overhead (OH) standards reflect the company's predetermined manufacturing overhead rate(s). As discussed in Chapter 4, the most appropriate costing information will result when (1) overhead is assigned to separate cost pools based on cost drivers and (2) allocations are made using activity drivers directly related to the overhead costs being assigned.

After the bill of materials, operations flow document, and predetermined OH rates per activity measure have been developed, a **standard cost card** is prepared that summarizes the standard quantities and costs needed to produce a unit. The standard cost card for Salinas Corporation's mountain bike is shown in Exhibit 7.4. For simplicity, it is assumed that Salinas Corporation uses only two predetermined overhead rates: one for variable manufacturing costs and one for fixed manufacturing costs.

Exhibit 7.4 Salinas Corporation's Standard Cost Card for a Mountain Bike

Product: Mountain Bike

Product # 15

Date Established: January 10, 2013

DIRECT MATERIAL

Component ID#	Quantity Required	Unit Cost	Total Cost
WF-05	1	$ 20.00	$ 20
WR-05	1	25.00	25
B-05	2	20.00	40
HB-05	1	23.00	23
B-21	16	0.75	12
S-18	12	1.25	15
SPS-05	1	17.00	17
P-05	2	14.00	28
F-05	1	200.00	200
Total cost			$380

DIRECT LABOR

Oper. ID#	Wage Rate/Hr	Total Hrs	Painting	Assembling	Oiling	Testing	Packaging	Total Cost
009	$12	3.00	$36					$ 36
012	15	5.00		$75				75
015	8	1.00			$8			8
018	20	0.50				$10		10
210	8	0.25					$2	2
Totals		9.75	$36	$75	$8	$10	$2	$131

MANUFACTURING OVERHEAD

Expected capacity for 2013: 5,000 bikes	
Expected capacity in DLHs for 2013 = 5,000 × 9.75 DLHs per bike = 48,750 DLHs	
Variable overhead ($682,500 ÷ 48,750 = $14; $14 × 9.75 DLHs per bike)	$136.50
Fixed overhead ($487,500 ÷ 48,750 = $10; $10 × 9.75 DLHs per bike)	97.50
Total overhead per bike	$234.00

Although both actual and standard costs are recorded in a standard cost system, only standard costs are shown in the Raw (Direct) Material, Work in Process, and Finished Goods Inventory accounts. The standard cost of each cost element (direct material, direct labor, variable overhead, and fixed overhead) is said to be "applied" or "allocated" to the goods produced. This terminology is the same as that used when overhead is assigned to inventory based on a predetermined rate. A **variance** is any difference between an actual cost and a standard cost.

3 How are material, labor, and overhead variances calculated and recorded?

GENERAL VARIANCE ANALYSIS MODEL

The difference between total actual cost for production inputs and total standard cost applied to the production output is the total variance for production. This variance can be diagrammed as follows:

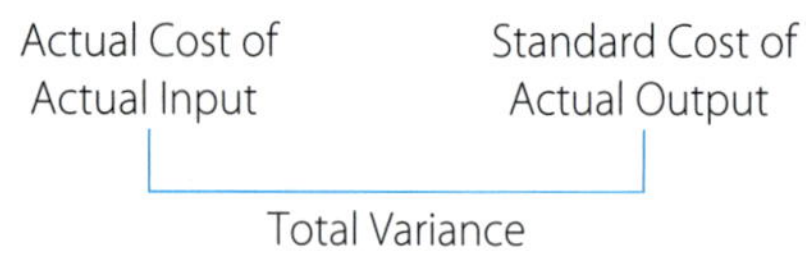

Total variances do not provide useful information for determining why standard and actual costs differed. For instance, the preceding variance computation does not indicate whether the variance was caused by price factors, quantity factors, or both. To provide additional information, total variances are subdivided into price and usage components. The total variance diagram can be expanded to provide the following general model indicating the two subvariances, using a middle column that reflects a combination of standard price and actual quantity:

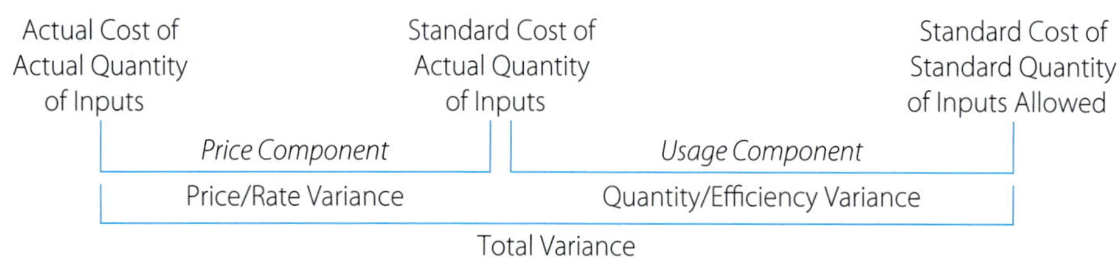

The price component indicates the difference between the actual cost of the inputs and cost expected to be paid for inputs. The price (or rate) variance is calculated as the difference between the actual price (AP) and the standard price (SP) per unit of input multiplied by the actual input quantity (AQ):

$$\text{Price (or rate) variance} = (\text{AP} \times \text{SP})(\text{AQ})$$

The usage component of the total variance shows the efficiency of results or the relationship of input to output. The change from input to output reflects the fact that the actual ratio of inputs to outputs will not necessarily equal the standard ratio of inputs to outputs. The model's far right column shows total standard cost, which reflects a measure of output known as the **standard quantity**. This quantity translates actual quantity of production output into the standard quantity of production input or the quantity of input that *should have been* used to achieve the actual output. For example, if five 8-ounce bottles of juice are produced, a standard quantity of 40 ounces of juice should have been used to manufacture the five bottles. However, if some juice had been spilled during the production process, the actual quantity of juice used to make the five 8-ounce bottles might have been 42 ounces.

The monetary amount shown in the right-hand column of the general variance analysis model is computed as the standard quantity multiplied by the standard input price. This usage component computation provides a monetary measure that can be recorded in the accounting records. The quantity/efficiency variance is calculated as the difference between the AQ and standard quantity of input allowed (SQ) multiplied by the standard price per unit of input:

$$\text{Quantity (or efficiency) variance} = (\text{AQ} - \text{SQ})(\text{SP})$$

If the actual price or quantity amounts are higher than the standard price or quantity amounts, the variance is unfavorable (U); if the actual amounts are lower than the standard amounts, the variance is favorable (F). The designation of unfavorable and favorable reflect the effect that the variances have on income as indicated in the following chart.

Actual to Standard Relationship	Variance	Effect on Income
Actual Price > Standard Price	Unfavorable	Negative
Actual Price < Standard Price	Favorable	Positive
Actual Quantity > Standard Quantity	Unfavorable	Negative
Actual Quantity < Standard Quantity	Favorable	Positive

It is important to note that *unfavorable* is not necessarily equated with bad nor is *favorable* equated with good. Determination of "bad" or "good" must be made after identifying the variance's cause and its implications for other cost elements.

The following sections illustrate variance computations for each cost element.

MATERIAL AND LABOR VARIANCE COMPUTATIONS

During January 2013, Salinas Corporation started and completed 400 mountain bikes. The top half of Exhibit 7.5 shows the standard quantities and costs for that production, while the bottom half of the exhibit shows actual quantities and costs. This information is used to compute the January 2013 variances.

Exhibit 7.5 Standard and Actual Cost Data for Salinas Corporation's January 2013 Production of 400 Mountain Bikes

STANDARD COST FOR 400 MOUNTAIN BIKES

Direct Material Component ID#	Quantity	Unit Cost	Total Cost
WF-05	400	$ 20.00	$ 8,000
WR-05	400	25.00	10,000
B-05	800	20.00	16,000
HB-05	400	23.00	9,200
B-21	6,400	0.75	4,800
S-18	4,800	1.25	6,000
SPS-05	400	17.00	6,800
P-05	800	14.00	11,200
F-05	400	200.00	80,000
Total standard direct material cost			$152,000

Direct Labor Department	Total Hours	Rate	Total Cost
Painting	1,200	$12.00	$14,400
Assembling	2,000	15.00	30,000
Oiling	400	8.00	3,200
Testing	200	20.00	4,000
Packaging	100	8.00	800
Total standard DLHs and cost	3,900		$52,400

Variable overhead ($136.50 per bike × 400 bikes)	$54,600
Fixed overhead ($97.50 per bike × 400 bikes)	39,000
Total standard overhead cost	$93,600

(Continued)

Exhibit 7.5 Standard and Actual Cost Data for Salinas Corporation's January 2013 Production of 400 Mountain Bikes (*Continued*)

ACTUAL JANUARY COST FOR 400 MOUNTAIN BIKES

Direct Material Component ID#	Quantity	Unit Cost	Total Cost
WF-05	413	$ 19.00	$ 7,847
WR-05	400	24.00	9,600
B-05	810	20.00	16,200
HB-05	400	24.00	9,600
B-21	6,700	0.74	4,958
S-18	4,850	1.20	5,820
SPS-05	400	18.00	7,200
P-05	800	15.00	12,000
F-05	400	197.00	78,800
Total actual direct material cost			$152,025

Direct Labor Department	Total Hours	Rate	Total Cost
Painting	1,100	$12.10	$13,310
Assembling	1,900	16.00	30,400
Oiling	390	7.90	3,081
Testing	200	19.50	3,900
Packaging	90	8.00	720
Total actual DLHs and cost	3,680		$51,411

Variable overhead	$50,784
Fixed overhead	38,500
Total actual overhead cost	$89,284

Material Variances

The general variance analysis model is used to compute price and quantity variances for each type of direct material. Since each bike uses one WF-05, the standard quantity of this part for 400 bikes is 400 units. To illustrate the calculations, direct material item WF-05 is used.

AP × AQ	SP × AQ	SP × SQ
$19 × 413	$20 × 413	$20 × 400
$7,847	$8,260	$8,000

$413 F — Material Price Variance

$260 U — Material Quantity Variance

$153 F — Total Material Variance

The **material price variance (MPV)** indicates whether the amount paid for material was less or more than standard price. For item WF-05, the price paid was $19 rather than the standard price of $20 per unit, creating a favorable price variance. A favorable variance *reduces* the cost of production and, thus, a negative sign indicates a favorable variance. The MPV can also be calculated as follows:

MPV = (Actual price − Standard price) × Actual quantity
MPV = ($19 − $20) × 413 = −$1 × 413 = −$413 or $413 F

The purchasing manager should be able to explain why the price paid for item WF-05 was less than standard.

The **material quantity variance (MQV)** indicates whether the actual quantity used was less or more than the standard quantity allowed for the *actual* output. This difference is multiplied by the standard price per unit of material because quantities cannot be entered into the accounting records. Production used 13 more units of WF-05 than the standard allowed, resulting in a $260 unfavorable (positive) material quantity variance. The MQV can be calculated as follows:

MQV = Standard price × (Actual quantity − Standard quantity)
MQV = $20 × (413 − 400) = $20 × 13 = $260 U

The production manager should be able to explain why the additional WF-05 components were used in January.

The total material variance (TMV) is the summation of the individual variances or can also be calculated by subtracting the total standard cost for component WF-05 from the total actual cost of WF-05:

TMV = MPV + MQV = −$413 + $260 = −$153 or $153 F

or

TMV = Total actual cost − Total standard cost = $7,847 − $8,000 = −$153 or $153 F

Price and quantity variance computations must be made for each direct material component, and these component variances are summed to obtain the total price and quantity variances. Such a summation, however, does not provide useful information for cost control.

Point-of-Purchase Material Variance Model

A total variance for a cost component generally equals the sum of the price and usage variances. An exception to this rule occurs when the quantity of material purchased is different from the quantity of material placed into production. Because the material price variance relates to the purchasing (rather than the production) function, the point-of-purchase model calculates the material price variance using the quantity of materials purchased (Q_p) rather than the quantity of materials used (Q_u). The general variance analysis model is altered slightly to isolate the variance as early as possible to provide more rapid information for management control purposes.

Assume that Salinas Corporation purchased 450 WF-05s at $19 per unit during January, but only used 413 for the 400 bikes produced that month. Using the point-of-purchase variance model, the computation for the material price variance is adjusted, but the computation for the material quantity variance remains the same as previously shown. The point-of-purchase material variance model is a "staggered" one as follows:

$AP \times AQ_p$		$SP \times AQ_p$		
$19 × 450		$20 × 450		
$8,550		$9,000		
	$450 F Material Price Variance			
		$SP \times AQ_u$		$SP \times SQ$
		$20 × 413		$20 × 400
		$8,260		$8,000
			$260 U Material Quantity Variance	

The material quantity variance is still computed on the actual quantity used and, thus, remains at $260 U. However, because the price and quantity variances have been computed using different bases, they should not be summed. Thus, no total material variance can be meaningfully determined when the quantity of material purchased differs from the quantity of material used.

Labor Variances

The labor variances for mountain bicycle production in January 2013 would be computed on a departmental basis and then totaled. To illustrate the computations, the Painting Department data are used. Each mountain bike requires three hours in the Painting Department; thus, the standard labor time allowed for 400 bikes is (400 × 3) or 1,200 direct labor hours (DLHs). Exhibit 7.5 shows the actual labor time used in the Painting Department as 1,100 hours. Calculations of the labor variances are as follows:

AP × AQ	SP × AQ	SP × SQ
$12.10 × 1,100	$12 × 1,100	$12 × 1,200
$13,310	$13,200	$14,400

$110 U
Labor Rate Variance

$1,200 F
Labor Efficiency Variance

$1,090 F
Total Labor Variance

The **labor rate variance (LRV)** is the difference between the actual wages paid to labor for the period and the standard cost of actual hours worked. In January, the actual wage rate was $0.10 greater than the standard wage rates per hour, giving a $110 unfavorable labor rate variance. An unfavorable variance might be created by a raise granted within the period to employees; a favorable variance would be generated if employees in a particular period opted to take a reduced hourly rate rather than having some of the workers laid off.

The **labor efficiency variance (LEV)** indicates whether the amount of time worked was less or more than the standard quantity allowed for the actual output. This difference is multiplied by the standard rate per hour of labor time. In January, the Painting Department worked 100 fewer hours than the standard allowed to produce 400 mountain bikes.

The LRV and LEV can also be computed as follows:

LRV = (Actual price − Standard price) × Actual quantity
LRV = ($12.10 − $12.00) × 1,100 = $0.10 × 1,100 = $110 U

LEV = Standard price × (Actual quantity − Standard quantity)
LEV = $12 × (1,100 − 1,200) = $12 × −100 = −$1,200 or $1,200 F

The total labor variance for the Painting Department can be calculated as $1,090 F by either

1. subtracting the total standard labor cost ($14,400) from the total actual labor cost ($13,310) or
2. summing individual labor variances ($110 + −$1,200 = −$1,090).

Overhead Variances

As discussed in Chapter 3, total variable overhead changes in direct relationship with changes in activity and fixed overhead per unit changes inversely with changes in activity. Thus, to develop a predetermined overhead (OH) rate, a specific capacity level must be selected to compute budgeted overhead costs.

To compute the variable and fixed predetermined OH rates, managers at Salinas Corporation used an annual capacity level of 5,000 mountain bikes, which corresponds to 48,750 direct labor hours (5,000 bikes × 9.75 hours per bike). At that level of DLHs, budgeted annual variable and fixed overhead costs were calculated, respectively, as $682,500 and $487,500 (as shown earlier in Exhibit 7.4). Company accountants decided to set both the variable overhead (VOH) rate and the fixed overhead (FOH) rate using number of direct labor hours as follows:

$$\text{VOH rate} = \frac{\text{Budgeted VOH}}{\text{Budgeted DLHs}} = \$682{,}500 \div 48{,}750 = \$14 \text{ per DLH}$$

$$\text{FOH rate} = \frac{\text{Budgeted FOH}}{\text{Budgeted DLHs}} = \$487{,}500 \div 48{,}750 = \$10 \text{ per DLH}$$

Because Salinas Corporation uses separate variable and fixed overhead application rates, separate price and usage components can be calculated for each type of overhead. This four-variance approach provides managers with the greatest detail and, thus, the greatest flexibility for control and performance evaluation.

Variable Overhead

The computations for VOH variances are as follows:

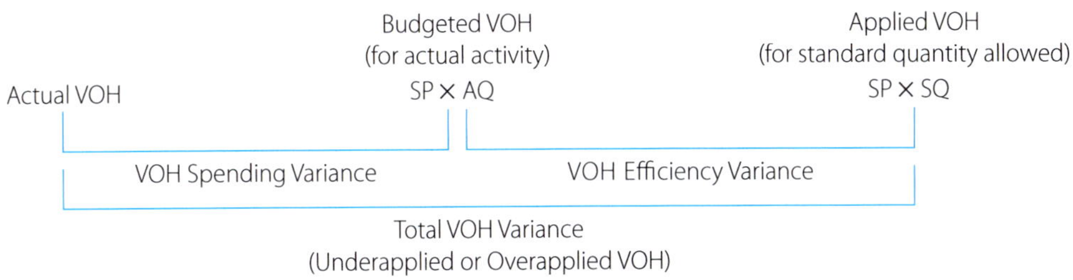

Because VOH increases with increases in activity, the budgeted amount of VOH will change with changes in actual production. In this case, Salinas Corp. worked a total of 3,680 DLHs; at a predetermined VOH rate of \$14 per DLH, the company would have budgeted a total of \$51,301 in VOH costs. The amount of applied VOH reflects the \$14 standard predetermined OH rate multiplied by the standard quantity of time required for the period's actual output (400 bikes × 9.75 DLHs per bike or 3,900 DLHs). Using the actual January 2013 VOH cost information from Exhibit 7.5, the VOH variances for mountain bike production are calculated as follows:

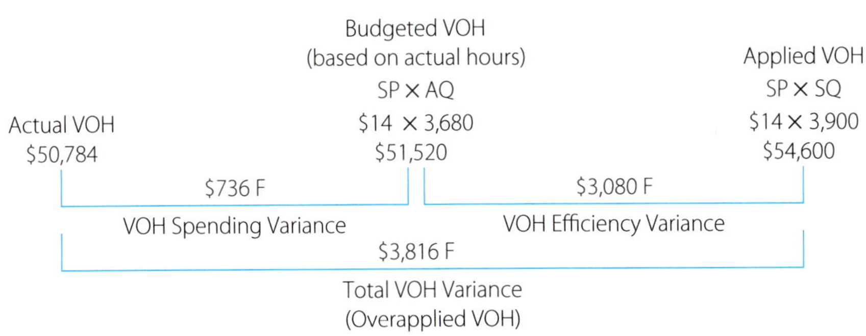

The difference between actual VOH and budgeted VOH based on actual hours is the **variable overhead spending variance**. VOH spending variances are caused by both component price and volume differences. For example, an unfavorable variable overhead spending variance could be caused by either paying a higher price or using more indirect material than the standard allows. Variable overhead spending variances associated with price differences can occur because, over time, changes in VOH prices have not been included in the standard rate. For example, average indirect labor wage rates or utility rates could have changed since the predetermined VOH rate was computed. Managers usually have little control over prices charged by external parties and should generally not be held accountable for variances arising because of such price changes. In these instances, the standard rates should be adjusted.

Variable overhead spending variances associated with quantity differences can be caused by waste or shrinkage of production inputs (such as indirect material). For instance, deterioration of material during storage or from lack of proper handling can be recognized only

Gvictoria/Dreamstime.com

Nurseries have to be careful about the storage of seeds, which can rapidly deteriorate with high temperature or humidity. Spoiled seeds will create a higher variable overhead spending variance for future greenhouse operations.

after the material is placed into production. Such occurrences usually have little relationship to the input activity basis used, but they do affect the VOH spending variance. If waste or spoilage is the cause of the VOH spending variance, managers should be held accountable and encouraged to implement more effective controls.

The difference between budgeted VOH for actual hours and applied VOH is the **variable overhead efficiency variance**. This variance quantifies the effect of using more or less of the activity or resource that is the base for VOH application. For example, Salinas Corporation applies VOH to mountain bikes using direct labor hours. If Salinas uses direct labor time inefficiently, higher variable overhead costs will occur. When actual input exceeds standard input allowed for the output achieved, production operations are considered to be inefficient. Excess input also indicates that an increased VOH budget is needed to support the additional activity base being used.

The total VOH variance for the period is equal to actual VOH minus applied VOH. This total variance is also the amount of underapplied or overapplied VOH for the period.

Fixed Overhead

The total fixed overhead (FOH) variance is divided into price and volume components by inserting budgeted FOH in the middle column of the general variance analysis model as follows:

Actual FOH | Budgeted FOH | Applied FOH (for standard quantity allowed) SP × SQ

FOH Spending Variance | Volume Variance

Total FOH Variance (Underapplied or Overapplied FOH)

The left column is the total actual fixed overhead incurred. Budgeted FOH is a constant amount throughout the relevant range of activity and was the amount used to develop the predetermined FOH rate; thus, the middle column is a constant figure *regardless of the actual quantity of input or the standard quantity of input allowed*. Applied FOH reflects the standard predetermined FOH rate multiplied by the standard quantity of activity for the period's actual output. The total FOH variance at the end of the period equals the amount of underapplied or overapplied FOH.

Total 2013 budgeted FOH for Salinas Corporation is given in Exhibit 7.4 as $487,500. Assuming that FOH is incurred steadily throughout the year, the monthly budgeted FOH is $40,625. As indicated in the computation for applied VOH, 3,900 DLHs is the standard quantity of time allowed for January's production of 400 bikes. Using the information in Exhibit 7.5, the FOH variances for mountain bike production are calculated as follows:

Actual FOH $38,500 | Budgeted FOH $40,625 | Applied FOH SP × SQ $10 × 3,900 $39,000

$2,125 F FOH Spending Variance | $1,625 U Volume Variance

$500 F Total FOH Variance (Overapplied FOH)

The difference between actual and budgeted FOH is the **fixed overhead spending variance**. This amount normally represents the differences for the numerous FOH components, although it can also reflect resource mismanagement. Individual FOH components would be shown in the company's flexible overhead budget, and individual spending variances should be calculated for each component.

As with variable overhead, applied FOH is related to the predetermined rate and the standard quantity for the actual production level achieved. Relative to FOH, the standard input allowed for the achieved production level measures capacity utilization for the period. The fixed overhead **volume variance (VV)** is the difference between budgeted and applied FOH. This variance is caused *solely* by producing at a level that differs from the level that was used to compute the predetermined FOH rate. In the case of Salinas Corporation, the $10 predetermined FOH rate was computed by dividing $487,500 of budgeted FOH cost by a capacity level of 48,750 DLHs for 5,000 bikes. Had any other capacity level been chosen, the predetermined FOH rate would have been a different amount, even though the $487,500 budgeted fixed overhead would have remained the same. For example, if 4,800 bikes (rather than 5,000) had been chosen as the expected capacity for 2013, Salinas would have expected to produce 400 each month and total expected capacity in direct labor hours would have been (4,800 × 9.75 DLHs = 46,800 DLHs). At that level of expected capacity, the predetermined FOH would have been

$$\text{Predetermined FOH rate} = \frac{\$487{,}500}{46{,}800} = \$10.41667$$

Since the actual volume for January was 400 bikes and the expected volume for January was 400 bikes, there would be no volume variance as shown in the following calculation:

Applied FOH for January (400 bikes × 9.75 DLHs × $10.41667 per bike)	$40,625
Budgeted FOH for January ($487,500 ÷ 12)	40,625
Volume variance	$ 0

However, if actual capacity usage differs from the capacity used in determining the predetermined FOH rate, a volume variance will arise because, by using a predetermined rate per unit of activity, fixed overhead is treated as if it were a variable cost even though it is not.

Although capacity utilization is controllable to some degree, the volume variance is the variance over which production managers have the least influence and control, especially in the short run. Thus, a volume variance is also called a **noncontrollable variance**. Although managers cannot control the capacity level chosen to compute the predetermined FOH rate, they do have the ability to control capacity utilization. Capacity utilization should be viewed in relation to inventory level and sales demand. Underutilization of capacity is not always undesirable; it is more appropriate to properly regulate production than to produce inventory that ends up in stockpiles. Producing unneeded inventory generates substantial costs for material, labor, and overhead as well as storage and handling costs. The positive impact that such unneeded production will have on the volume variance is insignificant because this variance is of little or no value for managerial control purposes.

Management is usually aware, as production occurs, of capacity utilization even if a volume variance is not reported. The volume variance merely translates under- or overutilization into a dollar amount. An unfavorable volume variance indicates less-than-expected utilization of capacity. If available capacity is commonly being used at a level higher (or lower) than that which was anticipated or is available, managers should recognize that condition, investigate the reasons for it, and (if possible and desirable) initiate appropriate action. Managers can influence capacity utilization by

- modifying work schedules,
- taking measures to relieve any obstructions to or congestion of production activities,
- carefully monitoring the movement of resources through the production process, and
- acquiring needed, or disposing of unneeded, space and equipment.

Preferably, such actions should be taken *before* production starts rather than *after* it is completed. Efforts made after production is completed might improve next period's operations but will have no impact on past production.

Alternative Overhead Variance Approaches

If the accounting system does not separate variable and fixed overhead costs, insufficient data will be available to compute four overhead variances. Use of a combined (variable and fixed) predetermined OH rate requires alternative overhead variance computations. One approach is to calculate only the **total overhead variance**, which is the difference between total actual overhead and total overhead applied to production. The amount of applied overhead is found by multiplying the combined rate by the standard quantity allowed for the actual production. The one-variance approach is as follows:

Actual Overhead	Applied Overhead
Variable OH + Fixed OH	SP × SQ
Total Overhead Variance	

Like other total variances, the total overhead variance provides limited information to managers. For Salinas Corporation, the total overhead application rate is \$24 per DLH (or \$14 per DLH for VOH + \$10 per DLH for FOH). The total OH variance is calculated as follows:

Actual Overhead	Applied Overhead
VOH + FOH	SP × SQ
\$50,784 + \$38,500	\$24 × 3,900
\$89,284	\$93,600
\$4,316 F	
Total Overhead Variance	

Note that this amount is the same as the summation of the \$3,816 F total VOH variance and the \$500 F total FOH variance computed under the four-variance approach.

A two-variance analysis is performed by inserting a middle column in the one-variance model:

Actual Overhead	Budgeted Overhead	Applied Overhead
VOH + FOH	(based on standard output measure)	SP × SQ
Budget Variance (or Controllable Variance)		Volume Variance (or Noncontrollable Variance)
Total Overhead Variance		

The middle column in the two-variance OH computation is the expected total overhead cost for the period's actual output. This amount represents total budgeted VOH at the standard quantity measure allowed plus the budgeted FOH, which is constant at all activity levels in the relevant range.

The **budget variance** equals total actual OH minus budgeted OH for the period's actual output. This variance is also referred to as the **controllable variance** because managers are able to exert some degree of influence on this amount during the short run. The difference between budgeted overhead for the period's actual output and total applied overhead is the volume (or noncontrollable) variance; this variance is the same as would be computed under the four-variance approach.

For Salinas Corporation, the two-variance OH computations are as follows:

Actual Overhead	Budgeted Overhead (based on standard output measure)	Applied Overhead
VOH + FOH	($14 × 3,900) + $40,625	SP × SQ
$50,784 + $38,500	$54,600 + $40,625	$24 × 3,900
$89,284	$95,225	$93,600

$5,941 F	$1,625 U
Budget Variance (or Controllable Variance)	Volume Variance (or Noncontrollable Variance)

$4,316 F
Total Overhead Variance

Note that the budget variance amount is the same as the summation of the $736 F VOH spending variance, the $3,080 F VOH efficiency variance, and the $2,125 F FOH spending variance computed under the four-variance approach. The $1,625 U volume variance is the same as the volume variance computed under the four-variance approach.

Inserting another column between the left and middle columns of the two-variance model provides a three-variance analysis by separating the budget variance into spending and efficiency variances. The new column represents the flexible budget based on the actual input measure(s).[8] The three-variance model is as follows:

Actual Overhead	Budgeted Overhead (based on actual input measure)	Budgeted Overhead (based on standard output measure)	Applied Overhead
VOH + FOH			SP × SQ

OH Spending Variance	OH Efficiency Variance	Volume Variance

Total Overhead Variance

The total **overhead spending variance** is computed as total actual overhead minus total budgeted overhead at the actual input activity level. Because FOH is the same at any level of activity, the **overhead efficiency variance** is related solely to variable overhead and is the difference between total budgeted overhead at the actual input activity level and total budgeted overhead at the standard activity level. This variance measures, at standard cost, the effect on VOH from using more or fewer inputs than standard for the actual production.

For Salinas Corporation, the three-variance computations are as follows:

Actual Overhead	Budgeted Overhead (based on actual input measure)	Budgeted Overhead (based on standard output measure)	Applied Overhead
VOH + FOH			SP × SQ
$50,784 + $38,500	($14 × 3,680) + $40,625	($14 × 3,900) + $40,625	$24 × 3,900
	$51,520 + $40,625	$54,600 + $40,625	
$89,284	$92,145	$95,225	$93,600

$2,861 F	$3,080 F	$1,625 U
OH Spending Variance	OH Efficiency Variance	Volume Variance

$4,316 F
Total Overhead Variance

Note that the OH spending variance amount is the same as the $736 F VOH spending variance plus the $2,125 F FOH spending variance computed under the four-variance approach. The $3,080 F OH efficiency variance is the same as the VOH efficiency variance computed under the four-variance approach. The sum of the overhead spending and overhead efficiency variances of the three-variance analysis equals the budget variance of the two-variance

[8] Flexible budgets are discussed in Chapter 3.

analysis. The $1,625 U volume (noncontrollable) variance is the same as was calculated using the two-variance or the four-variance approach.

If VOH and FOH are applied using a combined rate, the one-, two-, and three-variance approaches will have the relationships shown in Exhibit 7.6. The amounts in the exhibit represent the data provided for Salinas Corporation. Managers should select the method that provides the most useful information and that conforms to the company's accounting system. As more companies begin to recognize the existence of multiple cost drivers for overhead and to use multiple bases for applying overhead to production, computation of the one-, two-, and three-variance approaches will diminish.

Exhibit 7.6 Interrelationships of Overhead Variances

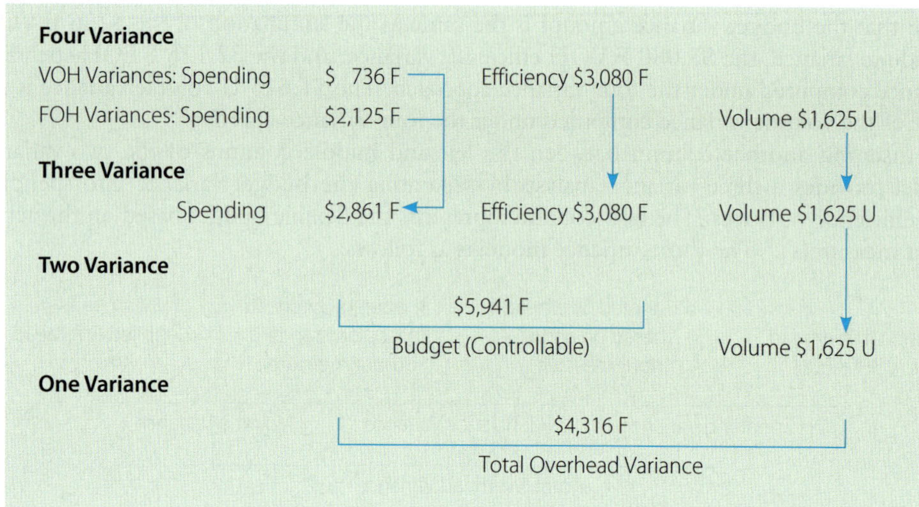

STANDARD COST SYSTEM JOURNAL ENTRIES

Using the information about material purchases from the point-of-purchase material variance model section as well as the labor and overhead actual cost information from Exhibit 7.5, Salinas Corporation's January 2013 journal entries for the information previously presented are shown in Exhibit 7.7. Remember that, in a standard costing system, the inventory accounts contain only standard cost information. The following explanations apply to the numbered journal entries:

1. The debit to Raw Material Inventory is for the standard price of the actual quantity of component WF-05 purchased in January. The credit to Accounts Payable is for the actual price of the actual quantity of component WF-05 purchased. The variance credit reflects the favorable material price variance for that component. Similar entries would be made for purchases of all other components.
2. The debit to Work in Process Inventory is for the standard price of the standard quantity of the WF-05 component used in January. The Raw Material Inventory credit is for the standard price of the actual quantity of WF-05 components used in production. The debit to the Material Quantity Variance account reflects the overuse (by 13 units) of WF-05s, valued at the standard price. Similar entries would be made for issuances of all other components to production.
3. The debit to Work in Process Inventory is for the standard hours to produce 400 mountain bikes in the Painting Department multiplied by the standard wage rate. The Wages Payable credit is for the actual amount of direct cost for painters during the period. The Labor Efficiency Variance credit reflects the difference between actual and standard hours multiplied by the standard wage rate. Similar entries would be made for wages incurred and standard direct labor wages allowed for all other departments.

Exhibit 7.7 Selected Journal Entries for Salinas Corporation's Mountain Bike Production, January 2013

	Debit	Credit
(1) Raw Material Inventory ($20 × 450)	9,000	
Material Purchase Price Variance [($19 – $20) × 450]		450
Accounts Payable		8,550
To record the acquisition of 450 WF-05s		
(2) Work in Process Inventory ($20 × 400)	8,000	
Material Quantity Variance [$20 × (413 – 400)]	260	
Raw Material Inventory ($20 × 413)		8,260
To record issuance of WF-05s to Production Department		
(3) Work in Process Inventory ($12 × 1,200 DLHs)	14,400	
Labor Rate Variance [($12.10 – $12.00) × 1,100]	110	
Labor Efficiency Variance [$12 × (1,100 – 1,200)]		1,200
Wages Payable ($12.10 × 1,100)		13,310
To record incurrence of direct labor costs by the Painting Department		
(4) Variable Manufacturing Overhead Control	50,784	
Fixed Manufacturing Overhead Control	38,500	
Various accounts		89,284
To record actual overhead costs		
(5) Work in Process Inventory	93,600	
Variable Manufacturing Overhead Control ($14 × 400 × 9.75)		54,600
Fixed Manufacturing Overhead Control ($10 × 400 × 9.75)		39,000
To apply overhead to the month's production		
(6) Variable Manufacturing Overhead Control	3,816	
Variable Overhead Spending Variance		736
Variable Overhead Efficiency Variance		3,080
To close the VOH Control account and recognize the VOH variances		
(7) Volume Variance [(10 × 400 × 9.75) – ($487,500 ÷ 12)]	1,625	
Fixed Manufacturing Overhead Control	500	
Fixed Overhead Spending Variance [$38,500 – ($487,500 ÷ 12)]		2,125
To close the FOH Control account and recognize the FOH variances		

4. This entry reflects the incurrence of all company overhead for the month. During January, actual costs incurred for variable and fixed overhead are debited to the Manufacturing Overhead Control accounts. For convenience, credits to all actual overhead items are not shown; instead, "Various accounts" are indicated. In reality, credits would be provided to accounts representing the overhead items (such as indirect material inventory, wages payable, accumulated depreciation, and utility payables).
5. Overhead is applied to production using the predetermined rates multiplied by the standard input allowed. Applied overhead is debited to Work in Process Inventory and credited to Manufacturing Overhead Control accounts. Overhead application is recorded at completion of production or at the end of the period, whichever occurs first. The difference between actual debits and applied credits in each overhead account represents the total variable and fixed overhead variances and is also the under- or

overapplied overhead for the period. For January, variable overhead and fixed overhead are applied at the respective $14 per DLH and $10 per DLH predetermined rates.

6. & 7. These entries assume an end-of-month closing of the Variable Manufacturing Overhead Control and Fixed Manufacturing Overhead Control accounts. These entries close the manufacturing overhead accounts and recognize the appropriate overhead variances. This entry is provided for illustration only. This process would typically not be performed at month-end but rather at year-end because an annual period was used to calculate the predetermined OH rates.

Note that all unfavorable variances have debit balances and favorable variances have credit balances. Unfavorable variances represent excess production costs; favorable variances represent savings in production costs. Standard production costs are shown in inventory accounts (which have debit balances); therefore, excess costs are also debits.

DISPOSITION OF STANDARD COST VARIANCES

Although standard costs are useful for internal reporting, they can be used in financial statements only if the amounts are substantially equivalent to those that would have resulted from using an actual cost system. If standards are achievable and current, this equivalency should exist. Standard costs in financial statements should provide fairly conservative inventory valuations because the effects of excess price and/or inefficient operations are eliminated.

At year-end, adjusting entries are made to eliminate standard cost variances. The entries depend on whether the variances are, in total, insignificant or significant. If the combined impact of the variances is insignificant, unfavorable variances are closed as debits (increases) to Cost of Goods Sold (CGS); favorable variances are credits (decreases) to CGS. Thus, unfavorable variances decrease operating income because of the higher-than-expected costs; favorable variances increase operating income because of the lower-than-expected costs. Even if the year's entire production has not been sold yet, this variance treatment is based on the immateriality of the amounts involved.

In contrast, large variances are prorated at year-end among ending inventories and Cost of Goods Sold so that the balances in those accounts approximate actual costs. Proration is based on the relative size of the account balances. Disposition of significant variances is similar to the disposition of large amounts of under- or overapplied overhead as shown in Chapter 3.

To illustrate the disposition of significant variances, assume that Nailz Company has a $20,000 unfavorable (debit) year-end Material Purchase Price Variance. The company considers this amount significant. Nailz makes one type of product, which requires a single raw material input. During the period, some of the raw material purchased by Nailz was placed into production; however, some purchased raw material remains in ending inventory at the end of the period. Of the material placed into production, some was used in goods that were completed and were either sold or remain in ending FG inventory; some of the raw material placed into production, though, remains in process with goods not yet completed. Thus, raw material may be in any of the three inventory accounts or in CGS. Prorating the material price variance requires allocating the favorable or unfavorable price to all of these accounts, using the following year-end account balances for Nailz Company:

Raw Material Inventory	$ 49,126
Work in Process Inventory	28,072
Finished Goods Inventory	70,180
Cost of Goods Sold	554,422
Total of affected accounts	$701,800

The theoretically correct allocation of the material price variance would use actual material cost in each account at year-end. However, as was mentioned in Chapter 3 with regard to overhead, after the conversion process has begun, cost elements within account balances are commingled and tend to lose their identity. Thus, unless a significant misstatement would result, disposition of the variance can be based on the proportions of each account balance to the total, as follows:

Raw Material Inventory	7%	($ 49,126 ÷ $701,800)
Work in Process Inventory	4	($ 28,072 ÷ $701,800)
Finished Goods Inventory	10	($ 70,180 ÷ $701,800)
Cost of Goods Sold	79	($554,422 ÷ $701,800)
Total	100%	

Applying these percentages to the $20,000 unfavorable material purchase price variance gives the amounts in the following journal entry to assign to the affected accounts:

Raw Material Inventory ($20,000 × 0.07)	1,400	
Work in Process Inventory ($20,000 × 0.04)	800	
Finished Goods Inventory ($20,000 × 0.10)	2,000	
Cost of Goods Sold ($20,000 × 0.79)	15,800	
Material Purchase Price Variance		20,000
To dispose of the material purchase price variance at year-end		

All material and labor variances other than the material price variance occur as part of the conversion process. Because conversion includes only the raw material put into production (rather than raw material purchased), all remaining variances are prorated only to Work in Process Inventory, Finished Goods Inventory, and Cost of Goods Sold. Thus, using the same account balances for Nailz Company, other significant variances would be allocated using the following (rounded) proportions:

Work in Process Inventory	$ 28,072	$ 28,072 ÷ $652,674 = 4%
Finished Goods Inventory	70,180	$ 70,180 ÷ $652,674 = 11%
Cost of Goods Sold	554,422	$554,422 ÷ $652,674 = 85%
Total of affected accounts	$652,674	

Thus, if Nailz had a $13,000U labor efficiency variance, it would be allocated as a $520 increase to Work in Process Inventory, $1,430 increase to Finished Goods Inventory, and an $11,050 increase to Cost of Goods Sold. Overhead variances are closed through the Overhead Control account and the ending over- or under-applied overhead balances are closed as discussed in Chapter 3.

CHANGES IN STANDARDS USAGE

4 How have the setting and use of standards changed over time?

Many accountants and managers believe that variance analysis is not currently being used as wisely for control and performance evaluation purposes as it could be. For example, material standards generally include a factor for waste, and labor standards are commonly set at the expected level of attainment even though this level includes downtime and human error. The use of standards that are not aimed at the highest possible (ideal) level of attainment is now being questioned in business environments concerned with world-class operations.

Use of Ideal Standards and Theoretical Capacity

The Japanese influence on Western management philosophy and production techniques has been significant. Both total quality management (TQM) and just-in-time (JIT) production systems evolved as a result of an upsurge in Japanese productivity. These two concepts are inherently based on ideal standards. Traditional standards build waste and inefficiency into the standards and then additional waste and spoilage are accepted under the management-by-exception principle. Both TQM and JIT begin with the premises of zero defects, zero inefficiency, and zero downtime. Thus, under TQM and JIT, ideal standards become expected standards, and there is no (or only a minimal) level of allowable deviation from the standards.

Workers may, at first, resent the introduction of standards set at a "perfection" level, but it is in their own and management's best long-run interest to have such standards for the following reasons.

- When a standard is set at a less-than-ideal level, managers are allowing and encouraging inefficient resource utilization.

- If no inefficiencies are built into or tolerated in the system, deviations from standard should be minimized and overall organizational performance improved.
- Higher standards for efficiency automatically mean lower costs because of the elimination of non-value-added activities such as waste, idle time, and rework.
- Ideal standards require that employees communicate and work together to improve performance.
- Ideal standards result in the most useful information for managerial purposes as well as the highest-quality products and services at the lowest possible cost.

Implementing ideal standards begins with identifying where and why problems are occurring. The answers to these issues help determine what changes are needed. For example, if variances are caused by the equipment, facility, or workers, management must be ready to invest in plant and equipment, workplace reorganization, or worker training so that the standards are amenable to the operations. Training is essential if workers are to perform at the high levels of efficiency demanded by ideal standards. If variances are related to external sources (such as poor quality material), management must be willing to change suppliers and/or pay higher prices for higher-grade input.

Setting standards at the ideal level in part assigns the responsibility for quality to workers. Thus, management must also give those workers the authority to react to problems. Additionally, requiring people to work at their maximum potential demands recognition, which means that management must provide rewards for achievement. The process of implementing ideal standards is illustrated in Exhibit 7.8.

In addition to setting standards at an ideal level, world-class companies can also use theoretical capacity to set fixed OH rates. If a company were totally automated or if people

Exhibit 7.8 Implementing Ideal Standards

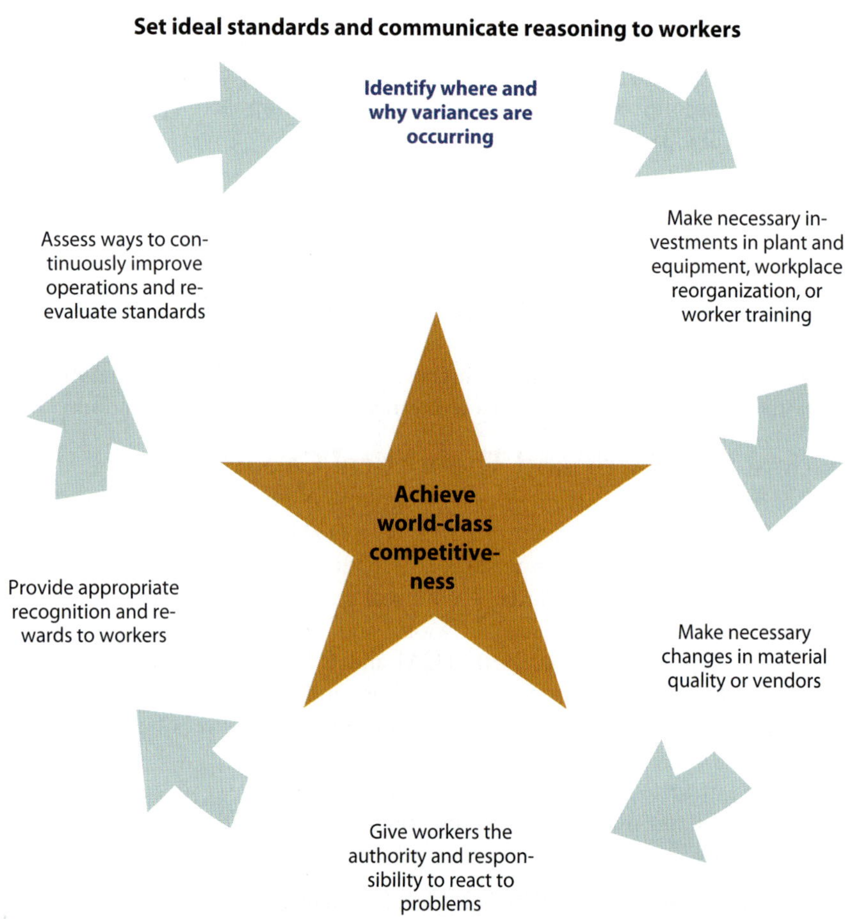

consistently worked at their full potential, such a capacity measure would provide the lowest and most appropriate predetermined OH rate. Any underapplied OH resulting from a difference between theoretical and actual capacity would indicate capacity that should be either used or eliminated. The underapplied OH could also indicate human capabilities that have not been fully developed. Also, any end-of-period underapplied OH would be viewed as a period cost and closed to a loss account (such as Loss from Inefficient Operations) on an internal income statement. Showing the underapplied OH in this manner should attract managerial attention to the inefficient and ineffective use of resources.

Whether setting standards at the ideal level and using theoretical capacity to compute predetermined fixed OH rates will become norms for non-Japanese companies cannot be determined at this time. However, standards are slowly moving from the expected or practical closer to the ideal, if only because of the competitive business environment in which organizations operate. The company that produces goods based on the highest possible standards and determines costs based on the highest level of capacity is more likely to have lower costs and higher quality—which, in turn, will often result in lower prices.

Adjusting Standards

Standards should be set only after comprehensive investigation of prices and quantities for the various cost elements. Standards were traditionally retained for at least one year and, sometimes, for multiple years. However, the current operating environment (which includes suppliers, technology, competition, product design, and manufacturing methods) changes so rapidly that a standard may no longer be useful for management control purposes for an entire year.

Company management must decide if standards should be modified during a year when significant cost or quantity changes occur. Ignoring the changes is a simplistic approach that allows the same type of cost to be recorded at the same amount all year. Thus, for example, any material purchased during the year would be recorded at the same standard cost regardless of when it was purchased. Although making recordkeeping easy, this approach eliminates any opportunity to adequately control costs or evaluate performance. Additionally, such an approach could create large differentials between standard and actual costs, making standard costs unacceptable for external reporting.

Adjusting standards to reflect price or quantity changes would make some aspects of management control and performance evaluation more effective, and others more difficult. For instance, budgets prepared using the original standards would need to be adjusted before appropriate actual comparisons could be made against them. Changing standards also creates a problem for recordkeeping and inventory valuation. Accountants would have to decide whether products should be valued at the standard cost that was in effect when they were made or at the standard cost in effect when the financial statements were prepared. Although standards that were modified during the period would be more closely related to actual costs, the use of such standards might undermine many of the benefits discussed earlier in the chapter.

If possible, management should consider combining these two choices in the accounting system. The original standards can be considered "frozen" for budget purposes and a revised budget can be prepared using the new current standards. Differences between these two budgets would reflect variances related to operating environment cost changes. These variances could be designated as uncontrollable (such as those related to changes in the market price of raw material) or internally initiated (such as changes in standard labor time resulting from employee training or equipment rearrangement). Comparing the budget based on current standards with actual costs incurred would provide variances that more adequately reflect internally controllable causes, such as excess material and/or labor time usage caused by inferior material purchases. A combined "frozen" and revised budget system for variance analysis is depicted in Exhibit 7.9.

Material Price Variance Based on Usage Rather Than on Purchases

The material price variance computation has traditionally been based on the quantity purchased rather than on quantity used so that the variance could be calculated as quickly as

Exhibit 7.9 Combined "Frozen" and Revised Budget System for Variance Analysis

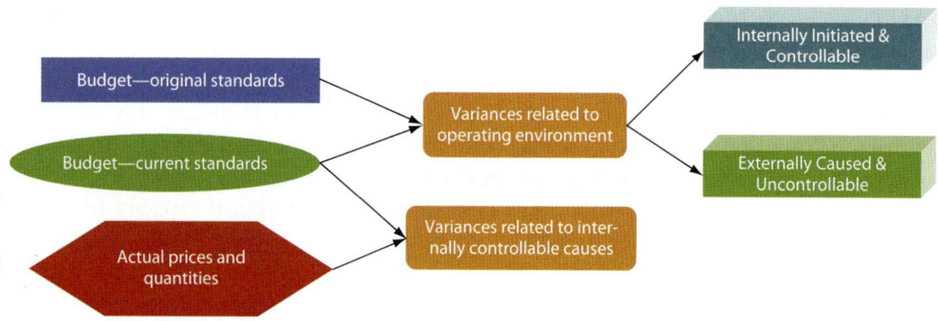

possible relative to the cost incurrence. Although computing the material price variance at the purchase point allows managers to see the impact of buying decisions rapidly, such information might not be most relevant in a JIT environment. Buying material that is not needed for current production requires that the material be stored and moved, both of which are non-value-added activities. The trade-off in price savings should be measured against the additional costs to determine the cost–benefit relationship of such a purchase.

Additionally, computing a material price variance on purchases rather than on usage can reduce the probability of recognizing a relationship between a favorable material price variance and an unfavorable material quantity variance. If a favorable price variance resulted from buying low-grade material, the potential negative effects of that purchase on material usage and labor efficiency will not be known until the material is actually used.

Decline in Direct Labor

As the proportion of product cost comprised of direct labor declines, the necessity for direct labor variance computations is minimized. Automation often relegates labor to an indirect category because workers become machine overseers rather than producers of goods. Accordingly, direct labor can be combined with overhead to become viewed as the "conversion cost" of a product.

CONVERSION COST AS AN ELEMENT IN STANDARD COSTING

5 How does the use of a single conversion element (rather than the traditional labor and overhead elements) affect standard costing?

As discussed in Chapter 2, conversion cost consists of direct labor and manufacturing overhead. The traditional view of separating product cost into three categories (direct material, direct labor, and overhead) is appropriate in labor-intensive production settings. However, in automated factories, direct labor cost often represents only a small part of total product cost. In such circumstances, one worker might oversee a large number of machines and deal more with troubleshooting machine malfunctions than with converting raw material into finished products. Within these new production operations, all production workers may be considered indirect labor, and therefore, their wages would be part of overhead.

Many automated companies have adapted their standard cost systems to provide for only two elements of product cost: direct material and conversion. In these situations, conversion cost is likely to be separated into variable and fixed components. Conversion cost can also be separated into direct and indirect categories based on the ability to trace such costs to a machine rather than to a product. Overhead can be applied under an activity-based costing methodology (see Chapter 4) using a variety of cost drivers such as number of machine hours, material cost, number of production runs, number of machine setups, or throughput time.

Variance analysis for conversion cost in automated plants normally focuses on the following:

- spending variances for overhead costs,
- efficiency variances for machinery and production costs rather than labor costs, and
- a volume variance for production.

These categories are similar to the traditional three-variance overhead approach. In an automated system, managers are better able to control not only the spending and efficiency variances but also the volume variance. The idea of planned output is essential in a JIT system. Variance analysis under a conversion cost approach is illustrated in Exhibit 7.10. Regardless of how variances are computed, managers must analyze those variances and use them for cost control purposes to the extent that such control can be exercised.

Exhibit 7.10 Variances under Conversion Approach

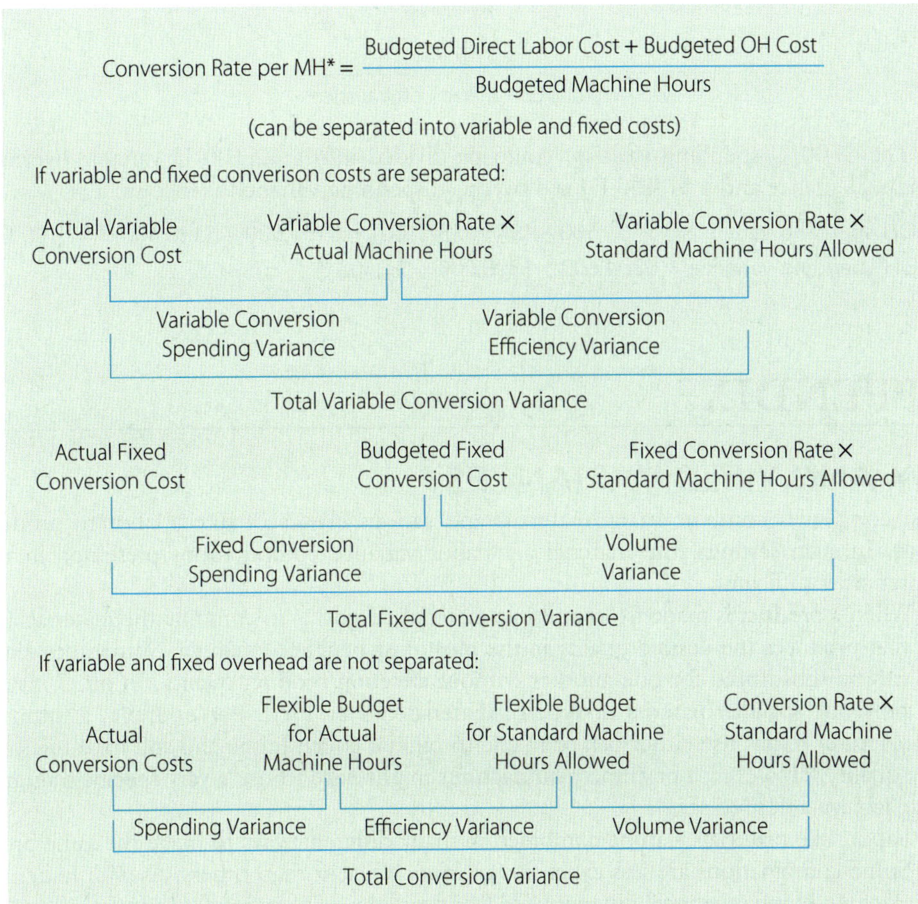

*Other cost drivers could be more appropriate than MHs. If such drivers are used to determine the rate, they must also be used to determine the variances.

Assume that Kalinda Corp. makes bike frames in a fully automated production facility; all labor required for this product is considered indirect. For simplicity, it is assumed that all overhead is applied on the basis of budgeted machine hours. Necessary 2013 production and cost information for bike frames is as follows:

Expected production	48,000 units
Actual production	50,000 units
Actual machine time	37,100 MHs
Standard machine time allowed per unit	0.75 MH
Budgeted variable conversion cost	$144,000
Budgeted fixed conversion cost	$306,000
Actual variable conversion cost	$150,500
Actual fixed conversion cost	$304,600

Expected production time for 2013 = 48,000 × 0.75 = 36,000 MHs
Variable conversion rate: $144,000 ÷ 36,000 MHs = $4.00 per MH
Fixed conversion rate: $306,000 ÷ 36,000 MHs = $8.50 per MH
Standard machine hours allowed: 50,000 units × 0.75 MH per unit = 37,500 MHs

The three-variance computations for conversion costs follow.

Actual Conversion Cost	Flexible Budget at Actual Hours	Flexible Budget at Standard Hours	Standard Cost
	[($4 × 37,100) + $306,000]	[($4 × 37,500) + $306,000]	
($150,500 + $304,600)	($148,400 + $306,000)	($150,000 + $306,000)	($12.50 × 37,500)
$455,100	$454,400	$456,000	$468,750

$700 U Spending Variance | $1,600 F Efficiency Variance | $12,750 F Volume Variance

$13,650 F Total Conversion Cost Variance

The $700 U spending variance could be divided into a $2,100 U variable overhead spending variance and a $1,400 F fixed overhead spending variance as follows:

VOH spending variance = $150,500 – ($4 × $37,100) = $150,500 – $148,400 = $2,100 U
FOH spending variance = $304,600 – $306,000 = $1,400 F

APPENDIX

MIX AND YIELD VARIANCES

6 How are variances affected by multiple material and labor categories?

Most companies combine many materials and various classes of direct labor to produce goods. In such settings, the material and labor variance computations presented in this chapter are insufficient.

When a product is made from multiple materials, a goal is to combine the materials in a way that produces the desired quality in the most cost-beneficial manner. Sometimes materials can be substituted for one another without affecting product quality. In other instances, only one specific material or type of material can be used. For example, a furniture manufacturer might use either oak or maple to build a couch frame and still have the same basic quality. However, a perfume manufacturer might have to use a very specific fragrance oil to achieve a desired scent.

Labor, like materials, can be combined in many different ways to make the same product. Some combinations are less expensive or more efficient than others. As with materials, some degree of interchangeability between labor categories is assumed. However, all potential combinations could not be viable; for example, unskilled workers could not be substituted for skilled craftspeople in making Baccarat crystal. The goal is to find the most effective and efficient selection of workers to perform specific tasks.

Each possible combination of materials or labor is called a **mix**. Experience, judgment, and experimentation are used to set the standards for the material mix and labor mix. Process **yield** is the output quantity that results from a specified input. Mix standards are used to calculate mix and yield variances for material and labor. An underlying assumption in product mix situations is that there can be substitution between the material and labor components. If this assumption is invalid, changing the mix cannot improve the yield and could even prove wasteful. In addition to mix and yield variances, price and rate variances are still computed for material and labor.

Rizzo's Fish Market is used to illustrate the computation of price/rate, mix, and yield variances. The company recently began selling one-pound packages of seafood mix containing crab, shrimp, and oysters. Ingredients are mixed in 200-pound batches, and because seafood is purchased fully cleaned, there is no waste in processing. To some extent, one ingredient can be substituted for another. In addition, the company uses two direct labor categories (A and B), and there is a labor rate differential between these two categories. Exhibit 7.11 provides standard and actual information for the company for December 2013.

Exhibit 7.11 Standard and Actual Information for December 2013

Material standards for one batch (200 1-pound packages):		
Crab (30%)	60 pounds at $7.20 per pound	$ 432
Shrimp (45%)	90 pounds at $4.50 per pound	405
Oysters (25%)	50 pounds at $5.00 per pound	250
Total	200 pounds	$1,087
Labor standards for one batch (200 1-pound packages):		
Category A workers (3/4)	9 hours at $10.50 per hour	$ 94.50
Category B workers (1/4)	3 hours at $14.30 per hour	42.90
Total	12 hours	$137.40

Actual production and cost data for December:		
Production	40 batches	
Material:		
Crab	Purchased and used	2,285.7 pounds at $7.50 per pound
Shrimp	Purchased and used	3,649.1 pounds at $4.40 per pound
Oysters	Purchased and used	2,085.2 pounds at $4.95 per pound
Total		8,020.0 pounds
Labor:		
Category A workers	450 hours at $10.50 per hour	
Category B workers	50 hours at $14.40 per hour	
Total	500 hours	

Material Price, Mix, and Yield Variances

A material price variance shows the dollar effect of paying prices that differ from the raw material standard. The **material mix variance** measures the effect of substituting a nonstandard mix of material during the production process. The **material yield variance** measures the difference between the actual total quantity of input and the standard total quantity allowed based on output; this difference reflects standard mix and standard prices. Summing the material mix and yield variances provides a material quantity variance similar to the one discussed in the chapter; the difference is that the sum of the mix and yield variances is attributable to multiple ingredients rather than to a single one. A company can have a mix variance without experiencing a yield variance. Computations for the price, mix, and yield variances are given in a format similar to that used in the chapter:

Actual Mix × Actual Quantity × Actual Price	Actual Mix × Actual Quantity × Standard Price	Standard Mix × Actual Quantity × Standard Price	Standard Mix × Standard Quantity × Standard Price
Material Price Variance (columns 1–2)	Material Mix Variance (columns 2–3)	Material Yield Variance (columns 3–4)	

Given the information in Exhibit 7.11, Rizzo's Fish Market used 8,020 total pounds of ingredients to make forty 200-pound batches of seafood mix. The standard quantity necessary to produce this quantity is 8,000 total pounds of ingredients. The actual mix of crab, shrimp, and oysters was 28.5, 45.5, and 26.0 percent, respectively:

Crab	2,285.7 ÷ 8,020 = 28.5%
Shrimp	3,649.1 ÷ 8,020 = 45.5%
Oysters	2,085.2 ÷ 8,020 = 26.0%

As with material price variances, separate rate variances should be calculated for each class of labor. Because category A does not have a labor rate variance, the total labor rate variance for December relates solely to category B.

Rizzo's Fish Market saved $285 by using the actual mix of labor rather than the standard. A higher proportion of the less expensive, unskilled class of labor (category A) than specified in the standard mix was used. One result of substituting a higher proportion of lower-paid workers seems to be that an unfavorable yield occurred because total actual hours were 20 hours higher than standard. However, the company saved a net of $51 by using the actual mix (even with the higher pay to category B workers) than the standard.

Because there are trade-offs in mix and yield when component qualities and quantities are changed, management should observe the integrated nature of price, mix, and yield. The effects of changes of one element on the other two need to be considered for managing cost efficiency and output quality. If mix and yield can be increased by substituting less expensive resources while maintaining quality, managers and product engineers should change the standards and the proportions of components. If costs are reduced but quality is maintained, selling prices could be reduced to gain a larger market share.

Comprehensive Review Module

KEY TERMS

bill of materials, p. 248
budget variance, p. 260
controllable variance, p. 260
expected standard, p. 247
fixed overhead spending variance, p. 259
ideal standard, p. 247
labor efficiency variance (LEV), p. 256
labor mix variance, p. 273
labor rate variance (LRV), p. 256
labor yield variance, p. 273
management-by-exception, p. 245
material mix variance, p. 271
material price variance (MPV), p. 254
material quantity variance (MQV), p. 255
material yield variance, p. 271
methods-time measurement (MTM), p. 249
mix, p. 270
noncontrollable variance, p. 259
operations flow document, p. 250
overhead efficiency variance, p. 261
overhead spending variance, p. 261
practical standard, p. 247
standard cost card, p. 250
standard quantity, p. 252
standard, p. 244
total cost of ownership (TCO), p. 249
total overhead variance, p. 260
variable overhead efficiency variance, p. 258
variable overhead spending variance, p. 257
variance analysis, p. 245
variance, p. 252
volume variance (VV), p. 259
yield, p. 270

CHAPTER SUMMARY

1 Uses of Standard Costing Systems

- A standard cost system is used to
  - provide clerical efficiency.
  - assist management in its planning, controlling, decision making, and evaluating performance functions.
  - motivate employees when the standards are
    - set at a level to encourage high-quality production and promote cost control.
    - seen as expected performance goals.
    - updated periodically so that they reflect actual economic conditions.

2 Setting Material, Labor, and Overhead Standards

- Material standards require that management identify the
  - types of material inputs needed to make the product or perform the service.
  - quality of material inputs needed to make the product or perform the service.
  - quantity of material inputs needed to make the product or perform the service.
  - prices of the material inputs, given normal purchase quantities.
- A bill of materials contains all quantity and quality raw material specifications to make one unit (or batch) of output.
- Labor standards require that management identify the
  - types of labor tasks needed to make the product or perform the service.
  - amount of labor time needed to make the product or perform the service.
  - skill levels of personnel needed to make the product or perform the service.
  - wage rates or salary levels for the classes of labor skills needed.
- An operations flow document contains all labor operations necessary to make one unit (or batch) of output or perform a particular service.
- Overhead standards require that management identify the
  - variable and fixed overhead costs incurred in the organization.
  - estimated level of activity to be used in computing the predetermined overhead rate(s).
  - estimated variable and fixed overhead costs at the estimated level of activity.
  - predetermined overhead rate(s) used to apply overhead to production or service performance.
- A standard cost card summarizes the standard quantities and costs needed to complete one unit of product or perform a particular service.

3 Calculating and Recording Material, Labor, and Overhead Variances

- Direct material variances are calculated as follows:
  - Material price variance = (Actual price × Actual quantity) − (Standard price × Actual quantity); generally calculated using quantity of material purchased
  - Material quantity variance = (Standard price × Actual quantity) − (Standard price × Standard quantity); calculated using quantity of material used
  - Total material variance = Material price variance + Material quantity variance; generally not calculated if the material price and quantity variances have been computed using different measures (purchased and used)
- Direct labor variances are calculated as follows:
  - Labor rate variance = (Actual price × Actual quantity) − (Standard price × Actual quantity)
  - Labor efficiency variance = (Standard price × Actual quantity) − (Standard price × Standard quantity)
  - Total labor variance = Labor rate variance + Labor efficiency variance
- Variable overhead variances are calculated as follows:
  - VOH spending variance = Actual VOH − (Standard price × Actual quantity)
  - VOH efficiency variance = (Standard price × Actual quantity of overhead application base) − Applied VOH
    - ➢ Note: Applied VOH = (Standard price × Standard quantity of overhead application base)
  - Total VOH Variance = VOH spending variance + VOH efficiency variance
- Fixed overhead variances are calculated as follows:
  - FOH spending variance = Actual FOH − Budgeted FOH
    - ➢ Note: Budgeted FOH = Expected FOH amount for the period
  - Volume variance = Budgeted FOH − Applied FOH
    - ➢ Note: Applied FOH = (Standard price × Standard quantity of overhead application base)
  - Total FOH variance = FOH spending variance + Volume variance
- A variance is the difference between an actual and a standard cost.
  - Only standard costs are recorded in the inventory accounts.
  - Variances are recorded as either debit (unfavorable) or credit (favorable) differences between the standard cost and the actual cost incurred.
  - Variances are closed at the end of each accounting period.
    - ➢ Insignificant material and labor variances are closed to Cost of Goods Sold.
    - ➢ Significant material and labor variances are allocated among Cost of Goods Sold and the appropriate ending inventory accounts; the material price variance is the only one allocated to the Raw Material Inventory account.

4 Changes in Standard Cost Setting and Usage

- In automated companies, the standard cost system may
  - use only two elements of production cost: direct material and conversion.
  - use ideal standards rather than expected or practical standards.
  - use predetermined fixed overhead rates based on theoretical capacity rather than expected, normal, or practical capacity.
  - compute material price variances based on usage rather than purchases.

5 Standard Costing Using a Conversion Element

- If a conversion category is used rather than the traditional labor and overhead categories,
  - overhead will commonly be separated into its variable and fixed categories.
  - overhead may be applied using activity-based costing.
  - the focus will be on
    - ➢ spending variances for variable and fixed overhead.
    - ➢ efficiency variances for machinery and production equipment rather than labor.
    - ➢ volume variance for production.

SOLUTION STRATEGIES

Actual Costs (AC), p. 247

1. Direct material:

Actual price (AP) × Actual quantity purchased or used (AQ)

$$\text{DM: AP} \times \text{AQ} = \text{AC}$$

2. Direct labor:

Actual price (rate) × Actual quantity of hours worked

$$\text{DL: AP} \times \text{AQ} = \text{AC}$$

Standard Costs (SC), p. 250

1. Direct material:

Standard price × Standard quantity

$$\text{DM: SP} \times \text{SQ} = \text{SC}$$

2. Direct labor:

Standard price (rate) × Standard quantity of hours

$$\text{DL: SP} \times \text{SQ} = \text{SC}$$

General Variance Format, p. 252

AP × AQ	SP × AQ	SP × SQ
Material Price Variance Labor Rate Variance VOH Spending Variance		Material Quantity Variance Labor Efficiency Variance VOH Efficiency Variance

Variances in Formula Format, p. 256

The following abbreviations are used:

AFOH = actual fixed overhead
AM = actual mix
AP = actual price or rate
AQ = actual quantity or hours
AVOH = actual variable overhead
BFOH = budgeted fixed overhead (remains at constant amount regardless of activity level as long as within the relevant range)

(*Continued*)

SM = standard mix
SP = standard price
SQ = standard quantity
TAOH = total actual overhead

Material price variance = (AP × AQ) – (SP – AQ)
Material quantity variance = (SP × AQ) – (SP × SQ)
Labor rate variance = (AP × AQ) – (SP × AQ)
Labor efficiency variance = (SP × AQ) – (SP × SQ)

Four-Variance Approach:

Variable OH spending variance = AVOH – (VOH rate × AQ)
Variable OH efficiency variance = (VOH rate × AQ) – (VOH rate × SQ)
Fixed OH spending variance = AFOH – BFOH
Volume variance = BFOH – (FOH rate × SQ)

Three-Variance Approach:

Spending variance = TAOH – [(VOH rate × AQ) + BFOH]
Efficiency variance = [(VOH rate × AQ) + BFOH] – [(VOH rate × SQ) + BFOH]
Volume variance = [(VOH rate × SQ) + BFOH] – [(VOH rate × SQ) + (FOH rate × SQ)]
(This is equal to the volume variance of the four-variance approach.)

Two-Variance Approach:

Budget variance = TAOH – [(VOH rate × SQ) + BFOH]
Volume variance = [(VOH rate × SQ) + BFOH] – [(VOH rate × SQ) + (FOH rate × SQ)]
(This is equal to the volume variance of the four-variance approach.)

One-Variance Approach:

Total OH variance = TAOH – (Combined OH rate × SQ)

Variances in Diagram Format, p. 255

Direct Material

Point of Purchase

Actual Price × Actual Quantity Purchased | Standard Price × Actual Quantity Purchased

Material Price Variance

Standard Price × Actual Quantity Used | Standard Price × Standard Quantity

Material Quantity Variance

Point of Usage

Actual Price × Actual Quantity Used	Standard Price × Actual Quantity Used	Standard Price × Standard Quantity
Material Price Variance	Material Quantity Variance	
Total Material Variance		

Direct Labor

Actual Price × Actual Quantity of Hours Worked	Standard Price × Actual Quantity of Hours Worked	Standard Price × Standard Quantity of Hours
Labor Rate Variance	Labor Efficiency Variance	
Total Labor Variance		

Overhead Four-Variance Approach:

Variable Overhead

Actual VOH	VOH Rate × Actual Quantity	Applied VOH VOH Rate × Standard Quantity
(a) VOH Spending Variance	(b) VOH Efficiency Variance	
Total VOH Variance		

Fixed Overhead

Actual FOH	Budgeted FOH	Applied FOH FOH Rate × Standard Quantity
FOH Spending Variance	Volume Variance	
Total FOH Variance		

Overhead One-, Two-, and Three-Variance Approaches:

Actual	**Budget Based on Actual Input Measure**	**Budget Based on Standard Output Measure**	**Applied**
Actual VOH + Actual FOH	(VOH Rate × AQ) + Budgeted FOH	(VOH Rate × SQ) + Budgeted FOH	(VOH Rate × SQ) + (FOH Rate × SQ)
(a) + (c) Spending Variance	(b) Efficiency Variance	(d) Volume Variance	
(a) + (b) + (c) Budget Variance		(d) Volume Variance	
(a) + (b) + (c) + (d) Total Overhead Variance (Total Underapplied/Overapplied Overhead)			

DEMONSTRATION PROBLEM

Filano Corp. has the following standards for one unit of product:

Direct material: 80 pounds × \$6	\$480
Direct labor: 3 hours × \$16 per hour	48
Variable overhead: 1.5 hours of machine time × \$50 per hour	75
Fixed overhead: 1.5 hours of machine time × \$30 per hour	45

The predetermined OH rates were developed using a capacity of 6,000 units per year. Production is assumed to occur evenly throughout the year.

During May 2013, the company produced 525 units. Actual data for May 2013 are as follows:

Direct material purchased: 45,000 pounds × \$5.92 per pound
Direct material used: 43,020 pounds (all from May's purchases)
Total labor cost: \$24,955 for 1,550 hours
Variable overhead incurred: \$43,750 for 800 hours of machine time
Fixed overhead incurred: \$22,800 for 800 hours of machine time

Required:

a. Calculate the following:
1. Material price variance based on quantity purchased
2. Material quantity variance
3. Actual rate per direct labor hour
4. Labor rate variance
5. Labor efficiency variance
6. Variable overhead spending and efficiency variances
7. Budgeted annual and monthly fixed overhead
8. Fixed overhead spending and volume variances
9. Combined variable and fixed overhead rate
10. Overhead variances using a three-variance approach
11. Overhead variances using a two-variance approach
12. Overhead variance using a one-variance approach

b. Record the entries to recognize the variances.

Solution to Demonstration Problem

a. 1.

$AP \times AQ_p$	$SP \times AQ_p$
\$5.92 × 45,000	\$6.00 × 45,000
\$266,400	\$270,000

\$3,600 F
MPV

2. SQ = 525 × 80 pounds = 42,000 pounds

$SP \times AQ_u$	$SP \times SQ$
\$6 × 43,020	\$6 × 42,000
\$258,120	\$252,000

\$6,120 U
MQV

3. AR = \$24,955 ÷ 41,550 hours = \$16.10 per DLH

4. & 5. SQ = 525 × 3 hours = 1,575 DLHs

AP × AQ	SP × AQ	SP × SQ
$16.10 × 1,550	$16 × 1,550	$16 × 1,575
$24,955	$24,800	$25,200

$155 U	$400 F
LRV	LEV

6. SQ = 525 × 1.5 = 787.5 MHs

Actual VOH	SP × AQ	SP × SQ
	$50 × 800	$50 × 787.5
$43,750	$40,000	$39,375

$3,750 U	$625 U
VOH Spending Variance	VOH Efficiency Variance

7. Annual BFOH = 6,000 × 1.5 hours × $30 = $270,000
   Monthly BFOH = $270,000 ÷ 12 months = $22,500
8. SQ = 787.5 machine hours [from (5)]

Actual FOH	Budgeted FOH	SP × SQ
		$30 × 787.50
$22,800	$22,500	$23,625

$300 U	$1,125 F
FOH Spending Variance	Volume Variance

9. Combined OH = $50 + $30 = $80 per MH
10. SQ = 787.5 MHs [from (5)].
11.

Actual VOH + Actual FOH	(VOH Rate × AQ) + Budgeted FOH	(VOH Rate × SQ) + Budgeted FOH	Applied OH (SP × SQ)
$ 43,750	$50 × 800 = $ 40,000	$50 × 787.5 = $ 39,375	$ 50 × 787.5 = $39,375
+ 22,800	+ 22,500	+ 22,500	+ 30 × 787.5 = 23,625
$ 66,550	$ 62,500	$ 61.875	$ 80 × 787.5 = $63,000

$4,050 U	$625 U	$1,125 F
Spending Variance	Efficiency Variance	Volume Variance

Actual OH	(VOH Rate × SQ) + Budgeted FOH	Applied OH (SP × SQ)
	$50 × 787.5 = $ 39,375	
	+ 22,500	
$66,550	$ 61,875	$80 × 787.5 = $63,000

$4,675 U	$1,125 F
Budget Variance	Volume Variance

12.

Actual OH	Applied OH SP × SQ
$66,550	$80 × 787.5 = $63,000

$3,550 U
Total Overhead Variance
(Total Underapplied Overhead)

b. All amounts are taken from the computations shown in (a).

Account	Debit	Credit
Raw Material Inventory	270,000	
Material Purchase Price Variance		3,600
Accounts Payable		266,400
To record acquisition of material		
Work in Process Inventory	252,000	
Material Quantity Variance	6,120	
Raw Material Inventory		258,120
To record issuance of material to production		
Work in Process Inventory	25,200	
Labor Rate Variance	155	
Wages Payable		24,955
Labor Efficiency Variance		400
To record direct labor costs in all departments		
Work in Process Inventory	39,375	
Variable Overhead Efficiency Variance	3,750	
Variable Overhead Spending Variance	625	
Variable Manufacturing Overhead Control		43,750
To close variable OH		
Work in Process Inventory	23,625	
Fixed Overhead Spending Variance	300	
Fixed Manufacturing Overhead Control		22,800
Volume Variance		1,125
To close fixed OH		

POTENTIAL ETHICAL ISSUES

ETHICS

1. Setting labor time standards extremely high so that variances on which performance is evaluated are consistently favorable
2. Evaluating each manager on the variances generated in his or her production area without regard for potential implications on other production areas
3. Estimating production at levels significantly higher than is necessary to meet current and anticipated sales, thereby lowering the predetermined fixed OH rate per unit and inventory cost, while increasing reported operating income
4. Producing unnecessary inventory to generate a high, favorable volume variance
5. Not adjusting standards for changed production conditions so that favorable variances will result
6. Using inappropriate material or labor mixes that create favorable price or rate variances but result in a lower-quality product

QUESTIONS

1. What are the three primary uses of a standard cost system? In a business that routinely manufactures the same products or performs the same services, why are standards helpful?
2. What is management by exception? Why is a standard cost system useful when managers control "by exception"?
3. What is a standard cost card? What information does it contain? How does it relate to a bill of materials and an operations flow document?
4. How is the material standard developed? Why are the quantities shown in the bill of materials not always the same quantities shown in the standard cost card?
5. A total variance can be calculated for each product cost component. Into what variances can this total be separated and to what does each relate?

6. What is meant by the term *standard hours*? Does the term refer to inputs or outputs?
7. When Domino's Pizza began operations in 1960, it had a "30 Minutes or It's Free" campaign. In making that promise, the company set a standard time to prepare and deliver a pizza. In 1993, Domino's completely removed that campaign. Discuss how setting such a standard might have been problematic for Domino's. Can you think of any other organizations in which guaranteeing specific labor time standards might create problems?
8. The overhead spending and overhead efficiency variances are said to be controllable, but the volume variance is said to be noncontrollable. Explain.
9. Discuss the following statement: Since standard costs are recorded in the inventory accounts in a standard cost system, actual costs are ignored.
10. How are insignificant variances closed at the end of an accounting period? How are significant variances closed at the end of an accounting period? Why is there a difference in treatment?
11. Why do managers care about capacity utilization? Are managers controlling costs when they control utilization?
12. Why should the use of ideal standards result in lower production costs?
13. When would adjusting standards within a period be reasonable?
14. (Appendix) What variances can be computed for direct material and direct labor when some materials or labor inputs are substitutes for others? What information does each of these variances provide?

EXERCISES

15. **LO.1 (Ethics; writing)** Hotel rooms have become more extravagant over the past decade and the time needed to clean a room has increased. eHow says that housekeepers generally have to clean 15 to 20 rooms per day; occupied rooms should take about 15 minutes to complete, while a room cleaned at check-out should take no more than 30 minutes. A good housekeeper should be able to make a bed in about one minute (http://www.ehow.com/about_4612024_hotel-housekeeping.html; last accessed 10/14/11).

    According to a study entitled "Creating Luxury, Enduring Pain" by Unite Here (the primary union representing hotel workers in the United States), housekeepers have the most dangerous jobs at hotels and have an injury rate of more than one in ten workers—almost twice that of other hotel employees. At one pricey hotel chain, it was estimated that a housekeeper who cleaned 15 rooms stripped approximately 500 pounds of soiled linens and replaced those with 500 pounds of clean linens ... resulting in back and shoulder injuries, carpal tunnel syndrome, and bursitis.

    Two articles relating to this situation are "New Study on Hotel Housekeeper Health and Safety," *Hotel News Resource* (April 25, 2006) (http://www.hotelnewsresource.com/article22006.html; last accessed 10/14/11) and Frumin et al., "Workload-Related Musculoskeletal Disorders among Hotel Housekeepers: Employer Records Reveal a Growing National Problem" (April 19, 2006) (http://www.hotelworkersrising.org/pdf/hskpr_analysis0406.pdf; last accessed 10/14/11).

    a. Why is it necessary for hotels to establish a standard for number of rooms to be cleaned by housekeepers?
    b. The average annual wages of housekeepers is $20,250, although this may be higher at the larger hotel chains. The large hotel chains are, however, attempting to eliminate health-care benefits with the wage increases. Given the rate of job injuries, do you believe that the housekeepers are better off with the lower wage and health-care benefits or a higher wage and no health-care benefits? Explain.
    c. In an eight-hour day (480 minutes), cleaning 15 rooms amounts to approximately 32 minutes per room. What makes it difficult for a housekeeper to strip and remake a bed, vacuum, lightly dust, and clean a bathroom in that period of time?

16. **LO.1 (DL & OH; use of standard cost systems; ethics; writing)** Many companies face the prospect of paying workers overtime wages; some of these payments are at time-and-a-half wages.

a. How does overtime pay affect direct labor cost? Variable overhead?
b. Obviously, paying overtime to already employed workers makes better financial business sense than does hiring additional workers. If workers would prefer not to work overtime but do so to maintain their jobs, how does overtime affect the ethical contract between employers and employees?
c. What effects might overtime have on job efficiency? On job effectiveness (such as quality of production)?
d. Would you be in favor of limiting allowable hours of overtime to have more individuals employed? Discuss this question from the standpoint of (1) the government, (2) the employer, (3) a currently employed worker, and (4) an unemployed individual.

17. **LO.1 (Cost control evaluation)** HardHead makes precast concrete steps for use with manufactured housing. The company had the following 2013 budget based on expected production of 6,400 units:

	Standard Cost	Amount Budgeted
Direct material	$22.00	$140,800
Direct labor	12.00	76,800
Variable overhead		
Indirect material	4.20	26,880
Indirect labor	1.75	11,200
Utilities	1.00	6,400
Fixed overhead		
Supervisory salaries		80,000
Depreciation		30,000
Insurance		19,280
Total		$391,360

Cost per unit = $391,380 ÷ 6,400 = $61.15

Actual production for 2013 was 7,000 units, and actual costs for the year were as follows:

Direct material used	$161,000
Direct labor	84,600
Variable overhead	
Indirect material	28,000
Indirect labor	13,300
Utilities	7,700
Fixed overhead	
Supervisory salaries	82,000
Depreciation	30,000
Insurance	17,600
Total	$424,200

Cost per unit = $424,200 ÷ 7,000 = $60.60

The plant manager, Tanzi Palate, whose annual bonus includes (among other factors) 20 percent of the net favorable cost variances, states that he saved the company $3,850 [($61.15 – $60.60) × 7,000]. He has instructed the plant cost accountant to prepare a detailed report to be sent to corporate headquarters comparing each component's actual per-unit cost with the per-unit amounts in the preceding annual budget to prove the $3,850 cost savings.

a. Is the actual-to-budget comparison proposed by Palate appropriate? If his comparison is not appropriate, prepare a more appropriate comparison.
b. How would you, as the plant cost accountant, react if Palate insisted on his comparison? Suggest what alternatives are available to you.

18. **LO.1 (Ethics; writing)** Most hospitals are reimbursed according to diagnostic-related groups (DRGs). Each DRG has a specified standard "length of stay." If a patient leaves the hospital early, the hospital is financially impacted favorably, but a patient staying longer than the specified time costs the hospital money.
    a. From the hospital administrator's point of view, would you want favorable length-of-stay variances? How might you try to obtain such variances?
    b. From a patient's point of view, would you want favorable length-of-stay variances? Answer this question from the point of view of (1) a patient who has had minor surgery and (2) a patient who has had major surgery.
    c. Would favorable length-of-stay variances necessarily equate to high-quality care?

19. **LO.1 (Behavioral implications of standard costing; research)** Contact a local company that uses a standard cost system. Make an appointment with a manager at that company to interview her or him on the following issues.
    - the characteristics that should be present in a standard cost system to encourage positive employee motivation
    - how a standard cost system should be implemented to positively motivate employees
    - the meaning of management by exception and how variance analysis often results in the use of this concept
    - how employee behavior could be adversely affected when "actual to standard" comparisons are used as the basis for performance evaluation

    Prepare a short report and an oral presentation based on your interview.

20. **LO.2 (Developing standard cost card; discussion)** One of Sure-Bet Sherbet's best-selling products is raspberry sherbet, which is manufactured in 10-gallon batches. Each batch requires six quarts of raspberries. The raspberries are sorted by hand before entering the production process, and because of imperfections, one quart of berries is discarded for every four quarts of acceptable berries. The standard direct labor sorting time to obtain one quart of acceptable raspberries is three minutes. After sorting, raspberries are blended with other ingredients; blending requires 12 minutes of direct labor time per batch. During the blending process, some sherbet is lost because it adheres to the blending vats. After blending, the sherbet is packaged in quart containers. The following cost information is relevant:
    - Raspberries are purchased for $0.80 per quart.
    - All other ingredients cost a total of $0.45 per gallon.
    - Direct labor is paid $9.00 per hour.
    - The total cost of material and labor required to package the sherbet is $0.38 per quart.

    a. Develop the standard cost for the direct cost components of a 10-gallon batch of raspberry sherbet. The standard cost should identify standard quantity, standard price/rate, and standard cost per batch for each direct cost component.
    b. Discuss the possible causes of unfavorable material price variances, and identify the individual(s) who should be held responsible for these variances.
    c. Discuss the possible causes of unfavorable labor efficiency variances, and identify the individual(s) who should be held responsible for these variances.

CMA ADAPTED

21. **LO.2 (Standard setting; team project)** As a three-person team, choose an activity that is commonly performed every day, such as taking a shower/bath, preparing a meal, or doing homework. Have each team member time him- or herself performing that activity for two days and then develop a standard time for the team. Now have the team members time themselves performing the same activity for the next five days.
    a. Using an assumed hourly wage rate of $12, calculate the labor efficiency variance for your team.
    b. Prepare a list of reasons for the variance.
    c. How could some of the variance have been avoided?

22. **LO.3 (Variance journal entries)** At year-end 2013, the trial balance of Pennopscott Corp. showed the following accounts and amounts:

	Debit	Credit
Raw Material Inventory	$ 73,200	
Work in Process Inventory	87,840	
Finished Goods Inventory	131,760	
Cost of Goods Sold	1,171,200	
Material Price Variance	14,500	
Material Quantity Variance		$21,930
Labor Rate Variance		2,200
Labor Efficiency Variance	8,780	

Assume that, taken together, the variances are believed to be significant. Prepare the journal entries to close the variances at year-end. Round any necessary calculations to one decimal point.

23. **LO.3 (OH variances)** KrisKross Inc.'s total predetermined overhead rate is $50 per hour based on a monthly capacity of 59,400 machine hours. Overhead is 30 percent variable and 70 percent fixed.

During September 2013, KrisKross produced 5,100 units of product and recorded 60,000 machine hours. September's actual overhead cost was $2,927,000. Each unit of product requires 12 machine hours.

a. What were standard hours for September?
b. What is total monthly budgeted fixed overhead cost?
c. What is the controllable overhead variance?
d. What is the noncontrollable overhead variance?

24. **LO.3 (Missing data; three OH variances)** Li Corporation's flexible budget formula for total overhead is $360,000 plus $8 per direct labor hour. The combined overhead rate is $20 per direct labor hour. The following data have been recorded for 2013:

Actual total overhead	$580,000
Total overhead spending variance	16,000 F
Volume variance	24,000 U

Use a three-variance approach to determine the following:

a. Standard hours for actual production
b. Actual direct labor hours worked

25. **LO.3 (Three OH variances)** Berlin Ltd. uses a combined overhead rate of $2.90 per machine hour to apply overhead to products. The rate was developed at an annual expected capacity of 264,000 machine hours; each unit of product requires two machine hours to produce. At 264,000 machine hours, expected fixed overhead for Munich Ltd. is $250,800.

During November, the company produced 11,960 units and used 24,700 machine hours. Actual variable overhead for the month was $47,100 and fixed overhead was $20,000. Calculate the overhead spending, efficiency, and volume variances for November.

26. **LO.3 (Four OH variances; journal entries)** Kemp Manufacturing set 70,000 direct labor hours as the 2013 capacity measure for computing its predetermined variable overhead rate. At that level, budgeted variable overhead costs are $315,000. Kemp will apply budgeted fixed overhead of $140,400 on the basis of 3,900 budgeted machine hours for the year. Both machine hours and fixed overhead costs are expected to be incurred evenly each month.

During March 2013, Kemp incurred 5,900 direct labor hours and 300 machine hours. Actual variable and fixed overhead were $26,325 and $11,400, respectively. The standard times allowed for March production were 5,980 direct labor hours and 290 machine hours.

a. Using the four-variance approach, determine the overhead variances for March 2013.
b. Prepare all journal entries related to overhead for Kemp Manufacturing for March 2013.

27. **LO.3 (OH variances)** The manager of the Texas Department of Transportation has determined that it typically takes 30 minutes for the department's employees to register a new car. In Bexar County, the predetermined fixed overhead rate was computed on an estimated 10,000 direct labor hours per month and is $9 per direct labor hour, whereas the predetermined variable overhead rate is $3 per direct labor hour.

During July, 18,800 cars were registered in Bexar County, and 9,500 direct labor hours were worked in registering those vehicles. For the month, variable overhead was $27,700 and fixed overhead was $90,800.

a. Compute overhead variances using a four-variance approach.
b. Compute overhead variances using a three-variance approach.
c. Compute overhead variances using a two-variance approach.

28. **LO.3 (OH variances)** Nelson Co. manufactures a product that requires 3.5 machine hours per unit. The variable and fixed overhead rates were computed using expected capacity of 144,000 units (produced evenly throughout the year) and expected variable and fixed overhead costs, respectively, of $2,016,000 and $3,528,000. In October, Nelson manufactured 11,900 units using 41,800 machine hours. October variable overhead costs were $165,000; fixed overhead costs were $294,500.

a. What are the standard variable and fixed overhead rates?
b. Compute the variable overhead variances.
c. Compute the fixed overhead variances.
d. Explain the volume variance computed in (c).

29. **LO.3 (DM & DL variances)** Green Tee produces 100 percent cotton t-shirts, with the following standard direct material and labor quantities and costs:

Direct material	2.0 yards × $3.00
Direct labor	0.7 hour × $7.50

Actual September production and costs for the company to produce 10,000 t-shirts were as follows:

	Quantity	Cost
Direct material		
Purchased	30,000 yards	$89,700
Requisitioned into production	20,120 yards	
Direct labor	7,940 hours	58,756

a. What is the standard quantity of material and the standard labor time for September's production?
b. Compute the direct material and direct labor variances.
c. How might the sales and production managers explain the direct material variances?
d. How might the production and human resources managers explain the direct labor variances?
e. Record the year-end adjusting entry to close the material and labor variances, assuming that they are insignificant.

30. **LO.3 (DM & DL variances; journal entries)** Madzinga's Draperies manufactures curtains. Curtain #4571 requires the following:

Direct material standard	10 square yards at $5 per yard
Direct labor standard	5 hours at $10 per hour

During the second quarter, the company purchased 17,000 square yards at a cost of $83,300 and used 16,500 square yards to produce 1,500 Curtain #4571s. Direct labor totaled 7,600 hours for $79,800.

a. Compute the material price and usage variances.
b. Prepare the journal entries for the purchase and use of direct material.
c. Compute labor rate and labor efficiency variances.
d. Prepare the journal entry to accrue direct labor cost and record the labor variances for the quarter.
e. Comment on the above variances. Identify possible causes and relationships among the variances that you computed.

CPA ADAPTED

31. **LO.3 (DM & DL variances; journal entries)** In July 2013, Zinger Corp. purchased 20,000 gallons of Numerol for $61,000 to use in the production of product #43MR7. During July, Zinger Corp. manufactured 3,900 units of product #43MR7. The following information is available about standard and actual quantities and costs:

	Standard for One Unit	Actual Usage for July
Direct material	4.8 gallons @ $3 per gallon	18,350 gallons
Direct labor	20 minutes @ $9 per DLH	1,290 DLHs @ $9.02 per DLH

a. Compute the material purchase price variance and the material quantity variance.
b. Compute the labor rate, labor efficiency, and total labor variance.
c. Prepare the journal entries for the material and labor variances.

32. **LO.3 (Missing information for DL)** For each independent case, fill in the missing figures.

	Case A	Case B	Case C	Case D
Units produced	1,000	?	240	1,500
Standard hours per unit	3.5	0.9	?	?
Standard hours	?	900	600	?
Standard rate per hour	$ 7.25	?	$10.50	$ 7.00
Actual hours worked	3,400	975	?	4,900
Actual labor cost	?	?	$6,180	$ 31,850
Labor rate variance	$850 F	$975 F	$300 U	?
Labor efficiency variance	?	$765 U	?	$2,800 U

33. **LO.3 (DM & DL variances)** In December, Sam Antari, president of Antari Inc., received the following information from Denise Sweet, the new controller, in regard to November production of travel bags:

EXCEL

November production	4,800 bags
Actual cost of material purchased and used	$14,550
Standard material allowed	0.5 square yard per bag
Material quantity variance	$600 U
Standard price per yard of material	$6
Actual hours worked	9,760 hours
Standard labor time per bag	2 hours
Labor rate variance	$1,464 F
Standard labor rate per hour	$17

Antari asked Sweet to provide the following information:

a. Standard quantity of material allowed for November production
b. Standard direct labor hours allowed for November production
c. Material price variance
d. Labor efficiency variance
e. Standard prime (direct material and direct labor) cost to produce one travel bag
f. Actual cost to produce one travel bag in November
g. An explanation for the difference between standard and actual cost; be sure that the explanation is consistent with the pattern of the variances

34. **LO.3 (DL variances; journal entries)** Calista & Lane, CPAs, set the following standard for its inventory audit of Triumph Co.: 350 hours at an average hourly rate of $250. The firm actually worked 330 hours during the inventory audit process. The total labor variance for the audit was $3,500 unfavorable.

a. Compute the total actual payroll.
b. Compute the labor efficiency variance.
c. Compute the labor rate variance.
d. Prepare the entry to assign labor costs to inventory, record the labor variances, and accrue payroll costs.
e. Provide a brief explanation of these variances that is consistent with the labor rate and efficiency variances.

EXCEL

35. **LO.3 (OH variances)** FUN Inc. has a fully automated production facility in which almost 97 percent of overhead costs are driven by machine hours. As the company's cost accountant, you have computed the following overhead variances for May:

Variable overhead spending variance	$34,000 F
Variable overhead efficiency variance	41,200 F
Fixed overhead spending variance	28,000 U
Fixed overhead volume variance	20,000 U

The company's president is concerned about the variance amounts and has asked you to show her how the variances were computed and to answer several questions. Budgeted fixed overhead for the month is $1,000,000; the predetermined variable and fixed overhead rates are, respectively, $20 and $40 per machine hour. Budgeted capacity is 20,000 units.

a. Using the four-variance approach, prepare an overhead analysis in as much detail as possible.
b. What is the standard number of machine hours allowed for each unit of output?
c. How many actual hours were worked in May?
d. What is the total spending variance?
e. What additional information about the manufacturing overhead variances is gained by inserting detailed computations into the variable and fixed manufacturing overhead variance analysis?
f. How would the overhead variances be closed if the three-variance approach were used and the variances are considered insignificant?

36. **LO.3 (DL variances; journal entries)** Information on Hanley's direct labor costs for January 2013 is as follows:

Actual direct labor rate	$7.50
Standard direct labor hours allowed	9,000
Actual direct labor hours	10,000
Labor rate variance	$5,500 F

a. Compute the standard direct labor rate in January.
b. Compute the labor efficiency variance in January.
c. Prepare the journal entry to accrue direct labor cost and to record the labor variances for January.

CPA ADAPTED

37. **LO.3 (DL variances)** Logen Construction builds standard prefabricated wooden frames for walls. Each frame requires five direct labor hours and the standard hourly direct labor rate is $18. During July, the company produced 670 frames and worked 3,310 direct labor hours. Payroll records indicate that workers earned $60,407.50.

a. What were the standard hours for July production?
b. What was the actual hourly wage rate?
c. Calculate the direct labor variances.

38. **LO.3 (DM variances)** McHenry Corp. makes wrought iron garden sculptures. During April, the purchasing agent bought 25,600 pounds of scrap iron at $0.64 per pound. During the month, 21,400 pounds of scrap iron were used to produce 600 sculptures. Although each sculpture is slightly different, McHenry uses a standard quantity per sculpture of 35 pounds of scrap iron at a standard cost of $0.70 per pound.

a. For April, compute the direct material price variance (based on the quantity purchased) and the direct material quantity variance (based on quantity used).

b. Identify the titles of individuals in the firm who would be responsible for each of the variances.
c. Provide some possible explanations for the variances computed in (a).

39. **LO.3 (DM variances)** Bell Inc. manufactures a product that requires five pounds of material. The purchasing agent has an opportunity to purchase the necessary material at a vendor's bankruptcy sale at $1.40 per pound rather than the standard cost of $2.10 per pound. The purchasing agent purchases 100,000 pounds of material on May 31. During the next four months, the company's production and material usage was as follows:

	Production	Quantity Used
June	3,000	16,400 lbs.
July	3,400	17,640 lbs.
August	2,900	14,950 lbs.
September	2,500	13,100 lbs.

a. What is the material price variance for this purchase?
b. What is the material quantity variance for each month for this material?
c. What might be the cause of the unfavorable material quantity variances?

40. **LO.3 (DM variances; journal entries)** Skip Company produces a product called Lem. The standard direct material cost to produce one unit of Lem is four quarts of raw material at $2.50 per quart. During May 2013, 4,200 quarts of raw material were purchased at a cost of $10,080. All the purchased material was used to produce 1,000 units of Lem.

a. Compute the actual cost per quart and the material price variance for May 2013.
b. Assume the same facts except that Skip Company purchased 6,000 quarts of material at the previously calculated cost per quart, but used only 4,200 quarts. Compute the material price variance and material usage variance for May 2013, assuming that Skip identifies variances at the earliest possible time.
c. Prepare the journal entries to record the material price and usage variances calculated in (b).
d. Which managers at Skip Company would most likely assume responsibility for control of the variance computed in requirement (b)? CPA ADAPTED

41. **LO.3 (DM variances)** In November 2013, DayTime Publishing Company's costs and quantities of paper consumed in manufacturing its 2014 Executive Planner and Calendar were as follows:

Actual unit purchase price	$0.13 per page
Standard unit price	$0.14 per page
Standard quantity for good production	97,900 pages
Actual quantity purchased during November	115,000 pages
Actual quantity used in November	100,000 pages

a. Calculate the total cost of purchases for November.
b. Compute the material price variance (based on quantity purchased).
c. Calculate the material quantity variance.

42. **LO.5 (Variances and conversion cost category)** Svenson Technology considers direct labor cost too insignificant to separately account for and, therefore, uses a $22.50 per machine hour predetermined conversion cost rate (of which $16 is related to fixed overhead costs). The conversion rate was established based on expected capacity of 1,008,600 machine hours. One of Svenson Technology's products requires 4.1 machine hours to manufacture.

In September 2013, the company manufactured 21,000 units of product and used 83,000 machine hours and 840 direct labor hours. Variable and fixed conversion costs incurred for September were $551,230 and $1,330,000, respectively.

a. What is the expected capacity per month in units and machine hours?
b. Prepare a four- and three-variance analysis of conversion costs for September 2013.

43. **LO.5 (Variances and conversion cost category)** Auto Brakes Inc. manufactures brake rotors and has always applied overhead to production using direct labor hours. Recently, company facilities were automated, and the accounting system was revised to show only two cost categories: direct material and conversion. Estimated variable and fixed conversion costs for the current month were $170,000 and $76,000, respectively. Expected output for the current month was 5,000 rotors, and the estimated number of machine hours was 10,000. During July 2013, the firm actually used 9,000 machine hours to make 4,800 rotors while incurring $228,000 of conversion costs. Of this amount, $150,000 was variable cost.

    a. Using the four-variance approach, compute the variances for conversion costs.
    b. Evaluate the effectiveness of the firm in controlling the current month's costs.

44. **LO.6 (Appendix; labor variances)** Taglia Law Office has three labor classes: administrative assistants, paralegals, and attorneys. Standard wage rates are as follows: administrative assistants, $30 per hour; paralegals, $60 per hour; and attorneys, $125 per hour. For October, the numbers of actual direct labor hours worked and of standard hours for probate cases were as follows:

	Actual DLHs	Number of Standard Hours Allowed
Administrative assistant	900	1,008
Paralegal	2,520	2,772
Attorney	1,500	1,260

    a. Calculate October's direct labor efficiency variance as well as the direct labor mix variance and the direct labor yield variance.

CMA ADAPTED

    b. Discuss whether management used an efficient mix of labor.

45. **LO.6 (Appendix; material variances)** Hennessey Company produces 12-ounce cans of mixed pecans and cashews. Standard and actual information follows.

Standard Quantities and Costs (12-oz. can)	
Pecans: 6 ounces at $6.00 per pound	$2.25
Cashews: 6 ounces at $8.00 per pound	3.00

Actual Quantities and Costs for Production of 36,000 Cans

Pecans: 15,554 pounds at $5.80 per pound
Cashews: 12,726 pounds at $8.50 per pound

Determine the material price, mix, and yield variances.

46. **LO.6 (Appendix; labor variances)** Coffen Corp. employs engineers and draftspeople. The average hourly rates are $60 for engineers and $30 for draftspeople. For one project, the standard was set at 400 hours of engineer time and 600 hours of draftsperson time. Actual hours worked on this project were:

Engineers—500 hours at $65 per hour
Draftspeople—500 hours at $32 per hour

Determine the labor rate, mix, and yield variances for this project.

PROBLEMS

47. **LO.3 (OH variances; journal entries)** N Joy makes wooden picnic tables, swings, and benches. Standard hours for each product are as follows:

Picnic table	10 standard direct labor hours
Swing	3 standard direct labor hours
Bench	7 standard direct labor hours

The standard variable overhead rate is $4 per direct labor hour. The standard fixed overhead rate, computed using an expected annual capacity of 36,000 direct labor hours, is $2 per direct labor hour. The company estimates stable fixed overhead costs and direct labor hours each month of the annual period. March production was 100 picnic tables, 400 swings, and 60 benches; production required 2,780 actual direct labor hours. Actual variable and fixed overhead for March were $12,800 and $5,900, respectively.

a. Prepare a variance analysis using the four-variance approach. (Hint: Convert the production of each type of product into standard hours for all work accomplished for the month.)
b. Prepare journal entries to record actual overhead costs, application of overhead to production, and closing of the overhead variance accounts (assuming those variances are immaterial).
c. Evaluate the effectiveness of the managers in controlling costs.

48. **LO.3 (OH variances with unknowns)** During December 2013, Amin Corp. manufactured products requiring 8,000 standard labor hours. The following variance and actual information is available:

Labor rate variance	$ 4,500 U
Labor efficiency variance	12,000 U
Actual variable overhead	162,000
Actual fixed overhead	84,000

Amin Corp.'s standard costs for labor and overhead were set at the beginning of 2013 and have remained constant through the year as follows:

Direct labor (4 hours × $12 per hour)	$ 48
Factory overhead (10,000 DLHs expected capacity)	
Variable (4 hours × $16 per direct labor hour)	64
Fixed (4 hours × $9 per direct labor hour)	36
Total unit conversion cost	$148

Calculate the following unknown amounts:

a. Number of units manufactured
b. Total applied factory overhead
c. Volume variance
d. Variable overhead spending variance
e. Variable overhead efficiency variance
f. Total actual overhead

49. **LO.3 (Incomplete data; variances)** Quinan Carpentry Co. makes wooden shelves. A small fire on October 1 partially destroyed the records relating to September's production. The charred remains of the standard cost card appear here.

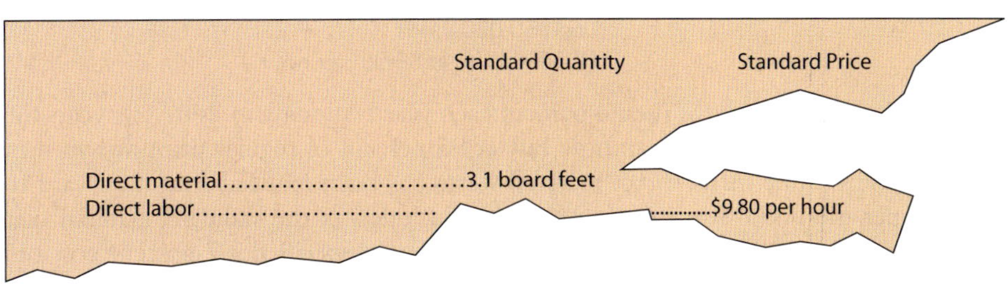

From other fragments of records and several discussions with employees, you learn the following:

- The purchasing agent's files showed that 50,000 board feet had been purchased on account in September at $1.05 per board foot. He was proud of the fact that this price was $0.05 below standard cost per foot.
- There was no beginning inventory of raw material on September 1, and since the raw material storage location is apart from the production facility, the fire caused no

damage to the remaining raw material. Fourteen hundred board feet of raw material were on hand on October 1.

- The standard quantity of material allowed for September's production was 49,600 board feet.
- The September payroll for direct labor was $39,494 based on 4,030 actual hours worked.
- The production supervisor distinctly remembered being held accountable for 30 more hours of direct labor than should have been worked. She was upset because top management failed to consider that she saved hundreds of board feet of material by creative efforts that required extra time.

a. How many units were produced during September?
b. Calculate direct material variances for September.
c. What is the standard number of hours allowed for the production of each unit?
d. Calculate all direct labor variances for September.
e. Prepare general journal entries reflecting direct material and direct labor activity and variances for September, assuming a standard cost, perpetual inventory system.

50. **LO.3 (One-, two-, and three-variance approaches to OH variances)** Terkelsen Mfg. produces comforter sets with the following standard cost information:

- Each comforter set requires 0.5 hours of machine time to produce.
- Variable overhead is applied at the rate of $9 per machine hour.
- Fixed overhead is applied at the rate of $6 per machine hour, based on an expected annual capacity of 30,000 machine hours.

Production Statistics for 2013

Number of comforter sets produced	62,000 units
Actual number of machine hours	33,300 hours
Variable overhead cost incurred	$265,400
Fixed overhead cost incurred	$177,250

a. Calculate variances using the one-variance approach.
b. Calculate variances using the two-variance approach.
c. Calculate variances using the three-variance approach.

51. **LO.3 (Adjusting standards)** ALOHA Corp., started in January 2007, manufactures Hawaiian muumuus. At that time, the following material and labor standards were developed:

Material	3.0 yards at $4 per yard
Labor	1.5 hours at $6 per hour

In January 2013, ALOHA Corp. hired a new cost accountant, Anulu Haoki. At the end of the month, Haoki was reviewing the production variances and was amazed to find that the company's material and labor standards had never been revised. Actual material and labor data for January, when 17,200 muumuus were produced, follow.

Material	Purchased, 50,000 yards at $4.90
	Used 50,000 yards
Labor	17,800 hours at $9.05 per hour

Material prices have risen 4 percent each year beginning in 2007 (six years through 2012), but the company can now buy at 95 percent of regular price due to increased purchase volume. Also, direct material waste has been reduced from 1/4 yard to 1/8 yard per muumuu; waste has always been included in the standard material quantity. Beginning in 2007, each annual labor contract has specified a 7 percent cost-of-living adjustment. Revision of the plant layout and acquisition of more efficient machinery has decreased the labor time per muumuu by one-third since the company began.

a. Determine the material and labor variances based on the company's original standards.
b. Determine the new standards against which Haoki should measure the January 2013 results. (Round adjustments annually to the nearest cent.)
c. Compute the variances for material and labor using the revised standards.

52. **LO.3 (Comprehensive; all variances; all methods)** Hellier Contractors paints interiors of residences and commercial structures. The firm's management has established cost standards per 100 square feet of area to be painted.

Direct material ($18 per gallon of paint)	$1.50
Direct labor	2.00
Variable overhead	0.60
Fixed overhead (based on 600,000 square feet per month)	1.25

Management has determined that 400 square feet can be painted by the average worker each hour. During May, the company painted 600,000 square feet of space and incurred the following costs:

Direct material (450 gallons purchased and used)	$ 8,300.00
Direct labor (1,475 hours)	12,242.50
Variable overhead	3,480.00
Fixed overhead	7,720.00

a. Compute the direct material variances.
b. Compute the direct labor variances.
c. Use a four-variance approach to compute overhead variances.
d. Use a three-variance approach to compute overhead variances.
e. Use a two-variance approach to compute overhead variances.
f. Reconcile your answers for (c) through (e).
g. Discuss other cost drivers that could be used as a basis for measuring activity and computing variances for this company.

53. **LO.3 (OH variances)** Pier Corp. has an expected monthly capacity of 9,000 units but only 5,700 units were produced and 6,000 direct labor hours were used during August 2013 due to a flood in the manufacturing facility. Actual variable overhead for August was $48,165, and actual fixed overhead was $140,220. EXCEL

Standard cost data follow:

	Standard Cost per Unit (One Unit Takes One Labor Hour)
Direct material	$ 9.00
Direct labor	15.00
Variable overhead	8.00
Fixed overhead	16.00
Total	$48.00

a. Compute and compare the actual overhead cost per unit with the expected overhead cost per unit.
b. Calculate overhead variances using the four-variance method.
c. Explain why the volume variance is so large.

54. **LO.3 (Variance disposition)** The following variances existed at year-end 2013 for Muckstadt Production Company:

Material price variance	$23,400 U
Material quantity variance	24,900 F
Labor rate variance	5,250 F
Labor efficiency variance	36,900 U
Variance overhead spending variance	3,000 U
Variance overhead efficiency variance	1,800 F
Fixed overhead spending variance	6,600 F
Volume variance	16,800 U

In addition, the following inventory and Cost of Goods Sold account balances existed at year-end 2013:

Raw Material Inventory	$ 320,600
Work in Process Inventory	916,000
Finished Goods Inventory	641,200
Cost of Goods Sold	2,702,200

a. Prepare the journal entry at December 31 to dispose of the variances, assuming that all are insignificant.
b. After posting your entry in (a), what is the balance in Cost of Goods Sold?
c. Prepare the journal entries at December 31 to dispose of the variances, assuming that all are significant. (Round to the nearest whole percentage.)
d. After posting your entries in (c), what are the balances in each inventory account and in Cost of Goods Sold?

55. **LO.3 (Incomplete data; variances; journal entries)** Surgical Products produces latex surgical gloves. Machines perform the majority of the processing for 1,000 pairs of gloves per hour. Each pair of gloves requires 0.85 square foot of latex, which has a standard price of $0.80 per square foot. Machine operators are considered direct labor and are paid $15 per hour.

During one week in May, Surgical Products produced 300,000 pairs of gloves and experienced a $1,440 unfavorable material quantity variance. The company had purchased 2,500 more square feet of material than had been used in production that week. The unfavorable material price variance for the week was $5,186. A $288 unfavorable total labor variance was generated based on 315 total actual labor hours to produce the gloves.

a. Determine the following amounts:
   (1) Standard quantity of material for production achieved
   (2) Actual quantity of material used
   (3) Actual quantity of material purchased
   (4) Actual price of material purchased
   (5) Standard hours for actual production
   (6) Labor efficiency variance
   (7) Labor rate variance
   (8) Actual labor rate
b. Prepare the journal entries for the above information.

56. **LO.3 (Variances and variance responsibility)** Namathe Industries manufactures children's footballs with the following standard costs per unit:

Material: one square foot of leather at $2.00	$ 2.00
Direct labor: 1.6 hours at $9.00	14.40
Variable overhead cost	3.00
Fixed overhead cost	3.00
Total cost per unit	$22.40

Per-unit overhead cost was calculated from the following annual overhead budget for 180,000 footballs.

Variable Overhead Cost		
Indirect labor—90,000 hours @ $7.00	$630,000	
Supplies (oil)—180,000 gallons @ $0.50	90,000	
Allocated variable service department costs	90,000	
Total variable overhead cost		$ 810,000
Fixed Overhead Cost		
Supervision	$ 81,000	
Depreciation	135,000	
Other fixed costs	45,000	
Total fixed overhead cost		261,000
Total budgeted overhead cost @ 180,000 units		$1,071,000

Following are the charges to the manufacturing department for November when 15,000 units were produced:

Material (15,900 square feet @ \$2.00)	\$ 31,800
Direct labor (24,600 hours @ \$9.10)	223,860
Indirect labor (7,200 hours @ \$7.10)	51,120
Supplies (oil) (18,000 gallons @ \$0.55)	9,900
Allocated service department variable OH costs	9,600
Supervision	7,425
Depreciation	11,250
Other fixed costs	3,750
Total	\$348,705

Purchasing normally buys about the same quantity as is used in production during a month. In November, the company purchased 15,600 square feet of material at a price of \$2.10 per foot.

a. Calculate the following variances from standard costs for the data given:
   1. Material purchase price
   2. Material quantity
   3. Direct labor rate
   4. Direct labor efficiency
   5. Overhead budget
b. The company has divided its responsibilities so that the Purchasing Department is responsible for the purchase price of materials and the Manufacturing Department is responsible for the quantity of materials used. Does this division of responsibilities solve the conflict between price and quantity variances? Explain your answer.
c. Prepare a report detailing the overhead budget variance. The report, which will be given to the Manufacturing Department manager, should only show that part of the variance that is her responsibility and should highlight the information in ways that would be useful to her in evaluating departmental performance and when considering corrective action.
d. Assume that the departmental manager performs the timekeeping function for this manufacturing department. From time to time, analyses of overhead and direct labor variances have shown that the manager has deliberately misclassified labor hours (i.e., listed direct labor hours as indirect labor hours and vice versa) so that only one of the two labor variances is unfavorable. It is not feasible economically to hire a separate timekeeper. What should the company do, if anything, to resolve this problem? **CMA ADAPTED**

57. **LO.3 (DM & DL variances)** Aquatica uses a standard cost system for materials and labor in producing small fishing boats. Production requires three materials: fiberglass, paint, and a purchased trim package. The standard costs and quantities for materials and labor are as follows:

Standards for One Fishing Boat

2,000 pounds of fiberglass × \$1.80 per pound	\$3,600
6 quarts gel coat paint × \$15.00 per quart	90
1 trim package	200
40 hours of labor × \$25.00 per hour	1,000
Standard cost for DM and DL	\$4,890

The following actual data related to the production of 600 boats was recorded for July:

Material Purchased on Account

Fiberglass—2,100,000 pounds × \$1.83 per pound
Paint—1,000 gallons × \$55.50 per gallon
Trim packages—640 × \$205 per package

Material Used
Fiberglass—1,380,000 pounds
Paint—924 gallons
Trim packages—608

Direct Labor Used
23,850 hours × $23.50 per hour

Calculate the material and labor variances for Aquatica for July. The material price variance should be computed for each type of material and on the quantity of material purchased.

EXCEL

58. **LO.3 (Comprehensive)** Piedmont Manufacturing produces metal products with the following standard quantity and cost information:

Direct Material		
Aluminum	4 sheets @ $4	$ 16
Copper	3 sheets @ $8	24
Direct labor	7 hours @ $16	112
Variable overhead	5 machine hours @ $6	30
Fixed overhead	5 machine hours @ $4	20

Overhead rates were based on normal monthly capacity of 6,000 machine hours.

During November, the company produced only 850 units because of a labor strike, which occurred during union contract negotiations. After the dispute was settled, the company scheduled overtime to try to meet regular production levels. The following costs were incurred in November:

Material	
Aluminum	4,000 sheets purchased @ $3.80; used 3,500 sheets
Copper	3,000 sheets purchased @ $8.40; used 2,600 sheets
Direct Labor	
Regular time	5,200 hours @ $16 (pre-contract settlement)
Regular time	900 hours @ $17 (post-contract settlement)
Variable Overhead	
$23,300 (based on 4,175 machine hours)	
Fixed Overhead	
$18,850 (based on 4,175 machine hours)	

Determine the following and prepare the journal entries to record the standard costing information for November:

a. Total material price variance
b. Total material usage (quantity) variance
c. Labor rate variance
d. Labor efficiency variance
e. Variable overhead spending variance
f. Variable overhead efficiency variance
g. Fixed overhead spending variance
h. Volume variance
i. Budget variance

59. **LO.3 (DM & DL variances; journal entries)** Triscuit-Biscuit Corp. makes small plastic dog toys with the following material and labor standards:

	Standard Quantity	**Standard Cost**
Material	0.25 pound	$3.00 per pound
Labor	3 minutes	9.00 per hour

During October, 60,000 pounds of material were acquired on account at $3.08 per pound. During October, 24,800 pounds of that were used in production during the month to make 100,000 toys. Factory payroll for October showed 5,320 direct labor hours at a total cost of $46,816.

a. Compute material and labor variances, basing the material price variance on the quantity of material purchased.
b. Assuming a perpetual inventory system is used, prepare the relevant general journal entries for October.

60. **LO.3 (Comprehensive OH variances)** For 2013, Riguilio Inc. set predetermined variable and fixed overhead rates, respectively, at $6.50 and $9.35 based on an expected monthly capacity of 4,000 machine hours. Each unit of product requires 1.25 machine hours.

During August 2013, the company produced 3,360 units and incurred $27,000 of variable overhead costs and $41,400 of fixed overhead costs. The firm used 4,100 machine hours during August 2013.

a. Using separate overhead rates, calculate overhead variances using the four-variance approach.
b. Using a combined overhead rate, calculate variances using the three-variance approach.
c. Using a combined overhead rate, calculate variances using the two-variance approach.
d. Using a combined overhead rate, calculate variances using the one-variance approach.

61. **LO.3 (DM & DL variances; journal entries)** Schmidt Co. has the following standard material and labor quantities and costs for one unit of Product SWK#468:

Material	1.85 pounds @ $3.50 per pound
Labor	0.04 hour @ $12 per hour

During July, the purchasing agent found a "good deal" on the raw material needed for Product SWK#468 and bought 100,000 pounds of material at $3.15 per pound. In July, the company produced 48,000 units of Product SWK#468 with the following material and labor usage:

Material	95,000 pounds
Labor	2,200 hours @ $12.10 (due to a renegotiated labor contract)

a. What is the standard quantity of material and the standard labor time for July?
b. Calculate the material and labor variances for July.
c. Prepare the material and labor journal entries for July.
d. Did the purchasing agent make a "good deal" on the raw material? Explain.

62. **LO.4 (Standards revision; writing)** Ripper Corp. uses a standard cost system for its aircraft component manufacturing operations. Recently, the company's direct material supplier went out of business, but Ripper's purchasing agent found a new source that produces a similar material. The price per pound from the original supplier was $7.00; the new source's price is $7.77. The new source's material reduces scrap, and thus, each unit requires only 1.00 pound rather than the previous standard of 1.25 pounds per unit. In addition, use of the new source's material reduces direct labor time from 24 to 22 minutes per unit because there is less machine setup time. At the same time, the recently signed labor contract increased the average direct labor wage rate from $12.60 to $14.40 per hour.

The company began using the new direct material on April 1, the same day that the new labor agreement went into effect. However, Ripper Corp. is still using the following standards that were set at the beginning of the calendar year:

Direct material	1.2 pounds @ $6.80 per pound	$ 8.16
Direct labor	20 minutes @ $12.30 per DLH	4.10
Standard DM and DL cost per unit		$12.26

Steve Wenskel, cost accounting supervisor, had been examining the following April 30 variance report.

PERFORMANCE REPORT
STANDARD COST VARIANCE ANALYSIS FOR APRIL 2013

Standard		Price Variance	Quantity Variance	Actual
DM	$ 8.16	($0.97 × 1.0) = $0.97 U	($6.80 × 0.2) = $1.36 F	$ 7.77
DL	4.10	[$2.10 × (22/60)] = 0.77 U	[$12.30 × (2/60)] = 0.41 U	5.28
	$12.26			$13.05

COMPARISON OF 2013 ACTUAL COSTS

	Average 1st Quarter Costs	April Costs	Percent Increase (Decrease)
DM	$ 8.75	$ 7.77	(11.2)
DL	5.04	5.28	4.8
	$13.79	$13.05	(5.4)

When Cynthia Dirope, assistant controller, came into Wenskel's office, he said, "Cynthia, look at this performance report! Direct material price increased 11 percent, and the labor rate increased over 14 percent during April. I expected greater variances, yet prime costs decreased over 5 percent from the $13.79 we experienced during the first quarter of this year. The proper message just isn't coming through."

Dirope said, "This has been an unusual period. With all the unforeseen changes, perhaps we should revise our standards based on current conditions and start over."

Wenskel replied, "I think we can retain the current standards but expand the variance analysis. We could calculate variances for the specific changes that have occurred to direct material and direct labor before we calculate the normal price and quantity variances. What I really think would be useful to management right now is to determine the impact the changes in direct material and direct labor had in reducing our prime costs per unit from $13.79 in the first quarter to $13.05 in April—a reduction of $0.74."

a. Discuss the advantages of (1) immediately revising the standards and (2) retaining the current standards and expanding the analysis of variances.
b. Prepare an analysis that reflects the impact of the new direct material and new labor contract on reducing Ripper Corp.'s standard costs per unit from $13.79 to $13.05. The analysis should show the changes in direct material and direct labor costs per unit that are caused by (1) the use of the new direct material and (2) the labor rates of the new contract. This analysis should be in sufficient detail to identify the changes due to direct material price, direct labor rate, the effect of direct material quality on direct material usage, and the effect of direct material quality on direct labor usage.

CMA ADAPTED

63. **LO.5 (Conversion cost variances)** Kieffer Company makes men's suit alterations for a major clothing store chain. No direct materials are used in the alterations process and overhead costs are primarily variable and relate very closely to direct labor charges. The company owner has decided to compute variances on a conversion cost basis. Standards for 2013 are as follows:

Expected direct labor hours (DLHs; to be incurred evenly throughout the year)	60,000
Number of suits altered in October	1,800
Standard DLHs per suit	3
Actual DLHs worked in October 2013	5,490
Budgeted variable conversion cost per DLH	$ 18
Budgeted annual fixed conversion cost	$ 72,000
Actual variable conversion cost for October 2013	$103,100
Actual fixed conversion cost for October 2013	$ 5,750

a. How many suits does Kieffer Company expect to alter during 2013?
b. What is the predetermined fixed OH rate for Kieffer Company?
c. How many standard direct labor hours were allowed for October 2013?
d. Calculate the four conversion cost variances assuming that variable and fixed costs are separated.
e. Calculate the three conversion cost variances assuming that fixed and variable costs are combined.

64. **LO.5 (Conversion cost variances)** The May budget for the Auberage Company shows $1,080,000 of variable conversion costs, $360,000 of fixed conversion costs, and 72,000 machine hours for the production of 24,000 units of product. During May, 76,000 machine hours were worked and 24,000 units were produced. Variance and fixed conversion costs for the month were $1,128,800 and $374,500, respectively.
    a. Calculate the four conversion cost variances assuming that variable and fixed costs are separated.
    b. Calculate the three conversion cost variances assuming that fixed and variable costs are combined.

65. **LO.6 (Appendix)** Haddas Ltd. makes Healthy Life, a nutritional aid. For a 50-pound batch, standard material and labor costs are as follows:

	Quantity	Unit Price	Total
Wheat	25.0 pounds	$ 0.20 per pound	$5.00
Barley	25.0 pounds	0.10 per pound	2.50
Corn	10.0 pounds	0.05 per pound	0.50
Skilled labor	0.8 hour	12.00 per hour	9.60
Unskilled labor	0.2 hour	8.00 per hour	1.60

During June, the following materials and labor were used in producing 600 batches of Healthy Life:

Wheat	18,000 pounds @ $0.22 per pound
Barley	14,000 pounds @ $0.11 per pound
Corn	10,000 pounds @ $0.07 per pound
Skilled labor	400 hours @ $12.25 per hour
Unskilled labor	260 hours @ $9.00 per hour

a. Calculate the material quantity, mix, and yield variances.
b. Calculate the labor efficiency, mix, and yield variances.

66. **LO.6 (Appendix)** Polermo Inc. produces three-topping, 18-inch frozen pizzas and uses a standard cost system. The three pizza toppings (in addition to cheese) are onions, olives, and mushrooms. To some extent, discretion may be used to determine the actual mix of these toppings. The company has two classes of labor, and discretion also may be used to determine the mix of the labor inputs. The standard cost card for a pizza follows:

Onions	3 ounces @ $0.10 per ounce
Olives	3 ounces @ $0.35 per ounce
Mushrooms	3 ounces @ $0.50 per ounce
Labor category 1	5 minutes @ $12 per hour
Labor category 2	6 minutes @ $8 per hour

During May 2013, the company produced 48,000 pizzas and used the following inputs:

Onions	8,000 pounds
Olives	12,000 pounds
Mushrooms	8,000 pounds

Labor category 1	5,200 hours
Labor category 2	4,000 hours

During the month there were no deviations from standards on material prices or labor rates.

a. Determine the material quantity, mix, and yield variances.
b. Determine the labor efficiency, mix, and yield variances.
c. Prepare the journal entries to record the above mix and yield variances.

Apdesign/Shutterstock.com

8

The Master Budget

LEARNING OBJECTIVES

After completing this chapter, you should be able to answer the following questions:

1. How are strategic planning and tactical planning related to budgeting?
2. What is the starting point of a master budget, and why?
3. What are the various components of a master budget, and how are they prepared?
4. Why is the cash budget so important in the master budgeting process?
5. How and why are budgeted financial statements prepared at the end of the budgeting process?
6. What benefits are provided by a budget?
7. (*Appendix*) How does a budget manual facilitate the budgeting process?

INTRODUCTION

In virtually any endeavor, organizing and coordinating behavior involves visualizing the future, specifying the desired outcomes, and determining the activities and resources needed to achieve those results. The last part of the behavioral process is essential because, as stated in *The Little Prince*, "a goal without a plan is just a wish."

Planning is the cornerstone of effective management, and in the complex business environment, successful planning requires that managers predict, with reasonable precision, the key variables that affect company performance. Such predictions provide managers with the foundation for effective problem solving, control, and resource allocation. Planning (especially in financial terms) is important even if future conditions are expected to approximate current ones; planning is critical when future conditions are expected to change.

This chapter covers the budgeting process and master budget preparation. Budgeting is important for organizations of all sizes, especially those with large quantities of monetary, human, and physical resources.

THE BUDGETING PROCESS

1 How are strategic planning and tactical planning related to budgeting?

Unlike a computer, human beings often have difficulty processing many facts and relationships simultaneously and also have a tendency to forget. Thus, as plans become more intricate, they should be documented in writing and include qualitative narratives of goals, objectives, and means of accomplishing the objectives. However, if plans consisted only of qualitative narratives, comparisons between expected and actual results would be vague generalizations that would not provide the ability to measure whether the organization succeeded. The process of formalizing plans and translating qualitative narratives into a documented, quantitative format is called **budgeting**. The end result of this process is a **budget**, which quantitatively expresses an organization's commitment to planned activities, resource acquisition, and resource usage. Although budgets are typically expressed in financial terms, the budgeting process must begin by considering nonquantitative factors and all organizational resources, such as raw material, inventory, supplies, personnel, and facilities.

The budgeting process indicates a direction or path that management has chosen from many alternatives. Inclusion of quantifiable amounts provides specific criteria against which future performance (also recorded in accounting terms) can be compared. Thus, a budget is a type of standard that allows variances to be computed and feedback about those variances to be given to appropriate individuals. Budgets can be viewed from a long-term (strategic) or a short-term (tactical) perspective.

Strategic Planning

Top-level managers, generally with the assistance of key staff members, who plan on a long-range basis (5–10 years) are engaged in **strategic planning**. The result is a statement of long-range organizational goals as well as the strategies and policies that will help achieve those goals. The strategic plan should identify key variables that will be the direct causes of the achievement (or nonachievement) of organizational goals and objectives. Key variables (shown in Exhibit 8.1) can be internal (under the control of management) or external (normally noncontrollable by management). Effective strategic planning requires that managers build plans and budgets that integrate the key internal and external variables. This information is used to adjust the previously gathered historical information for any changes in the key variables for the planning period.

During the strategic planning process, managers set organizational goals and objectives and agree on how to achieve them. Typically, goals are stated as desired abstract achievements (such as "to become a market leader for a particular product") and objectives are stated as desired quantifiable results for a specified time (such as "to manufacture 200,000 units of Product X with fewer than 1 percent defects next year"). Achieving goals and objectives requires organizing complex activities, managing diverse resources, and formalizing plans.

Tactical Planning

After identifying key variables, management should gather information useful for managing or reacting to changes in these variables. Often this information is historical and qualitative and provides a useful starting point for tactical planning activities. **Tactical planning**

Exhibit 8.1 Key Internal and External Variables

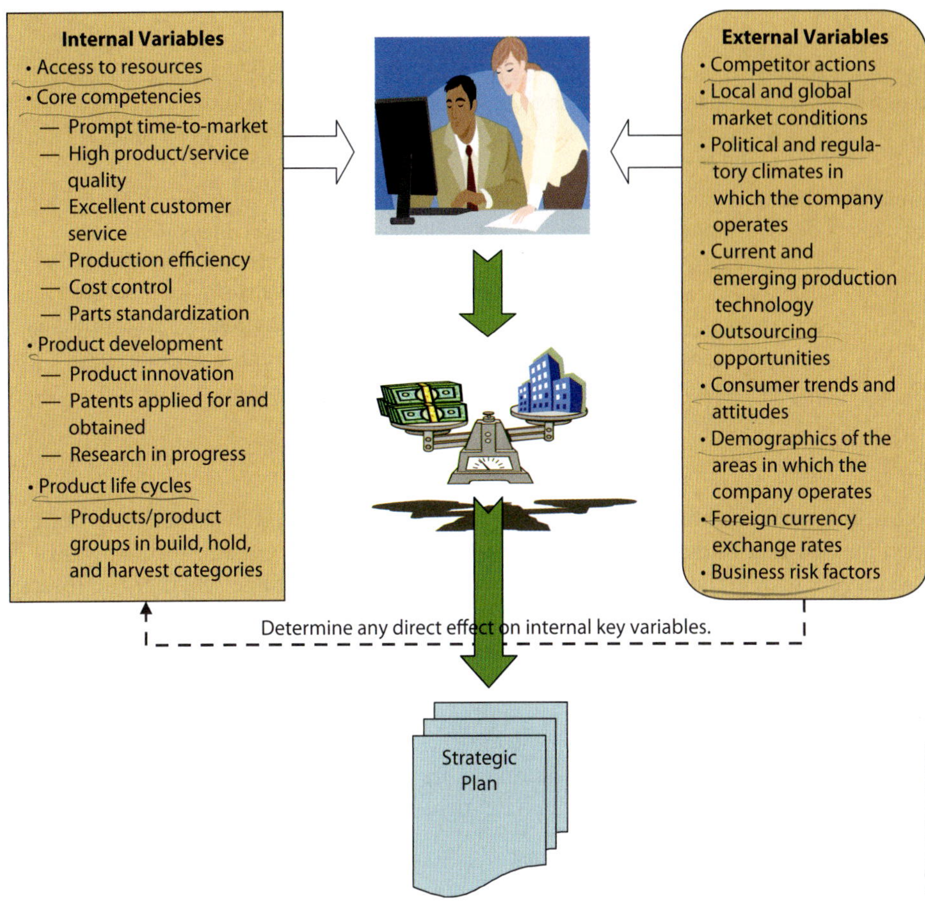

determines how the strategic plans will be achieved. Some tactical plans, such as corporate policy statements, exist for the long term and address repetitive situations. Most tactical plans, however, are short term (1–18 months). They are considered "single-use" plans and are developed to address a given set of circumstances or to cover a specific period of time.

The annual budget is an example of a single-use tactical plan. Shorter-term (quarterly and monthly) plans should also be included, so the budget contains the details necessary for the plan to work effectively. The monetary budget is the end product of the predictions and assumptions underlying organizational goals and objectives. Financial performance targets could include net income, earnings per share, or sales revenue. Nonfinancial performance targets could include a designated customer satisfaction level, defect reduction rates, and percentage of on-time deliveries. Quantifying potential difficulties in achieving organizational targets makes those difficulties visible. Thus, budgets help managers find ways to overcome problems before they are realized. Exhibit 8.2 (page 304) illustrates the relationships among strategic planning, tactical planning, and budgeting.

A well-prepared budget serves as a guide for company activities and is an effective tool for communicating objectives, constraints, and expectations to organizational personnel. Communication promotes understanding of

- what is to be accomplished,
- how those accomplishments are to be achieved, and
- the manner in which resources are to be allocated.

Resource allocations are made, in part, from a process of obtaining information, justifying requests, and negotiating compromises.

Employee participation is needed to effectively integrate information from various sources and to obtain individual managerial commitment to the resulting budget. Participation helps to produce a spirit of cooperation, motivate employees, and instill teamwork. However, the greater the employee participation in the budgeting process, the greater the time

Exhibit 8.2 Relationships among Planning Processes

Who?	What?	How?	Why?
Top management	Strategic planning	State organizational mission, goals, and strategies; long range (5–10 years)	Establish a long-range organizational vision and provide a sense of unity and commitment to specified purposes
Top management and mid-management	Tactical planning	State organizational plans; short range (1–18 months)	Provide direction for achievement of strategic plans; state strategic plans in terms for which managers can act; furnish a basis against which results can be measured
Top management, mid-management, and operational management	Budgeting	Prepare quantitative and monetary statements that coordinate company activities for a year or less	Allocate resources effectively and efficiently; indicate a commitment to objectives; provide a monetary control device

and cost involved. Traditionally, to say that a company uses a highly participative budgeting process implied that budgets were built from the bottom of the organization upward.

Managers review the budget prior to its approval to determine whether the forecasted results are acceptable. The budget could indicate that results expected from the planned activities do not achieve the desired objectives. In this case, planned activities are reconsidered and revised so that they more effectively achieve the desired outcomes expressed in the tactical planning stage.

After a budget is approved, it is implemented and becomes a performance benchmark. The budget sets the resource constraints under which managers must operate for the upcoming budget period. The control phase includes

- making actual-to-budget comparisons,
- determining variances,
- investigating variance causes,
- taking necessary corrective action, and
- providing feedback to operating managers.

Feedback, both positive and negative, is essential to the control process and must be provided in a timely manner. This cyclical process is illustrated in Exhibit 8.3.

Exhibit 8.3 Cyclical Nature of Budgeting Process

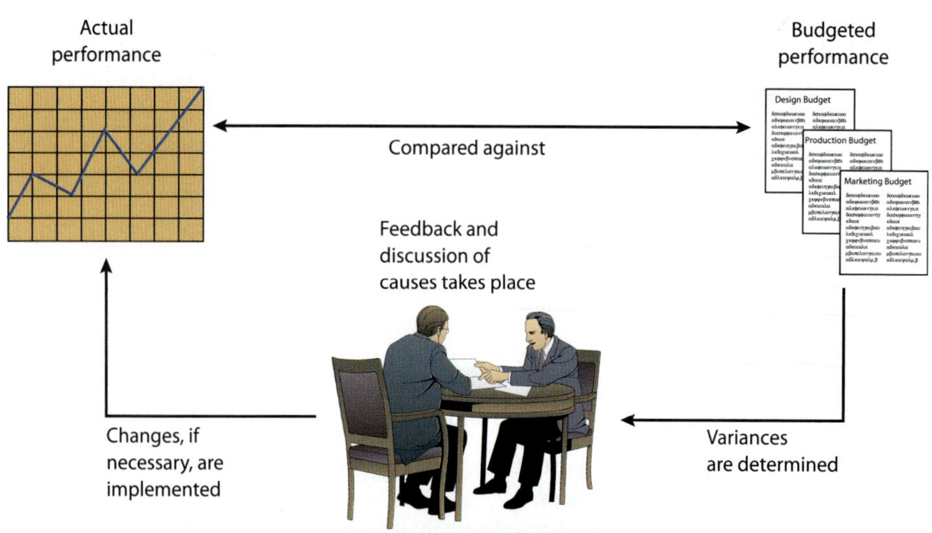

Source: From Raiborn/Barfield/Kinney *Managerial Accounting*, 2E. © 1996 South-Western, a part of Cengage Learning, Inc. Reproduced by permission. www.cengage.com/permissions.

The preceding discussion describes a budgeting process but, as with many other business practices, budgeting is unique to individual organizations and within individual countries. For example, the lengthy and highly specific budgeting process used by many U.S. businesses differs dramatically from that used by many Japanese businesses. Japanese companies tend to view the budget more as a device to help focus personnel and resources on achieving group and firm-level targets than as a control device by which to gauge individual performance. But, regardless of how it is carried out, the budgeting process results in a **master budget**. This "budget" is actually a comprehensive set of budgets, budgetary schedules, and budgeted (pro forma) organizational financial statements.

THE MASTER BUDGET

Budgeting allows managers to effectively communicate organizational goals and objectives while producing a spirit of cooperation and participation in the planning process.

As shown in Exhibit 8.4, operating and financial budgets compose the master budget. An **operating budget** is a budget that is expressed in both units and dollars. When an operating budget relates to revenues, the units are those expected to be sold, and the dollars reflect selling prices. In contrast, when an operating budget relates to costs, the input units are those expected to be either transformed into output units or consumed, and the dollars reflect costs.

Monetary details from the various operating budgets are combined to prepare **financial budgets**, which indicate the funds to be generated or consumed during the budget period. Financial budgets include cash and capital budgets as well as the budgeted financial statements that are the ultimate focal points for top management.

2 What is the starting point of a master budget, and why?

The master budget is prepared for a specific period and is static in the sense that it is based on a single level of output demand.[1] Developing the budget using a single demand level is necessary to identify the specific input quantities to be acquired. Arrangements must be made to assure that an adequate number of personnel are hired, needed production and/or storage space is available, and suppliers, prices, delivery schedules, and quality of resources are confirmed.

Exhibit 8.4 Components of a Master Budget

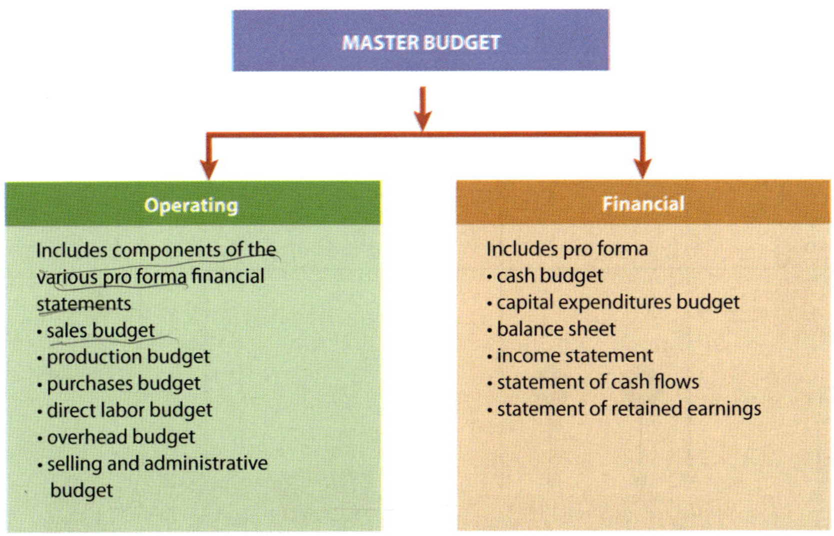

[1] Companies can engage in contingency planning, providing for multiple budgeting paths. For example, a company could construct three budgets, such as for a high level of activity, an expected level of activity, and a low level of activity. If actual activity turns out to be either higher or lower than expected, management has a budget ready.

In manufacturing or retail companies, the sales demand level selected for use in the master budget affects all other budget components. In not-for-profits, the primary inflows would be contributions, interest on endowments, fees, and allocations from other entities; in governmental entities, the primary inflows are usually taxes and fees. Regardless of the organizational source of inflows, all departmental budgets must interact in a coordinated manner because of the many budgetary relationships. A budget developed by one department is often an essential ingredient in developing another department's budget. Exhibit 8.5 presents an overview of the budget preparation sequence, indicates departmental budget preparation responsibility, and illustrates how the budgets interrelate. Departments involved in the budgeting process both generate and use information. If top management encourages participation of lower-level managers in the budgeting process, each department either prepares its own budget or provides information for inclusion in a budget. The budget is typically prepared for a year and then subdivided into quarterly and monthly periods.

Estimating sales is a complex process that incorporates a wide variety of external and internal information, such as that shown in Exhibit 8.6. That information is then used to

Exhibit 8.5 The Master Budget: An Overview

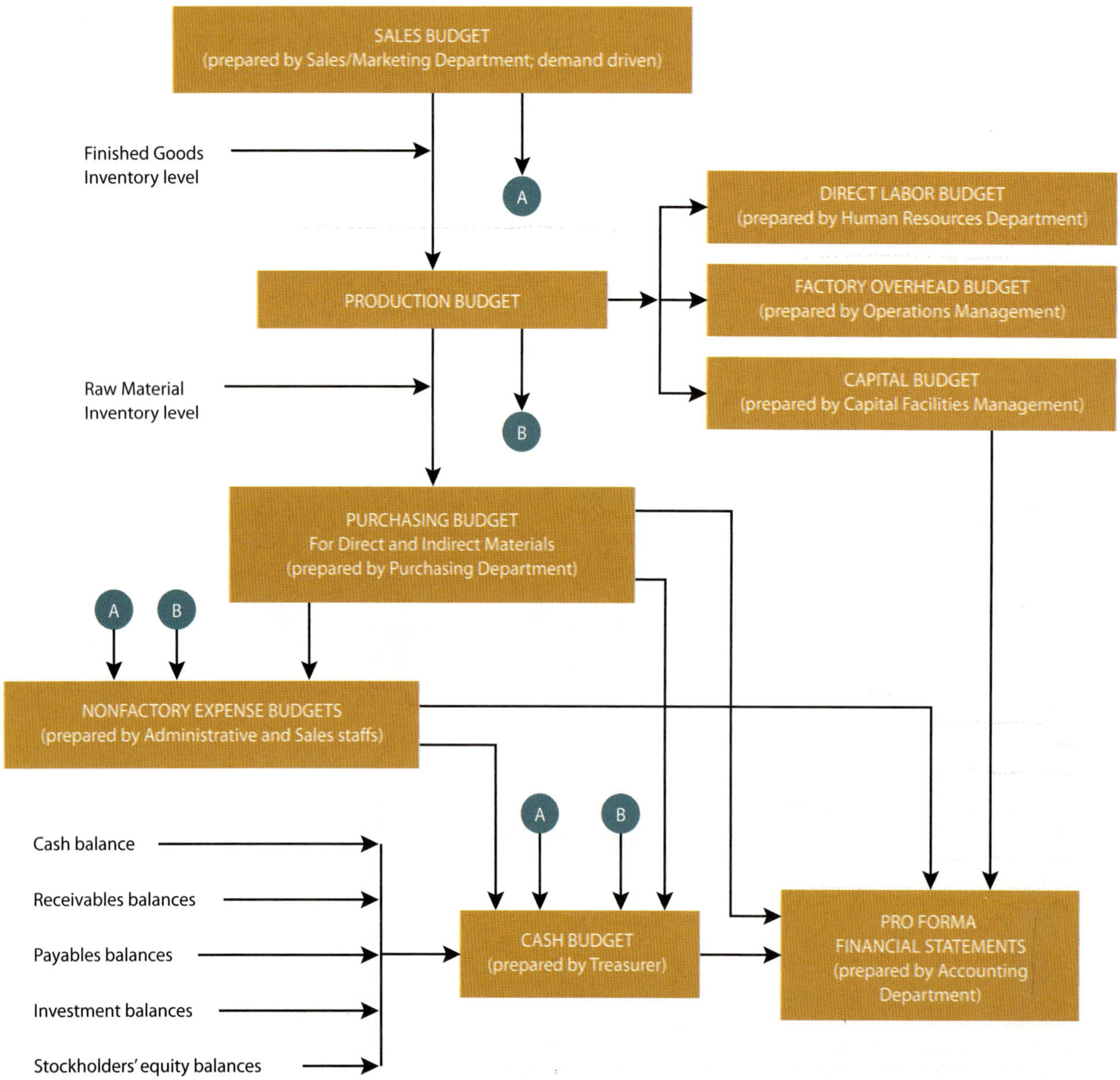

Exhibit 8.6 Information for Sales Forecasting

Internal	**External**
Seasonality of the product/service	Local, domestic and global economic conditions (including employment rates, tax rates, interest rates, consumer purchasing power, age of population, and credit policy changes)
Production capability and capacity	Competition and market share levels
Advertising plans and media usage	Political changes
Sales bonus plans	Style or fashion trends
Capital availability	Selling price changes and add-on fees (such as those made by the airlines)
Distribution methods relied upon	Industry growth
Adjustments to product lines (new, modified, eliminations)	
Utilization of technology	
Operational efficiency	
Changes in client base	
Historical data (modified by known changes such as cancelled contracts or pending new contracts)	
Life cycle of products	

project the Sales Department's estimates of the types, quantities, and timing of sales for the company's products. A production manager combines sales estimates with information from Purchasing, Human Resources, Operations, and Capital Facilities to specify the types, quantities, and timing of products to be manufactured. Sales estimates, in conjunction with estimated cash collection patterns, are used to determine the amounts and timing of cash receipts. Resource consumption budgets are then integrated into budgeted financial statements. To properly manage the organization's funds, the treasurer needs cash receipts and disbursements information from all areas so that cash is available when, and in the amount, needed. Exhibit 8.5 depicts information flow but not the necessary details; thus, this chapter discusses the specifics of preparing a master budget next. This in-depth example focuses on a manufacturing company; a shorter retail company example is provided in the demonstration problem at the end of the chapter.

THE MASTER BUDGET ILLUSTRATED

3 What are the various components of a master budget, and how are they prepared?

Dresdill Corp. has been in business for several years. The company, which produces a single type of commercial stainless steel lock, is preparing its 2014 budget and has estimated total annual sales at 350,000 locks. Although annual sales would be detailed on a monthly basis, Dresdill focuses on the budgets for only the first quarter of 2014. The process of developing the master budget is the same regardless of whether the time frame is one year or one quarter.

The December 31, 2013, balance sheet presented in Exhibit 8.7 provides account balances needed to begin preparation of the master budget. The December 31, 2013, balances are estimates rather than actual figures because the budget process for 2014 must begin significantly before December 31, 2013. The company's budgetary time schedule depends on many factors, including company size, degree of forecasting sophistication, and cyclical nature of the business. For example, in May and June, Dresdill Corp. begins analyzing historical November sales patterns to project the seasonal labor that will need to be hired before the holiday season over a half year away.[2] Assume that Dresdill Corp. begins its budgeting

[2] D. Amato-McCoy, "Holiday Preparations," *Chain Store Age* (August/September 2010), pp. 28, 30.

Exhibit 8.7 Beginning Balance Sheet for Dresdill Corp.

Drisdell Corp.
Balance Sheet
December 31, 2013

Assets			**Liabilities & Stockholders' Equity**		
Current Assets			Current Liabilities		
Cash		$ 10,000	Accounts Payable		$ 42,504
Accounts Receivable	$ 69,840		Dividends Payable (payment scheduled for March 31)		45,000
Less Allowance for Uncollectibles	(1,248)	68,592	Total Current Liabilities		$ 87,504
Inventories					
Raw Material (3,289 pounds)	$ 7,565*				
Finished Goods (1,500 units)	4,800	12,365			
Total Current Assets		$ 90,957			
Plant Assets			**Stockholders' Equity**		
Property, Plant, and Equipment	$370,000		Common Stock	$180,000	
Less Accumulated Depreciation	(90,000)	280,000	Retained Earnings	103,453	283,453
Total Assets		$370,957	Total Liabilities and Stockholders' Equity		$370,957

*This amount is actually $7,564.70, or 3,289 pounds of steel multiplied by $2.30 per pound. It has been rounded for simplicity in this exhibit. Retained Earnings has been similarly rounded.

process in November 2013, when the 2014 sales forecast is received by management or a committee designated to oversee the budgeting process.

The sales budget is prepared in both units and sales dollars. The selling price set for 2014 is $5 per lock, regardless of sales territory or customer. Monthly demand and its related revenue impact for the first four months of 2014 are shown in Exhibit 8.8. April information is presented because some elements of the master budget for March require the subsequent month's information.

Exhibit 8.8 Sales Budget for the Three Months and Quarter Ending March 31, 2014

	January	February	March	Total for Quarter	April*
Sales in units	30,000	28,000	33,000	91,000	32,000
Selling price per unit	× $5	× $5	× $5	× $5	× $5
Sales in dollars	$150,000	$140,000	$165,000	$455,000	$160,000

*Information for April is needed for subsequent computations.

Production Budget

For a manufacturing company, the production budget follows from the sales budget and is based on information about the type, quantity, and timing of units to be sold. (A retail or service company would not prepare a production budget.) Sales information is combined with beginning and ending Finished Goods (FG) Inventory information so that managers can schedule necessary production. The following formula provides the computation for units to be produced:

Number of units to be sold (from sales budget)	XXX
+ Number of units desired in ending FG Inventory	XXX
= Total units needed during period	XXX
− Number of units in beginning FG Inventory	(XXX)
= Units to be produced	XXX

Company management determines ending inventory policy. Desired ending FG Inventory balance is generally a function of the quantity and timing of demand in the upcoming period as related to the firm's capacity and speed to produce particular units. Frequently, management wants ending FG Inventory to equal a given percentage of the next period's projected sales. Other alternatives include

- a constant amount of inventory,
- a buildup of inventory for future high-demand periods, or
- near-zero inventory under a just-in-time system (discussed in depth in Chapter 18).

The decision about ending inventory levels often relates to whether a firm wants to have constant production with varying inventory levels or variable production with constant inventory levels.

Managers should consider the high costs of stockpiling inventory before making a decision about how much inventory to keep on hand. Demand for Dresdill's products is relatively constant year-round. Because most sales are to recurring customers, Dresdill's policy is that ending FG Inventory should be 5 percent of the next month's unit sales. Considering this policy and using the sales information from Exhibit 8.8, the production budget shown in Exhibit 8.9 is prepared.

Exhibit 8.9 Production Budget for the Three Months and Quarter Ending March 31, 2014

	January	February	March	Total
Sales in units (from Exhibit 8.8)	30,000	28,000	33,000	91,000
+ Desired ending inventory	1,400	1,650	1,600	1,600
= Total needed	31,400	29,650	34,600	92,600
− Beginning inventory	(1,500)	(1,400)	(1,650)	(1,500)
= Units to be produced	29,900	28,250	32,950	91,100

January's beginning FG Inventory is the 1,500 units on hand at December 31, 2013, or 5 percent of January's estimated sales of 30,000 units. Desired March ending inventory is 5 percent of the April sales of 32,000 units (given in Exhibit 8.8). Dresdill does not have any Work in Process Inventory because all units placed into production are assumed to be fully completed during each period.[3]

Purchases Budget

Direct material must be purchased each period in quantities sufficient to meet production needs and to conform to the company's desired ending inventory policies. Companies may have different policies for the raw material associated with different products or for different seasons of the year. For example, a company may maintain only a minimal ending inventory of a raw material that is consistently available in the quantity and quality desired.

[3] Most manufacturing entities do not produce only whole units during the period. Normally, partially completed beginning and ending Work in Process inventories will exist. These inventories create the need to use equivalent units of production (discussed in Chapter 6) when computing the production budget.

Alternatively, if a material is difficult to obtain at certain times of the year, a company may stockpile that material for use in future periods.

Dresdill Corp.'s management aligns its policy for ending Raw Material Inventory with its production needs for the following month. Because of occasional difficulty in obtaining the high quality of stainless steel needed, Dresdill's ending inventory for raw material is set at 10 percent of the quantity needed for the following month's production.

The purchases budget is first stated in whole units of finished products and then converted to direct material component requirements and dollar amounts. Production of a Dresdill lock requires only one direct material: stainless steel. The cost of the appropriate grade of stainless steel has been estimated by the purchasing agent at $2.30 per pound, and it takes 1.1 pounds of steel to produce one lock. Exhibit 8.10 shows Dresdill's purchases cost for each month of the first quarter of 2014. Note that beginning and ending inventory quantities are expressed first in terms of locks and then are converted to the appropriate material quantity measure (pounds of steel). Total budgeted cost of direct material purchases for the first quarter of 2014 is $231,646.80.

Exhibit 8.10 Purchases Budget for the Three Months and Quarter Ending March 31, 2014

	January	February	March	Quarter
Units to be produced (from Exhibit 8.9)	29,900	28,250	32,950	91,100
× Pounds needed per unit	× 1.1	× 1.1	× 1.1	× 1.1
= Total pounds needed	32,890.0	1,075.0	36,245.0	100,210
+ Desired EI (10% of next month's needs)	3,107.5	3,524.5	3,795.0[a]	3,795
− Beginning inventory	(3,289)[b]	(3,107.5)	(3,524.5)	(3,289)
= Total pounds of steel to purchase	32,708.5	31,492.0	36,515.5	100,716
× Price per pound	× $2.30	× $2.30	× $2.30	× $2.30
= Total cost of steel purchases	$75,229.55	$72,431.60	$83,985.65	$231,646.80

[a]April production is assumed to be 34,500 units, which would require 37,950 pounds.
[b]From Exhibit 8.7.

Personnel Budget

Given expected production, the Engineering and Human Resources Departments can work together to determine the necessary labor requirements for the factory, sales force, and office staff. A variety of issues must be considered in preparing the personnel budget.

Labor Requirement Considerations	Labor Cost Considerations
Total number of people	Union labor contracts
Specific number of worker "types" (skilled vs. unskilled labor; setup helpers; salespeople; clerical personnel; etc.)	Minimum-wage laws
	Fringe benefit costs
Production hours needed	Payroll taxes
Vacation time provided	Bonus arrangements
	Commission arrangements

The various personnel amounts are shown, as appropriate, in the direct labor budget, manufacturing overhead budget, or selling and administrative budget.

Direct Labor Budget

Dresdill's management has reviewed the staffing requirements and has developed the direct labor cost estimates shown in Exhibit 8.11 for the first quarter of 2014. Factory direct labor costs are based on standard hours of labor needed to produce the units in the production budget. The average wage rate includes the direct labor payroll rate, payroll taxes, and fringe benefits; these items usually add between 25 and 30 percent to the base labor cost.

Exhibit 8.11 Direct Labor Budget for the Three Months and Quarter Ending March 31, 2014

	January	February	March	Total
Units to be produced	29,900	28,250	32,950	91,100
× Standard hours allowed	× 0.025	× 0.025	× 0.025	× 0.025
= Total hours allowed	747.50	706.25	823.75	2,277.50
× Average wage rate (including fringe benefits)	× $14.00	× $14.00	× $14.00	× $14.00
= Direct labor cost	$ 10,465	$ 9,888	$ 11,532	$ 31,885

All compensation is paid in the month in which it is incurred. Because of a union contract, the labor rate for production workers will increase from $9 per hour in 2013 to $14 per hour in 2014.

Est OH
Activity Rate

Overhead Budget

Overhead costs are the third production cost that must be budgeted by month and for the quarter. Dresdill has determined that machine hours are the best predictor of overhead costs and has prepared the overhead budget shown in Exhibit 8.12. Ten units can be produced per machine hour.

Exhibit 8.12 Overhead Budget for the Three Months and Quarter Ending March 31, 2014

			January	February	March	Total
Estimated machine hrs (X) (Units of production ÷ 10)			2,990	2,825	3,295	9,110
	VALUE OF					
	(Fixed) a	(Variable) b				
Overhead item						
Depreciation	$1,700	$0.00	$ 1,700	$ 1,700	$ 1,700	$ 5,100
Indirect material	0	0.20	598	565	659	1,822
Indirect labor	6,000	1.50	10,485	10,238	10,942	31,665
Utilities	500	0.10	799	783	829	2,411
Property tax	500	0.00	500	500	500	1,500
Insurance	450	0.00	450	450	450	1,350
Maintenance	575	0.30	1,472	1,423	1,563	4,458
Total cost (y)	$9,725	$2.10	$16,004	$15,659	$16,643	$48,306
Total cost net of depreciation			$14,304	$13,959	$14,943	$43,206

Note: The costs for February have been rounded up to the next whole dollar, and the costs for March have been rounded down to balance to the appropriate quarter total.

In estimating overhead, all fixed and variable costs must be specified, and mixed costs must be separated into their fixed (a) and variable (b) components. Each overhead amount shown is calculated using the $y = a + bX$ formula discussed in Chapter 3. For example, March maintenance cost is $575 fixed cost plus $988.50 ($0.30 × 3,295 estimated machine hours) variable cost for a total of $1,563 (rounded). Both total cost and cost net of depreciation are shown in the budget. The net of depreciation cost is expected to be paid in cash during the month and will affect the cash budget.

Selling and Administrative Budget

Selling and administrative (S&A) expenses can be predicted in the same manner as overhead costs. Exhibit 8.13 presents Dresdill's first-quarter 2014 S&A budget. Sales figures, rather than production levels, are the activity measure used to prepare this budget. The company has two salespeople who are paid $1,000 per month plus a 2 percent commission on sales. Administrative salaries total $9,000 per month.

Exhibit 8.13 Selling and Administrative Budget for the Three Months and Quarter Ending March 31, 2014

	VALUE OF (Fixed) a	VALUE OF (Variable) b	January	February	March	Total
Predicted sales (from Exhibit 8.8)			$150,000	$140,000	$165,000	$455,000
S&A item						
Supplies	$ 0	$0.02	$ 3,000	$ 2,800	$ 3,300	$ 9,100
Depreciation	500	0.00	500	500	500	1,500
Miscellaneous	100	0.01	1,600	1,500	1,750	4,850
Compensation						
Salespeople	2,000	0.02	5,000	4,800	5,300	15,100
Administrative	9,000	0.00	9,000	9,000	9,000	27,000
Total cost (*y*)	$11,600	$0.05	$ 19,100	$ 18,600	$ 19,850	$ 57,550
Total cost net of depreciation			$ 18,600	$ 18,100	$ 19,350	$ 56,050

Capital Budget

The master budget focuses on the short-term or upcoming fiscal period. Managers, however, must also assess and budget for long-term needs such as plant and equipment purchases. Determining the current planned expenditures for long-term assets is referred to as capital budgeting.[4] A capital budget is prepared separately from the master budget, but the asset purchases included in the capital budget will impact cash outflows and periodic depreciation expense. Thus, results of the capital budgeting process affect the master budget.

As shown in Exhibit 8.14, Dresdill's managers have decided to purchase a $28,000 machine in January and pay for the machine in February. The machine will be placed into

Exhibit 8.14 Capital Budget for the Three Months and Quarter Ending March 31, 2014

	January	February	March	Total
Acquisition—machinery	$28,000	$ 0	$0	$28,000
Cash payment for machinery	0	28,000	0	28,000

[4]Capital budgeting is discussed in depth in Chapter 15.

service in April after installation, testing, and employee training. Depreciation on the new machine will not be included in the overhead calculation until installation is complete.

Cash Budget

4 Why is the cash budget so important in the master budgeting process?

After the preceding budgets have been developed, a cash budget can be constructed. The cash budget might be the most important schedule prepared during the budgeting process because a company cannot survive without cash.

The following model can be used to summarize cash receipts and disbursements in a way that assists managers in devising appropriate financing measures to meet company needs:

Cash Budget Model

Beginning cash balance		XXX
+ Cash receipts (collections)		XXX
= Cash available for disbursements exclusive of financing		XXX
− Cash needed for disbursements (purchases, direct labor, overhead, S&A, taxes, bonuses, etc.)		(XXX)
= Cash excess or deficiency (*a*)		XXX
− Minimum desired cash balance		(XXX)
= Cash needed or available for investment or loan repayment		XXX
Financing methods		
± Borrow (repay)	XXX	
± Issue (reacquire) capital stock	XXX	
± Sell (acquire) investments	XXX	
± Sell (acquire) plant assets	XXX	
± Receive (pay) interest or dividends	XXX	
Total impact (+ or −) of planned financing (*b*)		XXX
= Ending cash balance (*c*), where [(*c*) = (*a*) ± (*b*)]		XXX

Cash Receipts and Accounts Receivable Because some sales are not made on a cash basis, managers must translate sales information into cash receipts through the use of an expected collection pattern. This process considers the collection patterns experienced in the recent past and management's judgment about changes that could disturb current collection patterns. For example, changes that could weaken current collection patterns include recessionary conditions, increases in interest rates, less strict credit-granting policies, and ineffective collection practices.

In specifying collection patterns, managers should recognize that different types of customers pay in different ways. Any sizable, unique category of clientele should be segregated. Dresdill Corp. has two types of customers:

- cash customers who never receive a discount and
- credit customers.

Of the credit customers, manufacturers and wholesalers are allowed a 2 percent cash discount; retailers are not allowed the discount.

Dresdill has determined from historical data that the collection pattern diagrammed in Exhibit 8.15 is applicable to its customers. Of each month's sales, 20 percent will be for cash and 80 percent will be on credit. The 40 percent of the credit customers who are allowed the discount pay in the month of the sale. Collections from the remaining credit customers are as follows: 20 percent in the month of sale, 50 percent in the month following the sale, and 29 percent in the second month following the sale. Uncollectible accounts amount to 1 percent of the credit sales that do not take a discount.

Using the sales budget, information on November and December 2013 sales, and the collection pattern, management can estimate cash receipts from sales during the first three months of 2014. Management must have November and December sales information because collections for credit sales extend over three months, meaning that collection of some of the previous year's sales occurs in the budget year. Dresdill's November and December sales were $125,000 and $135,000, respectively. Using Dresdill's expected collection pattern, projected monthly collections in the first quarter of 2014 are shown in Exhibit 8.16.

Exhibit 8.15 Collection Pattern for Sales

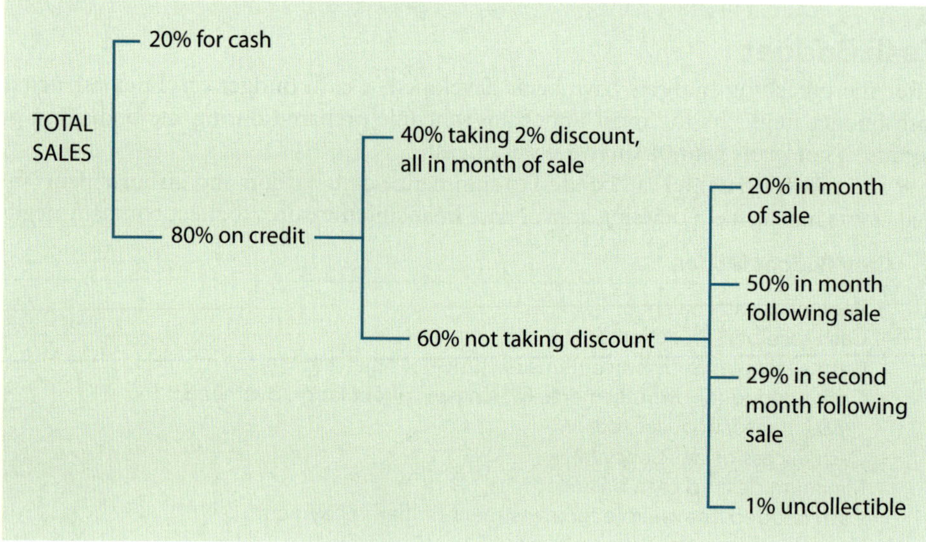

Exhibit 8.16 Cash Collections for the Three Months and Quarter Ending March 31, 2014

From	January	February	March	Total	Discount	Uncollectible
November 2013 sales						
$125,000(0.8)(0.6)(0.29)	$ 17,400			$ 17,400		
$125,000(0.8)(0.6)(0.01)						$ 600
December 2013 sales						
$135,000(0.8)(0.6)(0.5)	32,400			32,400		
$135,000(0.8)(0.6)(0.29)		$ 18,792		18,792		
$135,000(0.8)(0.6)(0.01)						648
January 2014 sales						
$150,000(0.2)	30,000			30,000		
$150,000(0.8)(0.4)(0.98)	47,040N*			47,040	$ 960	
$150,000(0.8)(0.6)(0.2)	14,400			14,400		
$150,000(0.8)(0.6)(0.5)		36,000		36,000		
$150,000(0.8)(0.6)(0.29)			$ 20,880	20,880		
$150,000(0.8)(0.6)(0.01)						720
February 2014 sales						
$140,000(0.2)		28,000		28,000		
$140,000(0.8)(0.4)(0.98)		43,904N		43,904	896	
$140,000(0.8)(0.6)(0.2)		13,440		13,440		
$140,000(0.8)(0.6)(0.5)			33,600	33,600		
March 2014 sales						
$165,000(0.2)			33,000	33,000		
$165,000(0.8)(0.4)(0.98)			51,744N	51,744	1,056	
$165,000(0.8)(0.6)(0.2)			15,840	15,840		
Totals	$141,240	$140,136	$155,064	$436,440	$2,912	$1,968

*N stands for "net of discount." To determine the gross amount, divide the net amount by 0.98 (i.e., 100% – 2%).

The amounts for November and December collections can be reconciled to the December 31, 2013, balance sheet (Exhibit 8.7), which indicated a balance of $69,840 in Accounts Receivable. This amount appears in the collection schedule as follows:

December 31, 2013, Balance in Accounts Receivable	
January collections of November sales	$17,400
Estimated November bad debts	600
January collections of December sales	32,400
February collections of December sales	18,792
Estimated December bad debts	648
December 31, 2013, Accounts Receivable balance	$69,840

January 2014 sales of $150,000 are used to illustrate the collection calculations in Exhibit 8.16. The first line for January represents cash sales equal to 20 percent of total sales, or $30,000. The next line represents the 80 percent of the customers who buy on credit and who take the discount:

Sales to credit customers (80% of $150,000)	$120,000
Sales to customers allowed discount (40% × $120,000)	$ 48,000
− Discount taken by customers (0.02 × $48,000)	(960)
= Net collections from customers allowed discount	$ 47,040

The third line for January in Exhibit 8.16 reflects the 60 percent of credit customers who paid in the month of sale but were not allowed the discount. The remaining amounts for February and March in Exhibit 8.16 are computed similarly.

After the cash collections schedule has been prepared, balances for Accounts Receivable, Allowance for Uncollectibles, and Sales Discounts can be projected. These T-accounts for Dresdill follow. Balances will be used to prepare budgeted, quarter-end 2014 financial statements. For illustrative purposes only, all sales are initially recorded as Accounts Receivable. Immediate cash collections are then deducted from the Accounts Receivable balance.

Accounts Receivable (A/R)

Debit		Credit	
12/31/13 Balance (Exhibit 8.7)	69,840	Collections in January from beginning A/R ($17,400 + $32,400)	49,800
January 2014 sales (Exhibit 8.8)	150,000	Cash sales in January (Exhibit 8.16)	30,000
		Credit collections subject to discount (cash received, $47,040)	48,000
		Credit collections not subject to discount	14,400
February 2014 sales (Exhibit 8.8)	140,000	Collections in February from beginning A/R	18,792
		Cash sales in February (Exhibit 8.16)	28,000
		Collections in February from Jan. sales	36,000
		Credit collections subject to discount (cash received, $43,904)	44,800
		Credit collections not subject to discount	13,440
March 2014 sales (Exhibit 8.8)	165,000	Cash sales in March (Exhibit 8.16)	33,000
		Collections in March from January sales	20,880
		Collections in March from February sales	33,600
		Credit collections subject to discount (cash received, $51,744)	52,800
		Credit collections not subject to discount	15,840
3/31/14 Balance	85,488		

Allowance for Uncollectible Accounts

		12/31/13 Balance (Exhibit 8.7)	1,248
		January estimate (Exhibit 8.16)	720
		February estimate [$140,000 × (80%) × (60%) × (1%)]	672
		March estimate [$165,000 × (80%) × (60%) × (1%)]	792
		3/31/14 Balance	3,432

Sales Discounts

January discounts	960		
February discounts	896		
March discounts	1,056		
3/31/14 Balance	2,912		

Note that the estimated uncollectible accounts from November 2013 through March 2014 have not been written off as of the end of the first quarter of 2014. Companies continue to make collection efforts for a substantial period before accounts are acknowledged as worthless. Thus, these receivables may remain on the books for six months or more from the original sales date. When accounts are written off, Accounts Receivable and the Allowance for Uncollectibles will both decrease; however, there will be no income statement impact relative to the write-off.

Cash Disbursements and Accounts Payable Using the purchases information from Exhibit 8.10, management can prepare a cash disbursements schedule for Accounts Payable. Dresdill buys all raw material on account. The company pays for 40 percent of each month's purchases in the month of purchase and is allowed a 2 percent discount for prompt payment. The remaining 60 percent is paid in the month following purchase, and no discounts are taken.

Exhibit 8.17 presents the first-quarter 2014 cash disbursements information for purchases. The December 31, 2013, Accounts Payable balance of $42,504 (Exhibit 8.7) represents 60 percent of December purchases of $70,840. All amounts have been rounded to whole dollars.

Exhibit 8.17 Cash Disbursements for Accounts Payable for the Three Months and Quarter Ending March 31, 2014

Payment for Purchases of	January	February	March	Total	Discount
December 2013	$42,504			$ 42,504	
January 2014 (from Exhibit 8.10)					
$75,229.55(0.40)(0.98)	29,490N*			29,490	$ 602
$75,229.55 (0.60)		$45,138		45,138	
February 2014 (from Exhibit 8.10)					
$72,431.60(0.40)(0.98)		28,393N		28,393	580
$72,431.60(0.60)			$43,459	43,459	
March 2014 (from Exhibit 8.10)					
$83,985.65(0.40)(0.98)			32,922N	32,922	672
Total disbursements for A/P	$71,994	$73,531	$76,381	$221,906	$1,854

*N stands for "net of discount." The total amount of gross purchases paid for in the month of purchase is the sum of the net of discount payment plus the amount shown on the same line in the Discount column.

Accounts payable activity is summarized in the following T-account. The March 31 balance represents 60 percent of March purchases that will be paid during April.

Accounts Payable

Debit		Credit	
		12/31/13 Balance (Exhibit 8.7)	42,504
		January 2014 purchases (Exhibit 8.10)	75,230
January payments for December purchases (Exhibit 8.7)	42,504		
January payments for January purchases subject to discount (cash paid, $29,490)	30,092		
February payments for January purchases (Exhibit 8.17)	45,138	February 2014 purchases (Exhibit 8.10)	72,432
February payments for February purchases subject to discount (cash paid, $28,393)	28,973		
March payments for February purchases (Exhibit 8.17)	43,459	March 2014 purchases (Exhibit 8.10)	83,986
March payments for March purchases subject to discount (cash paid, $32,922)	33,594		
		3/31/14 Balance	50,391

Purchases Discounts

Debit		Credit	
		January discounts	602
		February discounts	580
		March discounts	672
		3/31/14 Balance	1,854

Given the cash receipts and disbursements information for Dresdill, the cash budget model is used to formulate the cash budget shown in Exhibit 8.18 (page 318). The company has established $10,000 as its desired minimum cash balance. There are two primary reasons for having a desired minimum cash balance: one is internal and the other is external. The first reason reflects the uncertainty associated with the budgeting process. Because managers cannot budget with absolute precision, they maintain a "cushion" to protect the company from potential errors in forecasting collections and payments. The second reason is that the company's bank may require a minimum cash balance in relation to an open line of credit.

For simplicity, it is assumed that any investments or sales of investments are made in end-of-month $1,000 increments. Interest on company investments at 3 percent per year (or 0.0025 percent per month) is added to the company's bank account at month's end.

Exhibit 8.18 indicates that Dresdill expects $35,877 excess of cash available over disbursements in January. Such an excess, however, does not consider the need for the $10,000 minimum balance. Thus, the company has $25,877 available. It will use $25,000 of that amount to purchase temporary investments at the end of January.

In February, Dresdill will meet its desired minimum cash balance, but will have to sell $3,000 of its investments to pay for the machine. In March, Dresdill will have enough excess cash available, coupled with the liquidation of $12,000 of investments, to pay the $45,000 dividend declared in 2013.

Cash flow provides the short-run source of power in a business to negotiate and act. In addition to preparing and executing a sound cash budget, a business can take other measures. Exhibit 8.19 (page 319) offers some suggestions in this regard for small businesses, although the same prescriptions are applicable to businesses of all sizes.

Budgeted Financial Statements

5 How and why are budgeted financial statements prepared at the end of the budgeting process?

The final step in the budgeting process is development of budgeted financial statements that reflect the achieved results if the estimates and assumptions used for all previous budgets actually occur. Such statements allow management to determine whether the projected

Exhibit 8.18 Cash Budget for the Three Months and Quarter Ending March 31, 2014

	January	February	March	Total
Beginning cash balance	$ 10,000	$ 10,877	$ 10,598	$ 10,000
Cash collections (Exhibit 8.16)	141,240	140,136	155,064	436,440
Cash available exclusive of financing	$151,240	$151,013	$165,662	$446,440
Disbursements				
Accounts payable (for purchases, Exhibit 8.17)	$ 71,994	$ 73,531	$ 76,381	$221,906
Direct labor (Exhibit 8.11)	10,465	9,888	11,532	31,885
Overhead (Exhibit 8.12)*	14,304	13,959	14,943	43,206
S&A expenses (Exhibit 8.13)*	18,600	18,100	19,350	56,050
Total disbursements	$115,363	$115,478	$122,206	$353,047
Cash excess (inadequacy)	$ 35,877	$ 35,535	$ 43,456	$ 93,393
Minimum balance desired	(10,000)	(10,000)	(10,000)	(10,000)
Cash available (needed)	$ 25,877	$ 25,535	$ 33,456	$ 83,393
Financing				
Borrowings (repayments)	$ 0	$ 0	$ 0	$ 0
Issue (reacquire) stock	0	0	0	0
Sell (acquire) investments	(25,000)	3,000	12,000	(10,000)†
Sell (acquire) plant assets	0	(28,000)	0	(28,000)
Receive (pay) interest‡	0	63	55	118
Receive (pay) dividends	0	0	(45,000)	(45,000)
Total impact of planned financing	$ (25,000)	$ (24,937)	$ (32,945)	$ (82,882)
Ending cash balance	$ 10,877	$ 10,598	$ 10,511	$ 10,511

*These amounts are net of depreciation.
†This is the net result of investments and disposals of investments.
‡Interest is calculated assuming a 3 percent annual rate (0.25 percent per month); investments and disposals of investments are made at the end of the month in $1,000 increments.

results are acceptable. If results are not acceptable, management has the opportunity to make adjustments before the beginning of the period for which the budget is being prepared.

When expected net income is unacceptably low, management can investigate the possibility of raising selling prices or finding ways to decrease costs. Any changes considered by management might have related effects that must be included in the revised projections. For example, raising selling prices could decrease volume. Alternatively, cost reductions from using lower-grade material could increase spoilage during production or cause a decline in demand. With the availability of computer software, changes in budget assumptions and their resultant effects can be simulated quickly and easily.

Cost of Goods Manufactured Schedule In a manufacturing environment, management must prepare a schedule of cost of goods manufactured before it can prepare an income statement. This schedule is necessary to determine cost of goods sold. Using information from previous budgets, Dresdill's budgeted cost of goods manufactured schedule is shown in Exhibit 8.20 (page 320). Because it was assumed that no beginning or ending Work in Process Inventories exist, cost of goods manufactured equals the manufacturing costs of the period. Had a partially completed Work in Process Inventory existed, the computations would be more complex and would have involved the use of equivalent units of production (discussed in Chapter 6).

Exhibit 8.19 Ten Ways to Improve Small Business Cash Flow

Cash flow is the lifeblood of any small business. A healthy stream is essential if a business is to succeed. In general, the key is to accelerate the flow of money coming in and delay what goes out. Having written credit and collection policies can also help. Here are 10 tips a business can use to improve cash flow.

1. **Establish sound credit practices.** Before dealing with a new customer, always get at least three trade references and one bank reference. Credit reports, available from Dun and Bradstreet and others, report on a company's general financial health as well as how quickly—or slowly—it pays its bills. Never give credit until you are comfortable with a customer's ability to pay.
2. **Expedite fulfillment and shipping.** Fill orders accurately and efficiently, and then use the quickest means available to deliver products and services to customers. Unnecessary delays can add days or weeks to customer payments.
3. **Bill promptly and accurately.** The faster you mail an invoice, the faster you will be paid. When possible, send an invoice with the order. If deliveries do not automatically trigger an invoice, establish a set billing schedule, preferably weekly. Check invoices for accuracy before mailing them. All invoices should include a payment due date. An invoice without payment terms may fall to the bottom of a customer's pile of bills.
4. **Offer discounts for prompt payment.** Given an incentive, some customers will pay sooner rather than later. Trade discounts typically give 1–2 percent off the total amount due if customers pay in 10 days.
5. **Aggressively follow up on past due accounts.** As soon as a bill becomes overdue, call the customer and ask when you can expect payment. Keep a record of the conversation and the customer's response. Set a follow-up date in the event the promised payment is not received. Ask delinquent customers with genuine financial problems to try to pay at least a small amount every week. When necessary, don't hesitate to seek professional help from an attorney or collection agency
6. **Deposit payments promptly.** Don't let checks sit in a drawer waiting to be deposited. The sooner you make a deposit, the sooner you can put the money to work for your business. If you are really serious about speeding up your cash flow, a post office box or bank lockbox can accelerate receipt of checks.
7. **Seek better payment terms from suppliers and banks.** Better payment terms from suppliers are the simplest way to slow down a company's cash outflow. Whereas most suppliers provide 30-day terms, 60 or 90 days are sometimes available, though it might mean changing suppliers. Better credit terms translate into borrowing money interest free. Some banks also could be willing to restructure business loans to make them easier to repay.
8. **Keep a tight control on inventory.** Less cash tied up in inventory generally means better cash flow. Although some suppliers offer deeper discounts on volume purchases, if inventory sits on the shelf too long, it ties up money that could be put to better use elsewhere.
9. **Review and reduce expenses.** Take a critical look at all expenses. If you're not sure an expense is necessary, hold back until you are confident it will have a favorable impact on the bottom line. Consider ways to decrease operating costs, such as switching from a weekly to a biweekly payroll to reduce payroll processing costs. Be careful not to cut costs that could hurt profits. For instance, rather than cutting the marketing budget, redirect the money to areas where it will have a more positive impact.
10. **Pay bills on time, but never before they are due.** The basic rule is to take as long as you are allowed to pay bills—without incurring late fees or interest charges. Make an exception to this rule only when you are offered a trade discount for early payment.

Source: "10 Ways to Improve Small Business Cash Flow," *Journal of Accountancy* March 1, 2000.

Income Statement Dresdill's budgeted income statement for the first quarter of 2014 is presented in Exhibit 8.21 (page 321). This statement uses much of the information previously developed in determining the revenues and expenses for the period.

Balance Sheet On completion of the income statement, a March 31, 2014, balance sheet (Exhibit 8.22, page 322) can be prepared.

Statement of Cash Flows Information found on the income statement, balance sheet, and cash budget is also used to prepare a statement of cash flows (SCF). This statement can assist managers in performing the following functions:

- judging the company's ability to handle fixed cash outflow commitments,
- adapting to adverse changes in business conditions,
- undertaking new commitments, and
- assessing the quality of company earnings by indicating the relationship between net income and net cash flow from operations.

Whereas the cash budget is essential to current cash management, the budgeted SCF gives managers a more comprehensive view of cash flows by rearranging them into three

Exhibit 8.20 Budgeted Cost of Goods Manufactured Schedule

Dresdill Corp. Budgeted Cost of Goods Manufactured Schedule For Quarter Ending March 31, 2014			
Beginning Work in Process Inventory			$ 0
Cost of raw material used			
Beginning balance (Exhibit 8.7)		$ 7,565	
Net purchases (from Exhibit 8.10 and Purchases Discounts account, p. 317)		229,793	
Total raw material available		$237,358	
Ending balance of raw material (Note A; rounded)		(8,729)	
Cost of raw material used		$228,629	
Direct labor (Exhibit 8.11)		31,885	
Factory overhead (Exhibit 8.12)		48,306	
Total costs to be accounted for			308,820
Ending Work in Process Inventory			(0)
Cost of goods manufactured			$308,820
Note A: Steel			
Ending balance (Exhibit 8.10)	3,795		
Price per pound	× $2.30		
Ending balance of raw material	$8,728.50		

distinct major activities (operating, investing, and financing). Such a rearrangement permits management to judge whether the specific anticipated flows are consistent with the company's strategic plans. In addition, the SCF would incorporate a schedule or narrative about significant noncash transactions if any have occurred, such as an exchange of stock for land.

The operating section (prepared on either a direct or an indirect basis) of the SCF is acceptable for external reporting. The direct basis uses pure cash flow information (cash receipts and cash disbursements) for operating activities. The operating section of an SCF prepared on an indirect basis begins with net income and makes reconciling adjustments to arrive at cash flow from operations. Exhibit 8.23 (page 323) provides a statement of cash flows for Dresdill using the information from the cash budget in Exhibit 8.18. The bottom of Exhibit 8.23 shows the indirect method of presenting operating cash flows and uses the information from the budgeted income statement in Exhibit 8.21 and the balance sheets in Exhibits 8.7 and 8.22.

Dresdill's cash flow from operations ($83,373) is low compared to net sales revenue of $455,000, as is its net income per net sales dollar (18.3 percent). Dresdill may want to review the sales price for its locks and its production costs, especially given the very large increase (from $9 to $14 per hour) in the direct labor wage rate. Another issue that might be discussed is whether such a high proportion of retained earnings should be paid out as dividends.

USING BUDGETS FOR MANAGEMENT CONTROL

6 What benefits are provided by a budget?

A well-prepared master budget can act as a:

- guide to help managers align activities and resource allocations with organizational goals;
- vehicle to promote employee participation, cooperation, and departmental coordination;
- tool to enhance conduct of the managerial functions of planning, controlling, problem solving, and performance evaluating;

Exhibit 8.21 Budgeted Income Statement

Drisdell Corp.
Budgeted Income Statement
For Quarter Ending March 31, 2014

Sales (Exhibit 8.8)					$ 455,000
Less sales discounts (p. 316)					(2,912)
Net sales					$ 452,088
Cost of goods sold					
Finished goods—12/31/13 (Exhibit 8.7)				$ 4,800	
Cost of goods manufactured (Exhibit 8.20)				308,820	
Cost of goods available for sale				$313,620	
Finished goods—3/31/14 (Note A)				(5,280)	(308,340)
Gross margin					$ 143,748
Expenses					
Uncollectible accounts expense (Note B)				$ 2,184	
S&A expenses (Exhibit 8.13)				57,550	(59,734)
Income from operations					$ 84,014
Other revenue—interest earned (Exhibit 8.18)					118
Income before income taxes					$ 84,132
Income taxes (assumed rate of 40%)					(33,653)
Net income					$ 50,479
Note A					
Beginning finished goods units			1,500		
Production (Exhibit 8.9)			91,100		
Units available for sale			92,600		
Sales (Exhibit 8.9)			(91,000)		
Ending finished goods units			1,600		
Cost per unit:					
Material ($2.30 × 1.1)		$2.53			
Conversion (assumed)		0.77	×$3.30		
Cost of ending inventory			$5,280		
Note B					
Total sales	$455,000				
× % credit sales	× 0.80				
= Credit sales	$364,000				
× % not taking discount	× 0.60				
= Potential bad debts	$218,400				
× % estimated uncollectible	× 0.01				
= Estimated bad debts	$ 2,184				

- basis on which to sharpen management's responsiveness to changes in both internal and external factors; and
- model that provides a rigorous view of future performance of a business in time to consider alternative measures.

Exhibit 8.22 Budgeted Balance Sheet

Drisdell Corp.
Budgeted Balance Sheet
March 31, 2014

Assets		
Current Assets		
Cash (Exhibit 8.18)		$ 10,511
Accounts Receivable (p. 315)	$ 85,488	
Less Allowance for Uncollectibles (p. 316)	(3,432)	82,056
Inventories		
Raw Material (3,795 pounds) (Exhibit 8.20, Note A, rounded)	$ 8,729	
Finished Goods (1,600 units) (Exhibit 8.21, Note A)	5,280	14,009
Investment		10,000
Total Current Assets		116,576
Plant Assets		
Property, Plant, and Equipment (Note A)	$398,000	
Less Accumulated Depreciation (Note B)	(96,600)	301,400
Total Assets		$417,976

Liabilities and Stockholders' Equity		
Current Liabilities		
Accounts Payable (p. 317)		$ 50,391
Income Tax Payable (Exhibit 8.21)		33,653
Total Current Liabilities		$ 84,044
Stockholders' Equity		
Common Stock	$180,000	
Retained Earnings (Note C)	153,932	333,932
Total Liabilities and Stockholders' Equity		$417,976

Note A	
Beginning balance (Exhibit 8.7)	$370,000
Purchased new machine	28,000
Ending balance	$398,000

Note B	
Beginning balance (Exhibit 8.7)	$ 90,000
Factory depreciation (Exhibit 8.12)	5,100
S&A depreciation (Exhibit 8.13)	1,500
Ending balance	$ 96,600

Note C	
Beginning balance (Exhibit 8.7)	$103,453
Net income (Exhibit 8.21)	50,479
Ending balance	$153,932

Because of its fundamental role in the budgeting process, sales demand has a pervasive impact on the master budget. Projected sales must be predicted as accurately and with as many details as possible. Sales forecasts should indicate type and quantity of products to be sold, geographic locations of the sales, types of buyers, and timing of sales. Such detail is necessary because different products require different production and distribution facilities and channels; different customers have different credit terms and payment schedules; and different seasons or months can necessitate different shipping schedules or methods. Managers should use as much information as is available and can combine several estimation

Exhibit 8.23 Budgeted Statement of Cash Flows

Drisdell Corp.
Budgeted Statement of Cash Flows
For Quarter Ending March 31, 2014

Operating activities			
Cash collections from sales		$ 436,440	
Interest earned		118	
Total		$ 436,558	
Cash payments			
For inventory:			
Raw material	$221,906		
Direct labor	31,885		
Overhead	43,206	(296,997)	
For S&A costs		(56,050)	
Net cash inflow from operating activities			$ 83,511
Investing activities			
Purchase of plant asset		$ (28,000)	
Short-term investment		(10,000)	
Net cash outflow from investing activities			(38,000)
Financing activities			
Dividends paid		$ (45,000)	
Net cash outflow from financing activities			(45,000)
Net increase in cash			$ 511
Beginning balance of cash (1/1/14)			10,000
Ending balance of cash (3/31/14)			$ 10,511
Alternative (indirect) basis for operating activities			
Net income		$ 50,479	
+ Depreciation (Exhibit 8-12 and Exhibit 8.13)	$ 6,600		
– Increase in net Accounts Receivable ($68,592 – $82,056)	(13,464)		
– Increase in total inventory ($12,365 – $14,009)	(1,644)		
+ Increase in Taxes Payable ($0 – $33,653)	33,653		
+ Increase in Accounts Payable ($42,504 – $50,391)	7,888	33,032	
= Net cash inflow from operating activities		$ 83,511	

approaches. Combining prediction methods provides managers a way to confirm estimates and reduce uncertainty. Some ways of estimating future demand are

- canvassing sales personnel for a subjective consensus,
- making simple extrapolations of past trends,
- using market research, and
- employing statistical and other mathematical models.

Care should be taken to use realistic, rather than optimistic or pessimistic, forecasts of revenues and costs. Firms can develop computer models that allow repetitive simulations to be run after changes are made to one or more factors. These simulations permit managers to review results that would be obtained under various circumstances.

The master budget is normally prepared for a year and is detailed by quarters and months within those quarters. Some companies (such as **American Express**, **tw telecom**, **Group Health Cooperative**, **Park Nicollet Health Services**, and **Unilever**)[5] use a **continuous budget** (or **rolling budget**), which means that an ongoing 12-month budget is presented by successively adding a new budget month (12 months into the future) as each current month expires. Such a process allows management to work, at any time, within the present one-month component of a full 12-month annual budget. Continuous budgets make the planning process less sporadic. Rather than having managers "go into the budgeting period" at a specific time, they are continuously involved in planning and budgeting. Benefits of a continuous budget include

- eliminating a fiscal year mind-set by recognizing that business is an ongoing operation and should be managed accordingly;
- allowing management to take corrective steps as forecasted business conditions change;
- eliminating the unrealistic "gap" that occurs with the first iteration of each annual budget; and
- reducing or eliminating the budget planning process that occurs at the end of each fiscal year.[6]

A survey jointly conducted by the American Productivity Quality Center and IBM Global Business Services found that companies focusing on "planning, budgeting and forecasting as a business strategy are higher performers in all areas than those that focus on cost accounting, control and cost management."[7] The study also showed that high-performing organizations tend to complete their budgeting cycle in 30 days compared to 90 days in low-performing organizations—and most of the high-performers used rolling budgets.

If actual results differ from plans, managers should find the causes of the differences and then consider budget revisions. Arrangements usually cannot be made rapidly enough to revise the current month's budget. However, managers could revise future months' budgets under certain circumstances (such as if actual and expected performance deviated substantially).

If budget variance causes are beyond the organization's control and are cost related, management can decide to revise budget cost estimates upward or downward to be more realistic. If the causes are internal (such as the sales staff not selling the product), management can leave the budget in its original form so that the effects of operational control are visible in the comparisons. Regardless of whether the budget is revised, managers should commend those individuals responsible for positive performance and communicate the effects of such performance to other related departments. For example, if the sales force has sold significantly higher quantities of product than expected in the original budget, production and purchasing must be notified to increase the number of units manufactured and amount of raw material purchased.

Budget revisions, however, may not occur because the system in use is too complex or detailed. However, given new budgeting software and the fact that Wall Street tends to "punish the stock of any company with errant finance forecasts," some companies are beginning to view budgets as "living documents" that are revised as necessary throughout the year.[8] For example, Southwest Airlines "updates its revenue forecast daily and its fuel forecast weekly. But other items may be forecast bimonthly, monthly or quarterly."[9]

When budgets are used for performance evaluations, management often encounters the problem of **budget slack**, which is the intentional underestimation of revenues and/or overestimation of expenses. Slack can be incorporated into the budget during the development process in a participatory budget. A **participatory budget** is developed through joint decision making by top management and operating personnel. However, slack is not often found in **imposed budgets**, which top management prepares with little or no input from

[5] M. Lamoreaux, "Planning for Uncertainty," *Journal of Accountancy* (October 2011), pp. 32–36.

[6] S. Hunt and P. Klein, "Budgets Roll with the Times," *Optimize* (August 2003), p. 85.

[7] L. Brannen, "Focus on Control, Cost Management Falls Short," *Business Finance* (March 2007), p. 11.

[8] R. Whiting, "Budget Planning: The Next Generation," *InformationWeek* (September 25, 2000), pp. 160ff.

[9] M. Lamoreaux, "Planning for Uncertainty," *Journal of Accountancy* (October 2011), pp. 32–36.

operating personnel. After the budget has been developed, operating personnel are informed of the budget goals and constraints. The budgeting process can be represented by a continuum with participatory budgets on one end and imposed budgets on the other. Only rarely is a budget either purely participatory or purely imposed. The budget process in a company is usually defined by the degree to which the process is either participatory or imposed.

Having budget slack allows subordinate managers to achieve their objectives with less effort than would be necessary without the slack. Slack also creates problems because of the significant interaction of the budget factors. For example, if sales volumes are understated or overstated, problems in the production, purchasing, and personnel areas can arise.

Managers may also "pad" the budget by increasing budget amounts in areas that may be approved rather than in areas in which the funds are actually desired. For instance, the repair and maintenance budget is increased when the manager actually desires—and will use the funds for—computer upgrades. "Diverting corporate funds for purposes not sanctioned by higher management can result in lower profit overall, less return for shareholders, difficulty meeting debt covenants, and fewer bonuses being paid."[10]

Top management can try to reduce slack or padding by tying actual performance to the budget through a bonus system. Operating managers are rewarded with large bonuses for budgeting relatively high performance levels and achieving those levels. If performance expectations are low, achievement of that performance is either not rewarded or only minimally rewarded. Top management must be aware that budget slack and padding have a tremendous negative impact on organizational effectiveness and efficiency.

Managers could consider expanding their budgeting process to recognize the concepts of activities and cost drivers in a manner consistent with activity-based management. An activity budget can be created by mapping the line items in the conventional budget to a list of activities. This type of budget can increase managerial awareness of non-value-added (NVA) activities and make managers question why such costs are being incurred. Based on this enhanced awareness, managers can plan to reduce or eliminate some of these NVA activities.

Managers in not-for-profit organizations (NFPs) must recognize that their budgeting process is often more difficult than in for-profit entities. Because contribution or fee inflows are often tied closely to general economic conditions, estimates of these amounts may be less reliable than sales revenue estimates. Costs in NFPs may be less reasonably tied to inflows and more tied to the service activities of the NFPs. There is a strong emphasis in NFPs on stewardship responsibility so budget versus actual comparisons are critical as is cash management. Cash flows in NFPs often fluctuate greatly during the year even though expense items remain constant; thus, managers at NFPs must keep a close eye on whether sufficient cash is available to provide client services. "An increase in demand for a not-for-profit's services can lead to a management crisis" should insufficient funds exist.[11]

APPENDIX

BUDGET MANUAL

7 How does a budget manual facilitate the budgeting process?

To be useful, a budget requires a substantial amount of time and effort from the persons who prepare it. This process can be improved by the availability of an organizational **budget manual**, which is a detailed set of information and guidelines about the budgetary process. These materials are frequently maintained on a company's intranet so they are available continuously and can be economically updated. The manual should include:

- statements of the budgetary purpose;
- a listing of specific budgetary activities to be performed;
- a calendar of scheduled budgetary activities;
- sample budgetary forms; and
- original, revised, and approved budgets.

[10] T. Stephenson and J. Porter, "Part 6 of 6: Really Using an Excel-Based Budget You've Created," *Strategic Finance* (July 2010), pp. 38–43.

[11] M. Piché, "Planning and Budgeting in Non-Profit Organizations," *CMA Magazine* (March 2009), pp. 22–27.

The statements of budgetary purpose and desired results communicate the reasons behind the process. These statements should flow from general to specific details. An example of a general statement of budgetary purpose might be as follows: "The cash budget provides a basis for planning, reviewing, and controlling cash flows from and to various activities; this budget is essential to the preparation of a pro forma statement of cash flows." Specific statements could include references to minimum desired cash balances and periods of intense cash needs.

Budgetary activities should be listed by position rather than by person because the responsibility for actions should be assigned to the individual holding the designated position at the time the budget is being prepared. The manual's activities section should indicate who has the final authority for revising and approving the budget. Budget approval can be delegated to a budget committee or reserved by one or several members of top management.

The budget calendar helps coordinate the budgetary process by providing a timetable for all budget activities. The larger the organization, the more time that will be needed to gather and coordinate information, identify weak points in the process or the budget itself, and take corrective action. The calendar should also indicate control points for the upcoming periods at which budget-to-actual comparisons are to be made and feedback provided to managers who are responsible for operations.

Sample forms and templates are extremely useful because they provide for consistent presentations of budget information from all individuals, making summarization of information easier and quicker. Templates should be easy to understand and may include standardized worksheets or programmed spreadsheets that allow managers to update historical information to arrive at budgetary figures. This section of the budget manual may also provide standard cost tables for items on which the organization has specific guidelines or policies. For example, in estimating employee fringe benefit costs, the company rule of thumb could be 25 percent of base salary. Or, if company policy states that each salesperson's per diem meal allowance is $70, meal expenses would be budgeted as estimated travel days multiplied by $70.

The final section of the budget manual contains the budgets generated during the budgeting process. Numerous budgets may be proposed and rejected prior to actual budget acceptance and implementation. Understanding this revision process and why changes were made is helpful for future planning. The final approved master budget is included in the budget manual as a control document.[12]

Comprehensive Review Module

KEY TERMS

budget, p. 302
budget manual, p. 325
budget slack, p. 324
budgeting, p. 302
continuous budget, p. 324
financial budget, p. 305
imposed budget, p. 324
master budget, p. 305
operating budget, p. 305
participatory budget, p. 324
rolling budget, p. 324
strategic planning, p. 302
tactical planning, p. 302

[12] In the event of changes in economic conditions or strategic plans, the "final" budget can be revised during the budget period.

CHAPTER SUMMARY

1 Relationship of Strategic and Tactical Planning to Budgeting

- Strategic planning focuses on the long term (5–10 years).
- Tactical planning focuses on the short term (1–18 months).
- Both strategic and tactical planning need qualitative and quantitative information.
- Budgeting helps in the planning process by having management
  - visualize the future and move in a focused direction.
  - agree on and communicate organizational goals and objectives.
  - translate strategic goals and objectives into quantifiable, monetary information.
  - tie the long-term and short-term (tactical) plans together.
  - harmonize external considerations and internal factors.
  - determine how to commit resources to desired activities.
  - establish financial performance indicators of success.
  - engage people to participate in the planning process.
  - produce a spirit of cooperation among employees and organizational departments or divisions.
  - control operations and resource usage.

2 Sales as the Starting Point of a Master Budget

- Determination of a sales projection requires current information regarding
  - the economy,
  - business environment,
  - technological developments, and
  - available resources.
- The sales projection provides a single level of output demand that is used as a base throughout the budget process.
- The use of a specific sales projection provides a static base to facilitate the numerous arrangements (employees, suppliers, prices, resource quality, capacity availability, etc.) that must be in place before operations begin.

3 Components and Preparation of a Master Budget

- The sales budget (prepared first) reflects unit sales volume and sales prices.
- The production budget adds unit sales to desired units in ending Finished Goods Inventory and subtracts units in beginning Finished Goods Inventory.
  - Retail and service companies do not have a production budget.
- The purchases budget adds production requirements to desired ending raw material or component inventories and subtracts beginning raw material or component inventories.
  - Purchases quantities are multiplied by raw material or component costs.
- The personnel budget indicates
  - the number and types of employees needed as well as salary amounts and wage rates.
- The direct labor budget multiplies units of production by standard hours allowed and then by average wage rate.
- The overhead budget indicates the type and amount of variable and fixed manufacturing overhead costs.
- The selling and administrative budget indicates the type and amount of variable and fixed nonmanufacturing costs.
- The capital budget contains fixed asset purchases and payment points for those assets.
- The cash budget reflects all cash received from and spent on items included in the other budgets.
- All of the individual budgets are combined to prepare budgeted financial statements.

4 Importance of the Cash Budget in Master Budgeting

- Cash is essential for an organization to survive.
- The cash budget
  - translates accrual-based information (such as sales revenues and purchases) into cash flows.
  - helps management assess the effectiveness of credit practices (i.e., whether customers are paying for purchases within the designated credit period).
  - indicates when cash borrowings might be necessary or when cash investments might be made (and for how long).
  - provides important information for preparing the budgeted statement of cash flows.

5 Reasons for Preparing Budgeted Financial Statements

- Such statements
  - indicate the results that will be achieved if the estimates and assumptions used actually occur.
  - allow management to determine if the budgeted results are acceptable.
  - provide management an opportunity, if necessary, to make adjustments to budget assumptions.
  - assess the effects of a change in one budget assumption on related budget assumptions or amounts.

6 Budgeting Benefits

- Guide management to align organizational goals with activities and resource commitments.
- Promote employee participation and departmental coordination.

- Enhance the managerial functions of planning, controlling, and problem solving.
- Allow management to forecast future performance to determine acceptability and, if necessary, provide an opportunity for change.
- Provide a benchmark against which to judge how effectively and efficiently organizational goals were met.

SOLUTION STRATEGIES

Sales Budget, p. 308

Units of sales
× Selling price per unit
= Dollars of sales

Production Budget, p. 309

Units of sales
+ Units desired in ending inventory
− Units in beginning inventory
= Units to be produced

Purchases Budget, p. 310

Units to be produced*
+ Units desired in ending inventory
− Units in beginning inventory
= Units to be purchased

*Converted to direct material component requirements, if necessary

Direct Labor Budget, p. 311

Units to be produced
× Standard time allowed per unit
= Standard labor time allowed
× Per-hour direct labor cost
= Total direct labor cost

Overhead Budget, p. 311

Predicted activity base
× Variable overhead rate per unit of activity
= Total variable overhead cost
+ Fixed overhead cost
= Total overhead cost

Selling and Administrative Budget, p. 312

Predicted sales dollars (or other variable measure)
× Variable S&A rate per dollar (or other variable measure)
= Total variable S&A cost
+ Fixed S&A cost
= Total S&A cost

Cash Budget, p. 313

Beginning cash balance
+ Cash receipts (collections)
= Cash available for disbursements
− Cash needed for disbursements:
  Cash payments for accounts payable for month
  Cost of compensation
  Total cost of overhead minus depreciation
  Total S&A cost minus depreciation

= Cash excess or deficiency
− Minimum desired cash balance
= Cash needed or available for investment or financing
± Various financing measures
= Ending cash balance

Schedule of Cash Receipts (Collections) from Sales, p. 314

Dollars of credit sales for month
× Percent collection for month of sale
= Credit to accounts receivable for month's sales
− Allowed and taken sales discounts
= Receipts for current month's credit sales
+ Receipts from cash sales
+ Current month's cash receipts for prior months' credit sales
= Cash receipts for current month

Schedule of Cash Payments for Purchases, p. 316

Units to be purchased
× Cost per unit
= Total cost of purchases
× Percent payment for current purchases
= Debit to accounts payable for month's purchases
− Purchase discounts taken
= Cash payments for current month's purchases
+ Cash purchases
+ Current month's payments for prior months' purchases
= Cash payments for accounts payable for current month

DEMONSTRATION PROBLEM

The July 31, 2013, balance sheet for World Windows Inc. includes the following information:

Cash	$ 40,000 debit
Accounts Receivable	270,000 debit
Merchandise Inventory of R#850 units	8,750 debit
Merchandise Inventory of R#925 units	7,200 debit

The firm's management has designated $35,000 as the firm's monthly minimum cash balance. Because a piece of equipment was sold at the end of July, the beginning cash balance was greater than the minimum desired amount. Other information about World Windows is as follows:

- Projected sales (all on account) for the following three months are

	August	September	October
R#850 units (unit selling price = $250)	1,000	800	1,100
R#925 units (unit selling price = $480)	500	700	1,300

- Cost of Goods Sold (CGS) for R#850 and R#925 units approximate 70 and 60 percent, respectively, of sales revenues.
- Management wants to end each month with 5 percent of the following month's sales in units. Unit costs are assumed to be stable.
- The collection pattern for accounts receivable is 55 percent in the month of sale, 44 percent in the month following the sale, and 1 percent uncollectible.
- All accounts payable for inventory are paid in the month of purchase.
- Other monthly expenses are $28,000, which includes $6,000 of depreciation but does not include uncollectible accounts expense.
- Investments of excess cash are made in $5,000 increments.

Required:

a. Prepare a sales budget for August, September, and October.
b. Prepare a purchases budget for August and September.

c. Forecast the August cash collections.
d. Prepare the cash budget for August including the effects of financing (borrowing or investing).

Solution to Demonstration Problem

a.

	August	September	October
R#850 units	1,000 × $250 = $250,000	800 × $250 = $200,000	1,100 × $250 = $275,000
R#925 units	500 × $480 = 240,000	700 × $480 = 336,000	1,300 × $480 = 624,000
	$490,000	$536,000	$899,000

b. R#850 units: Cost = 70% of sales revenue = 0.70 × $250 = $175 per unit
R#925 units: Cost = 60% of sales revenue = 0.6 × $480 = $288 per unit
R#850 units in beginning inventory = 5% of 1,000 = 50; 50 × $175 = $8,750 (as shown in beginning merchandise inventory)
R#925 units in beginning inventory = 5% of 500 = 25; 25 × $288 = $7,200 (as shown in beginning merchandise inventory)

R#850 units	August	September
Sales	1,000	800
Ending inventory	40	55
Beginning inventory	(50)	(40)
Units to purchase	990	815
Cost per unit	× $250	× $250
Purchases of R#850	$247,500	$203,750

R#925 units	August	September
Sales	500	700
Ending inventory	35	55
Beginning inventory	(25)	(35)
Units to purchase	510	720
Cost per unit	× $480	× $480
Purchases of R#925	$244,800	$345,600

Total purchases in August = $247,500 + $244,500 = $495,500
Total purchases in September = $203,750 + $345,600 = $549,350

c. A/R on July 31 = 0.45 July sales
$270,000 = 0.45X
X = $600,000 = total July sales

August Collections	
From July ($600,000 × 0.44)	$264,000
From August ($490,000 × 0.55)	269,500
Total	$533,500

d. **August Cash Budget**

Beginning cash balance		$ 40,000
August collections		533,500
Total cash available for disbursements		$ 573,500
Disbursements		
Purchase of merchandise	$495,500	
Other monthly expenses ($28,000 – $6,000)	22,000	(517,500)
Cash excess or deficiency (*a*)		$ 56,000
Less minimum cash balance desired		(35,000)
Cash available		$ 21,000
Financing:		
Acquire investment (*b*)		(20,000)
Ending cash balance (*c*); (*c* = *a* − *b*)		$ 36,000

POTENTIAL ETHICAL ISSUES

ETHICS

1. Using a single budgeting system globally that may conflict with national cultures
2. Knowingly introducing, or allowing employees to introduce, budget slack into the process that will misallocate resources or generate inequitable performance rewards
3. Treating short-term conditions as long-term conditions (or vice versa) to intentionally distort the effects of those conditions on the budgeting process
4. Pressuring employees to meet or exceed budget goals through the use of fraudulent accounting techniques
5. Encouraging employee participation in the budgeting process only to disregard that input
6. Engaging in "backwards budgeting" that justifies management decisions that have been previously determined—especially relative to employee layoffs and plant closures
7. Disregarding contingencies during budget preparation because those conditions cannot be quantified with extreme accuracy
8. Ignoring external performance measures and benchmarks (such as comparisons with competitors or customer satisfaction levels) and concentrating only on meeting internally selected financial targets
9. Allowing lower-level managers to participate in the budgeting process but not communicating necessary "big picture" assumptions—causing participatory budgets to be unrealistic and managers to fail to achieve targets
10. Promoting a "spend-it-or-lose-it" attitude, whereby organizational units reducing expenditures are punished, and units that spend unnecessarily are rewarded, in future periods
11. Mandating a uniform "across-the-board" organizational budget cut without giving employees the opportunity to justify current expenditures or to suggest alternative methods of achieving the desired cost reduction

QUESTIONS

1. How does budgeting provide important information to managers and operating personnel?
2. How does the strategic plan influence preparation of the master budget?
3. Distinguish between a strategic plan and a tactical plan. How are these plans related?
4. After a master budget has been prepared, what is its role in managerial control?
5. Differentiate between the operating and financial budgets that are contained in a master budget. Why are both types needed?
6. Discuss the sequence in which the major components of the master budget are prepared. Why is it necessary to prepare the components in such a sequence?
7. Why is a firm's production budget influenced by the finished goods inventory policy?
8. Assume that in preparing the cash budget, the accountant discovers that a cash shortage will likely occur in a specific month. What actions might the accountant recommend to management to deal with the cash shortage?
9. The cash budget and the budgeted statement of cash flows both provide information about cash. What information about cash is common to these two sources, and what information is unique to the two sources?
10. Why is continuous (rolling) budgeting becoming more popular than it was in the past for organizational managers?
11. If the majority of companies find that their forecasts are inaccurate, why should managers engage in budgeting at all?
12. What is budgetary slack, and what might top managers do to rid their firms' budgets of slack?
13. (*Appendix*) Why is it helpful for a company to prepare a budget manual?

EXERCISES

14. **LO.1 (Tactical planning; writing)** People, as well as businesses, need to budget. Assume that you and your spouse are having difficulties living within your combined incomes. Prepare a list of at least 10 recommendations on how to "do things differently" to help manage your finances.

15. **LO.1 (Strategic planning; writing)** Before a budget can be prepared, company management considers "what if" changes that might occur during the forecast period. Prepare a list of five possible questions about changes that you might want to consider if you were a manager in a
    a. global manufacturing company.
    b. local retailer.

16. **LO.1 (Strategic planning; research)** When engaging in strategic planning, company management often prepares a SWOT analysis.
    a. What is a SWOT analysis, and why is it useful in the planning process?
    b. Choose an organization with which you are familiar and develop a SWOT analysis for that organization.

17. **LO.6 (Planning; writing)** High-level executives have often indicated that competitors' actions are the top external factor affecting their businesses and their business plans.
    a. Why are competitors' actions so important to business planning?
    b. How would competitors' actions affect a business's internal planning?
    c. What other internal and external factors are key elements in a business's budgeting process?

18. **LO.2 (Sales budget)** Pataky Co.'s sales manager estimates that 2,000,000 units of product RI#698 will be sold in 2014. The product's selling price is expected to decline as the result of technology changes during the year and estimates of the sales price are as follows:

1st Quarter	2nd Quarter	3rd Quarter	4th Quarter
$17	$16	$14	$12

In talking with customers, the sales department discovered that sales quantities per quarter could vary substantially. Thus, the sales manager has prepared the following three sets of quarterly sales projections:

	1st Quarter	2nd Quarter	3rd Quarter	4th Quarter	Total
Scenario A	600,000	300,000	640,000	460,000	2,000,000
Scenario B	400,000	700,000	250,000	650,000	2,000,000
Scenario C	530,000	480,000	800,000	190,000	2,000,000

If Pataky's sales department is able to influence customers, which of the potential sales scenarios would be most profitable for the company? Would that scenario possibly cause the company any difficulties?

19. **LO.2 (Revenue budget)** In 2013, Grand Falls Bank (GFB) had $4,000,000 in business loans at an average interest rate of 3.5 percent as well as $3,200,000 in consumer loans with an average rate of 8 percent. GFB also has $750,000 invested in government securities that pay interest at an average rate of 2.5 percent.

    For 2014, GFB estimates that the volume of business loans will increase to $6,000,000, and the interest rate will rise to 5 percent. It projects that consumer loans will be $4,000,000 and have an average interest rate of 11 percent. The bank's government security investment will be $1,600,000 and will bear an average interest rate of 4.5 percent. What is GFB's projected revenue for 2014?

20. **LO.3 (Production, direct materials, and direct labor budgets)** Gerrad Manufacturing has projected sales of its product for the next six months as follows:

January	300 units
February	700 units
March	1,000 units
April	900 units
May	400 units
June	300 units

The finished product requires 3 pounds of raw material and 10 hours of direct labor. Gerrad tries to maintain a Finished Goods ending inventory equal to the next two months of sales and a Raw Material ending inventory equal to one-half of the current month's production needs. January's beginning inventories are expected to conform to company policy.

a. Prepare a production budget for February, March, and April.
b. Prepare a forecast of the units and cost of raw material that will be required for February, March, and April. The expected cost per pound of raw material is expected to be $2 in February, $2.30 in March, and $2.40 in April.
c. Prepare a direct labor budget (assuming a $12 per hour rate) for February, March, and April.

21. **LO.3 (Material purchases budget)** Gap'O has projected sales of 325,000 hospital gowns in October. Each gown requires 2.5 yards of fabric. The beginning inventory of fabric and gowns, respectively, are 5,000 yards and 21,000 gowns. Gap'O wants to have 4,550 yards of fabric and 15,800 gowns on hand at the end of October. The fabric comes in 15-yard bolts. If Gap'O has no beginning or ending Work in Process Inventory, how many bolts of fabric must the company purchase in October?

22. **LO.3 (Production budget)** Nafari Company's sales budget has the following unit sales projections for each quarter of calendar year 2014:

January–March	1,080,000
April–June	1,360,000
July–September	980,000
October–December	1,100,000
Total	4,520,000

Sales for the first quarter of 2015 are expected to be 1,200,000 units. Ending inventory of finished goods for each quarter is scheduled to equal 10 percent of the next quarter's budgeted sales. The company's ending inventory on December 31, 2013, is estimated at 94,500 units. Develop a quarterly production budget for 2014 and for the year in total.

23. **LO.3 (Material purchases budget)** Hard Core had budgeted sales of 190,000 feet of its concrete culvert products for June 2013. Each foot of product requires 4 pounds of concrete ($0.10 per pound) and 7.5 pounds of gravel ($0.04 per pound). Actual beginning inventories and projected ending inventories follow.

	June 1	June 30
Finished Goods Inventory (in feet)	12,250	10,000
Concrete (in pounds)	41,000	34,300
Gravel (in pounds)	32,650	46,250

a. How many pounds of concrete did Hard Core plan to purchase in June? What was the cost of those purchases?
b. How many pounds of gravel did Hard Core plan to purchase in June? What was the cost of those purchases?

24. **LO.3 (Production budget)** Seguin Inc. has the following projected unit sales for the first four months of 2014:

January	102,400
February	96,000
March	128,000
April	153,600

Company policy is to have an ending monthly inventory equal to 5 percent of next month's estimated sales; however, this criterion was not in effect at the end of 2013. Ending inventory at that time was 7,000 units. Determine the company's production requirements for each month of the first quarter of 2014.

EXCEL

25. **LO.3 (Production and related schedules)** Goldstein Inc. manufactures and sells plastic boxes and trays. Sales are projected to be evenly spread over the annual period. Estimated product sales and material needs for each unit of product follow.

	Boxes	Trays
Annual sales	42,000	30,000
Material A	2.0 pounds	1.0 pound
Material B	1.5 pounds	0.8 pound
Direct labor	0.3 hour	0.2 hour

Overhead is applied at a rate of $1.60 per direct labor hour.

	Expected Beginning Inventories	Desired Ending Inventories
Material A	1,780 pounds	1,500 pounds
Material B	5,000 pounds	1,400 pounds
Boxes	1,200 units	1,800 units
Trays	800 units	650 units

Material A costs $0.05 per pound, and Material B costs $0.07 per pound. Prepare the following information:

a. Production schedule by product and in total.
b. Purchases budget in units by raw material, in total, and in dollars.
c. Direct labor budget in hours by product, in total, and in dollars. The average direct labor wage rate is $9.50 per hour.
d. Overhead to be charged to production by product and in total.

26. **LO.3 & LO.4 (Budgeted purchases; budgeted cash payments)** Grenfell Company is preparing a cash budget for 2014 for purchases of Calvos. Budgeted data are as follows:

Cost of goods sold for the year 2014	$600,000
Accounts payable, 1/1/14	40,000
Inventory, 1/1/14	60,000
Desired inventory, 12/31/14	84,000

Purchases will be made in 12 equal monthly amounts and paid for in the following month. Compute the budgeted cash payment for purchases of Calvos for 2014.

27. **LO.3 & LO.4 (Direct material purchases and budgeted payments)** Campbell Manufacturing intends to start business on January 1, 2014. Production plans for the first four months of operations are as follows:

January	20,000 units
February	50,000 units
March	70,000 units
April	70,000 units

Each unit requires two pounds of material. The firm would like to end each month with enough raw material to cover 25 percent of the following month's production needs. Raw material costs $7 per pound. Management pays for 40 percent of purchases in the month of purchase and receives a 10 percent discount for these payments. The remaining purchases are paid in the following month, with no discount available.

a. Prepare a purchases budget for the first quarter of 2014 in units, in total, and in dollars.
b. Determine the budgeted payments for purchases of raw material for each of the first three months of operations and for the quarter in total.
c. Where in the budgeted financial statements do the purchase discounts appear?

28. **LO.4 (Cash collections)** Ridenour Ltd. is preparing its first-quarter monthly cash budget for 2014. The following information is available about actual 2013 sales and expected 2014 sales:

EXCEL

November	December	January	February	March
$83,000	$76,000	$79,000	$88,000	$59,000

Tracing collections from prior year monthly sales and discussions with the credit manager helped develop a profile of collection behavior patterns.

Of a given month's sales, 40 percent is typically collected in the month of sale. Because the company terms are 1 percent (end of month) net 30, all collections within the month of sale are net of the 1 percent discount. Of a given month's sales, 30 percent is collected in the month following the sale. The remaining 30 percent is collected in the second month following the month of the sale. Bad debts are negligible and should be ignored.

a. Prepare a schedule of cash collections for Ridenour Ltd. for January, February, and March 2014.
b. Calculate the Accounts Receivable balance at March 31, 2014.

29. **LO.4 (Cash collections, accounts receivable)** The October 1, 2013, Accounts Receivable balance for Darin Landscaping is $632,500. Of that balance, $480,000 represents remaining accounts receivable from September billings. The normal collection pattern for the firm is 20 percent of billings in the month of service, 55 percent in the month after service, and 22 percent in the second month following service. The remaining billings are uncollectible. October billings are expected to be $750,000.

a. What were August billings for Darin Landscaping?
b. What amount of September billings is expected to be uncollectible?
c. What are the firm's projected cash collections in October?

30. **LO.4 (Cash balance)** The following budgeted May 2013 cash information is available for Salado Corp.:

Net after-tax income	$336,000
Depreciation expense	56,200
Accrued income tax expense	82,000
Increase in Accounts Receivable for month	8,000
Decrease in Accounts Payable for month	7,000
Estimated bad debts expense	4,100
Dividends declared in May	35,000
Dividends paid in May	47,000

If Salado's May 1, 2013, cash balance is $23,000, what is the company's budgeted May 31, 2013, cash balance?

31. **LO.4 (Cash collections, accounts receivable)** Total June 2013 sales for Roy's Catering are expected to be $450,000. Of each month's sales, 80 percent is expected to be on credit. The Accounts Receivable balance at May 31 is $119,600, of which $90,000 represents the remainder of May credit sales. There are no receivables from months prior to April 2013. The collection pattern of Roy's Catering credit sales is 70 percent in the month of sale, 20 percent in the month following the sale, and 10 percent in the second month following the sale. Roy's Catering has no uncollectible accounts.

a. What were total sales for April 2013?
b. What were credit sales for May 2013?
c. What are projected cash collections for June 2013?
d. What is the expected balance of Accounts Receivable at June 30, 2013?

32. **LO.4 (Cash disbursements)** The following budgeted information about Reeves Co. is available for September 2013:

Sales for September	$2,700,000
Gross profit on sales	40%
Decrease in Merchandise Inventory during September	$ 43,750
Wages expense for September	$ 325,500
Increase in Wages Payable for September	$ 42,000
Other cash expenses for September	$ 245,000
Decrease in Accounts Payable during September	$ 35,000

Reeves Co. only uses its Accounts Payable for inventory purchases.

a. How much does Reeves Co. expect to pay for inventory in September 2013?
b. What are total budgeted cash disbursements for September 2013?

33. **LO.4 (Cash collections)** Miriam Irby is president of MI Corp. Irby has decided to take a month's vacation with her family to South Africa, Zimbabwe, and Angola. Irby has researched the trip and determined that the total cost of the trip for her family will be approximately $50,000—she wants to go first class on everything! Her travel agent says that a 10 percent discount can be obtained if Irby can write a check for the cost of the trip by the end of November. Irby says she sees no problem in doing that given that the company's expected billings for October, November, and December, respectively, are $100,000, $65,000, and $15,000 (Irby will leave on vacation in December).

As of September 30, 2013, MI Corp.'s accountant has estimated cash collections from billings to be 15 percent in the month of sale, 55 percent in the month following sale, and 30 percent in the second month following sale. The September 30, 2013, Accounts Receivable balance is $11,000; that amount is expected to be collected in October. Average monthly business costs are $22,500.

a. What are MI Corp.'s expected cash collections for October, November, and December?
b. Can Irby pay for her trip in November and obtain the 10 percent discount? Explain.
c. What would you suggest that Irby do?

34. **LO.4 (Cash budget)** The following cash budget is for the third quarter of 2014. Solve for the missing numbers on the cash budget, assuming that the accountant has requested a minimum cash balance of $7,000 at the start of each month. All borrowings, repayments, and investments are made in even $1,000 amounts. No borrowings or investments exist at the beginning of July.

	July	August	September	Total
Beginning cash balance	$ 7,400	$?	$?	$?
Cash receipts	16,400	20,200	?	?
Total cash available	$?	$?	$41,000	$ 77,800
Cash disbursements				
Payments on account	$?	$ 7,800	$11,400	$?
Wages expense	10,000	?	12,400	34,600
Overhead costs	8,000	9,200	?	26,000
Total disbursements	$20,600	$?	$32,600	$?
Cash excess (deficiency)	$?	$?	$?	$?
Minimum cash balance	(7,000)	(7,000)	?	?
Cash available (needed)	$?	$ (8,800)	$?	$(11,600)
Financing				
Borrowings (repayments)	$ 4,000	$?	$ (1,000)	$?
Acquire (sell) investments	0	0	?	?
Receive (pay) interest	0	0	?	(20)
Ending cash balance	$ 7,200	$?	$?	$ 7,380

35. **LO.4 (Cash collections)** The treasurer of Homeyra Corp. needs to estimate cash collections from accounts receivable for September, October, and November 2014. Forty percent of the company's customers pay in cash, and the rest are credit customers. The collection pattern for the credit customers is 20 percent in the month of sale and

80 percent in the following month. Because of Homeyra's established client base, the company experiences almost zero uncollectible accounts. Estimated total sales for August, September, October, and November 2014 follow.

August	$78,000
September	80,000
October	95,000
November	91,000

Determine Homeyra Corp.'s cash collections for September, October, and November 2014.

36. **LO.3 & LO.4 (Various budgets)** Compute the required answer for each of the following independent situations.

a. For next year, Penny Suits projects $8,000,000 of sales and total fixed manufacturing costs of $2,000,000. Variable manufacturing costs are estimated at 65 percent of sales. Assuming no change in inventory, what is the company's projected cost of goods sold?

b. Tommy's Company has projected the following information for October:

Sales	$800,000
Gross profit (based on sales)	25%
Increase in Merchandise Inventory in October	$ 20,000
Decrease in Accounts Payable for October	$ 45,000

What are expected cash disbursements for inventory purchases for October?

c. Buda Corp. is attempting to budget its overhead costs for March 2014. Overhead is a mixed cost with the following flexible budget formula: $y = \$250,000 + \$17.50X$, where X represents machine hours. Fixed overhead includes $95,000 of depreciation. If Buda Corp. expects to utilize 7,500 machine hours in March, what is the company's budgeted March overhead cost? How much cash will the company pay for budgeted overhead in March?

d. Elizabeth Enterprises expects to begin 2014 with a cash balance of $15,000. Cash collections from sales and on account during the year are expected to be $470,500. The firm wants to maintain a minimum cash balance of $5,000. Budgeted cash disbursements for the year are as follows:

Payoff of note payable	$ 52,500
Interest on note payable	4,700
Purchase of computer system	17,900
Payments for operating costs and inventory purchases	193,500
Direct labor payments	110,000
Cash overhead payments	106,400
Cash selling and administrative payments	94,800

The company can, if necessary, borrow in $1,000 amounts. Prepare a cash budget for 2014.

37. **LO.5 (Budgeted income statement)** The operating results in summarized form for a retail computer store for 2013 are:

Revenue:	
Hardware sales	$ 4,800,000
Software sales	2,000,000
Maintenance contracts	1,200,000
Total revenue	$ 8,000,000
Costs and expenses:	
Cost of hardware sales	$ 3,360,000
Cost of software sales	1,200,000
Marketing expenses	600,000
Customer maintenance costs	640,000
Administrative expenses	1,120,000
Total costs and expenses	$(6,920,000)
Operating income	$ 1,080,000

The computer store is in the process of formulating its operating budget for 2014 and has made the following assumptions:

- The selling prices of hardware are expected to increase 10 percent but there will be no selling price increases for software and maintenance contracts.
- Hardware unit sales are expected to increase 5 percent with a corresponding 5 percent growth in the number of maintenance contracts; growth in unit software sales is estimated at 8 percent.
- The cost of hardware and software is expected to increase 4 percent.
- Marketing expenses will be increased 5 percent in the coming year.
- Three technicians will be added to the customer maintenance operations in the coming year, increasing the customer maintenance costs by $120,000.
- Administrative costs will be held at the same level.

CIA ADAPTED

Compute the computer retail store's budgeted operating income for 2014.

38. **LO.5 (Budgeted income statement)** Last year's income statement for Cooper Company is as follows:

Sales (100,000 × $10)		$1,000,000
Cost of goods sold		
Direct material	$400,000	
Direct labor	200,000	
Overhead	100,000	(700,000)
Gross profit		$ 300,000
Expenses		
Selling	$104,000	
Administrative	120,000	(224,000)
Income before taxes		$ 76,000

This year, unit sales are expected to increase by 25 percent; material and labor costs are expected to increase by 10 percent per unit. Overhead is applied to production based on a percentage of direct labor costs. Fixed selling expenses total $24,000; the remainder varies with sales dollars. All administrative costs are fixed.

Management desires to earn 10 percent on sales this year and will adjust the unit selling price if necessary. Develop a budgeted income statement for the year for Cooper Company that incorporates the indicated changes.

39. **LO.3, LO.4, & LO.5 (Budgeted accounts receivable; cash; and income statement)** In preparing its budget for July, Wade Inc. has the following information available:

Accounts Receivable at June 30	$750,000
Estimated credit sales for July	900,000
Estimated collections in July for credit sales in July and prior months	660,000
Estimated write-offs in July for uncollectible credit sales	27,000
Estimated provision for uncollectible accounts for credit sales in July	20,000

a. What is the projected balance of Accounts Receivable at July 31?
b. Which of these amounts (if any) will affect the cash budget?
c. Which of these amounts (if any) will affect the budgeted income statement for July?

CPA ADAPTED

40. **LO.5 (Budgeted income statement)** The following budget information is available for Sluyter Corp. for May 2014:

- Sales are expected to be $400,000. All sales are on account, and a provision for bad debts is accrued monthly at 3 percent of sales.
- Inventory was $35,000 on April 30, and an increase of $10,000 is planned for May.
- All inventory is marked to sell at cost plus 60 percent.
- Estimated cash disbursements for selling and administrative expenses for the month are $55,000.
- Depreciation for May is projected at $8,000.

CPA ADAPTED

Prepare a budgeted income statement for Sluyter Corp. for May 2014.

41. **LO.5 (Budgeted income statement)** Alyssa Co. is planning to purchase a new piece of production equipment. The equipment will increase fixed overhead by $700,000 per year in depreciation but reduce variable expenses per unit by 20 percent. Budgeted 2014 sales of the company's products are 240,000 units at an average selling price of $25. Variable expenses are currently 65 percent of sales, and fixed costs total $1,400,000 per year.
    a. Prepare an income statement assuming that the new equipment is not purchased.
    b. What is the current variable cost per unit? What will be the new variable cost per unit if the equipment is purchased?
    c. Prepare an income statement assuming that the new equipment is purchased.
    d. Should the equipment be acquired?

42. **LO.6 (Budgeting attitudes; writing)** Many managers believe that if all amounts in their spending budgets are not spent during a period, they will lose allocations in future periods and that they will receive little or no recognition for the cost savings.

    Prepare an essay that discusses the behavioral and ethical issues involved in a spend-it-or-lose-it attitude. Include in your discussion the issue of negotiating budget allocation requests prior to the beginning of the period.

ETHICS

43. **LO.6 (Continuous budgeting; writing)** You own a small boat manufacturing company. At a recent manufacturers' association meeting, you overheard one of the other company owners say that he liked using a continuous budgeting process. Discuss in a report to your top management group what you believe are the advantages and disadvantages of continuous budgeting for your company.

44. **LO.6 (Management control; writing)** You are a managing partner for a 50-person CPA firm. What important detail items would you want to review in making a budget and year-end analysis in each of the following areas?
    a. Human resources
    b. Information technology
    c. Marketing/Business development
    d. Accounts receivable

45. **LO.6 (Research; writing)** Find the Web page for a charitable organization that operates internationally as well as domestically.
    a. Prepare a list of activities in which this organization is currently involved.
    b. What would be the greatest challenges in budgeting for such an organization?
    c. Do you think not-for-profits should be as concerned as for-profit organizations with budgeting? Explain the rationale for your answer.

INTERNET

PROBLEMS

46. **LO.3 (Production and purchases budgets; writing)** Narisho Supply is in the process of preparing the budget for the first quarter of 2014. The following projections for unit sales have been made:

	January	February	March	Total
Sales	72,000	64,000	60,000	196,000

Each finished unit requires three direct materials: 4 pounds of Material M, 2.5 pounds of Material N, and 2 pounds of Material O. Based on company policies, the following estimates of finished units and pounds of direct material inventories are made:

	December	January	February	March
Finished units	18,000	16,000	15,000	14,000
Direct material M	13,500	12,000	11,250	10,500
Direct material N	9,000	8,000	7,500	7,000
Direct material O	7,300	9,400	8,200	8,500

a. Prepare a monthly production and purchases budget for the first quarter of 2014.
b. The production supervisor wants to purchase new production equipment for 2014. Such equipment would largely replace the current labor-intensive production system. Write a memo to corporate management explaining why new production equipment could affect the production and purchases budget.
c. Who should be consulted to determine the new material requirements per unit if the new production equipment is installed?

47. **LO.3 (Production and purchases budgets)** Caleb Corp. has prepared the following unit sales forecast for 2014:

	January–June	July–December	Total
Sales	1,160,000	1,440,000	2,600,000

Estimated ending Finished Goods Inventories are 50,000 units at December 31, 2013; 72,000 units at June 30, 2014; and 120,000 units at December 31, 2014.

In manufacturing a unit of this product, Caleb Corp. uses 3 pounds of Material A and 0.75 gallons of Material B. Materials A and B cost, respectively, $2.50 per pound and $1.80 per gallon.

The company carries no Work in Process Inventory. Ending inventories of direct material are projected as follows:

	December 31, 2013	June 30, 2014	December 31, 2014
Material A (in pounds)	240,000	270,000	284,000
Material B (in gallons)	90,000	70,000	76,000

Prepare a production and purchases budget for each semiannual period of 2014.

EXCEL

48. **LO.3 & LO.4 (Production; purchases; cash disbursements)** So Sweet! has budgeted sales of 600,000 cans of diet iced tea mix during June 2013 and 750,000 cans during July. Production of the mix requires 14.5 ounces of tea and 1.5 ounces of sugar substitute. June 1 inventories of tea and sugar substitute are as follows:

Iced tea mix	24,600 cans of finished product
Tea	750 pounds
Sugar substitute	200 pounds

So Sweet! generally carries a finished goods inventory equal to 5 percent of the following month's needs; raw material ending inventories should equal 10 percent of Finished Goods Inventory. Assuming that the ending inventory policy is met, answer the following questions.

a. How many cans of iced tea mix will be produced in June?
b. How many pounds of tea will be purchased in June?
c. How many pounds of sugar substitute will be purchased in June?
d. Tea and sugar substitute cost $3.50 and $0.40 per pound, respectively. What dollar amount of raw material purchases is budgeted for June?
e. If the company normally pays for 40 percent of its budgeted purchases during the month of purchase and takes a 2 percent discount, what are budgeted cash disbursements in June for June purchases? How much will So Sweet! owe for June purchases in July?

49. **LO.3 (Production; purchases; direct labor & OH budgets)** Atkinson's Reliable Tools makes two products that use similar raw materials: #587Q and #253X. Estimated production needs for a unit of each product follow.

	#587Q	#253X
Steel (in pounds)	3	5
Wood (in board feet)	0.5	0.2
Direct labor (in hours)	2	3
Machine hours	0.5	0.7

Estimated sales in units by product for 2014 are 80,000 of #587Q and 30,000 of #253X. Additionally, estimated beginning and desired ending inventory quantities for 2014 are as follows.

	Beginning	Ending
#587Q (units)	800	640
#253X (units)	1,200	900
Steel (in pounds)	2,000	1,400
Wood (in board feet)	800	600

Overhead is applied to production at the rate of $15 per machine hour and the direct labor wage rate is $10.50 per hour. Prepare the production, purchases, direct labor, and overhead budgets for 2014.

50. **LO.3 & LO.4 (Budgeted sales and S&A; other computations)** Butler Inc. has projected Cost of Goods Sold (CGS) for June 2014 of $1,500,000. Of this amount, $80,000 represents fixed overhead costs. Total variable costs for the company each month average 70 percent of sales. The company's cost to retail (CGS to sales) percentage is 60 percent, and the company normally generates net income equal to 15 percent of sales. All purchases and expenses (except depreciation) are paid 65 percent in the month incurred and 35 percent in the following month. Depreciation is $45,000 per month.

    a. What are Butler Inc.'s expected sales for June?
    b. What are Butler Inc.'s expected variable selling and administrative costs for June?
    c. What are Butler Inc.'s total fixed costs? How much of this is fixed selling and administrative cost?
    d. Butler Inc. normally collects 55 percent of its sales in the month of sale and the rest in the next month. What are expected cash receipts and disbursements related only to June's transactions?

51. **LO.3 & LO.4 (Production; purchases; cash budgets)** Corner Brook Furniture Co. makes bookstands and expects sales and collections for the first three months of 2014 to be as follows:

	January	February	March	Total
Sales quantity (units)	6,400	5,200	7,400	19,000
Revenue	$128,000	$104,000	$148,000	$380,000
Collections	$116,200	$ 81,300	$101,500	$299,000

The December 31, 2013, balance sheet revealed the following selected account balances: Cash, $18,320; Direct Material Inventory, $8,230; Finished Goods Inventory, $23,200; and Accounts Payable, $5,800. The Direct Material Inventory balance represents 1,580 pounds of scrap iron and 1,200 bookstand bases. The Finished Goods Inventory consists of 1,220 bookstands.

Each bookstand requires two pounds of scrap iron, which costs $3 per pound. Bookstand bases are purchased from a local lumber mill at a cost of $2.50 per unit. Company management decided that, beginning in 2014, the ending balance of Direct Material Inventory should be 25 percent of the following month's production requirements and that the ending balance of Finished Goods Inventory should be 20 percent of the next month's sales. Sales for April and May are expected to be 8,000 bookstands per month.

The company normally pays for 75 percent of a month's purchases of direct material in the month of purchase (on which it takes a 1 percent cash discount). The remaining 25 percent is paid in full in the month following the month of purchase.

Direct labor is budgeted at $0.70 per bookstand produced and is paid in the month of production. Total cash manufacturing overhead is budgeted at $14,000 per month plus $1.30 per bookstand. Total cash selling and administrative costs equal $13,600 per month plus 10 percent of sales revenue. These costs are all paid in the month of incurrence. In addition, the company plans to pay executive bonuses of $35,000 in January 2014 and make an estimated quarterly tax payment of $5,000 in March 2014.

Management requires a minimum cash balance of $10,000 at the end of each month. If the company borrows funds, it will do so only in $1,000 multiples at the beginning of a month at a 12 percent annual interest rate. Loans are to be repaid at the end of a month in multiples of $1,000. Interest is paid only when a repayment is made. Investments are made in $1,000 multiples at the end of a month, and the return on investment is 8 percent per year.

a. Prepare a production budget by month and in total for the first quarter of 2014.
b. Prepare a direct material purchases budget by month and in total for the first quarter of 2014.
c. Prepare a schedule of cash payments for purchases by month and in total for the first quarter of 2014.
d. Prepare a combined payments schedule for manufacturing overhead and selling and administrative cash costs for each month and in total for the first quarter of 2014.
e. Prepare a cash budget for each month and in total for the first quarter of 2014.

52. **LO.3 (Budgeted cash collections; budgeted accounts receivable; bad debts)** Cute and Cuddly Inc. sells teddy bears in walk-by kiosks in shopping malls. The company's balance sheet on March 31, 2013, showed the following balances related to Accounts Receivable and inventories:

Accounts Receivable	$346,000
Allowance for doubtful accounts	$35,000
Inventory	208,000
Accounts payable to suppliers	$455,000

The company's controller, Brad Jones, is making budget projections for the second quarter of 2013 and has made the following assumptions:

- Budgeted sales: April—60,000 units, May—140,000 units, June—46,000 units
- Selling price per bear—$12
- Cost per bear—$8

Expected cash collections from 3/31/13 Accounts Receivable:

In April:	$ 36,000
In May:	295,000
To be written off:	15,000

Other information:

The Accounts Receivable balance at March 31 consists of $36,000 from February sales and $310,000 from March sales.

Eighty percent of sales are on credit. The remaining sales are cash sales. Twenty-five percent of credit sales are collected in the month of sale, with 55 percent in the month following and 18 percent in the second month following. The remaining 2 percent are uncollectible. The company expects to write off $15,000 of accounts receivable during the second quarter.

Thirty percent of purchases are paid for in the month of purchase with the remainder in the month following.

The company budgets ending inventory equal to 40 percent of the following month's sales in units. July's sales are budgeted at 30,000 units.

a. Prepare a sales budget for the quarter ended June 30, 2013.
b. Compute budgeted cash collections for the quarter ending June 30, 2013.
c. Compute budgeted Accounts Receivable at June 30, 2013.
d. Compute the estimated bad debt expense that will appear in the budgeted income statement for the quarter ending June 30, 2013.
e. How would the Accounts Receivable be presented on the budgeted balance sheet at June 30, 2013?
f. Compute budgeted purchases for the quarter ended June 30, 2013.
g. Compute budgeted cash payments for inventory for the quarter ended June 30, 2013.
h. Compute budgeted accounts payable at June 30, 2013.

53. **LO.4 (Cash budget)** Collegiate Management Education (CME) Inc. is a nonprofit organization that sponsors a wide variety of management seminars throughout the Southwest. In addition, it is heavily involved in research into improved methods of teaching and motivating college administrators. Its seminar activity is largely supported by fees, and the research program is supported by membership dues.

CME operates on a calendar-year basis and is finalizing the budget for 2014. The following information has been taken from approved plans, which are still tentative at this time:

Seminar Program

Revenue

The scheduled number of programs should produce $12,000,000 of revenue for the year. Each program is budgeted to produce the same amount of revenue. The revenue is collected during the month the program is offered. The programs are scheduled during the basic academic year and are not held during June, July, August, or December. Of the revenue, 12 percent is generated in each of the first five months of the year and the remainder is distributed evenly during September, October, and November.

Direct expenses

The seminar expenses are of three types:

- Instructors' fees are paid at the rate of 70 percent of seminar revenue in the month following the seminar. The instructors are considered independent contractors and are not eligible for CME employee benefits.
- Facilities fees total $5,600,000 for the year. They are the same for each program and are paid in the month the program is given.
- Annual promotional costs of $1,000,000 are spent equally in all months except June and July, when there is no promotional effort.

Research Program

Research grant

The research program has a large number of projects nearing completion. The main research activity this year includes feasibility studies for new projects to be started in 2015. As a result, the total grant expense of $3,000,000 for 2014 is expected to be incurred at the rate of $500,000 per month during the first six months of the year.

Salaries and Other CME Expenses

- Office lease—annual amount of $240,000 paid monthly at the beginning of each month.
- General administrative expenses—$1,500,000 annually, or $125,000 per month, paid in cash as incurred.
- Depreciation expense—$240,000 per year.
- General CME promotion—annual cost of $600,000, paid monthly.
- Salaries and benefits are as follows:

Number of Employees	Annual Cash Salary	Total Annual Salaries
1	$50,000	$ 50,000
3	40,000	120,000
4	30,000	120,000
15	25,000	375,000
5	15,000	75,000
22	10,000	220,000
50		$960,000

Employee benefits are $240,000, or 25 percent of annual salaries. Except for the pension contribution, the benefits are paid as salaries are paid. The annual pension payment of $24,000, based on 2.5 percent of total annual salaries, is due on April 15, 2014.

Other Information

- Membership income—CME has 100,000 members, each of whom pays a $100 annual fee. The fee for the calendar year is invoiced in late June.
- Collection schedule—July, 60 percent; August, 30 percent; September, 5 percent; and October, 5 percent.
- Capital expenditures—this program calls for a total of $510,000 in cash payments to be spread evenly over the first five months of 2014.
- Cash and temporary investments at January 1, 2014, are estimated at $750,000.

a. Prepare a budget of the annual cash receipts and disbursements for 2014.
b. Prepare a cash budget for CME for January 2014.
c. Using the information developed in (a) and (b), identify two important operating problems of CME.

CPA ADAPTED

EXCEL

54. **LO.4 (Cash budget)** Vassar Corp. has incurred substantial losses for several years and has decided to declare bankruptcy. The company petitioned the court for protection from creditors on March 31, 2013, and submitted the following balance sheet:

Vassar Corp.
Balance Sheet
March 31, 2013

	Book Value	Liquidation Value
Assets		
Accounts Receivable	$100,000	$ 50,000
Inventories	90,000	40,000
Plant Assets (net)	150,000	160,000
Totals	$340,000	$250,000

Vassar's liabilities and stockholders' equity at this date are as follows:

Accounts Payable—General Creditors	$ 600,000
Common Stock	60,000
Retained Earnings Deficit	(320,000)
Totals	$ 340,000

Vassar's management informed the court that the company has developed a new product and that a prospective customer is willing to sign a contract for the purchase of 10,000 units during the year ending March 31, 2014, and 12,000 units during the year ending March 31, 2015, at a price of $90 per unit. Vassar expects to sell 15,000 units during the year ending March 31, 2015. This product can be manufactured using Vassar's present facilities. Monthly production with immediate delivery is expected to be uniform within each year. Receivables are expected to be collected during the calendar month following sales. Unit production costs of the new product are estimated as follows:

Direct material	$20
Direct labor	30
Variable overhead	10

Fixed costs of $130,000 (excluding depreciation) are incurred per year. Purchases of direct material will be paid during the calendar month following purchase. Fixed costs, direct labor, and variable overhead will be paid as incurred. Inventory of direct material will equal 60 days' usage. After the first month of operations, 30 days' usage will be ordered each month.

The general creditors have agreed to reduce their total claims to 60 percent of their March 31, 2013, balances under the following conditions:

- Existing accounts receivable and inventories are to be liquidated immediately, with the proceeds turned over to the general creditors.
- The reduced balance of accounts payable is to be paid as cash is generated from future operations but no later than March 31, 2015. No interest will be paid on these obligations.

Under this proposed plan, the general creditors would receive $110,000 more than the current liquidation value of Vassar's assets. The court has engaged you to determine the feasibility of this plan.

Ignoring any need to borrow and repay short-term funds for working capital purposes, prepare a cash budget for the years ending March 31, 2014 and 2015, showing the cash expected to be available for paying the claims of the general creditors, the amount of payments to general creditors, and the cash remaining after payment of claims.

CPA ADAPTED

55. **LO.4 (Cash budget)** Blackman Corp., a rapidly expanding crossbow distributor, is in the process of formulating plans for 2014. Cara Jordan, director of marketing, has completed her 2014 forecast and is confident that sales estimates will be met or exceeded. The following forecasted sales figures show the growth expected and will provide the planning basis for other corporate departments.

	Sales		Sales
January	$3,600,000	July	$6,000,000
February	4,000,000	August	6,000,000
March	3,600,000	September	6,400,000
April	4,400,000	October	6,400,000
May	5,000,000	November	6,000,000
June	5,600,000	December	6,800,000

George Moore, assistant controller, has been given the responsibility for formulating the cash flow projection, a critical element during a period of rapid expansion. The following information will be used in preparing the cash analysis.

- Blackman has experienced an excellent record in accounts receivable collections and expects this trend to continue. The company collects 60 percent of its billings in the month after the sale and 40 percent in the second month after the sale. Uncollectible accounts are insignificant and should not be considered in the analysis.
- The purchase of crossbows is Blackman's largest expenditure; the cost of these items equals 50 percent of sales. The company receives 60 percent of the crossbows one month prior to sale and 40 percent during the month of sale.
- Prior experience shows that 80 percent of accounts payable is paid by Blackman one month after receipt of the purchased crossbows, and the remaining 20 percent is paid the second month after receipt.
- Hourly wages, including fringe benefits, are a function of sales volume and are equal to 20 percent of the current month's sales. These wages are paid in the month incurred.
- Administrative expenses are projected to be $5,280,000 for 2014. All of these expenses are incurred uniformly throughout the year except the property taxes. Property taxes are paid in four equal installments in the last month of each quarter. The composition of the expenses is:

Salaries	$ 960,000
Promotion	1,320,000
Property taxes	480,000
Insurance	720,000
Utilities	600,000
Depreciation	1,200,000
Total	$5,280,000

- Income tax payments are made by Blackman in the first month of each quarter based on income for the prior quarter. Blackman's income tax rate is 40 percent. Blackman's net income for the first quarter of 2014 is projected to be $1,224,000.
- Blackman has a corporate policy of maintaining an end-of-month cash balance of $200,000. Cash is invested or borrowed monthly, as necessary, to maintain this balance.

Blackman uses a calendar year reporting period.

a. Prepare a budgeted schedule of cash receipts and disbursements for Blackman Corp., by month, for the second quarter of 2014. Ignore interest expense and/or interest income associated with the borrowing/investing activities.

b. Discuss why cash budgeting is particularly important for a rapidly expanding company such as Blackman Corp.

CPA ADAPTED c. Do monthly cash budgets ignore the pattern of cash flows within the month? Explain.

56. **LO.4 (Cash budget)** Stabler Co.'s projected March 31, 2014, balance sheet follows.

Assets		Liabilities and Stockholders' Equity		
Cash	$ 24,000	Accounts Payable		$140,400
Accounts Receivable (net of Allowance for Uncollectibles of $2,880)	69,120			
Merchandise Inventory	104,800	Common Stock	$50,000	
Plant Assets (net of Accumulated Depreciation of $120,000)	72,000	Retained Earnings	79,520	129,520
Total Assets	$269,920	Total Liabilities and Stockholders' Equity		$269,920

Additional information about the company is as follows:

- Expected sales for April and May are $240,000 and $260,000, respectively. All sales are made on account.
- The monthly collection pattern from the month of sale forward is 50 percent, 48 percent, and 2 percent uncollectible. Accounts Receivable and the Allowance for Uncollectibles reflect only accounts for March.
- Cost of goods sold is 65 percent of sales.
- Purchases each month are 60 percent of the current month's sales and 30 percent of the next month's projected sales. All purchases are paid for in full in the month following purchase.
- Dividends of $20,000 will be declared and paid in April 2014.
- Selling and administrative expenses each month are $43,000, of which $8,000 is depreciation.
- Investments and borrowings must be made in $1,000 amounts.

a. What were March 2014 budgeted sales?
b. What will be budgeted cash collections for April 2014?
c. What will be the Merchandise Inventory balance at April 30, 2014?
d. What will be the projected balance in the Retained Earnings account at April 30, 2014?
e. If the company wishes to maintain a minimum cash balance of $16,000, how much will be available for investment, or be borrowed at the end of April 2014?

57. **LO.3 & LO.4 (Comprehensive budgets)** Shredder Manufacturing has the following projected unit sales (at $18 per unit) for four months of operations:

January	25,000
February	30,000
March	32,000
April	35,000

Twenty-five percent of the customers are expected to pay in the month of sale and take a 3 percent discount; 70 percent of the customers are expected to pay in the month following sale. The remaining 5 percent will never pay.

It takes two pounds of raw material (costing $0.75 per pound) to produce a unit of product. In January, no raw material is in beginning inventories, but management wants to end each month with enough material for 20 percent of the next month's production. (April's production is assumed to be 34,000 units.) Shredder Manufacturing pays for 60 percent of its material purchases in the month of purchase and 40 percent in the following month.

Each unit of product requires 0.5 hours of labor time. Labor is paid $15 per hour and is paid in the same month as worked. Overhead is estimated to be $2 per unit plus $25,000 per month (including depreciation of $12,000). Overhead costs are paid as incurred.

Shredder will begin January with no Work in Process or Finished Goods Inventory. Inventory policy for these two accounts is set at zero ending WIP and 25 percent of the following month's sales for FG.

a. Prepare a sales budget for January, February, and March.
b. Prepare a production budget for January, February, and March.
c. Prepare a purchases budget for January, February, and March.
d. Prepare a direct labor budget for January, February, and March.
e. Prepare an overhead budget for January, February, and March.
f. Prepare a cash receipts schedule for sales and a cash payments schedule for material purchased.

58. **LO.4 & LO.5 (Cash budget; budgeted income statement)** Davide's Arrangements purchases, wholesales, and retails fresh flowers. Company estimates reveal the following for the first three months of the company's 2014 fiscal year:

	Purchases	Sales
June	$132,000	$204,000
July	116,000	184,000
August	160,000	232,000

Davide's pays 60 percent of any month's purchases in the month of purchase, receiving a 2 percent discount on those payments. The remaining amount is paid in the following month, with no discount given. Other monthly payments for expenses are $48,000 plus 12 percent of sales revenue. Depreciation is $8,000 per month. Davide's maintains a minimum cash balance of $28,000. Borrowings and repayments must be made in $1,000 amounts.

All sales transactions are on credit. Experience indicates the following expected collection pattern for credit sales: 25 percent in the month of sale, 60 percent in the month following the sale, and 15 percent in the second month following the sale. The company has no debt other than what is currently owed for purchases on account.

a. Calculate the July 31 balances for Accounts Receivable and Accounts Payable.
b. Calculate the expected total cash collections in August.
c. Calculate the expected total cash disbursements in August.
d. Prepare a cash budget for August, assuming that the beginning balance of cash was $28,470.
e. Prepare a budgeted income statement for August. Assume an average gross profit rate of 45 percent and ignore income taxes.
f. Explain how and why inventory management must be different for perishable commodities than for nonperishable commodities.

59. **LO.5 (Budgeted income statement and balance sheet)** The projected October 31, 2014, balance sheet for Blanco Co. follows:

ASSETS	
Cash	$ 28,000,000
Accounts Receivable (net of Allowance for Uncollectibles of $3,000,000)	57,000,000
Inventory	52,500,000
Property, Plant, and Equipment (net of Accumulated Depreciation of $37,500,000)	112,500,000
Total Assets	$250,000,000
LIABILITIES AND STOCKHOLDERS' EQUITY	
Accounts Payable	$165,000,000
Common Stock	120,000,000
Retained Earnings (deficit)	(35,000,000)
Total Liabilities and Stockholders' Equity	$250,000,000

Additional information is as follows:

- Sales for November and December are budgeted at $330,000,000 and $360,000,000, respectively.
- Collections are expected to be 70 percent in the month of sale, 28 percent in the following month, and 2 percent uncollectible.
- The company's gross profit is projected at 30 percent of sales.

- Purchases each month are 70 percent of the following month's projected sales. Purchases are paid in full in the month following the purchase.
- Other monthly cash expenses are $46,500,000. Monthly depreciation is $15,000,000.

a. Prepare a budgeted income statement for November 2014.
b. Prepare a budgeted balance sheet at November 30, 2014.
c. Describe any special problems this company may encounter because of its weak balance sheet. Recommend actions the firm might take to improve the balance sheet.

60. **LO.5 (Budgeted results)** GJO Corp. manufactures decorative, high-quality nutcrackers. Selling price of a nutcracker is full production cost plus 25 percent (rounded to the nearest dollar). Variable production cost is $55 per unit, and total fixed costs are $2,600,000. Fixed manufacturing costs are 80 percent of total fixed costs and are allocated to the product based on the number of units produced. Variable selling and administrative costs are 8 percent of sales. Variable and fixed costs are expected to increase by 15 and 7.5 percent, respectively, next year. Estimated production and sales are 400,000 units.

a. What is the expected full production cost per unit of GJO Corp.'s nutcrackers for next year?
b. What is the product's expected selling price?
c. What is budgeted income before tax using the selling price computed in (b)?
d. What is the required selling price (rounded to the nearest dollar) for the company to earn income before tax equal to 25 percent of sales?

61. **LO.2-LO.5 (Master budget preparation)** Kalogridis Corp. manufactures industrial dye. The company is preparing its 2014 master budget and has presented you with the following information:

a. The projected December 31, 2013, balance sheet for the company is as follows:

Assets			Liabilities		
Cash		$ 5,080	Notes Payable		$ 25,000
Accounts Receivable		26,500	Accounts Payable		2,148
Raw Material Inventory		800	Dividends Payable		10,000
Finished Goods Inventory		2,104	Total Liabilities		$ 37,148
Prepaid Insurance		1,200	Common Stock	$100,000	
Building	$300,000		Paid-in Capital	50,000	
Accum. Depreciation	(20,000)	280,000	Retained Earnings	128,536	278,536
Total Assets		$315,684	Total Liabilities and Stockholders' Equity		$315,684

b. The Accounts Receivable balance at 12/31/13 represents the remaining balances of November and December credit sales. Sales were $70,000 and $65,000, respectively, in those two months.

c. Estimated sales in gallons of dye for January through May 2014 are as follows:

January	8,000
February	10,000
March	15,000
April	12,000
May	11,000

Each gallon of dye sells for $12.

d. The collection pattern for accounts receivable is as follows: 70 percent in the month of sale, 20 percent in the first month after the sale, and 10 percent in the second month after the sale. Kalogridis Corp. expects no bad debts and gives no cash discounts.

e. Each gallon of dye has the following standard quantities and costs for direct material and direct labor:

1.2 gallons of direct material (some evaporation occurs during processing) × $0.80 per gallon	$0.96
0.5 hour of direct labor × $6 per hour	3.00

f. Variable overhead (VOH) is applied to the product on a machine-hour basis. Processing one gallon of dye takes five hours of machine time. The variable overhead rate is $0.06 per machine hour; VOH consists entirely of utility costs. Total annual fixed overhead is $120,000; it is applied at $1 per gallon based on an expected annual capacity of 120,000 gallons. Fixed overhead per year is composed of the following costs:

Salaries	$78,000
Utilities	12,000
Insurance—factory	2,400
Depreciation—factory	27,600

Fixed overhead is incurred evenly throughout the year.

g. There is no beginning Work in Process Inventory. All work in process is completed in the period in which it is started. Raw Material Inventory at the beginning of the year consists of 1,000 gallons of direct material at a standard cost of $0.80 per gallon. There are 400 gallons of dye in Finished Goods Inventory at the beginning of the year carried at a standard cost of $5.26 per gallon: direct material, $0.96; direct labor, $3.00; variable overhead, $0.30; and fixed overhead, $1.00.

h. Accounts Payable relates solely to raw material and is paid 60 percent in the month of purchase and 40 percent in the month after purchase. No discounts are received for prompt payment.

i. The dividend will be paid in January 2014.

j. A new piece of equipment costing $9,000 will be purchased on March 1, 2014. Payment of 80 percent will be made in March and 20 percent in April. The equipment has a useful life of three years, will have no salvage value, and will be placed into service on March 1.

k. The note payable has a 12 percent interest rate; interest is paid at the end of each month. The principal of the note is repaid as cash is available to do so.

l. Kalogridis Corp.'s management has set a minimum cash balance at $5,000. Investments and borrowings are made in even $100 amounts. Interest on any borrowings is expected to be 12 percent per year, and investments will earn 4 percent per year.

m. The ending Finished Goods Inventory should include 5 percent of the next month's sales. This situation will not be true at the beginning of 2014 due to a miscalculation in sales for December. The ending inventory of raw materials also should be 5 percent of the next month's needs.

n. Selling and administrative costs per month are as follows: salaries, $25,000; rent, $7,000; and utilities, $800. These costs are paid in cash as they are incurred.

o. The company's tax rate is 35 percent. (Round to the nearest dollar.)

Prepare a master budget for each month of the first quarter of 2014 and pro forma financial statements as of the end of the first quarter of 2014.

62. **LO.2-LO.5 (Comprehensive)** Clarenville Kitchen Products produces and sells upscale mixers and breadmakers. In October 2013, Clarenville's budget department gathered the following data to meet budget requirements for 2014.

2014 PROJECTED SALES

Product	Units	Price
Mixers	60,000	$ 90
Breadmakers	40,000	140

2014 INVENTORIES (UNITS)

Product	Expected 1/1/14	Desired 12/31/14
Mixers	15,000	20,000
Breadmakers	4,000	5,000

To produce one unit of each product, the following major internal components are used (in addition to the plastic housing for products, which is subcontracted in a subsequent operation):

Component	Mixer	Breadmaker
Motor	1	1
Beater	2	4
Fuse	2	3

Projected data for 2014 with respect to components are as follows:

	Anticipated Purchase Price	Expected Inventory 1/1/14	Desired Inventory 12/31/14
Motor	$18.00	2,000	3,600 units
Beater	1.75	21,000	24,000 units
Fuse	2.40	6,000	7,500 units

Projected direct labor requirements for 2014 and rates are as follows:

Product	Hours per Unit	Rate per Hour
Mixers	2	$ 8
Breadmakers	3	10

Overhead is applied at a rate of $7.50 per direct labor hour.

Based on these projections and budget requirements for 2014 for mixers and breadmakers, prepare the following budgets for 2014:

a. Sales budget (in dollars)
b. Production budget (in units)
c. Internal components purchases budget (in units and dollars)
d. Direct labor budget (in dollars)
e. The total production cost, excluding subsequent departments, per mixer and per breadmaker

63. **LO.3, LO.5, & LO.6 (Revising and analyzing an operating budget)** Attala Co., a division of Jackson Industries (JI), offers consulting services to clients for a fee. JI's corporate management is pleased with the performance of Attala Co. for the first nine months of the current year and has recommended that Attala Co.'s division manager, Jason Newport, submit a revised forecast for the remaining quarter because the division has exceeded the annual year-to-date plan by 20 percent of operating income. An unexpected increase in billed hour volume over the original plan is the main reason for this gain in income. The original operating budget for the first three quarters for Attala Co. is as follows:

2014 OPERATING BUDGET

	1st Quarter	2nd Quarter	3rd Quarter	Total 9 Months
Consulting fees				
Management consulting	$ 315,000	$ 315,000	$ 315,000	$ 945,000
EDP consulting	421,875	421,875	421,875	1,265,625
Total	$ 736,875	$ 736,875	$ 736,875	$ 2,210,625
Other revenue	10,000	10,000	10,000	30,000
Total	$ 746,875	$ 746,875	$ 746,875	$ 2,240,625
Expenses				
Consultant salaries	$(386,750)	$(386,750)	$(386,750)	$(1,160,250)
Travel and entertainment	(45,625)	(45,625)	(45,625)	(136,875)
Administrative	(100,000)	(100,000)	(100,000)	(300,000)
Depreciation	(40,000)	(40,000)	(40,000)	(120,000)
Corporate allocation	(50,000)	(50,000)	(50,000)	(150,000)
Total	$(622,375)	$(622,375)	$(622,375)	$(1,867,125)
Operating income	$ 124,500	$ 124,500	$ 124,500	$ 373,500

When comparing the actuals for the first three quarters to the original plan, Newport analyzed the variances and will reflect the following information in his revised forecast for the fourth quarter.

The division currently has 25 consultants on staff, 10 for management consulting and 15 for EDP consulting, and has hired 3 additional management consultants to start work at the beginning of the fourth quarter to meet the increased client demand.

The hourly billing rates for consulting revenues will remain at $90 for each management consultant and $75 for each EDP consultant. However, due to the favorable increase in billing hour volume when compared to the plan, the hours for each consultant will be increased by 50 hours per quarter. New employees are equally as capable as current employees and their time will be billed at the same rates.

The annual budgeted salaries and actual salaries, paid monthly, are $50,000 for a management consultant and 8 percent less for an EDP consultant. Corporate management has approved a merit increase of 10 percent at the beginning of the fourth quarter for all 25 existing consultants, but the new consultants will be compensated at the planned rate.

The planned salary expense includes a provision for employee fringe benefits amounting to 30 percent of the annual salaries; however, the improvement of some corporate-wide employee programs will increase the fringe benefit allocation to 40 percent.

The original plan assumes a fixed hourly rate for travel and other related expenses for each billing hour of consulting. These expenses are not reimbursed by the client, and the previously determined hourly rate has proven to be adequate to cover these costs.

Other revenues are derived from temporary rentals and interest income and remain unchanged for the fourth quarter.

Administrative expenses are 7 percent below the plan; this 7 percent savings on fourth-quarter expenses will be reflected in the revised plan.

Depreciation for office equipment and computers will stay constant at the projected straight-line rate.

Due to the favorable experience for the first three quarters and the division's increased ability to absorb costs, JI corporate management has increased the corporate expense allocation by 50 percent.

a. Prepare a revised operating budget for the fourth quarter for Attala Co. that Jason Newport will present to Jackson Industries. Be sure to furnish supporting calculations for all revised revenue and expense amounts.
b. Discuss the reasons that an organization would prepare a revised forecast.
c. Discuss your feelings about the 50 percent increase in corporate expense allocations. CPA ADAPTED

64. **LO.3, LO.5, & LO.6 (Preparing and analyzing a budget)** Norton Weymer & Collins, LLP, a local accounting firm, has a formal budgeting system. The firm has five partners, two managers, four seniors, two secretaries, and two bookkeepers. The budgeting process has a bottom-line focus; that is, the budget and planning process continues to iterate and evolve until an acceptable budgeted net income is obtained. The determination of an acceptable level of net income is based on two factors: (1) the amount of salary the partners could generate if they were employed elsewhere and (2) a reasonable return on the partners' investment in the firm's net assets.

For 2014, after careful consideration of alternative employment opportunities, the partners agreed that the best alternative employment would generate the following salaries:

Partner 1	$150,000
Partner 2	225,000
Partner 3	110,000
Partner 4	90,000
Partner 5	125,000
Total	$700,000

The second input to determining the desired net income level is more complex. This part of the desired net income is based on the value of the net assets owned by the accounting firm. The partners have identified two major categories of assets: tangible and intangible. The partners have agreed that the net tangible assets are worth $230,000. The intangible assets, consisting mostly of the accounting practice itself, are worth 1.1 times gross fees billed in 2013, which totaled $1,615,000. The partners have also agreed that a reasonable rate of return on the net assets of the accounting firm is 12 percent. Thus, the partners' desired net income from return on investment is as follows:

Tangible assets	$ 230,000
Intangible assets ($1,615,000 × 110 percent)	1,776,500
Total investment	$2,006,500
Rate of return	× 0.12
Required dollar return	$ 240,780

The experience of the accounting firm indicates that other operating costs are incurred as follows:

Fixed expenses (per year)	
Salaries (other than partners)	$300,000
Overhead	125,000
Variable expenses	
Overhead	15 percent of gross billings
Client service	5 percent of gross billings

Source: Adapted from Jerry S. Huss, "Better Budgeting for CPA Firms," *Journal of Accountancy* (November 1977), pp. 65–72. Reprinted with permission from the *Journal of Accountancy*.

a. Determine the minimum level of gross billings that would allow the partners to realize their net income objective. Prepare a budget of costs and revenues at that level.
b. If the partners believe that the level of billings you have projected in (a) is not feasible given the time constraints at the partner, manager, and senior levels, what changes can they make to the budget to preserve the desired level of net income?

65. **LO.6 (Budgeting internationally; writing)** Preparing budgets for a multinational organization is significantly more complex than doing so for a solely domestic organization. What costs might managers find in budgets for international companies that might not commonly be included (or included at similar amounts) in budgets for domestic companies?

9

Break-Even Point and Cost-Volume-Profit Analysis

LEARNING OBJECTIVES

After completing this chapter, you should be able to answer the following questions:

1. What is the break-even point (BEP), and why is it important?
2. How is the BEP determined, and what methods are used to identify BEP?
3. What is cost-volume-profit (CVP) analysis, and how do companies use CVP information in decision making?
4. How do break-even and CVP analysis differ for single-product and multiproduct firms?
5. How are margin of safety and operating leverage concepts used in business?
6. What are the underlying assumptions of CVP analysis?

Formula Approach to Breakeven

The formula approach to break-even analysis uses an algebraic equation to calculate the BEP. In this analysis, sales volume, rather than production activity, is the focus of the relevant range. The equation represents the variable costing income statement and shows the relationships among revenue, fixed cost, variable cost, volume, and profit as follows:

$$R(X) - VC(X) - FC = P$$

where

$$\begin{aligned} R &= \text{revenue (selling price) per unit} \\ X &= \text{volume (number of units)} \\ R(X) &= \text{total revenue} \\ VC &= \text{variable cost per unit} \\ VC(X) &= \text{total variable cost} \\ FC &= \text{total fixed cost} \\ P &= \text{total profit} \end{aligned}$$

Because this equation simply represents an income statement, P can be set equal to zero to solve for the break-even point. At the point where P = \$0, total revenue equals total cost, and break-even point (BEP) in units can be found by solving the equation for X.

$$\begin{aligned} R(X) - VC(X) - FC &= \$0 \\ R(X) - VC(X) &= FC \\ (R - VC)(X) &= FC \\ X &= FC \div (R - VC) \\ X &= FC \div CM \end{aligned}$$

Break-even volume equals total fixed cost divided by contribution margin per unit (revenue per unit minus the variable cost per unit). Using the Calispell information given in Exhibit 9.1 (\$40 selling price per clock, \$29 variable cost per clock, and \$4,400,000 of total fixed cost), the company's BEP is calculated as

$$\begin{aligned} \$40(X) - \$29(X) - \$4{,}400{,}000 &= \$0 \\ \$40(X) - \$29(X) &= \$4{,}400{,}000 \\ \$11(X) &= \$4{,}400{,}000 \\ X &= \$4{,}400{,}000 \div \$11 \\ X &= 400{,}000 \text{ clocks} \end{aligned}$$

BEP can be expressed in either units or dollars of revenue. One way to convert a unit BEP to dollars is to multiply the number of units by the selling price per unit. For Calispell, the BEP in sales dollars is \$16,000,000 (400,000 clocks × \$40 per clock).

Another method of computing BEP in sales dollars uses **contribution margin ratio (CM%)**, which is calculated as contribution margin divided by revenue. This ratio indicates the proportion of revenue remaining after variable cost has been deducted from sales, or that portion of the revenue dollar that can be used to cover fixed cost and provide profit. The CM% can be calculated using either per-unit or total revenue and variable cost information. Dividing total fixed cost by the CM% gives the BEP in sales dollars.

For Calispell Company, the break-even sales dollars are

$$\begin{aligned} X &= FC \div [(R - VC) \div R] \\ X &= \$4{,}400{,}000 \div [(\$40 - \$29) \div \$40] \\ X &= \$4{,}400{,}000 \div (\$11 \div \$40) \\ X &= \$4{,}400{,}000 \div 0.275 \\ X &= \$16{,}000{,}000 \end{aligned}$$

BEP in units can be determined by dividing the BEP in sales dollars by the unit selling price, or

$$\begin{aligned} X &= \$16{,}000{,}000 \div \$40 \\ X &= 400{,}000 \text{ clocks} \end{aligned}$$

The CM% allows the BEP to be determined even if unit selling price and unit variable cost are not known. Subtracting the contribution margin ratio from 100 percent gives the **variable cost ratio (VC%)**, which represents variable cost as a proportion of revenue.[3]

Graphing Approach to Breakeven

Although solutions to BEP problems can be determined using equations, sometimes the information is more effectively conveyed to managers in a visual format. Exhibit 9.2 graphically presents each income statement item for Calispell's original budgeted data (see Exhibit 9.1) to provide visual representations of revenue, cost, and contribution margin behaviors.

Exhibit 9.2 Calispell Company Graphing Presentation of Income Statement Items

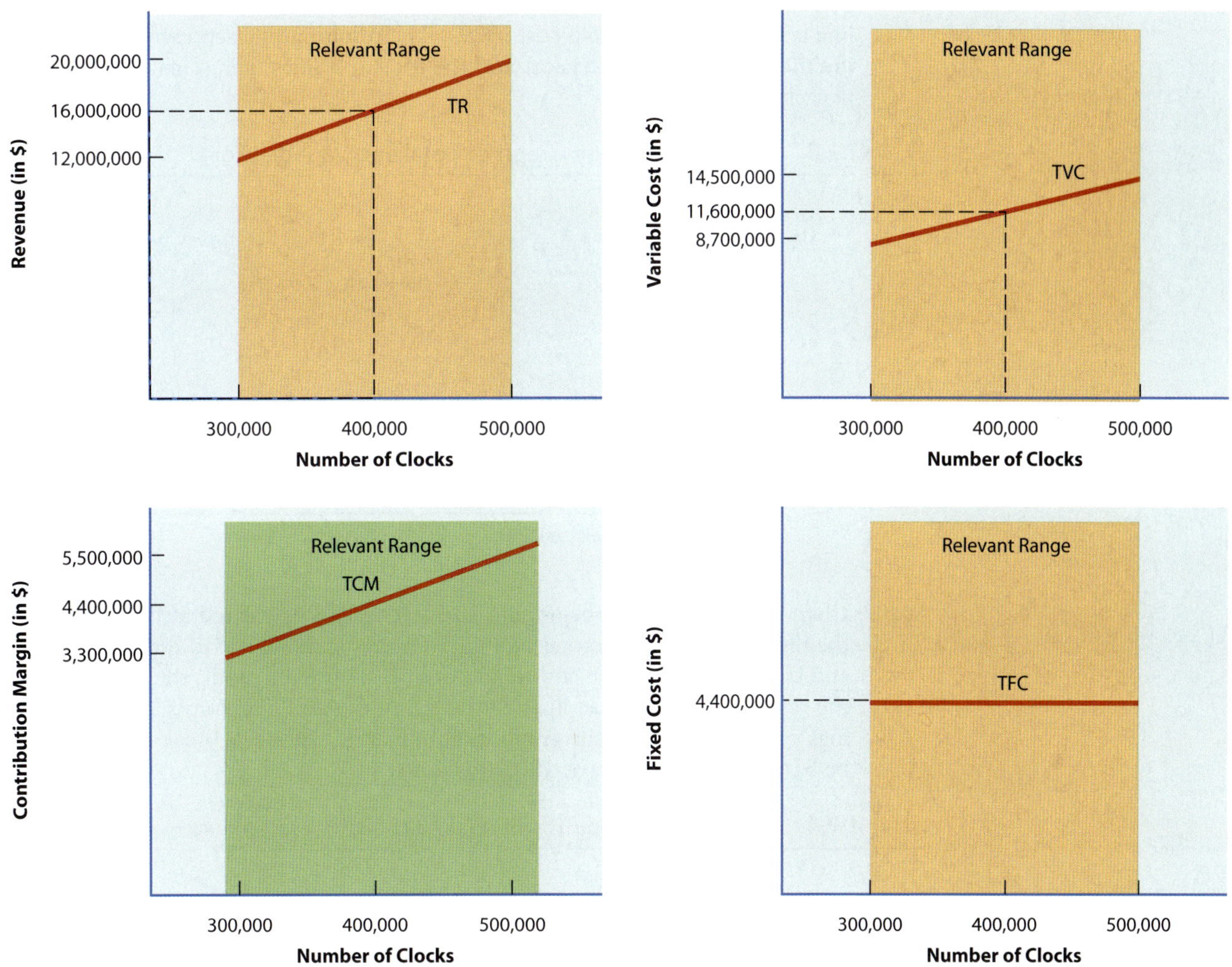

TR = Total Revenue TCM = Total Contribution Margin TVC = Total Variable Cost TFC = Total Fixed Cost

Note: Linear functions are always assumed for total revenue, total variable cost, and total fixed cost. These functions are reflected in the basic assumptions given on pp. 371–372.

[3] Derivation of the contribution margin ratio formula is as follows:

$$\text{Sales} - [(\text{VC\%})(\text{Sales})] = \text{FC}$$
$$(1 - \text{VC\%})\text{Sales} = \text{FC}$$
$$\text{Sales} = \text{FC} \div (1 - \text{VC\%})$$
$$\text{because } (1 - \text{VC\%}) = \text{CM\%}$$
$$\text{then Sales} = \text{FC} \div \text{CM\%}$$

where VC% = variable cost ratio or variable cost as a percentage of sales,
CM% = contribution margin ratio or contribution margin as a percentage of sales

Thus, the VC% plus the CM% is equal to 100 percent.

The graphs shown in Exhibit 9.2 illustrate individual behaviors but are not very useful for determining the relationships among the income statement amounts. A **break-even chart** can be prepared to graph the relationships among revenue, volume, and cost. The BEP on a break-even chart is located at the point where the total cost and total revenue lines intersect. Two approaches to graphing can be used to prepare break-even charts: the traditional approach and the profit-volume graph approach.

Traditional Approach The traditional break-even graph shows the relationships among revenue, cost, and profit/loss, but does not show contribution margin. A traditional break-even graph for Calispell Company is prepared by completing the following steps.

Step 1: As shown in Exhibit 9.3, label each axis and graph the total cost and fixed cost lines. The fixed cost line is drawn parallel to the *x*-axis (volume). The variable cost line begins where the fixed cost line intersects the *y*-axis. The slope of the variable cost line is the per-unit variable cost ($29). The resulting line represents total cost. The distance between the fixed cost and the total cost lines represents total variable cost at each activity level.

Exhibit 9.3 Calispell Company Graph of Total and Variable Cost

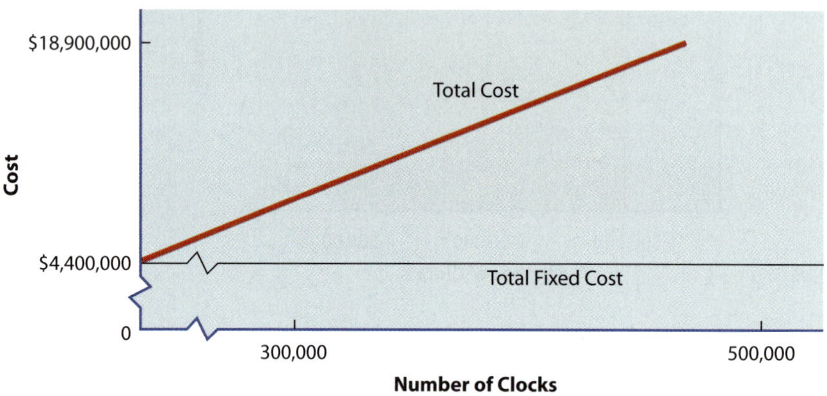

Step 2: Chart the revenue line, beginning at $0. The BEP is located at the intersection of the revenue line and the total cost line. The vertical distance to the right of the BEP and between the revenue and total cost lines represents profit; the distance between the revenue and total cost lines to the left of the BEP represents loss. If exact readings could be taken on the graph in Exhibit 9.4. Calispell's break-even point would be $16,000,000 of sales, or 400,000 clocks.

Exhibit 9.4 Calispell Company Traditional Approach of Graphing

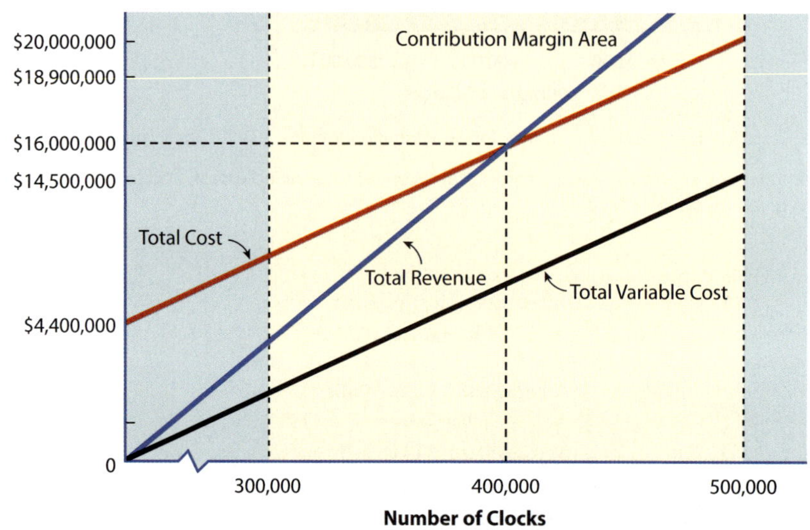

Profit-Volume Graph The **profit-volume (PV) graph** depicts the profit or loss associated with each sales level. The horizontal, or *x*, axis on the PV graph represents sales volume; the vertical, or *y*, axis represents dollars of profit or loss. Amounts shown above the *x*-axis are positive and represent profits; amounts shown below the *x*-axis are negative and represent losses.

Two points can be located on the graph: total fixed cost and break-even point. Total fixed cost is shown on the *y*-axis below the sales volume line as a negative amount. If no products were sold, the fixed cost would still be incurred and a loss of that amount would result. Location of the BEP in units may be determined algebraically and is shown at the point where the profit line intersects the *x*-axis; at that point, there is no profit or loss. The amount of profit or loss for any sales volume can be read from the *y*-axis. The slope of the profit (diagonal) line is determined by the unit contribution margin ($11), and the points on the line represent the contribution margin earned at each volume level. The line shows that no profit is earned until total contribution margin covers total fixed cost.

The PV graph for Calispell Company is shown in Exhibit 9.5. The diagonal line reflects profits (or losses) at any level of volume. For example, at the BEP of 400,000 clocks, the line crosses the horizontal line to indicate zero profit or loss. The original Exhibit 9.1 income statement data indicating a profit of $2,200,000 at a sales volume of 600,000 clocks is also visible on the graph.

Exhibit 9.5 Calispell Company Profit-Volume Graph

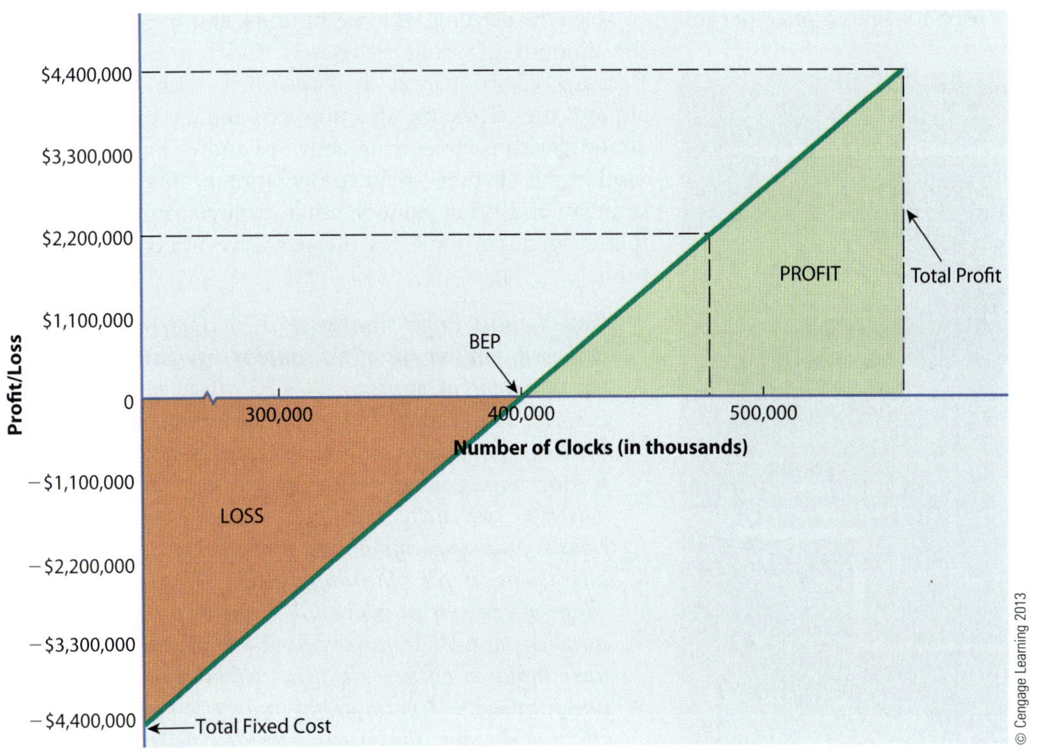

The graphing approach to breakeven provides a detailed visual display of the BEP. It does not, however, provide a precise solution because exact points cannot be determined on a graph. A definitive computation of the BEP can be found algebraically using the formula approach or a computer software application. A third approach to illustrating breakeven is the income statement approach.

Income Statement Approach

The income statement approach to finding the BEP allows accountants to prepare budgeted statements using available revenue and cost information. Income statements can also be used to prove the accuracy of computations made using the BEP formulas or graphs.

Because the formula, graphing, and income statement approaches are based on the same relationships, each should align with the other.

The BEP provides a starting point for planning future operations. Managers want to earn operating profit rather than simply cover costs. Substituting an amount other than zero for the profit (P) term in the break-even formula converts break-even analysis to cost-volume-profit analysis.

CVP ANALYSIS

3 What is cost-volume-profit (CVP) analysis, and how do companies use CVP information in decision making?

Because profit cannot be achieved until the BEP is reached, the starting point of CVP analysis is the break-even point. Examining shifts in cost and volume and the resulting effects on profits is called **cost-volume-profit (CVP) analysis**. CVP analysis can be used to calculate the sales volume necessary to achieve a target profit, stated as either a fixed or variable amount on a before- or after-tax basis.

Managers use CVP analysis to effectively plan and control by concentrating on the relationships among revenues, cost, volume changes, taxes, and profit. The CVP model can be expressed mathematically or graphically. The CVP model considers all costs, regardless of whether they are product, period, variable, or fixed. The analysis is usually performed on a companywide basis. The same basic CVP model and calculations can be applied to a single- or multiproduct business.

CVP analysis requires substitution of known amounts in the formula to solve for an unknown amount. The formula mirrors the income statement when known amounts are used for selling price per unit, variable cost per unit, volume of units, and fixed cost to find the amount of profit generated under given conditions. Because CVP analysis is concerned with relationships among the elements affecting continuing operations, in contrast with nonrecurring activities and events, profits—as used in this chapter—refer to operating profits before extraordinary and other nonoperating, nonrecurring items. The following quote indicates the pervasive utility of the CVP model:

> *Cost Volume Profit analysis (CVP) is one of the most hallowed, and yet one of the simplest, analytical tools in management accounting. [CVP] allows managers to examine the possible impacts of a wide range of strategic decisions [in] such crucial areas as pricing policies, product mixes, market expansions or contractions, outsourcing contracts, idle plant usage, discretionary expense planning, and a variety of other important considerations in the planning process. Given the broad range of contexts in which CVP can be used, the basic simplicity of CVP is quite remarkable. Armed with just three inputs of data—sales price, variable cost per unit, and fixed cost—a managerial analyst can evaluate the effects of decisions that potentially alter the basic nature of a firm.*[4]

An important application of CVP analysis allows managers to set a desired target profit and focus on the relationships between it and other known income statement amounts to find an unknown. One common unknown in such applications is the sales volume that is needed to generate a particular profit amount.

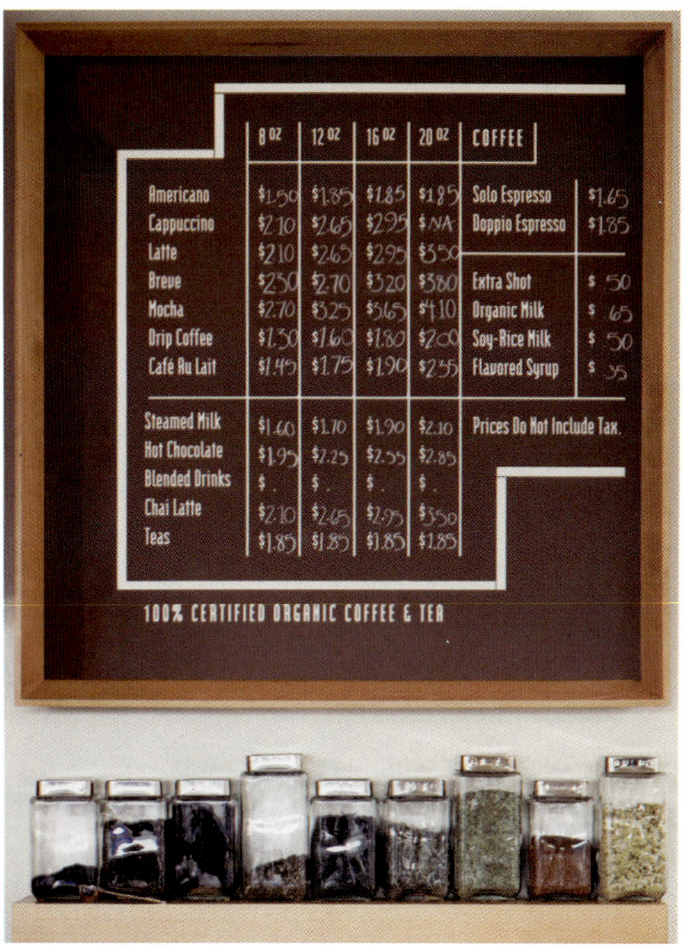

Corbis/Jupiter Images

A product's selling price is often market-related rather than being a management decision variable.

[4] Flora Guidry, James O. Horrigan, and Cathy Craycraft, "CVP Analysis: A New Look," *Journal of Managerial Issues* (Spring 1998), pp. 74ff.

In many organizations, selling price is often market determined and not a management decision variable. Additionally, selling price and volume are often directly related, and fixed costs are assumed to be constant within a period. Thus, variable cost is the amount in a CVP computation that can most likely be affected in the short-run. Managers often use CVP analysis to determine how high variable cost can rise and still allow the company to generate a desired amount of profit. Variable cost can be affected by modifying product specifications or material quality as well as by being more efficient or effective in the production, service, and/or distribution processes.

The following examples continue using the Calispell Company data with different amounts of target profit.

Fixed Amount of Profit

Because contribution margin represents the sales dollars remaining after variable cost is covered, each dollar of CM generated by product sales goes first to cover fixed cost and then to produce profits. After the BEP is reached, each dollar of CM is a dollar of before-tax profit.

Before Tax Profit can be treated in the break-even formula as an additional cost to be covered. Inclusion of a target profit changes the break-even formula to a CVP equation.

$$R(X) - VC(X) - FC = PBT$$
$$R(X) - VC(X) = FC + PBT$$
$$X = (FC + PBT) \div (R - VC)$$
or
$$X = (FC + PBT) \div CM$$

where PBT = fixed amount of profit before tax

Assume that Calispell's management desires a $3,300,000 before-tax profit. The calculations in Exhibit 9.6 show that to achieve this profit before tax, the company must sell 700,000 clocks and generate $28,000,000 of revenue.

Exhibit 9.6 Calispell Company CVP Analysis—Fixed Amount of Profit before Tax

In units:

Profit before tax (PBT) desired = $3,300,000

$$R(X) - VC(X) = FC + PBT$$
$$CM(X) = FC + PBT$$
$$(\$40 - \$29)X = \$4,400,000 + \$3,300,000$$
$$\$11X = \$7,700,000$$
$$X = \$7,700,000 \div \$11 = \underline{\underline{700,000}} \text{ clocks}$$

In sales dollars:

$$Sales = (FC + PBT) \div CM\%$$
$$Sales = \$7,700,000 \div 0.275^*$$
$$Sales = \underline{\underline{\$28,000,000}}$$

*From Exhibit 9.1.

After Tax In choosing a target profit amount, managers must recognize that income tax represents a significant influence on business decision making. A company wanting a particular amount of profit after tax must first determine, given the applicable tax rate, the

Thus, the following relationship exists:

$$R(X) - VC(X) = FC + [P_uAT \div (1 - TR)](X)$$
$$CM(X) = FC + P_uBT(X)$$
$$CM(X) - P_uBT(X) = FC$$
$$X = FC \div (CM - P_uBT)$$

Calispell's managers desire to earn an after-tax profit of 10 percent of revenue and the company has a 25 percent tax rate. The necessary sales in units and dollars are given in Exhibit 9.9.

Exhibit 9.9 Calispell Company CVP Analysis—Set Amount of Profit per Unit after Tax

In units:

$$P_uAT \text{ desired} = 10\% \text{ of revenue; tax rate} = 25\%$$
$$P_uAT = 0.10(\$40)$$
$$P_uAT = \$4$$
$$P_uBT = \$4 \div (1.00 - 0.25)$$
$$P_uBT = \$4 \div 0.75$$
$$P_uBT = \$5.33 \text{ (rounded)}$$

$$CM(X) - P_uBT(X) = FC$$
$$\$11.00X - \$5.33X = \$4,400,000$$
$$\$5.67X = \$4,400,000$$
$$X = \$4,400,000 \div \$5.67$$
$$X = 776,014 \text{ clocks (rounded)}$$

	Per Clock	Percentage
Selling price	$ 40.00	100.00
Variable cost	(29.00)	(72.50)
Set amount of profit before tax	(5.33)	(13.33) (rounded)
"Adjusted" contribution margin	$ 5.67	14.17

Sales = FC ÷ "Adjusted" CM ratio

Sales = $4,400,000 ÷ 0.1417

Sales = $31,051,517 (rounded)

Exhibit 9.10 (p. 365) proves each of the computations made in Exhibits 9.6 through 9.9 for Calispell Company. The answers provided by break-even or CVP analysis are valid only in relation to specific selling price and cost relationships. Any change that occurs in the company's selling price or cost structure will cause a change in the BEP or in the sales needed to obtain a desired profit. However, the effects of revenue and cost changes on a company's BEP or sales volume can be determined through incremental analysis.

Incremental Analysis for Short-Run Changes

The break-even point can increase or decrease, depending on revenue and cost changes. Other things being equal, the BEP will increase if there is an increase in the total fixed cost or a decrease in the unit (or percentage) contribution margin. A decrease in contribution margin could arise because of a reduction in selling price, an increase in variable cost per unit, or a combination of the two. The BEP will decrease if total fixed cost decreases or unit (or percentage) contribution margin increases. A change in the BEP will also cause a shift in total profit or loss at any level of activity.

Incremental analysis is a process that focuses on factors that change only from one course of action or decision to another. In CVP situations, incremental analysis is focused on revenue, cost, and/or volume changes. Following are some examples of changes that

Exhibit 9.10 Calispell Company's Income Statement Approach to CVP— Proof of Computations

Previous computations:
Break-even point: 400,000 clocks
Fixed profit ($3,300,000) before tax: 700,000 clocks
Fixed profit ($3,300,000) after tax: 800,000 clocks
Set amount of profit (15% on revenues) before tax: 880,000 clocks
Set amount of profit (10% on revenues) after tax: 776,014 clocks
R = $40 per clock; VC = $29 per clock; FC = $4,400,000
Tax rate = 25% for Exhibits 9.3 and 9.5

Clocks Sold	Basic Data 400,000	Exh. 9.6 700,000	Exh. 9.7 800,000	Exh. 9.8 880,000	Exh. 9.9 776,014
Sales	$ 16,000,000	$ 28,000,000	$ 32,000,000	$ 35,200,000	$ 31,040,560
Total variable cost	(11,600,000)	(20,300,000)	(23,200,000)	(25,520,000)	(22,504,406)
Contribution margin	$ 4,400,000	$ 7,700,000	$ 8,800,000	$ 9,680,000	$ 8,536,154
Total fixed cost	(4,400,000)	(4,400,000)	(4,400,000)	(4,400,000)	(4,400,000)
Profit before tax	$ 0	$ 3,300,000	$ 4,400,000	$ 5,280,000[a]	$ 4,136,154
Tax (25%)			(1,100,000)		(1,034,039)
Profit after tax (NI)			$ 3,300,000		$ 3,102,115[b]

[a]Desired profit before tax = 15% on revenue; 0.15 × $35,200,000 = $5,280,000.
[b]Desired profit after tax = 10% on revenue; 0.10 × $31,040,560 = $3,104,056 (differs from $3,102,115 only because of rounding error).

could occur in a company and the incremental computations used to determine the effects of those changes on BEP or on profit. In most situations, incremental analysis is sufficient to determine the feasibility of contemplated changes, and a complete income statement need not be prepared. The basic facts presented for Calispell Company in Exhibit 9.1 are continued. All of the following examples use before-tax information to simplify the computations. After-tax analysis would require the application of the (1 − Tax rate) adjustment to all profit figures.

Case 1 Calispell wants to earn a before-tax profit of $2,750,000. How many clocks must the company sell to achieve that profit? The incremental analysis relative to this question addresses the number of clocks above the BEP that must be sold. Because each dollar of contribution margin after BEP is a dollar of profit, the incremental analysis focuses only on the profit desired:

$2,750,000 ÷ $11 = 250,000 clocks above BEP

Because the BEP has already been computed as 400,000 clocks, the company must sell a total of 650,000 clocks.

Case 2 Calispell estimates that spending an additional $425,000 on advertising will result in an additional 50,000 clocks being sold. Should the company incur this extra fixed cost? The contribution margin from the additional clock sales must first cover the additional fixed cost before additional profits can be generated.

Increase in contribution margin (50,000 clocks × $11 CM per clock)	$ 550,000
− Increase in fixed cost	(425,000)
= Net incremental benefit	$ 125,000

Because there is a net incremental profit of $125,000, the company should undertake the advertising campaign.

An alternative computation is to divide the additional fixed cost of $425,000 by the $11 contribution margin. The result indicates that 38,636 clocks (rounded) would be

Exhibit 9.11 Calispell Company CVP Analysis—Multiple Products

Product Cost Information	Clocks	(Percentage)	Clock Wall-Mounting Kits	(Percentage)
Selling price	$ 40	100.0	$10	100
Total variable cost	(29)	(72.5)	(4)	(40)
Contribution margin	$ 11	27.5	$ 6	60

Total fixed cost (FC) = $4,400,000 previous + $514,000 additional = $4,914,000

	Clocks		Clock Wall-Mounting Kits		Total	Percentage
Number of products per bag	3		1			
Revenue per product	$ 40		$10			
Total revenue per "bag"		$120		$10	$130	100
Variable cost per product	(29)		(4)			
Total variable cost per "bag"		(87)		(4)	(91)	(70)
Contribution margin—product	$ 11		$ 6			
Contribution margin—"bag"		$ 33		$ 6	$ 39	30

BEP in units (where B = number of "bags" of products)

CM(B) = FC

$39B = $4,914,000

B = 126,000 bags

Note: Each "bag" consists of 3 clocks and 1 clock wall-mounting kit; therefore, it will take sales of 378,000 clocks and 126,000 clock wall-mounting kits to break even, assuming the constant 3:1 mix.

BEP in sales dollars (where S$ = sales dollars; CM% = weighted average CM per "bag")

S$ = FC ÷ CM%

S$ = $4,914,000 ÷ 0.30

S$ = $16,380,000

Note: The break-even sales dollars also represent the assumed constant sales mix of $120 of clocks to $10 of clock wall-mounting kits to represent a 92.3% to 7.7% ratio (both percentages are rounded). Thus, the company must have $15,120,000 ($16,380,000 × 0.923) in sales of clocks and $1,260,000 in sales of clock wall-mounting kits to break even.

Proof of these computations using the income statement approach:

	Clocks	Clock Wall-Mounting Kits	Total
Sales	$ 15,120,000	$1,260,000	$ 16,380,000
Variable cost	(10,962,000)	(504,000)	(11,466,000)
Contribution margin	$ 4,158,000	$ 756,000	$ 4,914,000
Fixed cost			(4,914,000)
Income before tax			$ 0

The MS calculations allow management to determine how close to a "danger level" the company is operating and, as such, provide an indication of risk. The lower the MS, the more carefully management must watch revenue and control cost to avoid operating losses. At low margins of safety, managers are less likely to take advantage of opportunities that, if incorrectly analyzed or forecasted, could put the company in a loss position.

Exhibit 9.12 Calispell Company's Effects of Product Mix Shift

		Clocks		Clock Wall-Mounting Kits	Total	Percentage
Number of products per bag	2.5		1.5			
Revenue per product	$ 40		$10			
Total revenue per "bag"		$100.00		$15	$115.00	100.0
Variable cost per product	(29)		(4)			
Total variable cost per "bag"		(72.50)		(6)	(78.50)	(68.3)
Contribution margin—product	$ 11		$ 6			
Contribution margin—"bag"		$ 27.50		$ 9	$ 36.50	31.7

BEP in units (where B = number of "bags" of products)

CM(B) = FC

$36.50B = $4,914,000

B = 134,631 bags (rounded up)

Actual results: 126,000 "bags" with a sales mix ratio of 2.5 clocks to 1.5 clock wall-mounting kits; thus, the company sold 315,000 clocks and 189,000 clock wall-mounting kits.

	315,000 Clocks	189,000 Clock Wall-Mounting Kits	Total
Sales	$12,600,000	$1,890,000	$14,490,000
Variable cost	(9,135,000)	(756,000)	(9,891,000)
Contribution margin	$ 3,465,000	$1,134,000	$ 4,599,000
Fixed cost			(4,914,000)
Net loss			$ (315,000)

Exhibit 9.13 Calispell Company's Margin of Safety

In units: 600,000 actual − 400,000 BEP = 200,000 clocks

In sales $: $24,000,000 actual sales − $16,000,000 BEP sales = $8,000,000

As a percentage: 200,000 ÷ 600,000 = 33.33%

or

$8,000,000 ÷ $24,000,000 = 33.33%

Operating Leverage

Another measure that is closely related to the MS and provides useful management information is the company's degree of operating leverage. The relationship between a company's variable and fixed costs is reflected in its **operating leverage**. Typically, highly labor-intensive organizations have high variable cost and low fixed cost; these organizations have low operating leverage.[7]

Conversely, organizations that are highly capital intensive or automated have cost structures that include low variable and high fixed cost, providing high operating leverage. Because variable cost is low relative to selling price, the contribution margin is high.

[7] An exception to this rule is a sports team, which is highly labor intensive, but its labor cost is fixed rather than variable.

However, high fixed cost means that the BEP also tends to be high. If the market determines selling prices, volume has the primary impact on profitability. Greater automation creates such a cost structure and companies become more dependent on volume increases to raise profits. Thus, cost structure strongly influences the degree to which its profits respond to sales volume changes.

Companies with high operating leverage have high contribution margin ratios. Although such companies must establish fairly high sales volumes to initially cover fixed cost, once that cost is covered, each unit sold after breakeven adds significantly to profits. Thus, a small increase in sales can have a major impact on a company's profits.

The **degree of operating leverage (DOL)** measures how a percentage change in sales from the current level will affect company profits. DOL indicates how sensitive the company's profit is to sales volume increases and decreases. The computation for DOL follows.

$$\text{DOL} = \text{CM} \div \text{Profit before tax}$$

This calculation assumes that fixed costs do not increase when sales increase.

Assume that Calispell Company is currently selling 600,000 clocks. The income statement in Exhibit 9.14 reflects this sales level and shows that the company has a DOL of 3.00. If Calispell increases sales by 20 percent, the 60 percent change in profits equals the DOL multiplied by the percentage change in sales or (3.00 × 20%). If sales decrease by the same 20 percent, the impact on profits is a negative 60 percent. These amounts are confirmed in Exhibit 9.14.

Exhibit 9.14 Calispell Company's Degree of Operating Leverage

	Current (600,000 clocks)	20 Percent Increase (720,000 clocks)	20 Percent Decrease (480,000 clocks)
Sales	$ 24,000,000	$ 28,800,000	$ 19,200,000
Variable cost ($29.00 per clock)	(17,400,000)	(20,880,000	(13,920,000)
Contribution margin	$ 6,600,000	$ 7,920,000	$ 5,280,000
Fixed cost	(4,400,000)	(4,400,000)	(4,400,000)
Profit before tax	$ 2,200,000	$ 3,520,000[a]	$ 880,000[b]
Degree of operating leverage = Contribution margin ÷ Profit before tax			
($6,600,000 ÷ $2,200,000)	3.00		
($7,920,000 ÷ $3,520,000)		2.25	
($5,280,000 ÷ 880,000)			6.00

[a]Profit increase = $3,520,000 − $2,200,000 = $1,320,000 (or 60.00% of the original profit).
[b]Profit decrease = $880,000 − $2,200,000 = ($1,320,000) (or −60% of the original profit).

The DOL decreases as sales move upward from the BEP. Thus, when the margin of safety is low, the degree of operating leverage is high. In fact, at the BEP, the DOL is infinite because any increase from zero is an infinite percentage change. If a company is operating close to BEP, each percentage increase in sales can make a dramatic impact on net income. As sales increase from the BEP, margin of safety increases, but the degree of operating leverage declines. The relationship between the MS percentage (MS%) and DOL is as follows:

$$\text{MS\%} = 1 \div \text{DOL}$$
$$\text{DOL} = 1 \div \text{MS\%}$$

This relationship is proved in Exhibit 9.15 using the 600,000-clock sales level information for Calispell. Therefore, if one of the two measures is known, the other can be easily calculated.

Exhibit 9.15 Calispell Company's Margin of Safety and Degree of Operating Leverage Relationship

Break-even sales = 400,000 units; Current sales = 600,000 units

Margin of safety % = Margin of safety in units ÷ Actual sales in units
= [(600,000 – 400,000) ÷ 600,000]
= 0.33, or 33% (rounded)

Degree of operating leverage = Contribution margin ÷ Profit before tax
= $6,600,000 ÷ $2,200,000
= 3

Margin of safety = (1 ÷ DOL) = (1 ÷ 3) = 0.33, or 33% (rounded)

Degree of operating leverage = (1 ÷ MS%) = (1 ÷ 0.33) = 3 (rounded)

UNDERLYING ASSUMPTIONS OF CVP ANALYSIS

6 What are the underlying assumptions of CVP analysis?

CVP analysis is a short-run model that focuses on relationships among selling price, variable cost, fixed cost, volume, and profit. This model is a useful planning tool that can provide information about the impact on profit when changes are made in the cost structure or in the sales level. Although limiting the accuracy of the results, several important but necessary assumptions are made in the CVP model. These assumptions follow:

1. All revenue and variable cost behavior patterns are constant per unit and linear within the relevant range.
2. Total contribution margin (Total revenue – Total variable cost) is linear within the relevant range and increases proportionally with output. This assumption follows directly from assumption 1.
3. Total fixed cost is constant within the relevant range. This assumption, in part, indicates that no capacity additions will be made during the period under consideration.
4. Mixed costs can be accurately separated into fixed and variable elements. Although accuracy of separation can be questioned, reliable estimates can be developed from the use of regression analysis or the high–low method (as discussed in Chapter 3).
5. Sales and production are equal; thus, there is no material fluctuation in inventory levels. This assumption is necessary because fixed cost can be allocated to inventory at a different rate each year. Thus, variable costing information must be available. Because CVP and variable costing both focus on cost behavior, they are distinctly compatible with one another.
6. In a multiproduct firm, the sales mix remains constant. This assumption is necessary so that a weighted average contribution margin and CM% can be computed.
7. Labor productivity, production technology, and market conditions will not change. If any of these changes were to occur, cost would change correspondingly, and selling prices might change. Such changes would invalidate assumptions 1 through 3.

These assumptions limit the activity volume for which the calculations can be made as well as the time frame for the usefulness of the calculations. If changes occur in selling price or cost, new computations must be made for break-even and CVP analyses.

The preceding seven assumptions are the traditional ones associated with CVP analysis. An additional assumption must be noted with regard to the distinction between variable and fixed cost. Accountants have generally assumed that cost behavior, once classified, remains constant as long as operations remain within the relevant range. Thus, for example, once a cost was determined to be "fixed," it would be fixed next year, the year after, and 10 years from now.

It is more appropriate, however, to regard fixed cost as long-term variable cost. Over the long run, through managerial decisions, companies can change fixed cost; thus, a fixed cost is not fixed forever. Generating cost information in a manner that yields a longer-run perspective is presented in Chapter 4 on activity-based costing/management. Part of the traditional "misclassification" of fixed cost has been caused by improperly specifying drivers of cost. As production and sales volumes are less often viewed as cost drivers, companies will begin to recognize that a "fixed cost" exists only in a short-term perspective.

Such a reclassification of cost simply means that cost drivers for long-term variable cost must be specified in break-even and CVP analyses. The formula will need to be expanded to include these additional drivers, and more information and a longer time frame will be needed to make the calculations. No longer will sales volume necessarily be the overriding nonmonetary force in the computations.

These adjustments to the CVP formula will force managers to take a long-run, rather than a short-run, view of product opportunities. Such a perspective could produce better organizational decisions. As the time frame is extended, both the time value of money and life cycle costing become necessary considerations. Additionally, the traditional income statement becomes less useful for evaluating projects that will take several years to mature. A long-run perspective is important in a variety of circumstances, such as when variable or fixed costs arise only in the first year that a product or service is provided to customers.

Comprehensive Review Module

KEY TERMS

break-even chart, p. 358
break-even point (BEP), p. 355
contribution margin ratio (CM%), p. 356
cost-volume-profit (CVP) analysis, p. 360
degree of operating leverage (DOL), p. 370
incremental analysis, p. 364
margin of safety (MS), p. 367
operating leverage, p. 369
profit-volume (PV) graph, p. 359
variable cost ratio (VC%), p. 357

CHAPTER SUMMARY

1 Determining the Break-Even Point (BEP)

- BEP identifies the volume level separating losses from profits.
- BEP requires organizing costs by behavior.
- BEP requires assumptions, relative to volume, of linear revenue and linear cost behavior.
- BEP relies on the existence of a relevant range of activity.

2 Identifying the Break-Even Point

- BEP can be determined using the
  - following formulas where X = BEP:
    - X = Fixed cost ÷ Contribution margin per unit, where X = BEP in units
    - X = Fixed cost ÷ Contribution margin ratio, where X = BEP in sales dollars
  - graphing approach
    - by reading the *y*-axis at the point where the total revenue and total cost lines intersect using the traditional CVP graph.
    - by reading where the profit line intersects the *x*-axis using the profit-volume graph.
  - income statement approach, which
    - requires developing complete income statements showing total revenue minus total cost as being equal to a profit figure.
    - is often used to prove the solutions found with other approaches.

3 CVP Analysis

- CVP analysis can be used by a company to
  - determine BEP by assigning a zero value to the profit figure.
  - study the interrelationships of
    - price,
    - volume,
    - fixed and variable cost, and
    - contribution margin.
  - calculate the level of sales volume necessary to achieve specific before- or after-tax target profit objectives.
  - enhance a manager's ability to positively influence current operations and to predict future operations, thereby reducing the risk of uncertainty.

4 BEP and CVP Analysis for Single-Product and Multi-Product Firms

- In a multiproduct environment, break-even and CVP analysis
  - require that a constant product sales mix or "bag" assumption be used for the various products.
  - require that a weighted average contribution margin or CM ratio be calculated for each "bag" of product sold.
  - state solutions in terms of "bags" of product, which means the solutions must be converted (using the original product sales mix) to actual units (or sales dollars) of individual products.

5 MS and DOL

- Companies use the margin of safety (MS) and degree of operating leverage (DOL) concepts as follows:
  - the MS indicates how far (in units, in sales dollars, or as a percentage) a company is operating from its BEP; the MS% is equal to (1 ÷ DOL).
  - the DOL shows the percentage change that would occur in profit given a specified percentage change in sales from the current level; the DOL is equal to (1 ÷ MS%).

6 Underlying Assumptions of CVP Analysis

- The break-even and CVP models are based on several assumptions that limit their ability to reflect reality. Underlying assumptions are that
  - revenue and variable cost per unit are constant and linear within the relevant range.
  - contribution margin is linear within the relevant range.
  - total fixed cost is constant within the relevant range.
  - mixed cost can be accurately separated into its variable and fixed components.
  - sales and production levels are equal.
  - sales mix is constant in a multiproduct setting.
  - labor productivity, production technology, and market conditions will not change during the period under consideration.

SOLUTION STRATEGIES

Cost-Volume-Profit (CVP), p. 360

The fundamental equation for break-even and CVP problems is

$$\text{Total revenue} - \text{Total cost} = \text{Profit}$$

CVP problems can also be solved by using a numerator/denominator approach. All numerators and denominators and the types of problems that each relates to follow. The formulas relate to both single- and multiproduct firms, but results for multiproduct firms are per bag and should be converted to units of individual products.

Problem Situation	Numerator	Denominator
Simple BEP in units	FC	Unit CM
Simple BEP in dollars	FC	CM%
CVP with fixed profit in units	FC + P	Unit CM
CVP with fixed profit in dollars	FC + P	CM%
CVP with specified profit in units	FC	Unit CM − P_u
CVP with profit specified as percentage of sales	FC	CM% − P_u%

where FC = fixed cost
CM = contribution margin
CM% = contribution margin percentage
P = total profit (on a before-tax basis)
P_u = profit per unit (on a before-tax basis)
P_u% = profit percentage per unit (on a before-tax basis)

To convert after-tax profit to before-tax profit, divide after-tax profit by (1 − tax rate).

Margin of Safety (MS), p. 367

Margin of safety in units = Actual sales in units − Break-even sales in units
Margin of safety in dollars = Actual sales $ − Break-even sales $
Margin of safety % = (Margin of safety in units or $) ÷ (Actual sales in units or $)

Degree of Operating Leverage (DOL), p. 370

Degree of operating leverage = Contribution margin ÷ Profit before tax
Predicted profit = [1 + (DOL × Percent change in sales)] × Current profit

DEMONSTRATION PROBLEM

SunnyVale makes small plant stands that sell for $25 each. The company's annual level of production and sales is 120,000 units. In addition to $430,500 of fixed manufacturing overhead and $159,050 of fixed administrative expenses, the following per-unit costs have been determined for each plant stand:

Direct material	$ 6.00
Direct labor	3.00
Variable manufacturing overhead	0.80
Variable selling expense	2.20
Total variable cost	$12.00

Required:

a. Prepare a variable costing income statement at the current level of production and sales.
b. Calculate the unit contribution margin in dollars and the contribution margin ratio for a plant stand.
c. Determine the break-even point in number of plant stands.
d. Calculate the dollar break-even point using the contribution margin ratio.
e. Determine SunnyVale's margin of safety in units, in sales dollars, and as a percentage.
f. Compute the company's degree of operating leverage. If sales increase by 25 percent, by what percentage will before-tax income increase?
g. How many plant stands must the company sell to earn $996,450 in before-tax income?
h. If the company wants to earn $657,800 after tax and is subject to a 20 percent tax rate, how many units must be sold?
i. How many plant stands must be sold to break even if SunnyVale's fixed manufacturing cost increases by $7,865? (Use the original data.)
j. The company has received an offer from a Brazilian company to buy 4,000 plant stands at $20 per unit. The per-unit variable selling cost of the additional units will be $2.80 (rather than $2.20), and $18,000 of additional fixed administrative cost will be incurred. This sale would not affect domestic sales or their costs. Based on quantitative factors alone, should SunnyVale accept this offer?

Solution to Demonstration Problem

a.

SunnyVale
Variable Costing Income Statement

Sales (120,000 × $25.00)		$ 3,000,000
Variable production cost		
Direct material (120,000 × $6.00)	$720,000	
Direct labor (120,000 × $3.00)	360,000	
Overhead (120,000 × $0.80)	96,000	
Variable selling expenses (120,000 × $2.20)	264,000	(1,440,000)
Contribution margin		$ 1,560,000
Fixed cost		
Manufacturing overhead	$430,500	
Administrative	159,050	(589,550)
Income before income tax		$ 970,450

b. CM = SP – VC = \$25 – \$12 = \$13 per unit
CM% = CM ÷ SP = \$13 ÷ \$25 = 52 percent
c. BEP = FC ÷ CM = \$589,550 ÷ \$13 = 45,350 plant stands
d. BEP = FC ÷ CM% = \$589,550 ÷ 0.52 = \$1,133,750 in sales
e. MS_u = Current unit sales – BEP unit sales = 120,000 – 45,350 = 74,650 plant stands
MS\$= Current sales in dollars – BEP sales in dollars = \$3,000,000 – \$1,133,750 = \$1,866,250
MS% = MS in units ÷ Current unit sales = 74,650 ÷ 120,000 = 62 percent (rounded)
f. DOL = Current CM ÷ Current Pre-Tax Income = \$1,560,000 ÷ \$970,450 = 1.61 (rounded)
Increase in Income = DOL × % Increase in Sales = 1.61 × 0.25 = 40.25 percent
Proof:

New sales = 120,000 × 1.25 = 150,000
New CM = 150,000 × \$13.00 = \$1,950,000
New pre-tax profit = New CM – FC = \$1,950,000 – \$589,550 = \$1,360,450
Increase = New pre-tax profit – Old pre-tax profit = \$1,360,450 – \$970,450 = \$390,000
Increase in % terms = \$390,000 ÷ \$970,450 = 40.19 percent (rounded)

g. \$13X = \$589,550 + \$996,450
X = \$1,586,000 ÷ \$13
X = 122,000 plant stands
h. PBT = PAT ÷ (1 – Tax rate) = \$657,800 ÷ (1 – 0.20) = \$657,800 ÷ 0.80 = \$822,250
\$13X = \$589,550 + \$822,250
X = \$1,411,800 ÷ \$13
X = 108,600 plant stands
i. X = Increase in FC ÷ CM
X = \$7,865 ÷ \$13
X = 605 units over BEP
New BEP = 45,350 + 605 = 45,955 plant stands
j. New CM for each additional unit = \$20.00 – \$12.60 = \$7.40
Total new CM = \$7.40 × 4,000 = \$29,600
Increase in pre-tax profit = Increase in CM – Increase in FC = \$29,600 – \$18,000 = \$11,600
Yes, the company should accept the offer.

POTENTIAL ETHICAL ISSUES

1. Ignoring the relevant range when setting assumptions about cost behavior to disregard the implications of cost changes on the calculation of BEP or CVP analysis
2. Treating some or all fixed costs as per-unit costs (i.e., using absorption costing) in calculating BEP or performing CVP analysis
3. Using untested or inaccurate assumptions about the relationship between variables such as advertising and sales volume or sales price and sales volume to assure a particular decision outcome
4. Assuming a constant sales mix ratio while ignoring expected changes in demand for individual products when conducting CVP analysis for multiproduct firms
5. Using CVP analyses to support long-term cost management strategies
6. Visually distorting BEP graphs to project improper conclusions
7. Including irrelevant information in incremental analysis to manipulate calculation results

QUESTIONS

1. What information provided by a variable costing income statement is used in computing the break-even point? Is this information on an absorption costing income statement? Explain your answer.
2. How is "break-even point" defined? What are the differences among the formula, graph, and income statement approaches for computing breakeven?
3. What is the contribution margin ratio? How is it used to calculate the break-even point?
4. Why is CVP analysis generally used as a short-run tool? Would CVP ever be appropriate as a long-run model?
5. How is the "bag" assumption used in CVP analysis for a multiproduct firm? What additional assumption must be made in multiproduct CVP analysis that does not pertain to a single-product CVP situation?
6. A multiproduct company has a sales mix of nine widgees to three squigees. Widgees have a contribution margin ratio of 45 percent, and squigees have a contribution margin ratio of 80 percent. If the sales mix changes to six widgees to six squigees, will the company have a higher or lower weighted average contribution margin ratio and a higher or lower break-even point (in sales dollars)? Explain the rationale for your answer.
7. Define and explain the relationship between margin of safety and degree of operating leverage.

EXERCISES

8. **LO.1 (Variable costing income statement)** Sports Drinks, Inc. began business in 2013 selling bottles of a thirst-quenching drink. Production for the first year was 104,000 bottles, and sales were 98,000 bottles. The selling price per bottle was $3.10. Costs incurred during the year were as follows:

Ingredients used	$ 56,000
Direct labor	26,000
Variable overhead	48,000
Fixed overhead	5,200
Variable selling expenses	10,000
Fixed selling and administrative expenses	28,000
Total actual cost	$173,200

For 2013:

a. What was the production cost per bottle under variable costing?
b. What was variable cost of goods sold?
c. What was the contribution margin per bottle?
d. What was the contribution margin ratio?

EXCEL

9. **LO.1 (Variable costing income statement)** Top Disc manufactures frisbees. The following information is available for 2013, the company's first year in business when it produced 325,000 units. Revenue of $450,000 was generated by the sale of 180,000 frisbees.

	Variable Cost	Fixed Cost
Production		
Direct material	$150,000	
Direct labor	100,000	
Overhead	75,000	$112,500
Selling and administrative	90,000	100,000

a. What is the variable production cost per unit?
b. What is the total contribution margin per unit?
c. Prepare a variable costing income statement.

10. **LO.2 (Formula; graph; income statement)** Pittsburg Tar Co. had the following income statement for 2013:

Sales (30,000 gallons × $8)		$ 240,000
Variable cost		
Production (40,000 gallons × $3)	$120,000	
Selling (30,000 gallons × $0.50)	15,000	(135,000)
Contribution margin		$ 105,000
Fixed cost		
Production	$ 46,000	
Selling and administrative	6,200	(52,200)
Income before tax		$ 52,800
Income tax (40%)		(21,120)
Net income		$ 31,680

a. Compute the break-even point using the equation approach.
b. Prepare a CVP graph to reflect the relationships among cost, revenue, profit, and volume.
c. Prepare a profit-volume graph.
d. Prepare a short explanation for company management about each of the graphs.
e. Prepare an income statement at break-even point using variable costing.

11. **LO.2 (Break-even point)** Diamond Jim's makes and sells class rings for local schools. Operating information is as follows:

Selling price per ring	$600
Variable cost per ring	
Rings and stones	$220
Sales commissions	48
Overhead	32
Annual fixed costs	
Selling	$180,000
Administrative	105,000
Manufacturing	60,000

a. What is Diamond Jim's break-even point in rings?
b. What is Diamond Jim's break-even point in sales dollars?
c. What would Diamond Jim's break-even point be if sales commissions increased to $54?
d. What would Diamond Jim's break-even point be if selling expenses decreased by $6,000?

12. **LO.2 (Break-even point)** Llano Lamps has the following revenue and cost functions:

Revenue = $70 per unit
Cost = $90,000 + $40 per unit

a. What is the break-even point in units?
b. What is the break-even point in dollars?

13. **LO.2 (Cost and revenue behavior)** The following financial data have been determined from analyzing the records of Joe's Ceramics (a one-product firm):

Contribution margin per unit	$25
Variable cost per unit	$21
Annual fixed cost	$90,000

How does each of the following measures change when product volume goes up by one unit at Joe's Ceramics?

a. Total revenue
b. Total cost
c. Income before tax

14. **LO.3 (CVP)** Salina Sports Wear has designed a new athletic suit. The company plans to produce and sell 30,000 units of the new product in the coming year. Annual fixed

EXCEL

costs are $600,000, and variable costs are 70 percent of selling price. If the company wants a pre-tax profit of $300,000, at what minimum price must it sell its product?

15. **LO.3 (CVP; taxes)** Use the information for Hamlet House in Exercise 16 and assume a tax rate for the company of 35 percent.
    a. If Hamlet House wants to earn an after-tax profit of $182,000, how many garden sheds must be sold?
    b. How much revenue is needed to yield an after-tax profit of 8 percent of revenue? How many garden sheds does this revenue amount represent?

16. **LO.3 (CVP)** Hamlet House makes portable garden sheds that sell for $1,800 each. Costs are as follows:

	Per Unit	Total
Direct material	$800	
Direct labor	90	
Variable production overhead	60	
Variable selling and administrative cost	50	
Fixed production overhead		$200,000
Fixed selling and administrative		60,000

    a. How many garden sheds must the company sell to break even?
    b. If Hamlet House's management wants to earn a pre-tax profit of $200,000, how many garden sheds must be sold?
    c. If Hamlet House's management wants to earn a pre-tax profit of $280,000, how many garden sheds must be sold?

17. **LO.3 (CVP)** Austin Automotive sells an auto accessory for $180 per unit. The company's variable cost per unit is $30 for direct material, $25 per unit for direct labor, and $17 per unit for overhead. Annual fixed production overhead is $37,400, and fixed selling and administrative overhead is $25,240.
    a. What is the contribution margin per unit?
    b. What is the contribution margin ratio?
    c. What is the break-even point in units?
    d. Using the contribution margin ratio, what is the break-even point in sales dollars?
    e. If Austin Automotive wants to earn a pre-tax profit of $51,840, how many units must the company sell?

18. **LO.3 (Incremental sales)** Pantene Paints has annual sales of $2,250,000 with variable expenses of 60 percent of sales and fixed expenses per month of $25,000. By how much must annual sales increase for Pantene Paints to have pre-tax income equal to 30 percent of sales?

19. **LO.3 (CVP analysis)** Following are abbreviated income statements for two companies, Ainsley and Bard:

	Ainsley	Bard
Sales	$ 2,000,000	$ 2,000,000
Variable cost	(1,400,000)	0
Contribution margin	$ 600,000	$ 2,000,000
Fixed cost	0	(1,400,000)
Operating income	$ 600,000	$ 600,000

    Ainsley and Bard produce an identical product and both sell that product at $40. Both companies are searching for ways to increase operating income. Managers of both companies are considering three identical strategies. Consider each of the following strategies, and discuss which company is best situated to adopt that strategy.
    a. Decrease sales price 30 percent to increase sales volume 60 percent.
    b. Increase sales price per unit 30 percent, which will cause sales volume to decline by 15 percent.
    c. Increase advertising by $200,000 to increase sales volume by 15,000 units.

20. **LO.3 (CVP; taxes)** Use the information for Austin Automotive in Exercise 17 and assume a tax rate for the company of 30 percent.

   a. If Austin Automotive wants to earn an after-tax profit of $135,800, how many units must the company sell?
   b. If Austin Automotive wants to earn an after-tax profit of $7.20 on each unit sold, how many units must the company sell?

21. **LO.3 (Writing; Internet)** A significant trend in business today is the increasing use of outsourcing. Go to the Internet and search Web sites with the objective of gaining an understanding of the vast array of outsourcing services that are available. Prepare a presentation in which you discuss the extensive use of outsourcing today and how it could be used as a tool to manage a firm's cost structure and in CVP planning.

INTERNET

EXCEL

22. **LO.3 (Volume and pricing)** Dim Witt is the county commissioner of Clueless County. He decided to institute tolls for local ferry boat passengers. After the tolls had been in effect for four months, Astra Astute, county accountant, noticed that collecting $1,450 in tolls incurred a daily cost of $2,000. The toll is $0.50 per passenger.

   a. How many people are using the ferry boats each day?
   b. If the $2,000 cost is entirely fixed, how much must each passenger be charged for the toll process to break even? How much must each passenger be charged for the toll process to make a profit of $250 per day?
   c. Assume that only 80 percent of the $2,000 is fixed and the remainder varies by passenger. If the toll is raised to $0.60 per person, passenger volume is expected to fall by 10 percent. If the toll is raised and volume falls, will the county be better or worse off than it is currently and by what amount?
   d. Assume that only 80 percent of the $2,000 is fixed and the remainder varies by passenger. If passenger volume will decline by 5 percent for every $0.20 increase from the current $0.50 rate, at what level of use and toll amount would the county first make a profit?
   e. Discuss the saying "We may be showing a loss, but we can make it up in volume."

23. **LO.3 (CVP; taxes)** Golf Glider makes gasoline-powered golf carts. The selling price is $5,000 each, and costs are as follows:

Cost	Per Unit	Total
Direct material	$2,000	
Direct labor	625	
Variable overhead	325	
Variable selling	50	
Annual fixed production overhead		$250,000
Annual fixed selling and administrative		120,000

   Golf Glider's income is taxed at a 40 percent rate.

   a. How many golf carts must Golf Glider sell to earn $600,000 after tax?
   b. What level of revenue is needed to yield an after-tax income equal to 20 percent of sales?

24. **LO.4 (Multiproduct)** Green Rider makes three types of electric scooters. The company's total fixed cost is $1,080,000,000. Selling prices, variable cost, and sales percentages for each type of scooter follow:

	Selling Price	Variable Cost	Percent of Total Unit Sales
Mod	$2,200	$1,900	30
Rad	3,700	3,000	50
X-treme	6,000	5,000	20

   a. What is Green Rider's break-even point in units and sales dollars?
   b. If the company has an after-tax income goal of $1 billion and the tax rate is 50 percent, how many units of each type of scooter must be sold for the goal to be reached at the current sales mix?

c. Assume the sales mix shifts to 50 percent Mod, 40 percent Rad, and 10 percent X-treme. How does this change affect your answer to (a)?
d. If Green Rider sold more X-treme scooters and fewer Mod scooters, how would your answers to (a) and (b) change? No calculations are needed.

25. **LO.4 (CVP; multiproduct)** Mel's Male Accessories sells wallets and money clips. Historically, the firm's sales have averaged three wallets for every money clip. Each wallet has an $8 contribution margin, and each money clip has a $6 contribution margin. Mel's incurs fixed cost in the amount of $180,000. The selling prices of wallets and money clips, respectively, are $30 and $15. The corporate-wide tax rate is 40 percent.
    a. How much revenue is needed to break even? How many wallets and money clips does this represent?
    b. How much revenue is needed to earn a pre-tax profit of $150,000?
    c. How much revenue is needed to earn an after-tax profit of $150,000?
    d. If Mel's earns the revenue determined in (b) but does so by selling five wallets for every two money clips, what would be the pre-tax profit (or loss)? Why is this amount not $150,000?

26. **LO.5 (Leverage factors; writing)** A group of prospective investors has asked for your help in understanding the comparative advantages and disadvantages of starting a company that is either labor intensive or, in contrast, one that uses significant cutting-edge technology and is therefore capital intensive. Prepare a report addressing the issues. Include discussions regarding cost structure, BEP, CVP, MS, DOL, risk, customer satisfaction, and the relationships among these concepts.

27. **LO.5 (Operating leverage; margin of safety; income statement)** Titan Foods makes a high-energy frozen meal. The selling price per package is $7.20, and variable cost of production is $4.32. Total fixed cost per year is $316,600. The company is currently selling 125,000 packages per year.
    a. What is the margin of safety in packages?
    b. What is the degree of operating leverage?
    c. If the company can increase sales in packages by 30 percent, what percentage increase will it experience in income? Prove your answer using the income statement approach.
    d. If the company increases advertising by $41,200, sales in packages will increase by 15 percent. What will be the new break-even point? The new degree of operating leverage?

28. **LO.5 (CVP; margin of safety)** Farmer Ned wants to cash in on the increased demand for ethanol. Accordingly, he purchased a corn farm in Iowa. Ned believes his corn crop can be sold to an ethanol plant for $9.60 per bushel. Variable cost associated with growing and selling a bushel of corn is $7.60. Ned's annual fixed cost is $264,000.
    a. What is the break-even point in sales dollars and bushels of corn? If Ned's farm is 1,200 acres, how many bushels must he produce per acre to break even?
    b. If Ned actually produces 174,000 bushels, what is the margin of safety in bushels, in dollars, and as a percentage?

29. **LO.5 (CVP; operating leverage; income statement)** Racine Tire Co. manufactures tires for all-terrain vehicles. The tires sell for $60, and variable cost per tire is $30; monthly fixed cost is $450,000.
    a. What is the break-even point in units and sales dollars?
    b. If Ronnie Rice, the company's CEO, wants the business to earn a pre-tax profit of 25 percent of revenues, how many tires must be sold each month?
    c. If the company is currently selling 20,000 tires monthly, what is the degree of operating leverage?
    d. If the company can increase sales volume by 15 percent above the current level, what will be the increase in net income? What will be the new net income? Prove your calculations with an income statement.

30. **LO.6 (Product cost; writing)** A friend of yours, attending another university, states she learned that CVP is a short-run-oriented model and is, therefore, of limited usefulness. Your professor, however, has often discussed CVP in presentations about long-run planning to your cost accounting class. You decide to investigate your friend's allegation by preparing a report addressing your friend's contention. Your professor is also asking you to prepare a separate report for internal management's use that addresses how the CVP model could be adapted to become more useful for making long-run decisions. Prepare these two reports, one for your friend's understanding and one for your professor.

31. **LO.2-LO.4 (Comprehensive)** Compute the answers to each of the following independent situations.
    a. Orlando Ray sells liquid and spray mouthwash in a sales mix of 1:2, respectively. The liquid mouthwash has a contribution margin of $10 per unit; the spray's CM is $5 per unit. Annual fixed cost for the company is $100,000. How many units of spray mouthwash would Orlando Ray sell at the break-even point?
    b. Piniella Company has a break-even point of 4,000 units. At BEP, variable cost is $6,400 and fixed cost is $1,600. If one unit over breakeven is sold, what will be the company's pre-tax income?
    c. Montreal Company's product sells for $10 per bottle. Annual fixed costs are $216,000 and variable cost is 40 percent of selling price. How many units would Montreal Company need to sell to earn a 25 percent pre-tax profit on sales?
    d. York Company has a BEP of 2,800 units. The company currently sells 3,200 units at $65 each. What is the company's margin of safety in units, in sales dollars, and as a percentage?

32. **LO.6 (CVP assumptions; writing)** A local businesswoman, Jane Aire, has hired you and a colleague, Joanna, from your cost accounting class to advise her regarding her small manufacturing business that makes leather valises. The business was organized just two years ago and has failed to become profitable, which is why the business owner has hired you and Joanna. After analyzing the client's books, Joanna prepared the following simple income statement for the current year.

Sales	$ 200,000
Variable cost	(120,000)
Contribution margin	$ 80,000
Fixed cost	(140,000)
Operating loss	$ (60,000)

After studying the income statement, Joanna worked out the break-even point for the firm and advised the client, "Ms. Aire, you will need to achieve sales of $350,000 before this business is producing enough revenues to cover all cost."

Ms. Aire replied, "That's a 75 percent increase over existing sales; I don't see any way this business will reach that level of sales."

"Then," said Joanna, "you should shut the business down today to cut your losses."

After considering Joanna's income statement and the conversation between Joanna and Aire, discuss whether you agree with Joanna's recommendation.

33. **LO.6 (Ethics; writing)** Niobrara Pesticide Company's new president has learned that, for the past four years, the company has been dumping its industrial waste into the local river and falsifying reports to authorities about the levels of suspected carcinogens in that waste. The plant manager says that there is no proof that the waste causes cancer and that only a few fishing villages are within 100 miles downriver. If the company must treat the substance to neutralize its potentially injurious effects and then transport it to a legal disposal site, the company's variable and fixed costs would rise to a level that might make the firm uncompetitive. If the company loses its competitive advantage, 10,000 local employees could become unemployed and the town's economy could collapse.

ETHICS

    a. What specific variable and fixed costs can you identify that would increase (or decrease) if the waste were treated rather than dumped? How would these costs affect product contribution margin?

b. What ethical conflicts does the president face?
c. What rationalizations can you detect that plant employees have devised?
d. What options and suggestions can you offer the president?

34. **LO.6 (CVP assumptions)** Identify which of the CVP assumptions is violated in each of the circumstances described below.

a. Price per unit declines as the volume of sales and production increase.
b. Labor productivity increases as the volume of production declines.
c. The sales mix in a multiproduct firm varies as the volume of total sales changes.
d. Mixed cost cannot be separated into variable and fixed components.
e. Costs behave according to a curvilinear function.
f. Sales and production volume differ.
g. Fixed cost and capacity can be adjusted within the period.

PROBLEMS

ETHICS

35. **LO.1 & LO.2 (Variable costing; ethics)** In its first year of operations, Utah Utility Trailers incurred the following costs:

Variable production cost	$2,800 per unit
Variable selling and administrative cost	$200 per unit
Fixed production cost	$200,000
Fixed selling and administrative cost	$80,000

For the year, the company reported the following results:

Sales ($5,000 per unit)	$ 500,000
Cost of goods sold	(400,000)
Gross margin	$ 100,000
Selling and administrative cost	(100,000)
Operating income	$ 0

a. Using the contribution margin ratio approach, compute the break-even point for this company.
b. How many units did the firm produce in its first year of operations?
c. Provide an explanation that reconciles your result in (a) to the income statement provided above.
d. Prepare a variable costing income statement for sales of 100 units.
e. Assume that Utah Utility Trailers is in need of a bank loan. Would it be unethical to use the income statement above, rather than the income statement compiled in (d), to present to the loan officer? Explain.

36. **LO.1-LO.3 (CVP)** Aqua Gear, in business for 20 years, makes swimwear for professional athletes. Analysis of the firm's financial records for the current year reveals the following:

Average swimsuit selling price	$70
Variable swimsuit expenses	
Direct material	$28
Direct labor	12
Variable overhead	8
Annual fixed cost	
Selling	$10,000
Administrative	24,000

The company's tax rate is 40 percent. Samantha Waters, company president, has asked you to help her answer the following questions. (Round CM% to the nearest tenth of a percent and BE in units to the nearest whole unit.)

a. What is the break-even point in number of swimsuits and in dollars?
b. How much revenue must be generated to produce $40,000 of pre-tax earnings? How many swimsuits would this level of revenue represent?

c. How much revenue must be generated to produce $40,000 of after-tax earnings? How many swimsuits would this represent?
d. What amount of revenue would be necessary to yield an after-tax profit equal to 20 percent of revenue?
e. Aqua Gear is considering purchasing a faster sewing machine that will save $6 per swimsuit in cost but will raise annual fixed cost by $40,000. If the equipment is purchased, the company expects to make and sell an additional 5,000 swimsuits. Should the company make this investment?
f. A marketing consultant told Aqua Gear managers that they could increase the number of swimsuits sold by 30 percent if the selling price was reduced by 10 percent and the company spent $10,000 on advertising. The company has been selling 3,000 swimsuits. Should the company make the changes advised by the consultant?

37. **LO.1-LO.3 & LO.5 (CVP single product; comprehensive)** Beantown Baseball Company makes baseballs that sell for $13 per two-pack. Current annual production and sales are 960,000 baseballs. Costs for each baseball are as follows:

Direct material	$2.00
Direct labor	1.25
Variable overhead	0.50
Variable selling expenses	0.25
Total variable cost	$4.00
Total fixed overhead	$1,250,000

a. Calculate the unit contribution margin in dollars and the contribution margin ratio for the company.
b. Determine the break-even point in number of baseballs.
c. Calculate the dollar break-even point using the contribution margin ratio.
d. Determine the company's margin of safety in number of baseballs, in sales dollars, and as a percentage.
e. Compute the company's degree of operating leverage. If sales increase by 30 percent, by what percentage would pre-tax income increase?
f. How many baseballs must the company sell if it desires to earn $1,096,000 in pre-tax profit?
g. If the company wants to earn $750,000 after tax and is subject to a 40 percent tax rate, how many baseballs must be sold?
h. How many baseballs would the company need to sell to break even if its fixed cost increased by $50,000? (Use original data.)
i. Beantown Baseball Company has received an offer to provide a one-time sale of 20,000 baseballs at $8.80 per two-pack to the Lowell Spinners. This sale would not affect other sales, nor would the cost of those sales change. However, the variable cost of the additional units would increase by $0.20 for shipping, and fixed cost would increase by $6,000. Based solely on financial information, should the company accept this offer? Show your calculations. What other factors should the company consider in accepting or rejecting this offer?

38. **LO.1-LO.3 (CVP)** Casper Karts manufactures a three-wheeled shopping cart that sells for $60. Variable manufacturing and variable selling cost are, respectively, $35 and $10 per unit. Annual fixed cost is $975,000.
a. What is the contribution margin per unit and the contribution margin ratio?
b. What is the break-even point in units?
c. How many units must the company sell to earn a pre-tax income of $900,000?
d. If the company's tax rate is 40 percent, how many units must be sold to earn an after-tax profit of $750,000?
e. If labor costs are 60 percent of the variable manufacturing cost and 40 percent of the fixed cost, how would a 10 percent decrease in both variable and fixed labor costs affect the break-even point?

f. Assume that the total market for three-wheeled shopping carts is 600,000 units per year and that Casper Karts currently has 18 percent of the market. The company wants to obtain a 25 percent market share and also wants to earn a pre-tax profit of $1,350,000. By how much must variable cost be reduced? Provide some suggestions for variable cost reductions.

39. **LO.1, LO.3, & LO.4 (CVP decision alternatives)** Mitch Weatherby owns a sports brokerage agency and sells tickets to major league baseball, football, and basketball games. He also sells sports travel packages that include game tickets, airline tickets, and hotel accommodations. Revenues are commissions based as follows:

Game ticket sales	8% commission
Airline ticket sales	10% commission
Hotel bookings sales	20% commission

Monthly fixed costs include advertising ($2,200), rent ($1,800), utilities ($500), and other costs ($4,400). There are no variable costs. A typical month generates the following sales amounts that are subject to the stated commission structure:

Game tickets	$60,000
Airline tickets	9,000
Hotel bookings	14,000
Total	$83,000

a. What is Weatherby's normal monthly profit or loss?
b. Weatherby estimates that airline bookings can be increased by 40 percent if he increases advertising by $1,200. Should he increase advertising?
c. Weatherby's friend Rusty has asked him for a job in the travel agency. Rusty has proposed that he be paid 50 percent of any additional commissions he can bring to the agency plus a salary of $400 per month. Weatherby has estimated that Rusty can generate the following additional bookings per month:

Game tickets	$ 8,000
Airline tickets	1,500
Hotel bookings	6,000
Total	$15,500

Hiring Rusty would also increase fixed cost by $600 per month inclusive of salary. Should Weatherby hire Rusty?
d. Weatherby hired Rusty and in the first month, Rusty generated an additional $13,000 of bookings for the agency. The bookings, however, were all airline tickets. Was the decision to hire Rusty a good one? Why or why not?

40. **LO.2 (Graph)** The Real Deal is a social organization that performs charitable work in its local community. The club has the following monthly cost and fee information: monthly membership fee per member, $60; monthly variable cost of service per member, $25; and monthly fixed service cost, $3,500. Costs are extremely low because volunteers provide almost all services and supplies. Excess of fees over service cost are used to support charitable activities.

a. Prepare a break-even chart for The Real Deal.
b. Prepare a profit-volume graph for The Real Deal.
c. At this time, The Real Deal has only 120 members. Which of the preceding items (break-even chart or profit-volume graph) would you use in a speech to the membership about the benefits of recruiting additional members? Why?

41. **LO.3 & LO.4 (Multiproduct firm)** The Glass Menagerie makes small, pressed-resin ducks and ducklings. For every duck sold, the company sells five ducklings. The following information is available about the company's selling prices and cost:

	Ducks		Ducklings
Selling price	$24		$12
Variable cost	12		8
Annual fixed cost		$288,000	

a. What is the average contribution margin ratio? (Round CM% to the nearest tenth of a percent.)
b. Calculate the monthly break-even point if fixed cost is incurred evenly throughout the year. At the BEP, indicate how many units of each product will be sold monthly.
c. If the company wants to earn $96,000 pre-tax profit monthly, how many units of each product must it sell?
d. Company management has specified $31,680 as monthly net income, and the company is in a 40 percent tax bracket. However, marketing information has indicated that the sales mix has changed to one duck to nine ducklings. How much total revenue and what number of products must be sold to achieve the company's profit objective?
e. Refer to the original information. If the company can reduce variable cost per duckling to $4 by raising monthly fixed cost by $8,500, how will the break-even point change? Should the company make these changes? Explain your answer.

42. **LO.3 & LO.4 (Multiproduct firm)** Yard Bird manufactures commercial and residential riding lawnmowers. The company sells one commercial mower per three residential mowers sold. Selling prices for the commercial and residential mowers are, respectively, $5,600 and $1,800, and variable selling and production cost are, respectively, $3,800 and $1,000. The company's annual fixed cost is $8,400,000. Compute the sales volume of each mower type needed to

a. break even.
b. earn $1,260,000 of income before tax.
c. earn $1,008,000 of income after tax, assuming a 40 percent tax rate.
d. earn 12 percent on sales revenue in pre-tax income.
e. earn 8 percent on sales revenue in after-tax income, assuming a 40 percent tax rate. (Round percentages and units to the nearest whole number.)

43. **LO.3-LO.5 (Multiproduct firm)** The Pink Flamingo, Inc., manufactures plastic lawn ornaments. Currently the firm manufactures three items: reindeer, snowmen, and flamingos. For each reindeer, two snowmen and four flamingos are sold.

	Reindeer	Snowmen	Flamingos
Variable product cost	$12.00	$15.00	$25.00
Variable selling expenses	6.00	4.50	8.00
Variable administrative expenses	3.00	5.50	6.00
Selling price	40.00	35.00	60.00
Annual fixed factory overhead		$420,000	
Annual fixed selling expenses		150,000	
Annual fixed administrative expenses		80,178	

The firm is in a 40 percent tax bracket.

a. What is the annual break-even point in revenues?
b. How many reindeer, snowmen, and flamingos are expected to be sold at the break-even point?
c. If the firm desires pre-tax income of $250,428, how much total revenue is required, and how many units of each product must be sold?
d. If the firm desires after-tax income of $155,718, how much total revenue is required, and how many units of each product must be sold?
e. If the firm achieves the revenue determined in (d), what is its margin of safety in dollars and as a percentage? (Round to the nearest tenth of a percent.)

44. **LO.2-LO.5 (Comprehensive; multiproduct)** Nature's Own makes three types of wood flooring: Oak, Hickory, and Cherry. The company's tax rate is 40 percent. The following costs are expected for 2014:

		Oak	Hickory	Cherry
Variable cost (on a per-square-yard basis)				
Direct material		$10.40	$6.50	$17.60
Direct labor		3.60	0.80	12.80
Production overhead		2.00	0.30	3.50
Selling expense		1.00	0.50	4.00
Administrative expense		0.40	0.20	0.60
Fixed overhead	$760,000			
Fixed selling expense	240,000			
Fixed administrative expense	200,000			

Per-square-yard expected selling prices are as follows: Oak, $32.80; Hickory, $16.00; and Cherry, $50.00. The expected sales mix is as follows:

	Oak	Hickory	Cherry
Square yards	9,000	72,000	6,000

a. Calculate the break-even point for 2014. (Round to the next highest whole unit.)
b. How many square yards of each product are expected to be sold at the break-even point? (Round CM% to the nearest tenth of a percent.)
c. If the company wants to earn pre-tax profit of $800,000, how many square yards of each type of flooring would it need to sell? How much total revenue would be required? (Round to the next highest whole unit.)
d. If the company wants to earn an after-tax profit of $680,000, determine the revenue needed using the contribution margin percentage approach. (Round CM% to the nearest tenth of a percent and amounts to the nearest whole dollar.)
e. If the company achieves the revenue determined in (d), what is the margin of safety (1) in dollars and (2) as a percentage? (Round to the nearest tenth of a percent.)

45. **LO2-LO.4 (CVP analysis; multiproduct)** Ted Tyner owns Sixth Man Hotel, a luxury hotel with 60 two-bedroom suites for coaches and their players. Capacity is 10 coaches and 50 players. Each suite is equipped with extra-long king-sized beds, super-tall and extended shower heads, extra-tall bathroom vanities, a laptop, and a printer. Each suite has a Pacific Ocean view. Hotel services include airport limousine pickup and drop-off, a daily fruit basket, champagne on the day of arrival, and a Hummer for transportation. Coaches and players are interviewed about their dietary restrictions and room service requirements before arrival. The hotel's original cost was $1,920,000, and depreciation is $160,000 per year. Other hotel operating costs include:

Labor	$320,000 per year plus $5 per suite per day
Utilities	$158,000 per year plus $1 per suite per day
Miscellaneous	$100,000 per year plus $6 per suite per day

In addition to these costs, costs are also incurred on food and beverage for each guest. These costs are strictly variable and (on average) are $40 per day for coaches and $15 per day for players.

a. Assuming that the hotel is able to maintain an average annual occupancy of 80 percent in both coach and player suites (based on a 360-day year), determine the minimum daily charge that must be assessed per suite per day to generate $240,000 of income before tax. (Round to the nearest cent.)
b. Assume that the per-day price Tyner charges is $240 for coaches and $200 for players. If the sales mix is 12:48 (12 coach days of occupancy for every 48 player days of occupancy), compute the following (rounding BEP to the nearest whole bag):
   1. The break-even point in total occupancy days.
   2. Total occupancy days required to generate $400,000 of income before tax.

3. Total occupancy days to generate $400,000 of after-tax income. Tyner's personal tax rate is 35 percent.

c. Tyner is considering adding a massage service for guests to complement current hotel services. He has estimated that the cost of providing such a service would largely be fixed because all necessary facilities already exist. He would, however, need to hire five certified masseurs at a cost of $500,000 per year. If Tyner decides to add this service, how much would he need to increase his daily charges (assume equal dollar increases to coach and player room fees) to maintain the break-even point computed in (b)? (Round to the nearest cent.)

46. **LO.3 (CVP analysis; advanced)** Fairbanks Express is a luxury passenger carrier in Alaska. All seats are first class, and the following data are available:

Number of seats per passenger train car	60
Average load factor (percentage of seats filled)	75%
Average full passenger fare	$140
Average variable cost per passenger	$60
Fixed operating cost per month	$2,400,000

a. What is the break-even point in passengers and revenues per month? (Round CM% to the nearest tenth of a percent and BEP to the nearest dollar.)

b. What is the break-even point in number of passenger train cars per month? (Round to the nearest whole unit.)

c. If Fairbanks Express raises its average passenger fare to $170, it is estimated that the load factor will decrease to 60 percent. What will be the monthly break-even point in number of passenger cars? (Round to the nearest whole unit.)

d. (Refer to original data.) Fuel cost is a significant variable cost to any railway. If crude oil increases by $16 per barrel, it is estimated that variable cost per passenger will rise to $80. What would be the new break-even point in passengers and in number of passenger train cars? (Round to the nearest whole unit.)

e. Fairbanks Express has experienced an increase in variable cost per passenger to $70 and an increase in total fixed cost to $3,000,000. The company has decided to raise the average fare to $160. If the tax rate is 40 percent, how many passengers per month are needed to generate an after-tax profit of $800,000? (Round to the nearest whole dollar and unit.)

f. (Use original data.) Fairbanks Express is considering offering a discounted fare of $100, which the company believes would increase the load factor to 80 percent. Only the additional seats would be sold at the discounted fare. Additional monthly advertising cost would be $160,000. How much pre-tax income would the discounted fare provide Fairbanks Express if the company has 40 passenger train cars per day, 30 days per month?

g. Fairbanks Express has an opportunity to obtain a new route that would be traveled 15 times per month. The company believes it can sell seats at $150 on the route, but the load factor would be only 60 percent. Fixed cost would increase by $200,000 per month for additional crew, additional passenger train cars, maintenance, and so on. Variable cost per passenger would remain at $60.

1. Should the company obtain the route?
2. How many passenger train cars must Fairbanks Express operate to earn pre-tax income of $101,000 per month on this route? (Round to the nearest whole unit.)
3. If the load factor could be increased to 75 percent, how many passenger train cars must be operated to earn pre-tax income of $101,000 per month on this route? (Round to the nearest whole unit.)
4. What qualitative factors should be considered by Fairbanks Express in making its decision about acquiring this route?

47. **LO.2, LO.3, & LO.5 (CVP; DOL; decision making)** Atlantic Fish Company is a wholesale distributor of cod. The company services restaurants in the Boston area. Small but steady growth in sales has been achieved by Atlantic Fish Company over the past few years, while cod prices have been increasing. The company is formulating its plans for 2013 and has gathered the following information:

Average selling price per pound	$9.00
Costs	
Cost of cod per pound	$5.60
Shipping expense per pound	0.40
Selling and administrative expense (rent and salaries)	$650,000
Sales commissions	10% of sales

Expected annual sales volume for 2013: 400,000 pounds of cod
The company's estimated tax rate is 40 percent.

a. What is the expected net income for the coming year? Prepare a contribution income statement.
b. Compute the contribution margin per unit and the contribution margin ratio. (Round to the nearest tenth of a percent.)
c. What is the break-even point in pounds sold and revenues? (Round to the nearest whole unit and dollar.)
d. Compute the degree of operating leverage and margin of safety expected for the coming year. (Round to the nearest tenth of a percent.)
e. Refer to the original data. Using the degree of operating leverage you computed in (d), compute the expected profit if sales are 20% above the expected level.
f. Refer to the original data. How many pounds of cod must be sold to earn an after-tax net income of $900,000? (Round to the nearest dollar.)

EXCEL

48. **LO.1-LO.3 & LO.5 (MS; DOL; PV graph)** You are considering buying one of two local firms (Olson Corp. and Miami Inc.). Olson Corp. uses a substantial amount of direct labor in its manufacturing operations, and its salespeople work on commission. Miami Inc. uses the latest automated technology in manufacturing; its salespeople are salaried. The following financial information is available for the two companies:

	OLSON CORP.		MIAMI INC.	
	2013	2014	2013	2014
Sales	$ 600,000	$ 960,000	$ 600,000	$ 840,000
Expenses including taxes	(528,000)	(823,200)	(528,000)	(667,200)
Net income	$ 72,000	$ 136,800	$ 72,000	$ 172,800

After examining cost data, you find that the fixed cost for Olson Corp. is $60,000; the fixed cost for Miami Inc. is $300,000. The tax rate for both companies is 40 percent.

a. Recast the income statements into a variable costing format.
b. What are the break-even sales for each firm for each year? (Round to the next highest whole dollar.)
c. Assume that you could acquire either firm for $1,200,000, and you want an after-tax return of 12 percent on your investment. Determine what sales level for each firm would allow you to reach your goal.
d. What is the margin of safety for each firm for each year? What is the degree of operating leverage?
e. Assume that product demand for 2015 is expected to rise by 15 percent from the 2014 level. What will be the expected net income for each firm?
f. Assume that product demand for 2015 is expected to fall by 20 percent from the 2014 level. What will be the expected net income for each firm?
g. Prepare a profit-volume graph for each firm.

49. **LO.5 (CVP; DOL; MS—two quarters; comprehensive)** Following is information pertaining to Dayton Co.'s operations of the first and second quarter of 2013:

	QUARTER	
	First	Second
Units		
Production	70,000	60,000
Sales	60,000	70,000
Expected activity level	65,000	65,000
Unit selling price	$ 75.00	$ 75.00
Unit variable costs		
Direct material	$ 34.50	$ 34.50
Direct labor	16.50	16.50
Factory overhead	7.80	7.80
Selling and administrative	5.70	5.70
Fixed costs		
Factory overhead	$195,000	$195,000
Selling and administrative	42,800	42,800

Additional Information

- There were no finished goods at January 1, 2013.
- Dayton Co. writes off any quarterly underapplied or overapplied overhead as an adjustment to Cost of Goods Sold.
- Dayton Co.'s income tax rate is 35 percent.

a. Prepare a variable costing income statement for each quarter.

b. Calculate each of the following for 2013 if 260,000 units were produced and sold:
   1. Unit contribution margin.
   2. Contribution margin ratio.
   3. Total contribution margin.
   4. Net income.
   5. Degree of operating leverage. (Round to the nearest tenth of a percent.)
   6. Annual break-even unit sales volume. (Round to the nearest whole unit.)
   7. Annual break-even dollar sales volume. (Round to the nearest dollar.)
   8. Annual margin of safety as a percentage. (Round to the nearest whole percent.)
   9. Annual margin of safety in units.

50. **LO.6 (CVP assumptions; writing)** You were talking to your roommate one day about CVP analysis and the approaches that are used to calculate the break-even point. You also described the assumptions that underlie this type of analysis.

Your roommate proclaimed, "Wow, you people in accounting are pretty simple. Do you realize how unrealistic it is to assume that, no matter how many units you sell, you will realize the same price per unit? And, I've never heard any serious person suggest that costs are linear. How can you possibly state that assumption with a straight face? In your world, profit maximization is simple … just produce the maximum amount possible."

Provide a written justification of the assumptions accountants make in conducting CVP analysis that will satisfy your critical economist roommate.

51. **LO.2, LO.3, & LO.5 (Incremental analysis)** Calypso Canvas makes canvas window awnings. You have been asked to predict the potential effects of some proposed company changes. The following information is available:

Variable cost per unit	
Direct material	$18.40
Direct labor	13.00
Production overhead	8.60
Selling expenses	4.60
Administrative expenses	3.00
Annual fixed cost	
Production overhead	$1,200,000
Selling	960,000
Administrative	480,000

The selling price is $94 per unit, and expected sales volume for the current year is 150,000 units. Following are some changes proposed by various members of the company.

1. Engineers suggest that adding color accents to each unit at a cost of $14.40 would increase product sales by 20 percent.
2. The sales manager suggests that a $520,000 increase in advertising will increase sales by 15 percent.
3. The sales force believes that lowering the price by 5 percent will increase demand in units by 10 percent.

a. Compute the current break-even point in units and dollars. (Round to the nearest unit.)
b. Compute the current margin of safety in dollars, in units, and as a percentage. (Round to the nearest whole percentage.)
c. Compute the independent effects on profit and dollar break-even point of each of the suggestions. For each proposal, advise company management about acceptability.

Yuri Arcurs/Shutterstock.com

10

Relevant Information for Decision Making

LEARNING OBJECTIVES

After completing this chapter, you should be able to answer the following questions:

1. What factors determine the relevance of information to decision making?
2. What are sunk costs, and why are they not relevant in making decisions?
3. What information is relevant in an outsourcing decision?
4. How can management achieve the highest return from use of a scarce resource?
5. What variables do managers use to manipulate sales mix?
6. How are special prices set, and when are they used?
7. How do managers determine whether a product line should be retained or discontinued?

INTRODUCTION

Relevant costing focuses managerial attention on a decision's relevant (or pertinent) information. Relevant costing techniques are applied in virtually all business decisions in both short- and long-term contexts. This chapter examines the application of relevant costing techniques to recurring business decisions, such as replacing an asset, outsourcing a product or part, allocating scarce resources, manipulating sales mix, and evaluating special pricing of orders. Discussion of analysis tools that are applied to longer-term decisions is deferred to Chapter 15. Long-term decisions generally require consideration of costs and benefits that are mismatched in time; that is, the cost is incurred currently, but the benefit is derived in future periods.

The concepts of relevant costing are applied in the process of making decisions and using a step-wise approach to select the best decision choice. There are four steps in this decision process.

Step 1: The necessity of making a decision becomes evident. To illustrate, assume a machine crucial to a manufacturing firm suffers a major breakdown. This event triggers the need to make a decision to choose an action that will restore the machine's productive function.

Step 2: Decision choices or alternatives are identified. Continuing with the broken machine example, two obvious choices would be to repair or replace the machine. However, less obvious choices might also be considered, such as outsourcing the work normally performed on the broken machine to a third-party vendor that possesses and operates this type of machine.

Step 3: The relevant costs and benefits associated with each decision alternative identified in step 2 are calculated. This chapter is largely dedicated to this step in the decision process.

Step 4: The decision alternative providing the largest net benefit to the organization is selected. This step naturally follows from the pursuit of profit maximization in business organizations and efficient cost management in governmental and not-for-profit entities.

THE CONCEPT OF RELEVANCE

1 What factors determine the relevance of information to decision making?

In decision making, managers should consider only relevant costs and revenues associated with each decision alternative. For information to be relevant, it must possess three characteristics:

- be associated with the decision under consideration;
- be important to the decision maker; and
- have a connection to, or bearing on, some future endeavor.

There is a relationship between time and relevance. As the decision time horizon is reduced, fewer costs and revenues are relevant because the majority of such amounts cannot be changed by short-term management actions. In the longer term, management action can influence virtually all costs. Regardless of whether the decision is a short- or long-term one, all decision making requires analysis of relevant information.

Association with Decision

Cost accountants assist managers in determining which costs and revenues are decision relevant. Costs or revenues are relevant when they are logically related to a decision and vary (incrementally or differentially) from one decision alternative to another. **Incremental revenue** (or **differential revenue**) is the amount of revenue that varies across decision choices; **incremental cost** (or **differential cost**) is the amount of cost that varies across decision choices. For example, if the annual operating cost of an existing machine is $30,000 and that of a potential replacement machine is $22,000, the incremental annual cost to operate the existing machine is $8,000 ($30,000 – $22,000). Stated differently, $22,000 of operating cost is in common between the two machines, but $8,000 is incremental or differential. Only the incremental cost is relevant to a decision.

The process of relevant costing requires comparing the incremental revenues and incremental costs of alternative choices. Although incremental costs can be variable or fixed, a general guideline is that most variable costs are relevant but most fixed costs are not.

The logic of this guideline is that, as an activity measure (such as sales or production volume) changes within the relevant range, total variable cost changes but total fixed cost remains constant. However, there are exceptions to this general rule, particularly in the long-run.

The difference between the incremental revenue and incremental cost of a particular alternative is the incremental profit (incremental loss) of that course of action. Management can compare incremental effects of alternatives in choosing the most profitable (or least costly) alternative. Although such a comparison sounds simple, for two reasons often it is not. First, the concept of relevance is an inherently individualistic determination; second, technological changes have increased the amount of available information to consider in making a decision. One challenge is to get as much information as possible that reflects relevant costs and benefits.

Some relevant factors, such as sales commissions or direct production costs, are easily identified and quantified because they are captured by the accounting system. Other factors are relevant and quantifiable but are not captured by the accounting system. Such factors cannot be ignored merely because they are difficult to obtain or require the use of estimates. For example, an **opportunity cost** represents the benefit forgone because one course of action is chosen over another. These costs are extremely important in decision making but are not directly obtainable from the accounting records.

To illustrate the concept of opportunity cost, assume that on August 1, Joey bought a ticket for $90 to attend a concert in December. In October, Joey's friend offers to buy the ticket for $120. Joey now must make a decision in which there are two mutually exclusive choices: attend the concert or sell the ticket. The $120 price offered by Joey's friend is an opportunity cost or the benefit that Joey will sacrifice if he chooses to attend the concert rather than sell the ticket.

Importance to Decision Maker

The need for specific information depends on how important that information is relative to achieving managerial objectives. Additionally, precise information is given more credence in the decision process over less precise information. However, if information is extremely important, but less precise, a manager must weigh importance against precision.

Bearing on the Future

Information may pertain to past or present events but is relevant only if it pertains to a future decision choice. All managerial decisions are made to affect future events, so the information on which decisions are based should reflect future effects. The future can be the short run (two hours from now, or next month) or the long run (three years from now).

Only future costs and revenues can be influenced by current decisions and, as the time horizon lengthens, a larger set of future costs are differential, avoidable, and relevant. The challenge in relevant costing is to remove from consideration those costs that are not relevant, such as **sunk costs** which have been incurred in the past. One common misconception or error in decision making is treating a sunk cost, such as a previously purchased asset's acquisition cost or book value, as though it were relevant.

SUNK COSTS

2 What are sunk costs, and why are they not relevant in making decisions?

Sunk costs cannot be changed no matter what future course of action is taken because historical transactions cannot be reversed. For example, managers could find that a previously acquired asset is no longer adequate for its intended purpose, does not perform to expectations, is technologically obsolete, or is no longer marketable. Managers must then decide whether to keep the asset. This decision uses the current or future selling price that can be obtained for the asset, but that price is the result of current or future conditions and does not "recoup" the historical or sunk cost. The historical cost is irrelevant to the decision.

Although asset acquisition decisions are covered in depth in Chapter 15, they provide an excellent setting to introduce the concept of relevant information. The following illustration includes simplistic assumptions regarding asset acquisitions but demonstrates why sunk costs are not relevant costs.

Assume that Landry Mechanical purchases a robotic warehouse management system for $12,000,000 on December 9. This "original" system is expected to have a useful life of five years and no salvage value. Five days later, on December 14, Jill Landry, vice president of production, notices an advertisement for a similar system for $10,800,000. This "new" system also has an estimated life of five years and no salvage value, but it has features that enable it to perform better than the original system as well as save $355,000 per year in labor costs. On investigation, Landry discovers that the original system can be sold currently for $8,900,000. Exhibit 10.1 provides data on the original and new robotic warehouse management systems.

Exhibit 10.1 Landry Mechanical: Robotic Warehouse Management System Replacement Decision Data

	Original System (Purchased December 9)	New System (Available December 14)
Cost	$12,000,000	$10,800,000
Life in years	5	5
Salvage value	$0	$0
Current resale value	$8,900,000	Not applicable
Annual operating cost	$855,000	$500,000

Landry Mechanical has two options:

- use the original system or
- sell the original system and buy the new system.

Exhibit 10.2 indicates the relevant costs Landry should consider in making her decision. As the computations show, the original system's $12,000,000 purchase cost does not affect the decision outcome. This amount was sunk when the company bought the system. However, by selling the original system, the company would have net cash outlay for the new system of only $1,900,000, calculated as follows:

Cash cost of new system	$10,800,000
Less cash from sale of old system	(8,900,000)
Incremental cash outlay	$ 1,900,000

Exhibit 10.2 Relevant Costs Related to Landry Mechanical's Alternatives

Alternative (1): Use original system		
Operating cost over life of original system ($855,000 × 5 years)		$ 4,275,000
Alternative (2): Sell original system and buy new		
Cost of new system	$10,800,000	
Resale value of original system	(8,900,000)	
Effective net outlay for new system	$ 1,900,000	
Operating cost over life of new system ($500,000 × 5 years)	2,500,000	
Total cost of new system		(4,400,000)
Benefit of keeping the original system		$ 125,000
The alternative incremental calculation follows:		
Savings from operating the new system for five years		$ 1,775,000
Less effective incremental outlay for new system		(1,900,000)
Incremental advantage of keeping the original system		$ 125,000

Using either system, Landry Mechanical will incur operating costs over the next five years, but will spend $355,000 less each year using the new system for lifetime operating savings of $1,775,000.

A common analytical tendency is to include the $12,000,000 sunk cost of the old system in the analysis. However, this cost does not differ between the decision alternatives. If Landry keeps the original system, the company will deduct the $12,000,000 as depreciation expense over the system's life. Alternatively, if the system is sold, Landry will charge the $12,000,000 against the revenue realized from the system's sale. Thus, the $12,000,000 depreciation charge or its equivalent loss is the same in magnitude whether the company retains the original system or sells it and buys the new one. Because the amount is the same under both alternatives, it is not relevant to the decision process.

Landry must consider only the following relevant factors in deciding whether to purchase the new system:

- cost of the new system ($10,800,000);
- current resale value of the original system ($8,900,000); and
- annual savings of the new system ($355,000) and the number of years (five) such savings would be enjoyed.[1]

This example demonstrates the difference between relevant and irrelevant costs, including sunk costs. The next section discusses how the concepts of relevant costing, incremental revenues, and incremental costs are applied in making routine, recurring managerial decisions.

RELEVANT COSTS FOR SPECIFIC DECISIONS

In evaluating courses of action, managers should select the alternative that provides the highest incremental benefit to the company. In doing so, managers must compare the net benefits of all courses of action against a baseline alternative. One course of action that is often used as the baseline alternative is the "change nothing" or "do nothing" option.

Although certain incremental revenues and incremental costs are associated with other alternatives, the "change nothing" alternative has a zero incremental benefit because it reflects the status quo. Some situations involve specific government regulations or mandates in which a "change nothing" alternative does not exist. For example, assume a regulatory governmental agency issues an injunction against a company for polluting river water. Delays in the installation of pollution control devices could create fines that management should consider as incremental costs of the decision to delay. Not installing the devices would result in company closure, creating an opportunity cost equal to the lifetime income that would have been generated had sales continued.

Rational decision-making behavior includes a comprehensive evaluation of the monetary effects of all alternative courses of action. The chosen course should be one that provides the greatest benefit to the business relative to all other possible choices. In making decisions, managers must also find a way to include any inherently nonquantifiable considerations. Inclusion can be made by attempting to quantify those items or by simply making instinctive value judgments about nonmonetary benefits and costs.

Outsourcing Decisions

3 What information is relevant in an outsourcing decision?

Deciding how to source required inputs is an important decision for every business. Traditionally, many companies ensured the availability as well as the desired level of quality of parts and services by controlling all functions internally. However, there is a growing trend to purchase more of the required materials, components, and services through an outsourcing process. **Outsourcing** refers to having work performed for one company by an off-site, nonaffiliated supplier; this process allows a company to buy a product (or service) from an outside supplier rather than making the product or performing the service in-house.

The outsourcing trend is global in scope and has become a hotly debated topic in the United States. Central to the debate is the effect on U.S. employment that outsourcing has

[1] In addition, two factors that were not discussed are important: the potential tax effects of the transactions and the time value of money. The authors have chosen to defer consideration of these factors to Chapter 15, which covers capital budgeting. Because of the time value of money, both systems were assumed to have zero salvage values at the end of their lives—a fairly unrealistic assumption.

when it involves **offshoring**, which sends work formerly performed in the home country to other countries.

While offshoring might cause potential job losses in the United States, an alternative viewpoint is that foreign companies are also "offshoring" from their countries to the United States, possibly resulting in more job creation than job loss.[2] According to one research study, the industries with the highest total contract values for outsourced and offshored work in 2010 were financial services ($25.2 billion), manufacturing ($17.1 billion), and energy ($8.5 billion).[3]

An **outsourcing decision** (or **make-or-buy decision**) is made only after comparing internal production and opportunity costs to external purchase cost and then assessing the best use of facilities. Having an insourcing (make) option implies that the company has the capacity available for that purpose or has considered the cost of obtaining the necessary capacity. Relevant information for this type of decision includes both quantitative and qualitative factors. Exhibit 10.3 summarizes the primary motivations for companies to pursue

Exhibit 10.3 Benefits of Outsourcing

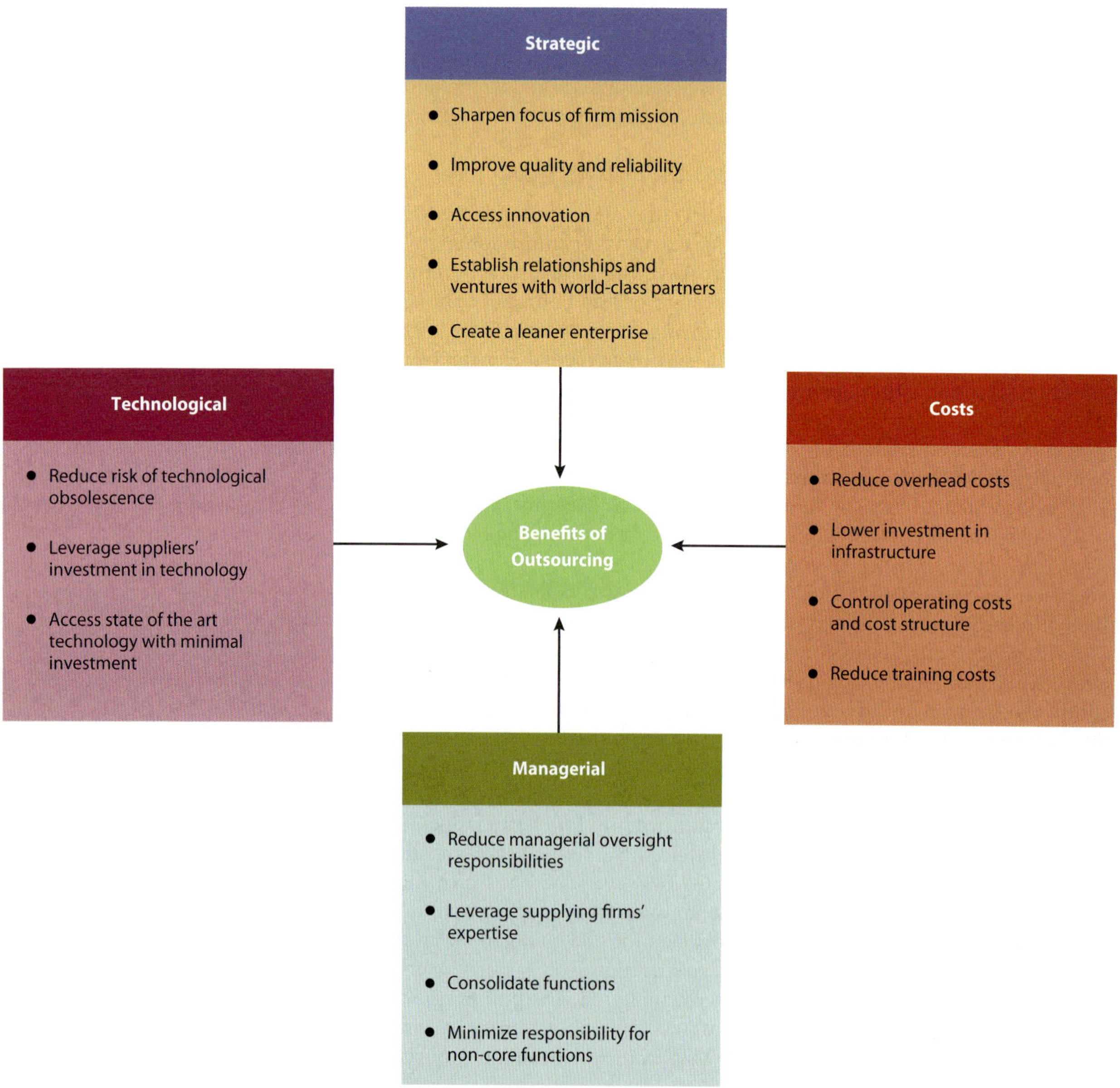

[2] See Benjamin Wright, "Employment, Trends, and Training," *Occupational Outlook Quarterly* (Spring 2009), p. 38; http://www.bls.gov/opub/ooq/2009/spring/art04.pdf (accessed 12/16/11).

[3] See Plunkett Research Ltd., Outsourcing & Offshoring Industry Overview (2011); http://www.plunkettresearch.com/outsourcing-offshoring-bpo-market-research/industry-statistics (accessed 12/16/11).

outsourcing. Most outsourcing is not related to an organization's strategic core but to the management of operating costs and the desire to free personnel from "drudge work."[4]

Thus, routine activities such as information processing are more often outsourced than activities that constitute core competencies or new strategies.

Numerous factors, such as those included in Exhibit 10.4, should be considered in the outsourcing decision. Several quantitative factors, such as incremental direct material and direct labor costs per unit, are known with a high degree of certainty. Other factors, such as variable overhead per unit and opportunity cost for production facilities, must be estimated. Qualitative factors should be evaluated by more than one individual so personal biases do not distort business judgment.

Exhibit 10.4 Outsource Decision Considerations

Relevant Quantitative Factors

- Incremental production costs for each unit
- Unit cost of purchasing from outside supplier (price less any discounts available plus shipping, etc.)
- Number of available suppliers
- Production capacity available to manufacture components
- Opportunity costs of using facilities for production rather than for other purposes
- Amount of space available for storage
- Costs associated with carrying inventory
- Increase in throughput generated by buying components

Relevant Qualitative Factors

- Reliability of supply sources
- Ability to control quality of inputs purchased from outside
- Nature of the work to be subcontracted (such as the importance of the part to the whole)
- Impact on customers and markets
- Future bargaining position with supplier(s)
- Perceptions regarding possible future price changes
- Perceptions about current product prices (are the prices appropriate or, in some cases with international suppliers, is product dumping involved?)

Although companies can access better knowledge, experience, and process methodology through outsourcing, they also lose some control. Thus, company management should carefully evaluate the activities to be outsourced. The pyramid in Exhibit 10.5 is one model for assessing outsourcing risk. Factors to consider include whether

- a function is considered critical to the organization's long-term viability (such as product research and development);
- the organization is pursuing a core competency relative to this function; and
- issues such as product/service quality, time of delivery, flexibility of use, or reliability of supply can be resolved to the company's satisfaction.

Exhibit 10.6 provides information about hinges for a door casing manufactured by Landry Mechanical. The total cost to manufacture one hinge set is $7.90, or a set can be purchased externally for $7.00. Landry's cost accountant is preparing an analysis to determine whether the company should continue making the hinges or purchase them from the outside supplier.

[4] See Paul Brent, "The Third-Party Solution," *CA Magazine* (May 2009), p. 26.

goal or purpose. **Linear programming (LP)** is one method used to find the optimal allocation of scarce resources in a situation involving one objective and multiple limiting factors.[6]

In addition to considering the monetary effects related to scarce resource decisions, managers must remember that all factors cannot be readily quantified and that a situation's qualitative aspects must be evaluated in addition to the quantitative ones. For example, before choosing to produce only drills, Landry Mechanical's managers should assess the potential damage to the firm's reputation and customer markets if the company were to limit its product line to a single item. Such a choice severely restricts a company's customer base and is especially important if the currently manufactured products are competitively related. For example, if Landry Mechanical stopped manufacturing table saws, customers wanting a drill and a table saw might decide to make their purchase from a company that could supply both products.

Concentrating on a single product can also create market saturation or company stagnation. Some products, such as refrigerators and Rolex watches, are purchased infrequently; other products, such as exercise equipment, may be purchased only in single units. Making products that are purchased infrequently or only in single units limits the company's opportunity for repeat business. If a company concentrates on the wrong single product (such as video telephones or laser video disks), that exclusionary choice can be the beginning of the company's end.

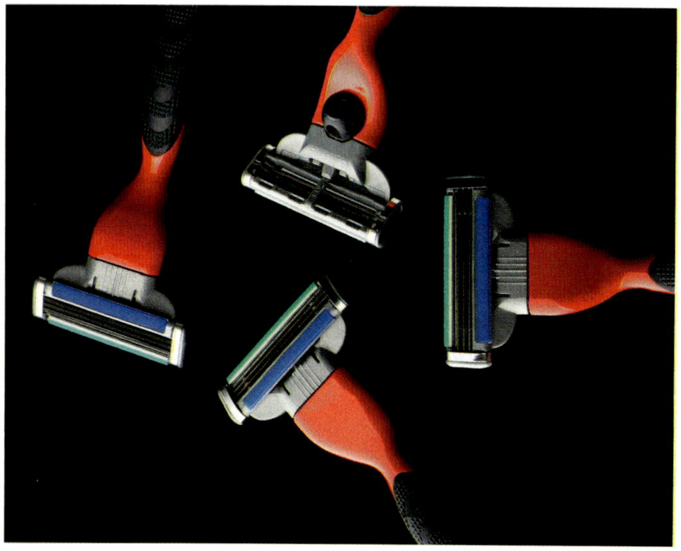
Enrico Jose/Dreamstime.com

Companies that produce related or complementary products, like razors and razor blades, may group the revenues and expenses associated with the products.

In some cases, the revenues and expenses of a group of products must be considered as a set in allocating scarce resources. Multiple products could be complementary or part of a package in which one product cannot be used effectively without another product or is the key to revenue generation in future periods. To illustrate these possibilities, consider the following products: **Gillette**'s Atra razor and razor blades, **Hewlett Packard**'s ink jet printers and printer cartridges, and **Mattel**'s Barbie "family" of products. Would it be reasonable for Gillette to make only razors, HP to make only printers, or Mattel to make only Barbie dolls? In the case of Gillette, the company is known for giving away its razors—simply because of the future benefit of razor blade purchases. Mattel's management would probably choose to manufacture and sell Barbie dolls at zero contribution margin because of the profits that Barbie accessories generate.

Thus, company management could decide that production and sale of some number of less profitable products is necessary to maintain either customer satisfaction or sales of other products. The revenue side of production mix is sales mix.

Sales Mix Decisions

5 What variables do managers use to manipulate sales mix?

Managers continuously strive to achieve a variety of company objectives such as maximization of profit, maintenance of or increase in market share, and generation of customer goodwill and loyalty. Managers must be effective in selling products or performing services to accomplish these objectives. Regardless of whether the company is a retailer, manufacturer, or service organization, **sales mix** refers to the relative product quantities composing a company's total sales. Some important factors affecting a company's sales mix are

- product selling prices,
- sales force compensation, and
- advertising expenditures.

Because a change in one or all of these factors could cause sales mix to shift, managing these factors is fundamental to managing profit.

[6] Finding the best allocation of resources when multiple goals exist is called goal programming. This topic is beyond the scope of this text.

Assume that Landry Mechanical has a line of meat slicers in addition to drills and table saws. Exhibit 10.9 provides information on that line; the information is used to illustrate the effects of the three factors—selling prices, sales compensation, and advertising—on sales mix. The product line includes standard, home deluxe, and professional slicers; each type of slicer has different features and is targeted at a different market segment. All slicers compete on the basis of high quality and are priced at the high end of their market niches.

Exhibit 10.9 Landry Mechanical—Meat Slicer

Product Information		Standard	Home Deluxe	Professional
Unit selling price (SP)		$80	$450	$900
Variable costs				
Direct material		$33	$185	$425
Direct labor		12	75	245
Variable factory overhead		15	45	90
Total variable production cost		$60	$305	$760
Product contribution margin		$20	$145	$140
Variable selling expense (10% of SP)		(8)	(45)	(90)
Contribution margin per unit		$12	$100	$ 50
Total fixed costs:				
Production	$4,200,000			
Selling & administrative	1,100,000			
Total	$5,300,000			

Sales Price Changes and Relative Profitability of Products A company must continually monitor the sales prices of its products, with respect to both each other and competitors. Such monitoring can provide information that causes management to change one or more sales prices. Factors that might influence price changes include

- fluctuations in demand,
- changes in production/distribution cost,
- changes in economic conditions, and
- changes in competition.

Any shift in the selling price of one product in a multiproduct firm normally causes a change in sales mix of that firm because of the economic law of demand elasticity with respect to price.[7]

For Landry Mechanical, profit maximization is the primary corporate objective. This strategy does not necessarily translate into maximizing unit sales of the product with the highest selling price and minimizing unit sales of the product with the lowest selling price; the highest selling price per unit does not necessarily yield the highest contribution margin per unit or per dollar of sales. In Landry Mechanical's case, the slicer with the highest sales price (the professional model) yields the second-highest unit CM of the three products but the lowest CM as a percent of sales. The company generates more profit by selling a dollar's worth of the home deluxe slicer than a dollar's worth of either the standard or the professional model. A dollar of sales of the home deluxe slicer yields $0.22 (rounded) of CM compared to $0.15 for the standard and $0.06 (rounded) for the professional.

[7] The law of demand elasticity indicates how closely price and demand are related. Product demand is highly elastic if a small price reduction generates a large demand increase. If demand is less elastic, large price reductions are needed to bring about moderate sales volume increases. In contrast, if demand is highly elastic, a small price increase results in a large drop in demand.

If profit maximization is the goal, managers should consider each product's sales volume and unit contribution margin. Total company CM is the sum of the contribution margins provided by the sale of all products. Exhibit 10.10 shows product sales volumes and the respective total CMs from the three slicer types. To maximize profits from the slicers, Landry's management must maximize total contribution margin rather than per-unit CM.

Exhibit 10.10 Landry Mechanical—Relationship between Contribution Margin, Sales Volume, and Profit

	Unit Contribution Margin (from Exhibit 10.9)	Current Sales Volume in Units	Income Statement Information
Standard slicers	$ 12	52,000	$ 624,000
Home deluxe slicers	100	39,000	3,900,000
Professional slicers	50	15,000	750,000
Total contribution margin of product sales mix			$ 5,274,000
Fixed expenses (from Exhibit 10.9)			(5,300,000)
Product line income at present volume and sales mix			$ (26,000)

A product's sales volume typically is related to its selling price. Generally, when a product's or service's price increases and demand is elastic with respect to price, demand for that product decreases.[8] Thus, if Landry Mechanical's management decides to raise the standard slicer price to $100, the company should experience some decline in demand for that product. Landry's marketing researchers have indicated that a $20 price increase would cause product demand to drop from 52,000 to 30,000 slicers per period. The effect of this pricing decision on Landry Mechanical's slicer product line income is shown in Exhibit 10.11.

Exhibit 10.11 Landry Mechanical—Relationship between Sales Price Change, Sales Volume, and Profit

	Unit Contribution Margin (from Exhibit 10.9)	New Sales Volume in Units	Income Statement Information
Standard slicers	$ 30*	30,000	$ 900,000
Home deluxe slicers	100	39,000	3,900,000
Professional slicers	50	15,000	750,000
Total contribution margin of product sales mix			$ 5,550,000
Fixed expenses (from Exhibit 10.9)			(5,300,000)
Product line income at new volume and sales mix			$ 250,000

*New $100 price minus [total $60 variable production costs + $10 variable selling expense (10% of new selling price)]

Because CM per unit of the standard slicer increased, the total dollar contribution margin generated by sales of that product increased despite the decrease in unit sales.

[8] Such a decline in demand would generally not occur when the product in question has no close substitutes or is not a major expenditure in consumers' budgets.

This example assumed that customers did not switch their purchases from the standard slicer to other Landry Mechanical products when the price of the standard slicer went up. When some product prices in a product line remain stable and others increase, customers might substitute one product for another. This example ignored switching between company products, but some customers might purchase a more expensive slicer after the standard slicer price increased. For example, customers might believe that the difference in functionality between the standard and home deluxe slicers is worth the price difference and make such a purchasing switch.

In making decisions to raise or lower prices, relevant quantitative factors include

- new contribution margin per unit of product,
- short-term and long-term changes in product demand and production volume because of the price change, and
- best use of the company's scarce resources.

Some relevant qualitative factors involved in pricing decisions are

- impact of changes on customer goodwill toward the company,
- customer loyalty toward company products, and
- competitors' responses to the firm's new pricing structure.[9]

Also, changes in the competitive environment create opportunities for producing new products; exploiting such opportunities leads to sales mix changes.

When determining prices for proposed new products, management should take a long-run view of the product's life cycle. This view should include assumptions about consumer behavior, competitor behavior, pace of technology changes, government posture, environmental concerns, size of the potential market, and demographic changes. These considerations would affect product price estimates at various stages in the product's life cycle.

Sales Compensation Changes Many companies compensate salespeople by paying a fixed rate of commission on gross sales dollars. This approach motivates salespeople to sell the highest-priced product rather than the product providing the highest contribution margin to the company. If the company has a profit maximization objective, such a compensation policy will be ineffective in achieving that objective.

Assume that Landry Mechanical has set a price structure for its slicers as follows: standard, \$100; home deluxe, \$450; and professional, \$900. The company's current policy is to pay sales commissions equal to 10 percent of selling price. This commission structure encourages sales of professional slicers rather than home deluxe or standard slicers. Landry is considering a new compensation structure that would provide base salaries for all salespeople totaling \$925,000 per period.[10] In addition, Landry would pay salespeople a commission equal to 15 percent of product contribution margin (selling price minus total variable production cost). The per-unit product CMs of the slicers are \$40, \$145, and \$140, respectively, for standard, home deluxe, and professional slicers. The new compensation policy should motivate sales personnel to sell more of the slicers that produce the highest commission, which would correspondingly be the company's most profitable products.[11]

Exhibit 10.12 (page 406) compares Landry Mechanical's total contribution margin using the current sales mix and commission structure with that of the new compensation structure focused on total CM. The new structure increases profits by shifting sales from slicers with a lower CM ratio to those with a higher CM ratio. Salespeople also benefit from the new pay structure through higher total compensation. Reflected in the sales mix change

[9]With regard to competitor reactions, consider what occurs when one airline lowers its fares on a particular route. Typically, all other airlines flying that route rapidly adjust their fares accordingly. Thus, any competitive advantage lasts only for a short time.

[10]The revised compensation structure should allow the sales personnel to achieve the same or higher income as before the change given a similar level of effort.

[11]This statement relies on the assumption that the salespersons' efforts are more highly correlated with unit sales than dollar sales. If this assumption is accurate, the commission structure should encourage sales of products with higher CM ratios.

Exhibit 10.12 Landry Mechanical—Impact of Change in Commission Structure

	Product Contribution Margin	–	Commission	=	Contribution Margin after Commission	×	Volume	=	Total Contribution Margin
Old Policy—Commissions Equal 10% of Selling Price									
Standard	$ 40		(0.1 × $100) = $10		$ 30.00		30,000		$ 900,000
Home deluxe	145		(0.1 × $450) = $45		100.00		39,000		3,900,000
Professional	140		(0.1 × $900) = $90		50.00		15,000		750,000
Total contribution margin for product sales							84,000		$5,550,000
New Policy—Commissions Equal 15% of Product Contribution Margin per Unit and Incremental Base Salaries of $925,000									
Standard	$ 40		(0.15 × $40) = $ 6.00		$ 34.00		40,000		$1,360,000
Home deluxe	145		(0.15 × $145) = $21.75		123.25		49,000		6,039,250
Professional	140		(0.15 × $140) = $21.00		119.00		10,000		1,190,000
Total contribution margin for product sales							99,000		$8,589,250
Less sales force base salaries									(925,000)
Contribution margin adjusted for sales force base salaries									$7,664,250

is the fact that standard slicers can be sold with substantially less salesperson effort per unit than that required for the other models.

Fixed expenses would not be considered in setting compensation structures unless those expenses were incremental relative to the new policy or to changes in sales volumes. The new base salaries were an incremental cost of Landry Mechanical's proposed compensation plan.

Advertising Budget Changes Adjusting the advertising budgets of specific products or increasing the company's total advertising budget could lead to shifts in the sales mix. This section uses the data for Landry Mechanical from Exhibit 10.11 and examines a proposed increase in the company's total advertising budget.

Landry Mechanical's advertising manager, Joe Malanga, has proposed increasing the advertising budget from $500,000 to $650,000 per year. He believes the increased advertising will result in the following additional slicer sales during the coming year: standard, 2,500; home deluxe, 1,500; and professional, 750. Company management wants to know whether spending the additional $150,000 for advertising to generate the additional 4,750 units of sales will produce higher profits than the slicer line is currently generating.

The original fixed costs, as well as the CM generated by the current sales levels, are irrelevant to the decision. The relevant items are the increased sales revenue, increased variable costs, and increased fixed cost—the incremental effects of the advertising change. The difference between incremental revenues and incremental variable costs is the incremental contribution margin from which the incremental fixed cost is subtracted to obtain the incremental benefit (or loss) of the decision.[12]

See Exhibit 10.13 for calculations of the expected increase in contribution margin if the company makes the increased advertising expenditure. Because the $262,500 additional CM more than covers the $150,000 incremental cost for advertising, company management should increase advertising by $150,000. Increased advertising can cause changes in the sales mix or in the number of units sold by targeting advertising efforts at specific products. Sales can also be influenced by opportunities that allow companies to obtain business at a sales price that differs from the normal price.

[12] This same type of incremental analysis is shown in Chapter 9 in relation to cost-volume-profit computations.

Exhibit 10.13 Landry Mechanical—Analysis of Increased Advertising Cost

	Standard	Home Deluxe	Professional	Total
Increase in volume	2,500	1,500	750	4,750
Contribution margin per unit	× $30	× $100	× $50	
Incremental contribution margin	$75,000	$150,000	$37,500	$ 262,500
Incremental fixed cost of advertising				(150,000)
Incremental benefit from increased advertising expenditure				$ 112,500

Special Order Decisions

6 How are special prices set, and when are they used?

In a **special order decision**, management computes sales prices for production or service jobs that are not part of the company's normal operations. Special order situations include

- jobs that require a bid,
- are accepted during slack periods, or
- are made to a particular buyer's specifications.

Typically, the sales price quoted on a special order job should be high enough to cover the job's variable and incremental fixed costs and generate a profit.

Sometimes companies depart from their price-setting routine and offer "low-ball" selling prices. A low-ball price could cover only costs and produce no profit or even be below cost. The rationale of low-ball bids is to obtain the job and have the opportunity to introduce company products or services to a particular market segment. Special pricing of this nature could provide work for a period of time, but cannot be continued over the long run. To remain in business, a company must set selling prices to cover total costs and provide a reasonable profit margin.[13]

Special pricing also arises for private-label orders in which the buyer's (rather than the producer's) name is attached to the product. Companies may accept these jobs during slack periods to more effectively use available capacity. Fixed costs are typically not allocated to special order, private-label products. Some variable costs (such as sales commissions) can be reduced or eliminated by the very nature of the private-label process. Prices on this type of special order are typically set high enough to generate a positive contribution margin.

Special prices can also be justified when orders are of an unusual nature (because of the quantity, method of delivery, or packaging) or when products are tailor-made to customer instructions. Last, special pricing is used when goods are produced for a one-time job, such as an overseas order that will not affect domestic sales.

Assume that Landry Mechanical has the opportunity to bid on a special order for 60,000 private-label slicers for a major kitchen products retailer. Company management wants to obtain the order if the additional business will provide a satisfactory contribution to profit. Landry has unused production capacity available and can obtain the necessary components and raw material from suppliers. Also, Landry has no immediate opportunity for its currently unused capacity, so there is no opportunity cost associated with the unused capacity.

Management has gathered the information shown in Exhibit 10.14 (page 408) to determine a price to bid on the private-label slicers. Direct material and components, direct labor, and variable factory overhead costs are relevant to setting the bid price because these costs will be incurred for each slicer produced. Although all variable costs are normally relevant to a special pricing decision, variable selling expense is irrelevant in this instance because no sales commission will be paid on this sale. Fixed manufacturing overhead and

[13] An exception to this general rule can occur when a company produces related or complementary products. For instance, an electronics company can sell a video game at or below cost and allow the ancillary software program sales to be the primary source of profit.

Exhibit 10.14 Landry Mechanical—Private-Label Slicer Product Information

	Normal Costs	Relevant Costs
Per-unit cost for slicers:		
Direct material and components	$ 90	$ 90
Direct labor	25	25
Variable overhead	35	35
Variable selling expense (commission)	20	0
Total variable cost	$170	$150
Fixed factory overhead (allocated)	30	
Fixed selling & administrative expense	20	
Total cost per slicer	$220	

fixed selling and administrative expenses are not expected to increase because of this sale, so these expenses are not relevant in the pricing decision.

Using the available cost information, the relevant cost for determining the bid price for each slicer is $150 (direct material and components, direct labor, and variable overhead). This cost is the minimum price at which the company should sell one slicer. Any price higher than $150 will provide some incremental contribution margin and profit.

Assume that Landry Mechanical's slicer line is currently experiencing a $3,100,000 net loss. Any price set above the $150 variable cost will contribute toward reducing the product line loss. If company managers want to set a bid price that would cover the net loss and create a $200,000 before-tax profit, Landry would spread the total $3,300,000 desired contribution margin over the 60,000-unit special order at $55 per slicer. This approach would indicate a bid price of $205 per slicer ($150 variable cost + $55).

In setting the bid price, management may specify a "reasonable" profit on the special order. Landry's management believes that a normal profit margin of $25 per slicer, or 11.4 percent (rounded) of the $220 full cost. is reasonable. Setting the special order bid price at $167.10 would cover the $150 variable production cost and provide the 11.4 percent profit margin ($17.10) on incremental unit cost. This computation illustrates a simplistic cost-plus approach to pricing but ignores both product demand and market competition. Landry's bid price should also reflect these considerations. In addition, company management should consider any effects that the additional job will have on normal company activities and whether this job will create additional, unforeseen costs. As discussed in Chapter 4, activities create costs, so management must be aware of the company's cost drivers.

When setting a special order price, management must consider qualitative as well as quantitative issues. For instance, management should answer questions such as the following:

- Will setting a low bid price establish a precedent for future prices?
- Will the contribution margin on a bid, set low enough to acquire the job, be sufficient to justify the additional burdens placed on management and employees by this activity?
- Will the additional production activity require the use of bottleneck resources and reduce company throughput?
- How will special order sales affect the company's normal sales?
- If production of the special order is scheduled during a period of low business activity (off-season or recession), is management willing to take the business at a lower contribution or profit margin simply to keep a trained workforce employed?

A final consideration in making special pricing decisions in the United States is the **Robinson-Patman Act**, which prohibits companies from pricing the same product at different levels when those amounts do not reflect related cost differences. Cost differences must result from actual variations in the cost to manufacture, sell, or distribute a product because of different methods of production or quantities sold.

Companies may, however, give **ad hoc discounts**, which are price concessions that relate to real (or imagined) competitive pressures rather than to where a buyer is located or the quantity of goods purchased. Such discounts are not usually subject to detailed justification because they are based on a competitive market environment. Although ad hoc discounts do not require intensive justification under the law, other types of discounts do because they could reflect some type of price discrimination. Prudent managers must understand the legalities of special pricing and the factors that allow for its implementation. For normally stocked merchandise, the only support for pricing differences is a difference in distribution or service costs.

In making pricing decisions, managers typically first analyze the market environment, including the degree of industry competition and competitors' prices. Then managers consider full production cost in setting normal sales prices. Full production cost includes an allocated portion of fixed manufacturing costs, which in a multiproduct environment could include common costs of production relating to more than one type of product. Allocations of common costs can distort the results of operations shown for individual products.

Product Line and Segment Decisions

7 How do managers determine whether a product line should be retained or discontinued?

Operating results of multiproduct environments are often disaggregated to show results by product lines. In reviewing these disaggregated statements, managers must distinguish relevant from irrelevant information regarding individual product lines. If all costs (variable and fixed) are allocated to product lines, a product line or segment could be perceived as operating at a loss when actually it is not. The commingling of relevant and irrelevant information on the statements could cause such perceptions.

Exhibit 10.15 provides basic earnings information for Landry Mechanical's Steel Door Division, which manufactures three product lines: Economy, Standard, and Deluxe. The data suggest that the Deluxe line is operating at a net loss of $165,000. Managers reviewing such results might reason that the division would be $165,000 more profitable if the Deluxe line were dropped. Such a conclusion could be premature because relevant and irrelevant information are combined within the income statement.

Exhibit 10.15 Steel Door Division of Landry Mechanical Product Line Income Statements (in $000s)

	Economy	Standard	Deluxe	Total
Sales	$ 8,000	$ 9,800	$ 3,000	$ 20,800
Total direct variable expenses	(5,400)	(5,700)	(2,200)	(13,300)
Total contribution margin	$ 2,600	$ 4,100	$ 800	$ 7,500
Total fixed expenses	(2,100)	(3,700)	(965)	(6,765)
Net income (loss)	$ 500	$ 400	$ (165)	$ 735
Details of fixed expenses				
(1) Avoidable fixed expenses	$ 1,200	$ 3,000	$ 450	$ 4,650
(2) Unavoidable fixed expenses	600	420	300	1,320
(3) Allocated common expenses	300	280	215	795
Total	$ 2,100	$ 3,700	$ 965	$ 6,765

All fixed expenses have been allocated to the individual product lines in Exhibit 10.15. Such allocations are traditionally based on one or more measures of "presumed" equity for each product line, such as the following:

- square footage occupied in the manufacturing plant,
- number of machine hours incurred for production, and
- number of direct labor employees.

In all cases, however, allocations could force fixed expenses into specific product line operating results even though some of those expenses were not actually incurred for the benefit of the specific product line.

Based on the data at the bottom of Exhibit 10.15, Exhibit 10.16 segregates the Steel Door Division's fixed expenses into three subcategories:

- avoidable if the particular product line is eliminated (these expenses can also be referred to as *attributable expenses*),
- directly associated with a particular product line but not avoidable, and
- incurred for the benefit of the company as a whole (i.e., **common expenses**) but that are allocated to individual product lines.

Exhibit 10.16 Steel Door Division of Landry Mechanical Segment Margin Income Statements (in $000s)

	Economy	Standard	Deluxe	Total
Sales	$ 8,000	$ 9,800	$ 3,000	$ 20,800
Total direct variable expenses	(5,400)	(5,700)	(2,200)	(13,300)
Total contribution margin	$ 2,600	$ 4,100	$ 800	$ 7,500
(1) Avoidable fixed expenses	(1,200)	(3,000)	(450)	(4,650)
Segment margin	$ 1,400	$ 1,100	$ 350	$ 2,850
(2) Unavoidable fixed expenses	(600)	(420)	(300)	(1,320)
Product line result	$ 800	$ 680	$ 50	$ 1,530
(3) Allocated common expenses	(300)	(280)	(215)	(795)
Net income (loss)	$ 500	$ 400	$ (165)	$ 735

The latter two subcategories are irrelevant in deciding whether to eliminate a product line. If one product line is eliminated, an unavoidable expense merely shifts to another product line. Common expenses will be incurred regardless of which product lines are eliminated. An example of a common cost is the insurance premium on a manufacturing facility that houses all product lines.

If the Steel Door Division eliminates the Deluxe line, total divisional profit will decline by the $350,000 segment margin of that line. **Segment margin** represents the excess of revenues over direct variable expenses and avoidable fixed expenses. It is the amount remaining to cover unavoidable direct fixed expenses and common expenses and to provide profit.[14] The appropriate figure on which to base the continuation or elimination decision is segment margin because it measures the segment's contribution to the coverage of indirect and unavoidable expenses. The new net income of $385,000 that would result from having only two product lines (Economy and Standard) is in the following alternative computations:

	(In $000s)
Current net income	$ 735
Decrease in income due to elimination of Deluxe (segment margin)	(350)
New net income	$ 385
Proof:	
Total contribution margin of Economy and Standard lines	$ 6,700
Less avoidable fixed expenses of the Economy and Standard lines	(4,200)
Segment margin of Economy and Standard lines	$ 2,500
Less all remaining unavoidable and allocated expenses in Exhibit 10.16 ($1,320 + $795)	(2,115)
Remaining income with two product lines	$ 385

[14] All common expenses are assumed to be fixed; this is not always the case. Some common costs could be variable, such as expenses of processing purchase orders or computer time-sharing expenses for payroll or other corporate functions.

Based on the information in Exhibit 10.16, the Steel Door Division should not eliminate the Deluxe product line because it is generating a positive segment margin and covering its relevant expenses.

In classifying product line costs, managers should be aware that some costs can appear to be avoidable but are actually not. For example, the salary of a supervisor working directly with a product line appears to be an avoidable fixed cost if the product line is eliminated. However, if such supervisors are transferred to other areas upon disposition of a product line, their salaries will continue and must be treated as unavoidable. These types of determinations must be made before costs can be appropriately classified in product line elimination decisions.

Depreciation on factory equipment used to manufacture a specific product is an irrelevant cost in product line decisions. But if the equipment can be sold, the selling price is relevant to the decision because the sale increases the benefit of discontinuing the product line. Even if the equipment will be kept in service and used to make other products, the depreciation expense is unavoidable and irrelevant to the decision.

Before deciding to discontinue a product line, management should carefully consider what resources would be required to make the product line profitable as well as the long-term ramifications of product line elimination. For example, product line elimination shrinks market assortment, which could cause some customers to seek other suppliers that maintain a broader market assortment. And, as in other relevant costing situations, decisions have qualitative as well as quantitative factors that must be analyzed. Individual customers also should be assessed (in the same manner as product lines) for profitability. When necessary, ways to improve the cost–benefit relationship should be determined.

Management's task is to effectively and efficiently allocate its finite stock of resources to accomplish its objectives. A cost accountant must learn what uses management will make of requested information to ensure that it is relevant and provided in the appropriate form. Managers must have a reliable quantitative basis on which to analyze problems, compare viable solutions, and choose the best course of action. Because management is a social rather than a natural science, it has no fundamental "truths," and few related problems are susceptible to black-or-white solutions. Relevant costing is a process of making human approximations of the costs of alternative decision results.

Comprehensive Review Module

KEY TERMS

ad hoc discount, p. 409
common expense, p. 410
differential cost, p. 392
differential revenue, p. 392
incremental cost, p. 392
incremental revenue, p. 392
linear programming (LP), p. 402
make-or-buy decision, p. 396
mathematical programming, p. 401
offshoring, p. 396
opportunity cost, p. 393
outsourcing, p. 395
outsourcing decision, p. 396
relevant costing, p. 392
Robinson-Patman Act, p. 408
sales mix, p. 402
scarce resource, p. 400
segment margin, p. 410
special order decision, p. 407
sunk cost, p. 393

CHAPTER SUMMARY

1 Decision Making

- Because of their association with the decision, importance to the decision maker, and bearing on the future, the following items are relevant in decision making:
  - costs that vary between decision choices (incremental or differential costs) and
  - benefits sacrificed by pursuing one decision choice rather than another (opportunity costs).

2 Sunk Costs

- Sunk costs are
  - incurred in the past to acquire assets or resources.
  - not relevant to decision making because they cannot be changed regardless of which decision choice is selected.
  - not recoverable regardless of current circumstances.

3 Outsourcing

- Relevant considerations in outsourcing (or offshoring) decisions include
  - quantitative factors such as
    - ➢ incremental/differential production costs,
    - ➢ opportunity costs,
    - ➢ external purchase costs, and
    - ➢ cash flow.
  - qualitative factors such as
    - ➢ capacity availability,
    - ➢ quality control,
    - ➢ technology availability,
    - ➢ organizational core competencies,
    - ➢ employee skill levels in-house and externally,
    - ➢ business risk, and
    - ➢ supplier availability and reliability.

4 Scarce Resources

- A scarce resource
  - is essential to production but is available only in limited quantity.
  - includes machine hours, skilled labor hours, raw materials or components, and production capacity.
  - requires management to base decisions on the contribution margin per unit of scarce resource available from alternative uses of the scarce resources; organizational profitability will be maximized by producing and selling the product or service that has the highest contribution margin per unit of scarce resource.

5 Sales Mix

- Sales mix is a key determinant of organizational profitability.
- Sales mix can be managed by manipulating
  - sales prices,
  - sales compensation methods, or
  - advertising budgets.

6 Special Prices

- Special prices for products or services
  - are generally set based on relevant variable production and selling costs and, if any, incremental fixed costs.
  - may or may not include a profit amount.
  - are used when companies bid on special order jobs, such as those that
    - ➢ require a bid,
    - ➢ are accepted during slack periods,
    - ➢ are made to a particular buyer's specifications, or
    - ➢ are of an unusual nature because of the order quantity, method of delivery, or packaging.

7 Product Line Decisions

- Segment margin
  - is the excess of revenues over direct variable expenses and avoidable fixed expenses for a specific product/service line.
  - measures the segment's contribution to the coverage of indirect and unavoidable expenses and profit.
  - is used to decide whether a product line should be retained or eliminated; a positive segment margin indicates retention and a negative segment margin indicates elimination.

SOLUTION STRATEGIES

General rule of decision making: Choose the alternative that yields the greatest incremental benefit.

  Incremental (additional) revenues
– Incremental (additional) costs
  Incremental benefit (positive or negative)

Relevant Costs, p. 392

- Direct material
- Direct labor
- Variable production overhead
- Variable selling expenses related to each alternative (can be greater or less than the "change nothing" alternative)
- Avoidable fixed production overhead
- Avoidable fixed selling/administrative costs (if any)
- Opportunity cost of choosing some other alternative (either increases the cost of one alternative or reduces the cost of another alternative)

Relevant Cost Analysis of Specific Decisions, p. 400

Single Scarce Resource

1. Identify the scarce resource.
2. Determine the per-unit consumption of the scarce resource for each product.
3. Determine the contribution margin per unit of the scarce resource for each product.
4. Produce and sell the product with the highest contribution margin per unit of scarce resource to maximize profits.

Product Line Analysis

Sales
– Direct variable expenses
= Product line contribution margin
– Avoidable fixed expenses
= Segment (product line) margin*
– Unavoidable fixed expenses
= Product line operating results

*Make decision to retain or eliminate based on this line item.

DEMONSTRATION PROBLEM

HD Video produces various equipment for home theatre and sound systems. One key component in all of the company's products is a module requiring two speakers configured in custom combinations. The firm currently incurs the following costs to make each speaker module:

Direct material	$24
Direct labor	16
Variable overhead	10
Fixed overhead	20

Of the per-unit fixed overhead, the firm could avoid $8 if the modules were purchased from a company that has offered to sell an equivalent module for $56. HD Video produces 20,000 modules annually.

Required:

(Consider each requirement to be independent of the others.)

a. Should HD Video outsource the production of the module? Show calculations.
b. HD Video's vice president, Fred Flick, estimates that the company can rent out the facilities used to make the modules for $120,000 annually. What should the company do? Show calculations.
c. What are some qualitative factors that HD Video should consider in making the speaker module outsourcing decision?

Solution to Demonstration Problem

a. Relevant cost of making:

Direct material	$24
Direct labor	16
Variable overhead	10
Avoidable fixed overhead	8
Total	$58
Cost to outsource	$56

The cost to outsource is below the relevant cost to manufacture. Therefore, HD Video should outsource the speaker module.

b. $120,000 rental income ÷ 20,000 modules = $6 opportunity cost per module

Relevant cost to insource [from (a)]	$58
Opportunity cost	6
Total	$64

The cost to insource is now even more inferior to outsourcing. Therefore, HD Video should outsource the item.

c. Some qualitative factors include the following:

- HD Video's future control of quality, supply, cost, and price of the speaker module;
- supplier's long-run going concern prospects;
- existence and number of qualified suppliers;
- impact on customers and markets;
- impact on employees; and
- reaction of financial and business press.

POTENTIAL ETHICAL ISSUES

ETHICS

1. Ignoring important qualitative factors in making relevant decisions, such as the impact on domestic employees, when companies choose to offshore operations
2. Choosing to move production offshore to a developing country to exploit lax environmental and labor regulations
3. Making decisions based on how they will impact reported financial earnings rather than by using relevant information
4. Using bait-and-switch advertising techniques to manage sales mix
5. Pricing products or services at amounts that violate the Robinson-Patman Act or other jurisdictional pricing regulations, especially if the prices are meant to be discriminatory against any type of protected group
6. Handling a scarce material circumstance by substituting materials that pose high risks to human health or the environment

QUESTIONS

1. What does the term *relevance* mean in the context of making management decisions?
2. How does the passage of time affect the set of costs that is relevant to a decision?
3. What are opportunity costs, and why are they often the most difficult costs to analyze in decision making?
4. Describe sunk costs. Are there circumstances in which sunk costs are relevant to decisions? Discuss.
5. What is outsourcing? Why is the practice fervently debated in the United States?
6. What is a scarce resource? Why is an organization's most scarce resource likely to change from time to time?

7. What is the objective of managing the sales mix of products? What are the major factors that influence sales mix?
8. What is a special order decision? Under what circumstances would a company refuse to accept a special order?
9. What is segment margin? How is segment margin used in the quantitative analysis of a decision to drop or keep a product line?

EXERCISES

10. **LO.1-LO.3 (Relevant costs; sunk costs)** Prior to the 2012 Super Bowl, a Boston-area retailer ordered 50,000 T-shirts that read: New England Patriots—2012 Super Bowl Champs. The company paid $11.75 for each of the custom T-shirts. Following the loss of New England to the New York Giants, the retailer found itself with 15,000 unsold T-shirts after the Super Bowl. Before the Super Bowl, the retailer was able to sell 35,000 of the T-shirts at an average per-unit price of $25. The company is currently deciding how to dispose of the 15,000 remaining T-shirts. The retailer has learned from one of its suppliers that each shirt could be reworked at an average cost of $5.50 per shirt (which involves removing the Super Bowl reference from the shirts). Management of the retailer believes the reworked shirts could be sold at an average price of $10.25 during the coming football season. Alternatively, the company could sell the shirts at an average price of $2.60 as scrap material.
    a. Identify at least three alternative courses of action management could take with regard to the leftover T-shirts.
    b. Which costs are sunk in this decision?
    c. Identify the relevant costs of each alternative you listed in (a).
    d. Based on your answer to (c), what is the best alternative and what is the relative financial advantage of the best alternative over the second-best alternative?

11. **LO.1 & LO.2 (Asset replacement)** On April 1, 2013, Topeka Brake Mfg. purchased new computer-based production scheduling software for $480,000. On May 15, 2013, a representative of a computerized manufacturing technology company demonstrated new software that was clearly superior to that purchased by the firm in April. The price of this software is $840,000. Corporate managers estimate that the new software would save the company $32,000 annually in schedule-related costs compared to the recently installed software. Both software packages should last 10 years (the expected life of the computer hardware) and have no salvage value at that time. The company can sell its existing software for $356,000 if the new software is purchased. Should the company keep and use the software purchased earlier or buy the new software? Show computations to support your answer.

12. **LO.1 & LO.2 (Asset replacement)** Certain production equipment used by Dayton Mechanical has become obsolete relative to current technology. The company is considering whether it should keep or replace its existing equipment. To aid in this decision, the company's controller gathered the following data:

	Old Equipment	New Equipment
Original cost	$350,000	$396,000
Remaining life	5 years	5 years
Accumulated depreciation	$158,000	$0
Annual cash operating costs	$64,000	$16,000
Current salvage value	$88,000	NA
Salvage value in five years	$0	$0

    a. Identify any sunk costs in the data.
    b. Identify any irrelevant (nondifferential) future costs.
    c. Identify all relevant costs to the equipment replacement decision.
    d. What are the opportunity costs associated with the alternative of keeping the old equipment?

e. What is the incremental cost to purchase the new equipment?
f. What qualitative considerations should be considered before making any decision?

13. **LO.1 & LO.2 (Relevant vs. sunk costs; writing)** Your roommate, Jill Catanac, purchased a new portable DVD player just before this school term for $95. Shortly after the semester began, her new DVD player was crushed by an errant "flying plant" during a party at her apartment. Returning the equipment to the retailer, Catanac was informed that the estimated cost of repairs was $75 because the damage was not covered by the manufacturer's warranty.

    Pondering the figures, Catanac was ready to decide to make repairs; after all, she had recently paid $95 for the equipment. However, before making a decision, she asked for your advice.

    a. Using concepts from this chapter, prepare a brief presentation outlining factors that Catanac should consider in making her decision.
    b. Continue the presentation in (a) by discussing the options Catanac should consider in making her decision. Start by defining a base case against which alternatives can be compared.

14. **LO.1 & LO.2 (Relevant costs)** Assume that you are about to graduate from your university and are deciding whether to apply for graduate school or enter the job market. To help make the decision, you have gathered the following data:

Costs incurred for the bachelor's degree	$163,000
Out-of-pocket costs for a master's degree	$94,000
Estimated starting salary with B.A.	$49,400
Estimated starting salary with M.A.	$66,800
Estimated time to complete master's degree	2 years
Estimated time from the present to retirement	40 years

    a. Which of these factors is relevant to your decision?
    b. What is the opportunity cost associated with earning the master's degree?
    c. What is the out-of-pocket cost to obtain the master's degree?
    d. What other factors should you consider before making a decision?

15. **LO.1 & LO.2 (Relevant costs)** High Frequency manufactures and sells MP-3 players. Information on last year's operations (sales and production of the 2013 model) follows.

Sales price per unit	$70
Costs per unit	
Direct material	$16
Direct labor	14
Overhead (50% variable)	12
Selling costs (40% variable)	20
Production in units	10,000
Sales in units	9,500

    At this time (April 2014), the 2014 model is in production, and it renders the 2013 model obsolete. If the remaining 500 units of the 2013 model MP-3 players are to be sold through regular channels, what is the minimum price the company would accept for the players?

16. **LO.1 & LO.2 (Relevant costs; writing)** Because of a monumental error committed by its purchasing department, Corner Grocery ordered 5,000 heads of lettuce rather than the 1,000 that should have been ordered. The company paid $0.65 per head for the lettuce. Although management is confident that it can sell 2,000 units through regular sales, the market is not large enough to absorb the other 3,000 heads. Management has identified two ways to dispose of the excess heads of lettuce. First, a wholesaler has offered to purchase them for $0.25 each. Second, a restaurant chain has offered to purchase the lettuce if Corner Grocery will agree to convert it into packaged lettuce for salads. This option would require Corner Grocery to incur $2,500 for conversion, and the heads of lettuce could then be sold for the equivalent of $1.05 each.

a. Which costs are sunk in this decision?
b. Actually, Corner Grocery can consider three alternatives in this decision. Describe the alternative that is not mentioned in the problem.
c. What are the relevant costs of each decision alternative, and what should the company do?

17. **LO.3 (Outsourcing)** Glass Tech manufactures fiberglass housings for portable generators. One part of the housing is a metal latch. Currently, the company produces the 120,000 metal latch units required annually. Company management is considering purchasing the latch from an external vendor. The following data are available for making the decision:

ETHICS

EXCEL

Cost per Unit to Manufacture	
Direct material	$1.40
Direct labor	1.36
Variable overhead	0.72
Fixed overhead—applied	1.12
Total cost	$4.60

Cost per Unit to Purchase	
Purchase price	$3.92
Freight charges	0.08
Total cost	$4.00

a. Assuming that all of Glass Tech's internal production costs are avoidable if the company purchases rather than makes the latch, what would be the net annual cost advantage to purchasing the latches?
b. Assume that some of Glass Tech's fixed overhead costs could not be avoided if it purchases rather than makes the latches. How much of the fixed overhead must be avoidable for the company to be indifferent as to making or buying the latches?

18. **LO.3 (Outsourcing)** Pneu Shoe Company manufactures various types of athletic shoes. Several types require a built-in air pump. Presently, the company makes all air pumps it requires. However, management is evaluating an offer from Ram Air Co. to provide air pumps at a cost of $3.60 each. Pneu Shoe's management has estimated that the variable production costs of the air pump total $2.70 per unit and that the company could avoid $27,000 per year in fixed costs if it purchased rather than produced the air pumps.

a. If 25,000 pumps per year are required, should Pneu Shoe make them or buy them from Ram Air Co.?
b. If 60,000 pumps per year are required, should Pneu Shoe make them or buy them?
c. Assuming that all other factors are equal, at what level of production would the company be indifferent between making and buying the pumps?

19. **LO.3 (Outsourcing)** Tuff Tach produces pickup truck bumpers that are sold on a wholesale basis to new car retailers. The average bumper sales price is $170. Normal annual sales volume is 300,000 units, which is the company's maximum production capacity. At this capacity, the company's per-unit costs are as follows:

Direct material	$ 53 (including mounting hardware @ $15 per unit)
Direct labor	17
Overhead (2/3 is fixed)	45
Total	$115

A key component in producing bumpers is the mounting hardware used to attach the bumpers to the vehicles. Birmingham Mechanical has offered to sell Tuff Tach as many mounting units as the company needs for $20 per unit. If Tuff Tach accepts the offer, the released facilities currently used to produce mounting hardware could be used to produce an additional 4,800 bumpers. What alternative is more desirable and by what amount? (Assume that the company is currently operating at its capacity of 300,000 units.)

20. **LO.4 (Allocation of scarce resources)** Sierra Sound Systems makes electronic products. Because the employees of one of the company's plants are on strike, the Chicago plant is operating at peak capacity. It makes two electronic products: MP3 players and PDAs. Presently, the company can sell as many of each product as can be made, but making a PDA takes twice as long in production labor time as an MP3 player. The company's production capacity is 100,000 labor hours per month. Data on each product are as follows:

	MP3 Players	PDAs
Sales	$ 72	$108
Variable costs	(58)	(88)
Contribution margin	$ 14	$ 20
Labor hours required	1	2
Fixed costs are $240,000 per month.		

a. How many of each product should the Chicago plant make? Explain your answer.
b. What qualitative factors would you consider in making this product mix decision?

EXCEL

21. **LO.4 (Allocation of scarce resources)** LaNora White received her accounting degree in 1992. Since graduating, she has obtained significant experience in a variety of job settings. Her skills include auditing, income and estate taxation, and business consulting. White currently has her own practice, and her skills are in such demand that she limits her practice to taxation issues. Most of her engagements are one of three types: individual income taxation, estate taxation, or corporate taxation. Following are data pertaining to the revenues and costs of each tax area (per tax return):

	Individual	Estate	Corporate
Revenue	$350	$1,200	$750
Variable cost	$ 50	$ 200	$150
Hours per return of White's time	2	8	5

Fixed costs of operating the office are $80,000 per year. White has such significant demand for her work that she must ration her time. She desires to work no more than 2,000 hours in the coming year. She can allocate her time so that she works only on one type of tax return or on any combination of the three types.

a. How should White allocate her time in the coming year to maximize her income?
b. Based on the optimal allocation, what is White's projected pre-tax income for the coming year?
c. What other factors should White consider in allocating her time?
d. What could White do to overcome the scarce resource constraint?

22. **LO.5 (Sales mix)** Cellular Communications manufactures cell phones and two cell phone accessories: ear buds and a 12-volt (automotive) battery charger. (Each ear bud package contains a set of ear buds.) The ear buds and charger are compatible only with the Matrix cell phone. Sales prices and variable costs for each product are as follows:

	Cell Phones	Set of Ear Buds	Charger
Sales	$ 75	$20	$20
Variable production costs	(60)	(4)	(5)
Variable selling costs	(4)	(1)	(2)
Contribution margin	$ 11	$15	$13
Unit sales (next year's budget)	1,400,000	400,000	200,000

The historical data of Cellular Communications suggest that, for each of the seven cell phones sold, two ear bud sets and one battery charger are sold. The company is currently exploring two options to increase overall corporate income for the upcoming year. The alternatives that follow would maintain the historical sales mix ratios:

1. Increase corporate advertising by $1,000,000. The company estimates doing so would increase total unit sales to 2,200,000.

2. Decrease the price of cell phones to $70. The company estimates doing so would increase cell phone sales to 3,150,000 units and have no effect on the other products.

a. Determine the effect of each proposal on budgeted profits for the coming year. Which alternative is preferred, and what is the relative financial benefit of that alternative?

b. How could the firm's management increase the ratio of ear buds and chargers to cell phone unit sales?

23. **LO.5 (Sales mix)** Pet Palace provides two types of services to dog owners: grooming and training. All company personnel can perform each service equally well. To expand sales and market share, Pet Palace's manager, Jim Jones, relies heavily on radio and billboard advertising, but the 2014 advertising budget is expected to be very limited. Information on projected operations for 2014 follows.

	Grooming	Training
Revenue per billable hour	$50	$70
Variable cost of labor	$20	$41
Material cost per billable hour	$6	$7
Allocated fixed cost per year	$250,000	$260,000
Projected billable hours for 2014	30,000	20,000

a. What is Pet Palace's projected pre-tax profit (or loss) for 2014?

b. If $1 spent on advertising could increase grooming revenue by $20 or training revenue by $20, on which service should the advertising dollar be spent?

c. If $1 spent on advertising could increase either grooming billable time or training billable time by one hour, on which service should the advertising dollar be spent?

24. **LO.5 (Sales mix)** One product produced and sold by Big Boy Toys is an ATV gun rack for which 2014 projections are as follows:

Projected volume in units	120,000
Sales price per unit	$60
Variable production cost per unit	$25
Variable selling cost per unit	$12
Fixed production cost	$805,000
Fixed selling and administration costs	$435,000

a. Compute the projected pre-tax profit to be earned on the ATV gun rack during 2014.

b. Corporate management estimates that unit volume could be increased by 20 percent if sales price were decreased by 10 percent. How would such a change affect the profit level projected in (a)?

c. Rather than cutting the sales price, management is considering holding the sales price at the projected level and increasing advertising by $185,000. Such a change would increase volume by 20 percent. How would the level of profit under this alternative compare to the profit projected in (a)?

25. **LO.6 (Special order)** For The Ages Inc. produces solid-oak umbrella stands. Each stand is handmade and hand finished using the finest materials available. The firm has been operating at capacity (2,000 stands per year) for the past three years. Based on this capacity of operations, the firm's costs per stand are as follows:

Direct material	$ 50
Direct labor	40
Variable overhead	10
Fixed overhead	30
Total cost	$130

All selling and administrative expenses incurred by the firm are fixed. The average selling price of stands is $230. Recently, a large retailer approached Bill Wood, the president of For The Ages, about supplying three special stands to give as gifts to CEOs of key suppliers. Wood estimates that the following per-unit costs would be incurred to make the three stands:

Direct material	$250
Direct labor	350
Variable overhead	90
Total direct costs	$690

To accept the special order, the firm would have to sacrifice production of 20 regular units.

a. Identify all relevant costs that Wood should consider in deciding whether to accept the special order.
b. Assume the retailer offers to pay For The Ages a total of $3,800 for the three stands. How would accepting this offer affect For The Ages' pre-tax income?

26. **LO.6 (Special order)** Wyoming Wire produces 12.5-gauge barbed wire that is retailed through farm supply companies. Presently, the company has the capacity to produce 100,000 tons of wire per year. It is operating at 80 percent of annual capacity, and at this level of operations, the cost per ton of wire is as follows:

Direct material	$560
Direct labor	40
Variable overhead	50
Fixed overhead	190
Total	$840

The average sales price for the output produced by the firm is $900 per ton. The State of Texas has approached the firm to supply 200 tons of wire for the state's prisons for $670 per ton. No production modifications would be necessary to fulfill the order from the State of Texas.

a. What costs are relevant to the decision to accept this special order?
b. What would be the dollar effect on pre-tax income if this order were accepted?

27. **LO.7 (Product line)** Lakeland Financial Services provides outsourcing services for three areas: payroll, general ledger (GL), and tax compliance. The company is currently contemplating the elimination of the GL area because it is showing a pre-tax loss. An annual income statement follows.

Lakeland Financial Services
Income Statement by Service Line
For the Year Ended July 31, 2013
(in thousands)

	Payroll	GL	Tax	Total
Sales	$ 4,400	$ 3,200	$ 3,600	$11,200
Cost of sales	(2,800)	(2,000)	(2,160)	(6,960)
Gross margin	$ 1,600	$ 1,200	$ 1,440	$ 4,240
Avoidable fixed and variable costs	$ 1,260	$ 1,470	$ 1,040	$ 3,770
Allocated fixed costs	180	140	210	530
Total fixed costs	$ 1,440	$ 1,610	$ 1,250	$ 4,300
Operating profit	$ 160	$ (410)	$ 190	$ (60)

a. Should corporate management drop the GL area? Support your answer with appropriate schedules.
b. If the GL area were dropped, how would the company's pre-tax profit be affected?

28. **LO.7 (Product line)** Operations of Borderland Oil Drilling Services are separated into two geographical divisions: United States and Mexico. The operating results of each division for 2013 are as follows:

	United States	Mexico	Total
Sales	$ 7,200,000	$ 3,600,000	$10,800,000
Variable costs	(4,740,000)	(2,088,000)	(6,828,000)
Contribution margin	$ 2,460,000	$ 1,512,000	$ 3,972,000
Direct fixed costs	(800,000)	(490,000)	(1,290,000)
Segment margin	$ 1,660,000	$ 1,022,000	$ 2,682,000
Corporate fixed costs	(1,900,000)	(890,000)	(2,790,000)
Operating income (loss)	$ (240,000)	$ 132,000	$ (108,000)

Corporate fixed costs are allocated to the divisions based on relative sales. Assume that all of a division's direct fixed costs could be avoided by eliminating that division. Because the U.S. division is operating at a loss, Borderland's president is considering eliminating it.

a. If the U.S. division had been eliminated at the beginning of the year, what would have been Borderland's pre-tax income?
b. Recast the income statements into a more meaningful format than the one given. Why would total corporate operating results change from the $108,000 loss to the results determined in (a)?

PROBLEMS

29. **LO.1 & LO.2 (Asset replacement)** Arizona Mechanical recently created a new product, a computer-controlled, laser-precise lathe, and Ohio Ornamental Metals is considering purchasing one. Ohio's CFO received the following information from the accounting department regarding the company's existing lathe and the new Arizona Mechanical lathe. The savings in operating costs offered by the new lathe would mostly derive from reduced waste, reduced labor, and energy cost savings.

Old Machine	
Original cost	$875,000
Present book value	$150,000
Annual cash operating costs	$450,000
Market value now	$200,000
Market value in five years	$0
Remaining useful life	5 years

New Machine	
Cost	$1,600,000
Annual cash operating costs	$155,000
Market value in five years	$0
Useful life	5 years

a. Based on financial considerations alone, should Ohio Ornamental Metals purchase the new lathe? Show computations to support your answer.
b. What qualitative factors should Ohio Ornamental Metals consider before making a decision about purchasing the new lathe?

30. **LO.1 & LO.2 (Asset replacement)** Missouri River Energy Company provides electrical services to several rural counties in Nebraska and South Dakota. Its efficiency has been greatly affected by changes in technology. The company is currently considering the replacement of its main steam turbine, which was put in place in the 1980s but is now technologically obsolete. The turbine's operation is very reliable, but it is much less efficient than newer, computer-controlled turbines. The controller presented the following financial information to corporate management:

	Old Turbine	New Turbine
Original cost	$4,000,000	$6,000,000
Market value now	$400,000	$6,000,000
Remaining life	8 years	8 years
Quarterly operating costs	$210,000	$45,000
Salvage value in eight years	$0	$0
Accumulated depreciation	$800,000	N/A

a. Identify the costs that are relevant to the company's equipment replacement decision.
b. Determine whether it is more financially sound to keep the old turbine or replace it. Provide your own computations based on relevant costs only.
c. For this part only, assume that the acquisition cost of the new technology is unknown. What is the maximum amount that the company could pay for the new technology and be in the same financial condition as it is in currently?
d. What other considerations would come into play if, rather than a new turbine, the company were considering solar-powered technology to replace the old turbine system?

31. **LO.1 & LO.2 (Relevant costs; writing)** Janet Cosgrove is the manager of Saratoga Sporting Goods, a division of Global Sports. Cosgrove's division sells a variety of sporting goods and supplies to wholesalers and retail chains throughout the Pacific Northwest and Latin America. Saratoga Sporting Goods has a single manufacturing facility located in Florida. As the manager of Saratoga Sporting Goods, Cosgrove is paid a salary and a bonus based on the profit she generates for the company. Recently, Cosgrove has been contemplating selling a warehouse owned by the division in Jacksonville. She has gathered the following information regarding the warehouse.

Acquisition date	10/10/1997
Acquisition price	$ 17,500,000
Accumulated depreciation	$ 5,300,000
Current market value	$ 7,000,000

Because the company has adopted JIT-based inventory management, the warehouse is no longer needed to store finished goods inventory. Furthermore, if the warehouse were sold, the $7,000,000 of current market value would be realized on the sale. Cosgrove has consulted you, the CFO of the division, about the effect of the warehouse sale on divisional profits. You provided Cosgrove the following calculation:

Sales price	$ 7,000,000
Less net book value ($17,500,000 – $5,300,000)	(12,200,000)
Projected profit (loss) on sale	$ (5,200,000)

a. Discuss whether the loss that would be recognized on the sale is relevant to the decision to sell the warehouse.
b. What would you recommend that Cosgrove do with respect to the warehouse?

ETHICS

32. **LO.3 (Outsourcing; ethics; writing)** Tate Electronics manufactures computers and all required components. Its purchasing agent informed the company owner, Mervin Tate, that another company had offered to supply keyboards for Tate computers at prices below the variable costs at which Tate can make them. Incredulous, Tate hired an industrial consultant to explain how the supplier could offer the keyboards at less than Tate's variable costs.

The consultant suspects the supplier is using many undocumented laborers to work in its plant. These people are poverty stricken and will take work at substandard wages. Tate's purchasing agent and the plant manager recommend to Mervin Tate that the company should outsource the keyboards because "no one can blame us for the supplier's hiring practices and if those practices come to light, no one will be able to show that we knew of those practices."

a. What are the ethical issues involved in this case?
b. What are the advantages and disadvantages of buying from this supplier?
c. What do you think Tate should do and why?

33. **LO.3 (Outsourcing)** Structural Steel Systems manufactures steel buildings for agricultural and home applications. Currently, managers are trying to decide between two alternatives regarding a major overhead door assembly for the company's buildings. The alternatives are as follows:

- Purchase new equipment with a five-year life and no salvage value at a cost of \$10,000,000. The company uses straight-line depreciation and allocates that amount on a per-unit-of-production basis.
- Purchase the assemblies from an outside vendor who will sell them for \$480 each under a five-year contract.

Following is Structural Steel Systems' present cost to produce one door assembly based on current and normal activity of 50,000 units per year.

Direct material	\$278
Direct labor	132
Variable overhead	86
Fixed overhead*	72
Total	\$568

*The fixed overhead includes \$14 supervision cost, \$18 depreciation, and \$40 general company overhead.

The new equipment would be more efficient than the old equipment and would reduce direct labor costs and variable overhead costs by 25 percent. Supervisory costs of \$700,000 would be unaffected. The new equipment would have a capacity of 75,000 assemblies per year. Structural Steel Systems could lease the space occupied by current assembly production to another firm for \$228,000 per year if the company decides to buy from the outside vendor.

a. Show an analysis, including relevant unit and total costs, for each alternative of producing or buying the assemblies. Assume 50,000 assemblies are needed each year.
b. How would your answer differ if 60,000 assemblies were needed?
c. How would your answer differ if 75,000 assemblies were needed?
d. In addition to quantitative factors, what qualitative factors should be considered?

34. **LO.3 (Outsourcing)** Louisiana Luggage Components manufactures handles for suitcases and other luggage. Depending on the size of the luggage piece, attaching each handle to the luggage requires between two and six standard fasteners, which the company has historically produced. The costs to produce one fastener (based on capacity operation of 4,000,000 units per year) are:

Direct material	\$0.08
Direct labor	0.06
Variable factory overhead	0.04
Fixed factory overhead	0.07
Total	\$0.25

Fixed factory overhead includes \$100,000 of depreciation on equipment for which there is no alternative use and no market value. The balance of the fixed factory overhead pertains to the salary of the production supervisor, Jeff Wittier. Wittier has a lifetime employment contract and the skills that could be used to replace Brenda Gibbons, supervisor of floor maintenance. She draws a salary of \$50,000 per year but is due to retire from the company.

Saratoga Suitcase Co. recently approached Louisiana Luggage Components with an offer to supply all required fasteners for \$0.19 per unit. Anticipated sales demand for the coming year will require 4,000,000 fasteners.

a. Identify the costs that are relevant in this outsourcing decision.
b. What is the total annual advantage or disadvantage (in dollars) of outsourcing the fasteners rather than making them?
c. What qualitative factors should be taken into account in making this decision?

35. **LO.4 & LO.7 (Scarce resource; discontinued product lines; negative contribution margin)** The officers of Bardwell Company are reviewing the profitability of the company's four products and the potential effects of several proposals for varying the product mix. The following is an excerpt from the income statement and other data.

	Total	Product P	Product Q	Product R	Product S
Sales	$ 62,600	$10,000	$18,000	$ 12,600	$ 22,000
Cost of goods sold	(44,274)	(4,750)	(7,056)	(13,968)	(18,500)
Gross profit	$ 18,326	$ 5,250	$10,944	$ (1,368)	$ 3,500
Operating expenses	(12,004)	(1,990)	(2,968)	(2,826)	(4,220)
Income before taxes	$ 6,322	$ 3,260	$ 7,976	$ (4,194)	$ (720)
Units sold		1,000	1,200	1,800	2,000
Sales price per unit		$10.00	$15.00	$7.00	$11.00
Variable cost of goods sold		2.50	3.00	6.50	6.00
Variable operating expenses		1.17	1.25	1.00	1.20

Each of the following proposals is to be considered independently of the other proposals. Consider only the product changes stated in each proposal; the activity of the other proposals remains stable.

a. What is the effect on income if Product P is discontinued?
b. What is the effect on income if Product R is discontinued?
c. What is the effect on income if Product R is discontinued and a consequent loss of customers causes a decrease in sales of 200 units of Product Q?
d. What is the effect on income if the sales price of product R is increased to $8.00 with a decrease in the number of units sold to 1,500?
e. Janet Poole, marketing manager at Bardwell Company, approaches Pamela Bardwell, the company's president. She proposes that Bardwell Company drop production of Product S to produce Product T, which is made on the same production equipment. Product T has a selling price of $14.00, variable manufacturing costs of $9.00, and variable selling expenses of $2.46. Poole estimates that 2,100 units of Product T could be sold annually; she feels that this would be good for the company, as total sales revenue will increase by $7,400 and Product T would be replacing a product that is currently losing money for the company. Poole also believes that this would be good for the morale of the sales department, as total sales commissions will increase. Should Bardwell consider Poole's suggestion? Why or why not?
f. Explain why traditional cost accounting sometimes leads managers to make incorrect decisions.

AICPA ADAPTED

36. **LO.3 (Outsourcing; opportunity cost)** Yoto Heavy Industrial uses ten units of Part No. T305 each month in the production of large diesel engines. The cost to manufacture one unit of T305 is presented below:

Direct material	$ 2,000
Material handling (20% of direct materials)	400
Direct labor	16,000
Manufacturing overhead (150% of direct labor)	24,000
Total manufacturing cost	$42,400

Material handling, which is not included in the manufacturing overhead, represents the direct variable costs of the receiving department that are applied to direct materials and purchased components on the basis of their cost. Yoto's annual manufacturing overhead budget is one-third variable and two-thirds fixed. Workman Hydraulic Company, one of Yoto's reliable vendors, has offered to supply T305 at a unit price of $30,000.

a. If Yoto Heavy Industrial purchases the ten T305 units from Workman Hydraulic Company, the capacity Yoto used to manufacture these parts would be idle. Compute the change in the out-of-pocket cost per unit to Yoto if it decided to purchase the parts from Workman Hydraulic Company.
b. Assume that Yoto Heavy Industrial is able to rent all idle capacity for $50,000 per month. If Yoto decides to purchase the ten units from Workman Hydraulic Company, what would be the change in the total monthly cost for T305?

CMA ADAPTED

37. **LO.3 & LO.4 (Outsourcing; scarce resources)** Callahan Manufacturing has assembled the data appearing below pertaining to two products. Past experience has shown that the unavoidable fixed factory overhead included in the cost per machine hour averages $10. Direct labor is paid $18 per hour. Callahan has a policy of filling all sales orders, even if it means purchasing units from outside suppliers at the same selling price per unit that Callahan currently charges.

	Blender	Electric Mixer
Direct material	$6	$11
Direct labor	$4	$9
Factory overhead at $16 per machine hour	$16	$32
Selling price per unit	$20	$38
Annual demand in units	20,000	28,000

a. Assume Callahan Manufacturing has 50,000 machine hours available. What would be the optimal production of each product to maximize Callahan's profits?
b. Refer to the original information. With all other things constant, if Callahan is able to reduce direct materials cost for the electric mixer by $6 per unit, what strategy should Callahan pursue?
c. Refer to the original information. Assume that an outbreak of swine flu has left Callahan shorthanded on direct labor personnel. Approximately one-half of the workforce will be out of work for one month. During the month, what strategy should Callahan pursue?

CMA ADAPTED

38. **LO.2 & LO.6 (Relevant costs; special order pricing)** Kantrovitz Company is a manufacturer of industrial components. One of its products, AP110, is used as a subcomponent in appliance manufacturing. This product has the following information per unit:

Selling price	$150
Costs:	
Direct material	$ 20
Direct labor	15
Variable manufacturing overhead	12
Fixed manufacturing overhead	30
Shipping and handling	3
Fixed selling and administrative	10
Total per-unit cost	$ 90

a. Kantrovitz has received a special, one-time order for 1,000 AP110 parts. Assuming Kantrovitz has excess capacity, what is the minimum price that is acceptable for beginning negotiations on this order?
b. Kantrovitz has 5,000 units of AP110 in inventory that have some defects. The units cannot be sold through regular channels without a significant price reduction. What per-unit cost figure is relevant for setting a minimum selling price on these units?
c. During the next year, sales of AP110 are expected to be 10,000 units. All costs will remain the same except that fixed manufacturing overhead will increase by 20 percent and direct material will increase by 10 percent. The selling price per unit for next year will be $160. Based on these data, calculate the total contribution margin generated by part AP110.
d. Referring to (a), Kantrovitz has received a special, one-time order for 1,000 AP110 parts. Assume that Kantrovitz is operating at full capacity, and that the contribution of the output would be displaced by the one-time special order. Using the original data, compute the minimum acceptable selling price for this order.

CMA ADAPTED

39. **LO.1, LO.2, & LO.5 (Relevant costs; sales mix; writing)** In November 2005, Microsoft introduced its highly anticipated new video game player, the Xbox 360. In early July 2007, Microsoft announced it was extending the warranty on its Xbox 360 to three years for a certain type of malfunction indicated by three flashing red lights on the game console. The warranty extension would apply to previously sold units; however, the warranty for any other type of failure would not be extended beyond the original one-year warranty term. In making this announcement, Microsoft indicated it

would take a charge of $1.05–1.15 billion in the quarter ending June 30, 2007, for the costs of the warranty extension. [Source: Nick Wingfield, "Microsoft's Videogame Efforts Take a Costly Hit," *Wall Street Journal* (July 6, 2007), p. A3.]

INTERNET

ETHICS

a. What relevant costs were likely considered by Microsoft management in reaching the decision to extend the warranty on the Xbox 360 and, in so doing, incur in excess of $1 billion of additional costs?
b. Conduct research to determine how Microsoft's stock price was affected by the announcement of the warranty extension and its associated costs on July 6, 2007. Explain why the stock price reacted as it did.
c. Assume that one of the rationalizations for Microsoft to extend the warranty on the Xbox 360 was to manage sales mix. How could the extension of the Xbox warranty affect the sales mix of Microsoft's entertainment and devices division?
d. Comment on whether Microsoft was ethically obligated to extend the warranty on the Xbox 360 to three years.

40. **LO.5 (Sales mix)** Leather Accessories produces leather belts and key fobs that sell for $40 and $10, respectively. The company currently sells 100,000 units of each type with the following operating results:

Belts

Sales (100,000 × $40)		$ 4,000,000
Variable costs		
Production (100,000 × $25)	$2,500,000	
Selling (100,000 × $6)	600,000	(3,100,000)
Contribution margin		$ 900,000
Fixed costs		
Production	$ 400,000	
Selling and administrative	180,000	(580,000)
Income		$ 320,000

Key Fobs

Sales (100,000 × $10)		$1,000,000
Variable costs		
Production (100,000 × $6)	$600,000	
Selling (100,000 × $1)	100,000	(700,000)
Contribution margin		$ 300,000
Fixed costs		
Production	$100,000	
Selling and administrative	80,000	(180,000)
Income		$ 120,000

Corporate management has expressed its disappointment with the income being generated from the sales of these two products. Managers have asked for your help in analyzing three alternative plans to improve operating results.

1. Change the sales commission to 12 percent of sales price less variable production costs for each product from the current 5 percent of selling price. The marketing manager believes that the sales of the belts will decline by 5,000 units but those of key fobs will increase by 15,000 units.
2. Increase the advertising budget for belts by $75,000. The marketing manager believes this will increase the sales of belts by 19,000 units but will decrease the sales of key fobs by 9,000 units.
3. Raise the per-unit price of belts by $5 and of key fobs by $3. The marketing manager believes this will cause a decrease in the sales of belts by 6,000 units and of key fobs by 10,000 units. Variable costs per units will not change with the sales price increase.

a. Determine the effects on the income of each product line and the company in total if each alternative plan is put into effect.
b. What is your recommendation to the management of Leather Accessories?

41. **LO.4 & LO.5 (Sales mix with scarce resources)** San Fran Cycles manually manufactures three unique bicycle models: racing, touring, and basic. All of the skilled craftspeople employed at San Fran can make each of the three models. Because it takes about a year to train each craftsperson, labor is a fixed production constraint over the short term. For 2013, the company expects to have available 34,000 labor hours. The average hourly labor rate is $30. Data regarding the current product line follow.

EXCEL

		Racing	Touring	Basic
Selling price		$3,600	$2,720	$960
Variable costs				
Direct material		$ 880	$ 640	$240
Direct labor		1,500	1,050	300
Variable factory overhead		720	480	164
Variable selling		80	60	40
Fixed costs				
Factory	$400,000			
Selling and administrative	100,000			

The company pays taxes at the rate of 50 percent of operating income.

a. If an unlimited amount of any product can be sold, how many of each product should the company make? What pre-tax income will the company earn given your answer?

b. How many (rounded to the nearest whole unit) of each product must the company make if it has the policy to devote no more than 50 percent of its available skilled labor capacity to any one product but at least 20 percent to every product? What pre-tax income will the company earn given your answer?

c. Given the nature of the three products, is it reasonable to believe that there are market constraints on the mix of products that can be sold? Explain.

d. How does the company's tax rate enter into the calculation of the optimal labor allocation?

42. **LO.6 (Special order)** Layton Ironworks manufactures a variety of industrial valves and pipe fittings sold primarily to customers in the United States. Currently, the company is operating at 70 percent of capacity and is earning a satisfactory return on investment.

Prince Industries Ltd. of Scotland has approached Layton's management with an offer to buy 120,000 pressure valves. Prince manufactures an almost identical pressure valve, but a fire in Prince's valve plant has closed its manufacturing operations. Prince needs the 120,000 valves over the next four months to meet commitments to its regular customers; the company is prepared to pay $19 each for the valves.

Layton's product cost for the pressure valve based on current attainable standards is

Direct material	$ 5
Direct labor	6
Manufacturing overhead	9
Total cost	$20

Manufacturing overhead is applied to production at the rate of $18 per standard direct labor hour. This overhead rate is made up of the following components:

Variable factory overhead	$ 6
Fixed factory overhead—direct	8
Fixed factory overhead—allocated	4
Applied manufacturing overhead rate	$18

Additional costs incurred in connection with sales of the pressure valve include 5 percent sales commissions and $1 freight expense per unit. However, the company does not pay sales commissions on special orders that come directly to management.

In determining selling prices, Layton adds a 40 percent markup to product cost, which provides a $28 suggested selling price for the pressure valve. The marketing department, however, has set the current selling price at $27 to maintain market share.

Production management believes that it can handle Prince Industries' order without disrupting its scheduled production. The order would, however, require additional fixed factory overhead of $12,000 per month for supervision and clerical costs.

If management accepts the order, Layton will manufacture 30,000 pressure valves and ship them to Prince Industries each month for the next four months.

a. Determine how many additional direct labor hours would be required each month to fill the Prince Industries order.
b. Prepare an incremental analysis showing the impact of accepting the Prince Industries order.
c. Calculate the minimum unit price that Layton Valves' management could accept for the Prince Industries order without reducing net income.
d. Identify the factors, other than price, that Layton Valves should consider before accepting the Prince Industries order.

CMA ADAPTED

43. **LO.7 (Product line)** You have been hired to assist the management of Great Bend Office Systems in resolving certain issues. The company has its home office in Montana and leases facilities in Montana, Idaho, and North Dakota, where it produces a high-quality bean bag chair designed for residential use. Great Bend management has provided you a projection of operations for fiscal 2014, the forthcoming year, as follows:

	Total	Montana	Idaho	North Dakota
Sales	$ 17,600,000	$ 8,800,000	$ 5,600,000	$ 3,200,000
Fixed costs				
Factory	$ 4,400,000	$ 2,240,000	$ 1,120,000	$ 1,040,000
Administration	1,400,000	840,000	440,000	120,000
Variable costs	5,800,000	2,660,000	1,700,000	1,440,000
Allocated home office costs	2,000,000	900,000	700,000	400,000
Total costs	$(13,600,000)	$(6,640,000)	$(3,960,000)	$(3,000,000)
Pre-tax profit from operations	$ 4,000,000	$ 2,160,000	$ 1,640,000	$ 200,000

The sales price per unit is $100.

Due to the marginal results of operations in North Dakota, Great Bend has decided to cease operations there and sell that factory's machinery and equipment by the end of 2014. Managers expect proceeds from the sale of these assets to exceed their book value by enough to cover termination costs.

Great Bend would like to continue serving its customers in that area if it is economically feasible. It is considering the following three alternatives:

1. Expand the operations of the Idaho factory by using space that is currently idle. This move would result in the following changes in that factory's operations:

	Increase over Factory's Current Operations
Sales	50%
Fixed costs	
Factory	20%
Administration	10%

   Under this proposal, variable costs would be $32 per unit sold.
2. Enter into a long-term contract with a competitor that will serve the area's customers and pay Great Bend a royalty of $16 per unit based on an estimate of 30,000 units being sold.
3. Close the North Dakota factory and not expand the Idaho factory's operations.
   Note: Total home office costs of $2,000,000 will remain the same under each situation.

To assist the company's management in determining which alternative is most economically feasible, prepare a schedule computing its estimated pre-tax profit from total operations that would result from each of the following alternatives:

a. Expansion of the Idaho factory.
b. Negotiation of a long-term contract on a royalty basis.
c. Closure of the North Dakota operations with no expansion at other locations.

AICPA ADAPTED

44. **LO.7 (Product line)** Gilfeather Food Service sells high-quality ice cream and steaks via overnight delivery. Income statements showing revenues and costs of fiscal year 2013 for each product line are as follows.

	Ice Cream	Steaks
Sales	$ 4,000,000	$ 2,000,000
Less: Cost of merchandise sold	(2,600,000)	(1,500,000)
Commissions to salespeople	(200,000)	(150,000)
Delivery costs	(600,000)	(120,000)
Depreciation on equipment	(200,000)	(100,000)
Salaries of division managers	(80,000)	(75,000)
Allocated corporate costs	(100,000)	(100,000)
Net income (loss)	$ 220,000	$ (45,000)

Management is concerned about profitability of steaks and is considering dropping the line. The equipment currently used to process steaks could be rented to a competitor for $8,500 annually. If the steaks line is dropped, allocated corporate costs would decrease from a total of $200,000 to $170,000, and all employees, including the product line manager, would be dismissed. Equipment depreciation would be unaffected by the decision, but $105,000 of the delivery costs charged to the steaks line could be eliminated if it is dropped.

a. Recast the preceding income statements in a format that provides more information in making this decision regarding the steaks product line.
b. What is the net advantage or disadvantage (change in total company pre-tax profits) of continuing sales of steaks?
c. Should the company be concerned about losing ice cream sales if the steaks line is dropped? Explain.
d. How might the layoffs occurring from dropping the steaks line adversely affect the whole company?

45. **LO.1, LO.2, & LO.7 (Comprehensive)** Louisville Jar Co. has processing plants in Kentucky and Pennsylvania. Both plants use recycled glass to produce jars that a variety of food processors use in food canning. The jars sell for $10 per hundred units. Budgeted revenues and costs for the year ending December 31, 2014, in thousands of dollars, are:

EXCEL

	Kentucky	Pennsylvania	Total
Sales	$1,100	$2,000	$3,100
Variable production costs			
Direct material	$ 275	$ 500	$ 775
Direct labor	330	500	830
Factory overhead	220	350	570
Fixed factory overhead	350	450	800
Fixed regional promotion costs	50	50	100
Allocated home office costs	55	100	155
Total costs	$1,280	$1,950	$3,230
Operating income (loss)	$ (180)	$ 50	$ (130)

Home office costs are fixed and are allocated to manufacturing plants on the basis of relative sales levels. Fixed regional promotional costs are discretionary advertising costs needed to obtain budgeted sales levels.

Because of the budgeted operating loss, Louisville Jar Co. is considering ceasing operations at its Kentucky plant. If it does so, proceeds from the sale of plant assets will exceed asset book values and exactly cover all termination costs; fixed factory overhead costs of $25,000 would not be eliminated. Louisville Jar Co. is considering the following three alternative plans:

PLAN A: Expand Kentucky's operations from its budgeted 11,000,000 units to a budgeted 17,000,000 units. It is believed that this can be accomplished by increasing Kentucky's fixed regional promotional expenditures by $120,000.

PLAN B: Close the Kentucky plant and expand the Pennsylvania operations from the current budgeted 20,000,000 to 31,000,000 units to fill Kentucky's budgeted production of 11,000,000 units. The Kentucky region would continue to incur promotional costs to sell the 11,000,000 units. All sales and costs would be budgeted by the Pennsylvania plant.

PLAN C: Close the Kentucky plant and enter into a long-term contract with a competitor to serve the Kentucky region's customers. This competitor would pay a royalty of $1.25 per 100 units sold to Louisville, which would continue to incur fixed regional promotional costs to maintain sales of 11,000,000 units in the Kentucky region.

a. Without considering the effects of implementing Plans A, B, and C, compute the number of units that the Kentucky plant must produce and sell to cover its fixed factory overhead costs and fixed regional promotional costs.
b. Prepare a schedule by plant and in total of Louisville's budgeted contribution margin and operating income resulting from the implementation of each of the following:
   1. Plan A.
   2. Plan B.
   3. Plan C.

AICPA ADAPTED

46. **LO.1, LO.2, & LO.7 (Comprehensive; product line)** Clean-N-Brite is a multiproduct company with several manufacturing plants. The Cincinnati plant manufactures and distributes two household cleaning and polishing compounds, regular and heavy-duty, under the HouseSafe label. The forecasted operating results for the first six months of 2014, when 100,000 cases of each compound are expected to be manufactured and sold, are presented in the following statement:

HouseSafe Compounds—Cincinnati Plant
Forecasted Results of Operations
For the Six-Month Period Ending June 30, 2014

	(IN $000s)		
	Regular	**Heavy-Duty**	**Total**
Sales	$ 2,000	$ 3,000	$ 5,000
Cost of sales	(1,600)	(1,900)	(3,500)
Gross profit	$ 400	$ 1,100	$ 1,500
Selling and administrative expenses			
Variable	$ 400	$ 700	$ 1,100
Fixed*	240	360	600
Total selling and administrative expenses	$ (640)	$(1,060)	$(1,700)
Income (loss) before taxes	$ (240)	$ 40	$ (200)

*The fixed selling and administrative expenses are allocated between the two products on the basis of dollar sales volume on the internal reports.

The sales price per case for the regular compound will be $20 and for the heavy-duty will be $30 during the first six months of 2014. The manufacturing costs by case of product follow.

	COST PER CASE	
	Regular	**Heavy-Duty**
Raw material	$ 7.00	$ 8.00
Direct labor	4.00	4.00
Variable manufacturing overhead	1.00	2.00
Fixed manufacturing overhead*	4.00	5.00
Total manufacturing cost	$16.00	$19.00
Variable selling and administrative costs	$ 4.00	$ 7.00

*Depreciation charges are 50 percent of the fixed manufacturing overhead of each line.

Each product is manufactured on a separate production line. Annual normal manufacturing capacity is 200,000 cases of each product. However, the plant is capable of producing 250,000 cases of regular compound and 350,000 cases of heavy-duty compound annually.

The following schedule reflects top management consensus regarding the price/volume alternatives for the HouseSafe products for the last six months of 2014, which are essentially the same as those during its first six months.

REGULAR COMPOUND		HEAVY-DUTY COMPOUND	
Alternative Prices (per case)	Sales Volume (in cases)	Alternative Prices (per case)	Sales Volume (in cases)
$18	120,000	$25	175,000
20	100,000	27	140,000
21	90,000	30	100,000
22	80,000	32	55,000
23	50,000	35	35,000

Top management believes the expected loss for the first six months reflects a tight profit margin caused by intense competition and that many competitors will be forced out of this market by next year, so the company's profits should improve.

a. What unit selling price should Clean-N-Brite select for each HouseSafe compound for the remaining six months of 2014? Support your answer with appropriate calculations.

b. Without prejudice to your answer for (a), assume that the optimum price/volume alternatives for the last six months will be a selling price of $23 and volume level of 50,000 cases for the regular compound and a selling price of $35 and volume of 35,000 cases for the heavy-duty compound.

   1. Should Clean-N-Brite consider closing its Cincinnati operations until 2015 to minimize its losses? Support your answer with appropriate calculations.
   2. Identify and discuss the qualitative factors that should be considered in deciding whether the Cincinnati plant should be closed during the last six months of 2014.

CMA ADAPTED

47. **LO.1, LO.2, & LO.7 (Sales and profit improvement)** Classic Clothes is a retail organization in the Northeast that sells upscale clothing. Each year, store managers (in consultation with their supervisors) establish financial goals; a monthly reporting system captures actual performance.

One of the firm's sales districts, District A, has three stores but has historically been a very poor performer. Consequently, the district supervisor has been searching for ways to improve the performance of her three stores. For May, she set performance goals with the managers of Stores 1 and 2. The managers will receive bonuses if the stores exceed certain performance measures. The manager of Store 3 decided not to participate in the bonus scheme. Because the district supervisor is unsure what type of bonus will encourage better performance, she offered the manager of Store 1 a bonus based on sales in excess of budgeted sales of $670,000; the manager of Store 2 was offered a bonus based on net income in excess of budgeted net income. The company's net income goal for each store is 12 percent of sales. Budgeted sales for Store 2 are $630,000.

Other pertinent data for May follow.

- At Store 1, sales were 40 percent of total District A sales; sales at Store 2 were 35 percent of total District A sales. The cost of goods sold at both stores was 45 percent of sales.
- Variable selling expenses (sales commissions) were 8 percent of sales for all stores and districts.
- Variable administrative expenses were 3 percent of sales for all stores and districts.
- Maintenance cost including janitorial and repair services is a direct cost for each store. The store manager has complete control over this outlay; however, it should not be below 1 percent of sales.

- Advertising is considered a direct cost for each store and is completely under the store manager's control. Store 1 spent two-thirds of District A's total outlay for advertising, which was 10 times more than Store 2 spent on advertising.
- The rental expense at Store 1 is 40 percent of District A's total and at Store 2 is 30 percent of District A's total.

District A expenses are allocated to the stores based on sales.

a. Will Store 1 or Store 2 generate more profit under the new bonus scheme?
b. Will Store 1 or Store 2 generate more revenue under the new bonus scheme?
c. Why would Store 1 have an incentive to spend so much more on advertising than Store 2?
d. Which store manager has the most incentive to spend money on regular maintenance? Explain.
e. Which bonus scheme appears to offer the most incentive to improve the profit performance of the district in the short term? Long term?

CMA ADAPTED

11

Allocation of Joint Costs and Accounting for By-Product/Scrap

LEARNING OBJECTIVES

After completing this chapter, you should be able to answer the following questions:

1. How are the outputs of a joint process classified?
2. What management decisions must be made before beginning a joint process?
3. How is the joint cost of production allocated to joint products?
4. How are by-product and scrap accounted for?
5. How should retail and not-for-profit organizations account for the cost of a joint activity?

INTRODUCTION

Most companies produce and sell multiple products. Some companies engage in multiple production processes to manufacture a variety of products; other companies have a single process that simultaneously generates different outputs. For example, a chicken processing plant generates whole chickens, chicken parts, ground chicken, and fertilizer from a single input. Similarly, crude oil refining can produce gasoline, motor oil, heating oil, and kerosene; mining can produce copper, silver, and gold.

In a **joint process**, one product line cannot be manufactured without producing others. Such processes are common in the food, extractive, agricultural, and chemical industries. Additionally, the process of producing first-quality merchandise and factory seconds in a single operation can be viewed as a joint process. For example, if a manufacturing process is unstable in that it cannot "maintain output at a uniform quality level, [then] ... the products that emerge from the [process] vary across one or more quality dimensions."[1]

This chapter discusses joint manufacturing processes, their related product outputs, and the accounting treatment of those processing costs. The total cost incurred for material, labor, and overhead during a joint process is called the **joint cost** of the production process. Joint cost is allocated only to the primary products of a joint process using either a physical or a monetary measure. Although joint cost allocations are necessary to determine financial statement valuations, such allocations should *not* be used in making internal decisions.[2] For example, in evaluating a specific joint product's profitability, the decision maker must understand that profitability is determined largely by the method used to allocate the joint cost to the product and that allocation process is an arbitrary one. In later production stages, additional **separate costs** may be incurred and these costs are assignable to the specific products to which those costs relate.

In addition, advertising and marketing expenditures can be joint costs. For example, a not-for-profit (NFP) organization could produce a brochure that serves the concurrent purposes of providing public service information and requesting donations. Joint costs for retail companies and NFPs are covered in the last section of the chapter.

OUTPUTS OF A JOINT PROCESS

1 How are the outputs of a joint process classified?

A joint process inevitably produces more than one product line. Products that result from a joint process and that have a sales value are classified as

- joint products (also called primary products, main products, or co-products),
- by-products, or
- scrap.

Joint products are the key outputs of a joint process. Joint products have substantial revenue-generating ability and, as such, provide the financial motive for the company entering into the production process. Some joint products are dissimilar, while other joint products may be similar products that are finished in alternative ways or similar products of differing quality. For example, a poultry processor generates different grades of turkeys that, depending on certain characteristics defined by the U.S. Department of Agriculture, are graded as A, B, or C quality.

In contrast, **by-product** and **scrap** are incidental outputs of a joint process. Both are salable (with by-products being the more valuable); however, the sales values of these products alone would not be sufficient for management to undertake the joint process. For example, **Corn Products International** would never undertake corn processing simply to generate the corn cob by-product that is ground and used in cosmetics and vitamins. **Krispy Kreme** would not manufacture doughnuts simply to generate the doughnut holes sold to customers. **Weyerhaeuser** would never process lumber merely to obtain the bark that is burned to produce power and steam.

[1] James F. Gatti and D. Jacque Grinnell, "Joint Cost Allocations: Measuring and Promoting Productivity and Quality Improvements," *Cost Management* (July–August 2000), pp. 13–21.

[2] Sometimes correctly pricing a product depends on knowledge of the full cost of making the product, particularly when contractual agreements require cost-plus pricing. Joint cost allocation is also necessary to the costing of products for financial reporting.

Jason Alan/iStockphoto.com

Instead of throwing away day-old bread or bagels, a bakery may decide to use them to make croutons, allowing what would have been waste to be reclassified as a by-product or scrap.

A final residual output from a joint process is **waste**, which has no sales value. In some cases, the expense incurred in disposing of waste may exceed its production cost. Many companies, though, have learned either to minimize their production waste by changing their processing techniques or to reclassify waste as by-product or scrap by finding a use that generates some minimal amount of revenue.

Over time, a product's classification may change because of technology advances, consumer demand, or ecological factors. New joint products may be developed from a production process, as illustrated in the ever-growing list for soybeans (Exhibit 11.1). Some products originally classified as by-products may be reclassified as joint products, and some joint products may be reduced to the by-product category. Even products originally viewed as scrap or waste can be upgraded to joint product or by-product status. For example, years ago, poultry processors considered chicken litter, bones, beaks, and feet to be waste. These items are now recycled and processed further to produce valuable organic fertilizer and, therefore, may be classified as either by-product or scrap. Furthermore, chicken litter can, when gasified, be used to produce electricity.

Joint process output is classified based on management's judgment about the relative sales values of outputs. Classifications are unique to each company. For example, assume

Exhibit 11.1 Products from Soybeans

Soy Foods	Nonedible Products
Animal feed	Adhesives
Butter	Biodiesel fuel
Cereals	Building materials
Chocolate coatings	Candles
Coffee	Cosmetics
Flour	Crayons
Milk and creamers	Disinfectants
Oil	Fiber (Yarn)
Sauce	Foam for furniture
Sausage casings	Electrical insulation
Salad dressing	Leather substitute
Tofu	Lubricants and hydraulic fluids
	Paints and coatings
	Pesticides and herbicides
	Pharmaceuticals
	Plastics
	Printing inks
	Road materials
	Rubber
	Shampoo and detergent
	Solvents

that Companies A and B are both poultry processors. Company A might classify whole chickens and breast meat as joint products and all other chicken parts as by-product, whereas Company B might classify whole chickens, breasts, thighs, legs, and wings as joint products and all other chicken parts as by-product. These classifications could be based on the fact that Company A's processing facilities are only large enough to clean the chickens and remove the breast section; any additional processing would require a capital investment that would not be cost beneficial. Company B could have significantly larger facilities that allow further processing at costs substantially below the sales values of the multiple products.

THE JOINT PROCESS

Joint products are typically manufactured in companies using mass production processes and a process costing accounting method. Exhibit 11.2 shows that the outputs of steer processing include a wide variety of meat cuts for retail sales (joint products); fat, entrails, bones, horns, and hooves that are classified as by-product or scrap; and some nonusable waste (primarily blood) that is discarded.

Exhibit 11.2 Illustration of Joint Process Output

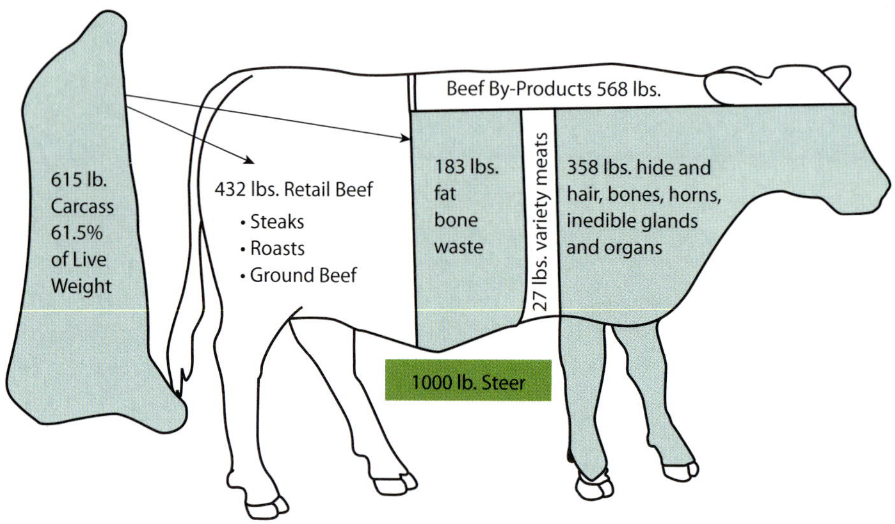

Beef By-Products and Scrap

Fats and Fatty Acids	Intestines	Hide and Hair	Bones, Horns, and Hooves	Manure
• Explosives • Chewing gum • Paints • Dog food • Tires	• Sausage casings • Instrument strings • Surgical sutures • Tennis racquet strings	• Clothing • Saddles • Insulation • Luggage • Artist's brushes	• Combs & toothbrushes • Dog biscuits • Piano keys • Ice cream • Shampoo & conditioner	• Methane gas • Urea fertilizer

Source: http://www.cdfa.ca.gov/ahfss/Meat_and_Poultry_Inspection/By_Products.html (accessed 12/20/11).

The point at which joint process outputs are first identifiable as individual products is called the **split-off point**. A joint process can have one or more split-off points, depending on the number and types of output produced. Output may be sold at the split-off point (if a market exists for products at that degree of completion) or may be processed further and then sold.

Joint cost includes all direct material, direct labor, and overhead costs incurred up to the split-off point. Financial reporting requires that all necessary and reasonable costs of production be attached to products. The following table indicates why joint cost is allocated only to joint products rather to all outputs of the joint process.

Joint Cost	Rationale
Allocated only to joint products	Necessary for financial statement valuations at split-off point Underlying financial motivation for undertaking the production process Not relevant for internal decision making because, at split-off, joint cost is a sunk cost
Not allocated to "other" output	Not cost beneficial Not significant to production process decision

If joint output is processed beyond the split-off point, additional separate costs will be incurred and must be assigned to the specific products for which those costs were incurred. Exhibit 11.3 illustrates a joint process with multiple split-off points and the allocation of costs to products. For simplicity, the joint process shows no by-product production. Even if created

Exhibit 11.3 Model of a Joint Process

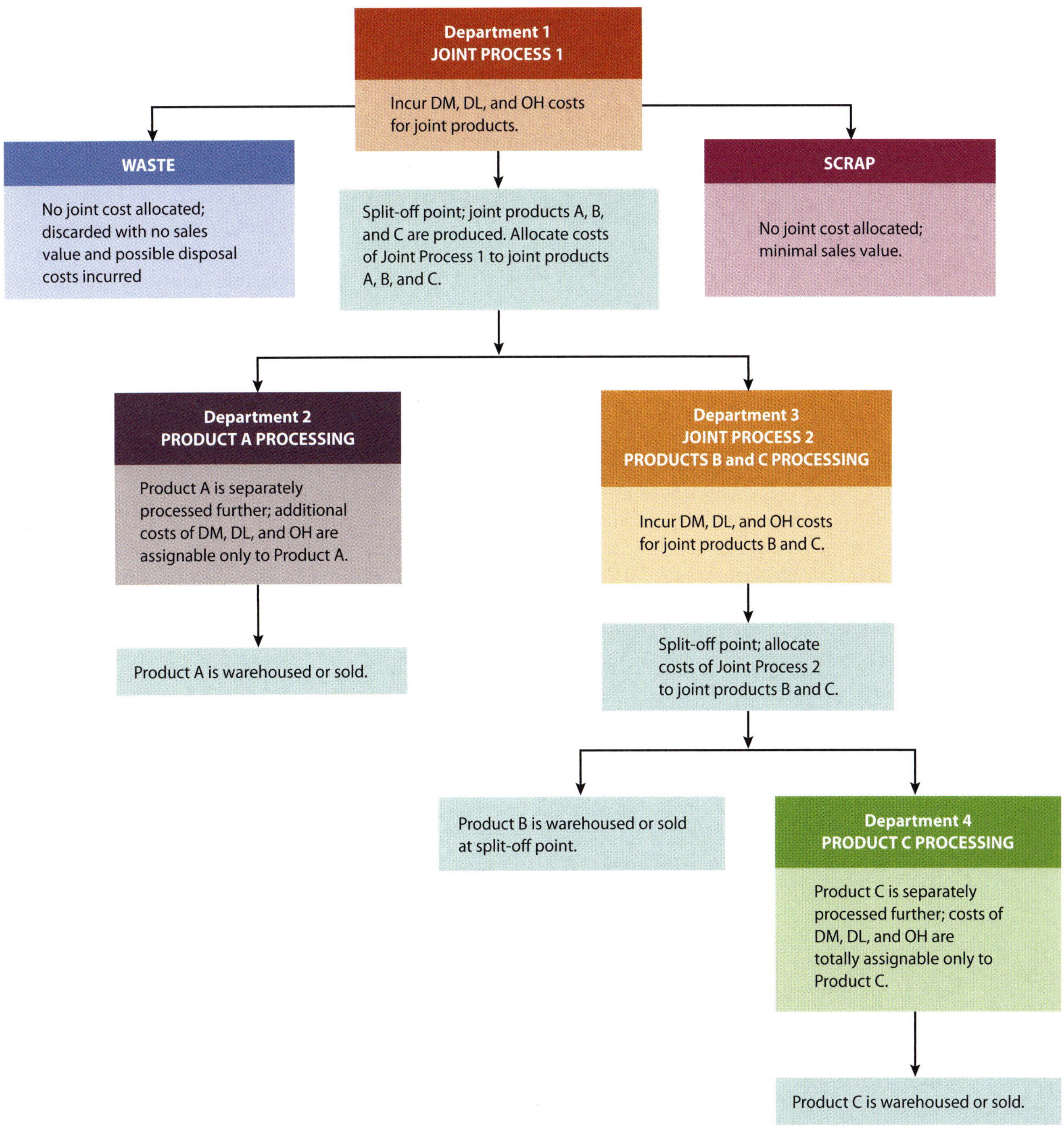

in the joint process, a by-product (such as the scrap and waste produced from Joint Process 1) would not receive any joint cost allocation. Note that joint products B and C of Joint Process 1 become direct material for Joint Process 2. For accounting purposes, joint cost allocations will follow products B and C into Joint Process 2, but these allocated costs should *not* be used in making decisions about further processing in Departments 2, 3, or 4. Such decisions should be made only after considering whether the expected additional revenues from further processing are greater than the expected additional costs of further processing.

2 What management decisions must be made before beginning a joint process?

THE JOINT PROCESS DECISION

Exhibit 11.4 indicates the four management decision points in a joint production process. Before committing resources to a joint process, management's first decision is whether total expected revenue from selling the joint output "basket" of products is likely to exceed total expected processing cost, which includes

- joint cost,
- separate processing costs after split-off,
- selling expenses for the goods, and
- disposal costs for any waste materials.

If total anticipated revenue exceeds total anticipated costs, managers should next decide whether this production process is the best use of the facilities. The income from this use of company resources would be compared to the income provided by the best alternative use. If the joint process income exceeds that of the best alternative, management would begin production.

The next two decisions are made at split-off. The third decision is to determine how to classify joint process outputs. This classification decision is necessary because joint cost is assigned only to joint products. Prior to allocation, however, the joint cost may be reduced by the sales value of any by-product or scrap (as discussed later in the chapter).

The fourth decision is the most complex. Management must decide whether to sell any or all joint output at split-off or to process it further. If joint products are salable at split-off, further processing should be undertaken only if the value added to the product, as reflected by the incremental revenue, exceeds the incremental cost.[3] If a primary product cannot be sold at split-off, additional costs must be incurred to make that product salable. For other output, management must also estimate whether the incremental revenue from additional processing will exceed the additional processing cost. By-product and scrap should also be processed further only if additional processing provides a net monetary benefit.

The following example illustrates a further processing decision. Assume that a whole chicken sells for \$0.96 per pound at split-off. The minimum selling price for edible chicken parts after further processing is \$1.06 per pound.

Incremental revenue = Revenue after additional processing − Revenue at split-off
Incremental revenue = \$1.06 − \$0.96 = \$0.10

If no weight is lost in additional processing and the cost is less than \$0.10 per pound, additional processing should occur.

In making decisions at any potential sales point, managers must have a reasonable estimate of each joint output's selling price. Expected selling prices should be based on both cost and market factors. In the long run, the product selling prices and volumes must be sufficient to cover their total costs. However, current economic influences, such as competitors' prices and consumers' sensitivity to price changes, must be considered when estimating selling prices and forecasting revenues.

3 How is the joint cost of production allocated to joint products?

ALLOCATION OF JOINT COST

Gobble Gobble, Inc. is used to demonstrate alternative methods of allocating joint cost. The company manufactures three primary products from a joint process: turkey breasts, ground turkey, and whole turkeys. (All remaining parts are considered by-products of the joint process.) Joint products can be either sold at split-off or processed further at an

[3] See Chapter 10 for a detailed discussion of incremental and relevant costs.

Exhibit 11.4 Decision Points in a Joint Production Process

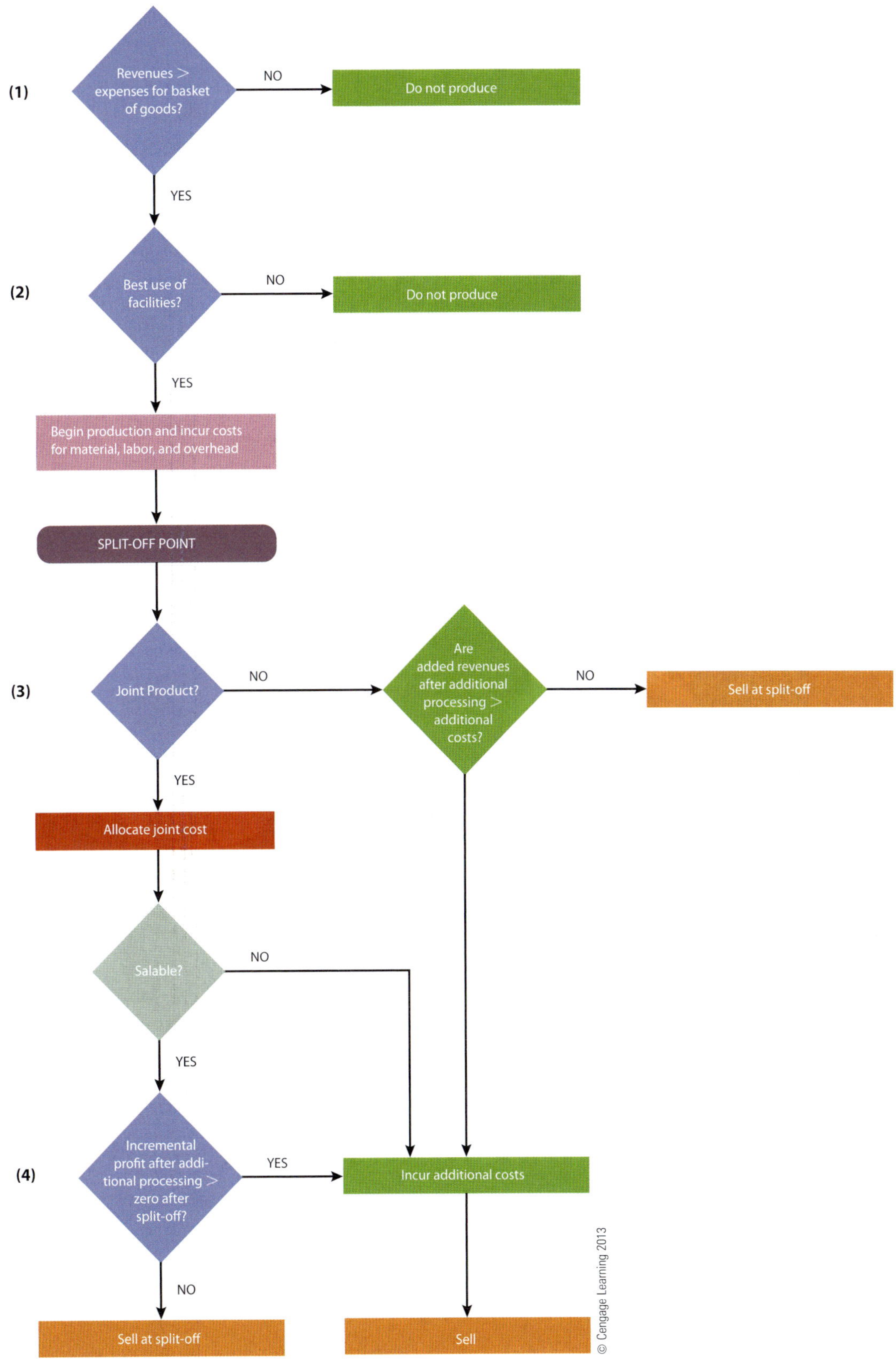

additional cost. Breasts can be processed further to produce deli meats; ground turkey can be processed further into turkey sausage; whole turkeys can be processed further into precooked or marinated roasters. Certain marketing and disposal costs for advertising, commissions, and transportation are incurred regardless of when the products are sold.

Exhibit 11.5 provides assumed information on Gobble Gobble's processing operations and joint products for October 2013. The company started processing 10,000 tons of turkey during that month. Approximately 10 percent of the tonnage started will become a by-product to be used in fertilizer pellets. Thus, the 10,000 tons of input results in 9,000 tons of joint product output and 1,000 tons of by-product.

Exhibit 11.5 Joint Cost Information for Gobble Gobble

Joint processing cost for period: $5,400,000

(1) Joint Product	(2) Tons Produced	(3) Sales Price per Ton at Split-Off	(4) Marketing Cost per Ton Regardless of When Sold	(5) Separate Cost per Ton If Processed Further	(6) Final Sales Price per Ton
Breast	3,800	$2,800	$200	$100	$3,200
Ground	2,400	1,800	100	100	2,100
Whole	2,800	1,200	50	60	1,500

Diagram of problem assuming products are sold at split-off

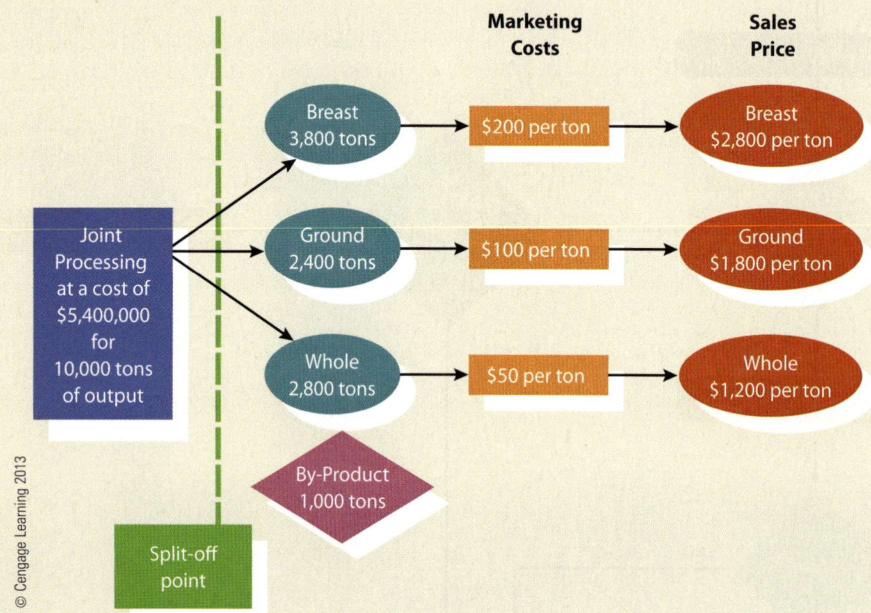

Physical Measure Allocation

An easy, objective way to prorate joint cost at the split-off point is to use **physical measure allocation** or proration using a common physical characteristic of the joint products such as:

- tons of meat, bone, and hide in the meat packing or turkey processing industry,
- pounds of milk in the dairy industry,
- linear board feet in the lumber milling industry,
- barrels of oil in the petroleum refining industry, or
- number of computer chips in the semiconductor industry.

Physical measures provide an unchanging yardstick of output. Assuming that it is agreed that the word *ton* means "short ton" or 2,000 pounds (rather than a "long" or "metric ton"), a ton of output produced from a process 10 years ago is the same measurement as a ton produced from that process today. Physical measures are useful in allocating joint cost to products that have highly variable selling prices. These measures are also necessary in rate-regulated industries that use cost to determine selling prices. For example, assume that a rate-regulated company has the right to set the selling price of its product at 20 percent above cost. It would be circular logic to allocate joint cost using selling prices that were set based on production cost.

Allocating joint cost based on a physical measure, however, ignores the revenue-generating ability of individual joint products. Products that weigh the most or that are produced in the largest quantity will receive the highest proportion of joint cost allocation—regardless of their ability to bear that cost when they are sold.

Using the physical measure allocation, the $5,400,000 of joint cost is assigned as shown in Exhibit 11.6. This allocation process treats each weight unit of output as equally desirable and assigns each ton the same per-unit cost. For Gobble Gobble, physical measure allocation assigns a cost of approximately $600 ($5,400,000 ÷ 9,000 tons) per ton of turkey, regardless of type. However, the computations in Exhibit 11.6 show that, by allocating the same amount of joint cost to each ton of joint product, whole turkeys generate the lowest gross profit per ton of the three joint products.

Exhibit 11.6 Gobble Gobble's Joint Cost Allocation Based on Physical Measure

Cost per physical measure = Total joint cost ÷ Total units of physical measurement
= $5,400,000 ÷ 9,000 tons = $600 per ton

Joint Product	Tons Produced	Sales Price per Ton at Split-Off	Total Sales Value at Split-Off	Allocated Joint Cost per Ton	Total Allocated Joint Cost
Breast	3,800	$2,800	$10,640,000	$600	$2,280,000
Ground	2,400	1,800	4,320,000	600	1,440,000
Whole	2,800	1,200	3,360,000	600	1,680,000
Total	9,000		$18,320,000		$5,400,000

The journal entries for incurring the joint cost, allocating it to the joint products, and recognizing the separate processing cost (assuming that all joint products are processed further) follow. The marketing costs shown in Exhibit 11.5 are not recorded until the products are sold.

	Debit	Credit
Work in Process Inventory—Turkey Processing	5,400,000	
Various accounts		5,400,000
To record joint cost		
Work in Process Inventory—Breast	2,280,000	
Work in Process Inventory—Ground	1,440,000	
Work in Process Inventory—Whole	1,680,000	
Work in Process Inventory—Turkey Processing		5,400,000
To allocate joint cost		
Work in Process Inventory—Breast (3,800 tons × $100)	380,000	
Work in Process Inventory—Ground (2,400 tons × $100)	240,000	
Work in Process Inventory—Whole (2,800 tons × $60)	168,000	
Various accounts		788,000
To record separate processing costs (from Ex. 11.5)		

Monetary Measure Allocation

The primary benefit of monetary over physical measure allocations is that the former recognizes the relative revenue generation of each product.[4] A problem with monetary measure allocations is that the allocation basis being used is a dynamic one. Because of fluctuations

[4] Monetary measures are more reflective of the primary reason a joint process is undertaken: profit. Physical measure allocations are sometimes of dubious value because they are based on the flawed assumption that all physical units are equally desirable.

in general and specific price levels, a dollar of output today is different from a dollar of output from the same process five years ago. However, accountants customarily ignore price-level fluctuations when recording or processing data, so this particular flaw of monetary measures is manageable.

All allocation methods employ a proration process. Because the physical measure allocation process is so simplistic, a detailed proration scheme is unnecessary. However, more complex monetary measure allocations use the following steps to prorate joint cost to joint products:

1. Choose a monetary allocation base.
2. List each joint product's base values.
3. Add the values in Step 2 to obtain total.
4. Divide each individual Step 2 value by the Step 3 total to obtain numerical proportions. These proportions should add to 100 percent.
5. Multiply the joint cost by each proportion to obtain the allocation for each product.
6. Divide each product's prorated joint cost by the number of product units[5] to obtain a cost per unit for valuation purposes.

Many different monetary measures can be used to allocate joint cost to primary output. The three presented in this text are sales value at split-off, net realizable value at split-off, and approximated net realizable value at split-off.

Sales Value at Split-Off The **sales value at split-off allocation** method assigns joint cost to joint products based on the relative split-off point sales values for the products. To use this method, all joint products must be salable at split-off. Exhibit 11.7 presents the assignment of Gobble Gobble's joint cost to production using the sales value at split-off method. This allocation method uses a weighting technique based on both quantity produced and product selling price. The low selling price per ton of whole turkeys compared to the selling prices of other joint products results in a lower allocated cost than was obtained using physical measure allocation. Account titles used in journal entries to record joint cost incurrence, allocate joint cost to joint products, and recognize separate processing cost are the same as those used earlier; however, the allocated cost amounts would be changed to those shown in Exhibit 11.7.

Exhibit 11.7 Gobble Gobble's Joint Cost Allocation Based on Sales Value at Split-Off

Joint Product	Tons Produced	Sales Price per Ton at Split-Off	Total Sales Value at Split-Off	% of Total Sales Value*	Joint Cost	Total Allocated Joint Cost	Allocated Joint Cost per Ton
Breast	3,800	$2,800	$10,640,000	58%[a]	$5,400,000	$3,132,000	$824.21
Ground	2,400	1,800	4,320,000	24[b]	5,400,000	1,296,000	540.00
Whole	2,800	1,200	3,360,000	18[c]	5,400,000	972,000	347.14
Total	9,000		$18,320,000	100%		$5,400,000	

*Proportions = Total sales value of joint product ÷ Total sales value

[a]$10,640,000 ÷ $18,320,000 = 0.58 (rounded)

[b]$4,320,000 ÷ $18,320,000 = 0.24 (rounded)

[c]$3,360,000 ÷ $18,320,000 = 0.18 (rounded)

Net Realizable Value at Split-Off The **net realizable value at split-off allocation** method assigns joint cost based on an inventory valuation amount for the joint products at the split-off point. **Net realizable value (NRV)** is equal to sales value at split-off minus any expected completion and disposal costs.[6] This method requires that all joint products

[5]Given that joint products are generated in process costing environments, the units in this computation will actually be equivalent units of production as discussed in Chapter 6. The issue of EUP is ignored in this chapter.

[6]A complete discussion of net realizable value would also include the issues of "ceiling" and "floor" values. These issues are beyond the scope of this text and can be found in any intermediate accounting book.

be salable at split-off and considers the costs that must be incurred at split-off to realize the estimated sales value. The marketing costs (shown in the fourth column of Exhibit 11.5) for Gobble Gobble's products are considered disposal costs and are incurred whether the product is sold at split-off or after further processing. Exhibit 11.8 provides the joint cost allocations based on each product's relative proportion of total NRV. Results in Exhibits 11.7 and 11.8 are very similar because marketing costs incurred for each primary product are relatively low. When disposal costs are high, cost allocations based on sales values and on NRVs at split-off can differ substantially.

Exhibit 11.8 Gobble Gobble's Joint Cost Allocation Based on Net Realizable Value at Split-Off

Joint Product	Tons Produced	NRV per Ton at Split-Off*	Total NRV at Split-Off	% of Total NRV**	Joint Cost	Total Allocated Joint Cost	Allocated Joint Cost per Ton
Breast	3,800	$2,600[a]	$ 9,880,000	57%[d]	$5,400,000	$3,078,000	$810.00
Ground	2,400	1,700[b]	4,080,000	24[e]	5,400,000	1,296,000	540.00
Whole	2,800	1,150[c]	3,220,000	19[f]	5,400,000	1,026,000	366.43
Total	9,000		$17,180,000	100%		$5,400,000	

*NRV per ton = Sales price at split-off − Marketing cost at point of sale

[a]NRV = $2,800 − $200 = $2,600
[b]NRV = $1,800 − $100 = $1,700
[c]NRV = $1,200 − $50 = $1,150

**Proportion = Total NRV of respective joint product ÷ Total NRV

[d]$9,880,000 ÷ $17,180,000 = 0.57 (rounded)
[e]$4,080,000 ÷ $17,180,000 = 0.24 (rounded)
[f]$3,220,000 ÷ $17,180,000 = 0.19 (rounded)

Approximated Net Realizable Value at Split-Off Often, some or all of the joint products are not salable at split-off. Thus, these products must be processed at an additional separate cost beyond the split-off point. This lack of marketability at split-off means that neither the sales value at split-off nor the NRV at split-off approach can be used. The **approximated net realizable value at split-off allocation** uses simulated NRVs for the joint products at split-off to calculate the joint cost allocation. For each product, this value is the final selling price minus all incremental processing, marketing, and disposal costs incurred between split-off and point of sale. An underlying assumption of this method is that the incremental revenue from further processing is equal to or greater than the incremental costs of further processing and selling. For all Gobble Gobble's products, this assumption is true as shown by the following computations. Thus, Gobble Gobble should process all joint products beyond the split-off point.

Joint Product	Final Sales Price per Ton	Sales Price per Ton at Split-Off	Marketing Cost per Ton at Point of Sale	Further Processing Cost + Marketing Cost = Separate Cost per Ton after Split-Off
Breast	$3,200	$2,800	$200	$200 + $100 = $300
Ground	2,100	1,800	100	$100 + $100 = $200
Whole	1,500	1,200	50	$ 60 + $ 50 = $110

Joint Product	Incremental Revenue	−	Incremental Cost	=	Incremental Profit
Breast	$400		$100		$300
Ground	300		100		200
Whole	300		60		240

The same "process further" conclusion can be reached by comparing the final sales prices with the approximated NRVs at split-off:

Joint Product	(a) Final Sales Price per Ton	–	Separate Cost per Ton after Split-Off	=	(b) Approximated NRV at Split-Off	Difference = a – b
Breast	$3,200		$200 + $100 = $300		$2,900	+$300
Ground	2,100		$100 + $100 = $200		1,900	+$200
Whole	1,500		$ 60 + $ 50 = $110		1,390	+$240

Decisions made about further processing affect the values used to allocate joint cost with the approximated NRV method. If it is not economical to process one or more products beyond split-off, the base used for allocating joint cost will become a mixture of actual and approximated NRVs at split-off. Products that will not be processed further will be valued at their actual NRVs at split-off, whereas products that will be processed further are valued at approximated NRVs at split-off. Given that all products will be processed further, the joint cost allocation using the approximated NRV method is shown in Exhibit 11.9.

Exhibit 11.9 Gobble Gobble's Joint Cost Allocation Based on Approximated Net Realizable Value at Split-Off

Joint Product	Tons Produced	Approximated NRV per Ton	Total Approximated NRV	% of Total Approximated NRV*	Joint Cost	Total Allocated Joint Cost	Allocated Joint Cost per Ton
Breast	3,800	$2,900	$11,020,000	57%[a]	$5,400,000	$3,078,000	$810.00
Ground	2,400	1,900	4,560,000	23[b]	5,400,000	1,242,000	517.50
Whole	2,800	1,390	3,892,000	20[c]	5,400,000	1,080,000	385.71
Total	9,000		$19,472,000	100%		$5,400,000	

*Proportion = Total approximated NRV of respective joint product ÷ Total approximated NRV

[a]$11,020,000 ÷ $19,472,000 = 0.57 (rounded)
[b]$4,560,000 ÷ $19,472,000 = 0.23 (rounded)
[c]$3,892,000 ÷ $19,472,000 = 0.20 (rounded)

Gobble Gobble decides to further process its 1,000 tons of breast meat into deli meat, 900 tons of ground turkey into turkey sausage, and 1,200 tons of whole turkey into marinated turkeys (see Exhibit 11.10). For purposes of these calculations, the allocations are assumed to be the ones computed in Exhibit 11.9. At the split-off point, the joint cost cannot be recouped and must be considered a "sunk" cost. Thus, the only relevant items in the decision to process further are the incremental revenue and incremental cost.

Each allocation method assigns a different amount of joint cost to the joint products and results in a different per-unit cost for each product. Each method has advantages and disadvantages. For most companies, approximated NRV at split-off provides the most logical joint cost assignment because this method captures the

- intended level of separate processing,
- costs of separate processing,
- expected selling costs of each joint product, and
- expected selling price of each joint product.

Thus, approximated NRV measures the expected contribution of each product line to the coverage of joint cost. This method is, however, more complex than the others because estimations must be made about additional processing costs and potential future sales values.

Exhibit 11.10 Gobble Gobble's Further Processing Diagram

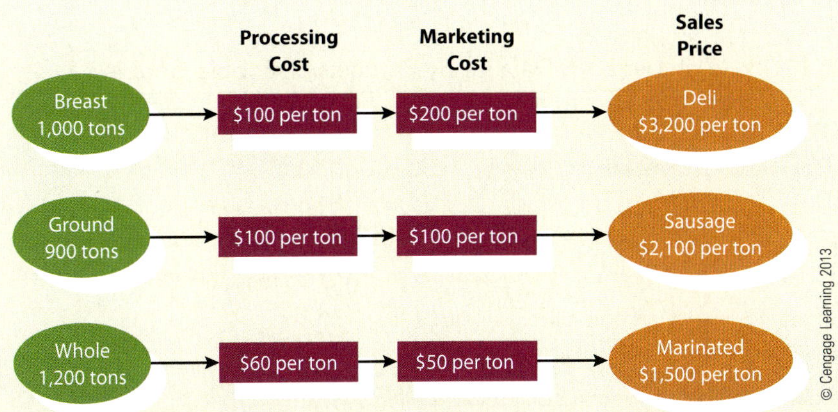

Further processing does not change the joint cost allocations previously made. The new products are allocated some of the original joint cost and absorb their own separate processing costs, as shown in the following journal entries. The marketing costs have not been recorded because the products have not yet been sold.

Work in Process Inventory—Deli (1,000 tons × $810.00)	810,000	
Work in Process Inventory—Sausage (900 tons × $517.50)	465,750	
Work in Process Inventory—Marinated (1,200 tons × $385.71)	462,852	
Work in Process Inventory—Breast		810,000
Work in Process Inventory—Ground		465,750
Work in Process Inventory—Whole		462,852
To transfer allocated costs to new product inventories		
Work in Process Inventory—Deli (1,000 tons × $100)	100,000	
Work in Process Inventory—Sausage (900 tons × $100)	90,000	
Work in Process Inventory—Marinated (1,200 tons × $60)	72,000	
Various accounts		262,000
To record separate processing costs		

ACCOUNTING FOR BY-PRODUCT AND SCRAP

4 How are by-product and scrap accounted for?

The distinction between by-product and scrap is merely one of degree. Thus, in the following discussion, "scrap" can be substituted anywhere that "by-product" is used. Similar to the accounting for joint cost, a variety of methods exist in practice to account for a by-product. The choice of method should depend on the magnitude of the net realizable value of the by-product and the need for additional processing after split-off. As the sales value of the by-product increases, so does the need for inventory recognition. By-product sales value is generally recorded under either the NRV approach or realized value approach.[7] The net *realizable* value approach reflects the *expected* amount to be received from the by-product sale; the net *realized* value approach reflects the *actual* amount that was received from by-product sale. Thus, the NRV approach can be used in advance of revenue realization, whereas the realized value approach cannot be used until revenue is realized. Regardless of whether a company uses the NRV or the realized value approach, the specific method that will be used to account for by-product must be determined before the joint cost is allocated to the joint products.

[7] Other alternative presentations include showing the realized value from the sale of by-product as (1) an addition to gross margin, (2) a reduction of the Cost of Goods Manufactured, or (3) a reduction of the Cost of Goods Sold. The major advantage of these simplistic approaches is clerical efficiency.

These approaches are discussed in the following sections using additional data for Gobble Gobble, which produces fertilizer pellets as a by-product. Exhibit 11.11 provides the October 2013 data.

Exhibit 11.11 October 2013 Data for By-Products of Gobble Gobble

Total processing for month:	10,000 tons of turkey
Total tons of output:	9,000 tons of joint products
By-products (fertilizer pellets) from joint product production:	1,000 tons (2,000,000 pounds)
Selling price per pound of fertilizer pellets:	\$0.30
Processing costs per pound of fertilizer pellets:	\$0.08 for labor and \$0.02 for overhead
Net realizable value per pound of fertilizer pellets:	\$0.20

Net Realizable Value Approach

The **net realizable value approach** (or **offset approach**) reduces joint product cost for the NRV that will be created by the by-product's sale. When by-product is generated, the NRV is debited to inventory and credited to one of two accounts (Work in Process Inventory—Joint Products or Cost of Goods Sold for the joint products). Using the Work in Process Inventory account allows the joint cost to be reduced immediately when the by-product is produced and before the joint cost is allocated to the joint products. However, recording the reduction in WIP Inventory or CGS immediately upon by-product production is less conservative than waiting until the by-product is actually sold. Additionally, the by-product could have sales potential beyond that currently known by management.

The journal entries to record Gobble Gobble's by-product production and the additional processing, completion, and sale of the by-product are as follows:

Work in Process Inventory—Fertilizer Pellets (2,000,000 × \$0.20)	400,000	
Work in Process Inventory—Joint Products		400,000
To record production of by-product; an alternative credit could have been made to Cost of Goods Sold from the sale of the joint products		
Work in Process Inventory—Fertilizer Pellets (2,000,000 × \$0.10)	200,000	
Various accounts		200,000
To record additional separate processing costs for the by-product		
Finished Goods Inventory—Fertilizer Pellets (2,000,000 × \$0.30)	600,000	
Work in Process Inventory—Fertilizer Pellets		600,000
To record completion of by-product		
Cash (or Accounts Receivable) (2,000,000 × \$0.30)	600,000	
Finished Goods Inventory—Fertilizer Pellets		600,000
To record sale of by-product		

The choice of reducing WIP Inventory-Joint Products or Cost of Goods Sold creates alternative income statement presentations and balance sheet information. A reduction in WIP Inventory-Joint Products lowers the production cost per unit of the joint products. To illustrate, assume that Gobble Gobble used a physical measure joint cost allocation. If by-product NRV were used to reduce WIP Inventory-Joint Products, the company's joint cost to allocate would have been \$5,000,000 rather than \$5,400,000: the difference is the 2,000,000 pounds of by-product multiplied by \$0.02 NRV per pound. The reduction in WIP Inventory-Joint Products would create a corresponding reduction in cost of goods manufactured. Thus, the allocated joint cost per ton would have been approximately \$555 (or \$5,000,000 ÷ 9,000) per ton for any joint product rather than the \$600 joint cost per ton allocation shown in Exhibit 11.6. The reduced cost per ton would affect not only the amount of CGS upon joint product sale but also the amount shown in the inventory account. Alternatively, reducing CGS by the NRV would not affect the \$600 per ton allocated cost of the joint products. Exhibit 11.12 shows the presentation of these two NRV approaches; a zero balance in beginning finished goods inventory is used to highlight the differences in the CGS computation. All other figures are assumed amounts. Note that the $22,500 difference in income before taxes is equal to the 500 tons of finished goods inventory multiplied by the $45 difference in cost per ton.

Exhibit 11.12 Gobble Gobble's Comparative Income Statements—NRV Approach to By-Products

(a) Net Realizable Value Approach: Reduce WIP-Joint Products

Sales		$ 7,200,000
Cost of goods sold		
Beginning FG	$ 0	
CGM ($5,400,000 – $400,000)	5,000,000	
CGA	$5,000,000	
Ending FG (assumed to be 500 tons @ $555 per ton)	(277,500)	(4,722,500)
Gross margin		$ 2,477,500
Operating expenses		(1,600,000)
Income from principal operations		$ 877,500
Other income		
Royalties		80,000
Income before income taxes		$ 957,500

(b) Net Realizable Value Approach: Reduce Cost of Goods Sold

Sales		$ 7,200,000
Cost of goods sold		
Beginning finished goods (FG)	$ 0	
Cost of goods manufactured (CGM)	5,400,000	
Cost of goods available (CGA)	$5,400,000	
Ending FG (assumed to be 500 tons @ $600 per ton)	(300,000)	
Unadjusted CGS	$5,100,000	
NRV of by-product	(400,000)	(4,700,000)
Gross margin		$ 2,500,000
Operating expenses		(1,600,000)
Income from principal operations		$ 900,000
Other income		
Royalties		80,000
Income before income taxes		$ 980,000

Although commonly used to account for such goods, the NRV method is not necessarily best for internal decision making or by-product management. This method does not indicate the revenues, expenses, or profits from the by-product and, thus, does not provide sufficient information to induce management to maximize the inflows from by-product sales.

Realized Value Approach

When management considers by-product to be a moderate source of income, the accounting and reporting methods used should help managers monitor by-product production and further processing as well as make effective decisions regarding this resource. The **realized value approach** (or **other income approach**) is the easiest approach to accounting for by-product because no value is recognized for the by-product until it is sold.

One income statement presentation of the realized value approach shows total sales of by-product under the Other Revenue caption. Costs of additional processing or disposal of the by-product are included as part of the cost of producing the joint products. This presentation provides little useful information to management because it does not match the costs of producing the by-product with its revenues.

A second presentation for the realized value approach reflects by-product sales as Other Income. This method requires that an inventory account be established for the by-product processing costs; the inventory account will be removed from the balance sheet upon sale of the by-product. By-product revenue, net of additional costs of processing and disposal, is then shown on the income statement. This presentation allows management to recognize the monetary benefit realized from managing the costs and revenues related to by-product. The entries using the Other Income method for the incurrence of labor and overhead costs and sale of by-product for Gobble Gobble follow.

Account	Debit	Credit
Work in Process Inventory—Fertilizer Pellets (2,000,000 × $0.10)	200,000	
Various accounts		200,000
To record the labor and overhead costs of by-product processing		
Cash (or Accounts Receivable)	600,000	
Work in Process Inventory—Fertilizer Pellets		200,000
Other Income		400,000
To record sale of by-product net of processing/disposal costs		

Exhibit 11.13 shows income statements using two different realized value presentations for accounting for by-product/scrap income for Gobble Gobble. The top section (a) of this exhibit assumes the use of physical measure joint cost allocation. Note that the cost per ton for joint products has increased to approximately $622 (or $5,600,000 ÷ 9,000) per ton from the $600 per ton shown in Exhibit 11.6 because of the assignment of by-product costs to the joint products. In contrast, the bottom section (b) of this exhibit shows no effect on the allocated joint cost per joint product from the original computation because the processing costs for the by-product are netted from its sales value.

The Other Income method matches by-product revenue with related storage, further processing, transportation, and disposal costs. As such, this method

- presents detailed information on financial responsibility and accountability for disposition of these secondary outputs,
- provides better control opportunities than the realized value approach, and
- could improve performance because managers are more apt to look for new or expanded sales potential given that the net benefits of doing so are provided on the income statement.

By-product, scrap, and waste are created in all types of businesses, not just by manufacturers. Managers might not see the need to determine the cost of these secondary types of outputs. However, with the trend toward more emphasis on cost and quality control, companies are becoming more aware of the potential value of by-product, scrap, and waste and are devoting time and attention to developing those innovative revenue sources.

BY-PRODUCT AND SCRAP IN JOB ORDER COSTING

Although joint products are not normally associated with job order costing systems, accounting for by-product or scrap is common in these systems. Either the NRV or the realized value approach can be used to recognize the value of by-product/scrap.

In a job order system, the value of by-product/scrap is appropriately credited to either manufacturing overhead or the specific jobs in process. Overhead is credited if by-product/scrap is typically created by most jobs undertaken. This method reduces the

Exhibit 11.13 Gobble Gobble's Comparative Income Statements—Realized Value Approaches to By-Products

(a) Net Realized Value Approach: Present as Other Revenue

Sales		$ 7,200,000
Other revenue		
By-product sales (at total selling price)		600,000
Total revenue		$ 7,800,000
Cost of goods sold		
Beginning FG	$ 0	
CGM (main products)	5,400,000	
CGM (by-product processing costs)	200,000	
CGA	$5,600,000	
Ending FG (assumed to be 500 tons @ $622 per ton)	(311,000)	(5,289,000)
Gross margin		$ 2,511,000
Operating expenses		(1,600,000)
Income from principal operations		$ 911,000
Other income		
Royalties		80,000
Income before income taxes		$ 991,000

(b) Net Realized Value Approach: Present as Other Income

Sales		$ 7,200,000
Cost of goods sold		
Beginning FG	$ 0	
CGM	5,400,000	
CGA	$5,400,000	
Ending FG (assumed to be 500 tons @ $600 per ton)	(300,000)	(5,100,000)
Gross margin		$ 2,100,000
Operating expenses		(1,600,000)
Income from principal operations		$ 500,000
Other income		
Royalties	$ 80,000	
By-product sales ($600,000 – $200,000)	400,000	480,000
Income before income taxes		$ 980,000

amount of overhead that is applied to all products for the period. In contrast, if only a few or specific jobs generate substantial amounts of by-product/scrap, the individual jobs causing this output should be credited with its value. This method reduces the total costs assigned to those jobs.[8]

To illustrate, assume that Gobble Gobble occasionally prepares special turkey products for large institutional clients. Every special order generates scrap meat that is sold to Canine Catering Corporation. In October 2013, Gobble Gobble received an order for 20,000

[8]Conceptually, the treatment of the profitability of by-product/scrap in a job order system is similar to the treatment of the costs of spoilage in a job order system, as discussed in Chapter 5.

turkey casseroles from the Hays County Public School District. The casseroles are prepared using a combination of breast, thigh, and wing meat. After production of the casseroles, Gobble Gobble sold $250 of scrap meat. Using the realized value approach, the entry to record the sale of the scrap is:

Cash	250	
Manufacturing Overhead		250
To record the sale of scrap		

In contrast, assume that Gobble Gobble seldom has salable scrap on its special order jobs. However, during October 2013, the company contracted with Green Cove Convalescent Centers to prepare 25,000 frozen chicken croquettes. Because Gobble Gobble normally does not process chicken, it must acquire specific raw material for the job and will charge the cost of all raw material directly to Green Cove. Preparation of the chicken croquettes generates some scrap that can be sold for $375 to Tortilla Soup Cannery. Because the raw material is directly related to the Green Cove job, sale of scrap from that raw material also relates to that job. Under these circumstances, the production and sale of the scrap are recorded (using the net realizable value approach) as follows:

Scrap Inventory—Chicken	375	
Work in Process Inventory—Green Cove Convalescent Centers		375
To record the NRV of scrap produced by Green Cove job		
Cash	375	
Scrap Inventory—Chicken		375
To record sale of the scrap		

In this case, the NRV approach is preferred because of the timing of recognition. The need to affect the specific job cost that caused an unusual incidence and quantity of scrap makes it essential to recognize the scrap at the point of production. Without prompt recognition, the job could be completed before the scrap could be sold, and thus, the reduction in the actual cost of the job would not be known.

JOINT COSTS IN RETAIL BUSINESSES AND NOT-FOR-PROFIT ORGANIZATIONS

5 How should retail and not-for-profit organizations account for the cost of a joint activity?

Allocation of joint costs is not unique to manufacturing organizations. Some costs incurred in retail businesses and in not-for-profit organizations are considered joint costs in that such costs may need to be allocated among product lines, organizational locations, or types of organizational activities. For example, retail businesses and NFPs incur joint costs for advertising multiple programs, printing multipurpose documents, or holding multipurpose events. Additionally, NFPs often develop and distribute brochures providing information about the organization, its purposes, and its programs as well as appealing to readers for funds.

A retail business can choose either a physical or a monetary allocation base to allocate joint costs. For example, a local bicycle and lawn mower repair company could advertise a sale and list all store locations in a single newspaper advertisement. The ad cost could be allocated equally to all locations or be allocated on sales volume for each location during the period of the sale. As another example, a grocery delivery service could deliver several customers' orders on the same trip. The cost of the trip could be allocated based on the number of bags or pounds of food delivered for each customer.

Although retail businesses may decide that allocating joint cost is not necessary, financial accounting requires that NFPs (and state and local government entities) meeting three tests allocate the costs of "joint activities" among fund-raising, organizational program (program activities), and administrative functions (management and general activities).[9] If

[9] American Institute of Certified Public Accountants, *Statement of Position 98-2: Accounting for Costs of Activities of Not-for-Profit Organizations and State and Local Governmental Entities That Include Fund Raising* (March 11, 1998); Section 10,730; http://www.fasb.org/cs/BlobServer?blobcol=urldata&blobtable=MungoBlobs&blobkey=id&blobwhere=1175820927486&blobheader=application%2Fpdf (accessed December 21, 2011).

all three tests are not met, the entire cost associated with the "joint activity" must be charged to fund-raising.[10] The tests relate to the following concepts:

Criterion	Meaning
Purpose	The activity includes accomplishing some program or management/general function.
Audience	The audience is suitable for accomplishing the activity's program or management/general functions.
Content	The content supports program or management/general functions.

The commonality among the criteria is that each creates some type of "call for action." Thus, a brochure that simply informs the audience about the NFP's purpose or a particular disease is not considered a call for action.

A critical element under the purpose criterion is the compensation test. If a majority of compensation or fees for anyone performing a part of the activity is tied to contributions raised, the activity automatically fails the purpose criterion and all costs of the activity must be charged to fund-raising. Thus, if professional fund-raisers are used and paid a percentage of the amount raised, all costs of the activity must be charged to fund-raising.

No specific allocation method is prescribed for the joint cost. The SOP merely states that the method must be

- rational and systematic,
- result in reasonable allocations, and
- applied in the same manner under similar situations.

A major purpose of this allocation process is to ensure that financial statement users are able to clearly determine amounts spent by the organization for various activities—especially fund-raising. High fund-raising costs may harm an NFP's credibility with donors who measure an organization's effectiveness by the percentage of funds that goes to programs furthering the entity's mission rather than the percentage going to raise more funds. High fund-raising percentages may also jeopardize an NFP's standing with charity regulators.

[10] An exception to the rule is that costs for goods and services provided in exchange transactions (such as a meal provided at a function that failed to meet the three required criteria) that are part of joint activities should not be reported as fund-raising costs; such costs should be reported as cost of sales for the activity.

Comprehensive Review Module

KEY TERMS

approximated net realizable value at split-off allocation, p. 443
by-product, p. 434
joint cost, p. 434
joint process, p. 434
joint product, p. 434
net realizable value (NRV), p. 442
net realizable value approach, p. 446
net realizable value at split-off allocation, p. 442
offset approach, p. 446
other income approach, p. 448
physical measure allocation, p. 440
realized value approach, p. 448
sales value at split-off allocation, p. 442
scrap, p. 434
separate cost, p. 434
split-off point, p. 436
waste, p. 435

CHAPTER SUMMARY

1 Classification of Joint Process Output

- Joint products are the output with a relatively high sales value.
  - These products provide the primary incentive for undertaking production.
  - These products are identified at the split-off point.
  - These products are assigned the joint cost of the production process.
  - These products could have the related joint cost reduced by the net realizable value or realized value of by-product and scrap.
- By-products have a higher sales value than scrap but less than joint products.
- Scrap is output with the lowest sales value.
- Waste is the residual output with no sales value.

2 Management Decisions about a Joint Process

- Two questions must be answered before the joint process is started:
  - Do total revenues exceed total (joint and separate) costs?
  - Is this process the best use of available facilities?
- Two questions must be answered at the split-off point:
  - Which products will be classified as joint products, by-product, scrap, or waste?
  - Which products will be sold at split-off, and which will be processed further?

3 Allocation of Joint Cost to Joint Products

- There are two common methods of allocating joint cost to joint products.
  - Physical measures may be used. These measures
    - ➢ provide an unchanging yardstick of output over time and
    - ➢ treat each unit of product as equally desirable.
  - Monetary measures may be used. These measures consider different valuations of the individual joint products; these valuations can be based on
    - ➢ sales value at split-off,
    - ➢ net realizable value at split-off, or
    - ➢ approximated net realizable value at split-off.
- Allocated joint cost is a "sunk" cost and should not be used in decisions about further processing.
- Regardless of the method used to allocate joint cost to joint products, products should only be processed beyond split-off if the incremental revenue exceeds the incremental costs.

4 Accounting for By-Product and Scrap

- There are two common methods of accounting for by-product and scrap.
  - The net realizable value approach uses the expected NRV of the by-product to reduce either
    - ➢ Work in Process Inventory of the joint products when the by-product/scrap is produced or
    - ➢ Cost of Goods Sold of the joint products when the by-product/scrap is produced.
  - The realized value approach shows the actual value of the by-product/scrap on the income statement as either
    - ➢ other revenue when the by-product/scrap is sold or
    - ➢ other income when the by-product/scrap is sold.
- In a job order costing system, by-product and scrap may be accounted for using either the NRV or realized value approach.
  - The value of the by-product or scrap should be credited to manufacturing overhead if such items are created by most jobs.
  - The value of the by-product or scrap should be credited to individual jobs if by-product or scrap is not normally created; the net realized value approach is more appropriate because of timing of recognition.

5 Accounting for the Cost of a Joint Activity in a Retail or Not-for-Profit Organization

- Retail business may choose to allocate joint costs incurred for certain activities such as advertising; either a physical or monetary measure may be used.
- There are two alternatives for accounting for the cost of a joint activity by not-for-profit organizations:
  - The activity must meet three tests for its cost to be allocated:
    - ➢ purpose
    - ➢ audience
    - ➢ content
  - If all of the criteria are met, the cost is allocated among three categories:
    - ➢ fund-raising,
    - ➢ program, and/or
    - ➢ management/general activities.
  - If all of the criteria are not met, the entire cost is allocated to fund-raising.

SOLUTION STRATEGIES

Allocation of Joint Cost, pp. 438–445

Joint cost is allocated only to joint products; however, joint cost can be reduced by the value of by-product/scrap before the allocation process begins.

For physical measure allocation: Divide joint cost by the products' total physical measurements to obtain a cost per unit of physical measure.

For monetary measure allocation:

1. Choose an allocation base.
2. List the values that compose the allocation base for each joint process.
3. Sum the values in Step 2.
4. Calculate the percentage of the total base value associated with each joint product.
5. Multiply the joint cost by each percentage calculated in Step 4 to obtain the amount to be allocated to each joint product.
6. Divide the prorated joint cost for each product by the number of equivalent units of production (EUP) for each product to obtain a cost per EUP for valuation purposes.

Allocation bases, measured at the split-off point, by which joint cost is prorated to the joint products include the following:

Type of Measure	Allocation Base
Physical output	Physical measure of units of output (e.g., tons, feet, barrels, liters)
Monetary	Currency units of value
Sales value	Revenues of the several products
Net realizable value	Sales value minus incremental processing and disposal costs
	Final sales price minus incremental separate costs
	Approximated net realizable value

DEMONSTRATION PROBLEM

Circle City Inc. produces two joint products—Primero and Segundo—from a single input. Further processing of product Primero results in a by-product designated Más. A summary of production and sales for 2013 follows.

- Circle City Inc. input 600,000 pounds of raw material into the Processing Department. Total joint processing cost was $520,000. During the joint processing, 90,000 pounds of material were lost.
- After joint processing, 60 percent of the joint process output was transferred to Division 1 to produce Primero, and 40 percent of the joint process output was transferred to Division 2 to produce Segundo.
- Further processing in Division 1 resulted in 70 percent of the input pounds becoming Primero and 30 percent of the input pounds becoming Más. The separate processing cost for Primero in Division 1 was $649,026.
- Total packaging costs for Primero were $122,094. After Division 1 processing and packaging, product Primero is salable at $8.00 per pound.
- Each pound of Más can be sold for $0.25 after incurring total selling cost of $5,000. The company accounts for Más using the net realizable value method and showing the NRV as a reduction in the cost of goods sold of the joint products.
- In Division 2, Segundo was further processed at a separate cost of $387,600. A completed pound of Segundo sells for $4.70.
- Selling (marketing) costs for Primero and Segundo are, respectively, $0.80 per pound and $0.15 per pound.

Required:

a. Prepare a process diagram similar to the one shown in Exhibit 11.5 or 11.10.
b. Record the journal entry to
    1. recognize incurrence of joint cost.
    2. allocate joint costs to the joint products using pounds as a physical measure and transfer the products into Divisions 1 and 2.
    3. record incurrence of separate processing costs for products Primero and Segundo in Divisions 1 and 2.
    4. record incurrence of packaging cost for product Primero.
    5. transfer completed products Primero and Segundo to finished goods.
c. Allocate the joint cost to products Primero and Segundo using approximated net realizable values at split-off. (Round proportions to nearest whole percentage.)
d. Circle City Inc. had no Work in Process or Finished Goods Inventory at the beginning of 2013. Prepare an income statement through gross margin for Circle City Inc. assuming that
    - 80 percent of the Primero and 90 percent of the Segundo produced in 2013 were sold.
    - all the Más that was produced during the year was sold.
    - joint cost was allocated using the physical measurement method in (b).

Solution to Demonstration Problem

a.

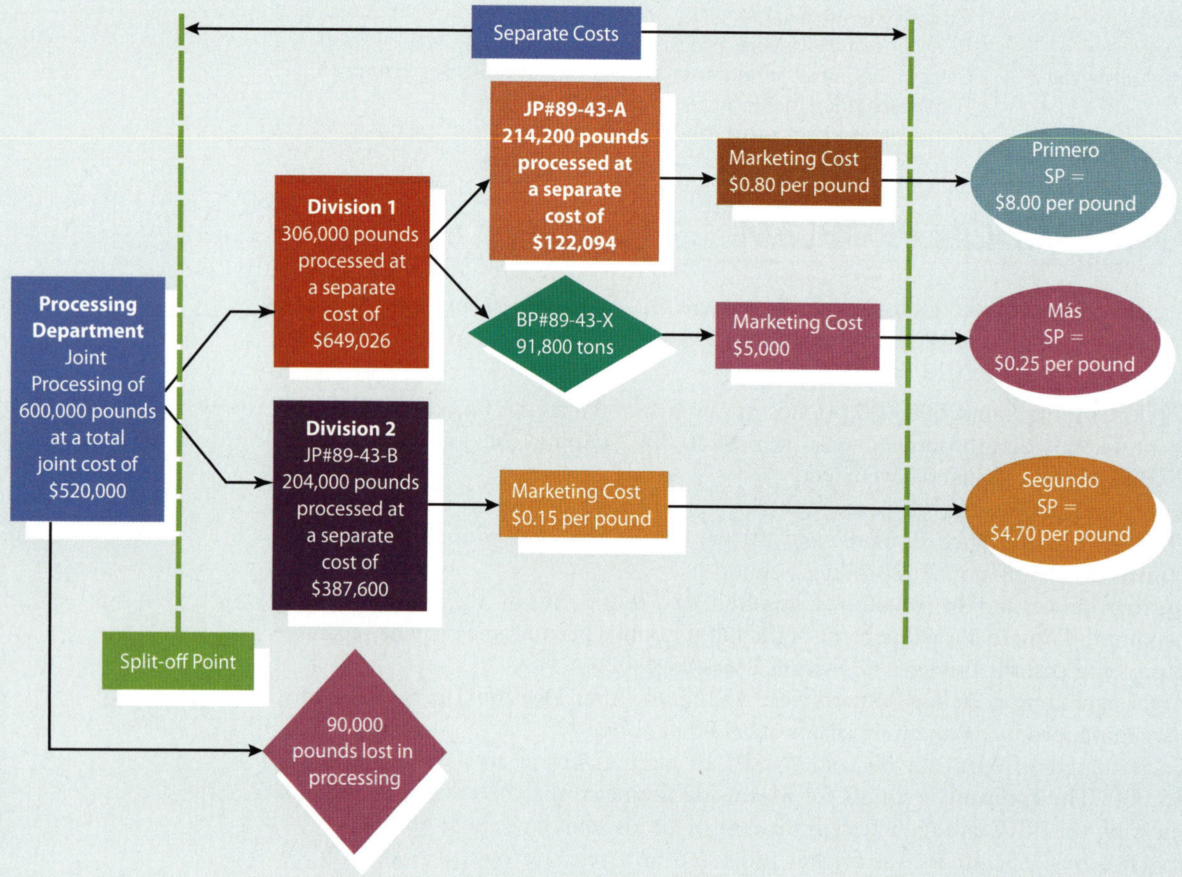

b. 1.	Work in Process Inventory—Processing	520,000	
	Various accounts		520,000
	To record 2013 joint processing costs		

2.	Work in Process Inventory—Division 1 (60%)	312,000	
	Work in Process Inventory—Division 2 (40%)	208,000	
	Work in Process Inventory—Processing		520,000
	To allocate joint cost to joint products		
3.	Work in Process—Division 1	649,026	
	Work in Process—Division 2	387,600	
	Various accounts		1,036,626
	To record separate processing costs		
4.	Work in Process Inventory—Division 1	122,094	
	Various accounts		122,094
	To record packaging costs for Primero		
5.	Finished Goods Inventory—Primero	1,083,120	
	Finished Goods Inventory—Segundo	595,600	
	Work in Process Inventory—Division 1		1,083,120
	Work in Process Inventory—Division 2		595,600
	To transfer completed production to finished goods		

c. Approximated NRV Method

Div. 1 = 0.6 × 510,000 lbs. = 306,000 lbs.; 306,000 × 0.7 = 214,200 lbs. Primero
Div. 2 = 0.4 × 510,000 lbs. = 204,000 lbs. Segundo
Más = 306,000 × 0.3 = 91,800 lbs.

Product	Pounds Produced	NRV per Lb. at Split-Off*	Total NRV	Proportion	Joint Cost	Allocated Joint Cost
Primero	214,200	$3.60	$ 771,120	59%	$520,000	$306,800
Segundo	204,000	2.65	540,600	41	520,000	213,200
			$1,311,720	100%		$520,000

	Primero	Segundo
*Selling price per pound	$ 8.00	$ 4.70
Separate costs		
Division 1 ($649,026 ÷ 214,200)	(3.03)	
Packaging ($122,094 ÷ 214,200)	(0.57)	
Division 2 ($387,600 ÷ 204,000)		(1.90)
Selling	(0.80)	(0.15)
Approximated net realizable value	$ 3.60	$ 2.65

d.

Circle City Inc.
Income Statement
For the Year Ended December 31, 2013

Sales		
Primero (214,200 × 0.80 × $8.00)	$1,370,880	
Segundo (204,000 × 0.90 × $4.70)	862,920	$ 2,233,800
Cost of Goods Sold		
Beginning finished goods inventories	$ 0	
Cost of goods manufactured [from (b5)]		
Primero	1,083,120	
Segundo	595,600	
Available for sale	$1,678,720	
Ending finished goods inventories		
Primero ($1,083,120 × 0.20)	(216,624)	
Segundo ($595,600 × 0.10)	(59,560)	
Unadjusted cost of goods sold	$1,402.536	
NRV of Más [(91,800 × $0.25) – $5,000]	(17,950)	(1,384,586)
Gross margin		$ 849,214

POTENTIAL ETHICAL ISSUES

ETHICS

1. Classifying a joint product as a by-product or scrap so that no joint cost will be allocated to that product and, thereby, increasing that product's appearance of profitability
2. Classifying a salable product as "waste" and then selling that product "off the books" for the personal benefit of a manager
3. Using the NRV approach for unsold by-products as a means to increase organizational income
4. Manipulating the assignment of joint costs such that joint products in inventory at period-end are assigned a disproportionately higher cost than joint products sold during the period so that higher income and higher inventory values are reported at period-end
5. Using the sales value of by-product/scrap generated by specific jobs to offset total manufacturing overhead and, thus, lowering the overhead allocation rate on all production rather than using that sales value to reduce the cost of the job specifically generating the by-product/scrap
6. Reducing or not incurring expenses by disposing of hazardous waste in a manner that causes harm to the environment or threatens humans and wildlife
7. Misallocating the cost of an activity to program and management/general activities solely to reduce the fund-raising cost of a not-for-profit organization

QUESTIONS

1. How does management determine how to classify each type of output from a joint process? Is this decided before or after production?
2. In a company that engages in a joint production process, will all processing stop at the split-off point? Discuss the rationale for your answer.
3. By what criteria would management determine whether to proceed with processing at each decision point in a joint production process?
4. Why is cost allocation necessary in accounting? Why is it necessary in a joint process?
5. Compare the advantages and disadvantages of the two primary methods used to allocate joint cost to joint products.
6. Why are approximated, rather than actual, net realizable values at split-off sometimes used to allocate joint cost?
7. Which of the two common approaches used to account for by-product/scrap provides better information to management? Discuss the rationale for your answer.
8. When is by-product/scrap cost considered in setting the predetermined overhead rate in a job order costing system? When is such cost not considered?
9. Why must not-for-profit organizations determine when it is appropriate to allocate any cost for a joint activity among fund-raising, program, and administrative activities?

EXERCISES

INTERNET

10. **LO.1 (Research; writing)** Use the Internet to find five examples of businesses that have joint processes.
    a. For each business, describe the various outputs from the processes; using logic, determine whether each output would be classified as a joint product, a by-product, scrap, or waste.
    b. Recommend the most appropriate methods of allocating joint cost to the outputs you described in (a); express, in nontechnical terms, your justification for each of your recommendations.
    c. For one of the businesses, diagram the flow of costs.

11. **LO.2 (Joint process decision making)** Triscuit Co. makes a variety of products from a joint process. The joint cost per batch run is $120,000 and each batch produces the following products:

Product	# of Units	Sales Value per Unit at Split-Off
Boco	1,200	$6.000
Loco	1,000	$1.750
Roco	5,000	$2.500
Soco	3,800	$4.200
Moco	4,100	$1.900
Coco	200	$0.250
Doco	300	$1.800
Joco	1,000	$0.020
Voco	6,000	$0.001

How would you classify each product (joint, by-product, scrap, or waste)? Provide rationale for your answer.

12. **LO.2 (Joint process decision making; writing)** Bethany Lutrell's uncle has asked her to take over the family poultry processing plant. Provide Lutrell, who graduated in engineering, answers to the following issues:

    a. What are the important questions to be answered about joint processes in a poultry processing plant? Also indicate the points in a joint process at which these questions should be answered.
    b. How should joint costs be used in managerial decision making? When and why might a joint cost be used inappropriately in decision making?
    c. How are joint process outputs similar and dissimilar?

13. **LO.3 (Physical and sales value allocations)** Indianola Beef buys sides of beef to convert into three products: steaks, roasts, and ground beef. In April 2013, Indianola bought multiple sides of beef for $20,000 that were converted into the following products at a cost of $6,400:

Product	# of Pounds	Sales Value at Split-Off
Steaks	3,312	$4.25 per pound
Roasts	6,210	$3.80 per pound
Ground beef	4,278	$0.90 per pound

The remaining 1,200 pounds were lost as waste.

    a. Allocate the joint cost to the three products using the physical units method. What problem do you find with this method?
    b. Allocate the joint cost to the three products using the sales value at split-off method. (Round proportions to the nearest whole percentage.) Does this allocation eliminate the problem identified in (a)?
    c. Assume that the ground beef could be processed into sausage that could be sold for $2.10 per pound to a distributor that wants a special label costing $0.15 per pound attached to the sausage. If Indianola Beef uses the sales value at split-off method to allocate joint cost, what is the maximum separate cost of processing that the company could incur to still appear to earn $0.40 per pound upon the sale? If this separate cost were incurred, would you consider the $0.40 per pound a "real" profit amount?

14. **LO.3 (Allocating joint cost)** Keiffer Production manufactures three joint products in a single process. The following information is available for August 2013:

Product	Gallons	Sales Value at Split-Off per Gallon	Cost after Split-Off	Final Selling Price
JP-4539	4,500	$14	$4	$24
JP-4587	18,000	8	5	15
JP-4591	13,500	18	2	22

Allocate the joint cost of $558,000 to the production based on the

a. number of gallons.
b. sales value at split-off.
c. approximated net realizable values at split-off.

(Round all percentages to the nearest whole percentage.)

15. **LO.3 (Processing beyond split-off and cost allocations)** All-A-Buzz makes three products from a joint production process using honey. Joint cost for the process in 2013 is $123,200.

Product	Units of Output	Per Unit Selling Price at Split-Off	Incremental Processing Cost	Final Sales Price
Honey butter	10,000	4.00	$3.00	$ 6.00
Honey jam	20,000	6.40	4.00	14.00
Honey syrup	1,000	3.00	0.40	3.60

Each container of honey butter, jam, and syrup, respectively, contains 16 ounces, 8 ounces, and 3 ounces of product.

a. Determine which products should be processed beyond the split-off point.
b. Assume honey syrup should be treated as a by-product. Allocate the joint cost based on units produced, weight, and sales value at split-off. Use the net realizable value method in accounting for the by-product. (Round to nearest whole percentage.)

16. **LO.3 (Sell or process further)** Winnovia Mills processes cotton in a joint process that yields two joint products: fabric and yarn. May's joint cost is $120,000, and the sales values at split-off are $360,000 for fabric and $300,000 for yarn. If the products are processed beyond split-off, the final sales value will be $540,000 for fabric and $420,000 for yarn. Additional costs of processing are expected to be $120,000 for fabric and $102,000 for yarn.

a. Should the products be processed further? Show computations.
b. Were any revenues and/or costs irrelevant to the decision? If so, what were they and why were they irrelevant?

17. **LO.3 (Sell or process further)** Storey Corp. manufactures three products in a joint process. Each of the products can be sold at split-off or may be processed further. Using the following per unit information, determine which of the products should undergo further processing.

	JP#1	JP#2	JP#3
Sales value at split-off	$360	$290	$585
Sales value after further processing	410	330	650
Joint costs allocated at split-off	215	185	380
Costs of further processing	55	25	45

EXCEL

18. **LO.3 (Approximated net realizable value method)** Scent of Money makes three products that can be sold at split-off or processed further and then sold. The joint cost for April 2013 is $1,080,000.

Product	Bottles of Output	Sales Price at Split-Off	Separate Cost after Split-Off	Final Sales Price
Perfume	20,000	$7.00	$2.50	$16.50
Eau de toilette	32,000	5.00	1.50	13.00
Body splash	28,000	5.00	2.00	12.00

The number of ounces in a bottle of each product is: perfume, one; eau de toilette, two; and body splash, three. Assume that all products are processed further after split-off.

a. Allocate the joint cost based on the number of bottles, weight, and approximated net realizable values at split-off. (Round to the nearest whole percentage.)

b. Assume that all products are processed further and completed. At the end of the period, the inventories are as follows: perfume, 600 bottles; eau de toilette, 1,600 bottles; and body splash, 1,680 bottles. Determine the values of the inventories based on answers obtained in (a). (Round per-unit costs to the nearest cent.)

c. Do you see any problems with the allocation based on approximated net realizable value?

19. **LO.3 (Sell or process further)** Bright Red Cannery makes three products from a single joint process. For 2013, the cannery processed all three products beyond split-off. The following data were generated for the year:

Joint Product	Incremental Separate Cost	Total Revenue
Candied apples	$26,000	$690,000
Apple jelly	32,000	775,000
Apple jam	15,000	271,000

Analysis of 2013 market data reveals that candied apples, apple jelly, and apple jam could have been sold at split-off for $670,000, $730,000, and $260,000, respectively.

a. Based on hindsight, evaluate management's production decisions in 2013.

b. How much additional profit could the company have generated in 2013 if it had made optimal decisions at split-off?

20. **LO.3 (Net realizable value allocation)** MediaForum has three operating groups: Games, News, and Documentaries. In May, the company incurred $24,000,000 of joint cost for facilities and administration. May revenues and separate production costs of each group are as follows:

	Games	News	Documentaries
Revenue	$34,040,000	$30,720,000	$189,320,000
Separate costs	31,040,000	16,320,000	110,720,00

a. What amount of joint cost is allocated to each operating group using the net realizable value approach? Compute the profit for each operating area after the allocation. (Round to nearest whole percentage.)

b. What amount of joint cost is allocated to each operating group if the allocation is based on revenues? Compute the profit for each operating group after the allocation. (Round to nearest whole percentage.)

c. Assume you are head of the Games Group. Would the difference in allocation bases create significant problems for you when you report to the top management of the company? Develop a short presentation for top management if the allocation base in (b) is used to determine each operating group's relative profitability. Be certain to discuss important differences in revenues and cost figures for the Games and Documentaries groups.

21. **LO.3 (Sell or process further)** In a joint process, Wear Art produces precut fabrics for three products: dresses, jackets, and blouses. Joint cost is allocated on the basis of relative sales value at split-off. The company can choose to process each of the products further rather than sell the fabric at split-off. Information related to these products follows.

	Dresses	Jackets	Blouses	Total
Number of units produced	10,000	16,000	6,000	32,000
Joint cost allocated	?	$138,000	?	$360,000
Sales values at split-off point	?	$230,000	$ 80,000	$600,000
Additional costs of processing further	$ 26,000	$ 20,000	$ 78,000	$124,000
Sales values after all processing	$300,000	$268,000	$210,000	$778,000

a. What amount of joint cost should be allocated to dresses and blouses?

b. What is the sales values at the split-off point for dresses?

c. Should any of the products be processed beyond the split-off point? Show computations.

d. If 12,000 jackets are processed further and sold at the regular selling price, what is the gross profit on the sale?

22. **LO.3 (Physical and sales value allocations)** FINS produces three products from its fish farm: fish, fish oil, and fish meal. During July 2013, FINS produced the following average quantities of each product from each pound (16 ounces) of fish processed:

Product	Obtained from Each Pound of Fish
Fish	8 ounces
Fish oil	4
Fish meal	2
Total	14 ounces

Of each pound of fish processed, two ounces are waste. In July, FINS processed 37.5 tons of fish (1 ton equals 2,000 pounds). Joint cost amounted to $142,800. On average, each pound of product has the following selling prices: fish, $4.50; fish oil, $6.50; and fish meal, $2.

a. Allocate the joint cost using weight as the basis. (Round to nearest whole percentage.)
b. Allocate the joint cost using sales value as the basis. (Round to nearest whole percentage.)
c. Discuss the advantages and disadvantages of the answers to (a) and (b).

23. **LO.3 (Sales value and physical value allocation)** To-Go produces milk and sour cream from a joint process. During June, the company produced 240,000 quarts of milk and 190,000 pints of sour cream (there are two pints in a quart). Sales value at split-off point was $377,400 for the milk and $177,600 for the sour cream. The milk was assigned $125,800 of the joint cost. (Round proportions to the nearest whole percentage and dollar amounts to the nearest whole dollar.)

a. Using the sales value at split-off approach, determine the total joint cost for June.
b. Assume, instead, that the joint cost was allocated based on the number of quarts produced. What was the total joint cost incurred in June?

24. **LO.3 (Physical measure allocation)** Oregon Forests uses a joint process to manufacture two grades of wood: A and B. During October 2013, the company incurred $16,200,000 of joint production cost in producing 27,000,000 board feet of Grade A and 9,000,000 board feet of Grade B lumber. The company allocates joint cost on the basis of board feet of lumber produced. The company can sell Grade A lumber at the split-off point for $0.70 per board foot. Alternatively, Grade A lumber can be further processed at a cost of $0.75 per board foot and then sold for $1.50 per board foot. No opportunity exists for processing Grade B lumber after split-off.

a. How much joint cost should be allocated to Grade A and to Grade B lumber?
b. If Grade A lumber is processed further and then sold, what is the incremental effect on Oregon Forest' net income? Should the additional processing be performed?

25. **LO.3 & LO.4 (Joint cost allocation; by-products)** Go-Go Co., which began operations in 2013, produces gasoline and a gasoline by-product. Go-Go accounts for the by-product at the time of production through a reduction in joint product cost of goods sold. The following information is available pertaining to 2013 sales and production:

Total production costs to split-off point	$240,000
Gasoline sales	540,000
By-product sales	60,000
Gasoline inventory, 12/31/2013	30,000
Additional by-product costs:	
Marketing	$ 20,000
Production	30,000

a. Compute Go-Go's cost of sales for gasoline and for the by-product for 2013.
b. If Go-Go had used the by-product's NRV to reduce the joint cost of the gasoline, how (if at all) would the gross margin for 2013 changed? No calculations are necessary.

CPA ADAPTED

26. **LO.4 (Accounting for by-product)** You Carve Me Up manufactures wood statues, which yields sawdust as a by-product. Selling costs associated with the sawdust are $250 per ton sold. The company accounts for sawdust sales by deducting the sawdust's net realizable value from the major products' cost of goods sold. Sawdust sales in 2013 were 1,200 tons at $335 each. If You Carve Me Up changes its method of accounting for sawdust sales to show the net realizable value as Other Revenue (presented at the bottom of the income statement), how would its gross margin be affected?

27. **LO.4 (Accounting for by-product)** The Bishop's Falls Lumber Corporation harvests lumber and prepares it for sale to wholesalers of lumber and wood products. The main product is finished lumber, which is sold to wholesale construction suppliers. A by-product of the processs is wood pellets, which are sold to wholesalers of wood pellet stoves. During December 2013, the manufacturing process incurred $664,000 in total costs; 160,000 board feet of lumber were produced and sold along with 40,000 pounds of pellets. The finished lumber sold for $10 per board foot and the pellets sold for $4 per 100-pound bag. There were no beginning or ending inventories.

    a. Compute the December 2013 gross margin for Bishop's Falls Lumber Corporation assuming that by-product revenues reduce joint production costs.
    b. How would your answer change if by-products are accounted for as revenue when sold?

28. **LO.4 (By-product and cost allocation)** Dover Studios shot hundreds of hours of footage that cost $20,000,000. From this footage, the company produced two movies: *Greedy CEOs* and *Greedy CEOs: The Sequel.* The sequel used better sound effects than the original and was significantly more expensive to produce. However, audiences seemed to be more interested in the careers of Erin Sacks and Henry Whalen, discussed in the sequel, than the CEOs portrayed in the original movie and the sequel was much better received at the box office.

    Dover Studios also generated revenue from admissions paid by numerous forensic accountants who wanted to tour the movie production set. The company accounted for this revenue as a by-product and used it to reduce joint cost before making allocations to the two feature-length movies.

    The following information pertains to the two movies:

Products	Total Receipts	Separate Costs
Greedy CEOs	$10,000,000	$ 6,800,000
Greedy CEOs: The Sequel	58,000,000	41,200,000
Studio tours	800,000	480,000

    a. If joint cost is allocated based on net realizable value, how much of the joint cost is allocated to each movie?
    b. Based on your allocations in (a), how much profit was generated by each movie?

29. **LO.4 (Accounting for by-product)** Potato skins are generated as a by-product in making potato chips and frozen hash browns at Zeena Foods. The skins are sold to restaurants for use in appetizers. Processing and disposal costs associated with by-product sales are $0.06 per pound of potato skins. During May 2013, Zeena Foods produced and sold 135,000 pounds of potato skins for $20,250. In addition, the joint cost for producing potato chips and hash browns was $82,000; separate costs of production were $48,000. In May, 90 percent of all joint production was sold for $319,000. Nonfactory operating expenses for May were $47,850.

    a. Prepare an income statement for Zeena Foods assuming that by-product sales are shown as Other Revenue and the processing and disposal costs for the by-product are shown as additional cost of goods sold of the joint products.
    b. Prepare an income statement for Zeena Foods assuming that the net realizable value of the by-product is shown as Other Income.

c. Prepare an income statement for Zeena Foods assuming that the net realizable value of the by-product is subtracted from the joint cost of the main products.
d. Would the presentation in (a), (b), or (c) be most helpful to managers? Why?

30. **LO.4 (By-product accounting method selection; writing)** Your employer engages in numerous joint processes that produce significant quantities and types of by-product. You have been asked to give a report to management on the best way to account for by-product. Develop criteria for making such a choice and provide reasons for each criterion selected. On the basis of your criteria, along with any additional assumptions you wish to provide about the nature of the company you work for, recommend a particular method of accounting for by-product and explain why you consider it to be better than the alternatives.

31. **LO.4 (Accounting for scrap)** Hammatt Inc. provides a variety of services for commercial clients. Hammatt destroys any paper client records after seven years and the shredded paper is sold to a recycling company. The net realizable value of the recycled paper is treated as a reduction to operating overhead. The following data pertain to 2013 operations:

Budgeted operating overhead	$415,200
Actual operating overhead	$410,500
Budgeted net realizable value of recycled paper	$ 9,200
Actual net realizable value of recycled paper	$ 9,700
Budgeted billable hours	70,000
Actual billable hours	70,900

a. Assuming that number of billable hours is the allocation base, what was the company's predetermined overhead rate?
b. Record the journal entry for the sale of the recycled paper.
c. What was the company's underapplied or overapplied overhead for 2013?

EXCEL

32. **LO.4 (By-product; net realizable value method)** Weinberg Canning produces fillet, smoked salmon, and salmon remnants in a single process. The same amount of disposal cost is incurred whether a product is sold at split-off or after further processing. In October 2013, the joint cost of the production process was $142,000.

Product	Pounds Produced	Separate Cost	Final Selling Price
Fillet	18,000	$3.00	$16.00
Smoked	20,000	5.20	13.00
Remnants	2,000	0.30	1.50

a. The remnants are considered a by-product of the process and are sold to cat food processors. Allocate the joint cost based on approximated net realizable value at split-off. Use the net realizable value method to account for the by-product.
b. Determine the value of ending Finished Goods Inventory, assuming that 4,000 pounds of salmon fillets, 2,400 pounds of smoked salmon, and 350 pounds of salmon remnants were sold. (Round cost per pound to the nearest penny.)

33. **LO.4 (Accounting for scrap)** Renaissance Creations restores antique stained glass windows. All jobs generate some breakage or improper cuts. This scrap can be sold to stained glass hobbyists. Renaissance Creations expects to incur approximately 45,000 direct labor hours during 2013. The following estimates are made in setting the predetermined overhead rate for 2013:

Overhead costs other than breakage		$297,200
Estimated cost of scrap	$25,200	
Estimated sales value of scrap	(7,400)	17,800
Total estimated overhead		$315,000

One job that Renaissance Creations completed during 2013 was a stained glass window of the Pierce family crest that took 125 hours, and direct labor is invoiced at

$20 per hour. Total direct material cost for the job was $890. Scrap that was generated from this job was sold for $93.

a. What was the predetermined overhead rate (set on the basis of direct labor hours) for 2013?
b. What was the cost of the Pierce stained glass window?
c. Prepare the journal entry to record the sales value of the scrap from the Pierce stained glass window.
d. Assume instead that only certain jobs generate scrap. What was the cost of the Pierce stained glass window?

34. **LO.4 (By-product and cost allocation)** Georgia Fresh raises peaches that, at harvest, are separated into three grades: premium, good, and fair. Joint cost is allocated to products based on bushels of output. The $337,500 joint cost for one harvest yielded the following output quantities.

Product	Output in Bushels
Premium	16,500
Good	43,560
Fair	5,940

The joint process also created a by-product that had a total net realizable value of $65,000. The company records the by-product inventory at the time of production. Allocate the joint cost to the joint products using bushels of output.

35. **LO.4 (Accounting for scrap)** Mae-Doff Designs uses a job order costing system to account for the various architectural services offered to commercial clients. For each major job, architectural models of the completed structures are built for client presentations. At the completion of a job, models not wanted by clients are sold to an arts and crafts retailer. Mae-Doff Designs uses the realized value method of accounting for model sales. The sales value of each model is credited to the cost of the specific job for which the model was built. During 2013, the model for the Hedge Fund Extraordinaire building was sold for $8,500.

a. Using the net realizable value approach, give the entry to record the sale.
b. Independent of your answer to (a), assume that a model's sales value is *not* credited to specific jobs. Give the entry to account for the sale of the Hedge Fund Extraordinaire model.
c. Which method would be preferable for Mae-Doff Designs to use, and why?

36. **LO.4 (By-product/scrap; net realizable value vs. realized value)** Indicate whether each item that follows is associated with (1) the realized value approach or (2) the net realizable value approach.

a. Is less conservative
b. Has the advantage of better timing
c. Uses an actual value for by-product sales
d. Is easier to apply
e. Presents proceeds from sale of the by-product as other revenue or other income
f. Ignores value of by-product/scrap until it is sold
g. Is used to reduce the cost of main products in the period the by-product is produced
h. Should be used when the by-product's net realizable value is large
i. Credits either cost of goods sold of main products or the joint cost when the by-product inventory is recorded
j. Is appropriate if the by-product's net realizable value is small
k. Has a greater likelihood for earnings management
l. Is the most clerically efficient
m. Uses an expected value for by-product sales

37. **LO.3 (Retail organization joint cost)** Wilke Realty separates its activities into two operating divisions: Rentals and Sales. In March 2013, the firm spent $32,500 for general company promotions (as opposed to advertisements for specific properties). The

corporate controller has decided to allocate general promotion costs to the two operating divisions. He is considering whether to base his allocations on the (1) expected increase in divisional revenue from the promotions or (2) expected increase in divisional profit from the promotions (before allocated promotion costs). General promotions had the following effects on the two divisions:

	Rentals	Sales
Increase in divisional revenue	$770,000	$105,000
Increase in profit (before allocated promotion costs)	104,500	85,500

a. Allocate the total promotion cost to the two divisions using change in revenue.
b. Allocate the total promotion cost to the two divisions using change in profit before joint cost allocation.
c. Which of the two approaches is more appropriate? Explain.

38. **LO.5 (NFP program and support cost allocation)** Memphis Jazz Company is preparing a pamphlet that will provide information on the types of jazz, jazz terminology, and biographies of some of the better-known jazz musicians. In addition, the pamphlet will include a request for funding to support the jazz company. The company has tax-exempt status and operates on a not-for-profit basis.

    The 10-page pamphlet cost $261,000 to design and print. Only 200,000 copies of the pamphlet were printed because the company director will be leaving and the pamphlet will soon be redesigned. One page of the pamphlet is devoted to fund solicitation; however, 98 percent of the design time was spent on developing and writing the jazz information.

    a. If space is used as the allocation measure, how much of the pamphlet's cost should be assigned to program activities? To fund-raising activities?
    b. If design time is used as the allocation measure, how much of the pamphlet's cost should be assigned to program activities? To fund-raising activities?

39. **LO.5 (Retail organization joint cost)** Abrula Archery provides archery training for children and adults. During 2013, the camp had the following operating data:

	Children	Adults
Training hours taught	4,000	2,000
Hourly tuition	$35	$65

Direct instructional costs for 2013 were $120,000; overhead costs for the two programs were $55,500. Camp owners want to know the cost of each program.

a. Determine each program's cost using a physical measure base.
b. Determine each program's cost using the sales value at split-off method.
c. Make a case for the allocation method in (a) and (b).

INTERNET

40. **LO.5 (NFP; research)** Look up three not-for-profit organization's Web sites and find a recent annual report or IRS filing. Many charities are also listed at http://www.charitynavigator.org.

    a. How much did each of the organizations spend on program, administrative, and fundraising costs during the period?
    b. What were the fundraising expenses percentages and fundraising efficiency amounts?
    c. Go to the same organizations' home pages and find financial information. In what types of activities were the organizations engaged that might have generated joint costs needing to be allocated?

PROBLEMS

ETHICS

INTERNET

41. **LO.2 (Joint product decision; ethics; research)** Production of ethanol, made from corn, is on the rise. Some states are even requiring that ethanol be blended in small amounts with gasoline to reduce pollution. The problem is that there is not enough corn being produced: the consumption of corn either as a food product (in all of its

many forms) or as a fuel product will have to suffer. Research the issues regarding ethanol production from corn, and discuss what must be considered by farmers when determining whether corn output should be sold for consumption or for fuel.

42. **LO.3 (Joint costs; journal entries)** Natural Beauty Corp. uses a joint process to make two main products: Forever perfume and Fantasy lotion. Production is organized in two sequential departments: Combining and Heating. The products do not become separate until they have been through the heating process. After heating, the perfume is removed from the vats and bottled without further processing. The residue remaining in the vats is then blended with aloe and lanolin to become the lotion.

EXCEL

The following costs were incurred in the Combining Department during October 2013: direct material, $42,000; direct labor, $11,340; and applied manufacturing overhead, $6,375. Prior to separation of the joint products, October costs in the Heating Department were direct material, $9,150; direct labor, $3,225; and applied manufacturing overhead, $4,860. After split-off, the Heating Department incurred separate costs for each product line as follows: bottles in which to package the Forever perfume, $3,180; and direct material, direct labor, and applied manufacturing overhead of $2,940, $4,680, and $6,195, respectively, for Fantasy lotion.

Neither department had beginning Work in Process Inventory balances, and all work that started in October was completed in that month. Joint costs are allocated to perfume and lotion using approximated net realizable values at split-off. For October, the approximated net realizable values at split-off were $238,365 for perfume and $79,455 for lotion.

a. Determine the joint cost allocated to, and the total cost of, Forever perfume and Fantasy lotion.
b. Prepare journal entries for the Combining and Heating Departments for October 2013.
c. Post the entries to the accounts.

43. **LO.3 (Physical measure joint cost allocation)** Powisett Farms Dairy began operations at the start of May 2013. Powisett Farms operates a fleet of trucks to gather whole milk from local farmers. The whole milk is then separated into two joint products: skim milk and cream. Both products are sold at the split-off point to dairy wholesalers. For May, the firm incurred the following joint costs:

Whole milk purchase cost	$400,000
Direct labor costs	180,000
Overhead costs	292,000
Total product cost	$872,000

During May, the firm processed 2,000,000 gallons of whole milk, producing 1,555,500 gallons of skim milk and 274,500 gallons of cream. The remaining gallons of the whole milk were lost during processing. There was no Raw Material or Work in Process Inventory at the end of May.

After the joint process, the skim milk and cream were separately processed at costs, respectively, of $67,660 and $83,310. Of the products produced, Powisett Farms Dairy sold 1,550,000 gallons of skim milk for $1,472,500 and 274,000 gallons of cream for $282,220 to wholesalers.

a. Powisett uses a physical measure (gallon) to allocate joint costs. Allocate the joint cost to production.
b. Calculate ending Finished Goods Inventory cost, Cost of Goods Sold, and gross margin for May.
c. A manager at Powisett Farms Dairy noted that the milk fat content of whole milk can vary greatly from farmer to farmer. Because milk fat content determines the relative yields of skim milk and cream from whole milk, the ratio of joint products can be partly determined based on the milk fat content of purchased whole milk. How could Powisett Farms Dairy use information about milk fat content in the whole milk it purchases to optimize the profit realized on its joint products?

44. **LO.3 (Physical measure joint cost allocation)** Illinois Soybeans operates a processing plant in which soybeans are crushed to create soybean oil and soybean meal. The company purchases soybeans by the bushel (60 pounds). From each bushel, the normal yield is 11 pounds of soybean oil, 44 pounds of soybean meal, and 5 pounds of waste. For March, Illinois Soybeans purchased and processed 5,000,000 bushels of soybeans. The yield in March on the soybeans was equal to the normal yield. The following costs were incurred for the month:

Soybeans	$47,500,000
Conversion costs	2,300,000

At the end of March, there was no in-process or raw material in inventory. Also, there was no beginning Finished Goods Inventory. For the month, 60 percent of the soybean oil and 75 percent of the soybean meal was sold.

a. Allocate the joint cost to the joint products on the basis of pounds of product produced.
b. Calculate the cost of goods sold for March.
c. Calculate the cost of Finished Goods Inventory at the end of March.

45. **LO.3 (Monetary measure joint cost allocation)** Refer to the information in Problem 43. (Round to the nearest whole percentage and cent.)

a. Calculate the sales price per gallon for skim milk and cream.
b. Using relative sales value, allocate the joint cost to the joint production.
c. Calculate ending Finished Goods Inventory cost, Cost of Goods Sold, and the gross margin for the month.

46. **LO.3 (Monetary measure joint cost allocation)** Refer to the information in Problem 44.

a. Assume the net realizable values of the joint products are as follows:

Soybean oil	$0.50 per pound
Soybean meal	$0.20 per pound

Allocate the joint cost incurred in March on the basis of net realizable value.
b. Calculate the cost of goods sold for March using the answer to (a).
c. Calculate the cost of Finished Goods Inventory at the end of March based on the answer to (a).
d. Compare the answers to (b) and (c) of Problem 44 to the answers to (b) and (c) of this problem. Explain why the answers differ.

EXCEL

47. **LO.3 & LO.4 (Joint cost allocation; by-product; income determination)** Schneider Bank offers two primary financial services: commercial checking and credit cards. The bank also generates some revenue from selling identity fraud insurance as a by-product of its two main services. The monthly joint cost for conducting the two primary services is $800,000 and includes expenses for facilities, legal support, equipment, record keeping, and administration. The joint cost is allocated on the basis of total revenues generated from each primary service.

The following table presents the results of operations and revenues for June:

Service	Number of Accounts	Total Revenues
Commercial checking	12,000	$1,914,000
Credit cards	28,000	1,386,000
Identity theft insurance	3,000	26,000

To account for revenues from the identity theft insurance, management reduces Cost of Services Rendered for primary services. The commissions are accounted for on a realized value basis as the policies are received.

For June, separate costs for commercial checking accounts and credit cards were $850,000 and 380,000, respectively.

a. Allocate the joint cost.
b. Determine the income for each primary service and the company's overall gross margin for June.

c. Assume instead that Schneider Bank uses the net realizable value approach for by-product revenue. How much joint cost would have been allocated to the commercial checking and the credit card products during June? Will the gross margin be the same as in (b)? Why or why not?

48. **LO.3 & LO.4 (Joint cost allocation; by-products)** Buchan's Junction Manufacturing Corporation uses a joint production process that produces three products at the split-off point. Joint production costs during March were $720,000. The company uses the sales-value method for allocating joint costs. March production information was as follows:

	PRODUCT		
	Alpha	**Beta**	**Gamma**
Units produced	2,500	5,000	7,500
Units sold	2,000	6,000	7,000
Sales prices:			
At the split-off point	$100	$80	$20
After further processing	$150	$115	$30
Costs to process after split-off point	$150,000	$150,000	$100,000

a. Compute the amount of joint costs allocated to each product assuming that joint cost allocation is based on sales value at the split-off point. (Rounding is not needed.)
b. Assume that all three products are main products and that they can be sold at the split-off point or processed further, whichever is economically beneficial to the company. Compute the total cost of product Beta in March if joint cost allocation is based on sales value at split-off.
c. Assume that product Gamma is treated as a by-product and that the company accounts for the by-product at net realizable value as a reduction of joint cost. Products Beta and Gamma must be processed further before they can be sold. Compute the total cost of production of products Alpha and Beta in March if joint cost allocation is based on net realizable values. (Round proportions to the nearest whole percentage.) CIA ADAPTED

49. **LO.3 & LO.4 (Joint cost allocation; scrap)** DD's Linens produces terrycloth products for hotels. The company buys fabric in 60-inch-wide bolts. In the first process, the fabric is set up, cut, and separated into pieces. Setup can be for either robes and beach towels, or bath towels, hand towels, and washcloths.

During July, the company set up and cut 6,000 robes and 12,000 beach towels. Because of the irregular pattern of the robes, the process produces scrap that is sold to various prisons and hospitals for rags at $0.45 per pound. July production and cost data for DD's Linens are as follows:

Fabric used, 25,000 feet at $1.50 per foot	$37,500
Labor, joint process	$12,000
Overhead, joint process	$11,000
Pounds of scrap produced	3,600

DD's Linens assigns the joint processing cost to the robes and beach towels based on approximated net realizable value at split-off. Other data gathered include these:

	Per Robe	Per Beach Towel
Final selling prices	$20.00	$7.00
Costs after split-off	6.80	1.60

The selling price of the scrap is treated as a reduction of joint cost.

a. Determine the joint cost to be allocated to the joint products for July.
b. How much joint cost is allocated to the robes in July? To the beach towels? Prepare the journal entry necessary at the split-off point.
c. What amount of cost for robes is transferred to Finished Goods Inventory for July? What amount of cost for beach towels is transferred to Finished Goods Inventory for July?

50. **LO.3 & LO.4 (By-product/joint product journal entries)** Arguillo Inc. is a 5,000-acre farm that produces two products: Zilla and Corma. Zilla sells for $3.50 per bushel (assume that a bushel weighs 60 pounds). Without further processing, Corma sells for $30 per ton (a ton equals 2,000 pounds). If the Corma is processed further, it can be sold for $45 per ton. In 2013, total joint cost up to the split-off point was $875,000. In 2013, Arguillo produced 70 bushels of Zilla and 1 ton of Corma per acre. If all the Corma were processed further, separate costs would be $50,000.

    Prepare the 2013 journal entries for Corma if it is:

    a. transferred to storage at sales value as a by-product without further processing with a corresponding reduction of Zilla's production costs.
    b. further processed as a by-product and transferred to storage at net realizable value with a corresponding reduction of the manufacturing costs of Zilla.
    c. further processed and transferred to finished goods with joint cost allocated based on relative sales value at the split-off point. (Round to the nearest whole percent.)

51. **LO.3 & LO.4 (Joint cost allocation; ending inventory valuation; by-product)** During March 2013, the first month of operations, Oink Oink's Pork Co. had the operating statistics shown in the following table.

Products	Weight in Pounds	Sales Value at Split-Off	Pounds Produced	Pounds Sold
Tenderloin	8,600	$132,000	6,440	5,440
Roast	13,400	86,000	16,740	14,140
Ham	10,800	22,400	8,640	7,640
Hooves	4,600	4,600	9,200	8,000

Costs of the joint process were direct material, $40,000; direct labor, $23,400; and overhead, $10,000. The company's main products are pork tenderloin, roast pork, and ham; pork hooves are a by-product of the process. The company recognizes the net realizable value of by-product inventory at split-off by reducing total joint cost. Neither the main products nor the by-product requires any additional processing or disposal costs, although management could consider additional processing.

    a. Calculate the ending inventory values of each joint product based on (1) relative sales value and (2) pounds. (Round to nearest whole percentage.)
    b. Discuss the advantages and disadvantages of each allocation base for (1) financial statement purposes and (2) decisions about the desirability of processing the joint products beyond the split-off point.

52. **LO.3 & LO.4 (Joint cost allocation; by-product)** Tangy Fresh produces orange juice and orange marmalade from a joint process. Second-stage processing of the marmalade creates an orange pulp by-product that can be sold for $0.05 per gallon. Expenses to distribute pulp total $90.

    In May 2013, 140,000 pounds of oranges costing $44,200 were processed in Department 1, with labor and overhead costs of $33,800 incurred. Department 1 processing resulted in 56,000 gallons of output, of which 40 percent was transferred to Department 2 to become orange juice and 60 percent was transferred to Department 3. Of the input going to Department 3, 20 percent resulted in pulp and 80 percent resulted in marmalade. Joint cost is allocated to orange juice and marmalade on the basis of approximated net realizable values at split-off.

    The orange juice in Department 2 was processed at a total cost of $9,620; the marmalade in Department 3 was processed at a total cost of $6,450. The net realizable value of pulp is accounted for as a reduction in the separate processing costs in Department 3. Selling prices per gallon are $5.25 and $3.45 for orange juice and marmalade, respectively.

    a. Diagram Tangy Fresh's process in a manner similar to Exhibits 11.5 and 11.10.
    b. How many gallons leaving Department 1 were sent to Department 2 for further processing? To Department 3?
    c. How many gallons left Department 3 as pulp? As marmalade?

d. What is the net realizable value of pulp?
e. What is the total approximated net realizable value of the orange juice? The marmalade?
f. What joint cost is assigned to each main product? (Round to the nearest whole percent.)
g. If 85 percent of the final output of each main product was sold during May and Tangy Fresh had no beginning inventory of either product, what is the value of the ending inventory of orange juice and marmalade?

53. **LO.3 & LO.4 (Process costing; joint cost allocation; by-product)** GetAhead provides personal training services for, and sells apparel products to, its clients. GetAhead also generates some revenue from protein drink sales. The net realizable value from drink sales is accounted for as a reduction in the joint cost assigned to the Personal Training Services and Apparel Products. Protein drinks sell for $2.50 per bottle. The costs associated with making and packaging the drinks are $1.00 per bottle.

The following information is available for 2013 on apparel products, which are purchased by GetAhead:

Beginning inventory	$ 35,000
Ending inventory	21,500
Purchases	181,350

Joint cost is to be allocated to Personal Training Services and Apparel Products based on approximated net realizable values. For 2013, total revenues were $753,000 from Personal Training Services and $289,000 from Apparel. The following joint costs were incurred:

Rent	$36,000
Insurance	43,750
Utilities	3,000

Separate costs were as follows:

	Personal Training	Apparel
Labor	$231,000	$33,250
Supplies	151,300	700
Equipment depreciation	165,000	1,200
Administration	103,000	3,700

For the year, 2,500 bottles of protein drinks were sold.

a. What is the total net realizable value of protein drinks used to reduce the joint cost assigned to Personal Training and Apparel?
b. What is the joint cost to be allocated to Personal Training and Apparel?
c. What is the approximated pre-tax realizable value of each main product or service for 2013?
d. How much joint cost is allocated to each main product or service?
e. Determine the net income produced by each main product or service.

54. **LO.3 & LO.4 (Joint products; by-product)** Fredericksburg Vegetable is a fruit-packing business. The firm buys peaches by the truckload in season and separates them into three categories: premium, good, and fair. Premium peaches can be sold as is to supermarket chains and to specialty gift stores. Good peaches are sliced and canned in light syrup and sold to supermarkets. Fair peaches are considered a by-product and are sold to Altas Company, which processes the peaches into jelly.

Fredericksburg Vegetable has two processing departments: (1) Cleaning and Sorting (joint cost) and (2) Cutting and Canning (separate costs). During the month, the company paid $15,000 for one truckload of fruit and $700 for labor to sort the fruit into categories. Fredericksburg Vegetable uses a predetermined overhead rate of 40 percent of direct labor cost. The following yield, costs, and final sales value resulted from the month's truckload of fruit.

	Premium	Good	Fair
Yield in pecks	1,500	2,000	500
Cutting and canning costs	$0	$2,000	$0
Total packaging and delivery costs	$1,500	$2,200	$500
Total final sales value	$30,000	$15,000	$4,500

a. Determine the joint cost.
b. Diagram Fredericksburg Vegetable's process in a manner similar to Exhibits 11.5 and 11.10.
c. Allocate joint cost using the approximated net realizable value at split-off method, assuming that the by-product is recorded when realized and is shown as Other Income on the income statement. (Round to the nearest whole percent.)
d. Using the allocations from (c), prepare the necessary entries assuming that the by-product is sold for $4,500 and that all costs were as shown.
e. Allocate joint cost using the approximated net realizable value at split-off method, assuming that the by-product is recorded using the net realizable value approach and that the joint cost is reduced by the net realizable value of the by-product. (Round to the nearest whole percent.)
f. Using the allocations from (d), prepare the necessary entries, assuming that the estimated realizable value of the by-product is $4,000.

ETHICS

55. **LO.4 (Scrap; ethics; writing; research)** Some waste, scrap, and by-product materials have little value. In fact, for many meat and poultry producers, animal waste represents a significant liability because it is considered hazardous and requires significant disposal costs. Some companies, such as **Smithfield Foods Inc.** (the largest hog processor in the United States), gather the animal waste in "lagoons" and allow it to be used as "liquid fertilizer."

INTERNET

a. Review "Smithfield Foods: A Corporate Profile" at http://www.citizen.org/documents/Smithfield.pdf as well as the environmental policies at the company's Web site (http://www.smithfieldcommitments.com/core-reporting-areas/environment/; accessed 3/15/12). Discuss the ethical and legal implications of disposing of industrial waste in this manner.
b. What actions can people take to reduce this type of disposal?
c. Ethically, what obligation does the vendor/manufacturer of potentially toxic pollutants have to the consumer of the company's products?

INTERNET

56. **LO.4 (By-product; research)** Choose a fairly common product that you believe would generate multiple by-products.

a. Without doing any research, prepare a list of some items that you believe would be by-products from the common product you have chosen.
b. After you have completed your list, use the web to find what by-products are actually associated with the product you have chosen.

57. **LO.5 (NFP joint cost)** Debra's Diabetes Foundation was started by a family whose mother had died after suffering for many years with diabetes. A lecture that cost the foundation $360,000 was held on the fourth Tuesday in March, which is American Diabetes Alert Day. Advertisements were placed in all local newspapers and were broadcast on local media channels. During the lecture, information was provided about the causes, symptoms, and treatment of diabetes, about help available for caregivers, and about the foundation and its mission. In addition to requesting contributions, members of the foundation asked attendees to take a quiz about diabetes, volunteer to distribute pamphlets about the disease to local businesses, write letters to their insurance companies about additional coverage availability, and participate in the Medicare Advocacy Program to gather information and identify problems encountered by beneficiaries and providers.

a. Did the lecture meet the audience criterion? Why or why not?
b. Did the lecture include a call for action? Explain.

c. Assume that 65 percent of the lecture time was related to the disease, 25 percent of the lecture was related to the foundation, and 10 percent was related to fund-raising. Allocate the joint cost to the three activities.

d. Assume that the topics discussed at the lecture were not in specific order, and often, discussion was in response to questions that were asked by the attendees. How else might the joint cost be allocated among program, management, and fund-raising activities?

e. Debra's Diabetes Foundation hired a consultant to help with the lecture. The consultant was paid $40,000 but has been informed that, if the lecture raised between $400,001 and $500,000, the fee would increase to $50,000; if the lecture raised over $500,000, the consultant would be paid $70,000. The consultant's fee was not included in the $360,000 joint cost. The Foundation was excited to find that the lecture raised $540,000. The time allocation given in (c) was representative of the time spent on topics during the lecture. How much of the $430,000 ($360,000 + $70,000) should be allocated to the three activities?

58. **LO.5 (NFP joint cost)** WeeCare is a not-for-profit that provides food, clothing, and medical care to children in developing countries. U.S. television programs are sponsored by WeeCare to describe its programs, show the needy children, and ask for contributions. WeeCare's operating policies and internal management memos state that these programs are designed to educate the public about the needs of children in developing countries and to raise contributions. The employees producing the programs are familiar with WeeCare's programs; the executive producer is paid $25,000 plus will receive a $5,000 bonus is the aired program raises over $1,000,000 in contributions. Discuss whether the cost of the programs should be considered an allocable joint cost or if the entire cost should be considered fundraising. AICPA ADAPTED

59. **LO.5 (NFP joint cost)** Delores' Place is a not-for-profit that has a mission of helping parents prevent their children from abusing drugs. The NFP sends materials that discuss the dangers of drug abuse to parents of high school students. The materials encourage parents to discuss the dangers of drug use with children, explain how such abuse might be detected, and request contributions to continue the organization's mission. The materials sent to parents cost approximately $8,000 to produce. Similar materials are sent to other individuals without a contribution request. Discuss whether the $8,000 should be considered an allocable joint cost or if the entire cost should be considered fundraising. AICPA ADAPTED

60. **LO.5 (NFP joint cost)** Get-Up-N-Go! is a not-for-profit organization with a mission of improving the quality of life for senior citizens; one objective within that mission is to increase seniors' physical activity. One four-page brochure distributed to over-65ers uses the first two pages to discuss a self-supervised exercise program and to encourage the undertaking of such a program. The remaining two pages of the brochure explain the Get-Up-N-Go! program and solicit contributions. Production of this brochure costs $10,000. A second four-page brochure provides specific information on exercise techniques for seniors; no contribution requests are made. Development and production of this brochure cost $14,000. The brochures are distributed to people over 65, regardless of their ability to contribute, and were developed by a public relations firm that was aware of the objectives of Get-Up-N-Go! through a letter requesting the help of the PR firm.

a. How much, if any, of the brochure costs should be considered allocable? Explain your reasoning.

b. If you have determined that any of the brochure costs should be allocated, should the allocation be to fund-raising, program, or administrative functions? How would you allocate the joint cost?

c. How, if at all, would your answer change if Get-Up-N-Go! employs a fund-raising consultant to develop the first brochure and pays that consultant 30 percent of the contributions received? AICPA ADAPTED

INTERNET

61. **LO.5 (NFP joint cost; ethics; research; writing)** Read Joseph McCafferty's article entitled "Misgivings" at *CFO.com* (January 2007); http://www.cfo.com/article.cfm/8477078?f=search (accessed 12/23/11).

  a. Discuss your thoughts about not-for-profits claiming to raise funds without incurring any costs.
  b. What would you consider a "reasonable" cost of fund-raising ratio, and why?
  c. Why would some types of not-for-profits (such as educational institutions) have different types of fund-raising ratios than others (such as museums or health-related organizations)?

ETHICS

62. **LO.1-LO.3 & LO.5 (NFP joint cost; joint revenues; ethics; writing)** Accounting for certain breast cancer walks has been criticized by one author as providing misleading information. Read the article entitled "The Avon and Komen Breast Cancer Walks: Case Studies in Questionable Special Events Reporting" at http://aaahq.org/GNP/information/activities/2007MYM/Session10_Tinkelman.pdf (last accessed 12/23/11) and discuss whether you believe the author is correct or incorrect in his criticism of the walks' costs.

ETHICS

63. **LO.1-LO.3 & LO.5 (NFP joint cost; joint revenues; decision making; writing)** Throughout your college career, you have been employed on a part-time basis by the Center for Entrepreneurship of your business college. The Center for Entrepreneurship provides executive training and consulting for a fee to individuals and organizations located throughout the state. For 2013, the condensed income statement that follows summarizes the operating results of the center.

Fees	$ 2,625,000
Faculty and staff salaries	(1,050,000)
Facilities cost	(550,000)
Training materials	(375,000)
Marketing and promotions	(400,000)
Other costs of operations	(500,000)
Net operating loss	$ (250,000)

Given that the center operated at a loss in 2013, the dean of the business college has asked the director to provide a justification for not closing the center. As the dean stated, "We're charged with a fundamental obligation of being good stewards of the state's resources. We cannot justify spending net resources to subsidize educational programs to corporations and other profit-oriented organizations."

The center director has made the dean's comments known to all employees and faculty of the center, and all are concerned about losing their employment should the center be closed.

Having just completed a chapter in your accounting course addressing joint products, you become curious as to whether the preceding income statement fairly reflects the value of all outputs of the center. Particularly, you believe that the center plays a crucial role in the generation of contributions made to the college by alumni and friends of the business college and university.

  a. Discuss how the existence of joint products of the Center for Entrepreneurship would potentially modify the preceding income statement.
  b. Discuss how you could use the concepts of joint products and joint cost allocation to demonstrate to the dean that the Center for Entrepreneurship is not consuming "net resources" of the state or college and that the center should continue its operations.

12

Introduction to Cost Management Systems

LEARNING OBJECTIVES

After completing this chapter, you should be able to answer the following questions:

1. Why do organizations have management control systems?
2. What is a cost management system?
3. What are the organizational roles of a cost management system?
4. What factors influence the design of a cost management system?
5. What are the three groups of elements that comprise a cost management system, and what are the purposes of these elements?
6. What is gap analysis, and how is it used to update a cost management system?

INTRODUCTION

A fundamental concern of managers is identifying factors that affect organizational costs and benefits. This concern arises from the managerial focus on revenue growth and profit generation. Managers use financial models and information systems to improve their understanding of costs and benefits and to identify drivers of costs and revenues. Many models used by managers are comparative analyses of costs and benefits. Financial experts, especially accountants, bear the primary responsibility for providing managers with information about measurements of those costs and benefits.

The field of accounting is divided into separate, sometimes competing roles which are often dominated by financial accounting influences. Chapter 1 discussed the differences and similarities among the disciplines of financial, management, and cost accounting. Cost accounting is described as being part of both internal and external reporting. Even though directly linked to the managerial functions of planning, controlling, decision making, and performance evaluation, cost accounting information is frequently found to be of limited value to managers because that information is shaped by financial reporting demands.

The problem is that financial reporting needs are very different from those of cost management. For financial reporting purposes, cost information is usually highly aggregated, focused on historical data, and must be consistent with GAAP. In contrast, cost information used for management purposes may be segmented, takes a current or prospective focus, and is relevant only for a particular purpose. Consequently, information provided by the financial reporting system is often of little value for cost management purposes.[1] In designing cost accounting systems, the general internal use and specific application of information to manage costs are receiving increased attention. The first section of this chapter introduces management information and control systems, which offer a foundation and context for understanding the roles of the cost management system (CMS) first introduced in Chapter 2. This chapter then discusses concepts and approaches to designing information systems that support the internal use of accounting and other information to manage costs. A CMS is presumed to be an integral part of an organization's overall management information and control systems. The discussion emphasizes the primary factors that determine the structure and success of a CMS, that influence the design of such a system, and that compose the system.

INTRODUCTION TO MANAGEMENT INFORMATION AND CONTROL SYSTEMS

1 Why do organizations have management control systems?

A CMS is part of an overall management information and control system. Exhibit 12.1 illustrates the types of information an organization needs to meet the requirements of internal parties performing managerial functions as well as requirements of external parties performing investment and credit-granting functions. A **management information system (MIS)** is a structure of interrelated elements used to collect, organize, and communicate data to managers so they can plan, control, make decisions, and evaluate performance. An MIS emphasizes satisfying internal, rather than external, demands for information. Most organizations have computerized the MIS for ease of access to information, reliability of input and processing, and ability to simulate outcomes of alternative situations.

The accounting function is charged with providing information about monetary receipts from, as well as purchases and payments to, interested internal parties (such as managers) and external parties (such as creditors and suppliers). In addition, government bodies such as the Internal Revenue Service and Securities and Exchange Commission receive mandatory reports from the accounting function. Because managers need external intelligence to govern their organizations, information to be included in the MIS is also gathered from various external parties, including competitors.

[1] Robin Cooper and Regine Slagmulder, "Strategic Cost Management: Introduction to Enterprisewide Cost Management," *Management Accounting* (August 1998), p. 17.

Exhibit 12.1 Information Flows and Types of Information

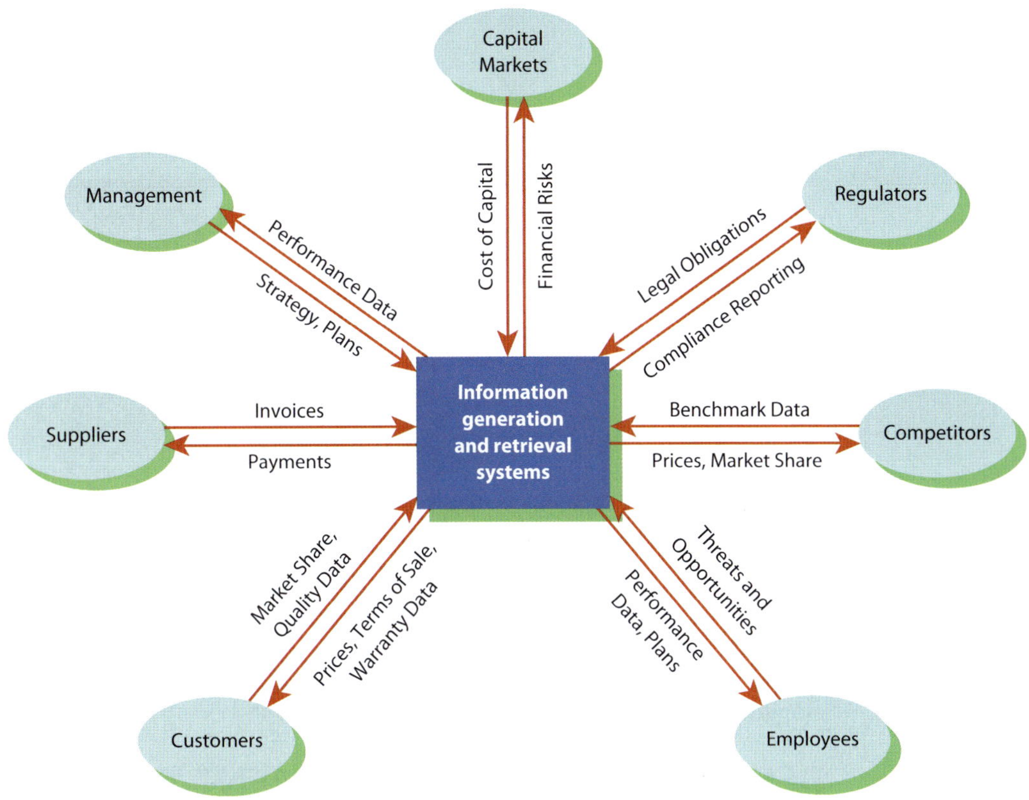

Because one managerial function requiring information is control, the MIS is part of the **management control system (MCS)**. As illustrated in Exhibit 12.2 (page 476), a control system has the following four primary components:

1. A detector or sensor, which is a measuring device that identifies what is actually happening in the process being controlled.
2. An assessor, which is a device for determining the significance of what is happening. Usually, significance is assessed by comparing the information about what is actually happening with some standard or expectation of what should be happening.
3. An effector, which is a device that alters behavior if the assessor indicates the need for doing so. This device is often called feedback.
4. A communications network, which transmits information between the detector and the assessor and between the assessor and the effector.[2] The arrows in Exhibit 12.2 depict the communication network.

Through these system components, information about organizational occurrences is gathered, comparisons are made against plans, changes are made when necessary, and communications take place among appropriate parties. For example, source documents (detectors) gather sales information that is compared to the budget (assessor). If sales revenues are below budget, management can issue (communications network) a variance report (effector) to encourage the sales staff to increase volume or prices.

However, different managers could interpret and respond differently to the same information. In this respect, development of an MCS is not merely a mechanical process but requires expert judgment. Thus, an MCS can be referred to as a **black box**, which is defined as an operation whose exact nature cannot be observed.[3] Regardless of the specific actions taken, an MCS should serve to guide entities in designing and implementing strategies to achieve organizational goals and objectives.

[2] Robert N. Anthony and Vijay Govindarajan, *Management Control Systems*, 9th ed. (Burr Ridge, IL: Irwin/McGraw-Hill, 1998), pp. 1–2.

[3] Ibid., p. 5.

Exhibit 12.2 Elements of a Control System

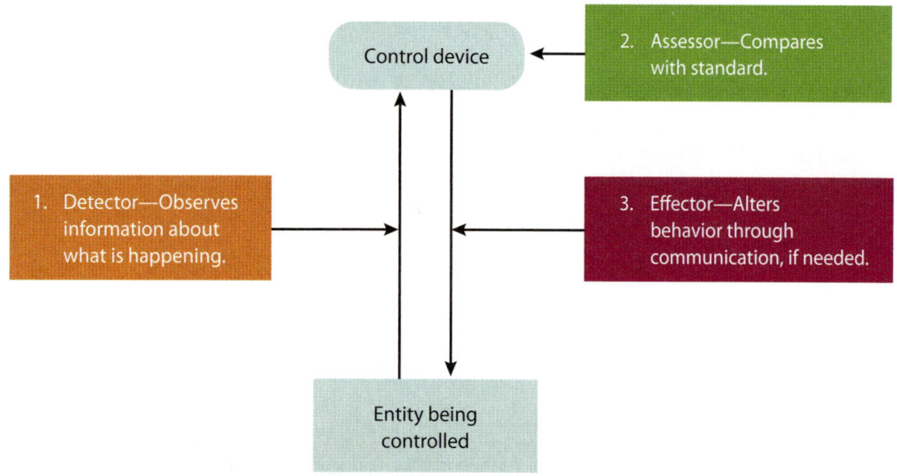

Source: From Robert N. Anthony and Vijay Govindarajan, "Management Control Systems," 9th ed. (Burr Ridge, IL: Irwin/McGraw-Hill, 1998), p. 2. Copyright © 1998 The McGraw-Hill Companies, Inc.

Most businesses have a variety of control systems in place. For example, a control system could reflect a set of procedures for screening potential suppliers or employees, a set of criteria to evaluate potential and existing investments, or a statistical control process to monitor and evaluate product quality.

2 What is a cost management system?

DEFINING A COST MANAGEMENT SYSTEM

A cost management system consists of a set of formal methods developed for planning and controlling an organization's cost-generating activities relative to its short-term objectives and long-term strategies. Business entities face two major challenges:

- achieving profitability in the short run, and
- maintaining a competitive position in the long run.

An effective CMS provides managers the information needed to meet both challenges.

Exhibit 12.3 illustrates the organizational role of a cost management system. The CMS helps provide information useful to managing an organization's core competencies, so the organization can exploit perceived opportunities in the marketplace and develop tactics and

Exhibit 12.3 Organizational Role of a Cost Management System

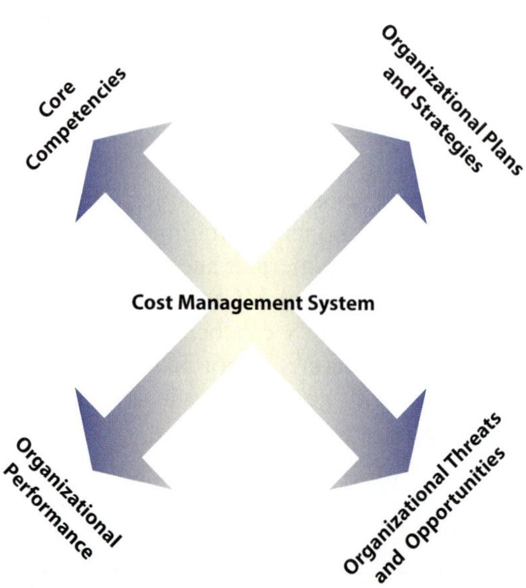

strategies to fend off threats. Similarly, the CMS links plans and strategies to actual organizational performance.

Refer to Exhibit 12.4 for a summary of differences in the information requirements for organizational success in the short run relative to the long run. In the short run, organizational revenues must exceed costs and efficient use must be made of resources relative to revenues. Specific cost information is needed and must be delivered in a timely fashion to someone who can influence that cost. Short-run information requirements are often described as relating to organizational efficiency.

Meeting the long-run objective of survival depends on acquiring the right inputs from the right suppliers, selling the right product mix to the right customers, and using the right distribution channels. These decisions require only periodic information that is reasonably accurate.

Exhibit 12.4 Dual Focus of a Cost Management System

	Short Run	Long Run
Objective	Organizational efficiency	Survival
Focus	Specific costs: • manufacturing • service • marketing • administration	Cost categories: • customers • suppliers • products • distribution channels
Important characteristics of information	Timely Accurate Highly specific Short term	Periodic Reasonably accurate Broad focus Long term

Source: Adapted from Robin Cooper and Regine Slagmulder, "Operational Improvement and Strategic Costing," *Management Accounting* (September 1998), pp. 12–13. Copyright 1998 by Institute of Management Accountants. Reproduced with permission of Institute of Management Accountants in the format Textbook via Copyright Clearance Center.

The information generated from the CMS should benefit all an entity's functional areas. Thus, as shown in Exhibit 12.5 (page 478), a CMS should integrate information from all areas of the organization and provide managers faster access to more cost information that is relevant, detailed, and appropriate for short- and long-term decision making.

THE ROLES OF A COST MANAGEMENT SYSTEM

3 What are the organizational roles of a cost management system?

Crossing all functional areas, a CMS can be viewed as having six primary goals:

- Develop reasonably accurate product costs, especially through the use of cost drivers (or activities that have direct cause-and-effect relationships with costs);
- Assess product/service life cycle performance;
- Improve understanding of processes and activities;
- Control costs;
- Measure performance; and
- Allow the pursuit of organizational strategies.

Primarily, a CMS should provide the means of developing accurate product or service costs; thus, the system must be designed to use cost driver information to trace costs to products and services. The system is not required to be the most accurate, but it should weigh the benefits of additional accuracy against costs of achieving such accuracy. Traceability has been made easier by improved information technology, including bar coding and **radio frequency identification (RFID)**, which uses exceptionally small "flakes" of silicon to transmit a code for the item to which it is attached. Bar coding, although patented in 1952, was not used commercially until 1966 when a system was installed in a Kroger store and did not become popular until Walmart required the codes to be used by suppliers

Exhibit 12.5 An Integrated Cost Management System

in the early 1980s. Now, because of the cost savings potential, Walmart is currently the largest proponent of RFID technology and has been subsidizing some of the RFID costs of its suppliers to gain their support.[4] This technology is also used in passports and credit cards as well as to identify pets and commercial livestock.

The product/service costs generated by the CMS are the inputs to managerial processes. These costs are used to

- plan,
- prepare financial statements,
- assess individual product/service profitability and periodic profitability,
- establish prices for cost-plus contracts, and
- create a basis for performance measurements.

If the costs generated by the CMS are not reasonably accurate, the execution of the preceding processes will be inappropriate for control and decision-making purposes.

Although product/service profitability may be calculated periodically (possibly as a requirement for external reporting), the financial accounting system does not provide profitability information over a product's entire life; the financial accounting system provides only a period-by-period look at product profitability. The CMS should provide information about a product's or service's life cycle performance. Without life cycle information, managers will not have a basis to relate costs incurred in one part of the life cycle to costs and profitability of other parts. For example, managers might not recognize that strong investment

[4] M. Bustillo, "Wal-Mart Radio Tags to Track Clothing," *Wall Street Journal* (7/23/10).

early in a product's life could provide significant returns later by reducing engineering change and quality-related costs. Further, if development/design cost is not traced to the related product or service, managers could be unable to recognize organizational investment "disasters."

A CMS should also help managers understand business processes and organizational activities. Only by understanding how an activity is accomplished and the reasons for cost incurrence can managers make cost-beneficial improvements in the production and processing systems. Managers desiring to implement new technology or production systems must be able to identify the costs and benefits that will arise from such actions. Such assessments can be made only if the managers understand how the processes and activities will differ after the change.

A cost accounting system's original purpose was to control costs and, given the current global competitive environment, this is still an important CMS function. As discussed in Chapter 4, a cost can be controlled only when the related activity is monitored, the cost driver is known, and information is available. For example, if units are spoiled during a process, the CMS should provide information on spoilage quantity and cost rather than "burying" that information in other cost categories. Additionally, the cost management system should allow managers to determine the underlying spoilage causes so that the cost of fixing the process can be compared with the benefits to be gained.

Information generated from a CMS should also help managers measure and evaluate performance. The measurements can be used to evaluate human or equipment performance as well as future investment opportunities.

Finally, to maintain a competitive position, a firm must generate the information necessary to define and implement its organizational strategies. Strategy is the link among an organization's goals, objectives, and operational activities. In the current global market, firms must be certain that such a linkage exists. Information provided by a CMS enables managers to perform strategic analyses on issues such as determining core competencies and organizational constraints from a cost–benefit perspective and assessing the positive and negative financial and nonfinancial factors linked to strategic and operational plans. Thus, the CMS generates information for effective strategic resource management.

The world of business competition is dynamic and creative managers are constantly devising new business practices and innovative approaches to competition. Adapting to change requires that a CMS be flexible.

DESIGNING A COST MANAGEMENT SYSTEM

4 What factors influence the design of a cost management system?

A generic cost management system cannot be taken "off the shelf" and applied to any organization. A CMS should be tailored to each firm's specific situation; thus, when designing or revising a CMS, managers and accountants must be attune to their firm's unique characteristics. However, the overriding factors shown in Exhibit 12.6 (page 480) are important in designing and revising any CMS and are described in this section.

Organizational Form, Structure, and Culture

An entity's legal nature reflects its **organizational form**. Selecting the organizational form is a critically important business decision because this choice affects the costs of raising capital, operating the business (including taxation issues), and possibly, litigating.

The most popular organizational form for large, publicly traded businesses is the corporation. Smaller businesses or cooperative ventures between large businesses use general partnerships, limited partnerships, limited liability partnerships (LLPs), and limited liability companies (LLCs). Both the LLP and LLC provide more liability protection for an investor's personal assets and better control over legal costs than a general partnership does in the event of litigation that leads to the firm's liquidation.

Organizational form also helps determine who has the statutory authority to make decisions for the firm. Unless specified to the contrary in the partnership agreement, all partners in a general partnership are allowed to make business decisions as a mere incidence of ownership. Alternatively, in a corporation, individual shareholders act through a board of directors who, in turn, typically hire professional managers. This ability to "centralize"

Exhibit 12.6 Design of a Cost Management System

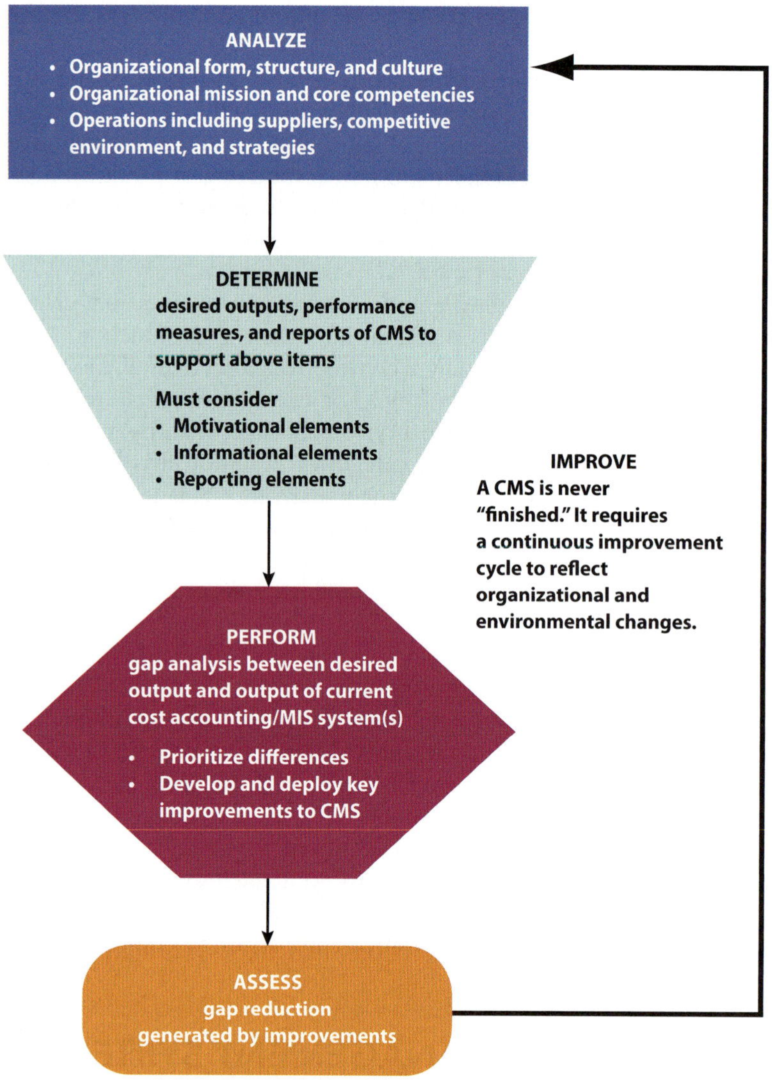

authority is regarded as a primary advantage of the corporate organizational form and, to some extent, is available in limited partnerships, LLPs, and LLCs.

After the organizational form has been selected, top managers are responsible for creating a structure that is best suited to achieving the firm's goals and objectives. Organizational structure, introduced in Chapter 1, refers to how authority and responsibility for decision making are distributed in an entity. Top managers decide how to organize subunits and the extent to which authority will be distributed among managers and employees. Although the current competitive environment is conducive to a high degree of delegation, top managers usually retain authority over operations that can be performed more economically centrally because of economies of scale. For instance, financing, human resources, research and development, and certain accounting functions typically are maintained "at headquarters" rather than being delegated to organizational subunits.

In designing the organizational structure, top managers normally try to group subunits either geographically or by similar missions or natural product clusters. Such an aggregation process provides effective cost management because of proximity or similarity of the subunits under a single manager's control. To illustrate, relative to mission similarity, business subunits could pursue one of the three generic missions described in Exhibit 12.7:

- build,
- harvest, or
- hold.

Exhibit 12.7 Depiction of Organizational Generic Missions

BUILD	HOLD	HARVEST

BUILD	HOLD	HARVEST
Denoted by: • Rapid market expansion and growth • Internal changes to improve (or find new uses for) products/services and gain market share • External related acquisitions (upstream or downstream) or diversification • Possible lack of competitors	Denoted by: • Stability of market • Dominance in market • Internal changes to create new demand for product and retain market share	Denoted by: • Mature or declining market (low expected growth rate) • Strategically "unimportant" product/service • Product/service is a "cash cow"

Subunits pursuing a "build" mission use more cash than they generate. Such subunits invest cash today with an expectation of future returns. These are the firm's high-growth-oriented subunits. At the other extreme, subunits pursuing a "harvest" mission are expected to generate excess cash and have a much shorter investment horizon. Between the build and harvest missions is the hold mission, which applies to subunits that are pursuing a balance between growth and profit generation.

Different cost management tools are used for different subunit missions. Thus, top management would not be able to design proper incentives or performance evaluation measures for a manager who was placed in charge of multiple subunits with differing missions. If one specific cost management tool is applied to a subunit with a mix of missions, there is high potential for making poor decisions and inadequately judging cost management effectiveness and efficiency.

The extent to which managers delegate authority to make decisions also determines who will be held accountable for cost management and organizational control. An information system must provide relevant and timely information to the individuals who are making decisions that have cost control implications, and a control system must be in place to evaluate the quality of those decisions.

An entity's culture also plays an important role in setting up a CMS. **Organizational culture** refers to the underlying set of assumptions about the entity and the goals, processes, practices, and values that its members share. To illustrate the effect of organizational culture on the CMS, consider AT&T in the early 1980s prior to its breakup. AT&T was characterized by "bureaucracy, centralized control, nepotism, a welfare mentality in which workers were 'taken care of,' strong socialization processes, [and] little concern for efficiency...."[5] Such a culture would have limited the requirements of a CMS because few individuals needed information. Decisions were made at the top of the organization, and cost control was not a consideration because costs were passed on to customers through the rate structure. After breakup, AT&T and the spin-off companies changed to embrace decision making at multiple organizational levels, cost efficiency, and individual responsibility and accountability. Supporting such a changed culture requires different types, quantities, and distributions of cost management information.

The values-based aspects of organizational culture are also extremely important in assessing the CMS. For example, a part of Walmart's mission statement "is to help people save money so they can live better."[6] Without a well-designed CMS, Walmart could not

[5] Thomas S. Bateman and Scott A. Snell, *Management Building Competitive Advantage* (Burr Ridge, IL: Irwin, 1996), p. 268.

[6] Wal-Mart Stores, Inc., "Frequently Asked Questions," http://walmartstores.com/Investors/7614.aspx (last accessed 12/16/11).

evaluate its progress toward accomplishing that mission. Thus, a CMS is instrumental in providing a foundation for companies with an organizational culture emphasizing cost savings and continuous improvement.

Organizational Mission and Core Competencies

Knowledge of the organization's mission and core competencies is a key consideration in the CMS design. The mission provides a long-term goal toward which the organization wishes to move. If the entity's mission is unknown, it does not matter what information is generated by the CMS—or any other information system!

In pursuing the business mission, companies can either avoid or confront competition. For example, companies could try to avoid competition by attempting to be more adept than other entities in some way. Product differentiation as defined in Chapter 1 is the most common approach to avoiding competition. Products can be differentiated based on quality, functionality, or markets served.

In the current global environment, it is often difficult to maintain a competitive advantage under a differentiation strategy. Competitors are becoming skilled at duplicating the specific competencies that gave rise to the original competitive advantage. For many companies, the key to future success is to confront competition by identifying and exploiting temporary opportunities for advantage. In a confrontation strategy, companies "still try to differentiate their products by introducing new features, or try to develop a price leadership position by dropping prices, ... [but the companies] assume that their competitors will rapidly bring out products that are equivalent and match any price changes."[7] Although sometimes necessary, a confrontation strategy is, by its very nature, less profitable than differentiation or cost leadership.

See Exhibit 12.8 for an illustration of how a firm's strategy, together with product life cycle stages, determines what a firm must do well to be successful. This exhibit illustrates how the managerial information requirements change over time as the life cycle evolves and, thus, depend on the strategy being pursued.

Exhibit 12.8 Critical Organizational Activities by Strategy and Life Cycle Stage

	PRODUCT STRATEGY		
Life Cycle Stage	**Cost Leadership**	**Product Differentiation**	**Confrontation**
Build	Research and development Parts standardization Efficient distribution channels	Research and development Advertising Product customization Customer relationship management	Time to market Activity-based management Process flexibility Business intelligence
Hold	Process standardization Engineering change elimination Kaizen costing	Advertising Distribution channels Customer relationship management	Process dependability Service emphasis Advertising Engineering changes
Harvest	Cost control Product changeover speed Capacity control Outsource Distribution cost management	Product replacement Continued marketing efforts Exit strategy Enhance service	Distribution channel development Service differentiation Distribution network focus

[7] Robin Cooper, *When Lean Enterprises Collide* (Boston, MA: Harvard Business School Press, 1995), p. 11.

In many industries, globalization of markets has created competition among equals. Today, many firms are capable of delivering products and services that are qualitatively and functionally equivalent. Without being able to make quality or functionality differentiations between competitors' products, the consumer's focus switches to price. In turn, price-based competition changes the internal focus to costs.

An organization can clarify its mission by identifying core competencies or the operational dimensions that are instrumental to survival. Most organizations would consider timeliness, quality, customer service, cost control, and responsiveness to change as five critical competencies. Once managers have reached consensus on an entity's core competencies, the CMS can be designed to

- gather information related to measurement of those items,
- collect external intelligence on competitor performance in competency areas,
- track performance in competency areas through time, and
- generate output about those competencies in a useful format for interested parties.

Operations and Competitive Environment and Strategies

Once the organizational "big picture" has been established, managers can assess internal specifics related to the design of a CMS. A primary consideration is the firm's **cost structure**. Traditionally, cost structure has been defined in terms of relative proportions of fixed and variable costs and, thus, how costs change relative to changes in production or sales volume.[8]

Manufacturing and service firms have aggressively adopted advanced technology, which creates substantial costs associated with the plant, equipment, and infrastructure investments that provide the capacity to produce goods and services. These costs are higher in industries that depend on technology for competing on the basis of quality and price. Thus, technology dependence has made it more difficult for firms to control costs.

This shift in cost structure has significant implications for cost management. Most importantly, because most technology costs are not susceptible to short-run control, cost management efforts are increasingly directed toward the longer term. Also, managing costs is increasingly a matter of managing capacity: high capacity utilization (if accompanied by high sales volume) allows a firm to reduce its per-unit costs in pursuing a cost leadership strategy. A second consequence of the changed cost structure relates to a firm's ability to respond to changing short-term conditions. As the proportion of costs relating to technology investment increases, a firm has less flexibility to take short-term cost reduction actions without generating long-term adverse consequences.

In pursuing either a differentiation or cost leadership strategy, the management of high technology costs requires beating competitors to the market with new products. Being first to market can enable a company to set a price that leads to a larger market share and, in turn, an industry position of cost leader. Alternatively, the leading-edge company can set a product price that provides a substantial per-unit profit for all sales generated before competitors are able to offer alternative products. For example, when first introduced, Apple's iPhone had no direct competing product. However, by 2009, offerings from Blackberry were competing head-to-head with the iPhone. By late 2011, the field of competing phones had grown dramatically to include Droids by Samsung and Motorola, Samsung Nexis, Windows Phone Mango, HTC Vigor, and others. Time to market is critical in the high-tech industry because profitability depends on selling an adequate number of units at an acceptable price. Because per-unit prices in the technology sector have been falling steadily for years, getting a new product to the market late can be disastrous.

Monitoring the external environment is a key activity to manage revenues and costs over the longer term. For instance, the evolution of social media has created new channels for product distribution, advertising, customer outreach, and market intelligence. Failure to stay abreast of market and technology trends may lead to business model stagnation and lost opportunities to improve cost management and generate new revenues.

[8] An organization's cost structure reflects its operating leverage as discussed in Chapter 9.

"Faster time to market and shorter product life cycles are pushing companies into more frequent product transitions, requiring managers to confront the potential rewards and challenges associated with product introductions and phaseouts."[9] Missing the "right" time to provide a product to customers may also mean missing the "best" price at which that product can be sold.

Reducing time to market is one way a company can cut costs; other techniques are indicated in Exhibit 12.9. Most actions to reduce product cost are associated with the early product life cycle stages. Thus, product profitability is largely determined by an effective design and development process.

Exhibit 12.9 Actions to Substantially Reduce Product Costs

- Reduce non-value-added activities
- Standardize product parts and processes
- Reduce variability of processes
- Increase product and process quality
- Manufacture products to order
- Design products to limit engineering change orders
- Implement new technologies
- Increase capacity utilization
- Minimize investment in inventories
- Outsource non-core competencies
- Find and eliminate process bottlenecks
- Redesign factory layout
- Reduce setup time
- Train employees to obtain learning curve effects
- Engage in benchmarking to find better methodologies
- Develop long-term and sole-source supplier relationships
- Stress the importance of a quality culture
- Encourage employee suggestions
- Engage in life cycle and target costing

Getting products to market quickly and profitably requires a compromise between product innovation and superior product design. Rapid time to market could mean that a firm incurs costs (such as engineering changes) associated with design flaws that could have been avoided if more time had been allowed for the product's development. This situation was evident in General Motors' release of the Chevrolet Volt in 2010. Although innovative and widely anticipated by the marketplace, the hybrid electric car was found to have some problems with its battery compartments. GM was expected to spend about $1,000 per car to fix the problem or a total of $9 million, but the company will need "to convince buyers that the vehicle poses no safety threat."[10] When a flawed product is marketed, costs will likely be incurred for returns, warranty work, or customer "bad will" regarding the firm's reputation for product quality. Time to market is important because of the competitive advantages it offers and because of compressed product life cycles. The faster a product gets to market, the fewer competitive products will exist; consequently, a greater market share can be captured (see Exhibit 12.10).

Supplier relationships constitute another aspect of an organization's operating environment. Many companies that have formed strategic alliances with suppliers have found such relationships to be effective cost control mechanisms. For example, by involving suppliers early in the design and development stages of new products, a company should achieve a

[9] Feryal Erhun, Paulo Conçalves, and Jay Hopman, "The Art of Managing New Product Transitions," *MIT Sloan Management Review* (Spring 2007), p. 73.

[10] J. Korzeniewski, "Chevy Volt Battery Fix May Cost $1,000 per Car, Will Hang on to Top IIHS Rating," *Autoblog* (12/7/11); http://www.autoblog.com/2011/12/07/chevy-volt-battery-fix-may-cost-1-000-will-hang-on-to-top-iihs/ and T. Spangler, "GM's Akerson to Lawmakers in D.C.: 'We Did Not Design the Volt to Become a Political Punching Bag," *Detroit Free Press* (1/25/12); http://www.freep.com/article/20120125/BUSINESS0101/120125008/GM-s-Akerson-lawmakers-D-C-We-did-not-design-Volt-become-political-punching-bag- (accessed 2/11/12).

Exhibit 12.10 Relationship of Time to Market and Market Share

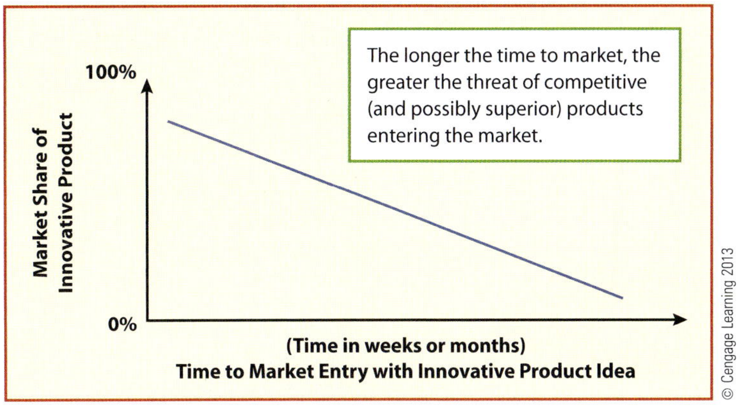

better design for manufacturability and improve the likelihood of meeting cost targets. Additionally, if the information systems of customers and suppliers are linked electronically, the capabilities and functions of these systems must be considered in designing the CMS.

An internal operating environment consideration in CMS design is the need to integrate the organization's current information systems. The "feeder" systems (such as payroll, inventory valuation, budgeting, and costing) that are in place should be evaluated to answer the following questions:

In the high-tech industry, companies must balance product innovation and development costs with the need to minimize time to market.

- What input data are being gathered and in what form?
- What outputs are being generated and in what form?
- How do the current systems interact with one another, and how effective are those interactions?
- Is the current chart of accounts appropriate for the cost management information desired?
- What significant information issues (such as yield, spoilage, and cycle time) are not currently being addressed by the information system, and could those issues be integrated into the current feeder systems?

With knowledge of the preceding information, management must analyze the cost–benefit trade-offs that relate to CMS design. As the costs of gathering, processing, and communicating information decrease, or as the quantity and intensity of competition increase, more sophisticated CMSs are required. Additionally, as companies focus on customer satisfaction and expand their product or service offerings, more sophisticated CMSs are needed. In these conditions, the generation of "better" cost information is essential to long-run organizational survival and short-run profitability.

Even with appropriate information systems in place, there is no guarantee that managers' decisions will be consistent with organizational strategies. Proper incentives and reporting systems must be incorporated into the CMS for managers to make appropriate decisions, as discussed in the following section.

DETERMINE DESIRED COMPONENTS OF CMS

5 What are the three groups of elements that comprise a cost management system, and what are the purposes of these elements?

A CMS is composed of three primary elements: motivational, informational, and reporting. These elements are detailed in Exhibit 12.11 (on page 486). The elements as a whole must be internally consistent, and the individually selected elements must be consistent with the strategies and missions of the subunits. Different aspects of these elements can be used for different purposes. For example, numerous measures of performance can be specified, but only certain measures will be appropriate for specific subunit missions.

Exhibit 12.11 Cost Management System Elements

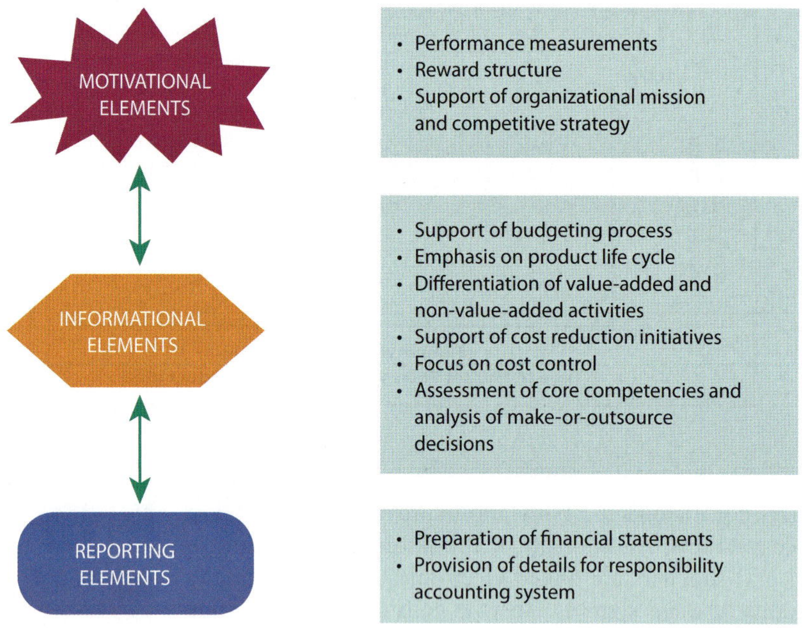

Motivational Elements

Performance assessments are chosen to be consistent with organizational goals and objectives and to motivate or "drive" managers toward designated achievements. These assessments can be

- quantitative or nonquantitative,
- financial or nonfinancial, and
- short term or long term.

For example, if a subunit is expected to generate a specified annual profit amount, the performance measure has been set to be quantitative, financial, and short term. A longer-term performance measure might be an average increase in profit or change in stock price over a five-to-ten year period.

Motivational elements create a linkage between the internal information systems (CMS information elements) and the firm's performance as perceived by the stockholders. Exhibit 12.12 indicates how this linkage typically is operationalized. Top managers' compensation contracts are based on two elements: earnings as measured by the financial accounting system and stock price performance. In turn, top managers drive lower-level managers' performance by relating compensation to actual compared to budgeted performance. Thus, the motivational elements link all managerial performance to stockholder welfare through compensation contracting that cascades down through the organizational hierarchy. These motivational elements create the incentive for managers to outperform the budget, increase earnings, and raise stock price.

The motivational elements can also create dysfunctional behaviors if the performance pressure placed on managers is too intense. Among possible dysfunctional behaviors are the intentional misstatements of transactions and inappropriate accruals or deferrals made by managers to distort accounting system performance measurements. Numerous examples of such occurrences have appeared in the financial press in recent years.

Firms develop internal controls to protect the integrity of financial reports and to safeguard assets. The Sarbanes-Oxley Act of 2002 (Section 404) brought control systems to the forefront of managerial focus: companies must now take responsibility for establishing and maintaining an "adequate" system of internal controls over financial reporting and report on any material weaknesses within that system.

Exhibit 12.12 Managerial Contracting Process

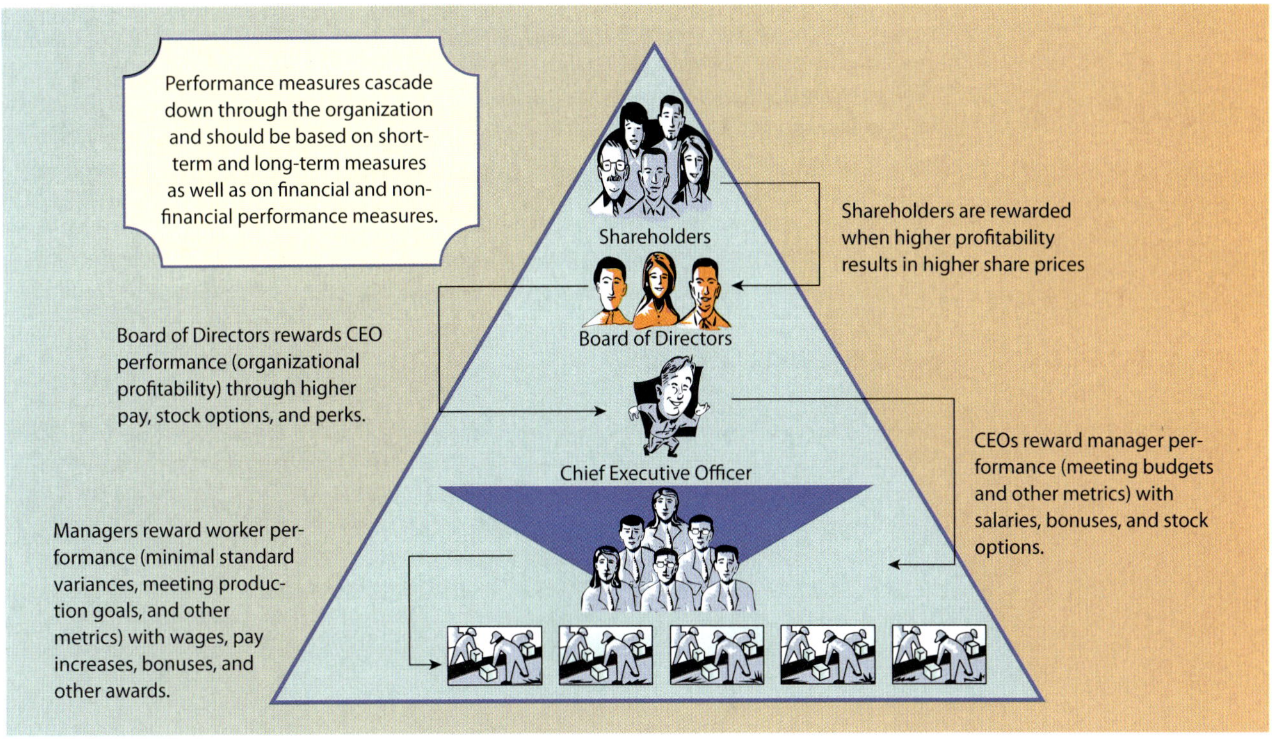

Performance measures and rewards should be designed to

- support organizational missions and competitive strategies,
- motivate employees and managers to act in the best interest of the organization and its subunits, and
- help recruit and retain qualified employees.

Once defined, the criteria used to measure performance should be linked to the organizational incentive system because "you get what you measure." This linkage sends the message to managers that they will be rewarded based on the quality of their organizational and subunit decisions and, thereby, their contributions to achieving the organizational mission.

In addition to performance measures, different forms of rewards have different incentive effects and can reflect different time orientations. In general, longer-term incentives encourage managers to be more long-term oriented in their decisions whereas short-term incentives encourage managers to be focused on the near future.

To illustrate, cash is the most obvious reward for short-term performance. All managers receive some compensation in cash to provide for living expenses. However, once a manager receives a cash reward, its value does not depend on the firm's future performance. In contrast, a stock option that is not exercisable until a future time provides a manager with an incentive to be more concerned about long-term performance. A stock option's ultimate value is determined when the option is exercised rather than when it is received. Thus, the option's value is related more to long-term than to short-term organizational performance.

Performance rewards for top management can consist of both short-and long-term incentives. Normally, a major incentive is performance-based pay that is tied to the firm's stock price. Rewards for subunit managers should be based on that subunit's mission. For example, managers of subunits charged with a "build" mission should receive long-term incentives and be evaluated based on longer-term performance measures. These managers need to be concerned about long-term success and be willing to make short-term sacrifices for long-term gains. In contrast, managers of subunits charged with a "harvest" mission must be more oriented to the short term. These subunits are expected to generate as much cash and profit as possible from their operations. Accordingly, incentives should be in place to encourage these managers to have a short-term focus in decision making.

Today's companies experiment with a variety of incentives as "carrots" to induce employees and managers to act in the best interest of customers and shareholders. **Profit sharing** refers to compensation that is contingent on the level of organizational profit generated. This type of pay is a powerful incentive and is now used in virtually every U.S. industry.

Selection of performance measurements and the reward structure is important because managers evaluate decision alternatives based on how the outcomes could impact the selected performance (measurement and reward) criteria.[11] Because higher performance equals a larger reward, the CMS must have specified performance "yardsticks" and provide measurement information to the appropriate individuals for evaluation purposes. Performance measurement is meaningful only in a comparative or relative sense. Typically, current performance is assessed relative to past or expected performance, relative to customer expectations or to competitor performance.

Informational Elements

An organization's accounting function is expected to support managers' abilities to plan, control, make decisions, and evaluate performance. These functions converge in a system designed for cost management. Relative to the planning role, the CMS should provide a sound foundation for the financial budgeting process.

Budgets provide both a specification of expected achievement and a benchmark against which to compare actual performance. A CMS should both supply the financial information needed for budget preparation and disclose the cost drivers of activities so that more useful simulations of alternative scenarios can be made. The system should help identify any activities that have a poor cost–benefit relationship so that they can be reduced or eliminated and, in turn, reduce organizational costs and improve profits.

As firms find it more difficult to maintain a competitive advantage, they must place greater emphasis on managing the product life cycle. As discussed earlier in this chapter, most actions available to managers to control costs are concentrated in the earliest stages of the product life cycle. Accordingly, information relevant to managing costs must be focused on decisions made during those stages. That information will be provided by a well-designed and integrated CMS.

Product life cycles are getting shorter as firms become more adept at duplicating their competitors' offerings. In the future, managers will confront the fact that products will spend less time in the maturity stage of the product life cycle. Firms will be forced to find ways to continue to "squeeze" cash from mature products to support new product development. Additionally, the future will place greater emphasis on a firm's ability to adapt to changing competitive conditions. Flexibility will be an important organizational attribute and cause managers to change the emphasis of control systems (see Exhibit 12.13).

To provide information relevant to product design and development, the CMS must be able to relate resource consumption and cost to alternative product and process designs. Computer simulation models are useful in relating products to activities. In addition to focusing information on the front end of the product life cycle, capital spending is becoming an increasingly important tool in cost management, especially relative to new technology acquisition decisions. Decisions about capital investments affect a firm's future cost structure and, hence, the extent to which short-term actions can effect a change in total costs.

Finally, the system should produce cost information with minimal distortions from improper or inaccurate allocations or from improper exclusions. Improper exclusions, such as the mandate to expense product development and distribution costs, usually relate to financial accounting's influence. If the system minimizes cost distortions, cost assignments are more relevant for control and internal decision making purposes.

The information required to support decisions depends on the unique situational factors of the firm and its subunits. The information system must enable the decision maker to evaluate how alternative decision choices would impact the items used to measure and evaluate the decision maker's performance. Techniques, such as relevant costing, quality cost management, job order and process costing, and cost-volume-profit analysis, discussed in other chapters relate to cost information's role in decision making. Many decisions involve

[11] Performance measurements and rewards are discussed in greater depth in Chapter 14.

Exhibit 12.13 Shift in Control Emphasis in Future Competitive Environments

Activity	From		To
Product design	Releasing early to gain market share	→	Designing for manufacturability and reliability
Product offerings	Developing a limited number of product styles	→	Engaging in mass customization to entice a wide variety of customers
Budgeting	Developing annual budgets	→	Developing rolling budgets
Cost standards	Using expected standards	→	Using ideal standards
Overhead allocation	Using expected capacity	→	Using theoretical capacity
Quality	Inspecting for quality problems	→	Building quality into the production system
Outsourcing	Turning product and process control over to the outsource provider	→	Working in partnership with the outsource provider
Strategy	Focusing on the short term as the primary indicator of success	→	Focusing on the short term as a means for long-term success
Employee involvement and procedures	Emphasizing the need to comply with policies	→	Encouraging participation in change and understanding functions
Performance measurement	Concentrating on financial results	→	Concentrating on multiple types of critical success measurements
Product marketing	Selling what the firm makes	→	Focusing on sales mix that maximizes customer value

comparing the benefit received from some action (such as serving a given customer) to the costs of that action. Only if the cost data contain minimal distortion can managers make valid cost–benefit assessments.

Reporting Elements

The reporting elements of a cost management system refer to methods of providing information to persons in evaluative roles. First and foremost, the CMS must be effective in generating fundamental financial statement information such as inventory valuations and cost of sales. Regardless of whether such information is used for internal planning, control, decision making, or performance evaluation, there should be little difficulty generating an "external" product or service cost if the feeder systems to the CMS have been appropriately integrated and the system itself is designed to minimize distortions.

In addition to financial statement valuations, reporting elements of the CMS must address internal needs of a responsibility accounting system that provides performance information on organizational subunits and their managers to top management.[12] Such a system should separately track costs and, if appropriate, revenues for each organizational subunit.

Performance reports are useful only to the extent that a manager's or subunit's actual performance can be compared to a meaningful baseline, such as a measure of expected

[12] Responsibility accounting concepts are discussed in detail in Chapter 13.

performance. Expected performance can be denoted in financial terms, such as budgetary amounts, or in nonfinancial terms, such as throughput, customer satisfaction measures, lead time, capacity utilization, and research and development activities. As illustrated by balanced scorecards, performance reports can be multidimensional. By comparing actual to expected performance, top managers are able to determine which managers and subunits performed according to expectations and which exceeded or failed to meet expectations. Using the information that has been processed and formulated by the CMS, top managers link decisions about managerial rewards to performance.

Decentralization, or the movement toward delegation of more authority to lower levels, has increased the importance of an effective reporting system. Top managers must depend on the reporting system to keep all organizational subunits aligned with their subunit missions as well as with organizational goals and objectives. A CMS is not designed to "cut" costs, but to ensure that a satisfactory yield (revenue) is realized from cost incurrence. Accordingly, cost management begins with an understanding that different costs are incurred for different purposes. Some costs are incurred to yield immediate benefits; others are expected to yield benefits in the near or distant future.

Only by linking costs to activities and activities to strategies can the yield on costs be understood. Thus, to achieve effective cost management, organizational activities must first be sorted according to their strategic roles. This logic suggests that organizational management is made easier by breaking down operations into subunits. By so doing, top managers can assign responsibility and accountability for distinct subunit missions to a particular manager. In turn, by creating the proper incentives for each subunit manager, top management will have set the stage for those managers to act in the overall organization's best interest. This linkage is the start of a process that focuses a specific subunit manager's attention on a set of costs and activities that uniquely relates to that unit's organizational mission.

Costs can be effectively managed only when subunit managers are provided with relevant information. Because the nature and time horizon of decisions made by managers vary across subunits, each manager requires unique information. Accountants face the task of providing information that is tailored to each subunit manager's decision needs. In addition to information about decision alternatives, managers must know how their expected rewards will be impacted by the choices made.

A reporting system's role is to compare each manager's actual and benchmark performance. Based on this comparison, the relative rewards of subunit managers are determined. Accordingly, this comparison is a key source of motivation for subunit managers to act in the organization's best interest. Optimal organizational performance is realized only if there is consistency for each subunit across the motivational, informational, and reporting elements. Managers of subunits with a "build" mission need information tailored to competitive strategies and focused on the early product life cycle stages. Incentives to manage costs must be relatively long term, and reward structures should emphasize success in product development, design, and market share growth. Alternatively, subunit managers of mature businesses need information that pertains more to short-term competition. The reward and reporting structures for these managers should emphasize near-term profit and cash flow.

One evolving challenge in today's business environment is the management of activities across an entire supply chain. Competition is prevalent among supply or "value" chains as well as individual businesses. Thus, future financial specialists will develop CMSs that include activities not only occurring within a single firm but occurring within a supply chain involving multiple firms.

Because most businesses have some type of CMS in place, design and implementation issues primarily relate to modifications of the current system. The analysis of existing systems is discussed next.

PERFORM GAP ANALYSIS AND ASSESS IMPROVEMENTS

6 What is gap analysis, and how is it used to update a cost management system?

After the organization and its subunits have been structured and the CMS elements have been determined, the current information system(s) should be evaluated. **Gap analysis** is the study of the differences between two information systems, often a current system and a proposed system, or the current system and an ideal system. To assess existing system deficiencies, gap analysis compares the currently available information with the information that is needed. Any differences represent deficiencies or "gaps" to be overcome. In many situations, all system gaps cannot be eliminated in the short term, often because of software or hardware capability or availability or because of budgetary constraints. Methods of reducing or eliminating the gaps, including all related technical requirements and changes to existing feeder systems, should be specified in detail. These details should be expressed, qualitatively and quantitatively, in terms of costs and benefits.

In the common circumstance of limited resources, top management can prioritize which gap issues should be addressed and in what order. As system implementation proceeds, management should assess the effectiveness of the improvements and determine the need for others. Once the CMS has been established, previously identified gaps can become irrelevant or can rise in rank of priority. Only through continuous improvement efforts can the CMS provide an ongoing, viable network of information to users.

Technological impact on CMS design and implementation is significant. With advancements in technology, it is becoming possible to link a company's feeder systems into a truly integrated CMS. **Enterprise resource planning (ERP) systems** are packaged and customized business software systems that, through information systems standardization, allow companies to:

- manage and coordinate a myriad of organizational activities;
- present complex project information in a way that indicates current status;
- improve operational efficiencies and timeliness of information;
- work effectively by running inventory, supply chain, and distribution functions globally;
- take advantage of cost savings from shared service centers; and
- contribute substantially to competitive advantage and strategic value.[13]

ERP software often involves many separate modules that collect data from individual organizational processes (sales, shipping, distribution, and so forth) and assemble those data in a form accessible by all managers. ERP is discussed in detail in Chapter 19.

APPENDIX

COST MANAGEMENT SYSTEM CONCEPTUAL DESIGN PRINCIPLES

"In 1986, Computer Aided Manufacturing-International Inc. (CAM-I) formed a consortium of progressive industrial organizations, professional accounting firms, and government agencies to define the role of cost management in the new advanced manufacturing environment."[14] One outcome of this consortium was a conceptual framework of principles (listed in Exhibit 12.14 on page 492) for designing a cost management system. If a CMS provides the suggested information relating to costs, performance measurements, and investment management, that system will be relevant to management's decision-making needs. Although compatible with existing cost accounting systems, the set of principles as a whole suggests a radical departure from traditional practices. The approach focuses management attention on

- organizational activities,
- product life cycles,
- integrating cost management and performance measurement, and
- integrating investment management and strategic management.

[13] Alan Cane, "The Incredible Shrinking System," *Financial Times* (London) (May 14, 2009), p. 1.

[14] Callie Berliner and James A. Brimson, eds., *Cost Management for Today's Advanced Manufacturing* (Boston, MA: Harvard Business School Press, 1988), p. vii.

Exhibit 12.14 CMS Conceptual Design Principles

Cost Principles

- Costs of non-value-added activities should be identified to improve use of resources.
- Holding costs should be recognized as a non-value-added activity traceable directly to a product.
- Significant costs should be directly traceable to management reporting objectives.
- Separate cost centers should be established for each homogeneous group of activities consistent with organizational responsibility.
- Activity-based cost accumulation and reporting will improve cost traceability.
- Separate bases for allocations should be developed to reflect causal relations between activity costs and management reporting objectives.
- Costs should be consistent with the requirement to support life cycle management.
- Technology costs should be assigned directly to products.
- Actual product cost should be measured against target cost to support elimination of waste.
- Cost-effective approaches for internal control should be developed as a company automates.

Performance Measurement Principles

- Performance measures should establish congruence with a company's objectives.
- Performance measures should be established for significant activities.
- Performance measures should be established to improve visibility of cost drivers.
- Financial and nonfinancial activities should be included in the performance measurement system.

Investment Management Principles

- Investment management should be viewed as more than the capital budgeting process.
- Investment management decisions should be consistent with company goals.
- Multiple criteria should be used to evaluate investment decisions.
- Investments and attendant risks should be considered interrelated elements of an investment strategy.
- Activity data should be traceable to the specific investment opportunity.
- Investment management decisions should support the reduction or elimination of non-value-added activities.
- Investment management decisions should support achieving target cost.

Source: From Callie Berliner and James A. Brimson, eds., *Cost Management for Today's Advanced Manufacturing* (Boston, MA: Harvard Business School Press, 1988), pp. 13–18. Reprinted by permission of Harvard Business School Press.

Comprehensive Review Module

KEY TERMS

black box, p. 475
cost structure, p. 483
enterprise resource planning (ERP) system, p. 491
gap analysis, p. 490
management control system (MCS), p. 475
management information system (MIS), p. 474
organizational culture, p. 481
organizational form, p. 479
profit sharing, p. 488
radio frequency identification (RFID), p. 477

CHAPTER SUMMARY

1 Management Control Systems

- Organizations have management control systems to
  - implement strategic and operating plans.
  - provide a means for comparison of actual to planned results for management control purposes.

2 Cost Management System (CMS)

- A CMS is a set of formal methods developed for planning and controlling an organization's cost-generating activities relative to its short-term objectives and long-term strategies.
- A CMS has a short-term goal of making efficient use of organizational resources.
- A CMS has a long-term goal of ensuring the organization's survival.

3 CMS Roles in an Organization

- CMS design is influenced by
  - organizational form through, for example, laws that determine who within the organization is entitled to be a decision maker.
  - organizational structure because it
    - ➢ determines how authority and responsibility are distributed in an organization.
    - ➢ indicates who is accountable, what they are accountable for, and the nature of information needed by each decision maker.
  - organizational culture because it determines
    - ➢ how people interact with each other in the organization.
    - ➢ the extent to which individuals take authority and assume responsibility for organizational outcomes.
  - organizational mission.
  - organizational core competencies.
  - the organization's external environment because it determines the
    - ➢ nature and extent of competitive pressures bearing on the organization.
    - ➢ industry's competitive dimensions and the bases on which organizations compete.
  - organizational strategies that influence the
    - ➢ variable and fixed cost structure.
    - ➢ managerial preferences in responding to competitive pressures.

4 Elements Affecting CMS Design

- Motivational elements are used to influence managers and employees to exert high effort and to act in the organization's interests.
- Informational elements are selected to provide the appropriate information to managers who are responsible for making decisions and for making the organization effective and efficient in its operations.
- Reporting elements are selected to provide feedback to, and to provide consequences for, managers and employees.

5 Gap Analysis

- Gap analysis is a tool that can help identify and prioritize necessary changes in a CMS.
- Gap analysis assesses differences between an organization's ideal CMS and the organization's existing CMS.

POTENTIAL ETHICAL ISSUES

ETHICS

1. Using the financial accounting system rather than an integrated cost management system to support management functions of planning, controlling, decision making, and performance evaluation
2. Failing to balance long-run and short-run concerns when designing the cost management system and the motivational, informational, and reporting elements
3. Using the motivational elements in the CMS to create high payoffs for fraudulent or deceptive behavior—for example, overstating earnings
4. Designing motivational elements that do not align with the authority of individual managers

QUESTIONS

1. How can a company evaluate whether it is effectively managing its costs?
2. What is a control system? What purpose does a control system serve in an organization?
3. Why does a cost management system necessarily have both a short- and long-term focus?
4. Why is it not possible simply to take a cost management system "off the shelf"?
5. How does the choice of organizational form influence the design of a firm's cost management system?
6. What information could be generated by a cost management system that would help an organization manage its core competencies?
7. How could an organization's culture be used as a control mechanism?
8. How does a product's life cycle stage influence the nature of information required to successfully manage costs of that product?
9. In the present highly competitive environment, why has cost management risen to such a high level of concern, whereas price management has declined in importance?
10. (Appendix) What is CAM-I, and why was it organized?

EXERCISES

11. **LO.1 (Management control systems)** Following are activities that are components of a management control system in a production department. For each item listed, discuss whether it is a detector, assessor, effector, or communications network:

    a. Comparing actual costs to budgeted costs and calculating cost variances
    b. Reporting variances
    c. Implementing changes in production systems to correct the largest negative variances
    d. Measuring actual costs

12. **LO.1 (Management control systems; writing)** A few years after graduation, Ibrahim and four of his friends from college organized an engineering consulting business called 5Q. All five individuals had earned degrees in engineering fields and were anxious to pool their expertise and work together in a successful business venture. Even though the business was very successful in attracting clients, the business failed within two years of its founding because the entrepreneurs were unable to control their costs. Discuss how the adoption of management controls could have improved the odds that the business would have been successful.

EXCEL

13. **LO.2 & LO.3 (Cost management and strategy)** As a financial analyst, you have just been handed the 2012 financial report of Firm A, a large, global pharmaceutical company. Firm A competes in both traditional pharmaceutical products and in evolving

biotechnology products. The following data (in billions) on Firm A and the pharmaceutical industry are available:

	Firm A	Industry Average
Sales	$2.00	$0.960
Net income	0.54	0.096
Advertising	0.04	0.160
Research and development	0.16	0.240
New investment in facilities	0.20	0.240

Given these data, evaluate the cost management performance of Firm A.

14. **LO.2 & LO.3 (Cost management and strategy)** Following are descriptions of three businesses. For each, assume that you are the CEO. Identify the most critical information you would need to manage the strategic decisions of that business.
    a. Private hospital that competes on the basis of delivering high-quality services to an upscale clientele
    b. Small, high-technology firm that has just developed its first product, will begin sales in the coming quarter, and has five other products under development
    c. American Sugar Company, which is a large firm that competes in the commodity refined sugar industry.

15. **LO.4 (Cost management and organizational objectives; discussion)** Prepare an oral presentation discussing how accounting information can (a) help and (b) hinder an organization's progress toward its mission and objectives. Be sure to differentiate between the effects of what you perceive as "traditional" versus "nontraditional" accounting information.

16. **LO.4 (Cost management and organizational culture; research; writing)** Use Internet resources to gather information on any two firms in the same industry. The following examples are possible pairs to compare.

INTERNET

- American Airlines and Southwest Airlines
- ChevronTexaco and Shell
- Nordstrom's and Walmart
- Oracle and Microsoft
- Hewlett-Packard and Dell Computer

In your discussion, address the following questions:
    a. Compare and contrast the organizational cultures of the firms.
    b. Compare and contrast the operating performance of the firms.
    c. Which of each pair is the better operating performer? Discuss the criteria used to make this determination.
    d. Do you believe that organizational culture has any relationship to the differences in operations? Why?

17. **LO.4 (Cost management and technology; research; writing)** Many firms now engage in some form of B2B (business-to-business) Internet-based commerce. A specific type is B2B buy-side, which is Internet technology that allows firms to solicit bids on inputs that firms require to support production, sales, and administration. Interested and qualified vendors can view the bid specifications and then electronically submit offers to sell the firms the needed inputs. Search the Internet to learn about B2B buy-side systems, and then discuss how a small firm could use a B2B buy-side system to reduce its supply chain costs.

INTERNET

18. **LO.4 (Organizational strategy; research; writing)** Use Internet resources to find a company (regardless of where it is domiciled) whose managers have chosen to (a) avoid competition through differentiation, (b) avoid competition through cost leadership, and (c) confront competitors head on. Analyze each of these strategies and discuss your perception of how well each strategy has worked.

INTERNET

19. **LO.4 (Organizational culture; writing)** Write a paper describing the organizational culture at a job you have held or the organizational culture at the college or university you attend. Be sure to include a discussion of the value system and how it was communicated to new employees or new students.

20. **LO.4 (Organizational form; writing)** Write a paper that compares and contrasts the corporate, general partnership, limited partnership, LLP, and LLC forms of business. At a minimum, discuss issues related to formation, capital generation, managerial authority and responsibility, taxation, ownership liability, and implications for success in mission and objectives.

ETHICS

21. **LO.5 (Elements of management control system; ethics; research; writing)** The use of stock options to compensate executives has become much more common in recent years. The increased use of options is based on efforts by boards of directors to align managerial and stockholder interests. Prior to the implementation of FAS 123R, firms would often report the stock options expense only in a footnote: thus, the expense did not flow through the income statement.
    a. Discuss why managers would desire to report the expense of stock options in financial statement footnotes rather than within the income statement.
    b. Discuss whether the practice of reporting stock option expense only in the footnotes was unethical or misleading.
    c. Research the topic "backdating stock options." Discuss the motivation for backdating options and whether such backdating would be considered an ethical practice.

ETHICS

22. **LO.5 (Elements of management control system; ethics; writing)** In recent years, many firms have been forced to restate the earnings previously reported in public financial reports. A number of these restatements have been linked to attempts by top management to manipulate the reported accounting information for the purpose of achieving higher compensation. For example, some firms accelerated the recognition of revenue (in a manner not consistent with GAAP) so that the profit on sales could be reported in an earlier, rather than a more appropriate later, period. These reporting anomalies often required manual intervention in the firm's normal reporting policies.
    a. Discuss which elements in the management control system might cause the manipulative behavior described.
    b. Is the described behavior ethical? Discuss.

INTERNET

23. **LO.6 (Gap analysis; writing)** Susan Cheng is the CFO of Automotive Solutions, a small company that makes specialized lighting equipment for the car industry. Because of intensified competition from foreign companies, Automotive Solutions has experienced extreme price pressure for its products. In response to this pressure, top management has decided to focus more intently on product quality to improve the company's competitive position.

    With this change in competitive focus, Cheng recognizes that the company must revise its CMS to better manage product quality. As an intern working for Cheng, write her a memo describing how gap analysis could be used to revise the CMS.

24. **LO.6 (Gap analysis; writing)** Star International manufactures after-market parts for lawn mowers and recreational all-terrain vehicles (ATVs). Because of ATV market growth, sales of Star International's products have grown at double-digit rates over the past five years, and the firm's information systems no longer adequately provide the information managers need to run the business. For example, the accounting system cannot provide information needed to control the high rate of growth in costs, or even to relate the growth in costs to the growth in sales. As a consultant hired by Star International, discuss how you could use gap analysis to identify the deficiencies in the firm's CMS and to prioritize the firm's efforts to close the gaps.

PROBLEMS

25. **LO.1 (Information and cost management)** A product's or service's price is a function of its total production or performance costs. In turn, the total production or performance cost reflects the aggregate costs incurred throughout the supply chain.

    Higher education is one industry that has been characterized by rapidly rising costs and prices. Study your college's or university's supply chain and prepare a table identifying specific ways in which improved communications with suppliers and customers could result in specific cost savings for the educational institution, its suppliers, or its customers (students). Organize your table in three columns as follows:

Specific Information to Be Obtained	Information Source	Specific Cost to Be Reduced

26. **LO.1 (Management control systems)** In many organizations, the operating budget is the primary control tool. Using a budget to control activities is more appropriate in some circumstances than in others, and a key criterion in evaluating a control's efficacy is always whether that control helps to implement the firm's strategy. Consider the following activities and circumstances, and discuss whether use of a budget as a primary control is appropriate:

    a. research and development department of a mature manufacturing firm
    b. marketing expense of a start-up technology company
    c. travel expense for the salesforce of an insurance company
    d. energy costs for a public utility company
    e. costs of environmental remediation for a chemical manufacturer
    f. production costs in a car manufacturing company
    g. operational costs of classroom buildings in a public university

27. **LO.2 & LO.3 (Alternative cost management strategies; writing)** In 1993, Procter & Gamble (P&G) management tried to control costs by eliminating many of its brands' coupons while increasing print advertising. Only a miniscule portion of the hundreds of billions of coupons distributed annually by P&G were ever redeemed by customers. Eliminating coupons allowed P&G to reduce its prices on most brands. After testing a market in the northeastern United States, P&G found that it lost 16 percent of its market share because competitors did not follow P&G in this move. Instead, P&G's decrease in price promotions was countered by competitors that increased their price promotions. Although price promotions had been unprofitable, discontinuing them while competitors did not was even more unprofitable for the company. P&G probably anticipated losing some market share in exchange for more profitability and equity for its brands but not to the degree that occurred. Advertising was expected to reverse the damage to competitor market penetration.

    Source: Raju Narisetti, "P&G Ad Chief Plots Demise of the Coupon," *Wall Street Journal* (April 17, 1996), pp. B1, B5A; and Tim Ambler, "P&G Learnt the Hard Way from Dropping Its Price Promotions," *Marketing* (June 7, 2001), pp. 22–23.

    a. What costs and benefits did P&G likely consider in its discontinuance of coupons?
    b. What was P&G's apparent strategy in deciding to lower prices? Explain.

28. **LO.2 & LO.3 (Cost management and customer service; writing)** Companies sometimes experience difficult financial times—often so drastic that bankruptcy is declared. If a firm does not invest sufficient resources in its growth, then at some point it will experience diminishing revenues as its product revenues decline. Alternatively, if a firm invests too heavily in growth, costs can spiral out of control. Commonly, companies striving to maintain profitability vacillate between a focus on cost management or cost reduction and a focus on revenue growth. Often cost reduction is achieved by tactics such as across-the-board cost cutting. Seldom do companies maintain a balance of focus on cost management and revenue generation; however, one company, Alcoa, has taken a more strategic approach to both revenue growth and cost management. Even

while in the middle of an effort to reduce costs by $1 billion per year, the company was focused on generating significant revenue growth. To achieve growth, the company breaks down its current revenue streams into five categories, including sales from existing customers and sales won from competitors' customers. By segmenting its revenue streams, the company can better evaluate the profitability of obtaining additional sales from different streams and focus on cost management and revenue growth simultaneously. The underlying idea is that growth in costs should occur only where there is a significant opportunity to increase profitability. Further, the company believes that cost management and revenue generation must be managed jointly so that managers understand how cost cutting affects customer value and revenue growth.

Source: Joseph McCafferty, "Testing the Top Line: Analyzing a Company's Sources of Revenues Can Bring Insights into Growth," *CFO Magazine* (October 19, 2004), http://www.cfo.com/article.cfm/3219980/2/c_2984272?f=archives (last accessed 12/16/11).

a. When are across-the-board spending cuts a rational approach to cost management?
b. How can a cost management system help avoid adverse effects from cost cutting?
c. Why is it necessary for managers to focus attention on both generating new revenue and managing costs to be successful?

29. **LO.2 & LO.3 (Cost management and strategy; writing)** You are the product manager at a silicone chip manufacturer. One of your products is a commodity chip widely used in cell phones, printers, digital cameras, and computers. As product manager, you have full profit responsibility for the commodity chip.

The commodity chip is a "cash cow" for your company and enjoys an enviable market share in the industry. Because your company's chip has approximately the same features and functionality as chips available from competitors, market competition for this product is primarily based on price.

Because of your success in managing the commodity chip, you were recently promoted to product manager of ZX chip, your company's most innovative chip based on its data-processing speed, miniature size, and incredible functionality. The ZX chip has just completed final testing and will be ready to be presented to the market in two weeks.

You were successful in managing the commodity chip because you kept unit production cost low by achieving high volume and efficient production. Identify and discuss the key variables you will try to manage to make the ZX chip as successful as the commodity chip. Discuss whether your efforts to manage costs will be similar to or different from your efforts to manage costs of the commodity chip.

30. **LO.4 (Cost management and profitability)** After graduating last year from an Ivy League university, Joe Tyler was hired as a stock analyst. Wanting to make his mark on the industry, Tyler issued a scathing report on a major discount department store retailer, Smart-Mart. The basis of his attack was a comparative analysis between Smart-Mart and Tracy's Department Store, an upscale, full-service department store. Some of the information cited in Tyler's report follows.

Items as Percent of Sales	Smart-Mart	Tracy's
Cost of goods sold	65%	55%
Gross margin	35	45
Selling and administrative	27	33
Profit	8	12

Based on the comparative analysis, Tyler issued to his clients a "sell" recommendation for Smart-Mart and a "buy" recommendation for Tracy's. The gist of Tyler's rationale for the recommendations was that Tracy's Department Store was outperforming Smart-Mart in the crucial area of cost management as evidenced by both a higher profit as a percent of sales and a higher gross margin as a percent of sales.

a. Evaluate Tyler's recommendations given the limited evidence available.
b. Because the two firms contrasted by Tyler have different strategies, what performance criteria would you use to evaluate their competitiveness in the industry?

31. **LO.4 (Stakeholders; cost management; writing)** Laura Thompson, newly appointed controller of Allied Networking Services Inc. (ANSI), a rapidly growing company, has just been asked to serve as lead facilitator of a team charged with designing a cost management system (CMS) at ANSI. Also serving on the team are Tom Weiss, company president; Susan Turner, vice president of finance; and George Wipple, vice president of marketing.

At the team's organizational meeting, Weiss suggested that the performance measurements to be built into the CMS should have a primary focus on ANSI's ultimate goal. Thompson advised the team that it needed to arrive at a consensus as to the appropriate goal to emphasize in the CMS's primary measurements.

Weiss indicated that he thought ANSI's goal should be maximization of company profits. At this, Wipple chimed in that because sales are the company's lifeblood, the team should think about making customer satisfaction ANSI's ultimate goal.

Turner, who had been silently listening to the discussion, was prompted by Thompson to give her opinion on the issue. Turner said that professional literature often advocates maximization of shareholder wealth as the ultimate business goal and she believed that should be ANSI's goal. After all, the stockholders provide the financial capital, take the ultimate risk, and are responsible for organizing the company. Therefore, she asserted, the primary emphasis of measurements in the CMS should focus on whether stockholder wealth was being maximized.

A heated debate ensued. Wipple said, "Look, without customers, the company has no reason for existence—how profitable is a company without customers, and how well off would its managers and stockholders be without revenues?" To this, Turner replied, "Without stockholder funds, you have no company!" Weiss responded, "Unless we manage ANSI profitable, there'll be no company to provide customers with products and services or to provide a basis for stockholder wealth!" The team decided to reconvene after everyone had a chance to assess what had been said.

a. Should the CMS design team be deciding the company's ultimate goal? If not, who should make such a decision?
b. What do you believe should be the ultimate goal for a business? Defend your answer.
c. Can one group of stakeholders effectively be served at the expense of the other stakeholders? Discuss.

32. **LO.4 (Cost management; product life cycle; research; writing)** In August 2007, **Heelys**, a Texas-based maker of wheeled shoes, reported quarterly profits that beat the street estimates by three cents per share. Upon receiving the news, the market price of Heelys dropped 48 percent. Why? Although the profit reported for the current quarter was better than the market expected, the company simultaneously informed the market that sales for the balance of the year were being revised downward because the company's shoes were piling up in retail stores.

INTERNET

Source: Rob Curran, "Anthracite, DGSE Rise; Heelys Slip," *The Wall Street Journal* (August 9, 2007), p. C2.

a. Using Internet resources, identify the economic reasons cited by Heelys' management for the profit warning issued in August 2007.
b. Applying your understanding of product life cycle, explain why Heelys' stock price dropped so significantly following the profit warning.
c. Following the profit warning in August 2007, what specific actions did managers take to improve profitability? Do any of these actions suggest that Heelys had revised its strategy in August 2007?

33. **LO.4 (Cost management and profitability)** Ohio Steel produces steel products for a variety of customers. One division of the company is the Garage Door Division, created in the late 1940s. Since that time, this division's principal products have been galvanized steel components used in garage door installations. The division has been continuously profitable since 1950, and, in 2013, it generated $20 million of profits on $500 million of sales.

However, over the past 10 years, divisional growth has been slow; profitability has become stagnant, and few new products have been developed, although the garage door components market has matured. Company president Kendra Lawson has asked her senior staff to evaluate operations of the Garage Door Division and to recommend changes that would improve its operations. The staff uncovered the following facts:

- Tonya Calley, age 53, has been division president for the past 15 years. Her compensation package includes an annual salary of $375,000 plus a cash bonus based on achievement of the budgeted level of annual profit.
- Growth in sales in the residential metal products industry has averaged 12 percent annually over the past decade. Most of the growth has occurred in ornamental products used in residential privacy fencing.
- Nationally, the division's market share in the overall residential metal products industry has dropped from 12 percent to 7 percent during the past 10 years and has dropped from 40 percent to 25 percent for garage door components.
- The division maintains its own information systems, which are essentially the same systems that were in place 15 years ago; however, some of the manual systems have been computerized (e.g., payroll, accounts payable, accounting).
- The division has no customer service department. A small sales staff solicits and takes orders by phone from national distribution chains.
- The major intra-division communication tool is the annual operating budget. No formal statements have been prepared in the division regarding strategies, mission, values, goals and objectives, or identifying core competencies.

Given this information, identify the major problems in the Garage Door Division and develop recommendations to address the problems you have identified.

ETHICS

34. **LO.1 & LO.5 (CMS; MIS; ethics; writing)** An oil and gas company's value is tied to two fundamental facts. The first is the amount of oil and gas the company is presently producing. This amount, along with unit prices, determines the revenue and cash inflow that the company generates. The second is the level of oil and gas reserves controlled by the company. Over the long run, the reserve level is a constraint on the amount and cost of current oil and gas production. Accordingly, the capital markets evaluate the performance of oil and gas companies as much on management of reserves as on management of current production. Because investors use information about reserves to value oil and gas companies, the SEC has developed rules for classifying and reporting reserves.

In a series of several announcements in early 2004, **Shell Oil** (Royal Dutch/Shell Group of Cos.) downgraded its proven oil and gas reserves by more than 20 percent, or about 4.5 billion barrels. Most of the misstatements of reserves, which were revealed to the public in 2004, had been booked in the years 1997–2000. Following the 2004 disclosures, regulatory bodies, including the SEC and the U.S. Justice Department, opened inquiries into the misreporting of reserves to determine if there had been violations of reporting rules or other laws.

a. Assume that the misreporting of reserves by Shell resulted from the MIS's generation of unintentional but inaccurate information. From a cost management perspective, how might the CMS, built on inaccurate data, have caused managers to take actions that were not in the company's best long-run interests? What actions could managers have taken to ensure the reliability of the data?
b. Assume that Shell intentionally misreported reserves. Discuss how the CMS, if not properly designed, could have contributed to the misreporting.
c. Discuss the ethics of manipulating financial and fundamental data to manage (mislead) perceptions of investors and other interested users of company information.

ETHICS

35. **LO.5 (Cost management; social responsibility; writing)** Through its three sets of elements (motivational, informational, and reporting), a CMS focuses the attention of a given decision maker on the data and information that are crucial to that decision maker's responsibilities in the organization. However, the nature and scope of information generated by the CMS for that decision maker are often limited by traditions of financial reporting and the imaginations of CMS designers. A common omission from a CMS is information useful in meeting a firm's social responsibility.

Consider the possibility that a CMS could be developed that would be informative relative to organizational performance from the following perspectives: minorities, local community, customers, employees, and the environment. Discuss how this information could be used to manage the following specific expenses:

a. product liability costs
b. local property taxes
c. pollution remediation
d. costs associated with employee turnover
e. warranty expense

36. **LO.4-LO.6 (CMS design; writing)** New England Bottling was founded in the late 1800s and was owned by the same family until 1960 when the firm went public. Throughout its life as a public firm, the company has been continuously profitable and recorded slow, but steady, growth. Historically, the company has maintained a steady focus on cost control as the key to profit generation. However, since about 2005 the company has struggled to significantly increase profits. In 1980, the firm bottled merely five brands of product and sold its output through four large wholesalers. Today, the firm bottles 40 brands of product, and product life averages only four years. Consequently, the firm is constantly adding and deleting brands in its product line. Further, to market the 40 brands of product, the company sells to dozens of wholesalers, brokers, and large retail chains. The company uses multiple pricing models to accommodate the various outlets.

a. Discuss how the changes in the operating environment of New England Bottling could negatively affect its ability to generate profit.
b. The firm's cost management system has not evolved with the changing complexity of the business environment. Discuss how gap analysis could be used to update the cost management system.

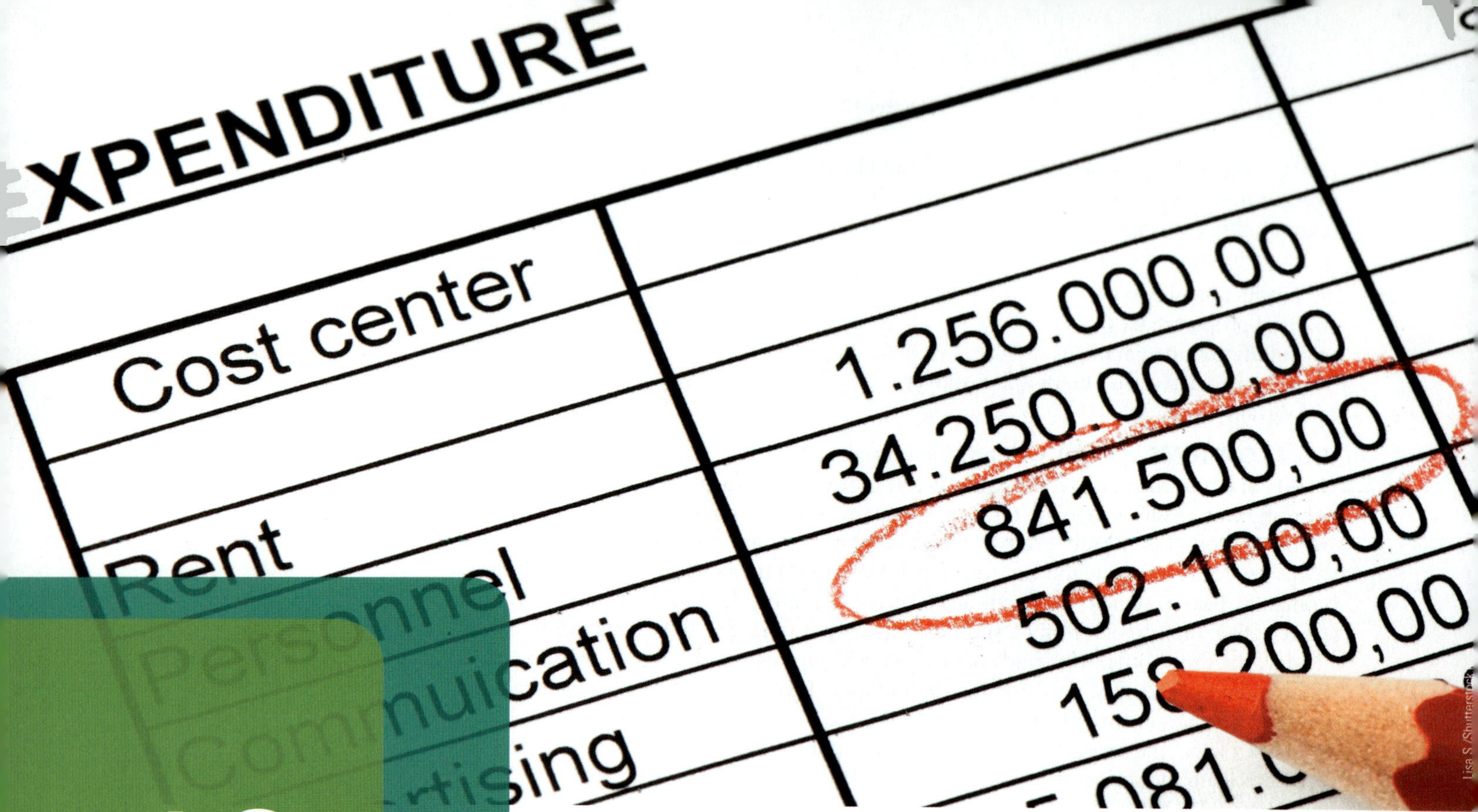

Lisa S./Shutterstock

13

Responsibility Accounting, Support Department Cost Allocations, and Transfer Pricing

LEARNING OBJECTIVES

After completing this chapter, you should be able to answer the following questions:

1. Which factors determine whether a firm should be decentralized or centralized?
2. How are decentralization and responsibility accounting related?
3. What are the four primary types of responsibility centers, and what distinguishes them from each other?
4. How are revenue variances computed?
5. Why and how are support department costs allocated to operating departments?
6. What types of transfer prices are used in organizations, and why are such prices used?
7. What difficulties can be encountered by multinational companies using transfer prices?

INTRODUCTION

As an organization grows, its customer-base size and locations, product and service offerings, level of technology, distribution channels, and number of employees change. To cope with such changes, managers must recognize when and how the company's authority structure should be altered to support decision making, communication, and employee motivation. Global operations demand that managers in all regions effectively use corporate human and physical resources; product customization demands that managers be in close touch with customers; and coordination of larger and more diverse workforces demands that managers be more adept at employee training and development. Decisions often need to be made rapidly at a "grass-roots" level rather than at "the top" of the organizational hierarchy. Thus, one of the most common progressions made by high-growth companies is from highly centralized organizational structures to highly decentralized structures. When an organization has a centralized structure, top management retains the majority of decision-making authority. When top management delegates decision-making authority to subunit managers, decentralization exists. This chapter describes the accounting methods—responsibility accounting, support department cost allocations, and transfer pricing—that are appropriate in decentralized organizations.

DECENTRALIZATION

1 Which factors determine whether a firm should be decentralized or centralized?

The degree of centralization can be viewed as a continuum. With **centralization**, a single individual (usually the company owner or president) makes all major decisions and retains full authority and responsibility for that organization's activities. Alternatively, a purely decentralized organization would have virtually no central authority, and each subunit would act as a totally independent entity. **Decentralization** is a transfer of authority, responsibility, and decision-making rights from the top to the bottom of the organizational structure. Decentralization has both advantages and disadvantages, which are summarized in Exhibit 13.1.

Exhibit 13.1 Advantages and Disadvantages of Decentralization

Advantages

- Help top management recognize and develop managerial talent
- Allow managerial performance to be comparatively evaluated
- Can often lead to greater job satisfaction and provide job enrichment
- Make the accomplishment of organizational goals and objectives easier
- Reduce decision-making time
- Allow the use of management by exception

Disadvantages

- Can result in a lack of goal congruence or in suboptimization by subunit managers
- Require more effective communication abilities because decision making is removed from the home office
- Can create personnel difficulties upon introduction, especially if managers are unwilling or unable to delegate effectively
- Can be extremely expensive, including costs of training and of making poor decisions

Either extreme of the centralization–decentralization continuum represents a clearly undesirable arrangement. In a totally centralized organization, a single individual would have neither the expertise nor sufficient and timely information to make effective decisions in all functional areas. In a totally decentralized organization, subunits could act in ways that are inconsistent with the whole entity's goals. Organizations tend to structure themselves according to the pure centralization versus pure decentralization factors in Exhibit 13.2.

Most businesses are somewhere along the continuum. An organization usually determines the appropriate degree of decentralization based on a combination of the

- managers' personal preferences,
- nature of decisions required for organizational growth, and
- types of activities in which the organization is engaged.

Exhibit 13.2 Degree of Decentralization in an Organizational Structure

FACTOR	CONTINUUM		
	Pure Centralization	→	Pure Decentralization
Age of organization	Young	→	Mature
Size of organization	Small	→	Large
Stage of product development	Stable	→	Growth
Growth rate of organization	Slow	→	Rapid
Expected impact on profits of incorrect decisions	High	→	Low
Top management's confidence in subordinates	Low	→	High
Historical degree of control in organization	Tight	→	Moderate or loose
Geographical diversity of operations	Local	→	Widespread
Cost of communications	Low	→	High
Ability to resolve conflicts	Easy	→	Difficult
Level of employee motivation	Low	→	Moderate to high
Level of organizational flexibility	Low	→	High
Time of response to changes	Slow	→	Rapid

Decentralization does not necessarily mean that a unit manager has the authority to make all decisions for that unit. Top management selectively determines the types of authority to delegate to, and withhold from, lower-level managers. Even highly decentralized companies often have certain organizational functions made centrally. The provision of a "back office" or support function for various organizational units from a central location is often referred to as a **shared service**. Typical back-office functions are accounting/cash management, human resources, information technology, legal, and procurement. Whereas such services may be performed in-house at headquarters for decentralized units, organizations may also opt to outsource these functions to consultants or independent contractors. Positive answers to the following questions may indicate that a particular organizational function should be centralized rather than being performed at multiple locations:

- Should the function be performed in a consistent manner throughout the organization?
- Are specialized skills/expertise, coordinated training, and/or a "best practices" model needed to perform the function effectively?
- Can the function be performed effectively without detailed interactions or coordination between the performers and the organizational units?
- Is there a high risk of negative impact to the organization if the function is performed incorrectly or improperly?
- Are there substantial monetary economies of scale if the function is performed centrally?
- Will the process be completed more rapidly if the function is performed centrally?
- Is there a distinct need (such as an ethical or a legal purpose) for organizational accountability for the function's performance?

Exhibit 13.3 provides some points for management to consider when deciding to centralize or decentralize the responsibility for environmental issues.

Exhibit 13.3 Decentralization/Centralization Considerations for Environmental Issues

Decentralize Responsibility and Decision Making

- Local management is better informed and aware of local environmental problems, concerns, and requirements.
- Local management is more attuned to local laws related to environmental use.
- Decentralized responsibility will result in a higher motivation for management's more efficient and effective usage of natural resources.
- Decision making will be more reflective of local population input; local information is less likely to be "lost" in organizational aggregation of data.
- Decisions about problems can be made rapidly and without organizational bureaucracy.
- Greater opportunity may exist for governmental negotiation in the event of environmental failures because decision making was local rather than "external."
- Distrust of external influence may exist in the local population and/or political organizations.

Centralize Responsibility and Decision Making

- Decentralized units may make conflicting environmental decisions, especially if there is a difference in local laws.
- Decentralized units may lack environmental expertise, creating a need for additional communication and coordination.
- Lack of a standardized organizational environmental policy or enforcement of such a policy could result in high costs for the organization in the event of environmental failures.
- A greater level of transparency is likely because all environmental decisions will be made based on similar rules and policies.
- Fewer conflicts of interest relative to performance evaluation can exist among decentralized managers.
- More proactive decisions may be made if local influence differences are eliminated.
- Environmental protection is more likely to be seen as part of the organizational culture if established and monitored centrally.

Regardless of whether a function and the decision-making authority for that function is retained centrally or delegated to decentralized units or external parties, top management retains ultimate responsibility for decision outcomes. Thus, a sophisticated accounting and reporting system must be implemented to provide top management information about overall subunit accountability as well as the ability to measure it. A **responsibility accounting system** facilitates decentralization by providing information about the performance, efficiency, and effectiveness of organizational subunits and their managers. Responsibility accounting is the key management control tool in a decentralized organization.

RESPONSIBILITY ACCOUNTING SYSTEMS

2 How are decentralization and responsibility accounting related?

A responsibility accounting system produces **responsibility reports** that assist each successively higher level of management in evaluating the performances of subordinate managers and their respective organizational units. The reports should be tailored to fit the subordinate managers' planning, controlling, and decision-making needs and should include both monetary and nonmonetary information. Exhibit 13.4 on page 506 provides examples of information that is shown in responsibility reports. Depending on the type of responsibility unit for which the report is being generated, all types of information shown are not necessarily available.

A manager's responsibility report should reflect his or her degree of influence and should include only the revenues and/or costs under that manager's control. Normally, some of an organizational unit's revenues or costs are noncontrollable (or only partially or indirectly controllable) by the unit manager. In such instances, the responsibility accounting

Exhibit 13.4 Information for Responsibility Reports

Monetary

- Budgeted and actual revenues
- Budgeted and actual costs (computed on a comparable basis)
- Variance computations for revenues and costs
- Asset investment base

Nonmonetary

- Capacity measures (theoretical and that used to compute predetermined overhead rates)
- Target rate of earnings on investment base
- Desired and actual market share
- Departmental or divisional throughput
- Number of defects (by product, product line, and supplier)
- Number of orders backlogged (by date, cost, and selling price)
- Number of customer complaints (by type and product); method of complaint resolution
- Percentage of orders delivered on time
- Manufacturing (or service) cycle efficiency
- Percentage of reduction of non-value-added time from previous reporting period (broken down by idle time, storage time, move time, and quality control time)
- Number and percentage of employee suggestions considered significant and practical
- Number and percentage of employee suggestions implemented
- Number of unplanned production interruptions or schedule changes
- Number and significance of environmental "instances"
- Number of engineering change orders; percentage change from previous period
- Number of safety violations; percentage change from previous period
- Number of days of employee absences; percentage change from previous period

report should separately classify all reported monetary information as controllable or noncontrollable by the manager. Alternatively, separate reports should be prepared for the organizational unit (showing all monetary amounts) and for the unit manager (showing only those monetary amounts under his or her control).

A responsibility accounting system helps organizational unit managers to conduct the five basic control activities:

1. Prepare a plan (e.g., using budgets and standards) and use it to communicate output expectations and delegate authority.
2. Gather, record, summarize, and classify actual data for the unit in accordance with the organizational plan's specified activities and categories.
3. Compare and monitor the differences between planned and actual data at scheduled intervals. To assess performance, comparisons should be made using both flexible budgets at the actual activity level as well as the master budget.
4. Exert managerial influence in response to significant differences. Because of day-to-day contact with operations, unit managers should be aware of any significant variances before they are reported, identify the variance causes, and attempt to correct any problems. In contrast, top management might not know about operational variances until responsibility reports are received. By that time, subordinate managers should have corrected the problems causing the variances or have explanations as to why the problems were not or could not be resolved.
5. Continue comparing data and responding; at the appropriate time, the process will begin again.

Responsibility reports reflect the upward flow of information from operational units to company top management and illustrate the broadening scope of responsibility. Managers receive detailed information on the performance of their immediate control areas and summary information on all organizational units for which the managers are responsible. Summarizing results causes a pyramiding of information. Reports at the lowest-level units are highly detailed, whereas more general information is reported to the top of the organization. Upper-level managers desiring more detail than is provided in summary reports can obtain it by reviewing subordinates' responsibility reports.

Exhibit 13.5 illustrates the June 2013 responsibility report for Kemp Company. Each area's budget is presented for comparative purposes. Production department data are aggregated or "rolled up" with data of the other departments under the production vice president's control. Similarly, the total costs of the production vice president's responsibility area are combined with other costs for which the company president is responsible.

Exhibit 13.5 Kemp Company Responsibility Report (June 2013)

President's Performance Report

	Budget	Actual	Variance Fav. (Unfav.)
Administrative office—president	$1,192,000	$1,196,800	$ (4,800)
Financial vice president	944,000	936,400	7,600
Production vice president	2,951,984	2,977,600	(25,616) ←
Sales vice president	1,100,000	1,105,600	(5,600)
Totals	$6,187,984	$6,216,400	$(28,416)

Production Vice President's Performance Report

	Budget	Actual	Variance Fav. (Unfav.)
Administrative office—vice president	$ 720,000	$ 728,800	$ (8,800)
Distribution and storage	498,800	504,000	(5,200) ←
Production department	1,733,184	1,744,800	(11,616) ←
Totals	$2,951,984	$2,977,600	$(25,616)

Distribution and Storage Manager's Performance Report

	Budget	Actual	Variance Fav. (Unfav.)
Direct material	$ 144,000	$ 141,600	$ 2,400
Direct labor	218,000	221,200	(3,200)
Supplies	18,800	21,200	(2,400)
Indirect labor	94,400	95,200	(800)
Repairs and maintenance	14,000	14,800	(800)
Other	9,600	10,000	(400)
Totals	$ 498,800	$ 504,000	$ (5,200)

Production Department Manager's Performance Report

	Budget	Actual	Variance Fav. (Unfav.)
Direct material	$ 477,200	$ 490,000	$(12,800)
Direct labor	763,520	752,108	11,412
Supplies	70,624	74,000	(3,376)
Indirect labor	185,152	188,080	(2,928)
Depreciation	154,612	154,612	0
Repairs and maintenance	49,628	51,600	(1,972)
Other	32,448	34,400	(1,952)
Totals	$1,733,184	$1,744,800	$(11,616)

Variances are itemized in performance reports at the lower levels so that the appropriate manager has the necessary details to take any required corrective action related to significant variances.[1] Under the management-by-exception principle, major deviations from

[1] In practice, the variances presented in Exhibit 13.5 would be further separated into the portions representing price and quantity effects as shown in Chapter 7 on standard costing.

expectations are highlighted under the subordinate manager's reporting section to assist upper-level managers in determining whether they need to become involved in subordinates' operations. In addition, such detailed variance analyses alert operating managers to items that require explanations for superiors. For example, the unfavorable direct material and favorable direct labor amounts in the production department manager's section of Exhibit 13.5 would probably be considered significant and require explanations to the production vice president.

Responsibility accounting creates some managerial issues. For example, aggregation of information to each successively higher level allows potentially important details to be buried. If different units within the responsibility accounting system compete with each other for resources, managers could try to "promote their own agendas" by blaming problems on other organizational units. Alternatively, the competition could lead to a lack of goal congruence between or among organizational units. (**Goal congruence** exists when the personal and organizational goals of decision makers throughout the firm are consistent and mutually supportive.) Additionally, partitioning each responsibility unit as a separate part of the report might obscure interdependencies among units. As mentioned in Chapter 4, organizational processes are typically horizontal and, thereby, the activities in one unit often affect activities in other responsibility accounting units.

Responsibility accounting's focus is on the manager who has control over a particular cost object. In a decentralized company, the cost object is an organizational unit or **responsibility center**, such as a division, department, or geographical region.

TYPES OF RESPONSIBILITY CENTERS

3 What are the four primary types of responsibility centers, and what distinguishes them from each other?

Responsibility accounting systems identify, measure, and report on the performance of responsibility centers and their managers. Responsibility centers are generally classified according to their manager's scope of authority and type of financial responsibility: costs, revenues, profits, and/or asset base. The four primary types of responsibility centers are illustrated in Exhibit 13.6 and discussed in the following sections.

Exhibit 13.6 Types of Responsibility Centers

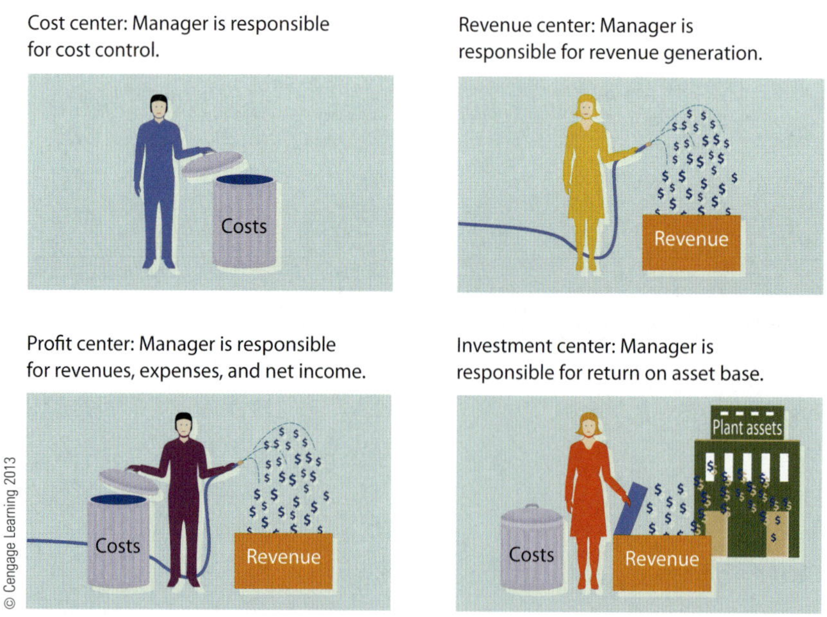

Cost Center

A **cost center** is an organizational unit whose manager has the authority only to incur costs and is specifically evaluated on the basis of how well costs are controlled. Such units (usually service and administrative departments) do not generate revenues or charge for services, but they do incur costs.[2] The human resources, customer service, and accounting

[2] Controlling costs in these areas is discussed in Chapter 16.

departments of most companies would likely be considered cost centers. In a traditional manufacturing environment, the production department is the largest cost center; individual assembly lines within the production department could also be viewed as separate cost centers. In a hospital, nursing, housekeeping, security, and medical records are typically designated as cost centers.

In some instances, a cost center can generate revenues, but the revenues are either not under the manager's control or not effectively measurable. The first situation exists in a community library that is provided a specific proration of property tax dollars but has no authority to levy or collect the related taxes. The second situation is reflected in research and development centers in which the outputs (revenues or benefits generated from the cost inputs) are not easily measured.[3] In these two types of situations, revenues should *not* be included in the manager's responsibility accounting report.

Cost center managers often concentrate only on unfavorable standard cost variances and ignore the efficient performance indicated by favorable variances. However, significant favorable variances should not be disregarded if the management-by-exception principle is applied properly. Using this principle, top management should investigate all variances (both favorable and unfavorable) that fall outside the range of acceptable deviations.

Revenue Center

4 How are revenue variances computed?

A **revenue center** is strictly defined as an organizational unit that is responsible for generating revenues and has no control over setting selling prices or budgeting costs. For instance, in many retail stores, each sales department is considered an independent unit, and managers are evaluated based on their departments' total revenues. Departmental managers, however, might have no authority to adjust selling prices to affect volume, and often they do not participate in the budgeting process. Additionally, the departmental managers might have no ability to affect costs. In a hospital, revenue centers might include the radiology, newborn intensive care, cancer care, and sleep disorders centers; a revenue center classification is likely if the hospital receives the majority of its funding from governmental sources that limit service payments to specific amounts based on the indicated DRG (diagnostic-related group) classification.

In a revenue center, performance evaluations are limited because the manager has control over only one item: revenue. Actual performance in revenue centers (as well as in any other area that has revenue control) should be compared against budgeted performance to determine variances from expectations. Budgeted and actual revenues may differ because of either volume of units sold or price of units sold. To compare budgeted and actual revenues, the price and volume components of revenue must be distinguished from one another.[4] The **sales price variance (SPV)** is calculated by multiplying the actual number of units sold by the difference between actual and budgeted sales prices. This variance indicates the portion of the total revenue variance that is related to a change in selling price. The **sales volume variance (SVV)** is calculated by multiplying the budgeted sales price by the difference between the actual and budgeted sales volumes. The model for computing revenue variances is as follows:

ASP × ASV	BSP × ASV	BSP × BSV
Sales Price Variance	Sales Volume Variance	
Total Revenue Variance		

where ASP = actual sales price
ASV = actual sales volume
BSP = budgeted sales price
BSV = budgeted sales volume

[3] Such a cost center involves discretionary costs, which are discussed in Chapter 16.

[4] Separating the price and volume elements of a revenue variance is similar to the separation of the price and usage elements of cost variances discussed in Chapter 7.

In most instances, pure revenue centers do not exist because managers are also responsible for managing some costs in their centers. A more appropriate term for such organizational units is a *revenue and limited cost center.*

Profit Center

A **profit center** is an organizational unit whose manager is responsible for generating revenues and managing expenses related to current activity. Thus, profit centers should be independent organizational units whose managers

- have the ability to obtain resources at the most economical prices,
- sell products at prices that will maximize revenue, and
- have a goal of maximizing the center's profit.

Costs not under a profit center manager's control are those related to long-term investments in plant assets; as such, separate evaluations should be made for the unit and its manager.

Investment Center

An **investment center** is an organizational unit whose manager is responsible for managing both revenues and expenses. In addition, the center's manager has the authority to acquire, use, and dispose of plant assets to earn the highest feasible rate of return on the center's asset base. Many investment centers are independent, freestanding divisions or corporate subsidiaries. This independence gives investment center managers the opportunity to make decisions about all matters affecting their organizational units and to be judged on the outcomes of those decisions. Because of their closeness to daily divisional activities, investment center managers should have more current and detailed knowledge than top management has about sales prices, costs, and other market information.

Regardless of the type of responsibility center overseen, managers will be evaluated on their performance. Thus, each manager may not always act harmoniously to accomplish the organization's goals and may instead act to optimize only his or her own isolated performance and that of his or her responsibility center. Losing sight of the organizational goals while working to achieve an independent responsibility center's conflicting goal results in **suboptimization**, which refers to the pursuit of goals and objectives that reflect personal, rather than organizational, best interests.

A unique challenge for the design of responsibility centers arises from the instance in which one responsibility center supplies its outputs largely to other internal responsibility centers. In determining a unit's responsibility classification, top management often makes judgments about the nature and extent of the costs and revenues to include in those responsibility centers. Frequently, rather than attempting to make performance assessments about cost centers, management assigns costs incurred in cost centers to operating areas through a process of support department cost allocation. Alternatively, management can attempt to "create" revenues for the cost center by using an internal transfer pricing system for the center's tangible or intangible output that is used by other company units.

SUPPORT DEPARTMENT COST ALLOCATION

5 Why and how are support department costs allocated to operating departments?

Organizations incur two types of overhead costs: those directly related to the operating (or primary revenue-generating) activities and those indirectly related to operating activities. Typically, as the number of product lines or service types increases, so does the need for additional indirectly related activities. **Support departments** include both service and administrative departments. A **service department** is an organizational unit (such as central purchasing, maintenance, engineering, security, or warehousing) that performs specific functional tasks for other internal units. **Administrative departments** perform management activities that benefit the entire organization and include the human resources, accounting, legal, and insurance departments as well as organizational headquarters.

All support department costs must be covered in the long run by sales of products and services. These costs may be allocated to operating departments to meet the objectives of full cost computation, managerial motivation, and managerial decision making. Exhibit 13.7 identifies reasons for and against allocating support department costs in relationship to each allocation objective.

Exhibit 13.7 Allocating Service Department Costs: Pros and Cons

Objective: To Compute Full Cost

Reasons *for*:

1. Provides for cost recovery.
2. Instills a consideration of support costs in production managers.
3. Reflects production's "fair share" of support costs.
4. Meets regulations in some pricing instances.

Reasons *against*:

1. Provides costs that are beyond production manager's control.
2. Provides arbitrary costs that are not useful in decision making.
3. Confuses the issues of pricing and costing. Prices should be set high enough so that product sales provide a profit margin large enough to cover all nonproduction costs.

Objective: To Motivate Managers

Reasons *for*:

1. Instills a consideration of support costs in production managers.
2. Relates individual production unit's profits to total company profits.
3. Reflects usage of services on a fair and equitable basis.
4. Encourages production managers to help support departments control costs.
5. Encourages the usage of certain services.

Reasons *against*:

1. Distorts production division's profit figures because allocations are subjective.
2. Includes costs that are beyond production manager's control.
3. Will not materially affect production division's profits.
4. Creates interdivisional ill will when there is lack of agreement about allocation base or method.
5. Is not cost beneficial.

Objective: To Compare Alternative Courses of Action

Reasons *for*:

1. Provides relevant information in determining corporate-wide profits generated by alternative actions.
2. Provides best available estimate of expected cost changes due to alternative actions.

Reasons *against*:

1. Is unnecessary if alternative actions will not change costs.
2. Presents distorted cash flows or profits from alternative actions because allocations are arbitrary.

Source: Adapted from *Statements on Management Accounting Number 4B: Allocation of Service and Administrative Costs* (June 13, 1985), pp. 9–10. Copyright by Institute of Management Accountants. Reproduced with permission of Institute of Management Accountants.

Allocation Bases

If support department costs are to be assigned to revenue-generating areas, a rational and systematic means by which to make the assignment must be developed. An improper cost allocation base will yield distorted cost allocations. A valid allocation base should

- measure the benefit the operating department receives from the support department;
- capture the causal relationship existing between factors in the operating department and costs incurred in the support department;
- reflect the fairness or equity of the allocations among operating departments; and
- measure the ability of operating departments to bear the allocated costs.

The first two criteria are used most often to select allocation bases because these criteria are reasonably objective and will produce rational allocations. Fairness is a valid theoretical basis for allocation, but its use can cause dissension because everyone does not agree on what is fair or equitable. The ability-to-bear criterion often results in unrealistic or profit-detrimental actions: managers might manipulate operating data related to the allocation base to minimize support department allocations. Exhibit 13.8 indicates some appropriate bases for assigning various types of support department costs.

Exhibit 13.8 Appropriate Service/Administrative Cost Allocation Bases to Divisions/Departments

Type of Cost	Acceptable Allocation Bases
Research and development	Estimated sales; assets employed; new products developed
Personnel functions	Number of employees; number of new hires
Accounting/treasury functions	Estimated time or usage; assets employed; payroll checks issued
Public relations and corporate promotion	Sales; number of advertisements developed; number of advertisements placed
Purchasing function	Dollar value of purchase orders; number of purchase orders; estimated time of usage; percentage of material purchases
Corporate executives' salaries	Sales; assets employed; pretax operating income
Legal, tax, or governmental affairs	Estimated time or usage; sales; assets employed
Property taxes	Square feet; real estate valuation
Data processing	Time of service; volume; storage capacity used; number of data mining searches run
Information technology	Number of service calls; number of computers or other IT devices; dollar value of technology employed
Custodial services	Square footage occupied; total labor hours

PictureNet/Corbis/Jupiter Images

Under the direct method, costs associated with a cafeteria, which provides services for operating and other service departments, would be charged only to operating departments.

Methods of Allocating Support Department Costs

The idea underlying support department cost allocations is that the responsibility centers benefiting from the services provided by support units should bear the costs of such units. Therefore, all the allocation methods intend to accomplish the same result: assign the cost of support departments to their customers. The methods differ merely in their complexity and reliability of results.

The **direct method** assigns support department costs only to operating areas. For example, the human resources department costs can be assigned to production departments based on number of employees, and purchasing department costs can be assigned to production departments based on number of purchase orders generated for each department's manufacturing operations. The direct method is the simplest allocation method, but it may result in distorted cost allocations if there is significant exchange of services between support departments as well as between support and operating departments.

In assigning costs, the **step method** allows a partial recognition of the effects of interactions among support departments. This method ranks the quantity of services provided by each support department to other support areas. A **benefits-provided ranking** begins with the support department providing the most service to all other support areas and ends with the support department providing the least service to all other support areas. Then, support department costs are sequentially allocated down the ranking until all costs have been assigned to the operating areas. For example, the human resources department might be the first department listed in the ranking because it provides assistance to all company areas. All other areas, including support areas, would receive an allocation of the human resources department's costs based on the proportion of human resources services used. Many approaches are used to implement the benefits-provided ranking; two common methods are the dollar volume of services provided and the percentage of total assistance to other support areas.

The **algebraic method** of allocating support department costs considers all departmental interrelationships and reflects these relationships in simultaneous equations. These equations provide for reciprocal allocation of total support costs among the support departments as well as to the operating departments. No benefits-provided ranking is needed. The algebraic method is the most complex of all the allocation techniques, but it is also the most theoretically correct and, if relationships are properly formulated, provides the most accurate and reliable allocations.

SERVICE DEPARTMENT COST ALLOCATION ILLUSTRATION

Data for McNally Supplements Co. (MNSC) illustrate the three methods of allocating budgeted support department costs. MNSC has two operating divisions: nutritionals and diet aids. MNSC's support departments are corporate administration, human resources, and maintenance. Budgeted costs of each support department are first allocated to each operating division using one of the three methods of support area cost allocation and are then added to the budgeted overhead costs of those divisions to determine an appropriate divisional overhead application rate. Exhibit 13.9 provides an abbreviated 2014 budget of the direct and indirect costs for each support department and operating division of MNSC.

Exhibit 13.9 McNally Supplements Co. 2014 Budgeted Departmental and Divisional Costs

	Administration	Human Resources	Maintenance	Nutritionals	Diet Aids	Total
Direct departmental costs:						
Material	$ 0	$ 0	$ 0	$1,275,600	$ 669,600	$1,945,200
Labor	1,350,000	150,000	360,000	736,200	864,000	3,460,200
Total	$1,350,000	$150,000	$360,000	$2,011,800	$1,533,600	$5,405,400
Departmental overhead*	1,651,200	69,750	238,200	1,677,000	267,600	3,903,750
Total initial departmental costs	$3,001,200	$219,750	$598,200	$3,688,800	$1,801,200	$9,309,150

*Would be specified by type and cost behavior in actual budgeting process.

Exhibit 13.10 (page 514) presents the bases selected for allocating MNSC's support department costs. These bases are proxies for the quantity of services consumed by each service area and operating division. The support departments are listed in a benefits-provided ranking. Management determined that administration provides the most assistance to all other support areas, human resources is second in the rank ordering, and maintenance supports only the operating areas (equipment used in other areas is under a lease maintenance arrangement and is not serviced by the company's maintenance department). All product research and development is conducted in a separate subsidiary company.

Direct Method Allocation

In the direct method of allocation, support department costs are assigned using the specified bases only to the operating areas. The direct method cost allocation for McNally Supplement Co. is shown in Exhibit 13.11.

Exhibit 13.10 Service Department Allocation Bases

Administration costs—allocated based on dollars of assets employed
Human resources costs—allocated based on number of employees
Maintenance costs—allocated based on machine hours used

	Dollars of Assets Employed	Number of Employees	Number of Machine Hours Used
Administration	$12,000,000	24	0
Human resources	3,600,000	6	0
Maintenance	6,000,000	18	0
Nutritionals	30,000,000	75	258,000
Diet aids	24,000,000	21	64,500

Exhibit 13.11 Direct Allocation of Service Department Costs

	Base	Proportion of Total Base	Amount to Allocate	Amount Allocated
Administration costs (dollars of assets employed)				
Nutritionals	$30,000,000	30,000,000 ÷ 54,000,000 = 56%*	$3,001,200	$1,680,672
Diet aids	24,000,000	24,000,000 ÷ 54,000,000 = 44*	3,001,200	1,320,528
Total	$54,000,000	100%		$3,001,200
Human resouces costs (number of employees)				
Nutritionals	75	75 ÷ 96 = 78%*	$ 219,750	$ 171,405
Diet aids	21	21 ÷ 96 = 22*	219,750	48,345
Total	96	100%		$ 219,750
Maintenance costs (number of machine hours used)				
Nutritionals	258,000	258,000 ÷ 322,500 = 80%	$ 598,200	$ 478,560
Diet aids	64,500	64,500 ÷ 322,500 = 20	598,200	119,640
Total	322,500	100%		$ 598,200

*Rounded.

Use of the direct method of support department allocation produces the total budgeted costs for nutritionals and diet aids (Exhibit 13.12). If budgeted revenues and costs equal actual revenues and costs, nutritionals would show a 2014 profit of $1,730,563, or 22.3 percent on revenues, and diet aids would show a profit of $1,210,287, or 26.9 percent.

Step Method Allocation

To apply the step method allocation, the benefits-provided ranking specified in Exhibit 13.10 is used. Costs are assigned using an appropriate, specified allocation base to the departments receiving support. After costs have been assigned from a department, no costs are charged back to that department. Step method allocation of MNSC support costs is shown in Exhibit 13.13 (page 516).

Exhibit 13.12 Direct Method Allocation to Revenue-Producing Areas

	Nutritionals	Diet Aids	Total
Total (assumed) budgeted revenues *(a)*	$7,750,000	$4,500,000	$12,250,000
Allocated overhead			
From administration	$1,680,672	$1,320,528	$ 3,001,200
From human resources	171,405	48,345	219,750
From maintenance	478,560	119,640	598,200
Subtotal	$2,330,637	$1,488,513	$ 3,819,150
Departmental overhead (from Exhibit 13.9)	1,677,000	267,600	1,944,600
Total overhead (for OH application rate determination)	$4,007,637	$1,756,113	$ 5,763,750
Direct costs	2,011,800	1,533,600	3,545,400
Total budgeted costs *(b)*	$6,019,437	$3,289,713	$ 9,309,150
Total budgeted pretax profits *(a – b)*	$1,730,563	$1,210,287	$ 2,940,850

VERIFICATION OF ALLOCATION TO

	Administration	Human Resources	Maintenance	Nutritionals	Diet Aids	Total
Initial costs	$ 3,001,200	$ 219,750	$ 598,200			$3,819,150
Costs from						
Administration	(3,001,200)			$1,680,672	$1,320,528	
Human resources		(219,750)		171,405	48,345	
Maintenance			(598,200)	478,560	119,640	
Totals	$ 0	$ 0	$ 0	$2,330,637	$1,488,513	$3,819,150

In this case, the amount of support department costs assigned to each operating area differs only slightly between the step and direct methods. However, in many situations, the difference can be substantial. If budgeted revenues and costs for 2014 equal the actual revenues and costs for that year, the step method allocation process will cause nutritionals and diet aids to show the following profits:

	Nutritionals	Diet Aids
Revenues	$ 7,750,000	$ 4,500,000
Direct costs	(2,011,800)	(1,533,600)
Indirect departmental costs	(1,677,000)	(267,600)
Allocated support department costs	(2,420,270)	(1,398,880)
Profit	$ 1,640,930	$ 1,299,920

These profit figures reflect rates of return on revenues of 21.2 percent and 28.9 percent, respectively.

The step method is a hybrid between the direct and the algebraic methods. This allocation approach is more realistic than the direct method in that the step method partially recognizes the exchange of services among support departments. Under this allocation process, a support department is "eliminated" once its costs have been assigned. Assistance provided by a support department further down the ranking sequence is not recognized as being given to departments higher in the benefits-provided ranking.

Algebraic Method Allocation

By recognizing all interrelationships among departments and making no decision about a rank ordering of support departments, the algebraic method of allocation eliminates the step method's two disadvantages. The algebraic method requires a set of equations be

Exhibit 13.13 Step Method Allocation to Revenue-Producing Areas

	Base	Proportion of Total Base		Amount to Allocate	Amount Allocated
Administration costs (dollars of assets employed)					
Human resources	$ 3,600,000	3,600,000 ÷ 63,600,000 =	6%[a]	$3,001,200	$ 180,072
Maintenance	6,000,000	6,000,000 ÷ 63,600,000 =	9[a]	3,001,200	270,108
Nutritionals	30,000,000	30,000,000 ÷ 63,600,000 =	47[a]	3,001,200	1,410,564
Diet aids	24,000,000	24,000,000 ÷ 63,600,000 =	38[a]	3,001,200	1,140,456
Total	$63,600,000		100%		$3,001,200
Human resources costs (number of employees)					
Maintenance	18	18 ÷ 114 =	16%[a]	$ 399,822[b]	$ 63,972
Nutritionals	75	75 ÷ 114 =	66[a]	399,822	263,882
Diet aids	21	21 ÷ 114 =	18[a]	399,822	71,968
Total	114		100%		$ 399,822
Maintenance costs (number of machine hours used)					
Nutritionals	258,000	258,000 ÷ 322,500 =	80%	$ 932,280[c]	$ 745,824
Diet aids	64,500	64,500 ÷ 322,500 =	20	932,280	186,456
Total	322,500		100%		$ 932,280

[a]Rounded.
[b]Human resources = Original cost + Allocated from administration = \$219,750 + \$180,072 = \$399,822.
[c]Maintenance costs = Original cost + Allocated from administration + Allocated from human resources = \$598,200 + \$270,108 + \$63,972 = \$932,280.

VERIFICATION OF ALLOCATION TO

	Administration	Human Resources	Maintenance	Nutritionals	Diet Aids	Total
Initial costs	$ 3,001,200	$ 219,750	$ 598,200			$3,819,150
Costs from						
Administration	(3,001,200)	180,072	270,108	$1,410,564	$1,140,456	
Human resources		(399,822)	63,972	263,882	71,968	
Maintenance			(932,280)	745,824	186,456	
Totals	$ 0	$ 0	$ 0	$2,420,270	$1,398,880	$3,819,150

formulated to reflect reciprocal service among departments. Solving these equations simultaneously recognizes the fact that support departments both give and receive services.

The algebraic method's starting point is choosing which base to use for measuring each department's consumption of services. A schedule is created to show each department's proportionate usage of the other departments' services. These proportions are then used to develop equations that, when solved simultaneously, give cost allocations that fully recognize the reciprocal services provided.

Using the bases shown in Exhibit 13.10, the allocation proportions for all departments of MNSC are shown in Exhibit 13.14. The human resources department allocation is discussed to illustrate the derivation of these proportions. The allocation basis for human resources cost is number of employees. MNSC has 138 employees, excluding those in the human resources department. Human resources employees are ignored because costs are

Exhibit 13.14 Interdepartmental Proportional Relationships

	ADMINISTRATION (DOLLARS OF ASSETS EMPLOYED)		HUMAN RESOURCES (NUMBER OF EMPLOYEES)		MAINTENANCE (NUMBER OF MACHINE HOURS USED)	
	Base	Percent*	Base	Percent*	Base	Percent*
Administration	N/A	N/A	24	18%	0	0%
Human resources	$ 3,600,000	6%	N/A	N/A	0	0
Maintenance	6,000,000	9	18	13	N/A	N/A
Nutritionals	30,000,000	47	75	54	258,000	80
Diet aids	24,000,000	38	21	15	64,500	20
Total	$63,600,000	100%	138	100%	322,500	100%

*Rounded.

being removed from that department and assigned to other areas. Because maintenance has 18 employees, the proportionate amount of human resources services used by maintenance is 18 ÷ 138 or 13 percent (rounded).

By using the calculated percentages, algebraic equations representing the interdepartmental usage of services can be formulated. The departments are labeled A (Administration), H (Human Resources), and M (Maintenance) in the equations. Initial costs of each support department are shown first in the formulas:

$$A = \$3{,}001{,}200 + 0.18H + 0.00M$$
$$H = \$\ \ 219{,}750 + 0.06A + 0.00M$$
$$M = \$\ \ 598{,}200 + 0.09A + 0.13H$$

These equations are solved simultaneously by substituting one equation into the others, gathering like terms, and reducing the unknowns until only one unknown exists. The value for this unknown is then computed and substituted into the remaining equations. This process is continued until all unknowns have been eliminated.

1. Substituting the equation for A into the equation for H gives the following:

$$H = \$219{,}750 + 0.06(\$3{,}001{,}200 + 0.18H)$$

Multiplying and combining terms produces the following results:

$$H = \$219{,}750 + \$180{,}072 + 0.01H$$
$$H = \$399{,}822 + 0.01H$$
$$H - 0.01H = \$399{,}822$$
$$0.99H = \$399{,}822$$
$$H = \$403{,}861$$

2. The value for H is substituted in the administration equation:

$$A = \$3{,}001{,}200 + 0.18(\$403{,}861)$$
$$A = \$3{,}001{,}200 + \$72{,}695$$
$$A = \$3{,}073{,}895$$

3. Substituting the values for A and H into the maintenance equation M gives the following:

$$M = \$598{,}200 + 0.09(\$3{,}073{,}895) + 0.13(\$403{,}861)$$
$$M = \$598{,}200 + \$276{,}651 + \$52{,}502$$
$$M = \$927{,}353$$

The amounts provided by these equations are then allocated among all the departments; costs are allocated both to and from the support areas. The resulting allocations are shown in Exhibit 13.15. Note that the net amount assigned to all support areas is $0.

Exhibit 13.15 Algebraic Solution of Service Department Costs

Costs are allocated based on percentages computed in Exhibit 13.14.

	ADMINISTRATION		HUMAN RESOURCES		MAINTENANCE	
	Percent	Amount	Percent	Amount	Percent	Amount
Administration	N/A	N/A	18%	$ 72,695	0%	$ 0
Human resources	6%	$ 184,434	N/A	N/A	0	0
Maintenance	9	276,650	13	52,502	N/A	N/A
Nutritionals	47	1,444,731	54	218,085	80	741,882
Diet aids	38	1,168,080	15	60,579	20	185,471
Total*	100%	$3,073,895	100%	$403,861	100%	$927,353

*Total costs are the solution results of the set of algebraic equations.

The $3,073,895 of administration costs is used to illustrate the computation of the amounts in Exhibit 13.15. Administration costs are assigned to the other areas based on dollars of assets employed. Exhibit 13.15 indicates that human resources has 6 percent of MNSC's total asset dollars; thus, $184,434 (0.06 × $3,073,895) is assigned to that area. A similar proration process is used for the other departments. Allocations from Exhibit 13.15 are used in Exhibit 13.16 to determine the reallocated costs and finalize the total budgeted overhead of nutritionals and diet aids.

Exhibit 13.16 Algebraic Method Allocation to Revenue-Producing Areas

	Human Department Cost (from equations)	Administration	Human Resources	Maintenance	Nutritionals	Diet Aids
Administration	$3,073,895	$ 0	$ 184,434	$ 276,650	$1,444,731	$1,168,080
Human resources	403,861	72,695	0	52,502	218,085	60,579
Maintenance	927,353	0	0	0	741,882	185,471
Total costs	$4,405,109	$ 72,695	$ 184,434	$ 329,152	$2,404,698	$1,414,130
Less reallocated costs	(586,281)	(72,695)	(184,434)	(329,152)		
Budgeted costs	$3,818,828	$ 0	$ 0	$ 0		
Departmental OH costs of operating areas					1,677,000	267,600
Total budgeted cost for OH application rate determination					$4,081,698	$1,681,730

When a company has few support department interrelationships, the algebraic method can be solved by hand. If a large number of support area interactions exist, this method must be performed by a computer. Results obtained from the algebraic method provide the most rational and appropriate means of allocating support department costs, but a substantial amount of time is needed to accurately determine the proportional relationships.

Determining Overhead Application Rates

Regardless of the method used to allocate support department costs, the final step is to determine the overhead application rates for the operating areas. After support department costs have been assigned to production, they are included as part of production overhead and allocated to products or jobs through normal overhead assignment procedures.

As shown in Exhibit 13.16, the total allocated overhead costs of $4,081,698 and $1,681,730 for nutritionals and diet aids, respectively, will be divided by an appropriate overhead allocation base to assign both manufacturing and nonmanufacturing overhead to products. For example, assume that MNSC has chosen total ounces of diet aid products as the overhead allocation base for diet aids. The division expects to produce 2,250,000 ounces of diet aid products in 2014. Thus, the support department overhead cost assigned to each ounce of diet aid product is:

$$\begin{aligned}\text{Allocated OH cost per ounce} &= \text{Total support cost} \div \text{Total ounces of products}\\ &= \$1{,}681{,}730 \div 2{,}250{,}000\\ &= \$0.75\end{aligned}$$

For simplicity, cost behavior in all departments has been ignored. A more appropriate allocation process would specify different bases in each department for the variable and fixed costs. Such differentiation would not change the allocation process but would change the results of the three methods (direct, step, or algebraic). Separation of variable and fixed costs would provide a more accurate allocation; use of the computer makes this process more practical than relying on manual calculations.

Before making any allocations, management should be certain that the allocation bases are reasonable. Allocations are often based on the easiest available measure, such as the number of people employed or number of documents processed. Use of such measures can distort the allocation process and result in inappropriate performance evaluations. However, regardless of the allocation method selected, the process of allocation does not change the organization's final profitability—but will change the "profitability" of individual divisions.

Allocating support department costs to operating divisions makes managers more aware of, and responsible for, controlling support service usage. However, if such allocations are made, evaluation of the operating division managers' performance should exclude these allocations. Operating division managers can control their usage of support services but not the actual incurrence of support department costs. The financial performance of an operating department manager should be evaluated using an incremental, rather than a full allocation, approach. For example, the diet aid manager's performance should be evaluated using a predetermined overhead rate based only on the incurrence of departmental overhead cost rather than total overhead cost. Thus, rather than being based on the $0.75 rate calculated earlier, the rate for the manager's performance evaluation would be:

$$\begin{aligned}\text{Diet aid departmental OH rate} &= \$267{,}600 \div 2{,}250{,}000\\ &= \$0.12 \text{ per ounce (rounded)}\end{aligned}$$

An alternative to using cost allocation is to "sell" support service to user departments using a **transfer price** or an internal charge for services (or goods) transferred between organizational units. The practice of using transfer prices for products is well established; using transfer prices for services is becoming more prevalent. Often transfer pricing systems are used when the selling unit offers services both inside and outside of the organization. Using transfer prices for services between organizational units has several advantages, as described in Exhibit 13.17. Top management must determine which method (allocation or transfer pricing) produces the most useful information.

Exhibit 13.17 Advantages of Transfer Prices for Services

	Revenue Departments	Service Departments
User Involvement	Encourage ways to improve services to benefit users	Promote development of services more beneficial to users
Cost Consciousness	Relate to services used; restrict usage to those that are necessary and cost beneficial	Relate to cost of services provided; must justify transfer price established
Performance Evaluations	Include costs for making performance evaluations if control exists over amount of services used	Promote making a service department a profit center rather than a cost center and thus provide more performance evaluation measures

TRANSFER PRICING

Transfer prices are established for a variety of reasons:

- help promote goal congruence;
- ensure optimal resource allocation;
- promote operating efficiency;
- make comparable performance evaluations among segments; and
- motivate managers to be more entrepreneurial.

In addition, transfer prices are used to "transform" a cost center into a **pseudo-profit center**.[5] Use of transfer prices allows a selling segment to create "artificial" revenue and a buying segment to create "artificial" costs.

Although transfer prices can be used for services or products, for simplicity the following discussion will assume that a product is being transferred from a production department.[6] Transfer prices can be calculated in a number of ways, but the following general rules are appropriate:

- The *maximum* price should be no higher than the lowest market price at which the buying segment can acquire the goods or services externally.
- The *minimum* price should be no less than the sum of the selling segment's incremental costs associated with the goods or services plus the opportunity cost of the facilities used.[7]

To illustrate these rules, assume that a product is available from external suppliers at a price below the internal supplier's minimum price. The immediate short-run decision could be for the internal selling division to stop production and for the purchasing division to buy the product externally. This decision might be reasonable because, compared with the external suppliers, the selling division's activities do not appear to be cost efficient and elimination of the activity would release the facilities, people, and funds for other, more profitable purposes. A longer-run solution could be to have the selling division improve efficiency so that the internal cost of making the product is reduced. This solution could be implemented without stopping internal production, but some external purchases might be made until costs are reduced.

[5] Pseudo-profit centers have been discussed for many years. One article by Ralph L. Benke, Jr., and James Don Edwards, "Should You Use Transfer Pricing to Create Pseudo-Profit Centers?" appeared in *Management Accounting* (now *Strategic Finance*) in February 1981. Such centers (termed microprofit centers) were also discussed at great length by Robin Cooper in *When Lean Enterprises Collide* (Boston, MA: Harvard Business School Press, 1995).

[6] Thus, all references to "products" or "goods" and "production" are equally applicable to "services" and "service performance."

[7] Incremental costs are typically variable ones, and companies often ignore opportunity costs in calculating the minimum price because these are not included in the accounting records. Opportunity cost is discussed in Chapter 10.

The difference between the upper and lower transfer price limits is the corporate "profit" (or savings) generated by producing internally rather than buying externally. Transfer prices act to "divide the corporate profit" between the buying and selling segments. Because they are internally set, transfer prices (and their "divided profits") are always eliminated for external reporting purposes, leaving only the actual cost of the items on balance sheets or income statements.[8]

In contrast, these "profits" can be extremely important for internal reporting. If performance is evaluated on a competitive basis, both buying and selling segment managers want to maximize their financial results in the responsibility accounting reports. The supplier-segment manager tries to obtain the highest transfer (selling) price, whereas the buying-segment manager tries to acquire the goods or services at the lowest transfer (purchase) price. Thus, the company's selling and buying segments should agree on the amount of a transfer price.

Types of Transfer Prices

6 What types of transfer prices are used in organizations, and why are such prices used?

There are three traditional types of transfer prices: cost-based, market-based, and negotiated; some companies may also use a dual pricing structure. Each type of transfer price is applicable to products or services. Exhibit 13.18 lists some questions that should be addressed for each type of transfer price. A discussion of each method and its advantages and disadvantages follows. Numerical examples of transfer price calculations are given in the Demonstration Problem at the end of the chapter.

Cost-Based Transfer Prices A cost-based transfer price would seem simple to implement until one realizes there are many definitions of the term *cost,* ranging from variable

Exhibit 13.18 Types of Transfer Prices and Related Questions of Use

Cost-Based

1. What should be included in cost?
   - Variable production or performance costs
   - Total variable cost
   - Absorption production or performance costs
   - "Adjusted" absorption production or performance costs
2. Should cost be actual or standard?
3. Should a profit margin for the selling division be included?

Market-Based

1. What if there is no exact counterpart in the market?
2. What if internal sales create a cost savings (such as not having bad debts) that would not exist in external sales?
3. What if the market price is currently depressed?
4. Which market price should be used?

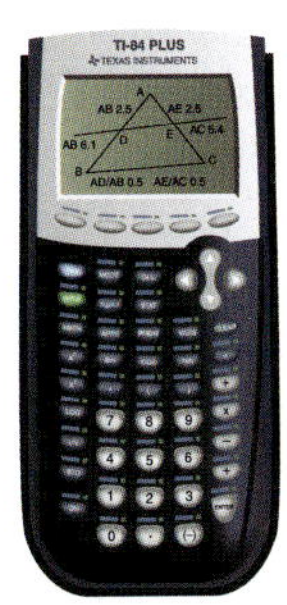

Negotiated

1. Do both parties have the ability to bargain with autonomy?
2. How will disputes be handled?
3. Are comparable product substitutes available externally?

[8]Elimination of transfer prices within a company is similar to the elimination of any markup on the sale of inventory between a company and its subsidiaries (or among the subsidiaries of a single company) in preparing consolidated financial statements.

production cost to absorption cost plus additional amounts for selling and administrative costs (and, possibly, opportunity cost) of the selling division. If only variable costs are used to set a transfer price, the production division has little incentive to "sell" to another internal division because no contribution margin is generated on the transfer to help cover fixed costs. Transfer prices based on absorption cost at least provide a contribution toward covering the production division's fixed overhead. In the services area, cost-based transfer prices are commonly used for low-cost and low-volume services such as temporary maintenance and temporary office staff assistance.

Modifications can be made to reduce the problems of cost-based transfer prices. When variable cost is used as a base, an additional amount can be added to cover some fixed costs and provide a measure of profit to the production division. This adjustment is an example of a cost-plus arrangement. Some managers think cost-plus arrangements are acceptable substitutes for market-based transfer prices, especially when market prices for comparable substitute products are unavailable. Absorption cost can be modified by adding an amount for nonproduction costs associated with the product and/or an amount for profit to the production division. In contrast, a transfer price could be set at less than absorption cost if there were no other use for the capacity or if estimated savings (such as reduced packaging) in production costs were created by internal transfers.

Another consideration in a cost-based transfer price is whether actual or standard cost is used. Actual costs can vary according to the season, production volume, and other factors, whereas standard costs can be specified in advance and are stable measures of efficient production costs. Standard costs provide a superior basis for transfer pricing. Any variances from standard are borne by the selling division; if actual costs are used, the selling division's efficiencies or inefficiencies are passed on to the buying division.

Market-Based Transfer Prices To eliminate the problems of defining "cost," some companies use a market price approach to set transfer prices. Market price is believed to be an objective, arm's-length measure of value that simulates the selling price that would be offered and paid if the selling and buying divisions were independent companies. If operating efficiently relative to the competition, a selling division should be able to show a profit when transferring products or services at market prices. Similarly, an efficiently operating buying division would have to pay market price if the alternative of buying internally did not exist. Market-based transfer prices are effective for common high-cost and high-volume standardized services such as storage and transportation.

Several problems can exist, however, with the use of market prices for intracompany transfers:

- Transferred products may have no exact counterpart in the external market, which means there is no established market price.
- Internal sales reduce packaging, advertising, or delivery expenditures and eliminate bad debts; thus, market price is generally not entirely appropriate.
- In instances of a temporary downturn in market demand, the transfer price might be set at the artificially "depressed" price, which could cause inappropriate performance evaluations or decisions to be made.
- Different prices, discounts, and credit terms are allowed to different buyers, so there is a question of which is the "right" market price to use.

Negotiated Transfer Prices Because of the problems associated with both cost- and market-based prices, **negotiated transfer prices** are often set through a process of bargaining between the selling and buying unit managers. Such prices are typically below the normal market price paid by the buying unit but above the selling unit's combined incremental and opportunity costs. If internal sales would eliminate any variable selling costs, such costs are not considered. If external sales do not exist or a division cannot downsize its facilities, no opportunity cost is involved. To encourage cooperation between divisions, top management can consider joint divisional profits as one performance measurement for both the selling and the buying unit managers.

Negotiated transfer prices are often used for services because their value—as shown through expertise, reliability, convenience, or responsiveness—is often qualitative and can be assessed only judgmentally from the perspective of the parties involved. The transfer price should depend on the service's cost and volume level as well as whether comparable substitutes are available. Negotiated transfer prices are commonly used for customized high-cost and high-volume services such as risk management and specialized executive training.

Ability to negotiate a transfer price implies that segment managers have the autonomy to sell or buy products externally if internal negotiations fail. Because such extensive autonomy could lead to dysfunctional behavior and suboptimization, top management can provide a means of arbitrating a price in the event that the units cannot agree. Another way of reducing the difficulties in establishing a transfer price is simply to use a dual pricing approach.

Dual Pricing A **dual pricing arrangement** provides different transfer prices for the selling and buying segments by allowing the seller to record the transfer of goods at a market or negotiated market price and the purchaser to record the transfer at a cost-based amount. This arrangement provides a profit margin on the goods transferred from the selling division but a minimal cost to the buying division. Dual pricing eliminates the problem of having to artificially divide the profits between the selling and buying segments and allows managers to have the most relevant information for decision making and performance evaluation. However, an internal reconciliation (similar to that used in preparing consolidated statements when intercompany sales are made at an amount other than cost) is needed to adjust revenues and costs when company external financial statements are prepared.

Selecting a Transfer Pricing System

Setting a reasonable transfer price is not an easy task. Everyone involved in the process must be aware of both positive and negative aspects of each type of transfer price and be responsive to suggestions for change. The type of transfer pricing system selected should reflect the organizational units' characteristics as well as corporate goals. No single method of setting a transfer price is best in all instances, and all organizational units may not be able to use transfer pricing. For example, support departments that do not provide measurable benefits or cannot show a distinct cause-and-effect relationship between cost behavior and service use by other departments should not attempt to use transfer prices.

Transfer prices are not intended to be permanent; they are frequently revised in relation to changes in costs, supply, demand, competitive forces, and other factors. Flexibility by the selling segment to increase a transfer price when reduced productive capacity is present or to decrease a transfer price when excess productive capacity exists is a strong management lever. A company should evaluate the following potential negative and positive outcomes of transfer prices before instituting such a system.

Negative transfer pricing system outcomes:	Positive transfer pricing system outcomes:
• Disagreement between unit managers as to how the transfer price should be set • Additional organizational costs and employee time • The potential for dysfunctional behavior among organizational units and for underutilization or overutilization of services • The need for year-end entries to eliminate the transfer prices	• An appropriate basis for calculating and evaluating segment performance • Information to make rational acquisition decisions about transfers of goods and services between corporate divisions • The flexibility to respond to changes in demand or market conditions • A means of encouraging and rewarding goal congruence by managers in decentralized operations

7 What difficulties can be encountered by multinational companies using transfer prices?

TRANSFER PRICES IN MULTINATIONAL SETTINGS

A common use of transfer prices is to determine the tax effects created by moving products between organizational units located in different tax jurisdictions. Because of differences in tax systems, customs duties, freight and insurance costs, import/export regulations, and foreign-exchange controls, setting transfer prices for products and services becomes extremely difficult when a company has multinational operations.[9] To gain the best outcome, a multi-disciplinary team (see Exhibit 13.19) should be involved in establishing a transfer pricing system.

Exhibit 13.19 Cross-Discipline Approach to Transfer Pricing

Tax

- Acts as project driver
- Ensures objectives are met
- Makes sure all tax requirements are met
- Handles notifications to tax authorities
- Provides documentation/defense

Finance

- Advises on and develops solutions for management systems
- Addresses the ability of the financial reporting system to handle implications of transfer pricing
- Provides required financial data, including segmented data and budgets
- Assists in (or takes primary responsibility for) developing and running transfer pricing models

Accounting

- Provides information on accounting systems, accounting rules, consolidation of accounts
- Administers invoicing/booking/settlement of intercompany payments

Legal

- Oversees development of intercompany legal agreements and legal pricing requirements

Information Technology

- Assists in developing software, a programming interface with the transfer pricing model, and an internal financial system

Customs

- Assesses valuation, duty impacts, and representation and notification requirements

Operations: Members with Global Business Experience

- Assist in determining foreign implications of transfer pricing policy
- Act as intermediaries between local and foreign businesspeople
- May be structured similarly to local core team

Outside Advisers

- Bring industry best practices to the internal team
- Provide access to global expertise in international tax, transfer pricing, valuation, VAT, and customs
- Offer insight into expectations of auditors with respect to tax provisions, including FAS 109, FIN 48, and Sarbanes-Oxley requirements for U.S. Securities and Exchange Commission registrants

Source: KPMG LLP (U.S.), *Improving Transfer Pricing Risk Management in High-Technology Companies* (2008), p. 10; http://www.kpmg.com/Ca/en/IssuesAndInsights/ArticlesPublications/Documents/Improving%20Transfer%20Pricing%20Risk%20Management%20in%20High-Technology%20Companies.pdf (accessed 12/30/11).

[9] Similar to international settings, multistate firms can employ transfer pricing strategies to move profits from state to state. The various states have different income tax rates—and some have no tax at all.

Although multinational enterprises (MNEs) can use different transfer prices for the same product being sent to, or received from, different countries, the company's transfer pricing policies should be followed consistently. For example, a parent company should not price services performed for foreign subsidiaries in a way that sends the greatest cost amount to the subsidiary in the country with the highest tax rate *unless* that method of pricing is reasonable and equitable to all subsidiaries. The general test of reasonableness is that a transfer price should reflect an arm's-length transaction or what the price would be on the open market.[10] Thus, although the cost-plus approach is used most commonly by MNEs for products and services, tax authorities prefer market-based methods.[11]

As shown in Exhibit 13.20, the internal and external objectives of transfer pricing policies differ in multinational entities. In addition to MNE objectives, countries have specific goals in relation to transfer prices: to protect the country tax base and to encourage foreign direct investment and cross-border trade. Thus, tax authorities in both the home and host countries carefully scrutinize multinational transfer prices because such prices determine which country taxes the income from the transfer. The U.S. Congress is concerned about both U.S. multinationals operating in low-tax-rate countries and foreign companies operating in the United States. In either situation, Congress believes that companies could avoid paying U.S. corporate income taxes because of misleading or inaccurate transfer pricing. Thus, the Internal Revenue Service (IRS) can be quick to investigate U.S. subsidiaries that operate in low-tax areas and have unusually high profits.

Exhibit 13.20 Multinational Company Transfer Pricing Objectives

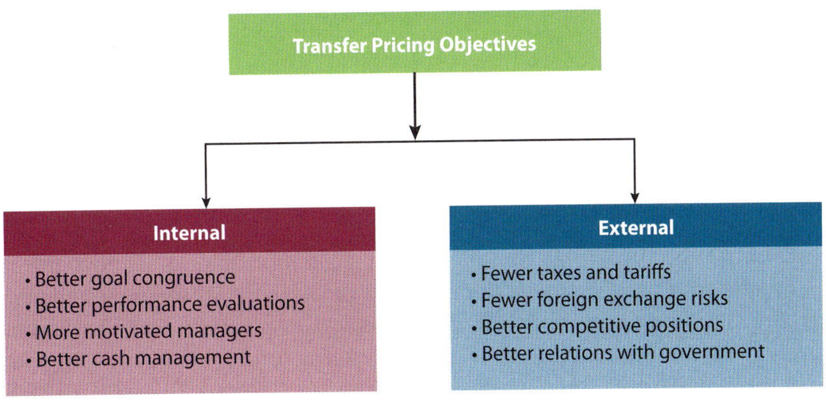

Source: Wagdy M. Abdallah, "Guidelines for CEOs in Transfer Pricing Policies," *Management Accounting* (September 1988), p. 61. Copyright 1988 by Institute of Management Accountants. Reproduced with permission of Institute of Management Accountants in the format Textbook via Copyright Clearance Center.

Advance pricing agreements (APAs) are binding contracts between the IRS and a company that provide details of how a transfer price is to be set. An APA establishes that no adjustments or penalties will be made if the agreed-upon methodology is used. These agreements usually run for three to five years and may be renewed if no major changes occur. APAs also help eliminate the possibility of double taxation on the exchange of goods or services. One disadvantage of seeking an APA is that, because of a scarcity of resources, IRS approval of the APA often took substantial time (an average of 37.2 months for all new and renewal applications in 2010).[12] In 2011, the IRS made a significant change in the APA program to streamline the time needed to execute an APA and to resolve transfer

[10] Another method, referred to as global formulary apportionment, is also acceptable in the United States. However, the OECD views this methodology as contrary to the arm's-length principle. A discussion of this issue can be found in multiple articles, including R. Feinschreiber and M. Kent, "Behind the OECD's Attack on Global Formulary Apportionment," *Journal of International Taxation* (September 2011), pp. 45–51.

[11] Ernst & Young, *2010 Global Transfer Pricing Survey*; http://www.ey.com/Publication/vwLUAssets/2010_Global_transfer_pricing_survey_low_res/$FILE/2010_Global_transfer_pricing_survey_lowres.pdf (last accessed 12/30/11).

[12] J. Hinding, *Announcement and Report Concerning Advance Pricing Agreements* (March 29, 2011), p. 11; http://www.irs.gov/pub/irs-utl/2010statutoryreport.pdf (last accessed 12/30/11).

pricing disputes.[13] An important advantage of APAs is that they may fulfill documentation requirements under the Sarbanes-Oxley Act of 2002 (SOX) to substantiate "proper allocation of revenues and expenses" making the "development of effective, SOX-compliant internal controls more attainable and acceptable."[14] Transfer pricing is viewed as the most important international tax issue for parent company MNEs.[15] Additionally, one 2010 survey found that 68 percent of respondents had their transfer pricing policy examined by tax authorities.[16] Exhibit 13.21 indicates some of the items that may trigger transfer pricing audits or reviews in MNEs. Different countries have different triggers and may target specific industries.

Exhibit 13.21 Potential Transfer Pricing Audit/Review Triggers (in Parent Companies)

- Related party transactions
- Royalties, intellectual property, and other intangibles
- Management service fees
- Financing arrangements
- Business reorganizations/restructurings
- Use of tax havens or low-tax rate jurisdictions
- Sustained past losses
- Unusual pricing methods or transactions
- Limited, poor, or highly aggregated transfer pricing documentation
- Gross profit increases at parent company with no change or lowered net profit
- High profits in foreign subsidiaries relative to parent company profits
- Unusual statistical benchmarks compared with industry
- Prior transfer pricing issues with tax authorities

Source: Based on information in the "audit risk/transfer pricing scrutiny" sections of the Ernst & Young, *Transfer Pricing Global Reference Guide* (November 2010); http://www.ey.com/Publication/vwLUAssets/2011_Transfer_pricing_reference_guide/$File/2011_Transfer_pricing_global_reference_guide.pdf (accessed 12/30/11).

More countries are adopting transfer pricing legislation and, as MNEs begin doing business in a new country, they must comply with that country's tax requirements relative to transfer pricing. The Organization for Economic Cooperation and Development has been actively involved in helping to establish internationally accepted procedures for APAs.[17] In February 2007, the European Commission adopted EU-wide guidelines on APAs to "simplify or prevent costly and time-consuming tax examinations into the transactions included in the APA" and eliminate double taxation within the EU.[18]

[13] Ernst & Young, "Advance Pricing Agreement Program Moves to Large Business & International Division," *International Tax Alert* (July 29, 2011); http://www.ey.com/Publication/vwLUAssets/ITA_29July_2011/$FILE/ITA_29July2011.pdf (last accessed 12/29/11).

[14] Mitch McGhee, "SOX and APAs: A Look at Their Compatibility," *Strategic Finance* (May 2007), pp. 15ff.

[15] Ernst & Young, *2010 Global Transfer Pricing Survey.*

[16] Ernst & Young, *2010 Global Transfer Pricing Survey.*

[17] The OECD issued new *Transfer Pricing Guidelines for Multinational Enterprises and Tax Administrations* in August 2010.

[18] Commission of the European Communities, *Communication from the Commission to the Council, the European Parliament and the European Economic and Social Committee on the Work of the EU Joint Transfer Pricing Forum in the Field of Dispute Avoidance and Resolution Procedures and on Guidelines for Advance Pricing Agreements within the EU* (February 2, 2007), Section 1; http://www.transferpricing.com/pdf/EU%20-%20Dispute%20Avoidance.pdf (last accessed 12/30/11).

Comprehensive Review Module

KEY TERMS

administrative department, p. 510
advance pricing agreement (APA), p. 525
algebraic method, p. 513
benefits-provided ranking, p. 512
centralization, p. 503
cost center, p. 508
decentralization, p. 503
direct method, p. 512
dual pricing arrangement, p. 523
goal congruence, p. 508
investment center, p. 510
negotiated transfer price, p. 522
profit center, p. 510
pseudo-profit center, p. 520
responsibility accounting system, p. 505
responsibility center, p. 508
responsibility report, p. 505
revenue center, p. 509
sales price variance (SPV), p. 509
sales volume variance (SVV), p. 509
service department, p. 510
shared service, p. 504
step method, p. 512
suboptimization, p. 510
support department, p. 510
transfer price, p. 519

CHAPTER SUMMARY

1 Decentralization

- Decentralization is generally appropriate for companies that
  - are mature.
  - are large.
  - are in a growth stage of product development.
  - are growing rapidly.
  - can financially withstand incorrect decisions.
  - have high confidence in the employees' decision-making ability.
  - have widespread operations.
  - want to challenge, motivate, and mentor employees.
  - require rapid response to changing conditions or opportunities.

2 Relationship Between Decentralization and Responsibility Accounting

- Decentralization is made to work effectively through the use of responsibility accounting, which provides information about the
  - performance,
  - efficiency, and
  - effectiveness of organizational responsibility centers and their managers.
- Decentralization implies the acceptance of authority by subordinate managers, and the responsibility accounting system produces reports that indicate the "rolling up" of that authority back to upper management.
- Decentralization requires each responsibility center to report on the activities under its manager's immediate control.
- Decentralization uses the principle of management by exception, which is reflected in the successively aggregated responsibility reports.
- Decentralization seeks goal congruence and uses responsibility reports to highlight any suboptimal use of resources.

3 Types of Responsibility Centers

- Cost centers are organizational units in which managers are primarily responsible for controlling costs.
- Revenue centers are organizational units in which managers are primarily responsible for generating revenues, although in some instances, managers have control over revenues and some costs.
- Profit centers are organizational units in which managers are responsible for generating revenue, controlling costs, and maximizing their units' incomes.
- Investment centers are organizational units in which managers are responsible for generating revenue, controlling costs, and producing a satisfactory return on the asset base under their control.

4 Revenue Variances

- Revenue centers calculate variances created by price or volume of units sold.
- The sales price variance is calculated as actual volume × (actual sales price − budgeted sales price).
- The sales volume variance is calculated as budgeted sales price × (actual volume − budgeted volume).
- The total revenue variance is calculated as sales price variance + sales volume variance.

5 Support Department Cost Allocations

- Support departments are service and administrative departments (i.e., non-revenue generating).
- Support department costs are allocated to producing departments to meet one or more objectives:
  - full cost computation,
  - managerial motivation, and/or
  - managerial decision making.
- Support department costs are allocated using the direct, step, or algebraic method:
  - The direct method assigns support department costs only to operating departments but does not consider assistance that can be provided from one support department to another.
  - The step method uses a benefits-provided ranking that lists support departments from the one providing the most assistance to other departments to the one providing assistance primarily to the operating areas. Costs are assigned from each department in order of the ranking.
  - The algebraic method recognizes the interrelationships among all departments through the use of simultaneous equations. This method provides the best allocation information and is readily adaptable to computer computations.

6 Transfer Prices

- Transfer prices are intracompany charges for goods or services bought and sold between segments of a decentralized company.
- Transfer prices may be cost based, market based, or negotiated; a dual pricing system can also be used to assign different transfer prices to the selling and buying units.
- Transfer prices are set between two boundaries:
  - The upper price boundary is the lowest market price at which the product/service can be acquired externally.
  - The lowest price boundary is the incremental cost of production or performance plus the opportunity cost of the facilities used.
- Transfer prices are used in organizations to
  - enhance goal congruence.
  - make performance evaluations among segments more comparable.
  - change a cost center into a pseudo-profit center.
  - ensure optimal resource allocations.
  - promote responsibility center autonomy.
  - encourage motivation and communication among responsibility center managers.

7 Transfer Prices in Multinational Companies

- Multinational companies using transfer prices encounter difficulties, including differences in
  - tax systems,
  - customs duties,
  - freight and insurance costs,
  - import/export regulations, and
  - foreign-exchange controls.
- Multinational companies must attempt to determine what transfer price would be considered "reasonable" as if generated in an arm's-length transaction.
- Multinational companies face an increase in transfer pricing audits by tax authorities.
- Advanced pricing agreements are binding contracts with tax authorities that indicate no adjustments or penalties will be assessed if the agreements are followed.

SOLUTION STRATEGIES

Revenue Variances, p. 509

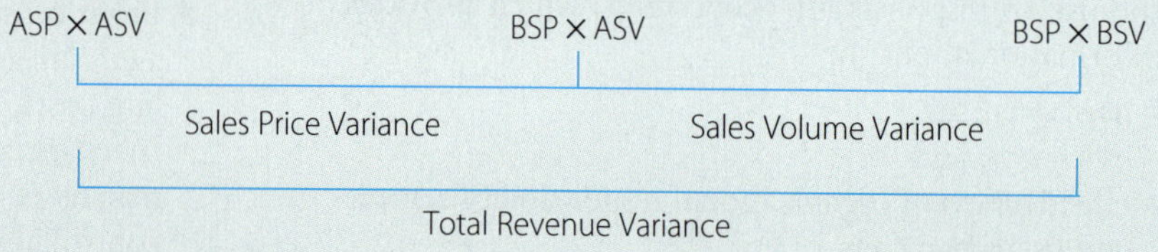

Transfer Prices (Cost Based, Market Based, Negotiated, Dual), p. 520

Upper limit: Lowest price available from external suppliers

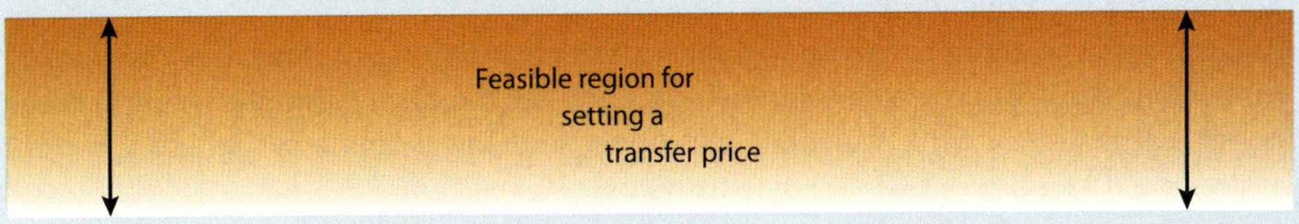

Lower limit: Incremental costs of producing and selling the transferred goods or services plus the opportunity cost of the facilities used

Service Department Cost Allocation, p. 513

Direct Method, p. 513

1. Determine rational and systematic allocation bases for each support department.
2. Assign costs from each support department directly to operating areas using specified allocation bases. No costs are assigned to support areas.

Step Method, p. 514

1. Determine rational and systematic allocation bases for each support department.
2. List support departments in a benefits-provided ranking from the one that provides the most assistance to all other areas (both operating and support) to the one that provides assistance only to operating areas.
3. Beginning with the first support department listed, allocate the costs from that department to all remaining departments; repeat the process until only operating departments remain.

Algebraic Method, p. 515

1. Determine rational and systematic allocation bases for each department.
2. Develop equations that express the costs of, and service relationships among, support areas.
3. Solve the simultaneous equations for the support departments through an iterative process or by computer until all values are known.
4. Allocate costs using allocation bases developed in step 2. Eliminate "reallocated" costs from consideration.

DEMONSTRATION PROBLEM

RaceFest Inc. has two operating divisions. The Ski Division makes water and snow skis, and the Binding Division makes rubber boots for water skis. The Binding Division estimates that 800,000 pairs of boots will be produced in 2013; of those, 600,000 pairs will be sold to the Ski Division and 200,000 pairs will be sold externally. Managers of the two divisions are in the process of determining a transfer price for a pair of boots. The following information for the Binding Division is available:

Direct material	$27	
Direct labor	12	
Variable overhead	7	
Variable S&A (both for external and internal sales)	4	
Total variable cost		$50
Fixed overhead (rate based on estimated annual production)	$10	
Fixed selling and administrative (rate based on estimated annual sales)	5	
Total fixed cost		15
Total cost per pair of boots		$65
Markup on total variable cost (40%)		20
List price to external customers		$85

Required:

a. Determine a transfer price based on variable production cost.
b. Determine a transfer price based on total variable production cost plus normal markup.
c. Determine a transfer price based on full production cost.

d. Determine a transfer price based on total cost per pair of boots.
e. Prepare the journal entries for the Binding (selling) and Ski (buying) segments if the transfer is made at the external selling price for the selling division and the full production cost for the buying division.
f. Assume that the Binding Division has no alternative use for the facilities that make the rubber boots for internal transfer. Also assume that the Ski Division can buy equivalent boots externally for $80. Calculate the upper and lower limits for which the transfer price should be set.
g. Using the information in (f), compute a transfer price that divides the "profit" between the two divisions equally.
h. Assume that a large portion of the facilities in which boots are produced can be rented for $600,000 if the Binding Division makes boots only for external sale. Determine the lower limit of the transfer price.

Solution to Demonstration Problem

a.	Direct material	$27
	Direct labor	12
	Variable overhead	7
	Transfer price	$46
b.	Total variable cost	$50
	Markup (40%)	20
	Transfer price	$70
c.	Variable production cost	$46
	Fixed production cost	10
	Transfer price	$56
d.	Total variable cost	$50
	Total fixed cost	15
	Transfer price	$65

e. Binding Division:

Accounts Receivable—Ski Division (600,000 × $56)	33,600,000	
Intracompany Profits* (600,000 × $29)	17,400,000	
Intracompany Sales* (600,000 × $85)		51,000,000
Intracompany Cost of Goods Sold (CGS)* (600,000 × $56)	33,600,000	
Finished Goods (600,000 × $56)		33,600,000

**Note: When company income statements are prepared, these amounts would be eliminated as follows:*

Intracompany Sales	51,000,000	
Intracompany CGS		33,600,000
Intracompany Profits		17,400,000

In addition, any remaining amounts of intracompany Accounts Receivable and Accounts Payable shown by the two divisions would be eliminated

Ski Division:

Inventory (600,000 × $56)	33,600,000	
Accounts Payable—Binding Division		33,600,000

In addition, any remaining amounts of intracompany Accounts Receivable and Accounts Payable shown by the two divisions would be eliminated

f. Upper limit: Ski Division's external purchase price = $80
Lower limit: Total variable cost of Binding Division = $50
g. (Lower limit + Upper limit) ÷ 2 = ($50 + $80) ÷ 2 = $130 ÷ 2 = $65
h. $600,000 ÷ 600,000 pairs of boots = $1 opportunity cost per pair
Lower limit: Incremental variable cost of Binding Division + Opportunity cost = $50 + $1 = $51

POTENTIAL ETHICAL ISSUES

ETHICS

1. Having managers engage in suboptimization acts that benefit themselves to the detriment of the overall firm
2. Creating responsibility reports that "bury" important details needed to accurately evaluate managerial performance in summary data
3. Allocating support department costs using an "ability-to-bear" criterion that results in profit-detrimental actions
4. Improperly estimating the benefits provided between departments to shift support department costs inappropriately
5. Establishing a transfer pricing system that does not allow managers who will be judged on profitability performance to buy or sell externally
6. Engaging in transfer pricing techniques that improperly shift costs to low- or no-tax locations
7. Using non-arm's-length transfer pricing techniques that create losses through aggressive tax planning

QUESTIONS

1. Wayne Litcomb is the president and chief operating officer of Litcomb Electronics. He founded the company and has led it to prominence in the electronics field. He has manufacturing plants or retail outlets in 40 states. Litcomb is finding, however, that he cannot "keep track" of things the way he did previously. Discuss the advantages and disadvantages of decentralizing the firm's decision-making activities among the various local and regional managers. Also discuss what functions Litcomb might want to be performed centrally and why he would choose these functions.
2. Why are responsibility reports prepared? Is it appropriate for a single responsibility report to be prepared for a division of a major company? Why or why not?
3. What is suboptimization, and what factors contribute to it in a decentralized firm?
4. Why are support department costs often allocated to operating departments? Is such an allocation process always useful from a decision-making standpoint? How might support department cost allocation create a feeling of cost responsibility among managers of operating departments?
5. "The four criteria for selecting an allocation base for support department costs should be applied equally." Discuss the merits of this statement.
6. Compare and contrast the direct, step, and algebraic methods of allocating support department costs. What are the advantages and disadvantages of each method?
7. When the algebraic method of allocating support department costs is used, total costs for each support department increase from what they were prior to the allocation. Why does this occur, and how are the additional costs treated?
8. What are transfer prices, and why do companies use them? How could the use of transfer prices improve or impair goal congruence?
9. What problems might be encountered when attempting to implement a cost-based transfer pricing system? A market-based transfer pricing system?
10. What type of transfer price would you recommend be used in each of the following selling and buying responsibility centers: cost, revenue, profit, and investment? How and why would such prices be set?
11. What is dual pricing? What is the intended effect of dual pricing on the performance of each division affected by the dual price?
12. How can support departments use transfer prices, and what advantages do transfer prices have over cost allocation methods?
13. Explain why the determination of transfer prices is more complex in a multinational, rather than in a domestic, setting.
14. How are transfer prices involved in cap-and-trade schemes for carbon and other emissions?

EXERCISES

15. **LO.1 (Decentralization advantages and disadvantages)** Indicate whether each of the following is a potential advantage (A) or disadvantage (D) of decentralization. If an item is neither an advantage nor a disadvantage, use N.
    a. Promotion of goal congruence
    b. Use of management-by-exception principle by top management
    c. Development of leadership qualities
    d. Support of training in decision making
    e. Provision of increased job satisfaction
    f. Intricacies of communication process
    g. Cost of developing the planning and reporting system
    h. Speed of decisions
    i. Delegation of ultimate responsibility
    j. Placement of decision maker closer to time and place of problem

16. **LO.1 (Centralization vs. decentralization)** Indicate whether a firm exhibiting each of the following characteristics would more likely be centralized (C) or decentralized (D).
    a. Few employees
    b. Wary of financial impacts of incorrect subordinate management decisions
    c. Subordinates highly trained and mentored in decision-making skills
    d. Slow growth rate
    e. Two years old
    f. Stable market environment
    g. Growth stage of product development
    h. High level of organizational flexibility
    i. Large number of employees who telecommute
    j. Tight management control
    k. Widely dispersed operating units
    l. High cost of gathering information
    m. Redundancy of functions is minimized
    n. Few interdependencies among organizational units

INTERNET

17. **LO.1 (Centralization vs. decentralization; research; writing)** Many companies are trying to determine the best organizational structure for information technology (IT) operations. Although IT operations had been decentralized in the past, there has been a growing trend to bring such operations back to a central location. Use the Internet to gather research to compare and contrast the advantages and disadvantages of centralized and decentralized IT operations. What other important information would you need to make a decision on such an organizational structure?

INTERNET

18. **LO.1 & LO.6 (Decentralization; transfer prices; research; writing)** Search the Internet to identify three highly decentralized companies. Based on the information you find on each, either determine directly or infer the types of responsibility centers used by these companies. Also, determine or speculate about whether the companies use transfer prices or allocation of costs for intracompany transfers of services. Prepare a report on your findings and inferences. In cases for which you had to infer, explain what information or reasoning led you to that inference. Why is decentralization appropriate for some companies but not for others?

19. **LO.3 (Profit centers and allocations; research)** Multiple-doctor medical practices are often structured with each doctor acting as a profit center.
    a. Discuss why such an organizational structure would be appropriate.
    b. Go to the web and find some software packages that could be used to account for such an organizational structure.
    c. List some costs of a medical practice that would be directly traceable to each physician.
    d. List some costs of a medical practice that might not be directly traceable to each physician. Provide possible allocation bases for such costs.

20. **LO.3 (Responsibility centers; research)** Go to your university's Web site and review the various organizational units within the university. Assuming no transfer pricing exists, make a list of the units that you believe would be classified as cost centers and profit centers.

INTERNET

21. **LO.3 (Responsibility centers)** For each of the following organizational units, indicate whether the unit would most likely be classified as a cost center (C), a revenue center (R), a profit center (P), or an investment center (I):

a. University-owned bookstore
b. Local public television station's fund-raising telethon staffed by volunteers
c. Corporate-owned local outlet of a fast-food restaurant
d. Bloodmobile of a local hospital
e. Beijing office of an international public accounting firm
f. Wildlife management department in a national or state park
g. Long-term parking lot at a regional airport
h. City ticket office of an airline
i. Cafeteria of a for-profit hospital
j. Fine jewelry counter in a local department store
k. Laundry of a large bed-and-breakfast
l. Sales representative for a college textbook publisher
m. Fraud investigation department of a major retailer

22. **LO.3 (Responsibility centers)** Nussbaum Inc. is a chemical company that is comprised of five independent divisions, located in three different countries. Divisional managers are evaluated based on divisional profitability. Home office functions include human resources, accounting, and environmental management (EM). Projects of the EM group are solicited and paid for by the contracting operating divisions. Nussbaum's transfer pricing policy requires EM to charge the operating divisions a market-based price for services.

a. Is the EM group centralized or decentralized?
b. What type of responsibility center is the EM group?
c. What potential problems exist from having the EM group charge a market-based transfer price for its services?

23. **LO.4 (Revenue variances)** You have asked your sales manager to explain why budgeted revenues for your division are below expectations. The budget indicated \$472,500 of revenues based on a sales volume of 675,000 units. Sales records indicate that 682,000 product units were actually sold, but revenues were only \$463,760. Analyze revenues and explain what occurred.

24. **LO.4 (Revenue variances)** Ha-Chin Yi delivers two-day statistical process control seminars for manufacturing workers. For each program, a \$4,000 fee is normally paid. In 2012, Yi presented 30 seminars, and he budgeted a 30 percent increase in seminars for 2013. At the end of 2013, Yi is disappointed that his actual revenue is only \$154,350. He presented 42 seminars during the year.

a. What was Yi's expected revenue for 2013?
b. What were Yi's sales price and sales volume variances?
c. Discuss why Yi did not achieve his budgeted 2013 revenue.

25. **LO.4 (Revenue variances)** For 2013, Logitom planned to sell 460,000 units at a \$39 selling price. In early 2014, the marketing manager was asked to explain why budgeted revenue had not been achieved. Investigation revealed the following information:

Actual sales volume	473,000 units
Actual selling price	\$38 per unit

Analyze the information given and prepare the explanation that Logitom's marketing manager should present.

26. **LO.5 (Step method)** Leander Mfg. has three support departments (human resources, administration, and maintenance) and two revenue-generating departments (assembly and finishing). The company uses the step method to allocate support department costs to operating departments. In October 2013, human resources incurred \$360,000 of

costs, administration incurred $558,000, and maintenance incurred $170,000. Proportions of services provided to other departments for October 2013 follow.

	Human Resources	Administration	Maintenance
Human resources		10%	5%
Administration	10%		15
Maintenance	15	10	
Assembly	40	50	45
Finishing	35	30	35

a. Assuming that the departments are listed in a benefits-provided ranking, what amount of cost should be assigned from human resources to each of the other departments? From administration? From maintenance?
b. What total support department cost was assigned to assembly in October? To finishing?
c. Explain why the cost allocation is affected by the order in which costs are assigned.

EXCEL

27. **LO.5 (Direct method)** Prosperous Bank has three support areas (administration, human resources, and accounting) and three revenue-generating areas (checking accounts, savings accounts, and loans). Monthly direct costs and the interdepartmental support structure are shown in the following benefits-provided ranking:

		PERCENTAGE OF SERVICE USED BY					
Department	**Direct Costs**	**Admin.**	**Human Resources**	**Accounting**	**Checking**	**Savings**	**Loans**
Administration	$540,000		10	10	30	40	10
Human resources	360,000	10		10	30	20	30
Accounting	300,000	10	10		40	20	20
Checking	630,000						
Savings	337,500						
Loans	675,000						

Compute the total cost for each revenue-generating area of the bank using the direct method.

EXCEL

28. **LO.5 (Step method)** Use the information in Exercise 27 to compute total cost for each revenue-generating area if Prosperous Bank uses the step method of cost allocation.

29. **LO.5 (Direct method)** Andreka Inc. uses the direct method to allocate support department costs to production departments (fabricating and finishing). Information for June 2013 follows.

	Human Resources	Administration
Service department costs	$630,000	$450,000
Services provided to other departments		
Human resources		10%
Administration	20%	
Fabricating	35%	50%
Finishing	45%	40%

a. What amounts of human resources and administration costs should be assigned to Fabricating for June?
b. What amounts of human resources and administration costs should be assigned to Finishing for June?

EXCEL

30. **LO.5 (Algebraic method)** Use the information for Prosperous Bank in Exercise 27 to compute the total cost for each revenue-generating area using the algebraic method.

EXCEL

31. **LO.5 (Algebraic method)** The following chart indicates the percentage of support department services used by other departments. Service departments are designated S1, S2, and S3; operating departments are designated RP1 and RP2.

	SERVICES USED				
Department	**S1**	**S2**	**S3**	**RP1**	**RP2**
S1	N/A	10%	20%	30%	40%
S2	40%	N/A	30	20	10
S3	20	30	N/A	40	10

Direct costs of the period were $170,000, $360,000, and $600,000 for S1, S2, and S3, respectively. Allocate the support department costs to the operating departments using the algebraic method.

32. **LO.6 (Transfer pricing)** Walsdorf Company's information technology department is developing a support department transfer price based on minutes of computer time. For 2013, its expected capacity was 700,000 minutes, and theoretical capacity was 1,000,000 minutes. Costs of the IT department for 2013 were expected to total $665,000.

    a. What is the IT transfer price based on expected capacity?
    b. What is the IT transfer price based on full capacity?
    c. Actual operating costs of the IT department for 2013 were $689,400, and actual capacity usage was 730,000 minutes. What were the total variances from budget if the IT department used a transfer price based on expected capacity? On full capacity? What are some possible causes of that variance?

33. **LO.6 (Transfer pricing; management motivation; writing)** Great Taste Food Stores operates 20 large supermarkets in the East. Each store is evaluated as a profit center, and store managers have complete control over their purchases and inventory policy. Company policy is that transfers between stores will be made at cost if a store runs short of an item and another store has a sufficient supply.

    During a recent period of rapid increases in food prices, company managers noticed that interstore transfers had decreased sharply. Store managers indicated that it was almost impossible to find another store with sufficient inventory to make a transfer when one store ran short of inventory. However, more in-depth checking revealed that many of the other stores did actually have the inventory items on hand.

    a. Why would the store managers be reluctant to make the interstore transfers?
    b. How could the transfer pricing policy be changed to avoid this type of situation?

34. **LO.6 (Transfer pricing)** Peyvandi Co., a profit center of California Enterprises, manufactures Product BP3751-9S to sell internally to other company divisions as well as externally. One unit of Product BP3751-9S sells for $72. Production and selling costs for a unit of Product BP3751-9S follow.

Direct material	$ 9.00
Direct labor	11.40
Variable overhead	4.80
Fixed overhead (based on production of 1,400,000 units)	16.50
Variable selling expense	3.00

Andersen Co., another division of California Enterprises, wants to purchase 50,000 units of Product BP3751-9S from Peyvandi Co. during the next year. No selling costs are incurred on internal sales.

a. All the units of Product BP3751-9S that can be produced by Peyvandi Enterprises can be sold externally. What should the minimum transfer price be? Explain.
b. Assume that Peyvandi Co. is experiencing a slight slowdown in external demand and will be able to sell only 1,200,000 units of Product BP3751-9S externally next year at the $72 selling price. What should be the minimum selling price to Andersen Co. under these conditions? Explain.
c. Assume that Joe Dhir, the manager of Andersen Co., offers to pay Peyvandi Co.'s production cost plus 25 percent for each unit of Product BP3751-9S. Dhir receives an invoice for $2,606,250 but was planning on only $1,575,000. How were these amounts determined? What created the confusion? Explain.

35. **LO.6 (Transfer pricing)** Elba Division of Haimes Industries manufactures product #54B89. Three-fourths of the production is transferred to the Crete Division of Haimes Industries; the remainder is sold externally for $67 per unit. The following information is available about product #54B89:

Total production annually	1,200,000 units
Variable production costs	$40
Variable selling costs (includes $4 per unit in advertising cost)	$16
Fixed overhead (allocated on the basis of units of production)	$1,800,000
Fixed selling costs	$2,400,000

a. Determine the transfer price under each of the following methods:
   (1) total variable cost
   (2) full production cost
   (3) total variable production cost plus allocated fixed selling costs
   (4) market price

b. What transfer price do you think Elba Division should use to "sell" the units to Crete Division?

36. **LO.6 (Transfer pricing)** Qvat Division, a subsidiary of Imogene Ltd., manufactures a silicon chip with the following costs:

Direct material	$15.00
Direct labor	26.25
Variable overhead	12.75
Fixed overhead	18.00
Total	$72.00

Some of the chips are sold externally for $162; others are transferred internally to the Kwak Division. Qvat Division's plant manager wants to establish a reasonable transfer price for chips transferred to Kwak. The purchasing manager of Kwak Division has informed the plant manager that comparable chips can be purchased externally in a price range from $112.50 to $172.50.

a. Determine the upper and lower limits for the transfer price between Qvat Division and Kwak Division.
b. If Qvat Division is presently selling all the chips it can produce to external buyers, what minimum price should be set for transfers to Kwak Division?

37. **LO.6 (Transfer pricing)** Squish Corp. has two divisions: Production (which makes pillow foam) and Assembly (which makes pillows). Division managers can choose to purchase components internally or externally. For each pound of foam, the Production Division incurs $4 of variable cost and $1 of fixed cost with a production capacity of 30,000 pounds per month; the division recently increased its transfer price to Assembly to $5.50 to cover full production cost and provide a profit margin to the Production Division. Assembly's manager has decided to begin purchasing foam externally for $4.50 per pound.

a. Assume that Production Division has no alternative uses for its manufacturing facilities. Fixed costs could not be avoided by external purchases. What is the monthly advantage (or disadvantage) to Squish Corp. if the foam is purchased internally?
b. Assume that, rather than manufacturing foam, the Production Division manufacturing facilities can be rented for $25,000 per month. What is the monthly advantage (or disadvantage) to Squish Corp. if the foam is purchased internally?
c. Assume that Squish decides to stop internal foam production and rent out the facilities for $25,000 per month. Thus, Assembly Division begins buying all of its production needs externally at $4.50 per pound. What short- or long-term effects would these transactions have on Squish Corp.?

38. **LO.6 (Transfer pricing)** Mogi Corp. manufactures one primary product, which is processed through two divisions (P and R). Costs for each division are:

	P	R
Variable cost per gallon	$3	$15
Fixed cost per gallon	2	12

P Division produces 25,000 gallons per month. R Division uses 40,000 gallons per month; of that, 25,000 gallons are purchased internally and 15,000 are purchased externally at $10 per gallon. After processing through R Division, a gallon of final product can be sold for $55.

a. What would be P's transfer price to R Division if the price is set at 180 percent of variable cost?
b. What would be P's transfer price to R Division if the price is set at 130 percent of full cost?
c. What would be P's transfer price to R Division if the price is set at market value?
d. What is Mogi Corp.'s operating profit if all 40,000 gallons of product are transferred in a month? By how much would this profit increase if R Division could acquire all necessary gallons internally?

39. **LO.6 (Transfer pricing in support departments)** Indicate whether each of the following statements constitutes a potential advantage (A), disadvantage (D), or neither (N) of using transfer prices for support department costs.

a. Requires additional organizational data and employee time
b. Puts all support departments on an equal footing
c. Reduces goal congruence
d. Makes a support department into a profit center
e. Increases resource waste
f. Improves ability to evaluate performance
g. Increases communication about which additional services are needed and which ones can be reduced or eliminated
h. Increases disagreements among departments
i. Causes certain services to be under- or overutilized
j. Makes users and providers more cost conscious
k. Measures benefits provided to operating departments
l. Includes costs outside a manager's control

40. **LO.7 (International transfer pricing; research; writing)** Use the Internet to identify a multinational company encountering tax problems related to transfer pricing between its organizational units in different countries. Prepare a brief discussion of the issues and the actual or potential consequences.

INTERNET

PROBLEMS

41. **LO.1 (Decentralization; ethics; writing)** Although centralization and decentralization are commonly discussed in the context of business organizations and distinct, often "far-flung" subunits, the concepts are also applicable within a single building! Consider that, in the last 25 years, most hospitals began shifting from centralized nursing stations to decentralized stations that were close to patients' rooms. This trend was thought to make it easier for nurses to attend to patients and to maintain their charts.

a. Why did the shift from centralized stations to decentralized stations take place?
b. What problems could be created by the decentralized nurse stations that did not exist when centralized stations were more common?

42. **LO.1 (Decentralization; ethics; writing)** A large U.S. corporation participates in a highly competitive industry. Company management has decided that decentralization will best allow the company to meet the competition and achieve profit goals. Each responsibility center manager is evaluated on the basis of profit contribution, market penetration, and return on investment. Failure to meet the objectives established by corporate management for these measures is not acceptable and usually results in demotion or dismissal of a center manager.

ETHICS

An anonymous survey of company managers showed that they felt extreme pressure to compromise their personal ethical standards to achieve corporate objectives. For example, managers at certain plants felt it necessary, for cost control purposes, to reduce quality control to such a level that it was uncertain whether all unsafe products were being rejected. Also, sales and human resources were encouraged to use questionable tactics to obtain orders, including offering gifts and other incentives to purchasing agents.

The chief executive officer is disturbed by the survey findings. In her opinion, the company cannot condone such behavior. She concludes that the company should do something about this problem.

a. Discuss what might be the causes for the ethical problems described.
b. Outline a program that could be instituted by the company to help reduce the pressures on managers to compromise personal ethical standards in their work.

CMA ADAPTED

ETHICS

43. **LO.2 (Responsibility accounting reports)** Hippolito Inc. manufactures industrial tools and has annual sales of approximately $3.5 million with no evidence of cyclical demand. R&D is very important to Hippolito because its market share expands only in response to product innovation.

The company controller has designed and implemented a new annual budget system divided into 12 equal segments for use for monthly performance evaluations. The vice president of operations was upset upon receiving the following responsibility report for the Machining Department for October 2013:

Machining Department
Responsibility Report
For the Month Ended October 31, 2013

	Budget	Actual	Variance
Volume in units	3,000	3,185	185 F
Variable manufacturing costs			
Direct material	$ 27,000	$ 28,028	$1,028 U
Direct labor	28,500	30,098	1,598 U
Variable factory overhead	33,300	35,035	1,735 U
Total	$ 88,800	$ 93,161	$4,361 U
Fixed manufacturing costs			
Indirect labor	$ 3,300	$ 3,334	$ 34 U
Depreciation	1,500	1,500	0
Property tax	300	300	0
Insurance	240	240	0
Other	930	1,027	97 U
Total	$ 6,270	$ 6,401	$ 131 U
Corporate costs			
Research and development	$ 2,400	$ 3,728	$1,328 U
Selling and administration	3,600	4,075	475 U
Total	$ 6,000	$ 7,803	$1,803 U
Total costs	$101,070	$107,365	$6,295 U

a. Identify the weaknesses in the responsibility report for the Machining Department.
b. Prepare a revised responsibility report for the Machining Department that reduces or eliminates the weaknesses indicated in (a).
c. Deviations in excess of 5 percent of budget are considered material and worthy of investigation. Should any of the Machining Department's variances be investigated? Regardless of materiality, is there any area that the vice president of operations might wish to discuss with the manager of the Machining Department?

CMA ADAPTED

44. **LO.2 (Responsibility report; performance evaluation)** Swimmingly Corp. buys raw fish, cooks and processes it, and then cans it in single-portion containers. The canned fish is sold to several wholesalers, who specialize in providing food to school lunch programs in the northwest United States and western Canada. All processing is conducted in the firm's highly automated plant in Portland, Oregon. Amir Rigera, the production manager, is evaluated on the basis of a comparison of actual costs to standard costs. Only variable costs that Rigera controls are included in the comparison. Fish cost is noncontrollable. Standard costs per pound of fish for 2013 follow.

Direct labor	$0.25
Repairs	0.05
Maintenance	0.30
Indirect labor	0.05
Power	0.10

For 2013, Swimmingly Corp. purchased 2.5 million pounds of fish and canned 1.5 million pounds. There were no beginning or ending inventories of raw, in-process, or canned fish for the year. Actual 2013 costs were:

Direct labor	$300,000
Repairs	80,000
Maintenance	325,000
Indirect labor	77,500
Power	157,500

a. Prepare a responsibility report for Rigera for 2013.
b. As his supervisor, evaluate Rigera's performance based on the report in (a).
c. Rigera believes his 2013 performance is so good that he should be considered for immediate promotion to vice president of production operations. Do you agree? Discuss the rationale for your answer.
d. Do you believe that all of the costs shown on Rigera's responsibility report are truly under his control? Discuss the rationale for your answer.

45. **LO.2 (Responsibility reports)** To respond to increased competition and a reduction in profitability, the nationwide law firm of O'Brien New & Cave recently instituted a responsibility accounting system. One of the several responsibility centers established was the Civil Litigation Division. This division is treated as a cost center for control purposes. In the first year (2013) after the new system was established, the responsibility report for the Civil Litigation Division contained the following comparisons:

	Budget	Actual	Variance
Variable costs			
Professional labor	$3,000,000	$2,820,000	$180,000 F
Travel	150,000	120,000	30,000 F
Supplies	300,000	270,000	30,000 F
Fixed costs			
Professional labor	$1,200,000	$1,215,000	$ 15,000 U
Facilities	750,000	795,000	45,000 U
Insurance	240,000	234,000	6,000 F
Total	$5,640,000	$5,454,000	$186,000 F

For 2013, the division projected it would handle 3,000 cases, but its actual case load was 2,970.

a. What are the major weaknesses in the preceding responsibility report?
b. Recast the responsibility report in a more meaningful format for cost control evaluation.
c. If O'Brien New & Cave uses a management-by-exception philosophy, which costs are likely to receive additional investigation? Explain.

46. **LO.3 (Cost and profit centers; ethics; research; writing)** Many companies provide on-site child-care facilities for employees' children. In some situations, this service is provided free of charge; in other situations, employees are charged, usually on a sliding-scale basis relative to pay, for such services.

a. If a company provides, but does not charge for, employee child care, the cost of such facilities would be considered a cost center. What potential ethical issues might arise when child-care facilities are viewed as a cost center?
b. If a company charges for employee child care, do you think the company should establish a designated percentage of profitability that it wishes to earn on the facilities? Discuss the reason for your answer.

c. Find information on two companies that have child-care facilities for employees' families and determine whether employees are charged for such facilities. What benefits are gained from the companies' perspectives from having such on-site facilities?

INTERNET

47. **LO.3 (Responsibility centers; research; writing)** Organizational spending on outsourced contact centers (previously referred to as call centers) continues to increase. Contact centers are critical to organizational success because these units often have primary responsibility for interactions with customers. In some companies, the contact centers are established primarily for customer support; in other companies (especially in the financial services sector), these centers not only provide customer support but also sell additional services to customers who call. Use library, web, or interview research to gather information on contact centers.

a. Contact centers often have a large responsibility for customer relationship management (CRM). What is CRM, and why is it so important to companies?
b. List five well-known companies that use such centers and indicate the primary purpose of those contact centers.
c. For each company identified in (b), do you think that its contact center would primarily be considered a cost or a profit center? Discuss the rationale for your answers.
d. For each company in (b), list three possible methods of allocating the costs of contact centers to operating departments. Discuss the rationale for your answers.
e. Although outsourced contact centers (especially those that are offshore) may create cost reductions, what other measurements might be useful in gauging contact center performance and customer satisfaction?

48. **LO.3 (Profit center performance)** The accounting department at Kerrville College decided to offer a three-day ethics workshop for local CPAs in March 2013. Rose Morris supervised the seminar's planning process and submitted the following budget to the departmental chairperson:

Revenues ($900 per participant)		$ 90,000
Expenses		
Speakers ($2,500 each)	$15,000	
Rent on facilities	3,600	
Advertising	4,000	
Meals and lodging	33,390	
Departmental overhead allocation	23,560	(79,550)
Profit		$ 10,450

The $3,600 facilities rent is a fixed rental, which is to be paid to a local hotel for the use of a meeting room. Advertising is also a fixed cost. Meal expense is budgeted at $10 per person per meal (a total of nine meals to be provided for each participant and each speaker); lodging is budgeted at the rate of $75 per participant and speaker per night. Departmental overhead includes a $10 charge per participant and speaker for supplies as well as a general allocation of 25 percent of revenues for use of departmental secretarial and production resources. The budget was approved and Morris proceeded with the seminar.

a. Recast the budget in a segment margin income statement format.
b. The seminar's actual financial results were as follows:

Revenues (120 participants)		$102,000
Expenses		
Speakers ($2,950 each)	$17,700	
Rent on facilities	4,200	
Advertising	4,900	
Meals and lodging	41,391	
Departmental overhead allocation	26,760	(94,951)
Profit		$ 7,049

Because signups were below expectations, the seminar fee was reduced from $900 to $850, and advertising expense was increased. In budgeting for the speakers, Morris neglected to include airfare, which averaged $450 per speaker. With the increased attendance, a larger meeting room had to be rented from the local hotel. Actual lodging costs were as budgeted, but meals were 15 percent more expensive because of the gratuity. Recast the actual results in a segment margin income format.

c. Identify and discuss the factors that are primarily responsible for the difference between the budgeted and the actual profit on the ethics seminar.

49. **LO.4 (Revenue variances)** Folsom Fashions sells a line of women's dresses. Folsom's performance report for November 2013 is shown below. The company uses a flexible budget to analyze its performance and measure the effect on operating income of the various factors affecting the difference between budgeted and actual operating results.

	Actual	Budget
Dresses sold	5,000	6,000
Sales	$ 235,000	$ 300,000
Variable costs	(145,000)	(180,000)
Contribution margin	$ 90,000	$ 120,000
Fixed costs	(84,000)	(80,000)
Operating income	$ 6,000	$ 40,000

a. Compute the sales price variance and the sales volume variance for November 2013.
b. Determine the impact of the sales volume variance on Folsom's contribution margin for the month of November 2013.
c. What additional information is needed for Folsom to calculate the dollar impact of a change in the market share on operating income for November 2013? What would be the overall benefit to Folsom's sales managers of having such information?
d. Explain why performance evaluation at Folsom Fashions is limited if the company's evaluation of management is based solely on sales price and volume variances.

50. **LO.4 (Revenue variances)** Cardiff Sports sells footballs and shoulder pads. For 2013, company management budgeted the following:

	Footballs	Shoulder Pads
Sales revenue	$1,200,000	$1,800,000
Unit sales price	$60	$45

At the end of 2013, management was told that actual sales of footballs were 21,000 units and the sales price variance was $63,000 unfavorable. Sales of shoulder pads generated $1,680,000 of revenue, with an unfavorable sales volume variance of $360,000.

a. Compute the budgeted sales volume for each product.
b. Compute the sales volume variance for footballs.
c. Compute the sales price variance for shoulder pads.
d. What conditions might have contributed to the revenue variances?

51. **LO.4 (Revenue variances)** Kessla Taub manages the marketing department at Electronic Village. Company management has been concerned about the sales of three products and has informed Taub that, regardless of other sales, her performance in 2013 will be evaluated on whether she has met the sales budget for the following items:

	Sales Price per Unit	Budgeted Unit Sales
HD radio tuners	$120	1,600
Satellite radios	68	2,100
MP3 car decks	60	1,050

Actual sales for these three products, generated in 2013, were as follows:

	Sales Price per Unit	Sales Revenue
HD radio tuners	$115	$195,500
Satellite radios	70	141,400
MP3 car decks	55	228,250

a. For 2013, compute the sales price variances by product.
b. For 2013, compute the sales volume variances by product.
c. Assuming that the variances computed in (a) and (b) are controllable by Taub, discuss what actions she may have taken to cause actual results to deviate from budgeted results.
d. What problems might be caused by the manner in which Taub was evaluated during 2013?

52. **LO.5 (Comprehensive support department allocations)** Management at C. Pier Press has decided to allocate costs of the paper's two support departments (administration and human resources) to the two revenue-generating departments (advertising and circulation). Administration costs are to be allocated on the basis of dollars of assets employed; human resources costs are to be allocated on the basis of number of employees. The following costs and allocation bases are available:

Department	Direct Costs	Number of Employees	Assets Employed
Administration	$ 390,750	5	$ 193,550
Human resources	246,350	4	145,850
Advertising	478,900	6	381,200
Circulation	676,300	13	935,150
Totals	$1,792,300	28	$1,655,750

a. Using the direct method, allocate the support department costs to the revenue-generating departments. (Round to the nearest whole percent and dollar.)
b. Using your answer to (a), what are the total costs of the revenue-generating departments after the allocations?
c. Assuming that the benefits-provided ranking is the order shown in the table, use the step method to allocate the support department costs to the revenue-generating departments.
d. Using your answer to (c), what are the total costs of the revenue-generating departments after the allocations?
e. Using the algebraic method, allocate the support department costs to the revenue-generating departments.

53. **LO.5 (Direct and step methods)** Salado Inc. provides cleaning services through its Residential and Commercial divisions. Support services of the company are provided by Personnel and Administration areas. Costs of these two areas are allocated to the revenue producing departments. Personnel costs are allocated using number of employees; administration costs are allocated using direct department costs. The following 2013 budgeted information (presented in a benefits-provided ranking) is available:

	Personnel	Administration	Residential	Commercial
Direct costs	$140,000	$180,000	$480,000	$800,000
Number of employees	12	30	72	48
Direct labor hours			60,000	90,000
Square feet cleaned			450,000	570,000

a. Using the direct method, allocate the costs of Personnel and Administration to the Residential and Commercial divisions.
b. Using the step method, allocate the costs of Personnel and Administration to the Residential and Commercial divisions.
c. Salado prices jobs by the direct labor hour for Residential services and by the square foot cleaned for Commercial services. Compute the full cost of providing one direct labor hour of service for Residential and for one square foot cleaned for Commercial using (1) the direct method and (2) the step method. (Round cost per hour and cost per square foot to nearest cent.)

54. **LO.5 (Effect of support department allocations on reporting and evaluation; writing)** Kensington Corporation is a diversified manufacturing company with corporate headquarters in Easton, Massachusetts. The three operating divisions are Kennedy

Division, Consumer Products Division, and Outerspace Products Division. Much of Kennedy Division's manufacturing activity is related to work performed for the government space program under negotiated contracts.

Kensington Corporation headquarters provides general administrative support and computer services to the three operating divisions. Computer services are provided through a computer time-sharing arrangement. The central processing unit (CPU) is located in Boston, and the divisions have remote terminals connected to the CPU by telephone lines. One standard from the Cost Accounting Standards Board provides that the cost of general administration may be allocated to negotiated defense contracts. Furthermore, the standards provide that, in situations in which computer services are provided by corporate headquarters, the actual costs (fixed and variable) of operating the computer department may be allocated to the Kennedy Division based on a reasonable measure of computer usage.

The general managers of the three divisions are evaluated on divisional before-tax performance. The November 2013 performance evaluation reports (in millions of dollars) for each division follow.

	Kennedy Division	Consumer Products Division	Outerspace Products Division
Sales	$ 46	$ 30	$110
Cost of goods sold	(26)	(14)	(76)
Gross profit	$ 20	$ 16	$ 34
Selling and administrative			
Division selling and administration costs	$ 10	$ 10	$ 16
Corporate general administration costs	2	0	0
Corporate computing	2	0	0
Total	$ 14	$ 10	$ 16
Profit before taxes	$ 6	$ 6	$ 18

Without a charge for computing services, the operating divisions might not make the most cost-effective use of the computer systems resources. Outline and discuss a method for charging the operating divisions for computer services usage that would promote cost consciousness by the operating divisions and operating efficiency by the computer systems services. CMA ADAPTED

55. **LO.5 (Direct method)** Leyh Management Co. classifies its operations into three departments: commercial sales, residential sales, and property management. The owner, Ellen Leyh, wants to know the full cost of operating each department. Direct departmental costs and several allocation bases associated with each follow:

		AVAILABLE ALLOCATION BASES		
	Direct Costs	Number of Employees/ Salespersons	Assets Employed	Revenue
Administration	$ 1,500,000	20	$2,480,000	N/A
Accounting	990,000	15	1,364,000	N/A
Promotion	720,000	12	720,000	N/A
Commercial sales	10,490,000	45	900,000	$10,000,000
Residential sales	9,179,000	210	1,440,000	18,000,000
Property management	398,400	18	540,000	2,000,000

The support departments are shown in a benefits-provided ranking. Leyh has selected the following allocation bases for each department: number of employees/salespersons for administration, dollars of assets employed for accounting, and dollars of revenue for promotion.

a. Use the direct method to allocate the support department costs to the revenue-generating departments. (Round proportions to the nearest whole percentage.)
b. Determine the operating income for each division.

EXCEL

56. **LO.5 (Algebraic method)** Lombardi Printing has two support departments (administration and editorial) and two operating divisions (college texts and professional publications). Following are the direct costs and allocation bases for each of these areas:

		ALLOCATION BASES	
Department	**Direct Costs**	**Assets Employed**	**Number of Employees**
Administration	$ 225,000	$310,000	5
Editorial	175,000	75,000	4
College texts	2,250,000	600,000	25
Professional publications	950,000	525,000	15

Company management has decided to allocate administration and editorial costs using dollars of assets employed and number of employees, respectively. Use the algebraic method to allocate the support department costs and determine the total operating costs of college textbooks and professional publications.

57. **LO.5 (Step method)** Use the information for Leyh Management Co. in Problem 55.
    a. Allocate the support department costs to the revenue-generating departments using the step method.
    b. Which department is apparently the most profitable?

EXCEL

58. **LO.5 (Comprehensive support department allocations)** Wakowski Company's annual budget for its three support departments (administration, legal/accounting, and maintenance/engineering) and its two production departments (processing and finishing) is as follows:

ANNUAL BUDGET ($000 omitted)

	Administration	Legal/ Accounting	Maintenance/ Engineering	Processing	Finishing	Total
Direct labor	$1,400	$1,000	$1,800	$5,600	$4,000	$13,800
Direct material	140	400	180	800	2,400	3,920
Insurance	350	100	150	600	440	1,640
Depreciation	180	140	160	400	300	1,180
Miscellaneous	60	40	80	120	60	360
Total	$2,130	$1,680	$2,370	$7,520	$7,200	$20,900

ANNUAL BUDGET ($000 omitted)

	Administration	Legal/ Accounting	Maintenance/ Engineering	Processing	Finishing	Total
Number of employees	80	40	60	400	300	880
Sq. ft. of floor space	800	600	400	1,600	2,000	5,400
Maint./Eng. hours	30	40	30	136	204	440

a. Prepare a cost distribution that allocates support department costs using the step method. Assume the benefits-provided ranking is the order in which the departments are listed. The allocation bases for the support department are (1) administration: number of employees; (2) legal/accounting: floor space; and (3) maintenance/engineering: number of hours. Calculate the factory overhead (OH) rates using 400,000 direct labor hours in processing and 300,000 direct labor hours in finishing. Round OH rates to the nearest $0.10.

b. Calculate the factory overhead rates per direct labor hour using the direct method. Round OH rates to the nearest $0.10.

c. Calculate the factory overhead rates per direct labor hour using the algebraic method. Round percentages to three decimal points. Round OH rates to the nearest $0.10.

59. **LO.5 (Direct method)** Management of Shreveport Community Hospital has decided to allocate the budgeted costs of its three support departments (administration, public relations, and maintenance) to its three operating programs (surgery, in-patient care, and out-patient services). Budgeted information for 2013 follows.

Budgeted costs	
Administration	$5,400,000
Public relations	1,100,000
Maintenance & janitorial	1,700,000
Allocation bases	
Administration	Dollars of assets employed
Public relations	Number of employees
Maintenance & janitorial	Hours of equipment operation

EXPECTED UTILIZATIONS

	Assets Employed	Number of Employees	Hours of Equipment Operation
Administration	$1,480,180	8	2,040
Public relations	900,200	14	940
Maintenance & janitorial	1,651,360	10	3,060
Surgery	3,948,500	20	24,850
In-patient care	2,458,500	36	28,400
Out-patient services	1,043,000	44	17,750

Using the direct method, allocate the expected support department costs to the operating areas.

60. **LO.6 (Transfer pricing journal entries)** Worldly Traveler's Roll-Em-On Division makes computer bags. The bags are sold to another internal division, SkyWheels, for inclusion in a luggage set and to external buyers. During the month just ended, SkyWheels acquired 4,000 bags from the Roll-Em-On Division, whose standard unit costs follow.

Direct material	$40
Direct labor	12
Variable factory overhead	16
Fixed factory overhead	24
Variable selling expense	8
Fixed selling and administrative expense	12

SkyWheels can acquire comparable bags externally for $160 each. Give the entries for each division and for Roll-Em-On (assuming that no bags acquired by SkyWheels have been sold) for the past month if the transfer is to be recorded

a. at SkyWheels' external purchase price and no selling expenses were incurred on, or allocated to, internal transfers.
b. at a negotiated price of total variable cost plus 15 percent of full production cost.
c. by Roll-Em-On Division at SkyWheels' external price, and by SkyWheels at Roll-Em-On's variable production cost.
d. at Roll-Em-On's absorption cost.

61. **LO.6 (Transfer prices)** Cookie Delight Company has two divisions: Plain Cookies and Decorated Cookies. Lars Linden is the manager of Plain Cookies Division and Theresa Davis is the manager of Decorated Cookies Division. Company president Marie Strauss wants to develop a transfer pricing system that will instill goal congruence in the two division managers. Linden and Davis each get a bonus of 10 percent of the operating margins of his and her respective division. The following information is available:

	Plain Cookies	Decorated Cookies
Sales (market price)	$2.00 per cookie	$4.00 per cookie
Variable costs (excluding direct costs)	$0.50 per cookie	$0.75 per cookie
Fixed costs	$300 per month	$500 per month
Units sold to outside market	3,000 per month	800 per month
Capacity (in units)	4,000 per month	850 per month

a. Create a contribution margin income statement for each division and for the company in total, assuming that the Decorated Cookie Division buys cookies from outside suppliers. Show both Linden's and Davis's bonuses separately.

b. Assuming there are no cost savings associated with the Plain Cookie Division selling directly to the Decorated Cookie Division, what is the lowest transfer price Linden should charge? What is the highest transfer price?

c. Prepare contribution income statements for each division and the company as a whole using the lowest and highest transfer prices computed in (b). What effect does each transfer price have on the two division managers?

d. How can Strauss encourage the division managers to agree to an arrangement that will be acceptable to them and also be the best price for the benefit of the company as a whole? Explain your answer.

62. **LO.6 (Transfer price)** Ludmilla Corp. has two divisions: Engine and Mobile Systems. The Engine Division produces engines used by both the Mobile Systems Division and a variety of external industrial customers. External sales orders are generally produced in 50-unit lots. Using this typical lot size, the cost per engine is as follows:

Variable production cost	$4,200
Fixed manufacturing overhead	1,800
Variable selling expense	600
Fixed selling expense	840
Fixed administrative expense	1,280
Total unit cost	$8,720

An engine's external selling price is $10,464, providing the Engine Division with a normal profit margin of 20 percent. Because a significant number of sales are being made internally, Engine Division managers have decided that the external selling price should be used to transfer all engines to Mobile Systems.

When the Mobile Systems Division manager learned of the new transfer price, she became very upset because it would have a major negative impact on her division's profit. Mobile Systems has asked for a lower transfer price from the Engine Division so that it earns a profit margin of only 15 percent. Mobile Systems' manager has asked corporate management whether the division can buy engines externally. Faye Ryan, Ludmilla's president, has gathered the following information on transfer prices to help the two divisional managers negotiate an equitable transfer price:

Current external sales price	$10,464
Total variable production cost plus a 20% profit margin ($4,200 × 1.2)	5,040
Total production cost plus a 20% profit margin ($6,000 × 1.2)	7,200
Bid price from external supplier (if motors are purchased in 50-unit lots)	9,280

a. Discuss advantages and disadvantages of each of these transfer prices to both the selling and buying divisions and to Ludmilla Corp.

b. If the Engine Division could sell all of its production externally at $10,464, what is the appropriate transfer price and why?

63. **LO.6 (Internal vs. external sale)** The president of Charlottetown Inc. has given the managers of the company's three decentralized divisions (O'Leary, Alberton, and Summerside) the authority to decide whether to sell externally or internally at a transfer price the division managers determine. Market conditions are such that internal or external sales will not affect market or transfer prices. Intermediate markets will always be available for the divisions to purchase their manufacturing needs or sell their product. Division managers attempt to maximize their contribution margin at the current level of operating assets for their divisions.

The Alberton Division manager is considering the following two alternative orders:

- Summerside Division needs 1,500 units of a motor that Alberton Division can supply. To manufacture these motors, Alberton would purchase components from O'Leary Division at a transfer price of $600 per unit; O'Leary's variable cost for these components is $300 per unit. Alberton Division would further process these components at a variable cost of $500 per unit.

If Summerside cannot obtain the motors from Alberton, it will purchase the motors from Montague Company for $1,500 per unit. Montague Company would also purchase 1,500 components from O'Leary at a price of $400 for each motor; O'Leary's variable cost for these components is $200 per unit.

- New London Company wants to buy 1,750 similar motors from the Alberton Division for $1,250 per unit. Alberton would again purchase components from O'Leary Division, in this case at a transfer price of $500 per unit; O'Leary's variable cost for these components is $250 per unit. Alberton Division would further process these components at a variable cost of $400 per unit.

Alberton Division's plant capacity is limited, and therefore the company can accept either the New London contract or the Summerside order but not both. The president of Charlottetown Inc. and the manager of Alberton Division agree that it would not be beneficial in the short or long run to increase capacity.

a. If the Alberton Division manager wants to maximize the short-run contribution margin, determine whether Alberton Division should (1) sell motors to Summerside Division at the prevailing market price or (2) accept New London Company's contract. Support your answer with appropriate calculations.
b. Without prejudice to your answer to (a), assume that Alberton Division decides to accept the New London contract. Determine whether this decision is in the best interest of Charlottetown Inc. Support your answer with appropriate calculations. **CMA ADAPTED**

64. **LO.6 (Transfer prices)** In each of the following cases, the Speaker Division can sell all of its production of audio speakers externally or some internally to the Sound System Division and the remainder to outside customers. The Speaker Division's production capacity is 400,000 units annually. The data related to each independent case are as follows:

	Case 1	Case 2
Speaker Division		
Selling price to outside customers	$80	$65
Production costs per unit		
Direct material	32	22
Direct labor	12	10
Variable overhead	4	3
Fixed overhead (based on capacity)	1	1
Other variable selling and delivery costs per unit*	6	3
Sound System Division		
Number of speakers needed annually	40,000	40,000
Current unit price being paid to outside supplier	$70	$57

**In either case, $1 of the selling expenses will not be incurred on intracompany transfers.*

a. For each case, determine the upper and lower limits for a transfer price for speakers.
b. For each case, determine a transfer price for the Speaker Division that will provide a $12 contribution margin per unit.
c. Using the information developed for (b), determine a dual transfer price for Case 1 assuming that Sound System will acquire the speakers from the Speaker Division at $12 below Sound System's purchase price from outside suppliers.

65. **LO.5 & LO.6 (Direct method; transfer price)** Tobias & Barfield LLC has three revenue departments: litigation (Lit.), family practice (FP), and legal consulting (LC). In addition, the company has two support departments, administration and EDP. Administration costs are allocated to the three revenue departments on the basis of number of employees. EDP's fixed costs are allocated to revenue departments on the basis of peak hours of monthly service expected to be used by each revenue department. EDP's variable costs are assigned to the revenue departments at a transfer price of $80 per hour of actual service. Following are the direct costs and the allocation bases associated with each of the departments:

	Direct Costs (before transfer costs)	ALLOCATION BASES: NUMBER OF Employees	Peak Hours	EDP Hours Used
Administration	$900,000	4	30	290
EDP—Fixed	600,000	2	N/A	N/A
EDP—Variable	181,280	2	N/A	N/A
Lit.	400,000	10	80	1,220
FP	510,000	5	240	650
LC	680,000	3	25	190

a. Was the variable EDP transfer price of $80 adequate? Explain.
b. Allocate all support department costs to the operating departments using the direct method.
c. What are the total costs of the operating departments after the allocation in (b)?

66. **LO.6 (Transfer prices)** Des Moines Industries consists of eight divisions that are evaluated as profit centers. All transfers between divisions are made at market price. I-O-WoW, a division of Des Moines, sells approximately 20 percent of its output externally. The remaining 80 percent of I-O-WoW's output is transferred to other divisions within Des Moines. No other Des Moines Industries division transfers internally more than 10 percent of its output.

With respect to any profit-based measure of performance, I-O-WoW is the leading division within Des Moines Industries. Other divisional managers always find that their performance is compared to that of I-O-WoW. These managers argue that the transfer pricing situation gives I-O-WoW a competitive advantage.

a. What factors could contribute to any advantage that the I-O-WoW Division might have over the other divisions?
b. What alternative transfer price or performance measure might be more appropriate in this situation?

67. **LO.6 (Interdivisional transfers; deciding on alternatives)** Eekaydo Inc. is organized on a divisional basis with considerable vertical integration. Mary Sue Oehlke is the new controller of the CarryOn! Division of Eekaydo.

CarryOn! Division makes a variety of leather products, including a portfolio. Product sales have been steady, and the marketing department expects continued strong demand. Oehlke is looking for ways the CarryOn! Division can contain its costs and thus boost its earnings from future sales. She discovered that CarryOn! Division has always purchased its leather from HIDE, another part of Eekaydo. HIDE has been providing the three square feet of tanned leather needed for each portfolio for $9 per square foot.

Oehlke wondered whether it might be possible to purchase CarryOn!'s leather needs at comparable quality from an external supplier at a lower price. Top management at Eekaydo reluctantly agreed to allow the CarryOn! Division to consider purchasing outside the company.

CarryOn! Division management has issued an RFP (request for proposal) for the leather needed for 100,000 portfolios during the coming year. The two best supplier bids are $8 and $7 per square foot from Koenig and Thompson, respectively. Oehlke has been informed that another subsidiary of Eekaydo, Barrows Chemical, supplies Thompson the chemicals that are an essential ingredient of Thompson's tanning process. Barrows Chemical charges Thompson $2 for enough chemicals to prepare three square feet of leather. Barrows' profit margin is 30 percent.

HIDE Division wants to continue supplying CarryOn!'s leather needs at the same price per square foot as in the past. Tom Reed, HIDE's controller, believes the sales are necessary to maintain HIDE's healthy profit margin of 40 percent of sales.

As Eekaydo's finance vice president, you have called a meeting of the controllers of CarryOn! and HIDE. Oehlke is eager to accept Thompson's $7 bid. She points out that CarryOn!'s earnings will show a significant increase if the division can buy from Thompson.

Reed, however, wants Eekaydo to keep the business within the company and suggests that you require CarryOn! to purchase its needs from HIDE. He emphasizes that HIDE's profit margin should not be lost from the company.

From whom should the CarryOn! Division buy the leather? Consider both CarryOn!'s desire to minimize its costs and Eekaydo's corporate goal of maximizing profit on a companywide basis. CMA ADAPTED

68. **LO.6 (Transfer prices; writing)** Rowling Inc. is a decentralized company, and each investment center has its own sales force and production facilities. Top management uses return on investment (income divided by assets) for performance evaluation. Potter Division has just been awarded a contract for a product that uses a component manufactured by Gondorf Division and by outside suppliers. Potter used a cost figure of $15.20 for the component when the bid was prepared for the new product. Gondorf supplied this cost figure in response to Potter's request for the average variable cost of the component.

Gondorf has an active sales force that is continually soliciting new customers, and sales of the component are expected to increase. Gondorf's regular selling price is $26 for the component that Potter needs for the new product. Gondorf has the following costs associated with the component:

Standard variable manufacturing cost	$12.80
Standard variable selling and distribution cost	2.40
Standard fixed manufacturing cost	4.80
Total	$20.00

The two divisions have been unable to agree on a transfer price for the component. Corporate management has never established a transfer price because interdivisional transactions have never occurred. The following suggestions have been made for the transfer price:

- Regular selling price
- Regular selling price less variable selling and distribution expenses
- Standard manufacturing cost plus 15 percent
- Standard variable manufacturing cost plus 20 percent

a. Compute each suggested transfer price.
b. Discuss the effect that each of the transfer prices might have on the attitude of Gondorf Division management toward intracompany business.
c. Is the negotiation of a price between the Potter and Gondorf Divisions a satisfactory method for solving the transfer price problem? Explain your answer.
d. Should the corporate management of Rowling Inc. become involved in this transfer controversy? Explain your answer. CMA ADAPTED

69. **LO.7 (International transfer prices; writing)** Why would intangible assets create significant difficulties in international transfer pricing?

70. **LO.7 (International transfer prices; writing)** APAs are determined in advance of the time in which they are used. Discuss problems that may be generated in a recessionary business climate for companies that have preapproved APAs.

71. **LO.7 (International transfer prices; research)** Go to http://www.deloitte.com/assets/Dcom-Global/Local%20Assets/Documents/Tax/dttl_tax_strategymatrix_2011_180211.pdf to find Deloitte's 2011 *Global Transfer Pricing Desktop Reference.* Select ten countries and answer the following questions for each.

    a. What transfer pricing methods are acceptable?
    b. Are foreign comparables acceptable to local tax authorities?
    c. Are management fees deductible?
    d. Are APAs allowed?

72. **LO.7 (International transfer prices; research)** Go to the **Ernst & Young** Web site to find information on the 2011 *Transfer Pricing Global Reference Guide.* Choose five countries (other than the United States) and compare and contrast the transfer pricing penalties, penalty relief, documentation requirements, and return disclosures/related party disclosures for those countries. Which of the countries you selected seems to be the (1) most stringent and (2) most lenient?

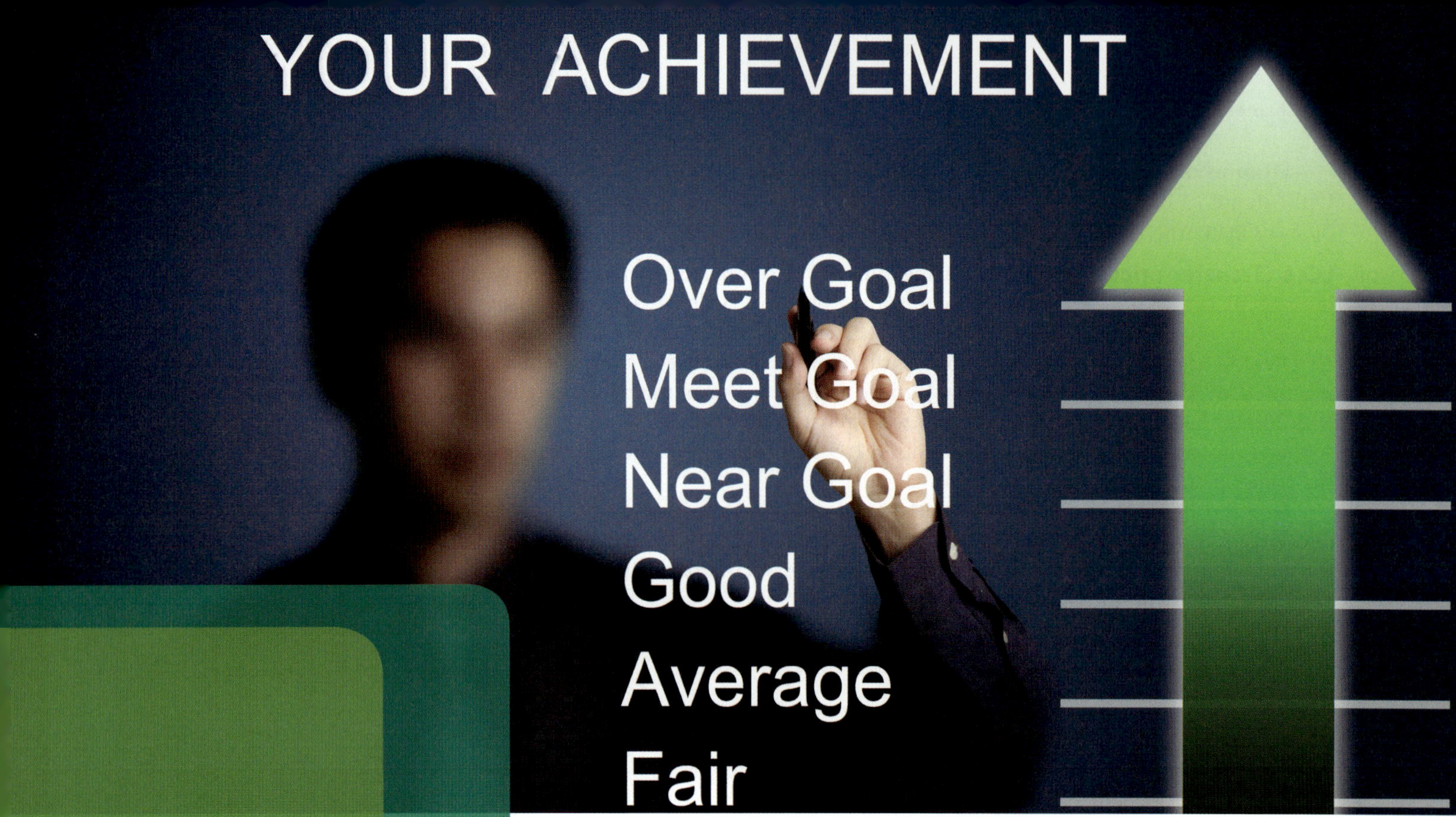

Dusit/Shutterstock.com

14

Performance Measurement, Balanced Scorecards, and Performance Rewards

LEARNING OBJECTIVES

After completing this chapter, you should be able to answer the following questions:

1. Why is a mission statement important to an organization?
2. What roles do performance measures serve in organizations?
3. What guidelines or criteria apply to the design of performance measures?
4. What are the common short-term financial performance measures, and how are they calculated and used?
5. Why should company management focus on long-run performance?
6. What factors should managers consider when selecting nonfinancial performance measures?
7. Why is it necessary to use multiple performance measures?
8. How can a balanced scorecard be used to measure performance?
9. What is compensation strategy, and what factors must be considered in designing the compensation strategy?
10. What difficulties are encountered in trying to measure performance and design compensation plans for multinational firms?

INTRODUCTION

To achieve profitability in the face of global competition, managers recognize that the most important tasks are to attract and satisfy customers. Historically, managers focused almost exclusively on short-run financial performance measures and often ignored the long-run and critical nonfinancial activities. Such tunnel vision was partially created by two circumstances:

- managers were commonly judged on a short-term basis, and
- long-run and nonfinancial performance data were often unavailable from the accounting system.

Because many recent accounting scandals resulted from intense pressure on managers to achieve short-term performance targets, more managers in the post-Enron era recognize the need to use a longer horizon to gauge performance. Additionally, with the ability of new technology to implement strategic cost management systems, world-class companies have begun implementing multiple types of performance measurement and reward systems.

An organization's performance evaluation and reward systems are key tools for aligning the efforts and goals of workers, managers, and owners.[1] The manager's primary function is to maximize stockholder value or stockholder wealth. When employees help control costs and profits increase, stockholders benefit through higher dividends and/or stock market prices. One of the most important ways of motivating employees to maximize stockholder wealth is through the design and implementation of effective employee performance metrics and remuneration structures.

ORGANIZATION MISSION STATEMENTS

1 Why is a mission statement important to an organization?

Every organization has a reason or mission for existing. The mission statement expresses an organization's purpose and should identify how the organization will meet targeted customers' needs through its products or services. For example, **Intel**'s mission statement is "Delight our customers, employees, and shareholders by relentlessly delivering the platform and technology advancements that become essential to the way we work and live."[2] Mission statements must be communicated not only externally to customers but also to all employees; internal communication can be made in numerous ways, including conference room posters and printed cards that employees can add to their identification badges.

In addition to a mission statement, many companies have developed a **values statement** that reflects the organization's culture by identifying fundamental beliefs about what is important to the organization. These values may be objective (such as profitability and increased market share) or subjective (such as ethical behavior and respect for individuals). Intel's values are:

- customer orientation,
- results orientation,
- risk taking,
- great place to work,
- quality, and
- discipline.

Mission and values statements are two of the underlying bases for setting organizational goals (abstract targets to be achieved) and objectives (quantified targets with expected completion dates). Goals and objectives can be short term or long term, but they are inexorably linked. Without achieving at least some short-run success, there will never be long-run success. Without engaging in long-run planning, short-run success will rapidly fade.

[1] The authors use the term *employees* to refer to all personnel of an organization. The terms *workers* and *managers* are used to identify mutually exclusive groups of employees.

[2] Intel, General Company Information; http://www.intel.com/intel/company/corp1.htm (accessed 1/27/12).

ORGANIZATIONAL ROLES OF PERFORMANCE MEASURES

2 What roles do performance measures serve in organizations?

In fulfilling organizational missions, managers design and implement strategies that apply organizational resources to activities. The organizational structure reflects the manner in which a firm assigns and coordinates its people to deploy strategies. Subunits can be created and charged with making specific contributions to the business strategy. The extent to which each subunit succeeds in its mission can be assessed using carefully designed performance measures that capture the subunit's important performance dimensions.

Management talent and time are dedicated to planning, controlling, decision making, and evaluating performance. For an organization to be successful, managers must devise appropriate information systems to track and gauge the effective and efficient use of organizational resources. Two conditions must exist to make such determinations:

1. the terms *effective* and *efficient* must be defined, and
2. measures consistent with those definitions must be formulated.

Definitions of *effective* and *efficient* may relate to historical organizational performance, competitive benchmarks, or stakeholder expectations. Once defined, effectiveness and efficiency can be assessed by comparing actual performance with defined and targeted performance goals.

As indicated in Exhibit 14.1, performance measures should exist for all elements that are critical to an organization's success in a competitive market. Management must recognize that progress toward a goal can be achieved only if the goal is specified and communicated to the organization's members. Thus, not setting performance measures for any of an

Exhibit 14.1 Critical Elements for Performance Measurement and Examples of Measurements

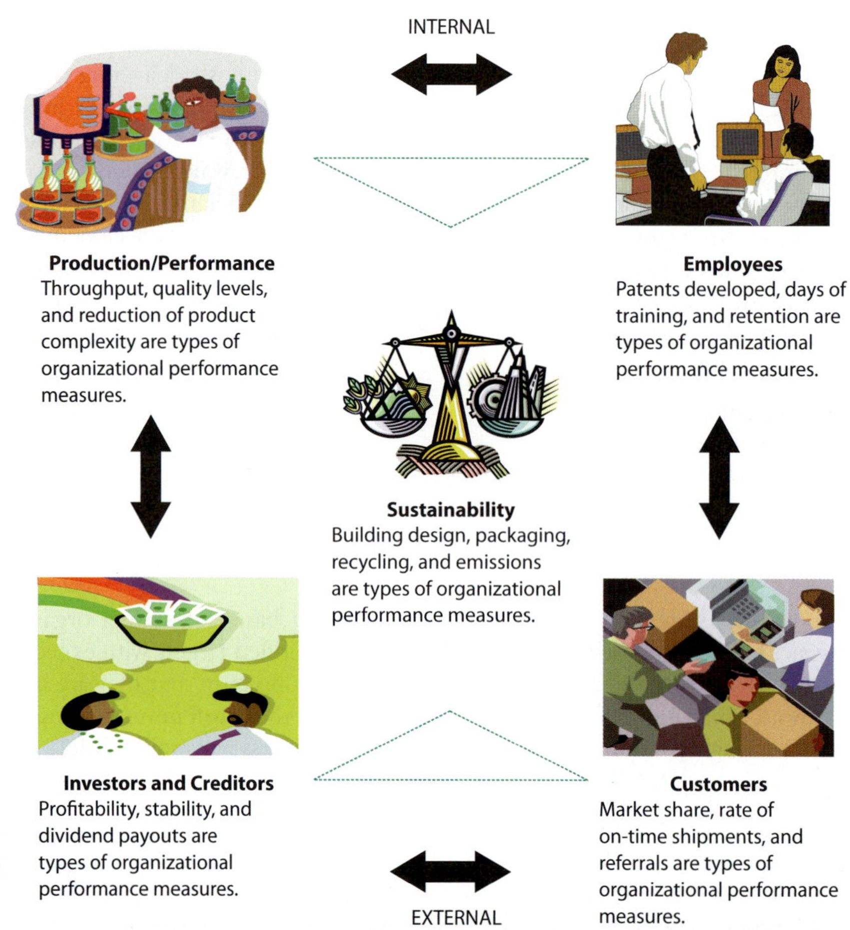

organization's critical elements is tantamount to stating that the ignored element is unimportant. All elements are linked because high performance in one element should lead to high performance in the others.

Internal Performance Measures

Management must develop internal measures that provide a focus on the efficiency and effectiveness of production processes. Inadequate processes make it more difficult for a company to manufacture a product or perform a service that will engender both employee pride and customer satisfaction. Internal process measures should reflect concern for streamlined production, high quality, minimization of product complexity, and reduction/elimination of negative environmental impacts. Products and services compete with others on the dimensions of price, quality, and product features (including aspects of sustainability). Superior performance in any of these three areas can provide the competitive advantage needed for success. Developing performance measures for each competitive dimension can help to identify alternative ways to leverage a firm's competencies.

Employee performance is also a critical element of organizational success. Each successive management level establishes target measures for subordinates. These measures communicate organizational mission, goals, and strategies and motivate subordinates to accomplish the stated targets. Measures, such as comparing actual to budgeted results in responsibility reports, are also used for implementing organizational control over activities. Employee performance comparisons are used for promotion and retention decisions. A firm searching for new ways to provide customers with more value at lower cost must develop an organizational culture that promotes employee learning, job satisfaction, and production efficiency.

Sustainability concerns may relate to product production or service performance. Company management must be aware of the organization's impact on the environment from the organization's building design, to resource (especially recycled ones) usage, to product packaging, to employee training, and to research and development activities related to sustainability processes and strategies.

External Performance Measures

Externally, performance measures must signal an organization's ability to satisfy its customers, investors/creditors, and other stakeholders. The quality and quantity of firms competing in the global market have placed consumers at the center of attention. Although profit may be the ultimate measure of success in serving customers, other measures that indicate relative accomplishment in specific areas of market performance can be developed. For example, performance measures must reflect characteristics, such as product/service reliability, value, quality, and on-time delivery, that customers highly value. Such performance measures should result in a high level of customer loyalty, as measured by customer retention. Meeting or exceeding the performance targets set for customers should result in the increased likelihood of meeting or exceeding the performance targets set for investors and creditors.

The most common organizational performance metric is profit, which can be measured as operating income or net income, and can be expressed on a gross or per-share basis. Generally accepted accounting principles are formulated to provide information that is comparable across firms. This comparability facilitates investor/creditor judgments about which firms are worthy of capital investments and which firms can provide appropriate returns relative to the investment risks borne. Financial performance measures typically determine whether top management is retained or dismissed. Meeting or exceeding the market's performance expectations should create capital inflows that fund improving processes, hiring more qualified employees, and creating more satisfied customers. Management must be careful to realize, after recent accounting scandals in the business community, that "good" financial performance should not be sought by improper accounting methods—whether in regard to "managing" revenues or expenses.

Sustainability must be measured from an external as well as internal perspective. In addition to the stakeholders already mentioned, an organization must be concerned with its local and more global communities. As such, an extremely common performance metric is level of (or reduction in level of) pollutant emissions into the air, water, and soil. But additional measures may also be important: proportion of suppliers that are "green," number of or fines from environmental "incidents," increase/decrease in percentage of local jobs from the organization, paid hours for community volunteer work, and dollars of investments in disaster relief projects. External sustainability metrics should reflect strategic organizational priorities.

DESIGNING A PERFORMANCE MEASUREMENT SYSTEM

3 What guidelines or criteria apply to the design of performance measures?

In creating any performance measurement system, it is important to remember that people focus on the items that are measured by superiors. Thus, an essential question to address when implementing a performance measurement system is, "What behavior will this metric encourage?" The performance measurement system should be designed to encourage behaviors that will result in outcomes that generate organizational success.

General Criteria

Regardless of the results that are being measured, the employee level at which the measurement is occurring, or the type (monetary or nonmonetary) of measure that is being used, five general criteria (Exhibit 14.2) should be considered in designing a performance measurement system:

- The measures should be established to assess progress toward the organizational mission and its related goals and objectives.
- The persons being evaluated should be aware of the measurements being used and have had some input in developing them.
- The persons being evaluated should have the appropriate skills, equipment, information, and authority to be successful under the measurement system.
- Feedback of accomplishment should be provided in a timely and useful manner.
- The system should be flexible enough to adapt to new conditions in the organization's environment.

Exhibit 14.2 Criteria for Designing a Performance Measurement System

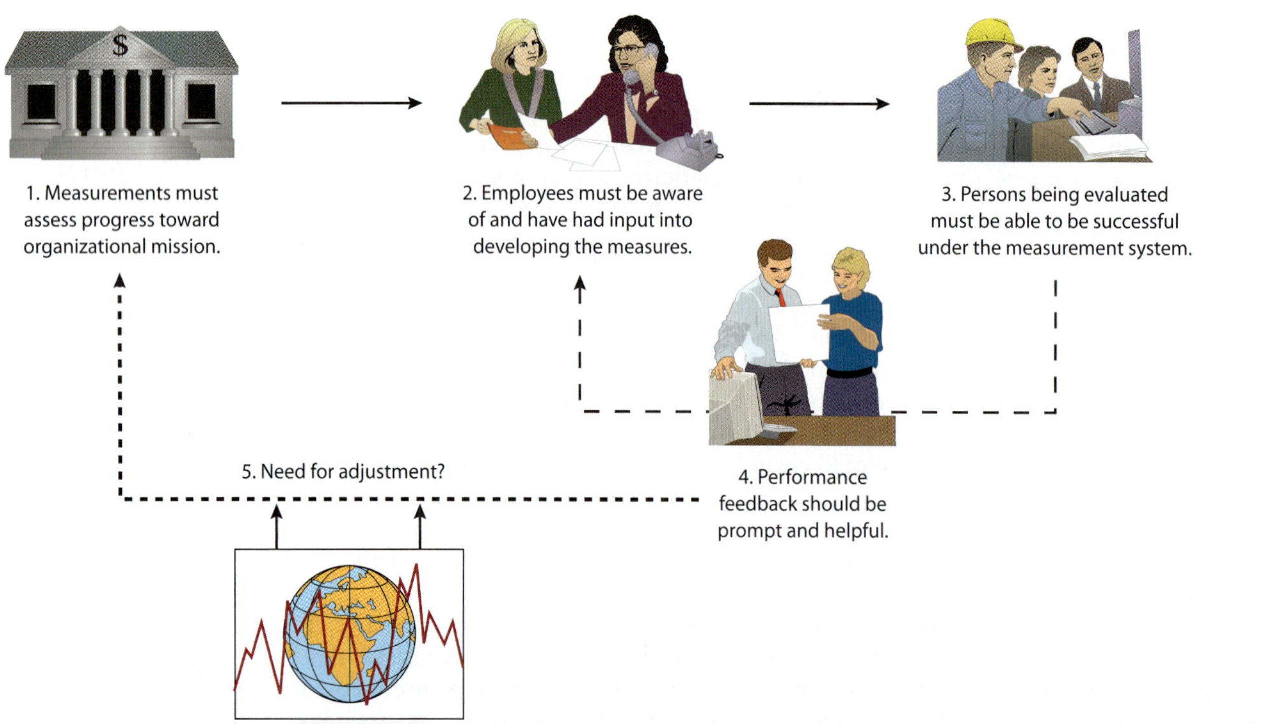

Assess Progress toward Mission

Organizations have a variety of objectives, including the need to be financially viable. Therefore, financial performance measures must be relevant for the type of organization or subunit being evaluated and must reflect an understanding of accounting information and its potential for manipulation. In addition to financial success, many companies are now establishing operational targets of total customer satisfaction, zero defects, lead time to market, and environmental and social responsibility. These goals generally cannot be measured directly using traditional, short-term financial methods. Alternative methods are needed to capture the nonfinancial performance dimensions. Nonfinancial performance measures (NFPMs) that indicate progress—or lack thereof—toward the achievement of a world-class company's critical success factors can be developed.

Awareness of and Participation in Performance Measures

Regardless of the number or types of measures chosen, top management must set high performance standards and communicate them to others. The measures should promote harmonious operations rather than suboptimization among organizational units. Because people are expected to act in accordance with the way they are measured, they must be aware of and understand the performance measures being used. Withholding measurement information does not allow people to perform at their highest level, which frustrates them and does not foster feelings of mutual respect and cooperation.

If standards or budget comparisons are used to assess performance, people should be involved in setting those standards or the budget. Participation results in a "social contract" between participants and evaluators by generating an understanding, and acceptance of, the standards or budget. Also, people who have participated in setting targets generally attempt to achieve the results to affirm that the plans were well founded.

Appropriate Tools for Performance

For performance measures to be fair, people must first possess or obtain the appropriate skills for their jobs. Given job competence, people must then be provided the necessary tools (equipment, resources, information, and authority) to perform their jobs in a manner consistent with the measurement process. If the appropriate support is unavailable, superiors cannot presume that subordinates will be able to reach their objectives.

In decentralized firms, there may be little opportunity to directly observe subordinates' actions and managers must make evaluations based on the outcomes that are captured by performance measures. Thus, the performance measures selected should

- highly correlate with the subunit mission,
- reflect fairly and completely the subunit manager's performance, and
- measure performance dimensions that are under the subunit manager's control.

To evaluate performance, benchmarks are established as reference points for performance measures. Benchmarks can be monetary (such as standard costs or budget appropriation amounts) or nonmonetary (such as zero defects or another organization's market share).

Need for Feedback

Performance should be monitored, and feedback (both positive and negative) should be provided to the appropriate individuals on a continuing basis. Waiting to give feedback on performance until a known evaluation point is reached does not allow employees an opportunity for early adjustment. Thus, if employee performance reviews and evaluations are performed at a certain date annually, feedback on performance should be provided periodically during the year so that employees are aware of how they are doing and have ample opportunities to maximize positive results and correct negative results, so those employees are not "blindsided" during performance reviews.

martin purmensky/iStockphoto.com

Managers should provide feedback on employee performance often so that employees are rewarded for successful results while having an opportunity to continually improve or correct poor results.

The ultimate feedback is that organizational stakeholders exhibit belief in the firm's viability. The primary determinant of this belief is typically provided by short-run financial performance measures.

SHORT-TERM FINANCIAL PERFORMANCE MEASURES FOR MANAGEMENT

4 What are the common short-term financial performance measures, and how are they calculated and used?

As discussed in Chapter 13 relative to responsibility centers and responsibility accounting, each manager in a firm is expected to make specific organizational contributions. Measurements selected to gauge managerial performance must be appropriate for the types of responsibility assigned and behavior desired. Traditionally, managerial performance was judged primarily on monetary measures such as profits, achievement of and variations from budget objectives, and cash flow.

The ability to use monetary measures is, however, affected by the type of responsibility center being evaluated because managers should be evaluated only with metrics that reflect authority and responsibility. In a cost center, the primary financial performance measurements are variances from budgeted or standard costs. Performance in a pure revenue center can be judged primarily by comparing budgeted with actual revenues. Profit and investment center managers are responsible for revenues, expenses, and return on investment; thus, a variety of measures are appropriate.

Divisional Profits

The segment margin of a profit or investment center is frequently used to measure divisional performance.[3] Segment margin is an appealing financial metric because it does not include allocated costs. Actual and budgeted margins are compared, and variances are computed to determine the points at which targets were exceeded or not achieved.

One problem with using segment margin to measure performance is that (as with many other accounting measures) individual components are subject to manipulations, such as the following:

- If a cost flow method other than first-in, first-out is used, inventory purchases can be accelerated or deferred at the end of the period to manage the period's Cost of Goods Sold for retailing and wholesaling firms. Managers in manufacturing firms can increase or decrease production to manage earnings. For example, production can be increased so that fixed cost per unit declines and earnings rise.
- Replacement of workers who have resigned or been dismissed can be deferred to minimize salary expense for the period.
- Routine maintenance can be delayed or eliminated to reduce perceived expenses in the short run.
- Sales recognition can be delayed or accelerated.
- Advertising expenses or other discretionary costs can be delayed or accelerated.
- Depreciation methods can be changed to affect depreciation expense.

These tactics can be used to "cause" reported segment margin to conform to budget expectations, but such manipulations are normally not in the center's long-run best interest and could even be improper accounting.

Cash Flow

To succeed, an entity or an investment center must meet two requirements:

- long-run profitability and
- continuous liquidity.

The statement of cash flows (SCF) provides information about the sources and uses of cash from operating, investing, and financing activities. Such information is useful when managing cash outflow commitments, adapting to adverse changes in business conditions, and assessing new cash commitments. Furthermore, because this statement identifies the

[3] The term *segment margin* is defined in Chapter 10 as segment sales minus (direct variable expenses and avoidable fixed expenses).

relationships between segment margin (or net income) and net cash flow from operations, the SCF assists managers in judging reliability of the entity's earnings. Analysis of the SCF in conjunction with budgets and other financial reports provides information on cost reductions, collection policies, impact of capital projects on total cash flows, and liquidity position. Many useful financial ratios (such as the current ratio, quick ratio, and number of days' collections in accounts receivable) involve cash flow and are useful to managers, aiding them in effectively conducting their responsibilities.

Return on Investment

Return on investment (ROI) is a ratio relating income generated by an investment center or organization to the resources (or asset base) used to produce that income. The return on investment formula is

$$\text{ROI} = \text{Income} \div \text{Assets invested}$$

To use ROI, both terms in the formula must be specifically defined; alternative definitions and preferred definitions are provided in Exhibit 14.3. Once definitions have been assigned to the terms, ROI can be used to evaluate individual entities and to make intracompany, intercompany, and multinational comparisons. However, managers making these comparisons must consider differences in the entities' characteristics and accounting methods.

Data for Nationwide Services (Exhibit 14.4 on page 558) are used to illustrate return on investment computations. The company has investment centers in Denver, San Diego, and Raleigh. All three divisions operate in the same industry, offer the same types of services to customers, and are charged with similar missions. Similarity in business lines and missions allows for comparisons among the three centers.

Exhibit 14.3 ROI Definitional Questions and Answers

Question	Preferable Answer
Is income defined as segment or operating income?	Segment income Because the manager does not have short-run control over unavoidable fixed expenses and allocated corporate costs.
Is income on a before-tax or after-tax basis?	Before-tax Because investment centers might pay higher or lower tax rates than the overall organization.
Should assets be defined as • total assets utilized; • total assets available for use; or • net assets (equity)?	Total assets available for use Because if duplicate or unused assets were eliminated from the formula, there would be no encouragement for managers to dispose of those assets and gain additional cash flow that could be used for more profitable projects. Alternatively, if the objective is to measure how well the segment is performing, given the funds provided for that segment, then net assets should be used to measure return on equity.
Should plant assets be included at • original cost; • depreciated book value; or • current value?	Current value Because as assets age and net book value declines, an investment center earning the same income each year would show a continuously increasing ROI. Although more difficult to obtain and possibly more subjective, current values measure the opportunity cost of using the assets.
Should beginning, ending, or average assets be used?	Average assets Because the numerator income amount is for a period of time, the denominator base should reflect for the same time frame.

Exhibit 14.4 Data for Nationwide Services

	IN THOUSANDS			
	Denver	San Diego	Raleigh	Total
Revenues	$ 3,200,000	$ 675,000	$ 430,000	$ 4,305,000
Direct costs				
Variable	(1,120,000)	(310,000)	(172,000)	(1,602,000)
Fixed (avoidable)	(550,000)	(118,000)	(60,000)	(728,000)
Segment margin	$ 1,530,000	$ 247,000	$ 198,000	$ 1,975,000
Unavoidable fixed and allocated costs	(372,000)	(78,000)	(50,000)	(500,000)
Operating income	$ 1,158,000	$ 169,000	$ 148,000	$ 1,475,000
Taxes (34%)	(393,720)	(57,460)	(50,320)	(501,500)
Net income	$ 764,280	$ 111,540	$ 97,680	$ 973,500
Current assets	$ 48,500	$ 33,120	$ 20,000	
Fixed assets	6,179,000	4,610,000	900,000	
Total asset cost	$ 6,227,500	$ 4,643,120	$ 920,000	
Accumulated Depreciation	(1,232,500)	(1,270,000)	(62,500)	
Total asset book value	$ 4,995,000	$ 3,373,120	$ 857,500	
Liabilities	(2,130,000)	(600,000)	(162,500)	
Net assets	$ 2,865,000	$ 2,773,120	$ 695,000	
Proportion of total assets utilized	100%	93%	85%	
Current value of fixed assets	$ 5,500,000	$ 2,400,000	$ 780,000	
Market value of invested capital (for EVA)	$18,250,000	$ 2,400,000	$ 500,000	

Note: A summarized corporate balance sheet would not balance with the investment center balance sheets because of the existence of general corporate assets and liabilities.

Exhibit 14.5 provides the return on investment rates (using a variety of bases) for Nationwide Services' investment centers. The rates vary because different numerator and denominator definitions are used in each case. These variations demonstrate why the income and assets involved must be defined before making computations or comparisons.

The ROI formula can be restated to provide useful information about two individual factors that compose the rate of return: profit margin and asset turnover. This restatement, called the **Du Pont model**, is

$$\text{ROI} = \text{Profit margin} \times \text{Asset turnover}$$
$$= (\text{Income} \div \text{Sales}) \times (\text{Sales} \div \text{Assets})$$

Profit margin is the ratio of income to sales and indicates what proportion of each sales dollar is *not* used for expenses (and, thus, becomes profit). Profit margin can be used to judge management's efficiency with regard to the relationship between sales and expenses. **Asset turnover** measures asset productivity and shows the number of sales dollars generated by each dollar of assets. This metric can be used to judge management's effective utilization of assets relative to revenue production.

Exhibit 14.6 shows the calculations of the ROI components for each of Nationwide Services' investment centers using segment margin and total historical cost as the income

Exhibit 14.5 ROI Computations

	Denver	San Diego	Raleigh
Operating income / Assets utilized	$1,158,000 / $4,995,000	$169,000 / $3,137,002	$148,000 / $728,875
ROI	23.2%	5.4%	20.3%
Operating income / Asset current value	$1,158,000 / $5,500,000	$169,000 / $2,400,000	$148,000 / $780,000
ROI	21.1%	7.0%	19.0%
Segment margin / Total asset cost	$1,530,000 / $6,227,500	$247,000 / $4,643,120	$198,000 / $920,000
ROI	24.6%	5.3%	21.5%
Segment margin / Asset book value	$1,530,000 / $4,995,000	$247,000 / $3,373,120	$198,000 / $857,500
ROI	30.6%	7.3%	23.1%
Segment margin / Asset current value	$1,530,000 / $5,500,000	$247,000 / $2,400,000	$198,000 / $780,000
ROI	27.8%	10.3%	25.4%
Segment margin / Net assets	$1,530,000 / $2,865,000	$247,000 / $2,773,120	$198,000 / $695,000
ROI	53.4%	8.9%	28.5%

Exhibit 14.6 ROI Components—Du Pont Formula

Denver

ROI = (Income ÷ Sales) × (Sales ÷ Assets)
= ($1,530,000 ÷ $3,200,000) × ($3,200,000 ÷ $6,227,500)
= 0.478 × 0.514
= 24.6%

San Diego

ROI = (Income ÷ Sales) × (Sales ÷ Assets)
= ($247,000 ÷ $675,000) × ($675,000 ÷ $4,643,120)
= 0.366 × 0.145
= 5.3%

Raleigh

ROI = (Income ÷ Sales) × (Sales ÷ Assets)
= ($198,000 ÷ $430,000) × ($430,000 ÷ $920,000)
= 0.460 × 0.467
= 21.5%

and asset base definitions. Thus, ROI is the same as that given in the third calculation of Exhibit 14.5.

The Denver investment center has both the highest profit margin and highest turnover. This center may be benefiting from scale economies relative to the other divisions, which could partially account for its superior performance. Additionally, Denver is better at leveraging its assets; as shown in Exhibit 14.4 (p. 558), the center's assets are 100 percent utilized.

The San Diego center is performing very poorly compared to the other two investment centers. Based on the relationship between the accumulated depreciation and fixed asset cost amounts, the San Diego center appears to be the oldest, which could be a factor driving its poor performance. San Diego's manager should consider purchasing more modern facilities to generate more sales and greater profits. Such an investment could, however, cause ROI to decline because the asset base would increase. Rate of return computations can encourage managers to retain and use old plant assets (especially when accumulated depreciation is deducted from the asset base) to keep ROIs high as long as those assets can keep revenues up and expenses down.

The Raleigh investment center is the newest of the three based on the low proportion of accumulated depreciation to fixed asset cost. With increased asset utilization, the Raleigh investment center should generate a higher asset turnover and raise its ROI.

Sales prices, volume and mix of products sold, expenses, and capital asset acquisitions and dispositions affect ROI. Return on investment can be increased through various management actions including

- raising sales prices if demand will not be impaired;
- decreasing expenses; and
- decreasing investment in assets, especially nonproductive ones.

Actions should be taken only after considering relationships among the factors that determine ROI. For instance, a sales price increase could reduce sales volume if demand is elastic with respect to price.

Profit margin, asset turnover, and ROI can be assessed as favorable or unfavorable only if each component is compared with a valid benchmark. Comparison bases include expected results, prior results, or results of other similar entities.

Residual Income

An investment center's **residual income (RI)** is the profit earned that exceeds an amount "charged" for funds committed to the center. The "charged" amount is equal to a specified target rate of return multiplied by the asset base and is comparable to an imputed rate of interest on the divisional assets used.[4] The rate can be changed to compensate for market rate fluctuations or for risk. The RI computation is:

$$\text{Residual income} = \text{Income} - (\text{Target rate} \times \text{Asset base})$$

Residual income yields a dollar figure rather than a percentage. Expansion (or additional investments in assets) should occur in an investment center if positive RI (dollars of return) is expected on the dollars of additional investment. Continuing the Nationwide Services example, Exhibit 14.7 illustrates the calculation of each investment center's RI.

Exhibit 14.7 Residual Income Calculations

Denver

RI = \$1,530,000 − (0.15 × \$6,227,500) = \$1,530,000 − \$934,125 = \$595,875

San Diego

RI = \$247,000 − (0.15 × \$4,643,120) = \$247,000 − \$696,468 = \$(449,468)

Raleigh

RI = \$198,000 − (0.15 × \$920,000) = \$198,000 − \$138,000 = \$60,000

[4]This target rate is similar to the discount rate used in capital budgeting (discussed in Chapter 15). For management to invest in a capital project, that project must earn at least a minimum specified rate of return. In the same manner, the ROI of an investment center must be equal to or higher than the target rate used to compute residual income.

Nationwide Services has established a 15 percent target return on total assets and has defined income as segment margin and asset base as total historical cost of assets. Denver and Raleigh show positive RIs, but San Diego's negative RI indicates that income is significantly low relative to asset investment.

Economic Value Added

A measure that has been developed to more directly align managerial interests with common stockholders' interests is **economic value added (EVA®)**.[5] Conceptually similar to RI, EVA measures the profit produced above the cost of capital. However, EVA applies the target rate of return to the market value of the capital invested rather than the asset book values that are used to calculate RI. Furthermore, EVA is calculated on net income, or the after-tax profits available to stockholders. The EVA calculation is as follows:

EVA = After-tax profits − (Cost of capital % × Market value of invested capital)

Using information on net income and market values given in Exhibit 14.4 (p. 558), calculations of EVA for each Nationwide Services investment center are given in Exhibit 14.8. The after-tax cost of capital is assumed to be 13 percent.

Exhibit 14.8 Economic Value Added Calculations

Denver

EVA = \$764,280 − (0.13 × \$18,250,000) = \$764,280 − \$2,372,500 = \$(1,608,220)

San Diego

EVA = \$111,540 − (0.13 × \$2,400,000) = \$111,540 − \$312,000 = \$(200,460)

Raleigh

EVA = \$97,680 − (0.13 × \$500,000) = \$97,680 − \$65,000 = \$32,680

As the difference between the market value of invested capital (total equity and interest-bearing debt) and the book value of assets increases, so do the relative benefits of using EVA rather than RI as a performance measure. The results given in Exhibit 14.8 show a different portrayal of performance than those given by ROI and RI. EVA shows the Raleigh center to be the stellar performer. By failing to capture the large difference between the market and book values of the Denver investment center, ROI and RI significantly overstate Denver's performance. San Diego still appears to be performing poorly, although better than Denver.

Despite its popularity, EVA cannot measure all dimensions of performance and is short-term focused. Accordingly, the EVA measure can discourage investment in long-term projects because such investments cause an immediate increase in the amount of invested capital, but only later in time do they increase after-tax profits. For greatest benefit, EVA should be supplemented with longer-term financial and nonfinancial performance measures.

Limitations of Return on Investment, Residual Income, and Economic Value Added

Each financial measure of performance discussed has certain limitations. For example, the limitations of divisional profit and cash flow are, respectively, their potential for income and cash flow manipulation.

ROI, RI, and EVA have three primary limitations. The first limitation reflects the use of accounting income. Income can be manipulated or managed in the short run, depending on the accounting methods selected to account for items such as inventory or depreciation.

[5] EVA is a registered trademark of Stern Stewart & Co. It was first discussed by Alfred Marshall, an English economist, in about 1890. More information about EVA can be found at http://www.sternstewart.com/?content=proprietary&p=eva (last accessed 1/28/12).

For valid comparisons to be made, all investment centers must use the same accounting methods. Because neither cash flows nor the time value of money are considered, income may not always provide the best basis for evaluating performance.

The second limitation of ROI, RI, and EVA relates to the asset investment base used. Asset investment can be difficult to properly measure and assign to center managers. Some investments (such as research and development costs) have value beyond the accounting period but are not capitalized and, thus, create an understated asset base. Previous managers could have acquired assets and, if those managers are no longer heading the center, current managers can potentially be judged on investment decisions over which the current managers had no control. If fixed assets and inventory are not restated for price-level increases, net income could be overstated (or understated, in the event of price-level decreases), and the investment base could be understated (or overstated). Managers who keep and use older assets can report much higher ROIs than managers using new assets. For EVA, this situation exists for the income measure, but not for the asset measure, because EVA focuses on the market value of capital employed.

The third limitation of these measures is a single, potentially critical problem: the measures direct attention to how well an investment center performed in isolation rather than relative to companywide objectives. Such a focus can result in resource suboptimization so that the firm is not maximizing its operational effectiveness and efficiency. Assume that the Raleigh investment center (shown in Exhibit 14.6, p. 559 to have an ROI of 21.5 percent) has an opportunity to increase income by $40,000 by installing a new $200,000 service kiosk. This specific investment has an ROI of 20 percent ($40,000 ÷ $200,000), and as shown in the following calculation, installing the kiosk would cause Raleigh's ROI to decline slightly:

$$\begin{aligned}\text{New Raleigh ROI} &= (\$198{,}000 + \$40{,}000) \div (\$920{,}000 + \$200{,}000)\\ &= \$238{,}000 \div \$1{,}120{,}000\\ &= 21.25\%\end{aligned}$$

If investment center managers are evaluated only on the basis of ROI, the Raleigh center manager will not accept this investment opportunity. However, if Nationwide Services has a 15 percent target rate of return on investment, the Raleigh manager's decision to reject the new opportunity suboptimizes companywide returns. This venture should be accepted because it provides a return higher than the firm's target rate. Top management should be informed of such opportunities, made aware of the effects that acceptance might have on divisional performance measurements, and be willing to reward such acceptance based on the impact on company performance.

DIFFERENCES IN PERSPECTIVES

5 Why should company management focus on long-run performance?

Concentrating solely on financial results is similar to a basketball coach focusing solely on the game score. Both the financial measures and the score are **lagging indicators**, or reflections of past decisions. Succeeding in business or sports requires that considerable attention be placed on actionable steps for effectively competing, whether in the global marketplace or on the court. Measurements for improving performance should involve tracking **leading indicators** or data about the actionable steps that will create the results desired. Thus, as illustrated in Exhibit 14.9, leading indicators reflect causes and lagging indicators reflect effects or outcomes.

Managing for the long run has commonly been viewed as managing a series of short runs. Theoretically, if a firm performs well in each successive short period, its future is secure. Although appealing, this approach fails when the firm does not keep pace with long-range technical and competitive trends. Thinking only of short-run performance and ignoring the time required to make long-term improvements can doom a firm in the globally competitive environment.

Short-run objectives focus on the effective and efficient management of current operating, investing, and financing activities. A firm's long-term objectives involve resource investments and proactive efforts, such as customer satisfaction, quality, delivery, price, service, and sustainability to enhance competitive position. Because competitive position results from the interaction of various factors, a firm must identify the most important drivers (not

Exhibit 14.9 Leading and Lagging Indicators

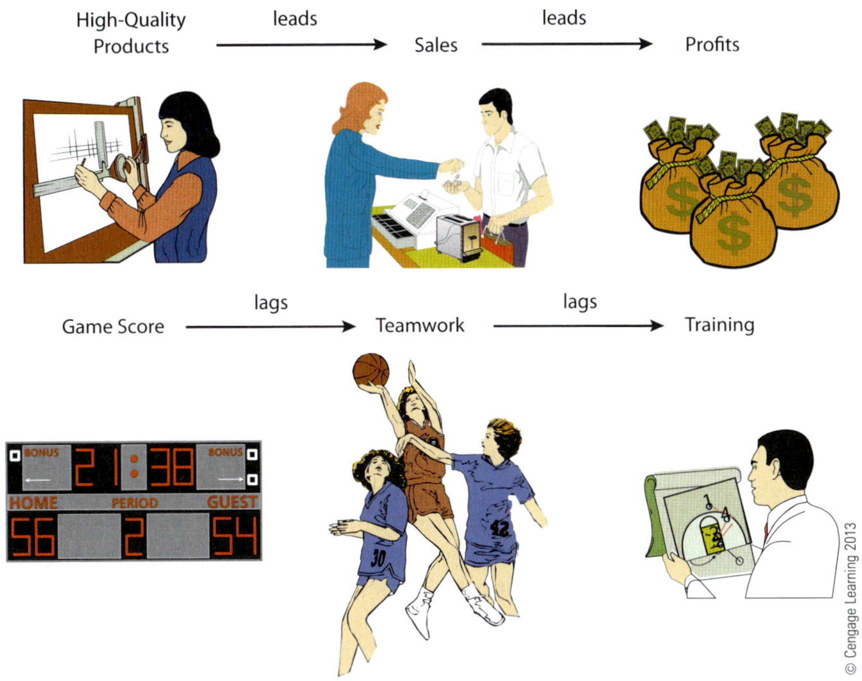

just predictors) for achieving a particular long-run objective. For example, predictors of increased market share might include increased spending on employee training, research and development, or capital improvements. The true drivers of a firm's increased market share, however, are likely to be product and service quality, speed of delivery, and reputation relative to the competitors. Measurements of success in these areas would be leading indicators of increased market share and profitability.

NONFINANCIAL PERFORMANCE MEASURES

6 What factors should managers consider when selecting nonfinancial performance measures?

Performance can be evaluated qualitatively and quantitatively. Qualitative measures are often subjective; for example, a manager could be evaluated using low-to-high rankings on job skills such as technical knowledge, quality of work, and need for supervision. Rankings can be given for an individual on a stand-alone basis, in relationship to other managers, or on a group or team basis. Although such measures provide useful information, at some point and in some way, performance should also be compared to a quantitative—but not necessarily financial—standard. People are generally more comfortable with, and respond better to, quantitative rather than qualitative measures of performance because quantitative measures provide a defined target at which to aim. Quantitative performance measures are of two types: financial (previously discussed) and nonfinancial.

Selection of Nonfinancial Measures

Nonfinancial performance measures use information contained in the cost management, rather than the financial accounting, system. Thus, NFPMs are based on nonmonetary details, such as time (e.g., manufacturing cycle time or setup time), quantities (e.g., number of patents generated or pounds of material moved), and ratios (e.g., percentage of good units to total units produced or percentage change in pollutant emissions from prior period). Appropriate nonfinancial metrics are those that

- can be clearly articulated and defined,
- are relevant to the objective,
- can trace responsibility,
- rely on valid data,
- have target objectives, and
- have established internal and/or external benchmarks.

As indicated in Exhibit 14.10, NFPMs have many distinct advantages over financial performance measures.

Using a very large number of NFPMs is counterproductive and wasteful. Additionally, there may be considerable dependence among some measures. For example, increased product quality should increase customer satisfaction, and additional worker training should decrease poor service performance. An organization must determine which factors are essential to long-term success and develop short- and long-run metrics for such factors to steer the company toward success. A short-run success measure for quality is the number of customer complaints in the current period; a long-range success measure for quality is the number of patents obtained for quality improvements of company products. Choosing appropriate performance measures can also help a company focus on the activities that cause costs to be incurred and, thus, control costs and improve processes. As discussed in Chapter 4 on activity-based management (ABM), if an activity is controlled, the cost resulting from that activity is controlled.

The following discussion addresses four important nonfinancial performance measures.

Throughput One significant NFPM is **throughput**, which reflects the movement of inputs through a process to become outputs. Throughput provides a measure of productive activity for firms. For example, **Kinder Morgan Energy Partners**' completion of a terminal facility project in Houston, Texas, will provide a throughput capacity of ten million tons of coal per year.[6] Top performing **Chipotle Mexican Grill** locations can serve 300 customers per hour: "that rate of service—'throughput'—is a Chipotle obsession."[7]

For a manufacturer, throughput could reflect the number of units that are produced during a period; for a service business, throughput could reflect the number of customers served during a period.[8] However, two additional factors should be considered in the actual

Exhibit 14.10 Advantages of Nonfinancial over Financial Performance Measures

Compared to financial measures, nonfinancial performance measures are more

- **relevant** to nonmanagement employees who are generally more familiar with nonfinancial items (such as times and quantities) than financial items (such as costs or profits).
- **timely** than historical financial data and, thus, more apt to identify problems or benefits.
- **reflective** of the leading indicators of activities, such as manufacturing and delivering quality goods and services and providing customer service, that create shareholder wealth.
- **causal** of goal-congruent behavior (rather than suboptimization) because they promote long-term success rather than the short-term success promoted by financial measures.
- **integrated** with organizational effectiveness because they can be designed to focus on processes rather than simply outputs.
- **indicative** of productive activity and the direction of future cash flows.
- **appropriate** for gauging teamwork because they can focus on outputs that result from organizational effort (such as quality) rather than inputs (such as costs).
- **cross-functional** than financial measures, which are generally related to one function.
- **comparable** for benchmarking externally than financial measures (which can be dramatically affected by differences in accounting methods).
- **aligned** with the reward system because they are more likely to be under the control of lower-level employees than are financial measures.

[6] Business Wire, "Kinder Morgan and Arch Coal Sign Throughput Agreement to Further Expand Coal Terminal Network," *Mining.com* (January 25, 2012); http://www.mining.com/2012/01/25/kinder-morgan-and-arch-coal-sign-throughput-agreement-to-further-expand-coal-terminal-network/ (last accessed 1/28/12).

[7] D. A. Kaplan, "Chipotle's Growth Machine," *Fortune* (September 26, 2011), p. 138.

[8] In computer technology, throughput is viewed as the quantity of data that a computer can process (as measured in bits, bytes, etc. per second) during a period. In data transmission, throughput is the amount of data that can be moved from one place to another during a period.

determination of throughput. First, organizations should not count units, services, or work performed as truly being throughput unless they would be deemed acceptable for purchase by customers. Second, because a firm's primary goal is to earn income, only goods or services that are actually sold should be considered throughput. Therefore, goods or services that are either unacceptable or produced only to be stored in inventory should not be viewed as throughput.

Throughput can be analyzed as a set of component elements (similar to the manner in which the Du Pont model includes components of ROI). Components of throughput include manufacturing cycle efficiency, process productivity, and process quality yield.[9] Throughput can be calculated as follows:

$$\text{Manufacturing cycle efficiency} \times \text{Process productivity} \times \text{Process quality yield} = \text{Throughput}$$

$$\frac{\text{Value-added processing time}}{\text{Total time}} \times \frac{\text{Total units}}{\text{Value-added processing time}} \times \frac{\text{Good units}}{\text{Total units}} = \text{Throughput}$$

Manufacturing cycle efficiency is the proportion of value-added (VA) processing time to total processing time. VA processing time reflects activities that increase the product's worth to the customer. Total units produced during the period divided by the VA processing time determine **process productivity**. Production activities can produce both good and defective units. The proportion of good units resulting from activities is the **process quality yield**. An example of these calculations is given in Exhibit 14.11.

Exhibit 14.11 Throughput Calculation Example

Total processing time	80,000 hours
Total value-added processing time	20,000 hours
Total quantity of product manufactured	100,000 tons
Total quantity of good production manufactured and sold	88,000 tons

Manufacturing cycle efficiency (MCE) = VA processing time ÷ Total processing time
= 20,000 ÷ 80,000 = 25%
(indicates 75% of processing time is non-value-added)

Process productivity (PP) = Total units ÷ VA processing time
= 100,000 ÷ 20,000 = 5
(indicates 5 tons can be produced per hour)

Process quality yield (PQY) = Good units ÷ Total units
= 88,000 ÷ 100,000 = 88%
(means that 88% of the tons were good, or 12% were defective)

Throughput = MCE × PP × PQY
= 0.25 × 5 × 0.88 = 1.1
(means that 1.1 good tons are produced per hour of total processing time, compared with the 5 tons actually produced per value-added hour)

or

Throughput = Good units ÷ Total time
= 88,000 ÷ 80,000 = 1.1

[9] These terms and formulas are based on the following article: Carole Cheatham, "Measuring and Improving Throughput," *Journal of Accountancy* (March 1990), pp. 89–91. One assumption that must be made with regard to this model is that the quantity labeled "throughput" is sold. Another assumption is that the units started are always completed before the end of the measurement period.

Management should strive to increase throughput by engaging in one or several of the following methods:

- decreasing non-value-added (NVA) activities,
- increasing total unit production and sales,
- decreasing the per-unit processing time, and/or
- increasing process quality yield.

Some companies have increased throughput significantly by the use of flexible manufacturing systems and, in some cases, by reorganizing production operations. Computer technologies such as bar coding, computer-integrated manufacturing, electronic data interchange, and sophisticated production scheduling technology have also enhanced throughput at many firms. Improved throughput means a greater ability to respond to customer needs and demands, reduce production costs, and reduce inventory levels, and therefore, the NVA costs of moving and storing goods.

Quality Measures Companies operating in the global environment are also generally concerned with high product and service quality and the need to develop measurements of quality such as those presented in Exhibit 14.12. For example, if a performance measurement is the cost of defective units produced during a period, the expectation is that defects will occur and management will accept some amount of defect cost. If, instead, the performance measurement is zero defects, the expectation is that no defects will occur and such a standard would create an atmosphere more conducive to eliminating defects than would the first. As quality improves, management's threshold of "acceptable" performance becomes more demanding and performance is evaluated against progressively more rigorous benchmarks.

Exhibit 14.12 Nonfinancial Quality Measurements

Element	Measure
Prevention	Design review (number of hours) Preventive maintenance (number of hours) Employee training (number of hours) Quality circles (number of hours) Quality engineering (number of hours)
Appraisal	Material inspection (number of inspections) Work in Process inspection (number of inspections) Finished Goods inspection (number of inspections) Sample preparation (number of samples) Product simulation (number of simulations)
Internal failure	Scrap (number of units) Rework (number of units) Spoilage (number of units) Quality-related downtime (number of hours) Inspection of rework (number of units)
External failure	Warranty claims (number of claims) Complaint processing (number of complaints) Loss of goodwill (percentage of nonreturning customers*) Liability suits (number of suits) Product recalls (number of recalls)

*Not as originally listed in article.

Source: Ronald C. Kettering, "Accounting for Quality with Nonfinancial Measures: A Simple No-Cost Program for the Small Company," *Management Accounting Quarterly* (Spring 2001), p. 17. Copyright 2001 by Institute of Management Accountants. Reproduced with permission of Institute of Management Accountants in the format Textbook via Copyright Clearance Center.

A detailed discussion of calculating the cost of quality is included in Chapter 17.

Lead Time A NFPM related to customer service is lead time, which reflects how quickly customers receive their goods after placing their orders. Measuring lead time should result in products becoming more rapidly available for customers. In addition, using fewer parts, interchangeable parts, and product designs that require few or no engineering changes after the start of production shortens lead time. Lead time incentives could also drive changes in facility layout to speed work flow, increase workforce productivity, and reduce defects and rework. Last, lead time incentives should cause managers to observe and correct any NVA activities or constraints that are creating production, performance, or processing delays. Some companies are implementing activity-based management techniques to remove any implied acceptance of NVA activities. ABM can provide information on the overhead impact created by reengineered processes meant to streamline activities and minimize nonquality work.

Carbon Footprint The environmental dimension of sustainability concerns an organization's impacts on the earth's ecosystems. To assess such impacts, one NFPM is the organization's **carbon footprint**, which reflects the total of all greenhouse gas emissions created by that organization's activities during a specified time. A variety of software programs and carbon footprint calculators are available, but measurement is still difficult. The Carbon Disclosure Project (CDP), a nongovernmental organization formed in the United Kingdom in 2000, collects and publishes carbon data from nearly 3,000 companies in over 60 countries. The information is used to set reduction targets and improve environmental impacts. To help encourage the use of this NFPM, companies such as **IBM** and **HP** require suppliers to disclose their greenhouse gas emissions or be removed from the supply chains of those companies.[10]

Establishment of Comparison Bases

Once the NFPMs are selected, benchmark performance levels should be established against which actual data are compared. These levels can be developed internally (such as from a world-class division) or determined from external sources (such as competitors, companies in other industries, or database reporting initiatives). In addition, a system of monitoring and reporting comparative performance levels should be established at appropriate intervals. Typically, lower-level results are monitored more frequently (continuously, daily, or weekly) than upper-level results (monthly, quarterly, and annually). Measures used by middle management are intermediate links between the lower- and upper-level performance measures and require monitoring at intermediate points (weekly, monthly, and annually). Annual measurements can be plotted to reveal long-run trends and progress toward long-run objectives.

A general model for measuring an activity's relative success compares a numerator representing number of successes with a logical and valid denominator representing total outcome volume. For example, delivery success could be measured for a period based on success or failure information. Assume that Nationwide Services made 1,000 deliveries during a period; of those, 922 were on time and 78 were late. The company's measurement of delivery success is 92.2 percent (922 ÷ 1,000), or its delivery failure rate is 7.8 percent (78 ÷ 1,000). Determination of how well or poorly the company performed for the period would require comparison with previous periods, a target rate of success (such as 100 percent on-time deliveries), or a benchmark with a world-class competitor. Analysis of the types and causes of the 78 late deliveries should allow management to determine what actions would eliminate these causes in the process of continuous long-term improvement.

USE OF MULTIPLE MEASURES

7 Why is it necessary to use multiple performance measures?

A performance measurement system should encompass a variety of measures, especially those that track factors considered necessary for mission achievement and long-run success. Although internal measures of performance are useful, only a company's customers can truly assess organizational performance. Good performance is typically defined as providing a product or service that equals or exceeds a customer's quality, price, and delivery expectations. This definition is totally unrelated to internal measurements such as standard

[10] A. Newell, "What Is the Carbon Disclosure Project?" *TriplePundit People, Planet, Profit* (November 12, 2010); http://www.triplepundit.com/2010/11/carbon-disclosure-project/ (accessed 1/28/2012).

cost variances or capacity utilization. Companies that cannot meet customer expectations will find themselves at some point without customers and without any need for financial performance measures.

Knowing that performance is to be judged using external criteria should cause companies to implement concepts such as just-in-time inventory, total quality management, and continuous improvement. Two common themes of these concepts are to make the organization, its products, and its processes (production as well as customer responsiveness) more effective and efficient and to generate higher value through lower costs.

Exhibit 14.13 provides ideas for judging managerial performance in five areas. Some of these measures should be monitored for both short-run and long-run implications. For

Exhibit 14.13 Examples of Performance Measurements

		QUANTITATIVE	
	Qualitative	**Nonfinancial**	**Financial**
Human Resources	Acceptance of additional responsibility Increased job skills Need for supervision Interaction with upper- and lower-level employees	Proportion of direct to indirect labor (low or high depending on degree of automation) Diversity of ethnic background in hiring and promotion Scores on standardized examinations	Comparability of personnel pay levels with those of competitors Savings from using part-time personnel
Market	Addition of new product features Increased product durability Improved efficiency (and/or effectiveness) of product	Number of sales transactions Percentage repeat customers Number of new ideas generated Number of customer complaints Delivery time	Increase in revenue from previous period Percent of total market revenue Revenue generated per advertising dollar (by product or product line)
Costs	Better traceability of costs Increased cost consciousness Better employee suggestions for cost reductions Increased usage of automated equipment for routine tasks	Time to design new products Number of engineering change orders issued Length of process time Proportion of products with defects Number of different product parts Number of days of inventory Proportion of material generated as scrap/waste Reduction in setup time since prior period	Reduction in production cost (DM, DL, & OH and in total) since prior period Reduction in distribution and scrap/waste cost since prior period Variances from standard Cost of engineering changes
Returns (Profitability)	Customer satisfaction Product brand loyalty	Proportion of on-time deliveries Degree of accuracy in sales forecasts of demand	Change in market price per share Return on investment Change in net income
Environmental Sustainability	Natural habitats that have been protected or restored Energy reduction initiatives Environmental protection training for employees ISO 14001 (environmental management system) certification status	Greenhouse gas emissions Proportion of inputs from recycled sources Number of sanctions for environmental noncompliance Number of environmental audits	Environmental protection expenditures by type Amount of environmental fines Savings from environmental initiatives (such as packaging reduction)

example, a short-run measure of market improvement is the growth rate of sales. A long-run measure is change in market share. Brainstorming about both short-run and long-run measures can be an effective approach to identifying measurements. Because measures should reflect the organization's mission and culture as well as management's expectations and philosophies, changes in any of these factors should also create changes in performance measures.

USING A BALANCED SCORECARD FOR MEASURING PERFORMANCE

8 How can a balanced scorecard be used to measure performance?

In recognition of the multiple facets of performance, some companies use a balanced scorecard (BSC) approach to performance measurement. The BSC provides a set of measurements that "complements financial measures of past performance with measures of the drivers of future performance."[11] The scorecard should reflect an organization's mission and strategy and typically includes performance measures from four perspectives:

- financial,
- internal business,
- customer, and
- learning and growth.

Managers choosing to apply the BSC demonstrate a belief that traditional financial performance measures alone are insufficient to assess how the firm is doing and how it is likely to do in the future.

One concern about the traditional four-box BSC diagram was that companies might select objectives for each perspective "without making sure they are linked or aligned... [which] could lead to silo activities" and noncohesive and nonintegrated strategies.[12] Many of the present BSCs are depicted as "strategy maps" rather than as the traditional four-box template. The strategy map indicates the linkages between and among the scorecard performance measurements and perspectives. Exhibit 14.14 (p. 570) provides such a strategy map presentation using the BSC from Crown Castle International, which owns and manages wireless infrastructures including towers for the communications industry.

Companies adapt the balanced scorecard to fit their own structures and environments. Financial measures of the BSC should reflect stakeholder-relevant issues of profitability, organizational growth, and market price of stock. Such measures are lagging indicators of the other perspectives and can include subunit operating income, net income, cash flow, change in market share, and return on assets. Customer measures lead financial perspective measures and should indicate how the organization is faring relative to customer issues of speed (delivery time), quality, service, and price (both at and after purchase). Internal process measures should focus on organizational actions designed to meet customer needs and expectations. Measures in this area are usually quantitative and could include process quality yields, manufacturing or service cycle efficiency, time to market on new products, on-time delivery, and cost variances. Learning and growth measures lead customer perspective measures and should focus on using the organization's intellectual capital to adapt to changing customer needs or influence new customer needs and expectations through product or service innovations. Learning and growth measures tend to be quantitative, long-term targets. These measures might include number of patents or copyrights applied for, percentage of research and development projects resulting in patentable products, average time of R&D project from conception to commercialization, and percentage of capital invested in "high-tech" projects. Learning and growth measures can help an organization ascertain its ability to learn, grow, improve, and survive.

BSCs may be used in organizations at multiple levels: top management, subunit, and even individual employees. When a BSC is implemented at lower levels of the organization, care should be taken to make certain that the measurements used can "roll up" into

[11] Robert S. Kaplan and David P. Norton, *The Balanced Scorecard* (Boston: Harvard Business School Press, 1996), p. 8.

[12] B. Marr, What Is a Modern Balanced Scorecard?, *Management Case Study*, The Advanced Performance Institute (2010), p. 4; http://www.ap-institute.com/media/3967/what_is_a_modern_balanced_scorecard.pdf (accessed 1/28/2012).

Exhibit 14.14 Using the Balanced Scorecard to Drive Strategy

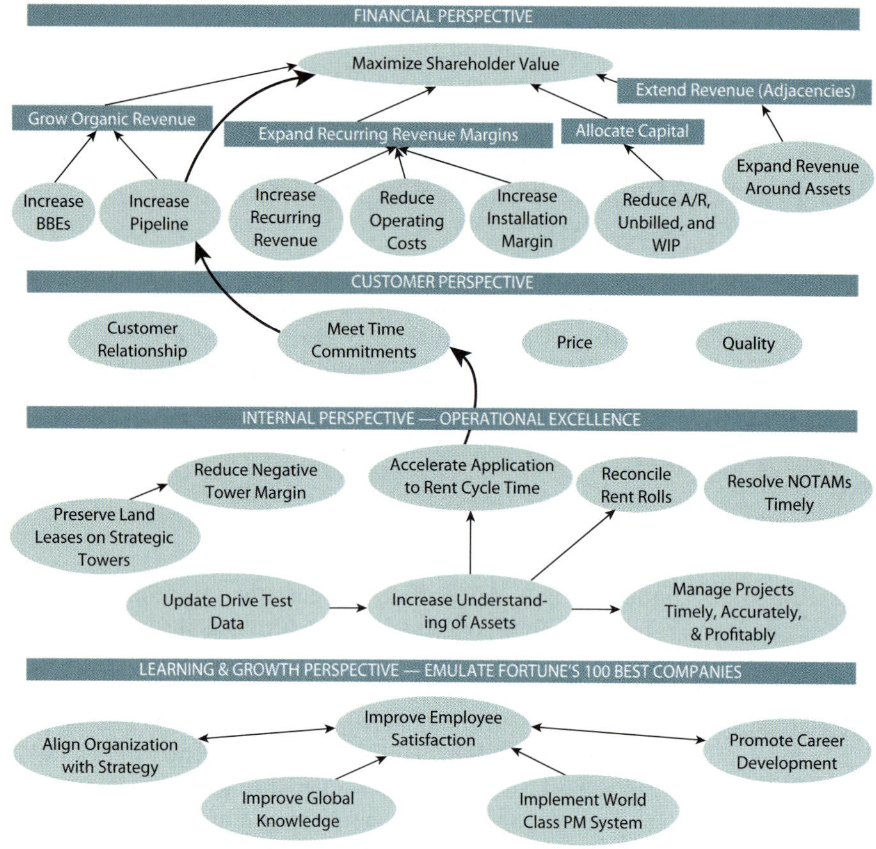

Source: Robert E. Paladino, "Balanced Forecasts Drive Value," *Strategic Finance* (January 2005) p. 36. Copyright 2005 by Institute of Management Accountants. Reproduced with permission of Institute of Management Accountants in the format Textbook via Copyright Clearance Center.

higher-level measurements that will ultimately provide the organizational results desired. Regardless of the managerial level at which the scorecard is used or the type of organization using the scorecard, this technique allows measurement data to be compiled in a way that reflects the organizational mission. "Taken together, the measures provide a holistic view of what is happening both inside and outside the organization or level, thus allowing all constituents of the organization to see how their activities contribute to attainment of the organization's overall mission."[13]

Because a clear trend in performance measurement is accounting for environmental impact and sustainability of operations, many firms are beginning to include sustainability metrics in BSCs. Three possible approaches to including such metrics are to incorporate them as a fifth dimension in a traditional BSC, develop a separate sustainability scorecard, or integrated them across the four existing BSC categories.[14] Exhibit 14.15 illustrates a framework that not only incorporates "green" information technology (IT) initiatives into the original four BSC perspectives but also includes a separate environmental and social sustainability perspective.

No single BSC, measurement system, or set of performance measurements is appropriate for all organizations or, possibly, even all responsibility centers within the same company. Although some performance measurements, such as financial viability, zero defects, and customer service, are important regardless of the type of organization or its location,

[13] Chee W. Chow, Denise Ganulin, Kamal Haddad, and Jim Williamson, "The Balanced Scorecard: A Potent Tool for Energizing and Focusing Healthcare Organization Management," *Journal of Healthcare Management* (May–June 1998), pp. 263–280.

[14] J. B. Butler, S. C. Henderson, and C. Raiborn, "Sustainability and the Balanced Scorecard: Integrating 'Green' Measures into Business Reporting," *Management Accounting Quarterly* (Winter 2011), pp. 1–10.

Exhibit 14.15 Green IT Initiatives and a Sustainability BSC

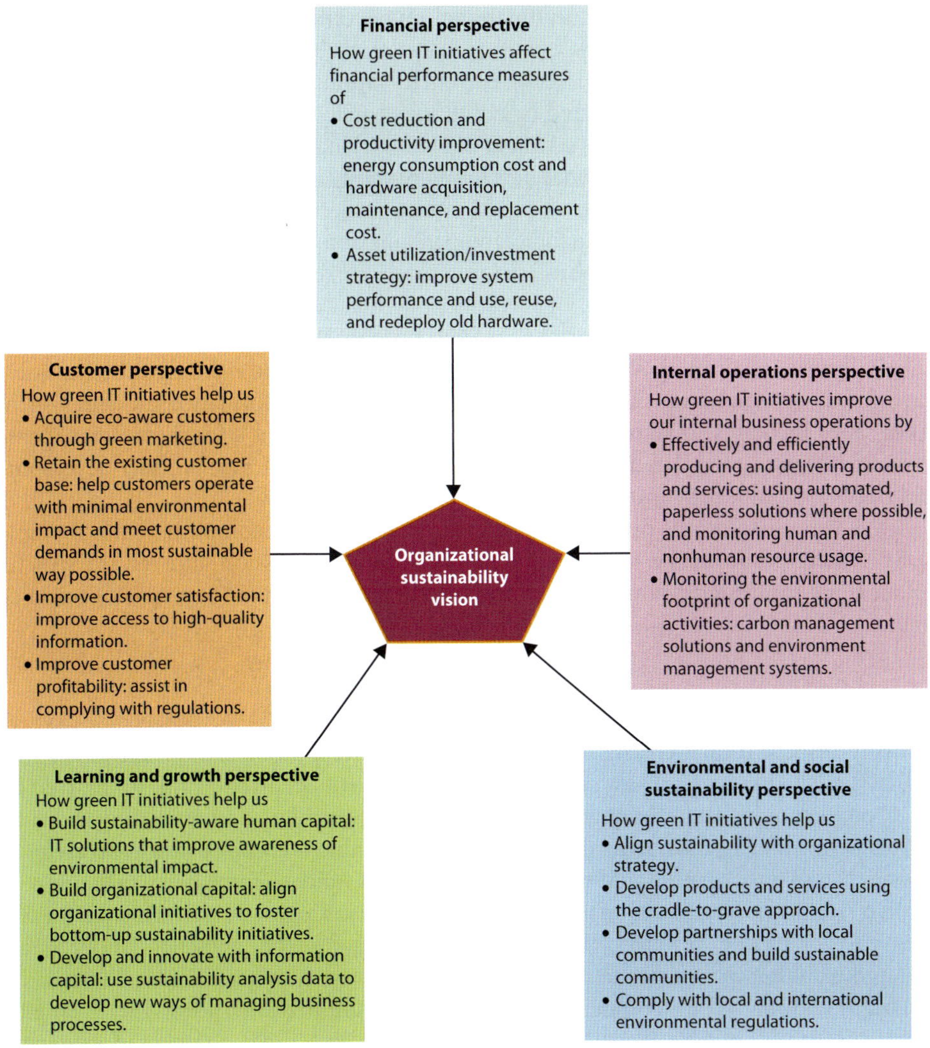

Source: Adapted from R. P. Jain, R. Benbunan-Fich, and K. Mohan, "Assessing Green IT Initiatives Using the Balanced Scorecard," *IT Pro* (January/February 2011), p. 27.

foreign operations may require some additional considerations in performance measurement and evaluation compared to domestic operations.

PERFORMANCE EVALUATION IN MULTINATIONAL SETTINGS

Many large companies have foreign operations in which performance must be measured and evaluated. Use of only one measurement criterion—especially a financial one such as income—is even less appropriate for multinational segments than it is for domestic responsibility centers.

The investment cost necessary to create the same type of organizational unit in different countries can differ substantially. For example, because of exchange rates and legal costs, it is significantly more expensive for a U.S. company to open a Japanese subsidiary than an Indonesian one. If performance were measured using residual income calculated with the same target rate of return, the Japanese unit would be placed at a distinct disadvantage because of its larger investment base. However, the company could believe that the possibility of future Japanese joint ventures or market inroads justifies the larger investment. One method of handling such a discrepancy in investment bases is to assign a lower target rate when computing residual income for the Japanese subsidiary than for the Indonesian one. This type of differential might also be appropriate because of the lower political, financial, and economic risks.

Income comparisons between multinational units could be invalid because of differences in trade tariffs, income tax rates, currency fluctuations, political risks, and the possibility of restrictions on the transfer of goods or currencies among countries. Income earned by a multinational unit can also be affected by conditions totally outside its control, such as protectionism of local companies, government aid, or varying wage rates caused by differing standards of living, levels of industrial development, and/or the amount of social services. If the multinational subunit adopts the local country's accounting practices, differences in international standards can make income comparisons among units difficult and inconvenient even after the statements are translated to a single currency basis.

Firms with multinational profit or investment centers (or subsidiaries) need to establish flexible systems of measuring performance. Such systems should recognize that differences in sales volumes, accounting standards, economic conditions, and risk might be outside the control of an international subunit's manager. Qualitative performance measures such as market share increases, quality improvements (defect reductions), inventory management improvements with the related reduction in working capital, and new product development could become significantly more useful.

Regardless of location, performance measures reflect on accomplishments of employees. By linking performance measures to an organization's mission and reward structure, employees are motivated to improve performance that will result in long-run organizational viability.

COMPENSATION STRATEGY

9 What is compensation strategy, and what factors must be considered in designing the compensation strategy?

The many organizational changes (technological advances, globalization, customer focus, product/service quality, and sustainability issues) that have occurred in the recent past have created opportunities and challenges in establishing responsibility and rewarding individuals for their performance. Each organization should determine a **compensation strategy** that addresses the role that pay should play in the firm. The foundation for the actual compensation plan should tie organizational goals, mission, and strategies to performance measurements and employee rewards. The relationships among the activities underlying an integrated planning, performance, and reward structure are shown in Exhibit 14.16.

The traditional U.S. compensation strategy differentiates among three employee groups: executives, middle management, and workers. Executive compensation generally includes a salary element and contingent pay tied to incentives for meeting or exceeding targeted objectives such as companywide net income or earnings per share. Middle managers are typically given salaries with the opportunity for future raises (and possibly bonuses) based on some performance measure such as segment income or divisional return on investment. Workers are paid wages (usually specified by union contract, established by skill level or seniority, or tied to the minimum-wage law) for the number of hours worked or production level achieved; current or year-end bonuses may be paid if performance exceeds some specified quantitative measure.

The most basic reward plan consists of hourly, weekly, monthly, or other periodic compensation, which is related to time spent at work rather than on tasks accomplished. This type of compensation provides no immediate link between performance and reward. The only motivational aspects of periodic compensation are the prospects for advancement to a higher periodic pay rate/amount, demotion to a lower pay rate/amount, or dismissal.

PAY-FOR-PERFORMANCE PLANS

Compensation plans should encourage higher levels of employee performance and loyalty, while lowering overall costs and raising profits. The plans must encourage behavior essential to achieving organizational goals and maximizing stockholder value. More than any other goal or objective, maximization of shareholder wealth (a long-term goal) drives the design of reward systems.

Exhibit 14.16 Planning–Performance–Reward Model

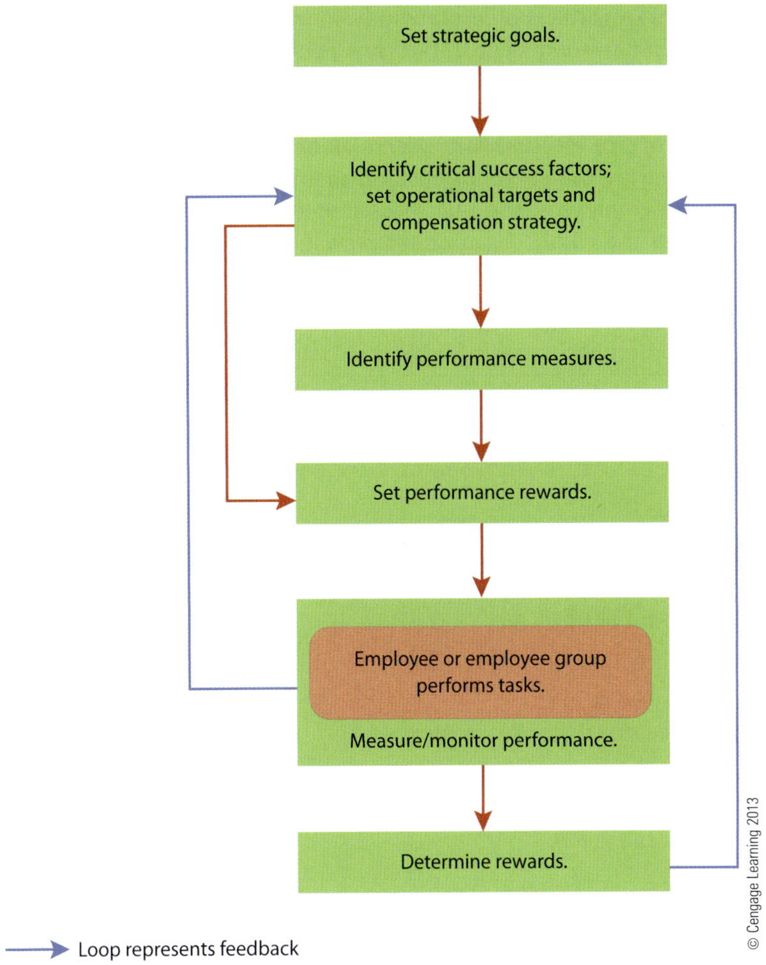

Approximately 83 percent of firms use some type of pay-for-performance plan for employees.[15] In a pay-for-performance plan, the defined performance measures must be highly correlated with the organization's operational targets. For example, because **Intel** has established sustainability as a corporate goal, part of every employee's pay-for-performance compensation is tied to the company's environmental performance to encourage employee support.[16] If such correlations do not exist, suboptimization can occur, and workers can earn incentive pay even though the organization's broader objectives are not achieved.

A second consideration when designing a performance-based reward system is that the measures should not focus solely on the short run. The most common short-run measure on which to base pay-for-performance is a financial one, such as income. However, such a linkage can encourage employees to forget to consider "risks to long-term sustainability, company brand or broader social concerns. The most successful reward strategies encourage long-term goals, and recognise [sic] the need for a balance [among] financial, operational and employee satisfaction measures."[17] In other words, short-run measures are not necessarily viable proxies for the long-run wealth maximization that is the primary objective of U.S. businesses.

[15] Incentive Research Foundation, *The State of Tangible Incentive Research: The Use of Tangible Incentives* (2011); http://theirf.org/.6079184.html (accessed 1/29/12).

[16] B. Chorn, "Case in Point: How Intel Engages Employees in Sustainability," *BSR Insight* (August 25, 2009), pp. 2–3; http://images.carbonrally.com/assets/BSR_Insight_Intel_Employee.pdf (accessed 1/29/12).

[17] Hay Group, "Bonuses Are Back...But Not As We Know Them," *News Release* (July 7, 2010); http://www.haygroup.com/ww/press/details.aspx?id=27567 (accessed 1/29/12).

Pay-for-performance criteria should encourage workers to adopt a long-range perspective. Many financial incentives now involve shares of corporate common stock or stock options. Employees (regardless of level) who become stockholders in their employing company tend to develop, to some degree, the same perspective as other stockholders: long-run wealth maximization.

Because each organizational subunit has a unique mission and possesses unique competencies, the performance measurement system and reward structure for subunit employees should be crafted with the subunit's mission in mind. What is measured and rewarded affects the focus of employees, and that focus should be directed toward factors that determine the success of the whole organization as well as its subunits. Exhibit 14.17 indicates how the form of reward is influenced by the subunit mission.

Exhibit 14.17 Different Strategic Missions: Compensation Implications

	← MISSION CONTINUUM →		
	Build	**Hold**	**Harvest**
Base salary	Low	⟶	High
Incentives tied to sales growth	High	⟶	Low
Incentives tied to profitability	Low	⟶	High
Incentives tied to cost control	Low	⟶	High
Incentives tied to nonfinancial performance measures	High	⟶	Low
Incentive compensation formula criteria	Subjective	⟶	Objective
Incentive compensation time horizon	Long term	⟶	Short term

Job commitment of employees can also be an important factor in designing employee incentive plans. It is possible that younger employees have a longer-term perspective than older employees, especially those who will retire from the firm within a few years.[18] In designing employee incentives, any difference in time-frame perspectives among employees should be considered. Soon-to-leave employees could suboptimize to see short-run, rather than long-run, benefits of investment projects.

Another consideration in designing worker incentives is balancing the incentives provided to individuals and groups (or teams). In automated production systems, workers devote more time to indirectly monitoring and controlling machinery and are less involved in hands-on production. Further, many organizational and managerial philosophies stress group or team performance. Group incentives are necessary to encourage cooperation among workers. However, if *only* group incentives are offered, the incentive system could be ineffective because the reward for an individual's effort goes to the group. The larger the group size, the smaller the individual's share of the group reward becomes. Eventually, some workers take a "free ride" on the group because they perceive their proportional shares of the group reward to be insufficient to compensate for their efforts.

[18] Although younger workers in the past were always presumed to have a longer time-frame perspective, such a presumption is no longer necessarily true. Today's workers tend not to have the same level of organizational commitment that workers of the past had. These workers often see their current job as merely a short-run "stepping stone" to their next position—meaning that their perspective is little different from the soon-to-retire employees. One study found that Millennials (generally considered to be born 1981 to 2000) will have an average of seven jobs by age 26. The same study said that 37 percent of Millennials switched jobs because they "just needed a change" rather than for a better salary, benefits, or position. [Mr. Youth and Intrepid, *Millennial Inc. What Your Company Will Look Like When Millennials Call the Shots* (New York: Chelsea Market, 2010), p. 9; http://www.millennialinc.com/viewPaper.html (accessed 1/29/12).]

LINKS BETWEEN PERFORMANCE MEASURES AND REWARDS

When the compensation strategy and target objectives are known, performance measures for individual employees or employee groups can be determined based on their required contributions to the operational plan. Performance measures should, directly or indirectly, link individual actions to basic business strategies. Rewards in a performance-based compensation plan should use monetary and nonmonetary as well as short-term and long-term measures. If an organization makes numerous measurements but only rewards financial outcomes, employees will quickly realize what is truly important in the work environment and what is being measured simply for the sake of measurement.

Degree of Control over Performance Output

Actual performance is a function of employee effort, employee skill, and random effects. Random effects include performance measurement error, problems or inefficiencies created by co-workers or adjacent workstations, illness, and weather-related production problems. After the actual performance is measured, determining the contributions of the controllable and noncontrollable factors to the achieved performance is impossible in many instances. Using performance-based pay systems causes employees to bear more risk than does the use of less comprehensive input–output measurements to determine compensation. Efforts should be made to identify performance measures that minimize the risk borne by employees.

At the worker level, performance measures should be specific and typically have a short-run focus—usually on cost and/or quality control. Each higher level in the organizational hierarchy should include increasingly more elements related to the critical success factors under an individual's control and responsibility. As the level of responsibility increases, performance measures should, by necessity, become less specific, focus on a longer time horizon, and be more concerned with organizational longevity than with short-run cost control or income. When the compensation strategy, operational targets, and performance measurements have been determined, appropriate target rewards can be specified. Rewards should motivate employees to contribute in a manner congruent with the operational objectives, and employees must be able to relate their performance to the reward structure.

Incentives Relative to Organizational Level

Individuals at different organizational levels typically view monetary rewards differently because of the relationship of pay to standard of living. Relative pay scales are essential to recognizing the value of monetary rewards to different employees. At lower employee levels, most incentives should be monetary and short term (to enhance current lifestyles), but some nonmonetary and long-term incentives should also be included so these individuals will take a long-run organizational ownership view. At higher levels, most incentives should be nonmonetary and long term (such as stock and stock options), so that top management will be more concerned about the organization's continuing well-being rather than their own short-term personal gains.

Performance Plans and Feedback

As employees perform their required tasks, performance related to the measurement standards is monitored. The two feedback loops in the model shown in Exhibit 14.16 (p. 573) exist so that problems identified in one period can be corrected in future periods. The first feedback loop relates to monitoring and measuring performance, which must be considered in setting targets for the following periods. The second feedback loop relates to the rewards given and the compensation strategy's effectiveness. Both loops are essential in the managerial planning process.

Worker Pay and Performance Links

The competitive environment in many industries has evolved to use more automation and less labor-intensive technology. Also, management philosophies now emphasize the need for workers to perform in teams and groups. An interesting paradox has been created by these changes. Workers are more detached from the production function and more involved with higher-technology tasks. Thus, the trend is to rely more on performance-based evaluation and less on direct supervision to control worker behavior. This trend is consistent with the movement to empower workers and decrease levels of supervision and layers of management. Research has indicated that pay-for-performance is increasing in large organizations for four primary reasons:

- to better align activities with business strategies;
- to create better linkages between corporate and individual performance;
- to improvement organizational or team performance; and
- to ensure market competitiveness.[19]

Promoting Overall Success

Many performance-based plans have the express goal of causing employees to act in the best interest of shareholders. One popular arrangement is profit sharing, which provides incentive payments to employees. These current and/or deferred incentive payments are contingent on organizational performance and can be in the form of cash or stock. Allocation of the total profit-sharing payment among individual employees is made on the basis of personal performance, seniority, team performance, managerial judgment, and/or specified formulas. One popular profit-sharing compensation program is the **employee stock ownership plan (ESOP)**, in which investments are made in the employer's securities.

An ESOP conforming to the Internal Revenue Code rules offers both tax and incentive advantages. Under an ESOP, the employer makes tax-deductible payments of cash or stock to a trust fund. If cash is contributed, it is used by the trust to purchase shares of the employing company's stock. Trust beneficiaries are the employees, and their wealth grows with both the employer contributions and advances in the stock price. Of course, as was so dramatically illustrated at Enron, employees are at risk of losing some or all of these benefits if the employing company goes bankrupt.

Nonfinancial Incentives

Besides various forms of monetary compensation, workers can also be motivated by nonfinancial factors. Although all employees value and require cash to satisfy basic human needs, other human needs cannot necessarily be fulfilled with monetary wealth. Employees are typically more productive when they think their efforts are appreciated. A 2011 survey of U.S. office workers showed that incentive programs made employees

- feel more valued (85 percent);
- happier and more motivated at work (70 percent);
- more loyal to their company (65 percent); and
- more productive and able to obtain better results (60 percent).[20]

Supervisors can formally recognize contributions of subordinates through simple gestures such as compliments and small awards. For example, because sustainability is a corporate goal, Intel employees can earn nonfinancial awards for community volunteering and engaging in environmental, energy-conservation, and pollution prevention programs.[21] Nonfinancial incentives contribute to making employment socially fulfilling and let employees know that superiors are attentive to, and appreciative of, their contributions.

TAX IMPLICATIONS OF COMPENSATION ELEMENTS

Differences in tax treatments of compensation components are important because taxes affect the take-home pay received by employees and the actual employer cost of the pay plan. There are three different tax treatments for employee compensation:

[19] WorldatWork, "Employers Increasing Proportion of Variable Pay in Employee Pay Programs," WorldatWork.org (July 8, 2010); http://www.worldatwork.org/waw/adimComment?id=39253 (accessed 1/29/12).

[20] SHRM Online Staff, "Survey: Noncash Rewards Boost Performance and Morale," *SHRM.org* (September 6, 2011); http://www.shrm.org/hrdisciplines/benefits/Articles/Pages/NoncashRewards.aspx (accessed 1/29/12).

[21] Chorn, *ibid.*, p. 3.

- full and immediate taxation,
- deferral of taxation, and
- exemption from taxation.

Tax deferral indicates that taxation occurs in the future rather than currently. **Tax exemption** is the most desirable form of tax treatment because the income is never subject to income taxation.

When analyzing the compensation plan, employers and employees must consider the entire package—not simply one element of the package. For employers, compensation beyond wages and salaries creates additional costs; for employees, such compensation creates additional benefits. Fringe benefits can include employee health insurance, child care, physical fitness facilities, and pension plans. However, different types of fringe benefits have different tax consequences. Certain employee fringe benefits are tax exempt to the employee but are fully deductible by the employer.[22]

GLOBAL COMPENSATION

10 What difficulties are encountered in trying to measure performance and design compensation plans for multinational firms?

As more companies engage in multinational operations, compensation systems should be developed that reward all employees and managers on a fair and equitable basis. A very important issue related to global compensation is the manner in which expatriates are compensated. **Expatriates** (expats) are parent-company and third-country nationals assigned to a foreign subsidiary or foreign nationals assigned to the parent company. Relocating individuals to foreign countries requires consideration of compensation. A fair and reasonable compensation package in one locale might not be fair and reasonable in another.

The compensation package paid to expats must reflect labor market factors, cost-of-living considerations, and currency fluctuations as well as recognize tax consequences. Typically, an expat's base salary and fringe benefits should reflect what he or she would have been paid domestically—adjusted for reasonable cost-of-living factors. These factors could be quite apparent (such as providing for housing, education, and security needs similar to those that would have been available in the home country or compensating for a spouse's loss of employment), or they could be less obvious (such as a need to hire someone in the home country to care for an elderly relative or to handle real estate investments).

Expats can be paid in the currency of the country in which they reside, in their home currency, or in a combination of both. Frequently, price-level adjustment clauses are built into the compensation system to counteract any local currency inflation or deflation. Regardless of the national currency that comprises the pay package, fringe benefits related to retirement must be related to the home country and should be paid in that currency.

Tying compensation to performance is essential because all workers recognize that what gets measured and rewarded determines what gets accomplished. Organizations must focus their reward structures to motivate employees to succeed at all activities that will create shareholder, stakeholder, and personal value. In this highly competitive age, the new paradigm of success is to provide quality products and services at a reasonable price while generating a reasonable profit margin. Top management compensation has traditionally been tied to financial measures of performance; more and more organizations are beginning to tie the compensation of all levels of workers to one or more nonfinancial performance measures.

ETHICAL CONSIDERATIONS OF COMPENSATION

ETHICS

A major issue of discussion and contention involves perceptions of disparity between the pay of ordinary workers and top managers. Plato argued that no one should earn more than five times the income earned by the lowest-paid worker. In the early 1900s, however, J. P. Morgan stated that the differential should be no more than 20 times. Today, numerous CEOs earn untold multiples of the pay of the average worker.[23]

[22] Information about fringe benefits and taxes can be found in IRS Publication 15-B; http://www.irs.gov/publications/p15b/ar02.html#en_US_2012_publink1000193627 (accessed 2/12/12).

[23] In April of each year, *The Wall Street Journal* provides a special report on executive pay.

In the recent global economic downturn, there has been considerable discussion about the gap between the income of management and the typical worker. It appears that the long-term trend of a growing gap between executives and workers may be in the process of reversing because of the recession. In 2009, the top 1 percent of income earners accounted for approximately 17 percent of adjusted gross income (AGI) in the United States; $343,927 was the lowest AGI to be included in the top 1 percent (compared to $424,000 in 2007).[24]

The greatest ethical compensation dilemmas involve circumstances that pit the welfare of employees against that of stockholders or the welfare of managers against the welfare of workers. Only if there is a perception of equity across the contributions and entitlements of labor, management, and capital will the organization be capable of achieving the efficiency to compete in global markets.

Comprehensive Review Module

KEY TERMS

asset turnover, p. 558
carbon footprint, p. 567
compensation strategy, p. 572
Du Pont model, p. 558
economic value added (EVA®), p. 561
employee stock ownership plan (ESOP), p. 576
expatriate, p. 577
lagging indicator, p. 562
leading indicator, p. 562
process productivity, p. 565
process quality yield, p. 565
profit margin, p. 558
residual income (RI), p. 560
tax deferral, p. 577
tax exemption, p. 577
throughput, p. 564
values statement, p. 551

CHAPTER SUMMARY

1 Mission Statement

- A mission statement is important to an organization because it
  - expresses the organization's purpose.
  - identifies how the organization intends to meet its customers' needs through its products/services.
  - communicates organizational purposes and goals to employees.
  - acts as a foundation for setting organizational strategy.

2 Performance Measures

- Performance measures in organizations serve to
  - assess organizational performance.
  - relate organizational goals and missions to managerial performance.
  - foster growth of subordinate managers.
  - motivate managers.
  - enhance organizational communication.
  - evaluate comparative managerial performance.
  - implement organizational control.

3 Designing Performance Measures

- The design of performance measures should be guided by
  - assessing progress toward organizational mission, goals, and objectives.
  - allowing the people being evaluated to participate in the development of the measures.
  - hiring people who have the appropriate skills and talents (or training people to have such) and

[24] T. Luhby, "Who Are the 1 Percent?" *CNNMoney* (October 29, 2011); http://money.cnn.com/2011/10/20/news/economy/occupy_wall_street_income/index.htm (last accessed 1/29/12).

providing those people with the necessary equipment, resources, information, and authority to be successful.
- providing feedback to people in a timely and useful manner.
- establishing a set of measures that will provide a variety of information about performance.

4 Short-Term Performance

- Common short-term financial performance measures include
  - divisional profits or segment margin, which is
    - calculated as segment sales minus (direct variable expenses and avoidable fixed expenses).
    - used to assess whether segmental profitability goals were achieved.
  - cash flow (by segment or responsibility unit), which is
    - calculated as cash provided (used) from operating activities, investing activities, and (if appropriate) financing activities.
    - used to assess the profitability of the responsibility unit, liquidity to pay debts as they arise, adaptability to adverse conditions, and ability to undertake new commitments.
  - return on investment, which is
    - calculated as profit margin multiplied by asset turnover.
    - used to assess the generation of income relative to the resources used to produce that income.
  - residual income, which is
    - calculated as income earned above a target rate on the unit's asset base.
    - used to assess the generation of income relative to the resources used to produce that income.
  - economic value added, which is
    - calculated as after-tax profits less the product of the market value of invested capital multiplied by the cost of capital percentage.
    - used to assess the generation of income relative to the market value of the resources used to produce that income.

5 Long-Term Performance

- Company management should focus on long-term performance because such a perspective reflects
  - leading indicators of future performance.
  - technical and competitive trends.
  - a more intensive investigation of resource allocations.
  - proactive efforts to enhance competitive position.

6 Nonfinancial Performance Measures

- When selecting nonfinancial performance measures, managers should consider that
  - people are more comfortable with quantitative rather than qualitative measures.
  - the measures must be clearly defined and communicated to those who will be evaluated by the measures.
  - the measures must be relevant to the objective, trace responsibility, and be evaluated against internal or external benchmarks.
  - the measures must use valid data that can be obtained in a cost-beneficial manner.
  - too many measures are counterproductive.

7 Multiple Measures of Performance

- Multiple measures of performance should be used because an organization's success depends on a variety of factors, each of which should be reviewed for contribution toward the organization's mission, goals, and objectives.

8 Balanced Scorecard

- A balanced scorecard can be used to measure performance by providing a set of measurements that reflect the organization's mission and strategy from a(n)
  - financial perspective.
  - customer perspective.
  - internal process perspective.
  - learning and growth perspective.
- Some companies are including a sustainability perspective in their BSCs.

9 Compensation Strategy

- The role compensation should play in an organization must be addressed.
- The underlying structure for the compensation plan includes consideration of
  - employees' control over performance output.
  - employees' positions in the organization.
  - employees' opportunities to gain feedback and adapt performance.
  - the alignment of organizational mission, goals, and objectives with the performance measurements and employee rewards.
  - tax and ethical implications of compensation.

10 Multinational Performance Measures and Design

- Measuring performance for multinational firms often creates difficulties because of differing
  - labor and tax laws.
  - employee work ethics.
  - market and political stability.
  - inflation, exchange, and labor rates.
  - consumer wealth and purchasing power.
  - financing costs.
  - accounting practices.

SOLUTION STRATEGIES

Performance Measures for Responsibility Centers, p. 555

- **Cost Center**

  Budgeted costs
  −Actual costs
  Variances (consider materiality)

- **Revenue Center**

  Budgeted revenues
  −Actual revenues
  Variances (consider materiality)

- **Profit Center**

  Budgeted profits
  −Actual profits
  Variances (consider materiality)

  Cash inflows
  −Cash outflows
  Net cash flow (adequate for operations?)

- **Investment Center**

  Budgeted profits
  −Actual profits
  Variances (consider materiality)

  Cash inflows
  −Cash outflows
  Net cash flow (adequate for operations?)

Return on investment = Income ÷ Assets (high enough rate?)

Du Pont model ROI = Profit margin × Asset turnover
= (Income ÷ Sales) × (Sales ÷ Assets)(high enough rate?)

Residual income = Income − (Target rate × Asset base) (positive or negative? amount?)

Economic value added = Income − (Cost of capital % × Market value of capital invested)
(positive or negative? amount?)

Throughput, p. 565

$$\text{Manufacturing cycle efficiency} \times \text{Process productivity} \times \text{Process quality yield} = \text{Throughput}$$

$$\frac{\text{Value-added processing time}}{\text{Total time}} \times \frac{\text{Total units}}{\text{Value-added processing time}} \times \frac{\text{Good units}}{\text{Total units}} = \text{Throughput}$$

Reward System, p. 573

The design of an effective reward structure depends heavily on each organization's unique characteristics. It is impossible to design a generic incentive model that would be effective in all firms. However, affirmative answers to the following questions provide guidance as to the applicability of a proposed incentive and reward plan for a particular organization.

1. Are the organizational objectives more likely to be achieved if the proposed compensation structure is implemented?
2. Is the proposed structure consistent with organizational design and culture as well as management philosophy?
3. Are there reasonable and objective performance measures that are good surrogates for the organizational objectives and subunit missions?
4. Are factors beyond employee/group control minimized under the performance measures of the proposed compensation structure?

5. Is the ability of employees to manipulate the performance measurements limited?
6. In light of the interests of managers, workers, and stockholders, is the proposed reward structure fair and does it encourage and promote ethical behavior?
7. Is the proposed reward structure arranged to take advantage of potential employee/employer tax benefits?
8. Does the proposed reward structure promote harmony among employee groups?
9. Is there an adequate balance between group and individual incentives?
10. Can the reward system be adapted to accommodate international constraints and considerations?

DEMONSTRATION PROBLEM 1

Household Products is a division of Delaware Electronics. The division had the following performance targets for 2013:

Asset turnover	3.1
Profit margin	6%
Target rate of return on investments for RI	15%
Cost of capital	9%
Income tax rate	35%

At the end of 2013, the following actual information concerning the company's performance is available:

Total assets at beginning of year	$24,800,000
Total assets at end of year	29,600,000
Average fair market value of invested capital for year	36,000,000
Sales	68,000,000
Variable operating costs	34,800,000
Direct fixed costs	27,440,000
Allocated fixed costs	2,700,000

Required:

a. Compute the 2013 segment margin and average assets for Household Products.
b. Based on segment margin and average assets, compute the profit margin, asset turnover, and ROI.
c. Evaluate the ROI performance of Household Products.
d. Using your answers from (b), compute the residual income for Household Products.
e. Compute the EVA for Household Products using after-tax segment margin. What causes EVA and RI to differ?
f. Based on the data given in the problem, discuss why ROI, EVA, and RI could be inappropriate measures of performance for Household Products.

Solution to Demonstration Problem 1

a.

Sales	$ 68,000,000
Variable operating costs	(34,800,000)
Direct fixed costs	(27,440,000)
Segment margin	$ 5,760,000

Average assets = ($24,800,000 + $29,600,000) ÷ 2 = $27,200,000

b. Profit margin = $5,760,000 ÷ $68,000,000 = 8.47%

Asset turnover = $68,000,000 ÷ $27,200,000 = 2.50

ROI = 8.47% × 2.5 = 21.18%

c. The target ROI for the division was 18.6 percent (6% × 3.1). The division generated an ROI of 21.18 percent. The division exceeded its target profit margin but fell short of its target asset turnover. Because the profit margin effect dominated the asset turnover effect, the achieved ROI was above the target ROI by more than 2.5 percent.

d. RI = \$5,760,000 − (0.15 × \$27,200,000)
 = \$5,760,000 − \$4,080,000
 = \$1,680,000

e. After-tax profits = Pre-tax segment income − Taxes
 = \$5,760,000 − (\$5,760,000 × 0.35)
 = \$5,760,000 − \$2,016,000
 = \$3,744,000

EVA = \$3,744,000 − (\$36,000,000 × 0.09)
 = \$3,744,000 − \$3,240,000
 = \$504,000

EVA and RI differ for three reasons. First, RI is based on pre-tax, rather than after-tax, income; RI is based on the book value of investment whereas EVA is based on the market value of investment; and the target rates of return differ between the methods.

f. ROI, RI, and EVA are all measures of short-term performance. These measures may be particularly inappropriate for divisions that have long-term missions (such as high growth). In this case, the relatively large growth (19.35 percent) in assets of Household Products from the beginning to the end of the period could indicate that this division is oriented toward growth. If so, the ROI, RI, and EVA measures will provide an incentive contrary to the growth mission.

DEMONSTRATION PROBLEM 2

Birmingham Hardwood Frames makes picture frames. During November 2013, managers compiled the following data:

Total frames manufactured	1,850,000
Good frames produced and sold	1,731,000
Total processing time (minutes)	21,120
Value-added processing time (minutes)	6,920

Required:

a. Calculate the manufacturing cycle efficiency (MCE).
b. Calculate the process productivity (PP).
c. Calculate the process quality yield (PQY).
d. Calculate throughput using one ratio.
e. Confirm your answer to (d) using the results of (a), (b), and (c).

Solution to Demonstration Problem 2

a. MCE = Value-added processing time ÷ Total processing time
 = 6,920 ÷ 21,120 = 32.77%

b. PP = Total frames manufactured ÷ Value-added processing time
 = 1,850,000 ÷ 6,920 = 267.34 frames per minute of VA time

c. PQY = Good frames manufactured ÷ Total frames manufactured
 = 1,731,000 ÷ 1,850,000 = 93.57%

d. Throughput = Good frames manufactured ÷ Total processing time
 = 1,731,000 ÷ 21,120 = 82 frames per minute

e. Throughput = MCE × PP × PQY
 = 0.3277 × 267.34 × 0.9357 = 82 frames per minute

POTENTIAL ETHICAL ISSUES

ETHICS

1. Creating an unbalanced performance measurement system that places excessive emphasis on short-term performance
2. Putting excessive emphasis on accounting earnings such that managers experience extreme pressure to manipulate financial reports
3. Reporting fraudulent or manipulated accounting numbers so that a higher bonus will be paid or the adverse effects of the actual performance on compensation will be avoided
4. Evaluating mid- and lower-level managers using performance criteria that are beyond the influence of such managers
5. Backdating managerial stock options so that the options are immediately "in the money"
6. Not informing or explaining fully all performance criteria by which employees and managers will be evaluated
7. Not providing timely feedback to employees and managers during the period so that corrective action can be taken on a timely basis
8. Rewarding only financial performance and ignoring other important performance criteria such as innovation and organizational learning
9. Engaging in suboptimization practices that are personally beneficial but detrimental to the organization as a whole
10. Compensating expats or employees in foreign operations in a manner that would be considered "inappropriate" from an external perspective because of the wage rate/salary being paid, work hours being demanded, or work conditions being provided

QUESTIONS

1. What are the benefits of organizational mission and values statements? How are organizational missions and strategies related to performance measures?
2. Why is performance measurement important to the success of businesses? Should performance measures be qualitative, quantitative, or both? Justify your answer. For performance measurements to be meaningful, why is it necessary to establish benchmarks?
3. What benefits can be gained by allowing a manager to participate in developing the performance measures that will be used to assess that manager's performance?
4. On what basis should the performance of a responsibility center be measured? What are the traditional financial performance measures for each type of responsibility center? Why can the same quantitative measures of performance *not* be used for all types of responsibility centers?
5. How can cash flow be used as a performance measure? In what ways is cash flow a relatively stronger or weaker performance measure than accrual measures such as segment income?
6. At Lockhart Inc., divisional managers are evaluated on the basis of a variety of net income measures. The controller informs the president that such measures could be misleading. What are the major concerns in defining the "income" measures? Are internal or external measures more susceptible to manipulation? Explain.
7. What is residual income, and how is it used to measure divisional performance? How is it similar to, and different from, the return on investment measure? How is residual income similar to, and different from, economic value added? How is economic value added superior to residual income as a performance measure?
8. In designing a performance measurement system, why should managerial rewards be linked to performance measures? Why would an effective compensation strategy treat top managers, middle managers, and other workers differently?
9. What is the balanced scorecard? What perspectives are considered in selecting performance measures for the balanced scorecard, and why is each of these perspectives important?

10. Why would a company want to include sustainability as a perspective in a balanced scorecard?
11. Why is the trend in U.S. business away from automatic pay increases and toward increased use of incentive compensation plans?
12. If worker performance measures used in a pay-for-performance plan are not highly correlated with corporate goals, what is the likely result for the organization? For the workers?
13. How does the time perspective of a performance-based plan affect the selection of performance measures?
14. Why should different missions for two subunits result in different performance reward structures for the managers of those subunits? How does the mission of an organizational subunit affect the mix of financial and nonfinancial, and short-term and long-term, rewards?
15. How can feedback, both positive and negative, be used to improve managerial performance? How is feedback used in a performance-based reward system?
16. Many pay structures involve compensation combining both cash and stock. Why do firms want employees to be holders of the firm's common stock? What additional performance measurement and reward issues are created when managers are not shareholders in their firms?
17. What are some of the important equity issues in designing reward structures? Why is the achievement of equity in the reward structure important?

EXERCISES

18. **LO.1-LO.3 (Performance measurement; writing)** Recall the various ways in which your academic performance has been measured and rewarded. Have the ways that your class grades were determined always provided the best indications of performance? Provide at least two positive and two negative examples. What would you have done to change the measurement system in the negative examples?

INTERNET

19. **LO.1-LO.3 & LO.6 (Selecting performance measures; research; writing)** Choose a company that has either gone out of business or is currently in poor financial condition. Use the Internet to research that company's history. Prepare a report on your findings, concentrating on indicators that might have provided a perspective of failure. Describe these indicators either as short-term or long-term and as leading or lagging.
20. **LO.1-LO.3 (Performance measurement; writing)** Research suggests that as people work over a certain number of hours, productivity goes down, stress goes up, and results are not as good. You have taken this observation to heart and want to establish some performance measures in your accounting firm to help indicate that there is a reasonable balance between work and leisure for employees. Use all resources available to research this topic and prepare your list of performance measures. How will you benchmark these measures? How will you react to employees who are "workaholics"?
21. **LO.1-LO.3 & LO.5 (Measuring long-run performance; writing)** The company president has asked you, as the new controller, to comment on any deficiencies of the firm. After saying you believe that the firm needs long-run performance measurements, the president says that the long run is really just a series of short runs. He says that if you do a good job of evaluating the short-run performance, the long run will take care of itself. He sees that you are unconvinced and agrees to keep an open mind if you can make a good case for measuring and evaluating long-run performance. He suggests that you prepare a report stating your case. Do so.
22. **LO.1-LO.3 (Selecting performance measures; writing)** Theta Property Management provides management services for commercial real estate development projects. The firm recently started a new division to market video game services to existing clients. The new division will purchase and maintain the video equipment placed in client buildings. Clients will be paid 25 percent of gross video equipment revenues.

Theta has hired you to report on recommended performance measures to be used in monitoring and evaluating the success of the new division and its manager. Begin your report with a discussion of your perception of the new division's strategic mission.

23. **LO.4 (ROI; RI)** The following 2013 information is available for Leffingwell Industries: average assets invested, \$8,200,000; sales, \$31,400,000; and expenses, \$27,600,000.
    a. Calculate return on investment. (Round to one decimal point.)
    b. Calculate profit margin. (Round to one decimal point.)
    c. Calculate asset turnover. (Round to one decimal point.)
    d. Using (b) and (c), prove your answer to (a). (Round to one decimal point.)
    e. Assuming Leffingwell's cost of capital is 14 percent, compute the 2013 residual income.

24. **LO.4 (RI)** Ribocon Corp. has established a 12 percent target ROI for 2013 for its Lynchfield Division. The following data have been gathered for the division's operations for 2013: average total assets, \$14,200,000; revenues, \$28,000,000; and expenses, \$26,500,000. What is the division's residual income? Did the division successfully meet the target ROI?

25. **LO.4 (ROI)** For the most recent fiscal year, the Southern Division of Fargo Corporation generated an asset turnover ratio of 5 and a profit margin (as measured by the segment margin) ratio of 6 percent on sales of \$3,950,000.
    a. Compute the average assets employed.
    b. Compute the segment margin.
    c. Compute the ROI.

26. **LO.4 (ROI; RI)** Schulz GmbH, a German company, set an 18 percent target rate of return for its U.S. division for 2013. For 2013, the U.S. division generated \$39,000,000 of revenue on average assets of \$25,000,000. The division's variable costs were 45 percent of sales, and fixed costs were \$6,750,000. Compute the following items for the U.S. division for 2013:
    a. ROI
    b. Residual income
    c. Profit margin (Round to one decimal point.)
    d. Asset turnover (Round to one decimal point.)

27. **LO.4 (ROI)** Data for the three autonomous divisions of Dakota Mining, Inc. for fiscal year 2013 follow.

	Division 1	Division 2	Division 3
Segment income	\$ 320,000	\$ 450,000	\$ 4,850,000
Asset investment	2,700,000	2,000,000	30,200,000

Compute the return on investment for each division. (Round to one decimal point.)

28. **LO.4 (RI)** Carrington Co. operates its two divisions as investment centers. Information about these divisions follows.

	Division 1	Division 2
Sales	\$5,200,000	\$1,850,000
Total variable costs	2,630,000	330,000
Total fixed costs	490,000	840,000
Average assets invested	7,180,000	875,000

a. What is the residual income of each division if the "charge" on invested assets is 13 percent? Which division is doing a better job?
b. If the only change expected for next year is a sales increase of 20 percent, what will be the residual income of each division? Which division will be doing a better job financially?
c. Why were the percentage changes in residual income determined in (b) so different for Divisions 1 and 2?

29. **LO.4 (EVA)** EVA is used by top management at College Learning Technologies to measure and evaluate the performance of segment managers. The company's cost of capital is 11 percent. In 2013, its Audio/Visual subsidiary generated after-tax income of $2,260,000, with $8,900,000 fair market value of invested capital.
   a. Compute the subsidiary's EVA.
   b. As the controller of College Learning Technologies, how would you determine the fair value of capital investment for a particular division?

30. **LO.4 (EVA)** Mountain Mist Inc.'s cost of capital is 11 percent. In 2013, one of the firm's divisions generated an EVA of $1,130,000. The fair market value of the capital investment in that division was $29,500,000. How much after-tax income was generated by the division in 2013?

31. **LO.4 (Performance measurement changes)** Following is a list of transactions that affected one division within a multiple-division company. Indicate, for the current fiscal year, whether each transaction would increase (I), decrease (D), have no effect (N), or have an indeterminate (?) effect on each of the following: asset turnover, profit margin, ROI, and RI. Each transaction is independent.
   a. In September, the division fired its R&D manager; the position will not be filled during the current fiscal year.
   b. At mid-year, the division manager increased scheduled annual production by 5,000 units. This decision has no effect on scheduled sales.
   c. Equipment with an original cost of $680,000 was sold for $139,000. At the time of sale, the book value of the equipment was $170,000. The equipment sale had no effect on production or sales activities.
   d. The division wrote down obsolete finished goods by debiting Cost of Goods Sold and crediting Finished Goods Inventory for $96,000.
   e. The division manager automated a previously labor-intensive operation. The action had no effect on sales, but total annual operating expenses declined by 17 percent.
   f. Because of significant changes in its cost of capital, the company lowered the division's target rate of return from 12 to 10 percent.
   g. A special overseas order was accepted at a selling price significantly less than that for domestic business. The selling price, however, was sufficient to cover all traceable costs of the order.
   h. During the year, the division manager spent an additional $165,800 on advertising, which sparked an immediate increase in sales.

EXCEL

32. **LO.4 (Throughput)** Completely Nuts, a macadamia nut cannery, is analyzing its throughput for September. The following statistics are obtained for the month:

Cans packed and sold	700,000
Total cans packed	742,040
Value-added processing time	650 hours
Total processing time	2,750 hours

   a. Calculate the manufacturing cycle efficiency. (Round to one decimal point.)
   b. Calculate the process productivity. (Round to one decimal point.)
   c. Calculate the process quality yield. (Round to one decimal point.)
   d. Calculate the throughput using only good units and total time. (Round to one decimal point.)
   e. Verify your answer to (d) by using your answers to (a), (b), and (c).

EXCEL

33. **LO.4 (Throughput)** Hernandez Corp. wants to compute its throughput for August 2013. The following production data are available:

Good units produced and sold	2,923,200
Total units produced	3,460,000
Total processing time	144,000 hours
Value-added time	50,300 hours

   a. Determine the manufacturing cycle efficiency. (Round to one decimal point.)
   b. Determine the process productivity. (Round to one decimal point.)
   c. Determine the process quality yield. (Round to one decimal point.)

d. Determine the throughput using only good units and total time.
e. What can company management do to raise hourly throughput?

34. **LO.4 (Throughput)** Management at Lantana Inc. has decided to begin using throughput as a divisional performance measure. The Carolina Division is a job shop that carefully crafts furniture to customer specifications. The following first quarter information is available for the division:

EXCEL

Good units started, completed, and sold	98,400
Total units completed	104,500
Total value-added hours of processing time	15,160
Total hours of divisional time	25,000

a. What is the division's manufacturing cycle efficiency? (Round to one decimal point.)
b. What is the division's process productivity? (Round to one decimal point.)
c. What is the division's process quality yield? (Round to one decimal point.)
d. What is the total hourly throughput? (Round to one decimal point.)
e. Discuss whether throughput is as useful a performance measurement in a job shop as in an automated plant. Why would you expect process quality yield to be high in a job shop? Why might a job shop such as Carolina Division have a low manufacturing cycle efficiency?

35. **LO.8 (Balanced scorecard)** Use the information from Exercise 38. What objectives and measurements for those objectives at Krazy Klothing do you think should be included for the internal perspective of the BSC?

36. **LO.8 (Balanced scorecard)** Use the information from Exercise 38. What objectives and measurements for those objectives at Krazy Klothing do you think should be included for the sustainability perspective of the BSC?

37. **LO.8 (Balanced scorecard)** Use the information from Exercise 38. What objectives and measurements for those objectives at Krazy Klothing do you think should be included for the customer perspective of the BSC?

38. **LO.8 (Balanced scorecard)** Management at Krazy Klothing wants to implement a balanced scorecard. The company has a single location in Seattle, Washington, and 15 employees. The primary customers are college students between 18 and 25. Clothing prices range from $10 to $150; most clothes are all-natural fibers, and all are made in the western part of the United States. The company is owned by Pam and Meg Pash. What objectives and measurements for those objectives at Krazy Klothing do you think should be included for the financial perspective of the BSC?

39. **LO.9 (Variable pay and incentives; writing)** In recent years, salaries for chief financial officers (CFOs) of large U.S. corporations averaged only about 20 percent of the total CFO compensation package; the other 80 percent was performance-based, variable compensation that included mostly stock options and short-term and long-term incentive bonuses. Among major corporate officers, typically, only CEOs had a higher percentage of pay that was variable.

a. What does the high portion of variable CFO pay indicate about the importance of CFOs to their organizations?
b. Discuss any concerns investors should have about such a high percentage of CFO pay being variable.

40. **LO.9 (Pay plan and suboptimization)** Thomas Owan is a division manager of Weatfarl Inc. He is in the process of evaluating a $4,000,000 investment. The following net annual increases, before depreciation, in divisional income are expected during the investment's five-year life:

Year 1	$ 300,000
Year 2	500,000
Year 3	760,000
Year 4	3,200,000
Year 5	2,900,000

All company assets are depreciated using the straight-line method. Owan receives an annual salary of $300,000 plus a bonus of 2 percent of divisional pre-tax profits. Before consideration of the potential investment project, he anticipates that his division will generate $4,000,000 annually in pre-tax profit.

a. Compute the effect of the new investment on the level of divisional pre-tax profits for years 1 through 5.
b. Determine the effect of the new project on Owan's compensation for each of the five years.
c. Based on your computations in (b), will Owan want to invest in the new project? Explain.
d. Would upper management likely view the new investment favorably? Explain.

PROBLEMS

41. **LO.4 (Statement of cash flows)** San Francisco Sea Salt's controller prepared the following cash flow statements (in thousands of dollars) for the past two years, the current year (2013), and the upcoming year (2014):

	2011	2012	2013	2014 Budget
Net cash flows from operating activities				
Net income	$ 41,700	$ 39,200	$ 43,700	$ 45,100
Add net reconciling items	2,200	4,300	3,000	4,000
Total	$ 43,900	$ 43,500	$ 46,700	$ 49,100
Net cash flows from investing activities				
Purchase of plant and equipment	$(18,700)		$(12,200)	$ (4,600)
Sale (purchase) of investments	8,700	$ (3,600)	(12,600)	(15,800)
Other investing inflows	1,200	800	600	2,400
Total	$ (8,800)	$ (2,800)	$(24,200)	$(18,000)
Net cash flows from financing activities				
Payment of notes payable	$(12,000)	$(24,000)	$(15,000)	$ (7,000)
Payment of dividends	(20,000)	(7,000)	(13,300)	(20,000)
Total	$(32,000)	$(31,000)	$(28,300)	$(27,000)
Net change in cash	$ 3,100	$ 9,700	$ (5,800)	$ 4,100

After preparation of the budgeted cash flow statement for 2014, Lana Kaslowski, the company president, asked you to recompile it based on a separate set of facts. She is evaluating a proposal to purchase a local area network (LAN) computer system for the company at a total cost of $50,000. The proposal has been deemed to provide a satisfactory rate of return. However, she does not want to issue additional stock and would prefer not to borrow any more money to finance the project.

Projecting the market value of the accumulated investments for 2012 and 2013 ($3,600 and $12,600) reveals an estimate that these investments could be liquidated for $18,400. Kaslowski said the investments scheduled for 2014 could be delayed indefinitely and that dividends could be reduced to 40 percent of the budgeted amount. These are the only changes that can be made to the original forecast.

a. Evaluate the cash trends for the company during the 2011–2014 period.
b. Giving effect to the preceding changes, prepare a revised 2014 budgeted statement of cash flows and present the original and revised versions in a comparative format.
c. Based on the revised budgeted SCF, can the LAN computer system be purchased if Kaslowski desires an increase in cash of at least $1,000?
d. Comment on the usefulness of the report prepared in (b) to Kaslowski.

42. **LO.4 (Divisional profit)** The Mergers & Acquisitions Division (M&A) of Global Financial Services is evaluated by corporate management based on a comparison of budgeted and actual pre-tax income. For 2013, M&A's budgeted income statement was as follows:

Sales	$ 36,000,000
Variable costs	(25,200,000)
Contribution margin	$ 10,800,000
Fixed costs	(7,200,000)
Pre-tax income	$ 3,600,000

At the end of 2013, M&A's actual results were as follows:

Sales	$ 39,000,000
Variable costs	(29,230,000)
Contribution margin	$ 9,770,000
Fixed costs	(7,230,000)
Pre-tax income	$ 2,540,000

a. Based on the preceding information, evaluate M&A's performance. What was the principal reason for the poor profit performance?

b. Why do complete income statements provide a more comprehensive basis for evaluating the profit performance of a manager than mere comparisons of the bottom lines of the budgeted and actual income statements?

43. **LO.3, LO.4, LO.6, & LO.7 (Cash flow; ethics)** Wayne Coyle, the controller of PEI Potato Co., is disillusioned with the company's system of evaluating the performance of divisional profit centers and their managers. The present system focuses on a comparison of budgeted to actual income from operations. Coyle's major concern with the current system is the ease with which profit center managers can manipulate the measure "Income from operations." Most corporate sales are made on credit, and most purchases are made on account. The profit centers are organized according to product line. Following is the second quarter 2013 income statement for one of the company's profit centers:

ETHICS

Sales	$ 31,500,000
Cost of goods sold	(25,500,000)
Gross profit	$ 6,000,000
Selling and administrative expenses	(4,500,000)
Income from operations	$ 1,500,000

Coyle has suggested that company management replace the accrual-based income from operations evaluation measure with a cash flow from operations measure. He believes this measure will be less susceptible to manipulation by profit center managers. To defend his position, he compiles a cash flow income statement for the same profit center:

Cash receipts from customers	$ 26,400,000
Cash payments for production labor, materials, and overhead	(21,600,000)
Cash payments for selling and administrative activities	(4,200,000)
Cash flow from operations	$ 600,000

a. If Coyle is correct that profit center managers are manipulating the income measure, where are manipulations likely taking place?

b. Explain whether the proposed cash flow measure would be less subject to manipulation than the income measure.

c. Explain whether manipulation would be reduced if both the cash flow and income measures were utilized.

d. Do the cash and income measures reveal different information about profit center performance? Explain.

e. How could the existing income statement be used more effectively in evaluating performance?

44. **LO.4 (ROI)** Evergreen Industries operates a chain of lumber stores. In 2013, corporate management examined industry-level data and determined the following performance targets for lumber retail stores:

EXCEL

Asset turnover	1.9
Profit margin	7.0%

The actual 2013 results for the company's lumber retail stores are as follows:

Total assets at beginning of year	$10,200,000
Total assets at end of year	12,300,000
Sales	28,250,000
Operating expenses	25,885,000

a. For 2013, how did the lumber retail stores perform relative to their industry norms? (Round percentages to one decimal point.)
b. Which, as indicated by the performance measures, are the most likely areas to improve performance in the retail lumber stores?
c. What are the advantages and disadvantages of setting a performance target at the start of the year compared with one that is determined at the end of the year based on actual industry performance?

45. **LO.4 (Decisions based on ROI and RI)** Miami Marine uses ROI to evaluate the performance of both its Powerboat and Sailboat Division managers. The following estimates of relevant measures have been made for the upcoming year:

	Powerboats	Sailboats	Total Company
Sales	$18,000,000	$48,000,000	$66,000,000
Expenses	16,200,000	42,000,000	58,200,000
Divisional assets	15,000,000	30,000,000	45,000,000

Both division managers have the autonomy to make decisions regarding new investments. The Powerboats manager is considering investing in a new asset that would generate a 14 percent ROI; the Sailboats manager is considering an investment that would generate an 18 percent ROI.

a. Compute the projected ROI for each division, disregarding the contemplated new investments.
b. Based on your answer in (a), which manager is likely to actually invest in the additional assets under consideration?
c. Are the outcomes of the investment decisions in (b) likely to be consistent with overall corporate goals? Explain.
d. If the company evaluated the division managers' performances using a residual income measure with a target return of 15 percent, would the outcomes of the investment decisions be different from those described in (b)? Explain.

46. **LO.4 (EVA)** As one of the division managers for Premier Inc., your performance is evaluated primarily on a single measure: after-tax divisional segment income less the cost of capital invested in divisional assets. The fair value of invested capital in your division is $20,000,000, the required return on capital is 10 percent, and the tax rate is 40 percent. Income projections for 2013 follow.

Sales	$ 30,000,000
Expenses	(26,250,000)
Segment income	$ 3,750,000
Taxes	(1,500,000)
After-tax segment income	$ 2,250,000

You are considering an investment in a new product line that would, according to projections, increase 2013 pre-tax segment income by $600,000. The investment cost is not yet determinable because negotiations about several factors are still under way.

a. Ignoring the new investment, what is your projected EVA for 2013?
b. In light of your answer in (a), what is the maximum amount that you would be willing to invest in the new product line?
c. Assuming that the new product line would require an investment of $3,100,000, what would be the revised projected EVA for your division in 2013 if the investment were made?

47. **LO.4 (Adjusting income for ROI purposes; ethics)** Imelda Sanchez, manager of the Arias Division of Poncé Chemical, is evaluated based on the division's return on investment and residual income. Near the end of November 2013, she was reviewing the division's financial information as well as some activities projected for the remainder of the year. The information she was reviewing follows.

ETHICS

1. Annual sales were projected at 100,000 units, each with a selling price of $30. Sanchez has received a purchase order from a new customer for 5,000 units. The purchase order states that the units should be shipped on January 3, 2011, for arrival on January 5.
2. The division's 2013 beginning inventory was 500 units, each with a cost of $11. Purchases of 99,500 units have been made steadily throughout the year, and the per-unit cost has been constant at $10. Sanchez intends to make a purchase of 5,200 units before year-end, providing a 200-unit balance in inventory after making the shipment to the new customer. Carrying costs for the units are quite high, but ordering costs are extremely low. The division uses a last-in, first-out (LIFO) cost flow assumption for inventory.
3. Shipping expenses are $0.50 per unit sold.
4. Sanchez has just received a notice from her primary supplier that he is going out of business and is selling his remaining stock of 15,000 units for $9 each. She makes a note to herself to place her final order for the year from this supplier.
5. Division advertising is $5,000 per month for newspaper inserts and television spots. No advertising has yet been purchased for December, but Sanchez intends to have her sales manager call the paper and TV station early next week.
6. Salaries through the end of the year are projected at $700,000. This amount assumes that the position to be vacated by the division's personnel manager will be filled on December 1. The personnel manager's job pays $66,000 per year. Sanchez has an interview on Monday with an individual who appears to be a good candidate for the position.
7. Other general and administrative costs for the full year are estimated to total $590,000.
8. As Sanchez was reviewing the divisional information, she received a phone call from the division's maintenance supervisor. He informed her that $10,000 of electrical repairs to the office heating system are necessary. When asked if the repairs were essential, the supervisor replied, "No, the office won't burn down if you don't make them, but they are advisable for energy efficiency and long-term operation of the system." Sanchez tells the supervisor to see her on Monday at 8:00 A.M.

Using her information, Sanchez prepared a budgeted income statement and was fairly pleased with the division's results. Although providing the 13 percent rate of return on investment desired by corporate management, the results did not reach the 16 percent rate needed for Sanchez to receive a bonus for the year.

a. Prepare a 2013 budgeted income statement for the Arias Division. Determine the division's residual income, assuming that the division has an asset investment base of $4,500,000.
b. Sanchez's less-than-scrupulous friend, John Greer, walked into the office at this time. When he heard that she was not going to receive a bonus, Greer said, "Here, let me take care of this for you." He proceeded to recompute the budgeted income statement and showed Sanchez that, based on his computation of $723,000 in income, she would receive her bonus. Prepare Greer's budgeted income statement.
c. What future difficulties might arise if Sanchez acts in a manner that will make Greer's pro forma income statement figures a reality?

48. **LO.4 (ROI; RI)** Morton Industrial produces stamping machinery for manufacturers. In 2009, the company expanded vertically by acquiring a supplier, Lancaster Company. Lancaster is now operated as a divisional investment center.

Morton monitors its divisions on the basis of both unit contribution and return on investment (ROI), with investment defined as average operating assets employed. Management bonuses are determined based on ROI. All investments in operating assets are expected to earn a minimum return of 10 percent before income taxes.

Lancaster's cost of goods sold is entirely variable, whereas the division's administrative expenses are totally fixed. Selling expenses are a mixed cost with 40 percent attributed to sales volume. Last year, Lancaster's ROI was 13.6 percent. During the fiscal year ended November 30, 2013, Lancaster contemplated a capital acquisition with an estimated ROI of 11.5 percent; however, division management decided that the investment would decrease Lancaster's overall ROI.

The division's operating assets employed were $15,750,000 at November 30, 2013, a 5 percent increase over the 2012 year-end balance. The division's 2013 income statement follows.

Lancaster Division
Income Statement
For the Year Ended November 30, 2013
($000 omitted)

Sales revenue		$ 25,000
Less expenses		
Cost of goods sold	$16,500	
Administrative expenses	3,955	
Selling expenses	2,700	(23,155)
Income from operations before income taxes		$ 1,845

a. Calculate the segment margin for the Lancaster Division, assuming that 1,484,000 units were produced and sold during the year ended November 30, 2013.

b. Calculate the following performance measures for 2013 for the Lancaster Division:

1. pre-tax ROI and
2. residual income calculated on the basis of average operating assets employed.

c. Explain why the management of the Lancaster Division would have been more likely to accept the contemplated capital acquisition if residual income rather than ROI were used as a performance measure.

d. Identify several items that Lancaster should control if it is to be evaluated fairly by either the ROI or residual income performance measures.

CMA ADAPTED

49. **LO.4 (ROI; RI)** Fashion Fabrics sells sewing and craft materials to specialty retail and department stores. For 2013, the company's New York Division had the following performance targets:

Asset turnover	3.0
Profit margin	5.5%

Actual information concerning the performance of the New York Division in 2013 follows.

Total assets at beginning of year	$ 8,400,000
Total assets at end of year	9,900,000
Sales	25,000,000
Operating expenses	23,160,000

a. For 2013, did the New York Division achieve its target objectives for ROI, asset turnover, and profit margin? (Round computations to one decimal point.)

b. Which, as indicated by the performance measures, are the most likely areas to improve performance?

c. If the company has an overall target return of 13 percent, what was the New York Division's residual income for 2013?

EXCEL

50. **LO.4 (Throughput)** Justin Fawber is a divisional manager within Monmouth GPS Guidance Systems. Haas is concerned about the amount of the division's production. The following production data are available for April 2013:

Total units completed	1,023,000
Total good units completed and sold	838,860
Total value-added hours of processing time	18,600
Total hours of processing time	62,000

Determine each of the following for this division for April.

a. What is the manufacturing cycle efficiency?
b. What is the process productivity?
c. What is the process quality yield?
d. What is the total throughput per hour? (Round to one decimal point.)
e. If only 660,000 of the units produced in April had been sold, would your answers to any of the preceding questions differ? If so, how? If not, why not? (Round to one decimal point.)
f. If Fawber can eliminate 20 percent of the NVA time, how would throughput per hour for these data differ? (Round to one decimal point.)
g. If Fawber can increase quality output to a yield of 90 percent and eliminate 20 percent of the NVA time, how would throughput per hour for these data differ? (Round to one decimal point.)
h. How would Fawber determine how the NVA time was being spent in the division? What suggestions do you have for decreasing NVA time and increasing yield?

51. **LO.2, LO.3, & LO.6 (Providing feedback on performance; writing)** Terry Travers is the manufacturing supervisor of the Aurora Manufacturing Company, which produces a variety of plastic products. Some of these products are standard items that are listed in the company's catalog, whereas others are made to customer specifications. Each month, Travers receives a performance report displaying the budget for the month, the actual activity for the period, and the variance between budget and actual. Part of Travers's annual performance evaluation is based on his department's performance against budget. Aurora's purchasing manager, Bob Christensen, also receives monthly performance reports and is evaluated in part on the basis of these reports.

The most recent monthly reports were just distributed when Travers met Christensen in the hallway outside their offices. Scowling, Travers began the conversation, "I see we have another set of monthly performance reports hand delivered by that not very nice junior employee in the budget office. He seemed pleased to tell me that I was in trouble with my performance again."

Christensen: "I got the same treatment. All I ever hear about are the things I haven't done right. Now, I'll have to spend a lot of time reviewing the report and preparing explanations. The worst part is that the information is almost a month old, and we spend all this time on history."

Travers: "My biggest gripe is that our production activity varies a lot from month to month, but we're given an annual budget that's written in stone. Last month, we were shut down for three days when a strike delayed delivery of the basic material used in our plastic formulation, and we had already exhausted our inventory. You know that, of course, since we had to ask you to call all over the country to find an alternate source of supply. When we got what we needed on a rush basis, we had to pay more than we normally do."

Christensen: "I expect problems like that to pop up from time to time—that's part of my job—but now we'll both have to take a careful look at the report to see where charges are reflected for that rush order. Every month, I spend more time making sure I should be charged for each item reported than I do making plans for my department's daily work. It's really frustrating to see charges for things I have no control over."

Travers: "The way we get information doesn't help, either. I don't get copies of the reports you get, yet a lot of what I do is affected by your department, and by most of the other departments we have. Why do the budget and accounting people assume that I should be told only about my operations even though the president regularly gives us pep talks about how we all need to work together as a team?"

Christensen: "I seem to get more reports than I need, and I am never asked to comment until top management calls me on the carpet about my department's shortcomings. Do you ever hear comments when your department shines?"

Travers: "I guess they don't have time to review the good news. One of my problems is that all the reports are in dollars and cents. I work with people, machines, and materials. I need information to help me solve this month's problems—not another report of the dollars expended last month or the month before."

a. Based on the conversation between Travers and Christensen, describe the likely motivation and behavior of these two employees resulting from Aurora Manufacturing Company's performance reporting system.

b. 1. When performance reporting systems have been properly implemented, both employees and companies should benefit from them. Describe the benefits that can be realized from using a performance reporting system.

2. Based on the situation presented here, recommend ways for Aurora Manufacturing Company to improve its performance system to increase employee motivation.

CMA ADAPTED

52. **LO.6-LO.8 (Performance measurement; BSC)** For each of the following items, indicate two performance measurements that could be obtained from a cost management system. Classify each item into one of the four balanced scorecard perspectives.

a. Quality
b. Cost
c. Production line flexibility
d. People productivity and development
e. Inventory management
f. Lead time
g. Responsive after-sales service
h. Customer satisfaction and retention
i. Product and process design
j. Manufacturing planning process
k. Procurement process
l. Manufacturing process
m. Management accomplishments
n. Marketing/sales and customer service
o. Delivery performance
p. Financial accounting services

53. **LO.8 (Balanced scorecard; writing)** You have been elected president of your university's newly chartered accounting honor society. The society is a chapter of a national organization that has the following mission: "To promote the profession of accountancy as a career and to imbue members with high ethical standards."

a. Determine the balanced scorecard categories that you believe would be appropriate for the honor society.

b. Under each category, determine between four and six important performance measures.

c. How would you choose benchmarks against which to compare your chapter to others of the national organization?

54. **LO.8 (Balanced scorecard; government)** As part of the mayor's advisory team, you are to develop a balanced scorecard for Hogwart City, which has a population of 65,000. The city's strategic themes are planning and community development, sustainability, resource management, and community safety. The city has decided that the perspectives its desires in its BSC are financial, customer, and internal processes. Prepare a BSC for Hogwart City that includes at least three goals and measurements in each category.

INTERNET

55. **LO.8 (Balanced scorecard; research; writing)** One of the fundamental performance measurements in an organization's balanced scorecard learning and growth perspective is the number of patents obtained. The following information from the U.S. Patent & Trademark Office indicates the total U.S. patents issued for 2008.

Company	Total Patents
1. IBM	6,180
2. Samsung	4,894
3. Canon	2,821
4. Panasonic	2,559
5. Toshiba	2,483
6. Microsoft	2,311

Company	Total Patents
7. Sony	2,286
8. Seiko Epson	1,533
9. Hon Hai Precision Industry	1,514
10. Hitachi	1,465

Source: V. Lotempio, "Top Ten List of Companies to Get US Patents in 2011," *LoTempio Law Blog* (January 11, 2012); http://www.lotempiolaw.com/2012/01/articles/patents/top-ten-list-of-companies-to-get-us-patents-in-2011/ (last accessed 1/29/12).

In a team of three or four people, research these companies on the web and prepare a written report on their financial performance, customers' perceptions of their service and product quality, and manufacturing operations (such as level of automation in plants).

56. **LO.8 (Balanced scorecard)** Assume that management at **Subway** has decided to implement a balanced scorecard for the organization. Visit the company's site map at http://www.subway.com/subwayroot/sitemap.aspx. Using the information there as well as other information you can obtain from the Internet, prepare a balanced scorecard for the organization.

57. **LO.2-LO.8 (Balanced scorecard; EVA; writing)** Chesterville Manufacturing makes a variety of glass products having both commercial and household applications. One of its newest divisions, ColOptics, manufactures fiber optic cable and other high-tech products. Recent annual operating results (in millions) for ColOptics and two older divisions follow.

	ColOptics	Industrial Glass	Kitchenware
Sales	$500	$1,800	$1,500
Segment income	50	184	170

Chesterville Manufacturing uses economic value added (EVA) as its only segment performance measure. Clare Cole, CEO of Chesterville, posed some serious questions in a memo to the controller, Doug Larsen, after studying the operating results.

> *Doug:*
> *I'm concerned about ColOptics. Its key competitor's sales and market share are growing at about twice the pace of ColOptics. I'm not comforted by the fact that ColOptics is generating substantially more profits than the competitor. The mission we have established for ColOptics is high growth. Do you think we should use EVA to measure the division's performance and as a basis to compensate ColOptics' divisional management? Do we need to change our performance criteria?*

After pondering the memo and studying the operating results, Larsen passed the memo and operating results to you, his newest employee in the controller's office, and asked you to respond to the following questions:

a. Why would the use of EVA discourage a high-growth strategy?
b. Could the concept of the balanced scorecard be used to encourage a higher rate of growth in ColOptics? Explain.

58. **LO.8 (Balanced scorecard; research; writing)** As the cost of health care continues to increase, hospital and clinic managers need to be able to evaluate the performance of their organizations. Numerous articles have been written on performance measurements for health-care organizations. Obtain some of these articles and prepare a report on what you believe to be the best set of balanced scorecard measures for such organizations.

INTERNET

59. **LO.8 (Balanced scorecard; sustainability)** Go to http://www.carbonfootprint.com/calculator.aspx to compute your approximate carbon footprint. What goals and measurements would you put on a balanced scorecard to reduce the size of that footprint?

60. **LO.8 (Balanced scorecard)** The Coca-Cola Company has taken sustainability to heart by specifying seven core areas in which to set goals and measure progress; the foundation of this framework is titled LIVE POSITIVELY. Review the company's 2009/2010 Sustainability Review at http://www.thecoca-colacompany.com/citizenship/pdf/SR09/2009-2010_The_Coca-Cola_Company_Sustainability_Review.pdf.
    a. Which three of the seven core areas do you think are most important to the company's long-term success? Why did you choose these three?
    b. At the time the report was issues, Coca-Cola operated in 206 countries. Do you think the LIVE POSITIVELY goals and measures might be more difficult to attain in some countries than in others? Explain your answer.

ETHICS

61. **LO.2, LO.3, & LO.9 (Performance evaluation; ethics; writing)** In September 2013, Lyon Precision Corporation (LPC) decided to launch an expansion plan for some product lines. To finance this expansion, the firm has decided to issue $400,000,000 of new common stock in November 2013.

    Historically, the firm's innovative cell phone was a significant contributor to corporate profits. However, a competitor has recently introduced a multifunctional cell phone that has rendered LPC's cell phone obsolete. The controller has informed LPC's president that the inventory value of the cell phones needs to be reduced to its net realizable value. Because LPC has a large inventory of the cell phones in stock, the write-down will have a very detrimental effect on both the balance sheet and income statement.

    The president, whose compensation is determined in part by corporate profits and in part by stock price, has suggested that the write-downs be deferred until January 2014. He argues that, by deferring the write-down, existing shareholders will realize more value from the shares to be sold in November because the stock market will not be informed of the pending write-downs.

    a. What effects are the performance evaluation measures of the president likely to have on his decision to defer the write-down of the obsolete inventory?
    b. Is the president's decision to defer the write-down of the inventory an ethical treatment of existing shareholders? Of potential new shareholders?
    c. If you were the controller of Lyon Precision Corporation, how would you respond to the president's decision to defer the write-down until after issuance of the new stock?

62. **LO.9 (Compensation; writing)** Relative to worker compensation, no topic is more hotly debated than the minimum-wage law. Using concepts from this chapter, prepare a report in which you explain why increases in the minimum wage are not desirable and how alternative mechanisms could be used to increase the compensation of low-paid workers.

63. **LO.7 & LO.9 (Pay plans and goal congruence)** In 2013, the lead story in your college newspaper reports the details of the hiring of the current football coach. The previous football coach was fired for failing to win games and attract fans. In his last season, his record was 1 win and 11 losses. The news story states that the new coach's contract provides for a base salary of $600,000 per year plus an annual bonus computed as follows:

Win less than five games	$ 0
Win five to seven games	75,000
Win eight games or more	150,000
Win eight games and conference championship	250,000
Win eight games, win conference, and get a bowl bid	350,000

The coach's contract has essentially no other features or clauses.

The first year after the new coach is hired, the football team wins three games and loses eight. In the second year, the team wins six games and loses five. In the third year, the team wins nine games, wins the conference championship, and is invited to a prestigious bowl. Shortly after the bowl game, articles appear on the front page of several national sports publications announcing that your college's football program has been cited by the National Collegiate Athletic Association (NCAA) for nine major rule violations including cash payoffs to players, playing academically ineligible players, illegal recruiting tactics, illegal involvement of alumni in recruiting, and so on. The national news publications agree that the NCAA will disband your college's football program. One article also mentions that during the past three years, only 13 percent of senior football players managed to graduate on time. Additional speculation suggests that the responsible parties, including the coaching staff, athletic director, and college president, will be dismissed by the board of trustees.

a. Compute the amount of compensation paid to the new coach in each of his first three years.
b. Did the performance measures in the coach's contract foster goal congruence? Explain.
c. Would the coach's actions have been different if other performance measures had been added to the compensation contract? Explain.
d. What performance measures should be considered for the next coach's contract, assuming the football program is allowed to continue?

64. **LO.5 & LO.9 (Compensation; ethics; research; writing)** Beginning in the 1990s, American firms increasingly adopted the practice of using stock options to compensate mid- to high-level managers. Companies were motivated to use stock options as a large portion of the compensation mix for two reasons. First, accounting rules allowed the expense of the stock options to be charged directly against Retained Earnings rather than against income of the period. Accordingly, reported income would be higher than if the compensation were paid in another form such as cash. Second, boards of directors viewed stock options as aligning manager and stockholder interests better than most other forms of compensation. Research the linkage between reported accounting abuses (e.g., manipulating reported earnings) and the increased use of stock options for managerial compensation. Discuss your findings.

ETHICS

65. **LO.5, LO.7, & LO.9 (Performance evaluation; compensation; ethics; writing)** A survey of U.S. chief financial officers provided compelling evidence that managers are willing to take extraordinary measures to achieve financial earnings targets. For example, the survey found 26 percent were willing to sacrifice some long-term value of the firm to achieve short-term earnings goals. Further, 55 percent were willing to delay the start of new projects to achieve higher earnings, and 80 percent indicated they would reduce spending on research and development to achieve short-term earnings targets.

ETHICS

Source: J. R. Graham, C. R. Harvey, and S. Rajgopal, "The Economic Implications of Corporate Financial Reporting," *Journal of Accounting and Economics* 40 (2005), pp. 3–73.

a. Discuss the ethics of managers forfeiting long-term value of their firms to achieve short-term earnings goals and earn higher short-term compensation.
b. How can boards of directors create incentives and performance measures that will discourage top managers from optimizing reported short-run performance at the expense of long-term performance?

66. **LO.4 & LO.9 (Performance evaluation; compensation; ethics; writing)** Anthem Manufacturing has just initiated a formula bonus plan that rewards plant managers for various achievements. One of the current criteria for bonuses is the improvement of asset turnover. The plant manager of the Eastern Plant asked Sam Jensen, his assistant, to meet him Saturday when the plant is closed. Without explanation, the plant manager specified that certain raw materials were to be loaded on one of the plant's dump trucks. When the truck was loaded, the plant manager and Jensen drove to a secluded mountain road where, to Jensen's astonishment, the plant manager flipped a switch

ETHICS

and the truck dumped the raw materials down a steep ravine. The plant manager grinned and said that these raw materials were obsolete and the company would run more smoothly without them. For the next several weekends, Jensen observed the plant manager do the same thing. The following month, the plant manager was officially congratulated for improving asset turnover.

a. How did the dumping improve asset turnover?
b. What are the ethical problems in this case?
c. What are Jensen's options? Which should he choose and why?

67. **LO.3, LO.5, & LO.9 (Performance and compensation)** Family Fun Vehicle Co. (FFV), a subsidiary of Drummondville Automotive, manufactures go-carts and other recreational vehicles. Family recreational centers that feature go-cart tracks, miniature golf, batting cages, paint ball wars, and arcade games have increased in popularity. As a result, FFV has been receiving some pressure from Drummondville Automotive top management to diversify into some of these other recreational areas. Great Games Inc. (GGI), one of the largest firms that leases arcade games to family recreation centers, is looking for a friendly buyer. Drummondville Automotive management believes that GGI's assets could be acquired for an investment of $6.4 million and has strongly urged Sam Peach, division manager of FFV, to consider acquiring GGI.

Peach has reviewed GGI's financial statements with his controller, Molly Howe, and they believe that the acquisition may not be in FFV's best interests. "If we decide not to do this, the Drummondville Automotive people are not going to be happy," said Peach. "If we could convince them to base our bonuses on something other than return on investment, maybe this acquisition would look more attractive. How would we do if the bonuses were based on residual income using the company's 15 percent cost of capital?"

Drummondville Automotive has traditionally evaluated all of its divisions on the basis of return on investment, which is defined as the ratio of operating income to total assets; the desired rate of return for each division is 20 percent. The management team of any division reporting an annual increase in the return on investment is automatically eligible for a bonus. The management of divisions reporting a decline in the return on investment must provide convincing explanations for the decline to be eligible for a bonus, and this bonus is limited to 50 percent of the bonus paid to divisions reporting an increase. Presented below are condensed financial statements for both FFV and GGI for the fiscal year ended May 31, 2013.

	FFV	GGI
Sales revenue	$ 21,000,000	
Leasing revenue		$ 5,600,000
Variable expenses	(14,000,000)	(2,000,000)
Fixed expenses	(3,000,000)	(2,400,000)
Operating income	$ 4,000,000	$ 1,200,000
Current assets	$ 4,600,000	$ 3,800,000
Long-term assets	11,400,000	2,600,000
Total assets	$ 16,000,000	$ 6,400,000
Current liabilities	$ 2,800,000	$ 1,900,000
Long-term liabilities	7,600,000	2,600,000
Shareholders' equity	5,600,000	1,900,000
Total liabilities and shareholders' equity	$ 16,000,000	$ 6,400,000

a. Under the present bonus system, how would the acquisition of GGI affect Peach's bonus expectations? (Round percentages to one decimal.)
b. If Peach's suggestion to use residual income as the evaluation criterion is accepted, how would acquisition of GGI affect Peach's bonus expectations?
c. Given the present bonus arrangement, is it fair for Drummondville Automotive management to expect Peach to acquire GGI?

d. Is the present bonus system consistent with Drummondville Automotive's goal of expansion of FFV into new recreational products?

68. **LO.10 (Global performance evaluation and compensation; ethics; research; writing)** Many domestic companies have chosen to "offshore" their production operations to countries with lower wage rates. Some of the countries being used have been accused of allowing sweatshops, child labor, and polluting conditions that would not be allowed domestically. Research the benefits of, and problems with, offshoring and answer the following items:

ETHICS

a. How should offshoring affect the establishment of performance measurements?
b. If you were an expat manager for a division in a developing country, how would you defend the fact that the wages being paid to your employees are so much less than the minimum wage required domestically?

69. **LO.10 (Expatriate compensation; writing)** Assume you are the newly appointed CFO of an international engineering services firm. As one of your first assignments you need to appoint a new controller for the branch of your firm located in Buenos Aires. You have identified an assistant controller in your New York office who has the requisite skills and knowledge to perform effectively in this assignment. You are aware of the candidate's current salary and that she owns an apartment in Manhattan, is married, and has three children. Discuss how you would assemble a compensation package for this candidate that would entice her to (1) accept the Buenos Aires assignment and (2) be motivated to perform at a high level in that assignment.

15

Capital Budgeting

LEARNING OBJECTIVES

After completing this chapter, you should be able to answer the following questions:

1. Why do most capital budgeting methods focus on cash flows?
2. How is payback period computed, and what does it measure?
3. How are the net present value and profitability index of a project computed, and what do they measure?
4. How is the internal rate of return on a project computed, and what does that rate measure?
5. How do taxation and depreciation affect project cash flows?
6. What are the underlying assumptions and limitations of each capital project evaluation method?
7. How do managers rank investment projects?
8. How is risk considered in capital budgeting analyses?
9. How and why should management conduct a postinvestment audit of a capital project?
10. (*Appendix 1*) How are present values calculated?
11. (*Appendix 2*) What are the advantages and disadvantages of the accounting rate of return method?

INTRODUCTION

Choosing the assets in which an organization will invest is one of the most important business decisions a manager will make. Organizations invest in working capital assets, such as merchandise inventory, supplies, and raw material. Organizations must also invest in **capital assets**, which are long-term assets used to generate future revenues or cost savings or to provide distribution, service, or production capacity. A capital asset can be a tangible fixed asset (such as a piece of machinery or a building), a partial or complete acquisition of another firm, or an intangible asset (such as a capital lease or drug patent).

Providing information about the estimated financial returns of potential capital projects is an important task of cost accountants. This chapter discusses techniques used in evaluating the expected financial costs and benefits of proposed capital projects. Several of these techniques are based on an analysis of the amounts and timing of investment cash flows.

CAPITAL ASSET ACQUISITION

Financial managers, assisted by cost accountants, are responsible for analyzing alternative investment opportunities through the process of capital budgeting. **Capital budgeting** involves evaluating and ranking alternative future investments to effectively and efficiently allocate limited capital. The process includes planning for and preparing the capital budget as well as reviewing past investments to assess the success of past decisions and to enhance future decisions. Planned annual expenditures for capital projects for the near term (five years or less) and summary information for the long term (six to ten years) are shown in the capital budget, which is a key instrument in implementing organizational strategies.

Capital budgeting involves comparing and evaluating alternative projects. Managers and accountants apply quantitative and qualitative criteria to evaluate the feasibility of alternative projects. Although financial criteria are used to judge virtually all projects, firms now also use nonfinancial criteria to critically assess activities that have benefits that are difficult to quantify. For example, high-technology and R&D investments as well as sustainability projects are often difficult to evaluate using only financial criteria.

Exhibit 15.1 provides quantitative and qualitative criteria used by the forest products industry to evaluate capital projects. These criteria were obtained from a survey of industry practices and are not presented in rank order in the exhibit; similar criteria are generally used by firms in other industries. Most firms evaluate projects using multiple criteria and include quantitative and qualitative considerations in their analyses. By evaluating potential capital projects using a portfolio of criteria, managers can be confident that they have carefully considered all project costs and contributions. Additionally, using multiple criteria allows for a balanced evaluation of short- and long-term benefits as well as the effects of capital spending on all significant organizational stakeholders.

Exhibit 15.1 Project Evaluation Criteria

Quantitative Criteria	Qualitative Criteria
1. Accounting rate of return	1. Employee morale
2. Payback period	2. Employee safety
3. Discounted payback period	3. Employee responsibility
4. Net present value	4. Corporate image
5. Internal rate of return	5. Social responsibility
6. Profitability index	6. Market share
	7. Growth
	8. Strategic planning
	9. Sustainability

Source: Liliya S. Hogaboam and Steven R. Shook, "Capital Budgeting Practices in the U.S. Forest Products Industry: A Reappraisal," *Forest Products Journal* (December 2004), p. 149.

1 Why do most capital budgeting methods focus on cash flows?

USE OF CASH FLOWS IN CAPITAL BUDGETING

All investments undertaken by organizations are expected to earn some type of return. For example, investments in bonds are expected to earn interest, and investments in other companies are expected to earn dividends. In general, such interest and dividends are cash returns. Similarly, investments in capital assets are evaluated from a financial perspective based on their cash costs and cash benefits. Accordingly, aside from the effects on cash tax flows, accounting accruals are typically not considered in capital budget analysis. Accrual accounting recognizes revenues when they are earned rather than when cash is received and recognizes expenses when they are incurred rather than when cash is paid. Using cash flow information puts all investment returns on an equivalent basis.

Capital budgeting investment decisions can be based on a variety of quantitative techniques (as indicated in Exhibit 15.1, p. 601) such as payback period, net present value, profitability index, internal rate of return, and accounting rate of return. All of these methods, except the accounting rate of return, focus on **cash flows** (cash receipts or disbursements). Cash receipts include revenues from a capital project that have been earned and collected, savings in cash operating costs, and any cash inflow from selling the asset at the end of its useful life. Cash disbursements include asset acquisition expenditures, incremental cash invested in working capital, and cash costs of project-related direct material, direct labor, and overhead.

In evaluating capital projects, a distinction is made between operating cash flows and financing cash flows. Interest expense is a cash outflow associated with debt financing and is *not* part of the project selection process. Project funding is a financing, not an investment, decision. A **financing decision** involves choices regarding the method of raising capital to fund an investment. Financing is based on an entity's ability to issue and service debt and equity securities. On the other hand, an **investment decision** is a judgment about which assets to acquire to accomplish an entity's mission. Cash flows generated by the two types of decisions should not be combined. Company management must justify an asset's acquisition and use prior to justifying the method of financing that asset.

Including financing receipts and disbursements with other project cash flows confuses the evaluation of a project's profitability because financing costs relate to all of an entity's projects rather than to a specific project. Assignment of financing costs to a specific project is often arbitrary, which causes problems in comparing projects that are acquired with different financing sources. In addition, including financing effects in an investment decision creates a problem in assigning responsibility. Divisional managers, or top managers with input from divisional managers, make investment decisions. An organization's treasurer in conjunction with top management typically makes financing decisions.

Cash flows from a capital project are received and paid at different points in time over the project's life. Some cash flows occur at the beginning of a period, some during the period, and others at the end. To simplify capital budgeting analysis, most analysts assume that all cash flows occur at a specific, single point in time—typically, either at the beginning or end of the time period in which they actually occur. The following example illustrates how cash flows are treated in capital budgeting situations.

CASH FLOWS ILLUSTRATED

Assume that various capital projects are being considered by Family One Stop, a retail chain selling consumer goods in 55 locations throughout the Midwest. One investment being considered by the firm is the acquisition of photovoltaic power technology to light all parking lots owned by the chain. In addition to long-term cost savings, this investment would reduce the company's carbon footprint.

The expected cost to purchase and install the technology as well as the operating cost savings appear in Exhibit 15.2. This detailed information can be simplified to a net cash flow for each year. For Family One Stop, the project generates a net negative flow in the first year and net positive cash flows thereafter. This cash flow information can be illustrated through the use of a time line.

Exhibit 15.2 Family One Stop's Photovoltaic Technology Decision Information

Cash Outflows	
Year 0	$13,500,000
Year 1	500,000
Year 2	300,000
Cash Inflows	
Electricity cost savings:	
Year 1	$2,700,000
Year 2	2,900,000
Year 3	3,200,000
Year 4	3,900,000
Year 5	4,200,000
Year 6	2,100,000
Year 7	1,000,000

Time Lines

A **time line** visually illustrates the points in time when projected cash flows are received or paid, making it a helpful tool for analyzing cash flows of a capital investment proposal. On a time line, cash inflows are shown as positive amounts and cash outflows are shown as negative amounts.

The following time line represents the cash flows (in thousands) associated with Family One Stop's potential photovoltaic technology investment:

End of period	0	1	2	3	4	5	6	7
Inflows	$ 0	$2,700	$2,900	$3,200	$3,900	$4,200	$2,100	$1,000
Outflows	(13,500)	(500)	(300)	(0)	(0)	(0)	(0)	(0)
Net cash flow	$(13,500)	$2,200	$2,600	$3,200	$3,900	$4,200	$2,100	$1,000

On a time line, the date of initial investment represents time point 0, which marks the start of the cash flows pertaining to a project. Each year after the initial investment is represented as a full time period; periods serve only to separate the timing of cash flows. Nothing is presumed to happen during a period. Thus, for example, cash inflows each year from product sales are shown as occurring at the end of, rather than during, the time period. A less conservative assumption would show the cash flows occurring at the beginning of, or middle of, the period.

PAYBACK PERIOD

2 How is payback period computed, and what does it measure?

Information on the timing of net cash flows is an input to a simple and often-used capital budgeting technique called **payback period**. This method measures the time required for a project's cash inflows to equal the original investment. A project's payback is complete when the organization has recouped its investment.

In one sense, payback period measures a dimension of project risk by focusing on the timing of cash flows. The assumption is that the longer it takes to recover the initial investment, the greater is the project's risk, because cash flows in the more distant future are more uncertain than relatively near-term cash flows. Another reason for concern about long payback periods relates to capital reinvestment. The faster that capital is returned from an investment, the more rapidly the capital can be invested in other projects.

Payback period for a project having unequal cash inflows is determined by accumulating cash flows until the original investment is recovered. Thus, using the information shown in Exhibit 15.2 and the time line presented earlier, the photovoltaic technology investment payback period is calculated using a yearly cumulative total of inflows (in thousands) as follows:

Year	Annual Cash Flow	Cumulative Total
0	$(13,500)	$(13,500)
1	2,200	(11,300)
2	2,600	(8,700)
3	3,200	(5,500)
4	3,900	(1,600)
5	4,200	2,600
6	2,100	4,700
7	1,000	5,700

At the end of the fourth year, all but $1,600,000 of the initial $13,500,000 investment has been recovered. The $4,200,000 inflow in the fifth year is assumed to occur evenly throughout the year. Therefore, it should take approximately 38 percent ($1,600,000 ÷ $4,200,000) of the fifth year to cover the balance of the original investment, giving a payback period for this project of 4.38 years (or 4 years and 4.6 months).

When equal periodic cash flows are generated from a project (an **annuity**), the payback period is determined as follows:

$$\text{Payback period} = \text{Investment} \div \text{Annuity amount}$$

Assume that another investment being considered by Family One Stop requires an initial investment of $200,000 and is expected to generate equal annual cash flows of $32,000 in each of the next 10 years. In this case, the payback period would equal the $200,000 net investment cost divided by $32,000, or 6.25 years (6 years and 3 months).

Family One Stop's management typically sets a maximum acceptable payback period as one of the capital project financial evaluation criteria. If the company has set five years as the longest acceptable payback period, the photovoltaic technology investment would be considered acceptable, but the second investment project would be considered unacceptable.

Most companies use payback period in conjunction with other quantitative criteria. After being found acceptable in terms of payback period, a project is then evaluated using other capital budgeting criteria. A second evaluation criterion is usually necessary because the payback period method ignores three things:

- cash inflows occurring after the payback period has been reached,
- the company's desired rate of return, and
- the time value of money.

These issues are considered in the decision process using discounted cash flow techniques.

DISCOUNTING FUTURE CASH FLOWS

A time value is associated with money because interest is paid or received on money.[1] For example, $1 received today has more value than $1 received one year from today because money received today can be invested to generate a return that will cause it to accumulate to more than $1 over time; this effect is referred to as the **time value of money**. Discounted cash flow techniques are used in most capital budgeting situations to account for the effect of the time value of money.

Discounting means reducing future cash flows by removing the portion of the future values representing interest. This "imputed" amount of interest is based on two considerations:

- the length of time until the cash flow is received or paid, and
- the rate of interest assumed.

After discounting, all future values associated with a project are stated in a common base of current dollars, known as **present values (PVs)**. Cash receipts and disbursements occurring at the beginning (time 0) of a project are already stated in their present values and are not discounted.

[1] The time value of money and present value computations are covered in Appendix 1 of this chapter. These concepts are essential to understanding the rest of this chapter; be certain they are clear before continuing.

Capital project evaluations require estimates of related cash flows. It is extremely important, therefore, to have the best possible estimates of all potential cash inflows and outflows, and the rate of return on capital required by the company. This rate of return, called the **discount rate**, is used to determine the imputed interest portion of future cash flows. The discount rate should equal or exceed the company's **cost of capital (COC)**, which is the weighted average cost of the various sources (debt and equity) of funds that compose a firm's financial structure.[2] For example, if a company has a COC of 10 percent, then each year an amount equal to 10 percent of investment capital is required to finance the company. To determine whether a capital project is a worthwhile investment, this company should generally use a minimum rate of 10 percent to discount its projects' future cash flows.

A distinction must be made between cash flows representing a return *of* capital and those representing a return *on* capital. A **return of capital** is the recovery of the original investment (or the return of principal), whereas a **return on capital** is income and equals the discount rate multiplied by the investment amount. For example, $1.00 invested in a project that yields a 10 percent rate of return will grow to a sum of $1.10 in one year. Of the $1.10, $1.00 represents the return of capital and $0.10 represents the return on capital. The return on capital is computed for each period of the investment life. For a company to benefit from making an investment, a project must produce cash inflows that exceed the investment made and the cost of capital. To determine whether a project meets a company's desired rate of return, one of several discounted cash flow methods can be used.

Three discounted cash flow techniques are the net present value method, the profitability index, and the internal rate of return. Each of these methods is defined and illustrated in the following sections.

Net Present Value Method

3 How are the net present value and profitability index of a project computed, and what do they measure?

The **net present value method** determines whether a project's rate of return is equal to, higher than, or lower than the desired rate of return. All cash flows from a project are discounted to their present values using the company's desired rate of return. Subtracting the total present value of all an investment project's cash outflows from the total present value of all cash inflows yields the project's **net present value (NPV)**. A 7 percent discount rate is used in Exhibit 15.3 to illustrate the net present value calculations for the cash flow data shown in Exhibit 15.2 (p. 603).

The factors used to compute NPV are obtained from the present value tables provided in Appendix A at the end of the text. Each period's cash flow is multiplied by a factor

Exhibit 15.3 Net Present Value Calculation for Photovoltaic Technology Investment

		DISCOUNT RATE = 7%				
		a	×	b	=	c
Cash Flow	**Time**	**Amount**		**Discount Factor**		**Present Value**
Initial investment	t_0	$(13,500,000)		1.0000		$(13,500,000)
Year 1 net cash flow	t_1	2,200,000		0.9346		2,056,120
Year 2 net cash flow	t_2	2,600,000		0.8734		2,271,840
Year 3 net cash flow	t_3	3,200,000		0.8163		2,612,160
Year 4 net cash flow	t_4	3,900,000		0.7629		2,975,310
Year 5 net cash flow	t_5	4,200,000		0.7130		2,995,600
Year 6 net cash flow	t_6	2,100,000		0.6663		1,399,230
Year 7 net cash flow	t_7	1,000,000		0.6228		622,800
Net present value						$ 1,433,060

[2]All examples in this chapter use an assumed discount rate or cost of capital. The computations required to estimate a company's cost of capital are discussed in any basic finance text.

obtained from Table 1 (PV of \$1) for 7 percent and the appropriate time period designated for the cash flow.

The net present value represents the net cash benefit (or, if negative, the net cash cost) of acquiring and using the proposed asset. If the NPV is zero, the project's actual rate of return is equal to the required rate of return. If the NPV is positive, the actual rate of return is more than the required rate of return. If the NPV is negative, the actual rate of return is less than the required rate of return. Note that the exact rate of return is not indicated under the NPV method, but its relationship to the desired rate can be determined. If all estimates about the investment are correct, the photovoltaic technology being considered by Family One Stop has an NPV of \$1,433,060 and will provide a rate of return of more than 7 percent.

If Family One Stop's management chose any rate other than 7 percent and used that rate in conjunction with the same facts, a different net present value would have resulted. For example, if the company set 9 percent as the discount rate, an NPV of \$469,310 would have resulted for the project (see Exhibit 15.4, which gives the project's net present values at other selected discount rates). The computations for these values are made in a manner similar to those at 7 and 9 percent. (To confirm your understanding of the NPV method, you may want to prove these computations.)

The information in Exhibit 15.4 indicates that the NPV is not a single, unique amount but is a function of two factors:

- Discount rate: changing the discount rate while holding the amounts and timing of cash flows constant affects the NPV. Increasing the discount rate causes NPV to decrease; decreasing the discount rate causes NPV to increase.
- Cash flows: changing the estimated amounts or timing of cash inflows and outflows affects a project's NPV. Effects of cash flow changes on NPV depend on the changes themselves. For example, decreasing the estimate of cash outflows causes NPV to increase; reducing the stream of cash inflows causes NPV to decrease. When amounts and timing of cash flows change, the effects of the changes on NPV can be determined only by calculation.

Although not providing a project's actual rate of return, the NPV method provides information on how the actual rate compares with the required rate. This information allows

Exhibit 15.4 Alternative Net Present Value Calculation for Photovoltaic Technology Investment

		DISCOUNT RATE = 9%				
		a	×	b	=	c
Cash Flow	**Time**	**Amount**		**Discount Factor**		**Present Value**
Initial investment	t_0	\$(13,500,000)		1.0000		\$(13,500,000)
Year 1 net cash flow	t_1	2,200,000		0.9174		2,018,280
Year 2 net cash flow	t_2	2,600,000		0.8417		2,188,420
Year 3 net cash flow	t_3	3,200,000		0.7722		2,471,040
Year 4 net cash flow	t_4	3,900,000		0.7084		2,762,760
Year 5 net cash flow	t_5	4,200,000		0.6499		2,729,580
Year 6 net cash flow	t_6	2,100,000		0.5963		1,252,230
Year 7 net cash flow	t_7	1,000,000		0.5470		547,000
Net present value						\$ 469,310

Net present value with a 5 percent discount rate: \$2,494,590
Net present value with an 8 percent discount rate: \$938,060
Net present value with a 10 percent discount rate: \$23,210

managers to eliminate from consideration any project producing a negative NPV because such a project would have an unacceptable rate of return. This method can also be used to select the best alternative among a set of competing projects. However, this method should *not* be used to compare competing projects requiring different levels of initial investment. Such a comparison favors projects having higher NPVs over those with lower NPVs without regard to the relative capital invested in the projects.

To illustrate, assume that Family One Stop could spend $200,000 on Investment A or $40,000 on Investment B. The net present values of Investments A and B are $4,000 and $2,000, respectively. If only NPVs were compared, the company would conclude that Investment A was a "better" investment because it has a higher NPV. However, relative to investment cost, Investment A provides an NPV of only 2 percent ($4,000 ÷ $200,000), whereas Investment B provides a 5 percent ($2,000 ÷ $40,000) NPV. Logically, organizations should invest in projects that produce the highest return per investment dollar. Comparisons of projects requiring different levels of investment are made using a variation of the NPV method known as the profitability index.

Profitability Index

The **profitability index (PI)** is a ratio of a project's net cash inflows to the project's net investment. The PI is calculated as

$$\text{PI} = \text{Present value of net cash inflows} \div \text{Net investment}$$

The present value (PV) of net cash inflows equals the PV of future cash inflows minus the PV of future cash outflows. The PV of net cash inflows represents an output measure of the project's worth, whereas the net investment represents an input measure of the project's cost. By relating these two measures, the PI gauges the efficiency of the firm's use of capital. The higher the index, the more efficient is the capital investment.

The following information illustrates the calculation and use of the profitability index. Family One Stop is considering two investments: a distribution warehouse costing $3,440,000 and distribution equipment costing $1,700,000 for an existing storage facility. Corporate managers have computed the present values of the investments by discounting all future expected cash flows at a rate of 12 percent. Present values of the expected net cash inflows are $4,200,000 for the distribution warehouse and $2,360,000 for the distribution equipment. Dividing the PV of the net cash inflows by net investment gives the PI for each investment. Subtracting asset cost from the present value of the net cash inflows provides the NPV. Results of these computations follow.

	PV of Inflows	Cost	PI	NPV
Warehouse	$4,200,000	$3,440,000	1.22	$760,000
Distribution equipment	2,360,000	1,700,000	1.39	660,000

Although the warehouse's NPV is higher, the profitability index indicates that the distribution equipment is a more efficient use of corporate capital.[3] The higher PI reflects a higher rate of return on the distribution equipment than on the warehouse. The higher a project's PI, the more profitable that project is per investment dollar.

If a capital investment is to provide a return on capital, the PI should be equal to or greater than 1.00. This criterion is the equivalent of an NPV equal to or greater than zero. Like the NPV method, the PI does not indicate the project's expected rate of return. However, another discounted cash flow method, the internal rate of return, provides the expected rate of return to be earned on an investment.

Internal Rate of Return

A project's **internal rate of return (IRR)** is the discount rate that causes the present value of the net cash inflows to equal the present value of the net cash outflows. The IRR is the project's expected rate of return. If the IRR is used as the discount rate to determine a

4 How is the internal rate of return on a project computed, and what does that rate measure?

[3] Two conditions must exist for the PI to provide better information than the NPV method. First, the decision to accept one project must require that the other project be rejected. Second, the availability of funds for capital acquisitions must be limited.

project's NPV, the NPV will be zero. Data in Exhibit 15.4 (p. 606) indicate that Family One Stop's photovoltaic technology investment would generate an IRR slightly above 10 percent because a discount rate of 10 percent produced an NPV of \$23,210, which is relatively close to \$0 relative to the initial investment cost is \$13,500,000.

The following formula can be used to determine NPV:

$$\begin{aligned} \text{NPV} &= -\text{Investment at } t_0 + \text{PV of future cash inflows} - \text{PV of future cash outflows} \\ &= -\text{Investment} + \text{Future cash inflows (PV factor)} - \text{Future cash outflows (PV factor)} \end{aligned}$$

Capital project information should include investment, cash inflow, and cash outflow amounts. Thus, the only missing data in the preceding formula are the PV factors. By inserting the known amounts into the formulas, the missing PV factors can be calculated and then located in the PV tables. The interest rate with which the factors are associated is the internal rate of return.

The IRR is most easily computed for projects having equal annual net cash inflows. When an annuity exists, the NPV formula can be restated as follows:

$$\begin{aligned} \text{NPV} &= -\text{Net investment} + \text{PV of annuity amount} \\ &= -\text{Net investment} + (\text{Cash flow annuity amount} \times \text{PV factor}) \end{aligned}$$

The investment and annual cash flow amounts are known from the expected data, and the NPV is known to be zero at the IRR. The IRR and its present value factor are unknown. To determine the internal rate of return, substitute known amounts into the formula, rearrange terms, and solve for the unknown (the PV factor):

$$\begin{aligned} \text{NPV} &= -\text{Net investment} + (\text{Annuity} \times \text{PV factor}) \\ \$0 &= -\text{Net investment} + (\text{Annuity} \times \text{PV factor}) \\ \text{Net investment} &= (\text{Annuity} \times \text{PV factor}) \\ \text{Net investment} \div \text{Annuity} &= \text{PV factor} \end{aligned}$$

The solution yields a present value factor for the number of annuity periods corresponding to the project's life at an interest rate equal to the IRR. Finding this PV factor in an annuity table and reading the interest rate at the top of the column in which the factor is found provides the internal rate of return.

To illustrate an IRR computation for a project with a simple annuity, assume that Family One Stop is considering the purchase of a warehouse distribution management system. The system would cost \$1,500,000, be installed immediately, and generate cost savings of \$600,000 per year over its seven-year life. The system has no expected salvage value.

The NPV equation is solved for the present value factor.

$$\begin{aligned} \text{NPV} &= -\text{Net investment} + (\text{Annuity} \times \text{PV factor}) \\ \$0 &= -\$1{,}500{,}000 + (\$300{,}000 \times \text{PV factor}) \\ \$1{,}500{,}000 &= (\$300{,}000 \times \text{PV factor}) \\ \$1{,}500{,}000 \div \$300{,}000 &= \text{PV factor} \\ 5.0000 &= \text{PV factor} \end{aligned}$$

The PV of an ordinary annuity table (Appendix A, Table 2) is examined to find the IRR. In the table, find the row representing the project's life (in this case, seven periods) and find the PV factor resulting from the equation solution. In row 7, a factor of 5.0330 appears under the column headed 9 percent. Thus, the internal rate of return for this investment is very near 9 percent. By using interpolation, a computer program, or a programmable calculator, the exact IRR can be found.[4] A computer program indicates that the warehouse distribution management system's IRR is 9.2 percent.

Refer to Exhibit 15.5 for a plot of the NPVs that result from discounting the warehouse distribution management system cash flows at various rates of return. For example, the NPV at 7 percent is \$109,146 and at 11 percent is \$(77,785). (These computations are

[4] *Interpolation* is the process of finding a term between two other terms in a series.

Exhibit 15.5 NPV of Warehouse Distribution Management System at Various Discount Rates

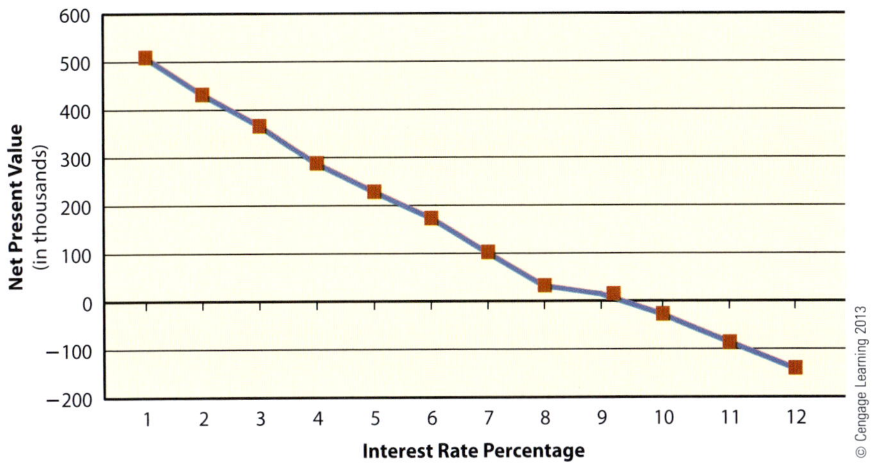

not provided here but can be performed by discounting the $300,000 annual cash flows and subtracting $1,500,000 of investment cost.)

The IRR is located on the graph's horizontal axis at the point where the NPV equals zero (or approximately 9.2 percent). Note that the graph reflects an inverse relationship between rates of return and NPVs. Higher rates yield lower present values because, at the higher rates, more of the future cash inflows is imputed interest.

Manually finding the IRR of a project that has unequal annual cash flows is more complex and requires an iterative trial-and-error process. An initial estimate is made of a rate believed to be close to the IRR, and the NPV is computed. If the resulting NPV is negative, a lower rate is estimated (because of the inverse relationship mentioned earlier), and the NPV is computed again. If the NPV is positive, a higher rate is selected, and the NPV is calculated. This process is continued until the NPV equals zero, at which time the IRR has been found.

The project's IRR is then compared with management's required **hurdle rate**, which is the rate of return specified as the lowest acceptable return on investment. Like the discount rate mentioned earlier, this rate should generally be at least equal to the cost of capital. In fact, the hurdle rate is commonly the discount rate used in computing NPV amounts. If a project's IRR is equal to or greater than the hurdle rate, the project is considered viable from a financial perspective.

The higher the IRR, the more financially attractive is the investment proposal. In choosing among alternative investments, however, managers cannot look solely at internal rates of return, because they do not reflect the dollars involved. An investor would normally rather have a 20 percent return on $1,000 than a 100 percent return on $5!

Using the IRR for capital project evaluation has three drawbacks.

- When uneven cash flows exist, the iterative process is inconvenient and time consuming.
- Unless PV tables provide factors for fractional interest rates, finding a project's precise IRR is difficult.
- Some projects can have several rates of return that will make the NPV of the cash flows equal zero. This phenomenon usually occurs when, at other than time 0, there are net cash inflows in some years and net cash outflows in other years of the investment project's life.

Note that the first two problems can be eliminated with the use of a computer or a programmable calculator.

In performing discounted cash flow analyses, accrual-based accounting information generally must be converted to cash flow data. One accrual that deserves special attention is depreciation. Although not a cash flow, depreciation has cash flow implications because it affects income tax payments—which *are* cash flows.

5 How do taxation and depreciation affect project cash flows?

EFFECT OF DEPRECIATION ON AFTER-TAX CASH FLOWS

Income taxes represent a significant cash expense for businesses and, therefore, are the subject of managerial planning and decision-making processes. Large organizations often have an individual designated "Director of Taxation" to oversee tax planning and tax compliance. This person typically has expertise in federal, state, and international tax laws. Tax considerations have a large impact on overall business profitability and managers typically make decisions only after examining how those decisions will affect company taxes. In evaluating capital projects, managers should use after-tax cash flows to determine project acceptability.

Depreciation expense is *not* a cash flow item: no funds are paid or received for it. However, depreciation on capital assets, like interest on debt, affects cash flows by reducing a company's income tax expense. Thus, depreciation provides a **tax shield** against the payment of taxes. The tax shield produces a **tax benefit** equal to the amount of taxes saved (the depreciation amount multiplied by the tax rate). The concepts of tax shield and tax benefit are shown on the following income statements. The tax rate is assumed to be 40 percent.

No Depreciation Deduction Income Statement

Sales	$ 500,000
Cost of goods sold	(350,000)
Gross margin	$ 150,000
Expenses other than depreciation	(75,000)
Depreciation expense	0
Income before taxes	$ 75,000
Tax expense (40%)	(30,000)
Net income	$ 45,000

Depreciation Deduction Income Statement

Sales	$ 500,000
Cost of goods sold	(350,000)
Gross margin	$ 150,000
Expenses other than depreciation	(75,000)
Depreciation expense	(75,000)
Income before taxes	$ 0
Tax expense (40%)	0
Net income	$ 0

In this example, the tax shield is the $75,000 depreciation expense, and the tax benefit is $30,000 (the difference between $30,000 of tax expense on the first income statement and $0 of tax expense on the second income statement). The tax benefit also equals the depreciation tax shield of $75,000 multiplied by the 40 percent tax rate. Because taxes are reduced by $30,000 because of the depreciation, the pattern of cash flows is improved.

It is the depreciation taken for income tax purposes rather than the depreciation taken for financial accounting purposes that is relevant in discounted cash flow analysis. Income tax laws regarding depreciation deductions are subject to frequent revision. For example, since the mid-1980s, Congress has allowed very rapid depreciation of certain assets to stimulate economic growth in the United States. In analyzing capital investments, managers should use the most current tax regulations for depreciation. Different depreciation methods can have significant impacts on after-tax cash flows. For a continuously profitable business, an accelerated method of depreciation, such as the modified accelerated cost recovery system (MACRS) allowed for U.S. tax computations, will produce higher tax benefits in the early years of an asset's life than will the straight-line method. These higher tax benefits will translate into a higher NPV for the investment's cash flows if the tax rate is constant across years.

Alternative depreciation methods and asset depreciable lives for tax purposes could dramatically affect projected after-tax cash flows, net present value, profitability index, and internal rate of return expected from a capital investment. Because capital projects are analyzed and evaluated before investments are made, managers should be aware of the inherent risk of tax law changes. Original assumptions made about the depreciation method or asset life could be invalid by the time an investment is actually made and an asset is placed into service. However, an asset can generally be depreciated using the method and tax life allowed when the asset was purchased and placed into service regardless of the tax law changes occurring after that time.

Relatively unpredictable changes may also occur in the tax rate structure. For example, the Tax Reform Act of 1986 lowered the maximum federal corporate tax rate from

46 percent to 34 percent; the present top U.S. tax rate is 35 percent.[5] With state income taxes added to the federal income tax, the combined rate for large U.S. corporations is approximately 40 percent.[6] A tax rate reduction lowers the tax benefit provided by depreciation by lessening the impact on cash flow.[7] Tax law changes (such as asset tax-life changes) can cause the expected outcomes of the capital investment analysis to vary from the project's actual outcomes.

To illustrate changes that would affect a project's cash flows, assume that Family One Stop is considering a $6 million investment in new point-of-sale store equipment that will have a 10-year economic life and produce expected net annual cash operating savings of $850,000. The company's after-tax cost of capital is 5 percent. Corporate assets are depreciated on a straight-line basis for tax purposes.[8] Recent tax law changes have dramatically accelerated the rate of cost recovery for many assets. Under current law, some asset costs can be deducted entirely in the year the asset is acquired.

Prior to making the point-of-sale equipment investment, Family One Stop's cost accountant, Sarah Brown, calculated the project's NPV. At the time of Brown's analysis, Family One Stop's tax rate was 30 percent, and the tax laws allowed a 10-year depreciable life on this equipment. See Situation A in Exhibit 15.6 (p. 612) for the results of Brown's calculations. Note that depreciation is added to income after tax to obtain the amount of after-tax cash flow. Even though depreciation is deductible for tax purposes, it is a noncash expense. The PV amounts are obtained by multiplying the after-tax cash flows by the appropriate PV of an annuity factor from Table 2 in Appendix A at the end of the text. The NPV evaluation technique indicates the acceptability of the capital investment.

Because Brown was concerned about proposed changes in the U.S. tax rate, she also analyzed the project assuming that tax rates changed. See Exhibit 15.6 for the different after-tax cash flows and NPVs that result if the same project is subjected to either a 25 percent (Situation B) or 40 percent (Situation C) tax rate. Using NPV as an investment criterion, a decrease in the tax rate makes the point-of-sale equipment a more acceptable investment; an increase has the opposite effect. Since multinational firms operate in countries having federal tax rates from 0 to nearly 40 percent, the tax jurisdiction in which a new asset is located can dramatically influence that asset's NPV.

Understanding how depreciation and taxes affect the various capital budgeting techniques allows managers to make the most informed decisions about capital investments. If the substantial resource commitment required can be justified, managers are more likely to have confidence in the company's capital investments. Justification is partially achieved by determining whether a capital project fits into an organization's strategic plans. To be confident of their conclusions, managers must also comprehend the assumptions and limitations of each capital budgeting method.

ASSUMPTIONS AND LIMITATIONS OF METHODS

6 What are the underlying assumptions and limitations of each capital project evaluation method?

As summarized in Exhibit 15.7 (p. 613), each capital budget evaluation method has underlying assumptions and limitations. To maximize benefits of the capital budgeting process, managers should understand the similarities and differences of the various methods and use multiple methods to evaluate projects.

All methods in Exhibit 15.7 have two similar limitations.

- Except to the extent that payback indicates promptness of investment recovery, none of the methods provides a mechanism to include management preferences with regard to

[5] Surtaxes that apply to corporations can drive the top marginal rate above 35 percent for certain income brackets.

[6] KPMG, Corporate and Indirect Tax Survey 2011; http://www.kpmg.com/Global/en/IssuesAndInsights/ArticlesPublications/Documents/corporate-and-indirect-tax-rate-survey-2011.pdf (accessed 2/15/12).

[7] Presently, the U.S. has one of the highest tax rates in the world. One implication of this fact is that the depreciation tax shield associated with an investment is worth more in the U.S. than other countries. This fact also means that any return on the investment is taxed at a higher rate in the U.S. than in most other countries.

[8] To simplify the presentation, the authors have elected to ignore a tax rule requirement called the *half-year* (or *mid-quarter*) *convention* that applies to personal assets and a mid-month convention that applies to most real estate improvements. Under tax law, only a partial year's depreciation may be taken in the year an asset is placed into service. The slight difference that such a tax limitation would make on the amounts presented is immaterial for purposes of illustrating these capital budgeting concepts.

Exhibit 15.6 Point-of-Sale Equipment Investment Analyses

Assumed Facts	
Initial investment	$6,000,000
Expected annual before-tax cash flows	850,000
Straight-line depreciation (10 years)	600,000
Expected economic life	10 years
Situation A: Tax rate of 30% (actual rate in effect)	
Situation B: Tax rate of 25%	
Situation C: Tax rate of 40%	

	SITUATION		
Years 1–10	**A**	**B**	**C**
Before-tax cash flow	$ 850,000	$ 850,000	$ 850,000
Depreciation	(600,000)	(600,000)	(600,000)
Income before tax	$ 250,000	$ 250,000	$ 250,000
Tax	(75,000)	(62,500)	(100,000)
Net income	$ 175,000	$ 187,500	$ 150,000
Depreciation	600,000	600,000	600,000
Cash flow after tax	$ 775,000	$ 787,500	$ 750,000

SITUATION A—NPV CALCULATIONS ASSUMING A 5% DISCOUNT RATE

Cash Flow	Time	Amount	Discount Factor	Present Value
Investment	t_0	$(6,000,000)	1.0000	$(6,000,000)
Annual inflows	t_1–t_{10}	775,000	7.7217	5,984,318
Net present value				$ (15,682)

SITUATION B—NPV CALCULATIONS ASSUMING A 5% DISCOUNT RATE

Cash Flow	Time	Amount	Discount Factor	Present Value
Investment	t_0	$(6,000,000)	1.0000	$(6,000,000)
Annual inflows	t_1–t_{10}	787,500	7.7217	6,080,839
Net present value				$ 80,839

SITUATION C—NPV CALCULATIONS ASSUMING A 5% DISCOUNT RATE

Cash Flow	Time	Amount	Discount Factor	Present Value
Investment	t_0	$(6,000,000)	1.0000	$(6,000,000)
Annual inflows	t_1–t_{10}	750,000	7.7217	5,791,275
Net present value				$ (208,725)

the timing of cash flows. This limitation can be partially overcome by discounting cash flows occurring further in the future at higher rates than those in earlier years, assuming that earlier cash flows are preferred.

- All methods use single, deterministic measures of cash flows rather than probabilities. This limitation can be minimized through the use of probability estimates of cash flows. Such estimates can be input into a computer program to determine a distribution of answers for each method under various conditions of uncertainty.

Exhibit 15.7 Assumptions and Limitations of Capital Budgeting Methods

ASSUMPTIONS	LIMITATIONS
Payback Method	
• Speed of investment recovery is the key consideration. • Timing and magnitude of cash flows are accurately predicted. • Risk (uncertainty) is lower for a shorter payback project.	• Cash flows after payback are ignored. • Cash flows and project life are treated as deterministic without explicit consideration of probabilities. • Time value of money is ignored. • Cash flow pattern preferences are not explicitly recognized.
Net Present Value	
• Discount rate used is valid. • Timing and size of cash flows are accurately predicted. • Project life is accurately predicted. • If the shorter lived of two projects is selected, the proceeds of that project will continue to earn the discount rate of return through the theoretical completion of the longer-lived project.	• Cash flows and project life are treated as deterministic without explicit consideration of probabilities. • Alternative project rates of return are not known. • Cash flow pattern preferences are not explicitly recognized. • IRR on project is not reflected.
Profitability Index	
• Assumptions are the same as NPV. • Size of PV of net future cash inflows relative to size of present value of investment measures efficient use of capital.	• Limitations are the same as NPV. • A relative answer is given but dollars of NPV are not reflected.
Internal Rate of Return	
• Hurdle rate used is valid. • Timing and size of cash flows are accurately predicted. • Project life is accurately predicted. • If the shorter lived of two projects is selected, the proceeds of that project will continue to earn the IRR through the theoretical completion of the longer-lived project.	• The IRR, rather than dollar size, is used to rank projects for funding. • Dollars of NPV are not reflected. • Cash flows and project life are treated as deterministic without explicit consideration of probabilities. • Cash flow pattern preferences are not explicitly recognized. • Multiple rates of return can be calculated on the same project.
Accounting Rate of Return (presented in Appendix 2 of this chapter)	
• Effect on accounting earnings relative to average investment is key consideration. • Timing and size of increase in earnings, investment cost, project life, and salvage value can be accurately predicted.	• Cash flows are not considered. • Time value of money is not considered. • Earnings, investment, and project life are treated as deterministic without explicit consideration of probabilities.

INVESTMENT DECISION

Management must identify the best asset(s) to acquire for fulfilling the company's goals and objectives; to do so requires answers to the questions appearing in the following four subsections.

Is the Activity Worthy of an Investment?

A company acquires assets when they have value in relation to specific current or desired organizational activities. For example, **Pioneer Hi-Bred International** invests heavily in product development because that activity is that firm's primary path to new revenues. Before making asset acquisition decisions, company management must be certain that the activity for which the assets are needed justifies an investment.

Greg Hinsdale/Corbis/Jupiter Images

Many companies today invest in implementing green workplace programs to reduce environmental impact, even though the costs may exceed the financial benefits of doing so.

An activity's worth is measured by cost–benefit analysis. For most capital budgeting decisions, costs and benefits are measured in monetary terms. If the monetary benefits exceed the monetary costs, the activity is potentially worthwhile. In some cases, though, the benefits provided by capital projects are difficult to quantify. Difficulty in quantification is no reason to exclude such benefits from capital budgeting analyses. Often surrogate quantifiable measures can be obtained for qualitative benefits. For example, benefits from investments in day-care centers for employees' children could be estimated through the reduction in employee time-off and turnover. At a minimum, managers should attempt to subjectively include qualitative benefits in the analytical process.

In other circumstances, management could know in advance that the monetary benefits of the capital project will not exceed the costs but that the project is essential for other reasons. For instance, a company could consider renovating the employee workplace with new carpet, furniture, paint, and artwork. The renovation would not make the employees' work any easier, faster, or safer but would make the workplace more comfortable. Such a project could be deemed "worthy" regardless of the results of a cost–benefit analysis. Companies could also invest in unprofitable products to maintain market share of a product group and, therefore, protect the market position of profitable products. Further, a company may invest in technology that reduces energy consumption and pollution even though the investment is not wholly justified on financial grounds alone.

Which Assets Can Be Used for the Activity?

Identifying appropriate assets to use for the proposed activity is closely related to an evaluation of the activity's worth. Management must determine how much the assets will cost to decide whether the activity should be pursued. Management should gather, for each asset being considered, the specific monetary and nonmonetary information shown in Exhibit 15.8 to make this determination.

As mentioned in the previous section, information used in a capital project analysis may include surrogate, indirect measures. Management must have both quantitative and qualitative information about each asset and recognize that some projects are simply more crucial to the firm's future than others.

Of the Available Assets for Each Activity, Which Is the Best Investment?

Using all available information, management should select the best asset from the candidates and end consideration of all others. In most instances, companies have committees that discuss, evaluate, and approve capital projects. In judging capital project

Exhibit 15.8 Capital Investment Information Expectations

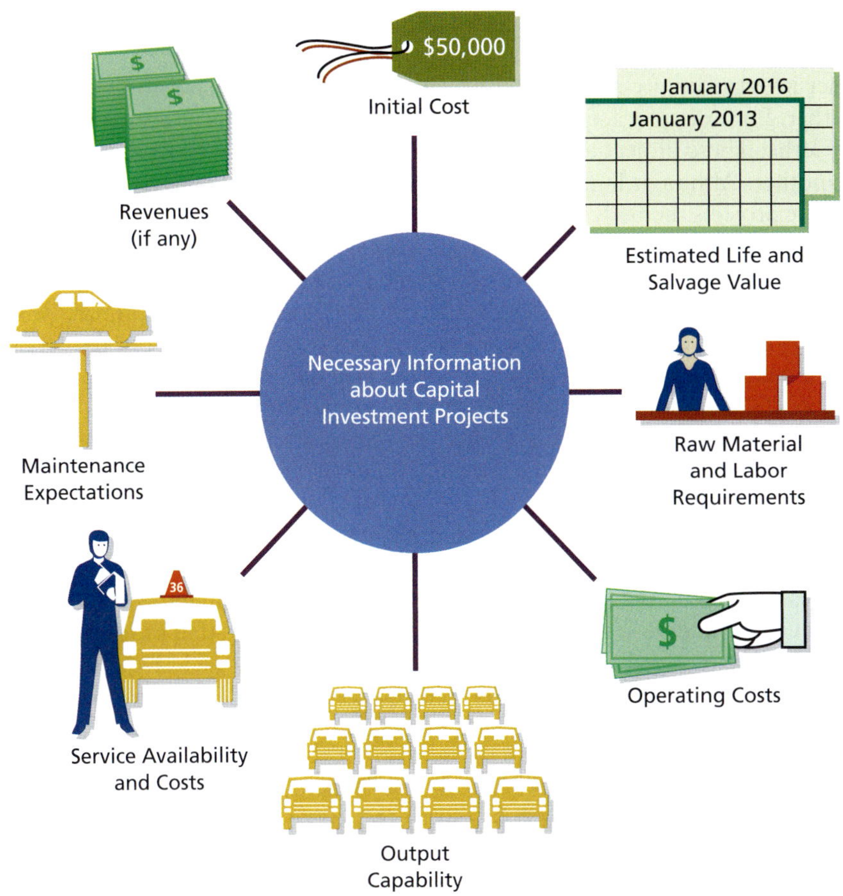

acceptability, a committee should recognize that two types of capital budgeting decisions must be made.

- A **screening decision** determines whether a capital project is desirable based on some previously established minimum criterion or criteria (i.e., NPV ≥ 0). A project that does not meet the minimum standard(s) is excluded from further consideration.
- A **preference decision** ranks projects according to their impact on the achievement of company objectives.

Deciding which asset is the best investment requires the use of one or more of the evaluation techniques discussed previously. Some techniques are used to screen project acceptability; other techniques are used to rank projects. Although different companies use different techniques for screening and ranking purposes, payback period is commonly used only for screening decisions because payback focuses on only the short run and does not consider the time value of money. The other techniques previously discussed can be used to screen or rank capital projects.

Of the "Best Investments" for All Worthwhile Activities, in Which Ones Should the Company Invest?

Although many worthwhile investment activities exist, each company has limited resources available and must allocate them in the most profitable manner. Therefore, after choosing the best asset for each activity, management must decide which activities and assets to fund. Investment projects are classified as mutually exclusive, independent, or mutually inclusive.

Mutually exclusive projects compete to fill the same function. One project will be chosen from such a group, excluding all others from further consideration. A proposal under consideration could be to replace a current asset with one that provides the same functionality. If the company keeps the old asset, the new one will not be purchased; if the new asset is purchased, the old asset will be sold. Thus, the two assets are mutually exclusive. For example, if a small bakery decides to buy a new delivery truck, it would no longer need the existing truck and would sell it to help finance the new truck.

Other investments are **independent projects** because they have no specific bearing on one another. For example, acquiring an office computer system is not related to purchasing a factory lathe. These project decisions are analyzed and accepted or rejected independently of one another. Although limited resources may preclude the acquisition of all acceptable projects, the projects themselves are not mutually exclusive.

Management may consider acquiring **mutually inclusive projects** in which multiple investments are linked to a primary project. In such a situation, if the primary project is chosen, all related projects are also selected. Alternatively, rejection of the primary project dictates rejection of the others. For example, when a firm chooses to invest in new technology, investing in an employee training program for the new technology would also be necessary.

Exhibit 15.9 illustrates a typical investment decision process in which a company is determining the best way to provide transportation for its sales force. Answers to the four questions asked in the subheadings to this section are provided for the transportation decision.

To ensure that capital funds are invested in the best projects available, managers must carefully evaluate all projects and decide which represent the most effective and efficient use of resources—a difficult determination. The evaluation process should consider activity priorities, cash flows, and project risk. Projects should then be ranked in order of acceptability. Ranking could be required for both independent and mutually exclusive projects. Ranking independent projects is required to efficiently allocate scarce capital to competing uses. Ranking mutually exclusive projects is required when selecting the best project from the set of alternatives.

Exhibit 15.9 Typical Investment Decision Process

Activity—Provide transportation for a sales force of 10 people.

1. Is the activity worthy of an investment?
   Yes; this decision is based on an analysis of the cost of providing transportation in relationship to the dollars of gross margin to be generated by the sales force.

2. Which assets can be used for the activity?
   Available: Bus passes, bicycles, motorcycles, automobiles (purchased), automobiles (leased), automobiles (currently owned), small airplanes.
   Infeasible: Bus passes, bicycles, and motorcycles are rejected because of inconvenience and inability to carry a reasonable quantity of merchandise; airplanes are rejected because of inconvenience and lack of landing sites near customers.
   Feasible: Various types of automobiles to be purchased (assume asset options A through G); various types of leasing arrangements (assume availability of leases 1 through 5); current fleet.
   Gather all relevant quantitative and qualitative information on all feasible assets (purchased assets; leased assets; current fleet).

3. Of the available assets for each activity, which is the best investment?
   Compare all relevant information and choose the best asset candidate from the purchase group (assume Asset D) and the lease group (assume Lease 2).

4. Of the "best investments" for all worthwhile activities, in which ones should the company invest?
   Comparing the best asset candidate from the purchase group (Asset D) and the lease group (Lease 2) represents a mutually exclusive, multiple-candidate project decision. The best candidate is found to be Type D assets. Comparing the Type D assets to the current fleet is a mutually exclusive project. The best investment is deemed to be the purchase of a new fleet of 10 Type D automobiles concurrently with the sale of the old fleet.

RANKING MULTIPLE CAPITAL PROJECTS

7 How do managers rank investment projects?

When managers must make an accept/reject decision for a single asset, all time value of money evaluation techniques normally point to the same decision alternative. A project is acceptable under the NPV method if its net present value is not negative. Acceptability of a capital investment is also indicated by a profitability index of 1.00 or more. Because the PI is an adaptation of the NPV method, these two evaluation techniques always provide the same screening result. To be acceptable using the IRR model, a project must have an internal rate of return equal to or greater than the specified hurdle rate. The IRR method gives the same accept/reject decision as the NPV and PI methods if the hurdle rate is used as the discount rate.

More often, however, managers must choose among multiple, mutually exclusive projects. Multiple project evaluation decisions require that a ranking be made, generally using net present value, profitability index, and/or internal rate of return. Payback period also can be used to rank multiple projects. However, the payback method does not provide as much useful information as do NPV, PI, and IRR because the payback method ignores both cash flows beyond the payback period and the time value of money.

Managers can use results from the evaluation techniques to rank projects in descending order of acceptability. For the NPV and PI methods, rankings are based on the magnitude of the NPV and PI index, respectively. Although based on the same figures, the NPV and PI methods do not always provide the same rank order because the former is a dollar measure and the latter is a percentage measure. When the IRR is used, rankings of multiple projects are based on expected rates of return. Rankings provided by the IRR method are not necessarily the same as those given by the NPV or PI methods.

Conflicting results arise, in part, among the three methods because of differing underlying **reinvestment assumptions**. The reinvestment assumption focuses on how the cash flows received during a project's life are assumed to be reinvested until the end of that project's life. The NPV and PI techniques assume that cash inflows are reinvested at the discount rate, which is typically the weighted average cost of capital. The IRR method assumes that cash inflows are reinvested at the expected internal rate of return, which is higher than the COC for projects with positive NPVs. In such a case, the IRR method could provide a misleading indication of project success because additional projects having the same high return might not be found.

In addition to ranking projects based on financial criteria, managers must evaluate whether there are differences in risks across potential projects.

COMPENSATING FOR RISK IN CAPITAL PROJECT EVALUATION

8 How is risk considered in capital budgeting analyses?

When choosing among multiple projects, managers must consider the risk or uncertainty associated with each project. In accounting, **risk** reflects uncertainty about differences between the expected and actual future returns from an investment. For example, the purchase of a \$100,000, 2 percent Treasury note would provide a virtually risk-free return of \$2,000 annually because such notes are backed by the full faith and credit of the U.S. government. If the same \$100,000 were used to purchase stock, the returns could range from −100 percent (losing the entire investment) to an abnormally high return. The potential for extreme variability makes the stock a much riskier investment than the Treasury note.

Managers considering a capital investment should understand and compensate for the degree of risk involved in that investment. There are three approaches to compensate for risk: the judgmental method, the risk-adjusted discount rate method, and sensitivity analysis. These methods do not eliminate risk, but they do help managers understand and evaluate risk in the decision-making process.

Judgmental Method

The **judgmental method** of risk adjustment allows decision makers to use logic and reasoning when deciding whether a project provides an acceptable rate of return in relation to its risk. The decision maker is presented all available information for each project, including the payback period, NPV, PI, and IRR. After reviewing the information, the decision maker chooses from among acceptable projects based on personal judgment of the risk-to-return relationship. The judgmental approach provides no formal process for adjusting data for the risk element. Although such a method sounds unorthodox, experienced business managers are generally able to use this method with a high level of reliability.

Risk-Adjusted Discount Rate Method

A more formal method of considering risk requires making adjustments to the discount (or hurdle) rate. Under the **risk-adjusted discount rate method**, the decision maker increases the rate used for discounting future cash inflows and decreases the rate used for discounting future cash outflows to compensate for increased risk. As the discount rate is increased (or decreased), the PVs of future cash flows are reduced (or increased). Therefore, larger cash inflows are required to "cover" the investment and provide an acceptable rate of return. Changes in the discount rate should reflect the degree of risk, other investment opportunities, and corporate objectives. If the internal rate of return were used for higher-risk project evaluation, the risk-adjusted discount rate method would increase the hurdle rate to which the IRR is compared.

Assume that Family One Stop's management is considering the purchase of an automated product-ordering system. The $1,500,000 system would be used for 10 years and then would be sold for $50,000. Exhibit 15.10 provides estimates of the cost for and annual cash savings from the automated system. Family One Stop's management generally uses its 10 percent cost of capital as the discount rate in evaluating capital projects using the NPV

Exhibit 15.10 Automated Ordering System Analyses

Initial installation cost	$1,500,000
After-tax net cash flows	
Years 1–5	260,000
Years 6–10	220,000
Year 10 (sale)	50,000

NPV USING 10% DISCOUNT RATE

Cash Flow	Time	Amount	Discount Factor	Present Value
Investment	t_0	$(1,500,000)	1.0000	$(1,500,000)
Annual inflows	t_1–t_5	260,000	3.7908	985,608
Annual inflows	t_6–t_{10}	220,000	2.3538[a]	517,836
Final inflow	t_{10}	50,000	0.3855	19,275
Net present value				$ 22,719

NPV USING 14% DISCOUNT RATE

Cash Flow	Time	Amount	Discount Factor	Present Value
Investment	t_0	$(1,500,000)	1.0000	$(1,500,000)
Annual inflows	t_1–t_5	260,000	3.4331	892,606
Annual inflows	t_6–t_{10}	220,000	1.7830[b]	392,260
Final inflow	t_{10}	50,000	0.2697	13,485
Net present value				$ (201,649)

[a]Factor for 10 periods at 10% – Factor for 5 periods at 10% = Factor for periods 6–10 at 10% = 6.1446 – 3.7908 = 2.3538

[b]Factor for 10 periods at 14% – Factor for 5 periods at 14% = Factor for periods 6–10 at 14% = 5.2161 – 3.4331 = 1.7830

method. However, Soloman Klatz, a capital projects committee member, believes that this project has substantially above-normal risk. First, the cost savings realized from the system could be significantly less than planned. Second, the system's salvage value in 10 years could vary substantially from the $50,000 estimate. Klatz wants to compensate for these risk factors by using a 14 percent discount rate rather than the 10 percent rate. Determining the adjustment of the discount rate (from 10 to 14 percent, for example) is most commonly an arbitrary one. Thus, even though a formal process is used to compensate for risk, the process still involves a degree of judgment on the part of the project evaluators. Exhibit 15.10 shows the NPV computations using both discount rates. When the discount rate is raised to 14 percent, the project's NPV is reduced and shows the project to be unacceptable.

The same type of risk adjustment can be used for payback period or accounting rate of return (ARR, which is discussed in Appendix 2 of this chapter). If the payback method is used, managers can choose to shorten the maximum allowable payback period to compensate for increased risk. This adjustment assumes that cash flows occurring in the more distant periods are riskier than cash flows occurring sooner. If the ARR method is used, managers can increase the hurdle rate against which the ARR is compared to compensate for risk. Another way in which risk can be included in the decision process is through the use of sensitivity analysis.

Sensitivity Analysis

Sensitivity analysis is a process of determining the amount of change that must occur in a variable before a different decision would be made. Sensitivity analysis examines what happens if a variable were different from that originally expected. In a capital budgeting situation, sensitivity analysis can be conducted for the discount rate, annual net cash flows, or project life. Except for the initial purchase price, all information used in capital budgeting is estimated. Use of estimates creates the possibility of introducing errors, and sensitivity analysis identifies an "error range" for the various estimated values over which the project will still be acceptable. The following sections consider how sensitivity analysis relates to the discount rate, cash flows, and asset life.

Range of the Discount Rate A capital project providing a rate of return equal to or greater than the discount or hurdle rate is considered an acceptable investment. A project's NPV will change, however, if the discount rate changes. Because the minimal discount and hurdle rates should be set at the organization's cost of capital, an increase in the COC would cause an increase in the discount rate—and a corresponding decrease in the project's NPV. The COC, for instance, can increase because of increases in interest rates on new issues of debt.

Sensitivity analysis allows a company to determine how much the estimated COC (and, therefore, the related discount rate) could increase before a project becomes unacceptable. The upper limit of increase in the discount rate (COC) is the project's internal rate of return. At the IRR, a project's NPV is zero; therefore, the PV of the cash inflows equals the PV of cash outflows. As long as the IRR for a project is equal to or greater than the COC, or alternative discount rate, the project is acceptable.

To illustrate the use of sensitivity analysis, assume that Family One Stop has an opportunity to invest $340,000 in new delivery equipment that has a 10-year life and will generate cost savings of $75,000 per year. Using a 10 percent COC rate for Family One Stop, the equipment's NPV is computed as follows:

After-tax cash flows for 10 years discounted at 10% ($75,000 × 6.1446)	$ 460,845
Initial investment	(340,000)
Net present value	$ 120,845

The equipment provides a positive NPV and is considered an acceptable investment candidate.

Family One Stop's management wants to know how high the discount rate can rise before the investment would become unacceptable. To find the upper limit of the discount rate, the PV factor for an annuity of 10 periods at the unknown interest rate is computed as follows:

$$\text{Cash flow} \times \text{PV factor} = \text{Investment}$$
$$\$75{,}000 \times \text{PV factor} = \$340{,}000$$
$$\text{PV factor} = 4.5333$$

Locating the PV factor in the discount tables, the IRR is found to be between 17 and 18 percent. As long as Family One Stop's COC is less than or equal to approximately 17.5 percent, this investment is acceptable. As the discount rate increases and approaches the IRR, the investment becomes less desirable. These calculations assume that the cash flows and equipment life have been properly estimated.

Range of the Cash Flows Another factor sensitive to changes in estimation is the investment's projected cash flows. Family One Stop's data for the delivery equipment are used to illustrate how to determine the range of acceptable cash flows. Company management wants to know how small the net cash inflows could be and still have the investment remain desirable. This determination requires that the present value of the cash flows for 10 periods, discounted at 10 percent, be equal to or greater than the investment cost. The PV factor for 10 periods at 10 percent is 6.1446. The equation from the preceding section can be used to find the lowest acceptable annuity:

$$\text{Cash flow} \times \text{PV factor} = \text{Investment}$$
$$\text{Cash flow} \times 6.1446 = \$340{,}000$$
$$\text{Cash flow} = \$340{,}000 \div 6.1446$$
$$\text{Cash flow} = \$55{,}333$$

As long as the net annual after-tax cash flow equals or exceeds $55,333, the delivery equipment will be financially acceptable.

Range of the Life of the Asset Asset life is related to many factors, some of which (such as the amount and timing of maintenance and equipment) are controllable. Other factors, such as technological advances and actions of competitors, are noncontrollable. Misestimating the project's life will change the number of periods from which cash inflows are to be derived. This change could affect the accept/reject decision for a project. The Family One Stop's delivery equipment example is used to demonstrate how to find the minimum length of time the cash flows must be received for the equipment to be acceptable. The solution requires setting the present value of the cash flows discounted at 10 percent equal to the investment. This computation yields the PV factor for an unknown number of periods:

$$\text{Cash flow} \times \text{PV factor} = \text{Investment}$$
$$\$75{,}000 \times \text{PV factor} = \$340{,}000$$
$$\text{PV factor} = 4.5333$$

Review the present value of an annuity table in Appendix A under the 10 percent interest column to find the 4.5333 factor. The investment life is between six and seven years. If the cash inflows were to stop at any point before approximately 6.5 years, the investment would be unacceptable.

Sensitivity analysis does not reduce the uncertainty about each variable. Such analysis does, however, provide management a sense of the tolerance for estimation errors by providing upper and lower ranges for selected variables. The preceding presentation simplistically focuses on single changes in each of the variables. If all factors change simultaneously, this type of sensitivity analysis is useless. More advanced treatments of sensitivity analysis, which allow for simultaneous ranging of all variables, can be found under the topic of simulation in an advanced mathematical modeling text.

POSTINVESTMENT AUDIT

9 How and why should management conduct a postinvestment audit of a capital project?

In a **postinvestment audit** of a capital project, information on actual project results is gathered and compared to expected results. This process provides a feedback or control feature to both the persons who submitted the original project information and those who approved it. Comparisons should be made using the same technique or techniques used originally to determine project acceptance. Actual data should be extrapolated to future periods in which such information would be appropriate. For cases in which significant learning or training is necessary, start-up costs of the first year may not be representative of future costs. Such projects should be given a chance to stabilize before making the project audit.

As the size of the capital expenditure increases, a postinvestment audit becomes more crucial. Although an audit cannot change a past investment decision, it can pinpoint project operations areas that are out of line with expectations so that problems can possibly be corrected before they get out of hand.

An audit can also provide feedback on the accuracy of the original project cash flow estimates. Sometimes project sponsors are biased in favor of their own projects and provide overly optimistic forecasts of future revenues or cost savings. Project sponsors should be required to explain all major variances. Knowing that postinvestment audits will be made could cause project sponsors to provide more realistic cash flow forecasts in their capital requests.

Performing a postinvestment audit is not an easy task. The actual information might be in a different form from the original estimates, and some project benefits can be difficult to quantify. Project returns fluctuate considerably over time, so results gathered at a single point might not be representative of the complete project results. Regardless of the difficulties involved, however, postinvestment audits provide information that can help managers make better capital investment decisions in the future.

Exhibit 15.11 provides information pertinent to a postinvestment audit of the photovoltaic technology investment presented in Exhibits 15.2 (p. 603) and 15.3 (p. 605). This postinvestment audit is occurring after all actual cash flows associated with the investment are known; i.e., after period t_7. Thus, none of the actual amounts are projected or estimated. As shown in Exhibit 15.3, the projected NPV of the investment was \$1,433,060. Exhibit 15.12 provides the NPV calculation on the actual data using the 7 percent discount rate.

As shown in Exhibit 15.12, the investment's actual NPV was \$47,947. Whereas the NPV is positive and the project generated a return in excess of 7 percent, the realized NPV was far less than the projected NPV of \$1,433,060. An examination of Exhibit 15.11 and the underlying facts reveals the difference between the planned and actual NPV is attributable to three primary factors:

1. The initial acquisition cost of \$14,250,000 exceeded the expected investment cost of \$13,500,000. This accounts for \$750,000 of the difference between the planned and actual NPVs.
2. The actual cash inflows in Years 1 through 4 exceeded the planned cash inflows. Further investigation revealed actual energy prices were higher than were anticipated in the project proposal. Hence, the energy savings were greater than originally estimated.
3. The actual cash inflows in Years 6 and 7 were far less than planned levels. The investigation revealed that actual repair and maintenance costs were much higher than planned. Simply put, extending the investment's actual life to the seven year planned life required extraordinary maintenance and repair activities. Accordingly, the cash inflows late in the investment's life were far below expectations.

Exhibit 15.11 Postinvestment Audit of Photovoltaic Technology Investment Presented in Exhibit 15.3

		DISCOUNT RATE = 7%	
Cash Flow	**Time**	**Planned Amount**	**Actual Amount**
Initial investment	t_0	\$(13,500,000)	\$(14,250,000)
Year 1 net cash flow	t_1	2,200,000	2,250,000
Year 2 net cash flow	t_2	2,600,000	2,650,000
Year 3 net cash flow	t_3	3,200,000	3,340,000
Year 4 net cash flow	t_4	3,900,000	4,200,000
Year 5 net cash flow	t_5	4,200,000	4,125,000
Year 6 net cash flow	t_6	2,100,000	1,000,000
Year 7 net cash flow	t_7	1,000,000	550,000

Exhibit 15.12 Net Present Value Calculation for Postinvestment Audit of Photovoltaic Technology Investment

		DISCOUNT RATE = 7%				
Cash Flow	**Time**	a **Amount**	×	b **Discount Factor**	=	c **Present Value**
Initial investment	t_0	$(14,250,000)		1.0000		$(14,250,000)
Year 1 net cash flow	t_1	2,250,000		0.9346		2,102,850
Year 2 net cash flow	t_2	2,650,000		0.8734		2,314,510
Year 3 net cash flow	t_3	3,340,000		0.8163		2,726,442
Year 4 net cash flow	t_4	4,200,000		0.7629		3,204,180
Year 5 net cash flow	t_5	4,125,000		0.7130		2,941,125
Year 6 net cash flow	t_6	1,000,000		0.6663		666,300
Year 7 net cash flow	t_7	550,000		0.6228		342,540
Net present value						$ 47,947

APPENDIX 1

TIME VALUE OF MONEY

10 How are present values calculated?

The time value of money can be discussed in relation to either its future or its present value. **Future value (FV)** refers to a cash flow occurring in the future. Alternatively, present value is the amount that future cash flows are worth currently given a specified rate of interest.[9] Thus, FVs and PVs depend on three things:

- amount of the cash flow,
- rate of interest, and
- timing of the cash flow.

Future and present values are related: a PV is an FV discounted to time 0. The rate of return used in PV computations is called the discount rate.

In computing FVs and PVs, simple or compound interest is used. **Simple interest** means that interest is earned only on the original investment or principal amount. **Compound interest** means that interest earned in prior periods is added to the original investment, so interest is earned in each successive period on both principal and previously accrued interest. The time between each interest computation is called the **compounding period**. The more often interest is compounded, the higher the actual interest rate being received relative to the stated rate. The following discussion is based on the use of compound interest because most analyses use this method. Additionally, only PVs are discussed because they are more relevant to the types of management decisions discussed in this text.

Interest rates are typically stated in annual terms, and compounding is assumed to occur annually. To compensate for more frequent compounding periods, the number of years is multiplied by the number of compounding periods per year, and the annual interest rate is divided by the number of compounding periods per year.

Present Value of a Single Cash Flow

Assume that Stevie Wild's investment account has an expected return of 10 percent per year, compounded annually. He wants to accumulate $100,000 in five years to attend graduate school and needs to know what amount to invest now to achieve that goal. The formula to solve for the present value is

[9] Interest can be earned or owed, received or paid. To simplify the discussion, the topic of interest is viewed only from the inflow standpoint.

$$PV = FV \div (1 + i)^n$$

where PV = present value of a future amount,
FV = future value of a current investment,
i = interest rate per compounding period, and
n = number of compounding periods.

Substituting known values into the formula gives the following:

$$PV = \$100{,}000 \div (1 + 0.10)^5$$
$$PV = \$100{,}000 \div 1.61051$$
$$PV = \$62{,}092$$

In capital budgeting analyses, many future value amounts must be converted to present values. Rather than using formulas to find PVs, a table of factors for the PV of $1 (Table 1) for various interest rates and time periods is provided in Appendix A at the end of the text for ease of computation. The discount factors for single period cash flows are obtained from the formula $[1 \div (1 + i)^n]$. Such factors are also built into programmable calculators, apps for smart phones and tablets, and electronic spreadsheets.

Present Value of an Annuity

An annuity is a cash flow (either positive or negative) that is repeated over consecutive periods. In an **ordinary annuity**, cash flows occur at the end of each period. In contrast, cash flows for an **annuity due** occur at the beginning of each period.

To illustrate the computation of the PV of an annuity, consider the following situation. Joe and Jenny Jones are planning for their daughter's college education. Their daughter, Bobbie, will need $25,000 per year for the next four years. The Joneses want to know how much to invest currently at 8 percent so that Bobbie can withdraw $25,000 per year. The following diagram presents the situation:

Time period	t_0	t_1	t_2	t_3	t_4
Future value		$25,000	$25,000	$25,000	$25,000
Present value	? ←				

The present value of each single cash flow can be found using 8 percent factors in Table 1 of Appendix A as follows:

PV of first receipt: $25,000 × 0.9259	$23,148
PV of second receipt: $25,000 × 0.8573	21,433
PV of third receipt: $25,000 × 0.7938	19,845
PV of fourth receipt: $25,000 × 0.7350	18,375
Total present value of future cash flows	$82,801

The PV factor for an ordinary annuity can also be determined by adding the PV factors for all periods having a future cash flow. Table 2 in Appendix A provides PV of ordinary annuity factors for various interest rates and time periods. From this table, the factor of 3.3121 can be obtained and multiplied by $25,000 to yield $82,803, or approximately the same result as just calculated. (The difference is caused by decimal-fraction rounding.)

APPENDIX 2

ACCOUNTING RATE OF RETURN

11 What are the advantages and disadvantages of the accounting rate of return method?

The **accounting rate of return (ARR)** measures the rate of earnings obtained on the average capital investment over a project's life. This evaluation method is consistent with the accounting model and uses profits from accrual-basis accounting. It is the one evaluation technique that is not based on cash flows. The formula for computing the accounting rate of return is

ARR = Average annual profits from project ÷ Average investment in project

Investment in project refers to project cost as well as working capital items (such as inventory) to support the project. Investment in project, salvage value, and working capital released at the end of the project's life are summed and divided by 2 to obtain the average investment over the life of the project.[10] The cost and working capital needed represent the initial investment, and the salvage value and working capital released represent the ending investment. The following information pertains to a new product line being considered by Family One Stop. The information is used to illustrate after-tax calculation of the ARR.

Beginning investment	
Initial cost of equipment and software	$4,000,000
Additional working capital needed for the product line	2,000,000
Return over life of project	
Average increase in profits after taxes	500,000
Return at end of project	
Salvage value of investment in 10 years (end of life of product line)	1,000,000
Working capital released at the end of 10 years	2,000,000

Solving the formula for the accounting rate of return gives

$$\begin{aligned} \text{ARR} &= \$500{,}000 \div [(\$6{,}000{,}000 + \$3{,}000{,}000) \div 2] \\ &= \$500{,}000 \div \$4{,}500{,}000 \\ &= 11.1\% \text{ (rounded)} \end{aligned}$$

The 11.1 percent ARR on this investment can be compared with a hurdle rate set in advance by management. This hurdle rate need not be the same as the desired discount rate because the data used in calculating the ARR are not strictly cash flows. The ARR hurdle rate can be set higher than the discount rate because the discount rate automatically compensates for the time value of money. In addition, the 11.1 percent ARR for this project should be compared with ARRs on other projects under investment consideration by Family One Stop to see which projects have the higher accounting rates of return.

Comprehensive Review Module

KEY TERMS

accounting rate of return (ARR), p. 623
annuity, p. 604
annuity due, p. 623
capital asset, p. 601
capital budgeting, p. 601
cash flow, p. 602
compound interest, p. 622
compounding period, p. 622
cost of capital (COC), p. 605
discount rate, p. 605
discounting, p. 604
financing decision, p. 602
future value (FV), p. 622
hurdle rate, p. 609
independent project, p. 616
internal rate of return (IRR), p. 607
investment decision, p. 602
judgmental method, p. 617
mutually exclusive project, p. 615
mutually inclusive project, p. 616
net present value (NPV), p. 605
net present value method, p. 605
ordinary annuity, p. 623
payback period, p. 603
postinvestment audit, p. 620
preference decision, p. 615
present value (PV), p. 604
profitability index (PI), p. 607
reinvestment assumption, p. 617
return of capital, p. 605

[10] Sometimes ARR is computed using initial cost rather than average investment as the denominator. Such a computation ignores the return of funds at the end of the project's life and is less appropriate than the computation shown.

CHAPTER SUMMARY

1 Capital Budgeting and Cash Flows

- Most capital budgeting techniques focus on cash flows because
  - investors are ultimately interested in cash flows rather than accounting earnings.
  - cash flows from a capital project can be compared with the cash returns provided from debt investments (in the form of interest) and stock investments (in the form of dividends).

2 Payback Period

- The payback period
  - is computed by summing the annual net cash inflows until they total the original investment.
  - is the length of time required for cash inflows to recoup the initial cost of a capital project.

3 Net Present Value and Profitability Index

- Net present value (NPV) and profitability index (PI) use discounted cash flows to measure the expected returns on potential capital projects.
  - NPV is the present value (PV) of cash inflows minus the PV of cash outflows.
    - To be acceptable, a project must generate an NPV of $0 or more.
  - PI is the PV of cash inflows divided by the PV of cash outflows.
    - To be acceptable, a project must generate a PI of at least 1.

4 Internal Rate of Return

- The internal rate of return (IRR) of a project is the discount rate that causes the NPV to equal zero.
  - IRR can be calculated by trial and error. Using the NPV framework, a discount rate can be arbitrarily selected and an NPV calculated.
    - If the resulting NPV is positive, select a higher discount rate and again calculate the NPV.
    - If the resulting NPV is negative, select a lower discount rate and again calculate the NPV.
    - Repeat the process until the discount rate selected causes the NPV to equal zero.
  - IRR can be calculated by many handheld calculators and computers.
  - If the only cash inflow is an annuity, the IRR can be found by using the PV of an ordinary annuity table.

5 Taxation and Depreciation

- Taxation and depreciation impact a project's cash flows because
  - operating profit is subject to income tax, which reduces the cash inflows from capital projects.
  - depreciation reduces the amount of taxes paid because depreciation is deducted in determining taxable income from projects.

6 Evaluation Method Assumptions and Limitations

- Each capital project evaluation method has certain underlying assumptions and limitations.
  - Payback method
    - Assumptions
      - The speed of investment recovery is the most important investment criterion.
      - The timing and amounts of cash flows can be accurately predicted.
      - The risk is lower for projects with shorter paybacks.
    - Limitations
      - Cash flows occurring after payback are ignored.
      - All cash flows are treated as deterministic.
      - The time value of money is ignored.
      - Any managerial preferences in the pattern of cash flows are ignored.
      - This method should be used in conjunction with another method because it ignores both the cash flows after the payback period is reached and the time value of money.
  - NPV method
    - Assumptions
      - The discount rate used is valid for that project.
      - The timing and amounts of cash flows can be accurately predicted.
      - Cash flows received from projects can be reinvested at the discount rate for the life of the project. When comparing projects with unequal lives, the NPV method assumes that the cash inflows from the shorter project can be reinvested at the discount rate for the life of the longer project.
    - Limitations
      - All cash flows are treated as deterministic.

- The actual rate of return for projects is not revealed.
- Any managerial preferences in the pattern of cash flows are ignored.

- PI method
  - Assumptions
    - The discount rate used is valid for that project.
    - The timing and amounts of cash flows can be accurately predicted.
    - Cash flows received from projects can be reinvested at the discount rate for the life of the project. When comparing projects with unequal lives, the NPV method assumes that the cash inflows from the shorter project can be reinvested at the discount rate for the life of the longer project.
    - The present value of cash inflows relative to the present value of the investment measures the efficiency of capital projects.
  - Limitations
    - All cash flows are treated as deterministic.
    - The actual rate of return for projects is not revealed.
    - Any managerial preferences in the pattern of cash flows are ignored.
    - Actual dollars of net present value are ignored.
- IRR method
  - Assumptions
    - The hurdle rate used is a valid return benchmark.
    - The timing and amounts of cash flows can be accurately predicted.
    - The life of projects can be accurately predicted.
    - Cash flows received from projects can be reinvested at the internal rate of return for the life of the projects. When comparing projects with unequal lives, the IRR method assumes that the cash inflows from the shorter project can be reinvested at the internal rate of return for the life of the longer project.
  - Limitations
    - All cash flows are treated as deterministic.
    - The actual rates of return for projects are not revealed.
    - Any managerial preferences in the pattern of cash flows are ignored.
    - The dollar magnitude of return on projects is ignored.
    - Multiple IRRs can be generated on the same project.

7 Ranking Investment Projects

- Managers can rank capital projects using the following guidelines:
  - Shorter payback period is preferred to longer payback period.
  - Higher NPV is preferred to lower NPV.
  - Higher PI is preferred to lower PI.
  - Higher IRR is preferred to lower IRR.

8 Risk

- Capital budgeting analysis considers risk by
  - requiring a shorter payback period for riskier projects.
  - applying a higher discount rate for riskier projects when the NPV or PI method is used.
  - applying a higher discount rate for riskier cash flows when the NPV or PI method is used.
  - requiring a higher IRR for riskier projects.
  - applying sensitivity analysis to the original project assumptions and estimates.

9 Postinvestment Audits

- Postinvestment audits of projects should be conducted
  - after the project has stabilized rather than shortly after start-up.
  - to compare actual project performance against expected performance to
    - evaluate the accuracy of original projections.
    - diagnose problems with implementation.
    - assess credibility of project sponsors' information.
  - in greater depth for high-value investment projects.
  - using the same technique or techniques originally used to determine project acceptance.

SOLUTION STRATEGIES

Prepare a time line to illustrate all moments in time when cash flows are expected. The minimum discount rate used should be the cost of capital.

Payback Period, p. 603

1. For projects with an equal annual cash flow:

$$\text{Payback period} = \text{Investment} \div \text{Annuity}$$

2. For projects with unequal annual cash flows:

   Find the length of time required for the sum of the annual cash inflows to equal the initial investment cost. If the payback period is equal to or less than a preestablished maximum number of years, the project is acceptable.

Net Present Value, p. 605

− Investment made currently (no discounting required)
+ PV of future cash inflows or cost savings
− PV of future cash outflows
= NPV

If NPV is equal to or greater than zero, the project is expected to return a rate equal to or greater than the discount rate, and it is acceptable.

Profitability Index, p. 607

+ PV of future cash inflows or cost savings
− PV of future cash outflows
= PV of net cash flows

PI = PV of net cash flows ÷ Net investment

If PI is 1.00 or higher, the project is expected to return a rate equal to or greater than the discount rate, and the project is acceptable.

Internal Rate of Return, p. 607

1. For projects with equal annual cash flows:

   PV factor = Net investment ÷ Annuity

   Find the PV factor (or the one closest to it) in the annuity table on the row for the number of periods of the cash flows. The percentage at the top of the column where this factor is found will approximate the IRR. (*Note:* For projects with equal annual cash flows, this factor also equals the payback period.)
2. For projects with unequal annual cash flows:

   Make an estimate of the rate provided by the project; compute NPV. If NPV is positive (negative), try a higher (lower) rate until the NPV is zero. Compare IRR to the required hurdle rate. If the IRR is equal to or greater than the hurdle rate, the project is acceptable.

Tax Benefit of Depreciation, p. 610

Tax benefit = Depreciation amount × Tax rate

Accounting Rate of Return, p. 623

ARR = Average annual profits from project ÷ Average investment in project

Average investment = (Beginning investment in project + Recovery of investment at end of project life) ÷ 2

Compare calculated ARR to hurdle ARR. If the calculated ARR is equal to or greater than the hurdle ARR, the project is acceptable.

Basic Concepts of Capital Budgeting Techniques

	Payback	NPV	PI	IRR	ARR
Uses time value of money?	No	Yes	Yes	Yes	No
Indicates a specific rate of return?	No	No	No	Yes	Yes
Uses cash flow?	Yes	Yes	Yes	Yes	No
Considers returns during life of project?	No	Yes	Yes	Yes	Yes
Uses discount rate in calculation?	No	Yes	Yes	No*	No*

*Discount rate is not used in the calculation, but it can be used as the hurdle rate.

DEMONSTRATION PROBLEM

Elton Credit Co. is considering an investment in a web-based store front. The project would require an initial investment of $400,000 and have an expected life of six years with no salvage value. At the end of the fourth year, the firm anticipates spending $70,000 to update some hardware and software. This amount would be fully deductible for tax purposes in the year incurred.

Management requires that investments of this type be recouped in five years or less. Management also requires this project to generate an accounting rate of return of at least 8 percent. The pre-tax increase in income is expected to be $95,000 in each of the first four years and $80,000 in each of the next two years. The company's discount rate is 8 percent, its tax rate is 30 percent, and the investment would be depreciated for tax purposes using the straight-line method with no consideration of salvage value over a five-year period and for accounting purposes over a six-year period with no salvage value.

Required:

a. Prepare a time line for displaying cash flows. Be certain to consider the effects of taxes.
b. Calculate the after-tax payback period.
c. Calculate the after-tax NPV on the project.
d. Calculate the profitability index of the project.
e. Calculate the accounting rate of return of the project.
f. Discuss whether this is an acceptable investment.

Solution to Demonstration Problem

a.

End of period	0	1	2	3	4	5	6
Investment	$(400,000)						
Operating inflows[a]		$66,500	$66,500	$66,500	$ 66,500	$56,000	$56,000
Depreciation tax benefit[b]		24,000	24,000	24,000	24,000	24,000	
Operating outflows[c]					(49,000)		
Total cash flows	$(400,000)	$90,500	$90,500	$90,500	$ 41,500	$80,000	$56,000

[a]$95,000 × (1 – 0.30) = $66,500
$80,000 × (1 – 0.30) = $56,000
[b]($400,000 ÷ 5) × 0.30 = $24,000
[c]$70,000 × (1 – 0.30) = $49,000

b.

Year	Annual Flow	Cumulative Flow
0	$(400,000)	$(400,000)
1	90,500	(309,500)
2	90,500	(219,000)
3	90,500	(128,500)
4	41,500	(87,000)
5	80,000	(7,000)
6	56,000	49,000

The payback is complete in 5.125 years or in the middle of February in the sixth year. The portion of the sixth year (0.125) required to complete the payback equals $7,000 ÷ $56,000.

c.

Cash Flow	Time	Amount	Discount Factor	Present Value
Investment	t_0	$(400,000)	1.0000	$(400,000)
Annual flow	t_1–t_3	90,500	2.5771	233,228
Annual flow	t_4	41,500	0.7350	30,503
Annual flow	t_5	80,000	0.6806	54,448
Annual flow	t_6	56,000	0.6302	35,291
Net present value				$ (46,530)

d. The profitability index = Present value of net cash inflows ÷ Net investment
= ($400,000 – $46,530) ÷ $400,000 = 0.88

e.

Period	0	1	2	3	4	5	6
Investment	$(400,000)						
Income		$ 95,000	$ 95,000	$ 95,000	$ 25,000	$ 80,000	$ 80,000
Depreciation		(66,667)	(66,667)	(66,668)	(66,667)	(66,667)	(66,667)
Taxable income		$ 28,333	$ 28,333	$ 28,333	$(41,667)	$ 13,333	$ 13,333
Income taxes		(8,500)	(8,500)	(8,500)	12,500	(4,000)	(4,000)
Net income		$ 19,833	$ 19,833	$ 19,833	$(29,167)	$ 9,333	$ 9,333

Average income = ($19,833 + $19,833 + $19,833 − $29,167 + $9,333 + $9,333) ÷ 6
= 48,998 ÷ 6 = $8,166

Average investment = ($400,000 + $0) ÷ 2 = $200,000

Accounting rate of return = Average income ÷ Average investment
= $8,166 ÷ $200,000 = 4.1%

f. The project is unacceptable based on the payback period and accounting rate of return. The project also fails to qualify based on all the discounted cash flow criteria. Accordingly, from strictly a financial perspective, the project is not acceptable. However, nonquantitative factors, such as effects on competitive position and ability to adopt future technological advances, must be considered.

POTENTIAL ETHICAL ISSUES

ETHICS

1. Using only financial criteria to evaluate projects that enhance employee safety or reduce detrimental environmental impact
2. Changing assumptions or estimates for projects solely so that they will meet required criteria for investment approval
3. Using an inappropriately low discount rate relative to the risk of a project so that the project will generate a positive NPV and be acceptable
4. Failing to conduct postinvestment audits to hold project sponsors accountable for differences between the investment proposal and actual results achieved by projects
5. Choosing projects based only on their impact on accounting earnings and not on discounted cash flow analyses

QUESTIONS

1. What is a capital asset? How is it distinguished from other assets?
2. Why do capital budgeting evaluation methods use cash flows rather than accounting income?
3. How are time lines helpful in evaluating capital projects?
4. What does the payback method measure? What are its major weaknesses?
5. What is the distinction between a return *of* capital and a return *on* capital?
6. What is measured by the net present value (NPV) of a potential project? If the NPV of a project is $0, is it an acceptable project? Explain.
7. Will the NPV amount determined in the capital budgeting process be the same amount as that which actually occurs after a project is undertaken? Why or why not?
8. How is the profitability index (PI) related to the NPV method? What does the PI measure?
9. What is measured by the internal rate of return? When is a project considered acceptable using this method?
10. Because depreciation is not a cash flow, why is it important in capital budgeting evaluation techniques that use discounted cash flows?
11. What four questions should managers ask when choosing the investment proposals to fund?

12. How is risk defined in capital budgeting analysis? List several aspects of a project in which risk is involved and how risk can affect a project's net present value.
13. How is sensitivity analysis used in capital budgeting?
14. Why are postinvestment audits performed? When should they be performed?
15. (*Appendix 1*) What is meant by the term *time value of money?* Why is a present value always less than the future value to which it relates?
16. (*Appendix 2*) How is the accounting rate of return computed? How does this rate differ from the discount rate and the internal rate of return?

EXERCISES

17. **LO.1 (Cash flows vs. accounting accruals)** Lundholm Corp. is considering the purchase of a robotic machine that would replace a manual labor production task. The purchase and installation of this machine would require an upfront cash commitment of $3,000,000. The machine would have a five-year expected life (and zero salvage value) and generate annual labor cost savings of $900,000. The machine will be depreciated over its expected life. Prepare a time line for this purchase that shows both the cash flow and accounting earnings effects for the machine's five-year life. Ignore taxes.

18. **LO.1 (Application of discounting methods; writing)** Several capital budgeting techniques depend on discounted cash flow concepts, which are applied in business in a variety of settings. Select a business that relies on discounted cash flow analysis, such as a venture capital company, and prepare a brief report on how the firm applies discounting methods to manage the business.

19. **LO.1 (Application of discounting methods; writing)** In recent years, stock price averages (such as the Dow Jones Industrial Average) have shown sensitivity to changes in interest rates. Based on your understanding of the factors that determine stock prices and of how future cash flows are discounted, prepare a brief statement explaining why stock prices should be sensitive to changes in interest rates.

20. **LO.1 (Cash flows vs. accounting accruals; writing)** In discussing your cost accounting class with friends, you explained that you were currently studying methods of evaluating capital investments. You mentioned that most of these methods rely upon cash flow analysis. One particularly sophisticated friend was surprised to hear that these analyses used cash flows rather than accounting earnings. He said, "It seems to me that investors are only interested in accounting earnings and don't pay much attention to cash flows. In fact, you never hear market commentators talk about cash flow; they always talk about a firm's income and whether earnings will match investor and analyst expectations."

    Provide a written explanation to your friend that provides the rationale for capital budgeting techniques focusing on cash flows rather than accounting earnings.

21. **LO.2 (Payback period)** Houston Fashions is considering a new product line that would require an investment of $140,000 in fixtures and displays and $180,000 in working capital. Store managers expect the following pattern of net cash inflows from the new product line over the life of the investment.

Year	Amount
1	$70,000
2	78,000
3	72,000
4	56,000
5	50,000
6	48,000
7	44,000

a. Compute the payback period for the proposed new product line. Houston Fashions requires a four-year pre-tax payback period on its investments. (Round to one decimal point.) Should the company make this investment? Explain.

b. Should Houston Fashions use any other capital project evaluation method(s) before making an investment decision? Explain.

22. **LO.2 (Payback period)** Laredo Laminates is considering the purchase of new production technology equipment requiring an initial $3,000,000 investment and having an expected ten year life. At the end of its life, the equipment would have no salvage value. By installing the new equipment, the firm's annual labor and quality costs would decline by $600,000.

a. Compute the payback period for this equipment.

b. Assume instead that the annual cost savings would vary according to the following schedule:

Years	Annual Cost Savings
1–5	$300,000
6–10	400,000

Compute the payback period under the revised circumstances.

23. **LO.3 (NPV)** Commodity Copper is considering the installation of a $1,800,000 production conveyor system that would generate the following labor cost savings over its 10-year life:

EXCEL

Years	Annual Labor Cost Savings
1–2	$280,000
3–5	340,000
6–8	288,800
9–10	260,000

The system will have no salvage at the end of its 10-year life, and the company uses a discount rate of 12 percent. What is the pre-tax net present value of this potential investment?

24. **LO.3 (NPV)** Birmingham Bolt, Inc., has been approached by one of its customers about producing 800,000 special-purpose parts for a new home product. The customer wants 100,000 parts per year for eight years. To provide these parts, Birmingham would need to acquire a $500,000 new production machine. The new machine would have no salvage value at the end of its eight-year life.

EXCEL

The customer has offered to pay Birmingham $7.50 per unit for the parts. Birmingham's managers have estimated that, in addition to the new machine, the company would incur the following costs to produce each part:

Direct labor	$2.00
Direct material	2.50
Variable overhead	2.00
Total	$6.50

In addition, annual fixed out-of-pocket costs related to the production of these parts would be $20,000.

a. Compute the net present value of the machine investment, assuming that the company uses a discount rate of 9 percent to evaluate capital projects.

b. Based on the NPV computed in (a), is the machine a worthwhile investment? Explain.

c. In addition to the NPV, what other factors should Birmingham's managers consider when making the investment decision?

25. **LO.3 (PI)** Cedar City Public Transportation is considering adding a new bus route. To do so, the entity would be required to purchase a new $600,000 bus, which would have a 10-year life and no salvage value. If the new bus is purchased, Cedar City Public Transportation's managers expect net cash inflows from bus ridership would rise by $91,000 per year for the life of the bus. Cedar City Public Transportation uses a 9 percent required rate of return for evaluating capital projects.

a. Compute the profitability index of the bus investment. (Round to two decimal points.)
b. Should Cedar City Public Transportation buy the new bus?
c. What is the minimum acceptable value for the profitability index for an investment to be acceptable? Explain.

26. **LO.3 (PI)** A manager at Shannon's Custom Cabinets is interested in purchasing a computer, software, and peripheral equipment costing $240,000 that would allow company salespeople to demonstrate to customers how a finished carpet installation would appear. Using this cost, the manager has determined that the investment's net present value is $18,000. Compute the investment's profitability index. (Round to two decimal points.)

27. **LO.4 (IRR)** Latin Cuisine is considering the purchase of new food processing technology, which would cost $1,800,000 and would generate $300,000 in annual cost savings. No salvage is expected on the technology at the end of its 10-year life. The firm's cost of capital and discount rate are both 10 percent.
    a. Calculate the internal rate of return for the project. (Round to the closest one-half percent.) Does the IRR indicate the project is acceptable?
    b. What qualitative factors should the company consider in evaluating the investment?

28. **LO.4 (IRR; sensitivity analysis)** White Sands Resort is considering adding a new dock to accommodate large yachts. The dock would cost $700,000 and would generate $144,000 annually in new cash inflows. Its expected life would be eight years, with no salvage value. The resort's cost of capital and discount rate are 7 percent.
    a. Calculate the internal rate of return for the proposed dock addition (round to the nearest whole percent).
    b. Based on your answer to (a), should the resort add the new dock?
    c. How much annual cash inflow would be required for the project to be minimally acceptable?

29. **LO.3 & LO.4 (NPV; IRR)** Jenna Smith recently purchased an annuity contract that will pay her $375,000 per year for the next seven years. According to Smith's calculations, the estimated internal rate of return on this investment is 14 percent. If Smith's cost of capital is 10 percent, what is the estimated NPV of the annuity investment?

30. **LO.5 (Depreciation; PV)** Yankee Freight provides truck freight services throughout the northeast United States. The firm is considering an investment in improved logistics management requiring a mainframe computer and communications software, which would cost $1,000,000 and have an expected life of eight years. For tax purposes, the investment will be depreciated using the straight-line method, with no salvage value. The company's cost of capital and tax rates are 8 and 30 percent, respectively.
    a. Compute the present value of the depreciation tax benefit.
    b. Assume instead that Yankee Freight uses the double-declining-balance method of depreciation with a five-year life. Compute the present value of the depreciation tax benefit.
    c. Why is the depreciation tax benefit computed in (b) larger than that computed in (a)?

31. **LO.3 & LO.5 (Alternative depreciation methods; NPV; sensitivity analysis)** Kansas Salt Co. is considering an investment in computer-based production technology as part of a business reengineering process. The necessary equipment will cost $18,000,000, have a life of eight years, and generate annual net before-tax cash flows of $3,100,000 from operations. Cost of installation and training is considered nominal. The equipment will have no salvage value at the end of its eight-year estimated life. The company's tax rate and cost of capital are, respectively, 30 percent and 5 percent.
    a. If Kansas Salt Co. uses straight-line depreciation for tax purposes, is the project acceptable using the net present value method?

b. Assume that the tax law allows the company to take accelerated annual depreciation on this asset in the following manner:

Years 1–2	23% of cost
Years 3–8	9% of cost

What is the net present value of the equipment? Is it acceptable?

c. Recompute (a) and (b) assuming the tax rate is increased to 40 percent.

32. **LO.5 (Tax effects of asset sale)** Three years ago, Girston Gravel Pit purchased a material conveyor system. The company has decided to sell the system and acquire more advanced technology. Data relating to the existing system follow.

Current market value	$37,000
Original cost	99,000
Current book value for tax purposes	18,000
Current book value for financial accounting purposes	35,000
Corporate tax rate	30%

a. How much depreciation has been taken on the conveyor system for (1) tax and (2) financial accounting purposes?
b. What will be the after-tax cash flow from the sale of this asset?
c. What will be the after-tax cash flow from the sale of the asset if its market value is $9,000 rather than $37,000?

33. **LO.6 (Limitations of capital budgeting methods)** For each of the following limitations of the capital project evaluation methods, indicate to which method, or methods, the limitation applies. Consider all of the following methods: payback, NPV, PI, IRR, and ARR (from appendix).

a. Treats cash flows as deterministic.
b. Ignores some cash flows.
c. Ignores cash flows.
d. Ignores the time value of money.
e. Ignores effects on accounting earnings.
f. Does not specifically consider cash flow preferences.
g. Can provide multiple rates of return for the same project.
h. Ignores dollar value of project benefits.

34. **LO.6 & LO.11 (Assumptions of capital budgeting methods)** For each of the following assumptions that underlie the capital project evaluation methods, indicate to which method, or methods, the assumption applies. Consider all of the following methods: payback, NPV, PI, IRR, and ARR (from appendix).

a. Speed of investment recovery is a key investment criterion.
b. Cash inflows can be reinvested at the hurdle rate.
c. Cash inflows can be reinvested at the IRR.
d. Timing and size of cash flows can be accurately predicted.
e. Life of project can be accurately predicted.
f. Risk is higher for cash flows in the more distant future.
g. Key consideration in evaluating projects is their effects on accounting earnings.

35. **LO.7 (Capital rationing)** Management of Frisco Films is considering the following capital projects:

Project	Cost	Annual After-Tax Cash Flows	Number of Years
New film studios	$20,000,000	$3,100,000	15
Cameras and equipment	3,200,000	800,000	8
Land improvement	5,000,000	1,180,000	10
Motion picture #1	17,800,000	4,970,000	5
Motion picture #2	11,400,000	3,920,000	4
Motion picture #3	8,000,000	2,300,000	7
Corporate aircraft	2,400,000	770,000	5

Assume that all projects have no salvage value and that the firm uses a discount rate of 10 percent. Management has decided that only $25,000,000 can be spent in the current year for capital projects.

a. Determine the net present value, profitability index, and internal rate of return for each of the seven projects.
b. Rank the seven projects according to each method used in (a).
c. Indicate how you would suggest to the management of Frisco Films that the money be spent. What would be the total net present value of your selected investments?

36. **LO.2 & LO.8 (Uncertain annual cash flow)** Sepchek Oil Field Services is considering the installation of a new electronic surveillance system for its warehouse. The system has an initial cost of $160,000 and an expected life of five years. For its life, the system will save the company labor costs for security guards.

a. If the company's cost of capital is 10 percent, how much annual increase in cash flows is necessary to minimally justify the investment?
b. Based on your answer to (a), what would be the payback period for this investment?

37. **LO.3 & LO.8 (NPV; uncertain cost of capital)** Brenda's Bees is considering the purchase of new honey processing equipment. The equipment would cost $100,000, have an expected life of seven years, and save $28,000 annually in maintenance, operating, and cleanup costs. The firm's cost of capital is estimated to be 10 percent.

a. Calculate the NPV of the proposed project.
b. Because the company is fairly small, the CEO is uncertain about her firm's actual cost of capital. To the nearest whole percent, what is the maximum the firm's cost of capital could be for this project to be acceptable?

38. **LO.10 (PV)** You have just purchased a new car, making a down payment of $8,000 and financing the balance of the purchase cost on an installment credit plan. According to the credit agreement, you will pay $800 per month for a period of 48 months. If the credit agreement is based on a monthly interest rate of 1 percent, what is the cost of the car?

39. **LO.10 (PV)** Use the tables in Appendix A to determine the answers to the following questions. Ignore taxes in all circumstances.

a. Titus wishes to have $50,000 in six years. He can make an investment today that will earn 8 percent each year, compounded annually. What amount of investment should he make today to achieve his goal?
b. Jacob is going to receive $400,000 on his 50th birthday, 20 years from today. He has the opportunity to invest money today in a government-backed security paying 5 percent compounded annually. How much would he be willing to receive today instead of the $400,000 in 20 years?
c. Jason has $60,000 today that he intends to use as a down payment on a house. How much money did Jason invest 20 years ago to have $60,000 now if his investment earned 8 percent compounded annually?
d. Lonnie is the host of a television game show that gives away thousands of dollars each day. One prize on the show is an annuity, paid to the winner, in equal installments of $200,000 at the end of each year for the next five years. If a winner has an investment opportunity to earn 8 percent, annually, what present amount would he or she take in exchange for the annuity?
e. Keri is going to be paid modeling fees for the next ten years as follows: Year 1, $50,000; Year 2, $55,000; Year 3, $60,000; Years 4–8, $100,000; Year 9, $70,000; and Year 10, $45,000. She can invest her money at 7 percent compounded annually. What is the present value of her future modeling fees?
f. Dave has just won the lottery, which will pay him $200,000 per year for the next five years. If this is the only asset Dave owns, will he be a millionaire (one who has a net worth of $1,000,000 or more)? Explain.

40. **LO.10 (FV)** You just invested $80,000 in a mutual fund account that guarantees to pay you 6 percent interest, compounded annually. At the end of five years, how much money will have accumulated in your investment account? (Ignore taxes.)

41. **LO.11 (Payback; ARR)** Portsmouth Port Services creates and maintains shipping channels at various ports around the world. The company is considering the purchase of a \$72,000,000 ocean-going dredge that has a five-year life and no salvage value. The company depreciates assets on a straight-line basis. This equipment's expected annual cash flow on a before-tax basis is \$20,000,000. Portsmouth requires that an investment be recouped in less than five years and have a pre-tax accounting rate of return of at least 18 percent.
    a. Compute the payback period and accounting rate of return for this equipment. (Round to one decimal point.)
    b. Is the equipment an acceptable investment for Portsmouth? Explain.

42. **LO.2 & LO.11 (Payback; ARR)** Kurt's Office Services is evaluating the purchase of a state-of-the-art desktop publishing system that costs \$40,000, has a six-year life, and has no salvage value at the end of its life. The company's controller estimates that the system will annually generate \$15,000 of cash receipts and create \$3,000 of cash operating costs. The company's tax rate is expected to be 30 percent during the life of the asset, and the company uses straight-line depreciation.
    a. Determine the annual after-tax cash flows from the project.
    b. Determine the after-tax payback period for the project. (Round to one decimal point.)
    c. Determine the after-tax accounting rate of return for the project. (Assume tax and financial accounting depreciation are equal.) (Round to one decimal point.)

PROBLEMS

43. **LO.1 (Ethics; qualitative information; writing)** Joey Hernandez was reprimanded by the home office for recommending a pollution abatement project because the project did not meet the standard financial criterion of an 8 percent rate of return. However, Hernandez had concluded that the \$950,000 piece of equipment was necessary to prevent small amounts of arsenic from seeping into the city's water system. No EPA warnings have been issued to the company.
    a. Discuss the company requirement of an 8 percent rate of return on all projects.
    b. What might be the ultimate consequence to Hernandez's employer if it fails to prevent future arsenic seepage into the water system?
    c. How should Hernandez justify the purchase of the equipment to the home office?

ETHICS

44. **LO.1 (Financing decision; ethics; writing)** Although they should be considered independently, investing and financing decisions are often considered together. Consider the case of a consumer acquiring a new car. The consumer can purchase a car by either paying cash or borrowing money through the car dealer or a bank. Alternatively, the consumer can acquire the car through a lease arrangement. When the consumer compares the options of financing or leasing the car, the better option may not be obvious. Indeed, the consumer may not have sufficient information, or skill, to identify the better alternative, and the car dealer and/or manufacturer may exploit that circumstance.

    Complex lease contracts combined with hidden costs complicate the decision to lease or buy. Only recently have key lease terms such as the cost of the car been disclosed to consumers. Laws in some states, as well as Federal Reserve Board Regulation M and leasing data available on the Internet, are prompting dealers to make increased disclosures. Unfortunately, some fees, including the interest rate the dealer uses to calculate the lease payment (known in the industry as the *money factor*), still remain unknown to the consumer.
    a. Why might some consumers find leasing a car to be more appealing than purchasing one?
    b. Is the practice of not disclosing lease information ethical for car dealers and manufacturers even if such disclosure is not required by law? Discuss.
    c. As an accountant, how could you aid a client in a car-buying situation?

ETHICS

45. **LO.2 & LO.3 (Time line; payback; NPV)** Austin Audio Systems is considering the purchase of a new delivery truck to replace an existing unit. The truck would cost $45,000 and would have a life of seven years with no salvage value. The existing truck could be sold currently for $4,000, but if it is kept, it will have a remaining life of seven years with no salvage value. By purchasing the truck, Austin Audio Systems' managers would anticipate operating cost savings as follows:

Year	Amount
1	$5,900
2	8,100
3	8,300
4	8,000
5	8,000
6	8,300
7	9,200

Austin Audio Systems' cost of capital and capital project evaluation rate is 8 percent.

a. Construct a time line for the purchase of the truck.
b. Determine the payback period. (Ignore taxes.) (Round time to one decimal point.)
c. Calculate the net present value of the truck. (Ignore taxes.)

46. **LO.2 & LO.3 (Time line; payback; NPV)** Holly's Fashions is considering expanding its building so it can stock additional merchandise for travelers and tourists. Store manager Jill Eliason anticipates that building expansion costs would be $190,000. The firm's suppliers are willing to provide inventory on a consignment basis so there would be no additional working capital needed upon expansion. Annual incremental fixed cash costs for the store expansion are expected to be as follows:

Year	Amount
1	$20,000
2	27,000
3	27,000
4	27,000
5	30,000
6	30,000
7	30,000
8	33,000

Eliason estimates that annual cash inflows could be increased by $60,000 of contribution margin generated from the additional merchandise sales. Because of uncertainty about the future, Eliason does not want to consider any cash flows after eight years. The firm uses an 8 percent discount rate.

a. Construct a time line for the investment.
b. Determine the payback period. (Ignore taxes.)
c. Calculate the net present value of the project. (Ignore taxes.)

EXCEL

47. **LO.2 & LO.3 (NPV; PI; sensitivity analysis)** Westside Warehouse is considering reengineering some production operations with automated equipment. The new equipment would have an initial cost of $5,000,000 including installation. The vendor has indicated that the equipment has an expected life of seven years with an estimated salvage value of $400,000. Estimates of annual labor savings and incremental costs associated with operating the new equipment follow.

Annual labor cost savings (14 workers)	$950,000
Annual maintenance costs	40,000
Annual property taxes	28,000
Annual insurance costs	44,000

a. Assuming the company's cost of capital is 6 percent, compute the NPV of the automated equipment. (Ignore taxes.)
b. Based on the NPV, should the company invest in the new equipment?

c. Compute the profitability index for this potential investment. (Ignore taxes.) (Round to two decimal points.)
d. Assume Westside's managers are least confident of the estimates of labor cost savings. Calculate the minimum annual labor savings that must be realized for the project to be financially acceptable.
e. What other qualitative factors should the company consider in evaluating this investment?

48. **LO.2 & LO.4 (Payback; IRR)** Shelly's Tax Services prepares tax returns for individuals and small businesses. The firm employs four tax professionals. Currently, all tax returns are prepared on a manual basis. The firm's owner, Shelly Foster, is considering purchasing a computer system that would allow the firm to serve all its existing clients with only three employees. To evaluate the feasibility of the computerized system, Foster has gathered the following information:

Initial cost of the hardware and software	$140,000
Expected salvage value in four years	$0
Annual depreciation	$30,000
Incremental annual operating costs	$8,500
Incremental annual labor savings	$47,500
Expected life of the computer system	4 years

Foster has determined that she will invest in the computer system if its pre-tax payback period is less than 3.5 years and its pre-tax IRR exceeds 12 percent.

a. Compute the payback period for this investment. (Round time to one decimal point.) Does the payback meet Foster's criterion? Explain.
b. Compute the IRR for this project to the nearest percentage. Based on the computed IRR, is this project acceptable to Foster? Explain.
c. What qualitative factors should Foster consider in evaluating the project?

49. **LO.2-LO.4 (NPV; PI; payback; IRR)** Pete's Paving provides custom paving of sidewalks and driveways. One of the most labor-intensive aspects of the paving operation is preparing and mixing materials. Sharon Guillon, corporate engineer, has found new computerized equipment to mix (and monitor the mixing of) materials. According to information received by Guillon, the equipment's cost is $580,000 and has an expected life of eight years. If purchased, the new equipment would replace manually operated equipment. Data relating to the existing and replacement mixing equipment follow.

EXCEL

	Existing Equipment
Original cost	$56,000
Present book value	$32,000
Annual cash operating costs	$150,000
Current market value	$12,000
Market value in eight years	$0
Remaining useful life	8 years

	Replacement Equipment
Cost	$580,000
Annual cash operating costs	$30,000
Market value in eight years	$0
Useful life	8 years

a. Assume that the company's cost of capital is 10 percent, which is to be used in discounted cash flow analysis. Compute the net present value and profitability index of investing in the new equipment. Should Pete's Paving purchase the machine? Why or why not? (Ignore taxes and round PI to one decimal point.)
b. Compute the payback period for the investment in the new equipment. (Ignore taxes and round time to one decimal point.)
c. Rounding to the nearest whole percentage, compute the internal rate of return for the equipment investment.

50. **LO.3 & LO.5 (NPV; taxes; sensitivity analysis)** The owner of Midwest Grocer's Warehouse is considering a $195,000 installation of a new refrigerated storage room. The storage room has an expected life of 20 years with no salvage value. The storage room is expected to generate net annual cash revenues (before tax, labor, utility, and maintenance costs) of $46,000 and would increase annual labor, utility, and maintenance costs by $21,000. The firm's cost of capital is 9 percent, and its tax rate is 30 percent.

    a. Using straight-line depreciation, calculate the after-tax net present value of the storage room.
    b. Based on your answer to (a), is this investment financially acceptable? Explain.
    c. What is the minimum amount by which net annual cash revenues must increase to make this an acceptable investment?

51. **LO.2 & LO.5 (NPV; taxes)** Dave's Drilling is considering the acquisition of new manufacturing equipment that has the same capacity as the current equipment. The new equipment will provide $150,000 of annual operating efficiencies in direct and indirect labor, direct material usage, indirect supplies, and power during its estimated four-year life.

    The new equipment costs $300,000 and would be purchased at the beginning of the year. Given the time of installation and training, the equipment will not be fully operational until the second quarter of the year in which it is purchased. Thus, only 60 percent of the estimated annual savings can be obtained in the year of purchase. Dave's Drilling will incur a one-time expense of $80,000 to transfer the production activities from the old equipment to the new. No loss of sales will occur, however, because the plant is large enough to install the new equipment without disrupting operations of the current equipment.

    Although the current equipment is fully depreciated and carried at zero book value, its condition is such that it could be used an additional four years. A salvage dealer will remove the old equipment and pay Dave's Drilling $5,000 for it.

    The company currently leases its manufacturing plant for $60,000 per year. The lease, which will have four years remaining when the equipment installation would begin, is not renewable. The company must remove any equipment in the plant at the end of the lease term. Cost of equipment removal is expected to equal the salvage value of either the old or the new equipment at the time of removal.

    Dave's Drilling uses the sum-of-the-years'-digits depreciation method for tax purposes. A full year's depreciation is taken in the first year an asset is put into use. The company is subject to a 40 percent income tax rate and requires an after-tax return of at least 11 percent on new investment.

    a. Calculate the annual incremental after-tax cash flows for the company's proposal to acquire the new manufacturing equipment.
    b. Calculate the net present value of the new manufacturing equipment using the cash flows calculated in (a) and indicate what action Dave's management should take. Assume all recurring cash flows occur at the end of the year.

CMA ADAPTED

52. **LO.3, LO.7, & LO.8 (NPV; project ranking; risk)** West Coast Real Estate Management is expanding operations, and the firm's president, Mike Mayberry, is trying to make a decision about new office space. The following are the firm's options:

Maple Commercial Plaza	5,000 square feet; cost, $800,000; investment period, 10 years; salvage value in 10 years, $400,000
High Tower	20,000 square feet; cost, $3,400,000; investment period, 10 years; salvage value in 10 years, $1,500,000

    If Maple Commercial Plaza is purchased, West Coast Real Estate Management will occupy all of the space. If High Tower is purchased, West Coast Real Estate Management will rent the extra space for $620,000 per year. Both buildings will be depreciated on a straight-line basis for tax purposes using a 25-year life with no salvage value. Purchasing either building will save the company $210,000 annually in rental payments. All other costs of the two options (such as land cost) are expected to be the same. The firm's tax rate is 40 percent. Either building would be sold after 10 years.

    a. Determine the before-tax net cash flows from each project for each year.
    b. Determine the after-tax cash flows from each project for each year.

c. Determine the net present value for each project if West Coast Real Estate Management's cost of capital is 11 percent. Which purchase is the better investment based on the NPV method?

d. Mayberry questions whether the excess space in High Tower can be rented for the entire 10-year period. To compute the NPV for that portion of the project's cash flows, he has decided to use a discount rate of 20 percent to compensate for risk. Compute the NPV and determine which investment is more acceptable.

53. **LO.2, LO.5, & LO.8 (NPV; taxes; sensitivity analysis)** Georgia Properties is considering purchasing a 50-room motel outside of Atlanta as an investment. The current owners state that the motel's occupancy rate averages 80 percent each of the 300 days per year the motel is open. Each room rents for $70 per day, and variable cash operating costs are $20 per occupancy day. Fixed annual cash operating costs are $250,000.

Savannah Roe, Georgia Properties' owner, is considering paying $1,500,000 for the motel. Georgia Properties would keep the motel for 14 years and then dispose of it. Because the market for motels is difficult to predict, Roe estimates a zero salvage value at the time of disposal. Depreciation (rounded to the nearest dollar) will be taken on a straight-line basis for tax purposes. Roe's tax rate is estimated at 25 percent for all years.

a. Determine the after-tax net present value of the motel to Georgia Properties, assuming a cost of capital rate of 10 percent.

b. What is the highest discount rate that will allow this project to be considered acceptable to Georgia Properties?

c. What is the minimum amount the net after-tax cash flows must be to allow the project to be considered acceptable by Georgia Properties, assuming a cost of capital rate of 10 percent?

d. What is the fewest number of years for which the net after-tax cash flows can be received and the project still be considered acceptable?

54. **LO.2-LO.5 (After-tax cash flows; payback; NPV; PI; IRR)** Forester Fashions is considering the purchase of computerized clothes-designing software. The software is expected to cost $320,000, have a useful life of five years, and have no salvage value at the end of its useful life. Assume that tax regulations permit the following depreciation pattern for this software:

Year	Percent Deductible
1	20
2	32
3	19
4	15
5	14

The company's tax rate is 35 percent, and its cost of capital is 8 percent. The software is expected to generate the following cash savings and cash expenses:

Year	Cash Savings	Cash Expenses
1	$122,000	$18,000
2	134,000	16,000
3	144,000	26,000
4	120,000	18,000
5	96,000	10,000

a. Prepare a time line presenting the after-tax operating cash flows.

b. Determine the following on an after-tax basis: payback period, net present value, profitability index, and internal rate of return. (Round time and PI to one decimal point.)

55. **LO.7 (Postinvestment audit)** CXI has formal policies and procedures to screen and approve capital projects. Proposed capital projects are classified as one of the following types:

1. expansion requiring new plant and equipment,
2. expansion by replacement of present equipment with more productive equipment, or
3. replacement of old equipment with new equipment of similar quality.

All expansion and replacement projects that will cost more than $50,000 must be submitted to the top management capital investment committee for approval. The investment committee evaluates proposed projects considering the costs and benefits outlined in the supporting proposal and the long-range effects on the company.

Projected revenue and/or expense effects of projects, once they are operational, are included in the proposal. After a project is accepted, the committee approves an expenditure budget from the project's inception until the project becomes operational. Annual required expenditures for expansions or replacements are also incorporated into CXI's annual budget procedure. Budgeted revenue and/or cost effects of the projects for the periods in which they become operational are incorporated into the five-year forecast.

CXI does not have a procedure for evaluating projects once they have been implemented and become operational. The vice president of finance has recommended that CXI establish a postinvestment audit program to evaluate its capital expenditure projects.

a. Discuss the benefits a company could derive from a postinvestment audit program for capital expenditure projects.
b. Discuss the practical difficulties in collecting and accumulating information that would be used to evaluate a capital project once it becomes operational.

CMA ADAPTED

56. **LO.3 & LO.9 (Postinvestment audit)** Ten years ago, based on a pre-tax NPV analysis, Sante's Sporting Goods decided to add a new product line. The data used in the analysis were as follows:

Discount rate	10%
Life of product line	10 years
Annual sales increase	
Years 1–4	$115,000
Years 5–8	$175,000
Years 9–10	$100,000
Annual fixed cash costs	$20,000
Contribution margin ratio	40%
Cost of production equipment	$130,000
Investment in working capital	$10,000
Salvage value	$0

Because the product line was discontinued this year, corporate managers decided to conduct a postinvestment audit to assess the accuracy of their planning process. Actual cash flows generated from the product line were found to be as follows:

Actual Investment	
Production equipment	$110,000
Working capital	17,500
Total	$127,500

Actual Revenues	
Years 1–4	$120,000
Years 5–8	200,000
Years 9–10	103,000

Actual Fixed Cash Costs	
Years 1–4	$15,000
Years 5–8	17,500
Years 9–10	25,000
Actual contribution margin ratio	35%
Actual salvage value	$6,000
Actual cost of capital	10%

a. Determine the original projected NPV on the product line investment.
b. Determine the actual NPV of the project based on the postinvestment audit.
c. Identify the factors that are most responsible for the differences between the projected NPV and the actual postinvestment audit NPV.

57. **LO.2-LO.4 & LO.11 (Comprehensive; appendix 2)** Pittsburgh Pipe management is evaluating a proposal to buy a new turning lathe to replace a less efficient piece of similar equipment that would then be sold. The new lathe's cost, including delivery and installation, is $1,420,000. If the lathe is purchased, Pittsburgh Pipe will incur $40,000 to remove the current lathe and revamp service facilities. The current lathe has a book value of $800,000 and a remaining useful life of 10 years. Technical advancements have made this lathe outdated, so its current resale value is only $340,000.

The following comparative manufacturing cost tabulation is available:

	Current Lathe	New Lathe
Annual production in units	780,000	1,000,000
Cash revenue from each unit	$1.20	$1.20
Annual costs		
Labor	$160,000	$100,000
Depreciation (10% of asset book value or cost)	$80,000	$142,000
Other cash operating costs	$192,000	$80,000

Management believes that if it does not replace the lathe now, the company will have to wait seven years before the replacement is justified. The company uses a 10 percent discount rate in evaluating capital projects and expects all capital project investments to recoup their costs within five years.

Both lathes are expected to have a negligible salvage value at the end of 10 years.

a. Determine the net present value of the new lathe. (Ignore taxes.)
b. Determine the internal rate of return on the new lathe. (Ignore taxes.)
c. Determine the payback period for the new lathe. (Ignore taxes and round time to one decimal point.)
d. Determine the accounting rate of return for the new lathe. (Ignore taxes and round to one decimal point.)
e. Determine whether the company should keep the present lathe or purchase the new lathe. Provide discussion of your conclusion. CMA ADAPTED

58. **LO.2, LO.3, & LO.11 (Payback; NPV; appendix 2)** New England Metals is considering adding a new product line that has an expected life of eight years. Setup costs for the new product line would total $6,400,000. All product line revenues will be collected as earned. Variable costs will average 35 percent of revenues. All expenses, except for the amount of straight-line depreciation, will be paid in cash when incurred. Following is a schedule of annual revenues and fixed cash operating expenses (excluding $800,000 of annual depreciation on the investment) associated with the new product line.

Year	Revenues	Fixed Expenses
1	$3,000,000	$1,480,000
2	3,200,000	1,280,000
3	3,720,000	1,280,000
4	5,120,000	1,440,000
5	6,400,000	1,280,000
6	6,400,000	1,280,000
7	4,480,000	1,280,000
8	2,720,000	1,120,000

The company's cost of capital is 8 percent. Management uses this rate in discounting cash flows for evaluating capital projects.

a. Calculate the payback period. (Ignore taxes and round time to one decimal point.)
b. Calculate the net present value. (Ignore taxes.)
c. Calculate the accounting rate of return. (Ignore taxes and round to one decimal point.)
d. Should New England Metals invest in this product line? Discuss the rationale, including any qualitative factors, for your answer.

16

Managing Costs and Uncertainty

LEARNING OBJECTIVES

After completing this chapter, you should be able to answer the following questions:

1. What are the functions of a cost control system?
2. What factors cause costs to change from period to period or to deviate from expectations?
3. What are the generic approaches to cost control?
4. What are the two primary types of fixed costs, and what are the characteristics of each?
5. What are the typical approaches to controlling discretionary fixed costs?
6. What are the objectives managers strive to accomplish in managing cash?
7. How is technology reducing costs of supply-chain transactions?
8. Why is uncertainty greater in dealing with future events than with past events?
9. What are the four generic approaches to managing uncertainty?

INTRODUCTION

This chapter presents a variety of topics that explain some of the key contributions of accounting and finance specialists to business organizations. The discussion begins with a description of cost control systems and general cost management strategies. The discussion then turns to the responsibilities and tools of the treasury function including cash management, financial risk management, and supply-chain management. The chapter concludes with a presentation of methods and tools for dealing with uncertainty in budgeting and cost management.

COST CONTROL SYSTEMS

1 What are the functions of a cost control system?

An integral part of the overall organizational decision support system is the **cost control system**, which is the set of formal and informal tools and methods designed to manage organizational costs. This system focuses on intraorganizational information and contains the detector, assessor, effector, and network components discussed in Chapter 12. Relative to the cost management system, the cost control system provides information for planning and control from the point activities are being planned until after they are performed, as indicated in Exhibit 16.1.

Exhibit 16.1 Functions of an Effective Cost Control System

Control Point	Reason	Cost Control Method
Before an event	Preventive; reflects planning	Budgets; standards; policies concerning approval for deviations; expressions of quantitative and qualitative objectives; ethical guidelines
During an event	Corrective; ensures that the event is being pursued according to plans; allows management to correct problems as they occur	Periodic monitoring of ongoing activities; comparison of activities and costs against budgets and standards; avoidance of excessive expenditures
After an event	Diagnostic; guides future actions	Feedback; variance analysis; responsibility reports (discussed in Chapter 13)

The general planning and control model in Exhibit 16.2 (p. 644) illustrates that control is part of a management cycle that begins with planning. Without first preparing organizational plans (such as the budgets discussed in Chapter 8), control cannot be achieved because no operational targets and objectives have been established. The planning phase establishes performance targets that become the inputs to the control phase.

Exhibit 16.3 (p. 644) depicts a more specific cost control model. A good control system encompasses not only the managerial functions shown in Exhibit 16.2 but also the ideas about cost consciousness shown in Exhibit 16.3. **Cost consciousness** refers to a companywide employee attitude toward the topics of understanding cost changes, cost containment, cost avoidance, and cost reduction. Each of these topics is important for a particular stage of cost control.

Managers alone cannot control costs. An organization is composed of many individuals whose attitudes and efforts affect how an organization's costs are controlled. Cost control is a continual process that requires the support and involvement of all employees at all times.

Exhibit 16.2 General Planning and Control Model

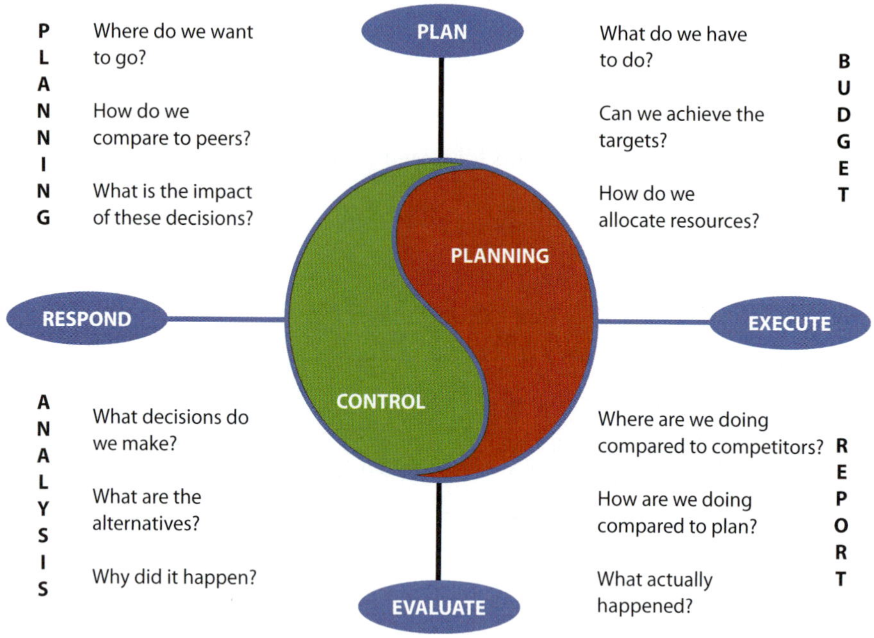

Source: Kathryn Jehle, "Budgeting as a Competitive Advantage," *Strategic Finance* (October 1999), p. 57. Copyright 1999 by Institute of Management Accountants. Reproduced with permission of Institute of Management Accountants in the format Textbook via Copyright Clearance Center.

Exhibit 16.3 Cost Control System

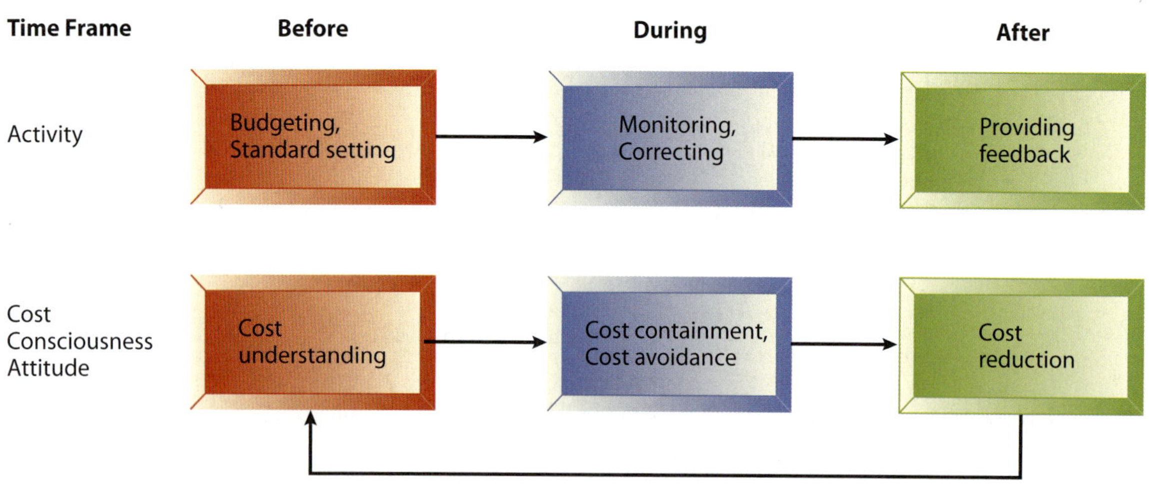

2 What factors cause costs to change from period to period or to deviate from expectations?

UNDERSTANDING COST CHANGES

Control requires that a set of expectations exists. Thus, cost control begins when the budget is prepared. However, budgets cannot be prepared without understanding why costs change from period-to-period, and cost control cannot be achieved without understanding why costs may differ between periods or from the budgeted amounts. Following is a discussion of common causes of cost changes, which include

- underlying cost behavior,
- inflation/deflation,
- supply/supplier cost adjustments, and
- quantity purchased.

In considering these factors, remember that an external price becomes an internal cost when a good or service is acquired.

Cost Changes Because of Volume Changes

Some costs change because of their underlying behavior. Total variable or mixed cost increases or decreases with, respectively, increases or decreases in activity. If the current period's actual activity differs from that of a prior period or from the budgeted activity level, total actual variable or mixed cost will differ from that of the prior period or from the budget. A flexible budget can compensate for such differences by providing expected costs at any activity level. By using a flexible budget, managers can make valid budget-to-actual cost comparisons to determine whether costs were properly controlled. For costs to be controlled most effectively relative to their cost behaviors, it is important that the driver of the cost (as discussed in Chapter 4) be determined as accurately as possible.

Cost Changes Because of Inflation/Deflation

Fluctuations in the value of money, called general price-level changes, cause the prices of goods and services to change. If all other factors are constant, general price-level changes affect prices approximately equally and in the same direction. In the United States, the Consumer Price Index (CPI) is the most often cited measure of general price-level changes. Inflation and deflation indexes by industry or commodity can be examined to obtain more accurate information about inflation/deflation effects on prices of particular inputs, such as energy resources. Among electrical energy sources, solar power is becoming more competitive relative to the alternatives because industry capacity to produce crystalline silicon (the active material used in many solar panels) has increased dramatically.[1] Thus there may be deflation in cost of solar energy versus inflation in alternative electrical energy sources.

Some companies include price-escalation clauses in sales contracts to cover the inflation occurring from order to delivery. Such escalators are especially prevalent in industries with production activities that require substantial lead time. Some government benefits and penalties are also inflation adjusted. For example, Congress passed the Debt Collection Improvement Act of 1996, which contained a provision to periodically adjust the Environmental Protection Agency's fines in the event of inflation. The law allows the EPA's penalties to keep pace with inflation and thereby maintain the deterrent effect that Congress intended when penalties were originally specified.[2]

Cost Changes Because of Supply/Supplier Cost Adjustments

The relationship between the availability of a good or service and the demand for that item affects its selling price. If supply is reduced but demand remains high, the selling price of the item increases. The higher price often stimulates greater production, which, in turn, increases supply. In contrast, if demand falls but supply remains constant, the price falls. This reduced price should motivate lower production, which lowers supply. Therefore, the relationship of supply and demand consistently and circularly influences price. Price changes resulting from independent causes are specific price-level changes, which can move in the same or opposite direction as a general price-level change. The relationship between price changes and supply and demand changes varies across products. **Price elasticity** is a numerical measure of the relationship of supply or demand to price changes. Price elasticities can be calculated for specific products using historical data by relating price changes to supply and demand changes. If price elasticity is low, then a large change in price will lead to only a small change in supply or demand; alternatively, if price elasticity is high, a large change in price leads to a large change in supply or demand.

Specific price-level changes are also caused by advances in technology. As a general rule, as suppliers advance the technology of producing a good or performing a service, the cost of that product or service to producing/performing firms declines. Assuming competitive market conditions, such cost declines are often passed along to consumers of that product or service in the form of lower prices. In January 2006, **Hallmark** introduced Sound Cards, which used technology to "deliver a multi-sensory experience" that was not feasible

[1] John Carey and Mark Scott, "Catching Rays Gets Cheaper," *Business Week* (June 22, 2009), p. 18.

[2] 61 FR 69360, Civil Monetary Penalty Inflation Adjustment Rule; http://www.gpo.gov/fdsys/granule/FR-1996-12-31/96-32972/content-detail.html (last accessed 2/22/12).

ten years prior; in that time, the "affordability and quality of technology" had been significantly enhanced.[3] This simple example illustrates the interaction between technological advances and cost reductions.

Alternatively, additional production or performance costs are typically passed on by suppliers to their customers as part of specific price-level changes. Such costs can be within or outside the supplier's control. For example, the increase in demand for corn to develop ethanol fuel caused corn prices to rise dramatically since 2006. As a result, the cost of many food products using inputs derived from corn (such as corn syrup) have increased.

The number of suppliers of a product or service can also affect selling prices. As the number of suppliers increases in a competitive environment, price tends to fall. Likewise, a reduction in the number of suppliers will, all else remaining equal, cause prices to increase. A change in the number of suppliers is not the same as a change in the quantity of supply. If the supply of an item is large, one normally expects a low price; however, if there is only one supplier, the price can remain high because the market is controlled by the supplier. For example, when drugs are first introduced under patent, the supply can be readily available, but the selling price is high because the prescription drug comes from only a single source. As patents expire and generic drugs become available, selling prices decline because more suppliers compete to produce and market the medication.

Sometimes, cost increases are caused by higher taxes or additional regulatory requirements. For example, airlines continually face more stringent noise abatement and safety legislation. Complying with these regulations increases airline costs. The companies can

- pass along the costs to customers as price increases to maintain the same income level,
- decrease other costs to maintain the same income level, or
- experience a decline in net income.

Cost Changes Because of Quantity Purchased

Suppliers normally give customers quantity discounts, up to some maximum level, when bulk purchases are made. Therefore, a cost per unit can change because quantities are purchased in lot sizes differing from those of previous periods or from the lot sizes projected. Involvement in group purchasing arrangements can make quantity discounts easier to obtain.

The preceding discussion indicates why costs change. Next, the discussion addresses actions firms can take to contain (control) costs.

COST CONTAINMENT

3 What are the generic approaches to cost control?

To the extent possible, period-by-period increases in per-unit variable and total fixed costs should be minimized through a process of **cost containment**. Cost containment is not possible for inflation effects, tax and regulatory changes, and supply and demand adjustments because these forces occur outside the organization.

In some circumstances, a significant exchange of information occurs among members of the supply chain, and members of one organization can actually be involved in activities designed to reduce costs of another organization. For example, **Motorola** has a facility called Motorola University which the company conducts workshops and offers training to employees, customers, and supplier chain partners so they can reduce product design and development costs. Concepts generated from this training helped an electronic device manufacturer redesign 12 products in four months, resulting in a \$6.8 million savings.[4] Motorola believes that such programs are essential for global marketplaces facing rising production costs.

Costs that rise because of reduced supplier competition, seasonality, and quantities purchased are, however, subject to cost containment activities. A company should look for ways to cap the upward changes in these costs. For example, purchasing agents should be aware of alternative suppliers for goods and services and determine which, if any, of those

[3] Mike Troy, "The Sounds of an Industry Evolving," *Retailing Today* (April 23, 2007), p. 22.

[4] Boothroyd Dewhurst Inc., "Case Study: Design in Cost Reduction," Quality Magazine (2/25/10); http://www.qualitymag.com/Articles/Departments/BNP_GUID_9-5-2006_A_10000000000000765846 (accessed 2/23/12).

suppliers can reliably provide items in the quantity, quality, and time desired. Comparing costs and finding new sources of supply can increase buying power and reduce costs.

If bids are used to select suppliers, the purchasing agent should remember that a bid is merely the first step in the negotiation process. Although a low bid may eliminate some competition from consideration, additional negotiations between the purchasing agent and the remaining suppliers could result in a purchase price even lower than the bid amount or other relevant concessions (such as faster and more reliable delivery) may be gained. Purchasing agents must also remember that the supplier offering the lowest bid is not necessarily the best supplier to choose because factors such as quality, service, and reliability are important.

A company can circumvent seasonal cost changes by postponing or advancing purchases of goods and services. However, such purchasing changes should not mean buying irresponsibly or incurring excessive carrying costs. Economic order quantities, safety stock levels, and materials requirements planning as well as the just-in-time philosophy should be considered when making purchases.[5]

As to services, seasonality is often important in cost control. It is often possible for employees to repair rather than to replace items that have seasonal cost changes. For example, maintenance workers might find that a broken heat pump can be repaired and used during spring and replaced in summer when the cost of servicing is lower.

COST AVOIDANCE AND COST REDUCTION

Cost containment can prove very effective if it can be implemented. However, when cost containment is not possible, cost avoidance strategies may be applied instead. **Cost avoidance** involves finding acceptable alternatives to high-cost items and/or not spending money for unnecessary goods and services. Avoiding one cost may require incurring an alternative, lower cost. For example, the older **Sam's Club** buildings are far less energy efficient than the newer ones. The latest Sam's Club buildings use natural and LED light in lieu of electrical lights and recycle rain water for property usage.[6]

Closely related to cost avoidance, the intent of **cost reduction** is to lower costs. Benchmarking is especially important in this area so that companies can become aware of excessively high costs. Companies can reduce costs by outsourcing functions such as data processing, legal, and distribution rather than maintaining internal departments.

Sometimes money must be spent to generate cost savings. For example, **Cisco** is currently developing software to manage energy costs. This technology may be linked to an employee ID card so that when the card is swiped, room lights are turned on or off and room temperature is adjusted up or down.[7] In another example, some of the large accounting firms (such as **PricewaterhouseCoopers**) have their own in-house studios and staffs and provide customized web-based training to new employees. Although the cost of producing an online presentation is high, the firms believe the cost is justified because the presentation can be used multiple times at very low cost.

Some companies are also beginning to look outside for information about how and where to cut costs. Consulting firms, such as Dallas-based **Ryan & Company**, review files for overpayment of state and local taxes. This firm often works on a contingent fee basis and gets paid only if tax overpayments are found.

Managers can adopt the five-step method of implementing a cost control system shown in Exhibit 16.4 (page 648):

- Step 1: Understand the type of costs incurred by an organization. Are the costs under consideration fixed or variable, product or period? What are the drivers of those costs? From whom were purchases made? When were purchases made? The generation of answers to these types of questions is generically referred to as **spend analysis**.

[5] These concepts are discussed in Chapter 18.

[6] John Martin, "Kudos to Wal-Mart," *Fleet Equipment* 35, no. 5 (May 2009), p. 12.

[7] Katie Fehrenbacher, "Cisco to Use the Network to Manage Energy of Devices," http://earth2tech.com/2009/01/27/cisco-to-use-the-network-to-manage-energy-of-devices/ (last accessed 2/09/12).

Exhibit 16.4 Implementing a Cost Control System

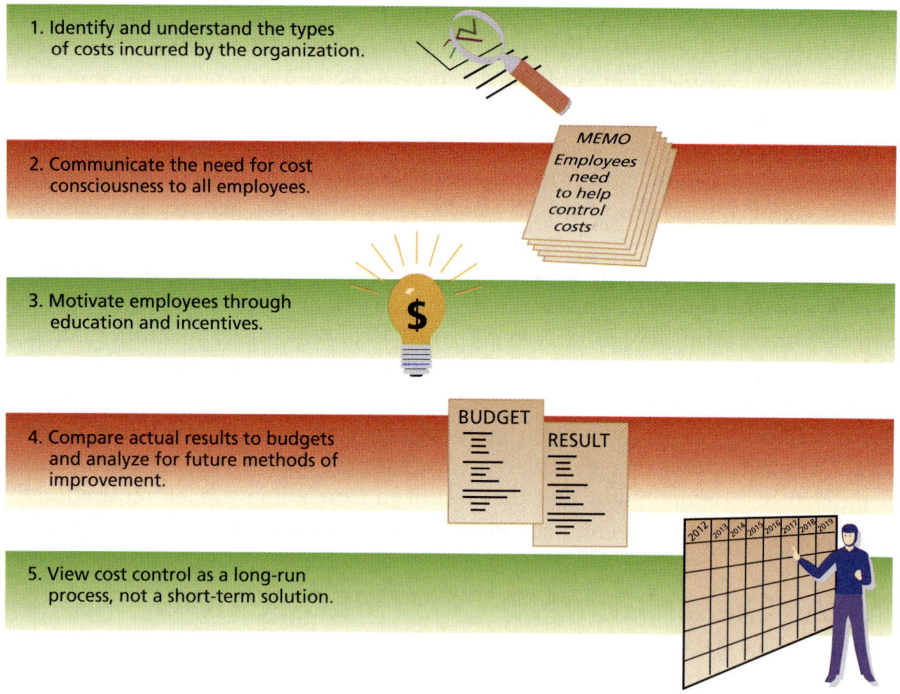

- Step 2: Communicate the need for cost consciousness to all employees. Employees must be aware of which costs need to be better controlled and why cost control is important individually and organizationally.
- Step 3: Educate employees in cost control techniques, encourage suggestions on ways to control costs, and motivate employees to take the concepts to heart. Incentives can range from simple verbal recognition to monetary rewards to time off with pay. Managers must also be flexible enough to allow for changes from the current method of operation.
- Step 4: Generate reports that indicate actual results, compare budget to actual, and calculate variances. Management must evaluate these costs to determine why costs were or were not controlled in the past. Such analysis can provide insight about cost drivers so that activities driving costs can be better controlled in the future.
- Step 5: Develop a view that the cost control system is a long-run process, not a short-run solution. Organizations need "to examine new kinds of questions, learn to experience time differently (long-term solutions versus quick fixes), [and] notice how systems work."[8] Proposed cost controls should be assessed using realistic circumstances rather than improbable assumptions.

Following these five steps will provide an atmosphere conducive to controlling costs as effectively as possible and to deriving the most benefit from costs incurrence. A cost–benefit analysis should be performed before a commitment is made to incur a cost. Costs should also be incorporated into the budgeting system because costs cannot be controlled after they have been incurred. Future costs, on the other hand, can be controlled based on information learned about past costs. Cost control should not cease at the end of a fiscal period or because costs were reduced or controlled during the current period. Managers are charged with planning and controlling the types and amounts of costs necessary to conduct business activities. Many activities required to achieve business objectives involve fixed costs. All fixed costs (and the activities that create them) can be categorized as either committed or discretionary. The difference between the two categories is primarily the time period for which management obligates itself to the activity and its cost.

[8] Sid Gardner and Alan Brown, "Cost Savings and Achievement Potential of Prevention Programs: Smart Cuts, Dumb Cuts, and a Process to Tell the Difference," *PM. Public Management* (March 2009), pp. 20–23.

COMMITTED FIXED COSTS

4 What are the two primary types of fixed costs, and what are the characteristics of each?

Costs associated with plant assets and human resources are known as **committed costs**. The amount of committed costs is normally dictated by long-run management decisions involving the desired scale and scope of operations. Committed costs include depreciation, lease rentals, property taxes, and staff salaries, all of which cannot be reduced easily even during temporarily diminished activity.

One method of controlling committed costs is to compare expected benefits of plant assets (or human resources) with expected costs of such investments. Managers must identify activities necessary to attain company objectives and what (and how many) assets are needed to support those activities. Once assets are acquired, managers are committed to both the activities and their related costs for the long run. But managers must understand how committed fixed costs could affect income in the event of changes in operations.

A second method of controlling committed costs is to compare actual and expected results from plant asset investments. During this process, managers are able to see and evaluate the accuracy of their cost and revenue predictions relative to the investment. This comparison is called a postinvestment audit and is discussed in Chapter 15.

An organization cannot operate without some basic plant and human assets. Considerable control can be exercised over the process of determining how management chooses fundamental assets and designs the human resources structure. The most logical point in time to control committed fixed costs is prior to making the investment in plant assets or hiring human resources. The benefits from committed costs generally can be predicted and commonly are compared with actual results in the future.

DISCRETIONARY COSTS

In contrast to a committed cost, a **discretionary cost** is one "that a decision maker must periodically review to determine if it continues to be in accord with ongoing policies."[9] Discretionary costs relate to company activities that are important, but the level of funding is subject to judgment. Discretionary cost activities are usually service-oriented and include

- employee travel,
- repairs and maintenance,
- advertising,
- research and development, and
- employee training and development.

Chris Schmidt/iStockphoto.com

Though costs associated with university recruitment are discretionary costs, they can have a direct impact on admissions.

There is no "correct" amount at which to set funding for discretionary costs because the relationship between the amount of cost incurred and the amount of benefit created can be determined only subjectively. Further, there are no specific activities for which all organizations consider the costs to be discretionary. A discretionary fixed cost reflects a management decision to fund a particular activity at a specified amount for a specified period of time. In the event of cash flow shortages or forecasted operating losses, discretionary fixed costs can be more easily reduced than committed fixed costs.

Discretionary costs, then, are generated by activities that vary in type and magnitude from day to day and whose benefits are often not measurable in monetary terms. Just as discretionary cost activities vary, performance quality can also vary according to the tasks involved and skill levels of the persons performing them. These two factors—varying activities and varying quality levels—usually cause discretionary costs not to be susceptible to the precise measures available to plan and control variable production costs or the cost–benefit evaluation techniques

[9] Institute of Management Accountants (formerly National Association of Accountants), *Statements on Management Accounting Number 2: Management Accounting Terminology* (Montvale, NJ, June 1, 1983), p. 35.

available to control committed fixed costs. Because the benefits of discretionary cost activities cannot be assessed definitively, these activities are often among the first to be cut when profits are lagging. Thus, proper planning for discretionary activities and costs can be more important than subsequent control measures. Control after the planning stage is often restricted to monitoring expenditures to ensure conformity with budget classifications and preventing managers from overspending budgets.

5 What are the typical approaches to controlling discretionary fixed costs?

Controlling Discretionary Costs

Described in Chapter 8 as both planning and controlling devices, budgets serve to officially communicate a manager's authority to spend up to a predetermined (**appropriation**) amount or rate for each budget item. Budget appropriations serve as a baseline for comparison with actual costs. Accumulated expenditures in each budgetary category are periodically compared with appropriated amounts to determine whether funds have been under- or overexpended.

Budgeting Discretionary Costs Before addressing control of discretionary costs, top management must translate company goals into specific objectives and policies that will contribute to organizational success. Cash flow and income expectations for a coming period need to be reviewed and discretionary cost activities must be prioritized before funding levels can be set. Management must then budget the types and quantities of discretionary activities to accomplish those objectives. Management tends to be more generous about making discretionary cost appropriations when the economic outlook for the organization is strong rather than weak.

Discretionary costs are generally budgeted on the basis of three factors:

- the related activity's perceived significance to achieving goals and objectives;
- the next period's expected level of operations; and
- the ability of managers to effectively negotiate during the budgetary process

For some discretionary costs, managers are expected to spend the full amount of their appropriations within the specified time frame. For other discretionary cost activities, the "less-is-better" adage is appropriate.

As an example of "less is *not* better," consider the cost of preventive maintenance. This cost can be viewed as discretionary, but reducing it could result in diminished quality, production breakdowns, or machine inefficiency. Although the benefits of maintenance expenditures cannot be precisely quantified, most managers believe that incurring less maintenance cost than budgeted is not effective cost control. In fact, spending (with supervisory approval) more than originally appropriated could be necessary or even commendable—assuming that positive results (such as a decline in quality defects or an extension of equipment life) are obtained. Such a perspective illustrates the perception mentioned earlier that cost control should be a long-run process rather than a short-run concern.

Alternatively, spending less than the amount budgeted on travel and entertainment (while achieving the desired results) would probably be considered positive performance, whereas spending on travel and entertainment in excess of budget appropriations might be considered irresponsible—especially in difficult economic times.

If revenues, profits, or cash flows are lower than expected, funding for discretionary expenditures should be evaluated, not simply in reference to reduced operations but also relative to activity priorities. Eliminating the funding for one or more discretionary activities altogether could be possible if other funding levels are maintained at the previously determined amounts. For example, faced with a downturn in product demand, a company often reduces its discretionary advertising budget—a potentially illogical reaction. Instead, increasing the advertising budget and reducing the corporate executives' travel budget might be more appropriate.

The difference in managerial attitude between committed and discretionary costs has to do with the ability to measure the benefits provided by those costs. Although benefits of committed fixed costs can be measured on a "before" and "after" basis (through the capital budgeting and postinvestment audit processes), the benefits from discretionary fixed costs are often not distinctly measurable in monetary terms, or the benefits may not even be identifiable.

Measuring Benefits from Discretionary Costs Because benefits from some activities traditionally classified as discretionary cannot be adequately measured, companies often assume that the benefits—and, thus, the related activities—are unimportant. However, many activities previously described as discretionary (repairs, maintenance, R&D, and employee training) are critical to survival in a world-class environment. In the long run, these activities create quality products and services; therefore, before reducing or eliminating expenditures in these areas, managers should attempt to more appropriately recognize and measure the benefits of these activities.

Funds are spent on discretionary activities to provide some desired output, but the value of discretionary costs must often be judged using nonmonetary, surrogate measures. Devising such measures sometimes requires substantial time and creativity. Exhibit 16.5 presents some useful surrogate measures for determining the effectiveness of various types of discretionary costs. Some of these measures are verifiable and can be gathered quickly and easily; others are abstract and require a longer time horizon before they can be obtained.

Exhibit 16.5 Examples of Nonmonetary Measures of Output from Discretionary Costs

Discretionary Cost Activity	Surrogate Measure of Results
Preventive maintenance	• Reduction in equipment failures • Reduction in unplanned downtime • Reduction in production interruptions caused by preventive maintenance activities
Advertising	• Increase in unit sales in the two weeks after an advertising effort relative to the sales two weeks prior to the effort • Number of customers referring to the ad • Number of coupons clipped from the ad and redeemed
University admissions recruiting trip	• Percentage of students met who requested an application • Number of students from area visited who requested to have ACT/SAT scores sent to the university • Number of admissions that year from that area
Prevention and appraisal quality activities	• Reduction in number of customer complaints • Reduction in number of warranty claims • Reduction in number of product defects discovered by customers
Staffing law school indigent clinic	• Number of clients served • Percentage of cases effectively resolved • Percentage of cases won
Executive retreat	• Proportion of participants providing positive feedback • Number of useful suggestions made • Values tabulated from an exit survey

Comparing input costs and output results can help determine whether there is a reasonable cost–benefit relationship. Managers can judge this cost–benefit relationship by how efficiently inputs (costs) were used and how effectively incurrence of the costs achieved the intended results. These relationships can be seen in the following model:

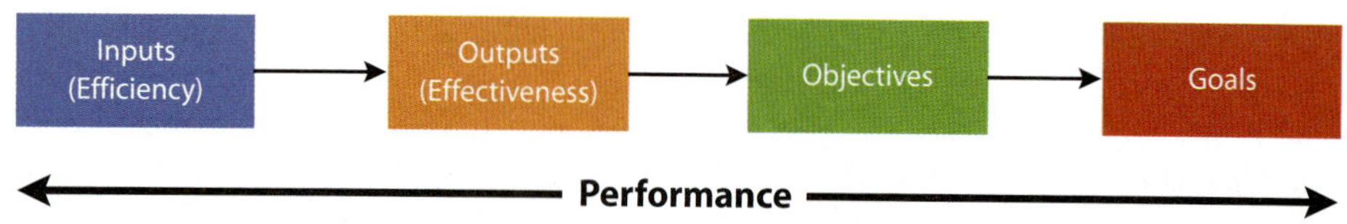

Efficiency The degree to which a satisfactory relationship occurs when comparing outputs to inputs reflects the activity's efficiency. Efficiency is a yield concept and is usually measured by a ratio of output to input. For instance, one measure of automobile efficiency is miles driven (output) per gallon of fuel consumed (input). The higher the miles per gallon, the greater is thc car's fuel efficiency.

Comparing actual output results to desired results indicates the effectiveness of an activity or how well the activity's objectives were achieved. When a valid output measure is available, efficiency and effectiveness can be determined as follows:

	Actual Result	**→ compared to →**	**Desired Result**
Efficiency =	$\frac{\text{Actual Output}}{\text{Actual Input}}$	→	$\frac{\text{Planned Output}}{\text{Planned Input}}$
or alternatively,			
Efficiency =	$\frac{\text{Actual Input}}{\text{Actual Output}}$	→	$\frac{\text{Planned Input}}{\text{Planned Output}}$
Effectiveness =	$\frac{\text{Actual Output}}{\text{Planned Output}}$	→	Preestablished Standard

A reasonable measure of efficiency can exist only when inputs and outputs can be matched in the same period and when a credible causal relationship exists between them. These two requirements make measuring the efficiency of discretionary costs very difficult. First, several years could pass before output occurs from some discretionary cost expenditures. Consider, for example, the length of time between expenditures made for research and development or a drug rehabilitation program and the time at which results of these expenditures are visible. Second, frequently a dubious cause-and-effect relationship exists between discretionary inputs and resulting outputs. For example, assume that you clip and use a cents-off coupon for breakfast cereal from a magazine advertisement (a discretionary cost of the cereal company). The company cannot be certain that it was the coupon that caused you to buy the product or whether you would have purchased the cereal without the coupon.

Effectiveness In contrast to the measurement of efficiency, measurement of effectiveness does not require the consideration of inputs. Effectiveness is determined for a particular period by comparing results achieved with results desired. Determination of an activity's effectiveness is unaffected by whether the designated output measure is stated in monetary or nonmonetary terms. Management can only subjectively attribute some or all of the effectiveness of the cost incurred to the results. Subjectivity is required because comparison of actual to planned output does not indicate a perfect causal relationship between activities and output results.

Assume that last month Precision Industrial increased its customer service training expenditures and, during this month, customer satisfaction ratings improved by 12 percent. The planned increase in customer satisfaction was 15 percent. Although management was 80 percent effective ($0.12 \div 0.15$) in achieving its goal of increased customer satisfaction, that result was not necessarily related to the customer service training expenditures. The increase in customer satisfaction could have resulted partially or entirely from other effects such as a reduction in complex customer orders. Therefore, management does not know for certain whether the customer service training program was the most effective way in which to increase customer satisfaction.

The relationship between discretionary costs and desired results is inconclusive at best, and the effectiveness of such costs can be inferred only from the relationship of actual to desired output. Because many discretionary costs result in benefits that must be measured on a nondefinitive and nonmonetary basis, exercising control of these costs is difficult. Therefore, planning for discretionary costs can be more important than subsequent control measures. Control after the planning stage is often limited to monitoring discretionary expenditures for conformity with the budget.

Control Using Engineered Costs Some discretionary activities are repetitive enough to allow the development of standards similar to those for manufacturing costs. Such activities result in **engineered costs**, which are costs that have been found to bear observable and known relationships to a quantifiable activity base. Such costs can be treated as either variable or fixed. Discretionary cost activities that fit into the engineered cost category are usually geared to a performance measure related to work accomplished. Budget appropriations for engineered costs are based on the static master budget. However, control can be exerted through the use of flexible budgets if the expected level of activity is not achieved.

To illustrate the use of engineered costs, assume that Precision Industrial has found that routine machine inspections of machining lathes can be treated as an engineered cost. Because Precision Industrial uses only one type of lathe, inspections are similar enough to allow management to develop a standard inspection time. Precision Industrial managers have found that inspection of each lathe averages slightly less than 20 minutes. Thus, each inspector is expected to perform approximately three inspections per hour. From this information, the company can obtain a fairly valid estimate of what inspection costs should be based on the inspection activity level and can compare actual cost against the standard cost each period. The activity base of this engineered cost is the number of inspections performed.

In May, Precision Industrial management predicts that 10,500 inspections will be performed, and thus, 3,500 hours is the expected total inspection time. If the standard average hourly pay rate for inspectors is $50, the May budget for this activity is $175,000. In May, 10,770 inspections are made at a cost of $176,400 for 3,600 actual hours (or $49 per hour). Using the generalized cost analysis model for variance analysis presented in Chapter 7, the following calculations can be made:

AP × AQ	SP × AQ	SP × SQ
$49 × 3,600	$50 × 3,600	$50 × (10,770 ÷ 3)
$176,400	$180,000	$179,500

$3,600 F	$500 U
Price Variance	Efficiency Variance

$3,100 F
Total Inspection Cost Variance

The price variance shows that, on average, Precision Industrial paid $1 less per hour ($50 – $49) for inspectors during May than was planned. The unfavorable efficiency variance results from using 10 hours more than standard [(10,770 ÷ 3) – 3,600] for May.

The preceding analysis is predicated on the company's willingness and ability to hire the exact number of inspection hours needed and a continual availability of lathes to inspect. If Precision Industrial can employ only full-time employees on a salary basis, analyzing inspection costs in the preceding manner is not very useful. In this instance, quality inspection cost becomes a discretionary fixed cost, and Precision Industrial might prefer the following type of fixed overhead variance analysis:

Actual Cost	Budgeted Fixed Cost	Standard Fixed Rate × Standard Hours Allowed

Spending Variance	Volume Variance

Total Inspection Cost Variance

The method of variance analysis and, thus, cost control must be appropriate to the cost category and management information needs. Regardless of the variance levels or the explanations provided, managers should always consider whether the activity itself and, therefore, its cost incurrence were sufficiently justified. Postincurrence audits of discretionary costs are often important in determining an expenditure's value.

Control Using the Budget After discretionary cost budget appropriations have been made, monetary control is provided through the use of budget-to-actual comparisons in the same manner as for other budgeted costs. Actual results are compared to expected results, and explanations should be provided for variances. Such explanations often can be found by recognizing cost consciousness attitudes. The following illustration involving two discretionary cost activities provides a budget-to-actual comparison that demonstrates employee cost consciousness.

Assume that Precision Industrial is one of many companies that outsource payroll processing activities to Payroll Financial Services (PFS). PFS has prepared the condensed budget shown in Exhibit 16.6 for the first quarter of 2014. Allison James, the controller for PFS, estimates 1,200,000 paychecks will be processed during that period; the company charges clients $0.75 per check processed.

Exhibit 16.6 Payroll Financial Services Budget—First Quarter 2014

Revenues		
Processing fees (1,200,000 × $0.75)		$ 900,000
Expenses		
Employee training	$ 80,000	
Maintenance	28,800	
Office	60,000	
Wages and fringe benefits	180,000	
Salaries and fringe benefits	120,000	
Depreciation	75,000	(543,800)
Operating income before tax		$ 356,200

In pursuing a strategy of total quality management and continuous improvement, PFS's management has chosen to fund employee training to improve employee and customer satisfaction. The company also considers maintenance a discretionary cost, and the budget allows a $1.20 processing fee per 50 checks processed. Office costs include utilities, phone service, supplies, and delivery. These costs are variable and are budgeted at $100 per office hour. PFS expects to operate at 600 office hours in the budget quarter. Wages are for ten employees, who are paid an average wage of $30 per hour. Salaries and fringe benefits are for management level personnel and, like depreciation, are fixed costs.

James collected the revenue and expense data shown in Exhibit 16.7 during the first quarter of 2014. Because of computer downtime during the quarter, PFS worked five extra hours on four different workdays. Additional contracts were responsible for the majority of the increase in checks processed.

After reviewing the actual results, PFS's board of directors requested a budget-to-actual comparison from James and explanations for the cost variances. Because most costs were higher than budgeted, the board questioned whether costs had been effectively controlled. James prepared the comparison presented in Exhibit 16.8 and provided the following explanations for the variances. Each explanation is preceded by the related budget item number.

Exhibit 16.7 Payroll Financial Services Actual Results—First Quarter 2014

Revenues		
Processing fees (1,300,000 × $0.75)		$ 975,000
Expenses		
Employee training	$ 70,000	
Maintenance	26,300	
Office	63,860	
Wages and fringe benefits	192,200	
Salaries and fringe benefits	116,450	
Depreciation	85,000	(553,810)
Operating income before tax		$ 421,190

Exhibit 16.8 Payroll Financial Services Budget-to-Actual Comparison for First Quarter 2014

	Budget Item No.	Original Budget	Budget for Actual Results	Actual	Variances
Revenues					
Processing fees		$900,000	$975,000	$975,000	$ 0
Expenses					
Training	(1)	$ 80,000	$ 80,000	$ 70,000	$ 10,000
Maintenance	(2)	28,800	29,760	26,300	3,460
Office	(3)	60,000	63,860*	63,860	0
Wages and fringe benefits	(4)	180,000	186,000	192,200	(6,200)
Salaries and fringe benefits	(5)	120,000	120,000	116,450	3,550
Depreciation	(6)	75,000	75,000	85,000	(10,000)
Total expenses		$543,800	$554,620	$553,810	$ 810
Operating income before tax		$356,200	$420,380	$421,190	$ 810

*This amount is based on the assumption that the higher hourly rate was attributable to an unforeseen utility rate increase: 620 hours × $103 = 63,860

1. The discretionary cost for employee training decreased because the vendor providing training services announced a new, higher price for its services. PFS chose to decrease training services while researching the pricing structure of other training service vendors. *Comment: This explanation reflects a cost containment approach to short-term management of training costs. In the long term, the company must provide at least the original level of training to avoid an eventual decline in quality and customer service. If a lower cost source of training services cannot be identified, the company may need to consider raising prices to maintain profitability.*
2. Maintenance cost decreased because managers obtained a favorable price on maintenance supplies obtained from a new Internet vendor. *Comment: This explanation reflects an understanding of how to reduce costs without adversely affecting quality. The*

company has found a way to reduce costs while maintaining high client service quality. Costs have been reduced by obtaining the maintenance inputs at a lower unit cost.

3. Office expenses were influenced by two factors: the additional 20 hours of operation and an increase in local utility rates, which caused PFS's costs to rise $3 per operating hour. *Comment: The first part of the explanation reflects an understanding of the nature of variable costs—working additional hours caused additional costs to be incurred. The second part of the explanation reflects an understanding of the nature of specific price-level adjustments. The increase in utility rates was caused by an increase in fuel prices paid by the utility company and passed along to customers through a higher rate.*
4. The increase in wages was caused by two factors: 20 additional operating hours and a $1 increase in the hourly cost of fringe benefits because of an increase in health insurance premiums.

10 employees × 620 hours × $30 per hour	$186,000
Increase in fringe benefit costs (10 × 620 × $1)	6,200
Total wages cost	$192,200

Comment: These cost changes reflect the nature of variable costs and an unavoidable increase caused by a vendor cost adjustment.

5. A new purchasing agent, hired at the beginning of the quarter, is being paid $14,200 less per year than the previous agent. *Comment: Salaries are usually higher for more experienced managers. The new manager is less experienced than the previous manager and, therefore, is being paid a lower salary.*
6. The depreciation increase was related to the purchase and installation of a new electronic data interchange (EDI) system. The purchase was made with board approval when a competitor went bankrupt during the quarter and had a distress liquidation sale. Purchase of this technology had been included in the capital budget for the fourth, not the first, quarter of 2014. *Comment: Acquiring the EDI technology is a good example of the cost containment concept. PFS wanted to buy the software and equipment and had an opportunity to buy it at a substantial savings, but earlier than anticipated. This purchase created an unfavorable cost variance for depreciation in the first quarter, but it shows an instance of planning, foresight, and flexibility. The long-run benefits of this purchase are twofold. First, the capital budget will show a favorable variance when this equipment's actual and expected costs are compared. Second, in future periods, the budgeted committed cost for depreciation will be less than it would have been had the purchase not been made at this time.*

Note that the variance computations in Exhibit 16.8 (p. 655) compare a revised budget using actual checks processed as the cost driver to actual revenues and costs. When comparing budgeted and actual expenditures, managers must be careful to analyze variances using an equitable basis of measurement. These variance computations illustrate the use of flexible budgeting. Comparisons between the original budget and actual results for the variable cost items would not have been useful for control purposes because variable costs automatically change with changes in cost driver volume levels.

In addition to effective cost control, management also must develop tools that are effective in managing a critical organizational resource: cash.

CASH MANAGEMENT

6 What are the objectives managers strive to accomplish in managing cash?

Of all organizational resources, cash is one of the most important and challenging to manage. Cash is the organizational resource that is the medium of exchange in most business transactions. Two key cash management tools were introduced in Chapter 8:

- the cash budget and
- budgeted (pro forma) cash flow statement.

This section provides an overview of cash management objectives and tools.

An organization's liquidity depends on having sufficient cash available to retire debts and other obligations as they come due. However, holding too much cash reduces a firm's profitability because the return on idle cash is below both the return that can be earned on other productive assets and the cost of capital.

Firms hold cash to liquidate transactions, to cover unexpected events, and for speculation. Objectives of managing cash are similar to objectives of managing inventories. Cash levels should be sufficient to cover all needs but low enough to constrain opportunity costs associated with alternative uses of the cash. Models useful in managing inventory (discussed in Chapter 18) are also useful for managing cash levels. Optimal cash management requires answers to the three questions posed in the following sections.

What Variables Influence the Optimal Level of Cash?

The cash budget and pro forma cash flow statement provide managers information about the amounts and timing of cash flows. These data are the primary inputs to determining the "inventory" of cash that should be available at a specific point in the budget year. However, the actual level of cash maintained can differ from that necessary to meet the cash flow requirements in the cash budget.

The level of confidence that managers have in the cash budget is a nonquantitative factor that influences the desired cash balance. For example, the less certain managers are of either the amount or timing of cash inflows or outflows, the higher is the amount of cash that managers will hold. If actual cash flows fail to match budgetary amounts, more cash could be required to satisfy transactions. Similarly, the greater the variability in cash requirements throughout the year, the more conservative managers must be in managing cash. To avoid liquidity problems, managers of firms with high variability in the operating cycle must hold a greater amount of cash than managers of firms with very stable, predictable operating cycles. Firms that would have difficulty arranging for short-term credit to cover unexpected cash shortages are forced to hold higher amounts of cash to cover contingencies.

Also, securities ratings (particularly bond ratings) can induce firms to hold larger cash balances than is justified based on all other considerations. A favorable bond rating is contingent on the organization paying interest and principal when these amounts are due. Security rating agencies encourage organizations to demonstrate conservative practices in managing cash. Related to bond ratings, firms with debt may be obligated by loan covenants to maintain minimum levels of cash.

What Are the Sources of Cash?

There are three usual sources of cash:

- sales of goods or services (the primary source);
- sale of equity or debt securities and other shorter-term instruments; and
- sale of assets that are no longer necessary or productive.

The capital budget is the key control tool for the last two sources of cash (as discussed in Chapter 15).

Management of cash consumed by and derived from the operating cycle is integral to the management of working capital. **Working capital** equals total current assets minus total current liabilities. In the operating cycle, cash is first invested in material and conversion costs, then in finished goods inventory, followed by (or concurrently with) marketing and administrative activities, and finally in accounts receivable. The cycle is completed when the accounts receivable are collected. Exhibit 16.9 (page 658) illustrates the cash collection cycle.

Effective management of the cash collection cycle can both reduce the demand for cash and increase its supply. For example, if cash invested (such as in inventories and receivables) during the operating cycle can be reduced by accelerating the cycle, the cash balance will increase. In the utopian case, raw material would be instantly obtained when a customer placed an order. That material would then be instantly converted into a finished product that would instantly be transferred to the customer who would instantly pay in cash. Even without achieving the utopian ideal, any reduction in the length of the operating cycle will reduce inventory and accounts receivable balances and increase the cash balance.

Managers can take explicit measures to accelerate inventory turnover. For example, inventory levels can be reduced if products can be manufactured more quickly after customer

Exhibit 16.9 Cash Collection Cycle

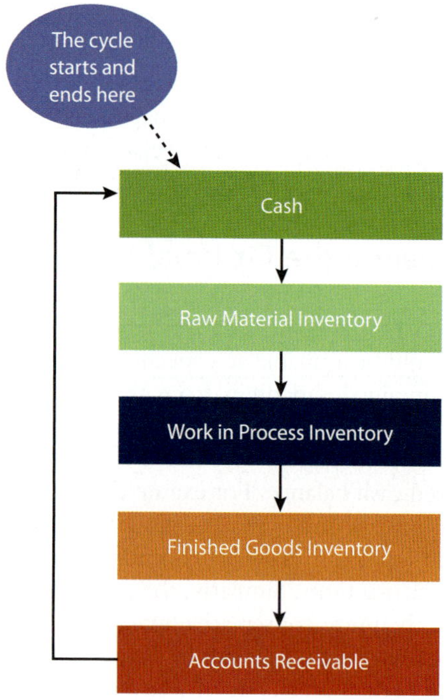

orders are received. In addition to reducing inventory, cash collections can be accelerated to increase cash levels. Accounts receivable turnover can be directly influenced by terms given on credit sales, policies governing credit approval, discounts given for early payment, and use of the services of financial intermediaries that specialize in purchasing (or "factoring") accounts receivable. Other practices can be implemented to accelerate customer payments including using

- electronic funds transfers,
- customer debit cards,
- lock boxes, and
- bank courier services.

Centralizing cash collection functions at organizational headquarters may also allow accounts receivable to be converted to cash more quickly.

Alternatively, the cash balance can be increased by slowing down payments for inputs. Managers can search among alternative vendors for the most desirable credit terms and policies. Credit rather than cash can be used to purchase inputs. Rather than paying factory employees weekly, a bimonthly or monthly pay plan can be instituted. Also, decentralizing cash disbursement functions can increase the interval from when a check is issued until it clears the financial banking system.

What Variables Influence the Cost of Carrying Cash?

The cost of carrying cash varies over time, and there are two classes of costs to manage: the cost of borrowing and the cost of issuing equity capital. For example, short-term borrowing costs will rise and fall with changes in inflation rates, creditworthiness of the borrower, and availability of funds for lending. The higher are short-term borrowing costs, the greater the incentive to minimize idle cash balances.

Second, there is an opportunity cost of holding cash. Excess cash can be invested in productive projects or returned to investors. Firms with mulitple investment opportunities have a greater incentive to convert idle cash to other assets. Even if few investment opportunities are available, managers can always return cash to investors by reducing debt or repurchasing stock. The higher a firm's cost of capital, the greater the opportunity cost of holding idle cash.

Banking Relationships

Managers depend on banks for most short-term liquidity and long-term loans. In turn, bankers depend on financial information from creditors to measure risk and determine loan eligibility. Accounting and cash flow information are key determinants of loan eligibility, loan limits, and credit terms.

From the bank's perspective, credit risk is a primary concern in determining whether, and how much, a bank will lend to an entity. Credit risk also is a key input in determining the borrower's interest rate. To assess credit risk, banks examine

- the borrower's credit history,
- the borrower's ability to generate cash flow,
- quality of collateral offered by the borrower,
- character of senior officers of the borrower, and
- the borrower's operational plans and strategies.

A loan agreement includes covenants or restrictions that prescribe minimal financial thresholds that the borrower must maintain over the loan term. For instance, covenants can stipulate minimum acceptable ratios for debt to assets, current assets to current liabilities, and interest coverage.

Accountants must monitor the firm's compliance with loan agreement covenants. By projecting revenues, expenses, and cash flows, accountants can identify potential problems before they are encountered and help develop plans to avoid covenant violations. If a covenant violation is inevitable, accountants can work with the bank to negotiate a solution to the situation. Furthermore, accountants should understand the bank's standard lending policies, such as margin requirements for short-term assets, and manage the firm's compliance with those policies.

Trust is an important element of a good relationship between a bank and a borrower. Development of trust depends on accountants providing the bank with accurate, conservative financial data as well as timely information about operating results. Accountants have the responsibility of preparing the reports provided to the bank and providing interpretations of the data to help bank personnel understand the financial and operating results.

Bankers abhor surprises. If a firm is facing bad news, such as the potential for missed loan payments or bankruptcy, the bank should be kept informed about the circumstances and efforts being made to overcome the challenge. By maintaining a trusting relationship with a bank and its officers, a firm will have a valuable partner in weathering financial storms.

In addition to building relationships with banks and other lenders, the trend is to build stronger ties to suppliers and providers of other necessary inputs as well.

SUPPLY-CHAIN MANAGEMENT

7 How is technology reducing costs of supply-chain transactions?

Today, competition in markets is as much between supply chains as between individual firms; thus, there is greater joint dependency among firms and their suppliers than previously existed. This dependency creates an incentive to share information and to manage costs across customers and suppliers. Exhibit 16.10 (page 660) depicts three significant supply-chain interactions and dependencies. The most obvious interaction is the downstream flow of goods and services. However, many supply-chain costs are associated with the other two arrows: the upstream flow of information and the upstream flow of payments.

Until recently, a significant amount of time and other resources was spent ordering parts and materials from suppliers and issuing payments for those inputs. The downstream firm typically prepared a material requisition form, purchase order, and receiving report. The upstream firm issued documents to control the production, shipping, and billing of the ordered goods. Collectively, these control processes and documents created significant supply-chain costs.

Exhibit 16.10 Supply-Chain Relationships

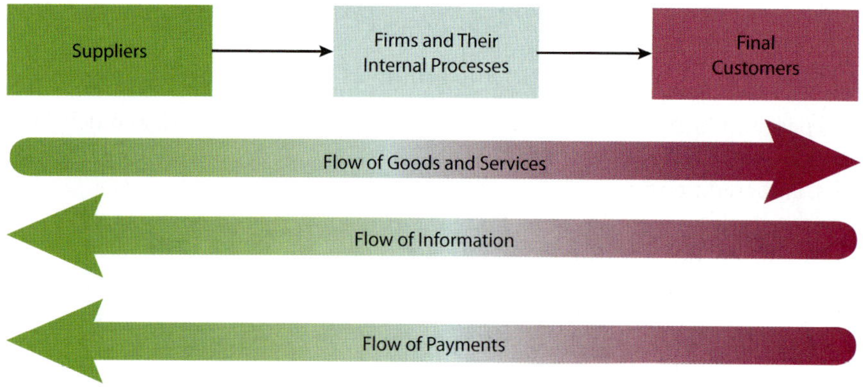

Today, firms increasingly use **e-procurement systems** to purchase goods and services over the Internet, exchange information and payments, and reduce purchasing transaction costs. Such systems are electronic B2B (business-to-business) applications that control the requisitioning, ordering, and payment functions for inputs. An **electronic data interchange (EDI) system** is often used in the process of e-procurement to precisely format communication messages "that represent documents other than monetary instruments" and are transmitted "via telecommunications or physically transported on electronic storage media."[10]

In a traditional purchasing system, buying a box of paper clips might require the same set of documents and procedures as required for buying $1,000,000 of raw materials. E-procurement saves significant time and money as well as results in fewer transaction errors between the buyer and supplier. One 2008 study of e-procurement activities indicated that requisition-to-order costs pre- and post-implementation of e-procurement were halved, from $54 to $27; cycle time dropped from 8.8 days to 2.7 days.[11] E-procurement arrangements are often governed by long-term supply agreements that involve interorganizational negotiations and detailed product specifications and engineering data.

One common configuration of such a system involves a large purchaser or a consortium of smaller purchasers, creating an electronic marketplace. Typically, the purchasing organization allows suppliers to make their electronic catalogs of products and materials available online. The e-procurement system then allows authorized personnel to order inputs from those catalogs and pay for the purchases electronically. Other systems allow competing vendors to bid for the right to sell inputs to the purchasing firm. An increasingly expanded group of global suppliers have become part of the e-procurement world, allowing greater flexibility and potential for cost efficiencies. Many firms also view their usage of e-procurement as a distinct part of their sustainability efforts because of its impact on diminishing paper usage.

COPING WITH UNCERTAINTY

8 Why is uncertainty greater in dealing with future events than with past events?

The world of the management and cost accountant is split into two spheres separated by time. The first sphere is the historical, in which the accountant is concerned with accounting accurately and fairly for events and activities that have already occurred; examples include determining the production cost for the period, determining the cost of equipment that has been purchased, and ascertaining a department's or division's operating costs. The focus of financial accounting is accurately reporting historical accounting data.

The second sphere is future oriented, in which accountants deal with events and activities yet to unfold; examples include budgeting future production costs for organizational

[10]National Institute of Standards and Technology, "Electronic Data Interchange (EDI)," *Federal Information Processing Standards Publication 161-2* (April 29, 1996); http://www.itl.nist.gov/fipspubs/fip161-2.htm (accessed 2/25/12).

[11]Aberdeen Group, *The Impact of E-Procurement in North America* (September 2008), p. 2; http://business.telus.com/en_CA/content/pdf/sector/Energy/5501-SI-e-procurement-north-america.pdf (accessed 2/25/12).

products, estimating the cost of equipment to be purchased, and projecting the impact of future events on departmental or divisional costs and revenues. Effectiveness of accountants in this second realm is determined in part by their abilities to cope with and manage uncertainty. **Uncertainty** reflects the doubt or imprecision in specifying future outcomes. Uncertainty arises from lack of complete knowledge about future events and is the reason accountants are less accurate in assigning costs to future events and activities than to historical events and activities. Much of management accountants' activity deals with uncertainty.

The Nature and Causes of Uncertainty

Before discussing specific strategies for dealing with effects of uncertainty in cost management, it is first necessary to understand the nature of uncertainty and its causes.

Understanding Uncertainty Causes and Effects Uncertainty in cost management has two main sources. First, uncertainty arises from a lack of identification or understanding of cost drivers. To estimate and budget future costs, accountants assess the relationship between a cost and its cost driver. In a simple and perfect world, each organizational cost would have a single driver that would perfectly explain every fluctuation in the related cost. However, in the real world, some costs may be predicted with accuracy based on the cost driver-to-cost relationship, but rarely is a cost predicted perfectly because cost is not entirely related to a single cost driver. In the context of cost prediction and cost understanding, **random** refers to the fact that some portion of a cost cannot be predicted from a specified cost driver or that a cost is stochastically, rather than deterministically, related to the cost driver.

For example, a cost accountant may use machine hours as the basis for predicting factory utility costs. Although changes in machine hour volume may account for nearly all of the change in factory utility cost, other factors, such as weather and number of employees, may account for some part of the cost. If machine hours alone are used as the basis for predicting utility costs, the prediction might be close to the actual cost, but the prediction will contain some error. This error is evidence that part of the utility cost is only randomly related to the machine-hour cost driver. Furthermore, logic suggests that whereas machine hours may explain with relative accuracy the quantity of kilowatt-hours of electricity consumed, machine hours may have no relationship to the price the utility company charges for each kilowatt-hour consumed.

Occurrence of Unforeseen Events A second source of uncertainty is unforeseen events. For example, the events of September 11, 2001, dealt a severe economic blow to most industries in the United States, but for the airline industry, the impact of 9/11 was nearly fatal. This industry is characterized by high fixed operating costs, and events that shock demand are a source of significant risk for any business, including the airlines. In the immediate aftermath of 9/11, the airlines lost 100 percent of their revenues for a brief period and a large portion of revenues for an extended period. Without significant aid from the U.S. government, this entire industry, at least as it existed prior to 9/11, might have vanished from the economy along with thousands of jobs and total disruption of the U.S. transportation system. Similarly, the recent economic downturn may have been anticipated by some firms; however, very few firms anticipated the severity of the downturn and how extensively the global economy would be affected.

When firms plan for unforeseen events, it is impossible to know the magnitude of all potential contingencies. Accordingly, no reasonable plan to deal with unforeseen events will provide solutions for all possible occurrences. Even so, managers must develop strategies for reducing the level of uncertainty to which firms are exposed.

Four Strategies for Dealing with Uncertainty

9 What are the four generic approaches to managing uncertainty?

There are four generic strategies applicable to cost management in the face of uncertainty:

- Uncertainty can be explicitly factored into estimates of future costs.
- Costs can be structured to automatically adjust to uncertain outcomes.

- Options and forward contracts can be used to mitigate effects of uncertainty.
- Insurance can be purchased to reimburse the firm in the event of unexpected occurrences.

Explicitly Considering Uncertainty When Estimating Future Costs Typically, the historical relationship between a cost and its cost driver is used to assess the extent to which the cost and its cost driver are related. Statistical tools are often used in this type of analysis. In the appendix to Chapter 3, ordinary least squares regression was introduced as a statistical tool to predict costs by estimating values for *a* and *b* in the following prediction equation, in which *y* is the cost or other item to be predicted (dependent variable); *a* and *b* are, respectively, the intercept and slope in the prediction equation; and *X* is the predictor variable (independent variable):

$$y = a + bX$$

When alternative independent variables exist, least squares regression can help select the independent variable that is the best predictor of the dependent variable. For example, managers can use least squares to decide whether machine hours, ambient temperature, factory production hours, or another variable best explains and predicts changes in factory utility expense.

Statistical software packages are often used to develop ordinary least squares estimates of the *a* and *b* values. These packages typically produce a variety of statistical information in addition to the estimates of *a* and *b*. For example, nearly all statistical packages as well as spreadsheet software produce a statistic called the **coefficient of determination**, which is the portion of the variance in the dependent variable (cost) explained by the movement in the independent variable (cost driver). The value of this statistic ranges between 0 and 1. A value of 0 indicates that the relationship between the predictor variable and the dependent variable is completely random. A value of 1 signifies that the variance of the independent variable explains completely the variance of the dependent variable. More important, a coefficient of determination value of 0 means the predictor variable is not useful in predicting the dependent variable, and a value of 1 means the predictor variable is ideal.

Although calculation of the coefficient of determination is beyond the scope of this text, the use of this measure in selecting predictor variables is straightforward and is readily available with even elementary statistical packages. Exhibit 16.11 illustrates a hypothetical relationship between factory utility costs and two possible predictor variables: machine hours and plant production hours. The exhibit features the relationships between dependent and independent variables based on six months of recent data. Ordinary least squares was used to estimate the exhibit's regression lines. The calculated coefficient of determination reflects the proximity of the data points to the fitted regression line. If the coefficient

Exhibit 16.11 Historical Relationship between Utility Costs and Alternative Explanatory Variables

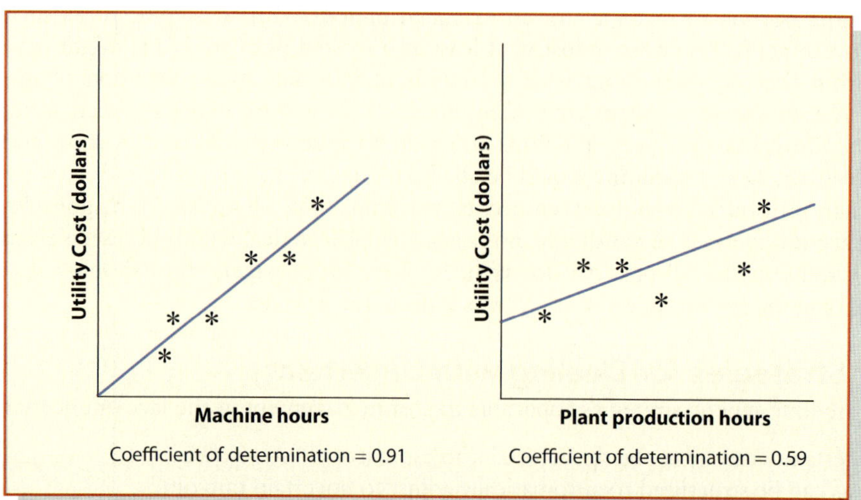

of determination is 1, all data points will fall on the ordinary least squares regression line. Given the relationships, neither of the candidate predictor variables provide a coefficient of determination of 1. However, the machine hour data points are much closer to the line than are the plant production hour data points. Thus, it follows that the coefficient of determination is higher for the machine hours regression (0.91) than for the plant production hours regression (0.59).

Using the coefficient of determination as a tool to select the best among candidate predictor variables will reduce the uncertainty regarding estimated costs or revenues. All other things being equal, the higher the coefficient of determination, the lower is the uncertainty regarding the resulting prediction or forecast. Other statistical techniques such as computer simulations and more elaborate regression models, which can include multiple independent variables as well as nonlinear relationships between independent and dependent variables, can also be used to select predictor variables. Use of these more advance techniques reduces the prediction error and the effects of uncertainty on prediction accuracy.

The alternative approach to explicitly considering the effects of uncertainty in cost estimates is to examine the sensitivity of costs and/or revenues to estimation errors. Because tools such as ordinary least squares regression provide predictions of a single value, it is useful to examine effects of errors in estimates. Sensitivity analysis, introduced in Chapter 15, is a tool commonly used for this purpose. To illustrate, assume that Precision Industrial predicts its factory maintenance costs (y) as a function of machine hours (X). Following is the prediction equation.

$$\text{Annual factory maintenance cost function: } y = \$60{,}000{,}000 + \$50X$$

If Precision Industrial expects to work 2,000,000 machine hours in the coming year, predicted factory maintenance cost would be $60,000,000 + $50(2,000,000) = $160,000,000. However, the possible range of activity is between 1,900,000 to 2,100,000 machine hours. The lower level reflects the most pessimistic level of customer demand, while the higher level reflects the most optimistic level of customer demand. As customer demand increases, more machine hours will have to be incurred to produce the demanded units. Inserting the minimum and maximum values of X into the maintenance cost equation yields a range for factory maintenance cost.

$$\begin{aligned}\text{Maintenance cost at most pessimistic demand} &= \$60{,}000{,}000 + \$50(1{,}900{,}000)\\ &= \$155{,}000{,}000\\ \text{Maintenance cost at most optimistic demand} &= \$60{,}000{,}000 + \$50(2{,}100{,}000)\\ &= \$165{,}000{,}000\end{aligned}$$

This approach yields very useful information in instances where there is uncertainty about volume of operations, perhaps because of uncertain customer demand. If Precision Industrial's managers are confident of the relationship between machine hours and factory maintenance costs as well as estimates of customer demand, the managers can be relatively confident that factory maintenance cost will fall between $155,000,000 and $165,000,000 for the coming year.

Structuring Costs to Adjust to Uncertain Outcomes As discussed earlier, the events of 9/11 were financially disastrous for the airline industry. Few other industries could be harmed as dramatically by a drop in service/product demand. The airline industry is characterized by very high levels of fixed costs, and in the short run, the level of costs is very insensitive to the level of customer demand. Consequently, if demand spikes, profits soar, and if demand falters, profits plummet and losses are quickly experienced. The greater the uncertainty about demand, the greater is the risk of allowing fixed costs to comprise a high proportion of total costs. In addition to experiencing revenue losses following 9/11, the airline industry also was dealt a blow by an increase in fuel prices (a variable operating cost) a few years after 9/11. Indeed, airline fuel costs today consume more than twice as much of revenue as they did a decade ago.[12]

[12] Source: IATA, "Airline Industry 2011 Profit Outlook Slashed to $4 Billion," *Press Release* (June 6, 2011);, http://www.iata.org/pressroom/pr/pages/2011-06-06-01.aspx (accessed 2/25/12).

Consider the cost and revenue graphs that are shown in Exhibit 16.12 for Companies A and B. Company A has a cost structure that is entirely variable, and Company B has a cost structure that is entirely fixed. The space between the revenue and total cost lines in the graphs represents profits or losses. Note how the amount of profit varies greatly with small changes in volume for Company B. Alternatively, Company A's profits change slowly as volume changes. Accordingly, Company A's profits are less exposed to the effects of uncertainty. General relationships between cost structure and profits are discussed in detail in Chapter 9 with regard to cost-volume-profit analysis.

Although fixed and variable costs are not completely substitutable, most companies have substantial opportunities to change their cost structures. For example, in the airline industry, managers could choose to lease rather than to purchase airplanes. The shorter the term of the lease, the more the cost of airplanes can approximate a variable cost. Thus, as demand changes, airplane leases can be added or cancelled.

Using Options and Forward Contracts to Mitigate Input Cost Risk Uncertainty about input costs arises from two sources: the quantity and cost of inputs consumed. Although input quantity is typically highly correlated with customer demand and production volume, input price can be influenced by many other factors. Accordingly, even though machine hours may, on a long-term basis, prove to be highly correlated with utility cost, machine hours are more highly correlated with the quantity, rather than the price, component of cost. Thus, although the uncertainty surrounding quantity of input usage may be best resolved by an improved understanding of volume drivers, other strategies will be necessary to deal with price uncertainty.

Some companies operate in industries that are intensely competitive, and if input costs unexpectedly increase, companies may be unable to increase prices sufficiently to cover the cost increases. Such companies in particular need effective strategies for dealing with input cost uncertainty. Two tools used in such strategies are options and forward contracts.

Options and **forward contracts** are agreements that give the holder the right to purchase a given quantity of a specific input at a specific price at a specific time. Generically, the use of options and forward contracts to manage risk is known as **hedging**. To illustrate, corn prices have increased more than 100 percent in the past five years.[13] Companies such as food and soft drink manufacturers are heavily exposed to risks of price changes for corn; these companies can use options and forward contracts to protect against such price

Exhibit 16.12 Relationship between Uncertainty and Cost Structure

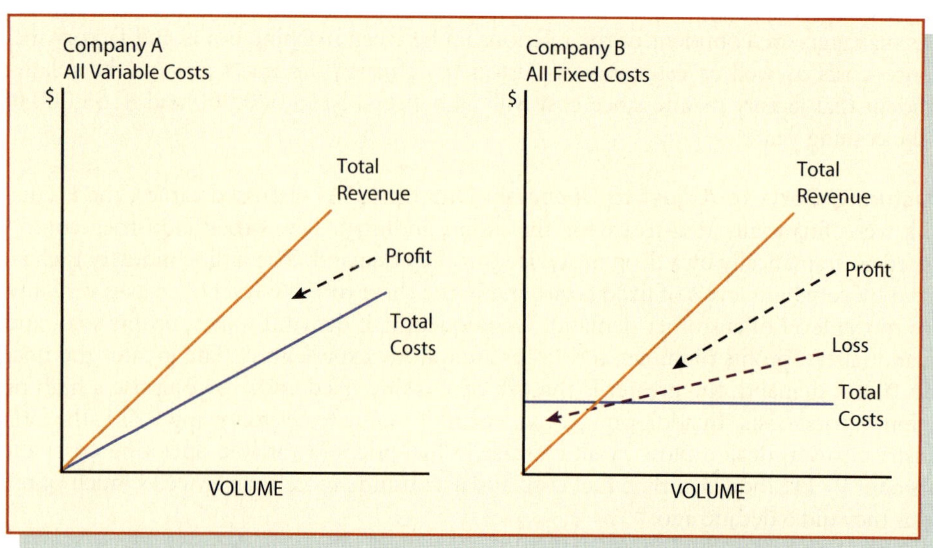

[13] Source: http://futures.tradingcharts.com/chart/CN/M (last accessed 2/09/11).

increases. The extent to which specific companies use these tools has varied widely in recent years. For example, **Sanderson Farms** chooses not to hedge its corn costs, but **Pilgrim's Pride** did use hedging—unfortunately, that company went bankrupt in 2009 because it hedged incorrectly on corn.[14]

Forward contracts or options can be executed between a company and a specific vendor, or options can be purchased on organized exchanges such as the Chicago Mercantile Exchange, Chicago Board of Trade, and New York Mercantile Exchange. Exhibit 16.13 lists items commonly traded on the organized exchanges. Just as the consumer of a commodity such as diesel fuel can use a forward contract or option to hedge against cost uncertainty, a producer of diesel fuel can use a forward contract or option to hedge against revenue uncertainty.

Exhibit 16.13 Examples of Items Commonly Hedged

Energy	***Metals***	***Interest Rates***
heating oil	*gold*	*short term*
crude oil	*silver*	*long term*
gasoline	*copper*	
natural gas	*aluminum*	***Agriculture***
electricity	*platinum*	*livestock*
coal		*meats*
propane	***Currencies***	*grains*
		cotton

Insuring against Occurrences of Specific Events The final strategy for coping with uncertainty involves use of insurance contracts, in which one party (an insurer) in exchange for a payment (premium) agrees to reimburse a second party (an insured) for the costs of certain occurrences. Whereas other strategies for dealing with uncertainty largely address uncertainty about costs deriving from quantity and price variability, insurance is purchased to cope with uncertainty about occurrences of specific events. The types of events are limited only by the imagination of the contracting parties, but are typically those that, in the absence of insurance, would dramatically increase costs (e.g., to rebuild a factory following a fire) or decrease revenues (e.g., business is interrupted by a labor strike in a company's only factory). Common types of occurrences for which insurance protection are sought include events often described as "acts of nature" such as tornados, hailstorms, floods, and earthquakes. Other types of common events covered by insurance include fire, theft, vandalism, accidental death of a key employee, and product failure. Companies can also obtain D&O (directors' and officers') insurance that can protect the board members and corporate officers from being personally liable while they are acting on the company's behalf. However, D&O insurance does not typically protect directors and officers who engage in dishonest, fraudulent, or illegal actions.

[14] M. Andrejczak, "A Steep Plunge in Commodities Sours Some Earnings Hopes," *Wall Street Journal* (1/23/09); http://articles.marketwatch.com/2009-01-23/news/30776246_1_hedges-commodities-bets.

Comprehensive Review Module

KEY TERMS

appropriation, p. 650
coefficient of determination, p. 662
committed cost, p. 649
cost avoidance, p. 647
cost consciousness, p. 643
cost containment, p. 646
cost control system, p. 643
cost reduction, p. 647
discretionary cost, p. 649
electronic data interchange system (EDI), p. 660
engineered cost, p. 653
e-procurement system, p. 660
forward contract, p. 664
hedging, p. 664
option, p. 664
price elasticity, p. 645
random, p. 661
spend analysis, p. 647
uncertainty, p. 661
working capital, p. 657

CHAPTER SUMMARY

1 Cost Control Systems

- An effective cost control system helps manage costs
  - prior to an event through
    - ➢ establishment of budgets and standards, or
    - ➢ other stated expectations of performance outcomes;
  - during an event by
    - ➢ identifying deviations from plans or budgets, or
    - ➢ monitoring other aspects of operations relative to expectations; and
  - following an event by providing feedback on performance.

2 Cost Changes and Deviations

- Costs can change from one period to the next, or deviate from expectations, as a result of
  - variable costs moving with changes in volume.
  - inflation or deflation of prices.
  - supplier-changed prices
    - ➢ in response to changes in demand or
    - ➢ due to changes in cost of production.
  - purchase volume changes, which affect purchase discounts related to volume.

3 Generic Approaches to Cost Control

- Three generic approaches to cost control include
  - cost containment, which is an approach to minimize cost increases;
  - cost avoidance, which means finding ways to avoid high-cost inputs by substituting lower-cost inputs; and
  - cost reduction, which involves finding ways to alter operations to lower costs.

4 Fixed Costs

- Two primary types of fixed cost are
  - committed fixed costs, which are associated with an organization's basic infrastructure and are determined by long-run strategy (examples include depreciation, lease payments, and property taxes); and
  - discretionary fixed costs, which are incurred for activities for which the level and nature are determined by management judgment (examples include research and development, advertising, and employee training).

5 Controlling Discretionary Fixed Costs

- Control of discretionary fixed costs can apply
  - before an event by the use of budgets or by treating those costs as engineered costs if they are associated with repetitive activities;
  - during an event by comparing budgets to actual expenditures; and
  - after an event by calculating variances for engineered costs.

6 Managing Cash

- The objectives in managing cash are to
  - maintain an organization's liquidity by making certain there is enough cash to cover cash expenses and to retire debt; and
  - invest any idle cash so that a return is generated on cash balances exceeding liquidity needs.

7 Technology and Cost Reduction in Supply-Chain Transactions

- Technology is reducing costs within supply chains by
  - reducing the need to generate paper documents for purchasing transactions;
  - automating payment transactions;
  - enhancing the exchange of information within the value chain; and
  - enhancing competition among alternative suppliers.

8 Uncertainty

- Uncertainty is greater for future events than for past events because
  - cause-and-effect relationships are incompletely understood.
  - events that are unforeseen can alter outcomes.

9 Managing Uncertainty

- Four generic strategies for dealing with uncertainty are to
  - explicitly consider uncertainty when estimates are generated by
    - ➢ using best predictor variables in generating estimates and
    - ➢ analyzing effects of estimation errors on estimates using sensitivity analysis;
  - structure costs to adjust to uncertain outcomes;
  - use options and forward contracts to manage price risks; and
  - use insurance to indemnify against occurrences of specific events such as
    - ➢ acts of nature or
    - ➢ fire, theft, and liability risks.

SOLUTION STRATEGIES

Efficiency: Relationship of input and output

Actual yield ratio = Actual output ÷ Actual input
or
Actual input ÷ Actual output

Desired yield ratio = Planned output ÷ Planned input
or
Planned input ÷ Planned output

Effectiveness: Relationship of actual output and desired output

Efficiency + Effectiveness = Performance

Cost Variances, p. 653

Comparison of actual costs with budgeted costs: allows management to compare discrepancies from the original plan

Comparison of actual costs with budgeted costs at actual activity level: allows management to determine how well costs were controlled; this approach requires a flexible budget

Variance analysis using standards for discretionary costs: allows management to compute variances for routine, structured discretionary costs

For discretionary costs susceptible to engineered cost treatment:

Actual Cost	Standard Price per Hour × Actual Hours	Standard Price per Hour × Standard Hours

Rate Variance | Efficiency Variance

Total Variance

For discretionary costs that are managed as lump-sum fixed costs:

Actual Cost | Budgeted Fixed Cost | Standard Fixed Rate per Hour × Standard Hours

Spending Variance | Volume Variance

Total Variance

For discretionary costs involving both fixed and variable elements:

Actual Cost | Flexible Cost Budget | Standard Price per Hour × Standard Hours

Spending Variance | Efficiency Variance

Total Variance

DEMONSTRATION PROBLEM

BigBiz, Inc., a firm with global operations, has developed a training program for compliance with company policy and international laws regarding hiring practices. The company believes it can treat the cost of this training as an engineered cost. The following data were extracted from documents addressing the training plan and from records regarding actual performance:

Planned volume of training	21,600 employees
Total budgeted trainer days	120
Actual volume of training	24,800 employees
Actual trainer days	130

Required:

a. Calculate the degree of effectiveness of the training program relative to number of employees trained.
b. Calculate planned efficiency for the trainers.
c. Calculate the actual efficiency of the trainers.
d. Comment on the performance of the trainers.

Solution to Demonstration Problem

a. Degree of effectiveness = Actual employees trained ÷ Budgeted employees trained
= 24,800 ÷ 21,600
= 1.148, or 115 percent (rounded)

b. Planned efficiency = Planned output ÷ Planned input
= 21,600 employees ÷ 120 trainer days
= 180 employees per trainer day

c. Actual efficiency = Actual output ÷ Actual input
= 24,800 employees ÷ 130 trainer days
= 191 employees per trainer day(rounded)

d. The performance of the trainers exceeded both effectiveness and efficiency expectations.

POTENTIAL ETHICAL ISSUES

ETHICS

1. Including price escalation clauses in sales contracts but refusing to grant sales price decreases in the event of substantial cost reductions
2. Artificially reducing the supply of a product or service to force an increase in price (or maintain an artificially high price) to customers
3. Acquiring raw material inputs in excessively high quantities to obtain a low price merely to generate a favorable variance for an individual manager or responsibility center (especially if that manager is primarily evaluated on the basis of price variances) while simultaneously ignoring the related non-value-added carrying costs related to the purchase
4. Engaging in cost avoidance by acquiring counterfeit goods at a lower price than their name-brand counterparts
5. Outsourcing production or procurement activities to companies that violate acceptable (as perceived from the firm's domicile country) labor or environmental laws
6. Delaying payments to suppliers simply to generate larger investment returns on cash balances, especially when those suppliers do a high, or the highest, percentage of their business with the company
7. Manipulating or falsifying financial statements to obtain additional credit or lower interest rates on borrowings

QUESTIONS

1. How does the cost control system interact with the overall cost management system?
2. Why does the general control model begin with planning activities?
3. At what points in time is cost control for any specific organizational activity exercised? Why are these points of cost control important?
4. What factors can cause costs to change? Which of these factors are subject to cost containment and which are not? What creates the difference in controllability?
5. Differentiate between committed and discretionary fixed costs. Could a cost be considered discretionary by one firm and committed by another? If so, discuss and give an example. If not, discuss why not.
6. Why is it often difficult to measure the output of activities funded by discretionary costs?
7. Define the terms *efficiency* and *effectiveness*, and distinguish one from the other. Why is measuring the efficiency of discretionary costs often difficult? Explain how the effectiveness of discretionary cost activities can be measured.
8. What types of discretionary costs are subject to control as engineered costs? Provide several examples.
9. Why do firms hold cash balances? Why do some firms hold larger cash balances than other firms?
10. How is technology affecting supply-chain purchasing practices and transaction costs?
11. What are the four generic approaches to reducing uncertainty? Describe the context in which each approach is typically used.
12. What factors create uncertainty when estimating future costs and revenues?

EXERCISES

13. **LO.2 (Cost control activities)** Rogal and Associates Legal Services hires full- and part-time professional employees. Full-time experienced staff can be hired for a salary of $60,000 per year; fringe benefit costs for each full-time employee amount to 20 percent of base salary. Rogal and Associates pays part-time professional employees $50 per hour but does not provide any fringe benefits. If a part-time employee has worked for the firm for more than 1,500 hours by year-end, he or she receives a $4,500 bonus.

    a. Does the firm's policy of hiring part-time professional staff represent an example of cost containment, cost avoidance, or cost reduction? Explain.

b. For a given professional position, at what level of annual hours worked should the firm consider hiring full-time rather than part-time professional staff?

14. **LO.1 & LO. 2 (Cost control; financial records; writing)** Idaho Industrial is a medium-size manufacturing corporation in a capital-intensive industry. Currently, actual profits are not meeting expectations. As a result, new investment funds are limited, and hiring is restricted. These consequences of the corporation's problems have placed a strain on the plant's repair and maintenance program. The result has been a reduction in work efficiency and cost control effectiveness in the repair and maintenance area.

The assistant controller proposes installing a maintenance work order system to overcome these problems. This system would require a work order to be prepared for each repair request and for each regular maintenance activity. The maintenance superintendent would record the estimated time to complete a job and send one copy of the work order to the department in which the work would be performed. The work order would also serve as a job cost sheet. Actual cost of parts and supplies used on the job as well as actual labor costs incurred in completing the job would be recorded directly on the work order. A copy of the completed work order would be the basis for the charge to the department in which the repair or maintenance activity occurred.

The maintenance superintendent opposes the program because the added paperwork will be costly and nonproductive. The superintendent states that the departmental clerk who now schedules repairs and maintenance activities is doing a good job without all the extra forms the new system would require. The real problem, in the superintendent's opinion, is that the department is understaffed.

a. Discuss how such a maintenance work order system would aid in cost control.
b. Explain how a maintenance work order system might assist the maintenance superintendent in getting authorization to hire more staff.

CMA ADAPTED

15. **LO.1 (Cost control systems; writing)** Lois Jilg, the CEO of Minnesota Manufacturing, was concerned about the amount the firm had spent on fuel and energy costs in the previous quarter. Jilg called Alice Briggs, the CFO, and expressed her concern, "Alice, according to our latest 10-Q, we spent $20 million on fuel and energy costs. Isn't that way too much?"

As an intern working for Briggs, how would you proceed to answer this query about control of quarterly fuel and energy costs at Minnesota Manufacturing?

INTERNET

16. **LO.2 (Cost consciousness; research; team activity; writing)** All organizations seek to be aware of and control costs. In a three- or four-person team, choose one of the following industries and do web research to identify methods that have been used to control costs:

- Internet e-tailers
- Automobile manufacturers
- Hospitals
- Software companies
- Government entities

Discuss the various methods of cost control, dollars of costs saved (if available), and your perceptions of the positive and negative implications of each cost control methodology. You may choose a particular company within the industry should you so desire.

17. **LO.1 & LO.3 (Cost control activities; writing)** Brenda Barnes has just been appointed the new director of Youth Hot-Line, a not-for-profit organization that operates a phone bank for teenage individuals experiencing emotional difficulties. The phones are staffed by qualified social workers and psychologists who are paid on an hourly basis. Barnes took the following actions in the first week on her new job. Indicate whether the actions represent cost understanding (CU), cost containment (CC), cost avoidance (CA), or cost reduction (CR). Some actions may have more than one control technique; if they do, indicate the reason.

a. Increased the advertising budget appropriation for the hotline.
b. Exchanged the more expensive push-button, cream-colored, designer telephones for regular push-button desk telephones.
c. Eliminated the call-forwarding feature installed on all telephones because Youth Hot-Line will now be staffed 24 hours a day.
d. Eliminated two paid clerical positions and replaced these individuals with volunteers.
e. Ordered blank notepads for the counselors to keep by their phones; the old notepads (stock now depleted) had the Youth Hot-Line logo and address printed on them.
f. Negotiated a new contract with the telephone company. Youth Hot-Line will now pay a flat rate of $100 per month regardless of the number of telephones installed. The previous contract charged the organization $10 for every telephone. At the time that contract was signed, Youth Hot-Line had only 10 telephones. With the increased staff, Barnes plans to install at least five additional telephones.

18. **LO.2 (Causes of cost changes; writing)** Identify in the following scenarios whether the cost change is attributable to effects of cost behavior (CB), inflation/deflation (I/D), supplier cost adjustment (CA), or quantity purchased (QP). Defend your answer.
a. Allison Mfg. experienced an increase in fuel costs following an increase in crude oil prices by members of OPEC.
b. Foremost Plastics experienced an increase in the cost of plastic resins when its main supplier merged with one of its competitors.
c. The amount Kimball Co. spent on raw materials declined when its sales volume dropped by 20 percent because of diminished overseas demand for its products.
d. Minerva Industrial reduced the price it paid for fasteners when it consolidated the purchases made from five vendors to just one vendor.
e. The price of corn syrup purchased by California Confectionary increased when the demand for corn-based ethanol jumped dramatically.
f. The amount Madison Beef Processing expended for direct labor jumped 25 percent when demand for the company's products jumped following the EU's removal of its U.S. beef import restrictions.
g. The price Villanova Steel paid for its metal products increased when it adopted JIT manufacturing practices and began purchasing steel in small lot sizes.
h. The cost of executive travel at Hudson Financial Services dropped by 20 percent when two new airlines began providing services at the airport nearest the firm's headquarters.

19. **LO.4 (Committed vs. discretionary costs; writing)** Choose letter C (for committed cost) or D (for discretionary cost) to indicate the type of each of the following described costs. Explain the rationale for your choice.
a. Control is first provided during the capital budgeting process.
b. Typical examples include advertising, research and development, and employee training.
c. This type of cost cannot be easily reduced even during temporary slowdowns in activity.
d. There is usually no "correct" amount at which to set funding levels.
e. Typical examples include depreciation, lease rentals, and property taxes.
f. This type of cost often provides benefits that are not monetarily measurable.
g. Temporary reductions can usually be made without impairing the firm's long-range capacity or profitability.
h. This cost is primarily affected by long-run decisions regarding desired capacity levels.
i. It often is difficult to ascribe outcomes as being closely correlated with this type of cost.
j. This cost usually relates to service-type activities.

20. **LO.4 (Committed vs. discretionary costs; writing)** A list of committed and discretionary costs follows.

Annual audit fees
Annual report preparation and printing
Building flood insurance
Charitable contributions
Corporate advertising
Employee continuing education
Equipment depreciation
Interest on bonds payable
Internal audit salaries
Marketing research
Preventive maintenance
Property taxes
Quality control inspection
Research and development salaries
Research and development supplies
Secretarial pool salaries

a. Classify each of these costs as normally being either committed (C) or discretionary (D).
b. Which of these costs can be either committed or discretionary based on management philosophy?
c. For the expenses marked discretionary in (a), provide a monetary or nonmonetary surrogate output measure. For each output measure, briefly discuss any objections that could be raised to it.

21. **LO.5 (Effectiveness and efficiency measures)** Allridge University formed a new department to recruit top out-of-state students. The department's funding for 2013 was $1,600,000, and the department was given the goal of recruiting 600 new nonresident students. By year-end 2013, the department was credited with recruiting 660 new students. The department actually consumed $1,873,200 in its recruiting efforts.

a. How effective was the newly formed department? Show calculations.
b. How efficient was the department? Show calculations.

22. **LO.5 (Effectiveness measures)** Houston Health Clinic has used funds during 2013 for the following purposes:

a. Sent two cost accounting staff members to seminars on activity-based costing.
b. Purchased a kidney dialysis machine.
c. Built an attached parking garage for the clinic.
d. Redecorated the main lobby.
e. Placed an advertisement on four local discount-priced web sites.
f. Acquired new software to track patient charges and prepare itemized billings.

Provide nonmonetary, surrogate measures that would help evaluate the effectiveness of the monies spent.

EXCEL

23. **LO.5 (Engineered cost variances)** Fred's Freight employs three drivers who are paid $20 per hour for regular time and $30 for overtime. A single pickup and delivery requires, on average, one hour of driver time. Drivers are paid for a 40-hour week because they must be on call all day. One driver stands by for after-hour deliveries. Analyze the labor cost variances for one week in which the company made 105 daytime deliveries and 12 after-hour deliveries. The payroll for drivers for that week was $2,780. The employees worked 120 hours of regular time and 15 hours of overtime.

EXCEL

24. **LO.5 (Engineered cost variances)** Management at Robo Weld Inc. has estimated that each quality control inspector should be able to make an average of 24 inspections per hour. Retired factory supervisors are excellent quality control inspectors because of their familiarity with the products and processes in the plant. Robo Weld management has decided to staff the quality control program with these individuals and has set $20 as the standard hourly rate. During the first month of the new program, 50,040 inspections were made, and the total pay to the inspectors was $38,950 for 2,050 hours of work.

a. Perform a variance analysis for management on the quality control labor cost.
b. Assume that management could hire eight full-time inspectors for a monthly salary of $4,500 each and hire part-timers for the overflow. Each full-time inspector would work 170 hours per month. How would the total cost of this alternative compare to the cost of a 2,050-hour month at the standard rate of $20 per hour?

ETHICS

EXCEL

25. **LO.5 (Variance analysis; ethics; writing)** Cost control in the human resources office of Eastern Wholesale is evaluated based on engineered cost concepts. The office incurs both variable and fixed costs. The variable costs are largely driven by the amount of employee turnover. For 2013, budgeted costs in the human resources office were:

Fixed	$400,000
Variable	800,000 (based on projected turnover of 2,000 employees)

For 2013, actual costs in the human resources office were:

Fixed	$440,000
Variable	900,000 (actual turnover of 2,100 employees)

Using traditional variance analysis, evaluate the control of fixed and variable costs in the office. Does this method of evaluation encourage the human resources office managers to hire low-quality workers? Explain.

26. **LO.6 (Cash management; writing)** New England Automotive manufactures aftermarket automobile parts that are sold in a variety of outlets including auto parts stores and discount retailers. The following account data (in millions) have been taken from a recent balance sheet:

Current Assets	
Cash	$ 20
Accounts Receivable	280
Finished Goods Inventory	50
Work in Process Inventory	340
Raw Material Inventory	180
Current Liabilities	
Accounts Payable	$44
Other Liabilities	14

Discuss recommendations that New England Automotive managers could use to improve its cash position. Focus your discussion on the operating cycle rather than on other means of raising cash.

27. **LO.7 (e-Procurement; writing)** You are employed by a firm engaging in heavy manufacturing. Its direct materials are sourced globally, but its nonoperating inputs are sourced from a variety of U.S. vendors. You have been charged with making a presentation to the CFO about the benefits of e-procurement for nonoperating inputs. Outline the benefits your firm could expect to realize if it replaced its paper controls with a state-of-the-art e-procurement system.

28. **LO.8 & LO.9 (Coping with uncertainty; writing)** Omaha Metal Products manufactures a variety of industrial products from stock metal components. The firm is engaged in its annual process of budgeting costs and revenues for the coming year. The cost of metal consumes approximately 50 percent of total revenues. Discuss which strategies for dealing with uncertainty would be appropriate for Omaha Metal Products to use in estimating and managing its metal costs for the coming year.

29. **LO.8 & LO.9 (Coping with uncertainty; writing)** Johnson Consumer Electronics operates in an industry in which the demand for products is cyclical and often unpredictable. Discuss a strategy for dealing with uncertainty associated with the cycles that would be appropriate for Johnson Consumer Electronics to employ to maintain its profitability throughout the cycles.

30. **LO.8 & LO.9 (Coping with uncertainty; writing)** You have been assigned the task of projecting the cost of 2014 employee fringe benefits for your firm and have identified number of employees, total labor hours, and total labor cost as candidate independent variables for use in the estimation equation. Using historical data and ordinary least squares regression, you calculate the coefficient of determination for each of the candidate variables. You get the following results:

Variable	Coefficient of Determination
Number of employees	0.87
Total labor hours	0.95
Total labor cost	0.81

a. Discuss how you would use the coefficient of determination to select the best predictor variable.
b. What are the highest and lowest possible values for the coefficient of determination? Explain.

PROBLEMS

31. **LO.1 (Cost control; writing)** The following graphic indicates where each part of the dollar that a student pays for a new college textbook goes:

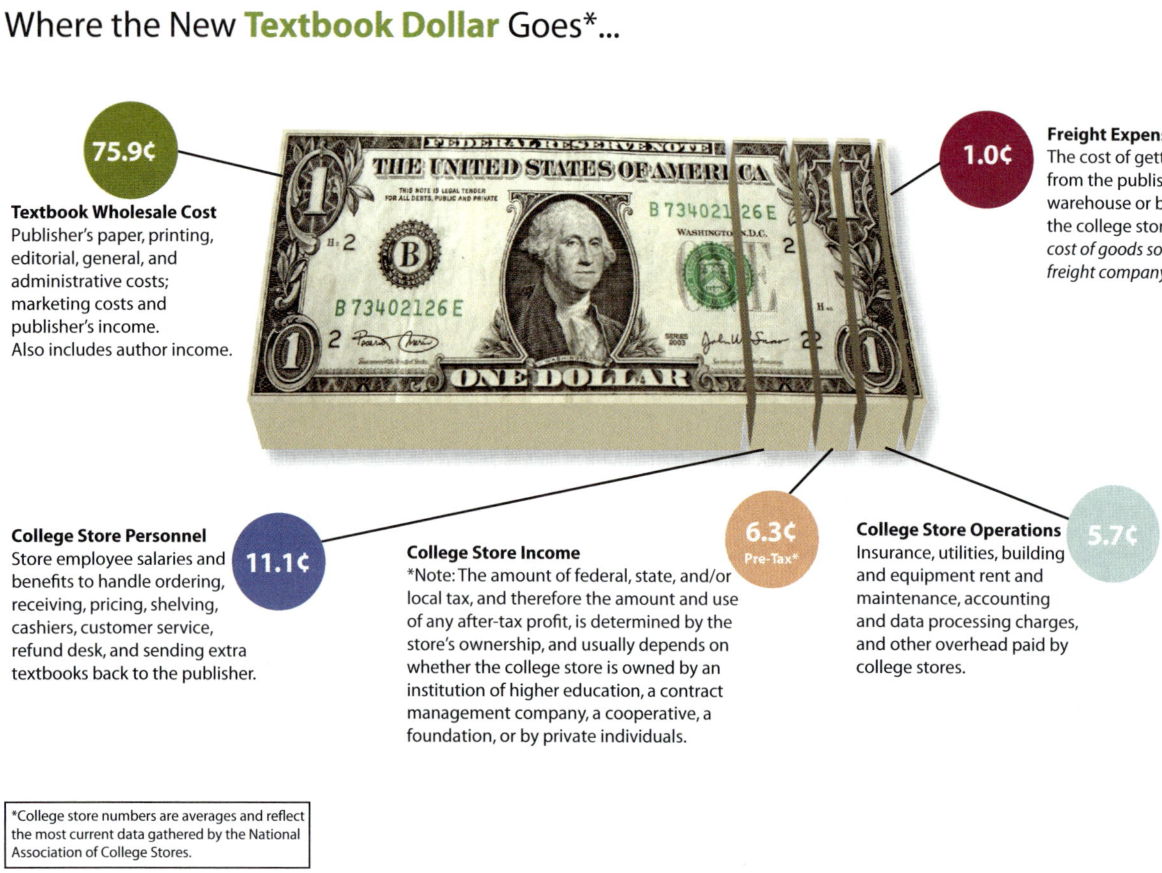

Students are frustrated with the cost of their textbooks, but most publishers would say that the selling prices have merely kept pace with inflation. Buying used books is an option, but publishers say that used books simply drive up the cost of future texts: if the publisher cannot sell as many of the new edition as are printed, the price is raised "to compensate for decreased sales volume, and the cycle starts again." Publishers also must cover the costs of many nonsalable faculty supplements such as instructor manuals, solutions manuals, videos, and test banks (hard copy and electronic). Additionally, as the books become "fancier" with multiple colors, photographs, and periodical cites, costs also increase.

a. Provide suggestions for ways the college/university bookstore could control costs.
b. Provide suggestions for ways the publisher could control costs.

c. Provide suggestions for ways students can legally control textbook expenditures (remember that substantial reproduction of the text is illegal).

d. Talk to someone who went to college 20 years ago and discuss how today's college textbooks differ from the textbooks he or she used. Are the current differences cost-beneficial from your perspective?

32. **LO.1 (Cost control; writing)** Temporary or part-time employees may be used rather than full-time employees in each of the following situations:

a. To teach undergraduate accounting courses at a university.
b. To serve as security guards.
c. To staff a health clinic in a rural area.
d. To write articles for a monthly technical magazine.
e. To clean the house when the regular maid is ill.
f. To answer questions on a tax help-line during tax season.
g. To work in department stores during the Christmas rush.
h. To do legal research in a law firm.
i. To perform quality control work in a car manufacturing plant.
j. To do seamstress work in a custom dress shop.
k. To work as a clerk/cashier in a small retail store. The store is a mom-and-pop operation, and the clerk is the only employee in the store when he or she works.

Indicate the potential advantages and disadvantages of the use of temporaries in each of these situations. These advantages and disadvantages can be viewed from the standpoint of the employer or the user of the employer's products or services.

33. **LO.1 (Cost control; writing)** Slydell Industries produces a variety of consumer goods including lamps, home office desks, and storage cabinets. Many products sold by the company are purchased disassembled and then assembled by the customer. To assist the customer with assembly, Slydell provides a free hotline staffed 24 hours daily and provides an assembly manual with each item sold. The firm produces the assembly manuals in-house and maintains very tight control over the production costs of the manuals. For the latest year, the company spent $9,000,000 writing, publishing, and packaging assembly manuals for its products. The manager tasked with managing the production of assembly manuals was speaking with the CEO and noted that "our actual production cost of $9,000,000 for assembly manuals was $700,000 under budget. I am very proud of my employees and their efforts to control costs for the company."

The CEO pondered the statement for a moment and then responded, "According to survey results that reached my desk only this morning, 65 percent of our customers use the hotline for assistance with product assembly; only 7 percent ever open their manual."

a. In light of the survey results, did the company effectively control costs of assembly manuals? Explain.

b. In the long term, why must cost control efforts be viewed through the eyes of the customer rather than through the accounting system only?

34. **LO.1 & LO.2 (Cost control; ethics; writing)** *The managers and partners [who] were interviewed listed reduced manpower costs as the major advantage for utilizing paraprofessionals [in CPA firms]. It seems that these savings were realized in a number of ways. First, there were significant savings in the salaries of paraprofessionals when compared with new staff professionals. Furthermore, since a large number of paraprofessionals were employed for less than 40 hours, many firms were realizing a significant savings in fringe benefit cost. As one manager indicated, "When we want to review inventory, we always try to get our paraprofessional because of his experience in the use of the audit guide, insights on inventory procedures, and level of training." Partners and managers indicated that the part-time nature of the employment agreement for most paraprofessionals offered the firm greater flexibility in scheduling work around peak business periods and aided in reducing hours that cannot be billed.*

ETHICS

Certainly, the savings discussed above can have a significant impact on dwindling profit margins or can be passed on to the client in the form of reduced fees. As indicated [in this article], the billing rate for accounting paraprofessionals [was much lower for paraprofessionals for both large and small firms].

Quality of work, especially on job assignments that require a large amount of detailed and repetitive tasks, was also cited on several occasions as a major consideration when employing accounting paraprofessionals. The fact that paraprofessionals are able to spend longer periods of time on jobs and their willingness to do repetitive tasks may explain the improved quality of work of paraprofessionals.

As one manager stated, "The quality of work of our paraprofessionals far exceeds that of our new staff professionals." Some of the practitioners who were interviewed still expressed concerns about utilizing paraprofessionals and the legal implications of using "less than qualified" individuals on audits. When considering using paraprofessionals on audit engagements, an argument could be advanced that the use of "less than competent audit personnel" is a violation of auditing standards. Of course the basic question is: Do these individuals possess the technical attributes one would normally expect of individuals working in that capacity?

Source: Adapted from Ted R. Compton, "Staffing Issues for the New Millennium—The Emerging Role of the Accounting Paraprofessional," *Ohio CPA Journal* (July–September 2000), pp. 56ff.

a. Discuss the use of part-timers and paraprofessionals from the perspective of controlling costs.
b. How could the use of part-timers and paraprofessionals impair the quality of work performed by public accounting firms?
c. Is it ethical for a CPA firm to bill the time of paraprofessionals at the same rate as fully qualified professionals? Discuss.
d. How could the use of part-timers and paraprofessionals affect the effectiveness and efficiency of work performed in public accounting firms?

35. **LO.2 (Cost consciousness)** Sue and Jim Hansen are preparing their household financial budget for December. They have started with their November budget and are adjusting it to reflect the difference between November and December in planned activities. The Hansens are expecting out-of-town guests for two weeks over the holiday season. The following list describes the budgetary changes from November to December that are contemplated by the Hansen family:

a. Increase the grocery budget by $165.
b. Decrease the commuter transportation budget by $70 to reflect the days off from work.
c. Change food budget to reflect serving pizza rather than steak and lobster each weekend.
d. Budget an extra $80 for utilities.
e. Reduce household maintenance budget by $90 to reflect the fact that outside maid services will not be used over the holiday period.
f. Buy generic breakfast cereal rather than name brand due to the quantity the guests will consume.
g. Use paper plates to avoid using the dishwasher as often.
h. Buy the institutional-size packages of paper plates rather than smaller-size packages.
i. Budget the long-distance phone bill at $40 less because there will be no need to call the relatives who will be visiting from England.
j. Budget movie costs at $2 per DVD rather than $12 per person to go to the movies.
k. Postpone purchasing of needed work clothes until the January sales.
l. Budget funds to repair the car. Sue plans to use part of her vacation time to make the repairs herself rather than take the car to a garage in January.

Indicate whether each of these items indicates cost understanding (CU), cost containment (CC), cost avoidance (CA), or cost reduction (CR). Some items may have more than one answer.

36. **LO.5 (Effectiveness vs. efficiency; writing)** *The founder and president of the Institute for Healthcare Improvement, Donald Berwick, is convinced that the U.S. health-care*

system can reduce costs by 30 percent while improving overall quality—just by getting health care professionals to adopt improvements others already have discovered.

- *Many children, possibly up to 30 percent, are being treated with new, broad spectrum, expensive, and potentially unsafe antibiotics despite national research and expert guidelines urging use of simple, inexpensive antibiotics as a far better initial treatment.*
- *MRI scans in the first week of back pain rarely produce useful information compared with "watchful waiting," but many doctors order MRIs for such patients.*
- *Simple, inexpensive medications such as aspirin and beta blocker drugs can significantly reduce the likelihood of dying from heart attacks, but only one in five eligible patients currently receives such medications.*
- *Inhaled steroid medications can prevent disability and complications among asthmatic patients, but fewer than one-third of eligible patients receive such medication.*
- *One HMO-based study showed an 80 percent decrease in hospital days and emergency room visits for asthma care among patients trained to avoid asthma triggers, measure their own lung function, follow a consistent treatment plan, and make adjustments in their own medications.*

Source: Ed Egger, "Best Outcomes May Be Salvation for Shriveling Managed Care Cost Savings," *Health Care Strategic Management* (March 1999), pp. 12–13.

Indicate whether each selected finding mentioned represents effectiveness (EFT), efficiency (EFC), or both. If the finding represents either efficiency or both, indicate whether you consider it to be primarily cost understanding (CU), cost containment (CC), cost avoidance (CA), or cost reduction (CR). Justify each of your answers.

37. **LO.5 (Effectiveness/efficiency; ethics; writing)** Top management of Capital Services observed that the budget for the EDP department had been growing far beyond what was anticipated for the past several years. Each year, the EDP manager would demonstrate that increased usage by the company's non-EDP departments would justify a larger appropriation. The administrative vice president commented that she was not surprised because user departments were not charged for the EDP department services, and EDP department personnel were creative and eager to continue expanding services. A review of the current year's statistics of the EDP department revealed the following:

ETHICS

EXCEL

Budgetary appropriation	\$2,000,000, based on 4,000 hours of run time; \$1,600,000 of this appropriation is related to fixed costs
Actual department expenses	Variable, \$370,500 (incurred for 3,900 hours of run time) Fixed, \$1,630,000

a. Did the EDP manager stay within his appropriation? Show calculations.
b. Was the EDP department effective? Show calculations. Comment.
c. Was the EDP department efficient? Show calculations. (Hint: Treat variable and fixed expenses separately.)
d. Using the formulas for analyzing variable and fixed costs, calculate the variances incurred by the EDP department.
e. Propose a rate per hour to charge user departments for EDP services. Do you think charging users will affect the demand for services by user departments? Why or why not?
f. Discuss whether it would be ethical to evaluate the EDP department manager based only on comparing budgeted versus actual costs and ignoring differences between budgeted and actual volume.

38. **LO.5 (Budget-to-actual comparison)** Birmingham Chemical evaluates performance in part through the use of flexible budgets. The selling expense budgets at three activity levels within the relevant range follow.

Activity Measures

Unit sales volume	15,000	17,500	20,000
Dollar sales volume	$15,000,000	$17,500,000	$20,000,000
Number of orders processed	1,500	1,750	2,000
Number of salespersons	100	100	100

Monthly Selling and Administrative Expenses

Advertising and promotion	$ 1,600,000	$ 1,600,000	$ 1,600,000
Administrative salaries	80,000	80,000	80,000
Sales salaries	100,000	100,000	100,000
Sales commissions	600,000	700,000	800,000
Salesperson travel	200,000	225,000	250,000
Sales office expense	445,000	452,500	460,000
Shipping expense	650,000	675,000	700,000
Total	$ 3,675,000	$ 3,832,500	$ 3,999,000

The following assumptions were used to develop the selling expense flexible budgets:

- The average size of the company's sales force during the year was planned to be 100 people.
- Salespersons are paid a monthly salary plus commission on gross dollar sales.
- The travel costs have both a fixed and a variable element. The fixed portion is related to the number of salespersons, and the variable portion tends to fluctuate with gross dollars of sales.
- Sales office expense is a mixed cost, with the variable portion related to the number of orders processed.
- Shipping expense is a mixed cost, with the variable portion related to the number of units sold. (An order consists of 10 units.)

A salesforce of 90 persons generated a total of 1,600 orders, resulting in a sales volume of 16,000 units during November. The gross dollar sales amounted to $14.9 million. The selling expenses incurred for November were as follows:

Advertising and promotion	$1,550,000
Administrative salaries	80,000
Sales salaries	101,000
Sales commissions	609,000
Salesperson travel	185,000
Sales office expense	500,000
Shipping expense	640,000
Total	$3,665,000

a. Explain why the selling expense flexible budget would not be appropriate for evaluating the company's November selling expense, and indicate how the flexible budget would have to be revised.

b. Determine the budgeted variable cost per salesperson and variable cost per sales order for the company.

c. Prepare a selling expense report for November that the company can use to evaluate its control over selling expenses. The report should have a line for each selling expense item showing the appropriate budgeted amount, the actual selling expense, and the monthly dollar variation.

d. Determine the actual variable cost per salesperson and variable cost per sales order processed for the company.

CMA ADAPTED

e. Comment on the effectiveness and efficiency of the salespersons during November.

39. **LO.5 (Efficiency standards)** Lucy Liu has been asked to monitor the efficiency and effectiveness of a newly installed machine. The machine has been guaranteed by the manufacturer to produce 2,000 engine gaskets per kilowatt hour (kWh). The rate of defects on production is estimated at 2 percent. The machine is equipped with a device to measure

the number of kWhs used. During the first month of use, the machine manufactured 350,000 gaskets, of which 5,000 packages were flawed, and used 180 kWhs.

a. What is the efficiency standard for flawless output?
b. Calculate the achieved efficiency for the first month and briefly comment on it.
c. Determine the achieved effectiveness and briefly comment on it.
d. Assume that the company was charged $4.50 per kWh during the first month this machine was in service. Estimate the company's savings or loss in power costs because of the machine's efficiency level in the first month of operations.
e. If you were a customer buying this company's gaskets for use in automobile production, what level of quality control would you want the company to have, and why?

40. **LO.6 (Cash management; research)** Multinational firms domiciled in the United States do not have to pay U.S. income taxes on foreign earnings, unless those earnings are returned to the United States. Accordingly, the U.S. income tax system acts as a deterrent to firms to bring cash earned abroad back to the United States. In 2004, the U.S. Congress passed the American Jobs Creation Act. One of the stated objectives of this act was to induce U.S. multinational firms to bring cash back to the United States to support growth of the domestic economy. Research the American Jobs Creation Act of 2004 and answer the following questions:

INTERNET

a. What was the incentive included in the Act to induce firms to bring cash earned abroad back to the United States?
b. Approximately how much cash was repatriated during the incentive period of the Act?

41. **LO.6 (Cash management; writing)** José Martin founded a firm that manufactures innovative toys. Since its founding in 2000, the firm has experienced steady growth. However, in the past six months, the firm's products were featured on two major network television shows. As a result of that exposure, the demand for the firm's products jumped dramatically. To meet demand, the firm ramped up production by adding a second shift of workers. With the added production capacity, the firm has been producing at 80 percent above levels of the prior year. One of the surprising side effects of this growth has been a severe cash crunch. Just this morning, Martin obtained the following balance sheet information from his CFO:

Current assets	
Cash	$ 200,000
Accounts receivable	950,000
Inventory	3,900,000
Current liabilities	
Accounts payable	$2,900,000
Wages payable	900,000
Taxes payable	300,000

a. Discuss how the high rate of growth has created the cash crunch Martin's firm is currently experiencing.
b. What strategies would you propose to Martin to deal with the cash shortage?

42. **LO.6 (Cash management; writing)** As the economy entered the new millennium, Internet companies were competing head to head in many markets with established, traditional retailers for the consumer's dollar. In comparing the financial statements of "e-tailers" relative to traditional retailing firms such as Walmart, one interesting difference is the comparatively large amount of cash held by the Internet firms. Using concepts presented in this chapter, discuss the most plausible explanations for the Internet companies holding such large sums of cash.

43. **LO.3-LO.5 (Comprehensive; analyzing cost control)** The financial results for the Business Education Department of Omega Educational Services Corporation for November 2013 are presented in the schedule at the end of this problem. Caroline Roper,

president of Omega Educational Services, is pleased with the final results but has observed that the revenue and most of the costs and expenses of this department exceeded the budgeted amounts. Bret Shulman, vice president of the Business Education Department, has been requested to provide an explanation for any amount that exceeded the budget by 5 percent or more.

Shulman has accumulated the following facts to assist in his analysis of the November results:

- The budget for calendar year 2013 was finalized in December 2012, and at that time, a full program of business education courses was scheduled to be held in St. Louis during the first week of November 2013. The schedule allowed eight courses to be run on each of the five days during the week. The budget assumed that there would be 425 participants in the program and 1,000 participant days for the week.
- Omega Educational Services charges a flat fee of $150 per day of course instruction, so the fee for a three-day course is $450. Omega grants a 10 percent discount to persons who subscribe to its publications. The 10 percent discount is also granted to second and subsequent registrants for the same course from the same organization. However, only one discount per registration is allowed.

  Historically, 70 percent of the participant day registrations are at the full fee of $150 per day, and 30 percent of the participant day registrations receive the discounted fee of $135 per day. These percentages were used in developing the November 2013 budgeted revenue.
- The following estimates were used to develop the budgeted figures for course-related expenses:

Food charges per participant day (lunch/coffee breaks)	$ 27
Course materials per participant	8
Instructor fee per day	1,000

- A total of 530 individuals participated in the St. Louis courses in November 2013, accounting for 1,280 participant days. This number included 20 persons who took a new, two-day course on pension accounting that was not on the original schedule; thus, on two of the days, nine courses were offered, and an additional instructor was hired to cover the new course. The breakdown of the course registrations follows.

Full fee registrations	704
Discounted fees	
Current periodical subscribers	128
New periodical subscribers	128
Second registration from the same organization	320
Total participant day registrations	1,280

  A combined promotional mailing was used to advertise the St. Louis program and a program in Boston that was scheduled for December 2013. The incremental costs of the combined promotion were $5,000, but none of the promotional expenses ($20,000) budgeted for the Boston program in December will have to be incurred. This earlier-than-normal promotion for the Boston program has resulted in early registration fees collected in November as follows (in terms of participant days):

Full fee registrations	140
Discounted registrations	60
Total participant day registrations	200

- Omega Educational Services includes $2,000 in each monthly budget for the purpose of updating courses or adding new ones. The additional amount spent on course development during November was for an unscheduled course that will be offered in February for the first time.

Shulman has prepared the following quantitative analysis of the November 2013 variances:

Omega Educational Services Corporation
Statement of Operations Business Education Department
For the Month Ended November 30, 2013

	Budget	Actual	Favorable (Unfavorable) Dollars	Favorable (Unfavorable) Percent
Revenue: Course fees	$145,500	$212,460	$ 66,960	46.0
Expenses				
Food charges	$ 27,000	$ 32,000	$ (5,000)	(18.5)
Course materials	3,400	4,770	(1,370)	(40.3)
Instructor fees	40,000	42,000	(2,000)	(5.0)
Instructor travel	9,600	9,885	(285)	(3.0)
Staff salaries and benefits	12,000	12,250	(250)	(2.1)
Staff travel	2,500	2,400	100	4.0
Promotion	20,000	25,000	(5,000)	(25.0)
Course development	2,000	5,000	(3,000)	(150.0)
Total expenses	$116,500	$133,305	$(16,805)	(14.4)
Revenue over expenses	$ 29,000	$ 79,155	$ 50,155	172.9

Omega Educational Services Corporation
Analysis of November 2013 Variances

Budgeted revenue		$145,500
Variances		
Quantity variance [(1,280 – 1,000) × $145.50]	$40,740 F	
Mix variance [($143.25 – $145.50) × 1,280]	2,880 U	
Timing difference ($145.50 × 200)	29,100 F	66,960 F
Actual revenue		$212,460
Budgeted expenses		$116,500
Quantity variances		
Food charges [(1,000 – 1,280) × $27]	$ 7,560 U	
Course materials [(425 – 530) × $8]	840 U	
Instructor fees (2 × $1,000)	2,000 U	10,400 U
Price variances		
Food charges [($27 – $25) × 1,280]	$ 2,560 F	
Course materials [($8 – $9) × 530]	530 U	2,030 F
Timing differences		
Promotion	$ 5,000 U	
Course development	3,000 U	8,000 U
Variances not analyzed (5% or less)		
Instructor travel	$ 285 U	
Staff salaries and benefits	250 U	
Staff travel	100 F	435 U
Actual expenses		$133,305

After reviewing Shulman's quantitative analysis of the November variances, prepare a memorandum addressed to Roper explaining the following:

a. The cause of the revenue mix variance.
b. The implication of the revenue mix variance.
c. The cause of the revenue timing difference.
d. The significance of the revenue timing difference.
e. The primary cause of the unfavorable total expense variance.
f. How the favorable food price variance was determined.
g. The impact of the promotion timing difference on future revenues and expenses.
h. Whether the course development variance has an unfavorable impact on the company.

CMA ADAPTED

44. **LO.7 (Supply-chain management; writing)** Your employer, Lawson Brake Systems, implemented an e-procurement system last year for purchasing nonoperating inputs. The installation has been such a success that the firm is now considering using the same system to acquire operating inputs (e.g., direct material and product components).

    However, some executives in the firm are reluctant to implement such a system for operating inputs because it does not support the rich collaboration that is necessary for effective supply-chain cost management. Current systems support exchange of only basic transactional information: price, product availability, shipping terms and dates, and routine transaction processing including electronic ordering and electronic payments.

    a. Assume that you are the firm's controller. Would you support the use of the e-procurement system for purchasing operating inputs? Why or why not?
    b. Assume that you are vice president of product development. Would you support installation of the e-procurement system? Why or why not?

45. **LO.8 & LO.9 (Coping with uncertainty; writing)** Wilson Ceramics manufactures holiday ornaments in its sole plant located in Wisconsin. Because the demand for the company's products is very seasonal, the company builds inventory throughout the first nine months of the year and draws down inventory the last three months of the year as demand in those months greatly exceeds production capacity. The company recently designated a member of management to be Chief Risk Officer (CRO). This individual has been charged with developing strategies to manage the effects of uncertainty on the business. The CRO has identified the following major sources of uncertainty:

    1. Financing costs of inventory.
    2. The cost of resin, which is the main material used in production.
    3. "Acts of nature" that could harm or destroy the production facility.
    4. The price to be realized for products.
    5. The level of demand for the company's products.

    As a risk consultant, you have been retained by the CRO to develop strategies to deal with each of these major sources of uncertainty. Identify the sources of risk for each of the five sources of uncertainty and provide recommendations on how to manage that uncertainty.

46. **LO.8 & LO.9 (Coping with uncertainty)** As an accounting intern working for your local police department, you learn that the department is considering starting a citizen's police academy. In recent years, there have been several events that have created friction between the police department and the citizens. The police academy is intended to create goodwill within the community and increase communication between the department and the community. You have been invited to advise the departmental management about managing the financial risk associated with the academy. You have learned that there is a federal program that provides grants to fund citizen police academies and that the program provides a reimbursement of costs up to $600 per participant. Following are estimated costs of the academy as determined by the departmental sponsors of the academy:

Variable costs	
Supplies	$200
Meals	$80
Equipment	$150
Fixed cost	
Rental for training facilities	$25,000

    Although the chief of police is very supportive of the police academy proposal, he is adamant that there is no slack in the department's budget to cover unreimbursed costs; thus, he has asked for assurance that the costs of the police academy will be covered by the federal grant program.

    a. How many citizens must participate in the program to reach the breakeven point?
    b. Is there financial risk in the proposed police academy for the police department? Explain.

c. What advice would you offer the proponents of the police academy to minimize losses the department could incur in offering the police academy?

47. **LO.8 & LO.9 (Coping with uncertainty; writing)** After reviewing financial results for 2013, Chicago Cannery's president sent the following e-mail to his CFO and controller, Willie Logan.

> *Dear Willie:*
> *I'm disappointed in the financial results for the year just completed. As you know, profits were $2 million below budget. In comparing the actual results to the budget, I note that the cost of natural gas exceeded budget by almost $1.3 million, and that cost alone accounts for 65 percent of the profit deficiency. This is the second year in a row that energy costs have dramatically reduced profits. I am calling a meeting on Tuesday to review our financial results, and I would like you to offer a presentation on the following topics:*
> 1. *Why our estimates of energy costs have been dramatically below actual costs.*
> 2. *What actions you intend to take to improve our ability to estimate these costs.*
> 3. *What actions the company could take to better manage these costs.*

As the most recent hire in the Financial Department of Chicago Cannery, Logan has asked you for help.

a. What suggestions will you give Logan to improve the estimates of energy costs for future budgeting cycles?
b. What suggestions will you give Logan to improve the management of energy costs in the future?

17

Implementing Quality Concepts

LEARNING OBJECTIVES

After completing this chapter, you should be able to answer the following questions:

1. What is quality, and from whose viewpoint should it be evaluated?
2. What is benchmarking, and why do companies engage in it?
3. What constitutes the total quality management philosophy?
4. How is the Baldrige Award related to quality?
5. What are the types of quality costs, and how are those types related?
6. How is cost of quality measured?
7. How are a cost management system and the balanced scorecard used to provide information on quality in an organization?
8. How is quality instilled as part of an organization's culture?
9. (*Appendix*) What international quality standards exist?

INTRODUCTION

Managers recognize that pursuit of high quality is a fundamental organizational strategy for competing in a global economy. Businesses, both domestic and foreign, compete to attract customers by offering more choices to satisfy customer needs and wants. Competition elicits the best in companies, and international competition has generated continuously higher-quality products and services.

Although consumers desire a wide variety of product and service choices, companies have resource constraints and must make trade-offs among price, quality, service, and promptness of delivery—thereby providing customers with a limited set of purchase options. Customers' ready access to multinational vendors has accelerated through the Internet marketplace and has motivated producers to improve quality and customer service. Vendors are continuously adopting more dynamic approaches to improve products, processes, and customer service.

This chapter discusses the issues of quality, benchmarking, total quality management, and quality costs and their measurement as well as how a cost management system and balanced scorecard are used to support quality initiatives. Many managers realize that current expenditures on quality improvements can be more than recouped through future material, labor, and overhead cost reductions and sales volume increases. Thus, regardless of the treatment for financial accounting purposes, quality improvement costs should be viewed not as expenses or losses but as recoverable investments with the potential for profit generation. Because of the potential financial consequences, accountants must understand the short- and long-run implications of the choice between higher and lower product/service quality.

WHAT IS QUALITY?

1 What is quality, and from whose viewpoint should it be evaluated?

Before an organization can improve its product or service quality, the term *quality* must be defined. After the Industrial Revolution helped manufacturers to increase output and decrease costs, quality was defined as conformity to designated specifications or requirements. The American Society for Quality Control (ASQC) considers requirements to be measurable written or verbal "specifications, product descriptions, procedures, policies, job descriptions, instructions, purchase/service orders, etc."[1] Thus, determination of conformity became the task of quality control inspectors.

In contrast, the late Joseph Juran, noted quality expert, defined quality as "fitness for use." Other quality authorities define quality in different ways, but a fairly inclusive definition of **quality** is the summation of all characteristics of a product or service that influence its ability to meet the stated or implied needs of the person acquiring that product or service.

Quality should be viewed as a production/performance, profitability, and longevity issue. All organizational processes (such as production, procurement, distribution, finance, and promotion) are involved in quality improvement efforts. Thus, two quality perspectives are

- the totality of internal processes making a product or performing a service and
- customer satisfaction with that product or service.

Production View of Quality

Productivity is measured by the quantity of good output generated from a specific amount of input during a time period. Any factor that either slows (or stops) a production process or causes unnecessary work reduces productivity. Activity analysis can be used to highlight such factors. As discussed in Chapter 4, the actions performed in making a product or providing a service can be classified into value-added (VA) and non-value-added (NVA) categories. VA activities increase the product's or service's worth to the customer; NVA activities consume time and generate costs but add no customer value. If impediments to good production are reduced or eliminated, managers can expect to realize productivity increases and production of higher-quality goods as indicated in Exhibit 17.1 (p. 686).

[1] American Society for Quality Control, *Finance, Accounting and Quality* (Milwaukee, WI: ASQC, 1990), p. 3.

Exhibit 17.1 Eliminating NVA Activities

NVA Activities	Reduce NVA Activities By	Reductions Create Positive Benefits Of
Reworking spoiled or defective units	Implementing better product design	Decreased product failure rates
Replacing spoiled or defective units	Using conforming materials	Decreased scrap and rework costs
Repairing spoiled or defective units	Instituting value-added production processes	Decreased product breakage rates
Producing and storing products with little demand	Using advanced production technology	Increased product life
Moving materials unnecessarily	Fitting machinery for mistake-proof operations	Increased manufacturing productivity
Experiencing unscheduled production interruptions	Hiring more skilled workers	Increased competitiveness
	Increasing worker training	Decreased time-to-market
	Having suppliers pre-inspect raw materials for conformity to specifications	Increased recyclability of products or product components
	Rearranging production areas for better work flow	
	Instituting a just-in-time inventory system	

Many companies focus on a **Six Sigma** production view of quality, which means that a process produces no more than 3.4 defects per million "opportunities" (that is, chances for failure or not meeting required specifications). Another way to view Six Sigma is that its purpose is to generate error-free products 99.9997 percent of the time. According to one global consulting firm, the average company in 2007 operated at approximately three sigma or 66,800 errors per million.[2] But some companies have made Six Sigma a bedrock of their processes: **American Express**, **Bank of America**, **Coca-Cola**, **General Electric**, **Starwood Hotels and Resorts**, and **Xerox** are some of the companies that have published web pages of their Six Sigma experiences.[3]

All attempts to reduce variability and product defects reflect the implementation of **quality control (QC)**. QC places the primary responsibility for product or service quality at the source: with the maker or provider. In implementing QC, many companies use **statistical process control (SPC)** techniques to analyze where variations (or fluctuations) occur in the process. SPC is based on the theory that a process has natural (common cause) variations over time and that these variations can cause errors that result in defective goods or poor service. These errors are typically produced at points of uncommon (nonrandom or special-cause) variations. Often these variations are eliminated after the installation of computer-integrated manufacturing systems, which have internal controls to detect production problems.

To analyze process variations, control charts are developed to record the occurrence of specified performance measures at preselected points in a process. **Control charts**, such as the one in Exhibit 17.2, graph actual process results and indicate upper and lower control limits. For example, a process is considered either "in" or "out of" control depending on whether

- results are within established limits and
- patterns reflect some nonrandom or special-cause variation.

[2]D. Rigby, *Management Tools 2007, An Executive's Guide* (Boston, MA: Bain & Company, 2007), p. 52; http://www.bain.com/bainweb/PDFs/cms/Public/Management_Tools_2007_Executive_Guide.pdf (accessed 1/22/12).

[3]asixsigma, *Six Sigma Business Improvement* (March 4, 2010); http://asixsigma.com/companies.php http://asixsigma.com/companies.php (accessed 1/22/12).

Exhibit 17.2 Control Chart

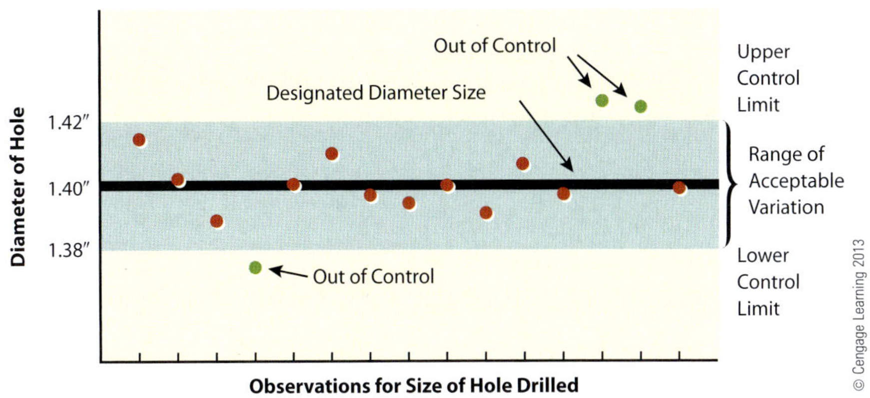

In effect, control charts use the management-by-exception principle and indicate the need for workers to respond to occurrences that are outside a predetermined limit or that form nonrandom, telltale patterns. Control charts help a process communicate to workers what is occurring in that process. If workers understand and react to that communication, potential product defects and process malfunctions can be prevented.

Control charts must be prepared consistently and accurately for a useful analysis of conditions to be made. Accountants are often directly involved in selecting appropriate performance measures and interpreting the charts. Often the measures selected to prepare control charts are nonfinancial, such as number of defective parts, quantity of waste created, and time consumed for task completion.[4]

Consumer View of Quality

Every consumer who acquires a product or service obtains a set of product/service characteristics and a set of organizational characteristics.

Product/Service Characteristics	Organizational Characteristics
Features and aesthetics	Convenience of access
Warranty and serviceability	Timeliness of delivery and service
Packaging	Reputation
Price (purchase and after-purchase)	Credit availability
Durability	Customer responsiveness
Ease of disposal and/or recyclability	
Performance	

The consumer's view of quality reflects more than whether the product or service delivers what was intended or the probability of purchasing a defective unit. The customer perceives quality as a product's or service's ability to meet and satisfy all specified needs at a reasonable cost. In other words, from a consumer's perspective, quality relates to both performance and value. This quality perspective derives from

- increased competition,
- public interest in product safety, and
- litigation relative to products and product safety.

When high-quality producers dominate a market, successful entering companies must understand both their own customers' quality expectations and their competitors' quality standards.

Exhibit 17.3 (page 688) lists eight characteristics that are commonly included in a customer's definition of product quality. An important difference between the first six and last two characteristics is level of objectivity. Characteristics A through F can be reasonably evaluated through objective methods, whereas G and H are strictly subjective. Thus, the first six are much more susceptible to organizational control than are the other two. Most,

[4]Selection of performance measures to assess quality is discussed in Chapter 14.

Exhibit 17.3 Characteristics of Quality

A. **Performance** refers to the operating features and relative importance of multiple characteristics such as ease of use and speed. Performance at The Ritz-Carlton might include comfortable beds, universal electronic charging stations for smart phones and laptops, and high-speed in-room Internet connections.
B. **Features** are the extras needed to customize a product. The Ritz-Carlton might include flowers in a customer's room at check-in, provide guests with spacious hotel rooms and fully equipped health club facilities, or offer electric vehicle charging stations in the hotel front drive.
C. **Reliability** refers to the likelihood that a product/service will perform on time as expected without a glitch. Ritz-Carlton customers expect on-time room cleanup and evening turn-down service with quality chocolates on the pillows.
D. **Conformance** is the extent to which products comply with prespecified standards. Ritz-Carlton guests may expect granite countertops on vanities and bathtubs with spa jets.
E. **Durability** refers to expected product life before deterioration and the need for replacement. Ritz-Carlton guests might expect hotel rooms to be refurbished every five years or a fresh fruit basket to be placed in the room every third day of a stay.
F. **Serviceability and Responsiveness** reflect the convenience, ease, and speed with which courteous and competent service staff complete work. Ritz-Carlton customers expect prompt responses to room service and maintenance requests.
G. **Aesthetics** refers to the environmental ambiance required by the discerning customer. The Ritz-Carlton might provide designer towels in the bathrooms and robes and slippers for in-room use.
H. **Perceived Value** is a customer's opinion of the product based on perceptions formed from advertising or product/service reputation. When customers stay at The Ritz-Carlton, they generally expect "royal" treatment.

Source: Adapted from David Garvin, "Eight Dimensions of Product Quality," http://www.1000ventures.com/business_guide/crosscuttings/bizsys_customer.html (last accessed 4/16/2012); and David Garvin, "What Does 'Product Quality' Really Mean?" *Sloan Management Review* (Fall 1984), pp. 25–43.

if not all, of the quality characteristics in Exhibit 17.3 apply equally to companies making tangible products and those providing services. For example, a hotel might consider the provision of in-room high-speed Internet access and luxury spas as "features" and low noise levels in guest rooms as high "performance." In the exhibit, illustrative examples are given for **The Ritz-Carlton**, an upscale hotel chain dedicated to service quality.

Service quality reflects the manner in which an output is delivered to a customer. Some firms use outside "secret shoppers" to assess the level of service provided. For example, an undercover hotel "guest" at an exclusive hotel could put a nonperforming light bulb in a room lamp to determine whether housekeeping detects the outage and replaces that bulb. Other companies simply reward customers for observations about service conditions: one large discount club pays customers $1 if the cashier does not address them by the name shown on their membership cards.

In addition to the quality characteristics in Exhibit 17.3 that apply to all organizations, the following additional quality characteristics apply to service organizations:

- assurance (customers expect employees to be knowledgeable, courteous, and trustworthy);
- tangibles (customers expect quality physical facilities, equipment, and appearance of personnel); and
- empathy (customers expect employees to express an appropriate level of caring and attention).

Not all customers can afford the same grade of product or service. **Grade** is the quality level that a product or service has relative to the inclusion or exclusion of characteristics (especially price) to satisfy customer needs. Customers try to maximize their satisfaction within the context of their willingness and ability to pay. They view a product or service as a **value** when it meets the highest number of their needs at the lowest possible total cost (which includes an item's purchase price plus its operating, maintenance, and disposal costs). Thus, although customers may have a collective vision of what constitutes "high quality," some choose to accept a lower grade of product or service because it satisfies their functional needs at a lower cost. Note that "high quality" is a more encompassing concept than "high grade." Someone with 20 minutes left for lunch can find more value in a fast-food hamburger than a sit-down restaurant's sirloin steak.

To illustrate the difference between quality and grade, assume that Ron Reeves is in the market for a new car for traveling to and from work, running errands, and going on vacation. He has determined that reliability, gas mileage, safety, and comfort are the most important features to him. He may believe the Lexus is the highest-quality car available, but his additional needs are that the car's price is within his budget and that repair and maintenance services are readily available at a reasonable cost. Thus, he will search for the highest-quality product that maximizes his set of quality-characteristic preferences within the grade of car he can afford.

Customers often make quality assessments by comparing a product or service to an ideal rather than to an actual product or service of the same type or in the same industry. For example, on business trips, Melanie Stringfellow frequently stays at The Ritz-Carlton hotels; the company has received all major awards from the hospitality industry and leading consumer groups as well as twice winning the U.S. Baldrige Award (discussed later in the chapter). On a recent trip, Stringfellow called a rental car company to arrange for a car. She could compare the service quality she received from the rental company with the high-quality service she receives from The Ritz-Carlton rather than how well this company compared to other rental car companies. Stringfellow is unconcerned that car company employees may not have received the same customer satisfaction training as Ritz-Carlton employees or that The Ritz-Carlton corporate culture is dedicated to high quality whereas the rental company may not have yet made such a quality commitment. Formally comparing one organization's quality levels to those of another company is called competitive benchmarking.

BENCHMARKING

2 What is benchmarking, and why do companies engage in it?

Because each company has its own unique philosophy, products, and people, "copying" such elements is neither appropriate nor feasible. Therefore, a company should attempt to imitate those ideas that are readily transferable but, more importantly, to upgrade its own effectiveness and efficiency by improving on methods used by others.[5] **Benchmarking** involves investigating, comparing, and evaluating a company's products, processes, and/or services against those of either competitors or companies believed to be the "best in class." Companies may be motivated by a variety of reasons (see Exhibit 17.4) to perform

Exhibit 17.4 Reasons to Benchmark

1. To increase awareness of the competition
2. To understand competitors' production and performance methods as well as cost structures
3. To identify areas of competitors' internal strengths and weaknesses
4. To identify external and internal threats and opportunities
5. To justify and accelerate a plan for continuous process improvement and change
6. To create a framework for program and process assessment and evaluation
7. To establish a focus for mission, goals, and objectives
8. To establish performance improvement targets
9. To understand customers' needs and expectations
10. To encourage creative thinking
11. To identify state-of-the-art business practices and new technologies

[5] The American Productivity and Quality Center has established a code of conduct for benchmarking activities. The code addresses issues such as equal exchange of information, confidentiality, avoidance of antitrust issues and illegalities, and inter-organizational courtesy; the code can be found at http://www.apqc.org/knowledge-base/download/33845/a%3A1%3A%7Bi%3A1%3Bs%3A1%3A%222%22%3B%7D/inline.pdf?destination=node/33845 (accessed 1/23/12).

benchmarking, but the end result is that an understanding of another company's production and performance methods is gained that allows the comparing company to identify its own strengths and weaknesses. As indicated in Exhibit 17.5, there are four primary types of benchmarking:

- internal,
- results (or performance),
- process, and
- strategic.

Exhibit 17.5 Types of Benchmarking

Type	Description	Advantages	Disadvantages
Internal	An approach to benchmarking that allows organizations to learn from "sister" companies, divisions, or operating units. Performance improvement may be 10 percent.	• Provides highest degree of process detail and simplified access to process information • Provides rapid and easy- to-adopt improvements • Is low cost • Provides a deeper understanding of in-house process	• Gives an internal focus that tends to be operational rather than strategic and bound by the organization's cultural norms • Creates an internal bias • Does not provide a significant stretch • May not find best-in-class practices
Results	An approach to benchmarking that targets specific product designs, process capabilities, or administrative methods used by one's direct competitors. Performance improvement may be 20 percent or better.	• Provides a strategic insight into marketplace competitiveness and can provide a "wake-up" call to action • Prioritizes areas of improvement according to competition • May create a possible partnership • Can show similar regulatory issues	• May generate legal issues regarding business relations between competitors • May provide study data that are insufficient for diagnosis • Could be threatening
Process	An approach to benchmarking that seeks information from the same functional area within a particular application or industry. Performance improvement may be 35 percent or better.	• Takes advantage of functional and professional networks to develop detailed process understanding • Provides industry trend information • Provides quantitative comparisons • Can review common business functions	• Tends to best support operational studies • Takes more time than internal or competitive studies, although it uses an external perspective • May be difficult to find common functions
Strategic	An approach to benchmarking that seeks process performance information from outside one's own industry. Enablers are translated from one organization to another through the interpretation of their analogous relationship. Performance improvement may be 35 percent or better.	• Provides the greatest opportunity for process breakthroughs • Generates reliable, detailed data because noncompeting organizations are used • Is innovative • Has high potential for discovery	• Is difficult to develop an analogy between dissimilar businesses • Is hard to determine which companies to benchmark • Has a high cost • Takes a long time to plan

Source: Adapted from U.S. Patent and Trademark Office, Office of Quality Management, *Benchmarking Workbook* (September 2000), p. 15; http://www.uspto.gov/web/offices/com/oqm-old/benchmarking_workbook_9_00.pdf (accessed 1/23/12).

Internal benchmarking addresses how and why one organizational unit is performing better than another. The techniques of the higher-performing unit are then implemented, to the extent possible, in the lower-performing units. The primary difficulty with internal benchmarking is that none of the organizational units may be performing on a quality level attained by external parties.

In **results benchmarking**, an end product or software program is examined using a process called **reverse engineering**. For a product, reverse engineering refers to disassembling the product to determine how it was designed and how it operates—generally so as to duplicate or enhance the product; for software, reverse engineering takes source code back to object code. The focus is on product/service specifications and performance results. Results benchmarking helps companies determine which other companies are "best in class" in a particular category. Many companies (such as **Pro-Weld**, **NVision**, and **M7 Technologies**) use technology such as lasers, CT scanning, and computer-aided-design systems to reverse engineer products for accuracy. For example, NVision Inc. reverse engineered a steam turbine core to perform simulations so that parts could be redesigned to improve energy efficiency.[6] However, if benchmarking leads to making an exact replica of another's product (especially for software), serious ethical and legal considerations exist.

Although benchmarking against direct competitors is necessary, it can also create the risk of becoming stagnant. For example, General Motors, Chrysler, and Ford historically competitively benchmarked among themselves and, over time, their processes became similar. When foreign competitors entered the U.S. market with totally different, and better, processes, the U.S. automotive companies were forced to change and improve their quality systems.

Because of potential stagnation, comparisons should also be made against companies that are the best in a specific characteristic rather than just the best in a specific industry. Focusing on how best-in-class companies achieve their results is called **process benchmarking**. The widespread applicability of process benchmarking is no better illustrated than when employees from a **General Mills** plant in California decided to go to a NASCAR track, videotape pit crews, study the tapes, and apply the principles of that process to reduce production changeover processes. Doing so enabled GM to reduce changeover processes from three hours to 17 minutes![7] Looking at noncompetitors is extremely valuable in process benchmarking. For example, many different types of companies have benchmarked **Walmart**'s world-class supply chain management practices, including logistics and distribution.[8] Many companies and organizations are now benchmarking environmental management and sustainability programs among peers and noncompetitors with an eye toward continuous improvement of operations, lowered emissions and resource conservation, green energy usage, and waste conservation.

Strategic benchmarking is also non–industry specific and focuses on strategy and how companies compete. This type of benchmarking is most important at many Japanese companies because their managers focus more on long-run performance than on the short-run benefits that can be gained from process and results benchmarking. In the United States, some network carrier airlines have tried to do strategic benchmarking against Southwest Airlines: the network carriers had some success in their benchmarking efforts relative to hedging activities against jet fuel costs but had some failures (United's Ted and Delta's Song) in starting up low-cost subsidiaries.[9] There has been some criticism aimed at strategic benchmarking with detractors referring to it as "a crutch" that results in a "herd mentality" rather than management concentrating on ways to be better competitors.[10]

[6] Anonymous, "Speedier Reverse Engineering," *Manufacturing Engineering* (January 2009), pp. 34–35.

[7] John Hackl, "New Beginnings: Change Is Here to Stay," *Quality Progress* (February 1998), p. 5.

[8] Cherie Blanchard, Clare Comm, and Dennis Mathaisel, "Adding Value to Service Providers: Benchmarking Wal-Mart," *Benchmarking* 15, no. 2 (2008), p. 166.

[9] Paul Muddle and Parvez Sopariwala, "Cost Restructuring and Revenue Building: A Strategic Benchmarking Analysis," *Cost Management* (January/February 2008), pp. 36ff.

[10] S. Ladd, "Business Performance: Are American Companies Benchmarking Their Way to Mediocity?" *Financial Executive* (November 2010), p. 11.

Benchmarking steps are detailed in Exhibit 17.6. Some companies have more steps than others but all have a structured approach. After the negative gap analysis (Step 6) is completed, everyone in the firm is expected to work toward both closing that gap and becoming a best-in-class organization. Through benchmarking, companies are working to improve their abilities to deliver high-quality products from the perspectives of how products are made and how customers perceive those products. Integrating these two perspectives requires involvement of all organizational members in the implementation of a total quality management system.

Exhibit 17.6 Steps in Benchmarking

1. Determine the specific area in which improvements are desired and/or needed.

2. Select the characteristic that will be used to measure quality performance.

3. Identify the best-in-class companies based on quality characteristics. Remember that these companies do not have to be industry, product, or service specific.

4. Ask for cooperation from the best-in-class companies. This may be handled directly or through a consulting firm. Be prepared to share information and respect requests for confidentiality.

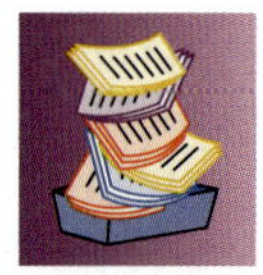

5. Have the people who are associated with the specific area being analyzed collect the needed information.

6. Analyze the "negative gap" between the company's product, process, or service and that of the best-in-class firm.

7. Act on the negative gap analysis and make improvements.

8. Do not become complacent. Strive for continuous improvement.

TOTAL QUALITY MANAGEMENT

3 What constitutes the total quality management philosophy?

Total quality management (TQM) is a "management approach of an organization, centered on quality, based on the participation of all its members and aiming at long-term success through customer satisfaction, and benefits to all members of the organization and to society."[11] Thus, TQM is based on four important tenets:

- Dictate continuous improvement for an internal managerial system of planning, controlling, and decision making;
- Require participation by everyone in the organization;
- Focus on improving goods and services from the customer's point of view; and
- Value long-term partnerships with suppliers.

Quality System

Effective quality management requires the implementation of a system that provides information about process quality so managers can plan, control, evaluate performance, and make decisions for continuous improvement. Traditionally, consideration of quality has not been part of the planning process. Most often, it has involved an after-the-fact measurement of errors because a certain level of defects was tolerated as part of the "natural" business process. Action was not triggered until a predetermined error threshold was exceeded. In contrast, a total quality system should be designed to reorient thinking:

[11] ISO 8402, *Total Quality Management* (Geneva: ISO, 1994), definition 3.7.

Old Way ⟶	New Emphasis ⟶	End Results
Ignored prior to occurrence	Planned for in every process and product	Ability to set goals and methods for quality improvements
Inspection	Prevention	System for measuring quality (or lack thereof) and providing feedback on quality enhancements
Tolerance of defects	Zero defects and continuous improvement	Encouragement of teamwork
		Move organizational attitude from product inspection and defect correction to proactive quality assurance

Employee Involvement

TQM recognizes that all organizational levels share responsibility for product/service quality. Workers should be viewed as effectors of success, not creators of problems. Training workers to handle multiple job functions helps improve efficiency and quality. Upper-level management must

- be involved in the quality process,
- develop an atmosphere that is conducive to quality improvements,
- set an example of commitment to TQM,
- provide constructive feedback about opportunities for improvement, and
- provide positive feedback when improvements are made.

Encouraging employee suggestions can produce substantial annual or, more commonly, enduring cost savings and increase productivity in all types and sizes of organizations. For example, a global manufacturer rewarded a team of ten employees $200,000 for saving the company $20 million.[12] The city of Phoenix, Arizona, saved almost $6 million in two years from employee suggestions.[13] Suggestions from three employees saved the University of St. Thomas about $220,000 in one year.[14]

Product/Service Improvement

Total quality management focuses attention on the relationship between the internal production/service process and the external customer whose satisfaction is the ultimate evidence of success. Therefore, TQM requires that companies first know who their customers are.

In analyzing their customers, companies must recognize that they may need to stop serving some groups of customers based on the results of cost–benefit analyses, activity-based costing, and data-mining techniques. Some customers simply cost more than they add in revenues and/or other benefits. Each revenue dollar does not contribute equally to organizational profitability because the cost to serve customers varies. The concept that shedding one or more sets of customers would be good for business is difficult to believe at first, but most organizations have some clients who drain, rather than improve, those organizations' ability to provide quality products and service. Managers should be attuned to customers that are not cost-beneficial and first attempt to find a way to make them profitable. If no solution is found, "nonperforming" customers should be sent to do business elsewhere so that the company can focus its attention on its current profitable customers and attract new, profitable customers. Organizations must recognize that customer loyalty and customer profitability are not the same thing. Consider that Netflix lost about 800,000 customers after a price hike, but many customers returned and the company's 2011 fourth quarter revenue was 47 percent greater than that of the same period in 2010—customers must have recognized that the new price was reasonable for Netflix services.[15]

[12] T. Lytle, "Give Employees a Say," *HRMagazine* (October 2011), pp. 68–72.

[13] A. Keim, "Employee Suggestions Saved Phoenix $6 Million in Two Years," *Ahwatukee Foothills News* (June 11, 2010); http://www.yourwestvalley.com/valleyandstate/article_bdf1b165-9a9c-5cb5-bbde-08788c6636b0.html (accessed 1/23/12).

[14] University of St. Thomas (Minnesota), "Employee Suggestions Are Win-Win Propositions," *Bulletin* (May 1, 2009); http://www.stthomas.edu/bulletin/2009/05/01/employee-suggestions-are-win-win-propositions/ (accessed 1/23/12).

[15] M. Liedtke, "Netflix Sees 4Q Customer Gains," *Tulsa World* (1/26/12); http://www.tulsaworld.com/business/article.aspx?subjectid=49&articleid=20120126_52_E2_SANFRA464041 (accessed 2/13/12).

Instituting customer service programs often produces valuable information. For example, many chains use plastic reward/loyalty key tag cards to develop databases of customer information. These systems typically contain information on purchases made, amounts spent, and customer likes/dislikes. A hotel chain may accumulate the same types of information as well as personal and family interests, preferred credit cards, and any previous difficulties encountered by a customer at a hotel. Such data can be used to sort customers and to decide whether a customer relationship merits additional investment. However, customer service programs should not be taken to the extreme: some customers, such as those that demand exorbitant service but are not willing to pay the related price, are not profitable to an organization.

After identifying its value-adding customers, a company must then understand what those customers want. The primary characteristics currently desired by customers are

- quality,
- value, and
- good service.

"Good" service is an intangible and means different things to different people. But most customers would agree that "good" service reflects the interaction between themselves and organizational employees—including response time in the event of problems or questions. Frequently, only service quality separates one product from its competition. The need for customer satisfaction information is essential to organizations embracing TQM because poor service can be disastrous. According to the U.S. Small Business Administration and U.S. Chamber of Commerce, 68 percent of customers lost by a business leave because of an employee's "attitude of indifference," while only 14 percent because of product or service dissatisfaction.[16]

Long-Term Supplier Relationships

Adopting TQM encourages companies to review their supply chain and establish long-term relationships with preferred suppliers. The TQM philosophy sees suppliers as a distinct part of a company's ability to either satisfy customers or create extreme dissatisfaction. For example, in 2010, Ford Motor Company had 90 key, long-term component and service suppliers in its Aligned Business Framework (ABF); these suppliers provide about half of Ford's global production purchases.[17] Use of a limited number of suppliers helps Ford to globally have commonality of parts and allows suppliers to take advantage of economies of scale. Ford views its ABF supplier partners as essential to helping the company deliver high-quality products to customers in a cost efficient manner.[18]

DamirK/iStockphoto.com

Suppliers can have a significant impact on a company's ability to offer customer satisfaction. Consider the negative implications to Microsoft's reputation when quality issues with the Xbox 360 were caused by a Microsoft supplier.

To ensure compliance with preferred supplier requirements, some companies often perform quality audits of their vendors. Such audits identify nonconformances in production, shipping, engineering changes, invoicing, and quality processes. After problems are identified, the parties agree on and implement effective changes; sometimes, cost recoveries are requested from suppliers. However, some companies that have adopted TQM and developed long-term supplier relationships have chosen to stop performing quality audits because they are viewed as non-value-added activities.

Given the extent to which outsourcing is currently used and the economic difficulties currently faced by many organizations, companies must be certain that they are "linking

[16] Business Automation Specialists, "Startling Statistics on Customer Retention & Acquisition," *Resources* (March 15, 2010); http://www.bautomation.com/resources/startling-statistics-on-customer-retention-acquisition (last accessed 1/23/12).

[17] Ford Motor Company, "Ford Expands List of Key Suppliers Selected for Long-Term Relationships, Collaboration," *@FordOnline* (April 26, 2010); http://www.at.ford.com/news/cn/Pages/FordExpandsListofKeySuppliersSelectedforLong-TermRelationships,Collaboration.aspx (accessed 1/24/12).

[18] International Automotive Components (IAC) Group, "Ford Recognizes IAC Group as ABF Supplier and for Consumer Satisfaction Performance," PRNewswire (June 15, 2011); http://www.prnewswire.com/news-releases/ford-recognizes-iac-group-as-abf-supplier-and-for-consumer-satisfaction-performance-123905624.html (accessed 1/24/12).

up" with suppliers that enhance product quality and customer satisfaction. Failure costs caused by defective materials or parts cannot be tolerated when companies are struggling to survive. For example, **Boeing** had significant problems with its suppliers in the production of the 787 Dreamliner, approximately 30 percent of the parts are made in other countries. Some parts made by outsourced foreign suppliers were incompatible; sufficient parts could not be provided in a timely manner; and many suppliers needed "hand-holding, which drained time and money"—all factors that contributed to the Dreamliner being three years late.[19]

Additionally, although suppliers can indirectly enhance customer satisfaction, some companies look for more direct ways to accommodate customers. For instance, The Ritz-Carlton has an agreement with **BMW** so that selected locations (such as Key Biscayne, Florida, and Doha, Qatar) could offer guests the use of a BMW during their stay: a Ritz manager commented that it was appropriate to link the hotel's "high-profile customer base" with "a premium automotive brand."[20]

Some TQM critics have called it nothing more than a management fad that does not work when practical attempts are made to implement its concepts. One rebuttal to such criticisms follows: "Poor management, not poor ideas, may be responsible for the inconsistency of TQM or other managerial interventions."[21] Companies using TQM have cited many positive outcomes and benefits, such as those included in Exhibit 17.7. In addition, dedication to total quality management may cause a company to strive for—and possibly win—the Baldrige (or other quality-based) Award.

Exhibit 17.7 Benefits of TQM

Internal

- Improved response time to change
- Increased ability to compete profitably in the marketplace
- Decreased cost through reduction/elimination of non-value-added activities and waste
- Increased profitability through reduced costs
- Improved products, services, and customer relations
- Increased employee morale, motivation, and retention
- Improved internal communications and organizational focus
- Enhanced employee decision-making abilities and teamwork
- Increased innovation and acceptance of new ideas
- Reduced number of errors
- Increased benchmarks for evaluating employee performance

External

- Increased customer trust and loyalty
- Enhanced customer satisfaction
- Improved response time to customer requests
- Decreased prices resulting from reduced internal costs

THE BALDRIGE AWARD

4 How is the Baldrige Award related to quality?

The embodiment of TQM in the United States is the Malcolm Baldrige National Quality Award (MBNQA or Baldrige Award), which focuses attention on management systems, processes, consumer satisfaction, and business results as the tools required to achieve product and service excellence. There are three versions of Baldrige criteria: business and

[19] K. Peterson, "Boeing's Billion-Dollar Outsourcing Problem," *MSN.com* (February 18, 2011); http://money.msn.com/top-stocks/post.aspx?post=15d4536f-db06-4fc6-a865-13efbdc7a94c (accessed 1/24/12).

[20] S. Pike, "Ritz-Carlton, BMW Team for Luxury Drives," Examiner.com (April 27, 2011); http://www.examiner.com/resort-spa-in-national/ritz-carlton-bmw-team-for-luxury-drives; Anonymous, "BMW 7 Series Fleet Adds Another Layer of Luxury to The Ritz-Carlton, Doha," Zawya.com (February 3, 2010); http://www.zawya.com/Story.cfm/sidZAWYA20100203130523/BMW%207%20Series%20fleet%20adds%20another%20layer%20of%20luxury%20to%20The%20Ritz-Carlton%2C%20Doha (accessed 1/24/12).

[21] 18 David Lemak, Neal Mero, and Richard Reed, "When Quality Works: A Premature Post-Mortem on TQM," *Journal of Business and Management* (Fall 2002), pp. 391ff.

not-for-profit, education, and health care. To win the award, applicants must show excellence in seven categories:

ETHICS

1. *Leadership* requires that the organization's senior managers' personal actions guide and sustain the organization. This section also addresses the organization's system of governance and how the organization fulfills legal, ethical, and societal responsibilities, and key stakeholders.
2. *Strategic planning* requires that the organization develop strategic objectives and action plans and manage how those items are implemented, adapt for changed circumstances, and measure progress toward achievement. Core competencies must be viewed as a strategic concept.
3. *Customer focus* requires that the organization establish methods to produce long-term marketplace success. The organization should have a culture that listens to customers, builds customer relationships, and uses the information those customers provide to improve and innovate.
4. *Measurement, analysis, and knowledge management* requires that the organization select, collect, analyze, manage, and continuously improve its information system and intellectual capital (both people and technology). Performance measurement and analysis are important aspects of this section as well as data management and integrity. This section addresses the issue of using internal and external benchmarking of best practices.
5. *Workforce focus* requires that the organization empower and develop its employees so that their full potential can be used in establishing and implementing organizational goals and objectives. This section requires the organization to analyze workforce capacity and capabilities as well as create a work environment that promotes high morale, job enrichment and job satisfaction, and ethical behavior among employees.
6. *Operations focus* requires that organizations examine how work systems and processes are designed, managed and improved so that customer value is provided. Four additional areas of consideration are cost control, sustainability, supply chain management, and emergency readiness.
7. *Results* requires that organizations monitor and improve performance in key business areas including product/process performance, customer satisfaction, workforce results, leadership and governance outcomes, and financial and marketplace performance.

Exhibit 17.8 illustrates the relationships among the Baldrige performance criteria categories. To achieve at least 70 percent of the points allocated within a category, the National Institute of Standards and Technology (which manages the Baldrige Award) must determine that the organization is effective and systematic in deploying and achieving the multiple requirements within each category and is innovative in continuously seeking improvement.

Corporate America has accepted the Baldrige Award because it represents excellence. Products and services of companies winning the award are regarded as some of the world's best. Such recognition invigorates workers, pleases stakeholders, and has caused the entire national economy to be strengthened by the enhanced awareness of and attention to quality and its benefits. Winning companies are asked to provide information about their performance excellence strategies so that they can be used as benchmarks for, and adapted to, other organizations for their own needs. Companies have indicated that the Baldrige criteria have been helpful in a variety of ways including better business results, systems thinking, better strategic planning, and organizational alignment.[22]

Putting quality management into practice in an organization can be very costly given the length of time needed to introduce and teach the philosophy and concepts throughout the company. Evidence indicates, however, that firms' operating performances during the process of implementing TQM are comparable to those of other companies. A 2011 study

[22]NIST, "What Were the Major Benefits to your Organization from Their [sic] Use of Baldrige?" *BPEP Program Review: Mission, Priorities, and Metrics* (2009 & 2010 Board of Examiners), slide 8; http://www.nist.gov/baldrige/enter/benefits_applying.cfm (accessed 1/24/12).

Exhibit 17.8 2011–2012 Baldrige Award Criteria

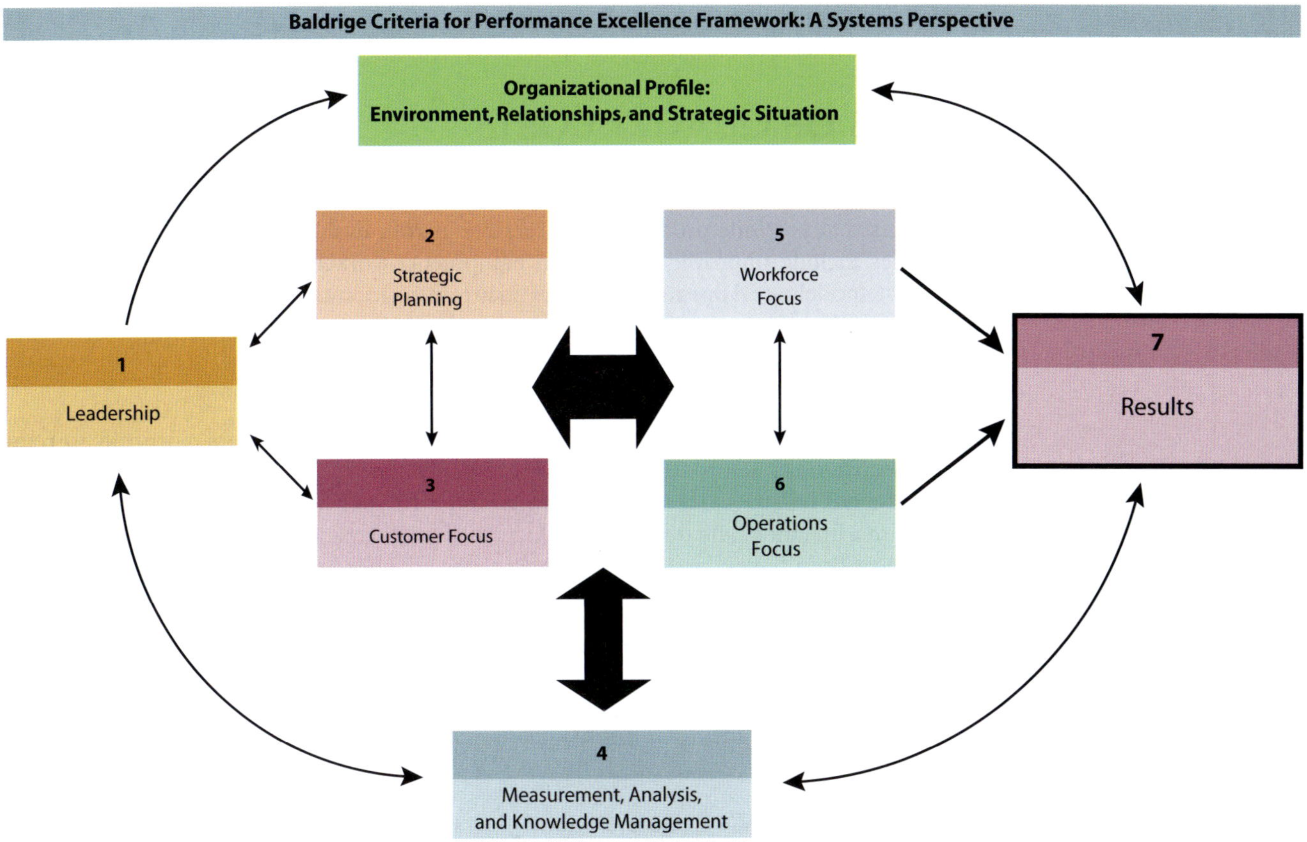

Source: Baldrige National Quality Program, National Institute of Standards and Technology, and United States Department of Commerce, 2011–2012 Criteria for Performance Excellence (Gaithersburg, MD: 2011), p. iv; http://www.nist.gov/baldrige/publications/upload/2011_2012_Business_Nonprofit_Criteria.pdf (accessed 1/24/12).

of quality award–winning firms found that the benefits of the Baldrige criteria, relative to cost savings, customer satisfaction, and financial gain, outweigh the overall cost of the program 820 to 1.[23]

Japan's equivalent of the Baldrige Award is the Deming Prize, named for the late Dr. W. Edwards Deming. There are three categories of the Deming Prize:

- The Deming Application Prize is for companies or company divisions that have achieved distinctive TQM performance in a particular year;
- The Deming Prize for Individuals is for people who have made great contributions to the field of TQM (or its dissemination) or statistical methodology; and
- The Quality Control Award for Operations is for organizational business units that have achieved distinctive operational improvements using TQM in a particular year.[24]

Three or more years after a company (or a company division) has received the Deming Application Prize, that company may apply for the Japan Quality Medal. When the applicant's implementation of TQM has been determined to have improved substantially beyond the level at the time when the Deming Application Prize was won, the company is awarded the Japan Quality Medal.

[23] NIST, "Economic Study Shows Value of Baldrige-Based Performance Excellence," *Quality Digest* (January 18, 2012); http://www.qualitydigest.com/inside/quality-insider-news/economic-study-shows-value-baldrige-based-performance-excellence.html# (accessed 1/24/12).

[24] More information about the Deming Prize, its winners, and the Japan Quality Medal can be found at http://deming.org/index.cfm?content=511 (accessed 1/23/12).

The Baldrige Award and Deming Prize are both designed to recognize quality achievements and increase awareness of TQM. However, the Baldrige Award is more focused on results and the importance of sharing information.

Other international quality standards are discussed in the appendix to this chapter.

TYPES OF QUALITY COSTS

5 What are the types of quality costs, and how are those types related?

Instituting TQM in an organization creates a new focus on costs and their incurrence. A company can increase its product and service quality by incurring **prevention costs** for activities that preclude product defects resulting from dysfunctional processing. Prevention activities include improved production equipment, worker training, and engineering and product modeling. **Appraisal costs** are incurred to monitor and compensate for mistakes not eliminated through prevention activities. Organizational spending for prevention and appraisal activities will reduce failure costs.

There are also two types of failure costs:

- **Internal failure costs** are expenditures, such as scrap or rework, incurred to remedy defective units before they are shipped to customers.
- **External failure costs** are expenditures for items, such as warranty work, customer complaints, litigation, and defective product recalls, that are incurred after a faulty unit of product has been shipped to (or an improper service has been performed for) the customer.

Although both types of failure costs can be expensive, an organization would prefer to incur internal, rather than external, failure costs.

The total quality management process will result in a cycle of benefit shown in Exhibit 17.9. This cycle will continue and produce a company that is profitable and secure in its market share—two primary goals of any organization.

Exhibit 17.9 TQM's Cycle of Benefit

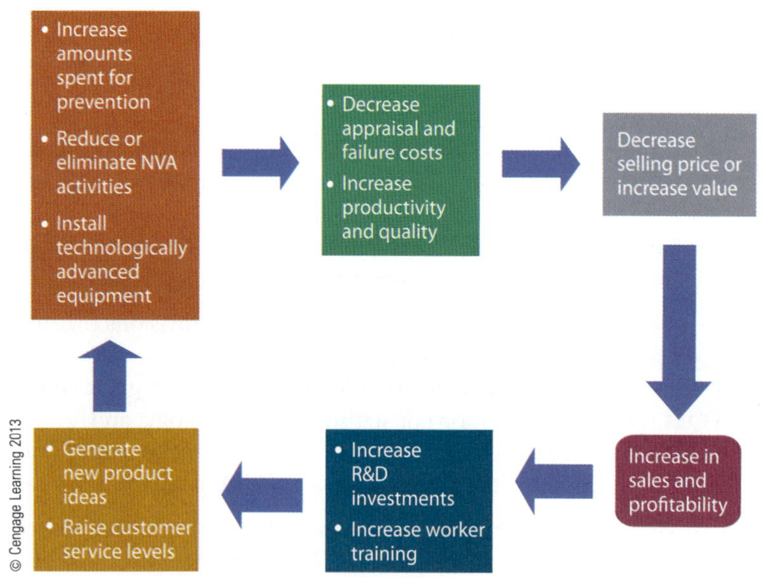

Thus, the TQM philosophy indicates that total costs decline, rather than increase, as an organization makes quality improvements. It seems that it is the *lack* of high quality, rather than the *pursuit* of high quality, that is expensive. Understanding the types and causes of quality costs helps managers prioritize improvement projects and provide feedback that supports and justifies improvement efforts.

Total quality costs can also be classified as compliance (or assurance) and noncompliance (or quality failure). The **cost of compliance** equals the sum of prevention and appraisal costs. Compliance costs are incurred to reduce or eliminate the present and future costs of failure; thus, expenditures for compliance are proactive. Furthermore, effective investments in prevention activities can even minimize the costs of appraisal. The **cost of noncompliance** results from production imperfections and is equal to internal and external failure costs. Exhibit 17.10 provides specific examples of each type of quality cost.

Inspection reports, SPC control charts, and customer returns or complaints contain information about production or service quality or lack thereof. Information about quality costs, on the other hand, is only partially contained in the accounting records and supporting documentation. Because accounting records are commonly kept primarily to serve financial accounting requirements, the quality cost behaviors relative to activity changes as well as the appropriate drivers for these costs must be separately developed or estimated for quality management purposes.

The need to estimate quality costs makes it essential for accountants to be involved in all activities from system design to accumulation of quality costs. A system in which quality costs are readily available or easily determined provides useful information to managers trying to make spending decisions by pinpointing areas having the highest cost–benefit

Exhibit 17.10 Types of Quality Costs

COSTS OF COMPLIANCE

Prevention Costs

Employees:
- Hiring for quality
- Providing training and awareness
- Establishing participation programs

Customers:
- Surveying needs
- Researching needs
- Conducting field trials

Machinery:
- Designing to detect defects
- Arranging for efficient flow
- Arranging for monitoring
- Incurring preventive maintenance
- Testing and adjusting equipment
- Fitting machinery for mistake-proof operations

Suppliers:
- Assessing for quality
- Educating suppliers
- Involving suppliers

Product Design:
- Developing specifications
- Engineering and modeling
- Testing and adjusting for conformity, effective and efficient performance, durability, ease of use, safety, comfort, appeal, and cost

Appraisal Costs

Before Production:
- Inspecting at receipt

Production Process:
- Monitoring and inspecting
- Keeping the process consistent, stable, and reliable
- Using procedure verification
- Automating

During and After Production:
- Conducting quality audits

Information Process:
- Recording and reporting defects
- Measuring performance

Organization:
- Administering quality control department

COSTS OF NONCOMPLIANCE

Internal Failure Costs

Product:
- Reworking
- Creating waste
- Storing and disposing of waste
- Reinspecting rework

Production Process:
- Reprocessing
- Creating unscheduled interruptions
- Experiencing unplanned downtime
- Retesting

Organization:
- Making inappropriate decisions because of lost or missing information
- Incurring non-value-added activities
- Losing revenue from selling items as "seconds"

External Failure Costs

Organization:
- Staffing complaint departments
- Staffing warranty claims departments

Customer:
- Losing future sales to current or potential customers
- Losing reputation
- Losing goodwill

Product:
- Repairing
- Replacing
- Reimbursing
- Recalling
- Litigating

Service:
- Providing unplanned service
- Expediting
- Serving after purchase

relationships. Additionally, quality cost information will indicate how a shift in one or more costs will affect the others. When quality costs are not reflected specifically in the accounting records, managers have no idea how large or pervasive these costs are and, therefore, have little incentive to reduce them.

Exhibit 17.11 indicates points in the production–sales cycle at which quality costs are usually incurred. An information feedback loop should be in effect to link the types and causes of failure costs to future prevention costs. Alert managers and employees continuously monitor failures to discover their causes and adjust prevention activities to close the gaps that allowed the failures to occur. These continuous rounds of action, reaction, and action are essential to continuous improvement initiatives for products currently in production and related products in the design stage.

Exhibit 17.11 Time-Phased Model for Quality Costs

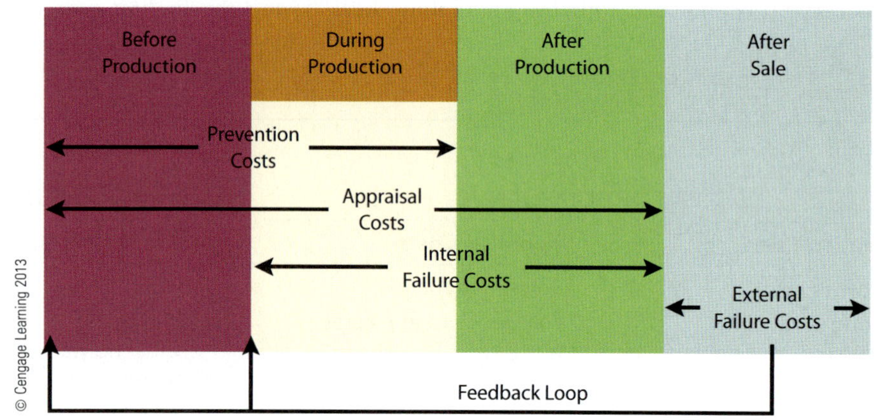

MEASURING THE COST OF QUALITY

6 How is cost of quality measured?

A company that wants to use TQM and continuous improvement should record and report its quality costs separately so that managers can plan, control, evaluate, and make decisions about the activities that cause those costs. However, merely generating quality cost information does not enhance quality. Managers and workers must consistently and aggressively use the information as a basis for creatively and intelligently advancing quality.

A firm's chart of accounts can be expanded to accommodate either tracing separately or allocating quality costs to new accounts. Exhibit 17.12 indicates some suggested accounts that will help management focus on quality costs. Opportunity costs, including lost future sales and a measure of the firm's loss of reputation, are also associated with poor quality. Although opportunity costs are real and may be estimated, they are not recorded in the accounting system because they do not result from specific transactions.

If a firm has a database management system, transactions can be coded so that reports can be generated without expanding the chart of accounts. Coding permits quality transaction types and amounts to be accessible and the generation of a cost of quality report such as the one shown on page 702 in Exhibit 17.13 (which uses assumed numbers). Two important assumptions underlie this report: stable production and a monthly reporting system. If wide fluctuations in production or service levels occur, period-to-period comparisons of absolute amounts may not be appropriate. Amounts might need to be converted to percentages to have valid meaning. Additionally, in some settings (such as the just-in-time environment discussed in Chapter 18), a weekly reporting system is more appropriate because of the need for continuous monitoring.

Theoretically, if prevention and appraisal costs were prudently incurred, failure costs would become \$0. However, because prevention and appraisal costs must still be incurred to identify and reduce failures, total quality costs can never actually be zero. But quality guru Philip Crosby proposes that, if the organizational benefits from increased sales and greater efficiency exceed the sum of compliance and noncompliance costs, then quality is

Exhibit 17.12 New Quality Accounts

Prevention Costs	Often "Buried" In
Quality training	Factory overhead (salaries/wages expense)
Quality market research	Marketing expense; Advertising expense
Quality technology	Assets; Factory overhead (depreciation)
Quality product design	Engineering salaries/Wages expense
Preventive maintenance	WIP inventory; FG inventory; Factory overhead
Appraisal Costs	
Quality inspections	Factory overhead (salaries/wages expense)
Procedure verifications	Factory overhead (salaries/wages expense)
Measurement equipment	Assets; Factory overhead (depreciation)
Internal Failure Costs	
Reworking products	WIP inventory; FG inventory; Factory overhead
Scrap and waste	WIP inventory; FG inventory
Storing and disposing of waste	Factory overhead; loss
Reprocessing	WIP inventory; FG inventory
Rescheduling and setup	Factory overhead
External Failure Costs	
Complaint handling	Salaries/Wages expense
Warranty handling	Warranty expense
Repairing or replacing returns	Warranty expense
Customer reimbursements after failure	Accounts Receivable credit
Expediting replacements	Shipping expense
Product recalls	Marketing expense; Advertising expense
Image improvements after failure	Marketing expense; Advertising expense

essentially free.[25] The following example indicates that quality may not only be "free" but even profit enhancing:

Expenditures on prevention	$ (450,000)
Expenditures on appraisal	(250,000)
Total quality compliance costs	$ (700,000)
Total failure costs eliminated	1,000,000
Addition to profit	$ 300,000

Management should analyze the quality cost relationships and spend money for quality in ways that balance costs and benefits. Such an analysis requires measuring the cost of quality to the extent possible and practical and estimating the benefits of quality costs.

Pareto analysis is a statistical technique based on the Pareto principle that can be used to separate the "vital few" from the "trivial many." Such an analysis reviews the causes of a problem so as to determine which ones occur most often. Data analysis has repeatedly shown that approximately 20–30 percent of the population (regardless of whether that population is inventory items, number of donors resulting from participants at a charity event, or sources of defects) accounts for 70–80 percent of the cost or values. Thus, a disproportionate benefit can be achieved by addressing a limited number of "problems." Pareto

[25] Philip Crosby, *Quality Is Free* (New York: Signet, 1979).

Exhibit 17.13 Cost of Quality Report

	Cost of Current Period	Cost of Prior Period	Percent Change from Prior Period	Current Period Budget	Percent Change from Budget
Prevention Costs					
Quality training	$ 5,800	$ 5,600	+4	$ 6,000	−3
Quality participation	8,200	8,400	−2	8,000	+3
Quality market research	9,900	7,700	+29	11,000	−10
Quality technology	9,600	10,800	−11	15,000	−36
Quality product design	16,600	12,200	+36	16,500	+1
Total	$ 50,100	$ 44,700	+12	$56,500	−11
Appraisal Costs					
Quality inspections	$ 3,300	$ 3,500	−6	$ 3,000	+10
Procedure verifications	1,200	1,400	−14	1,500	−20
Measurement equipment	2,700	3,000	−10	3,200	−16
Test equipment	1,500	1,200	+25	1,500	0
Total	$ 8,700	$ 9,100	−4	$ 9,200	−5
Internal Failure Costs					
Reworking products	$ 8,500	$ 8,300	+2	N/A*	
Scrap and waste	2,200	2,400	−8	N/A*	
Storing and disposing of waste	4,400	5,700	−23	N/A*	
Reprocessing	1,800	1,600	+13	N/A*	
Rescheduling and setup	900	1,200	−25	N/A*	
Total	$ 17,800	$ 19,200	−7		
External Failure Costs					
Complaint handling	$ 5,800	$ 6,200	−6	N/A*	
Warranty handling	10,700	9,300	+15	N/A*	
Repairing or replacing returns	27,000	29,200	−8	N/A*	
Customer reimbursements	12,000	10,700	+12	N/A*	
Expediting	1,100	1,300	−15	N/A*	
Total	$ 56,600	$ 56,700	0		
Total quality costs	$133,200	$129,700	+3	$65,700	+103

*TQM advocates planning for zero defects; therefore, zero failure costs would be included in the budget.

analysis can be used by management to decide where to concentrate the quality prevention budget. This technique classifies the causes of process problems according to impact on an objective. For example, a computer and peripherals manufacturer might classify its warranty claim costs for the past year according to the type of product failure as follows:

WARRANTY COST BY TYPE OF FAILURE

Model	Monitor	CPU	Ports	Keyboard	Total Dollars
Desktop PCs	$15,000	$16,000	$12,000	$ 2,760	$ 45,760
Notebooks	10,360	15,000	7,000	3,000	35,360
Netbooks	6,000	8,880	3,000	5,000	22,880
Total	$31,360	$39,880	$22,000	$10,760	$104,000
Percent (rounded)	30	38	21	11	100

Model	Dollars	Percent of Total	Cumulative Percent of Total
Desktop PCs	$ 45,760	44	44
Notebooks	35,360	34	78
Netbooks	22,880	22	100
Total	$104,000	100	

Listing the total failure costs of all models in descending order of magnitude indicates that desktop PCs and notebooks account for 78 percent of total warranty costs. Also, CPU problems are the largest source of warranty costs. Therefore, management should focus efforts on identifying the causes of CPU problems for all models. This type of information allows management to devote the appropriate portion of its prevention efforts to minimizing or eliminating specific problems. This analysis should be conducted sufficiently often to detect trends quickly and make adjustments rapidly. As another example, a large restaurant chain could use Pareto analysis to prioritize service problems and thus determine where to devote the majority of its training efforts.

Exhibit 17.14 provides formulas for calculating an organization's total quality cost, using the prevention, appraisal, and failure categories. Some amounts used in these computations are, by necessity, estimates. It is more appropriate for businesses to use reasonable estimates of quality costs than to ignore such costs because of a lack of verifiable or

Exhibit 17.14 Formulas for Calculating Total Quality Cost

Calculating Lost Profits

Profit lost by selling units as defects = (Total defective units − Number of units reworked) × (Profit for good unit − Profit for defective unit)

$$Z = (D - Y)(P_1 - P_2)$$

Calculating Total Internal Costs of Failure

Rework cost = Number of units reworked × Cost to rework defective unit

$$R = (Y)(r)$$

Calculating Total External Costs of Failure

Cost of processing customer returns = Number of units returned × Cost of a return

$$W = (D_r)(w)$$

Total failure cost = Profit lost by selling units as defects + Rework cost + Cost of processing customer returns + Cost of warranty work + Cost of product recalls + Cost of litigation related to products + Opportunity cost of lost customers

$$F = Z + R + W + PR + L + O$$

Calculating the Total Quality Cost

Total quality cost = Total compliance cost + Total failure cost

T = (Prevention cost + Appraisal cost) + Total failure cost

$$T = K + A + F$$

Prevention and appraisal costs are total estimated amounts; no formulas are appropriate. As the cost of prevention rises, the number of defective units should decline. Additionally, as the cost of prevention rises, the cost of appraisal should decline; however, appraisal cost should never become zero.

Source: Adapted from James T. Godfrey and William R. Pasewark, "Controlling Quality Costs," *Management Accounting* (March 1988), p. 50.

precise amounts. Consider the following April 2013 operating information for O'Reilly Company:

Defective units (D)	5,000	Units reworked (Y)	2,400
Profit for good unit (P_1)	\$50	Profit for defective unit (P_2)	\$30
Cost to rework defective unit (r)	\$10	Units returned (Dr)	800
Cost of return (w)	\$15	Prevention cost (K)	\$80,000
Appraisal cost (A)	\$14,400		

Substituting these values into the cost of quality formulas provided in Exhibit 17.14 gives the following results:

$$Z = (D - Y)(P_1 - P_2) = (5{,}000 - 2{,}400)(\$50 - \$30) = 2{,}600 \times \$20 = \underline{\underline{\$52{,}000}}$$

$$R = (Y)(r) = (2{,}400)(\$10) = \underline{\underline{\$24{,}000}}$$

$$W = (D_r)(w) = (800)(\$15) = \underline{\underline{\$12{,}000}}$$

$$F = Z + R + W = \$52{,}000 + \$24{,}000 + \$12{,}000 = \underline{\underline{\$88{,}000}} \text{ total failure cost}$$

$$T = K + A + F = \$80{,}000 + \$14{,}400 + \$88{,}000 = \underline{\underline{\$182{,}400}} \text{ total quality cost}$$

Of the \$182,400 total quality cost, O'Reilly's managers need to identify the causes of the \$88,000 failure costs and work to eliminate those causes. Eliminating the failure causes should also affect the planned amounts of prevention and appraisal costs for future periods.

OBTAINING INFORMATION ABOUT QUALITY FROM THE CMS AND BSC

7 How are a cost management system and the balanced scorecard used to provide information on quality in an organization?

Today's business strategy of focusing on customers and quality requires a firm to manage costs so that a reasonable value-to-price relationship can be achieved. Although prices are commonly set in reference to the competitive market rather than to costs, companies lacking appropriate cost management skills cannot expect to succeed in the long run. Thus, organizations need to engage in cost management.

Cost management can be viewed as the use of management accounting information for the purpose(s) of

- setting and communicating organizational strategies;
- establishing, implementing, and monitoring the success of methods to accomplish the strategies; and
- assessing the level of success in meeting the promulgated strategies.

An organization's cost management system (CMS) should accumulate and report information related to organizational success in meeting or exceeding customer needs and expectations as well as quality-related goals and objectives. Managers can analyze and interpret such information to plan and control current activities and to make decisions about current and future courses of action.

In designing a CMS, consideration must be given to cost accumulation and process measurement activities. Cost accumulation for financial accounting purposes can be inadequate for strategy-based decisions. For instance, financial accounting requires that research and development (R&D) costs be expensed as incurred, but a product's cost is largely determined during the design stage. Design has implications for perceived product value, necessary production technology, ease of product manufacturability, product durability, and likelihood of product failure. Consequently, a CMS should accumulate design costs as part of product cost. This cost need not appear on the financial accounting statements, but it must exist for decision-making purposes in the cost management system.

In contrast to its treatment of R&D costs, financial accounting requires all production costs to be inventoried and does not distinguish whether they add customer value. A useful CMS differentiates between costs that add value and those that do not so that managers and employees can work to reduce the NVA costs and enhance continuous improvement.

Another CMS function relates to the production process. Financial accounting is monetarily based and, therefore, does not directly measure nonfinancial organizational activities. For example, the percent of automated production, percent of reworked units, number of customer complaints, and percent of repeat customers are not recorded in financial accounting. Additionally, many activities critical to success in a quality-oriented, global marketplace are related to time—a nonmonetary characteristic. A truly useful CMS ensures the availability of information related to nonmonetary occurrences (such as late deliveries or defect rates) and incorporates that information into a balanced scorecard (BSC) so that management can achieve TQM and profitability goals. The BSC allows TQM strategy to be viewed from four perspectives that are directly compatible with, and reflective of, four of the Baldrige Award categories:

Balanced Scorecard Perspective	Baldrige Category
Learning and Growth	Workforce focus
Internal Business	Operations focus
Customer Value	Customer focus
Financial Performance	Results

Also, both the BSC and the Baldrige criteria emphasize the use of nonfinancial performance measurements as indicators of progress toward organizational goals. Goals and measurements for the BSC perspectives are shown in Exhibit 17.15.[26]

Exhibit 17.15 Quality Measures of a Balanced Scorecard

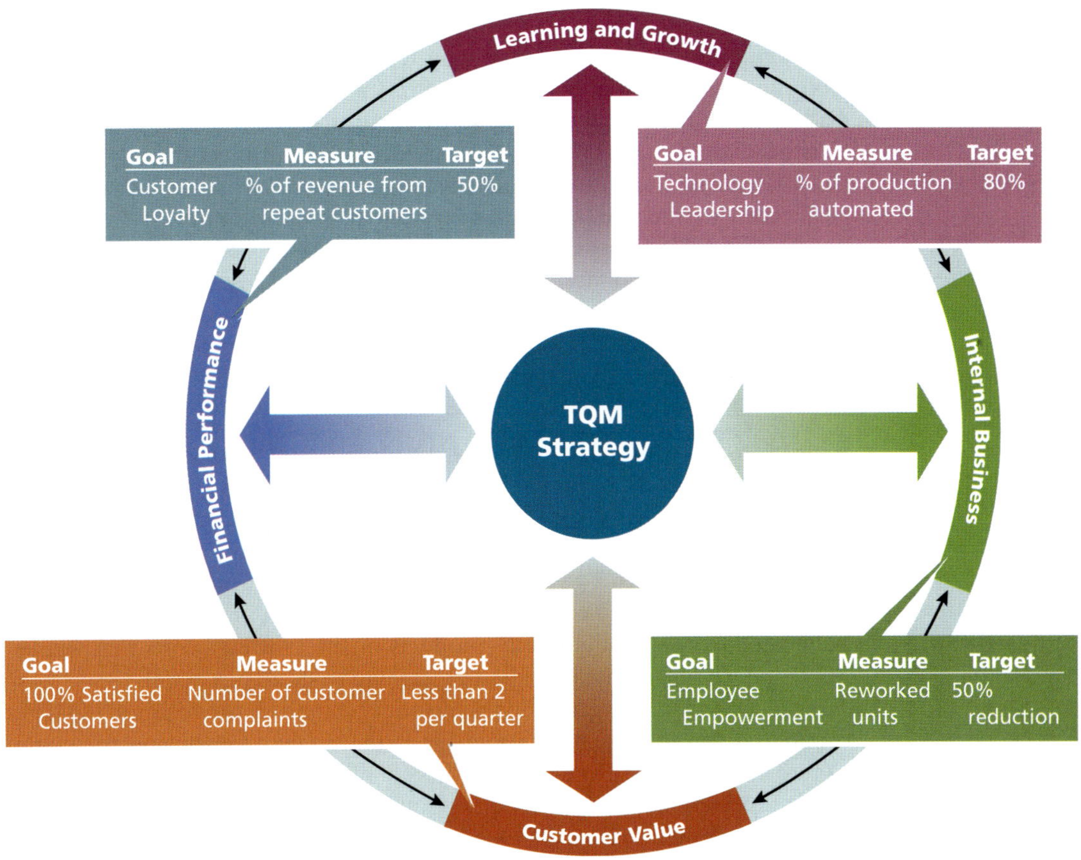

The following discussion illustrates how the BSC can be used to provide information on quality and help frame management decision processes. Assume that a company wants to fully automate its fiber-optic production line by year-end to reduce the number of product defects.

[26]Chapter 14 provides more discussion of the BSC.

Perspective	Process
Learning and Growth	Train employees to use new technologies and evaluate those employees on their success. Focus performance measurements on employee satisfaction, retention, and productivity.
Internal Business	Empower employees to troubleshoot production problems and manage quality. Monitor stoppages and compare NVA wait times and product defects before and after employee empowerment.
Customer Value	Ensure that all employees are focused on important customer criteria, such as speed (lead time), quality, service, and price (both original and after-purchase amounts). Empower sales staff to satisfy customers by offering discounts and allowances when production time is longer than expected or by servicing a product for a short time after the warranty period ends. Survey customers on satisfaction levels and compare with prior performance. Compare customer retention rates before and after new technologies were implemented.
Financial Performance	Analyze changes in revenues, sales returns, and cost of goods sold from prior periods. Compare market share before and after new technologies were implemented.

Continuous improvement is a long-term, rather than a short-term, organizational goal. Unfortunately, financial accounting reflects a short-term perspective of operating activity. Gathering monetary information and forcing it into a specific 12-month period does not clearly indicate to managers how today's decisions will affect the organization's long-run financial success. For instance, not investing in R&D would cause a company's short-run profitability to improve but could be disastrous in the long run.

Thus, a CMS should report more of the costs and benefits of organizational activities than do financial accounting reports. Having strategy-based information included in a BSC allows managers to make informed assessments of the company's performance in the value chain, its position of competitive advantage (or disadvantage), and its progress toward achieving the organization's mission.

QUALITY AS AN ORGANIZATIONAL CULTURE

8 How is quality instilled as part of an organization's culture?

Quality, propelled by changing customer needs and better competition, must be viewed as a moving target; thus, TQM is inseparable from the concept of continuous improvement. To provide the sense of working toward a common goal, continually higher performance standards must be set for everyone in the organization (not just for people in the production or service area). The TQM philosophy provides a new focus. In the future, it will not be the company with the "best" products or the "lowest" costs that will be successful; it will be the company that is the best at learning to do things better.[27]

The behavior of organizational personnel comprises the basis for TQM. Consistent and committed top management leadership is the catalyst for moving the company toward a culture in which all individuals, regardless of rank or position, are focused on exceeding customer expectations. Such an attitude should permeate all areas of the company, from R&D to product design, production, marketing, and distribution to customer and supplier relations to accounting and information processing. Management can effectively change its organizational culture by providing an environment in which employees know that the company cares about them, is responsive to their needs, and will appreciate and reward excellent results. This knowledge goes a long way in motivating employees to increase cooperation and making them feel trusted, respected, and comfortable. Such employees are more likely to treat customers in a similar manner.

The firm must empower employees to participate fully in the quest for excellence by providing the means by which employees gain pride, satisfaction, and substantive

[27] Tom Richman, "What Does Business Really Want from Government?" *The State of Small Business* (1995), p. 96.

involvement. The new corporate work environment involves the effective and appropriate use of teams and employees should be recognized and rewarded for being involved in

- team problem solving,
- contributing ideas for improvement,
- monitoring work processes,
- developing new skills, and
- sharing their knowledge and enthusiastic attitudes with their colleagues.

With its focus on process and customers, TQM is founded on one very obvious and simple principle:

Do the right things right the first time, all the time, on time, and continuously improve.

The heart of this principle is zero defects now and in the future. For example, a non-TQM production policy statement might read: "Defective production cannot be greater than one percent of total production." In contrast, TQM would state: "Zero-defect production will be achieved." Such a statement necessitates that management provide employees with the proper

- training,
- equipment,
- materials quality,
- encouragement,
- empowerment opportunities, and
- work environment to achieve the goal.

Exhibit 17.16 indicates how organizations have moved along the quality path—from passing information on "good" techniques within guilds of craftspeople to assuring quality through the inspection of goods and assessment of conformity with standards to installing in-process quality control techniques to competing for quality awards to focusing on long-term methods of continuous improvement. Companies have found that creating a quality

Exhibit 17.16 Moving toward True Quality

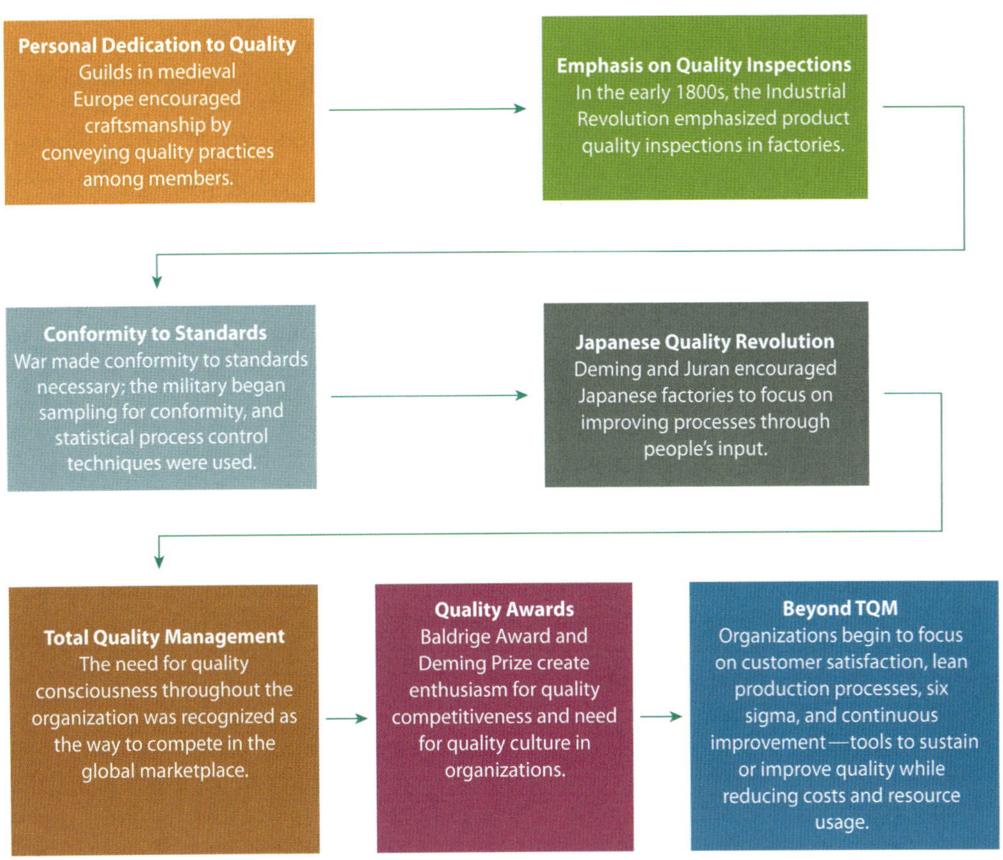

culture within all employees is a key to long-term customer satisfaction. When the firm has an imbedded "quality consciousness," it can be viewed as having achieved world-class status and will become the benchmark that others seek to emulate.

"High quality" is not a static concept; when one problem has been solved, another one is always waiting for a solution. The TQM philosophy cannot be integrated into an organization quickly; according to Dr. W. Edwards Deming, organizational changes take at least seven years. Therefore, in the time it takes for the changes necessitated by TQM implementation to be effected, today's organizations are bombarded with numerous technological innovations that require a reassessment of how customers view quality and how competitors are addressing quality issues. Achieving world-class status does not mark an ending point; it is only a resting point until the competition catches up and tries to race ahead.

APPENDIX

ASSESSING QUALITY INTERNATIONALLY

9 What international quality standards exist?

Most large companies view their markets on an international rather than a domestic basis. To compete effectively in a global environment, companies must recognize the need for, and be willing to initiate, compliance with a variety of international standards. Standards are essentially the international language of trade; they are formalized agreements that define the various contractual, functional, and technical requirements to assure customers that product, services, processes, and/or systems do what they are expected to do.

ISO

A primary international guideline for quality standards is the **ISO 9000 series**. This series was developed by the International Organization for Standardization (ISO), based in Geneva, Switzerland. Topics of the ISO 9000 "family" of standards are listed in Exhibit 17.17.

The ISO quality standards are written in a general manner and prescribe the generic design, material procurement, production, quality control, and delivery procedures necessary to achieve quality assurance. The directive is not a product standard and does not imply that ISO-certified companies have better products than competitors. The family of standards articulates what must be done to ensure quality, but management must decide how to meet the standards.

Compliance with ISO standards is required for regulated products sold in the European Union; however, there is no single organization that administers the program. Thus, companies seeking ISO certification must qualify under an internationally accepted registration program that is administered by a national registrar. Examples of such registrars in the United States and Great Britain are, respectively, Underwriters Laboratories and the British Standards Institution. After an internal review, a company deciding that it can meet the standards may apply for ISO registration. To be registered, a company must first submit to a **quality audit** by a third-party reviewer. Such an audit encompasses a review of product design activities, manufacturing processes and controls, quality documentation and records, and management quality policy and philosophy. After registration, teams visit the company biannually to monitor compliance.

Although registration costs are high, certified companies believe the benefits are even higher. Internally, certification helps ensure higher process consistency and quality and should help to reduce costs. Externally, ISO-certified companies have an important distinguishing characteristic from their noncertified competitors. Additionally, certified companies are listed in a registry of "approved" suppliers, which should increase business opportunities. The cost–benefit relationships of the quality system must be measured, documented, and reported under ISO requirements—all jobs for accountants.

ISO certification is not required for doing business in the United States, but many U.S. companies are ISO certified because of international sales. Even companies that do not sell overseas may seek ISO certification because of the operational and competitive benefits. If a company's competitors are in compliance with and registered under ISO standards, good business sense would recognize the necessity of becoming ISO certified.

Exhibit 17.17 ISO 9000 Family of Standards

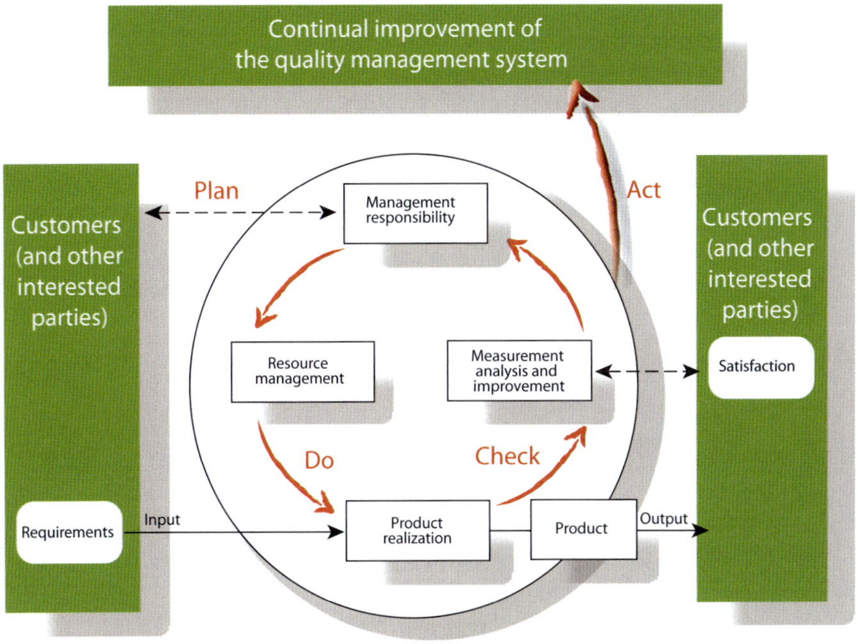

ISO 9001 provides guidance to establish a quality management system to fulfill customer needs and expectations.

ISO 9004 extends guidance on objectives of a quality management system beyond ISO 9001 (particularly for long-term organizational success) to all parties interested in or affected by operations; such parties include employees, owners, suppliers, partners and society in general.

ISO 19011 covers the area of auditing of quality management systems and environmental management systems.

Source: ISO, *The ISO 9000 Family—Core Standards* (Geneva, Switzerland: ISO, 2009); http://www.iso.org/iso/iso_catalogue/management_and_leadership_standards/quality_management/iso_9000_selection_and_use/iso_9000_family_core_standards.htm (accessed 1/23/12).

EFQM

The EFQM (formerly the European Foundation for Quality Management) was founded in 1988 by the presidents of 14 major European companies and with the endorsement of the European Commission. The EFQM's purpose was to develop a European framework for quality improvement similar to the Malcolm Baldrige National Quality Award in the United States and the Deming Prize in Japan. By 2012, the EFQM had over 500 members. The EFQM Excellence Model was originally introduced in 1991 and served as the basis of assessing applications for the European Quality Award. The first award was presented to Xerox in 1992 and the model has become the framework for many national and regional quality awards across Europe.[28] A revised model (shown in Exhibit 17.18, p. 710) was launched in September 2009. Each of the eight fundamental concepts are shown as "electrons" around an inner circle nucleus referred to as RADAR (Results, Approach, Deployment, and Assess & Refine). RADAR constitutes the assessment framework for the model.

The model is based on the premise that leadership is delivered through people, policy and strategy, and partnerships and resources, which all impact organizational processes. These factors enable organizations to achieve excellent results relative to people, customers, society, and performance. Thus, enablers describe what an organization does, whereas results describe what an organization achieves. Enablers cause results; feedback from results allows innovation and learning to take place, which, in turn, improves the enablers.

[28] Past winners of awards can be found at http://www.efqm.org/en/PdfResources/History%20of%20past%20winners.pdf (accessed 1/24/12).

Exhibit 17.18 EFQM Excellence Model

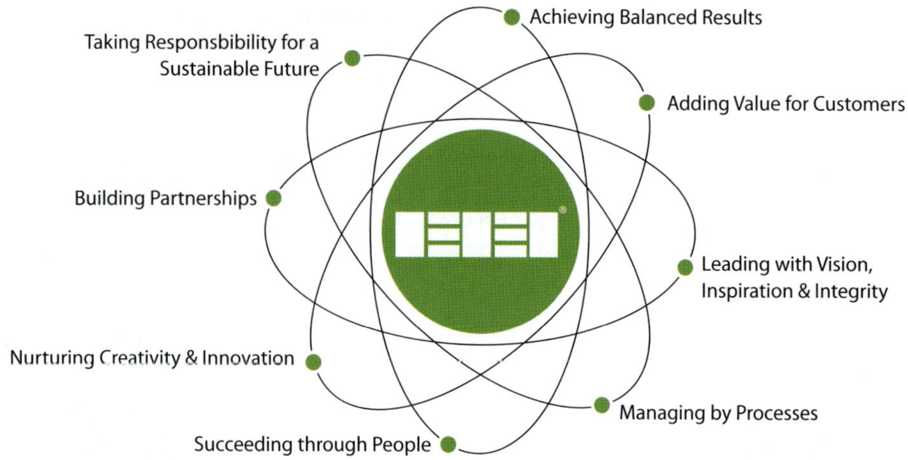

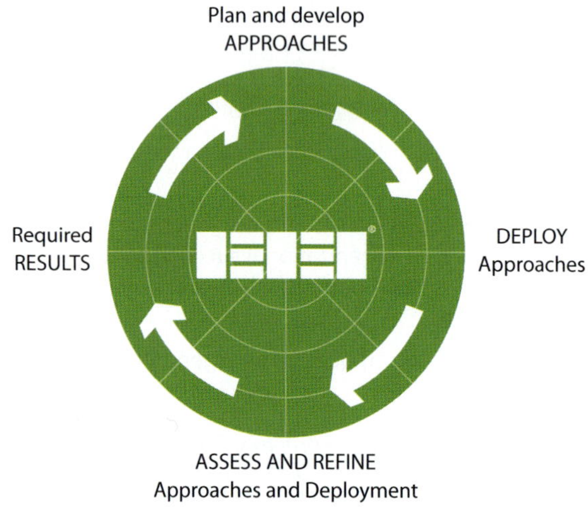

Source: EFQM, "Introducing the EFQM Excellence Model 2010," http://www.efqm.org/en/PdfResources/EFQMModel_Presentation.pdf (accessed 1/24/12).

The EFQM model's effectiveness is indicated by its widespread use as a management system and a means of organizational self-assessment. The model indicates gaps between where companies are and where they want to be so that management can take the necessary steps to minimize those gaps. The model is nonprescriptive in that it does not provide a road map for the path to organizational excellence, but the following fundamental concepts provide the foundation for improvement. These concepts are not listed in a particular order, and the listing is seen as flexible and subject to change as companies develop and improve.[29]

- *Achieving balanced results:* Focus is on developing a key set of results to monitor progress against the vision, mission, and strategy so that leaders can made effective and timely decisions.
- *Adding value for customers:* Focus is on clearly defining and communicating the value proposition and engaging customers in product and service design processes.
- *Leading with vision, inspiration, and integrity:* Focus is on the ability of leaders to adapt, react, and gain stakeholder commitment for organizational success.
- *Managing by processes:* Focus is on how processes are designed to deliver organizational strategy beyond the "classic" boundaries.
- *Succeeding through people:* Focus is on balancing organizational strategic needs and people's personal expectations and aspirations to gain their commitment.

[29] EFQM, "Introducing the EFQM Excellence Model 2010," http://www.efqm.org/en/PdfResources/EFQMModel_Presentation.pdf (last accessed 1/23/12).

- *Nurturing creativity and innovation:* Focus on the need to develop and engage stakeholders as potential sources of creativity and innovation.
- *Building partnerships:* Focus is on building partnerships, including those beyond the supply chain, and basing these on sustainable mutual benefits to succeed.
- *Taking responsibility for a sustainable future:* Focus is on taking responsibility for the organization's conduct and activities and managing its impact on the wider community by striving for economic, social, and ecological sustainability.

These underpinnings of this model relate to both the Baldrige criteria and the balanced scorecard perspectives.

Comprehensive Review Module

KEY TERMS

appraisal cost, p. 698
benchmarking, p. 689
control chart, p. 686
cost of compliance, p. 698
cost of noncompliance, p. 699
external failure cost, p. 698
grade, p. 688
internal benchmarking, p. 691
internal failure cost, p. 698
ISO 9000 series, p. 708
Pareto analysis, p. 701
prevention cost, p. 698
process benchmarking, p. 691
quality, p. 685
quality audit, p. 708
quality control (QC), p. 686
results benchmarking, p. 691
reverse engineering, p. 691
Six Sigma, p. 686
statistical process control (SPC), p. 686
strategic benchmarking, p. 691
total quality management (TQM), p. 692
value, p. 688

CHAPTER SUMMARY

1 Quality Definition and Perspective

- Quality is the sum of all characteristics of a product or service that influence its ability to meet the needs of the person acquiring that product or service.
- Quality, from a production viewpoint, is defined as conformity with requirements and, from this viewpoint, can be improved by
  - increasing the good output generated from a specific amount of input during a period.
  - reducing variability, often by adding automation in the process.
  - reducing the product's or service's failure rate.
- Determination of conformity to standards is often made using statistical process control techniques, including control charts.
- Many companies focus on a Six Sigma production view of quality, which means that a process produces no more than 3.4 defects per million "opportunities."
- Quality, from a consumer viewpoint, is defined as the ability to meet and satisfy all specified needs at a reasonable cost.
- Characteristics of product quality from a consumer viewpoint include
  - performance,
  - features,
  - reliability,
  - conformance,
  - durability,
  - serviceability and responsiveness,
  - aesthetics, and
  - perceived value.

- A consumer viewpoint is typically seen as the better perspective and should encompass
  - making certain that the product or service delivers what was intended.
  - ascertaining that the product or service fulfills consumer needs relative to a grade versus value perspective.

2 Benchmarking Definition, Rationale, and Types

- Benchmarking refers to investigating, comparing, and evaluating a company's products, processes, and/or services against those of competitors or companies believed to be "best in class."
- A company benchmarks to obtain an understanding of another's production and performance methods so that the company can identify its strengths and weaknesses.
- Benchmarking may be one of four types:
  - internal benchmarking, in which organizational units are compared to each other, with the lower performers "learning" from the higher performers;
  - results benchmarking, in which an end product or service is examined using reverse engineering to focus on product/service specifications and performance results; this type of benchmarking is performed on competitors' products or services;
  - process benchmarking, in which a specific process is examined to determine how a "best-in-class" company achieves its results; this type of benchmarking is often performed on noncompetitors although competitors may also be used; and
  - strategic benchmarking, in which the focus is on understanding how successful companies compete.

3 Total Quality Management (TQM)

- TQM involves all organizational employees and places the customer at the center of focus.
- TQM is defined as seeking continuous improvement in processes so as to meet or exceed customer expectations.
- TQM requires the following conditions to yield full benefits:
  - sharing planning and decision making among personnel;
  - eliminating non-value-added activities;
  - enhancing technology in hardware, production processes, and management systems that increase productivity;
  - increasing consumer awareness of the numerous types and grades of products available; and
  - using competitive benchmarking to close any performance gaps.

4 Malcolm Baldrige National Quality Award (Baldrige Award)

- The Baldrige Award is the highest award for quality given in the United States.
- The Baldrige Award focuses attention on management systems, processes, consumer satisfaction, and business results as the tools required to achieve product and service excellence.
- There are three versions of Baldrige criteria: business and not-for-profit, education, and health care.
- To win the award, applicants must show excellence in seven categories.
- Japan's equivalent of the Baldrige Award is the Deming Prize. Deming Prize winners may also apply for the Japan Quality Medal.

5 Types and Relationships of Quality Costs

- Quality costs include costs of compliance (or assurance), which are expenditures incurred to reduce or eliminate the current costs of quality failure and to continuously improve in the future. Compliance costs include
  - prevention costs that are incurred to minimize or eliminate the production of nonconforming products and services. The incurrence of prevention costs tend to reduce the costs of appraisal and failure.
  - appraisal costs that are incurred to identify units of output that do not conform to product specifications. The incurrence of appraisal costs tends to reduce the costs of external failure and increase the costs of internal failure.
- Quality costs include the costs of noncompliance (or quality failure), which include
  - internal failure costs that are incurred to remediate a nonconforming product that is detected through appraisal activities before that product is shipped to a customer. Incurrence of internal failure costs tends to reduce external failure costs.
  - external failure costs that are incurred to remediate a nonconforming product that is not detected until after being shipped to the customer.
- Compliance and noncompliance costs are inversely related. As compliance costs increase, noncompliance costs will fall.

6 Measurement of the Cost of Quality

- The total cost of quality is equal to prevention cost plus appraisal cost plus failure cost.
- The cost of failure includes the following costs:
  - profits lost by selling defective units,
  - rework of defective goods,
  - processing customer returns,
  - warranty work,
  - product recalls,
  - litigation related to products, and
  - opportunity cost of lost customers.

7 Use of Cost Management System (CMS) and Balanced Scorecard (BSC) to Provide Information on Quality in an Organization

- The CMS can be used to compute the
  - quality costs incurred for production/service activities,
  - costs of non-value-added activities,
  - product/service life cycle costs, and/or
  - rework costs.
- A CMS can be used to excerpt quality information that is typically "buried" in traditional financial accounting cost categories.
- The BSC can be used to develop measurements to compute
  - manufacturing cycle efficiency,
  - time to market for new products,
  - customer satisfaction levels,
  - on-time deliveries,
  - defect rates, and/or
  - success rates of research and development activities.
- Measurements developed for the BSC fit into four of the Baldrige Award categories.

8 Quality as Part of Organizational Culture

- Quality can be instilled as part of an organization's culture by
  - having committed and consistent top management leadership.
  - developing an esprit de corps among all employees so that they are eager to meet and exceed customer expectations.
  - making certain that a work environment is provided in which employees know that the company cares about and will reward efforts to achieve high quality.
  - empowering employees.
  - providing job and quality training.
  - encouraging the pursuit of quality awards.

SOLUTION STRATEGIES

Cost of Quality Components, p. 698

Total Cost of Quality = Cost of Compliance + Cost of Noncompliance

Cost of Compliance: Prevention Costs; Appraisal Costs

Cost of Noncompliance: Internal Failure Costs; External Failure Costs

Costs of noncompliance are inversely related to the costs of compliance and are a direct result of the number of defects.

Dimensions of product quality include

- conformity to specifications,
- effective and efficient performance,
- durability,
- ease of use,
- safety,
- comfort of use, and
- appeal.

Cost of Quality Formulas, p. 713

Profit lost by selling units as defects = (Total defective units − Number of units reworked) × (Profit for good unit − Profit for defective unit)

$$Z = (D - Y)(P_1 - P_2)$$

Rework cost = Number of units reworked × Cost to rework defective unit

$$R = (Y)(r)$$

Cost of processing customer returns = Number of units returned × Cost of a return

$$W = (D_r)(w)$$

Total failure cost = Profit lost by selling units as defects + Rework cost + Cost of processing customer returns + Cost of warranty work + Cost of product recalls + Cost of litigation related to products + Opportunity cost of lost customers

$$F = Z + R + W + PR + L + O$$

Total quality cost = Total compliance cost + Total failure cost

T = (Prevention cost + Appraisal cost) + Total failure cost

T = K + A + F

DEMONSTRATION PROBLEM

Burrow Corp.'s quality report for October 2013 showed the following information:

Profit for a good unit	$76
Profit for a defective unit	$44
Cost to rework a defective unit	$14
Cost to process a returned unit	$20
Total prevention cost	$54,000
Total appraisal cost	$32,000
Litigation related to product failure	$140,000
Opportunity cost of lost customers while litigation is being settled	$100,000
Total defective units	4,000
Number of units reworked	2,800
Number of customer units returned	1,300

Required:

Compute the following:

a. Profit lost by selling unreworked defects
b. Total rework cost
c. Cost of processing customer returns
d. Total failure cost
e. Total quality cost

Solution to Demonstration Problem

a. $Z = (D - Y)(P_1 - P_2) = (4{,}000 - 2{,}800)(\$76 - \$44) = 1{,}200(\$32) = \underline{\underline{\$38{,}400}}$

b. $R = (Y)(r) = (2{,}800)(\$14) = \underline{\underline{\$39{,}200}}$

c. $W = (D_r)(w) = (1{,}300)(\$20) = \underline{\underline{\$26{,}000}}$

d. $F = (Z + R + W + L + O) = \$38{,}400 + \$39{,}200 + \$26{,}000 + \$140{,}000 + \$100{,}000 = \underline{\underline{\$343{,}600}}$

e. $T = (K + A + F) = \$54{,}000 + \$32{,}000 + \$343{,}600 = \underline{\underline{\$429{,}600}}$

POTENTIAL ETHICAL ISSUES

ETHICS

1. Ignoring the actual range of acceptable variation on control charts to accept a higher level of defects than allowed and thus creating a higher possibility of external failure costs
2. Using lower-grade raw material and components than specified for production activities to reduce costs while continuing to promote the company's high-quality products
3. Using the benchmarking process as an opportunity to illegally gain information or product designs from competitors
4. Creating a set of preferred supplier characteristics that fosters discrimination against minority suppliers
5. Consciously choosing to discount internal information about product defects and failures that could result in significant consumer or environmental harm
6. Minimizing estimates of internal and external failure costs to justify retaining current practices rather than engaging in expenditures that would, in the long run, be cost beneficial

7. Communicating the importance of implementing total quality management within the firm while simultaneously encouraging practices that will cause TQM to fail (i.e., talking the talk, but not walking the walk)
8. "Low-ball" pricing a product to encourage consumer purchases, only to charge exorbitant repair costs when the product breaks after the warranty period (which the company was aware would happen given internal testing)

QUESTIONS

1. What is meant by the term *quality*? In defining quality, from what two perspectives can a definition be formulated? Why are both important?
2. In conducting activity analyses, the presence of certain activities indicates low production process quality. List five of these activities.
3. Compare and contrast the eight characteristics that constitute overall quality from the customer's perspective with the three additional characteristics that constitute service quality from the customer's perspective.
4. Locate a well-described product on the Internet. Discuss how that product exemplifies the eight overall quality characteristics. Prepare a balanced scorecard for this product assuming that its manufacturer has a total quality management strategy.
5. Describe four types of benchmarking. Use the Internet to find a company that has engaged in benchmarking. Describe the type of benchmarking used and the benefits and costs of the company's experience.
6. What is TQM? What are the four important tenets of TQM, and why are they important?
7. What is the Malcolm Baldrige National Quality Award? Why would an organization apply for that award?

INTERNET

8. In the production–sales cycle, what are the four points at which quality costs are incurred? How are these costs interrelated through these points?
9. How can Pareto analysis help focus managerial efforts on reducing the costs of quality-related problems?
10. How does strategic cost management link information to corporate strategies?
11. (Appendix) Why might a common set of global quality standards be needed or desirable?
12. (Appendix) What is a quality audit?
13. (Appendix) Compare and contrast the EFQM Excellence Model with the Malcolm Baldrige National Quality Award criteria.

EXERCISES

14. **LO.1 (Quality definition; research; writing)** Use the Internet to find four definitions of quality.
    a. Compare and contrast each of the four definitions with specific emphasis on whether the definition includes conformity or customer orientation.
    b. Assume that you are the manager of (1) a copy store and (2) a kitchen blender manufacturer. Prepare definitions of quality to distribute to your employees and discuss how you would measure service/product adherence to those definitions.

INTERNET

15. **LO.1, LO.2, & LO.5 (True/False)** Mark each of the following statements as true or false and explain why the false statements are incorrect.
    a. Appraisal cost is used to monitor and correct mistakes.
    b. Total quality management focuses on production processes rather than on customer satisfaction.
    c. Results benchmarking relies only on comparisons to firms within the same industry.
    d. Pareto analysis is used to help managers identify areas in which to focus quality-improvement efforts.
    e. SPC control charts are used to plot the costs of quality over time.
    f. Higher quality yields lower profits but higher productivity.

g. Traditional accounting systems have separate accounts to capture quality costs.
h. As the number of defective products manufactured rises, internal failure costs also rise but external failure costs are expected to decline.
i. Quality is free.
j. The total quality cost is the sum of prevention cost plus failure cost.

16. **LO.2 (Benchmarking)** The call center of Wobegon Electric Company handles 1.2 million calls per year. The average call requires six minutes of operator time, and 40 percent of the calls require a supervisor to be involved for at least half of the call time. Operators are paid $9 per hour, and supervisors are paid $15 per hour. After Wobegon Electric engaged in process benchmarking, call times were reduced by one minute, and the number of supervisor-involved calls were reduced by 15 percent. The benchmarking study cost Wobegon Electric Company $200,000.

    a. What was Wobegon Electric's total labor cost and labor cost per call at the call center prior to benchmarking?
    b. What was Wobegon Electric's total labor cost and labor cost per call at the call center after benchmarking? (Round up to the nearest penny.)
    c. If the new results are expected to continue for three years, was engaging in the benchmarking study profitable to Wobegon Electric Company? Show calculations.

17. **LO.1 (Statistical process control; writing)** Statistical process control (SPC) can be used in any process with identified errors, defects, or problems. Assume that you are in charge of analyzing defect at a software manufacturing facility.

    a. What is the primary goal of SPC?
    b. How would you define a defect in your organization?
    c. What defect information would you want to record in such an organization?
    d. Why would you want to record the types of defects?
    e. How do severity and priority of the defect affect your actions?

INTERNET

18. **LO.1 (Product defects)** According to the 2011 J.D. Power and Associates Reports, **Lexus** models have the fewest quality problems in the industry, with just 73 problems per 100 vehicles. **Honda** and **Acura** products follow with 86 and 89 problems per 100 vehicles.

    Source: J.D. Power and Associates, "J.D. Power and Associates Reports: Initial Quality of Recent Vehicle Launches is Considerably Lower than in 2010, while Carryover Model Quality is Better than Ever," Press Release 6/ 23/11); http://businesscenter.jdpower.com/JDPAContent/CorpComm/News/content/Releases/pdf/2011089-uiqs.pdf (accessed 1/24/12).

    a. Using the calculator at http://www.databison.com/index.php/six-sigma-calculator-in-excel/ (last accessed 1/24/12), calculate failure rate, accuracy rate, and current and long-term sigma levels for each of the three companies.
    b. Why would the sigma levels tend to be higher in the long-term?
    c. Why is the information provided by these calculations not totally helpful?

EXCEL

19. **LO.1 (Control chart)** Johnny Cantalore, owner of Ba-Da-Bing Pizza, has a policy to put 36 slices of pepperoni on a large pizza. Cantalore recently hired two college students to work part-time making pizzas and decided to observe them at their jobs for a few days. Cantalore gathered the following data on number of pepperoni slices being used on the pizzas:

    11:00 A.M. to 5:00 P.M.

    Thirteen pizzas were made containing the following number of pepperoni slices:
    36, 35, 41, 33, 35, 36, 34, 39, 44, 38, 32, 36, 35

    5:00 P.M. to 11:00 P.M.

    Twenty-five pizzas were made containing the following number of pepperoni slices:
    36, 36, 41, 42, 37, 39, 44, 40, 44, 37, 48, 36, 35, 40, 39, 41, 31, 36, 36, 42, 45, 44, 37, 37, 36

    a. Prepare a control chart for pepperoni slices.
    b. What information does the chart provide to Cantalore?

20. **LO.1 (Definition of quality; quality characteristics; writing)** In a three-person team, role-play the following individuals who are visiting a local car dealership: (1) a 19-year-old college student, (2) one-half of a young married couple with two children, and (3) a retired person. Each individual is interested in purchasing a new automobile.

  a. How does each customer define quality in an automobile? Explain the reasons for the differences.
  b. What vehicle characteristics are important to each type of buyer? Which vehicle characteristics are unique to each buyer?

21. **LO.1 (Quality characteristics; writing)** Choose one product and one service with which you are well acquainted. Indicate how the product and service each meet (or do not meet) the eight overall quality characteristics. For the service, indicate how it meets (or does not meet) the three additional characteristics for service quality.

22. **LO.2 (Benchmarks; research; writing)** In 2002, a green engineering case study about automobile emissions and saving energy was performed. The study generated designs for both gasoline- and diesel-powered automobiles with the following characteristics: a mid-size sedan that would get 52 miles per gallon when equipped with a gasoline engine and 68 miles per gallon when equipped with a diesel engine. The automobiles were also designed to be capable of achieving a "Five-Star" crash safety rating based on the anticipated 2004 safety standards, and would cost no more to build than traditionally engineered mid-size sedans.

INTERNET

Source: William Obenchain, Marcel van Schaik, and Pete Peterson, "Green Engineering Case Study: Reducing Automobile Emissions and Saving Energy" (4/11/02); http://www.epa.gov/oppt/greenengineering/pubs/ulsab-avc.pdf (accessed 1/24/12).

  a. Use the Internet to obtain miles per gallon and crash test ratings for five new automobiles (either gasoline or diesel). How do these automobiles compare to the benchmarks of the 2002 case study?
  b. What might cause the differences between the ratings for the automobiles selected and the benchmarks?

23. **LO.2 & LO.5 (Benchmarks; quality costs; writing)** For a benchmark, assume that the average firm incurs quality costs in the following proportions:

Prevention	30%
Appraisal	25%
Internal failure	15%
External failure	30%
Total costs	100%

Why might each of the following industries be inclined to have a spending pattern on quality costs that differs from the benchmark?

  a. Pharmaceutical company
  b. Department store
  c. Computer manufacturer
  d. Used-car retailer
  e. Lawn service company

24. **LO.3 (Cost and benefit of TQM; writing)** Colleges and universities have a variety of internal and external customers. Use a team of three or four individuals to answer the following:

  a. Who are three internal and two external customers of a college or university?
  b. How would each of the customers from (a) define product or service quality at a college or university? Do any of these views conflict and, if so, how?
  c. Are a college or university's internal customers as important as external customers? Explain the rationale for your answer.

25. **LO.3 (TQM; writing)** Different sources indicate differing key elements of total quality management, but integrity, training, leadership, and communication are four items that

seem to be essential. Discuss why you think that these four elements are critical to an effective TQM program and why disregard of each could invalidate such a program.

26. **LO.3 (Supplier quality; writing)** **Honda Motor Co. Ltd.** has paid for full-page advertisements in *The Wall Street Journal* that did not discuss any Honda products, refer to year-end earnings, or announce a new stock issuance. Instead, the ads informed readers that "buying quality parts is important to this company." The ads named Honda suppliers and identified their locations. Prepare a brief essay to answer the following questions:

   a. Why would Honda want newspaper readers to know what suppliers it uses?
   b. Do you think these advertisements would have any benefit for Honda itself? Discuss the rationale for your answer.

INTERNET

27. **LO.3 (Research; supplier relationships; writing)** Find a company's Web site that provides information on the characteristics that are desired for that company when establishing long-term/preferred supplier relationships.

   a. What characteristics are listed? Why do you think each of these is important?
   b. Did the characteristics within the list or elsewhere on the Web site address supplier diversity? Do you believe that supplier diversity is necessary? Why or why not?

28. **LO.3 (TQM; sustainability; writing)** Discuss how corporate sustainability programs are similar in direction and implementation to total quality management programs.

29. **LO.5 (Quality costs)** Harmon's Hardware has gathered the following data on its quality costs for 2012 and 2013:

Defect Prevention Costs	2012	2013
Quality training	$4,500	$6,250
Quality technology	4,750	5,200
Quality production design	2,000	4,700

External Failure Costs	2012	2013
Warranty handling	$7,500	$4,600
Customer reimbursements	5,500	3,900
Customer returns handling	3,500	1,900

   a. Compute the percentage change in the two quality cost categories from 2012 to 2013.
   b. Write a brief explanation for the pattern of change in the two categories.

30. **LO.5 & LO.6 (Quality costs)** The accounting system for Dolment Co. reflected the following quality costs for 2012 and 2013:

	2012	2013
Customer refunds for poor product quality	$37,000	$29,000
Fitting machines for mistake-proof operations	9,400	11,800
Supply chain management activities	9,000	10,000
Waste disposal	44,000	36,000
Quality training	26,000	30,000
Litigation claims for product defects	81,000	64,000

   a. Which of these are costs of compliance, and which are costs of noncompliance?
   b. Calculate the percentage change in each cost and for each category. (Round to the nearest whole percentage.)
   c. Discuss the pattern of the changes in the two categories.

31. **LO.5 (Quality costs; writing)** Sometimes a company, in its efforts to reduce costs, might also reduce quality.

   a. What kinds of costs could an organization reduce that would almost automatically lower product/service quality?
   b. If quality improvements create cost reductions, why would cost reductions not create quality improvements?
   c. Are there instances in which cost reductions would create quality improvements? Explain.

32. **LO.5 (Quality costs; writing)** Seymour Inc. has prepared the following summary quality cost report for 2013:

Prevention costs	$1,560,000
Appraisal costs	1,800,000
Internal failure costs	2,280,000
External failure costs	1,680,000
Total quality costs	$7,320,000

The company is actively striving to reduce total quality costs. Its current strategy is to increase spending in one or more quality cost categories in the hope of achieving greater spending cuts in other quality cost categories. Prepare a presentation that answers the following questions.

a. Which spending categories are most susceptible to control by managers? Why?
b. Why is it more logical for the company to increase spending in the prevention cost and appraisal cost categories than in the failure cost categories?
c. Which cost category is the most likely target for an increase in spending? Explain.
d. How would the adoption of a TQM philosophy affect the focus in reducing quality costs?

33. **LO.5 (Quality costs; ethics; writing)** By building quality into a process rather than having quality inspections at the end of the process, certain job functions (such as that of quality control inspector) can be eliminated. Additionally, the installation of automated equipment to monitor product processing could eliminate some line worker jobs.

ETHICS

In a company facing bankruptcy, would attempts to implement quality improvements that resulted in employee terminations be appreciated or condemned? Discuss your answer from the standpoint of a variety of concerned constituencies, including the consumers who purchase the company's products.

34. **LO.5 (Quality costs; writing)** Hartigay Manufacturing is evaluating its quality control costs for 2013 and preparing the budget for 2014. Quality costs incurred at the company for 2013 are as follows:

Prevention costs	$ 450,000
Appraisal costs	150,000
Internal failure costs	525,000
External failure costs	150,000
Total	$1,275,000

Prepare a memo to the company president on the following issues:

a. Which categories of quality costs would be affected by the decision to spend $2,250,000 on new computer chip–making equipment that would replace older equipment? Why?
b. If projected external failure costs for 2014 can be reduced 60 percent (relative to 2013 levels) by spending either $75,000 more on appraisal or $120,000 more on prevention, why might the firm opt to spend the $120,000 on prevention rather than the $75,000 on appraisal?

35. **LO.6 (Cost of quality)** Customer returns were getting out of control at The Electronic Toy Shack. Approximately 65 percent of the toys carried by the company are made in China or Taiwan. Customers were queried by sales personnel when goods were returned about the reason for the return. After six months of gathering information from customers who provided responses, Toy Shack management had the following data.

Type of Complaint	Number of Complaints
Did not perform as expected	28
Found item cheaper elsewhere	125
Instructions too complicated	59
Instruction wording unclear	85
Missing parts/manual	14
Changed mind	17

(Continued)

Type of Complaint	Number of Complaints
Used too many batteries too quickly	31
Wasn't fun	19
Other	12

a. Determine the percentage of complaints in each category and the cumulative percentage beginning with the largest complaint category.
b. Create a Pareto chart. (Directions on doing this with Microsoft Excel can be found at http://www.ehow.com/way_5798817_do-pareto-chart-microsoft-excel_.html.) Are these data consistent with the Pareto principle?
c. What actions would you suggest to Toy Shack's management to help resolve customer compliant issues?

36. **LO.6 (Cost of quality)** Managers at Walla-Walla LTD want to determine the company's cost of quality. The following information has been gathered from the records for August 2013:

Defective units	6,000
Units reworked	1,200
Defective units returned	400
Appraisal costs	$17,500
Cost per unit for rework	$18
Prevention costs	$85,000
Profit per good unit produced and sold	$85
Profit per defective unit sold	$43
Cost per unit for customer returns	$14
Cost of warranty work	$9,000

Compute the following:

a. Lost profits from selling defective work
b. Total costs of failure
c. Total quality cost

37. **LO.6 (Cost of quality)** Management at Goliath Corp. (located in Birmingham, Alabama) wants to use Pareto analysis to determine what issues to address relative to customer service at its call center. A survey was taken of customers and the following information was gathered about customer complaints.

Type of Complaint	Number of Complaints
Placed on hold for too long	391
No one available on weekends	63
Rude	49
Too many transfers	30
Hard to understand representative	124
Representative didn't understand problem	91
Other	18

a. Determine the percentage of complaints in each category and the cumulative percentage beginning with the largest complaint category.
b. Create a Pareto chart. (Directions on doing this with Microsoft Excel can be found at http://www.ehow.com/way_5798817_do-pareto-chart-microsoft-excel_.html.) Are these data consistent with the Pareto principle?
c. What actions would you suggest to Goliath's management to help resolve customer compliant issues?

EXCEL

38. **LO.6 (Cost of quality)** The following production information about quality costs has been gathered for June 2013:

Total defective units	720
Number of units reworked	595
Number of units returned	85
Total prevention cost	$27,600
Total appraisal cost	$8,500

Per-unit profit for defective units	\$20
Per-unit profit for good units	\$55
Cost to rework defective units	\$18
Cost to handle returned units	\$14

Using these data, calculate the following:

a. Total cost to rework
b. Profit lost from not reworking all defective units
c. Cost of processing customer returns
d. Total failure costs
e. Total quality cost

39. **LO.7 (Quality information system; team activity; writing)** Your company is interested in developing information about quality but has a traditional accounting system that does not provide such information directly. In a three- or four-person team, prepare a set of recommendations about how to improve the company's information system to eliminate or reduce this deficiency. In your recommendations, also explain in what areas management would have the most difficulty satisfying its desire for more information about quality and why these areas were chosen.

40. **LO.7 (Balanced scorecard; writing)** Find The Benchmarking Exchange on the Internet.

INTERNET

a. What are the five most actively benchmarked business processes of members of the exchange?
b. Why do you think benchmarking processes related to managing human resources rank highly on the benchmarking interest list of companies? Why would information systems technology be ranked higher?
c. What are the top five organizations involved in benchmarking? Choose one and provide a brief description of that organization and why benchmarking would be important to that organization.
d. Explain how benchmarking can be used to implement balanced scorecard goals and targets for each of its four perspectives for a company with a total quality management strategy.

PROBLEMS

41. **LO.1 (Quality and strategy; writing)** Three possible goals for a business are to (1) maximize profits, (2) maximize shareholder wealth, and (3) satisfy customer wants and needs. If goal (1) or (2) is chosen, the primary measurements of "success" are organizational profitability or stock price.

a. Do you believe that one of these three goals can be chosen to the exclusion of the others? Discuss the rationale for your answer.
b. How can total quality management help an organization meet all of these goals?
c. How might the selection of goal (1) or (2) lead to quality problems in an organization? Would the selection of goal (3) be likely to lead to quality problems? Explain.

42. **LO.1 & LO.2 (Quality problems; benchmarking; research; ethics; writing)** In 2008, pharmaceutical company Genentech withdrew its psoriasis drug Raptiva from the market because it was linked to a rare but often fatal brain disorder (progressive multifocal leukoencephalopathy) in patients who used the medication. There were about 2,000 patients in the United States taking the drug. Genentech expected to record an approximate \$125 million cost of sales increase for the first half of 2009 for the withdrawal. Genentech was acquired in March 2009 by Roche Holding AG.

INTERNET

ETHICS

Source: Ron Winslow, "Genentech Pulls Raptiva Psoriasis Drug," *Wall Street Journal* (4/9/09), p. B3.

a. Find information on the web about problems in the pharmaceutical industry. Be certain to review Genentech's annual report information related to Raptiva. Discuss your findings.

b. Compare Genentech's 2008 profits with those of other firms in the industry.
c. Discuss why a total quality management system would be more important in pharmaceutical companies than in most other companies.

ETHICS

43. **LO.1 (Quality problems; research; ethics; writing)** In mid-2007, numerous products produced in China were found unsafe, including pet food, fish, toothpaste, toys, and fireworks. In early 2008, the FDA pointed to Chinese companies as the source of contaminated heparin, a widely used blood thinner. Reports of at least 81 deaths linked to contaminated heparin in the United States set off withdrawals of the product in 11 countries. "The key ingredient in heparin is made from slaughtered pig intestines, much of which comes from China, often from small family workshops." In early 2009, it was found that "two Chinese-based companies shipped contaminated heparin to the U.S. between 2007 and 2008 and one company lied to federal health regulators about [its] role in the matter."

Sources: Christopher Bowe, Geoff Dyer, and Andrew Jack, "China Hits at Baxter in Heparin Probe," *Financial Times* (5/6/08); Jared Favole and Alicia Mundy, "FDA Cites Two Chinese Heparin Makers," *Wall Street Journal* (4/18/09).

a. Research problems with Chinese products and write a short summary that identifies what prior or current products were or are involved and the problems experienced with those products.
b. What conditions in China might have contributed to the quality problems?
c. Do you think that all Chinese products of a similar type should be banned if significant quality problems are found in several like products? Explain the rationale for your answer.

INTERNET

44. **LO.4 (Baldrige Award; research; writing)** Go to the Web site for the Malcolm Baldrige National Quality Award and find the answers to the following questions:

a. When and why were the health and education categories established?
b. How do the criteria for the health, education, and manufacturing categories differ? Why are such differences necessary?
c. Choose one of the education recipients and review its profile and application summary. Consider the category of student/stakeholder satisfaction and relationships. Compare your educational institution with the winner.

INTERNET

45. **LO.4 (Baldrige Award; writing)** Go to the Web site for the Malcolm Baldrige National Quality Award and find the questionnaire titled "Are We Making Progress?"

a. Download the questionnaire and answer the questions relative to your place of employment or university. Ask four of your colleagues to independently do the same.
b. Compare and contrast the five sets of answers. How would you rank your organization's "progress" solely based on the information from these questionnaires?

EXCEL

46. **LO.5 (Quality costs; Pareto analysis)** Pierre-Paul Appliances identified the following failure costs during 2013:

	COST OF FAILURE BY TYPE				
Product	**Motor**	**Wiring**	**Housing**	**All Other**	**Total Dollars**
Blender	$28,000	$24,000	$ 56,000	$22,560	$130,560
Mixer	32,000	28,000	20,480	12,000	92,480
Breadmaker	4,000	3,920	32,000	9,040	48,960
Total	$64,000	$55,920	$108,480	$43,600	$272,000

a. Rearrange the rows in descending order of magnitude based on the Total Dollars column, and prepare a table using Pareto analysis with the following headings:

Product	Dollars	% of Total	Cumulative % of Total

b. Which products account for almost 80 percent of all failure costs?

c. Focusing on the products identified in (b), prepare a table using Pareto analysis to identify the types of failure causing the majority of failure costs. (Hint: Rearrange the cost of failure types in descending order of magnitude.) Use the following headings for your table:

Failure Type	Dollars	% of Total	Cumulative % of Total

d. Describe the problem areas for which to use preventive measures first. How, if at all, does this answer reflect the concept of leveraging expenditures?

47. **LO.5 (Quality costs; research; writing)** Nanotechnology may be the future of manufacturing. The term refers to any area of research that deals with objects that are one to 100 nanometers; 10 nanometers is 1,000 times smaller than the diameter of a human hair. According to the Center for Responsible Nanotechnology and given the current rate of development, general-purpose molecular manufacturing might become a reality by 2010, is likely by 2015, and almost certainly will be achieved by 2020. The last stage of nanoengineering is the ability to create "assemblers" (a device with a submicroscopic arm that is controlled by a computer) that can build consumer goods. For the new technology to become a reality, the assemblers need to be able to self-replicate.

    a. What implications would the introduction of nanotechnology and molecular manufacturing have on the four types of quality costs within the manufacturing process? Outside the manufacturing process?
    b. What implications would the introduction of nanotechnology and molecular manufacturing have on nonquality costs?

48. **LO.5 (Quality costs; Pareto analysis)** Altazar Electronics has identified the following 2013 warranty costs for one of the company products. The information has been categorized according to the type of product failure.

Model	Electrical	Motor	Structural	Mechanical	Total Dollars
Chic	$ 45,360	$ 50,000	$26,760	$11,200	$133,320
Elegant	57,640	64,000	52,200	12,000	185,840
Others	17,660	33,180	12,360	21,640	84,840
Total	$120,660	$147,180	$91,320	$44,840	$404,000

    a. Rearrange the rows in descending order of magnitude based on the Total Dollars column, and prepare a table using Pareto analysis with the following headings:

Model	Dollars	% of Total	Cumulative % of Total

    b. Which model(s) account for the vast proportion of all failure costs? Discuss.
    c. Devise a plan for Altazar Electronics to address the prioritization of preventive measures based on the findings in the Pareto analysis.

49. **LO.5 (External failure cost; research; writing)** Many companies' products have had flaws; some of these companies have been more forthcoming than others in publicly acknowledging such flaws.

INTERNET

    a. Do you think admitting that a product is defective hurts or helps a company's reputation? Explain the rationale for your answer.
    b. Discuss the costs and benefits of halting sales when product flaws are discovered.
    c. Use the Internet to find an example of a company that has continued to sell its product in spite of complaints and other negative feedback about quality. What have been the results?

50. **LO.6 (Cost of quality)** BreatheWell is very aware that its scuba diving tanks must be of the highest quality to maintain its reputation of excellence and safety. The company has retained you as a consultant, and you have suggested that quantifying the costs would be important to the understanding and management of quality. Your experience as a cost accountant helped you determine year 2013 costs of quality from the company's accounting records as follows:

Prevention Costs	
Foolproofing machinery	$20,000
Quality training	60,000
Educating suppliers	44,000
Appraisal Costs	
Quality inspections	$24,000
Recording defects	18,000
Procedure verifications	12,000
Internal Failure Costs	
Waste disposal	$9,000
Unplanned downtime	2,800
External Failure Costs	
Warranty handling	$12,800
Customer reimbursements/returns	10,200

You also determined that 2,400 of the 200,000 tanks made in 2013 had to be sold "for swimming pool use only" for $70 less profit per tank than regular tanks. BreatheWell also incurred $8,000 of rework costs that had been buried in overhead (in addition to the failure costs listed) in producing the tanks sold at the regular price.

a. BreatheWell's management has asked you to determine the 2013 "costs" of the following:

   1. Lost profit from the sale of the 2,400 units limited to use in swimming pools
   2. Total failure cost
   3. Total quality cost

b. Assume that the company is considering expanding its existing full two-year warranty to a full three-year warranty in 2013. How would such a change be reflected in quality costs?

EXCEL

51. **LO.6 (Cost of quality)** During 2013 (the first year of operations), Ridenour Company produced 39,800 portable navigation systems. Of total production, 1,000 were found defective by quality appraisers. Six hundred of the defective units were reworked and sold through regular channels at the original price; the rest were sold as seconds without rework. (The uncorrected defect did not pose a hazard to customers; it was a "voice flaw" that made the units sometimes sound as if they were yelling at the users.) The navigation systems are sold with a two-year warranty; seconds have a six-month warranty.

In 2013, Ridenour Company spent $450,000 for prevention measures and $196,000 on appraisal. Following is the firm 2013 income statement, which appropriately does not reflect any income taxes:

Ridenour Company
Income Statement
For Year Ended December 31, 2013

Regular sales (39,400 units)	$10,244,000	
Sales of seconds (400 units)	56,000	$10,300,000
Cost of goods sold		
Original production costs	$ 3,200,000	
Rework costs (600 units)	21,000	
Prevention and appraisal costs	646,000	(3,867,000)
Gross margin		$ 6,433,000
Selling and administrative expenses (all fixed)		(2,400,000)
Net income		$ 4,033,000

a. Compute the total profit lost by Ridenour Company in its first year of operation by selling defective units as seconds rather than reworking them and selling them at the regular price.

b. Compute the company's total failure cost in 2013.

c. Compute the company's total quality cost in 2013.
d. Assume that selling and administrative expenses include $300,000 to operate a customer complaint center. How should this cost be categorized relative to quality costs?
e. Are the costs included in the 2013 income statement completely reflective of Ridenour's quality costs?

52. **LO.6 (Cost of quality)** Golf courses are demanding in their quest for high-quality carts because of the critical need for lawn maintenance. Antaris Co. manufactures golf carts and is a recognized leader in the industry for quality products. In recent months, company managers have become more interested in trying to quantify the company's cost of quality. As an initial effort, the company identified the following 2013 costs by categories that are associated with quality:

Prevention Costs	
Quality training	$ 30,000
Quality technology	100,000
Quality circles	64,000
Appraisal Costs	
Quality inspections	$36,000
Test equipment	28,000
Procedure verifications	18,000
Internal Failure Costs	
Scrap and waste	$13,000
Waste disposal	4,200
External Failure Costs	
Warranty handling	$19,000
Customer reimbursements/returns	15,200

Managers were also aware that in 2013, 500 of the 16,000 carts produced had to be sold as seconds. These 500 carts were sold for $160 less profit per unit than "good" carts. Also, the company incurred rework costs amounting to $12,000 to sell 400 other carts through regular market channels.

a. Using these data, calculate Antaris Co.'s 2013 expense for the following:
   1. Lost profit from the 500 units
   2. Total failure cost
   3. Total quality cost
b. Assume that the company is considering expanding its existing five-year warranty to a seven-year warranty in 2013. How would such a change be reflected in quality costs?

53. **LO.6 (Cost of quality)** Elijah Electronics makes PDAs. The firm produced 45,000 PDAs during its first year of operation. At year-end, it had no inventory of finished goods. Elijah sold 42,300 units through regular market channels, but 450 of the units produced were so defective that they had to be sold as scrap. The remaining units were reworked and sold as seconds. For the year, the firm spent $240,000 on prevention costs and $120,000 on quality appraisal. There were no customer returns. An income statement for the year follows.

Sales		
Regular channel	$8,460,000	
Seconds	213,750	
Scrap	15,750	$ 8,689,500
Cost of goods sold		
Original production costs	$2,876,400	
Rework costs	63,000	
Quality prevention and appraisal	360,000	(3,299,400)
Gross margin		$ 5,390,100
Selling and administrative expenses (all fixed)		(1,470,000)
Profit before income taxes		$ 3,920,100

a. Compute the total pre-tax profit lost by the company in its first year of operations by selling defective units as seconds or as scrap rather than selling the units through regular channels.
b. Compute the total failure cost for the company in its first year.
c. Compute total quality cost incurred by the company in its first year.
d. What evidence indicates that the firm is dedicated to manufacturing and selling high-quality products?

54. **LO.7 (Balanced scorecard; writing)** Assume that you are in the market for a new car. Since your promotion at work, price is no object. You are considering purchasing a **Porsche**, but your spouse has suggested the purchase of a **Kia**.

a. What do you perceive to be Porsche's strategy relative to value and grade of its automobiles?
b. How might Porsche modify its strategy to compete better against Kia vehicles? Do you think such a change in strategy would be profitable for Porsche? Explain.
c. If Porsche were to change its strategy, develop a balanced scorecard that would provide measurements of the new strategy.

ETHICS

55. **LO.7 (Balanced scorecard; writing; ethics)** Assume that you are in charge of Physicians Social Service Agency, which provides counseling services to low-income families. The agency's costs have been increasing with no corresponding increase in funding. In an effort to implement some cost reductions, you took the following actions:

- Empowered counselors to make their own decisions about the legitimacy of all low-income claims.
- Told counselors not to review processed claims a second time to emphasize the concept of "do it right the first time."
- Set an upper and lower control limit of 5 minutes on a standard 15-minute time for consultations to discourage "out-of-control" conditions.

a. Discuss the ethics as well as the positive and negative effects of each of the ideas listed.
b. Develop a balanced scorecard for Physicians Social Service Agency that incorporates the three changes listed.

INTERNET

56. **LO.8 (Quality culture; research; writing)** Choose an organization with which you have a solid familiarity (possibly even your fraternity, sorority, or college). You have been placed in charge of initiating a quality culture in that organization. Access at least four Web sites that refer to this subject; these sites may contain general information about creating a quality culture or specific information about how a quality culture was created (or enhanced) in a particular organization. Write a short paper to present to your organization's leaders with your suggestions on how such a culture should be established (or enhanced) in your organization.

57. **LO.9 (Appendix; ISO; writing)** Many companies are becoming ISO certified because of customer requests and because of the need to compete in the global marketplace.

a. Why do you think customers are insisting that suppliers meet the ISO 9001 series standards?
b. Does meeting the ISO 9001 series standards mean that a supplier's products or services are superior to those of competitors? Elaborate on what conformance to the standards means.
c. Why would the fact that a supplier's industry is moving toward the ISO 9001 series motivate the supplier to seek registration?
d. How would complying with the ISO 9001 series help a company improve quality?

INTERNET

58. **LO.9 (Appendix; EFQM Award; research; writing)** Go to the EFQM Web site and find the list of most-current award winners. Choose one of the companies listed and prepare a synopsis of the company. Gather additional information about the company and prepare a brief presentation on why you believe the company received an excellence award.

Marcin Balcerzak/Shutterstock.com

18

Inventory and Production Management

LEARNING OBJECTIVES

After completing this chapter, you should be able to answer the following questions:

1. What value chain relationships are important to organizations?
2. What costs are associated with buying, producing, and carrying inventory?
3. How do push and pull systems control production?
4. Why do product life cycles affect profitability?
5. What is target costing, and how does it influence production cost management?
6. What is the just-in-time philosophy, and what modifications does JIT require in accounting systems?
7. What are flexible manufacturing systems?
8. Why are lean enterprises important in today's business environment?
9. How can the theory of constraints help in determining production flow?
10. (*Appendix*) How are economic order quantity, order point, and safety stock determined and used?

INTRODUCTION

Manufacturing and retail firms face two significant challenges in managing inventory. First, these firms must have the inventory available to match the demand from their customers. To meet this challenge, firms must produce or order the right products at the right price and have them available when customers want those products. Second, to avoid excessive costs and remain competitive, firms must avoid producing or ordering inventory that is not demanded by their customers. No longer do firms hold inventory until a customer decides to make a purchase; they ardently strive to avoid investing cash in inventory until customers actually place orders. Efforts to avoid inventory investment are captured in the following quote:

> People who believe you can't have too much of a good thing obviously haven't worked with inventory! Operations managers know inventory dispels this adage and face the constant challenge of keeping inventory levels as low as possible without increasing overall costs or negatively impacting product availability. This isn't an easy job, especially since inventory rears its head throughout any organization—from raw materials, to work-in-process, to finished goods.[1]

Other than plant assets and human resource development, inventory is often the largest investment a company makes—although this investment yields no return until the inventory is sold. This chapter addresses ways companies minimize their monetary commitments to inventory while still satisfying customer demands. The chapter appendix covers the concepts of economic order quantity (EOQ), order point, safety stock, and Pareto inventory analysis.

IMPORTANT RELATIONSHIPS IN THE VALUE CHAIN

1 What value chain relationships are important to organizations?

Every company has upstream suppliers and downstream customers. Together, these parties comprise a supply chain, which can be depicted by the following model:

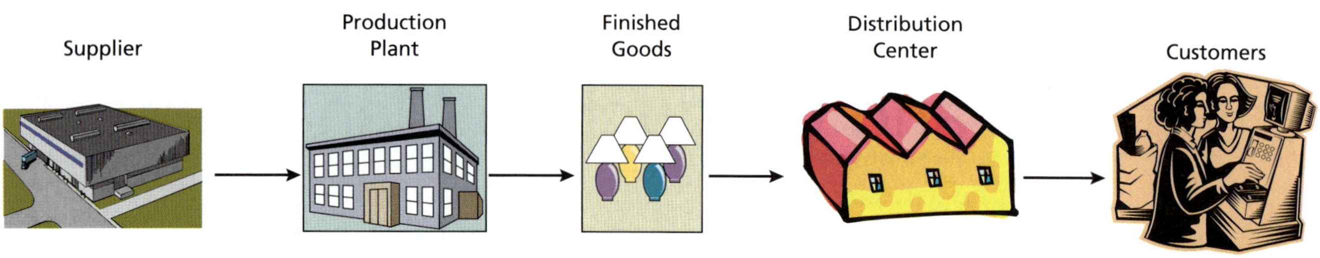

By improving cooperation, communication, and integration, entities within a value chain can treat each other as extensions of themselves and, thereby, increase quality, throughput, and cost efficiency. Entities can share expertise and engage in problem solving to reduce or eliminate non-value-added activities and enhance value-added activities. Firms can provide products and services faster and with fewer defects as well as perform activities more effectively and reliably with fewer errors and less redundancy. Consider the following areas in which opportunities for improvement between entities exist:

- communicating product/component requirements, specifications, and needs;
- clarifying requests for products or services;
- providing feedback about unsatisfactory products or services;
- planning, controlling, and problem solving; and
- sharing managerial and technical expertise, supervision, and training.

These same opportunities are also available to individuals and groups within an organization. Each employee or group of employees has internal suppliers and customers; these relationships form an intraorganizational value chain. When internal suppliers and customers are viewed as extensions of employees, teamwork enhancements and improvement

[1] Scott W. Hadley, "A Modern View of Inventory," *Strategic Finance* (July 2004), pp. 31–35.

opportunities are more likely to be found. Improved teamwork helps companies implement just-in-time systems, which are discussed later in the chapter. Improved productivity benefits all company stakeholders by

- reducing inventory investment,
- improving cash-to-cash cycle time,
- raising asset turnover,
- increasing inventory turnover, and
- lowering inventory risks.

BUYING OR PRODUCING AND CARRYING INVENTORY

2 What costs are associated with buying, producing, and carrying inventory?

In manufacturing organizations, production begins with the acquisition of raw material. Although not always the largest production cost, raw material purchases cause a continuous cash outflow. Similarly, retailers make significant investments in merchandise purchased for sale to customers. Profit margins in both types of organizations can benefit from reducing or minimizing inventory investments, assuming that product demand can still be met. The term *inventory* is used in this chapter to refer to direct material, work in process, finished goods, indirect material (supplies), and retail merchandise.

Efficient inventory management largely relies on cost-minimization strategies. As indicated in Exhibit 18.1, the primary costs associated with inventory are:

- purchasing/production,
- ordering/setup, and
- carrying/not carrying goods in stock.

Exhibit 18.1 Categories of Inventory Costs

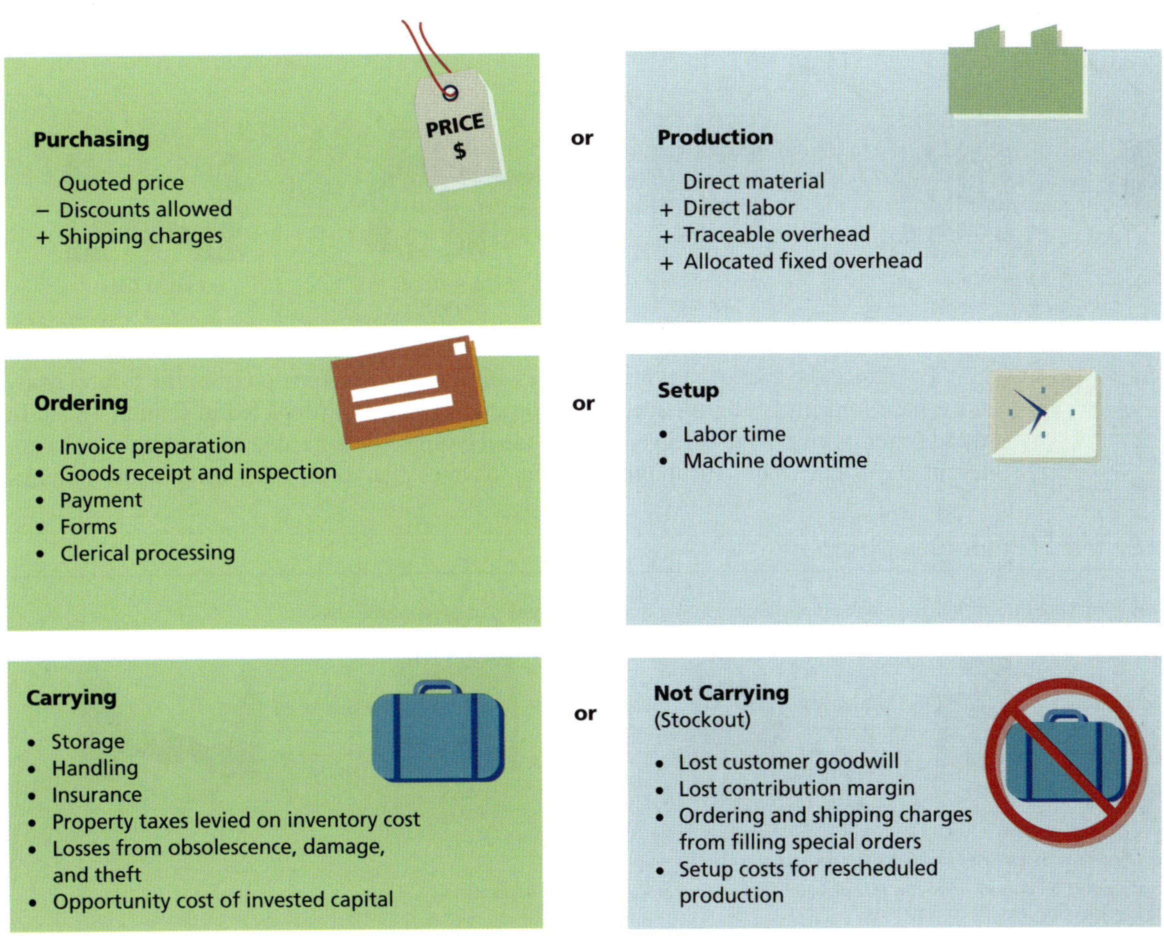

Inventory **purchasing cost** is the quoted purchase price minus any discounts allowed, plus shipping charges. For a manufacturer, production cost refers to the costs associated with purchasing direct material, paying for direct labor, and absorbing variable and fixed overhead. Of these production costs, fixed manufacturing overhead is the least susceptible to short-run cost minimization. An exception is that management is able to somewhat control the fixed component of unit product cost by managing production capacity utilization relative to short-run demand. Most efforts to minimize fixed manufacturing overhead costs involve long-run measures.

INVENTORY AND PRODUCTION MANAGEMENT PHILOSOPHIES

3 How do push and pull systems control production?

The two theoretical approaches to producing inventory are push systems and pull systems. In the traditional **push system** approach (illustrated in Exhibit 18.2), production occurs in anticipation of customer orders and, work centers buy or produce inventory according to lead time, economic order size, or production quantity requirements. Current sales demand and current production may be poorly correlated. Excess inventory is stored until it is needed by other work centers.

Exhibit 18.2 Push System of Production Control

Purchases and production are constantly *pushed* down into storage locations until need arises.

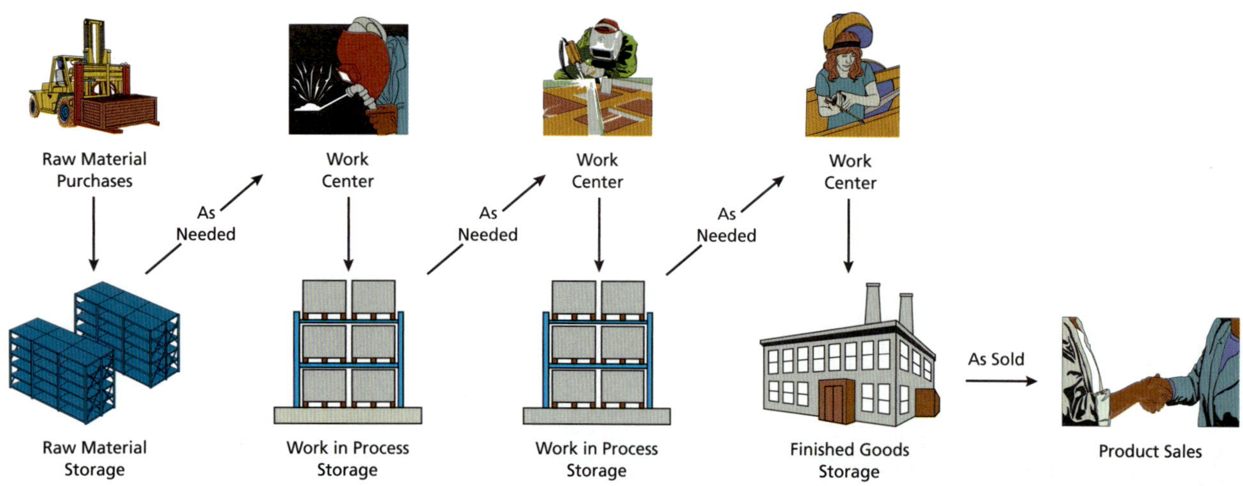

To reduce the cost of carrying inventory until needed at some point in the future, many firms have implemented **pull systems** of production control (depicted in Exhibit 18.3). In these systems, inventory is delivered or produced only as it is needed by the next work center in the value chain. Although necessity dictates that companies carry some minimal

Exhibit 18.3 Pull System of Production Control

Product sales dictate total production. Purchases and production are *pulled* through the system on an as-needed basis.

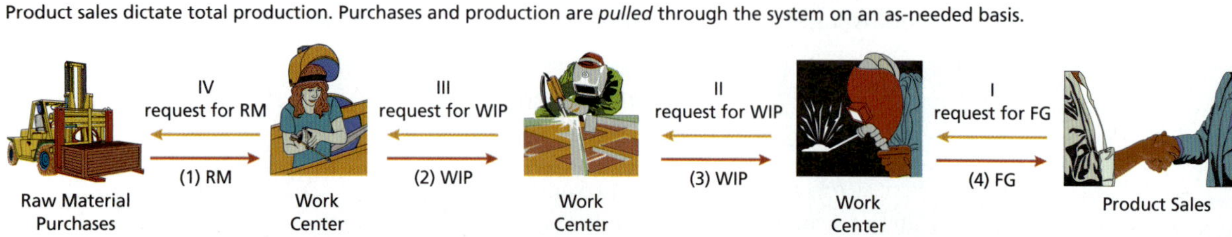

← Information flow that creates (pulls) demand at each successive operation

→ Physical production flow in which raw material (RM) and work in process (WIP) flow successively through work centers until completed (FG)

amount of inventory, work centers do not produce to compensate for lead times or to meet some economic production run model. The pull system approach to inventory management is more consistent with environmentally sustainable business models because there is a focus on both cost minimization and quality maximization. Matters such as managing inventory levels and optimum order size are discussed in the chapter appendix.

UNDERSTANDING AND MANAGING PRODUCTION ACTIVITIES AND COSTS

Managing production activities and costs requires an understanding of product life cycles and the various management and accounting models and approaches to effectively and efficiently engage in production planning, controlling, decision making, and evaluating performance.

Product Life Cycles

4 Why do product life cycles affect profitability?

Product profit margins are typically judged on a period-by-period basis without consideration of the product life cycle. However, products, like people, have life cycles. The **product life cycle** model depicts the stages through which a product class (not each product) passes from the time that an idea is conceived until production is discontinued. Those stages are development (which includes design), introduction, growth, maturity, and decline. Exhibit 18.4 illustrates a conventional sales trend line as the product class passes through each life cycle stage. Companies must be aware of where products are in their life cycles because, in addition to the sales effects, the life cycle stage can have a tremendous impact on costs and profits.

Exhibit 18.4 Product Life Cycle

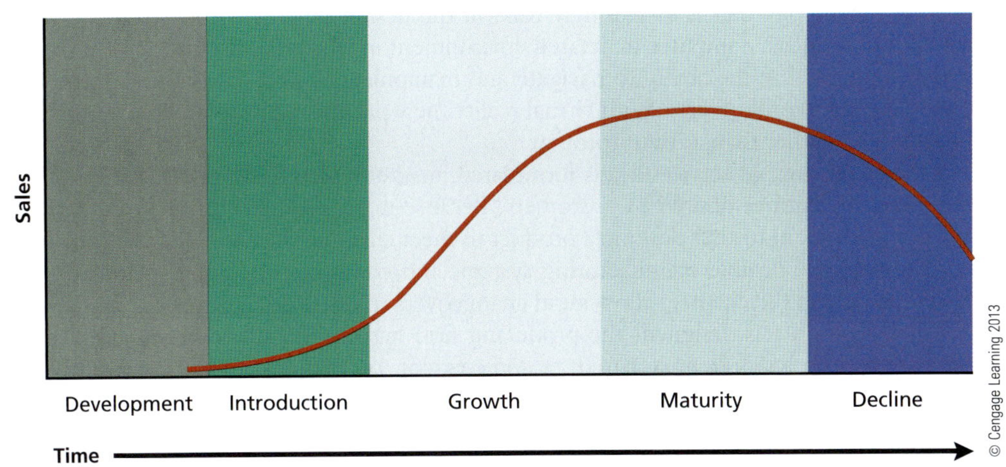

In the design stage, production methods, materials, and conversion operations are selected. Many of the product's quality, cost, and environmental impacts are set with the decisions made in this stage. During the product introduction stage, costs can be substantial and are typically related to engineering change orders, market research, and advertising/promotion. Sales are usually low and prices are often set in relationship to the market prices of similar or substitute goods, if any are available.

The growth stage begins when the product has gained market acceptance and starts to show increased sales. Product quality also can improve during this life cycle stage because of learning curve effects or if competitors have made cost efficient improvements to the original production design. Prices are fairly stable during the growth stage because many substitutes exist or because consumers have become "attached" to the product and are willing to pay a premium price for it rather than buy a substitute.

In the maturity stage, sales begin to stabilize or slowly decline, and firms often compete on selling price. Costs are often at their lowest level during this period because production techniques have become routine, so profits can be high. Some products remain at this stage for a long time; others pass through this stage quickly.

The decline stage reflects waning sales. Prices can be cut dramatically to stimulate business. Production cost per unit generally increases during this stage because fixed overhead is spread over a smaller production volume. The decrease in selling price and increase in fixed overhead cost per unit results in reduced profitability.

Life Cycle and Target Costing

5 What is target costing, and how does it influence production cost management?

From a cost standpoint, product development is an extremely important stage that the traditional financial accounting model almost ignores. Financial accounting requires that development costs be expensed as incurred—even though most studies indicate that decisions made by the time the production design team has completed only 25–50 percent of its work actually determine approximately 80–90 percent of a product's total life cycle costs.

Although technology and competition have tremendously shortened the time spent in the development stage, effective development efforts are critical to a product's life cycle profitability. Decisions made during this stage can

- reduce production and life cycle costs through material specifications,
- shorten manufacturing time through process design,
- increase quality by minimizing potential design defects, and
- add flexibility to product design or production processes.

Manufacturers are acutely aware of the need to focus attention on the product development stage, and the performance measure of time to market is becoming more critical. Thus, the length of the development process must reflect a balance between the short-term need for the product to be "first" and the longer-term need for the product to be "good."

One technology that is increasingly used in the design stage is virtual reality. **Virtual reality** is an artificial, computer-generated environment in which the user is a "part" of that environment and has the ability to navigate and manipulate objects (such as products) that behave like real-world objects. With virtual reality, new product testing can focus on a computer graphic, rather than a real, prototype.

Once a product or service idea is formulated, market research is typically performed to determine the features desired by customers. Because many products can now be customized, companies can further develop a product to meet customer tastes once it is in the market. Alternatively, flexible manufacturing systems and computer-integrated manufacturing (discussed later in the chapter) allow rapid changeovers to other designs.

After a product is designed, the producing firm has traditionally determined product cost and then set a selling price based, to some extent, on that cost. If the market will not bear the resulting selling price (possibly because competitors' prices are lower), the firm either earns less profit than desired or attempts to lower production costs. Because of intensified competition and surplus production capacity in many product markets, companies often have less discretion in setting prices now than in the past.

Today, most products are designed to be sold at a market price (the price point) that is associated with the preferences of a particular product market segment. To keep production costs in line with the price point, some companies use a technique called target costing. As expressed in the following formula, **target costing** develops an "allowable" product cost by using market research to estimate the price point for a product with specific characteristics.

$$TC = ESP - APM - S\&A$$

where TC = target production cost
ESP = estimated selling price
APM = acceptable profit margin
S&A = expected per-unit selling and administrative cost

Exhibit 18.5 Target Costing Process

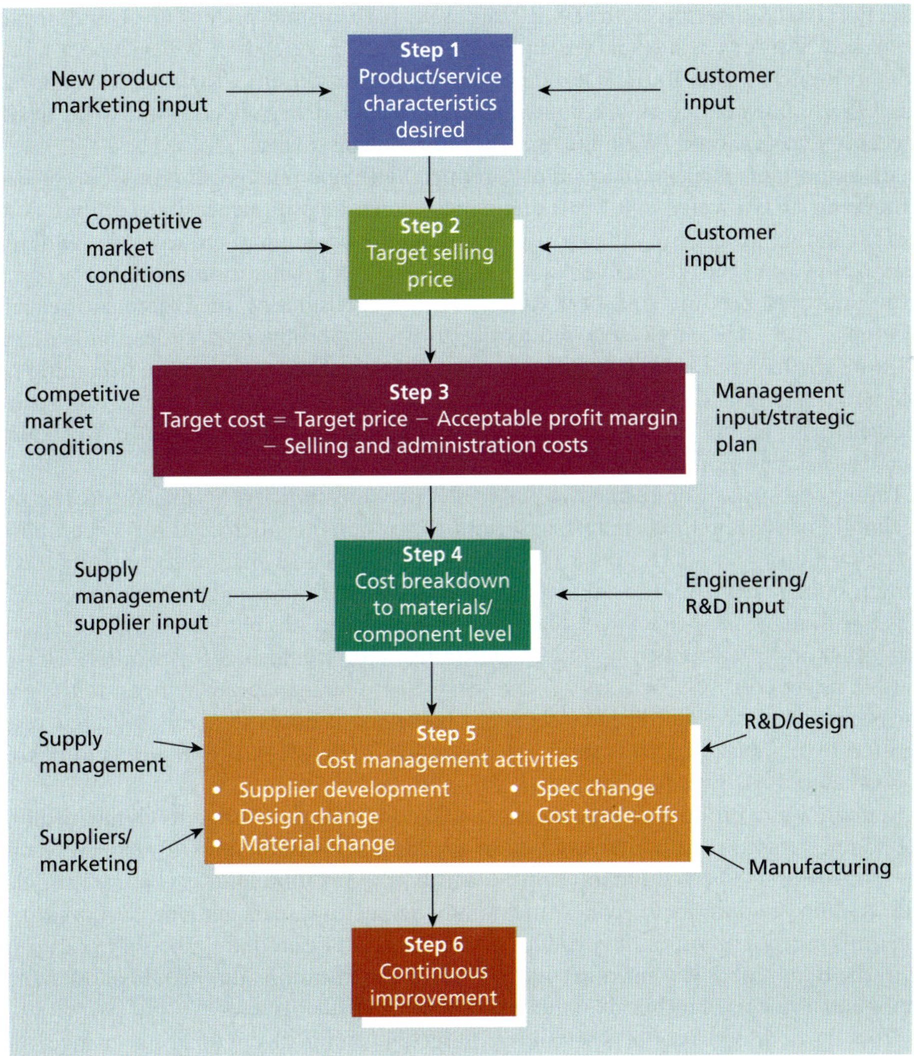

Source: From L.M. Ellram, "The Implementation of Target Costing in the United States: Theory versus Practice," *Journal of Supply Chain Management*, 42, no. 1, (Winter 2006), pp. 13ff. Copyright © 2006 Blackwell Publishing Ltd. Reproduced with permission of Blackwell Publishing Ltd.

Subtracting an acceptable profit margin and selling and administrative costs from the estimated selling price leaves an implied maximum per-unit target product cost, which is compared to an expected product cost. The target costing process is depicted in Exhibit 18.5.

If the expected product cost is higher than the target product cost, the company has several alternatives. First, cost tables can be used to help determine how the product design and/or production process can be adjusted to reduce costs. **Cost tables** are databases that provide information about the impact on product costs of using different input resources, manufacturing processes, and design specifications. **Honda**, for example, had to purchase the front engine/rear-whee-drive transmissions for its S2000s from **Toyota** to meet cost targets.[2] Second, a less-than-desired profit margin can be accepted. Third, the company can decide not to enter this particular product market at the current time because the desired profit margin cannot be obtained. If, for example, the target costing system used by **Canon** indicated that a product's life cycle costs were too high to make an acceptable profit, the product would be abandoned unless it were strategically necessary to maintain a comprehensive product line or to create a "flagship" product.

[2]The BRZ/FR-S/GT86 Transmissions and Driveline: What We Know So Far," Kaizen Factor (2/16/12); http://kaizenfactor.wordpress.com/ (accessed 2/29/12).

Target costing requires a shift in the way managers think about the relationships among cost, selling price, and profits. The traditional attitude has been that a product is developed, production cost is determined, a selling price is set (or a market price is met), and profits or losses result. Target costing takes a different perspective: a product is developed, a selling price and desired profit amount are determined, and maximum allowable costs are calculated. When allowable costs are constrained by selling price, all costs must be justified. Unnecessary costs should be eliminated without reducing quality.

An important step in successful product development is the process of **value engineering (VE)**, which involves a disciplined search for various feasible combinations of resources and methods that will increase product functionality and reduce costs. Multidisciplinary teams using various problem-solving tools such as brainstorming and Pareto analysis seek an improved product cost–performance ratio by considering such factors as reliability, conformity, and durability. Cost reduction, shortened production cycles, and increased quality are the major reasons to engage in VE. Additionally, companies are becoming more concerned about final disposal costs of products. As such, designing a product so that it can be recycled or will create a minimal environmental impact upon disposal has production cost and VE implications.

Target costing can be applied to services if they are sufficiently uniform to justify the modeling effort required. Assume that a print shop wants to offer customers the opportunity to buy a variety of items personalized with photographs. A market survey indicates that the metropolitan area could sustain an annual 500-order volume and that customers believe $18 is a reasonable fee per service. The print shop manager desires a $6 profit for each customer order and that marketing and administrative cost would be $3 per order. Thus, the allowable target cost is $9 per order ($18 – $6 – $3). The manager will invest in the equipment necessary to provide the new service if he or she believes that the indicated volume suggested by market research is sufficient to support the costs of production and depreciation on the newly acquired equipment.

In designing a product to meet an allowable cost, engineers strive to eliminate all non-value-added activities from the production process. Such reductions in activities will, in turn, reduce costs. The production process and types of components to be used should be discussed among appropriate parties (including engineering, management, accounting, and marketing) in recognition of the product quality and cost desired. Suppliers also can participate in the design phase by making suggestions for modifications that would allow standard components to be used rather than more costly special order items.

Properly designed products should require only minimal engineering change orders (ECOs) after being released to production. Each time an ECO is issued, one or more of the following situations can occur and create additional costs: production documents must be reprinted; workers must relearn tasks; machine dies, jigs, or setups must be changed; and parts in stock or currently ordered can be made obsolete. If costs are to be affected significantly, any design changes must be made early in the process—preferably before production begins.

If a company decides to enter a market, the target cost computed at the beginning of the product life cycle does not remain the final focus. Over the product's life, the target cost is continuously reduced in an effort to spur a process of continuous improvement in actual production cost. **Kaizen costing** involves ongoing efforts for continuous improvement to reduce product costs, increase product quality, and/or improve the production process *after* manufacturing activities have begun. These cost reductions are designed to keep the profit margin relatively stable as the product price is reduced over the product life cycle. Exhibit 18.6 compares target and kaizen costing. Kaizen initiatives often involve multifunctional teams that study specific production issues to lower costs or improve quality. For example, **Lexus** uses kaizen methods to reduce the time its dealerships require to change oil in customers' autos. The result is more satisfied customers who spend less time waiting for their vehicles to be serviced.[3] Kaizen methods are also being used by companies to reduce energy consumption and the environmental impacts of operations.

[3]Mark Rechtin, "Slimming Operations," *Automotive News* (February 6, 2006), pp. 31–32.

Exhibit 18.6 Comparison of Target and Kaizen Costing

	Target Costing	Kaizen Costing
What?	A procedural approach for determining a maximum allowable cost for an identifiable, proposed product, assuming a given target profit margin	A mandate to reduce costs, increase product quality, and/or improve production processes through continuous improvement efforts
Used for?	New products	Existing products
When?	Development stage (includes design)	Primary production stages (introduction and growth); possibly, but not probably, maturity
How?	Works best by aiming at a specified cost reduction objective; used to set original production standards	Works best by aiming at a specified cost reduction objective; reductions are integrated into original production standards to sustain improvements and provide new challenges
Why?	Extremely large potential for cost reduction because 80 to 90 percent of a product's lifelong costs are embedded in the product during the design and development stages	Limited potential for reducing cost of existing products, but may provide useful information for future target costing efforts
Focus?	All product inputs (material, labor, and overhead elements) as well as production processes and supplier components	Depends on where efforts will be most effective in reducing production costs; generally begins with the most costly component and (in more mature companies) ends with overhead components

JUST-IN-TIME SYSTEMS

6 What is the just-in-time philosophy, and what modifications does JIT require in accounting systems?

Just-in-time (JIT) is a philosophy about when to do something. The "when" is as needed and the "something" is a production, purchasing, or delivery activity. The JIT philosophy is applicable in all departments of all types of organizations. JIT's three primary goals follow:

- eliminating any production process or operation that does not add value to the product/service,
- continuously improving production/performance efficiency, and
- reducing the total cost of production/performance while increasing quality.

These goals are totally consistent with, and supportive of, the total quality management (TQM) program discussed in Chapter 17. Elements of the JIT philosophy are outlined in Exhibit 18.7 (page 736). A logical starting point for discussing JIT is in regard to manufacturing or production activities. JIT manufacturing originated in Japan where a card, or **kanban** (pronounced "kahn-bahn"), was used to communicate between work centers to control the flow of in-process products. A **just-in-time manufacturing system** attempts to acquire components and produce inventory units only as they are needed, minimize product defects, and reduce cycle/setup times for acquisition and production.

Production has traditionally been dictated by the need to smooth operating activities over time. Although allowing a company to maintain a steady workforce and continuous machine utilization, smooth production often creates products that must be stored until they are sold. Companies often filled warehouses with products that were not currently in demand, often while failing to meet promised customer delivery dates on other products. One cause of this dysfunctional behavior was management's preoccupation with spreading

Exhibit 18.7 Elements of a JIT Philosophy

- Quality is essential at all times; work to eliminate defects and scrap.
- Employees often have the best knowledge of ways to improve operations; listen to them.
- Employees generally have more talents than are being used; train them to be multiskilled and increase their productivity.
- Ways to improve operations are always available; constantly look for them, being certain to make fundamental changes rather than superficial ones.
- Creative thinking doesn't cost anything; use it to find ways to reduce costs before making expenditures for additional resources.
- Suppliers are essential to operations; establish and cultivate good relationships with suppliers and, if possible, use long-term contracts.
- Inventory is an asset that generates no revenue while it is held in stock, so it can be viewed as a "liability"; eliminate it to the extent possible.
- Storage space is directly related to inventories; eliminate it in response to the elimination of inventories.
- Long cycle times cause inventory buildup; keep cycle times as short as possible by using frequent deliveries.

overhead over the largest quantity of products possible. This obsession unwittingly resulted in much unnecessary inventory, huge inventory carrying costs, and other operating problems to be discussed subsequently.

Thus, raw material and work in process inventories were historically maintained at levels considered sufficient to compensate for inefficiencies in acquisition and/or production. Exhibit 18.8 depicts these inefficiencies or problems as "rocks" in a stream of "water" that represents inventory. The traditional philosophy is that the water should be kept high enough for the rocks to be so deeply submerged that there will be "smooth sailing" in production activity. The intent is to avoid the original problems, but in fact, new problems are actually created. By obscuring the problems, the excess "water" adds to the difficulty of making corrections. The JIT manufacturing philosophy is to lower the water level, expose the rocks, and eliminate them to the extent possible. The shallower stream will then flow more smoothly and rapidly than the deep river.

Changes Needed to Implement JIT Manufacturing

Implementation of a just-in-time system requires a long-term commitment. Consider that **Toyota** invested more than 20 years to develop the JIT system and realize significant benefits from it. However, any company—not simply a huge manufacturer—can now put a system in place and recognize benefits fairly rapidly. In a world in which managers work diligently to produce improvements of a percentage point or two, some numbers simply do not look realistic even though they are. One success story involves **Gamblin Artist's Oil Colors**, a small oil-paint manufacturer in Portland, Oregon. The company went from manufacturing three colors of paint to manufacturing 87 colors. Paint was previously produced in batches of 1,200 tubes that would remain in inventory for up to six months. After JIT implementation, inventory was cut in half; inventory storage was approximately three weeks; and cash was released for capital growth and advertising investment.[4]

For just-in-time production to be effective, certain modifications must be made to supplier relationships, distribution, product design, product processing, and plant layout. JIT depends on the ability of employees and suppliers to compress the time, distance, resources, and activities and to enhance interactions needed to produce a company's products and services. The methods currently being used successfully by many companies are discussed next.

Supplier Relationships and Distribution The optimal JIT situation is to contract with only one vendor for any given item. Such an ideal, however, creates the risk of not having

[4]Jane Applegate, "Just-in-Time Manufacturing," Entrepreneur.com (May 30, 2001); http://www.entrepreneur.com/management/operations/inventory/article40850.html (last accessed 3/01/12).

Exhibit 18.8 Depiction of Traditional and JIT Production Philosophies

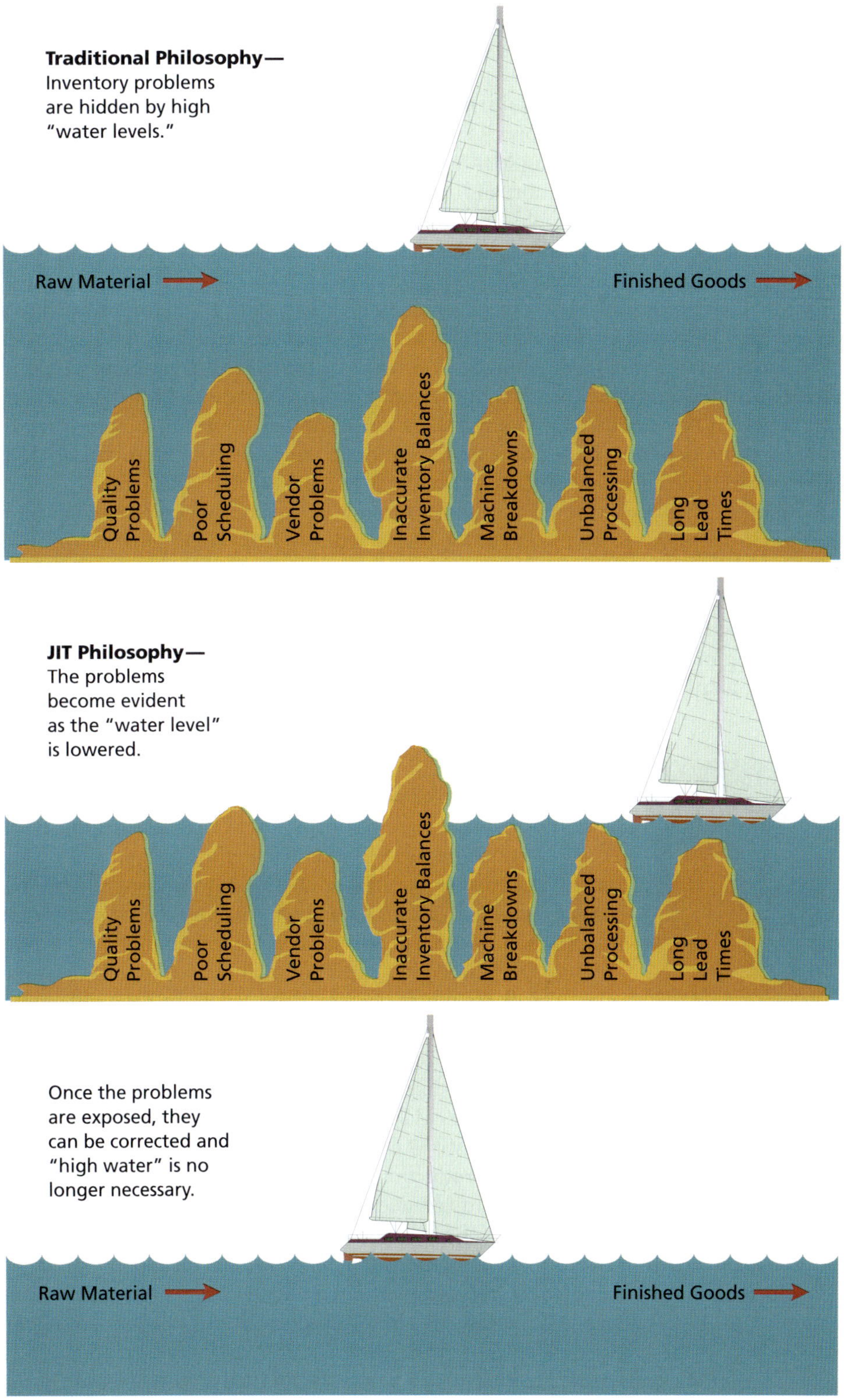

alternative sources (especially for critical inputs) in the event of vendor business failure, production strikes, unfair pricing, or shipment delays. Thus, it is often more realistic to limit the number of vendors to a select few that are recognized by the company for quality and reliability. The company then enters into long-term relationships with these suppliers, who become "partners" in the process. For example, in June 2011, **International Automotive**

Systems in Southfield, Michigan, was named to **Ford Motor Company**'s Aligned Business Framework preferred supplier network; these companies have long-term relationships with Ford that strengthen collaboration and drive "mutual profitability and technology development."[5] Some companies name suppliers to "preference" lists; others more formally "certify" the suppliers.

Vendor certification requires substantial efforts by the purchasing company, such as obtaining information on the supplier's operating philosophy, costs, product quality, environmental impact, and service. People from various functional areas must decide on the factors by which to rate the vendor and then must weight those factors as to relative importance. Rapid feedback should be given to potential vendors/suppliers so that they can, if necessary, make changes prior to the start of the relationship or understand why the relationship will not be established.

Factors commonly considered in selecting suppliers include a vendor's reliability and responsiveness, delivery performance, ability to provide service, human resources qualifications, research and development strength, production capacity, and environmental policies. Evaluations of new and infrequent vendors are more difficult because of the lack of a track record by which the purchaser's vendor analysis team can make informed judgments. Suppliers are often required to be certified under standards issued by the International Organization for Standardization (ISO). Quality standards are discussed in Chapter 17.

Forming partnerships with fewer vendors on a long-term basis provides the opportunity to continuously improve quality and substantially reduce costs. Such partnerships involve formal agreements in which both the vendor and the buying organization commit to specific responsibilities to each other for their mutual benefit. These agreements usually involve long-term purchasing arrangements according to specified terms and can provide for the mutual sharing of expertise and information. Such partnerships permit members of the supply chain to eliminate redundancies in warehousing, packaging, labeling, transportation, and inventories.

John Lund/Marc Romanelli/Blend Images/Jupiter Images

Making small changes in product design, such as using only one type of screw, can have a significant impact on the amount of production time required for assembly.

Product Design Products should be designed to use the fewest number of dissimilar parts and to minimize production steps and risks. For example, one company found that 29 different types of screws were being used to manufacture a single product. Downtime was excessive because screwdrivers were continuously being passed among workers. Changing to one type of screw significantly reduced production time. In another example, a printer acquired a new digital press so multiple jobs could be printed simultaneously and paper could be fed from four different stations. The investment allowed the company to increase the variety of print jobs it accepted and shortened delivery times.[6]

Parts standardization does not necessarily result in identical finished products. Many companies find they can produce a larger number of variations in finished products from just a few basic models. The production process is designed so that the vast proportion of parts or tasks can be standardized and added or performed prior to beginning the unique work that is performed near the end of the process. Such differentiation is aided by flexible manufacturing systems and computer-integrated manufacturing.

Products should be designed for the quality desired and should require no, or a minimal number of, ECOs after the design is released for production. An effective arrangement for a vendor–purchaser partnership is to have the vendor's engineers participate in the design phase of the purchasing company's product; an alternative is to provide product specifications and allow the vendor company to draft the design for approval.

If costs are to be significantly affected, design changes must be made early in the process. As discussed in Chapter 4, ECOs create activities generating significant non-value-added

[5] Ford, "Ford Adds 17 Companies to List of Preferred Suppliers Selected for Long-Term Relationships," *Press Release* (June 14, 2011); http://media.ford.com/article_display.cfm?article_id=34782 (accessed 2/29/12).

[6] Mike Ducey, "Lake County Merchants Bring Digital JIT," *Graphic Arts Monthly* (March 2006), p. 48.

(NVA) costs. Regardless of whether a company embraces JIT, time that is spent doing work that adds no value to the production process should be viewed as wasted time. Effective activity analysis eliminates such NVA work and its unnecessary cost.

From another point of view, good product design should address all the intended users' concerns, even product recyclability. For example, an automobile plant can be equipped to receive and take apart old models, remanufacture various parts, and send the cars back into the marketplace. Thus, companies are considering remanufacturing as part of their design and processing capabilities. The environmental effects of products can be dramatically altered if products are designed to be remanufactured or recycled at the end of their useful lives.

Environmental impact is likely to become a much more significant concern in coming years. Many countries are now considering placing caps on industrial emissions and taxing firms for the right to generate those emissions. Accordingly, the financial benefits of minimizing environmental implications generated by products and production activities are likely to be far greater in future years than in the past.

Product Processing In the product processing stage, one primary JIT consideration is the reduction of machine setup time so that processing can shift between products more often and at a lower cost. Costs of reducing setup time are more than recovered by the savings derived from reducing downtime, in-process inventory, and material handling as well as by increasing safety, process flexibility, and ease of operation. The following quote captures the value of reduced setup times. The quote is not from Toyota or a twenty-first-century management guru; it is from Henry Ford in 1926.

> One of the most noteworthy accomplishments in keeping the price of (our) products low is the gradual shortening of the production cycle. The longer an article is in the process of manufacture and the more it is moved about, the greater is its ultimate cost.[7]

Most companies implementing rapid tool-setting procedures have been able to obtain setup times of 10 minutes or less. Such companies use a large number of low-cost setups rather than the traditional approach of a small number of more expensive setups. Under JIT, setup cost is considered almost purely variable rather than fixed, as in the traditional manufacturing environment. One way to reduce machine setup time is to have workers perform as many setup tasks as possible while the machine is online and running. All unnecessary movements by workers or of material should be eliminated. Teams similar to pit-stop crews at auto races can be used to perform setup operations, with each team member handling a specialized task. Based on past results, with planning and education, setup times can be reduced by 50 percent or more.

Another essential part of product processing is the institution of high-quality standards because JIT has the goal of zero defects. Under JIT systems, quality is determined continuously rather than at quality control checkpoints. First, the quality of vendors' products is ensured at purchase. Then, workers and machines (such as optical scanners) monitor production quality. Controlling quality on an ongoing basis significantly reduces the assessment cost of obtaining high quality. The JIT philosophy recognizes that it is less costly *not* to make mistakes than to correct them after they have been made. Unfortunately, quality control and scrap costs are often buried in production cost standards, making such costs hard to identify.

The ability to standardize work so that every worker acts according to stated procedures without variation, on time, every time is important in any process. Standard procedures indicate the most efficient way to conduct a particular task as well as to allow planning, supervising, and training tasks to be more efficiently and effectively conducted. Standardization also provides the ability to improve processes because tasks are performed with consistency. It is nearly impossible to improve an unstable process because the high level of variation makes the cause-and-effect relationships hard to identify so that modifications can be made.

[7] Anonymous, *Reducing Setup Times: A Foundation for Lean Manufacturing*, http://www.imec.org/SS-Reducing-Setup-Times.cfm (last accessed 3/01/12).

Plant Layout Traditionally, manufacturing plants were designed to conform with functional areas; similar machines and workers with similar specialized skills were placed together. For JIT to work effectively, the physical plant must be conducive to the flow of goods and the location of workers as well as to increasing the value added per square foot of plant space. Manufacturing plants should be designed to minimize material handling time, lead time, and movement of goods from raw material input to completion of the finished product. This goal often requires that machines or workers be arranged in S- or U-shaped production groupings, commonly referred to as **manufacturing cells** (see Exhibit 18.9), to generate the most efficient and effective production process for a particular product type. This streamlined design allows for more visual controls to be instituted for problems such as excess inventory, production defects, equipment malfunctions, and out-of-place tools. The design also allows for greater teamwork and quicker exchange of vital information.

Exhibit 18.9 Depiction of a Manufacturing Cell

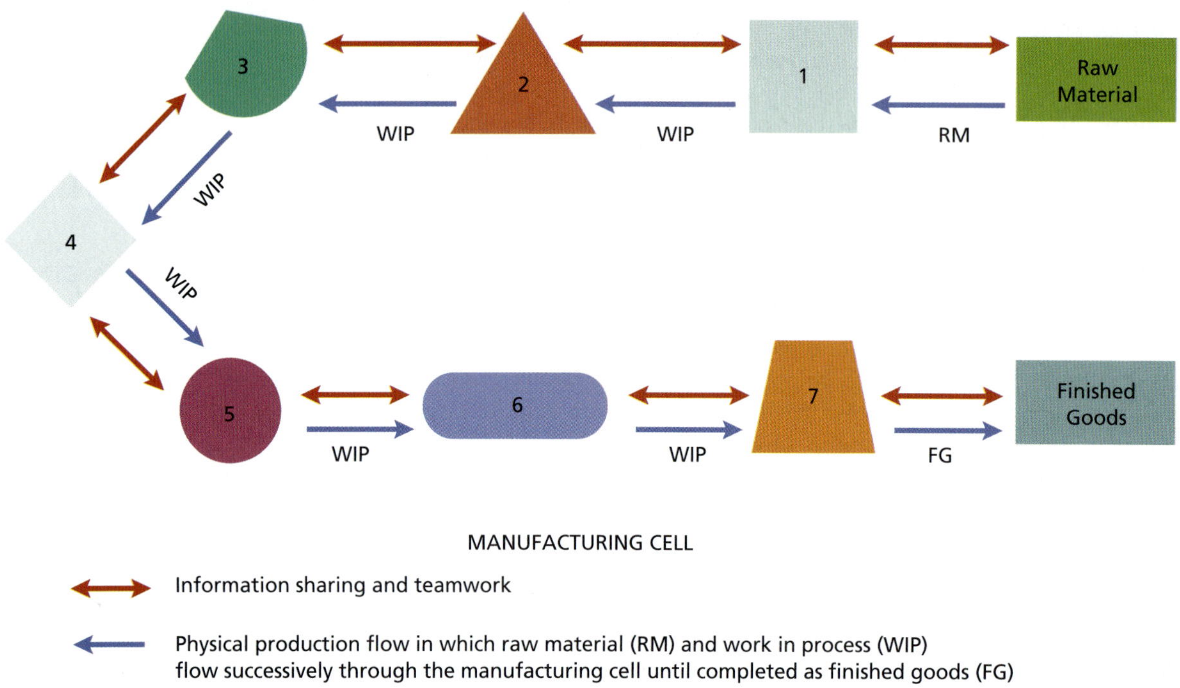

The informational arrows in Exhibit 18.9 indicate how production is "pulled" through the system as successive downstream work centers issue kanbans to acquire needed goods or services from upstream suppliers so that the goods or services demanded by downstream customers can be produced. Many pull systems today use electronic methods such as computer networks (rather than cards) to send requests for goods or services to upstream workstations.

Exhibit 18.10 illustrates the flow of three products through a factory before and after the redesign of factory floor space. In the "before" diagram, processes were grouped together by function, and products flowed through the plant depending on the type of processing that needed to be performed. Using JIT and a cellular design substantially reduces storage requirements because goods should be ordered only as needed. Products also flow through the plant more rapidly. Products 1 and 2 use the same flow, except that Product 2 skips the assembly process. When plant layout is redesigned to incorporate manufacturing cells, workers have the opportunity to broaden their skills and deepen their involvement in production because of multiprocess handling. Multiskilled workers are trained to monitor numerous machines, generally have more flexibility in work assignments, and are less bored because a variety of tasks are performed. The ability to oversee an entire process can prompt

Exhibit 18.10 Factory Floor Space Redesign

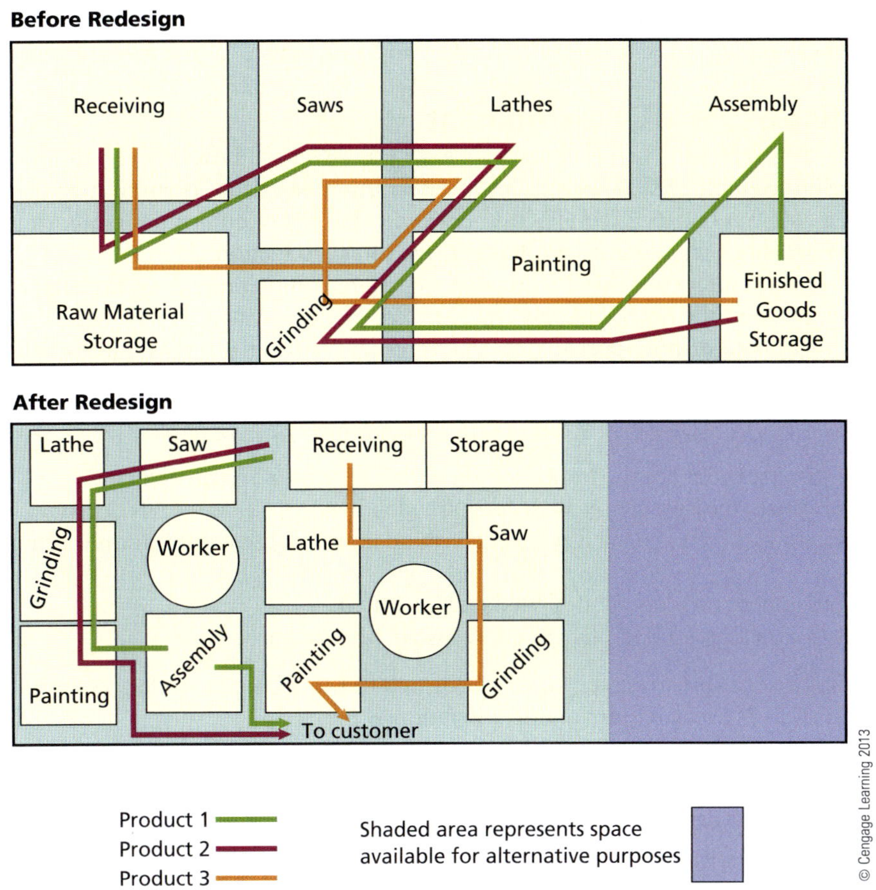

employee suggestions on improvement techniques that would not have been visible had the employee been working on a single facet of the process.[8]

Highly automated equipment can run without direct labor involvement but still requires monitoring. Employees must be available for oversight if an automated piece of equipment is programmed to stop when a given situation arises. The "situation" can be positive (a specified quantity of production has been reached) or negative (a quality defect has been indicated). Use of preprogrammed factory equipment is referred to as **autonomation** to distinguish it from automated factories in which the machinery is not programmed to stop when specified situations arise. Autonomation derives from the principle of "jidoka" in **Toyota**'s lean manufacturing philosophy, which calls for production to halt when there is a malfunction in the production process. Because machines "know" the conditions they are expected to sense, one worker is able to oversee several machines in a single manufacturing cell concurrently.

JIT companies often adopt **focused factory arrangements** that allow a closer connection between production operations and vendors. The vendors often supply a limited number of specified products or perform a limited number of unique services for the JIT company. Vendors can be other divisions of the same organization or separate, nonrelated companies. Focused factory arrangements can also involve relocation or plant modernization by a vendor, and financial assistance from the JIT manufacturer can be available to

[8] The average U.S. company receives about one suggestion per year from every six eligible employees. On the other hand, Japanese companies receive an average of 32 suggestions. See John Tschohl, "Be Bad: Employee Suggestion Program Cuts Costs, Increases Profit," *The Canadian Manager* (Winter 1998), pp. 23–24.

recoup such investments. In addition, the vendor benefits from long-term supply contracts. One downside, especially for small vendors, of focused factory arrangements is that they could create overreliance on a single customer. A decline in a primary customer's business or demands by that customer for lower prices can be disastrous for the focused factory.

Logistics of the JIT Environment

In a JIT environment, a certain degree of logistical assistance is developing in the areas of information technology (IT), new support services, and new value-chain relationships. Such advancements can enhance the effectiveness and efficiency of companies employing JIT in the preproduction stage, during production, and after production.

JIT can be employed within the context of more comprehensive management models such as TQM and the Six Sigma method. As discussed in Chapter 17, Six Sigma is a high-performance, data-driven approach to analyzing and solving the root causes of business problems. There are five steps for a successful application of the Six Sigma method:

Define → Measure → Analyze → Improve → Control

1. The company defines the projects and processes that need improvement.
2. Appropriate measurements for success are identified.
3. Data are gathered and analyzed to determine how well the organization is achieving its goals.
4. Improvement projects are designed and instituted.
5. Control measures are implemented to sustain performance.

It may not be possible to achieve the control step of the Six Sigma cycle process in a single iteration; steps 2-4 may require multiple iterations.

The **Internet business model** has become the new orthodoxy, transforming cost and service equations across the corporate landscape. This model refers to a business with

- few physical assets,
- little management hierarchy, and
- a direct pipeline to customers.

Internet business models have become specialized such that distinct models can be identified for Internet firms offering:[9]

- advertising—banner and direct marketing,
- subscription sites,
- customer services,
- directory services,
- content providers, or
- product sales.

In these new business models, electronic commerce has transformed supply-chain integration and delivered substantial cost savings.

Supply-chain management is the cooperative strategic planning, controlling, and problem-solving activities conducted by a company, its vendors, and its customers to generate efficient and effective transfers of goods and services within the supply chain. Three levels of business-to-business (B2B) relationships exist in e-commerce: transactional, information sharing, and collaboration.

The use of e-commerce has advanced more rapidly for the acquisition of certain types of inputs than for others. For example, administrative-type items such as travel arrangements, office supplies, and equipment are acquired much more frequently using e-purchasing than are manufacturing inputs, which are still most frequently acquired through traditional long-term supplier relationships.[10]

[9] C. S. Anajana, "Online Internet Business Models," http://stylusinc.com/website/business_models.htm (last accessed 3/01/12).

[10] Kip R. Krumwiede, Monte R. Swain, and Kevin D. Stocks, "10 Ways E-Business Can Reduce Costs," *Strategic Finance* (July 2003), pp. 25–29.

In addition to IT improvements in product design for manufacturability, simulation software is available for developing production systems that can enhance financial performance. The software can be used to observe the important organizational system interactions and dependencies as well as allow the testing of equipment reconfigurations, distribution channel changes, and quality enhancement programs. Benefits from such simulations include greater and faster throughput, lowered inventory levels, reduced waste or spoilage, error minimization, and cost savings from decreased run time, setup time, or transportation time.

Accounting Implications of JIT

Companies adopting a JIT inventory and/or flexible manufacturing system must be aware of the significant accounting implications created by such a system. A primary accounting impact occurs in variance analysis. The traditional standard cost accounting system discussed in Chapter 7 is primarily historical in nature, with a primary goal of reporting variances so they can be analyzed for cause-and-effect relationships to eliminate similar future problems.

In JIT systems, variance reporting and analysis essentially disappear because such information is untimely. Variances first appear physically (rather than financially); thus, JIT mandates immediate recognition of variances so that causes can be ascertained and, if possible, promptly remedied if unfavorable or exploited if favorable. JIT workers are trained to monitor quality and efficiency during, rather than at the end of, production. Further, if the firm is using statistical process controls, the potential for production defects can be predicted and measures taken to prevent the defects from occurring. Therefore, the number and monetary significance of end-of-period variances being reported for managerial control should be extremely rare.

Under a JIT system, long-term price agreements have been made with vendors, so material price variances should be minimal. The JIT accounting system should be designed so that purchase orders cannot be issued without manager approval for an amount higher than the designated price.[11] This practice assures that the variance amount and cause are known in advance, providing an opportunity to eliminate the excess expenditure before it occurs. The current vendor can be asked to negotiate the price, or other vendors can be contacted for quotes.

The ongoing use of specified or certified vendors also provides the ability to control material quality. It is becoming relatively common for companies to require that their vendors, regardless of global location, maintain certain quality standards and submit to quality assurance audits. Because better control of raw material quality is expected, few (if any) material quantity variances should be caused by substandard material. If usage standards have been accurately set based on established machine-paced efficiency, there should be virtually no favorable usage variance of material during production. Unfavorable use of material should be promptly detected because machines or humans are continuously observing production processes. When an unfavorable variance occurs, the manufacturing process is stopped to correct the error, causing an unfavorable material usage variance to be minimized.

One type of quantity variance is not caused by errors but by engineering changes made to the product specifications. A JIT system typically has two comparison standards: an annual standard and a current standard. Design modifications would change the current standard but not the annual one. The annual standard provides a basis for preparing and executing the company's master budget, and the annual standards are ordinarily kept intact because the annual financial plans and arrangements are predicated on the standards and plans used to prepare the master budget.

Using two standards allows comparisons to be made that indicate the cost effects of ECOs implemented after a product has begun to be manufactured. Exhibit 18.11 (p. 744) shows the calculation of a material quantity variance caused by an ECO. The portion of the total quantity variance caused by the ECO ($2,700 U) is shown separately from that caused by efficiency ($540 F). Labor, overhead, and/or conversion can also have ECO variances.

[11] This same procedure can be implemented under a traditional standard cost system as well as under a JIT system. However, whereas it is less commonly found in a traditional system, it is a requirement under JIT.

Exhibit 18.11 Material Variances under a JIT System

Annual standard	
Material M (8 feet × \$3.05)	\$24.40
Material N (5 feet × \$3.35)	16.75
	\$41.15
Current standard	
Material M (7 feet × \$3.05)	\$21.35
Material N (6 feet × \$3.35)	20.10
	\$41.45
Production during month	9,000 units
Usage during month	
Material M (64,800 feet × \$3.05)	\$ 197,640
Material N (52,200 feet × \$3.35)	174,870
Total cost of material used	\$ 372,510
Material quantity variance	
Material M (9,000 × 7 × \$3.05)	\$ 192,150
Material N (9,000 × 6 × \$3.35)	180,900
Material cost at current standard	\$ 373,050
Actual material cost	(372,510)
Material quantity variance	\$ 540 F
Engineering change variance for material	
Material M (9,000 × 8 × \$3.05)	\$ 219,600
Material N (9,000 × 5 × \$3.35)	150,750
Material cost at annual standard	\$ 370,350
Material cost at current standard	(373,050)
ECO variance	\$ 2,700 U

Labor variances in an automated just-in-time system should be minimal if standard rates and times have been set appropriately. If the plant is not entirely automated, redesigning the physical layout and minimizing any NVA labor activities should decrease the direct labor time component.

An accounting alternative that could occur in a JIT system is the use of a conversion cost category, rather than separate labor and overhead categories, for purposes of cost control. This category becomes more helpful as factories reduce the direct labor cost component through continuous improvements and automation. A standard departmental or manufacturing cell conversion cost per unit of product (or per hour of production time per manufacturing cell) can be calculated rather than individual standards for labor and overhead. Denominators for rate calculation for a conversion cost standard would be the practical or theoretical capacity of an appropriate activity base.[12] If time were used as the base, the conversion cost for a day's production would equal the number of units produced multiplied by the standard number of production hours multiplied by the standard cost per hour. Variances would be determined by comparing actual cost to the designated standard. However, direct labor is a very small part of production in a JIT environment. Use of efficiency variances to evaluate workers can cause excess inventory because these workers are

[12] Practical or theoretical capacity is the appropriate measure because the goal of JIT is virtually continuous processing. In a highly automated plant, these capacities more closely reflect world-class status than does expected annual capacity.

trying to "keep busy" to minimize this variance. Therefore, trying to reduce direct labor efficiency variances in a manufacturing cell setting could be counterproductive.

In addition to minimizing and adjusting the variance calculations, a JIT system can have a major impact on inventory accounting. Companies employing JIT production processes no longer require a separate raw material inventory classification because material is acquired only when needed for production; JIT companies could use a Raw and In-Process (RIP) Inventory account.

The focus of accounting in a JIT system is on the plant's output to the customer.[13] Each sequential activity in a production process depends on the previous activity; thus, any problems will quickly cause the production process to stop. Individual daily accounting for production costs is no longer necessary because all costs should be at standard, and variations will be observed and corrected almost immediately.

Additionally, fewer costs need to be allocated to products because more costs can be traced directly to their related output in a JIT system. Costs are incurred in specified manufacturing cells on a time (per-hour or per-minute) or per-unit basis. In a comprehensive JIT system, energy can be considered a direct production cost because there should be minimal machine downtime or unplanned time for idle workers. Virtually the only costs that need to be allocated are costs associated with the structure (building depreciation, rent, taxes, and insurance) and machinery depreciation.[14] The reduction in allocated costs provides better cost control and performance evaluation than has traditionally been available.

Backflush costing is a streamlined cost accounting method that speeds up, simplifies, and minimizes accounting effort in an environment that minimizes inventory balances, requires few allocations, uses standard costs, and has few variances from standard. During the period, this costing method records purchases of raw material and accumulates actual conversion costs. Then, at a predetermined trigger point, such as (1) at completion of production or (2) upon the sale of goods, an entry is made to allocate the total costs incurred to Cost of Goods Sold or to Finished Goods Inventory using standard production costs.

Information for Marshall Industrial, a ceramics producer, is used to illustrate JIT system backflush entries. To establish a foundation set of transactions from which to illustrate subsequent alternative recordings in a backflush costing system, entries for one of Marshall's products are presented in Exhibit 18.12 (page 746). The product's standard production cost is \$65.25. A long-term contract with Marshall's direct material supplier indicates a cost of \$19.25 per unit, so no material price variance occurs at purchase. Beginning inventories for July are assumed to be zero. Standard conversion cost per unit is \$46.00.

The following selected T-accounts summarize the activity presented in Exhibit 18.12:

Raw and In-Process Inventory

	Debit		Credit
(1)	392,500	(4)	1,305,000
(3)	920,000		
Bal.	7,500		

Conversion Cost Control

	Debit		Credit
(2)	921,750	(3)	920,000
Bal.	1,750		

Finished Goods Inventory

	Debit		Credit
(4)	1,305,000	(5)	1,291,950
Bal.	13,050		

Cost of Goods Sold

	Debit		Credit
(5)	1,291,950		

Accounts Receivable

	Debit		Credit
(5)	2,178,000		

Sales

	Debit		Credit
		(5)	2,178,000

Four alternatives to the entries presented in Exhibit 18.12 follow. First, if production time were extremely short, Marshall might not journalize raw material purchases until

[13] A company may wish to measure output of each manufacturing cell or work center rather than plant output. Such measurements can indicate problems in a given area but do not correlate with the JIT philosophy of the team approach, plantwide attitude, and total cost picture.

[14] A company using activity-based costing may not even need to allocate these costs because, under ABC, they would be considered nonallocable, organizational-level costs.

Exhibit 18.12 Basic Entries Used to Illustrate Backflush Costing

Marshall Industrial's standard production cost per unit:

Direct material	$19.25
Conversion	46.00
Total cost	$65.25

No beginning inventories exist.

	Debit	Credit
(1) Purchased $392,500 of direct material in July:		
Raw and In-Process (RIP) Inventory	392,500	
Accounts Payable		392,500
To record material purchased at standard cost under a long-term agreement with supplier		
(2) Incurred $921,750 of conversion costs in July:		
Conversion Cost Control	921,750	
Various accounts		921,750
To record conversion costs; various accounts include Wages Payable for direct and indirect labor, Accumulated Depreciation, Supplies, etc.		
(3) Applied conversion costs to RIP for 20,000 units completed:		
Raw and In-Process Inventory (20,000 × $46.00)	920,000	
Conversion Cost Control		920,000
To apply labor and overhead to units completed		
(4) Transferred 20,000 units of production in July:		
Finished Goods Inventory (20,000 × $65.25)	1,305,000	
Raw and In-Process Inventory		1,305,000
To transfer completed goods from RIP		
(5) Sold 19,800 units on account in July for $110 each:		
Accounts Receivable (19,800 × $110)	2,178,000	
Sales		2,178,000
To record goods sold on account		
Cost of Goods Sold (19,800 × $65.25)	1,291,950	
Finished Goods Inventory		1,291,950
To record cost of goods sold		

Ending inventories:

Raw and In-Process Inventory ($1,312,500 – $1,305,000)	$ 7,500
Finished Goods Inventory ($1,305,000 – $1,291,950)	$13,050

In addition, there are underapplied conversion costs of $1,750 ($921,750 – $920,000).

production is complete. In this case, and in addition to recording entries (2) and (5) in Exhibit 18.12, the entry to replace entries (1), (3), and (4) follows. Completion of the finished goods is the trigger point for this entry.

	Debit	Credit
Raw and In-Process Inventory	7,500	
Finished Goods Inventory (20,000 × $65.25)	1,305,000	
Accounts Payable		392,500
Conversion Cost Control (20,000 × $46.00)		920,000
To record completed production and accounts payable, and adjust RIP inventory account valuation		

Second, if completed goods were shipped immediately to customers, Marshall could use another alternative in which the entries to complete and sell products would be combined. Doing so would replace entries (3), (4), and the first element in (5) in Exhibit 18.12. Entries (1), (2), and the second element in (5) in Exhibit 18.12 would still be needed. Sale of the products is the trigger point for this entry.

Finished Goods Inventory (200 × \$65.25)	13,050	
Cost of Goods Sold (19,800 × \$65.25)	1,291,950	
Raw and In-Process Inventory (20,000 × \$19.25)		385,000
Conversion Cost Control (20,000 × \$46.00)		920,000
To record sale of products and adjust RIP and FG inventory account valuations		

The third alternative reflects the ultimate JIT system: other than entry (2) in Exhibit 18.12, the only entry made is to record product sales. All account adjustments would be made through this entry. For Marshall, the entry would be:

Raw and In-Process Inventory (minimal overpurchases)	7,500	
Finished Goods Inventory (minimal overproduction)	13,050	
Cost of Goods Sold	1,291,950	
Accounts Payable		392,500
Conversion Cost Control		920,000
To adjust inventory account valuations and record accounts payable		

A fourth alternative charges all costs to the Cost of Goods Sold account, with a subsequent backflush of costs to the Raw and In-Process Inventory and the Finished Goods Inventory accounts at the end of the period. The following entries replace entries (1), (3), (4), and (5) shown in Exhibit 18.12. Entry (2) in Exhibit 18.12 would still be made at the product sale trigger point.

Cost of Goods Sold	1,312,500	
Accounts Payable		392,500
Conversion Cost Control		920,000
To charge all material, labor, and overhead costs to CGS		
Raw and In-Process Inventory	7,500	
Finished Goods Inventory	13,050	
Cost of Goods Sold		20,550
To adjust inventory account valuations		

Implementing JIT can create significant cost reductions and productivity improvements. Management should consider the costs of, and benefits provided by, the inventory control alternatives before choosing a system. One qualitative benefit that must be quantified in the decision process is that JIT usage allows workers as well as managers to concentrate on providing quality service to customers.

Flexible Manufacturing Systems and Computer-Integrated Manufacturing

7 What are flexible manufacturing systems?

Many manufacturers have changed their processes and activities in the past few decades. Causes of change include the use of:

- automated equipment,
- a cellular plant layout,
- computer hardware and software technology, and
- new manufacturing systems and philosophies such as JIT and activity-based management.

Traditionally, most manufacturing firms employed long production runs to make thousands of identical products; this process was encouraged by the idea of economies of scale. After each run, the machines would be stopped and a slow and expensive setup would be made to prepare for the next massive production run. Now, many companies are using a new generation of manufacturing known as a **flexible manufacturing system (FMS)**.

An FMS involves a network of robots and material conveyance devices monitored and controlled by computers that allows for rapid production and responsiveness to changes in production needs. Exhibit 18.13 contrasts a traditional manufacturing system with an FMS.

Exhibit 18.13 Comparison of Traditional Manufacturing and Flexible Manufacturing System

Factor	Traditional Manufacturing	Flexible Manufacturing System
Product variety	Limited	Extensive
Response time to market needs	Slow	Rapid
Worker tasks	Specialized	Diverse
Production runs	Long	Short
Lot sizes	Massive	Small
Performance rewards basis	Individual	Team
Setups	Slow and expensive	Fast and inexpensive
Product life cycle expectations	Long	Short
Work area control	Centralized	Decentralized
Production activity	Labor intensive	Technology intensive
Information requirements	Batch based	Online, real-time
Worker knowledge of technology	Low to medium	High

Modular factories commonly employ FMSs and output can be customized upon request by customers because such systems can introduce new products quickly, produce in small lot sizes, make rapid machine and tool setups, and communicate and process large amounts of information. Information is transferred through an electronic network to computers that control the robots performing most of the production activities. The FMS functions with online, real-time production flow control using fiber optics and local-area networks. Companies are able to operate at high speeds and can quickly and inexpensively stop producing one item and start producing another, making it possible to minimize product costs while building a large assortment of high-quality products to offer customers.

An FMS can operate in a "lights-out" environment and never tire; thus, the need for direct labor is diminished. However, because workers perform a greater variety of tasks than the narrowly specialized workers of earlier manufacturing eras, workers in a company employing an FMS must be more highly trained than those working in traditional manufacturing environments. Managing manufacturing cells requires that workers have greater authority and responsibility because production and production scheduling changes happen so rapidly on the shop floor that an FMS relies on immediate decisions by people who "live there" and have a grasp of the underlying facts and conditions.

The connection of two or more FMSs via a host computer and an information networking system is generally referred to as **computer-integrated manufacturing (CIM)**. Although an FMS is typically associated with short-volume production runs, many companies (such as **Campbell Soup Co.**, **General Motors**, and **Cummins Engine**) use CIM for high-volume lines.

Lean Enterprises

8 Why are lean enterprises important in today's business environment?

Lean manufacturing refers to the process of making only those items demanded by customers and making those items without waste. Lean manufacturing originated in post–World War II Japan, when production managers were compelled to develop practices that minimized waste and resource consumption because access to material, factory equipment, and warehouse space was limited. Lean enterprises use many of the management tools, such as cellular manufacturing, JIT, Six Sigma, and autonomation, discussed earlier in this chapter. A major theme in lean enterprises is the same as that of JIT: inventory should be eliminated to the extent possible because it hides production problems and wastes resources.

Lean enterprises, such as **Toyota** and **Rockwell Automation Power Systems**, put pressure on the entire value chain to minimize waste, maximize quality, eliminate NVA activities, and shorten the lead time for delivering products and services. Two concepts are central to a lean enterprise's success and that of its value chain: leveraging technology and training employees. Technology allows for short cycle times, high-quality products, and quick changeovers of production lines. Well-trained employees manage the technology, identify ways to become more efficient, and focus on satisfying customer needs. With the ability to quickly develop and sell high-quality products having minimal defects, lean enterprises have raised the competitive bar in many industries. For some industries, these competitive pressures have led to reduced product life cycles and dramatically reduced new product time to market. Some performance benefits from implementing lean practices are shown in Exhibit 18.14.

Exhibit 18.14 Benefits of Being "Lean"

Estimated performance results accomplished by the implementation of lean principles	
Business process transaction cycle time	50 to 90% reduction
Manufacturing cycle time	0 to 95% reduction
Inventory	40 to 80% reduction
Manufacturing floor space/Office area	30 to 60% reduction
Productivity	25 to 60% improvement
New product development lead-time	0 to 50% improvement
Manufacturing/Operating costs	15 to 25% reduction
Cost of poor quality	30 to 50% reduction

Source: UCSD Extension, "Lean Enterprise: A Specialized Certificate Program," http://extension.ucsd.edu/programs/eng/lean.html.

The theory of constraints is another important production management tool that is used by lean enterprises.

THEORY OF CONSTRAINTS

9 How can the theory of constraints help in determining production flow?

The **theory of constraints (TOC)** can help management reduce cycle time. This theory indicates that the flow of goods through a production process cannot be at a rate faster than the slowest constraint in the process.[15] A **constraint** is anything that confines or limits the ability of a person or machine to perform a project or function.

Production limitations in a manufacturing environment are caused by human, material, and machine constraints. Some constraints relate to process speed, whereas others relate to absolute production limits such as availability of material or machine time. Still other constraints relate to people and any limitations those people have on their ability to understand, react, or perform at some particular rate of speed. These constraints cannot be totally overcome (because people will never be able to work at the speed of an automated machine), but can be reduced through proper hiring and training. Because the labor content contained in products is declining rapidly as automation increases, constraints caused by machines are often of more concern than human constraints in reducing cycle time.

[15] The theory of constraints was introduced to business environments by Eliyahu Goldratt and Jeff Cox in the book *The Goal* (New Haven, CT: North River Press, Inc./Spectrum Publishing Company, 1986).

Constraints, also called **bottlenecks**, are points at which the processing levels are sufficiently slow as to cause the other processing mechanisms in the network to experience idle time. Bottlenecks cause an activity's processing to be impeded. Even a totally automated, "lights-out" process will have some constraints because all machines do not operate at the same speed or handle the same capacity. Therefore, the constraints must be identified and corrected to the extent possible.

Exhibit 18.15 provides a simplistic illustration of a production process constraint. Although Machine 1 can process 90,000 pounds of raw material in an hour, Machine 2 can handle only 40,000 pounds. Of the 70,000 pounds of input, 30,000 pounds of processed material will be waiting at the constraining machine after an hour of processing. The constraint's effect on production is obvious, but the implications are not quite as clear. Managers have a tendency to want to see machines working, not sitting idle. Consider what this tendency would mean if the desired output were 450,000 pounds rather than 70,000. If Machine 1 were kept in continual use, all 450,000 pounds would be processed through Machine 1 in five hours. However, a backlog of 250,000 pounds [450,000 – 5(40,000)] of processed material would now be waiting at Machine 2! All of this material would require storage space and create additional NVA costs.

Exhibit 18.15 Production Constraint

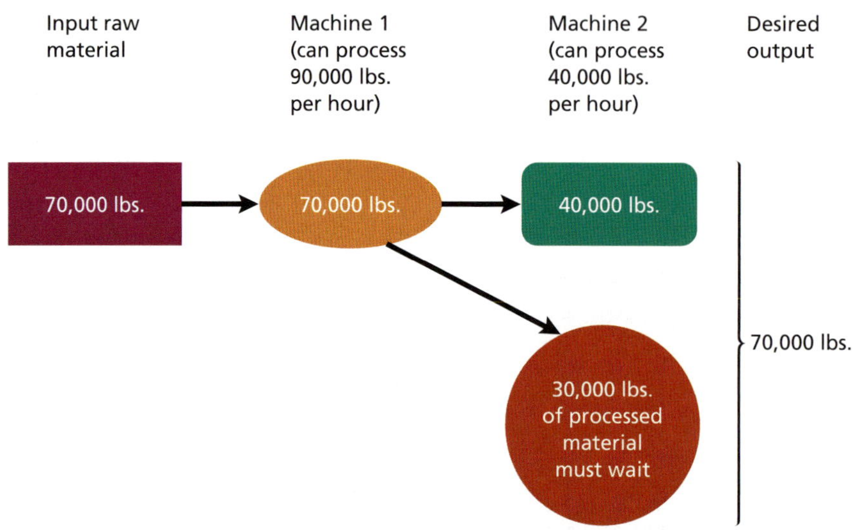

Machine constraints also impact quality control. Managers normally choose quality control points to follow completion of a particular process. When constraint points are known, quality control points should *always* be placed before a constrained process. "If you scrap a part before it reaches the bottleneck, all you have lost is a scrapped part. But if you scrap the part after it's passed through the bottleneck, you have lost time that cannot be recovered."[16]

As soon as constraints are known, managers should determine what is the best use of constrained process time or productive capacity and then limit the constraints' impacts on performance. Options such as adding more machines to perform the constrained activity or processing material through other machines that would reduce limitations should be investigated. Managing constraints is a process of continuous improvement.

[16] Ibid., p. 156.

APPENDIX

ECONOMIC ORDER QUANTITY AND RELATED ISSUES

The concepts of economic order quantity and economic production run are used, respectively, for purchasing and manufacturing decisions.

10 How are economic order quantity, order point, and safety stock determined and used?

Economic Order Quantity

Companies making purchasing (rather than production) decisions often compute the **economic order quantity (EOQ)**, which represents the least costly number of units to order. EOQ indicates the optimal balance between ordering and carrying costs by mathematically equating total ordering costs to total carrying costs. EOQ is a tool that is used in conjunction with traditional "push" production and inventory management systems. Because EOQ implies acquiring and holding inventory before it is needed, it is incompatible with "pull" systems such as JIT.

Purchasing managers should first determine which supplier can offer the appropriate quality of goods at the best price in the most reliable manner. After the supplier is selected, the most economical inventory quantity to order—at a single time—is determined. The EOQ formula is

$$EOQ = \sqrt{\frac{(2QO)}{C}}$$

where EOQ = economic order quantity in units
Q = estimated annual quantity used in units (can be found in the annual purchases budget)
O = estimated cost of placing one order
C = estimated cost to carry one unit in stock for one year

Note that unit purchase cost is not included in the EOQ formula. Purchase cost relates to the question of from whom to buy, which is considered separately from the question of how many to buy at a single time. Except to the extent that opportunity cost is calculated on the basis of investment, inventory unit purchase cost does not affect the other costs in the EOQ formula.

All inventory-related costs must be evaluated when purchasing or production decisions are made. The costs of ordering and carrying inventory oppose each other when estimating the economic order quantity: as more units are purchased at a time, fewer units must be kept in inventory.

Marshall Industrial uses 64,000 pounds of one material in producing ceramic products. The cost associated with placing each order is \$40. The carrying cost of one pound of the material is \$2 per year. Therefore, Marshall's EOQ for this material is calculated as follows:

$$EOQ = \sqrt{\frac{(2 \times 64{,}000 \times \$40)}{\$2}} = 1{,}600 \text{ pounds}$$

Economic Production Run

In a manufacturing company, managers are concerned not only with how many units of raw material to buy, but also with how many finished units to produce in a batch. The EOQ formula can be modified to calculate the appropriate number of units to manufacture in an **economic production run (EPR)**. This estimate reflects the production quantity that minimizes the total costs of setting up a production run and of carrying one unit in stock for one year. The only change in the EOQ formula is that the equation's terms are redefined as manufacturing rather than as purchasing costs. The formula is

$$EPR = \sqrt{\frac{(2QS)}{C}}$$

where EPR = economic production run in units
Q = estimated annual quantity to be produced in units (can be found in annual production budget)
S = estimated cost of setting up a production run
C = estimated cost to carry one unit in stock for one year

Marshall manufactures 183,750 ceramic sinks per year. Setup cost for a ceramic sink run is \$240, and the annual carrying cost for each sink is \$5. The economic production run quantity is determined as follows:

$$EPR = \sqrt{\frac{(2 \times 183{,}750 \times \$240)}{\$5}} = 4{,}200 \text{ sinks}$$

Cost differences among various run sizes around the EPR might not be significant. If such costs are insignificant, management would have a range of acceptable, economical production run quantities.

The critical step in using either an EOQ or an EPR model is to properly identify costs, especially carrying costs. This process is often very difficult, and some costs (such as those for facilities, operations, administration, and accounting) that were traditionally viewed as irrelevant fixed costs could, in actuality, be long-term relevant variable costs. Also, the EOQ or EPR model does not provide any direction for managers attempting to control all of the separate costs that collectively compose ordering and carrying costs. By considering only the trade-off between ordering (or producing) and carrying costs, these models do not lead managers to consider inventory management alternatives that can simultaneously reduce both categories of costs.

Additionally, as companies significantly reduce the necessary setup time (and thus cost) for operations and move toward a "stockless" inventory policy, a more comprehensive cost perspective will indicate a substantially smaller cost per setup and a substantially larger annual carrying cost. These changes will reduce the EOQ and EPR.

Order Point and Safety Stock

The EOQ or EPR model indicates how many units to order or produce, respectively. Managers are also concerned with the **order point**, which reflects the inventory level that triggers placement of an order for additional units; if the EPR model were being used, the concern would be about the inventory level that triggers production. Determination of order or production point is based on three factors: usage, lead time, and safety stock. **Usage** refers to the quantity of inventory used or sold each day. An order's **lead time** reflects the days between issuing an order (externally or internally) to obtaining or producing the necessary goods. Companies can often project a constant, average figure for both usage and lead time. The inventory quantity kept by a company in the event of fluctuating usage or unusual delays in lead time is called **safety stock**.

If usage is entirely constant and lead time is known with certainty, the order point equals daily usage multiplied by lead time:

$$\text{Order point} = \text{Daily usage} \times \text{Lead time}$$

As an example, Marshall uses 5,000 pounds of silica sand per day, and the supplier can have the material to Marshall in two days. When the stock of silica sand reaches 10,000 pounds, Marshall should place an order for additional silica sand.

The order point formula minimizes a company's inventory investment. Orders would arrive at precisely the time the inventory reached zero. This formula, however, does not take into consideration unusual events such as variations in production schedules, defective products being provided by suppliers, erratic shipping schedules of the supplier, and late arrival of units shipped. To provide for such events, managers carry a "buffer" safety stock of inventory to protect the company from being out of stock. When a safety stock is maintained, the order point formula becomes

Order point = (Daily usage × Lead time) + Safety stock

Safety stock size should be determined based on how crucial the item is to production or to retail sales, the item's purchase cost, and the amount of uncertainty related to both usage and lead time.

One way to estimate safety stock quantity is to allow one factor to vary from the norm. For example, either excess usage during normal lead time or normal usage with excess lead time can be considered in the safety stock calculation. Assume that Marshall never uses more than 8,000 pounds of silica sand in one day. Given this information, a revised estimate of the necessary safety stock is 6,000 pounds, computed as follows:

Maximum daily usage	8,000 pounds
Normal daily usage	(5,000) pounds
Excess usage	3,000 pounds
Lead time	× 2 days
Safety stock	6,000 pounds

Using this estimate of safety stock, Marshall would order silica sand when 16,000 pounds (10,000 original order point + 6,000 safety stock) was on hand.

Pareto Inventory Analysis

Unit cost commonly affects the degree of control that should be maintained over an inventory item. As unit cost increases, internal controls (such as inventory access) are typically tightened and a perpetual inventory system is more often used. Recognition of cost–benefit relationships can result in a **Pareto inventory analysis**, which separates inventory into three groups based on annual cost-to-volume usage.

Items having the highest value are referred to as A items; C items represent the lowest dollar volume of usage. All other inventory items are designated as B items. Exhibit 18.16 illustrates the results of a typical Pareto inventory analysis: 20 percent of the inventory items (A items) account for 80 percent of the cost; an additional 30 percent of the items

Exhibit 18.16 Pareto Inventory Analysis

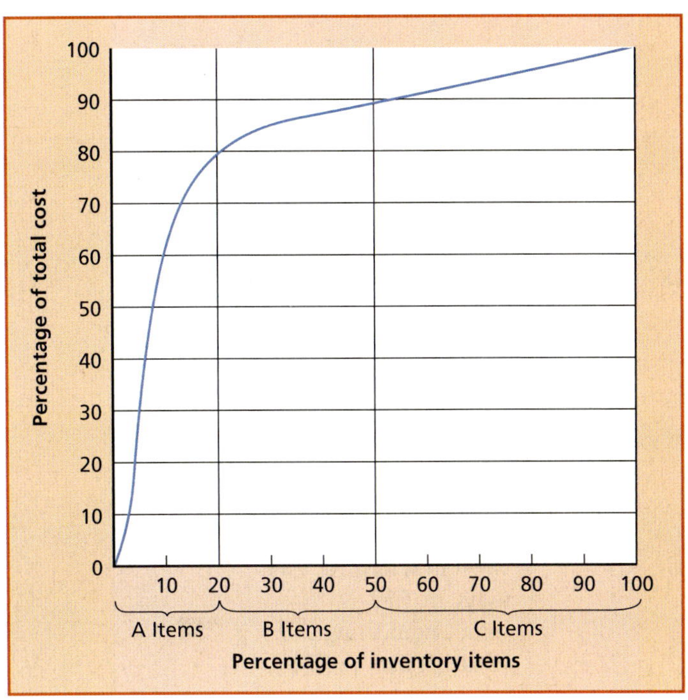

(B items), taken together with the first 20 percent (the A items), account for 90 percent of the cost; and the remaining 50 percent of the items (C items) account for the remaining 10 percent of the cost.

Once inventory is categorized as A, B, or C, management can determine the best inventory control method for items in each category. A-type inventory should require a perpetual inventory system and would be a likely candidate for JIT purchasing techniques to minimize the funds tied up in inventory investment. The highest control procedures would be assigned to these items. Such a treatment reflects the financial accounting concept of materiality.

Items falling into the C category need only periodic inventory control procedures and may involve a two-bin or red-line system. Under a **two-bin system**, two containers (or stacks) of inventory are available for production needs. When production begins to consume materials in the second container, a purchase order is placed to refill the first container. In a **red-line system**, a red line is painted on the inventory container at a level representing the order point. Both systems require that production needs and estimates of receipt time from suppliers be fairly accurate.

Having the additional container or stack of inventory on hand is considered to be reasonable based on the insignificant dollar amount of investment involved with C category items. The control placed on C items is probably minimal also because inventory cost is immaterial. The type of inventory system (perpetual or periodic) and the level of internal control associated with items in the B category will depend on management's judgment. Influencing characteristics include the item's significance to the production process, suppliers' response time, and estimates of benefits to be gained by increased accounting or access controls. Computers have made additional controls over inventory easier and more cost beneficial.

Comprehensive Review Module

KEY TERMS

autonomation, p. 741
backflush costing, p. 745
bottleneck, p. 750
computer-integrated manufacturing (CIM), p. 748
constraint, p. 749
cost table, p. 733
economic order quantity (EOQ), p. 751
economic production run (EPR), p. 751
flexible manufacturing system (FMS), p. 747
focused factory arrangement, p. 741
Internet business model, p. 742
just-in-time (JIT), p. 735
just-in-time manufacturing system, p. 735
kaizen costing, p. 734
kanban, p. 735
lead time, p. 752
lean manufacturing, p. 748
manufacturing cell, p. 740
order point, p. 752
Pareto inventory analysis, p. 753
product life cycle, p. 731
pull system, p. 730
purchasing cost, p. 730
push system, p. 730
red-line system, p. 754
safety stock, p. 752
supply-chain management, p. 742
target costing, p. 732
theory of constraints (TOC), p. 749
two-bin system, p. 754
usage, p. 752
value engineering (VE), p. 734
virtual reality, p. 732

CHAPTER SUMMARY

1 Important Value Chain Relationships

- Important value chain relationships for a firm are those
  - with suppliers—to get the highest-quality inputs, on time, at a competitive price.
  - with customers—to deliver the features, quality, and value that lead to customer satisfaction.
  - within the firm—to coordinate production activities.

2 Costs Associated with Inventory

- The primary cost associated with inventory is either the cost of purchasing or producing the goods.
  - Purchasing cost for inventory is the quoted purchase price minus any discounts allowed, plus shipping charges.
  - Production cost for inventory is the summation of costs associated with purchasing direct material, paying for direct labor, and absorbing variable and fixed overhead.
- Ordering costs include amounts for invoice preparation, receiving, inspection, and payment.
- Setup costs include labor costs and machine downtime costs.
- Carrying costs of inventory include storage, handling, insurance, property taxes, obsolescence losses, and the opportunity cost of invested capital.
- Stockout costs include loss of customer goodwill, special ordering expenses, and setup costs for rescheduled production.
- Managing inventory costs is important to the firm because inventory
  - produces no value for the firm until it is sold.
  - can hide inefficiencies in production activities.
  - is a significant investment.

3 Push and Pull Inventory Systems

- Push systems produce goods to satisfy a production schedule based on economic production run concepts.
- Pull systems produce goods only in response to current customer demand.

4 Product Life Cycles and Profitability

- Product life cycles affect profitability because costs vary across the product life cycle, although most costs are determined in the development stage of the life cycle.
- Product life cycle stages affect profitability because sales volume and selling prices vary across those stages.

5 Target Costing

- Target cost is calculated as expected selling price minus (acceptable profit margin + selling & administrative cost).
- Target costing is a tool to manage production costs
  - in the development stage of the product life cycle.
  - by developing an estimate of an "allowable" production cost (target cost) based on the estimated sales price of the product.
- Target costing forces managers to align the expected production cost with the target cost.
- Target cost is continually reduced over a product's life cycle to spur continuous improvement.

6 Just-in-Time (JIT) Inventory System

- JIT is a philosophy that states production should not occur until a customer demands the product.
- Successful implementation of JIT requires
  - elimination of non-value-added activities.
  - a focus on continuous improvement.
  - persistent efforts to reduce inventory.
  - a focus on improving quality of processes.
  - high-quality inputs from vendors.
- JIT can require modifications to the accounting system to recognize
  - variances immediately upon occurrence rather than at period end.
  - that inventories be sufficiently small to no longer justify separate accounting for raw, in-process, and finished goods. Simpler systems, such as backflush costing, can be adopted.

7 Flexible Manufacturing System (FMS)

- A flexible manufacturing system
  - integrates computer systems with automated production equipment.
  - is often used in plants organized for cellular manufacturing.
  - minimizes the time required to set up for production.
  - is ideal for low-volume, high-quality products.

8 Lean Enterprises

- Lean manufacturing refers to making only those items in demand by customers and making those items without waste.
- Lean enterprises put pressure on their entire value chains to minimize waste, maximize quality, eliminate activities that add product cost but not value, and shorten delivery lead time for products and services.
- Lean enterprises emphasize an organization's ability to leverage technology and train employees.
- Lean enterprises have raised the competitive bar in many industries by quickly developing and selling high-quality products that have few defects.

9 Theory of Constraints (TOC)

- TOC is a tool for reducing cycle time by
  - maximizing the flow of products through production bottlenecks.
  - overcoming constraints in the flow of goods through a production system.

SOLUTION STRATEGIES

Target Costing, p. 733

Target cost = Expected long-range selling price − Acceptable profit − Selling & administrative costs

Compare predicted total life cycle cost to target cost; if life cycle cost is higher, determine ways to reduce it.

Material and Labor Variances under JIT, p. 735

Two standards can exist:

1. an annual standard (set and held constant for the year), and
2. a current standard (based on design modifications or engineering change orders).

Generally, firms have minimal, if any, material price variances because prices are set by long-term contracts. A labor rate variance can occur and is calculated in the traditional manner.

Material Quantity Variance, p. 744

  Actual material cost
− Material cost at current standard
  Material quantity variance

Engineering Change Order Variance for Material, p. 744

  Material cost at annual standard
− Material cost at current standard
  ECO variance

Labor Efficiency Variance, p. 743

  (Actual labor hours × Current standard rate)
− (Standard labor hours × Current standard rate)
  Labor efficiency variance

Engineering Change Order Variance for Labor, p. 744

(Exists only if a change occurs in the mix of labor used to manufacture the product or through the automation of processes.)

  (Standard labor hours × Annual standard rate)
− (Standard labor hours × Current standard rate)
  ECO variance

DEMONSTRATION PROBLEM 1

NewMaid has designed a new consumer product, a floor cleaner and wax, that is expected to have a five-year life cycle. Based on market research, NewMaid's management has determined that the product should be packaged in 32-ounce containers and should be sold at $6 per container in the first three years and $4 per container during the last two years. Unit sales are expected to be as follows:

Year 1	300,000
Year 2	400,000
Year 3	600,000
Year 4	400,000
Year 5	250,000
Total	1,950,000

Variable selling costs are expected to be $1 per container throughout the product's life. Annual fixed selling and administrative costs are estimated to be $500,000. NewMaid management desires a 25 percent profit margin on selling price.

Required:

a. Compute the life cycle target cost to manufacture the product. (Round to the nearest cent.)

b. If NewMaid anticipates the new product will cost $3 per unit to manufacture in the first year, what is the maximum that manufacturing could cost in the last four years? (Round to the nearest cent.)

c. Suppose that NewMaid engineers determine that expected manufacturing cost per unit over the product life cycle is $2.25. What actions might the company take to reduce this cost?

Solution to Demonstration Problem 1

a. Step 1—Determine total product life cycle revenue:

Year 1	300,000 × $6 =	$ 1,800,000
Year 2	400,000 × $6 =	2,400,000
Year 3	600,000 × $6 =	3,600,000
Year 4	400,000 × $4 =	1,600,000
Year 5	250,000 × $4 =	1,000,000
Total revenue		$10,400,000

Step 2—Determine average unit revenue (AR) during product life:

AR = Total revenue ÷ Total product life cycle units
= $10,400,000 ÷ 1,950,000 units
= $5.33 (rounded)

Step 3—Determine average unit fixed selling and administrative cost (AFS&A):

AFS&A = (5 years × $500,000) ÷ 1,950,000 units
= $2,500,000 ÷ 1,950,000
= $1.28 (rounded)

Step 4—Determine unit selling and administrative cost (US&AC):

US&AC = AFS&A + Variable selling cost
= $1.28 + $1.00
= $2.28

Step 5—Calculate target cost (TC):

TC = AR – 0.25(AR) – US&AC
= $5.33 – (0.25 × $5.33) – $2.28
= $5.33 – $1.33 – $2.28
= $1.72

b. Step 1—Determine total allowable cost over product life:

1,950,000 units × $1.72 = $3,354,000

Step 2—Determine expected total production cost in first year:

$3 × 300,000 units = $900,000

Step 3—Determine allowable unit cost in last four years:

($3,354,000 – $900,000) ÷ 1,650,000 units = $1.49 (rounded)

c. The following actions are potential options for the company:

- Product design and/or production processes can be changed to reduce costs. Cost tables can be used to provide information on the impact of using different input resources, processes, or design specifications.
- The 25 percent acceptable profit margin can be reduced.
- NewMaid can suspend consideration of the project at the present time.

DEMONSTRATION PROBLEM 2

CAN-DO Inc. manufactures home-improvement products in a JIT environment. The annual and current material standards for one of the company's products follow.

Annual Material Standards	
Material 1: 4 pounds × $3.75	$15.00
Material 2: 12 pounds × $2.25	27.00
	$42.00

Current Material Standards	
Material 1: 8 pounds × $3.75	$30.00
Material 2: 8 pounds × $2.25	18.00
	$48.00

The current material standards differ from the original because an engineering change order was made near the end of August. During September, the company manufactured 1,000 units of product and used 7,500 pounds of Material 1 and 8,200 pounds of Material 2. All material is acquired at the standard cost per pound.

Required:

a. Calculate the material variance and the ECO material variance.
b. Explain the effect of the ECO on product cost.

Solution to Demonstration Problem 2

a.

Actual Material Usage	
Material 1: 7,500 × $3.75	$28,125
Material 2: 8,200 × $2.25	18,450
Total material cost	$46,575

Material Cost at Current Standard	
Material 1: 1,000 × 8 × $3.75	$30,000
Material 2: 1,000 × 8 × $2.25	18,000
Total material cost	$48,000

Material Cost at Annual Standard	
Material 1: 1,000 × 4 × $3.75	$15,000
Material 2: 1,000 × 12 × $2.25	27,000
Total material cost	$42,000

Variances	
Material cost at current standard	$ 48,000
Actual material cost	(46,575)
Material quantity variance	$ 1,425 F
Material cost at annual standard	$ 42,000
Material cost at current standard	(48,000)
ECO variance	$ (6,000) U

b. The effect of the ECO was to substitute the higher-priced Material 1 for the lower-priced Material 2. The financial effect of this change was to increase expected production cost for August by $6,000. However, the cost increase could have been offset by an increase in price, assuming the change in mix of materials increased product quality.

POTENTIAL ETHICAL ISSUES

ETHICS

1. Producing inventory that is not needed relative to current sales demand to increase reported operating profits
2. Avoiding the adoption of innovative production and inventory management methods because of short-run negative effects on profits
3. Blaming suppliers for inventory problems that are, in actuality, artifacts of in-house inventory management mistakes
4. Failing to write-down obsolete or spoiled inventory as soon as information regarding these conditions becomes known
5. Using coercion to force suppliers to yield price concessions so that the cost of manufacturing a product is kept in line with the product's market price
6. Using the adoption of evolving production and inventory management methods as a justification to dismiss workers

QUESTIONS

1. What are the three costs associated with inventory? Explain each and give examples.
2. Differentiate between the push and pull systems of production. Is JIT a push or a pull system?
3. How does a product's life cycle stage influence production cost management?
4. What is target costing, and how is it useful in assessing a product's total life cycle cost?
5. Why does the development stage have such a significant influence on a product's profitability over its life cycle?
6. What is kaizen costing, and how does it differ from target costing?
7. What are the primary goals of the JIT philosophy, and how does JIT attempt to achieve these goals?
8. What changes must occur in a production environment to effectively implement JIT? Why are these changes necessary?
9. How would switching from a traditional manufacturing system to a flexible manufacturing system affect a firm's inventory and production control systems?
10. What is the theory of constraints? How is this concept appropriate for manufacturing and service companies?
11. (*Appendix*) How are ordering costs and carrying costs related?
12. (*Appendix*) What is Pareto inventory analysis? Why do A items and C items warrant different inventory control methods? What are some methods that can be employed to control C items?

EXERCISES

INTERNET

13. **LO.2 (Inventory cost management; research)** Randomly select annual reports for ten publicly traded manufacturing companies. On the balance sheet, or in the related footnotes, for each firm, find the amounts for Raw Material, Work in Process, and Finished Goods Inventory accounts. Calculate the following ratios for each firm, and the average for the ten firms:
    - Raw Material Inventory to total assets
    - Work in Process Inventory to total assets
    - Finished Goods Inventory to total assets
    - total inventory to total assets

    a. On average, how large is total inventory as a percentage of total assets for your ten firms?
    b. On average, which inventory component comprises the largest percentage of total inventory?
    c. Do your answers to (a) and (b) suggest that effective inventory management is crucial to the success of these ten firms? Discuss.

14. **LO.2 & LO.10 (Inventory cost management)** Indicate whether each of the following costs would be considered an ordering cost (O), a carrying cost (C), or a cost of not carrying (N) inventory. For any costs that do not fit these categories, indicate N/A for "not applicable."
   a. Telephone call to supplier
   b. Stationery and purchase order forms
   c. Purchasing agent's salary
   d. Purchase price of product
   e. Customer goodwill lost due to unavailability of product
   f. Postage on purchase order
   g. Freight-in cost on product
   h. Insurance for products in inventory
   i. Wages of receiving clerks
   j. Preparing and issuing checks to suppliers
   k. Contribution margin lost due to unavailability of product
   l. Storage costs for products on hand
   m. Quantity discounts on products ordered
   n. Opportunity cost of funds invested in inventory
   o. Property taxes on warehouses
   p. Handling costs for products on hand
   q. Excess ordering and shipping charges for rush orders of standard product lines
   r. Spoilage of products awaiting use

15. **LO.1, LO.2, & LO.9 (Inventory cost management; EOQ; writing)** A plant manager and her controller were discussing the plant's inventory control policies. The controller suggested to the plant manager that the ordering policies should be reviewed because new technology had been implemented in the plant, including installation of (1) computerized inventory tracking, (2) electronic data interchange capabilities with the plant's major suppliers, and (3) in-house facilities for electronic fund transfers.
   a. As technology changes, why should managers update ordering policies for inventory?
   b. Write a memo to the plant manager describing the likely impact of the changes made in this plant on the economic order quantity of material input.

16. **LO.1 & LO.2 (Inventory cost management; writing)** The supply management director at Texas Oil Field Services has contracted to purchase $2 million of spare parts that are currently unneeded. His rationale for the contract was that the parts were currently available at a significantly reduced price from the standard price. The company just hired a new president who, on learning about the contracts, stated that the purchase contract should be canceled because the parts would not be needed for at least a year. The supply management director informed the president that the penalties for canceling the contracts would cost more than letting the orders go through. How would you respond to this situation from the standpoint of the president? From the standpoint of the supply management director?

17. **LO.3 (Push vs. pull systems; writing)** Everyone in your company seems excited about the suggestion that the firm implement a JIT system. Being a cautious person, however, your company president has asked you to write a report describing situations in which JIT will not work. Prepare such a report.

18. **LO.3 (Push vs. pull systems; writing)** Tonight you are going to dine at the restaurant of your choice. To choose the restaurant, you are going to consider the fact that some manage their food production on a push basis and others manage their food production on a pull basis.
   a. Discuss the difference between managing food production in a restaurant on a push versus a pull basis.
   b. Are there any circumstances in which you would prefer to dine at a restaurant that uses a push model of food production? Discuss.

c. Are there any circumstances in which you would prefer to dine at a restaurant that uses a pull model of food production? Discuss.

19. **LO.4 (Product life cycle; writing)** Joe Giles is a product engineer for a firm that makes various home and office electronic gadgets. Some of this company's products have long product life cycles and others have life cycles that are as short as nine months. Giles's company uses both target and kaizen costing to manage costs relative to the product life cycle of the firm's products. As an intern with the company, you recall a conversation in which Giles stated that kaizen cost management strategies were much more effective for products with longer life cycles than products with shorter life cycles, and that target costing techniques including value engineering were much more critical to products with short life cycles than to products with long life cycles. Do you agree with Giles? Why or why not?

20. **LO.4 (Product life cycle; writing)** Recently you read an article regarding a new product introduced late last year by 3G Inc., a consumer products company. The article's author, although praising 3G Inc. for providing the marketplace with this innovative product, simultaneously criticized the company because the product had generated a $50 million loss for the year due to low unit sales. The author concluded the article by suggesting that company management had "missed the boat" with this product and should "dump it" as soon as possible. After reading this article you recall the concept of product life cycle and after contemplating how sales volume behaves over the product life cycle, you believe you can rebut the author of the 3G Inc. story. Write the rebuttal.

21. **LO.5 (Target costing)** Utah Utensil has developed a new kitchen utensil. The firm has conducted significant market research and estimated the following pattern for sales of the new product:

Year	Expected Volume	Expected Price per Unit
1	48,000 units	$19
2	48,000 units	20
3	90,000 units	16
4	40,000 units	12

The firm wants to net a minimum of $3.50 per unit in profit over the product's life, and selling and administrative expenses are expected to average $50,000 per year. Calculate the target cost per unit to produce the new utensil.

22. **LO.4 & LO.5 (Target costing)** The marketing department at Cleveland Furniture Mfg. has an idea for a new product that is expected to have a six-year life cycle. After conducting market research, the company found that the product could sell for $800 per unit in the first four years of life and for $650 per unit for the last two years. Unit sales are expected to be as follows:

Year 1	4,000
Year 2	3,600
Year 3	4,700
Year 4	5,000
Year 5	1,500
Year 6	1,000

Per-unit variable selling costs are estimated at $140 throughout the product's life; total fixed selling and administrative costs over the six years are expected to be $3,700,000. Cleveland Furniture Mfg. desires a profit margin of 15 percent of selling price per unit.

a. Compute the life cycle target cost to manufacture the product. (Round to the nearest cent.)

b. If the company expects the product to cost $430 to manufacture in the first year, what is the upper bound for manufacturing cost in the following five years? (Round to the nearest cent.)

c. Refer to the original information. Assume that Cleveland Furniture Mfg. engineers indicate that the expected manufacturing cost per unit is $340. What actions might the company take to reduce this cost?

EXCEL

23. **LO.5 (Target costing; writing)** Mosquito MoJo is developing a propane-powered mosquito zapper for campers. Market research has indicated that potential purchasers would be willing to pay $145 per unit for this product. Company engineers have estimated that first-year production costs will amount to $120 per unit and selling and administrative expenses will be $20 per unit. On this type of product, Mosquito MoJo would normally expect to earn a $15 per unit profit. Using the concept of target costing, write a memo that (a) analyzes the prospects for this product and (b) discusses possible organizational strategies.

INTERNET

24. **LO.5 (Value engineering; research; writing)** Research the topic of value engineering on the Internet, and write a brief report on a company or an organization's experiences using this technique.

25. **LO.6 (Backflush costing)** Consider the following data pertaining to March 2013 for a firm that has adopted JIT.

Production	8,000 units
Sales ($20 per unit)	7,900 units
Standard production costs	
Direct material	$4
Conversion costs	8

Assume that there were no cost or usage variances for March, and the quantity of material used equaled the quantity purchased. All material is purchased on account, and all units started were completed.

a. Assuming that the company uses a traditional costing system, record the journal entries to recognize the following:
   1. purchase of material
   2. incurrence of conversion costs
   3. completion of the month's production
   4. sale of the month's production

b. Assuming that the company initially charges all costs to Cost of Goods Sold and then uses backflush costing to assign costs to inventories at the end of the period, record the journal entries to recognize the following:
   1. incurrence of conversion costs
   2. completion of production
   3. backflushing of costs to inventories

EXCEL

26. **LO.6 (Backflush costing)** Durham Denim uses backflush costing to account for production costs of its one-size-fits-all panchos. During August 2013, the firm produced 150,000 panchos and sold 149,000. The standard cost for each pancho is:

Direct material	$2
Conversion costs	4
Total cost	$6

The firm had no inventory on August 1. The following events took place in August:

- Purchased $302,000 of direct material
- Incurred $608,000 of conversion costs
- Applied $600,000 of conversion costs to Raw and In-Process Inventory
- Finished 150,000 panchos
- Sold 149,000 panchos for $10 each

a. Prepare journal entries using backflush costing with a minimum number of entries.
b. Post the amounts in (a) to T-accounts.
c. Explain any inventory account balances.

27. **LO.6 (JIT implementation; writing)** Duggan Mfg. began implementing a just-in-time inventory system several months ago. The production and purchasing managers, however, have not seen any dramatic improvements in throughput. The managers have decided that the problems are related to company suppliers. The company's three suppliers seem to send the wrong materials at the wrong times. Prepare a discussion of the problems that might exist in this situation. Be certain to address the following items: internal and external communications; possible engineering changes and their impacts; number, quality, and location of suppliers; and length of system implementation.

28. **LO.6 (JIT variances)** Oklahoma Pneumatic uses a JIT system. The following standards are related to materials A and B, which are used to make one unit of the company's final product:

Annual Material Standards	
3 pounds of Material A × $2.50	$ 7.50
4 pounds of Material B × $3.40	13.60
	$21.10

Current Material Standards	
2 pounds of Material A × $2.50	$ 5.00
5 pounds of Material B × $3.40	17.00
	$22.00

Current material standards differ from the original because of an engineering change made near the end of June. During July, the company produced 3,000 units of its final product and used 11,000 pounds of Material A and 10,000 pounds of Material B. All material is acquired at the standard cost per pound.

a. Calculate the material variance and the ECO material variance.
b. Explain the effect of the ECO on product cost.

29. **LO.6 (JIT variances)** Natural Gardens makes recyclable pots for plants and uses JIT to manage inventories and production. The following are standards for a typical one-gallon pot:

Annual Material Standards	
32 ounces of Component X × $0.02	$0.64
2 ounces of Component Y × $0.05	0.10
	$0.74

Current Material Standards	
27 ounces of Component X × $0.02	$0.54
4 ounces of Component Y × $0.05	0.20
	$0.74

In-house experiments indicated that changing the material standard would make the pots stronger, so the company issued an engineering change order for the product in February; this ECO established the current material standards. March production was 8,000 pots. Usage of raw material (all purchased at standard price) in March was 220,000 ounces of Component X and 31,000 ounces of Component Y.

a. Calculate the material quantity variance.
b. Calculate the ECO variance.
c. Summarize the company's effectiveness in managing March production costs.
d. Comment on the circumstances in which a company would institute an ECO that results in the expected product cost being unchanged.

30. **LO.7 (Flexible manufacturing systems; research; writing)** On the Internet, research the topic of manufacturing cells and write a brief report on company experiences using those cells.

INTERNET

31. **LO.7 & LO.8 (Flexible manufacturing systems; writing)** Installation of a flexible manufacturing system allows firms to make a variety of products in small batches. Assume Johnson Steel, a metal fabricating company, is considering switching from a traditional assembly line production process to an FMS. Provide answers to the following questions.

   a. How would the adoption of an FMS likely affect the inventory levels?
   b. How would the adoption of an FMS likely affect the quantity of production employees needed?
   c. Would the adoption of an FMS require employees to be retrained? Explain.

32. **LO.9 (Production constraints)** Xcaliber manufactures high-end flatware. One of the crucial processes in flatware production is polishing. The company normally operates three polishing machines to maintain pace with the upstream and downstream production operations. However, one of the polishing machines broke yesterday, and management has been informed that the machine will not be back in operation until repairs are completed in three weeks. Two machines cannot keep pace with the volume of product flowing to the polishing operation. You have been hired as a consultant to improve the throughput of the polishing operation. Discuss the tactics you would recommend Xcaliber to employ for handling the capacity limitation.

EXCEL

33. **LO.9 (Production constraints)** Promotional Products produces commercial banner flags in a two-department operation: Department 1 is labor intensive and Department 2 is automated. The average output of Department 1 is 45 units per hour. Units from Department 1 are transferred to Department 2 to be completed by a robot. The robot can finish a maximum of 45 units per hour. The company needs to complete 180 units this afternoon for an order that has been backlogged for four months. The production manager has informed the people in Department 1 that they are to work on nothing else except this order from 1:00 P.M. until 5:00 P.M. The supervisor in Department 2 has scheduled the same times for the robot to work on the order. Department 1's activity for each hour of the afternoon is as follows:

Time	1:00–2:00 P.M.	2:00–3:00 P.M.	3:00–4:00 P.M.	4:00–4:58 P.M.
Production	40 units	44 units	50 units	46 units

Each unit moves directly from Department 1 to Department 2 with no lag time. Did Promotional Products complete the 180 units by 5:00 P.M.? If not, explain and provide detailed computations.

34. **LO.10 (Appendix: multiproduct EOQs)** A retail cosmetics chain carries three types of skin products: face cream, lotion, and powder. Determine the economic order quantity for each, given the following information:

Product	Order Cost	Carrying Cost	Demand
Face cream	$12	$2.00	2,000 units
Lotion	40	1.45	1,000 units
Powder	15	1.25	900 units

Round each answer to the nearest whole unit.

35. **LO.10 (Appendix: carrying costs)** Farm Fresh manufactures a variety of animal food products from alfalfa "pellets." The firm has determined that its EOQ is 80,000 pounds of pellets. Based on the EOQ, the firm's annual ordering cost for pellets is $16,700. Given this information, what is the firm's annual carrying cost of pellets? Explain.

36. **LO.10 (Appendix: carrying costs)** Determine the carrying costs for an item costing $6.80, given the following per-unit cost information:

Storage cost	$0.24
Handling cost	0.28
Production labor cost	1.70
Insurance cost	0.44
Opportunity cost	8% of investment

37. **LO.10 (Appendix: EPR)** UpTown Mfg. custom manufactures machine parts used by other companies. The following data relate to production of Part #33:

Annual quantity produced in units	3,600
Cost of setting up a production run	$600
Cost of carrying one unit in stock for a year	$2

Calculate the economic production run for Part #33; round to the nearest whole unit.

38. **LO.10 (Appendix: EPR)** Rachelle Razer has taken a job as production superintendent in a plant that makes, among other products, jewelry cases. She is trying to determine how many cases to produce on each production run (EPR). Discussions reveal that last year the plant made 15,000 such cases, and this level of demand is expected for the coming year. The setup cost of each run is $400, and the cost of carrying a case in inventory for a year is estimated at $2.50.

   a. Calculate the EPR for jewelry cases and the total cost associated with it. Round the EPR to the nearest whole unit.
   b. Recalculate the EPR and total cost if the annual cost of carrying a case in inventory is $10 and the setup cost is $100. Round the EPR to the nearest whole unit.

39. **LO.10 (Appendix: product demand)** Compute annual estimated demand for a product if the economic order quantity is 1,600 units, carrying cost is $0.35 per unit, and ordering cost is $140.00 per order.

PROBLEMS

40. **LO.1 (Inventory cost management; ethics; writing)** In early 2007, Burger King, under pressure from animal rights activists including People for Ethical Treatment of Animals (PETA), announced it would start purchasing pork and eggs from suppliers that use cage-free animal management methods. In its announcement, Burger King stated it would also give purchasing preference to poultry suppliers that use or switch to "controlled atmosphere stunning," which is regarded by some to be a more humane method of slaughtering poultry.

ETHICS

Source: Associated Press, "Burger King to Serve up Cage-Free Food," CBS Money Watch (2/11/09); http://www.cbsnews.com/stories/2007/03/28/business/main2618928.shtml (last accessed 2/29/12).

   a. Discuss how the change in Burger King's pork and egg supplier policy might affect the prices Burger King pays for pork and eggs.
   b. Evaluate the ethics of the new supplier policy from the point of view of a Burger King patron, assuming that the new supplier policy will likely increase prices charged for pork and egg food products.
   c. Evaluate the ethics of the new policy from the point of view of a supplier who will now face higher costs in providing Burger King with pork or egg products.

41. **LO.2 (Identification of inventory costs)** Tyler Tubing's management has been evaluating company policies with respect to control of costs of corrugated metal, one of the firm's major component materials. The firm's controller has gathered the following financial data, which may be pertinent to controlling costs associated with the metal tubing:

Ordering Costs	
Annual salary of purchasing department manager	$61,500.00
Depreciation of equipment in purchasing department	$42,300.00
Cost per order for purchasing department supplies	$0.90
Typical phone expense per order placed	$6.06
Monthly expense for heat and light in purchasing department	$700.00

Carrying Costs

Annual depreciation on materials storage building	$30,000.00
Annual inventory insurance premium (per dollar of inventory value)	$0.15
Annual property tax on materials storage building	$7,500.00
Obsolescence cost per dollar of average annual inventory	$0.16
Annual salary of security officer assigned to the materials storage building	$38,000.00

a. Which of the ordering costs should Tyler Tubing's controller consider in performing short-run decision analysis? Explain.

b. Which of the carrying costs should Tyler Tubing's controller consider in performing short-run decision analysis? Explain.

42. **LO.2 (Inventory cost management; writing)** IMeg manufactures various electronic assemblies that are sold primarily to computer manufacturers. IMeg's reputation has been built on quality, timely delivery, and products that are consistently on the cutting edge of technology. IMeg's typical product has a short life; products are in development for about a year and in the growth stage, with sometimes spectacular growth, for about a year. Each product then experiences a rapid decline in sales as new products become available.

IMeg's competitive strategy requires a reliable stream of new products to be developed each year, which is the only way that the company can overcome the threat of product obsolescence. IMeg's products go through the first half of the product life cycle similar to products in other industries; however, differences occur in the second half of the products' life cycles. IMeg's products never reach the mature product or declining product stage. Near the end of the growth stage, products just "die" as new ones are introduced.

a. In the competitive market facing IMeg, what would be key considerations in production and inventory control?

b. How would the threat of immediate product obsolescence affect IMeg's practices in purchasing product components and materials?

CMA ADAPTED

c. How would the threat of product obsolescence affect the inventory carrying costs for a typical product produced by IMeg?

43. **LO.1 & LO.3 (Push vs. pull systems; writing)** Koss Corp. makes high-quality headphones for a variety of applications. Koss is a Milwaukee-based company but has significant manufacturing operations in China. When manufacturing operations were moved to China, CEO Michael Koss was a strong proponent of just-in-time inventory management. Although the company maintained significant orders of component parts, finished goods were produced only to satisfy customer orders. Accordingly, work in process and finished goods inventories were small. However, moving production offshore significantly increased the complexity of the firm's logistics. Unexpected changes in product mix and fluctuating demand for products caused the firm's backlog of orders to rise significantly. Koss responded by scrapping the JIT production and stacking finished goods on the factory floor pending receipt of customer orders.

Source: Paulette Thomas, "Case Study: Electronics Firm Ends Practice Just In Time," *Wall Street Journal* (October 29, 2002), p. B9.

a. Why does globalization of a firm's production operations increase the challenges in controlling inventories using the JIT philosophy (pull system)?

b. After scrapping JIT, Koss reported that the total investment in inventories dropped from $15 million to $8 million. How could this occur?

c. From the perspective of managing the risk of a stock outage, is Koss better off holding mostly finished goods inventory, or mostly component parts inventories? Explain.

44. **LO.3 (Push vs. pull systems; writing)** Assume that you are a management consultant who advises manufacturing firms regarding production technologies. One of the hot issues you often discuss with management is whether a pull system or a push system is superior in a particular situation. Consider the following circumstances and discuss whether you would recommend a push system or a pull system in each particular case:

a. The firm manufactures two consumer products; 75 percent of annual sales are made during the year-end holiday sales cycle.
b. The firm manufactures a variety of goods for the petroleum industry; most products are sold in low volumes and have a high unit cost.
c. The firm manufactures products subject to rapid obsolescence and that have relatively short product life cycles.
d. The firm manufactures products that have a limited shelf life.
e. The firm manufactures a limited line of products for which there is predictable, but seasonal, demand and the products have long life cycles.

45. **LO.4 (Product life cycles; writing)** Assume you are the CFO of an electronics manufacturer. Your firm is about to launch an extremely innovative new product. The product planning team has estimated life cycle sales of the product to be as follows (in thousands):

Year 1	35,000
Year 2	75,000
Year 3	125,000
Year 4	90,000
Year 5	15,000

The life cycle average sales price is projected by the product planning team to be \$80. The team has recommended to top management and the marketing team that the introductory product price be set at \$60.

a. As CFO, what is your reaction to the suggested introductory price of \$60 relative to the expected life cycle price of \$80?
b. Most of the profit of consumer electronic products is realized early in the product life cycle. How would this fact influence your recommendation about where the price for this product should be set for Year 1?
c. As CFO, are you concerned that a significant portion of the forecasted life cycle volume for this product is assigned to years 3 and 4? Explain.

46. **LO.4 (Product life cycles; writing)** Sony Corp. launched its PlayStation 3 in late 2006. It was introduced at a price point of \$599 for the top model. At the time of introduction, a California technology firm performed a tear-down of the PlayStation and estimated its cost of production to be \$839. Based on this cost estimate, the California tech firm estimated Sony was losing as much as \$240 per unit sold.

Source: Lee Gomes, "Talking Tech: A Peek under PlayStation 3's Hood Shows Sony Is Selling Units at a Loss," *Wall Street Journal* (November 21, 2006), p. B4.

a. Assume that Sony generates more profit on royalties from the games played on PlayStation than on the sales of PlayStation itself. In light of this explanation, is it rational for Sony to sell the PlayStation at a \$240 loss? Explain.
b. How would setting the price of the PlayStation at \$599, rather than the breakeven price of \$839, likely affect (1) early life cycle sales and (2) total life cycle sales of PlayStation 3?
c. Is Sony's pricing strategy (i.e., introductory price below production cost) more beneficial if the product's life cycle is long or short? Explain.

47. **LO.4 & LO.5 (Target costing)** Gourmet Grade has just completed its work on a new microwave entrée. After consumer research was conducted, the marketing group has estimated the following quantities of the product can be sold at the following prices over its life cycle: EXCEL

Year	Quantity	Selling Price	Year	Quantity	Selling Price
1	100,000	\$2.50	5	600,000	\$2.00
2	250,000	2.40	6	450,000	2.00
3	350,000	2.30	7	200,000	1.90
4	500,000	2.10	8	130,000	1.90

Initial engineering estimates of direct material and direct labor costs are $1.70 and $0.40, respectively, per unit. Variable overhead per unit is expected to be $0.50, and fixed overhead is expected to be $200,000 per year. Gourmet Grade's management strives to earn a 25 percent gross margin on products of this type.

a. Estimate the target cost for the new entrée.
b. Compare the estimated production cost to the target cost. Discuss this comparison and how management might use the comparison to manage costs.
c. Based on your answer in (b), should Gourmet Grade begin production of the new entrée? Explain.

48. **LO.5 (Target costing)** StatPro has just been presented the following market and production estimates on Product X27, which has been under development in the company.

Projected market price of X27		$215 (based on 180,000 life cycle unit sales over five-year life)
Projected gross margin per unit		35
Estimated selling and administrative costs per unit		40
Estimated production costs		
Direct material	$70	
Direct labor	40	
Variable overhead	15	
Fixed overhead	$360,000 annually	

Use the concept of target costing to integrate the marketing and engineering information and interpret the results for StatPro.

49. **LO.6 (JIT features)** Indicate by letter which of the three categories apply to the following features of just-in-time systems. Use as many letters as appropriate.

D = desired immediate result of using JIT
U = ultimate goal of JIT
T = technique associated with JIT

a. Reducing setup time
b. Reducing total cost of producing and carrying inventory
c. Using focused factory arrangements
d. Designing products to minimize design changes after production starts
e. Monitoring quality on a continuous basis
f. Using manufacturing cells
g. Minimizing inventory stored
h. Measuring variances caused by an engineering change order
i. Using autonomation processes
j. Pulling purchases and production through the system based on sales demand

50. **LO.6 (JIT journal entries; advanced)** Wisconsin Wire (WW) has implemented a just-in-time inventory system for the production of its insulated wire. Inventories of raw material and work in process are so small that WW uses a Raw and In-Process account. In addition, almost all labor operations are automated, and WW has chosen to cost products using standards for direct material and conversion costs. The following production standards are applicable at the beginning of 2013 for one roll of insulated wire:

Direct material (100 yards × $2)	$200
Conversion (4 machine hours × $35)	140
Total cost	$340

The conversion cost of $35 per machine hour was estimated on the basis of 500,000 machine hours for the year and $17,500,000 of conversion costs. The following activities took place during 2013:

1. Raw material purchased and placed into production totaled 12,452,000 yards. All except 8,000 yards were purchased at the standard price of $2.00 per yard. The other 8,000 yards were purchased at a cost of $2.06 per yard; the higher price was due to the placement of a rush order. The order was approved in advance by management. All purchases are on account.
2. From January 1 to February 28, WW manufactured 20,800 rolls of insulated wire. Conversion costs incurred to date totaled $3,000,000. Of this amount, $600,000 was for depreciation, $2,200,000 was paid in cash, and $200,000 was on account.
3. Conversion costs are applied to the Raw and In-Process account from January 1 to February 28 on the basis of the annual standard.
4. The Engineering Department issued a change order (ECO) to the operations flow document effective March 1, 2013. The change decreased the machine time to manufacture one roll of wire by five minutes per roll. However, the standard raised the amount of direct material to 100.4 yards per roll. The Accounting Department requires that the annual standard be continued for costing the Raw and In-Process Inventory for the remainder of 2013. The effects of ECOs should be shown in two accounts: Material Quantity ECO Variance and Machine Hours ECO Variance.
5. Total production for the remainder of 2013 was 103,200 rolls of wire. Total conversion costs for the remaining 10 months of 2013 were $14,442,000. Of this amount, $4,000,000 was depreciation, $9,325,000 was paid in cash, and $1,117,000 was on account.
6. The standard amount of conversion cost is applied to the Raw and In-Process Inventory for the remainder of the year.

Note: Some of the journal entries for the following items are not explicitly covered in the chapter. This problem challenges students regarding the accounting effects of the implementation of a JIT system.

a. Prepare entries for items 1, 2, 3, 5, and 6.
b. Determine the increase in material cost due to the ECO related to direct material.
c. Prepare a journal entry to adjust the Raw and In-Process Inventory account for the ECO cost found in (b).
d. Determine the reduction in conversion cost due to the ECO related to machine time.
e. Prepare a journal entry to reclassify the actual conversion costs by the savings found in (d).
f. Making the entry in (e) raises conversion costs to what they would have been if the ECO related to machine time had not been made. Are conversion costs under- or overapplied and by what amount?
g. Assume that the reduction in machine time could not have been made without the corresponding increase in material usage. Is the net effect of these ECOs cost beneficial? Why?

51. **LO.6 (JIT journal entries)** Cosmo Industries recorded the following transactions for its first month of operations:

		Debit	Credit
(1)	Direct Material Inventory	24,000	
	Accounts Payable		24,000
	To record purchase of direct material		
(2)	Work in Process Inventory	24,000	
	Direct Material Inventory		24,000
	To record distribution of material to production		
(3)	Conversion Cost Control	40,000	
	Various accounts		40,000
	To record incurrence of conversion costs		
(4)	Work in Process Inventory	40,000	
	Conversion Cost Control		40,000
	To assign conversion cost to WIP		

		Debit	Credit
(5)	Finished Goods Inventory	64,000	
	Work in Process Inventory		64,000
	To record completion of products		
(6)	Accounts Receivable	116,000	
	Sales		116,000
	To record sale of products		
	Cost of Goods Sold	62,000	
	Finished Goods Inventory		62,000
	To record cost of goods sold		

Because Cosmo employs JIT, the company's CEO has asked how the accounting system could be simplified.

a. Prepare the journal entries, assuming that no transactions are recognized until goods are completed.
b. Prepare the journal entries, assuming that goods are shipped to customers as soon as they are completed and that no journal entries are recorded until goods are completed.
c. Prepare the journal entries, assuming that sale of product is the trigger point for journal entries.
d. Prepare the journal entries, assuming that sale of product is the trigger point for journal entries and that the firm uses backflush costing.

ETHICS

52. **LO.8 & LO.9 (Lean manufacturing; TOC; ethics; writing)** Recent years have been characterized by high, and volatile, energy prices. Some critics of the energy industry suggest that the oil companies' use of JIT inventory management has contributed to the volatility in prices and the supply constraints. Further, oil and natural gas products are crucial inputs to other industrial products such as chemicals and plastics. These industries also have been rocked by both the volatility in energy prices and the availability of the oil- and gas-derived inputs to their products. To illustrate one of the negative outcomes of the supply volatility, **Citigroup** cut its stock rating of **Lear Corp.** in late 2005 because of fears of adverse effects on profits from shortages of materials and higher prices of materials derived from inputs produced by the oil and gas industry.

Source: Mary Ellen Lloyd, "Hurricanes' Effects on Oil, Gas Trickle Down to Other Products," *Wall Street Journal* (October 6, 2005), p. A2.

a. Is JIT management of inventories an ethical practice by the oil industry if it is true that JIT practices increase the volatility in energy prices for energy consumers?
b. How could application of the theory of constraints help alleviate the effects of material shortages experienced by firms that consume products derived from the oil and gas industry?
c. What actions could firms that are dependent on inputs from the oil and gas industry take to reduce supply chain risks?
d. In the United States, both federal and state governments increase the price of energy (particularly automotive fuels) to the consumer by assessing taxes on energy sold at the consumer level. Do governments have an ethical responsibility to reduce taxes on energy when prices spike upward? Discuss.

53. **LO.10 (Appendix: EPR)** Gale's Garden grows and sells a variety of indoor and outdoor plants and garden vegetables. One of the firm's more popular vegetables is a red onion, which has an annual sales quantity of approximately 30,000 pounds. Two of the major inputs in the growing of onions are seeds and fertilizer. Due to the poor germination rate, two seeds must be purchased for each onion plant grown (a mature onion plant provides 0.5 pound of onion). Also, 0.25 pound of fertilizer is required for each pound of onion produced. The following information summarizes costs for onions, seeds, and fertilizer. Carrying costs for onions are expressed per pound of onion; carrying costs for seeds are expressed per seed; and for fertilizer, carrying costs are expressed per pound of fertilizer. To plant onions, the company incurs a cost of $50 to set up the planter and the fertilizing equipment.

	Onions	Seeds	Fertilizer
Carrying cost	$ 0.25	$0.01	$0.05
Ordering cost	—	$4.25	$8.80
Setup cost	$50.00	—	—

a. What is the economic production run for onions? (Round to the nearest whole pound.)
b. How many production runs will Gale's Garden make for onions annually? (Round to the nearest whole production run.)
c. What are the economic order quantities for seeds and fertilizer? (Round to the nearest whole seed or whole pound.)
d. How many orders will be placed for seeds? For fertilizer? (Round to the nearest whole order.)
e. What is the total annual cost of ordering, carrying, and setting up for onion production?
f. How is the planting of onions similar to and different from a typical factory production run?
g. Are there any inconsistencies in your answers to (a)–(c) that need to be addressed? Explain.

54. **LO.10 (Appendix: EOQ)** Diane Delbert operates a health food bakery that uses a special type of ground flour in one of its high-margin products. The bakery operates 365 days a year. Delbert finds that she seems to order either too much or too little special flour and asks for your help. After some discussion, you find that she has no idea of when or how much to order. An examination of her records and answers to further questions reveal the following information:

Annual usage of special flour	7,000 pounds
Average number of days delay between initiating and receiving an order	12
Estimated cost per order	$32.00
Estimated annual cost of carrying a pound of special flour in inventory	$0.50

a. Calculate the economic order quantity for flour. (Round to the nearest whole pound.)
b. Assume that Delbert desires a safety stock cushion of seven days' usage. Calculate the appropriate order point. (Round the order point to the nearest whole pound.)

Maxstockphoto/Shutterstock.com

19

Emerging Management Practices

LEARNING OBJECTIVES

After reading this chapter, you should be able to answer the following questions:

1. How do business process reengineering initiatives cause radical changes in the way firms execute processes?
2. How are competitive forces driving decisions to downsize and restructure operations?
3. In what ways, and why, are operations of many firms becoming more diverse? How does the increasing diversity affect the roles of the firms' accounting systems?
4. Why are firms adopting enterprise resource planning systems, and how are such systems used?
5. What are strategic alliances, what forms do they take, and why do firms participate in them?
6. What are the characteristics of open-book management, and why does its adoption require changes in accounting methods and practices?
7. What are the three generic approaches that firms can take in controlling environmental costs?

INTRODUCTION

Firms are presently decentralizing information, authority, and responsibility to make decisions. This trend has created opportunities and challenges for the firms' accounting functions. To be effective, decision makers must have the skills to interpret a variety of information, including financial reports. However, not all employees are adequately trained to understand financial information. This circumstance has created some innovative approaches to developing the information skills of managers.

This chapter discusses innovation in management practices and the impact of innovation on accounting. The "age of change" is an apt description for the current environment in which managers and financial professionals must function. Although some changes have been driven by the fast pace of evolution in management practices and techniques, many changes have been driven by the even faster evolution of technology. These evolving management methods unite around a theme of focusing organizational resources on customers and maximizing the value that the firm delivers to its customers. The discussion begins with dramatic structural workplace changes that are affecting many employers and employees.

THE CHANGING WORKPLACE

The forces of global competition and technological advancements have caused profound changes in business organizations. To survive, managers must develop ways to achieve the competitive changes needed in organizations. Change may occur either immediately or gradually. Managers use both time frames to effect change.

Some overriding principles that managers should follow when implementing changes are presented in Exhibit 19.1. The roles for financial professionals in change management are discussed later in the chapter. When major operational improvements are mandated, managers completely revise the way activities are performed. Business process reengineering is one tool with which to achieve large, quick gains in effectiveness or efficiency through redesigning the execution of specific business functions.

Exhibit 19.1 Managerial Principles for Successfully Managing Change

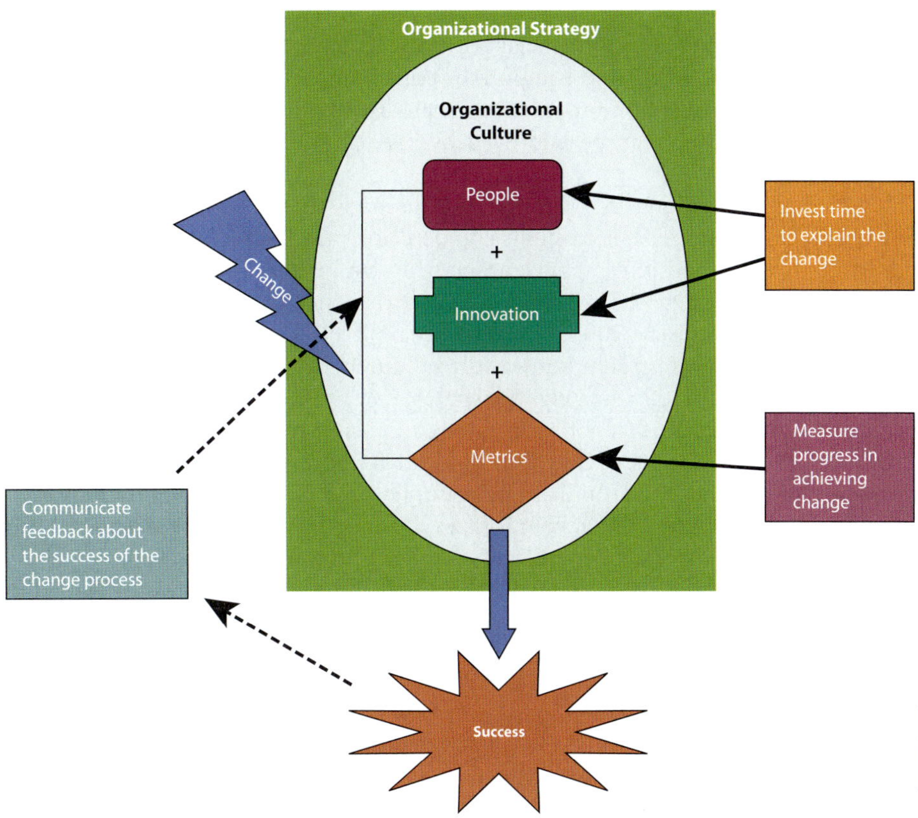

BUSINESS PROCESS REENGINEERING

1 How do business process reengineering initiatives cause radical changes in the way firms execute processes?

Business process reengineering (BPR) is a method of examining processes to identify and then eliminate, reduce, or replace functions and processes that add little customer value to products or services. The focus of BPR is on discrete initiatives to improve specific processes. Process examples include

- handling or storing purchased materials and components,
- issuing checks to pay labor and other production expenses,
- packaging finished products for shipment to customers,
- recording journal entries, and
- developing an organizational strategic plan.

BPR initiatives in a global enterprise could encompass the entire firm or only a single subunit. Thus, the initiatives can originate with managers at different organizational levels.

BPR is designed to bring radical changes to operations and is often associated with employee layoffs, outsourcing initiatives, and technology acquisition. Three major business trends are promoting the increased use of BPR in the twenty-first century. The first trend is the advancement of technology. Neither the electronic remittance for accounts payable nor the use of robotic equipment to move and assemble components in a manufacturing facility was possible 50 years ago. Both of these practices are common today, even in small companies. Because BPR focuses on alternative ways to execute required organizational functions, it is useful in automating processes that cannot be eliminated. Technology advancements have improved efficiencies throughout the supply chain. The feasibility of automating processes is constantly changing because technology is constantly evolving. For example, several U.S. airlines are currently experimenting with technology that would link up customer information that currently resides in separate databases. This technology will assume a major role in managing customer relationships. For example, the technology will identify patterns among fliers relative to vacation destinations, travel histories, and ticket purchasing habits.[1] If successful, this technology will allow airlines to reduce marketing and customer service staff while tailoring marketing strategies to each individual flier's tastes.

The second trend leading toward increased use of BPR is the pursuit of increased quality. As discussed in Chapter 17, global competition allows consumers to purchase the highest-quality products and services from best (relative to price, service, and dependability) providers regardless of their geographical location. In many product and service markets, quality has become one of the most important criteria applied by consumers in purchasing decisions. Because it focuses on processes associated with poor quality, BPR can help indicate ways in which quality can be improved by replacing, changing, or eliminating those processes.

The third trend resulting in expanded BPR usage is the increase in price competition caused by globalization. To successfully compete on price, firms must identify ways to become more efficient and, thus, reduce costs. BPR can be used to improve efficiency, particularly when a process needs to be overhauled or a new generation of technology is needed. For example, in early 2007, **Circuit City** replaced 3,400 highly paid workers with lower-paid workers. This restructuring was driven purely by the necessity of reducing costs to remain competitive.[2] Unfortunately, the strategy was unsuccessful, and Circuit City filed for bankruptcy in late 2008. In another example, soon after the turn of the twenty-first century, **EDS**, the giant IT outsourcing firm, laid off 5,000 employees in the United States and increased service capacity in India to increase the company's cost competitiveness.[3]

Because BPR methodically revolutionizes business practices, formal steps can be defined; however, creativity is an important element of the method. Exhibit 19.2 provides the steps for implementing BPR. Objectives of a BPR project represent the potential benefits to be realized from reengineering. All relevant technological innovations must be known so that all technological constraints and opportunities can be considered. Because

[1] Scott McCartney, "The Middle Seat: Your Airline Wants to Get to Know You," *Wall Street Journal* (March 24, 2009), p. D.1.

[2] Ylan Q. Mui, "Circuit City Cuts 3,400 'Overpaid' Workers," *Washington Post* (March 29, 2007), p. D01.

[3] Ritsuko Andu and Jim Finkle, "IBM to Cut 5,000 Jobs in U.S.—Sources," *Reuters.com* (March 25, 2009); http://www.reuters.com/article/rbssTechMediaTelecomNews/ idUSWEN647920090325 (last accessed 2/24/12).

Exhibit 19.2 Steps to Business Process Reengineering

Step 1: Define the project
The project is defined and authorized by senior management. The project team is established and gains an understanding of the desired reengineering project. Stakeholders are engaged.

Step 2: Review the business baseline
Hypotheses are developed about the underlying problem cause. Performance of the area under review is "business baselined" using process mapping to obtain an understanding of the area's activities to develop additional detailed cost modeling, problem identification, and solution.

Step 3: Identify opportunities
Until this point, the activity has been reflective: collecting data and formulating ideas. This step begins the development of process redesign and hypothesis testing and the emergence of a model that captures the new way of working using investigative or best practice benchmarking.

Step 4: Verify the opportunities
The solution is tested—using benchmarked data—against the problems to ensure that it effectively and efficiently solves the problem and meets the needs. Additionally, key stakeholders are consulted to make sure the solution is acceptable.

Step 5: Plan the achievement of the benefits
After the solution has been fully tested, project implementation begins. Implementation costs are identified, which may lead to a revision of the solution. Because there is likely to be resistance to change, a detailed discussion of costs and benefits should be provided to stakeholders so they are more likely to "get on board."

Step 6: Review and report
A project report and a project review ensure that all project details are recorded and that any learning is captured and shared.

Source: Adapted from: Anonymous, "Business Process Reengineering," http://ideamlp.wetpaint.com/page/business+process+reengineering (last accessed 2/20/12).

BPR is much more complicated than a mere automation or upgrade of existing processes, creativity and vision are needed to design a prototype of the revised process.

Accountants are important participants in the BPR process because they provide baseline performance measurements, help determine BPR objectives, and measure the achieved performance of the redesigned process. Accountants must also be aware of potential applications for newly developed software and hardware that may lead to BPR innovations. The following keys to a successful BPR implementation highlight the importance of involving customers, suppliers, and top-level managers in the process:

- Set "stretch" goals for the reengineered process, expressing them in the most appropriate performance measure, such as financial, time, or quality production.
- Make certain that the reengineering efforts have a "champion" and are supported by top management.
- To the extent possible, involve all constituents of the value chain, especially customers and suppliers, in the reengineering project.
- Assign both the authority and responsibility for the project to a single person.
- Use a pilot project to identify problems that might arise during full implementation.[4]

Involvement of customers ensures that their perspective drives process redesign. Top management involvement signals the project's importance to the organization and secures the resources necessary for execution.

[4] Gene Hall, Jim Rosenthal, and Judy Wade, "How to Make Reengineering Really Work," *Harvard Business Review* (November–December 1993), pp. 119–131.

BPR's focus is on improving organizational operations. Whether the issue is quality, cost, or customer value, BPR can help effect organizational improvements and change. Because BPR is designed to achieve radical changes, its impacts on employees—downsizing and restructuring—are potentially profound.

DOWNSIZING, LAYOFFS, AND RESTRUCTURING

2 How are competitive forces driving decisions to downsize and restructure operations?

Global competition is a fact of life in many industries, and survival requires firms to continually improve product quality while maintaining competitive prices. Not all firms are able to adapt and survive under the pressures of global competition. Just as global competition has driven firms to higher levels of quality and efficiency, the same competition drives some organizations out of business. The American auto industry exemplifies the consequences of failing to adapt to changing competitive conditions. American auto firms are now forced to evaluate which business operations to defend and which to sacrifice to the competition. Loss of market share to foreign competitors and loss of economic viability have been dramatic.

Many methods, including the use of automated technology to replace manual labor or equipment run by humans, discussed in this chapter have proven useful in improving process efficiency and effectiveness as well as product quality. However, in realizing improvements, firms also encounter additional problems. Foremost among them is how to deal with excess personnel. Businesses that are striving to remain viable as well as those that are retreating from the competition are forced into restructuring operations and reducing their workforces.

A grim reality of ever-improving efficiency is that fewer and fewer workers are required to achieve a given level of output. Using practices such as BPR, firms are constantly restructuring operations to maintain or gain competitive advantages. Each successful restructuring leverages employee work into more output, and therefore, a workforce reduction is required. **Downsizing** refers to any management action that reduces employment upon restructuring operations in response to competitive pressures. Following is a list of common motivations for downsizing:[5]

- Reduce costs.
- Rightsize resources relative to market demand.
- Signal that the company is taking proactive steps to adjust to changing business needs.
- Take advantage of cost synergies after a merger.
- Release the least-productive resources.

Although downsizing has greater risks for firms in some industries than in others, all firms face risk. For example, firms can find that layoffs have depleted the in-house talent pool. The collective workforce knowledge or **organizational memory** (the aggregation of data, facts, experiences, and lessons learned that is important to an organization's existence) may have been reduced to the point that the ability to solve problems creatively and generate innovative ideas for growth has been greatly diminished. Also, after downsizing, many firms have found that positions that once served as feeder pools for future top management talent have been eliminated.

To survive in the presence of global competition, trust and effective communication must exist between workers and managers. Successive rounds of layoffs

- diminish worker morale,
- cause worker mistrust of managers, and
- lead to a decrease in communication between workers and managers.

Workers often fear that sharing information could provide insights to management about how to further increase productivity and reduce costs by eliminating more of the workforce. Many management methods discussed in this chapter depend heavily on cooperation among all of a firm's employees. Firms that are downsizing should not concurrently attempt to implement other innovative practices. Downsizing can destroy a corporate culture that embraced long-term (or even lifetime) employment as a key factor in attracting

[5] Darrell Rigby, "Downsizing," Management Tools http://www.bain.com.au/management_tools/tools_downsizing.asp?groupCode=2 (last accessed 3/7/12).

new employees or that was perceived by employees as "nurturing." Significant negative change in an organization's culture is likely to have a similar negative impact on employee morale and trust.

Downsizing is an accounting issue because of its implications for financial reporting and its role in cost management. The financial consequences of downsizing can be highly significant. When restructuring and downsizing occur in the same year, the firm often reports a large, one-time loss in that year caused by the severance costs connected with employee layoffs and sale of unprofitable assets. From a cost management perspective, accountants must understand the full consequences, both monetary and nonmonetary, of downsizing. Before recommending downsizing to improve organizational efficiency, accountants should examine the likely impacts on customer service, employee morale and loyalty, and future growth opportunities.

Exhibit 19.3 demonstrates that strategic decisions affect the manner in which inputs, such as labor, technology, purchased material, and services, are converted into outputs for customers. Downsizing changes the mix of inputs used to produce outputs, increases the emphasis on technology-based conversion processes, and reduces the emphasis on manual conversion processes and, thus, the labor requirement. The two-directional arrow in Exhibit 19.3 shows increased outsourcing from suppliers and increased dependence on technology as substitutes for labor.

Exhibit 19.3 The Value Chain and Cost Management

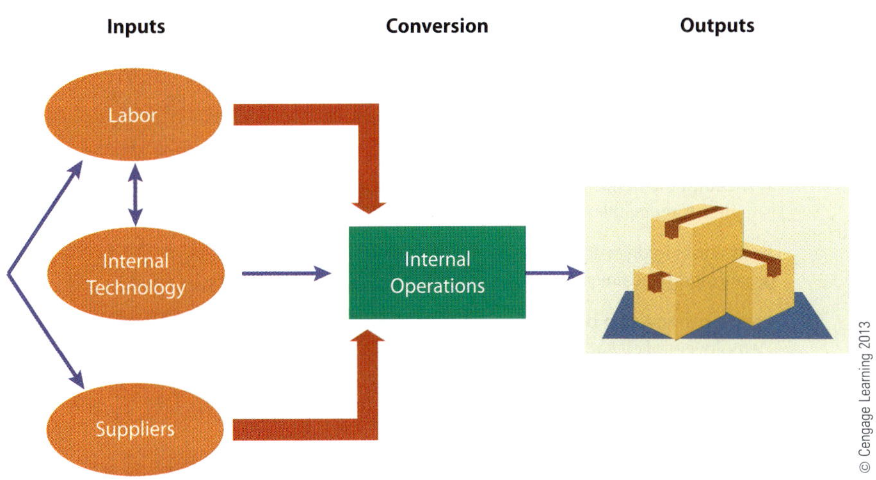

Financial analysis of the downsizing decision is complex because the analysis relies on comparing future labor cost savings to the current outlay for restructuring and acquiring additional technology. The capital budgeting methods discussed in Chapter 15 should be applied to this decision. If downsizing involves asset sales, the financial analysis must compare the cash to be realized from such sales against the annual net revenues or net cash flows that will *not* be realized in the future because of the reduced asset base. Capital budgeting tools provide managers information about how downsizing is likely to affect profitability and the return on invested capital.

WORKFORCE DIVERSITY

Under the pressure of global competition, many firms have expanded operations geographically. By sourcing and marketing worldwide, firms can develop new markets, reduce input costs, and manage the effects of peaks and valleys in local economies. Globalization of operations presents managers with new opportunities and challenges.

With widespread manufacturing and other operations, companies find that their employees have divergent religions, races, values, work habits, cultures, political ideologies, and education levels. Diversity across countries is evident within companies that operate

3 In what ways, and why, are operations of many firms becoming more diverse? How does the increasing diversity affect the roles of the firms' accounting systems?

globally. Corporate policies and information systems must adapt to the changing workforce and increasing operational diversity, which often result in the accounting function having a larger role in managing operations. Although different languages and cultures can impede communications within globally dispersed operations, accounting information can be a powerful coordinating mechanism: interpretation of accounting information need not depend on local culture or language.

Accounting concepts, tools, and measurements can be the medium through which people of diverse languages and cultures communicate. Accounting provides an ideal international technical language because it is a basic application of another universal language—mathematics. Managing a global business, as opposed to one that operates in a single country, involves many considerations in addition to coordinating employees. Global businesses must consider country differences in currency values, labor practices, political risks, tax rates, commercial laws, and infrastructure such as ports, airports, and highways. These considerations require development of new systems and controls with which to manage risks and exploit opportunities.

Within the United States, there is a trend toward increasing workplace diversity. The trend is driven partly by legal requirements and business initiatives to increase opportunities for minorities and partly by organizational self-interest. Refer to Exhibit 19.4 for reasons, other than legal requirements, that firms may seek a more diverse workforce. Unfortunately, this trend can be problematic in light of other business practices discussed in this

Exhibit 19.4 Why Self-Interested Firms Seek a Diverse Group of Employees

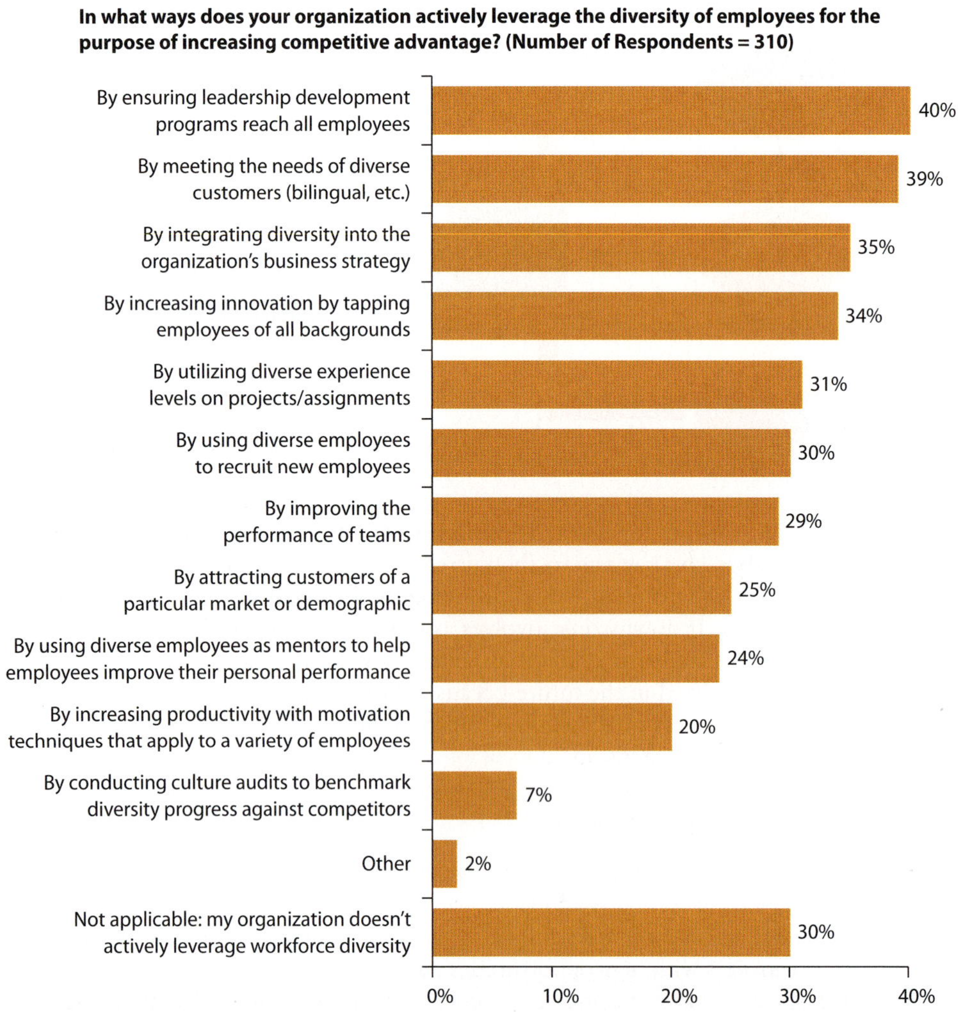

Source: Nancy R. Lockwood, "Workplace Diversity: Leveraging the Power of Difference for Competitive Advantage," *HR Magazine* 50 (6), pp. A1–A10.

chapter. BPR and downsizing diminish the opportunity to diversify and become more responsive to the marketplace.

Technology plays a major role in the communications that are necessary to harmonize employee actions to manufacture products and serve customers. Often the integration of information systems is accomplished with enterprise systems.

ENTERPRISE RESOURCE PLANNING SYSTEMS

4 Why are firms adopting enterprise resource planning systems, and how are such systems used?

Firms commonly use networked personal computers (PCs) and minicomputers to handle the information management requirements of specific business functions, such as finance, marketing, and manufacturing. PCs allow maximum user flexibility in accessing and manipulating data in real time. However, the increased use of PCs and local-area networks has resulted in the decentralization of information. As data management and storage have become more decentralized, firms have often lost the ability to integrate information across functions and to quickly access information that spans multiple functions. Exhibit 19.5 shows how internal processes and functions are distributed across the supply chain and the types of information that may reside in isolated databases.

Exhibit 19.5 Internal Supply Chain and Traditional Information Management

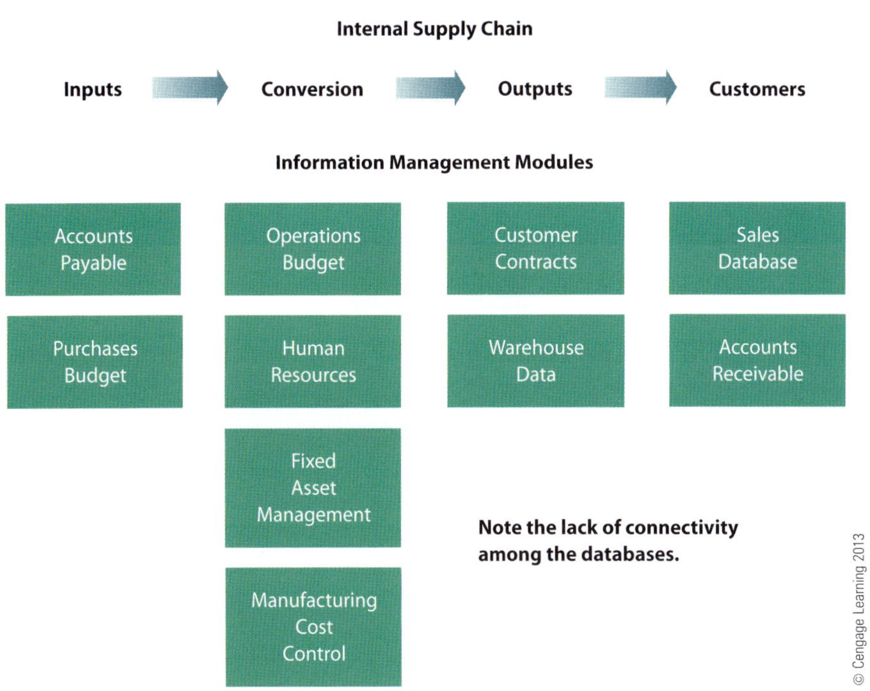

Enterprise resource planning (ERP) systems are packaged software programs that allow companies to

- have a single, comprehensive, enterprise-wide database;
- make quicker decisions based on real-time information and facts;
- improve decision-making quality because of the flexibility of information provided and the improved reports that are generated;
- reconcile and optimize conflicting organizational goals;
- standardize business processes;
- improve procedures that protect assets and prevent falsification of accounting records; and
- enhance the audit planning and execution process.[6]

[6]Leopoldo Colmenares, "Benefits of ERP Systems for Accounting and Financial Management," *Allied Academies International Conference, Academy of Information and Management Sciences Proceedings* (Vol. 13, Issue 1, 2009), pp. 3–7.

Implementing an ERP system should help a company to provide customers the highest-quality products and best possible service; Exhibit 19.6 illustrates an integrated, centralized information system. In theory, the ERP system should link the customer end of the supply chain with all functional areas responsible for the production and delivery of a product or service—all the way upstream to suppliers. Increasingly, businesses will allow customers to access all necessary data about their orders through the Internet.

Exhibit 19.6 Enterprise Resource Planning Information Management

The following lists expected benefits from ERP implementation for the whole business, its marketing function, and its customers:

- A single, integrated system
- Streamlined processes and workflows
- Reduced redundant data entry and processes
- Uniform processes that are based on recognized best business practices
- Information sharing across departments
- Improved access to information
- Improved workflow and efficiency
- Improved customer satisfaction based on improved on-time delivery, increased quality, shortened delivery times
- Reduced inventory costs resulting from better planning, tracking, and forecasting of requirements
- Faster collections based on better visibility into accounts and fewer billing and/or delivery errors
- Decreased vendor pricing by taking better advantage of quantity breaks and tracking vendor performance
- Tracking of actual costs of activities and performing activity-based costing
- Consolidated picture of sales, inventory, and receivables[7]

ERP's key concept is a central repository for all organizational data so that they are accessible in real time by, and in an appropriate format for, a decision maker. Data are entered into the central depository through a series of modules. Usually 30 or more modules are required to complete an ERP installation.[8] Exhibit 19.7 provides a list of typical modules

[7] Anonymous, "ERP FAQs," http://www.mosaic21.com/faq.htm (last accessed 2/20/12).

[8] Ibid.

Exhibit 19.7 Typical Modules in an ERP Installation

Finance (accounting-related tasks)

General ledger: Maintains charts of accounts and corporate finance balances

Accounts receivable: Tracks amounts owed to company

Accounts payable: Tracks amounts owed by company and schedules bill payments

Fixed assets: Manages costs and depreciation schedules related to property, plant, and equipment

Treasury management: Monitors and manages cash holdings and investment risks

Cost control: Analyzes costs related to overhead, products, and customers

Human Resources Management (personnel-related tasks)

Human resources: Automates processes such as recruitment, business travel management, vacation allotments, and absences

Payroll: Handles accounting and preparation of checks for employees for salary and bonuses

Training: Tracks training activities, both provided and needed

Self-service HR: Lets workers select benefits and manage personal information

Manufacturing and Logistics (production and distribution tasks)

Production planning: Performs capacity planning and creates a daily production schedule

Materials management: Maintains bills of materials, controls materials purchasing, and manages inventory

Order entry and processing: Tracks customer orders and their status

Warehouse management: Maintains inventory records and tracks flow of inventory through warehouses and production operations

Distribution management: Arranges, schedules, and monitors delivery of products to customers

Project management: Monitors costs and work schedules on a project-by-project basis

Plant maintenance: Sets plans and oversees upkeep of facilities

Customer service management: Administers service agreements and checks contracts and warranties when customers contact the company

Customer Relationship Management (customer-related tasks)

Customer portals: Allows customers to post service issues, place new orders, and view order histories

Commissions: Tracks salespersons' commissions from customers' orders

Contact center support: Tracks type and resolution of contact items

Marketing: Tracks promotions and related customer impacts

Service support: Administers service agreements and checks contracts and warranties when customers contact the company

included in a manufacturing company's ERP system. Exhibit 19.8 (p. 782) provides five motivations or justifications for implementing ERP systems.

Installation of an ERP system impacts the financial function in three significant ways. First, financial and system specialists become responsible for selecting and installing the software. ERP software includes brand names such as **SAP**, **Oracle**, **Great Plains**, and **Invensys**. Installing an ERP system in a large company involves thousands of hours of labor and millions of dollars of capital.

Exhibit 19.8 Five Reasons Firms Adopt ERP Systems

1. **Improve communication**—Older generation information technology solutions focused on singular organizational functions such as payroll, production, marketing, and human resources. Accordingly, any given manager was likely to develop a myopic view of the organization and have limited information about other organizational functions. With an ERP system, all managers see the same basic data repository, and communication within the organization is enhanced by each manager having a common view of basic transactions and facts.
2. **Expand organizational knowledge**—Organizational activity is defined around activities necessary to serve customers (e.g., marketing, producing, inbound logistics management, and shipping). An ERP system allows inquisitive managers to see the multifunctional impact of customers on the organization. Among other insights, managers may learn a great deal about the relative profitability of customers based on the specific manner in which those customers are served by the organization.
3. **Reduce redundancy**—In the legacy systems, in which data were organized and maintained by various functional areas in the organization, each function necessarily gathered, entered, stored, and processed data. With an ERP system, much of the data need be entered only once rather than redundantly, function by function. The ability to share data within an ERP system across functions eliminates significant amounts of data gathering and data entry cost.
4. **Improve efficiency of information management and processing**—ERP systems are built on platforms designed to be exploited by an infinite array of bolt-on modules, each drawing upon a common database. Thus, as new IT solutions are developed, they are integrated into an ERP system which saves time and resources in implementation. Further, the evolution of cloud computing has dramatically enhanced the ability of an ERP system to efficiently generate and distribute information to diverse users around the globe while preserving the integrity of the data.
5. **Develop a common language**—The use of a common database across organizational functions facilitates the development of a common vocabulary for communication. This reduces the noise in managers' communications resulting from differing definitions and measurements relating to cost objects, supply chain activities, customer service, and competitive threats and opportunities.

Second, financial specialists will be responsible for analyzing the data repository to support management decisions. Data analysis often involves "drilling down" from aggregate data (such as total sales for the firm) to detailed data (such as sales by store or sales by customer type) to identify market opportunities and to better manage costs. Such analysis can explain why a certain product moves well at some stores but not at others.

Analysis can also use **data mining**, which involves statistical techniques to uncover answers to important questions about business operations. Data mining is useful to uncover causality of quality problems, study customer retention, determine which marketing promotions generate the greatest sales impact, and identify cost drivers.

The modern evolution of data mining is reality mining. **Reality mining** refers to collecting and analyzing technology-based data as they relate to social behavior.[9] The web movements of individuals using their personal computers and mobile devices are noted and captured by a plethora of network servers. This voluminous body of data reveals information about individual preferences, personal habits, shopping tendencies, social interactions, and so forth that can be exploited for a variety of purposes. For example, these data could be used to identify social clusters, potential criminal activity, risk exposures, or emotional reactions to news and events and to product introductions. The breadth of potential applications of reality mining is mind boggling. However, firms such as **Facebook** and **Google** are under growing scrutiny by regulators for potential violation of individuals' rights to privacy. Increasingly

[9] Erica Orange, "Mining Information from the Data Clouds," *The Futurist* (July–August 2009), pp. 17–21.

Web users' social behaviors are observable to hosts of social media, and there is immense market value associated with this knowledge. The acceptable legal and ethical boundaries of buying and selling intelligence regarding individual behavior are not yet drawn.

Third, the ERP installation places a burden on financial specialists to maintain the integrity of the data depository. Fulfilling this obligation requires accountants and other specialists to monitor the ERP modules and be confident that the system successfully converts raw data into the main repository's standardized format.

Also, finance specialists are accountable for integrating externally purchased data (such as industry sales data and other external intelligence) with internally generated data. ERP systems represent a generational leap in the gathering, processing, and analysis of information. As ERP systems become increasingly integrated into Internet-based technology, customers will have ease of access to a worldwide marketplace.

In turn, customer-driven competition will cause firms to continually seek innovative ways to attract potential customers. These innovations are often obtained through strategic efforts that combine the talents and capabilities of two or more firms.

STRATEGIC ALLIANCES

5 What are strategic alliances, what forms do they take, and why do firms participate in them?

The traditional supply chain structure had clear distinctions between supplier and customer firms—there were no "fuzzy boundaries" that created an inability to determine where one firm ended its contribution to the supply chain and another began its contribution. Now, however, companies often have incentives to develop interorganizational agreements that go beyond normal supplier/customer arrangements. Generically, these agreements are called **strategic alliances**, which reflect agreements involving two or more firms with complementary core competencies to jointly contribute to the supply chain.

Strategic alliances can take many forms including joint ventures, equity investments, licensing, joint R&D arrangements, technology swaps, and exclusive buyer/seller agreements. A strategic alliance differs from the usual interactions between (or among) independent firms in that the output produced reflects a joint effort between (or among) the firms and the rewards of that effort are split between (or among) the allied firms. An unusual illustration of a strategic alliance is the 2003 agreement between the **Georgia Ports Authority** and the **Panama Canal Authority**. In the agreement, the two parties committed to jointly promote shipping routes between Asia and the Port of Savannah. The agreement also calls for sharing data, technology, and information as well as executing a joint marketing program.[10]

The strategic alliance is typical of many other business arrangements. It

- involves the exploitation of partner knowledge,
- includes partners with access to different markets, and
- allows sharing of risks and rewards.

The use of strategic alliances to exploit or create business opportunities is pervasive and economically significant, although the following quote indicates the challenges in measuring the frequency in use of alliances:

> In Hollywood and Silicon Valley, alliances are old hat: in a sense, almost every movie is an ad-hoc alliance, as is the development of every new computer chip. But, as in so much else, these two fashionable places are proving models for older industries. The most obvious change is in the sheer number of alliances.
>
> Mergers, like marriages, can be legally defined and therefore readily counted. Alliances are more like love affairs: they take many forms, may be transient or lasting, and live beyond the easy reach of statisticians.[11]

Dima Korotayev/Epsilon/Getty Images

Strategic alliances allow companies to collaborate and attract new customers, often resulting in the creation of a new entity.

[10] "Georgia Ports Authority, Panama Canal Sign Agreement," *Journal of Commerce* (June 20, 2003), p. 1.

[11] "Mergers and Alliances: Hold My Hand," *The Economist* (May 15, 1999), p. 73.

A typical strategic alliance involves the creation of a new entity. In structuring the new entity, the contributions required of the parent organizations must be determined. Beyond simply contributing cash, many new ventures will require inputs of human capital, technology, access to distribution channels, patents, and supply contracts. Furthermore, a governing board or set of directors must be established for the entity, and agreement must be reached as to how many directors can be appointed by each parent. Composition of the governing board determines which of the "parents" is more influential in managing the new entity. Simultaneous agreements must be executed to express the parent organizations' rights in sharing gains and to specify obligations for bearing losses. Such agreements will have significant implications for the risks borne by the parent companies.

An overriding concern in designing a strategic alliance is aligning the parents' and new entity's interests. The alliance is likely to work only if the parent organizations believe they are receiving adequate value for their contributions. This caveat is especially true today when many strategic alliances involve agreements between competitors.

Establishing strategic alliances involves a series of complex decisions that are based on inputs from many specialists. For example, financial professionals must assess risk and develop strategies for parent company management. These experts must also design a financial structure, develop management control systems, and install accounting and other information systems. Execution of a strategic alliance is as involved as the establishment of any new business. Managing an alliance requires the use of virtually every tool and concept discussed in this text including cost management systems, product costing systems, relevant costing, cost allocation, inventory management, decision making, and performance evaluation.

The technology evolution has been shown to have a significant impact on management practices and the activities of the financial professional. The next section discusses how technological and other organizational changes affect nonprofessional workers and how financial professionals have been pressured to develop ways in which to convey information to those without technical finance and accounting expertise.

OPEN-BOOK MANAGEMENT

6 What are the characteristics of open-book management, and why does its adoption require changes in accounting methods and practices?

Open-book management is a philosophy about increasing a firm's performance by involving all workers and by ensuring that all workers have access to operational and financial information necessary to achieve performance improvements. Although no specific definition of open-book management exists, it has some defined principles, as shown in Exhibit 19.9. Firms practicing open-book management typically disclose detailed financial information to employees, train them to interpret and use the information, empower them

Exhibit 19.9 Ten Common Principles of Open-Book Management

1. Turn the management of a business into a game that employees can win.
2. Open the books and share financial and operating information with employees.
3. Teach employees to understand the company's financial statements.
4. Show employees how their work influences financial results.
5. Link nonfinancial measures to financial results.
6. Target priority areas and empower employees to make improvements.
7. Review results together and keep employees accountable. Regularly hold performance review meetings.
8. Post results and celebrate successes.
9. Distribute bonus awards based on employee contributions to financial outcomes.
10. Share the ownership of the company with employees. Employee stock ownership plans (ESOPs) are routinely established in firms that practice open-book management.

Source: From Tim Davis, "Open-Book Management: Its Promises and Pitfalls," *Organizational Dynamics* (Winter 1997), pp. 6–20. Copyright 1997 by Elsevier Science & Technology Journals. Reproduced with permission of Elsevier Science & Technology Journals in the format Textbook via Copyright Clearance Center.

to make decisions, and tie a portion of their pay to the company's bottom line.[12] Application of this philosophy is appropriate in decentralized organizations that have empowered employees to make decisions. Proponents of open-book management argue that the approach helps employees understand how their work activities affect the firm's costs and revenues. With this understanding, employees can adopt or change work practices to either increase revenues or decrease costs.

However, merely opening the financial records to a firm's employees will not necessarily solve any problems or improve anyone's performance. Most employees, particularly nonmanagerial workers, have neither the skills necessary to interpret business financial information nor the understanding of accounting concepts and methods. Even many highly educated functional specialists have little knowledge of how profits are generated and performance is measured in financial terms. Additionally, the lack of information may lead to poor decisions. Salespeople may begin to offer large discounts when gross margins are down; engineers may want to redesign products or add more options when cash is stretched; and plant managers may lower quality when trying to meet production cost goals.[13]

The key to understanding is training. **Springfield Remanufacturing**, a recession-era spin-off of **General Motors**, first introduced the concept of open-book management. Gary Brown, human resources director at Springfield Remanufacturing, provides some insights about the learning curve for nonfinancial workers to become financially literate.

> Brown estimates that it generally takes two years for people to become financially literate (two iterations of the planning cycle). However, formal financial education and training is not the major expense, nor does training consume the most time, according to Brown. He emphasizes that the most valuable learning takes place in the "huddles" and when employees study the figures by themselves. An exceptionally motivated employee who does a great deal of self-study may become financially literate in six months.[14]

If financial information is to be the basis of employee decision making, the information must be structured with the level of sophistication of the decision maker in mind. Providing such information requires accountants to become much more creative in the methods used to compile and present financial data.

Effective open-book management requires sharing accounting and financial information with employees who have little knowledge of accounting concepts. Games can be used to teach these concepts to financially unsophisticated employees.

Using Games to Teach Open-Book Management

Games make learning both fun and competitive and can motivate employees to understand complex financial practices. To illustrate how games can be used, assume that Wolfson Industrial, a manufacturer of robotic equipment, has decided to implement open-book management concepts. One of Wolfson's key departments is Assembly, which combines mechanical and electronic components into finished products. Most components that are required for assembly are purchased from other manufacturers.

Assembly staff includes one manager and ten workers. Although highly skilled in the technical aspects of assembling electronic and mechanical components, workers know little about financial management or accounting techniques. For these workers, the game must begin with very simple accounting principles. Game outcomes, as determined by financial and nonfinancial performance measurements, must be both easy to comprehend and easily related to the motivation for establishing the game—such as profit maximization, customer satisfaction, or shareholder value.

Data in Exhibit 19.10 (p. 786) pertain to a major component of a production-line robotic welder. These data have been gathered from the most recent month's production and accounting records and have been provided by Wolfson's controller.

[12] Edward J. Stendardi and Thomas Tyson, "Maverick Thinking in Open-Book Firms: The Challenge for Financial Executives," *Business Horizons* (September–October 1997), p. 35.

[13] Karen Berman and Joe Knight, "What Your Employees Don't Know Will Hurt You," *Wall Street Journal* (February 27, 2012), p. R4.

[14] Tim Davis, "Open Book Management: Its Promises and Pitfalls," *Organizational Dynamics* (Winter 1997), p. 13.

Exhibit 19.10 Wolfson Industrial Assembly Department Cost Data for Robotic Welder

Item	Quantity	Unit Cost	Total Cost
Continuous-Rotation Servo	2	$25.00	$ 50.00
IR Receiver	2	11.00	22.00
Standard Servo	2	19.00	38.00
Wire Harness	1	90.00	90.00
Microcontroller	8	17.00	136.00
Chassis	1	48.00	48.00
Mini Sensors	8	7.00	56.00
Ultrasonic Range Finder	1	25.00	25.00
High-Current Motor Drivers	3	31.00	93.00
Fasteners	1 package	5.00	5.00
Total direct material cost			$563.00
Direct labor cost	6 hours	25.00	150.00
Total direct cost			$713.00

The starting point in designing a system for providing information to Assembly employees is to determine the system's objectives. Reasonable initial design objectives for this department include the following:

- Enabling employees to understand how their work affects the achievement of corporate objectives—to this end, it is important to measure what you want employees to do well;
- Helping employees understand how their work affects upstream and downstream departments; and
- Generating employee demand for information and training that leads to performance improvements.

Because overhead cost is more difficult to comprehend than direct material and direct labor cost, information on overhead costs can be excluded from the initial system developed for Assembly employees. Direct material and direct labor will be the information focus. Furthermore, employees cannot exert control over the price paid for material or labor; thus, these data could be presented as budgeted or standard, rather than as actual, cost. If actual costs are used, variations in purchase prices occurring throughout the year could disguise other more important information (such as quantities of materials consumed) from the financially unsophisticated workers. If desired, a more sophisticated system can be developed once the workers fully understand the initial system.

Providing information to Assembly workers should help them understand how their actions affect achievement of the overall corporate objectives. To initiate this understanding, management can establish an output (or transfer) price so that Assembly can measure its contribution to corporate profits. Assume that the initial price for the robot assembly is set at $950; it is not necessary for the established sales price to represent actual market value. The per-unit profit calculation for Assembly workers is as follows:

Sales	$ 950.00
Total direct cost (from Exhibit 19.10)	(713.00)
Profit contribution	$ 237.00

Total Assembly profit equals per-unit profit multiplied by the number of units produced. By analyzing this simple profit calculation, workers quickly realize that profits can be increased if costs are decreased or the number of units produced is decreased. However, some elementary quality information should be added so that the implication of defective production can be seen. For example, Assembly could be charged with a "defect cost" for products that are not of the quality specified. An income statement for the Assembly Department for a period would then appear as follows:

Sales	$ XXXXXX
Total direct cost	(XXXXXX)
Rework and defects	(XXXX)
Profit contribution	$ XXXX

With this profit calculation, workers will see that profit maximization requires maximization of output, minimization of direct costs, and minimization of quality defects.

One Japanese company, **Higashimaru Shoyu**, a maker of soy sauce, went so far as to create its own internal bank and currency.[15] Each department purchased its required inputs from other internal, upstream departments using the currency and established transfer prices. In turn, each department was paid in currency for its outputs. The flow of currency reinforced departmental profit calculations.

To exploit the financial information they receive, workers should be trained in ways to improve profits. The "game" of trying to increase profits serves as motivation for workers to learn about cost and operational management methods. Relating training to the game allows workers to see the relevance of training, and they will seek training to better understand how to read and comprehend a simple income statement and to identify approaches that can be used to improve results.

Motivating Employees

Wolfson's Assembly workers are not necessarily internally motivated to play the game well, so upper management should promote the game. An obvious motivation for profit improvements is establishing a linkage between department profits and worker compensation. Assembly workers could be paid bonuses if profits are above a target level. Alternatively, workers could be paid a percentage of profits as a bonus. In either case, linking compensation to profits motivates workers to have an interest in the game and to improve their performance.

Some companies offer performance-based bonuses to motivate employees and some offer employee stock ownership plans (ESOPs). Other companies do both. Pay and performance links can also be based on more specific data. For example, measures can be devised for on-time delivery rates (to the next downstream department), defect rates, output per labor hour, and other performance dimensions to make workers aware of how their inputs and outputs affect other departments and financial outcomes. All critical factors such as cost, quality, and investment management can be captured in performance measurements.

As soon as workers become accustomed to receiving financial and other information to manage their departments, more elaborate information systems can be developed as the sophistication of the information consumers (workers) evolves. For example, once the direct material, direct labor, and quality costs are understood, workers in Wolfson's Assembly Department can learn to evaluate overhead cost information.

Implementation Challenges

Open-book management can be difficult to implement. Characteristics of firms that are best suited to a successful implementation include

- small size,
- decentralized management,
- a history of employee empowerment, and
- trust between employees and managers.

In small firms, employees can more easily understand how their contributions influence the organization's bottom line. Firms with decentralized structures and empowered employees have workers who are accustomed to making decisions. Trust among employees and

[15] Robin Cooper, *When Lean Enterprises Collide* (Boston, MA: Harvard Business School Press, 1995).

managers is necessary for games to be devised that result in higher pay and greater job satisfaction for all employees.

Accountants face unique challenges in implementing open-book management in even the most favorable environments. The challenges are present in both the obstacles to be overcome and reporting innovations that need to be designed and implemented. One significant organizational obstacle in many firms is a history of carefully guarding financial information. Even in publicly held companies that are required to release certain financial information to the general public, top managers have historically limited employee access to financial data that the top managers regard as sensitive. Accountants have typically viewed themselves as the custodians of this sensitive information rather than its conveyors. To successfully implement open-book management, accountants must develop an attitude about information sharing that is as enthusiastic as the traditional attitude of information guarding.

Having been grounded in higher education courses and other appropriate training, accountants have generally operated under the assumption that financial information users have an adequate understanding of the rules used to compile financial data. However, open-book management requires the provision of accounting data to users who have little understanding of accounting conventions and rules. Thus, accountants must develop ways to convey accounting information so that unsophisticated users will understand it. Furthermore, by teaching users to have a better understanding of financial data, accountants help facilitate better organizational decision making.

Accountants must also be innovative when implementing open-book management. One significant requirement is the development of information systems that can generate segment information in a format that the segment's employees can understand. Thus, the information system must be designed to be sensitive to the user's financial sophistication.

Similarly, performance measures that employees can understand must be devised. Measures must capture the actual performance relative to the objectives of organizational segments and the organization as a whole. Objectives can be stated in terms of competitors' performance or industry norms. For example, a firm's objective might be to surpass the average quality level of products in the firm's industry. Measurement of actual achievement relative to this objective requires accountants to develop information systems that are focused on gathering nontraditional types of information—in this instance, quality level of output in the industry. The primary principle of measurement is to measure what is important.

> "The 'what' to measure comes from your mission statement, strategic business plan and the things that drive your business. If customer satisfaction is vital, measure customer satisfaction. If profit is vital, measure profit."[16]

Finally, because open-book management principles include involving all employees and evaluating and rewarding their performance, measures that can be integrated across segments and functional areas must be devised. For instance, if one of a firm's major objectives is to increase profitability, performance measures must be devised for engineers, accountants, production workers, administrators, janitors, and so forth that cause all of these functional groups to work toward a common end: increased profits.

An emerging area of concern for managers in nearly all entities is the impact of their operations on the environment. The concerns have arisen as a result of an increased consciousness of environmental issues and new governmental regulations enacted to protect the environment.

ENVIRONMENTAL MANAGEMENT SYSTEMS

7 What are the three generic approaches that firms can take in controlling environmental costs?

The environmental impact of businesses is of increasing concern to governments, citizens, investors, and managers. Accountants are increasingly concerned with both measuring business performance in regard to environmental issues and managing environmental costs. In the future, investors are likely to evaluate a company's environmental track record along with its financial record when making investment decisions.

[16]Matt Plaskoff, "Measure What You Want to Improve," *Professional Builder* (June 2003), p. 93.

Management of environmental costs requires the consideration of environmental issues in every operational aspect. For example, environmental effects are related to the scrap and byproduct from manufacturing operations, materials (recyclable or not) selected for product components, actions of suppliers providing necessary inputs, and product and packaging usage and disposition habits of customers. In short, environmental issues span the entire value chain. In addition to voluntary intentions to reduce pollution, many countries (not including the United States) agreed under the 1997 Kyoto Protocol to reduce the pollution (particularly greenhouse gases) generated by their industries. The Kyoto Protocol would go into effect only if two conditions were met. The first was that at least 55 countries ratified the agreement and the second was that the ratifying countries had to account for at least 55 percent of 1990 carbon dioxide emissions. Based on meeting these criteria, the Kyoto Protocol went into effect on February 16, 2005. This agreement includes three mechanisms to address greenhouse gases: emissions trading, clean development mechanism, and joint implementation. The Kyoto Protocol targets six specific greenhouse gases including carbon dioxide, methane, nitrous oxide, sulfur hexafluoride, HFCs, and PFCs. Kyoto Protocol provisions are legally binding on 37 industrialized nations as well as the European Union and stipulate target reductions in emissions for each industrialized nation, but the protocol does not set targets for developing countries. The goal of enacting the Kyoto Protocol is to reduce worldwide greenhouse gas emissions to 5.2 percent below 1990 levels between 2008 and 2012.[17] Unfortunately, as of 2011, many large nations were not meeting their target goals; the United States and China actually emitted "more than enough extra greenhouse gas to erase all the reductions made by other countries during the Kyoto period."[18]

Although some companies are striving to voluntarily reduce pollution because of a social consciousness, other companies are trying to do so to reduce the financial risks associated with generation of pollution. By avoiding these risks, companies may lower their cost of capital, as suggested in the following quote:

> A group of analysts at Innovest contend that a company's strategic response to environmental risk is a window into the company's management ability. The more "eco-efficient" a company is, the better its stock performance is likely to be compared with others in its industry—and that's true, apparently, whether the industry is oil, mining, or solar energy.[19]

There are three generic strategies for dealing with environmental effects of operations, and each has unique financial implications. First, an "end-of-pipe strategy" may be employed. With this approach, managers "produce the waste, or pollutant, and then find a way to clean it up."[20] Common tools used in this approach are wastewater cleaning systems and smokestack scrubbers, but this strategy can be ineffective in reducing the generation of greenhouse gases. A second strategy involves process improvements, which include changes to "recycle wastes internally, reduce the production of wastes, or adopt production processes that generate no waste."[21] A popular variant of this strategy is the purchase of renewable energy certificates or "carbon offsets." To illustrate, **Costa Del Mar** recently purchased renewable energy credits for 422,896 kilowatt hours of renewable energy. This action is intended to offset 100 percent of the carbon emissions associated with the electricity consumed at the company's Daytona Beach, Florida, headquarters.[22] A third strategy is

[17] United Nations Framework Convention on Climate Change, "Kyoto Protocol" http://unfccc.int/kyoto_protocol/items/2830.php (last accessed 2/24/12).

[18] Robert Henson, "What Is the Kyoto Protocol and Has It Made any Difference?" *The Guardian* (March 11, 2011); http://www.guardian.co.uk/environment/2011/mar/11/kyoto-protocol (last accessed 3/7/12).

[19] Abrahm Lustgarten, "Lean, Mean and Green?" *Fortune* (July 26, 2004), p. 210.

[20] Germain Böer, Margaret Curtin, and Louis Hoyt, "Environmental Cost Management," *Management Accounting* (September 1998), pp. 28ff.

[21] Ibid.

[22] Anonymous, "Costa Del Mar Buys Carbon Credits," *Orlando Business Journal*; http://www.bizjournals.com/orlando/stories/2009/06/15/daily24.html (last accessed 2/24/12).

pollution prevention, which involves "complete avoidance of pollution by not producing any pollutants in the first place."[23]

Although minimizing the environmental impact of operations can be a reasonable goal, some impact on the environment is unavoidable. For example, energy must be consumed to manufacture products; similarly, material must be consumed as goods are produced. Without energy and material consumption, no goods can be manufactured. In managing environmental costs, accountants must analyze the environmental dimensions of investment decisions:

> In the capital investment area, accountants can help managers by including quality and environmental benefits in the analysis. If a proposed project is more energy efficient or produces less pollution than an alternative, those factors should be included in the analysis. The financial data should include any cost savings from lower energy usage. If the company must control pollution, the financial impact should be recognized.[24]

Other business concerns related to environmental costs include managing quality, research and development, and technology acquisition. Although the relationship between quality costs and environmental costs is not fully understood, many examples can be cited suggesting that quality and environmental costs are highly, and positively, related. For example, the reduction in scrap and waste production (quality improvements) serves to reduce environmental costs and concerns (waste disposal).

Research and development identifies new products and new production processes, and develops new materials. New product design influences the

- types and quantities of materials used;
- types and quantities of waste, scrap, and by-products produced;
- amount of energy consumed in the production process; and
- potential for gathering and recycling products when they reach obsolescence.

For example, **Apple** has instituted recycling operations in 95 percent of the countries in which it operates. In 2011, the company achieved a recycling rate in excess of 70 percent; the company has recycled in excess of 115,000 metric tons of electronic waste since 1994.[25]

Technology acquisition also has many environmental impacts. For instance, technology affects

- energy consumption and conservation;
- environmental emissions;
- the quantity, types, and characteristics of future obsolete equipment (for instance, whether it is made of recyclable materials);
- the rate of defective output produced;
- the quantities of scrap, waste, and by-products produced; and
- the nature and extent of support activities necessary to keep the technology operating.

Exhibit 19.11 lists considerations for the financial professional to evaluate when determining whether a firm's information systems provide relevant information for managing environmental costs. An analysis of the checklist shows that the financial professional must effectively gather both quantitative and nonquantitative data both within and outside of the firm.

[23] Ibid., p. 18.

[24] Harold P. Roth and Carl E. Keller, Jr., "Quality, Profits, and the Environment: Diverse Goals or Common Objectives?" *Management Accounting* (July 1997), pp. 50–55.

[25] "Apple and the Environment," Apple, Inc.; http://www.apple.com/environment/ (last accessed 2/25/12).

Exhibit 19.11 Considerations for Environmental Cost Control

Cost Management Systems

How much does each of our divisions spend on environmental management?

Do we have consistent and reliable systems in place for measuring environmental costs?

How does our cost management system support good environmental management decisions?

How do we track compliance costs?

How do we connect line management decisions to the environmental costs they create?

Which divisions best manage environmental costs?

How do we compare with competitors in managing environmental costs?

What kinds of waste do we produce?

What are the proposed regulations that will affect our company?

Cost Reporting Systems

Who receives reports on environmental costs in our company?

Does our bonus plan explicitly consider environmental costs?

How do we charge internal environmental costs to managers?

How does the financial system capture environmental cost data?

Do our managers have all necessary tools to measure total costs of the waste generated?

Do our systems identify environmental cost reduction opportunities?

Source: Germain Böer, Margaret Curtin, and Louis Hoyt, "Environmental Cost Management," *Management Accounting* (September 1998), p. 32.

Comprehensive Review Module

KEY TERMS

business process reengineering (BPR), p. 774
data mining, p. 782
downsizing, p. 776
enterprise resource planning (ERP) system, p. 779
open-book management, p. 784
organizational memory, p. 776
reality mining, p. 782
strategic alliance, p. 783

CHAPTER SUMMARY

1 Business Process Reengineering

- Business process reengineering causes radical changes in ways firms execute processes by
  - using fewer employees.
  - making better use of technology.

2 Effects of Competition

- Global competition is forcing firms to downsize and restructure operations to
  - defend core competencies.
  - remain cost competitive.

3 Diversity

- Many organizations are becoming more diverse
  - as measured by the religion, race, values, work habits, cultures, political ideologies, and education level of employees.
  - because of globalization and proactive diversification programs.
  - and are placing more pressure on the accounting system for
    - ➢ communicating among employees and
    - ➢ measuring performance.

4 Enterprise Resource Planning (ERP) Systems

- Many firms are adopting ERP systems
  - which consist of a number of modules (such as payroll, fixed assets, accounts receivable, and cash management), each of which accounts for specific activities.
  - which facilitate data mining and the integration of financial and nonfinancial information across functional areas of the business.
  - to automate accounting processes.
  - to share data across the enterprise.
  - to provide real-time access to company data.

5 Strategic Alliances

- Strategic alliances are agreements involving two or more firms to jointly contribute to the supply chain.
- Strategic alliances often blur traditional boundaries between supplier and customer.
- Strategic alliances take many different forms such as
  - joint ventures,
  - equity investments,
  - licensing arrangements,
  - joint R&D arrangements,
  - technology swaps, and
  - exclusive buy/sell agreements.
- Strategic alliances allow the sharing of risks and rewards between/among firms.

6 Open-Book Management

- Open-book management increases the information transparency in an organization, which often means accountants must change from a mind-set of guarding to sharing information.
- Open-book management creates challenges and opportunities for accountants to make information understandable to financially unsophisticated employees, often through the use of games and meetings.
- Open-book management decentralizes both authority to make decisions and responsibility for decision results; the concept can be implemented by tying rewards to performance.

7 Controlling Environmental Costs

- The three generic approaches to controlling environmental costs include
  - cleaning up pollutants after they are produced (end-of-pipe strategy);
  - improving processes to reduce the amount of waste produced; and
  - preventing pollution by never producing polluting materials.

POTENTIAL ETHICAL ISSUES

ETHICS

1. Allowing executives to collect large bonuses and other perquisites while firing ordinary workers for the sake of remaining cost competitive
2. Firing highly paid long-term employees while hiring new, lower-paid employees to perform identical or similar work
3. Developing data repositories in ERP systems that contain sensitive data on employees, customers, and other stakeholders but not installing adequate systems to protect the privacy and integrity of that information
4. Adopting open-book management principles and holding employees accountable for financial results without first providing them training to understand financial reports
5. Making business decisions by considering only the costs of pollution that are borne by the company and ignoring the costs borne by society
6. Minimizing environmental costs by moving high-impact operations to countries that have lax environmental regulations

QUESTIONS

1. What is business process reengineering? Does it lead to radical or modest changes in business practices? Discuss.
2. Business process reengineering and downsizing often occur together. Why?

3. Describe "downsizing," its causes, and its primary risks.
4. How has the globalization of firms affected the diversity of their employees? Why has increased diversity put an additional burden on accounting systems?
5. Besides increasing globalization, what trends within the United States are causing firms to seek more diversified workforces?
6. What is an enterprise resource planning (ERP) system? How do ERP systems improve on prior generations of information systems?
7. New strategic alliances are formed every day. What are they, and why are they increasingly being used by businesses?
8. Open-book management is a relatively new philosophy about the use of information in organizations. Describe open-book management and how it differs philosophically from the traditional view of the management of financial information in an organization.
9. How does the implementation of open-book management require an organization's accountants to change their traditional practices?
10. Describe the three generic strategies for dealing with the environmental effects of operations. Is one of the strategies always preferred to the others? Discuss.

EXERCISES

11. **LO.1 (Business process reengineering; writing)** Process mapping and value analysis are tools often used in business process reengineering. As discussed in Chapter 4, a process map is a flowchart of the set of activities that compose a process. Value (or activity) analysis examines each of the activities identified in the flowchart and determines to what extent it provides "value" to the customer. Those activities that add no value are targets to be designed out of the process.

    Select a process at your college or university such as admissions or enrollment. Prepare a process map, and conduct a value analysis of the process map. Then develop a plan (using Exhibit 19.2 as a guide) to eliminate the process activities that add no value to the student customer.

12. **LO.1 (Technology acquisition; writing)** Acquisition of new technology is often a perilous event for firms. The successful acquisition and implementation of new systems require much more than merely purchasing hardware and software. For example, costs are likely to be incurred for the following:
    - research and consulting to select software and hardware vendors
    - software training
    - upgrading IT infrastructure to operate new hardware and software
    - continuing hardware and software support
    - implementing the new system

    a. Why should training be included as a cost of technology acquisition?
    b. How can the financial function of a business improve the internal process of technology acquisition?

13. **LO.1 (Business process reengineering; research; writing)** Business process reengineering (BPR) can be an effective tool to aid in achieving breakthroughs in quality improvement and cost management. Total quality management (TQM) is another philosophy about achieving organizational change. Conduct a library or Internet search to identify articles that discuss BPR and TQM, and write a report in which you compare and contrast the two methodologies.

INTERNET

14. **LO.1 (Technological change; writing)** Financial professionals are at the forefront in adopting new technologies, many of which comprise the core of business strategies. Discuss how the increasing reliance of business on technology coupled with the responsibility of the financial professional to manage technology has changed the skills required of corporate accountants.

INTERNET

15. **LO.2 (Downsizing; research; writing)** In the past decade, the Japanese economy has fallen from the lofty levels of previous decades. As a consequence, many Japanese companies have been forced to downsize. In most companies, one of two strategies can be pursued in downsizing. First, a company can lay off employees. Second, a company can cut employment through natural attrition and by reducing future hiring.

    Conduct a library or Internet search of "Japanese management culture" to identify attitudes of Japanese managers about employees. Then prepare a report in which you explain why Japanese companies might prefer one of these downsizing strategies to the other.

16. **LO.2 (Downsizing; writing)** In recent years, the financial press reported story after story regarding downsizing and layoffs in the U.S. auto industry. Indeed, since 2006, the U.S. auto industry lost more jobs than any other American industry, and from 2007 through mid-2010, **General Motors** led the nation in layoffs with over 107,000 jobs lost.

    Assume that you are a stock market analyst and are responsible for interpreting the economic significance of corporate layoffs. In general, would you interpret the auto industry layoffs as good news or bad news? Explain the rationale for your answer.

    Source: Douglas McIntyre, "The Layoff Kings: The 25 Companies Responsible for 700,000 Jobs Lost," *Daily Finance*; http://www.dailyfinance.com/2010/08/18/the-layoff-kings-the-25-companies-responsible-for-700-000-lost/ (last accessed, 2/24/12).

17. **LO.3 (Diversity and discrimination; writing)** In 2007, **Nike** settled a class action lawsuit filed on behalf of 400 African-American employees of the company's Niketown store in Chicago. One allegation in the suit was that the store segregated African-American employees into lower-paying jobs including cashiers and stockroom workers rather than sales positions. The settlement cost Nike $7.6 million to resolve the financial claims.

    Discuss the contributions that can be made by the accounting and finance professionals in an organization to actively promote diversification of the workforce while managing real and perceived discrimination in treatment of workers and managers.

18. **LO.3 (Diversity)** The issue of whether diversity is positive or negative for an organization has been hotly debated for many years. Some people argue that, because of its homogeneous workforce, Japan has an inherent advantage in competing with the United States. The benefits of a homogeneous workforce result from a common language, religion, work ethic, and so forth. Prepare a two-minute oral report in which you take a position and persuasively present an argument on whether diversity aids or hinders an organization.

19. **LO.4 (Enterprise resource planning; research; writing)** ERP software can facilitate the sharing of information throughout the supply chain. For example, an Internet storefront can be used to interact downstream operations with the final customer. Sales data gathered from the storefront can then be used as a basis for determining the quantity and mix of products to be produced. From this information, a production schedule can be prepared. Discuss how posting the production schedule on the Internet could result in improved coordination with the upstream (vendor) side of the supply chain.

20. **LO.4 (Enterprise resource planning; research; writing)** With an ERP system, a company can develop a "storefront" on the Internet. Through its storefront connection with customers, the company can gather much information about the market and the demand for specific products.

    Assume that you are employed by an automaker. How could you use the Internet storefront and data mining to learn more about the purchasers of your vehicles to improve the market share of future generations of your company's autos?

21. **LO.4 (Enterprise resource planning; writing)** ERP software programs allow tighter linkages within a supply chain than were possible with earlier generations of software. Consider the possibility of a tighter link between the marketing and engineering functions within a firm that makes consumer electronics. Discuss how the link between these two functions could improve the following:

a. customer satisfaction
b. time to bring new products to market
c. cost management

22. **LO.5 (Strategic alliances; research)** In their annual reports, companies provide brief descriptions of their most important contracts, including strategic alliances. Select a large publicly traded company and obtain a copy of its most recent annual report (in hard copy, on the company's Web site, or on the EDGAR portion of the SEC's Web site at http://www.sec.gov/edgar.shtml). Review the portions of the annual report that discuss strategic alliances. Based on your review, prepare an oral report in which you discuss the following points:

INTERNET

a. motivations for establishing strategic alliances
b. extent to which strategic alliances are used to conduct business
c. relative financial success of the strategic alliances

23. **LO.5 (Strategic alliances; research; writing)** Assume you are employed by a technology company that is considering entering into a strategic alliance with a communications company to provide certain innovative services delivered via the Internet. As a financial professional, how could you contribute to the organization and management of the strategic alliance?

24. **LO.6 (Open-book management)** You have been hired as a consultant by a company that manufactures plastic and resin toys. Company management is presently discussing ways to improve product quality. Evidence of quality problems is everywhere: high rates of product defects, many product returns from customers, poor rate of customer retention, and high warranty costs. Top management has traced virtually all quality-related problems to the production department.

    Production workers in the company are paid a flat hourly rate. No bonuses are paid based on corporate profits or departmental performance measures. As the outside consultant, prepare an oral report to present to your client's top management discussing how open-book management could be applied to address the quality problems. At a minimum, include in your report how quality information would be conveyed to workers, how workers would be trained to understand the information, and how incentives would be established for improved quality performance.

25. **LO.6 (Open-book management; writing)** MONOPOLY by Parker Brothers has been a popular board game for many years. Assume that you have just been hired by a multi-product company in the steel industry. Company management is examining the potential use of open-book management techniques. Prepare a written report discussing your recommendations for implementing open-book management for the company's top managers. In your report, discuss how you would use MONOPOLY as a training tool for workers who have little knowledge of accounting concepts.

26. **LO.7 (Environmental costs)** Dayton Industrial produces a variety of chemicals that are used in an array of commercial applications. One popular product, a chemical solvent, contains two very caustic acids, A and B, each of which can present a very serious environmental hazard if not disposed of properly. For every ton of chemical produced, 500 pounds of Acid A and 300 pounds of Acid B are required. Inefficiencies in the current production process allow 40 pounds of Acid A and 20 pounds of Acid B to remain as waste from each ton of chemical manufactured. Because of impurities, the waste acids cannot be used in the production of future batches of product. The company incurs a cost of $2 per pound to dispose of the waste acid produced.

    Recently, the company has become aware of new technology that reduces the amount of waste acids produced. This technology would generate only one pound of Acid A and five pounds of Acid B as waste from each ton of chemical manufactured. Corporate management has estimated that the new technology could be acquired and installed at a cost of $1,300,000. The technology would have a life expectancy of nine years. The new technology would not otherwise affect the cost of producing the chemical solvent.

a. Which environmental cost management strategy is Dayton Industrial considering in this example?
b. Why would the application of discounted cash flow methods (see Chapter 15) be appropriate for evaluating the new technology?

27. **LO.7 (Environmental costs; writing)** Following are descriptions of environmental waste situations. Identify the environmental strategy you would select to deal with each situation and discuss your logic.
   a. A relatively small amount of low-toxicity waste is produced. This waste is not easily recycled, nor is technology available to avoid its production. Disposal costs are relatively modest.
   b. The waste produced is highly toxic and is associated with several lethal diseases in humans. The cost of disposal is extraordinarily high.
   c. A moderate amount of waste, which is nearly identical to a chemical purchased and used in an etching operation, is produced. The waste differs from the purchased chemical only because of a small amount of contaminants introduced in the production process.

INTERNET

28. **LO.7 (Environmental cost management; research; writing)** Firms' increasing awareness of their impacts on the environment has led to the establishment of companies that specialize in all aspects of managing the environmental effects of operations. Search the Internet using the term "environmental cost management." Review the web pages of the vendors of environmental services identified by the search, and then write a brief report in which you describe the types of services that can be purchased to manage environmental costs.

PROBLEMS

INTERNET

29. **LO.1 (Business process reengineering; research)** The economic downturn beginning in 2007 claimed many victims in U.S. industries. However, no industry may have been hurt more than the auto industry. In 2009, two of America's largest auto firms, **General Motors** and **Chrysler**, each declared bankruptcy. Before and since their bankruptcy declarations, much attention has been focused on this industry, its competitive advantages and disadvantages, and its future prospects. The U.S. government invested funds to allow General Motors and Chrysler to emerge from bankruptcy. The fundamental theory of bankruptcy reorganization is that it allows a company a fresh start, a release from contractual entanglements, and a chance to reinvent itself to compete successfully.

    Conduct research on General Motors and Chrysler and assess whether the bankruptcy reorganizations of the two companies resulted in a successful reengineering of their business models. Also, write a paragraph for each company describing your expectations as to the global standing of each company in the global auto industry in the year 2020.

ETHICS

30. **LO.1 & LO.2 (Downsizing; outsourcing; ethics; writing)** One of the key drivers of downsizing and outsourcing is globalization. Recently, the Organization for Economic Cooperation and Development (OECD) acknowledged "growing unease about globalization." The organization expressed concerns that in some countries there may be a backlash against globalization because some workers have been victimized by the globalization trend. The conventional wisdom that globalization could be likened to a rising tide that would lift all boats is apparently not true. Particularly, many workers with low skills in developed countries are having difficulty finding work because of the offshoring of jobs to developing countries and the increased use of technology in the manufacturing sector.

    Source: Marcus Walker, "Free-Trade Alert: A Warning on Globalization Backlash," *Wall Street Journal* (June 20, 2007), p. A4.

a. Discuss the extent to which accounting systems capture the cost of downsizing incurred in a particular country. Do you think decisions to downsize would be different if all of the costs of downsizing borne by a society were captured by the accounting system of the reporting entity?
b. What ethical obligation, if any, do developed countries have to supply a safety net for workers who are displaced by effects of global competition? Explain.

31. **LO.1 & LO.2 (Accounting; downsizing; BPR)** Most accounting professionals would agree that the accounting profession has developed effective tools for measuring and reporting events involving tangible assets. Most might also agree that the profession has miles to go to report as effectively on events involving intangible assets. Examples of intangible assets are patents developed rather than purchased; customer and supplier relationships; and employee knowledge, skills, and abilities.

    Assume that a U.S.-based manufacturing company implemented a BPR that resulted in the layoff of 20 percent of production workers.

    a. How would the layoff impact the company's intangible assets?
    b. How would the BPR event be reflected in the company's financial statements?
    c. Given your answer to (a), do you think the financial reports reflect all significant effects of the layoffs? Explain.

32. **LO.2 (Restructuring and outsourcing; ethics; writing)** Automakers provide an interesting study in cost management strategies. **General Motors** often provides a contrast to other U.S. manufacturers. For example, **Chrysler** and **Ford** opted to outsource many product components, but GM continues to manufacture a much higher percentage of the parts needed to produce its cars. One of the variables driving GM's strategy is its high level of unionization. The unions have resisted attempts made by GM to restructure operations and outsource more components.

    ETHICS

    a. From the perspective of price-based competition, why would GM want the flexibility to outsource more of its parts and components?
    b. From the perspective of managing quality, how could outsourcing positively or negatively affect GM's ability to manage quality relative to its competitors?
    c. What ethical responsibility does GM bear to the union in seeking to restructure and outsource more of its parts manufacturing?
    d. In restructuring its operations following its 2009 bankruptcy, how did GM's unions influence the restructuring?

33. **LO.2 (Downsizing; writing)** *"Most experienced CEOs have seen command-and-control management come and go. They've been through downsizing and rightsizing. Now they're seeing most companies (their own included) working to recast themselves as 'high-performing' organizations, with streamlined, non-hierarchical, fast moving teams of 'knowledge workers' trying to generate the greatest possible return on 'human capital.' The New Economy has put that capital in high demand and short supply, particularly in IT and other high-tech fields. As a result, CEOs and their top executives find themselves facing a broad spectrum of new challenges: competing for top talent, designing jobs consistent with business goals, communicating strategy, sharing information, earning employees' trust and commitment, measuring and improving employee performance, moving them up and leading them onward."*

    Source: Hannele Rubin, "How CEOs Get Results," *Chief Executive* (February 2001), pp. 8ff.

    What can the accounting function in an organization do to help identify potential top management talent from internal operations?

34. **LO.1, LO.2, & LO.6 (Various)** Dayna Moore, CEO of Tennessee Transmissions, sat dejected in her chair after reviewing the 2013 first-quarter financial reports on one of the company's core products: a standard, five-speed transmission (product #2122) used in the heavy equipment industry in the manufacture of earth-moving equipment. Some of the information in the report follows.

MARKET REPORT, PRODUCT #2122, QUARTER 1, 2013

Sales Data	
Total sales (dollars), Quarter 1, 2013	$4,657,500
Total sales (dollars), Quarter 1, 2012	$6,405,000
Total sales (units), Quarter 1, 2013	3,450
Total sales (units), Quarter 1, 2012	4,200
Market Data	
Industry unit sales, Quarter 1, 2013	40,000
Industry unit sales, Quarter 1, 2012	32,000
Industry average sales price, Quarter 1, 2013	$1,310
Industry average sales price, Quarter 1, 2012	$1,640
Profit Data	
Tennessee Transmissions average gross profit per unit, Quarter 1, 2013	$ 45
Tennessee Transmissions average gross profit per unit, Quarter 1, 2012	160
Industry average gross profit per unit, Quarter 1, 2013	75
Industry average gross profit per unit, Quarter 1, 2012	140

Tennessee Transmissions' strategy for this transmission is to compete on the basis of price. The transmission offers no features that allow it to be differentiated from those of major competitors. Tennessee Transmissions' level of quality is similar to the average of the industry.

Also on Moore's desk was a report from her business intelligence unit, on which she underlined the following key pieces of information:

- Commodity transmission components (nuts, bolts, etc.), which all major transmission producers acquire from specialty vendors, decreased in price by approximately 5 percent from January 2012 to January 2013.
- Two major competitors moved their main assembly operations from the United States to China in early 2012. These competitors are believed to have the lowest unit production cost in the industry.
- A third major competitor ceased manufacturing major gear components and began outsourcing these parts from a Mexican firm in mid-2012. This firm increased its market share in 2012 from 10 to 14 percent following a major decrease in sales price.
- Tennessee Transmissions' production operations did not change in any material respect from 2012 to 2013.
- Tennessee Transmissions manufactures approximately 83 percent of the components used in the heavy industrial transmission. The industry norm is to make 57 percent of the components.
- For the balance of 2013, industry experts agree that quarterly demand for the heavy industrial transmission will be even higher than the levels posted for the first quarter of 2013.

a. Examine the information Moore has gathered. Analyze the data to identify as specifically as possible the problems that have led to Tennessee Transmissions' loss of profit and market share in the heavy industrial transmission market.

b. Based on your analysis in (a) and the information given to Moore, suggest specific alternatives that she should consider in making her firm more competitive in its market. Use concepts presented in the chapter as the basis of your recommendations.

ETHICS

35. **LO.2 & LO.6 (Downsizing; ethics; writing)** *Employees expect that all parties will honor their explicit and implicit obligations. Distrust occurs when these obligations are not met or when the parties have different expectations regarding the obligations. When downsizing is employed as an organizational strategy, it focuses on economic goals over the promotion of commitment, and as a result, the employees view the strategy with distrust.*

John A. Challenger notes, "It may be unrealistic to expect intense loyalty on the part of the worker when in many instances the employer cannot promise loyalty in return. The current spate of mergers in the banking, media, utilities, and other industries, major re-engineering efforts, and downsizings all have weakened the ties that spur employee commitment and productivity." Frederick Reichheld states, "The great betrayal of American workers is the failure of companies to let them know how much value they are creating, versus how much they are costing."

Source: Adapted from Larry Gross, "Downsizing: Are Employers Reneging on Their Social Promise?" *CPCU Journal* (Summer 2001), pp. 112ff.

a. In your opinion, does the achievement of high-quality operations mandate that a firm treat its employees ethically? Discuss.
b. Discuss how perceptions by employees of their employers mesh with the open-book management requirement to have honest exchanges of information between employees and managers.

36. **LO.5 (Strategic alliances; writing)** Strategic alliances and joint ventures are being used with increasing frequency to exploit market opportunities. Virtually all larger firms are involved in several to many strategic alliances.
    a. From the perspective of controlling the quality of production, discuss how a strategic alliance is significantly different from a typical vendor/customer relationship.
    b. How can the accounting function contribute to the management of quality for strategic alliances?

37. **LO.6 (Open-book management; writing)** Laura Johnson, Technical Instruments Division manager of Worldwide Electronics, attended a 30-minute seminar on open-book management recently. After the seminar, she decided to implement some open-book management practices in her division. She began the process today when she received her division's latest quarterly results.

    Joey Thompson, the production supervisor of the finishing department in Johnson's division, was surprised to receive the following note in his afternoon mail.

Dear Joey:

I've just finished reviewing the financial results for the last quarter. I am including some data from the financial reports below. Because our firm must identify ways to become more cost competitive, I intend to share data from the financial reports with you each quarter. I want you to use the information as the basis for making your department more efficient. By early in the coming year, I intend to put in place an incentive pay system that will replace your current salary. Accordingly, your income in the future will depend on your ability to manage the costs of your department.

To begin reducing costs, I suggest you concentrate on the cost items which I have circled below. Please give me a call if you have any questions.

Regards,
LJ

FINISHING DEPARTMENT COST ANALYSIS

	This Quarter	This Quarter Last Year	Last Quarter
Direct material	$ 95,000	$ 75,000	$ 90,000
Direct labor	925,000	840,000	940,000
Material-based overhead	27,000	22,000	23,000
Labor-based overhead	(413,000) circled	382,700	396,500
Machine-based overhead	(657,000) circled	589,000	617,000

As corporate controller of Worldwide Electronics, you are surprised when Joey Thompson calls your office and asks to meet with your staff to discuss the financial report and the meaning of "overhead." As you consider how to deal with him, you begin to contemplate the memo that you are going to write to Laura Johnson. Before any decisions are implemented, you realize that she can use your expertise to design and implement open-book management practices. As you write the memo, you know that your suggestions must be specific, positive, and informative. Write the memo to Johnson.

INTERNET

38. **LO.6 (Open-book management; transparency; research; writing)** Open-book management is consistent with another, larger trend in accounting—increased transparency of financial results. This trend follows a period in which many U.S. firms were guilty of generating misleading financial reports and hiding pertinent facts about financial performance. These practices led to the Sarbanes-Oxley Act of 2002 and other corporate reporting reforms. Conduct a library or Internet search on the topic of financial reporting transparency to address the following items:
    a. Discuss what is meant by the term "transparency" in the context of financial reporting.
    b. Discuss how open-book management is consistent with increased reporting transparency.

39. **LO.6 (Open-book management; writing)** In many large business organizations, financial experts are often physically located separately from operational personnel. One effect of this isolation is that the people with financial expertise often lack understanding of important facets of operations. At **SC Johnson**, financial experts intermingle in teams with production experts and much decision authority is delegated to cross-functional teams. Individuals with responsibilities for cost management, quality, safety, and so on rotate duties to learn about staffing, quality management, production processing, and production scheduling. Top management takes the view that every employee is essential to the success of the company—and the company has 12,000 employees in 70 countries and has never had a layoff!

    Source: Staff, "Springfield Remanufacturing, Behlen, and SC Johnson Deliver Outstanding 'Return on Individuals,'" *Control Engineering* (April 1, 2006); http://www.controleng.com/search/search-single-display/springfield-remanufacturing-behlen-and-sc-johnson-deliver-outstanding-return-on-individuals/e07e308257.html (last accessed 2/24/12).

    a. How could a financial specialist who is charged with designing an open-book management system benefit from serving a rotation in production, quality management, and other functional areas?
    b. Discuss how open-book management implementation would be affected by including, on cross-functional teams, a specialist in cost management.

ETHICS

40. **LO.7 (Environmental management; ethics; writing)** The chapter discusses three approaches to managing environmental costs. Some strategies deal with hazardous waste only after it has been produced.
    a. Does a firm have any ethical obligations *not* to produce hazardous waste regardless of how successfully it is dealt with by the firm?
    b. Assume that you are a key financial adviser in a firm that produces a large amount of toxic waste and that faces severe financial pressures and risks bankruptcy. By improperly disposing of certain waste materials, your firm could save millions of dollars, avoid bankruptcy, and preserve 10,000 local jobs. What action would you recommend your firm take? Explain the rationale for your answer.

41. **LO.7 (Environmental cost management; writing)** Horizon Resins has experienced serious problems as a result of attempts to manage its impacts on the environment. To illustrate the problems, consider the following events, which occurred during the past five years:
    - Horizon was assessed $75 million in fines and penalties for toxic emissions. These amounts related to several separate regulatory investigations.

- Horizon received reprimands from several regulatory bodies for failing to maintain required records regarding hazardous waste.
- Horizon is currently facing a class-action lawsuit filed by former employees of a subsidiary in Mexico alleging that management failed to disclose information to employees about the toxicity of certain materials. As a consequence, the health of the former employees has been permanently harmed.
- Horizon must submit bids to obtain most of its business. Managers have casually observed that the company is successful more frequently when it bids on jobs that require handling the most toxic chemicals.
- Horizon's accounting system tracks costs on a job order basis, but is not sensitive to quality or environmental costs.

Assume that you are an employee of the consulting firm that Horizon has hired to improve the management of all environmental effects. As the financial expert on the consulting team, you are expected to make recommendations as to how the information systems should be modified to reduce environmental costs. Prepare a report discussing your recommendations for Horizon.

APPENDIX

PRESENT VALUE TABLES

Table 1 Present Value of $1

Period	1.00%	2.00%	3.00%	4.00%	5.00%	6.00%	7.00%	8.00%	9.00%	9.50%	10.00%	10.50%	11.00%
1	0.9901	0.9804	0.9709	0.9615	0.9524	0.9434	0.9346	0.9259	0.9174	0.9132	0.9091	0.9050	0.9009
2	0.9803	0.9612	0.9426	0.9246	0.9070	0.8900	0.8734	0.8573	0.8417	0.8340	0.8265	0.8190	0.8116
3	0.9706	0.9423	0.9151	0.8890	0.8638	0.8396	0.8163	0.7938	0.7722	0.7617	0.7513	0.7412	0.7312
4	0.9610	0.9239	0.8885	0.8548	0.8227	0.7921	0.7629	0.7350	0.7084	0.6956	0.6830	0.6707	0.6587
5	0.9515	0.9057	0.8626	0.8219	0.7835	0.7473	0.7130	0.6806	0.6499	0.6352	0.6209	0.6070	0.5935
6	0.9421	0.8880	0.8375	0.7903	0.7462	0.7050	0.6663	0.6302	0.5963	0.5801	0.5645	0.5493	0.5346
7	0.9327	0.8706	0.8131	0.7599	0.7107	0.6651	0.6228	0.5835	0.5470	0.5298	0.5132	0.4971	0.4817
8	0.9235	0.8535	0.7894	0.7307	0.6768	0.6274	0.5820	0.5403	0.5019	0.4838	0.4665	0.4499	0.4339
9	0.9143	0.8368	0.7664	0.7026	0.6446	0.5919	0.5439	0.5003	0.4604	0.4419	0.4241	0.4071	0.3909
10	0.9053	0.8204	0.7441	0.6756	0.6139	0.5584	0.5084	0.4632	0.4224	0.4035	0.3855	0.3685	0.3522
11	0.8963	0.8043	0.7224	0.6496	0.5847	0.5268	0.4751	0.4289	0.3875	0.3685	0.3505	0.3334	0.3173
12	0.8875	0.7885	0.7014	0.6246	0.5568	0.4970	0.4440	0.3971	0.3555	0.3365	0.3186	0.3018	0.2858
13	0.8787	0.7730	0.6810	0.6006	0.5303	0.4688	0.4150	0.3677	0.3262	0.3073	0.2897	0.2731	0.2575
14	0.8700	0.7579	0.6611	0.5775	0.5051	0.4423	0.3878	0.3405	0.2993	0.2807	0.2633	0.2471	0.2320
15	0.8614	0.7430	0.6419	0.5553	0.4810	0.4173	0.3625	0.3152	0.2745	0.2563	0.2394	0.2237	0.2090
16	0.8528	0.7285	0.6232	0.5339	0.4581	0.3937	0.3387	0.2919	0.2519	0.2341	0.2176	0.2024	0.1883
17	0.8444	0.7142	0.6050	0.5134	0.4363	0.3714	0.3166	0.2703	0.2311	0.2138	0.1978	0.1832	0.1696
18	0.8360	0.7002	0.5874	0.4936	0.4155	0.3503	0.2959	0.2503	0.2120	0.1952	0.1799	0.1658	0.1528
19	0.8277	0.6864	0.5703	0.4746	0.3957	0.3305	0.2765	0.2317	0.1945	0.1783	0.1635	0.1500	0.1377
20	0.8195	0.6730	0.5537	0.4564	0.3769	0.3118	0.2584	0.2146	0.1784	0.1628	0.1486	0.1358	0.1240
21	0.8114	0.6598	0.5376	0.4388	0.3589	0.2942	0.2415	0.1987	0.1637	0.1487	0.1351	0.1229	0.1117
22	0.8034	0.6468	0.5219	0.4220	0.3419	0.2775	0.2257	0.1839	0.1502	0.1358	0.1229	0.1112	0.1007
23	0.7954	0.6342	0.5067	0.4057	0.3256	0.2618	0.2110	0.1703	0.1378	0.1240	0.1117	0.1006	0.0907
24	0.7876	0.6217	0.4919	0.3901	0.3101	0.2470	0.1972	0.1577	0.1264	0.1133	0.1015	0.0911	0.0817
25	0.7798	0.6095	0.4776	0.3751	0.2953	0.2330	0.1843	0.1460	0.1160	0.1034	0.0923	0.0824	0.0736
26	0.7721	0.5976	0.4637	0.3607	0.2812	0.2198	0.1722	0.1352	0.1064	0.0945	0.0839	0.0746	0.0663
27	0.7644	0.5859	0.4502	0.3468	0.2679	0.2074	0.1609	0.1252	0.0976	0.0863	0.0763	0.0675	0.0597
28	0.7568	0.5744	0.4371	0.3335	0.2551	0.1956	0.1504	0.1159	0.0896	0.0788	0.0693	0.0611	0.0538
29	0.7493	0.5631	0.4244	0.3207	0.2430	0.1846	0.1406	0.1073	0.0822	0.0719	0.0630	0.0553	0.0485
30	0.7419	0.5521	0.4120	0.3083	0.2314	0.1741	0.1314	0.0994	0.0754	0.0657	0.0573	0.0500	0.0437
31	0.7346	0.5413	0.4000	0.2965	0.2204	0.1643	0.1228	0.0920	0.0692	0.0600	0.0521	0.0453	0.0394
32	0.7273	0.5306	0.3883	0.2851	0.2099	0.1550	0.1147	0.0852	0.0634	0.0058	0.0474	0.0410	0.0355
33	0.7201	0.5202	0.3770	0.2741	0.1999	0.1462	0.1072	0.0789	0.0582	0.0500	0.0431	0.0371	0.0319
34	0.7130	0.5100	0.3660	0.2636	0.1904	0.1379	0.1002	0.0731	0.0534	0.0457	0.0391	0.0336	0.0288
35	0.7059	0.5000	0.3554	0.2534	0.1813	0.1301	0.0937	0.0676	0.0490	0.0417	0.0356	0.0304	0.0259
36	0.6989	0.4902	0.3450	0.2437	0.1727	0.1227	0.0875	0.0626	0.0449	0.0381	0.0324	0.0275	0.0234
37	0.6920	0.4806	0.3350	0.2343	0.1644	0.1158	0.0818	0.0580	0.0412	0.0348	0.0294	0.0249	0.0210
38	0.6852	0.4712	0.3252	0.2253	0.1566	0.1092	0.0765	0.0537	0.0378	0.0318	0.0267	0.0225	0.0190
39	0.6784	0.4620	0.3158	0.2166	0.1492	0.1031	0.0715	0.0497	0.0347	0.0290	0.0243	0.0204	0.0171
40	0.6717	0.4529	0.3066	0.2083	0.1421	0.0972	0.0668	0.0460	0.0318	0.0265	0.0221	0.0184	0.0154
41	0.6650	0.4440	0.2976	0.2003	0.1353	0.0917	0.0624	0.0426	0.0292	0.0242	0.0201	0.0167	0.0139
42	0.6584	0.4353	0.2890	0.1926	0.1288	0.0865	0.0583	0.0395	0.0268	0.0221	0.0183	0.0151	0.0125
43	0.6519	0.4268	0.2805	0.1852	0.1227	0.0816	0.0545	0.0365	0.0246	0.0202	0.0166	0.0137	0.0113
44	0.6455	0.4184	0.2724	0.1781	0.1169	0.0770	0.0510	0.0338	0.0226	0.0184	0.0151	0.0124	0.0101
45	0.6391	0.4102	0.2644	0.1712	0.1113	0.0727	0.0476	0.0313	0.0207	0.0168	0.0137	0.0112	0.0091
46	0.6327	0.4022	0.2567	0.1646	0.1060	0.0685	0.0445	0.0290	0.0190	0.0154	0.0125	0.0101	0.0082
47	0.6265	0.3943	0.2493	0.1583	0.1010	0.0647	0.0416	0.0269	0.0174	0.0141	0.0113	0.0092	0.0074
48	0.6203	0.3865	0.2420	0.1522	0.0961	0.0610	0.0389	0.0249	0.0160	0.0128	0.0103	0.0083	0.0067
49	0.6141	0.3790	0.2350	0.1463	0.0916	0.0576	0.0363	0.0230	0.0147	0.0117	0.0094	0.0075	0.0060
50	0.6080	0.3715	0.2281	0.1407	0.0872	0.0543	0.0340	0.0213	0.0135	0.0107	0.0085	0.0068	0.0054

Table 1 *(Continued)*

Period	11.50%	12.00%	12.50%	13.00%	13.50%	14.00%	14.50%	15.00%	15.50%	16.00%	17.00%	18.00%	19.00%	20.00%
1	0.8969	0.8929	0.8889	0.8850	0.8811	0.8772	0.8734	0.8696	0.8658	0.8621	0.8547	0.8475	0.8403	0.8333
2	0.8044	0.7972	0.7901	0.7832	0.7763	0.7695	0.7628	0.7561	0.7496	0.7432	0.7305	0.7182	0.7062	0.6944
3	0.7214	0.7118	0.7023	0.6931	0.6839	0.6750	0.6662	0.6575	0.6490	0.6407	0.6244	0.6086	0.5934	0.5787
4	0.6470	0.6355	0.6243	0.6133	0.6026	0.5921	0.5818	0.5718	0.5619	0.5523	0.5337	0.5158	0.4987	0.4823
5	0.5803	0.5674	0.5549	0.5428	0.5309	0.5194	0.5081	0.4972	0.4865	0.4761	0.4561	0.4371	0.4191	0.4019
6	0.5204	0.5066	0.4933	0.4803	0.4678	0.4556	0.4438	0.4323	0.4212	0.4104	0.3898	0.3704	0.3521	0.3349
7	0.4667	0.4524	0.4385	0.4251	0.4121	0.3996	0.3876	0.3759	0.3647	0.3538	0.3332	0.3139	0.2959	0.2791
8	0.4186	0.4039	0.3897	0.3762	0.3631	0.3506	0.3385	0.3269	0.3158	0.3050	0.2848	0.2660	0.2487	0.2326
9	0.3754	0.3606	0.3464	0.3329	0.3199	0.3075	0.2956	0.2843	0.2734	0.2630	0.2434	0.2255	0.2090	0.1938
10	0.3367	0.3220	0.3080	0.2946	0.2819	0.2697	0.2582	0.2472	0.2367	0.2267	0.2080	0.1911	0.1756	0.1615
11	0.3020	0.2875	0.2737	0.2607	0.2483	0.2366	0.2255	0.2149	0.2049	0.1954	0.1778	0.1619	0.1476	0.1346
12	0.2708	0.2567	0.2433	0.2307	0.2188	0.2076	0.1969	0.1869	0.1774	0.1685	0.1520	0.1372	0.1240	0.1122
13	0.2429	0.2292	0.2163	0.2042	0.1928	0.1821	0.1720	0.1625	0.1536	0.1452	0.1299	0.1163	0.1042	0.0935
14	0.2179	0.2046	0.1923	0.1807	0.1699	0.1597	0.1502	0.1413	0.1330	0.1252	0.1110	0.0986	0.0876	0.0779
15	0.1954	0.1827	0.1709	0.1599	0.1496	0.1401	0.1312	0.1229	0.1152	0.1079	0.0949	0.0835	0.0736	0.0649
16	0.1752	0.1631	0.1519	0.1415	0.1319	0.1229	0.1146	0.1069	0.0997	0.0930	0.0811	0.0708	0.0618	0.0541
17	0.1572	0.1456	0.1350	0.1252	0.1162	0.1078	0.1001	0.0929	0.0863	0.0802	0.0693	0.0600	0.0520	0.0451
18	0.1410	0.1300	0.1200	0.1108	0.1024	0.0946	0.0874	0.0808	0.0747	0.0691	0.0593	0.0508	0.0437	0.0376
19	0.1264	0.1161	0.1067	0.0981	0.0902	0.0830	0.0763	0.0703	0.0647	0.0596	0.0506	0.0431	0.0367	0.0313
20	0.1134	0.1037	0.0948	0.0868	0.0795	0.0728	0.0667	0.0611	0.0560	0.0514	0.0433	0.0365	0.0308	0.0261
21	0.1017	0.0926	0.0843	0.0768	0.0700	0.0638	0.0582	0.0531	0.0485	0.0443	0.0370	0.0309	0.0259	0.0217
22	0.0912	0.0826	0.0749	0.0680	0.0617	0.0560	0.0509	0.0462	0.0420	0.0382	0.0316	0.0262	0.0218	0.0181
23	0.0818	0.0738	0.0666	0.0601	0.0543	0.0491	0.0444	0.0402	0.0364	0.0329	0.0270	0.0222	0.0183	0.0151
24	0.0734	0.0659	0.0592	0.0532	0.0479	0.0431	0.0388	0.0349	0.0315	0.0284	0.0231	0.0188	0.0154	0.0126
25	0.0658	0.0588	0.0526	0.0471	0.0422	0.0378	0.0339	0.0304	0.0273	0.0245	0.0197	0.0160	0.0129	0.0105
26	0.0590	0.0525	0.0468	0.0417	0.0372	0.0332	0.0296	0.0264	0.0236	0.0211	0.0169	0.0135	0.0109	0.0087
27	0.0529	0.0469	0.0416	0.0369	0.0327	0.0291	0.0258	0.0230	0.0204	0.0182	0.0144	0.0115	0.0091	0.0073
28	0.0475	0.0419	0.0370	0.0326	0.0289	0.0255	0.0226	0.0200	0.0177	0.0157	0.0123	0.0097	0.0077	0.0061
29	0.0426	0.0374	0.0329	0.0289	0.0254	0.0224	0.0197	0.0174	0.0153	0.0135	0.0105	0.0082	0.0064	0.0051
30	0.0382	0.0334	0.0292	0.0256	0.0224	0.0196	0.0172	0.0151	0.0133	0.0117	0.0090	0.0070	0.0054	0.0042
31	0.0342	0.0298	0.0260	0.0226	0.0197	0.0172	0.0150	0.0131	0.0115	0.0100	0.0077	0.0059	0.0046	0.0035
32	0.0307	0.0266	0.0231	0.0200	0.0174	0.0151	0.0131	0.0114	0.0099	0.0087	0.0066	0.0050	0.0038	0.0029
33	0.0275	0.0238	0.0205	0.0177	0.0153	0.0133	0.0115	0.0099	0.0086	0.0075	0.0056	0.0043	0.0032	0.0024
34	0.0247	0.0212	0.0182	0.0157	0.0135	0.0116	0.0100	0.0088	0.0075	0.0064	0.0048	0.0036	0.0027	0.0020
35	0.0222	0.0189	0.0162	0.0139	0.0119	0.0102	0.0088	0.0075	0.0065	0.0056	0.0041	0.0031	0.0023	0.0017
36	0.0199	0.0169	0.0144	0.0123	0.0105	0.0089	0.0076	0.0065	0.0056	0.0048	0.0035	0.0026	0.0019	0.0014
37	0.0178	0.0151	0.0128	0.0109	0.0092	0.0078	0.0067	0.0057	0.0048	0.0041	0.0030	0.0022	0.0016	0.0012
38	0.0160	0.0135	0.0114	0.0096	0.0081	0.0069	0.0058	0.0049	0.0042	0.0036	0.0026	0.0019	0.0014	0.0010
39	0.0143	0.0120	0.0101	0.0085	0.0072	0.0060	0.0051	0.0043	0.0036	0.0031	0.0022	0.0016	0.0011	0.0008
40	0.0129	0.0108	0.0090	0.0075	0.0063	0.0053	0.0044	0.0037	0.0031	0.0026	0.0019	0.0013	0.0010	0.0007
41	0.0115	0.0096	0.0080	0.0067	0.0056	0.0046	0.0039	0.0033	0.0027	0.0023	0.0016	0.0011	0.0008	0.0006
42	0.0103	0.0086	0.0077	0.0059	0.0049	0.0041	0.0034	0.0028	0.0024	0.0020	0.0014	0.0010	0.0007	0.0005
43	0.0093	0.0077	0.0063	0.0052	0.0043	0.0036	0.0030	0.0025	0.0020	0.0017	0.0012	0.0008	0.0006	0.0004
44	0.0083	0.0068	0.0056	0.0046	0.0038	0.0031	0.0026	0.0021	0.0018	0.0015	0.0010	0.0007	0.0005	0.0003
45	0.0075	0.0061	0.0050	0.0041	0.0034	0.0028	0.0023	0.0019	0.0015	0.0013	0.0009	0.0006	0.0004	0.0003
46	0.0067	0.0054	0.0044	0.0036	0.0030	0.0024	0.0020	0.0016	0.0013	0.0011	0.0007	0.0005	0.0003	0.0002
47	0.0060	0.0049	0.0039	0.0032	0.0026	0.0021	0.0017	0.0014	0.0011	0.0009	0.0006	0.0004	0.0003	0.0002
48	0.0054	0.0043	0.0035	0.0028	0.0023	0.0019	0.0015	0.0012	0.0010	0.0008	0.0005	0.0004	0.0002	0.0002
49	0.0048	0.0039	0.0031	0.0025	0.0020	0.0016	0.0013	0.0011	0.0009	0.0007	0.0005	0.0003	0.0002	0.0001
50	0.0043	0.0035	0.0028	0.0022	0.0018	0.0014	0.0012	0.0009	0.0007	0.0006	0.0004	0.0003	0.0002	0.0001

Table 2 Present Value of an Ordinary Annuity of $1

Period	1.00%	2.00%	3.00%	4.00%	5.00%	6.00%	7.00%	8.00%	9.00%	9.50%	10.00%	10.50%	11.00%
1	0.9901	0.9804	0.9709	0.9615	0.0524	0.9434	0.9346	0.9259	0.9174	0.9132	0.9091	0.9050	0.9009
2	1.9704	1.9416	1.9135	1.8861	1.8594	1.8334	1.8080	1.7833	1.7591	1.7473	1.7355	1.7240	1.7125
3	2.9410	2.8839	2.8286	2.7751	2.7233	2.6730	2.6243	2.5771	2.5313	2.5089	2.4869	2.4651	2.4437
4	3.9020	3.8077	3.7171	3.6299	3.5460	3.4651	3.3872	3.3121	3.2397	3.2045	3.1699	3.1359	3.1025
5	4.8534	4.7135	4.5797	4.4518	4.3295	4.2124	4.1002	3.9927	3.8897	3.8397	3.7908	3.7429	3.6959
6	5.7955	5.6014	5.4172	5.2421	5.0757	4.9173	4.7665	4.6229	4.4859	4.4198	4.3553	4.2922	4.2305
7	6.7282	6.4720	6.2303	6.0021	5.7864	5.5824	5.3893	5.2064	5.0330	4.9496	4.8684	4.7893	4.7122
8	7.6517	7.3255	7.0197	6.7327	6.4632	6.2098	5.9713	5.7466	5.5348	5.4334	5.3349	5.2392	5.1461
9	8.5660	8.1622	7.7861	7.4353	7.1078	6.8017	6.5152	6.2469	5.9953	5.8753	5.7590	5.6463	5.5371
10	9.4713	8.9826	8.5302	8.1109	7.7217	7.3601	7.0236	6.7101	6.4177	6.2788	6.1446	6.0148	5.8892
11	10.3676	9.7869	9.2526	8.7605	8.3064	7.8869	7.4987	7.1390	6.8052	6.6473	6.4951	6.3482	6.2065
12	11.2551	10.5753	9.9540	9.3851	8.8633	8.3838	7.9427	7.5361	7.1607	6.9838	6.8137	6.6500	6.4924
13	12.1337	11.3484	10.6350	9.9857	9.3936	8.8527	8.3577	7.9038	7.4869	7.2912	7.1034	6.9230	6.7499
14	13.0037	12.1063	11.2961	10.5631	9.8986	9.2950	8.7455	8.2442	7.7862	7.5719	7.3667	7.1702	6.9819
15	13.8651	12.8493	11.9379	11.1184	10.3797	9.7123	9.1079	8.5595	8.0607	7.8282	7.6061	7.3938	7.1909
16	14.7179	13.5777	12.5611	11.6523	10.8378	10.1059	9.4467	8.8514	8.3126	8.0623	7.8237	7.5962	7.3792
17	15.5623	14.2919	13.1661	12.1657	11.2741	10.4773	9.7632	9.1216	8.5436	8.2760	8.0216	7.7794	7.5488
18	16.3983	14.9920	13.7535	12.6593	11.6896	10.8276	10.0591	9.3719	8.7556	8.4713	8.2014	7.9452	7.7016
19	17.2260	15.6785	14.3238	13.1339	12.0853	11.1581	10.3356	9.6036	8.9501	8.6496	8.3649	8.0952	7.8393
20	18.0456	16.3514	14.8775	13.5903	12.4622	11.4699	10.5940	9.8182	9.1286	8.8124	8.5136	8.2309	7.9633
21	18.8570	17.0112	15.4150	14.0292	12.8212	11.7641	10.8355	10.0168	9.2922	8.9611	8.6487	8.3538	8.0751
22	19.6604	17.6581	15.9369	14.4511	13.1630	12.0416	11.0612	10.2007	9.4424	9.0969	8.7715	8.4649	8.1757
23	20.4558	18.2922	16.4436	14.8568	13.4886	12.3034	11.2722	10.3711	9.5802	9.2209	8.8832	8.5656	8.2664
24	21.2434	18.9139	16.9355	15.2470	13.7986	12.5504	11.4693	10.5288	9.7066	9.3342	8.9847	8.6566	8.3481
25	22.0232	19.5235	17.4132	15.6221	14.0939	12.7834	11.6536	10.6748	9.8226	9.4376	9.0770	8.7390	8.4217
26	22.7952	20.1210	17.8768	15.9828	14.3752	13.0032	11.8258	10.8100	9.9290	9.5320	9.1610	8.8136	8.4881
27	23.5596	20.7069	18.3270	16.3296	14.6430	13.2105	11.9867	10.9352	10.0266	9.6183	9.2372	8.8811	8.5478
28	24.3164	21.2813	18.7641	16.6631	14.8981	13.4062	12.1371	11.0511	10.1161	9.6971	9.3066	8.9422	8.6016
29	25.0658	21.8444	19.1885	16.9837	15.1411	13.5907	12.2777	11.1584	10.1983	9.7690	9.3696	8.9974	8.6501
30	25.8077	22.3965	19.6004	17.2920	15.3725	13.7648	12.4090	11.2578	10.2737	9.8347	9.4269	9.0474	8.6938
31	26.5423	22.9377	20.0004	17.5885	15.5928	13.9291	12.5318	11.3498	10.3428	9.8947	9.4790	9.0927	8.7332
32	27.2696	23.4683	20.3888	17.8736	15.8027	14.0840	12.6466	11.4350	10.4062	9.9495	9.5264	9.1337	8.7686
33	27.9897	23.9886	20.7658	18.1477	16.0026	14.2302	12.7538	11.5139	10.4664	9.9996	9.5694	9.1707	8.8005
34	28.7027	24.4986	21.1318	18.4112	16.1929	14.3681	12.8540	11.5869	10.5178	10.0453	9.6086	9.2043	8.8293
35	29.4086	24.9986	21.4872	18.6646	16.3742	14.4983	12.9477	11.6546	10.5668	10.0870	9.6442	9.2347	8.8552
36	30.1075	25.4888	21.8323	18.9083	16.5469	14.6210	13.0352	11.7172	10.6118	10.1251	9.6765	9.2621	8.8786
37	30.7995	25.9695	22.1672	19.1426	16.7113	14.7368	13.1170	11.7752	10.6530	10.1599	9.7059	9.2870	8.8996
38	31.4847	26.4406	22.4925	19.3679	16.8679	14.8460	13.1935	11.8289	10.6908	10.1917	9.7327	9.3095	8.9186
39	32.1630	26.9026	22.8082	19.5845	17.0170	14.9491	13.2649	11.8786	10.7255	10.2207	9.7570	9.3299	8.9357
40	32.8347	27.3555	23.1148	19.7928	17.1591	15.0463	13.3317	11.9246	10.7574	10.2473	9.7791	9.3483	8.9511
41	33.4997	27.7995	23.4124	19.9931	17.2944	15.1380	13.3941	11.9672	10.7866	10.2715	9.7991	9.3650	8.9649
42	34.1581	28.2348	23.7014	20.1856	17.4232	15.2245	13.4525	12.0067	10.8134	10.2936	9.8174	9.3801	8.9774
43	34.8100	28.6616	23.9819	20.3708	17.5459	15.3062	13.5070	12.0432	10.8380	10.3138	9.8340	9.3937	8.9887
44	35.4555	29.0800	24.2543	20.5488	17.6628	15.3832	13.5579	12.0771	10.8605	10.3322	9.8491	9.4061	8.9988
45	36.0945	29.4902	24.5187	20.7200	17.7741	15.4558	13.6055	12.1084	10.8812	10.3490	9.8628	9.4163	9.0079
46	36.7272	29.8923	24.7755	20.8847	17.8801	15.5244	13.6500	12.1374	10.9002	10.3644	9.8753	9.4274	9.0161
47	37.3537	30.2866	25.0247	21.0429	17.9810	15.5890	13.6916	12.1643	10.9176	10.3785	9.8866	9.4366	9.0236
48	37.9740	30.6731	25.2667	21.1951	18.0772	15.6500	13.7305	12.1891	10.9336	10.3913	9.8969	9.4449	9.0302
49	38.5881	31.0521	25.5017	21.3415	18.1687	15.7076	13.7668	12.2122	10.9482	10.4030	9.9063	9.5424	9.0362
50	39.1961	31.4236	25.7298	21.4822	18.2559	15.7619	13.8008	12.2335	10.9617	10.4137	9.9148	9.4591	9.0417

Table 2 *(Continued)*

Period	11.50%	12.00%	12.50%	13.00%	13.50%	14.00%	14.50%	15.00%	15.50%	16.00%	17.00%	18.00%	19.00%	20.00%
1	0.8969	0.8929	0.8889	0.8850	0.8811	0.8772	0.8734	0.8696	0.8658	0.8621	0.8547	0.8475	0.8403	0.8333
2	1.7012	1.6901	1.6790	1.6681	1.6573	1.6467	1.6361	1.6257	1.6154	1.6052	1.5852	1.5656	1.5465	1.5278
3	2.4226	2.4018	2.3813	2.3612	2.3413	2.3216	2.3023	2.2832	2.2644	2.2459	2.2096	2.1743	2.1399	2.1065
4	3.0696	3.0374	3.0056	2.9745	2.9438	2.9137	2.8841	2.8850	2.8263	2.7982	2.7432	2.6901	2.6386	2.5887
5	3.6499	3.6048	3.5606	3.5172	3.4747	3.4331	3.3922	3.3522	3.3129	3.2743	3.1994	3.1272	3.0576	2.9906
6	4.1703	4.1114	4.0538	3.9976	3.9425	3.8887	3.8360	3.7845	3.7341	3.6847	3.5892	3.4976	3.4098	3.3255
7	4.6370	4.5638	4.4923	4.4226	4.3546	4.2883	4.2236	4.1604	4.0988	4.0386	3.9224	3.8115	3.7057	3.6046
8	5.0556	4.9676	4.8821	4.7988	4.7177	4.6389	4.5621	4.4873	4.4145	4.3436	4.2072	4.0776	3.9544	3.8372
9	5.4311	5.3283	5.2285	5.1317	5.0377	4.9464	4.8577	4.7716	4.6879	4.6065	4.4506	4.3030	4.1633	4.0310
10	5.7678	5.6502	5.5364	5.4262	5.3195	5.2161	5.1159	5.0188	4.9246	4.8332	4.6586	4.4941	4.3389	4.1925
11	6.0698	5.9377	5.8102	5.6869	5.5679	5.4527	5.3414	5.2337	5.1295	5.0286	4.8364	4.6560	4.4865	4.3271
12	6.3406	6.1944	6.0535	5.9177	5.7867	5.6603	5.5383	5.4206	5.3069	5.1971	4.9884	4.7932	4.6105	4.4392
13	6.5835	6.4236	6.2698	6.1218	5.9794	5.8424	5.7103	5.5832	5.4606	5.3423	5.1183	4.9095	4.7147	4.5327
14	6.8013	6.6282	6.4620	6.3025	6.1493	6.0021	5.8606	5.7245	5.5936	5.4675	5.2293	5.0081	4.8023	4.6106
15	6.9967	6.8109	6.6329	6.4624	6.2989	6.1422	5.9918	5.8474	5.7087	5.5755	5.3242	5.0916	4.8759	4.6755
16	7.1719	6.9740	6.7848	6.6039	6.4308	6.2651	6.1063	5.9542	5.8084	5.6685	5.4053	5.1624	4.9377	4.7296
17	7.3291	7.1196	6.9198	6.7291	6.5469	6.3729	6.2064	6.0472	5.8947	5.7487	5.4746	5.2223	4.9897	4.7746
18	7.4700	7.2497	7.0398	6.8399	6.6493	6.4674	6.2938	6.1280	5.9695	5.8179	5.5339	5.2732	5.0333	4.8122
19	7.5964	7.3658	7.1465	6.9380	6.7395	6.5504	6.3701	6.1982	6.0342	5.8775	5.5845	5.3162	5.0700	4.8435
20	7.7098	7.4694	7.2414	7.0248	6.8189	6.6231	6.4368	6.2593	6.0902	5.9288	5.6278	5.3528	5.1009	4.8696
21	7.8115	7.5620	7.3257	7.1016	6.8889	6.6870	6.4950	6.3125	6.1387	5.9731	5.6648	5.3837	5.1268	4.8913
22	7.9027	7.6447	7.4006	7.1695	6.9506	6.7429	6.5459	6.3587	6.1807	6.0113	5.6964	5.4099	5.1486	4.9094
23	7.9845	7.7184	7.4672	7.2297	7.0049	6.7921	6.5903	6.3988	6.2170	6.0443	5.7234	5.4321	5.1669	4.9245
24	8.0578	7.7843	7.5264	7.2829	7.0528	6.8351	6.6291	6.4338	6.2485	6.0726	5.7465	5.4510	5.1822	4.9371
25	8.1236	7.8431	7.5790	7.3300	7.0950	6.8729	6.6629	6.4642	6.2758	6.0971	5.7662	5.4669	5.1952	4.9476
26	8.1826	7.8957	7.6258	7.3717	7.1321	6.9061	6.6925	6.4906	6.2994	6.1182	5.7831	5.4804	5.2060	4.9563
27	8.2355	7.9426	7.6674	7.4086	7.1649	6.9352	6.7184	6.5135	6.3198	6.1364	5.7975	5.4919	5.2151	4.9636
28	8.2830	7.9844	7.7043	7.4412	7.1937	6.9607	6.7409	6.5335	6.3375	6.1520	5.8099	5.5016	5.2228	4.9697
29	8.3255	8.0218	7.7372	7.4701	7.2191	6.9830	6.7606	6.5509	6.3528	6.1656	5.8204	5.5098	5.2292	4.9747
30	8.3637	8.0552	7.7664	7.4957	7.2415	7.0027	6.7779	6.5660	6.3661	6.1772	5.8294	5.5168	5.2347	4.9789
31	8.3980	8.0850	7.7923	7.5183	7.2613	7.0199	6.7929	6.5791	6.3776	6.1872	5.8371	5.5227	5.2392	4.9825
32	8.4287	8.1116	7.8154	7.5383	7.2786	7.0350	6.8060	6.5905	6.3875	6.1959	5.8437	5.5277	5.2430	4.9854
33	8.4562	8.1354	7.8359	7.5560	7.2940	7.0482	6.8175	6.6005	6.3961	6.2034	5.8493	5.5320	5.2463	4.9878
34	8.4809	8.1566	7.8542	7.5717	7.3075	7.0599	6.8275	6.6091	6.4035	6.2098	5.8541	5.5356	5.2490	4.9898
35	8.5030	8.1755	7.8704	7.5856	7.3193	7.0701	6.8362	6.6166	6.4100	6.2153	5.8582	5.5386	5.2512	4.9930
36	8.5229	8.1924	7.8848	7.5979	7.3298	7.0790	6.8439	6.6231	6.4156	6.2201	5.8617	5.5412	5.2531	4.9930
37	8.5407	8.2075	7.8976	7.6087	7.3390	7.0868	6.8505	6.6288	6.4204	6.2242	5.8647	5.5434	5.2547	4.9941
38	8.5567	8.2210	7.9090	7.6183	7.3472	7.0937	6.8564	6.6338	6.4246	6.2278	5.8673	5.5453	5.2561	4.9951
39	8.5710	8.2330	7.9191	7.6268	7.3543	7.0998	6.8615	6.6381	6.4282	6.2309	5.8695	5.5468	5.2572	4.9959
40	8.5839	8.2438	7.9281	7.6344	7.3607	7.1050	6.8659	6.6418	6.4314	6.2335	5.8713	5.5482	5.2582	4.9966
41	8.5954	8.2534	7.9361	7.6410	7.3662	7.1097	6.8698	6.6450	6.4341	6.2358	5.8729	5.5493	5.2590	4.9972
42	8.6058	8.2619	7.9432	7.6469	7.3711	7.1138	6.8732	6.6479	6.4364	6.2377	5.8743	5.5502	5.2596	4.9976
43	8.6150	8.2696	7.9495	7.6522	7.3754	7.1173	6.8761	6.6503	6.4385	6.2394	5.8755	5.5511	5.2602	4.9980
44	8.6233	8.2764	7.9551	7.6568	7.3792	7.1205	6.8787	6.6524	6.4402	6.2409	5.8765	5.5517	5.2607	4.9984
45	8.6308	8.2825	7.9601	7.6609	7.3826	7.1232	6.8810	6.6543	6.4418	6.2421	5.8773	5.5523	5.2611	4.9986
46	8.6375	8.2880	7.9645	7.6645	7.3855	7.1256	6.8830	6.6559	6.4431	6.2432	5.8781	5.5528	5.2614	4.9989
47	8.6435	8.2928	7.9685	7.6677	7.3881	7.1277	6.8847	6.6573	6.4442	6.2442	5.8787	5.5532	5.2617	4.9991
48	8.6489	8.2972	7.9720	7.6705	7.3904	7.1296	6.8862	6.6585	6.4452	6.2450	5.8792	5.5536	5.2619	4.9992
49	8.6537	8.3010	7.9751	7.6730	7.3925	7.1312	6.8875	6.6596	6.4461	6.2457	5.8797	5.5539	5.2621	4.9993
50	8.6580	8.3045	7.9779	7.6752	7.3942	7.1327	6.8886	6.6605	6.4468	6.2463	5.8801	5.5541	5.2623	4.9995

GLOSSARY

A

abnormal loss decretion or spoilage of units in excess of that expected during a production process; the expectation is set by management

absorption costing a cost accumulation and reporting method that treats the costs of all manufacturing components (direct material, direct labor, variable overhead, and fixed overhead) as inventoriable or product costs; the traditional approach to product costing; must be used for external financial statements and tax reporting

accounting rate of return (ARR) the rate of earnings obtained on the average capital investment over the life of a capital project; computed as average annual profits divided by average investment; not based on cash flow

activity a repetitive action performed in fulfillment of business functions

activity analysis the process of detailing the various repetitive actions that are performed in making a product or providing a service, classifying them as value-added and non-value-added, and devising ways of minimizing or eliminating non-value-added activities

activity-based costing (ABC) a process using multiple cost drivers to predict and allocate costs to products and services; an accounting system collecting financial and operational data on the basis of the underlying nature and extent of business activities; an accounting information and costing system that identifies the various activities performed in an organization, collects costs on the basis of the underlying nature and extent of those activities, and assigns costs to products and services based on consumption of those activities by the products and services

activity-based management (ABM) a discipline that focuses on the activities incurred during the production/performance process as the way to improve the value received by a customer and the resulting profit achieved by providing this value

activity center a segment of the production or service process for which management wants to separately report the costs of the activities performed

activity driver a measure of the demands on activities and, thus, the resources consumed by products and services; often indicates an activity's output

actual cost system a valuation method that uses actual direct material, direct labor, and overhead charges in determining the cost of Work in Process Inventory

ad hoc discount a price concession made under competitive pressure (real or imagined) that does not relate to quantity purchased

administrative department an organizational unit that performs management activities benefiting the entire organization; includes top management personnel and organization headquarters

advance pricing agreement (APA) a binding contract between a company and one or more national tax authorities that provides details of how a transfer price is to be set and establishes that no regulatory adjustments or penalties will be made if the agreed-upon methodology is used

algebraic method a process of support department cost allocation that considers all interrelationships of the departments and reflects these relationships in simultaneous equations

allocate assign cost based on the use of a cost driver, a cost predictor, or an arbitrary method

allocation the systematic assignment of an amount to recipient cost objects

annuity a series of equal cash flows (either positive or negative) per period

annuity due a series of equal cash flows being received or paid at the beginning of a period

applied overhead the amount of overhead that has been allocated to Work in Process Inventory as a result of productive activity; credits for this amount are to an overhead account

appraisal cost a quality control cost incurred for monitoring or inspection; compensates for mistakes not eliminated through prevention activities

appropriation a budgeted maximum allowable expenditure

approximated net realizable value at split-off allocation a method of allocating joint cost to joint products using a simulated net realizable value at the split-off point; computed as final sales price minus incremental separate costs

asset turnover a ratio measuring asset productivity and showing the number of sales dollars generated by each dollar of assets

authority the right (usually by virtue of position or rank) to use resources to accomplish a task or achieve an objective

autonomation the use of equipment that has been programmed to sense certain conditions

B

backflush costing a streamlined cost accounting method that speeds up, simplifies, and reduces accounting effort in an environment that minimizes inventory balances, requires few allocations, uses standard costs, and has minimal variances from standard

balanced scorecard (BSC) an approach to performance measurement that uses performance measures from four perspectives: financial, internal business, customer, and innovation and learning

batch-level cost a cost that is caused by a group of things being made, handled, or processed at a single time

benchmarking the process of investigating how others do something well so that the investigating company can imitate, and possibly improve upon, the benchmarked company's techniques

benefits-provided ranking a listing of support departments in an order that begins with the one providing the most support to all other corporate areas and ends with the support department providing support primarily to revenue-producing areas

bill of materials a source document that contains information about a product's material components and their specifications (including quality and quantities needed)

black box a term for a management control system whose exact nature of operation cannot be observed

bottleneck any object or facility having a processing speed sufficiently slow to cause the other processing mechanisms in its network to experience idle time

break-even chart a graph that depicts the relationships among revenues, variable costs, fixed costs, and profits (or losses)

break-even point (BEP) the level of activity, in units or dollars, at which total revenues equal total costs

budget a financial plan for the future based on a single level of activity; the quantitative expression of a company's commitment to planned activities and resource acquisition and use

budgeting the process of formalizing plans and committing them to written, financial terms

budget manual a detailed set of documents that provides descriptive information and guidelines about the budgetary process

budget slack an intentional underestimation of revenues and/or overestimation of expenses in a budgeting process for the purpose of including deviations that are likely to occur so that results will meet expectations

budget variance the difference between total actual overhead and budgeted overhead based on standard hours allowed for the production achieved during the period; computed as part of two-variance overhead analysis; also referred to as the controllable variance

build mission an organizational mission of increasing market share even at the expense of short-term profits and cash flow; typically pursued by a business unit that has a small market share in a high-growth industry; appropriate for products that are in the early stages of the product life cycle

business process reengineering (BPR) the process of combining information technology to create new and more effective business processes that will lower costs, eliminate unnecessary work, upgrade customer service, and increase speed to market

business-value-added activity an activity that is necessary for the operation of the business but for which a customer would not want to pay; a non-value-added activity

by-product an incidental output of a joint process; is salable, but its sales value is not substantial enough for management to justify undertaking the joint process; has a higher sales value than scrap

C

capacity a measure of production volume or some other activity base

capital asset an asset used to generate revenues or cost savings by providing production, distribution, or service capabilities lasting for more than one year

capital budgeting a process of evaluating an entity's proposed long-range projects or courses of future activity for the purpose of allocating limited resources to desirable projects

capital rationing a process that allocates scarce or constrained monetary resources to capital asset acquisitions

carbon footprint a reflection of the total of all greenhouse gas emissions created by an organization's activities during a specified time

carrying cost the total variable cost of carrying one unit of inventory in stock for one year; includes the opportunity cost of capital invested in inventory

cash flow the receipt or disbursement of cash; when related to capital budgeting, cash flows arise from the purchase, operation, and disposition of a capital asset

centralization a management style that exists when top management makes most decisions and controls most activities of the organizational units from the company's central headquarters

coefficient of determination a measure of dispersion that indicates the "goodness of fit" of the actual observations to the least squares regression line; indicates what proportion of the total variation in *y* (the dependent variable) is explained by the regression model

committed cost a cost related to either the long-term investment in plant and equipment of a business or the organizational personnel who are deemed essential by top management; cannot be changed without long-run detriment to the organization

compensation strategy a foundation for the compensation plan that addresses the role compensation should play in the organization

competence a personal characteristic of developing, possessing, and maintaining the knowledge, skills, and qualifications necessary to perform a task or practice a profession

compounding period the time between each interest computation

compound interest a method of determining interest in which interest that was earned in prior periods is added to the original investment so that, in each successive period, interest is earned on both principal and interest

computer-integrated manufacturing (CIM) the integration of two or more flexible manufacturing systems through the use of a host computer and an information networking system

confidentiality a personal characteristic that reflects the discretion to refrain from disclosing company information to inappropriate parties, such as competitors; is often specifically defined or referred to in the company's code of ethics

confrontation strategy an organizational strategy in which company management decides to confront, rather than avoid, competition; an organizational strategy in which company management still attempts to differentiate company products through new features or to develop a price leadership position by dropping prices, even though management recognizes that competitors will rapidly bring out similar products and match price changes; an organizational strategy in which company management identifies and exploits current opportunities for competitive advantage in recognition of the fact that those opportunities are transitory

continuous budget a plan in which there is a rolling 12-month budget; a new budget month (12 months into the future) is added as each current month expires

continuous loss any reduction in units that occurs uniformly throughout a production process

contribution margin (CM) the difference between selling price and variable cost per unit or between total revenue and total variable cost at a specific level of activity; the amount of each revenue dollar remaining after variable costs have been covered that goes toward coverage of fixed costs and generation of profits

contribution margin ratio (CM%) the proportion of each revenue dollar remaining after variable costs have been covered; computed as contribution margin divided by selling price (per unit or in total)

control chart a graphical presentation of the results of a specified activity; indicates the upper and lower control limits and those results that are out of control

controllable cost a cost over which a manager has the ability to authorize incurrence or directly influence magnitude

controllable variance the budget variance of the two-variance approach to analyzing overhead variances

conversion cost the sum of direct labor and overhead cost; the cost necessary to transform direct material into a finished good or service

core competency a higher proficiency relative to competitors in a critical function or activity; a root of competitiveness and competitive advantage; anything that is not a core competency is a viable candidate for outsourcing

cost the cash or cash equivalent value necessary to attain an objective such as acquiring goods and services, complying with a contract, performing a function, or producing and distributing a product

cost accounting a discipline that focuses on techniques or methods for determining the cost of a project, process, or thing through direct measurement, arbitrary assignment, or systematic and rational allocation

Cost Accounting Standards Board (CASB) a body established by Congress in 1970 to promulgate cost accounting standards for defense contractors and federal agencies; disbanded in 1980 and reestablished in 1988

cost allocation the assignment, using some reasonable basis, of any indirect cost to one or more cost objects

cost avoidance the practice of finding acceptable alternatives to high-cost items and/or not spending money for unnecessary goods or services

cost-benefit analysis the analytical process of comparing the relative costs and benefits that result from a specific course of action (such as providing information or investing in a project); costs and benefits may be quantitative or qualitative and some may have to be analyzed using surrogate measures

cost center a responsibility center in which the manager has the authority to incur costs and is evaluated on the basis of how well costs are controlled

cost consciousness a company-wide attitude about the topics of cost understanding, cost containment, cost avoidance, and cost reduction

cost containment the practice of minimizing, to the extent possible, period-by-period increases in per-unit variable and total fixed costs

cost control system a logical structure of formal and/or informal activities designed to analyze and evaluate how well expenditures are managed during a period

cost driver a factor that has a direct cause-effect relationship to a cost; an activity creating a cost

cost driver analysis the process of investigating, quantifying, and explaining the relationships of cost drivers and their related costs

cost leadership a company's ability to maintain its competitive edge by undercutting competitor prices

cost management system (CMS) a set of formal methods developed for planning and controlling an organization's cost-generating activities relative to its goals and objectives

cost object anything to which costs attach or are related

cost of capital (COC) the weighted average cost of the various sources of funds (debt and stock) that comprise a firm's financial structure

cost of compliance the sum of prevention and appraisal costs

cost of goods manufactured (CGM) the total cost of the goods completed and transferred to Finished Goods Inventory during the period

cost of noncompliance the cost of production imperfections; equals the sum of internal and external failure costs

cost of production report a process costing document that details all operating and cost information, shows the computation of cost per equivalent unit, and indicates cost assignment to goods produced during the period

cost-plus contract a contract in which the customer agrees to reimburse the producer for the cost of the job plus a specified profit margin over cost

cost reduction the practice of lowering current costs, especially those that may be in excess of what is necessary

cost structure the relative composition of an organization's fixed and variable costs

cost table a database providing information about the impact on product costs of using different input resources, manufacturing processes, and design specifications

cost-volume-profit (CVP) analysis a procedure that examines the relationship among costs (both fixed and variable), sales volume, and profits (either before- or after-tax)

credibility a personal characteristic that indicates the provision of full, fair, and timely disclosure of all relevant information

critical success factor (CSF) any operational dimension (such as quality, customer service, efficiency, cost control, or responsiveness to change) so important that failure in that area could cause the organization to fail

customer value perspective a balanced scorecard perspective that addresses how well an organization is doing relative to important customer criteria such as speed (lead time), quality, service, and price (both at and after purchase)

cycle (lead) time the time elapsed between the placement of an order and the time the goods arrive for usage or are produced by the company; the sum of value-added time and non-value-added time

D

data mining a form of analysis in which statistical techniques are used to uncover answers to important questions about business operations

decentralization a management style that exists when top management grants subordinate managers a significant degree of autonomy and independence in operating and making decisions for their organizational units

defect a unit that, although rejected at inspection for failure to meet appropriate quality standards or designated product specifications, can be reworked and sold

degree of operating leverage (DOL) a factor that indicates how a percentage change in sales, from the existing or current level, will affect company profits; calculated as (contribution margin divided by net income); equal to (1 divided by margin of safety percentage)

dependent variable an unknown variable that is to be predicted using one or more independent variables

differential cost a cost that differs in amount among the alternatives being considered

differential revenue a revenue that differs in amount among alternatives being considered

direct cost a cost that is distinctly traceable to a particular cost object

direct costing see variable costing

direct labor the individuals who work specifically on manufacturing a product or performing a service; the time of individuals who work specifically on manufacturing a product or performing a service; the cost of the time of such individuals

direct material a readily identifiable input or component of a product; the cost of such an input or component

direct method a support department cost allocation approach that assigns support department costs directly to revenue-producing areas with only one set of intermediate cost pools or allocations

discounting the process of reducing future cash flows to present value amounts

discount rate the rate of return used to discount future cash flows to their present value amounts; should equal or exceed an organization's weighted average cost of capital

discrete loss a reduction in units that occurs at a specific point in a production process

discretionary cost a cost that is periodically reviewed by a decision maker in a process of determining whether it continues to be in accord with ongoing policies; arises from a management decision to fund an activity at a specified cost amount for a specified period of time, generally one year; can be reduced to zero in the short run if necessity so dictates

distribution cost a cost incurred to warehouse, transport, or deliver a product or service

downsizing any management action that reduces employment upon restructuring operations

downstream cost a cost related to marketing, distribution, or customer service

dual pricing arrangement a transfer pricing method that allows a selling division to record the transfer of goods or services at one price (e.g., a market or negotiated market price) and a buying division to record the transfer at another price (e.g., a cost-based amount)

Du Pont model a computation that indicates the return on investment as it is affected by profit margin and asset turnover

E

earnings management any accounting method or practice used by managers or accountants to deliberately "adjust" a company's profit amount to meet a predetermined internal or external target

economic order quantity (EOQ) an estimate of the number of units to purchase at one time that minimizes the total costs of ordering and of carrying inventory

economic production run (EPR) an estimate of the number of units to produce at one time that minimizes the total costs of setting up production runs and of carrying inventory

economic value added (EVA®) a measure of the extent to which income exceeds the dollar cost of capital; calculated as income minus (invested capital times the cost of capital percentage)

electronic data interchange (EDI) a system that allows for electronic data transmission between organizations; commonly used in the process of e-procurement

employee stock ownership plan (ESOP) a profit-sharing compensation program in which investments are made in an employer's stock(s)

employee time sheet a source document that indicates, for each employee, what jobs were worked on during a time period and for what amount of time

employee-to-capital cost ratio a measurement of the relative importance of human and financial capital to the industry

engineered cost a cost that has been found to bear an observable and known relationship to a quantifiable activity base

engineering change order (ECO) a business mandate that changes the way in which a product is manufactured or a service is performed by modifying the design, parts, process, or quality of the product or service

enterprise resource planning (ERP) system a packaged software program that allows a company to (1) automate and integrate the majority of its business processes, (2) share common data and practices across the entire enterprise, and (3) produce and access information in a real-time environment

environmental constraint any limitation on strategy options caused by external, cultural, fiscal, legal/regulatory, or political situations; a limiting factor that is not under the direct control of an organization's management; tends to be fairly long-run in nature

e-procurement system an electronic B2B (business-to-business) buy-side application controlling the requisitioning, ordering, and payment functions for inputs

equivalent units of production (EUP) an approximation of the number of whole units of output that could have been produced during a period from the actual effort expended during that period; used in process costing systems to assign costs to production

expatriate a parent company or third-country national assigned to a foreign subsidiary, or a foreign national assigned to the parent company

expected capacity a short-run concept that represents the anticipated level of capacity to be used by a firm in the upcoming period; is based on projected product demand

expected standard a standard set at a level that reflects what is actually expected to occur in the future period; anticipates future waste and inefficiencies and allows for them; is of limited value for control and performance evaluation purposes

expired cost an expense or a loss

external failure cost any expenditure for items such as warranty work, customer complaints, litigation, and defective product recalls incurred after a faulty unit of product has been shipped to the customer or an inadequate service has been performed for a customer

F

failure cost a quality control cost associated with goods or services that have been found not to conform or perform to the required standards as well as all related costs (such as that of the complaint department); may be internal or external

financial budget a plan that aggregates monetary details from the operating budgets; includes the cash and capital budgets of a company as well as the pro forma financial statements

financial performance perspective a balanced scorecard perspective that addresses the concerns of stockholders and other stakeholders about organizational profitability and growth

financing decision a judgment made regarding the method of raising funds that will be used to make acquisitions; is based on an entity's ability to issue and service debt and equity securities

finished goods the stage in the production or conversion process where units are fully completed and ready for sale to customers

first-in, first-out (FIFO) method (of process costing) the method of cost assignment that computes an average cost per equivalent unit of production for the current period; does not commingle the beginning inventory production and its cost with current period production and its cost

fixed cost a cost that remains constant in total within the relevant range of activity; cost varies inversely on a per-unit basis with changes in the level of activity

fixed overhead spending variance the difference between the total actual fixed overhead and budgeted fixed overhead; is computed as part of the four-variance overhead analysis

fixed overhead volume variance see volume variance

flexible budget a presentation of multiple budgets that show costs according to their behavior at different levels of activity

flexible manufacturing system (FMS) a production system in which a single factory manufactures numerous variations of products through the use of computer-controlled robots

focused factory arrangement an arrangement in which a vendor (which may be an external party or an internal corporate division) agrees to provide a limited number of products according to specifications or to perform a limited number of unique services to a company that is typically operating on a just-in-time system

Foreign Corrupt Practices Act (FCPA) a law passed by Congress in 1977 that makes it illegal for a U.S. company to engage in various "questionable" foreign payments and makes it mandatory for a U.S. company to maintain accurate accounting records and a reasonable system of internal control

forward contract see option

full costing see absorption costing

functional classification a separation of costs into groups based on a similar reason for the costs' incurrence; cost of goods sold and detailed selling and administrative expenses are examples of functional classifications

future value (FV) the amount to which one or more sums of money invested at a specified interest rate will grow over a specified number of compounding periods

G

gap analysis the study of the differences between the information provided by two information systems (often a current and a proposed system) to ascertain the deficiencies within the systems

goal congruence a circumstance in which the personal and organizational goals of decision makers throughout a firm are consistent and mutually supportive

grade (of a product or service) the assessment of product characteristics as to that product's ability to satisfy certain identified customer needs, especially price

H

harvest mission an organizational mission that attempts to maximize short-term profits and cash flow, even at the expense of market share; is typically pursued by a business unit that has a large market share in a low-growth industry; is appropriate for products in the final life cycle stages

hedging using options and forward contracts to manage price risk

high-low method a technique used to determine the fixed and variable portions of a mixed cost; uses only the highest and lowest levels of activity within the relevant range

hold mission an organizational mission that attempts to protect the business unit's market share and competitive position; is typically pursued by a business unit with a large market share in a high-growth industry

hurdle rate a preestablished rate of return against which other rates of return are measured; is usually the cost of capital rate when used in evaluating capital projects

hybrid costing system a costing system combining characteristics of both job order and process costing systems

I

ideal capacity see theoretical capacity

ideal standard a standard that provides for no inefficiencies of any type; is impossible to attain on a continuous basis

idle time the amount of time spent in storing inventory or waiting at a production operation for processing; is non-value-added time

imposed budget a budget developed by top management with little or no input from operating personnel; operating personnel are then informed of the budget objectives and constraints

incremental analysis a process of evaluating changes that focuses only on the factors that differ from one course of action or decision to another

incremental cost the cost resulting from the production or sale of an additional contemplated quantity of output

incremental revenue the revenue resulting from an additional contemplated sales quantity; a cost that must be allocated or assigned to products or services because of its non-traceability

independent project an investment project that has no specific bearing on any other investment project

independent variable a variable that, when changed, will cause consistent, observable changes in another variable; a variable used as the basis for predicting the value of a dependent variable

indirect cost a cost that cannot be traced explicitly to a particular cost object; a common cost; a cost that must be allocated or assigned to products or services because of its non-traceability

inspection time the time taken to perform quality control activities; generally considered as non-value-added time except in certain industries (such as food and pharmaceuticals)

integrity a personal characteristic that indicates non-participation in activities that would discredit their company or profession

intellectual capital the sum of the intangible assets of skill, knowledge, and information that exist in an organization; encompasses human, structural, and relationship capital

internal benchmarking a comparative technique that focuses on how and why one organizational unit is performing better than another

internal business perspective a balanced scorecard perspective that addresses those things an organization needs to do well to meet customer needs and expectations

internal control any measure used by management to protect assets, promote the accuracy of records, ensure adherence to company policies, or promote operational efficiency

internal failure cost an expenditure, such as scrap and rework, incurred on defective units before those units are shipped to the customer; an expenditure incurred for defective service before that service is accepted by the customer

internal rate of return (IRR) the expected or actual rate of return from a project based on, respectively, the assumed or actual cash flows; the discount rate at which the net present value of the cash flows equals zero

Internet business model a model that involves (1) few physical assets, (2) little management hierarchy, and (3) a direct pipeline to customers

intranet a mechanism for sharing information and delivering data from corporate databases to the local-area network (LAN) desktops

inventoriable cost see product cost

investment center a responsibility center in which the manager is responsible for generating revenues; planning and controlling expenses; and acquiring, disposing of, and operating assets to earn the highest rate of return feasible on those assets given the center's mission

investment decision a judgment about which assets will be acquired by an entity to achieve its stated objectives

ISO 9000 series a comprehensive series of international quality standards that define the various design, material procurement, production, quality control, and delivery requirements and procedures necessary to produce quality products and services; the series of three compliance standards (ISO 9001, 9002, and 9003) and two guidance standards (ISO 9000 and 9004) were integrated into ISO 9001:2000

J

job a single unit or group of units identifiable as being produced for a specific customer

job cost record see job order cost sheet

job order costing system a method of product costing used by an entity that provides limited quantities of products or services unique to a customer's needs; focus of recordkeeping is on individual jobs

job order cost sheet a source document that provides virtually all the financial information about a particular job; the set of all job order cost sheets for uncompleted jobs composes the Work in Process Inventory subsidiary ledger

joint cost the total of all costs (direct material, direct labor, and overhead) incurred in a joint process up to the split-off point; joint cost is assigned only to joint products

joint process a manufacturing process that simultaneously produces multiple product lines

joint product a primary output of a joint process; each joint product has substantial revenue-generating ability

judgmental method (of risk adjustment) an informal method of adjusting for risk that allows the decision maker to use logic and reason to decide whether a project provides an acceptable rate of return

just-in-time (JIT) a philosophy about when to do something; the when is "as needed" and the something is a production, purchasing, or delivery activity

just-in-time manufacturing system a production system that attempts to acquire components and produce inventory only as needed, to minimize product defects, and to reduce lead/setup times for acquisition and production

K

kaizen costing a costing technique to reflect continuous efforts to reduce product costs, improve product quality, and/or improve the production process after manufacturing activities have begun

kanban the Japanese word for card; the original name for a JIT system because cards were used to signal a work center's need for additional components during a manufacturing process

L

labor efficiency variance the number of hours actually worked minus the standard hours allowed for the production achieved multiplied by the standard rate; establishes a value for efficiency (favorable) or inefficiency (unfavorable) of the work force

labor mix variance (actual mix × actual hours × standard rate) minus (standard mix × actual hours × standard rate); presents the financial effect associated with changing the proportionate amounts of higher- or lower-paid workers in the production process

labor rate variance the actual rate (or actual weighted average rate) paid to direct labor for the period minus the standard rate multiplied by all hours actually worked during the period; can also be calculated as actual labor cost minus (actual hours × standard rate)

labor yield variance (standard mix × actual hours × standard rate) minus (standard mix × standard hours × standard rate); shows the monetary impact of using more or fewer total hours than the standard allowed in the production process

lag (or lagging) indicator a (generally) financial outcome assessed by historical data that has resulted from past actions or decisions

lead (or leading) indicator a financial or nonfinancial outcome (including opportunities and problems) that helps assess strategic progress and guide decision making before lag indicators are known; statistical data about the actionable steps that will create desired results

lead time see cycle time

lean manufacturing a concept that refers to making only those items in demand by customers and making those items without waste

learning and growth perspective a balanced scorecard perspective that focuses on using an organization's intellectual capital to adapt to changing customer needs or to influence new customers' needs and expectations through product or service innovations

least squares regression analysis a statistical technique that investigates the association between dependent and independent variables; determines the line of "best fit" for a set of observations by minimizing the sum of the squares of the vertical deviations between actual points and the regression line; can be used to determine the fixed and variable portions of a mixed cost

linear programming (LP) a method of mathematical programming used to solve a problem that involves an objective function and multiple limiting factors or constraints

line personnel employees (some of whom are in management positions) who work directly toward attaining organizational goals

M

make-or-buy decision a decision that compares the cost of internally manufacturing a component of a final product (or providing a service function) with the cost of purchasing it from outside suppliers (outsourcing) or from another division of the company at a specified transfer price

management by exception a management philosophy that indicates action is taken only when deviations are outside specified upper and lower tolerance limits

management control system (MCS) an information system that helps managers gather information about actual organizational occurrences, make comparisons against plans, effect changes when they are necessary, and communicate among appropriate parties; serves to guide organizations in designing and implementing strategies so that organizational goals and objectives are achieved

management information system (MIS) a structure of interrelated elements that collects, organizes, and communicates data to managers so they may plan, control, evaluate performance, and make decisions; emphasizes internal (rather than external) demands for information; commonly computerized for ease of access to information, reliability of input and processing, and ability to simulate outcomes of alternative situations

manufacturer a company engaged in a high degree of conversion that results in a tangible output

manufacturing cell a linear or U-shaped production grouping of workers or machines

manufacturing cycle efficiency (MCE) a ratio resulting from dividing the actual production time by total lead time; reflects the proportion of lead time that is value-added

margin of safety (MS) the excess of a company's budgeted or actual sales over its breakeven point; can be calculated in units or dollars or as a percentage; is equal to (1 ÷ degree of operating leverage)

mass customization a process of personalizing production that is generally accomplished through the use of flexible manufacturing systems; reflects an organization's increase in product variety from the same basic component elements

master budget the comprehensive set of all budgetary schedules and the pro forma financial statements of an organization

material mix variance (actual mix × actual quantity × standard price) minus (standard mix × actual quantity × standard price); is a measure of the monetary effect of substituting a nonstandard mix of material

material price variance total actual cost of material purchased minus (actual quantity of material × standard price); is the amount of money spent below (favorable) or in excess (unfavorable) of the standard price for the quantity of materials purchased; can be calculated based on the actual quantity of material purchased or the actual quantity used

material quantity variance (actual quantity × standard price) minus (standard quantity allowed × standard price); reflects the cost saved (favorable) or expended (unfavorable) due to the difference between the actual quantity of material used and the standard quantity of material allowed for the goods produced during the period

material requisition form a source document that indicates the types and quantities of material to be placed into production or used in performing a service; causes material to be released from the raw material inventory warehouse and sent to the production center as well as the cost of that material to be sent from Raw Material Inventory to Work in Process Inventory

material yield variance (standard mix × actual quantity × standard price) minus (standard mix × standard quantity × standard price); computes the difference between the actual total quantity of input and the standard total quantity allowed based on output and uses standard mix and standard prices to determine variance

mathematical programming a variety of techniques used to allocate limited resources among activities to achieve a specific objective

method of least squares see least squares regression analysis

method of neglect the treatment of spoiled units in an equivalent units of production schedule as if those units did not occur; is used for continuous normal spoilage

methods-time measurement (MTM) an industrial engineering process that analyzes work tasks to determine the time a trained worker requires to perform a given operation at a rate that can be sustained for an eight-hour workday

mission statement a written expression of organizational purpose that describes how the organization uniquely meets its targeted customers' needs with its products or services

mix any possible combination of material or labor inputs

mixed cost a cost that has both a variable and a fixed component; varies, but not proportionately, with changes in activity

multiple regression a statistical technique that uses two or more independent variables to predict a dependent variable

mutually exclusive projects a set of proposed capital projects from which one is chosen, causing all the others to be rejected

mutually inclusive projects a set of proposed capital projects that are all related and must all be chosen if the primary project is chosen

N

negotiated transfer price an intracompany charge for goods or services set through a process of negotiation between the selling and purchasing unit managers

net present value (NPV) the difference between the present values of all cash inflows and outflows for an investment project

net present value method a process that uses the discounted cash flows of a project to determine whether the rate of return on that project is equal to, higher than, or lower than the desired rate of return

net realizable value (NRV) the amount remaining after all costs necessary to prepare and dispose of a product are subtracted from product revenue at sales point or at split-off

net realizable value approach a method of accounting for by-product or scrap that requires that the net realizable value of these products be treated as a reduction in the cost of the primary products; primary product cost may be reduced by decreasing either (1) cost of goods sold when the joint products are sold or (2) the joint process cost before it is allocated to the joint products but after the by-product/scrap is produced

net realizable value at split-off allocation a method of allocating joint cost to joint products that uses, as the proration base, sales value at split-off minus all costs necessary to prepare and dispose of the products; requires that all joint products be salable at the split-off point

noncontrollable variance the fixed overhead volume variance; is computed as part of the two-variance approach to overhead analysis

non-value-added (NVA) activity an activity that increases the time spent on a product or service but that does not increase its worth or value to the customer

normal capacity the long-run (5–10 years) average production or service volume of a firm; takes into consideration cyclical and seasonal fluctuations

normal cost system a valuation method that uses actual costs of direct material and direct labor in conjunction with a predetermined overhead rate or rates in determining the cost of Work in Process Inventory

normal loss an expected decline in units experienced during the production process; the expectation is set by management

O

offset approach see net realizable value approach

offshoring an outsourcing of jobs formerly performed in the home country to foreign countries

open-book management a philosophy about increasing a firm's performance by involving all workers and by ensuring that all workers have access to operational and financial information necessary to achieve performance improvements

operating budget a budget expressed in both units and dollars

operating leverage the proportionate relationship between a company's variable and fixed costs; reflects the cost structure

operations flow document a source document listing all operations necessary to produce one unit of product (or perform a specific service) and the corresponding time allowed for each operation

opportunity cost a potential benefit that is forgone because one course of action is chosen over another

option an agreement that gives the holder the right to purchase a given quantity of a specific item (e.g., stock) at a specific price

ordering cost the variable cost associated with preparing, receiving, and paying for an order

order point the level of inventory that triggers the placement of an order for additional units; is determined based on usage, lead time, and safety stock

ordinary annuity a series of equal cash flows being received or paid at the end of a period

organizational culture the set of basic assumptions about the organization and its goals and ways of doing business; a system of shared values about what is important and beliefs about how things get accomplished; provides a framework that organizes and directs employee behavior at work; describes an organization's norms in internal and external, as well as formal and informal, transactions

organizational form an entity's legal nature (for example, sole proprietorship, partnership, corporation)

organizational-level cost a cost incurred to support the ongoing facility or operations

organizational memory the aggregation of data, facts, experiences, and lessons learned that is important to an organization's existence

organizational structure the manner in which authority and responsibility for decision making are distributed in an entity

other income approach see realized value approach

outlier an abnormal or nonrepresentative point within a data set

outsourcing the use, by one company, of an external provider of a service or manufacturer of a component

outsourcing decision see make-or-buy decision

overapplied overhead a credit balance in the Overhead Control account at the end of a period; exists when the applied overhead amount is greater than the actual overhead that was incurred

overhead any factory or production cost that is indirect to the product or service; does not include direct material or direct labor; any production cost that cannot be directly traced to the product or service

overhead application rate see predetermined overhead rate

overhead efficiency variance the difference between total budgeted overhead at actual hours and total budgeted overhead at standard hours allowed for the production achieved; is computed as part of a three-variance analysis; is the same as variable overhead efficiency variance

overhead spending variance the difference between total actual overhead and total budgeted overhead at actual hours; is computed as part of a three-variance analysis; is equal to the sum of the variable and fixed overhead spending variances

P

Pareto inventory analysis an analysis that separates inventory into three groups based on annual cost-to-volume usage

Pareto principle a rule that states that the greatest effects in human endeavors are traceable to a small number of causes (the vital few), while the majority of causes (the trivial many) collectively yield only a small impact; is often referred to as the 20:80 rule

participatory budget a budget that has been developed through a process of joint decision making by top management and operating personnel

payback period the time required to recoup an original investment through cash flows from a project

perfection standard see ideal standard

period cost a cost other than one associated with making or acquiring inventory

phantom profit a temporary absorption costing profit caused by producing more inventory than is sold; relates to fixed overhead allocations

physical measure allocation a method of allocating a joint cost to products that uses a common physical characteristic as the proration base

postinvestment audit the process of gathering information on the actual results of a capital project and comparing them to the expected results

practical capacity the physical production or service volume that a firm could achieve during normal working hours with consideration given to ongoing, expected operating interruptions

practical standard a standard that can be reached or slightly exceeded with reasonable effort by workers; allows for normal, unavoidable delays and for worker breaks; is often believed to be most effective in inducing the best performance from workers because it represents an attainable challenge

predetermined overhead rate an estimated constant charge per unit of activity used to assign overhead cost to production or services of the period; is calculated by dividing total budgeted annual overhead at a selected level of volume or activity by that selected measure of volume or activity; is also the standard overhead application rate

predictor an activity measure that, when changed, is accompanied by consistent, observable changes in another item

preference decision the second decision made in capital project evaluation in which projects are ranked according to their impact on the achievement of company objectives

present value (PV) the amount that one or more future cash flows is worth currently, given a specified rate of interest

present value index see profitability index

prevention cost a cost incurred to improve quality by preventing defects from occurring

price elasticity a numerical measure of the relationship of supply or demand to price changes

prime cost the total cost of direct material and direct labor for a product

process the combination of activities that, when performed together, satisfy a specific objective

process benchmarking a comparative technique that focuses on practices and how the best-in-class companies achieved their results

process complexity an assessment about the number of processes through which a product flows

process costing system a method of accumulating and assigning costs to units of production in companies producing large quantities of homogeneous products; accumulates costs by cost component in each production department and assigns costs to units using equivalent units of production

processing (service) time the actual time it takes to perform the functions necessary to manufacture a product; is value-added time

process map a flowchart or diagram indicating every step that goes into making a product or providing a service; includes value-added and non-value-added time

process productivity the total number of units produced during a period during value-added processing time

process quality yield the proportion of good units that resulted from the activities expended

product complexity an assessment about the number of components in a product

product contribution margin the difference between selling price and variable cost of goods sold

product cost a cost associated with making or acquiring inventory

product differentiation a company's ability to offer products superior to those of its competitors

productive processing time the proportion of total time that is value-added time; also known as manufacturing cycle efficiency

product-level (process-level) cost a cost that is caused by the development, production, or acquisition of specific products or services

product life cycle a model depicting the stages through which a product class (not necessarily each product) passes

product line margin see segment margin

product variety the number of different types of products produced (or services rendered) by a firm

profitability index (PI) a ratio that compares the present value of net cash flows to the present value of the net investment

profit center a responsibility center for which the manager is accountable for generating revenues and planning and controlling all expenses

profit margin the ratio of income to sales

profit sharing an incentive payment to employees that is contingent on organizational or individual performance

profit-volume (PV) graph a visual representation of the amount of profit or loss associated with each level of sales

pseudo-profit center a center created when one responsibility center uses a transfer price to artificially "sell" goods or services to another responsibility center

pull system a production system dictated by product sales and demand; a production system in which parts are delivered or made only as they are needed by the work center for which they are intended; requires only minimal storage facilities

purchasing cost the quoted price of inventory minus any discounts allowed plus shipping charges

push system the traditional production system in which work centers may produce inventory that is not currently needed because of lead time or economic production/order requirements; requires that excess inventory be stored until needed

Q

quality the condition of having all the characteristics of a product or service to meet the stated or implied needs of the buyer; relates to both performance and value; the pride of workmanship; conformity to requirements

quality audit a review of product design activities (although not for individual products), manufacturing processes and controls, quality documentation and records, and management philosophy

quality control (QC) the implementation of all practices and policies designed to eliminate poor quality and variability in the production or service process; places the primary responsibility for quality at the source of the product or service

R

radio frequency identification (RFID) an advanced information technology that uses exceptionally small "flakes" of silicon to transmit a code for the item to which the technology is attached

random the concept that some portion of a cost is not predictable based on the cost driver or the cost is stochastically, rather than deterministically, related to the cost driver

raw material the stage in the production or conversion process where work has not yet been started

realized value approach a method of accounting for by-product or scrap that does not recognize any value for such product until it is sold; the value recognized upon sale can be treated as other revenue or other income

red-line system an inventory ordering system in which a red line is painted on the inventory container at a point deemed to be the reorder point

regression line any line that goes through the means (or averages) of the set of observations for an independent variable and its dependent variable; mathematically, there is a line of "best fit," which is the least squares regression line

reinvestment assumption an assumption made about the rate of return that will be earned by intermediate cash flows from a capital project; the net present value and profitability index assume reinvestment at the discount rate; the internal rate of return assumes reinvestment at the IRR

relevant costing a process that compares, to the extent possible and practical, the incremental revenues and incremental costs of alternative decisions

relevant range the specified range of activity over which a variable cost per unit remains constant or a fixed cost remains fixed in total; is generally assumed to be the normal operating range of the organization

residual income (RI) the profit earned by a responsibility center that exceeds an amount "charged" for funds committed to that center

responsibility the obligation to accomplish a task or achieve an objective

responsibility accounting system an accounting system for successively higher-level managers about the performance of segments or subunits under the control of each specific manager

responsibility center a cost object or area under the control of a manager

responsibility report a report that reflects the revenues and/or costs under the control of a particular unit manager

results benchmarking a comparative technique in which an end product or service is examined; the focus is on product/service specifications and performance results

return of capital the recovery of the original investment (or principal) in a project

return on capital income from an investment in a project: is equal to the rate of return multiplied by the amount of the investment

return on investment (ROI) a ratio that relates income generated by an investment center to the resources (or asset base) used to produce that income

revenue center a responsibility center for which the manager is accountable only for the generation of revenues and has no control over setting selling prices, or budgeting or incurring costs

risk uncertainty; reflects the possibility of differences between the expected and actual future returns from an investment

risk-adjusted discount rate method a formal method of adjusting for risk in which the decision maker increases the rate used for discounting the future cash in flows to compensate for increased risk

Robinson-Patman Act a law that prohibits companies from pricing the same products at different amounts when those amounts do not reflect related cost differences

rolling budget see continuous budget

routing document see operations flow document

S

safety stock a buffer level of inventory kept on hand by a company in the event of fluctuating usage or unusual delays in lead time

sales mix the relative combination of the various products' sales quantities that comprise a company's total sales

sales price variance a revenue variance that indicates the financial difference between the actual and budgeted sales prices for the actual number of units sold

sales value at split-off allocation a method of assigning joint cost to joint products that uses the relative sales values of the products at the split-off point as the proration basis; use of this method requires that all joint products are salable at the split-off point

sales volume variance a revenue variance that indicates the difference caused by actually selling more or fewer units than budgeted multiplied by the budgeted sales price

scarce resource a resource that is essential to production activity, but is available only in some limited quantity

scrap an incidental output of a joint process; is salable but the sales value from scrap is not enough for management to justify undertaking the joint process; is viewed as having a lower sales value than a by-product; has a minimal but distinguishable disposal value

screening decision the first decision made in evaluating capital projects; indicates whether a project is desirable based on some previously established minimum criterion or criteria (see also preference decision)

segment margin the excess of revenues over direct variable expenses and avoidable fixed expenses for a particular segment

sensitivity analysis a process of determining the amount of change that must occur in a variable before a different decision would be made

separate cost a cost that follows incurrence of joint cost and that is related to a specific product or group of products; is assigned only to that product or group of products

service company a firm engaged in a high or moderate degree of conversion that results in service output

service cost the sum of all costs incurred to provide one unit of service to a customer

service cycle efficiency a ratio resulting from dividing total actual value-added service time by total cycle time; reflects the proportion of total time that is value-added

service department an organizational unit that provides one or more specific functional tasks for other internal units

service differentiation a company's ability to offer superior quality or more unique services than its competitors

shrinkage a decrease in units arising from an inherent characteristic of the production process; includes decreases caused by evaporation, leakage, and oxidation

simple interest a method of determining interest in which interest is earned only on the original investment (or principal) amount

simple regression a statistical technique that uses only one independent variable to predict a dependent variable

Six Sigma method a high-performance, data-driven approach to analyzing and solving the root causes of business problems; allows no more than 3.4 defects per million "opportunities"

special order decision a situation in which management must determine a sales price to charge for manufacturing or service jobs outside the company's normal production/service market

split-off point the point at which the outputs of a joint process are first identifiable or can be separated as individual products

spoilage a unit that has been rejected at inspection for failure to meet appropriate quality standards or designated product specifications and that cannot be reworked and sold

staff personnel employees who are responsible for providing advice, guidance, and service to line personnel; may be management

standard a model or budget against which actual results are compared and evaluated; a benchmark or norm used for planning and control purposes

standard cost card a document that summarizes the direct material, direct labor, and overhead standard quantities and prices needed to complete one unit of product

standard cost system a valuation method that uses predetermined norms for direct material, direct labor, and overhead to assign costs to the various inventory accounts and Cost of Goods Sold

standard quantity the standard quantity of input (in hours or some other cost driver measurement) required for the output actually achieved for the period

Statement on Management Accounting (SMA) a cost or management accounting pronouncement developed and issued by the Institute of Management Accountants; application of these statements is voluntary

statistical process control (SPC) the use of control techniques that are based on the theory that a process has natural variations in it over time, but uncommon variations are typically the points at which the process produces "errors," which can be defective goods or poor service

step cost a cost that increases in distinct amounts because of increased activity

step method a process of support department cost allocation that assigns support department costs to cost objects after considering the interrelationships of the support departments and revenue-producing departments

stockout the condition of not having inventory available upon need or request

strategic alliance an agreement between two or more firms with complementary core competencies to jointly contribute to the supply chain

strategic benchmarking a comparative technique that is non–industry specific and focuses on how companies compete, seeking to identify the winning strategies that have enabled high-performing companies to be successful in their marketplaces

strategic planning the process of developing a statement of long-range (5–10 years) goals for the organization and defining the strategies and policies that will help the organization achieve those goals

strategy the link between an organization's goals and objectives and the activities actually conducted by the organization

strict FIFO method (of process costing) the method of cost assignment that uses FIFO to compute a cost per equivalent unit and, in transferring units from a department, keeps the cost of the beginning inventory units separate from the cost of the units started and completed during the current period

suboptimization a situation in which an individual manager pursues goals and objectives that are in his/her own and his/her segment's particular interests rather than in the company's best interests

sunk cost a cost incurred in the past and not relevant to any future courses of action; the historical or past cost associated with the acquisition of an asset or a resource

supply-chain management the cooperative strategic planning, controlling, and problem solving by a company and its vendors and customers to conduct efficient and effective transfers of goods and services within the supply chain

support department the generic term for either a service or an administrative department

T

tactical planning the process of determining the specific means or objectives by which the strategic plans of the organization will be achieved; is short range in nature (usually 1–18 months)

target costing a method of determining what the cost of a product should be based on the product's estimated selling price less the desired profit

tax benefit (of depreciation) the amount of depreciation deductible for tax purposes multiplied by the tax rate; the reduction in taxes caused by the deductibility of depreciation

tax deferral a tax treatment in which income is subject to tax in a future period

tax exemption a tax treatment in which income is never subject to income taxation

tax shield (of depreciation) the amount of depreciation deductible for tax purposes; the amount of revenue shielded from taxes because of the depreciation deduction

theoretical capacity the estimated maximum production or service volume that a firm could achieve during a period

theory of constraints (TOC) a method of analyzing the bottlenecks (constraints) that keep a system from achieving higher performance; states that production cannot take place at a rate faster than the slowest machine or person in the process

throughput the total output that is completed and sold during a period

time line a representation of the amounts and timing of all cash inflows and outflows; is used in analyzing cash flow from a capital project

total contribution margin see contribution margin

total cost to account for the sum of the costs in beginning inventory and the costs of the current period

total overhead variance the difference between total actual overhead and total applied overhead; is the amount of underapplied or overapplied overhead

total quality management (TQM) a structural system for creating organization-wide participation in planning and implementing a continuous improvement process that exceeds the expectations of the customer/client; the application of quality principles to all company endeavors; is also known as total quality control

total units to account for the sum of the beginning inventory units and units started during the current period

total variance the difference between total actual cost incurred and total standard cost for the output produced during the period

transfer price an internal charge established for the exchange of goods or services between organizational units of the same company

transfer time the time consumed by moving products or components from one place to another; is non-value-added time

transferred-in cost a prior department cost that is carried forward to a successor department to obtain the full manufacturing or performance cost

two-bin system an inventory ordering system in which two containers (or stacks) of raw materials or parts are available for use; when one container is depleted, the removal of materials from the second container begins and a purchase order is placed to refill the first container

U

uncertainty the doubt or lack of precision in specifying future outcomes

underapplied overhead a debit balance in the Overhead Control account at the end of a period; exists when the applied overhead amount is less than the actual overhead incurred

unexpired cost an asset

unit-level cost a cost caused by the production or acquisition of a single unit of product or the delivery of a single unit of service

units started and completed the difference between the number of units completed for the period and the units in beginning inventory; can also be computed as the number of units started during the period minus the units in ending inventory

upstream cost a cost related to research, development, product design, or supply chain

usage the quantity of inventory used or sold each time interval

V

value the characteristic of meeting the highest number of customer needs at the lowest possible price

value-added (VA) activity an activity that increases the worth of the product or service to the customer; an activity for which the customer is willing to pay

value chain the set of processes that converts inputs into products and services for the firm's customers; includes the processes of suppliers as well as internal processes

value chart a visual representation indicating the value-added and non-value-added activities and time spent in those activities from the beginning to the end of a process

value engineering a disciplined search for various feasible combinations of resources and methods that will increase product functionality and reduce costs

values statement a statement reflecting an organization's culture by identifying fundamental beliefs about what is important to that organization

variable cost a cost that varies in total in direct proportion to changes in activity; is constant on a per-unit basis

variable costing a cost accumulation and reporting method that includes only variable production costs (direct material, direct labor, and variable overhead) as inventoriable or product costs; treats fixed overhead as a period cost; is not acceptable for external reporting and tax reporting

variable cost ratio (VC%) the proportion of each revenue dollar represented by variable costs; computed as variable costs divided by sales or as (1 − contribution margin ratio)

variable overhead efficiency variance the difference between budgeted variable overhead based on actual input activity and variable overhead applied to production

variable overhead spending variance the difference between total actual variable overhead and the budgeted amount of variable overhead based on actual input activity

variance a difference between an actual and a standard or budgeted cost; is favorable if actual is less than standard and is unfavorable if actual is greater than standard

variance analysis the process of categorizing the nature (favorable or unfavorable) of the differences between standard and actual costs and determining the reasons for those differences

virtual reality an artificial, computer-generated environment in which the user has the impression of being part of that environment and has the ability to navigate and manipulate objects (such as products) behaving like real-world objects

volume variance a fixed overhead variance that represents the difference between budgeted fixed overhead and fixed overhead applied to production of the period; is also referred to as the noncontrollable variance

W

waste a residual output of a production process that has no sales value and that must be disposed

weighted average (WA) method (of process costing) the method of cost assignment that computes an average cost per equivalent unit of production for all units completed during the current period; combines beginning inventory units and costs with current production and costs, respectively, to compute the average

working capital the amount remaining after total current liabilities are subtracted from total current assets; measures the amount of an organization's liquid assets; may also be referred to as "net working capital"

work in process the stage in the production or conversion process where work has been started but not yet completed

Y

yield the quantity of output that results from a specified input

ACRONYMS

ABC Activity-based costing
ABM Activity-based management
AP Actual price
APA Advance pricing agreement
AQ Actual quantity
ARR Accounting rate of return
ASP Actual sales price
ASQC American Society for Quality Control
ASV Actual sales volume
BEP Break-even point
BPR Business process reengineering
BSC Balanced scorecard
BSP Budgeted sales price
BSV Budgeted sales volume
BVA Business-value-added
CAM-I Computer Aided Manufacturing International
CASB Cost Accounting Standards Board
CEO Chief Executive Officer
CFO Chief Financial Officer
CGM Cost of goods manufactured
CGS Cost of goods sold
CM Contribution margin
CMA Certified Management Accountant
CMA-Canada Society of Management Accountants of Canada
CMS Cost management system
COC Cost of capital
CPA Certified Public Accountant
DL Direct labor
DM Direct material
DOL Degree of operating leverage
ECO Engineering change order
EFQM European Foundation for Quality Management
ERP Enterprise resource planning
ESOP Employee stock ownership plan
EUP Equivalent units of production
EVA Economic value added
FASB Financial Accounting Standards Board
FCA False Claims Act (1863; significant revisions 1986)
FCPA Foreign Corrupt Practices Act (1977)
FIFO First-in, first-out
FG Finished goods
FOH Fixed overhead
FV Future value
GAAP Generally accepted accounting principles
IASB International Accounting Standards Board
IMA Institute of Management Accountants
IRR Internal rate of return
ISO International Organization for Standardization
JIT Just-in-time
LEV Labor efficiency variance
LP Linear programming
LRV Labor rate variance
MAG Management Accounting Guideline
MBNQA Malcolm Baldrige National Quality Award
MCE Manufacturing cycle efficiency
MCS Management control system
MH Machine hour
MIS Management information system
MPV Material price variance
MQV Material quantity variance
MS Margin of safety
MTM Methods-time measurement
NFP Not-for-profit
NFPM Nonfinancial performance measure
NPV Net present value
NRV Net realizable value
NVA Non-value-added
OECD Organiaation of Economic Cooperation and Development
OH Overhead
PCAOB Public Company Accounting Oversight Board
PI Profitability index
PV Present value
QC Quality control
R&D Research & development
RFID Radio frequency identification
RI Residual income
ROI Return on investment
SCE Service cycle efficiency
SCF Statement of Cash Flows
SEC Securities & Exchange Commission
SKU Stock-keeping units
SMA Statement on Management Accounting
SOX Sarbanes-Oxley Act (2002)
SP Standard price
SPC Statistical process control
SPV Sales price variance
SQ Standard quantity
SRM Strategic resource management
SVV Sales volume variance
TCO Total cost of ownership
TQM Total quality management
TVC Total variable cost
VA Value-added
VOH Variable overhead
VV Volume variance
WA Weighted average
WIP Work in process

NAME INDEX

Note: Page numbers followed by "n" refer to footnotes.

SUBJECT INDEX

Note: Page numbers followed by "n" refer to footnotes.

T

X

Y